A Dictionary of Syriar
Englisl

Karl Stowasser
Moukhtar Ani

Georgetown University Press / Washington, D.C.

Georgetown Classics in Arabic Language and Linguistics

Karin C. Ryding and Margaret Nydell, series editors

For some time, Georgetown University Press has been interested in making available seminal publications in Arabic language and linguistics that have gone out of print. Some of the most meticulous and creative scholarship of the last century was devoted to the analysis of Arabic language, to producing detailed reference works and textbooks of the highest quality. Although some of the material is dated in terms of theoretical approaches, the content and methodology of the books considered for the reprint series is still valid and in some cases, unsurpassed.

With global awareness now refocused on the Arab world, and with renewed interest in Arab culture, society, and political life, it is essential to provide easy access to classic reference materials such as dictionaries and reference grammars and language teaching materials. The key components of this series of classic reprints have been chosen for quality of research and scholarship, and have been updated with new bibliographies and introductions to provide readers with resources for further study. Where possible, the original authors have been involved in the reproduction and republication process.

Georgetown University Press hopes hereby to serve the growing national and international need for reference works on Arabic language and culture, as well as provide access to quality textbooks and audiovisual resources for teaching Arabic language in its written and spoken forms.

Books in the series:

Arabic Language Handbook
Mary Catherine Bateson

Audio CD for A Reference Grammar of Syrian Arabic
Mark W. Cowell

A Basic Course in Iraqi Arabic with MP3 Audio Files
Wallace M. Erwin

A Basic Course in Moroccan Arabic
Richard S. Harrell with Mohammed Abu-Talib and William S. Carroll

A Basic Course in Moroccan Arabic *MP3 Files: Audio Exercises*
Richard S. Harrell

A Dictionary of Iraqi Arabic: English–Arabic, Arabic–English
B. E. Clarity, Karl Stowasser, and Ronald G. Wolfe, editors; D. R. Woodhead and Wayne Beene, editors

A Dictionary of Moroccan Arabic: Moroccan–English, English–Moroccan
Richard S. Harrell and Harvey Sobelman, editors

A Dictionary of Syrian Arabic: English–Arabic
Karl Stowasser and Moukhtar Ani

Formal Spoken Arabic FAST Course with MP3 Files
Karin C. Ryding and Abdelnour Zaiback

Modern Arabic: Structures, Functions, and Varieties, revised edition
Clive Holes

A Short Reference Grammar of Iraqi Arabic
Wallace M. Erwin

A Short Reference Grammar of Moroccan Arabic with Audio CD
Richard S. Harrell

The research reported herein was performed pursuant to a contract with the United States Office of Education, Department of Health, Education and Welfare.

Georgetown University Press, Washington, D.C.

Printed in the United States of America

10 9 8 7 6 5 4 3 2 1 2004

This book is printed on acid-free paper meeting the requirements of the American National Standard for Permanence in Paper for Printed Library Materials.

First published in 1964.

Library of Congress Cataloging-in-Publication Data

A dictionary of Syrian Arabic : English-Arabic / Karl Stowasser and Moukhtar Ani, editors.
p. cm. (Georgetown classics in Arabic language and linguistics)
ISBN 1-58901-105-8 (alk. paper)
1. Arabic language—dialects—Syria—Dictionaries—English. I. Stowasser, Karl. II. Ani, Moukhtar. III. Series.

PJ6816.D53 2004
492.7′321—dc22

2004040882

Contents

Arabic Research at Georgetown University

In the past forty years, the world of research in Arabic theoretical linguistics has expanded but the production of professional quality textbooks in colloquial Arabic has remained limited. Despite the passage of years, the Richard Slade Harrell Arabic series has consistently been in demand from Georgetown University Press because of the quality of research that went into its composition, the solid theoretical foundations for its methodology, and the comprehensive coverage of regional Arabic speech communities.

The Department of Arabic Language, Literature and Linguistics at Georgetown University (formerly Arabic Department) recognizes the need to sustain the tradition of research and publication in Arabic dialects and has continued dialectology field research and textbook production, most notably with Margaret (Omar) Nydell's *Syrian Arabic Video Course*, a three-year research project funded by Center for the Advancement of Language Learning from 1991 to 1994. Currently we are engaged in a four-year dialectology research project aimed at producing "conversion" courses to assist learners of Modern Standard Arabic in converting their knowledge and skills of written Arabic to proficiency in selected Arabic dialects. This project is part of a grant administered by the National Capital Language Resource Center under the directorship of Dr. James E. Alatis and Dr. Anna Chamot.

We pay tribute to the tradition initiated and led by Richard Harrell, the founder of this series, and of the original Arabic Research Program at Georgetown University. His scholarship and creative energy set a standard in the field and yielded an unprecedented and as-yet unsurpassed series of, as he put it, "practical tools for the increasing number of Americans whose lives bring them into contact with the Arab world." We hope that this series of reprints, and our continuing efforts in applied Arabic dialectology research, will yield a new crop of linguistic resources for Arabic language study.

Karin C. Ryding
Sultan Qaboos bin Said Professor of Arabic

The History of the Arabic Research Program
Institute of Languages and Linguistics, Georgetown University

The Arabic Research Program was established in June of 1960 as a contract between Georgetown University and the United States Office of Education under the provisions of the Language Development Program of the National Defense Education Act.

The first two years of the research program, 1960–1962 (contract number SAE-8706), were devoted to the production of six books, a reference grammar and a conversational English–Arabic dictionary in the cultivated spoken forms of Moroccan, Syrian, and Iraqi Arabic. The second two years of the research program, 1962–1964 (contract number OE-2-14-029), call for the further production of Arabic–English dictionaries in each of the three varieties of Arabic mentioned above, as well as comprehensive basic courses in the Moroccan and Iraqi varieties.

The eleven books of this series, of which the present volume is one, are designed to serve as practical tools for the increasing number of Americans whose lives bring them into contact with the Arab world. The dictionaries, the reference grammars, and the basic courses are oriented toward the educated American who is a layman in linguistic matters. Although it is hoped that the scientific linguist and the specialist in Arabic dialectolgy will find these books both of interest and of use, matters of purely scientific and theoretical importance have not been directly treated as such, and specialized scientific terminology has been avoided as much as possible.

As is usual, the authors or editors of the individual books bear final scholarly responsibility for the contents, but there has been a large amount of informal cooperation in our work. Criticism, consultation, and discussion have gone on constantly among the senior professional members of the staff. The contribution of more junior research assistants, both Arab and American, is also not to be underestimated. Their painstaking assembling and ordering of raw data, often in manners requiring considerable creative intelligence, has been the necessary prerequisite for further progress.

Staff work has been especially important in the preparation of the dictionaries. Although the contributing staff members are named on the title page of the individual dictionaries, special mention must be made of Mr. Karl Stowasser's work. His lexicographical experience, acquired in his work on the English version of Professor Wehr's *Arabisches Wörtenbuch für die Schriftsprache der Gegenwart* (Hans Wehr, *A Dictionary of Modern Written Arabic,* ed. J. Milton Cowan [Ithaca, N.Y.: Cornell University Press, 1961]), along with his thorough knowledge of Arabic, has been critically important for all our lexicographical work, covering the entire range from typography to substantive entries in the dictionaries.

In most cases the books prepared by the Arabic Research Program are the first of their kind in English, and in some cases the first in any language. The preparation of them has been a rewarding experience. It is hoped that the public use of them will be equally so. The undersigned, on behalf of the entire staff, would like to ask the same indulgence of the reader as Samuel Johnson requested in his first English dictionary: To remember that although much has been left out, much has been included.

Richard S. Harrell
Associate Professor of Linguistics
Georgetown University
Director,
Arabic Research Program

Foreword to the Georgetown Classics Edition

Georgetown University Press is pleased to reprint the *Dictionary of Syrian Arabic: English—Arabic*, edited by Karl Stowasser and Moukhtar Ani, in the Georgetown Classics in Arabic Language and Linguistics series. This work, as well as the other volumes in the series, can truly be called "classic." Since its publication in 1964, the *Dictionary of Syrian Arabic* has not gone out of print, and it continues to serve as a vital part of any research and reference library on spoken Arabic and on Arabic dialectology.

The *Dictionary of Syrian Arabic* is modest in size. At just under 300 pages, it contains some 15,000 main and subentries, representing the everyday usage of educated Arabic speakers in Damascus. It does not attempt to cover technical terminology from business, trade, or traditional crafts. Those 15,000 entries, however, contain a wealth of information.

The coverage of the *Dictionary* runs the gamut, from "abuse" to "zipper." A few entries provide only the Arabic equivalent of an English word. Most entries, however, include ample illustrations of Syrian usage, carefully distinguishing shades of meaning, as in the entry for the noun "check." English uses a single word to name a bank draft, a ticket or token showing ownership, and a bill. In contrast, Syrian has three separate words for these items. The *Dictionary* lists all of these. Other meanings of the same word are covered in a separate entry for the verb "to check." Another remarkable entry is that of the useful English word "get." The entry fills three columns and includes most of the common verb–preposition collocations based on "get," from "to get across" to "to get up."

Another unusual feature of the dictionary is its introduction, which opens with a brief but thorough outline of the sociolinguistic situation in Syria. That outline illustrates the point that Syrian Arabic differs systematically—not randomly—from Modern Standard Arabic. Examples cover phonology or the sound system of the language, morphology or the word-building system, syntax or grammar, and vocabulary. The introduction continues with a sketch of Syrian Arabic phonology. It does not stop, as many dictionaries do, with a list of the basic sounds of the language. Instead, it goes on to discuss other issues, among them emphasis and the spread of emphasis, stress, and assimilation.

The *Dictionary of Syrian Arabic* lacks only one thing, a thing that is sorely missed: its Syrian Arabic–English counterpart. The Syrian Arabic–English dictionary was planned as part of the larger Arabic language project, and much of the research for that dictionary was complete. Only the untimely death of Richard S. Harrell, who directed the project, prevented the completion of the Syrian Arabic–English dictionary and other works in the project. The project's completion would have complemented the other published dictionaries, grammars, and teaching materials for four major dialects of Arabic: Egyptian, Iraqi, Moroccan, and Syrian. Although the project remains unfinished, the published works of the Georgetown Classics series stand as testimony to the systematic and rigorous analyses of colloquial Arabic. It is hoped that this reprint will inform and inspire another generation of scholars.

Elizabeth M. Bergman
Language Resource Center, McNeil Technologies
Georgetown University

Introduction

The term "Syrian Arabic" actually comprises quite a number of distinct dialects and subdialects spoken by the sedentary population of Greater Syria, that is, of present-day Syria, Lebanon, Jordan and the Arab population of Israel. Yet these dialects share so many similar and identical features of phonology, grammar and vocabulary that there is a great deal of justification for referring to them as a unit. The degree of similarity among them is not necessarily determined by geographical location or political division. The urban dialects of Damascus, Beirut and Jerusalem, for instance, have much more in common than, let us say, the Arabic spoken in Damascus compared with that of some village thirty or forty miles away. Likewise, the dialects of two social or religious groups within the same community may show more points of dissimilarity in relation to each other than when compared with their counterparts in a community with a similar social or religious structure. Finally, the various dialects of the Bedouins living in the area do not belong to the Syrian-Arabic dialect group at all.

The dialect is the native language of an Arab, the language he learns as a child and speaks throughout his life, regardless of environment or social position. This is important for two reasons. First, the dialect, being the universal medium of oral communication, does not connote substandard and parochial usage in the sense that the speaker of a Western language might ascribe to it. Second, unlike the written language, which is an acquired skill and hence a matter of individual proficiency, it does not know correct and incorrect, only common and uncommon usage. Arabs can blunder in the written language, never in their native dialect.

The profound social upheaval which the Arab countries have experienced during the last two generations, the modernization movement and the concomitant spread of universal education on the one hand and of press, radio, television and film on the other, have engendered a remarkable and far-reaching socio-linguistic phenomenon: the blurring of the line between dialect and written language and the emergence of a spoken idiom containing so many features of written Arabic that it can almost be called a third language. The give and take between written and spoken language, the borrowing from one by the other, is, of course, nothing new. It is as old as diglossia in Arabic. In that process, the dialect has traditionally shown itself less reluctant to adopt features of the written language, for one thing because it has never known a purist or normative attitude, and secondly because, to an Arab's mind, the written language has always been the model, the "real Arabic," as it were, and hence implicitly superior and worth imitating. What is new, however, and what constitutes an unprecedented and significant aspect in the development over the past few decades is that the written language, by becoming accessible to an ever broader section of the population, has lost its exclusivity, its aura of the esoteric, the supernal, the solemn. This process of "democratization" combined with the increasing demands of our modern age has produced a distinctly practical, matter-of-fact, business-like style, a style with few or no literary and aesthetic ambitions, the language of a newspaper, for instance, or an official communiqué or a bill of lading or a textbook; the language spoken on radio and television, in a panel discussion and in the classroom. This style is handled by people who have neither the inclination nor the time to dwell on literary and philological niceties, whose primary concern is communication, not the elegance of the linguistic medium. It is this style rather than the classical literary language which affects and transforms the dialect, profoundly in vocabulary, considerably also in morphology, to a lesser extent in phonology and syntax. A few examples may serve to illustrate this point. The first column shows the pure dialectal forms, the second the variants under the influence of the written language.

In phonology:

ẓaabeṭ	*ḍaabeṭ*	'officer'
ḍann	*ẓann*	'thinking'
manṭiqa	*manṭiq̈a*	'area'
ṣaxaawe	*saxaawe*	'generosity'
sadaaqa	*ṣadaaq̈a*	'friendship'
matalan	*masalan*	'for example'
kədᵊb	*kəzᵊb*	'lie'
faayde	*faaʔide*	'benefit'
ryaase	*raʔaase*	'presidency'
məddə́ʕi	*muddáʕi*	'claimant'
məmken	*mumken*	'possible'

In morphology:

maa byənqaal	*laa yuq̈aal*	'it is not said'
byəstaʕᵊmlúu	*(b)yustaʕmal*	'it is used'
ḥarf ḥarf	*ḥarfiyyan*	'literally'
ʕala kəll ḥaal	*ʕala kullen*	'at any rate'
muu məqri	*ġeer maq̈ruuʔ*	'illegible'
məzdə́ḥem	*muzdáḥem*	'crowded'
ṣʕuube	*ṣuʕuube*	'difficulty'
tərbaaye	*tarbiye*	'education'
ʕəṭyaan	*ʔəʕṭaaʔ*	'giving'
tamriin	*tamarron*	'practice'
zabzabe	*tazabzob*	'vacillation'
barra	*barraʔ*	'he acquitted'
ʔəktə́fa	*ʔəktifaaʔ*	'contentment'
məbni	*mabni*	'built'
raḥle	*rəḥle*	'journey'
ʔəsara	*ʔasra*	'captives'

In syntax:

ẓ-ẓaaher	*ʕala maa yaẓhar*	'apparently'
maa fii šakk	*laa šakk*	'doubtless'
ʕtaraf ʔənno (kaan) ġalṭaan	*ʕtaraf bi-ʔənno (kaan) ġalṭaan*	'he admitted that he was wrong'
bada l-ḥarᵊb	*badet ᵊl-ḥarᵊb*	'the war began'
ʕaamleen muhəmmiin	*ʕaamleen muhəmmeen*	'two important factors'
ḍəbbaaṭ ᵊkbaar	*kibaar ᵊḍ-ḍəbbaaṭ*	'senior officers'
ʔaṣlo ləbnaani	*ləbnaani l-ʔaṣᵊl*	'of Lebanese origin'
baalo ṭawiil	*ṭawiil ᵊl-baal*	'patient'

In vocabulary:

ʔuuḍet ʔakᵊl	*ġərfet ṭaʕaam*	'dining room'
ʔəmḍa	*tawq̈iiʕ*	'signature'
staʕfa	*staq̈aal*	'he resigned'
faat	*daxal*	'he entered'
šaġġal maṣari	*stasmar ʔamwaalo*	'he invested his money'
šii yoom	*yawman maa*	'some day'
qayamaan	*ʔəstəʔṣaal*	'removal' (by surgery)
žarrab	*ḥaawal*	'he tried'
mətᵊl baʕḍo ʕandi	*sayyaan ʕandi*	'it's all the same to me'
ḍəġri	*mubaašaratan*	'directly'
ʕala ṭuul	*daaʔiman (daayman)*	'always'
ʔaxad	*ttaxaz*	'he took' (e.g., measures, a stand)

It must be emphasized that these variants have become part and parcel of the everyday language. To intersperse one's dialect with quasi-classicisms will rarely be interpreted as an attempt on the part of the speaker to parade his erudition. However, the extent to which a speaker incorporates features of the written language into his idiolect may still reveal his educational background. This may cover the whole span from a few random phrases in the speech pattern of the uneducated to the highly classicizing colloquial style of the intellectual which almost amounts to a mixed language.

* * * *

This dictionary is based on the dialect of Damascus, as spoken by educated Muslims. Within the dialect area outlined above, Damascus occupies a central position in more than the obvious geographical sense. The city is a major administrative center of the area and historically an important seat of Islamic culture and learning. Furthermore, a number of political, sociological and geographical factors have combined to mold there a dialect of uncommon uniformity and fixity. For all practical purposes, therefore, the speaker of Damascus Arabic will be perfectly understood and accepted in most of the Syrian-Arabic dialect area and — with some qualifications — a good deal beyond. On the other hand, given his ability and readiness to train his ear for phonological, grammatical and lexical variants, it will not take him long to understand native speakers of other Syrian dialects without undue difficulty.

The dictionary is an expression dictionary; that is, its format and presentation are geared exclusively to the needs of the native speaker of American English. Its corpus of approximately 15,000 main and subentries represents an essentially colloquial vocabulary intended for a fairly wide range of conversational usage.* A combination of synonymous and contextual definition was chosen as best suited for the practical purpose of the work. The contextual examples are, for the most part, intentionally simple in style and informational content and merely serve to bring out and illustrate a desired semantic or syntactical point. English homonyms are treated as separate main entries, but an English word belonging to different form classes is presented as one entry, merely the verb being set off as a subentry (cf. **light**).

The Arabic equivalent of an English entry is usually followed by a contextual example which is designed to illustrate and define its semantic range or syntactic behavior, or both. Several Arabic equivalents separated by commas are interchangeable within these confines. An English entry which has no word-for-word equivalent in Arabic is followed by a colon and, as a rule, by two or more contextual examples which demonstrate paraphrastic possibilities (cf. **bookworm**). A double asterisk (**) preceding an English sentence or an Arabic phrase signals idiomatic rendition.

---

*The English entries are based to a considerable extent on the English-German section of the *German-English English-German Dictionary of Everyday Usage,* ed. by J. Alan Pfeffer (New York: Henry Holt and Co.). Although the content of this dictionary is, in strictly legal terms, public domain since it was prepared as a part of the American war effort in World War II, we wish to express our thanks to the publishers for raising no copyright objections to our use of the material.

An Arabic noun is regularly followed by its sound and/or broken plural, the former in abbreviation (*-e/-a/-iyye* or *-iin/-iyyiin* or *-aat*). Plurals of the pattern *fƐuul* and an optional variant *fƐuule* are quoted as *fƐuul(e)*, e.g., *taxᵊt* pl. *txuut(e)*. The raised tilde (˜) at the end of a noun indicates annexion (*ʔiḍaafe*), as *mažles˜ wəzara;* the same symbol is occasionally used to distinguish the prepositional from the adverbial function of an Arabic word, as *taḥᵊt˜* 'under' and *taḥᵊt* 'down'.

With adjectives, only broken plurals are indicated; all others, unless they are marked "invariable," follow the predictable regular pattern, as *šaaṭer* f. *šaaṭra* pl. *šaaṭriin*. An asterisk after an adjective ending in *-i* indicates that it follows the pattern f. *-iyye* pl. *-iyyiin*, e.g., *fəƐli** f. *fəƐliyye* pl. *fəƐliyyiin*, *məstə́wi** f. *məstwiyye* pl. *məstwiyyiin*, as contrasted with the pattern *-i* f. *-ye* pl. *-yiin*, e.g., *ṃaaḍi* f. *ṃaaḍye* pl. *ṃaaḍyiin*, *məġri* f. *məġᵊrye* pl. *meġᵊryiin*.

An Arabic verb is quoted in the conventional third person singular (masculine) of the perfect. Triliteral verbs of the 1st Form (Stem I) are followed, in parentheses, by the stem vowel of the imperfect, the verbal noun or nouns and — set off by a double virgule — the passive, as *ḍarab (o ḍarᵊb//nḍarab)*. Alternate imperfect vowels are separated by a virgule: *e/o*, e.g., *tarak (e/o tarᵊk//ntarak)*, i.e., the imperfect of *tarak* is *byətrek* or *byətrok* without affecting the meaning. The symbol *ø* instead of a verbal noun signals that the verbal noun is uncommon in that particular sense of the verb, rather than nonexistent. As a space-saving device, the above grammatical information is furnished only once within a given English entry, namely with the first citation of the verb. Likewise, for reasons of economy, the grammatical information is omitted for a number of very common first-form verbs whenever they form part of a compound phrase. These verbs are:

ʔaxad (-yaaxod ʔaxᵊd//ttaaxad)	'to take'
ḥaṭṭ (ə ḥaṭaṭ, ḥaṭaṭaan//nḥaṭṭ)	'to put'
raaḥ (u rooḥa, rawaḥaan)	'to go'
ṣaar (i ṣayaraan)	'to become'
Ɛaṭa (-yaƐṭi Ɛəṭyaan//nƐaṭa)	'to give'
Ɛəmel (-yaƐmel Ɛamal//nƐamal)	'to do'
kaan (u koon)	'to be'

Since the augmented forms II to X of triliteral verbs and the quadriliteral verbs generally follow a predictable pattern, no information is needed other than the passive, as *Ɛammad//tƐammad*, *baxwaš//tbaxwaš*, and irregular verbal nouns, as *štaġal (šəġᵊl)* — for theoretical *ʔəštiġaal*. An obligatory prepositional complement is consistently quoted with the Arabic verb-definition, as *Ɛtaraf b-* 'to admit', *Ɛtamad Ɛala* 'to trust' whereas free prepositional complements are relegated to the illustrative sentences for demonstration.

* * * *

The system of transcription adopted for this book follows more or less conventional lines. The admittedly awkward and slightly misleading choice of *q* to represent the glottal catch corresponding to etymological *q̈aaf*, and *q̈* to stand for the voiceless postvelar stop was determined by limitations in the available type font. The other, no less undesirable, alternative would have been to disregard the distinction between *hamza* and *q̈aaf* entirely.

Transcription	Pronunciation	Corresponding Arabic Letter
a	A low vowel, somewhat like the a in 'pat', but usually a little more raised and retracted, toward the e in 'pet' and the u in (American) 'putt'. In the neighborhood of a velarized consonant and sometimes before back consonants, it is considerably retracted — more like the American pronunciation of o in 'pot'.	(*fatḥa*)
b, (*ḅ*)	Bilabial stop, usually voiced. Similar to English b.	ب
d	Voiced dental stop. Similar to English d, but with tongue tip against upper teeth.	د ، (ذ)[1]
ḍ	Like *d*, but velarized. (See below.)	ض ، (ظ)[1]
e	Higher-mid front vowel. Similar to French é as in 'été'. A closer, more even sound than the diphthongal English pronunciation of the a in 'date'.	(none)
ə, (*ᵊ*)	Higher-mid central vowel. Similar to the i in English 'pit', except in the neighborhood of velarized consonants, or before labial or back consonants or *w* or *r*, or before an *o* or *u* in the following syllable — all of which make it sound more like the u in 'put'. Before *ḥ* or *ε*, it sounds somewhat like the u in 'putt'.	(none)[2]
f	Labiodental spirant, usually voiceless. Like English f, except before certain voiced sounds, especially *ḍ* and *ẓ*, where it is often pronounced as a v.	ف
g	Voiced velar/mediopalatal stop. Like English g in 'give', 'sugar'.	(none)
ġ	Voiced postvelar spirant. A smooth "gurgle" produced in the back of the mouth, similar to the g in Spanish 'lago' but more strongly articulated.	غ
h	Glottal continuant. Similar to English h as in 'hill', 'cohort'.	هـ
ḥ	Voiceless pharyngeal spirant. A sharp fricative h-like sound produced entirely in the pharynx (upper throat).	ح
i	High front vowel. Similar to the i in 'machine'.	(*kasra*)
k	Voiceless velar/mediopalatal stop. Like English k in 'kick', 'ankle'.	ك
l, (*ḷ*)	Voiced lateral resonant. Plain *l* has a 'bright' or 'light' quality like the l in English 'leaf', or the standard French or German l. Velarized *ḷ* has a "dark" or "heavy" quality somewhat like the l in English 'bulk' or the "hard" Russian l.	ل

Transcription	Pronunciation	Corresponding Arabic Letter
m, (*ṃ*)	Voiced labial resonant. Like English m.	م
n, (*ṇ*)	Voiced dental/palatal/velar resonant. Similar to English n. Velar articulation before *g* or *k*, as in English 'single', 'rank'.	ن
o	Higher-mid back rounded vowel. Similar to the French ô in 'côte'. Closer, rounder, and more even than the diphthongal English pronunciation of o in 'note'.	(none)
p	Voiceless bilabial stop. Similar to English p.	(none)
q	Glottal catch. Pronounced the same as ʔ. See below.	(ق)[3]
q̈	Voiceless postvelar stop. A retracted k-like sound produced on the soft palate or uvula.	ق[3]
r, (*ṛ*)	Apico-alveolar trill, usually voiced. A single tap when short, and a multiple trill when long (*rr*). Like Spanish or Italian r.	ر
s	Voiceless alveolar sibilant. Generally somewhat sharper and stronger than English s as in 'set', 'miss'.	(ث)[1] ، س
ṣ	Like *s*, but velarized.	ص
š	Voiceless palatal slit spirant. Similar to English sh as in 'ship', 'hush'.	ش
t	Voiceless dental stop. Similar to English t, but with tongue against upper teeth.	(ث)[1] ، ت
ṭ	Like *t*, but velarized. Generally unaspirated (no puff of breath after it).	ط
u	High back rounded vowel. Similar to French ou in 'coupé' or German u in 'Huld'. More rounded than English oo in 'food'.	(*ḍamma*)
v	Voiced labiodental spirant. Like English v.	(none)
w	High back rounded semivowel. Similar to English w.	و
x	Voiceless postvelar spirant. A scraping sound in the back of the mouth, like the German ch in 'Bach'.	خ
y	High front semivowel. Similar to English y in 'yet', 'rayon'.	ى
z	Voiced alveolar sibilant. Similar to English z in 'Zen', 'fizz'.	(ذ)[1] ، ز
ẓ	Like *z*, but velarized.	(ض)[1] ، ظ
ž	Voiced palatal slit spirant. Similar to the French j, or to the English -si- in 'vision'.	ج

Transcription	Pronunciation	Corresponding Arabic Letter
ʔ	Glottal catch. Like the interruption in the middle of 'oh-oh!'.	ء
ɛ	Voiced pharyngeal spirant. A smooth, tense sound produced in the pharynx (upper throat), quite unlike anything in English or other European languages.	ع

Notes:

1. The Classical interdental spirants ذ , ث , and ظ are eliminated from the pronunciation of urban Syrian dialects. Classical ذ usually corresponds to *d* in colloquial words of genuine dialectal origin: *diib* 'wolf', *haada* 'this' — but to *z* in classicisms adapted to colloquial use: *ʔəzᵊn* 'permission', *zakkar* 'to remind'. Similarly, ث corresponds to dialectal *t*: *tlaate* 'three' — and to *s* in classicisms: *musallas* 'triangle'; while ظ most often corresponds to dialectal *ḍ* as in *ḍəhᵊr* 'noon', and to *ẓ* in classicisms, as in *ẓəher* 'to appear'.

2. The small raised letter ᵊ is pronounced the same as ə. While ə occurs as an integral part of words, ᵊ is merely a "helping vowel," used to keep consonants from coming together in unallowable or awkward combinations. For instance, while the combination *zn* may occur before a vowel, as in *ʔəznak* 'your (m./sg.) permission', it cannot occur before another consonant, hence *ʔəzᵊnkon* 'your (pl.) permission', *ʔəzᵊn ʔaxuuk,* your brother's permission'. (Between words, and between hyphenated parts of a word, the helping vowel is written after the space or the hyphen: *ʔarxaṣ ᵊktaab* 'the cheapest book' *hal-ᵊktaab* 'this book'.)

3. Although ق has merged with ء in urban Syrian pronunciation, the two letters are distinguished in our transcription (*q* = ق , ʔ = ء) as an aid in word-recognition for those who are familiar with literary Arabic or with other Arabic dialects. In certain classicisms, however, the true ق-sound is normally used in colloquial speech; this sound is represented here by the symbol *q̈*; *maq̈aal* 'article', *ḥuq̈uuq̈* 'law' (but this is also heard as *ḥquuq,* i.e. pronounced *ḥʔuuʔ*).

VELARIZATION

The velarized or "emphatic" consonants are transcribed with a dot under the letters: *ṣ, ṭ, ẓ, ḍ, ḷ, ṃ, ṇ, ṛ, ḅ*. These sounds are characterized by a "heavy" resonance, which contrasts with the "light" or "thin" sound of the corresponding plain consonants (transcribed without the dot). Velarization is produced mainly by humping up the back of the tongue to narrow the velar and pharyngeal passages. (The front of the tongue, however, must not be retracted.)

Examples of the contrast between plain and velarized sounds:

Plain	Velarized
seef 'sword'............	*ṣeef* 'summer'
tiin 'figs'............	*ṭiin* 'mud, clay'

Plain		Velarized	
diim	'perpetuate'..........	*ḍiim*	'injure'
buuz	'muzzle'..............	*buuẓ*	'ice'
walla	'he appointed'	*waḷḷa*	'by God'

Velarization usually affects more than one sound in a word, and often spreads over a whole word, e.g., *ṣeeḍ* 'hunting, game', *ṃabṣuuṭ* 'contented' Its effect on vowel sounds, especially the backing effect it has on *a* and *ə*, is considerable; compare *ḍall* 'he remained' with *dall* 'he showed', and *ṣəbb* 'pour' with *səbb* 'curse'.

Velarization is usually centered on one of the dental obstruents: *ṭ*, *ḍ*, *ṣ*, *ẓ*. The spread of velarization from these centers is vague but pervasive, and it is to be understood that other sounds in their neighborhood are generally also more or less velarized, even though only the one letter is written with a dot under it. Thus *ḍarb* is pronounced *ḍaṛb* (or *ḍaṛḅ*), *bəṭlaɛ* is pronounced *ḅəṭḷaɛ*, etc.

Only the front consonants — labials and dentals — are significantly affected by velarization. The subscript dot of *ḥ* (used to distinguish it from *h*) does not mean that *ḥ* is a velarized sound.

LONG AND SHORT SOUNDS

Single letters represent sounds that are clipped short, while doubled letters are held for a greater length of time. For example, the word *ˀasar* 'trace, effect' contains only short sounds, while *ˀassar* 'to affect' has a long middle consonant, and *ˀaasaar* 'ruins, antiquities' has two long vowels.

It is essential to distinguish clearly between long and short sounds. Note the contrasts between *marra* 'a time' and *mara* 'a woman', *saaɛa* 'hour' and *saɛa* 'capacity', *sabab* 'cause' and *sabbab* 'to cause', etc.

A doubled consonant before another consonant, however, is often pronounced short. Thus *mɛallme* '(female) teacher' may be pronounced *mɛalme*, while on the other hand *mɛallem* '(male) teacher' must always be pronounced with a long *ll*, since the *ll* is not followed immediately by another consonant.

This reduction in length does not in any case apply to doubled consonants involving a proclitic or an inflectional affix (e.g., the article, the demonstrative, the verbal person-affix *-t* 'you'). Thus the doubled consonant must always be pronounced long in *r-ržaal* 'the men' (as distinct from *ržaal* 'men'), *had-dyaane* 'this religion' (as distinct from *hadyaane* 'calm (f.)'), *baɛattni* 'you (m.) sent me' (as distinct from *baɛatni* 'he sent me').

At the end of a phrase, long sounds do not contrast significantly with short sounds, but a word-final doubled letter shows that the last syllable is accented. Thus, while *ˀamal* 'hope' is accented on the first syllable, *ˀamall* 'more boring' is accented on the last, and while *wara* 'behind' is accented on the first syllable, *waraa* 'behind him' is accented on the last.

All the sounds occur both long and short except *ə*, which is normally always short. Even a long *əə*, however, is transcribed in the expressions *byaano ˀakəə* 'grand piano' and *likəər* 'cordial', to represent the arabicized French sound of eu in 'piano à queue' and 'liqueur'.

ACCENTUATION

The accentuation of most words can be automatically determined by this rule:

The accented syllable is the last one whose vowel is long or followed by more than one (single) consonant. Examples:

Last Syllable Accented	Next-to-Last Accented	Second-from-Last Accented
mhandsíin	*mhándes*	*hándase*
tεalldmt	*tεállam*	*tεállamet*
biqə́ṣṣ	*qə́ṣṣa*	*qə́ṣaṣo*
saamaḥúu	*saamáḥtu*	*sáamaḥu*

If no vowel in the word is long or followed by more than one consonant, then usually the first syllable is accented: *dáras, fə́hem, lúġa, dáraso, báladi, másalan.* However, the accent is not in any case farther forward than the antepenult (second-from-last syllable): *mubaašáratan, ʔila ʔaaxírihi.*

Hyphenated suffixes consisting of *-l-* 'to, for' plus a pronoun count as part of the word they are attached to, and affect the accentuation accordingly: *fatáḥ-lak, fataḥt-ə́llo.* Pronoun objects formed with *-yáa-* are always accented, but they do not change the accentuation of the preceding word: *εaṭáani-yáahon, fatáḥ-lak-yáa.*

Other hyphenated elements (proclitics and enclitics) are never accented, and do not affect the accentuation of the word they are attached to: *bᵊl-bálad, εaṣ-ṣábi, la-had-dáraže, máṭraḥ-ma.*

The helping vowel ᵊ is never accented, and does not count in determining the accentuation of a word: *bə́ḍᵊrbak, fatáḥ-ᵊlkon, tεalldmᵊt* (accented as if the ᵊ were not there, as in *tεalldmt*).

The accent mark (´) is usually (though not always) omitted in the transcription of words that are accented according to the rules given above. Redundant accent marks are used regularly, for instance, in the case of final long vowels, as *maεnáa* 'its meaning', *qaalúu* 'they said it', in order to avoid possible confusion with *máεnaa* 'meaning', *qáaluu* 'they said', often encountered in other transcriptions.

The accentuation of certain kinds of words, however, does not follow these rules; their accented syllable is always marked with ´ over the vowel: *byəštə́ġel, məxtə́lef, muʔtámar, ḍarába, tεallamə́to, ḥaalə́ton.* These exceptional cases include verbs and participial adjectives or nouns of Forms VII and VIII; words with the pronoun suffixes *-a* 'her, it, its' and *-on* 'their, them'; and certain kinds of verb forms with *-ə́t-* 'she, it' plus pronoun object.

ASSIMILATION

The transcription of this dictionary ordinarily does not show partial or total assimilation of a radical to a following consonant. The general policy has been to leave the root consonants intact and recognizable for the reader. Hence, the dictionary transcribes *ʔəžtimaaε* (instead of *ʔəštimaaε*) 'meeting', *ʔaḥsán-lak* (instead of *ʔaḥsál-lak*) 'it is better for you', *saaεadtak* (instead of *saaεattak*) 'I helped you'. On the other hand, affixes, especially the inflectional and base-formative prefix *t-* and the *n*-prefix of Stem VII, are usually shown assimilated: *bədẓənn* (instead of *bətẓənn*) 'you think', *džazza*ʔ (instead of *tžazza*ʔ) 'to be divided', *mmaḥa* (instead of possible *nmaḥa*) 'to be erased'. The following list should enable the user of this dictionary to identify and reproduce the most common varieties of assimilation.

1. Devoicing:

žt → *št*: *məštdmaƐ* 'society', *štahad* 'he worked hard'
dt → *tt*: *ʔaxatto* 'I took it', *Ɛaatto* 'his habit', *məƐᵊtti* 'my stomach'
dx → *tx*: *tatxiin* 'smoking', *matxal* 'entrance'
ds → *ts*: *l-qəts* 'Jerusalem', *səts* 'one sixth'
ḍt → *ṭṭ*: *ʔuuṭṭi* 'my room', *ṭṭarr* 'he was compelled'
Ɛh → *ḥḥ*: *maḥḥa* 'with her'

2. Voicing:

tž → *dž*: *bədžiib* 'you bring', *byəndžu* 'they produce'
td → *dd*: *ddaaxal* 'he interfered', *bədduuq* 'you taste'
tz → *dz*: *bədziid* 'you add', *dzawwaž* 'he got married'
tḍ → *ḍḍ*: *byəḍḍaḥḥak* 'he laughs'
sž → *zž*: *mazžed* 'mosque', *tazžiil* 'registration'
sd → *zd*: *mazduud* 'clogged up'
ṣḍ → *ẓḍ*: *maẓḍar* 'verbal noun'
fž → *vž*: *tavžiir* 'explosion'
fd → *vd*: *navde* 'item'
fz → *vz*: *qavze* 'a jump'
fḍ → *vḍ*: *ʔavḍal* 'preferable', *ḍəvḍaƐa* 'frog'
fẓ → *vẓ*: *ʔavẓaƐ* 'ghastlier'
ḥƐ → *ƐƐ*: *raaƐ Ɛala* 'he went to'
qƐ → *ƐƐ*: *byəƐƐod* 'he sits'

3. Assimilations in position or manner of articulation:

nb → *mb*: *məmbiiƐ* 'we sell', *məm beeruut* 'from Beirut'
nf → *mf*: *mamfaƐa* 'benefit', *ʔəmfo* 'his nose'
nm → *mm*: *məmmuut* 'we die'
nr → *rr*: *mərruuḥ* 'we go'
nl → *ll*: *məllaaqi* 'we find', *ḥal-lak* 'its time for you'
rl → *ll*: *ṣal-lak* 'it happened to you'
bm → *mm*: *m-maḥallak* 'in your place', *mmiil* 'I lean'
bf → *ff*: *f-farᵊšti* 'in my bed', *ffuut* 'I enter'
ṭṣ → *ṣṣ*: *məṣṣaṭṭeḥ* 'lying'
dž → *žž*: *məžžawwez* 'married'
sž → *žž*: *ʔažžaƐ* 'more courageous'

For assimilation by velarization, as *mbaṣaṭt* → *mḅaṣaṭṭ* 'I had a good time', *tṣaṭṭaḥ* → *ṭṣaṭṭaḥ* 'he lay down', *taṣwiit* → *ṭaṣwiiṭ* 'voting', *ṣeed* → *ṣeeḍ* 'hunt', cf. VELARIZATION above.

* * * *

In compiling this dictionary, the authors were ably assisted by a competent staff of both Arabs and Americans. The Arab informants were all native Damascenes with a college background. Foremost mention among them must be made of Mr. Ziad H. Idilby, who made by far the greatest number of invariably reliable contributions. Special acknowledgments are also due to Miss Mary C. Chapple, who, with a fine understanding of the problems of bilingual lexicography and with painstaking accuracy, prepared a large portion of the English corpus, and to Dr. Barbara Freyer Stowasser, who, with great professional competence, did valuable preparatory work on a great number of entries and, in addition, undertook the onerous and traditionally thankless task of reading the proofs and seeing the manuscript through press. Contributions as part-time consultants were made by Mr. A. K. Jallad, Mr. Munir Jabban, Mr. Mouaffac Chatti, Mr. Sadalla Jouejati and Mr. Ali K. Bakri. Miss Alexandra Selim impeccably typed most of the approximately 23,000 slips of the original manuscript. To all of them, the authors wish to express their sincere gratitude for their dedication and for a job well done under sometimes rather strenuous conditions.

The authors are deeply indebted to a colleague and friend, Mr. Mark W. Cowell, who, through fruitful discussion, constructive criticism and knowledgeable advice, rendered invaluable help in clarifying many a difficult point of procedure and substance. Their heartfelt thanks also go to Georgetown University for providing an academic home, and to the authors and administrators of the National Defense Education Act, who made this project possible.

Washington, D. C. K.S.
February 1964 M.A.

Abbreviations

adj.	adjective
adv.	adverb
ap.	active participle
art.	article
cf.	compare
coll.	collective
def.	definite
e.g.	for instance
f.	feminine
fig.	figuratively
foll.	following
imperf.	imperfect
impv.	imperative
invar.	invariable
m.	masculine
n.	noun
perf.	perfect
pers.	personal
pl.	plural
pron.	pronoun, pronominal
sg.	singular
subj.	subject
suff.	suffix

A

a – No indefinite article in Arabic: Do you have a stamp and an envelope? *maεak ṭaabeε w-ẓarəf?* — These eggs are fifty piasters a dozen. *hal-beeḍaat xamsiin qərš əd-dazziine* or *hal-beeḍaat əd-dazziine (b-)xamsiin qərəš* or *b-xamsiin qərəš dazziint əl-beeḍ.* — He makes about a hundred pounds a week. *biṭaalśε-lo ḥawaali miit leera bəž-žəmεa.*

to **abandon** – 1. *hažar (o hažər//nhažar).* They abandoned the house a long time ago. *hažaru l-beet mən zamaan əktiir.* 2. *staġna εan, tarak (o/e tarək).* He has abandoned the whole idea. *staġna εan* (or *tarak) kəll əl-fəkra.*

to **abbreviate** – *xtaṣar.* "*šərke musaahime*" is abbreviated "*šiin miim*", isn't it? "*šərke musaahime*" *btəxtəṣśra "šiin miim", muu heek?*

abbreviation – *ʔəxtiṣaar* pl. *-aat.* I'm afraid these abbreviations will not be understood. *xaayśf-lak hal-ʔəxtiṣaaraat maa tənfśhem.*

ability – 1. *qaabliyye, maqədra.* I don't doubt his ability. *maa εandi šakk əb-qaabliito* (or *əb-maqdərto*). 2. *ʔəmkaaniyye* pl. *-aat, mawhibe* pl. *mawaaheb.* Everybody is aware of his great abilities. *kəll waaḥed byəšεor b-ʔəmkaaniyyaato* (or *b-mawaahbo*) *l-εaẓiime.*

able – *fahmaan, šaaṭeṛ.* Do you know of an able chemist? *btaεref šii kəmyaaʔi fahmaan?*

to be able – *qəder (e ə), ġəḍer (e ə), ḥəsen (e ə).* Will you be able to come? *btəqder təži?*

ablution – *wuḍuuʔ.*

aboard – (a ship) *εal-baaxra, εas-safiine,* (an airplane) *bəṭ-ṭayyaara.* They were all aboard by eight o'clock. *s-saaεa tmaane kaanu kəllon εal-baaxra (bəṭ-ṭayyaara).*

**All aboard! *yaḷḷa ṭlaεu!* or *yaḷḷa rkabu!*

to go aboard – *ṭəleε (a ṭluuε, ṭalεa) εas-safiine (εaṭ-ṭayyaara), rəkeb (a rəkəb, rkuub) bəs-safiine (bəṭ-ṭayyaara).* We went aboard an hour before the boat sailed. *ṭləεna εas-safiine qabəl-ma məšyet əb-saaεa.*

to **abolish** – *laġa (i laġi)* and *ʔalġa//ltaġa* and *nlaġa.* When was slavery abolished in the United States? *ʔeemta ltaġet l-əεbuudiyye bəl-wilaayaat əl-muttaḥide?*

abortion – *taṭriiḥ, ʔəžhaaḍ.*

to have an abortion – *ṭərḥet (a ṭərəḥ).*

to induce an abortion – (in a woman) *ṭarraḥ (əl-mara);* (in oneself) *ṭarraḥet ḥaala.*

abortive – *faašel.* It was an abortive revolution. *kaanet sawra faašle.*

about – 1. *ḥawaali, taqriiban.* There were about thirty people present. *kaan fii ḥawaali tlaatiin šaxəṣ ḥaaḍriin.* 2. *taqriiban.* It's about the same. *taqriiban nafs əš-šii.* 3. *ḥawaali.* We didn't see a living soul about the house. *maa šəfna d-doomari ḥawaali l-beet.* — The village ought to be located about here on this map. *ḍ-ḍeεa εala hal-xaarṭa laazem ətkuun mawžuude ḥawaali hal-manṭiq̌a.* — Her clothes were scattered all about the place. *ʔawaaεiiha kaanu mlaḥwašiin ḥawaali l-maḥall kəllo.* 4. *εan.* They were talking about the war. *kaanu εam yəḥku εan əl-ḥarəb.* — Oh, the letter is about the money he owes me. *ʔee, l-maktuub εan əl-maṣaari yalli bəddi-yaahon mənno.* 5. *b-* My husband is very particular about his food. *žoozi mʔannaf əktiir əb-ʔaklo.*

**Lunch is about ready. *l-ġada raḥa yəxloṣ baεd əšwayye.*

**It's about time you got here! *ḥallak təṣal!*

**What's it all about? *šuu fii?* or *šuu l-əḥkaaye?* or *šuu l-qəṣṣa?*

**How about going to a movie? *šuu raʔyak ənruuḥ εas-siinama?*

**How about your wife? Does she like the house? *kiif martak? ḥaabbe l-beet?*

**What about dinner? (invitation) *šuu raʔyak əb-εaša?* (inquiry) *šuu ṣaar bəl-εaša?*

**What about you? *šuu bən-nəsbe ʔəlak?*

to be about to – *kaan raḥa* or *kaan εala wašak* (with foll. imperf. without *b-*). I was about to send for you when ... *kənt raḥa ʔəbεat waraak lamma ...* — She was about to burst into tears. *kaanet raḥa təflat bəl-bəke.*

above – 1. *fooq˜.* The plane flew high above the clouds. *ṭ-ṭayyaara ṭaaret εaali fooq əl-ġeem.* — He is above suspicion. *huwwe fooq ʔayy šakk.* 2. *fooq.* The vultures were circling above in the sky. *n-nsuura kaanet ḥaayme fooq bəs-sama.* 3. *mən qabəl.* As we have already mentioned above ... *mətəl-ma ḥakeena mən qabəl ...* 4. *saabeq, mazkuur.* The above facts clearly demonstrate that ... *l-maεluumaat əs-saabqa bətwarži b-wuḍuuḥ ʔənno ...*

**He is above average height. *huwwe ʔaṭwal mn əl-muεaddal.*

**Attendance was above that of last week. *εadad əl-ḥaaḍriin kaan ʔaktar mn əž-žəmεa l-ṃaaḍye.*

**A major is above a captain in rank. *l-muq̌addam ʔaεla mn ər-raʔiis bər-rətbe.*

above all – *ʔahamm šii, qabəl kəll šii.* Above all, remember to be on time. *ʔahamm šii, dzakkar ʔənnak təži εal-waqət.*

to be above something – *kaan ʔaεla mən.* She's above such petty things. *hiyye ʔaεla mən ʔašyaaʔ əẓġiire mətəl hayy.* — He is above cheating people. *huwwe ʔaεla mən ʔənno yġəšš ən-naas.*

**He is not above cheating other people. *huwwe muu bεiid εalće yġəšš ən-naas.*

abroad – 1. *barraat˜ l-əblaad, bəl-xaarež.* How long did you stay abroad? *qaddeeš əbqiit barraat l-əblaad?* 2. *εal-xaarež, la-barraat˜ l-əblaad.* Is he going abroad? *raayeḥ εal-xaarež?*

abrupt – 1. *žəfeṣ.* He has a very abrupt manner. *ṭabεo žəfeṣ əktiir.* 2. *fəžaaʔi*.* We noticed an abrupt change in his attitude. *laaḥaẓna taġayyor fəžaaʔi b-taṣarrfo.*

abruptly – 1. *b-žafaaṣa.* He treated me rather abruptly. *εaamalni mətəl-ma tquul əb-žafaaṣa.* 2. *εala ġafle, fažʔatan.* The car stopped abruptly. *s-sayyaara waqqafet εala ġafle.*

absence – 1. *ġyaab, ġeebe.* His absence wasn't even noticed. *mạa ḥada ḥatta laaḥaẓ ġyaabo.* 2. *ġeebe* pl. *-aat.* How many absences have you had this month? *kam ġeebe kaan εandak əb-haš-šahər?*

absent – *ġaayeb, muu mawžuud.* Three members were absent because of illness. *tlətt ʔaεḍaaʔ kaanu ġaaybiin b-sabab əl-maṛaḍ.*

absent-minded – *msahhem, saareḥ əl-fəkər.* He's a regular absent-minded professor. *huwwe ʔəstaaz əmsahhem εal-maẓbuuṭ.*

absolute – 1. *maẓbuuṭ.* That's the absolute truth. *hayye l-ḥaqiiqa l-maẓbuuṭa.* 2. *ʔakiid.* That's an absolute fact. *haada šii ʔakiid* or ***haada ʔamər waaq̌eε.* 3. *məṭlaq̌, kaamel.* The dictator exercises absolute power. *d-dəktatoor bimaares ṣəlṭa məṭlaq̌a.* 4. *b-ḥadd zaato* (f. *zaata* pl. *zaaton*). Absolute moral law. *l-εərf əl-ʔaxlaaq̌i b-ḥadd zaato.*

absolutely – *miyye bəl-miyye, q̌aṭεan, tamaaman.* He's absolutely right. *maεo ḥaqq, miyye bəl-miyye.*

to **absorb** – 1. *ġabb (ə ġabb//nġabb), mṭaṣṣ.* The sponge absorbed the water quickly. *s-sfənže ġabbet əl-ṃayye b-εažale.* 2. *stạwεab.* You can't absorb all that material in a single lesson. *maa btəqder təstawεeb kəll hal-maεluumaat əb-dars waaḥed.*

absorbed in – *ġarqaan b-, ġaaṭeṣ b-, məltśhi* b-.* He was so absorbed in his book, he didn't hear me come in. *kaan ġarqaan b-əktaabo la-daraže ʔənno maa ḥass εaliyyi lamma ʔžiit.*

abuse – 1. *suuʔ˜ ʔəstəεmaal.* This looks like an abuse of his authority. *ẓ-ẓaaher ʔənno haada suuʔ ʔəstəεmaal la-ṣalaaḥiyyaato.* 2. *msabbe* pl. *-aat.* He heaped her with abuse. *ṭamḿra b-əmsabbaat.*

to abuse someone – *saaʔ (i ʔisaaʔa) mεaamalt˜ ḥada, qəsi (a qasaawe) εala ḥada.* He abuses his wife. *bisiiʔ əmεaamalt marto* or *byəqsa εala marto.*

to abuse something – *saaʔ (i ʔisaaʔa) ʔəstəεmaal˜ šii.* He's abusing his authority. *huwwe εam ysiiʔ ʔəstəεmaal ṣalaaḥiyyaato.*

academic – 1. *žaamiεi*.* This question is presently discussed in academic circles. *hal-masʔale btəndśres hallaq bəl-ʔawṣaaṭ əž-žaamiεiyye.* 2. *diraasi*.* The academic year will end on June 30. *s-səne d-diraasiyye btəxloṣ b-ətlaatiin ḥzeeraan.* 3. *naẓari*.* This is a purely academic question, of course. *haada maa fii šakk masʔale*

naẓariyye.
to **accelerate** - **1.** *Eaǧǧal, staEǧal.* The government is trying to accelerate its educational program. *l-ᵊḥkuume Eam ᵊtḥaawel ᵊtEaǧǧel bərnaamǝǧa s-saqaafi.* **2.** *daEas (a daEᵊs) banzin.* Don't accelerate in a curve. *laa tədEas banziin Eal-kuuE.* **3.** *ʔaxad lanṣ, lannaṣ.* The car accelerates with difficulty uphill. *s-sayyaara bəṭṭawwel la-taaxod lanṣ bᵊṭ-ṭluuE.*
acceleration - *taEǧiil;* (of a car) *lanṣ.*
accelerator - *daEset˜* (pl. *-aat˜*) *banziin.*
accent - **1.** *lahǧe* pl. *-aat, lakne* pl. *-aat.* He speaks Arabic with a Druse accent. *byəḥki Earabi b-lahǧe dərziyye.* **2.** *nabra* pl. *-aat.* Where is the accent in this word? *ween ᵊn-nabra b-hal-kəlme?*
to accent - *ḥaṭṭ ᵊn-nabra Eala, šaddad.* Accent the first syllable of this word. *ḥəṭṭ ᵊn-nabra Eal-maqṭaE ᵊl-ʔawwal b-hal-kəlme* or *šadded ʔawwal maqṭaE ᵊb-hal-kəlme.*
to **accept** - *qəbel (a qbuul).* Are you going to accept that position? *raḥa təqbal hal-markaz?*
access: He has access to the files. *ʔəlo ḥaqq bᵊl-ʔəṭṭilaaE Ead-doseeyaat.* -- The army blocked all the access routes into town. *ǧ-ǧeeš sadd kəll ᵊl-manaafed yalli bətwaddi ləl-balad.*
accident - *ḥaades* or *ḥaadse* pl. *ḥawaades,* (traffic, train, plane) *ʔaksidaan* pl. *-aat.* When did the accident happen? *ʔeemta ṣaar ᵊl-ḥaades?*
by accident - *b-ṭariiq˜ ᵊṣ-ṣədfe, bᵊṣ-ṣədfe.* I found it out by accident. *Eréfta b-ṭariiq ᵊṣ-ṣədfe.* -- That didn't happen by accident. *haada maa ḥaṣal ᵊb-ṭariiq ᵊṣ-ṣədfe.*
accidentally - **1.** *ġasban Ean* + pron. suff., *Eafwan.* I dropped the plate accidentally. *wəqeE ᵊṣ-ṣaḥᵊn ġaṣban Eanni.* **2.** *b-ṭariiq˜ ᵊṣ-ṣədfe, bᵊṣ-ṣədfe.* I accidentally learned the truth. *Erəft ᵊl-ḥaqiiqa b-ṭariiq ᵊṣ-ṣədfe.*
to **accommodate** - *ʔaxad (-yaaxod ʔaxᵊd//ttaaxad).* We can only accommodate three more people. *mnəqder naaxod tlətt ʔašxaaṣ taanyiin bass.*
accommodating - *xaduum, laṭiif* pl. *ləṭafa, mraḥḥeb.* The manager was very accommodating. *l-mudiir kaan xaduum ᵊktiir* or ***l-mudiir kaan kəllo ləṭᵊf.*
to **accompany** - **1.** *raafaq, ṣaaḥab.* He accompanied her to the station. *raafáqa ləl-ᵊmḥaṭṭa.* **2.** *raafaq.* She accompanies him on the piano. *bətraafqo Eal-byaano.*
to **accomplish** - **1.** *tammam, xallaṣ.* He accomplished what he set out to do. *tammam yalli kaan naawi yaEᵊmlo.* **2.** *ʔanha, tammam.* Did you accomplish anything in Beirut? *ʔanheet šii b-beeruut?* **3.** *saawa, Eəmel (-yaEmel Eamal//nEamal).* For one day he accomplished quite a lot. *la-yoom waaḥed saawa šii ktiir.* -- He accomplished a good deal in his life. *Eəmel šii ktiir ᵊb-mədđet ḥayaato.* **4.** *ḥaqqaq.* That has accomplished its purpose. *haada ḥaqqaq ġaayto.*
accomplished - *maaher, šaaṭer.* He's an accomplished musician. *huwwe musiiqaar maaher.*
accomplishment - *Eamal* pl. *ʔaEmaal.* His mother was proud of his accomplishments. *ʔəmmo kaanet faxuura b-ʔaEmaalo.* -- That is quite an accomplishment! *haada bsammi̇i Eamal Eaẓiim!*
accord - *ʔəttifaaq.* They acted in complete accord with him. *Eəmlu b-ʔəttifaaq taamm maEo.*
of one's own accord - *ḥasab ʔəxtiyaar-* + pron. suff. of subj., *ḥasab mašiiʔt-* + pron. suff. He did it of his own accord. *Eəmə́la ḥasab ʔəxtiyaaro* (or *ḥasab mašiiʔto*).
in **accordance with** - *ḥasab˜* ... In accordance with your request, we are sending you three more copies. *ḥasab ṭalabak mnəbEát-lak tlətt nəsax taanye.*
according to - *ḥasab˜* ... According to recent statistics, the population has increased by five percent. *ḥasab ᵊl-ʔəḥṣaaʔaat ᵊǧ-ǧdiide Eadad ᵊs-səkkaan zaad xamse bᵊl-miyye.* -- Everything was carried out according to instructions. *kəll šii tnaffaz ḥasab ᵊt-taEliimaat.*
accordingly - *b-muuǧə́b(h)a.* I acted accordingly. *təṣarraft ᵊb-muuǧə́ba.*
accordion - *ʔakordyoon* pl. *-aat.*
account - **1.** *ḥsaab* pl. *-aat.* I have an account in this bank. *Eandi ḥsaab b-hal-bank.* **2.** *waṣᵊf* pl. *ʔawṣaaf,* (official) *taqriir* pl. *taqariir.* His account of the accident isn't clear. *waṣfo ləl-ḥaades muu waaḍeḥ* or *taqriiro Ean ᵊl-ḥaades muu waaḍeḥ.*
**On no account must you open this drawer. *šuu-ma ṣaar laa təftaḥ had-dərᵊǧ.*

accounts - *ḥsaabaat* (pl.). The company's accounts were in good order. *ḥsaabaat ᵊš-šərke kaanu mantaẓmiin.*
on account of - *b-sabab˜* ... The game was postponed on account of rain. *l-ᵊmbaarda tʔaǧǧalet ᵊb-sabab ᵊl-maṭar.*
to call to account - *ḥaasab.* I'll call him to account. *raḥa ḥaasbo.*
to give an account of - **1.** *Eaṭa kašᵊf Eala.* You'll have to give an account of every penny you spend. *laazem taEṭi kašᵊf Eala kəll qərš ᵊbtəṣᵊrfo.* **2.** *waṣaf (-yuuṣef waṣᵊf).* Give me an account of what happened. *wṣə́f-li šuu ḥaṣal.*
to take into account - *ḥasab (e ø) ḥsaab˜ ...,* *raaEa.* You have to take all the factors into account. *laazem təḥseb ḥsaab kəll ᵊl-Eawaamel* or *laazem təḥseb ḥsaabak la-kəll ᵊl-Eawaamel.* -- You will have to take the following propositions into account. *laazem traaEi š-šruuṭ ᵊt-taalye.*
to account for - **1.** *fassar.* How do you account for that? *kiif bətfasser haš-šii?* **2.** *barrar.* You'll have to account for your actions. *laazem ᵊtbarrer taṣarrfaatak.*
accountant - *mḥaaseb* pl. *-iin.*
accurate - *daqiiq.* She's very accurate in her work. *hiyye daqiiqa b-šəġla ktiir.* -- He gave an accurate account of the situation. *Eaṭa waṣᵊf daqiiq ləl-waḍᵊE.*
accurately - *b-dəqqa, Eal-maẓbuuṭ.* She's figured it out accurately. *ḥasbə́ta b-dəqqa.*
accusation - *ʔəttihaam* pl. *-aat, təhme* pl. *təham.* He leveled a number of accusations against them. *waǧǧah Eəddet ʔəttihaamaat ḍəḍḍhon.* -- These are false accusations. *haadi təham baaṭle.*
to **accuse** - *taham (e/o tahᵊm, ʔəthaam//ntaham)* He was accused of theft. *ntaham bᵊs-sərqa* or *tahamúu bᵊs-sərqa.* -- You can't accuse me of being lazy. *maa fiik təthə́mni bᵊl-kaslane.*
accustomed - *mətEawwed, məEtaad.* I'm not accustomed to that. *maa-li mətEawwed Eala haš-šii.*
to get accustomed to - *tEawwad Eala, Etaad Eala.* He can't get accustomed to the strict discipline. *maa fii yətEawwad Ean-niẓaam ᵊl-qaasi.*
ace - *ʔaṣṣ* pl. *ʔṣuuṣ(a).* He has all four aces. *maEo l-ʔarbaE ᵊʔṣuuṣ.*
ache - *wažaE* pl. *ʔawžaaE.*
to ache - *wažaE (-yuužaE* and *-yəžaE wažaE).* My ear aches. *ʔədni Eam tuužaEni.*
to **achieve** - *ḥaqqaq.* He achieved his purpose. *ḥaqqaq ġaayto.*
achievement: Great achievements have been made in science in the course of this century. *l-Euluum ḥaqqaqet nataaʔeǧ Eaẓiime xilaal hal-qarᵊn.* -- Everybody recognized his achievements. *l-kəll qaddar ʔaEmaalo.*
acid - **1.** *ḥamᵊḍ* pl. *ḥawaameḍ, ʔasiid* pl. *-aat.* This solution has a high acid content. *hal-maḥluul fii nəsbet ḥamᵊḍ Eaalye.* **2.** *laadeE.* He made a few acid remarks. *Eəmel kam ᵊmlaaḥaẓa laadEa.*
acidity - *ḥmuuḍa.*
to **acknowledge** - *Etaraf b-.* I am sure all of us will acknowledge the great services he has rendered to our company. *ʔana mətʔakked kəllna raḥa nəEtə́ref ᵊb-xədmaato l-Eaẓiime la-šərkə́tna.*
acorn - *ḥabbet˜* (coll. *ḥabb˜* pl. *-aat˜*) *balluuṭ.*
to **acquaint with** - *Earraf Eala.* First, I want to acquaint you with the facts of the case. *ʔawwal šii bəddi Earrfak Eala ḥaqaayeq ᵊl-qaḍiyye* or ***ʔawwal šii bəddi xalliik təṭṭə́leE Eala ḥaqaayeq ᵊl-qaḍiyye.*
to acquaint oneself with - *ṭṭalaE Eala, tEarraf Eala.* It'll take me a week to acquaint myself with all the problems. *byaaxədni ǧəmEa la-ḥatta ʔəṭṭə́leE Eala kəll ᵊl-mašaakel.*
to get acquainted with - *tEarraf Eala.* You two should get acquainted with each other. *ʔəntu t-tneen laazem tətEarrafu Eala baEᵊḍkon.*
acquaintance - **1.** *maEᵊrfe.* I was very happy to make his acquaintance. *nsarreet ᵊktiir ᵊb-maErə́fto.* **2.** *maEᵊrfe* pl. *maEaaref.* I have many friends and acquaintances in this town. *ʔana Eandi ṣḥaab w-maEaaref ᵊktiir ᵊb-hal-balad.*
**He is an old acquaintance of mine. *maErə́fti fii qadiime* or *baEᵊrfo mən zamaan.*
to **acquire** - **1.** *ḥəṣel (a ḥṣuul//nḥaṣal) Eala.* We acquired the house when my uncle died. *ḥṣəlna Eal-beet baEᵊd-ma maat Eammi.* **2.** *ḥaṣṣal Eala.* He's acquired considerable skill in tennis. *ḥaṣṣal bᵊt-tanəs Eala mahaara laa baʔᵊs fiiha.*
acquisition - *tamallok, ḥṣuul (Eala), taḥṣiil (Eala).*

to **acquit** - *barra.* The jury acquitted him. *l-ᵊmḥal-lafiin barrúu.*
Acre - *ƹakke.*
across - *qaaṭeƹ.* He lives just across the street. *saaken qaaṭeƹ ᵊš-šaareƹ.* — The station is across the river. *l-ᵊmḥaṭṭa qaaṭeƹ ᵊn-nahᵊr.* — The restaurant is across the street from the hotel. *l-maṭƹam qaaṭeƹ ᵊš-šaareƹ mən ƹand ᵊl-ʔoteel.*
to go (walk, ride, etc.**) across** - *qaṭaƹ (a qaṭᵊƹ).* Let's walk across the bridge. *xalliina nəqṭaƹ ᵊž-žəsᵊr.* — This streetcar line goes (right) across town. *xaṭṭ hat-tramwaay byəqṭaƹ ᵊl-balad.*
act - **1.** *ƹamal* pl. *ʔaƹmaal.* That was a selfish act. *haada kaan ƹamal ʔanaani.* **2.** *faṣᵊl* pl. *fṣuul.* I don't want to miss the first act. *maa bəddi ḍawweƹ ᵊl-faṣl ᵊl-ʔawwal.*
**Don't put on an act! *ḥaaže tamsiil!* or *bala tamsiil!*
in the act - *bᵊž-žərm ᵊl-mašhuud.* The burglar was caught in the act. *məsku l-ḥaraami bəž-žərm ᵊl-mašhuud.*
to act - **1.** *tṣarraf.* He acted first and thought after. *ʔawwal šii tṣarraf baƹdeen fakkar.* -- You should act with more modesty. *laazem tətṣarraf ᵊb-tawaaḍoƹ ʔaktar.* -- Don't act like a child! *laa tətṣarraf mətᵊl walad* or ***ḥaažtak waldane!* **2.** *ḥaṭṭ ḥaalo.* I acted as mediator in the dispute. *ḥaṭṭeet ḥaali waaṣṭa bᵊl-xilaaf.* **3.** *massal.* Can she really act? *ṣaḥiiḥ byəṭlaƹ ᵊb-ʔiidha tmassel?*
**Now it's time to act. *hallaq waqt ᵊl-ƹamal.*
to act on - *ƹəmel (-yaƹmel ƹamal) b-, məši (i maši) b-.* I'll act on your advice. *raḥa ʔaƹmel ᵊb-naṣiiḥtak.*
action - **1.** *ƹamal* pl. *ʔaƹmaal.* This situation requires action. *hal-waḍᵊƹ byəṭṭallab ƹamal.* **2.** *ḥawaades* (pl.). The action of the novel takes place in Turkey. *ḥawaades ᵊr-riwaaye btəžri b-tərkiyya.*
**He is a man of action. *huwwe šaxᵊṣ faƹƹaal.*
actions - *taṣarrufaat* (pl.), *ʔaƹmaal* (pl.). His actions are hard to understand. *taṣarrufaato ṣaƹᵊb fəhma.*
to be killed in action - *nqatal bᵊl-maƹrake, ṣaqaṭ (o ṣquuṭ) šahiid.* Their son was killed in action. *ʔəbnon nqatal bᵊl-maƹrake.*
to bring action against - *rafaƹ (a rafᵊƹ) daƹwa ḍədd.* I'm afraid they will bring action against him. *xaayə́f-lak yərfaƹu daƹwa ḍəddo.*
to see action - *ḥaarab.* Where did he see action? *ween ḥaarab?*
to take action - *ƹəmel (-yaƹmel ƹamal).* Has any action been taken on my case? *ƹəmlu šii b-qaḍiiti?*
active - **1.** *ƹaamel.* Are you an active member? *ʔənte ƹəḍu ƹaamel?* **2.** *našiiṭ.* He's still very active for his age. *ləssaato našiiṭ ƹala ƹəmro.* **3.** *ḥarake* (invar.) He has always been very active. *huwwe ṭuul ƹəmro ḥarake.*
activity - **1.** *našaaṭ.* He has to give up all physical activity for a while. *laazem ywaqqef kəll našaaṭ jəsmaani la-mədde.* -- There's very little activity around here on Sundays. *n-našaaṭ hoon ᵊktiir qaliil ʔiyyaam ᵊl-ʔaḥad.* — She engages in a lot of social activities. *fii ƹanda našaaṭ ʔəžtimaaƹi waaseƹ.* **2.** *ḥarake.* Why all the feverish activity over there? *šuu fii la-kəll hal-ḥarake ṣ-ṣaaxbe hniik?*
actor - *mmassel* pl. *-iin.*
actress - *mmassle* pl. *-aat.*
actual - *ḥaqiiqi*.* The actual reason was an entirely different one. *s-sabab ᵊl-ḥaqiiqi kaan ġeer has-sabab.* — Little was known about his actual motives at that time. *b-hadaak ᵊl-waqᵊt šii qaliil kaan maƹruuf ƹan bawaaƹso l-ḥaqiiqiyye.*
actually - **1.** *ƹan ṣaḥiiḥ, fəƹlan.* Did he actually write this letter? *yaa-tə́ra katab hal-maktuub ƹan ṣaḥiiḥ?* **2.** *ƹan ḥaqa.* Do you actually believe that story? *laa yaa, ƹan ḥaqa bətsaddeq hal-qəṣṣa?* **3.** *bᵊl-ḥaqiiqa.* She works here, but her office is actually on the second floor. *btəštə́ġel hoon, laakən bᵊl-ḥaqiiqa maktə́ba bᵊṭ-ṭaabeq ᵊt-taani.* **4.** *fəƹlan.* No one expected it, but he actually spoke fluent Arabic. *maa kaan ḥada mentᵊẓə́ra laakənno fəƹlan ḥaka ƹarabi b-ṭalaaqa.*
acute - **1.** *ḥaadd.* She has acute appendicitis. *ṣaayə́r-lo ʔəltihaab ḥaadd bᵊz-zaayde.* — This triangle has two acute angles. *hal-musallas fii zaawiiteen ḥaaddiin.* **2.** *qawi*.* Dogs have an acute sense of smell. *l-ᵊklaab ƹandon ḥaasset šamm qawiyye.*
to become acute - *štadd, qəwi (a ø).* If the pain becomes acute, call a doctor. *ʔiza qəwi l-wažaƹ, ᵊbƹaat wara doktoor.*
ad - *ʔəƹlaan* pl. *-aat.* Why don't you put an ad in the paper? *leeš maa bəthəṭṭ ʔəƹlaan bᵊž-žariide?*
to **adapt** - *kayyaf.* When traveling in a foreign country, you will have to adapt your conduct to the manners and customs of the local population. *lamma bətsaafer b-balad ġariib laazem ᵊtkayyef taṣarrfak ḥasab ƹaadaat ᵊl-ʔahaali l-maḥalliyye.* — He adapts himself easily. *bikayyef ḥaalo b-ᵊshuule.*
adaptation - *qaabliyyet˜ takyiif.* This plant shows a remarkable degree of adaptation to its environment. *han-nabaat ƹam ywarži qaabliyyet takyiif məḍᵊhše la-waṣaṭo.*
**The play is an adaptation from a French novel. *t-tamsiiliyye məstawḥaaye mən qəṣṣa frənsaawiyye.*
to **add** - **1.** *zaad (i zyaade//nzaad), ḍaaf (i ʔiḍaafe //nḍaaf).* You'll have to add some more sugar, it is not sweet enough. *laazem ᵊdziid šwayyet səkkar, muu ḥəlu kfaaye.* -- I've nothing to add to that. *maa ƹandi šii ḍiif ƹala haada.* -- Add it to my bill. *ḍiifa ƹala ḥsaabi.* -- They added a number of amendments to the original document. *ḍaafu ƹəddet taƹdiilaat ƹas-sanad ᵊl-ʔaṣli.* **2.** *ḥaṭṭ (ə ḥaṭaṭ //nḥaṭṭ).* The soup will taste better if you add a little sugar. *š-šooraba bətṣiir ṭaƹmə́ta ʔaṭyab ʔiza bətḥəṭṭ-ə́lla šwayyet səkkar.*
**He added he would await further orders. *baƹdeen qaal ʔənno raḥa yəntə́ẓer ʔawaamer ᵊždiide.*
to add (up) - *žamaƹ (a žamᵊƹ//nžamaƹ).* Add up these figures! *žmaaƹ hal-ʔaƹdaad.*
to add up to - *ṭəleƹ (a ø).* How much does the bill add up to? *qaddeeš ṭaaleƹ l-ᵊḥsaab?*
**It all adds up to the same thing. *bᵊn-natiiže kəllo mətᵊl baƹḍo.*
addition - **1.** *ʔiḍaafe, zyaade, ḍamm.* The addition of geographical terms would make the dictionary even more useful. *ʔiḍaafet məṣṭalaḥaat žəġraafiyye ƹal-qaamuus ᵊbtaƹᵊmlo ḥatta ʔafyad w-ʔanfaƹ.* **2.** *žamᵊƹ.* Is my addition correct? *žamƹi maẓbuuṭ?*
in addition - *bᵊl-ʔiḍaafe.* In addition he asked for ten pounds. *bᵊl-ʔiḍaafe ṭalab ƹašᵊr leeraat.*
in addition to - *bᵊl-ʔiḍaafe la-, zyaade ƹala.* In addition to his fixed salary, he gets commissions. *bᵊl-ʔiḍaafe la-maƹaašo byaaxod ᵊƹmuule.*
additional - **1.** *ʔiḍaafi*, zaayed.* He gave me an additional amount for incidentals. *ƹaṭaani mablaġ ʔiḍaafi lən-natriyyaat.* **2.** *zyaade.* For an additional dollar, you get a better quality. *b-dolaar ᵊzyaade btaaxod ᵊbḍaaƹa ʔaṭyab.*
address - **1.** *ƹənwaan* pl. *ƹanawiin, ʔadrees* pl. *-aat.* Do you want to write down my address? *bətriid təktob ƹənwaani?* **2.** *xiṭaab* pl. *-aat.* The president delivered an important address. *r-raʔiis ʔalḍa xiṭaab ᵊmhəmm.*
to address - **1.** *ƹanwan//tƹanwan.* The letter is addressed to me. *l-maktuub ᵊmƹanwan ʔəli.* **2.** *ḥaaka, xaaṭab.* How shall I address him? *kiif laazem ḥaakii?* **3.** *waššah.* I would like to address a question to the speaker. *bəddi waššeh suʔaal ləl-xaṭiib.*
Aden - *ƹadan.*
adhesive tape - *ləzzeeqa* pl. *-aat.*
adjective - *ṣifa* pl. *-aat.*
to **adjoin** - *žaawar.* My garden adjoins his. *žneenti mžaawra la-žneento* or ***žneenti w-žneento l-ḥeeṭ bᵊl-ḥeeṭ.*
to **adjourn** - *faḍḍ (a faḍḍ//nfaḍḍ), ʔarža ʔ.* They adjourned the meeting till Tuesday. *faḍḍu l-ʔəžtimaaƹ la-yoom ᵊt-talaata.*
to **adjust** - **1.** *ẓabbaṭ, ƹaddal.* Did you adjust the opera glasses? *ẓabbaṭṭ ᵊn-naaḍuur?* **2.** *ƹaddal.* He only adjusted a screw. *huwwe ƹaddal bass bərġi.* **3.** *ẓabbaṭ, ṣaḥḥaḥ.* The manager will adjust your bill. *l-mudiir biṣaḥḥə́ḥ-lak ᵊḥsaabak.*
to adjust oneself to - *kayyaf ḥaalo la-, laaʔam ḥaalo la-.* I can't adjust myself to the climate here. *maa fiini kayyef ḥaali ləṭ-ṭaqᵊṣ hoon.*
adjustable - *qaabel lət-taƹdiil.* Is the seat adjustable? *l-kərsi qaabel lət-taƹdiil?*
adjustment - *taƹdiil* pl. *-aat.*
to **administer** - *daar (i ʔidaara//ndaar).* Who's administering his estate? *miin ƹam ydər-lo wərᵊtto?*
administration - **1.** *ʔidaara.* This project requires a well-organized administration. *hal-mašruuƹ byəḥtaaž la-ʔidaara mnaẓẓame.* **2.** *ḥkuume.* The present administration is about to take constructive measures in the unemployment situation. *l-ᵊḥkuume*

l-ḥaaḍra raḥa taaxod ʔəžraaʔaat ʔiižaabiyye b-ᵊxṣuuṣ ᵊl-baṭaale.

admiral – *ʔamiraal* pl. *-aat.*

admiration – *ʔᵊƐžaab (b-).*

to **admire** – *kaan məƐžab b-.* I admire your patience. *ʔana məƐžab b-ṭuulet baalak.*

admission – 1. *daxle, dxuuliyye, foote.* Admission is free. *d-dxuuliyye b-balaaš!* — How much is the admission? *b-qaddeeš ᵊd-daxle?* 2. *duxuul.* There will be no admission before 5 o'clock. *d-duxuul maa bikuun qabl ᵊs-saaƐa xamse.* 3. *ʔəƐtiraaf* pl. *-aat.* His admission proved my innocence. *ʔəƐtiraafo ʔasbat baraaʔti.*

admission charge – *rasᵊm~* (pl. *rsuum~*) *duxuul, dxuuliyye.* There is no admission charge. *maa fii rasᵊm duxuul.*

to **admit** – 1. *daxxal, fawwat.* Mention my name and they'll admit you. *zkoor ʔəsmi, bidaxxluuk.* 2. *qəbel (a qbuul//nqabal)* He was admitted to (membership in) the club. *nqabal la-Ɛəḍwiit ᵊn-naadi* or *nqabal bᵊn-naadi.* 3. *Ɛtaraf.* I admit that I was wrong. *bəƐtəref ʔənni kənt ğalṭaan.*

to **adopt** – 1. *tbanna.* My friend has adopted a little boy. *ṣaaḥbi tbanna walad ᵊẓğiir.* 2. *Ɛtanaq.* They adopted Islam toward the end of the first century. *Ɛtanaqu l-ʔəslaam ḥawaali ʔaaxer ᵊl-qarn ᵊl-ʔawwal.* 3. *waafaq Ɛala.* They adopted the measure unanimously. *waafaqu Ɛala hat-tadbiir bᵊl-ʔəžmaaƐ.* 4. *ttabaƐ.* Better results could be achieved if we adopted this method. *mnəṣal la-nataayež ʔaḥsan ʔiza ttabaƐna haṭ-ṭariiqa.*

adopted – *mətbanna.* He's an adopted child. *huwwe walad mətbanna.*

adult – *kbiir* pl. *kbaar.* There was milk for the children and coffee for the adults. *kaan fii ḥaliib ləẓ-ẓğaar w-qahwe ləl-ᵊkbaar.*

advance – 1. *taqaddom.* Great advances have been made in medicine during the last few years. *ṣaar fii taqaddom ᵊktiir bᵊṭ-ṭəbb b-hal-kam səne l-maaḍye.* 2. *səlfe* pl. *səlaf.* Can you give me an advance? *btəqder taƐṭiini səlfe?*

in advance – *qabl ᵊb-salaf.* Let me know in advance if you're coming. *xalliini ʔaƐref qabl ᵊb-salaf ʔiza kənt raḥa təži.*

to advance – 1. *raffaƐ//traffaƐ.* He was advanced rapidly. *traffaƐ ᵊb-sərƐa.* 2. *tqaddam.* We advanced twenty miles in one day. *tqaddamna Ɛəšriin miil b-yoom waaḥed.* 3. *sallaf//tsallaf.* Could you advance me some money? *btəqder tsallə́fni šwayyet maṣaari?*

advantage – *ḥasane* pl. *-aat* and *maḥaasen, faayde* pl. *fawaayed.* This method has advantages and disadvantages. *haṭ-ṭariiqa ʔəl(h)a maḥaasen w-masaawe ʔ.*

to one's advantage – *la-maṣlaḥto, la-ṣaalḥo.* This is to your advantage. *haada la-maṣlaḥtak.*

to have an advantage over – *mtaaz Ɛala.* You have an advantage over me in having a degree. *btəmtaaz Ɛaliyyi b-šahaadtak* or ***kafftak raažḥa Ɛala kaffti b-šahaadtak.*

to take advantage of someone – *staġall ḥada, ləƐeb (a ləƐᵊb) Ɛala ḥada.* Don't let people take advantage of you. *laa txalli n-naas təstaġəllak* (or *təlƐab Ɛaleek*).

to take advantage of something – *ntahaz šii, ğtanam šii.* He takes advantage of every opportunity. *byəntəhez kəll fərṣa.*

**Thanks, I'll take advantage of your offer. *šəkran, bəqbal Ɛarḍak ᵊb-kəll mamnuuniyye.*

advantageous – *mufiid, naafeƐ.*

adventure – *mġaamara* pl. *-aat, mxaaṭara* pl. *-aat, mžaazafe* pl. *-aat.*

adverb – *ẓarᵊf* pl. *ẓruufe.*

to **advertise** – *ʔaƐlan (Ɛan).* The store is advertising a sale. *l-maḥall Ɛam yaƐlen Ɛan rəxṣa.* — They're advertising for a cook. *Ɛam yaƐᵊlnu bəddon ṭabbaaxa.*

advertisement – 1. *ʔəƐlaan* pl. *-aat.* I saw your advertisement. *šəfᵊt ʔəƐlaanak.* 2. *diƐaaye.* Her clothes are a good advertisement for her dressmaker. *ʔawaƐiiha diƐaaye mniiḥa la-xayyaaṭə́ta.*

advertising – *diƐaaye.* Our company spends a lot on advertising. *šərkə́tna btəṣrof ᵊktiir Ɛad-diƐaaye.*

advice – *naṣiiḥa* pl. *naṣaayeḥ.* My advice is to leave immediately. *naṣiiḥti ʔənno tətrok ḥaalan.*

to ask someone's advice – *ṭalab (o ṭalab) naṣiiḥet~ ḥada, stašaar ḥada.* I asked his advice. *ṭalabᵊt naṣiiḥto.*

to give advice – *naṣaḥ (a nəṣᵊḥ), Ɛaṭa naṣiiḥa.* It's hard to give advice in this matter. *ṣaƐb ᵊl-waaḥed yənṣaḥ b-hal-mawḍuuƐ.*

advisable – 1. *ʔaḥsan.* I think it advisable that we stay home today. *bẓənn ʔənno ʔaḥsan nəbqa bᵊl-beet ᵊl-yoom.* 2. *məstaḥsan.* I don't think that's advisable at the moment. *maa bəƐtə́qed ʔənno haš-šii məstaḥsan bᵊl-waqt ᵊl-ḥaali.* — Would that be an advisable step to take? *btəƐtə́qed ʔənno hal-xaṭwe məstaḥsane?*

to **advise** – *naṣaḥ (a naṣᵊḥ* and *naṣiiḥa).* What do you advise me to do? *šuu btənṣaḥni ʔaƐmel?* — He advised me against it. *naṣaḥni ḍəḍḍa* or *naṣaḥni maa saawiiha.*

adviser – *məršed* pl. *-iin,* (official) *məstašaar* pl. *-iin.* Who is his adviser? *miin mərᵊšdo?*

advisory – *ʔəstišaari*.*

aerial – 1. *ʔanṭeen* pl. *-aat.* The aerial on our radio needs fixing. *ʔanṭeen ᵊr-raadyo tabaƐna bəddo taṣliiḥ.* 2. *žawwi*.* Aerial warfare. *ḥarᵊb žawwi.*

affair – 1. *ʔamᵊr* pl. *ʔmuur, šaʔᵊn* pl. *šʔuun.* I don't meddle in his affairs. *maa bəddaaxal b-ᵊʔmuuro.* 2. *šəğᵊl.* That's your affair. *haada šəğlak ʔənte.* 3. *šaʔᵊn* pl. *šʔuun.* He handled the affairs of the company badly. *daar ᵊšʔuun ᵊš-šərke b-šəkᵊl sayyeʔ.* 4. *šii* pl. *ʔašyaaʔ* and *ʔašya.* That dance was the most brilliant affair of the season. *l-ḥafle r-raaqṣa kaanet ʔalmaƐ šii bᵊl-muusem.* 5. *Ɛalaaqa.* The cook had an affair with the chauffeur. *ṭ-ṭabbaaxa kaan ʔəla Ɛalaaqa maƐ ᵊš-šofoor.*

to **affect** – 1. *ʔassar Ɛala* or *b-.* That damp climate affected his health. *haṭ-ṭaqṣ ᵊr-rəṭeb ʔassar Ɛala ṣaḥḥto.* — His wife's death affected him deeply. *moot marto ʔassar fii ktiir.* 2. *tṣannaƐ, ẓẓaahar.* He likes to affect indifference in a time of crisis. *biḥəbb yəṭṣannaƐ Ɛadam ᵊl-mubaalda bᵊl-ʔazmaaṭ.*

affected – 1. *məṭṣanneƐ.* Don't be so affected! *laa tkuun hal-qadd məṭṣanneƐ!* or ***ḥaaštak taṣannoƐ baqa!* 2. *məṣṭanaƐ, mətkallef.* Does he always write such an affected style? *šuu daayman byəktob ᵊb-ʔəsluub məstanaƐ matᵊl haada?*

to **afford**: I can't afford that. (financially) *maa byəṭlaƐ b-ʔiidi ʔəštə́ri haada* or *maaddiiti maa btəsmdḥ-li ʔəštə́ri haada;* (to do something) *maa fiyyi ʔaƐmel haš-šii.* — You can afford to laugh. *fiik təḍḥak ʔənte — šuu Ɛala baalak maa xaṣṣak.*

to be **afraid** – *xaaf (a xoof).* Don't be afraid. *laa txaaf.* — He's not afraid of anyone. *muu xaayef mən ḥada.* — I'm afraid it's too late for that. *xaayə́f-lak maḍa l-waqᵊt la-haš-šii.*

Africa – *ʔafriiqya.*

African – *ʔafriiqi*.*

after – 1. *baƐᵊd~.* Can you call me up after supper? *btəqder ᵊttalfə́n-li baƐd ᵊl-Ɛaša?* — Day after day he would come to the same place. *yoom baƐᵊd yoom kaan yəži la-nafs ᵊl-maḥall.* 2. *wara~.* They left, one after the other. *raaḥu, waaḥed wara t-taani.* 3. *Ɛala ʔəsᵊm~ ...* The building is named after the first president of the republic. *l-binaaye msammaaye Ɛala ʔəsᵊm ʔawwal raʔiis ləž-žamhuuriyye.* 4. *Ɛala.* Keep arranging the material after this pattern. *xalliik Ɛam ᵊtratteb ᵊl-mawaadd Ɛala han-namaṭ.* 5. *baƐᵊd-ma.* I answered immediately after I received his letter. *žaawabᵊt ḥaalan baƐᵊd-ma stalamt maktuubo.*

after all – 1. *bᵊn-natiiže.* You were right after all. *bᵊn-natiiže, kaan ᵊl-ḥaqq maƐak.* 2. *laa tənsa.* What can I do? After all, he's my friend? *šuu baƐmel? laa tənsa, huwwe ṣaaḥbi.*

after that – *baƐdeen, baƐᵊdha.* After that we went for a walk. *baƐdeen rəḥna məšwaar.*

after this – *mən hallaq w-raayeḥ.* After this, please let us know in advance. *mən hallaq w-raayeḥ ʔaržuuk xalliina naƐref qabl ᵊb-salaf.*

day after tomorrow – *baƐᵊd bəkra.* I'll see you day after tomorrow. *bšuufak baƐᵊd bəkra.*

to be after someone – *dawwar Ɛala ḥada.* The police are after him. *š-šərṭa Ɛam ᵊddawwer Ɛalée.*

to look after – *Ɛaṭa baalo Ɛala.* Is there anyone to look after the children? *fii ḥada yaƐṭi baalo Ɛaẓ-ẓğaar?*

to take after – *ṭəleƐ (a ṭalƐa) la-.* The boy takes after his father. *l-walad byəṭlaƐ la-ʔabúu.*

afternoon – *baƐd ᵊḍ-ḍəhᵊr.* The afternoon was rather dull. *baƐd ᵊḍ-ḍəhᵊr kaan ᵊšwayye mməll.* — You may set aside the afternoons for your own work. *fiik ᵊtxalli kəll yoom baƐd ᵊḍ-ḍəhᵊr mənšaan šəğlak.* — He goes home every afternoon at three. *biruuḥ Ɛal-beet kəll yoom ᵊs-saaƐa tlaate baƐd ᵊḍ-ḍəhᵊr.*

in the afternoon – *baƐd ᵊḍ-ḍəhᵊr.* I never have coffee in the afternoon. *maa bəšrab qahwe ʔabadan baƐd ᵊḍ-ḍəhᵊr.*

this afternoon - *l-yoom baЄd ᵊḍ-ḍəhᵊr.* Can you come this afternoon? *btəqder təži l-yoom baЄd ᵊḍ-ḍəhᵊr?*

afterward(s) - *baЄᵊdha, baЄdeen.* He came at ten and I left shortly afterwards. *ʔəža s-saaЄa Єašara, w-ʔana daššarᵊt baЄᵊdha b-ᵊšwayye.* -- I'll talk to you afterwards. *bəḥki maЄak baЄdeen.*

Agadir - *ʔaġadiir.*

again - **1.** *marra taanye, taani marra, kamaan.* I'll tell him again. *raḥa qəl-lo marra taanye.* -- Try again! *žarreb marra taanye!* **2.** *kamaan.* I'll pay you that and half as much again. *bədfəЄ-lak hadool w-nəṣṣon kamaan.* -- That's another matter again. *hauda mawḍuuЄ taani kamaan.* **3.** *mən žiha taanye.* Again, we should consider the other proposal too. *mən žiha taanye, laazem ᵊnsiin ᵊl-ʔəqtiraaḥ ᵊt-taani kamaan.*

to do something again - *radd* or *rəžeЄ (a) Єəmel šii.* She went to Beirut again. *raddet raaḥet la-beeruut.* -- We'll visit the castle again. *mənrədd mənzuur ᵊl-qalЄa (marra taanye).*

again and again - *marra baЄᵊd marra.* I told him again and again. *qəlt-əllo marra baЄᵊd marra.*

never ... again - *maa Єaad ... ʔabadan.* He never made that mistake again. *maa Єaad Єəmel hal-ġalṭa ʔabadan.*

over and over again - *marra baЄᵊd marra.* He tried over and over again. *ḍall yžarreb marra baЄᵊd marra.*

time and (time) again - *marra w-marrteen.* Time and again I told him not to play in the street. *marra w-marrteen qəlt-əllo laa təlЄab bᵊṭ-ṭariiq.*

against - **1.** *qəddaam˜.* Put the table against the wall. *ḥəṭṭ ᵊṭ-ṭaawle qəddaam ᵊl-ḥeeṭ.* **2.** *Єala.* Don't lean against the window. *laa təstə́ned Єaš-šəbbaak.* **3.** *Єakᵊs, ḍədd.* We had to swim against the current. *nžabarna nəsbaḥ Єaks ᵊt-tayyaar.* **4.** *ḍədd.* Are you for this plan or against it? *ʔənte maЄ hal-xəṭṭa wəlla ḍədda?* -- We must take measures against illiteracy. *laazem nəttə́xez tadabiir ḍədd ᵊl-ʔəmmiyye.* **5.** *mənšaan, məšaan.* He has been saving money against his retirement. *Єam yṣammed maṣaari mənšaan taqaaЄdo.* **6.** *mqaabel.* 50 ships went through the Canal as against 35 last month. *xamsiin baaxra maraqu bᵊl-qanaat ᵊmqaabel xamsda w-tlaatiin bᵊš-šahr ᵊl-maaḍi.*

age - **1.** *Єəmᵊr, sənn.* Tell me your age and occupation. *qəl-li Єəmrak w-məhᵊntak.* -- He's about my age. *Єəmro taqriiban qadd Єəmri.* **2.** *Єaṣᵊr* pl. *Єuṣuur.* This is the age of invention. *haada Єaṣr ᵊl-ʔəxtiraaЄ.*

in ages - *mən zamaanaat.* We haven't seen them in ages. *mən zamaanaat maa Єədna šəfnaahon.*

of age - *raašed.* Is he of age? *huwwe raašed?*

to come of age - *balaġ (o bluuġ) sənn ᵊr-rəšᵊd.* He'll come of age next year. *s-səne ž-žaaye raḥa yəbloġ sənn ᵊr-rəšᵊd.*

to age - **1.** *xatyar.* He has aged a great deal lately. *bᵊl-mədde l-ʔaxiira xatyar ᵊktiir.* **2.** *tЄattaq.* They let the wine age for a number of years. *bixallu l-xamr yətЄattaq la-Єəddet ᵊsniin.*

agency - **1.** *wakaale* pl. *-aat.* Our company has an agency in Beirut. *šərkətna ʔəlha wakaale b-beeruut.* **2.** *daaʔira* pl. *dawaaʔer.* All government agencies will be closed tomorrow for the holiday. *kəll dawaaʔer l-ᵊḥkuume msakkra bəkra məšaan ᵊl-Єiid.*

agent - **1.** *wakiil* pl. *wəkala.* Your agent has already called on me. *wakiilkon ʔəža w-zaarni.* **2.** *Єamiil* pl. *Єəmala.* He is said to be a communist agent. *biquulu Єanno huwwe Єamiil šiyuuЄi.*

to **aggravate** - *ʔazzam, šaddad.* These factors will probably aggravate the situation. *məḥtamal ʔənno hal-Єawaamel ᵊtʔazzem ᵊl-waḍᵊЄ.*

aggravation - *taʔazzom.* Their repeated demands only led to an aggravation of the present tension. *ṭalabaathon l-ᵊmkarrara maa ʔaddet ʔəlla la-taʔazzom ᵊt-tawattor ᵊl-ḥaali.*

aggression - *Єədwaan.*

agitation - *ʔəḍṭiraab* pl. *-aat, qalaq.*

ago - **1.** *mən, qabᵊl.* I was there two months ago. *kənt ᵊhniik mən šahreen.* **2.** *mən.* How long ago was that? *mən ʔeemta kaan haš-šii?* -- That was a long time ago. *haada kaan mən zamaan.*

(just) a moment ago - *qabᵊl laḥẓa.* Wasn't he here a moment ago? *maa kaan hoon qabᵊl laḥẓa?*

a while ago - *qabl ᵊšwayye.* He left a while ago. *tarak qabl ᵊšwayye.*

agony - *Єazaab.* You're just prolonging the agony. *ʔənte bass Єam ᵊṭṭawwel ᵊl-Єazaab.* -- It was agony just to watch him. *šoofto b-ḥadd zaatha kaanet Єazaab.*

to **agree** - **1.** *ṭṭaabaq, twaafaq.* The two statements don't agree. *t-taṣriiḥeen maa byəṭṭaabaqu.* **2.** *ttafaq.* We agreed to take turns. *ttafaqna nətbaadal ᵊd-door.* -- We've agreed on everything. *ttafaqna Єala kəll šii.* -- That's not what we agreed on. *haada muu yalli ttafaqna Єalée.* **3.** *waafaq.* Do you agree? *bətwaafeq?* -- Do you agree to these terms? *bətwaafeq Єala haš-šruuṭ?* -- Do you agree with me? *bətwaafəqni?* -- **4.** *waata, naasab.* This food doesn't agree with me. *hal-ʔakᵊl maa biwaatiini* (or ***maa byəmši maЄi*).

agreeable - *ẓariif.* She has an agreeable disposition. *ṭabЄa ẓariif.*

to be agreeable - *waafaq.* Is he agreeable to that? *huwwe mwaafeq Єala haš-šii?*

agreement - **1.** *ʔəttifaaqiyye* pl. *-aat.* The agreement has to be ratified by the Senate. *l-ʔəttifaaqiyye laazem tətsaddaq mən mažles ᵊš-šuyuux.* **2.** *mwaafaqa.* The contract was extended by mutual agreement. *l-Єaqd ᵊtmaddad b-ᵊmwaafaqa mətbaadle.*

to be in agreement - **1.** *ttafaq, kaan Єala ʔəttifaaq.* We're all in agreement on that. *kəllna məttəfqiin Єala haada* or *kəllna Єala ʔəttifaaq Єala haš-šii.* **2.** *waafaq.* Are you in agreement with me? *bətwaafəqni?* or *bətwaafeq maЄi?* **3.** *twaafaq, ṭṭaabaq.* This is definitely not in agreement with the original terms of the contract. *haada ḥatman maa byətwaafaq maЄ ᵊšruuṭ ᵊl-Єaqd ᵊl-ʔaṣliyye.*

to come to an agreement - *wəṣel (-yəṣal* and *yuuṣal wṣuul) la-ʔəttifaaq, twaṣṣal la-ʔəttifaaq, ttafaq.* I hope we can come to an agreement. *nšaaḷḷa nəṣal la-ʔəttifaaq.* -- We came to an agreement on that point. *wṣəlna la-ʔəttifaaq Єala han-nəqṭa.*

agricultural - *ziraaЄi**.

agriculture - *z(i)raaЄa.* Inquire at the Department of Agriculture. *sᵊʔaal wazaart ᵊz-ziraaЄa.* -- There isn't much agriculture in this region. *maa fii zraaЄa ktiir b-hal-manṭiqa.*

aground - see **run.**

ahead - **1.** *saabeq.* He's ahead of everybody. *huwwe saabeq ᵊl-kəll.* -- Who's ahead? *miin saabeq?* **2.** *qabᵊl.* Are you next? - No, he's ahead of me. *ʔənte t-taani? — laʔ, huwwe qabli.*

straight ahead - *dəġri.* Go straight ahead. *ʔəmši dəġri.*

to be way ahead in - *sabbaq ᵊktiir b-.* I'm way ahead in my work. *ʔana mṣabbeq ᵊktiir ᵊb-šəġli.*

to be way ahead of - *sabaq (e/o sabᵊq) ḥada b-ᵊktiir.* Hurry up, the others are way ahead of us already. *xəffa, l-baqaaya sabaquuna b-ᵊktiir.*

to get ahead - *tqaddam.* He doesn't seem to get ahead somehow. *ẓ-ẓaaher la-sabab mn ᵊl-ʔasbaab maa Єam yətqaddam.*

to go ahead - **1.** *kammal.* Just go ahead. Don't let me stop you. *kammel, laa txalliini waqqfak.* **2.** *sabaq (e/o sabᵊq).* You go ahead, I'll follow later. *sbəqni w-ʔana bə́lḥaqak baЄdeen.*

**Go ahead and take it! *ruuḥ xədha!*

**All right, go ahead and tell him! *ṭayyeb, qəl-lo la-šuuf!*

aid - **1.** *msaaЄade, maЄuune.* The country received quite a lot of economic aid in the past few years. *l-ᵊblaad ḥaṣlet Єala məqdaar ᵊkbiir mən l-ᵊmsaaЄade l-ʔəqtiṣaadiyye xilaal ᵊs-sniin ᵊl-maaḍye.* **2.** *ʔəsЄaaf.* I gave him first aid. *Єməlt-əllo ʔəsЄaaf ʔawwali.*

to aid - *saaЄad, Єaawan.* Can I aid you in any way? *fiini saaЄdak ᵊb-šii?*

aide - *mЄaawen* pl. *-iin, msaaЄed* pl. *-iin.* The Minister consulted his top aides before he made the decision. *l-waziir ᵊstašaar ʔahamm mЄaawniino qabᵊl-ma Єəmel qaraaro.*

ailing - *mariiḍ* pl. *mərada, ḍaЄfaan.* She's always ailing. *hiyye daayman mariiḍa.*

aim - **1.** *hadaf* pl. *ʔahdaaf.* His aim is to become a famous doctor. *hadafo yṣiir doktoor mašhuur.* **2.** *nišaan.* Is your aim good? *nišaanak maẓbuuṭ?*

to aim - **1.** *hadaf (o hadᵊf), neešan.* Aim higher. *hdoof la-ʔaЄla.* -- Aim at the upper right-hand corner of the target. *neešen Єala zaawiit ᵊl-hadaf ᵊl-yamiiniyye l-Єəlya.* **2.** *qaṣad (o qaṣᵊd).* What do you aim to do? *šuu qaaṣeḍ ᵊtsaawi?* -- That was aimed at me. *hayy kaanet maqṣuuḍe ʔəli* or ***hayy kənᵊt ʔana l-maqṣuuḍ fiiha.*

**You're aiming too high in life. *ṭumuuḥak muu maЄquul bᵊl-ḥayaat.*

air - **1.** *žaww.* The upper layers of the air. *ṭabaqaat ᵊž-žaww ᵊl-Єəlya.* **2.** *hawa.* The air in this room is bad. *l-hawa b-hal-ʔuuḍa ɛaaṭel.* -- I have to get some fresh air. *laazəmni šwayyet hawa naqi.*

**There's an air of mystery about the whole affair. *b-hal-qəṣṣa kəlla fii šii ğaameḍ.*

in the air - 1. *bəž-žaww.* A spirit of unrest was in the air. *kaan fii šuɛuur qalaq bəž-žaww.* **2.** *mɛallaq.* They left me in the air for some time. *daššaruuni mɛallaq la-mədde.*

to be on the air - *ʔazaaɛ (i ʔizaaɛa).* This station is on the air from six a.m. till midnight. *hal-əmḥaṭṭa bədziiɛ mn əs-sətte ṣ-ṣəbəḥ la-nəṣṣ əl-leel.*

to put on airs - *tɛanṭaẓ, tfašwar.* He loves to put on airs. *biḥəbb yətɛanṭaẓ.*

to air - *hawwa.* Would you please air the room while I'm out? *mən faḍlak hawwi l-ʔuuḍa b-əğyaabi.*

air base - *qaaɛde* (pl. *qawaaɛed) žawwiyye.*

to **air-condition** - *kayyaf hawa˜* ... They're going to air-condition the entire building. *laḥa ykayyfu hawa l-binaaye kəlla.*

air conditioning - *takyiif˜ hawa.* Do you have air conditioning at home? *fii ɛandkon takyiif hawa bəl-beet?*

aircraft - *ṭayyaara* pl. *-aat.*

aircraft carrier - *ḥaamlet˜* (pl. *-aat˜*) *ṭayyaaraat.*

airfield - *maṭaar.* We'll meet at the airfield. *mnəžtəməɛ bəl-maṭaar.*

Air Force - *silaaḥ əṭ-ṭayaraan, l-qùwwaat əž-žawwiyye.*

airline(s) - *xṭuuṭ žawwiyye* (pl.).

airliner - *ṭayyaara* (pl. *-aat*) *tižaariyye.*

air mail - *bariid žawwi.** Send the package by air mail. *bɛaat əṭ-ṭarəd bəl-bariid əž-žawwi.*

airplane - *ṭayyaara* pl. *-aat.* How long does it take by airplane? *qaddeeš əbtəthammal bəṭ-ṭayyaara?*

airport - *maṭaar* pl. *-aat.*

air pressure - *ḍağəṭ˜ hawa.*

air raid - *ğaara* (pl. *-aat*) *žawwiyye.*

air sick - *daayex (bəṭ-ṭayyaara).* I was airsick during most of the trip. *b-ʔaktar əl-ʔawqaat bəs-safra kənət daayex (bəṭ-ṭayyaara).*

to get airsick - *daax (u dawaxaan* and *dooxa) bəṭ-ṭayyaara.* I get airsick easily. *bduux qawaam bəṭ-ṭayyaara.*

airsickness - *dooxet˜ ṭayyaara.*

airtight: The jars have to be sealed airtight. *l-qaṭramiizaat laazem yətsakkaru b-ṣuura maa yfət-lon l-hawa.* -- It looked as if we had an airtight case against him. *ẓahər-əlna ʔənno kaan ɛanna qaḍiyye ḍəḍḍo bəl-miyye miyye raabḥa.*

aisle - *mamarr* pl. *-aat.* Our seats are in the second row close to the aisle. *maḥallaatna bəṣ-ṣaff əṭ-ṭaani žanb əl-mamarr.*

ajar - *mašquuq.* The door was ajar. *l-baab kaan mašquuq.*

alarm - 1. *ʔənzaar* pl. *-aat.* What's that alarm mean? *šuu byəɛni hal-ʔənzaar?* **2.** *mnabbeh* pl. *-aat.* Set the alarm for six. *rbooṭ l-əmnabbeh ɛas-sətte.*

**Who turned in the alarm? *miin xabbar əl-ʔəṭfaaʔiyye?*

to alarm - *nabbah.* Her screams alarmed the whole building. *ṣarxaata nabbahet əl-binaaye kəlla.*

to be alarmed - *qəleq (a qalaq).* Don't be alarmed. *laa təqlaq.*

alarm clock - *mnabbeh* pl. *-aat, saaɛa* (pl. *-aat*) *mnabbeh.* I bought myself a new alarm clock yesterday. *štareet əmnabbeh əždiid əmbaareḥ.*

Albania - *ʔalbaanya.*

Albanian - *ʔalbaani**.

alcohol - *sbeetro.* Use only pure alcohol. *staɛmel əsbeetro ṣərəf bass.* -- We have to cook by alcohol. *laazem nəṭbox ɛas-sbeetro.*

alcoholic - 1. *mədmen ɛal-xamər.* She's an alcoholic. *hiyye mədəmne ɛal-xamər.* **2.** *ruuḥi**. We don't carry alcoholic beverages. *maa mənbiiɛ mašruubaat ruuḥiyye.*

Aleppo - *ḥalab.*

alert - *fəteḥ.* He's an alert fellow. *huwwe (zalame) fəteḥ.*

on the alert - *ɛala ʔəstəɛdaad.* Be on the alert for a call from me. *kuun ɛala ʔəstəɛdaad la-mxaabara mənni.*

Alexandretta - *l-ʔəskandaroon(e).*

Alexandria - *l-ʔəskandariyye.*

Aley - *ɛaalée.*

Algeria - *ž-žazaaʔer.*

Algerian - *žazaaʔiri**.

Algiers - *ž-žazaaʔer.*

alien - *ʔažnabi** pl. *ʔažaaneb.* All aliens must register. *kəll əl-ʔažaaneb laazem yətsažžalu.*

alike - 1. *mətəl baɛḍ-* + pron. suff. These seats are all alike. *hal-maqaaɛed kəllon mətəl baɛḍon.* -- We treat all customers alike. *mənɛaamel kəll əz-zabaayen mətəl baɛḍon.* **2.** *sawa.* This law applies to men and women alike. *hal-qaanuun byəṭṭabbaq ɛar-ržaal wən-nəswaan sawa.*

alive - 1. *ɛaayeš.* Get him dead or alive! *žiibo ɛaayeš ʔaw mayyet.* **2.** *ṭayyeb.* Is your grandmother still alive? *səttak ləssaata ṭayybe?*

**I feel more dead than alive. *ʔana halkaan mn əṭ-taɛab.*

alive to - *ṣaḥyaan la-.* He's very much alive to the danger. *huwwe ṣaḥyaan tamaam ləl-xaṭar.*

alive with - *malaan˜* ... The pantry is alive with ants. *beet əl-muune malaane naməl.*

to keep alive - 1. *bəqi (a baqayaan) ɛaayeš, ḍall (a ḍall) ɛaayeš.* It's a miracle they kept alive. *məɛəžze ʔənnon bəqyu ɛaayšiin.* **2.** *xalla ɛaayeš.* He makes barely enough to keep his family alive. *doobo yaɛmel maṣaari kfaaye txalli ʔahlo ɛaayšiin.*

all - 1. *kəll˜.* That upsets all my plans. *haada bixarbeṭ kəll mašariiɛi.* -- Did you all go? *rəḥtu kəllkon?* -- That is beyond all doubt. *haada fooq kəll šakk.* -- That's all there is to it. *haada kəll maa fi l-ʔamər.* -- She was all happiness and joy. *kaanet kəlla faraḥ w-suruur.* -- My brother is all for fun and amusement. *ʔaxi kəllo ləl-baṣəṭ wəl-lahu.* -- The bread's all gone. *xalleṣ kəll əl-xəbəz.* -- The snow's all gone. *t-taləž kəllo daab.* **2.** *l-kəll.* All were convinced that ... *l-kəll kaanu məqtənɛiin ʔənno* ... **3.** *kəll šii.* That's all. *haada kəll šii.* **4.** *ṭuul˜.* I've been waiting all day. *ṣar-li ṭuul ən-nhaar ɛam ʔənṭəẓer.*

**He isn't all there. *huwwe maṣṭuul.*

**All's not well in their marriage. *fii šii b-əžwaazə́ton muu maaši.*

**If that's all there is to it, I'll do it. *ʔiza baṣiiṭa b-haš-šəkəl baɛməla.*

**That's all I needed! *haada lli kaan naaqə́ṣni!*

**She all but succeeded. *maa kaanet beenha w-been ən-nažaaḥ ʔəlla šaɛra* or *kaan baaqi-lha šaɛra ẓğiire la-tənžaḥ.*

**It's all but decided. *maa bəqi ʔəlla yəṭlaɛ əl-qaraar.*

**He comes home to lunch at all hours. *byəži ɛal-ğada ʔeemta-ma bəddo.*

**This place stays open till all hours. *hal-maḥall biḍall faateḥ la-ɛand əl-fažər.*

**He was creeping on all fours. *kaan maaši ɛal-ʔarbɛa.*

all along - *daayman, ṭuul əl-waqət.* We've suspected him all along. *šakkeena fii daayman.*

all in - *halkaan mn əṭ-taɛab.* I'm all in. *ʔana halkaan mn əṭ-taɛab.*

all in all - *ɛal-ʔəžmaal.* All in all, he's not a bad fellow. *ɛal-ʔəžmaal huwwe zalame muu ɛaaṭel.*

all of a sudden - *ɛala ğafle.* All of a sudden it got dark. *ɛala ğafle ṣaaret əd-dənye ɛəṭme.*

all over - 1. *kəll qərne, kəll maṭraḥ.* They came from all over. *ʔəžu mən kəll qərne.* **2.** *kəll˜.* He traveled all over the country. *daar l-əblaad kə̀lla.* -- He trembled all over. *kaan ɛam yərtažž kəllo.*

**It's all over. *kəll šii xalaṣ* or *xalṣet əš-šağle.*

all right - 1. *tamaam.* Is everything all right? *šuu kəll šii tamaam?* -- Don't worry, it'll be all right. *laa tənšə́ğel, kəll šii laḥa ykuun tamaam.* -- Is that all right with you? *haada tamaam maɛak?* **2.** *ṭayyeb.* All right, I'll do it. *ṭayyeb, laḥa saawiiha.* -- It's done all right, but how? *ṭayyeb, ənɛamlet əš-šağle, bass šuuf əšloon?!* -- That's true all right, but nevertheless ... *ṭayyeb, haada maẓbuuṭ, bass maɛ heek* ...

**That's all right! (in reply to an apology) *baṣiiṭa!* or *maɛleešii!*

**I think it's all right with him. *bẓənn maa ɛando maaneɛ.*

**He knows why, all right. *saddeq huwwe byaɛref leeš.*

**I'll get even with you all right! *saddeq ləssa bṣaffi ḥsaabi maɛak!*

**I'd like to go, all right, but it's impossible. *žaaye ɛala baali ruuḥ, bass məstaḥiil.*

**He'll be all right again in a few days. *biṭiib b-hal-kam yoom.*

all set - *mətḥaḍḍer.* We were all set to go to a movie. *kənna mətḥaḍḍriin ənruuḥ ɛas-siinama.*

all the - *kamaan.* When he'll get this news his

joy will be all the greater. *lamma laha yəṣalo hal-xabar farəhto laha tkuun kamaan ʔakbar.*

all the better - *bikuun ʔaḥsan.* If that is so, all the better. *ʔiza kaan heek, bikuun ʔaḥsan.*

all the same - 1. *kəllo waaḥed, mətəl baʕḍo.* That's all the same to me. *kəllo waaḥed bən-nəsbe ʔəli.* 2. *maʕ heek, maʕ zaalek.* All the same, you should do something about it. *maʕ heek, ʔaḥsán-lak taʕmel šii b-haš-šaġle.*

all the time - *daayman, ʕala ṭuul.* She's complaining all the time. *hiyye daayman btəštáki.* -- I've known about it all the time. *kənət ʕala ṭuul daryaan fiiha.*

all told - *ʕal-ʔəžmaal.* All told, he's not a bad fellow. *ʕal-ʔəžmaal, huwwe zalame muu ʕaaṭel.*

above all - *ʔahamm šii, qabəl kəll šii.* Above all, don't get discouraged. *ʔahamm šii maa tətxaazal.*

after all - 1. *bən-natiiže.* He's right, after all. *bən-natiiže, l-ḥaqq maʕo.* 2. *laa tənsa.* What can I do? After all, he's my friend. *šuu baʕmel? laa tənsa huwwe ṣaaḥbi.*

at all - *ʔabadan, bəl-marra, mnoob.* He has no patience at all. *maa ʕando ṣabər ʔabadan.*

**Do you know him at all? *ʔəlak ʔayy maʕərfe fii?*

**Do you know any English at all? *btaʕréf-lak ʔayy šii bəl-ʔəngliizi?*

in all - *bəl-ʔəžmaal.* How many are there in all? *qaddeeš əl-ʕadad bəl-ʔəžmaal?*

not at all - 1. *maa ... ʔabadan, maa ... bəl-marra, maa ... mnoob.* I don't know him at all. *maa baʕərfo ʔabadan.* -- I'm not at all tired. *maa-li taʕbaan ʔabadan.* 2. *ʔabadan.* But I told you so! - Not at all! *bass ʔana qəlt-əllak heek! - ʔabadan!* 3. (in reply to an apology) *baṣiiṭa!* or *maʕleešii!* 4. (in reply to thanks) *laa šəkər ʕala waažeb!* or *l-ʕafu* or *ʔahla w-sahla!* or *maa fii šii mən waažbak!* or *maa fii šii məhrez!* or *ʔastaġfiru ḷḷa!*

on all fours - *ʕal-ʔarbʕa.* He was creeping on all fours. *kaan maaši ʕal-ʔarbʕa.*

once and for all - *la-ʔawwal w-ʔaaxer marra.* Once and for all, let's get this over with. *la-ʔawwal w-ʔaaxer marra xalliina nəxṣom haš-šaġle.* -- I'm telling you once and for all, stop it! *ʕam qəl-lak la-ʔawwal w-ʔaaxer marra: xalaṣna baqa!*

Allah - *ʔaḷḷa.*

alley - *ṣqaaq* pl. *-aat.*

alliance - *ḥələf* pl. *ʔaḥlaaf* and *ḥluuf.* The two countries formed an alliance. *d-dawəlteen ʕəmlu ḥələf.*

to **allow** - 1. *samaḥ (a samaaḥ) b-.* He won't allow that. *maa byəsmaḥ əb-haš-šii.* 2. *qaam (i ø).* How much will you allow me for my old car? *qaddeeš laha tqəm-li sayyaarti l-qadiime?* -- How much should I allow for traveling expenses? *qaddeeš laazem qiim la-kəlfet əs-safar?* -- He doesn't allow himself a minute's rest. *maa biqiim la-ḥaalo w-laa daqiiqet raaḥa.*

allowance - 1. *xaržiyye* pl. *-aat.* How much allowance do you get a week? *qaddeeš btaaxod xaržiyye bəž-žəmʕa?* 2. *taʕwiiḍ* pl. *-aat.* They pay us a regular salary plus special allowances. *byədfaʕúu-lna maʕaaš maaši w-taʕwiiḍaat xaaṣṣa.*

to make allowance - *ḥasab (e ø) ḥsaab la-.* You've got to make allowance for his inexperience. *laazem təḥseb əḥsaab la-qəllet xəbərto.*

ally - *ḥaliif* pl. *ḥəlafa.* They are our allies. *hənne ḥəlafaaʔna.*

to ally oneself with - *tḥaalaf maʕ.* They allied themselves with their neighbors. *tḥaalafu maʕ žiiraanon.*

almond - *looze* coll. *looz* pl. *-aat.*

almost - 1. *taqriiban.* I'm almost finished. *taqriiban xalaṣət.* -- He's almost drunk. *huwwe taqriiban sakraan.* 2. *kaan ʕala wašak ʔənno ..., kaan laha* + imperf. without *b-.* We were almost ready to give up when ... *kənna ʕala wašak ʔənno nəstaslem lamma ...* or *kənna laha nəstaslem lamma ...* -- I'd almost come to the party if it hadn't been for my friend's unexpected arrival. *kənət ʕala wašak əž-žayye ʕal-ḥafle law-la waṣlet ərfiiqi ʕala ġafle* or *kənət laha ʔəži ʕal-ḥafle ...* -- He almost fell. *kaan laha yəqaʕ.*

alms - *ṣadaqa* pl. *-aat.* Traditionally, people distribute alms to the poor at the end of Ramadan. *l-ʕaade ʔənno n-naas bifarrqu ṣadaqaat ʕal-fəqara b-ʔaaxer ṛamaḍaan.*

almsgiving - *ʔəḥsaan.*

alone - *waḥd-* + pron. suff., *la-ḥaal-* + pron. suff. Do you live alone? *saaken waḥdak?* -- You alone can help me. *ʔənte waḥdak btəqder ətsaaʕədni.* -- Better leave it alone. *ʔaḥsán-lak tətrə́ka waḥda.* -- Leave me alone! *trəkni la-ḥaali!* or **ruuḥ ʕanni! or **fraqni!

along - 1. *ʕala ṭuul~ ...* We walked along the shore. *mšiina ʕala ṭuul əš-šaṭṭ.* 2. *maʕ.* The road runs along the river. *ṭ-ṭariiq byəmši maʕ ən-nahər.* -- What this job requires is diligence along with a sense of responsibility. *l-waẓiife hayye bədda ʔəžtihaad maʕ šuʕuur bəl-masʔuuliyye.*

all along - *ʕala ṭuul, daayman.* I said so all along. *haada yalli qəlto ʕala ṭuul.*

alphabet - *ḥruuf əl-hižaaʔ* (pl.), *ʔaleef bee.* The Arabic alphabet consists of 28 letters. *ḥruuf əl-hižaaʔ əl-ʕarabiyye* (or *l-ʔaleef bee tabaʕ əl-ʕarab*) *fiiha tmaanda w-ʕəšriin ḥarəf.*

alphabetical - *mhažžaʔ.* You find an alphabetical index at the end of the book. *bətlaaqi fahras əmhažžaʔ əb-ʔaaxer l-əktaab.*

alphabetically - *ʕala ḥasab ət-təhžaaye.* Arrange the cards alphabetically. *ratteb l-əkruute ʕala ḥasab ət-təhžaaye.*

already - 1. *sabaq* (uninflected) *w-* + verb in perf. Thank you, I've eaten already. *ṣaḥḥteen, sabaq w-ʔakalət* or **ṣaḥḥteen, ʔaakel. -- I've told you already, haven't I? *sabaq w-qəlt-əllak, muu heek?* -- They had already left when we arrived. *sabaq w-raaḥu lamma wṣəlna.* 2. *byəsboq* (inflected) *w-* + verb in imperf. So you'll be already there by the time I arrive? *šuu btəsboq w-bətkuun əhniik waqət-ma ʔuuṣal ʔana?* 3. *ṣaar* (inflected). It's already five o'clock. *ṣaaret əs-saaʕa xamse.* -- It's getting dark already. *ṣaaret əd-dənye ʕam ətʕattem.* -- It's already time to eat. *ṣaar waqt əl-ʔakəl.*

**I'm afraid it's too late already. *xaayə́f-lak ykuun faat əl-waqət.*

also - *kamaan.* May I have some of that also? *məmken ʔaaxod šwayye mən haad kamaan?*

altar - *mazbaḥ* pl. *mazaabeḥ.*

to **alter** - *ṣallaḥ//tṣallaḥ.* I'll have to have the suit altered. *laazem ṣalleḥ əl-badle.*

alteration - 1. *taṣliiḥ* pl. *-aat.* My overcoat needs a few alterations. *manṭooyi laazmo šwayyet taṣliiḥaat.* 2. *taʕdiil* pl. *-aat.* We'll have to make a few alterations in the text of the speech. *laazem naʕməl-lna šwayyet taʕdiilaat əb-naṣṣ əl-xəṭbe.*

alternative - 1. *taani.* I can't see any alternative solution. *maa-li šaayef ʔanu ḥall taani.* 2. *xiyaar.* They left us no alternative. *maa xallúu-lna xiyaar.*

**Both alternatives seem little attractive. *ṭ-ṭariiqteen ət-tənteen maa-lon məġəryiin əktiir.*

although - *maʕ ʔənno.* I'll be there, although I have very little time. *raḥa kuun əhniik, maʕ ʔənno waqti dayyeq.*

altitude - *ʔərtifaaʕ* pl. *-aat, ʕəlu.* The plane was flying at a very high altitude. *ṭ-ṭayyaara kaanet ṭaayra ʕala ʔərtifaaʕ ʕaali ktiir* (or *b-ʕəlu ʕaali ktiir*).

altogether - 1. *tamaam.* You're altogether right. *maʕak ḥaqq tamaam.* 2. *bəl-ʔəžmaal.* Altogether there are thirty books. *bəl-ʔəžmaal byəṭlaʕúu-lon tlaatiin əktaab.*

(taken) altogether - *ʕal-ʔəžmaal.* Taken altogether, this plan is good. *ʕal-ʔəžmaal, hayye xəṭṭa mniiḥa.*

aluminum - *ʔalamənyoom.*

always - *daayman, daaʔiman, ʕala ṭuul.* I'm always at home. *ʔana daayman bəl-beet.*

**She's always been rich. *mən ṭuul ḥayaata kaanet zangiile.*

amateur - *haawi* pl. *huwaat.* Frequently amateurs play better than professionals. *ʕal-ġaaleb əl-huwaat əbyəlʕabu ʔaḥsan mn əl-məḥtərfiin.* -- For an amateur he paints quite well. *ka-waaḥed haawi rasmo laa baʔəs.*

to **amaze** - *dahaš (e dahše).* His indifference amazed me. *qəllet əmbaalaato dahšətni.*

to be amazed at - *ndahaš mən.* I was amazed at the size of the town. *ndahašət mən kəbr əl-balad.*

amazing - *mədheš.* He told me an amazing story. *ḥakḍa-li ḥkaaye mədəhše.*

amazement - *dahše.*

ambassador - *safiir* pl. *səfara.*

amber - 1. *kahraba.* Are these rosary beads genuine amber? *šuu ḥabb hal-masbaḥa kahraba ʔaṣliyye?* 2. *ʕasali*.* She has beautiful amber hair. *ʕaleeha šaʕər ʕasali ḥəlu.*

ambergris - *ʕanbar.*

ambiguous - *məltəbes, ġaameḍ.*
ambition - *ṭmuuḥ.* There's no limit to his ambition. *maa fii ḥadd la-ṭmuuḥo.*
ambitious - *ṭamuuḥ.*
ambulance - *sayyaaret˜* (pl. *-aat˜*) *ʔəsƐaaf.* This man is hurt! Call an ambulance! *haz-zalame mažruuḥ! ṭləb-lo sayyaaret ʔəsƐaaf!*
ambush - *kamiin.* They lay in ambush. *kaanu mətrabbṣiin ᵊb-kamiin.*
to ambush - *kaman (o ø) la-, Ɛəmel kamiin la-.* The patrol was ambushed outside the village. *kamanu ləd-dawriyye barraat ᵊḍ-ḍeeƐa.*
America - *ʔameerka, ʔamariika.*
American - *ʔameerkaani** pl. *ʔameerkaan.* There were three Americans on the plane that crashed. *kaan fii tlaate ʔameerkaan bᵊṭ-ṭayyaara halli tḥaṭṭamet.*
Amman - *Ɛammaan.*
ammunition - *zaxiire* pl. *zaxaayer.*
amnesty - *Ɛafu Ɛaamm.*
among - *been, beenaat.* Look among the papers! *ṭalleƐ been l-ᵊwraaq!* -- He's popular among the masses. *huwwe maḥbuub been sawaad ᵊn-naas.* -- You're among friends. *ʔənte been rəfaqaatak.* -- We decided it among ourselves. *Ɛtamadna Ɛaleeha beenaatna* (or *been baƐᵊḍna*). -- They can't even agree among themselves. *maa byəqᵊdru ḥatta yəttəfqu beenaat baƐḍon.* -- Settle that among yourselves. *fəḍḍuuha beenaat baƐᵊḍkon.*
among other things - *w-bᵊž-žəmle.* Among other things he collects stamps. *w-bᵊž-žəmle byəžmaƐ ṭawaabeƐ.* -- Among other things he told me ... *w-bᵊž-žəmle qal-li ...*
amount - 1. *mablaġ* pl. *mabaaleġ.* What's the amount he paid? *qaddeeš ᵊl-mablaġ yalli dafaƐo?* 2. *kammiyye, məqdaar.* We'll never finish that amount of work in one day. *b-ḥayaatna maa mənxalleṣ hal-kammiyye mn ᵊš-šəġl ᵊb-yoom waaḥed.*
a certain amount of - *šwayyet˜* ... That work requires a certain amount of patience, of course. *ṭabƐan haš-šaġle bədda šwayyet ṣabᵊr.*
to amount to - 1. *ṭaleƐ (a ø).* How much does the bill amount to? *qaddeeš byəṭlaƐ l-ᵊḥsaab?* -- However you look at it, it amounts to the same thing. *kiif-ma ṭṭallaƐᵊt Ɛaleeha btəṭlaƐ mətᵊl baƐḍa.* 2. *səwi (a ø).* He doesn't amount to much. *maa byəswa (šii) ktiir.* -- His knowledge doesn't amount to a row of beans. *maƐrəfto maa btəswa nḥaase.*
**He allowed him to resign, but it amounted to a dismissal. *samḥ-lo yəstaƐfi, laaken bᵊl-ḥaqiiqa kaanet ᵊl-Ɛamaliyye ṣarf mən ᵊl-xədme.*
to **amputate** - *batar (o/e batᵊr//nbatar), qaṭaƐ (a qaṭᵊƐ//nqaṭaƐ).* His foot was amputated. *bataru rəžlo.*
amulet - (Muslim) *ḥžaab* pl. *-aat* and *ḥəžᵊb;* (Christian) *ḥərᵊz* pl. *ḥruuze.*
to **amuse** - *salla.* That amuses me very much. *haada bisalliini ktiir.* -- Do you find this play amusing? *šaayef hat-tamsiiliyye msallye?*
to amuse oneself - *salla nafso, tsalla.* He amuses himself by reading. *bisalli nafso bᵊl-ᵊqraaye.*
amusement - *təslaaye.* He did it only for amusement. *Ɛəməla bass lət-təslaaye.* -- What do you do for amusement here? *šuu fii Ɛandkon təslaaye hoon?*
amusement tax - *ḍariibet˜* (pl. *ḍaraayeb˜*) *malaahi.*
analogous - *ʕiyaasi**. Can you think of analogous verb forms? *btəqder ᵊtfakker ᵊb-ṣiyaġ ʔafƐaal ʕiyaasiyye?*
analogy - *ʕiyaas* pl. *-aat.* I arrived at this conclusion by simple analogy. *twaṣṣalᵊt la-hal-ʔəstəntaaž ᵊb-maḥḍ ᵊl-ʕiyaas.*
analysis - *taḥliil* pl. *-aat* and *taḥaliil.* A chemical analysis proved that the solution contained some 45% sulphuric acid. *t-taḥliil ᵊl-kiimaawi dall Ɛala wžuud xamsda w-ʔarᵊbƐiin bᵊl-miyye ḥamᵊḍ kəbriit bᵊl-maḥluul.*
in the final analysis - *xulaaṣt ᵊl-ḥaki.* In the final analysis, the problem is really not so complicated as it may look. *xulaaṣt ᵊl-ḥaki, l-məšᵊkle bᵊl-ḥaqiiqa maa-la mƐaqqade qadd-maa-la mbayyne.*
to **analyze** - *ḥallal.* When you analyze this case, you'll find two striking facts. *lamma tḥallel hal-masʔale laḥa tlaaqi ḥaqiiqteen mədᵊhšiin.*
anarchism - *fawḍawiyye.*
anarchist - *fawḍawi** pl. *-iyyiin* and *-iyye.*
anarchy - *fawḍa.*
Anatolia - *l-ʔanaḍool.*
anatomic(al) - *tašriiḥi**.
anatomy - *Ɛəlm˜ ᵊt-tašriiḥ.*
ancestor - *žədd* pl. *ʔažḍaad* and *žduud.* His ancestors came from the upper Jezirah. *ʔažḍaado byənḥədru mən ʔaƐaali ž-žaziire.*
anchor - *mərsaaye* pl. *maraasi.* The boat lost its anchor in the storm. *l-markab ḍawwaƐ mərsaayto bᵊl-Ɛaaṣfe.*
to cast (or **drop**) **anchor** - *rasa (i rasu).* The ship dropped anchor in the bay. *l-baaxra raset bᵊl-xaliiž.*
to lie (or **ride**) **at anchor** - *kaan raasi.* Our boat lay at anchor in the bay. *markabna kaan raasi bᵊl-xaliiž.*
to weigh anchor - *rafaƐ (a rafᵊƐ) ᵊl-mərsaaye.* We weighed anchor after the storm had passed. *rafaƐna l-mərsaaye baƐᵊd-ma raaḥet ᵊl-Ɛaaṣfe.*
to anchor - *rassa.* They anchored the ship out in the bay. *rassu s-safiine barra bᵊl-xaliiž.*
**He stood there as if he were anchored to the spot. *kaan waaqef ᵊhniik kaʔənno mbasmar bᵊl-ʔaṛᵊḍ.*
anchovy - *ʔaanšwa.*
ancient - 1. *Ɛatiiq* pl. *Ɛətaq.* Why did you invest so much money in that ancient building? *leeš ḥaṭṭeet kəll hal-maṣaari b-hal-binaaye l-Ɛatiiqa?* 2. *qadiim* pl. *qədama.* I'm very much interested in ancient art. *ʔana ktiir məhtamm bᵊl-fann ᵊl-qadiim.* -- Oh, that's ancient history! *haa, hayye qəṣṣa qadiime* or **haa, hayye qəṣṣa ʔakal Ɛaleeha d-dahᵊr w-šəreb.*
and - 1. *w-.* Only my brother and I were there. *bass ʔana w-ʔaxi kənna hniik.* 2. *u-.* Two and two is four. *tneen u-tneen ʔarᵊbƐa.* 3. *wiyyaa-* + pron. suff. You and I know about it, and nobody else. *bass ʔana wiyyaak mnaƐref Ɛanha, maa fii ḥada ġeerna.*
and so forth (or **on**) - *ʔila ʔaaxirihi, w-Ɛala heek.* I need paper, ink, and so on. *bəddi waraq w-ḥəbᵊr ʔila ʔaaxirihi.*
anesthetic - *banᵊž, mxadder* pl. *-aat.*
angel - *malaak* pl. *malaayke.*
anger - *zaƐal.* What's all this anger about? *leeš kəll haz-zaƐal?* -- In his anger, he said a lot of things he didn't really mean. *b-zaƐalo ḥaka ʔašyaaʔ ᵊktiire maa kaan byəqṣod fiiha šii.*
angle - 1. *zaawye* pl. *zawaaya.* Measure each angle of the triangle. *qiis kəll zaawye bᵊl-musallas.* 2. *naaḥye* pl. *nawaaḥi, žiha* pl. *-aat.* We considered the matter from all angles. *darasna l-mawḍuuƐ mən kəll ᵊn-nawaaḥi.* 3. *ʔəsluub* pl. *ʔasaliib.* Why, that's an entirely new angle of his! *haa, haada ʔəsluub ᵊždiid mənno!*
angry - 1. *zaƐlaan.* I haven't seen him so angry very often. *bᵊn-naader-ma šəfto zaƐlaan heek.* 2. *naašef.* His angry words must have hurt her more than he thought. *kalaamo n-naašef laazem ykuun žarḥha ʔaktar məmma tṣawwar.*
to be or **get angry about, at** or **with** - *zəƐel (a zaƐal) mən.* What are you angry about? *mən ʔeeš zaƐlaan?* -- Please don't be angry with me! *bətražžaak laa təzƐal mənni!* -- Why did you get so angry at him? *leeš ᵊzƐəlᵊt kəll hal-qadd mənno?*
to make angry - *zaƐal (e zaƐal)* This remark must have made him very angry. *hal-ᵊmlaaḥaẓa laazem ᵊtkuun zaƐᵊlto ktiir.*
animal - 1. *ḥaywaan* pl. *-aat* and *ḥawawiin, bahiime* pl. *bahaayem;* (hoofed farm animals) *daabbe* pl. *dawaabb.* Have you fed the animals yet? *ṭaƐmeet ᵊl-ḥaywaanaat wəlla ləssa?* 2. *ḥaywaani**. The doctor told me to avoid all animal fat for a while. *l-ḥakiim qal-li ʔəmtəneƐ Ɛan kəll ᵊd-dhuun ᵊl-ḥaywaaniyye la-mədde.*
Ankara - *ʔanqara.*
ankle - *kaaḥel* pl. *kawaaḥel.* Did she sprain her ankle? *šuu nfakaš kaaḥəla?*
anniversary - *Ɛiid* pl. *Ɛyaad.* They are celebrating their thirtieth anniversary. *məḥtəfliin ᵊb-Ɛiidon ᵊt-tlaatiini.*
to **announce** - 1. *ʔazaaƐ.* They just announced that on the radio. *mən šwayye ʔazaaƐuu bᵊr-raadyo.* 2. *ʔaƐlan.* They announced their engagement last night. *ʔaƐlanu xuṭuubəton ᵊl-leele l-maaḍye*
announcement - *ʔəƐlaan* pl. *-aat.* I want to make an important announcement. *bəddi ʔaƐmel ʔəƐlaan haamm.*
announcer - *muziiƐ* pl. *-iin.* The announcer has a pleasant voice. *l-muziiƐ ṣooṭo ẓariif.*
to **annoy** - 1. *zaƐaž (e ʔəzƐaaž//nzaƐaž).* Is this man annoying you? *har-rəžžaal Ɛam yəzƐžak?* 2. *daayaq.* Stop annoying the poor dog! *ḥaaže ddaayeq hal-kalb ᵊl-məskiin!*
annoying - *məzƐež.* That's very annoying. *haada šii məzƐež ᵊktiir!* -- She has the annoying habit of always sticking her nose into other people's business. *Ɛandha Ɛaade məzᵊƐže ʔənna daayman btəddaaxal*

b-ᵊšʔuun ᵊl-ġer.

to be annoyed with - *zəƐel (a zaƐal) mən.* I was terribly annoyed with him. *zƐəlᵊt mənno la-daraže.*

another - 1. *taani, kamaan* (invar.). Please give me another cup of coffee. *baḷḷaahi Ɛaṭiini fənžaan qahwe taani.* -- Another week's gone by, and still no news from him. *hayy ʔəsbuuƐ kamaan maḍa w-ləssa maa sməƐna mənno.* 2. *ġeer*~ ... I'd like another pattern. *bəddi ġeer batroon* or *bəddi batroon ġeero.* -- Give me another fork. This one's dirty. *Ɛaṭiini ġeer haš-šooke. hayy wəsxa.*

**I won't hear another word about it. *w-laa kəlme bəddi ʔəsmaƐ baqa Ɛan haš-šaġle!* or *qiimna mən has-siire baqa!*

one another - 1. *baƐḍ-* + pron. suff. of subj. (*ᵊl-baƐḍ*). They saw one another frequently. *šaafu baƐḍon miraaran* or *žtamaƐu maƐ baƐḍon miraaran.* -- They clung to one another, fighting the strong current of the river. *tmassaku b-baƐḍon ᵊl-baƐᵊḍ, w-hənne Ɛam yqaawmu tayyaar ᵊn-nahr ᵊl-qawi.* -- They don't play with one another any more. *maa Ɛaadu Ɛam yəlƐabu maƐ baƐḍon.* -- We depend on one another. *mnəƐtəmed Ɛala baƐᵊḍna ᵊl-baƐᵊḍ.* -- They don't trust one another. *maa fii siqa been baƐḍon.* 2. (sometimes expressed by stem VI of verb:). They're always fighting with one another. *hənne daayman mətƐaalqiin (maƐ baƐḍon).*

answer - 1. *žawaab* pl. *-aat* and *ʔažwibe.* I expect your answer by tomorrow. *ʔana mənṭəẓer žawaabak la-ḥadd bəkra.* 2. *ḥall* pl. *ḥluul.* Nobody can find the answer to that problem. *maa ḥada fii ylaaqi ḥall la-hal-məšᵊkle.*

**He thinks he knows all the answers. *byəƐtəqed ḥaalo byaƐref dawa la-kəll Ɛəlle.*

in answer to - *žawaaban Ɛala.* In answer to your question I would like to say that ... *žawaaban Ɛala suʔaalak ᵊbḥəbb quul ʔənno ...*

to answer - 1. *žaawab Ɛala, radd (ə radd) Ɛala.* Answer my question. *žaaweb Ɛala suʔaali.* -- Would you answer the telephone for me? *rədd Ɛat-talifoon Ɛawaaḍi Ɛmeel maƐruuf.* -- I called but nobody answered. *talfanᵊt bass maa ḥada radd.* 2. *žaawab, radd Ɛala.* Why didn't you answer me? *leeš maa žaawabᵊtni (or raddeet Ɛaliyyi)?* 3. *stažaab, labba.* God will answer your prayer. *ʔaḷḷa byəstažəb-lak (or bilabbi-lak) duƐaak.* 4. *ṭaabaq.* The police picked up three suspects who answer the description of the burglar. *l-booliis kamaš tlatt mašbuuhiin ʔawṣaafon bəṭṭaabeq ʔawṣaaf ᵊl-ḥaraami.* 5. *qaam (u ə) b-.* That should answer our immediate need. *l-maƐquul haada yquum ᵊb-ḥaažətna l-ʔaaniyye.*

**Does that answer your question? *bižiib haada Ɛala suʔaalak?*

ant - *namle* coll. *namᵊl* pl. *-aat.*

antagonism - *Ɛadaawe, xuṣuume.*

to antagonize - *Ɛaada, xaaṣam.* I don't want to antagonize him. *maa bəddi Ɛaadii.*

antelope - *ẓabi* pl. *ẓibaaʔ.*

antenna - *ʔanṭeen* pl. *-aat, hawaaʔi* pl. *-iyyaat.*

anthropologic(al) - *ʔantropolooži*.*

anthropologist - *ʔantropolooži* pl. *-iyyiin.*

anthropology - *ʔantropoloožiya.*

anti-aircraft gun - *madfaƐ muḍaaḍḍ* (pl. *madaafeƐ muḍaaḍḍa*) *ləṭ-ṭayyaraat.*

Anti-Atlas - *žbaal ᵊl-ʔaṭlaṣ ᵊṣ-ṣġiir.*

to anticipate - *twaqqaƐ, ntaẓar.* The attendance was larger than we had anticipated. *Ɛadad ᵊl-ḥaaḍriin kaan ʔaktar mənna twaqqaƐna.*

**He anticipates her every wish. *huwwe mətᵊl xaatem maared ᵊb-ʔiidha.*

Anti-Lebanon - *žbaal ləbnaan ᵊš-šarqiyye.*

Antioch - *ʔanṭaakye.*

antique - 1. *ʔantiika* (invar.). Look at this beautiful antique chair! *šuuf hal-kərsi l-ʔantiika l-ḥəlu!* 2. *ʔantiika* pl. *-aat.* Do they sell antiques too in that store? *fii Ɛandon kamaan ʔantiikaat ᵊb-hal-maxzan?*

anxiety - *qalaq.* Her face betrayed her great anxiety. *mbayyen Ɛala wəšša l-qalaq ᵊz-zaayed.*

anxious - 1. *mətšawweq.* I'm anxious to see the new book. *ʔana mətšawweq la-šuuf l-ᵊktaab ᵊž-ždiid.* -- I'm very anxious to see him. *ʔana ktiir mətšawweq la-šoofto.* -- He seemed very anxious for news. *kaan ᵊmbayyen Ɛalée ktiir mətšawweq lᵊl-ʔaxbaar.* 2. *mətḥarreq.* He was very anxious to sell the car. *kaan mətḥarreq ᵊktiir la-ybiiƐ ᵊs-sayyaara.* 3. *qalqaan.* He's anxious about his future. *huwwe qalqaan Ɛala məstaqbalo.*

**He showed himself anxious to please. *kaan kəllo rəġbe la-yərḍi n-naas.*

anxiously - *Ɛala naar.* They waited anxiously for about an hour until the news came in. *ntaẓaru Ɛala naar ḥawaali saaƐa la-ḥatta ʔəža l-xabar.*

any - 1. *ʔayy, ʔanu* f. *ʔani.* Have you any other questions? *fii Ɛandak ʔayy suʔaal taani?* -- Any job is better than none. *ʔani šaġle ʔaḥsan mən bala.* 2. *ḥayyaḷḷa, ʔayy, ʔanu (ʔani).* Any mechanic can fix that. *ḥayyaḷḷa miikaniiki byəqder yṣalləḥa.* -- Any child knows that. *ḥayyaḷḷa walad byaƐrəfa.* 3. *šii.* Did you find any books there? *šəft-əllak šii kətb ᵊhniik?* -- Do you have any money with you? *maƐak šii maṣaari?*

not ... any - *maa ... ʔabadan, maa ... mnoob, maa ... bᵊl-marra.* I don't have any bread. *maa Ɛandi xəbᵊz ʔabadan.*

anybody - 1. *ḥada.* Will anybody be at the station to meet me? *laḥa ykuun ḥada bᵊl-ᵊmḥaṭṭa la-ylaaqii-li?* -- If anybody leaves the house, let me know. *ʔiza ḥada daššar ᵊl-beet Ɛaṭiini xabar.* -- I don't know anybody here. *maa baƐref ḥada hoon.* 2. *ḥayyaḷḷa waaḥed, ʔayy waaḥed, ʔanu waaḥed.* Anybody can do that. *ḥayyaḷḷa waaḥed byəqder yaƐmel haš-šii.* -- We can't take just anybody. *maa mnəqder naaxod ḥayyaḷḷa waaḥed.*

**Everybody who's anybody was there. *kəll waaḥed maƐduud zalame kaan ᵊhniik.*

anyhow - 1. *w-maƐ heek, w-maa ṣaar ʔəlla ...* I said no, but he did it anyhow. *qəlt-əllo laʔ, w-maƐ heek saawaaha* or *qəlt-əllo laʔ, w-maa ṣaar ʔəlla saawaaha.* 2. *b-žamiiƐ*~ *ᵊl-ʔaḥwaal.* I would have gone anyhow. *b-žamiiƐ ᵊl-ʔaḥwaal kənᵊt raayeḥ.* 3. *kiif-ma kaan, Ɛala kəll ḥaal.* Anyhow, that's what she said. *kiif-ma kaan, haada yalli qaalto.*

**What's the use anyhow! *šuu l-faayde, qəl-li!*

anyone - 1. *ḥada.* If anyone needs help, send him to me. *ʔiza ḥada bəddo msaaƐade, bƐat-li-yda.* -- Has anyone asked for me while I was out? *fii ḥada saʔal Ɛanni b-ᵊġyaabi?* -- But I don't know anyone in that town. *bass maa baƐref ḥada b-hal-balad.* 3. *ḥayyaḷḷa waaḥed, ʔayy waaḥed, ʔanu waaḥed.* Anyone can do that. *ḥayyaḷḷa waaḥed byəqder ʔysaawi haš-šii.*

anything - 1. *šii.* Did he say anything? *qaal šii?* -- If anything goes wrong, you'll be responsible. *ʔiza šii ṣaar xaṭaʔ, bətkuun ʔənte l-masʔuul.* -- I can't do anything in this case. *maa bəqder ʔaƐmel šii b-hal-ḥaale.* -- I don't know anything about it. *maa baƐref šii Ɛan haš-šaġle.* 2. *ḥayyaḷḷa šii, ʔayy šii, ʔanu šii.* You can have anything you like here. *btəqder taaxod ʔayy šii byəƐžbak hoon.*

anything but - *kəll šii ʔəlla.* He can do anything but that. *byəqder yaƐmel kəll šii ʔəlla haš-šaġle.*

**I was anything but pleased with it. *ʔabadan maa kənᵊt raḍyaan Ɛan haš-šaġle.*

**She's anything but bright. *maa fiiha w-laa nəqṭet zaka.*

anything else - *ʔayy šii taani, ʔayy šii ġeero.* Would you like anything else? *bəddak ʔayy šii taani?*

not for anything - *maa ... (w-laa) b-ʔayy taman.* I wouldn't do that for anything. *maa baƐməla w-laa b-ʔayy taman.*

anyway - 1. *b-žamiiƐ*~ *ᵊl-ʔaḥwaal.* She didn't want to come anyway. *b-žamiiƐ ᵊl-ʔaḥwaal maa rəḍyet təži.* 2. *kiif-ma kaan, Ɛala kəll ḥaal.* Anyway, we're not responsible for his mistakes. *kiif-ma kaan, maa-lna masʔuuliin Ɛan ʔaxṭaaʔo.* -- Sooner or later you'll have to buy a car anyway. *Ɛala kəll ḥaal, n-kaan hallaq w-ᵊn-kaan baƐdeen laazmak təštəri sayyaara.* 3. *w-maƐ heek.* I didn't want to, but I did it anyway. *maa kaan bəddi saawiiha, w-maƐ heek saaweetha.*

anywhere - 1. *šii maḥall.* Are you going anywhere today? *raayəḥ-lak šii maḥall ᵊl-yoom?* -- If you have to go anywhere, I can give you a ride. *ʔiza laazmak ᵊtruuḥ šii maḥall ᵊbwaṣṣlak maƐi.* 2. *b-maḥall.* I haven't seen him anywhere. *maa šəfto b-maḥall.* 3. *ween-ma.* Anywhere you look there's dust. *ween-ma ṭṭallaƐᵊt bətlaaqi ġabra.*

**He'll never get anywhere. *b-ḥayaato maa byətwaffaq ᵊb-šii.*

**That won't get you anywhere. *haada maa biwaṣṣlak la-šii.*

apart - 1. *mənzəwi, mənfəred, mənfəṣel.* The house stands apart from the others. *l-beet mənzəwi Ɛan l-ᵊbyuut ᵊt-taanye.* 2. *la-waḥd-* + pron. suff. *la-ḥaal-* + pron. suff. Let's consider each argument apart. *xalliina nəbḥas ᵊb-kəll ḥəžže la-waḥda.*

**The two buses leave only five minutes apart.

been ᵊl-baaṣeen bass xamᵊs daqaayeq.
to take apart – *fakk (ə fakk//nfakk), fakfak//tfakfak.* Take it apart if necessary. *fəkka ʔiza ḍaruuri.*
to tell apart – *farraq been, mayyaz been.* How do you tell the two apart? *kiif btəqder ᵊtfarreq been ᵊt-tneen?*

apartment – *šaqqa* pl. *-aat, ʔabarṭmaan* pl. *-aat.* We're looking for an apartment. *ʕam ᵊndawwer ʕala šaqqa.*
apartment house – *binaayet˜* (pl. *-aat˜*) *sakan.* They're building a new apartment house on our street. *ʕam ᵊyʕammru binaayet sakan ᵊždiide b-šaarəʕna.*

ape – *qərᵊd* pl. *qruud(e).*

apiece – *l-waaḥed* f. *l-waaḥde.* My brother and I earned six pounds apiece. *ʔana w-ʔaxi ksəbna sətt leeraat ᵊl-waaḥed.*

to **apologize** – *ʕtazar.* You have to apologize! *laazem təʕtəzer.* -- Did you apologize to her? *ʕtazart-əlla?* -- I apologize. *bəʕtəzer* or ***laa tʔaaxəzni!* or ***ʕadam l-ᵊmʔaaxaze!*

apology – *ʔəʕtizaar* pl. *-aat.* She wouldn't accept his apology. *maa rəḍyet təqbal ʔəʕtizaaro.*

apostle – *rasuul* pl. *rəsol.*

apostolic – *rasuuli*.* Could you direct me to the Apostolic legation, please.. *baḷḷa btəqder ddəllni ʕal-ǧiṣaade r-rasuuliyye?*

apparatus – *ʕədde* pl. *ʕədad, žihaaz* pl. *ʔažhize, ʔaale* pl. *-aat.*

apparent – **1.** *ẓaaher, mbayyen.* It's apparent that he didn't understand the question. *ẓ-ẓaaher ʔənno maa fəhem ᵊs-suʔaal.* **2.** *waaḍeḥ, ẓaaher.* Then, for no apparent reason, he suddenly changed his mind. *baʕdeen, biduun sabab waaḍeḥ, fažʔatan ġayyar ʕaqlo.*

apparently – *ʕaẓ-ẓaaher.* He has apparently come to another conclusion. *ʕaẓ-ẓaaher twaṣṣal la-ʔəstəntaaž taani.*

appeal – **1.** *ʔəstəʔnaaf* pl. *-aat.* The appeal was denied. *l-ʔəstəʔnaaf ᵊnrafaḍ.* **2.** *nidaaʔ* pl. *-aat.* The head of the society made an appeal for contributions. *raʔiis ᵊž-žamʕiyye waššah nidaaʔ la-žamʕ ᵊt-tabarruʕaat.* **3.** *žaazbiyye.* The game has lost much of its appeal. *l-ləʕbe ḍayyaʕet ᵊktiir mən žaazbiita* or ***l-ləʕbe maa ʕaadet ᵊtšawweq ᵊktiir.*
to appeal to – **1.** *twassal la-.* Appeal to his conscience. *twassal la-ḍamiiro.* **2.** *ʕažab (e ø).* That type of humor doesn't appeal to me. *han-nooʕ ᵊmn ᵊl-mazᵊḥ maa byəʕžəbni.*
to appeal the case – *staʔnaf ᵊd-daʕwa.* The lawyer decided to appeal the case. *l-muḥaami ʕtamad yəstaʔnef ᵊd-daʕwa.*

to **appear** – **1.** *bayyan, baan (a ø).* He appeared at the last minute. *maa bayyan ʔəlla b-ʔaaxer daqiiqa.* **2.** *ṭələʕ (a ṭluuʕ).* This paper appears every Thursday. *haž-žariide btəṭlaʕ kəll xamiis.* **3.** *ẓəher (a ẓhuur), baan, bayyan.* He appears to be very sick. *byəẓhar* (or *bibaan*) *ʕalée ḍaʕfaan ᵊktiir.*

appearance – **1.** *ṭalʕa* pl. *-aat.* It's his first appearance on the stage. *hayye ʔawwal ṭalᵊʕto ʕal-masraḥ.* **2.** *ẓhuur.* His sudden appearance startled her. *ẓhuuro ʕala ġafle šahhdqa.* **3.** *maẓhar.* You have to pay more attention to your appearance. *laazem təʕtəni b-maẓharak ʔaktar.*
appearances – **1.** *maẓaaher* (pl.). I never judge by appearances. *maa bəḥkom ʕal-maẓaaher ᵊmnoob.* -- Appearances are deceiving. *l-maẓaaher bətġərr.* **2.** *ẓawaaher* (pl.). To all appearances he is a foreigner. *ḥasab kəll ᵊẓ-ẓawaaher huwwe ʔažnabi.*
to make (or **put in**) **an appearance** – *sabat (e sabataan) wžuudo.* At least make an appearance. *ʕal-ʔaqall, ruuḥ ᵊsbeet wžuudak.*

appendicitis – *ʔəltihaab˜ zaayde.*

appendix – **1.** *zaayde.* He had his appendix out when he was five. *qaamúu-lo z-zaayde lamma kaan ʕəmro xams ᵊsniin.* **2.** *məlḥaq* pl. *malaaḥeq.* Perhaps the word is in the appendix. *bižuuz ᵊl-kəlme mawžuude bᵊl-məlḥaq.*

appetite – *qaabliyye, šahiyye.* Our boy has a good appetite. *ʔəbᵊnna qaabliito mniiḥa.*

appetizers – *mšahhyaat, mqabblaat* (pl.).

appetizing – *mšahhi, mqabbel.*

to **applaud** – *saffaq.* We applauded heartily. *saffaqna b-ḥaraara.*

applause – *tasfiiq.* He was greeted by applause. *staqbalúu bət-tasfiiq.*

apple – *təffaaḥa* coll. *təffaaḥ* pl. *-aat.* Most of these apples are wormy. *ʔaktar hat-təffaaḥaat ᵊmdawwdiin.*

appliance – *žihaaz* pl. *ʔdžhize.* We carry all kinds of electrical appliances. *ʕanna kəll ʔanwaaʕ ᵊl-ʔažhize l-kahrabaaʔiyye.*

application – **1.** *taṭbiiq.* The application of his theory did not yield the results we had expected. *taṭbiiq naẓariito maa ʕaṭa n-nataayež yalli twaqqaʕnaaha.* **2** *ʔəžtihaad.* I admire his zeal and application in everything he does. *ktiir ʔana məʕžab ᵊb-ḥamaaso w-ʔəžtihaado b-kəll šii bisaawíi.* **3.** *ṭalab* pl. *-aat.* I mailed in my application too late. *baʕatᵊt ṭalabi baʕᵊd fawaat ᵊl-waqᵊt.* **4.** *šaašiyye* pl. *šawaaši.* Cold applications will relieve your pain. *š-šawaaši l-baarde bətkannen wažaʕak.*
application blank – *ʔəstimaaret˜* (pl. *-aat˜*) *ṭalab.* Fill out this application blank. *ʕabbi ʔəstimaaret haṭ-ṭalab hayy.*

to **apply** – **1.** *qaddam ṭalab.* I'd like to apply for the job. *bəddi qaddem ṭalab la-haš-šaġle.* **2.** *ṭabbaq.* You've applied this rule incorrectly. *ṭabbaqᵊt hal-qaaʕde ġalaṭ.* **3.** *staʕmal.* I had to apply all my strength. *nžabarᵊt ʔəstaʕmel kəll quwwti.* **4.** *ḥaṭṭ (ə ḥaṭaṭ//nḥaṭṭ).* Apply the wax evenly. *ḥəṭṭ ᵊš-šamᵊʕ ʕala swiyye waaḥde.* -- Apply a hot compress every two hours. *ḥəṭṭ šaašiyye ṣəxne kəll saaʕteen.* **5.** *štaġal, ṭṭabbaq.* The rule doesn't apply here. *l-qaaʕde maa btəštəġel hoon.*
to apply to – **1.** *ṭṭabbaq ʕala.* This order applies to everybody. *hal-ʔamᵊr byəṭṭabbaq ʕala kəll waaḥed.* **2.** *raažaʕ.* To whom do I apply? *miin laazem raažeʕ?*
to apply oneself to – *ḥaṭṭ žahdo b-.* I want you to apply yourself to this task. *bəddi-yaak ᵊtḥəṭṭ žahdak ᵊb-haš-šaġle.*

to **appoint** – *ʕayyan//tʕayyan.* He was appointed judge. *tʕayyan qaaḍi.*

appointment – **1.** *taʕyiin* pl. *-aat.* Congratulations on your appointment. *tahaaniina ʕala taʕyiinak.* **2.** *mawʕed* pl. *mawaʕiid.* I had to cancel all appointments for tomorrow. *ḍṭarreet ʔəlġi kəll mawaʕiidi tabaʕ bəkra.* -- I have an appointment with him. *ʕandi mawʕed maʕo.* -- I have an appointment at the dentist's for tomorrow morning. *ʕandi mawʕed maʕ doktoor ᵊs-snaan bəkra ʕala bəkra.*
to make an appointment – **1.** *ʕəmel mawʕed.* Did you make an appointment with the doctor? *ʕməlᵊt mawʕed maʕ ᵊd-doktoor?* **2.** *waʕad (-yuuʕed waʕᵊd).* I made an appointment with him for five o'clock. *waʕadto s-saaʕa xamse.*

appraisal – *taxmiin* pl. *-aat.* A careful appraisal of the property showed that ... *t-taxmiin ᵊd-daqiiq ləl-ʔamlaak warža ʔənno ...*

to **appraise** – *qaddar.* We want you to appraise the situation and to let us know your opinion. *bəddna-ydak ᵊtqadder ᵊl-maḍᵊʕ w-tqəl-lna šuu ṭaleʕ maʕak.*

to **appreciate** – *qaddar.* She doesn't seem to appreciate what we've done for her. *mbayyne maa-lha mqaddra kəll šii saaweenda mənšaanha.* -- I quite appreciate that it can't be done overnight. *(ʔana) mqadder tamaam ʔənno maa btəxloṣ haš-šaġle ma-been leele w-ḍəḥaaha.*
***I would appreciate it, if you could come. *bkuun mamnuun ʔəlak ʔiza ʔžiit.*
***He said he doesn't appreciate music. *qaal maa-lo maraaq bᵊl-muusiiqa.*

appreciation – **1.** *taqdiir.* I don't expect any appreciation. *maa-li məntəẓer ʔayy taqdiir.* **2.** *maraaq.* She has no appreciation for art. *maa-lha maraaq bᵊl-fann.*

appreciative: He doesn't seem very appreciative. *mbayyen maa biqadder ᵊl-maʕruuf.* -- It's a pleasure to wait on appreciative customers like you. *huwwe suruur ʔəli ʔiza bʕaawen zabaayen mətlak biqaddru l-xədme.*

apprentice – *ṣaaneʕ* pl. *ṣanaʕiyye* and *ṣannaaʕ.*

approach – **1.** *madxal* pl. *madaaxel.* The approaches to the bridge are under repair. *madaaxel ᵊž-žəsᵊr taḥt ᵊt-taṣliiḥ.* **2.** *ṭariiqa* pl. *ṭəroq.* I don't think you have the right approach to the problem. *maa bəʕtəqed ʔənnak maaši bᵊṭ-ṭariiqa l-maẓbuuṭa b-hal-məšᵊkle.* -- Am I using the wrong approach? *šuu ʔana maaši b-ṭariiqa ġalaṭ?*
to approach – **1.** *qarrab.* They approached cautiously. *qarrabu b-ḥaẓar.* **2.** *raažaʕ.* Who shall I approach about it? *miin halli laazem raažʕo b-hal-masʔale?* **3.** *ṭabbaq.* How shall I approach him? *kiif bəddi ṭabbqo?* **4.** *ʕaalaž.* How would you approach the problem? *kiif ʔənte bəddak tʕaalež ᵊl-mawḍuuʕ?*

appropriate – **1.** *b-maḥallo, mnaaseb, mlaaʔem.* The remark is quite appropriate. *l-ᵊmlaaḥaẓa tamaam* ᵊb-mahalla. 2. xarᵊž, mlaaᵓem, mnaaseb. I don't think his words were appropriate to the occasion. *maa bəčtəqed hakyo kaan xarᵊž hal-ᵊmnaasabe* (or *mlaaᵓem la-hal-ᵊmnaasabe*).

more appropriate – *ᵓansab*. We'll talk about that at a more appropriate time. *mnəhki čan haš-šağle b-waqᵊt ᵓansab*.

to appropriate – 1. *stawla čala*. My son has appropriated all my ties. *ᵓəbni stawla čala kəll ᵊgraafaati*. 2. *xaṣṣaṣ*. The city has appropriated fifty thousand pounds for a new library. *l-baladiyye xaṣṣaṣet xamsiin ᵓalf leera la-maktabe ždiide*.

approval – 1. *mwaafaqa*. You'll need your parents' approval. *laazem taaxod ᵊmwaafaqᵊt ᵓəmmak w-ᵓabuuk*. -- You'll have to get his approval on it. *laazem taaxod ᵊmwaafaqto čaleeha*. 2. *ᵓəstəhsaan*. This color will hardly find her approval. *maa bəčtəqed hal-loon byəhẓa b-ᵓəstəhsaana*.

**Does the suggestion meet with your approval? *šuu bətwaafeq čala hal-ᵓəqtiraah?*

on approval – *čala radad*. They sent me the book on approval. *bačatúu-li l-ᵊktaab čala radad*.

to **approve** – *saadaq//tsaadaq čala, waafaq//twaafaq čala*. Your application has been approved. *ṭalabak ᵊtwaafaq čalée*.

to approve of – *waafaq čala, stahsan*. Do you approve of my suggestion? *šuu bətwaafeq čala ᵓəqtiraahi?* -- He approves of my plans. *byəstahsen xəṭaṭi*.

approvingly – *bᵊl-ᵊmwaafaqa*. She nodded approvingly. *hazzet raasa bᵊl-ᵊmwaafaqa*.

approximate – *taqriibi**. The approximate length of the room is four meters. *ṭuul ᵊl-ᵓuuḍa t-taqriibi ᵓarbač ᵊmtaar*.

approximately – *taqriiban, hawaali*. He left approximately a month ago. *saafar taqriiban mən šahᵊr*.

apricot – *məšᵊmše* coll. *məšmoš* pl. *-aat*.

April – *niisaan, ᵓəbriil*.

apron – *maryuul* pl. *marayiil*.

apt – 1. *mṣiib, mnaaseb*. That was a very apt remark. *hayy kaanet ᵊmlaahaẓa ktiir ᵊmṣiibe*. 2. *šaaṭer*. He's a very apt pupil. *huwwe təlmiiz šaaṭer ᵊktiir*.

**He's apt to come in the middle of the night. *muu bčiid čalée yəži b-nəṣṣ ᵊl-leel*.

**He's apt to do anything. *muu məstağrab mənno ᵓayy šii*.

**I'm apt to be out when you call. *bižuuz kuun muu mawžuud lamma tačməl-li talifoon*.

**Such measures are apt to be resented by everybody. *heek tadabiir mən ṭabiičə́ta tənkə́reh mən kəll ᵊn-naas*.

Aqaba – *l-čaqabe*. Gulf of Aqaba. *xaliiž ᵊl-čaqabe*.

aquarium – *hooḍ˜* (pl. *ᵓahwaaḍ˜*) *samak*.

Arab – *čarabi** pl. *čarab*. As far as I know, he's an Arab from Bahrain. *hasab-ma bačref huwwe čarabi mn ᵊl-bahreen*. -- Have you studied the history of the Arabs? *darasᵊt šii taariix ᵊl-čarab?* -- We have three Arabs working in our lab. *fii čanna tlaate čarab byəštəğlu bᵊl-maxbar*. -- I like Arab food very much. *bhəbb ᵊl-ᵓakl ᵊl-čarabi ktiir*. -- We had quite a number of Arab students at the University. *kaan čanna čadad ᵊkbiir mn ᵊṭ-ṭəllaab ᵊl-čarab bᵊž-žaamča*.

Arabia – *žaziiret˜ ᵊl-čarab*.

Arabian Peninsula – *žaziiret˜ ᵊl-čarab*.

Arabian Nights – *ᵓalf leele w-leele*.

Arabian Sea – *bahr˜ ᵊl-čarab*.

Arabic – 1. *čarabi*. My wife doesn't speak Arabic. *marti maa btəhki čarabi*. -- Who translated the article into Arabic? *miin taržam ᵊl-maqaale ləl-čarabi?* -- Say that sentence in Arabic, please. *quul haž-žəmle bᵊl-čarabi balla*. 2. *čarabi**. I don't know very much about Arabic poetry. *maa bačref šii ktiir čan ᵊš-šəčr ᵊl-čarabi*.

Arabist – *məstačreb* pl. *-iin*.

Arab League – *žaaməčt˜ ᵊd-duwal ᵊl-čarabiyye*.

Aramaic – *ᵓaaraami**. Aramaic is still spoken in three villages north of Damascus. *l-ᵓaaraami ləssaato byəhkúu b-tlatt ḍiyač šamaal ᵊš-šaam*.

arch – 1. *qanṭara* pl. *qanaaṭer*. That bridge has a tremendous arch. *haž-žəsᵊr ᵓəlo qanṭara ḍaxme*. 2. *qooṣ* pl. *qwaaṣ*. They set up a number of triumphal arches along the road. *naṣabu čəddet ᵊqwaaṣ naṣᵊr čala ṭuul ᵊṭ-ṭariiq*.

fallen arches – *rəžᵊl baṭša* pl. *ražleen bəṭᵊš*. He has fallen arches. *ražlée bəṭᵊš*.

arched – *mqawweṣ*. The chapel has an arched ceiling. *l-mačbad saqfo mqawweṣ*.

archeological – *ᵓasari**.

archeologist – *čaalem˜* (pl. *čəlama˜*) *ᵓaasaar*.

archeology – *čəlm˜ ᵊl-ᵓaasaar*.

architect – *mhandes məčmaari* pl. *mhandsiin məčmaariyyiin*.

architecture – 1. *handase məčmaariyye, handast˜ ᵊl-binaaᵓ, handast˜ ᵊl-čamaar*. He studied architecture in Paris. *daras ᵊl-handase l-məčmaariyye b-baariiz*. 2. *fann məčmaari**. We admired the grandiose architecture of the cathedral. *kənna məčžabiin bᵊl-fann ᵊl-məčmaari l-baaher b-hal-katədraaᵓiyye*.

area – *manṭiqa* pl. *manaaṭeq*. The area around Damascus is more densely populated. *l-manṭiqa hawaali š-šaam ᵓaahle bᵊs-səkkaan ᵓaktar*.

Argentina – *l-ᵓaržantiin*.

to **argue** – 1. *tnaaqar, džaadal*. They argue all the time. *byətnaaqaru čala ṭuul*. 2. *žaadal b-*. I won't argue that point. *maa-li laha žaadel ᵊb-han-nəqṭa*. 3. *žaadal*. Don't argue with me. *laa džaadə́lni*. 4. *qanač (e ə)*. You can't argue me into going there again. *maa btəqder təqnəčni (ᵓənno) ruuh la-hniik marra taanye*.

**I argued that it would save us a lot of time. *kaanet həžžti ᵓənno haš-šağle laha twaffə́r-ᵊlna waqt ᵊktiir*.

argument – 1. *həžže* pl. *həžaž*. That's an argument in his favor. *hayy həžže la-ṣaalho*. -- I don't follow your argument. *maa-li fahmaan həžžtak*. 2. *xnaaqa* pl. *-aat* and *xanaayeq*. We had a violent argument. *txaanaqna xnaaqa kbiire ktiir*. 3. *xilaaf* pl. *-aat*. It was just a little argument. *kaan xilaaf baṣiiṭ bass*.

**I don't want any argument with you. *maa bəddi ᵓətčaalaq mačak*.

to **arise** – 1. *qaam (u qyaam), waqqaf*. They all arose at the same time. *kəllon qaamu sawa*. 2. *hadas (o hduus)*. The problem arose some time ago. *l-məšᵊkle hadset mən mədde*. 3. *sanah (a snuuh)*. As soon as the opportunity arises ... *b-ᵊmžarrad-ma təsnah l-fərṣa ...*

aristocracy – *ᵓarisṭuqraaṭiyye*.

aristocrat – *ᵓarisṭuqraaṭi** pl. *-iyyiin*.

aristocratic – *ᵓarisṭuqraaṭi**.

Aristotle – *ᵓarasṭo, ᵓarisṭəṭaaliis*.

arithmetic – *čəlᵊm˜ l-ᵊhsaab*.

arithmetical – *hsaabi**.

arm – *ᵓiid* (f.) dual *ᵓidteen* pl. *ᵓideen*. He has lost an arm. *faqad ᵓiido*. -- The arms on this chair are too low. *ᵓideen hal-kərsi ktiir waaṭyiin*. -- The arm of the crane swung outward. *ᵓiid ᵊr-raafča tharraket la-qəddaam*.

with open arms – *bᵊl-hafaawe*. They received him with open arms. *staqbalúu bᵊl-hafaawe*.

(to carry) under one's arm – *(hamal) tahᵊt baaṭo*. Can you carry the package under your arm? *btəqder təhmel ᵊl-baakeet tahᵊt baaṭak?*

arm – *slaah* pl. *ᵓə́sliha*. All arms have to be turned over to the police. *kəll ᵊl-ᵓə́sliha laazem tətsallam ləl-booliis*. -- He was arrested for the illegal possession of arms. *nhabas la-hyaazto ᵓasliha muu mraxxaṣ fiiha*.

under arms – *taht ᵊs-slaah*. All the able-bodied men were under arms. *kəll ᵊr-ržaal ᵊl-qaadriin kaanu taht ᵊs-slaah*.

to be up in arms – *hanaq (e hanᵊq)*. Everybody was up in arms. *kəll ᵊn-naas kaanet haanqa*.

to carry arms – *hamal (e hamᵊl) ᵊs-slaah*. Everybody who could carry arms was drafted. *kəll waahed kaan qaader čala haml ᵊs-slaah nṭalab*.

to arm – *sallah*. The rebel forces are beginning to arm the local population. *quwwaat ᵊs-suwwaar čam təbda tsalleh ᵊl-ᵓahaali l-mahalliyyiin*. -- He has armed himself with strong arguments before entering the debate. *sallah nafso b-həžaž qawiyye qabᵊl-ma yədxol bᵊl-ᵊmnaaqaše*.

armchair – *qəlṭoq* pl. *qalaaṭeq*.

armistice – *hədne* pl. *-aat*.

armor – *dərᵊč* pl. *druuč(a)*. These shells can't penetrate the heavy armor of the battleship. *hal-qanaabel maa fiiha təxtə́req ᵊd-druuča l-qawiyye tabač ᵊl-baarže*.

armored – *mdarrač*. Those tanks are heavily armored. *had-dabbaabaat ᵊmdarrača tqiile*. -- Armored units broke through the enemy lines. *fii wəhdaat ᵊmdarrača xtarqet ᵊxṭuuṭ ᵊl-čaduww*.

armpit – *baaṭ* pl. *-aat*.

army – 1. *žeeš* pl. *žyuuš*. Did you serve in the army or in the navy? *xadamᵊt bᵊž-žeeš walla bᵊl-bahriyye?* -- I'm joining the army. *laha ᵓəltə́heq bᵊž-žeeš*. -- The second and third armies are being concentrated along the southern border. *ž-žeešeen ᵊt-taani wᵊt-taalet εam yəḥᵊšduuhon εala ṭuul l-ᵊḥduud ᵊž-žanuubiyye.* 2. *xədme εaskariyye.* I know him from my days in the army. *baεᵊrfo mən ʔiyyaami bᵊl-xədme l-εaskariyye.*

around - 1. *daayer˜, ḥawaali˜.* They're building a wall around the garden. *εam yəbnu ḥeeṭ daayer ᵊž-žneene.* — The people around us were talking loudly. *n-naas daayərna* (or *ḥawaleena*) *kaan εam yəḥku bᵊl-εaali.* 2. *daayer˜.* He tied a rope around the tree. *rabaṭ ḥabᵊl daayer ᵊš-šažara.* 3. *ḥawaali.* I have around twenty pounds. *maεi ḥawaali εəšriin leera.* 4. *mawžuud, hoon.* Is she still around? *ləssaatha mawžuude?* — Is there anybody around? *fii ḥada hoon?*
  **We drove around the city to see the sights. *dərna bᵊl-balad la-nətfarraž εal-qaraani l-ᵊmhəmme.*
  **We drove around the city to avoid the heavy traffic. *laffeena daayer ᵊl-balad la-nəxloṣ mən εažqet ᵊs-seer.*
  around here (or **there**) - *b-han-nawaaḥi.* He lives somewhere around here. *(huwwe) saaken ᵊb-han-nawaaḥi.*
  around the clock - *leel w-nhaar, ʔarbεa εəšriin saaεa.* The store is open around the clock. *l-maxzan faateḥ leel w-nhaar.*
  around the corner - (literally) *bᵊl-lafte,* (generally nearby) *b-han-nawaaḥi.* She lives right around the corner. *saakne tamaam bᵊl-lafte.*

to **arouse** - 1. *fayyaq//faaq (i ə) εala.* I was aroused in the middle of the night by a terrible bang. *fəqᵊt εala ṣooṭ xabṭa qawiyye b-waṣṭ ᵊl-leel.* 2. *ʔasaar.* Her strange behavior aroused my suspicion. *taṣarrəfa l-ğariib ʔasaar šəbᵊhti (ḥawla).*

arrack - *εaraq.*

to **arrange** - 1. *rattab//trattab, ṣaff (ə ṣaff/nṣaff).* Who arranged the books? *miin rattab ᵊl-kətᵊb?* — The cards are arranged alphabetically. *l-ᵊkruut maṣfuufiin εala ḥasab ᵊt-təhžaaye.* 2. *dabbar, waḍḍab.* I arranged it in advance. *dabbárta salaf.*— Arrange it so that you'll be here tomorrow. *dabbəra la-tkuun bəkra hoon.*

arrangement - 1. *tartiib* pl. *-aat.* How do you like this arrangement of the furniture? *kiif bətšuuf hat-tartiib ləl-farᵊš?* — They made all arrangements to leave the following morning. *εəmlu kəll ᵊt-tartiibaat la-ysaafru taani yoom εala bəkra.* 2. *tadbiir* pl. *tadabiir.* They found an arrangement that solved the problem once and for all. *laqu tadbiir ḥall ᵊl-məšᵊkle bᵊl-marra.*

in **arrears** - *mətʔaxxer.* We're three months in arrears in the rent. *nəḥna mətʔaxxriin εan dafε ᵊl-ʔəžra tlətt əšhor.*

arrest - *tawqiif* pl. *-aat.* His arrest came as a total surprise. *tawqiifo ʔəžaana mfaažaʔa maa kənna ḥaasbiinha.* — You're under arrest! *ʔənte taḥt ᵊt-tawqiif!* or **ʔ*ənte mwaqqaf!*
  **The police made two arrests. *š-šərṭa waqqafu tneen.*
  to arrest - *waqqaf//twaqqaf.* Why was he arrested? *leeš ᵊtwaqqaf?* — Proper medical care can arrest leprosy in its early stages. *l-ᵊεnaaye ṭ-ṭəbbiyye l-ᵊmniiḥa btəqder ᵊtwaqqef maraḍ ᵊl-baraṣ ᵊb-maraaḥlo l-ʔuula.*

arrival - *wṣuul.* His arrival caused a lot of excitement. *wṣuulo sabbab hayažaan ᵊkbiir.*

to **arrive** - 1. *wəṣel (-yəṣal* and *-yuuṣal wṣuul).* When did the train arrive? *ʔeemta wəṣel ᵊt-treen?* 2. *twaṣṣal la-, wəṣel la-.* Did they arrive at a decision? *šuu twaṣṣalu la-q̈araar?*

arrogance - *εanṭaṣa, εažrafe.*

arrogant - *mεanṭaṣ, šaayef ḥaalo, mεažraf.* She has no reason to be so arrogant. *maa fii daaεi tkuun ᵊmεanṭaṣa* (or *šaayfe ḥaalha*) *kəll hal-qadd.*

arrow - 1. *sahᵊm* pl. *shuum(e).* The arrow points north. *s-sahᵊm biʔaššer εaš-šmaal.* 2. *naššaab* (coll.). Boys like to play with bows and arrows. *l-ᵊwlaad biḥəbbu yəlεabu bᵊl-qooṣ wᵊn-naššaab.*

art - *fann* pl. *fnuun.* He knows a lot about art. *byaεref šii ktiir εan ᵊl-fann.* — He's mastered the art of flattery. *huwwe baareε ᵊb-fann l-ᵊmmaalaqa.* — There's an art to it. *bəddha fann haš-šağle.*
  art gallery - *matḥaf˜* (pl. *mataaḥef˜*) *ᵊl-funuun ᵊž-žamiile.*
  work of art - *qəṭεa* (pl. *qəṭaε*) *fanniyye, təḥfe* pl. *təḥaf.* This building contains many works of art. *hal-binaaye fiiha qəṭaε fanniyye ktiire.*

arterial - *šəryaani**.

artery - *šəryaan* pl. *šarayiin.*

arthritis - *ʔəltihaab˜ mafaaṣel, nəq̈res.*

article - 1. *maq̈aale* pl. *-aat.* There was an interesting article about it in the newspaper. *kaan fii maq̈aale mhəmme εan ᵊl-mawḍuuε bᵊž-žariide.* 2. *maadde* pl. *mawaadd, banᵊd* pl. *bnuud(e).* I'm not clear on Article 3. *maa-li fahmaan ᵊl-maadde t-taalte.* 3. *ğaraḍ* pl. *ğraaḍ.* Many valuable articles were stolen. *fii ğraaḍ tamiine ktiire nsarqet.* 4. *ṣənᵊf* pl. *ʔaṣnaaf.* Our store doesn't carry these articles. *maxzanna maa byətεaamal ᵊb-hal-ʔaṣnaaf.*
  **He's a shrewd article. *huwwe waaḥed daahye.*
  definite article - *laam˜ ᵊt-taεriif.* Write the word with the definite article. *ktoob ᵊl-kəlme b-laam ᵊt-taεriif.*
  indefinite article - *ʔadaat˜ ᵊt-tankiir.*

artificial - 1. *ʔəṣṭinaaεi**. Are those flowers artificial? *šuu hal-ʔazhaar ʔəṣṭinaaεiyye?* — He has an artificial leg. *rəžlo ʔəṣṭinaaεiyye.* 2. *məṣṭanaε.* She has an artificial smile. *ʔəbtisaamə́ta məṣṭanaεa.*

artillery - 1. *madfaεiyye.* Are you in the infantry or in the artillery? *ʔənte bᵊl-mušaat wəlla bᵊl-madfaεiyye?* 2. *madaafeε* (pl.). The heavy artillery opened fire. *l-madaafeε ᵊt-tqiile fatḥet ᵊn-naar.*

artist - *fannaan* pl. *-iin,* f. *fannaane* pl. *-aat.*

as - 1. *mətᵊl-ma.* Leave it as it is. *trə́ka mətᵊl-ma hiyye.* — Do as you please. *saawi mətᵊl-ma bəddak.*— Everything stands as it was. *kəll šii baaqi mətᵊl-ma kaan* or **kəll šii baaqi εala ḥaalo.* 2. *lamma, waqᵊt.* Did you see anyone as you came in? *šəfᵊt ḥada lamma fətᵊt* or **šəfᵊt ḥada w-ʔənte faayet?* 3. *b-maa ʔənno, ṭaala-ma.* As he is leaving tomorrow, we must hurry. *b-maa ʔənno msaafer bəkra laazem nəstaεžel.*
  **I regard it as important. *bəεtə́bro mhəmm.*
  as ... as - 1. *qadd˜.* This crate is as big as that one. *has-saḥḥaara kbiire qadd hadiik.* — He's as old as you. *εəmro qadd εəmrak.* 2. *qadd-ma.* He's as bright as you can expect him to be. *huwwe zaki qadd-ma btəqder tətwaqqaε mənno zaka.*
  **I'd like to leave as soon as possible. *bəddi ruuḥ ᵊb-ʔasraε-ma yəmken.*
  **Try to make the price as low as possible. *žarreb ᵊtsaawi s-səεᵊr ʔaqall šii məmken.*
  **Write as many words as possible. *ktoob ʔakbar εadad məmken mn ᵊl-kəlmaat.*
  as far as - 1. *la-ḥadd.* The train goes only as far as Aleppo. *t-treen biwaṣṣel la-ḥadd ḥalab bass.* 2. *ḥadd-ma.* That's as far as we got yesterday. *hoon ḥadd-ma wəṣəlna mbaareḥ.* 3. *ḥasab-ma.* As far as I can see, he's right. *ḥasab-maa-li šaayef maεo ḥaqq.* — As far as I know, there's no mail for you. *ḥasab-ma baεref maa fii ʔəlak boosṭa.*
  as far as I'm concerned, etc. - *bᵊn-nəsbe ʔəli,* etc. As far as he's concerned it's all right. *bᵊn-nəsbe ʔəlo maa fii maaneε.* — As far as I'm concerned you can do as you like. *bᵊn-nəsbe ʔəli btəqder taεmel yalli bəddak-yáa.*
  as for - *bᵊn-nəsbe la-, ʔamma.* As for him, it's all right. *bᵊn-nəsbe ʔəlo* (or *ʔamma huwwe*) *maa fii maaneε.* — As for the books I lent you, you can keep them. *bᵊn-nəsbe ləl-kətᵊb yalli εərtak-yáahon btəqder təḥtə́feẓ fiihon.*
  as good as - *kaʔənn-* + pron. suff. The radio is as good as new. *r-raadyo kaʔənno ždiid* or **r-raadyo yuεtábar ᵊždiid.* — The work is as good as done. *š-šəğᵊl kaʔənno xalaṣ* or **š-šəğᵊl mnəḥᵊsbo xalaṣ.*
  as if - *kaʔənn-* + pron. suff. He acts as if it were very important. *εam yətṣarraf kaʔənnha š-šağle mhəmme ktiir.* — As if I hadn't told you before! *kaʔənni maa qəlt-ə́llak mən qabᵊl!*
  as it were - *mətᵊl-ma biquulu.* We're here as guests, as it were, of the city. *nəḥna hoon, mətᵊl-ma biquulu, ḍyuuf εal-balad.*
  as long as - *ma-daam, ṭaala-ma.* As long as you're here, let's finish the work. *ma-daam ʔənte hoon xalliina nxalleṣ ᵊš-šağle.*
  as soon as - *b-ᵊmžarrad-ma.* Let me know as soon as you get here. *b-ᵊmžarrad-ma tuuṣal εaṭiini xabar.*
  as such - *b-ḥadd zaat-* + pron. suff., *mən ḥaysu huwwe* (or *hiyye* respectively). The treaty as such is of no great importance. *l-ᵊmεaahade b-ḥadd zaata* (or *mən ḥaysu hiyye*) *maa-lha ʔahammiyye kbiire.*
  as though - *kaʔənn-* + pron. suff. He looks as though he didn't sleep well. *mbayyen εalée kaʔənno maa naam ᵊmniiḥ.*
  as usual - *mətl ᵊl-εaade.* He's late, as usual. *huwwe mətʔaxxer mətl ᵊl-εaade.*

as well – *kamaan.* He not only took care of his own work but he did hers as well. *huwwe maa štaġal šəġlo bass, kamaan štaġál-lha šəġla.*

as well as – 1. *w-kamaan.* He is a musician as well as a painter. *huwwe muusiiqi w-kamaan rassaam.* 2. *mniiḥ mətᵊl(-ma).* If you do this job as well as (you did) the other one, we'll give you a raise. *ʔiza ƐməlᵊT haš-šaġle mniiḥa mətᵊl yalli qabla* (or *mətᵊl-ma Ɛməlᵊt yalli qabla*) *mənzawwəd-lak maƐaašak.*

as yet – *la-hallaq, la-ḥadd hallaq, ləssa.* Nothing has happened as yet. *maa ṣaar šii la-ḥadd hallaq.* -- I don't know as yet. *ləssa maa baƐref.*

so as to – *la-ḥatta.* We'll have to start early so as to be on time. *laazem ᵊnruuḥ bakkiir la-ḥatta nkuun Ɛal-waqᵊt.*

**Would you be so kind as to close the door. *Ɛmeel maƐruuf sakkər-ᵊlna l-baab.*

ash – *šažaret~* (coll. *šažar~*) *ᵊlsaan ᵊl-Ɛaṣfuur.*

to be **ashamed** – *xəžel (a xažal), staḥa (-yəstəḥi ḥaya).* You needn't be ashamed of it. *maa fii daaƐi təxžal mənno.* -- He is not ashamed to work with his hands. *maa byəstəḥi yəštəġel ᵊb-ʔidée.*

ash can – *tanaket~* (pl. *-aat~*) *ᵊzbaale.*

ashes – *ṣafwe, ramaad.* The floor was covered with ashes. *l-ʔarᵊḍ kaanet ᵊmġaṭṭaaye ṣafwe.*

ash-gray – *rmaadi*.*

to go **ashore** – *nəzel (e nzuul) Ɛal-barr.* We weren't allowed to go ashore. *maa samaḥúu-lna nənzel Ɛal-barr.*

ash tray – *ṣaḥᵊn~* (pl. *ṣḥuunet~*) *sigaara.*

ash tree – *šažaret~* (coll. *šažar~*) *ᵊlsaan ᵊl-Ɛaṣfuur.*

Ash Wednesday – *ʔarbaƐet~ ᵊr-ramaad.*

Asia – *ʔaasya.*

Asia Minor – *ʔaasya ṣ-ṣəġra.*

Asian – *ʔaasyawi*.*

Asiatic – *ʔaasyawi*.*

aside – *Ɛala žanab.* All joking aside! I want my money! *l-mazᵊḥ Ɛala žanab! bəddi maṣaariyyi.* -- Let's leave those considerations aside for the moment. *xalliina nətrok hal-ʔəƐtibaarat Ɛala žanab hallaq.* -- Can you put the tie aside for me until tomorrow? *btəqder txallíi-li l-ᵊgraafe Ɛala žanab la-bəkra?* -- We also have to put aside a little money for a rainy day. *laazem kamaan nxalli šwayyet maṣaari Ɛala žanab la-yoom ᵊš-šədde.* -- Put the book aside now. *ḥəṭṭ l-ᵊktaab Ɛala žanab hallaq.*

aside from – *b-ṣarf ᵊn-naẓar Ɛan.* Aside from that, not much can be said in his favor. *b-ṣarf ᵊn-naẓar Ɛan haada, maa fii šii ktiir yənḥáka la-ṣaalḥo.*

to **ask** – 1. *saʔal (a suʔaal//nsaʔal).* Ask at the ticket office. *sʔaal ᵊb-maktab ᵊt-tazaaker.* -- Did you ask him his name? *saʔalto Ɛan ʔəsmo?* -- Why don't you ask her about her plans. *leeš maa btəsʔála Ɛan xəṭaṭa?* -- He asked about you when I saw him yesterday. *saʔalni Ɛannak lamma šəfto mbaareḥ.* -- May I ask a question? *məmken ʔəsʔal suʔaal?* 2. *ṭalab (o ṭalab//nṭalab).* He asked for permission. *ṭalab ʔəzᵊn.* -- He was asked to leave the house. *nṭalab mənno yətrok ᵊl-beet.* -- How much did he ask for it? *qaddeeš ṭalab fiiha?* 3. *daƐa (i daƐwe//ndaƐa), Ɛazam (e Ɛaziime//nƐazam).* Why don't you ask your friend to the party next week? *leeš maa btədƐi ṣaaḥbak lᵊl-ḥafle ž-žəmƐa ž-žaaye?*

**Ask him in. *qəl-lo yətfaḍḍal.*

**You asked for it! *xaržak!*

to ask back – *Ɛaad daƐa.* We never asked him back to our house again. *maa Ɛaad daƐeenda la-beetna bᵊl-marra.*

to ask for trouble – *Ɛarraḍ ḥaalo la-mašaakel.* You're asking for trouble if you do that. *bətƐarreḍ ḥaalak la-mašaakel ʔiza saaweet haš-šaġle.*

to ask someone's advice – *ʔaxad naṣiiḥet~ ḥada.* I'll ask your advice when I need it. *laḥa ʔaaxod naṣiiḥtak waqᵊt maa byəbqa ġeera.*

asleep – 1. *naayem.* I must have been asleep. *laazem ykuun kənᵊt naayem.* 2. *xadraan, mnammel.* My foot's asleep. *rəžli xadraane.*

to fall asleep – *ġəfel (a ġafle).* After ten minutes he fell asleep. *baƐᵊd Ɛašar daqaayeq ġəfel* (or ***ʔaxado n-noom*).

asparagus – *halyuun.*

aspect – *wažᵊh* pl. *wžuuh* and *ʔawžoh, ṭaraf* pl. *ʔaṭraaf, naaḥye* pl. *nawaaḥi.* We've considered every aspect of the problem. *baḥasna kəll wažᵊh mən ʔawžoh ᵊl-masʔale* or *baḥasna l-masʔale mən kəll wžuuha.*

asphalt – *ʔəsfalt, zəfᵊt.*

to asphalt – *zaffat.* When are they going to asphalt this road? *ʔeemta laḥa yzafftu haṭ-ṭariiq?*

aspirin – *ʔasbiriin.*

ass – *ḥmaar* pl. *ḥamiir.* He's a perfect ass. *huwwe ḥmaar Ɛan ḥaqa.*

assassin – *məġtaal* pl. *-iin, qaatel* pl. *-iin.*

to **assassinate** – *ġtaal.* Some fanatic assassinated the Prime Minister. *fii waaḥed məthawwer ᵊġtaal raʔiis ᵊl-wazaara.*

assault – 1. *hžuum* pl. *-aat, hažme* pl. *-aat.* The assault was repulsed with heavy losses for the enemy. *l-ᵊhžuum ᵊnradd maƐ xasaaʔer faadḥa lᵊl-Ɛaduww.* 2. *taƐaddi.* He was charged with assault and battery. *tahamúu bᵊt-taƐaddi wᵊḍ-ḍarᵊb.*

to assault – *tƐadda Ɛala, hažam (o hžuum) Ɛala.* The gang assaulted him in a dark alley. *l-Ɛiṣaabe tƐaddet Ɛalée b-ḥaara Ɛətme.*

to **assemble** – 1. *žtamaƐ, džammaƐ.* The guests assembled in the dining room. *ḍ-ḍyuuf ᵊžtamaƐu b-ġərfet ᵊṭ-ṭaƐaam.* 2. *žammaƐ.* The teacher assembled the students in the auditorium. *l-ʔəstaaz žammaƐ ᵊṭ-ṭəllaab ᵊb-qaaƐet ᵊl-ʔəḥtifaalaat.* 3. *rakkab.* He assembles airplane engines. *birakkeb ᵊmḥarrkaat ṭayyaara.*

assembly – 1. *žamᵊƐ* pl. *žmuuƐa, ʔəžtimaaƐ* pl. *-aat.* He spoke before a large assembly of lawyers. *xaṭab ᵊb-žamƐ ᵊkbiir mn ᵊl-muḥaamiin.* 2. *žamƐiyye* pl. *-aat.* The General Assembly of the United Nations met in an emergency session today. *ž-žamƐiyye l-Ɛumuumiyye tabaƐ ᵊl-ʔəmam ᵊl-məttəḥde žtamƐet ᵊb-žalse ʔəstəsnaaʔiyye l-yoom.* 3. *mažles* pl. *mažaales.* The National Assembly has finally passed the law. *mažles ᵊl-ʔəmme ʔaxiiran sann ᵊl-qaanuun.*

assembly line – *seer mətḥarrek* pl. *syuur mətḥarrke.* I work on the assembly line in an automobile factory. *bəštəġel bᵊs-seer ᵊl-mətḥarrek ᵊb-maṣnaƐ sayyaaraat.*

to **assess** – *xamman.* They assessed the property at 250,000 pounds. *xammanu l-ʔamlaak ᵊb-miiteen w-xamsiin ʔalf leera.*

asset – *maksab.* He is an asset to our organization. *huwwe maksab la-mnaẓẓamətna.*

assets – *mawžuudaat* (pl.). The Company's liabilities now exceed its assets. *dyuun ᵊš-šərke hallaq bədziid Ɛan mawžuudaatha.*

to **assign** – 1. *Ɛaṭa ... waẓiife.* The teacher has assigned us two poems for tomorrow. *l-ʔəstaaz Ɛaṭaana qaṣiidteen waẓiife la-bəkra.* 2. *Ɛayyan//tƐayyan.* He assigned two men to guard the prisoner. *Ɛayyan šaxṣeen la-yəḥᵊrsu s-sažiin.* 3. *naqal (o naqᵊl//ntaqal).* He was assigned to a different department. *ntaqal la-ġer daayre.*

assignment – *waẓiife* pl. *waẓaayef.* Our teacher gave us a big assignment over the weekend. *ʔəstaazna Ɛaṭaana waẓiife kbiire la-Ɛəṭlet ᵊl-ʔəsbuuƐ.* -- The boss gave me an interesting assignment. *r-raʔiis Ɛaṭaani waẓiife məġᵊrye.* 2. *tawziiƐ.* The assignment of the various jobs is taken care of by the foreman. *tawziiƐ ᵊl-ʔašġaal ᵊl-məxtəlfe byəržaƐ lᵊl-ᵊmnaaẓer.*

to **assist** – *saaƐad, Ɛaawan.* Who assisted you in that work? *miin saaƐadak ᵊb-haš-šəġᵊl?*

to assist one another – *tsaaƐadu, tƐaawanu.* They agreed to assist one another in case of war. *ttafaqu Ɛat-tasaaƐod waqt ᵊl-ḥarb.*

assistance – *msaaƐade, mƐaawane.* He did it without any assistance. *saawaaha biiduun ʔayy ᵊmsaaƐade.*

assistant – *msaaƐed* pl. *-iin, mƐaawen* pl. *-iin.*

associate – 1. *šriik* pl. *šəraka.* He's been my associate for many years. *huwwe šriiki mn ᵊsniin ᵊktiire.* 2. *məntəseb.* They are associate members of the club. *hənne ʔaƐḍaaʔ məntəsbiin bᵊn-naadi.*

associate professor – *ʔəstaaz* (pl. *ʔasaadze*) *bala kərsi.*

to associate – 1. *Ɛaašar, šaakal.* We never did associate with them very much. *bᵊl-ḥaqiiqa maa Ɛaašarnaahon ᵊktiir ʔabadan.* 2. *nasab (o nasᵊb) la-.* I associate the Arabs with hospitality and friendliness. *bənsob ləl-Ɛarab ᵊḍ-ḍyaafe wᵊl-karam.*

association – 1. *mƐaašara, mšaakale.* Everyone resents his association with that group of people. *kəll waaḥed byəkrah ᵊmƐaašarto la-haž-žamaaƐa.* 2. *žamƐiyye* pl. *-aat.* I don't think I'll join the association. *maa bəƐtəqed laḥa ʔəndamm la-haž-žamƐiyye.*

to **assort** – *ṣannaf.* Assort these buttons according to size. *ṣannef haz-zraar ᵊb-ḥasab l-ᵊqyaas.*

assorted – *mšakkal.* I want one pound of assorted chocolates. *bəddi nəṣṣ kiilo šakaleeṭa mšakkale.*

assortment – *taškiile* pl. *-aat.* We carry a large assortment of summer dresses. *Ɛanna taškiile kbiire mn ᵊl-malaabes ᵊṣ-ṣeefiyye.*

to **assume** - 1. *Ɛtaqad, ẓann (ə ẓann).* I assume that he'll be there too. *bəƐtəqed ʔənno laḥa ykuun əhniik kamaan.* 2. *ḥamal (e ḥaməl), ʔaxad.* I can't assume any responsibility for that. *maa bəqder ʔəḥmel ʔayy masʔuuliyye la-haš-šaǵle.*
**Don't assume such an air of innocence! *laa tətẓaahar kəll hal-qadd bəl-baraaʔa.*
assumption - *ʔəftiraaḍ* pl. *-aat.* This plan is based on the assumption that there will be no outside interference. *hal-xəṭṭa mabniyye Ɛala ʔəftiraaḍ ʔənno maa yṣiir tadaxxol xaarži.*
assurance - 1. *taʔkiid* pl. *-aat.* We can't rely on his assurance that he'll pay on time. *maa fiina nəƐtəmed Ɛala taʔkiido ʔənno raḥa yədfaƐ Ɛal-waqət.* 2. *siḡa bən-nafəs.* He tackled the job with assurance and efficiency. *Ɛaalaž əš-šaǵle bəs-siḡa b-nafso wəl-kafaaʔa.*
to **assure** - 1. *ʔakkad.* He assured us that he would be there. *ʔakkád-əlna ʔənno laḥa ykuun əhniik.* 2. *ḍəmen (a ḍamaan//nḍaman).* This government project will assure a considerable increase in the agricultural production. *hal-mašruuƐ tabaƐ l-əḥkuume laḥa yəḍman əzyaade laa baʔs fiiha bəl-ʔəntaaž əz-ziraaƐi.*
Assyria - *ʔaašuurya.*
Assyrian - *ʔaašuuri**.
asthma - *rabu.*
to **astonish** - *zahal (e zhuul//nzahal), dahaš (e dahše//ndahaš).* His courage astonished everyone. *šažaaƐto zahlet kəll waaḥed.*
to be astonished at - *ndahaš mən, nzahal mən.* We were astonished at the great number of people who attended the meeting. *ndahašna mən kətret ən-naas yalli ḥəḍru l-ʔəžtimaaƐ.*
astonishing - *mədheš.* What an astonishing story! *šuu qəṣṣa mədəhše!*
astonishment - *dahše.* He couldn't conceal his astonishment. *maa qəder yəxfi dahəšto.*
astronaut - *raaʔed~* (pl. *ruwwaad~*) *əl-faḍaaʔ.*
astronomer - *falaki** pl. *-iyyiin.*
astronomical - 1. *falaki**. The calendar contains a number of astronomical data. *r-roznaama fiiha Ɛəddet maƐluumaat falakiyye.* 2. *baaheẓ, žnuuni**. That lawyer charges astronomical fees. *hal-muḥaami byaaxod əʔžuur baahẓa.*
astronomy - *Ɛəlm~ əl-falak.*
Aswan - *ʔaswaan.*
asylum - 1. *məstašfa~* (pl. *məstašfayaat~*) *mažaniin.* People say she was in an asylum for two years. *biquulu ʔənna kaanet əb-məstašfa mažaniin la-məddet sənteen.* 2. *ḥaqq əl-lužuuʔ.* The refugees asked for political asylum. *l-laažʔiin ṭalabu ḥaqq əl-lužuuʔ əs-siyaasi.*
at - 1. *b-.* The streetcar stops at the next corner. *t-tramwaay biwaqqef bəl-qərne ž-žaaye.* -- The children are at school. *ẓ-ẓǵaar bəl-madrase.* -- It happened at night. *ḥadset bəl-leel.* -- He drove his car at full speed. *saaq sayyaarto b-ʔaḡṣa sərƐa.* 2. *Ɛand.* We were at the tailor's. *kənna Ɛand əl-xayyaaṭ.* -- I met him at the dentist's. *ṣaadafto Ɛand ḥakiim əs-snaan.* 3. *waqət, Ɛand.* We started out at daybreak. *mšiina waqt əṭluuƐ əl-fažər.* -- We reached the top of the mountain at sunset. *wṣəlna la-raas əž-žabal waqt əǵruub əš-šaməs.* 4. *waqət(-ma).* He could read and write at the age of four. *kaan yaƐref yeqra w-yəktob waqət kaan Ɛəmro ʔarbaƐ əsniin.* 5. *binaaʔan Ɛala.* I did it at his request. *saaweetha binaaʔan Ɛala ṭalabo.* 6. *mən.* At a word from him we changed our plans. *mən kəlme mənno ǵayyarna xəṭaṭna.*
**He came at three o'clock. *ʔəža s-saaƐa tlaate.*
**He generally comes home at noon. *Ɛaadatan byəži Ɛal-beet əḍ-ḍəhər.*
at all - see **all**.
at all costs - *mahma kaan ət-taman.* We must get it at all costs. *laazem nəḥṣal Ɛalée mahma kaan ət-taman.*
at best - *b-ʔaḥsan əl-ʔəḥtimaalaat.* At best it's an unpleasant job. *b-ʔaḥsan əl-ʔəḥtimaalaat hiyye šaǵle maa bətsərr.* -- He's an average student at best. *b-ʔaḥsan əl-ʔəḥtimaalaat huwwe təlmiiz waṣaṭ.*
at first - *bəl-ʔawwal.* At first we didn't like the town. *bəl-ʔawwal maa Ɛažbətna l-balad.*
at home - 1. *bəl-beet.* I'll be at home after five. *laḥa kuun bəl-beet baƐd əl-xamse.* 2. *ḍaliiƐ.* He is perfectly at home in that field. *huwwe ḍaliiƐ tamaam əb-hal-məḍmaar.*
**We like our guests to feel at home when they're with us. *mənḥəbb əḍyuufna yəšəƐru ʔənno l-beet beeton lamma ykuunu Ɛanna.*
**Make yourself at home. *tfaḍḍal, l-beet beetak.*
at it - *fiiha.* We've been at it for quite a while. *ṣar-əlna fiiha mən mədde.*
**He's at it again! *Ɛaadet ḥaliime la-Ɛaadəta l-qadiime.*
at last - *w-ʔaxiiran.* He's here at last. *w-ʔaxiiran ʔəža.*
at least - *Ɛal-ʔaqall, bəl-maqalli.* There were at least a hundred people present. *kaan fii Ɛal-ʔaqall miit zalame mawžuud.* -- You could thank him at least. *Ɛal-ʔaqall ətšakkaro.*
at most - *Ɛal-ʔaktar.* At most the bill will come to twenty pounds. *Ɛal-ʔaktar əl-faatuura raḥa təṭlaƐ la-Ɛəšriin leera.*
at once - 1. *ḥaalan, Ɛal-foor, Ɛal-ḥaarek.* Do it at once. *saawiiha ḥaalan.* 2. *b-waqət waaḥed.* I can't do everything at once. *maa bəqder saawi kəll šii b-waqət waaḥed.*
at random - *Ɛal-Ɛəmyaani.* He chose a glass at random from the shelf. *snaawal kaase Ɛal-Ɛəmyaani mən Ɛar-raff.*
at that - 1. *Ɛand hoon.* Let's leave it at that. *xalliina nətrəka Ɛand hoon.* -- We'll let it go at that for the time being. *mənxalliiha Ɛand hoon bəl-waqt əl-ḥaaḍer.* 2. *fooq haada.* And it will mean a lot of work at that. *w-fiiha kamaan šəǵl əktiir fooq haada.*
at times - 1. *ʔaḥyaanan, ʔawaqiit.* At times I'm doubtful. *ʔaḥyaanan bətlaaqiini šaakek.* -- At times he's very companionable, at others he seems moody. *ʔawaqiit huwwe məƐəšraani ktiir, w-ʔawaqiit byəẓhar nəked.* 2. *b-ʔawqaat.* At times like this I'm ready to quit my job. *b-ʔawqaat mətəl hayy məstƐədd ʔətrek šəǵli.*
at will - *mətəl-ma bədd-* + pron. suff. of subj. They come and go at will. *biruuḥu w-byəžu mətəl-ma bəddon.*
even at that - *ḥatta w-law kaan heek.* Even at that I wouldn't pay more. *ḥatta w-law kaan heek maa bədfaƐ ʔaktar.* -- Even at that it'll be too much. *ḥatta w-law kaan heek bikuun əktiir.*
atheist - *məlḥed* pl. *-iin.*
athlete - *riyaaḍi** pl. *-iyyiin.*
athletic - *riyaaḍi**.
athletic field - *malƐab riyaaḍi* pl. *malaaƐeb riyaaḍiyye.*
athletics - *riyaaḍa.*
Atlantic Ocean - *l-əmḥiiṭ əl-ʔaṭlaṣi.*
atlas - *ʔaṭlaṣ* pl. *ʔaṭaaleṣ.* You find a detailed map of Anatolia on page 23 of the atlas. *bətlaaqi xariiṭa tafṣiiliyye Ɛan əl-ʔanaḍool əb-ṣafḥa xamsṭa Ɛəšriin bəl-ʔaṭlaṣ.*
Atlas Mountains - *žbaal~ əl-ʔaṭlaṣ.*
atmosphere - *žaww.* The upper layers of the atmosphere. *ṭabaqaat əž-žaww əl-Ɛəlya.* -- The negotiations were held in a cordial atmosphere. *l-əmfaawaḍaat ṣaaret əb-žaww wəddi.*
atmospheric - *žawwi**. Atmospheric tests were resumed last week. *staʔnafu t-tažaareb əž-žawwiyye ž-žəmƐa l-maaḍye.*
atom - *zarra* pl. *-aat.*
atomic - *zarri**. Atomic energy. *ṭaaqa zarriyye.*
atrocious - *məkreb.* She wears atrocious clothes. *btəlbes ʔawaaƐi məkərbe.*
atrocity - 1. *faẓaaƐa, waḥšiyye, hamažiyye.* The atrocity of these acts is unbelievable. *faẓaaƐet hal-ʔaƐmaal maa btətsaddaq.* 2. *faẓiiƐa pl. faẓaayeƐ.* Many atrocities were committed during the war. *nƐamlet faẓaayeƐ əktiire ʔawqaat əl-ḥarəb.*
to **attach** - 1. *rabaṭ (o rabəṭ//nrabaṭ).* Is the belt attached to the dress? *šuu ẓ-ẓənnaar marbuuṭ bər-roob?* 2. *Ɛallaq.* You attach too much importance to it. *Ɛam ətƐalleq Ɛaleeha ktiir ʔahammiyye.* 3. *ʔalḥaq.* He is a liaison officer attached to the American Embassy. *huwwe ḍaabeṭ ʔəttiṣaal məlḥaq bəs-safaara l-ʔameerkaaniyye.* 4. *ḥažaz (e ḥažəz//nḥažaz).* We can attach his salary if he doesn't pay up. *mnəqder nəḥžəz-lo maƐaašo ʔiza maa saddad.*
attached - *məttəṣel.* The library is attached to the main building. *l-maktabe məttəṣle bəl-binaaye r-raʔiisiyye.*
to be or become attached to - *tƐallaq b-.* She is very much attached to her grandmother. *hiyye ktiir mətƐallqa b-sətta.* -- I've become very attached to that child. *tƐallaqt əktiir əb-hal-walad.*
attaché - *məlḥaq* pl. *-iin.*
attachment - 1. *taƐalloq.* His attachment to his friend became even stronger after the death of his brother. *taƐallqo b-ṣaaḥbo ṣaar kamaan ʔaqwa baƐəd-ma maat*

ʔaxúu. 2. *məlḥaq* pl. *-aat*. The machine and attachments are in perfect condition. *l-ʔaale w-məlḥaqaatha b-ʔaḥsan ḥaal.*

attack - 1. *həžuum* pl. *-aat, hažme* pl. *-aat*. The attack was beaten back. *l-əhžuum ənradd*. 2. *noobe* pl. *-aat*. He had another attack yesterday. *ṣar-lo noobe taanye mbaareḥ.*

to attack - 1. *haažam//thaažam*. He was violently attacked in the newspapers. *haažaməto ž-žaraayed əb-šədde*. 2. *haažam, hažam (o həžuum//nhažam) ƐaIa*. Enemy tanks attacked our position at daybreak. *dabbaabaat əl-Ɛaduww haažamet mawaaqəƐna Ɛand əl-faž ər.* 3. *Ɛaalaž, dabbar*. We must attack the problem immediately. *laazem ənƐaaleš əl-masʔale Ɛal-ḥaarek.*

attempt - *mḥaawale* pl. *-aat*. It was a brave attempt even if nothing came of it. *kaanet əmḥaawale mahuule ḥatta w-law maa ṭəleƐ mənha šii.* -- An attempt was made on his life. *ṣaaret əmḥaawale Ɛala ḥayaato.*

to make an attempt to - *ḥaawal, žarrab*. At least make an attempt to be nice. *Ɛal-ʔaqall ḥaawel ətkuun laṭiif.*

to attempt - *ḥaawal, žarrab*. Don't attempt too much at one time. *laa tḥaawel təmsek miit šaġle sawa* or ***laa təmsek baṭṭiixteen əb-ʔiid waaḥde.*

to **attend** - 1. *ḥəḍer (a ḥḍuur), ḥaḍar (o ḥḍuur)*. Did you attend the meeting? *ḥḍərt əl-ʔəžtimaaƐ?* 2. *ltaḥaq b-*. I attended business school. *ltaḥaqt əb-madrast ət-tižaara*. 3. *Ɛaalaž, ḥakkam, ṭabbab*. What doctor attended you? *ʔanu doktoor Ɛaalažak?* 4. *ṣaaḥab, ʔaḥaaṭ b-*. The peculiar circumstances attending his sudden departure caused a lot of raised eyebrows. *ṣ-ṣuruuf əš-šaažže yalli ṣaaḥabet safaro Ɛala ġafle sabbabet dahše kbiire.*

to attend to - *xallaṣ, dabbar*. I still have some things to attend to. *ləssa Ɛandi kam šaġle bəddi xalléṣa.*

attendance - 1. *ḥḍuur*. Attendance is compulsory. *l-əḥḍuur ʔəžbaari.* 2. *(Ɛadad˜) l-əḥḍuur*. The attendance at the last three meetings has been very poor. *b-ʔaaxer tlətt ʔəžtimaaƐaat kaan Ɛadad l-əḥḍuur əktiir qaliil.*

attention - *ʔəntibaah*. I tried to attract his attention. *ḥaawalət ʔəlfet ʔəntibaaho.* -- Can you do it without attracting attention? *btəqder ətsaawiiha biduun-ma təlfet ʔəntibaah ḥada?* -- Attention please! *ʔəntibaah mən faḍəlkon!*

**I asked that his letter be given special attention. *ṭalabət yaaxdu rsaalto b-Ɛeen əl-ʔəƐtibaar.*

to call attention to - *nabbah Ɛala*. I've called attention to that repeatedly. *nabbahət Ɛala haš-šaġle Ɛəddet marraat.*

to pay attention - 1. *Ɛaṭa baalo*. I told him again and again, but he didn't pay attention. *qəlt-éllo marra w-marraat, bass maa Ɛaṭa baalo.* -- Pay close attention. *Ɛaṭi baalak əmniiḥ.* 2. *ntabah la-*. Don't pay any attention to his griping. *laa təntébeh la-tašakkiyaato.* -- Pay no attention to him. *laa təntəbéh-lo.*

attentive - 1. *məltéfet*. The manager was very attentive and anxious to please. *l-mudiir kaan əktiir məltéfet w-raġbaan yərḍi n-naas.* 2. *məntébeh, ṣaaġi*. The speaker had an attentive audience. *l-xaṭiib xaṭab əb-žamhuur məntébeh.*

attentively - *b-ʔəntibaah*. The children listened attentively. *l-əwlaad səməƐu b-ʔəntibaah.*

attitude - *mawqef* pl. *mawaaqef*. I don't like his attitude. *maa Ɛaažəbni mawəqfo.* -- What's your attitude toward the man? *šuu mawəqfak ʔənte mən haz-zalame?*

attorney (at law) - *muḥaami* pl. *-iin*.

to **attract** - 1. *žaab (i žeeb, žayabaan//nžaab)*. What's attracting the flies here? *šuu Ɛam yžiib əd-dəbbaan la-hoon?* 2. *žalab (e/o žaləb//nžalab)*. The Chamber of Commerce is making plans to attract industry to this area. *ġərfet ət-tižaara Ɛam taƐmel xəṭaṭ la-təžleb əṣ-ṣinaaƐa la-hal-manṭiqa.* 3. *lafat (e lafət)*. Be quiet! You're attracting attention. *ʔəhda baqa! Ɛam təlfet əl-ʔanṣaar.*

attraction - 1. *žaləb*. The attraction of new customers is our main concern at present. *žalb əz-zabaayen əž-žədad ʔahamm ʔaġraaḍna bəl-waqt əl-ḥaaḍer.* 2. *žaaðbiyye, səḥər*. The town's attraction lies in its many historic buildings. *žaaðbiit əl-balad əb-kətret mabaaniiha t-taariixiyye.* 3. *šii žaazeb* pl. *ʔašya žaazbe*. Her dancing is the big attraction in the show. *raqṣa humme ʔaktar šii žaazeb bəl-ḥafle.*

attractive - 1. *žazzaab*. She is very attractive. *hiyye žazzaabe ktiir.* 2. *məġri*. He made me an attractive offer. *qaddám-li Ɛarəḍ məġri.*

attribute - *ṣifa* pl. *-aat*. Kindness is one of his many attributes. *l-laṭaafe waaḥde mən ṣifaato l-əktiire.* -- In "*ʔaḷḷaahu taƐaalaa*", "*taƐaalaa*" is the attribute of "*ʔaḷḷaah*". *b-qoolna "ʔaḷḷaahu taƐaalaa", "taƐaalaa" ṣifa la- "ʔaḷḷaah".*

to attribute - *Ɛaza (i Ɛazu//nƐaza)*. This year's poor cotton harvest can be attributed to drought and locusts. *ḍəƐəf maḥṣuul əl-qəṭən has-sene byəƐzúu ləl-maḥəl wəž-žraad.*

auction - *mazaad* pl. *-aat*. I bought the three armchairs at an auction. *štareet ət-tlətt qalaaṭeq bəl-mazaad.*

to auction off - *nazzal bəl-mazaad*. They're going to auction off his entire estate. *laḥa ynazzlu bəl-mazaad kəll tərəkto.*

audience - 1. *l-ḥaaḍriin*. The audience is asked to remain seated. *r-ražaaʔ mn əl-ḥaaḍriin yəbqu qaaƐdiin.* 2. *žamhuur* pl. *žamahiir*. The audience was enthusiastic. *ž-žamhuur kaan mətḥammes.* -- His poetry appeals to a limited audience only. *šəƐro maa byəƐžeb ʔəlla žamhuur maḥduud mn ən-naas.* 3. *mqaabale* pl. *-aat*. His majesty granted him a special audience. *žalaalto tkarram Ɛalée b-əmqaabale xaaṣṣa.*

auditorium - 1. *qaaƐet˜* (pl. *-aat˜*) *ʔəḥtifaalaat*. The graduation ceremony will be held in the auditorium. *ḥaflet ət-taxarrož laḥa tṣiir əb-qaaƐet əl-ʔəḥtifaalaat.* 2. *ṣaalya* pl. *-aat*. The orchestra pit is between the stage and the auditorium. *maṭraḥ əl-ʔorkestra been əl-marsaḥ wəṣ-ṣaalya.*

August - *ʔaab, ʔaġəsṭos.*

aunt - 1. (father's sister) *Ɛamme* pl. *-aat*. 2. (mother's sister) *xaale* pl. *-aat*. 3. (wife of father's brother) *mart˜ əl-Ɛamm*. 4. (wife of mother's brother) *mart˜ əl-xaal.*

auspices - *ʔəšraaf*. The program is being conducted under government auspices. *l-bərnaamež maaši taḥət ʔəšraaf l-əḥkuume.*

Australia - *ʔəstraalya.*

Australian - *ʔəstraali*.*

Austria - *n-neemsa.*

Austrian - *neemsaawi*.*

authentic - 1. *ʔaṣli**. Have you ever tasted authentic Arab food? *dəqt-əllak šii marra ʔakəl Ɛarabi ʔaṣli?* 2. *mawsuuq fii*. Are the reports authentic? *šuu hal-ʔaxbaar mawsuuq fiiha?*

author - *mʔallef* pl. *-iin*. He always wanted to be an author. *daayman kaan bəddo ykuun əmʔallef.* -- Who's the author of that book? *miin əmʔallef hal-əktaab?*

authority - 1. *ṣəlṭa* pl. *-aat*. He has no authority to do that. *maa Ɛando ṣəlṭa yaƐmel haš-šii.* -- Do you have the authority to sign this contract for him? *Ɛandak ṣəlṭa təmḍi hal-kontraat Ɛanno?* 2. *maržeƐ* pl. *maraažeƐ*. He's an authority on labor problems. *humme maržeƐ əb-šuʔuun əl-Ɛəmmaal.* -- Apply to the proper authorities. *tqaddam ləl-maraažeƐ əl-məxtaṣṣa.*

on one's own authority - *Ɛala masʔuuliito l-xaaṣṣa*. I'll do it on my own authority. *laḥa ʔaƐméla Ɛala masʔuuliiti l-xaaṣṣa.*

authorization - *tafwiiḍ* pl. *tafawiiḍ, rəxṣa* pl. *rəxaṣ*. He did this without my authorization. *Ɛəméla biduun tafwiiḍ mənni.*

to **authorize** - *xawwal, fawwaḍ*. Who authorized you to spend that money? *miin xawwalak təṣrof hal-maṣaari?*

authorized - 1. *mfawwaḍ*. He is authorized to search your baggage. *humme mfawwaḍ yfatteš Ɛafšak.* 2. *maʔzuun fii*. Is this an authorized translation of the book? *hayy taržame maʔzuun fiiha ləl-əktaab?*

auto - *sayyaara* pl. *-aat.*

autocracy - *ʔəstəbdaad.*

autocrat - *məstbədd* pl. *-iin.*

autocratic - *ʔəstəbdaadi*.*

automat - *ʔotomatiik.*

automatic - 1. *farəd* pl. *fruude*. He drew an automatic and fired. *saḥab farəd w-qawwaṣ.* 2. *ʔotomatiiki**. Is this an automatic pump? *hayye trəmbe ʔotomatiikiyye?* -- Her response was automatic. *kaan radd fəƐla ʔotomatiiki.*

automatically - *b-ṣuura ʔotomatiikiyye*. He reached automatically for his hat. *snaawal bərneeṭṭo b-ṣuura ʔotomatiikiyye.* -- The pistol ejects the shells automatically. *l-farəd byəntor əl-fašak əb-ṣuura ʔotomatiikiyye.*

automobile - *sayyaara* pl. *-aat.*

autonomy - *ḥəkəm saati*.*

autumn - *xariif*. I hope to stay through the autumn. *bətʔammal ḍall la-ʔaaxer əl-xariif.*

available - 1. *taḥt əl-ʔiid*. Every available car is

being used. *kəll sayyaara taḥt ᵊl-ʔiid məstaƐmale.* -- Those documents were not available to me. *hal-məstanadaat maa kaanu taḥᵊt ʔiidi.* 2. *mawǯuud.* Many of these articles are no longer available. *ktiir mən hal-ʔaṣnaaf maa Ɛaadet mawǯuude.* 3. *faaḍi.* When will the director be available? *ʔeemta l-mudiir bikuun faaḍi?*

to **avenge** - *ntaqam, ʔaxad taar.* He set out to avenge his brother's death. *raaḥ yəntəqem la-qatᵊl ʔaxúu* or *raaḥ yaaxod taar damm ʔaxúu.*

avenue - *šaareƐ* pl. *šawaareƐ.*

average - **1.** *waṣaṭ, mƐaddal.* He's better than the average. *huwwe fooq ᵊl-waṣaṭ.* **2.** *waṣaṭ, mətwaṣṣeṭ.* He's of average intelligence. *zakda waṣaṭ* (or *mətwaṣṣeṭ*) or *huwwe mətwaṣṣeṭ ᵊz-zaka.* **3.** *mƐaddal˜..., waṣaṭi˜...* What is the average temperature here? *šuu mƐaddal daraǯet ᵊl-ḥaraara hoon?*

on the average - *waṣaṭiyyan, b-ᵊmƐaddal.* On the average I go to the movies once a week. *bruuḥ Ɛas-siinama waṣaṭiyyan marra waaḥde bᵊǯ-ǯəmƐa.*

to average: He averages sixty dollars a week. *biṭaaleƐ waṣaṭiyyan səttiin dolaar bᵊǯ-ǯəmƐa.* -- We averaged forty miles an hour. *mšiina b-ᵊmƐaddal ʔarᵊbƐiin miil bᵊs-saaƐa.*

to **avoid** - *tḥaaša, dǯannab, btaƐad Ɛan.* Why is he avoiding me? *leeš Ɛam yətḥaašaani?* -- Avoid that, by all means. *btəƐed Ɛan haš-šii b-kəll ᵊẓ-ẓuruuf.*

**I avoid him as I would a plague. *bəhrob mənno mətᵊl-ma bəhrob mn ᵊṭ-ṭaaƐuun.*

Awaj River - *nahr˜ ᵊl-ʔaƐwaǯ.*

awake - *ṣaḥyaan.* I'm not fully awake yet. *ləssaani maa-li ṣaḥyaan tamaam.*

to awake - *faaq (i feeqa).* I awoke at seven o'clock. *fəqt ᵊs-saaƐa sabƐa.*

to **awaken** - *fayyaq.* I was awakened by a noise. *fayyaqə́tni ḍooǯe* or ***fəqᵊt mən ḍooǯe.*

award - *ǯaayze* pl. *ǯawaayez.* The film received a special award for good photography. *l-fəlᵊm ʔaxad ǯaayze xaaṣṣa mənšaan ᵊt-taṣwiir ᵊl-məmtaaz.*

to award - *manaḥ (a manᵊḥ/nmanaḥ).* They awarded her a cash prize. *manaḥuuha ǯaayze naqdiyye.*

aware - *Ɛarfaan.* We're aware of all that. *nəḥna Ɛarfaaniin ᵊb-kəll haš-šii.* -- He doesn't seem to be aware of the imminent danger. *mbayyen Ɛaléε maa-lo Ɛarfaan bᵊl-xaṭar yalli Ɛam ywaaǯho.*

away - **1.** *muu mawǯuud.* I was away when he called. *kənᵊt muu mawǯuud lamma talfán-li.* **2.** *msaafer.* Have you been away? *šuu kənt ᵊmsaafer?*

**Most of her life she lived away from home. *ʔaktar ḥayaata Ɛaašet bᵊl-ġərbe.*

**It's far away from here. *bƐiid ᵊktiir mən hoon.*

**Away with it! *xalləṣna mənha!*

awful - **1.** *mətl ᵊz-zəfᵊt.* The party was awful! *l-ḥafle kaanet mətl ᵊz-zəfᵊt!* **2.** *šaniiƐ.* I made an awful mistake. *Ɛməlᵊt ġalṭa šaniiƐa.*

**She looks awful after her long illness. *ṣaaret mətl ᵊš-šabaḥ baƐᵊd ḍaƐfə́ta ṭ-ṭawiile.*

awfully - *ǯəddan.* I'm awfully tired. *(ʔana) ǯəddan taƐbaan* or ***fazaaƐa šuu taƐbaan ʔana.*

awhile - *la-fatra ẓġiire.* He was here awhile this afternoon. *kaan hoon la-fatra ẓġiire baƐd ᵊḍ-ḍəhr ᵊl-yoom.*

awkward - **1.** *malxuum.* Is he so awkward in everything he does? *šuu kəll hal-qadd malxuum ᵊb-kəll šaġle bisaawiiha?* **2.** *məḥreǯ.* It was an awkward situation. *kaan mawqef məḥreǯ.*

awl - *maxraz* pl. *maxaarez.*

awning - *xeeme* pl. *-aat* and *xiyam, rwaaq* pl. *-aat.*

ax - *faas* pl. *-aat* and *fuus.*

axis - *məḥwar* pl. *maḥaawer.*

axle - *ʔakᵊs* pl. *-aat.*

B

Baalbek - *baƐᵊlbak, bƐalbak.*

Bab el Mandeb - *baab˜ ᵊl-mandab.*

baby - **1.** *beebée* pl. *beebiyaat, ṭəfᵊl* f. *ṭəfle* pl. *ṭfaal.* The baby is crying. *l-beebée Ɛam yəbki.* -- I won't let myself be treated like a baby. *maa bḥəbb nafsi ʔətƐaamal mətᵊl ṭəfl ᵊẓġiir.* **2.** *ʔaẓġar waaḥed.* She's the baby of the family. *hiyye ʔaẓġar waaḥde bᵊl-Ɛeele.* **3.** *ẓġiir* pl. *ẓġaar.* Children like baby animals. *l-ᵊwlaad biḥəbbu l-ḥaywaanaat ᵊẓ-ẓġaar.* **4.** *wallaadi*.* What's the best store in town for baby clothes? *ʔanu ʔaḥsan maxzan bᵊl-balad bibiiƐ ʔawaaƐi wallaadiyye?*

baby carriage - *Ɛarabiit˜ (pl. -iyyaat˜) ᵊwlaad.*

to baby - *dallal.* You baby your children too much. *Ɛam ᵊddallel ᵊwlaadak ᵊktiir.*

Babylon - *baabel.*

Babylonian - *baabili*.*

baccalaureate - *bakaloorya.*

bachelor - **1.** *Ɛəzzaabi* pl. *-iyye* and *-iyyiin.* My uncle is a confirmed bachelor. *Ɛammi Ɛəzzaabi ṣamiim* or ***Ɛammi mən ḥəzb ᵊl-Ɛəzzaabiyyiin.* **2.** *bakalooryus.* He's working on his bachelor's degree in engineering. *Ɛam yḥaḍḍer la-šahaadet ᵊl-bakalooryus bᵊl-handase.*

back - **1.** *ḍahᵊr* pl. *ḍhuura.* My back aches. *ḍahri Ɛam yəǯaƐni.* -- He was lying on his back. *kaan məṣṣaṭṭeḥ Ɛala ḍahro.* -- I wonder if you could mend this book. Its back is coming off. *yaa-tára btəqder ᵊtṣalláḥ-li hal-ᵊktaab. ḍahro Ɛam yənféreṭ.* -- They did it behind my back. *Ɛəmluuha wara ḍahri* or ***Ɛəmluuha b-qafaayi.* **2.** *qafa.* He was hit on the back of his head. *nəṣaab ᵊb-qafa raaso.* -- He slapped her with the back of his hand. *laṭáša b-qafa ʔiido.* **3.** *masnad* pl. *masaaned.* This chair has a higher back. *hal-kərsi haada masnado ʔaƐla.* **4.** *warraani*, xalfi*.* The back rooms are somewhat dark. *l-ʔuwaḍ ᵊl-warraaniyye mƐattme šwayye.* **5.** *maksuur.* I have one month's back pay coming to me. *ʔəli maƐaaš maksuur Ɛan šahᵊr waaḥed laḥa yəǯiini.*

**He isn't back yet. *ləssaato maa rəǯeƐ.*

**May I have it back? *məmken ʔəstarǯə́Ɛa?*

**The problem was in the back of my mind all day. *l-masʔale kaanet mətƐamᵊšqa b-Ɛaqli ṭuul ᵊn-nhaar.*

back and forth - *raayeḥ raaǯeƐ.* He walked back and forth in the room. *kaan Ɛam yəmši raayeḥ raaǯeƐ bᵊl-ʔuuḍa.* -- The trucks are moving back and forth between the station and our house. *l-kamyoonaat maašye raayḥa raaǯƐa been l-ᵊmḥaṭṭa w-beetna.*

in back - *bᵊl-qafa, wara.* Why don't you sit in back? *leeš maa btəqƐod bᵊl-qafa?*

in back of - *wara˜, b-qafa˜, xalf˜.* There's a garden in back of the house. *fii ǯneene wara l-beet.* -- I wonder who is in back of the plan. *yaa-tára miin b-qafa l-xəṭṭa.*

to turn one's back on - *daar (i ø) ḍahro la-.* He turned his back on me while I was still talking. *dar-li ḍahro w-ʔana ləssaani Ɛam ʔəḥki.* -- You turned your back on me when I needed you most. *waqt ᵊštaddet ḥaaǯti ʔəlak dərt-ə́lli ḍahrak* (or ***warǯeetni Ɛarḍ ᵊktaafak*).

to back - *ʔayyad, saanad, Ɛaaḍad.* All parties are backing him. *kəll ᵊl-ʔaḥzaab Ɛam ᵊtʔayydo.*

to back down - *traaǯaƐ.* We can't back down now. *maa fiina nətraaǯaƐ hallaq.*

to back out (of) - **1.** *ṭəleƐ (a ṭluuƐ) la-wara (mən).* I scraped the fender as I was backing out of the garage. *šaḥaṭᵊt rəfraaf ᵊs-sayyaara w-ʔana ṭaaleƐ la-wara mn ᵊl-karaaǯ.* **2.** *malaṣ (o malᵊṣ) mən, traaǯaƐ mən, nsaḥab mən.* They're trying to back out of the deal as usual. *Ɛam yḥaawlu yəmᵊlṣu mn ᵊl-Ɛamaliyye mətl ᵊl-Ɛaade.*

to back up - **1.** *rəǯeƐ (a rǯuuƐ) la-wara.* Back up a little. *rǯaaƐ šwayye la-wara.* **2.** *ʔayyad, saanad, Ɛaaḍad.* I'm depending on you to back me up in this controversy. *məƐtə́med Ɛaleek ᵊtʔayyədni b-hal-xilaaf haada.*

backbone - **1.** *sənsəlt˜ (pl. sanaasel˜) ᵊḍ-ḍahᵊr.* The car crushed the cat's backbone. *s-sayyaara faƐset sənsəlᵊt ḍahr ᵊl-qaṭṭa.* **2.** *Ɛamuud faqari.* They say he's the backbone of the company. *biquulu ʔənno huwwe l-Ɛamuud ᵊl-faqari ləš-šərke.*

**If she only had a little more backbone! *law Ɛanda šwayyet ḥeel bass!*

backgammon - *(ləƐbet˜) ṭaawle.*

background - **1.** *ʔarḍiyye.* The background is too dark. *l-ʔarḍiyye ktiir ᵊmƐattme.* -- The material has a black background with white dots. *l-ᵊqmaaš* *ˀarḍiito sooda mnaqqaṭa ɛala ˀabyaḍ.* 2. *ṃaaḍi.* Of course, they'll check your background before they hire you. *maɛluum bəddon yətḥarru ɛan ṃaaḍiik qabᵊl-ma yəstaxᵊdmuuk.*

**He kept in the background. *xalla ḥaalo wara l-kawaliis.*

backing - *taˀyiid.* Does the club have any financial backing? *fii šii taˀyiid maali lən-naadi?*

backside - *ṭiiẓ* (f.) pl. *ṭyaaẓ.*

back talk - *ˀəɛtiraaḍ, raddˇ žawaab.* I won't have any back talk! *bala ˀəɛtiraaḍ!*

backward - 1. *mətˀaxxer, mətxallef.* The people there are very backward. *n-naas ᵊhniik ᵊktiir mətˀaxxriin.* 2. *mqaṣṣer ᵊb-ɛaqlo.* Her boy is a bit backward. *ˀəbna mqaṣṣer šwayye b-ɛaqlo.*

backward(s) - 1. *la-wara.* He slipped and fell backwards. *zaḥlet rəžlo w-wəqeɛ la-wara.* 2. *bᵊl-maqluub.* The word, read forward or backward, is always the same. *l-kəlme ˀiza btəqraaha mən ˀawwalha wəlla bᵊl-maqluub, daayman mətᵊl baɛḍa.* 3. *ɛal-maqluub.* You've got that sweater on backwards. *(ˀənte) laabes hal-kanze ɛal-maqluub.*

bad - 1. *ɛaaṭel, baṭṭaal.* That's not a bad idea. *hayye fəkra muu ɛaaṭle.* — That's not bad. *haada muu baṭṭaal.* -- He's not a bad fellow. *huwwe zalame muu baṭṭaal.* 2. *ɛaaṭel.* Her cooking is very bad. *ṭabxa ktiir ɛaaṭel.* 3. *radi** pl. *ˀardiya* and *radaaya.* The child is not bad, he's just spoiled. *l-walad maa-lo radi, bass ᵊmdallal.* -- We have to take the bad along with the good. *laazem nəqbal bᵊl-ᵊmniiḥ wᵊr-radi.* 4. *bəšeɛ, sayyeˀ.* His remarks show his bad taste. *mlaaḥaẓaato bəddəll ɛala zooqo l-bəšeɛ.* -- He never tries to control his bad temper. *maa biḥaawel ᵊmnoob yəẓboṭ xəlqo s-sayyeˀ.* 5. *sayyeˀ.* His business is going from bad to worse. *tižaarto maašye mən sayyeˀ la-ˀaswaˀ.* 6. *məˀzi**. Drinking a lot of coffee is bad for the nerves. *šərb ᵊl-qahwe ktiir məˀzi ləl-ˀaɛṣaab.* -- Those neighborhood children are a bad influence on his boy. *hal-ᵊwlaad ᵊl-ḥaara ˀəlhon taˀsiir məˀzi ɛala ˀəbno.* 7. *qawi**. I have a bad cold. *ɛandi rašᵊḥ qawi.* 8. *ḍɛiif.* He has bad eyes. *naẓaro ḍɛiif.* 9. *manzuuɛ, mɛaffen.* Throw the bad eggs away. *kəbb ᵊl-beeḍ ᵊl-manzuuɛ.* 10. *mašˀuum.* She took the bad news calmly. *tlaqqet ᵊl-xabar ᵊl-mašˀuum ᵊb-hadaawe.* 11. *mzawwar, mzayyaf.* He was charged with passing a bad check. *tahamu b-tadaawol šakk ᵊmzawwar.*

**I feel bad today. *maa-li ɛala baɛḍi l-yoom.*

**Now he feels very bad about it. *hallaq šaaɛer bᵊn-nadam ɛala haš-šağle.*

**Just ignore his bad manners, that's all. *laa taɛṭi baalak ɛala qəllet ˀadabo wᵊs-salaam.*

too bad - *xṣaara.* Too bad that you couldn't come. *xṣaara maa qdərᵊt təži.*

**That's too bad! *šii məˀsef!*

badly - 1. *b-qəllet ˀadab.* She behaved badly in front of all those people. *tṣarrafet ᵊb-qəllet ˀadab qəddaam kəll han-naas.* 2. *b-ṣuura ɛaaṭle.* The laboratory is badly equipped for that kind of research. *l-maxbar ᵊmžahhaz ᵊb-ṣuura ɛaaṭle la-heek nooɛ ᵊmn ᵊl-ˀabḥaas.*

badge - *šiɛaar* pl. *-aat.*

badger - *ğreeri* pl. *-iyyaat.*

badminton - *(ləɛbetˇ) r-riiše ṭ-ṭaaˀira.*

to baffle - *ḥayyar//tḥayyar.* His answer baffled me. *žawaabo ḥayyarni.*

baffling - *mḥayyer.* His reply was rather baffling. *žawaabo kaan ᵊmḥayyer la-daraže.*

bag - 1. *šantaaye* pl. *šanaati, šanta* pl. *šənat.* She took some change out of her bag. *ṭaalaɛet šwayyet fraaṭa mən šantaayəta.* -- Where can I check my bags? *ween bəqder ˀuudaɛ šanatiyyi?* 2. *kiis (waraq)* pl. *kyaas (waraq).* Put these apples in(to) a bag. *ḥəṭṭ-əlli hat-təffaaḥaat ᵊb-kiis (waraq).*

**They moved in on us, bag and baggage. *ˀəžu ɛaleena b-žiibon w-žabaabon w-ɛafšon.*

**Who let the cat out of the bag? *miin faša s-sərr?*

**He has the money and I'm left holding the bag. *huwwe ˀaxad ᵊl-maṣaari w-ˀana bqiit laa mən wara w-laa mən qəddaam.*

baggage - *ɛafᵊš, ğraaḍ* (pl.). I want to send my baggage on ahead. *bəddi sabbeq ɛafši.*

Baghdad - *bəğdaad.*

Bahrein - *l-baḥreen.*

bail - *kafaale* pl. *-aat.* The court fixed his bail at two thousand dollars. *l-maḥkame ḥaddadet kafaalto ˀalfeen dolaar.*

on bail - *taḥᵊt kafaale.* He's out on bail now. *ṭəleɛ hallaq taḥᵊt kafaale.*

to put up bail - *kəfel (a kafaale).* Who's going to put up bail for him? *miin bəddo yəkfalo?*

to **bail** - *ğaraf (o ğarᵊf//nğaraf), žaraf (o žarᵊf//nžaraf).* We used our helmets to bail the water out of the boat. *staɛmalna xəwadna la-nəğrof ᵊl-mayy ᵊmn ᵊš-šaxtuura.*

bait - *ṭəɛᵊm* pl. *ṭɛuum(e).* What do you use for bait? *šuu ṭ-ṭəɛᵊm yalli bətḥəṭṭo?*

**They offered him a lot of money, but he wouldn't take the bait. *ɛaraḍu ɛaléea maṣaari ktiir, bass ᵊl-ḥiile maa məšyet ɛaléea.*

to bait - 1. *ḥaṭṭ ṭəɛᵊm b-.* They baited the trap with cheese. *ḥaṭṭu ṭəɛᵊm žəbne bᵊl-maṣyade.* 2. *ğara (i ˀəğraaˀ//nğara).* He tried to bait him with a big bribe. *ḥaawal yəğrii b-rašwe kbiire.* 3. *nakraz.* She likes to bait her sister. *bətḥəbb ᵊtnakrez ˀəxta.*

to **bake** - 1. *xabaz (e/o xabᵊz, xabiiz//nxabaz).* Mother baked bread yesterday. *ṃaaṃa xabzet xəbz ᵊmbarreḥ.* 2. *šawa (i šawi//nšawa).* That kiln over there is used for baking the pottery. *hal-fərᵊn hadaak ɛam yəstaɛᵊmlúu la-šawi l-fəxxaar.*

**I haven't baked a cake in all my life. *maa ɛməlᵊt gaato b-ḥayaati.*

baker - *xabbaaz* pl. *-e* and *-iin, farraan* pl. *-e.*

bakery - *maxbaz* pl. *maxaabez, fərᵊn* pl. *fraan, xabbaaz* pl. *-e* and *-iin.* The bakery is around the corner. *l-maxbaz wara s-suuke.*

baking powder - *karbonaat.*

balance - 1. *tawaazon.* I lost my balance. *ḍawwaɛᵊt tawaazni.* 2. *miizaan* pl. *mayaziin* and *mawaziin.* I used the grocer's balance to weigh my packages. *staɛmalᵊt miizaan ᵊl-baqqaal la-ziin bakeetaati.* 3. *raṣiid, baaqi.* Pay one third down and the balance in monthly installments. *dfaaɛ ᵊt-təlᵊt salaf wᵊr-raṣiid bᵊt-taqṣiiṭ šahri.*

**His life hung in the balance. *ḥayaato kaanet waaqfe ɛala šaɛra.*

to balance - 1. *waazan.* Can you balance a stick on your forehead? *btaɛref ᵊtwaazen ɛaṣaaye ɛala žbiinak?* 2. *ɛaadal.* His losses balance his gains. *maxaaṣro bətɛaadel maraabḥo.* 3. *twaazan, tɛaadal.* Does the account balance? *šuu l-ᵊḥsaab mətwaazen?*

balcony - *balkoon* pl. *-aat* and *balakiin.* I have an apartment with a balcony. *ɛandi šaqqa fiiha balkoon.* — We had seats in the first balcony. *kaanet maḥallaatna bᵊl-balkoon ᵊl-ˀawwalaani.*

bald - *ˀaṣlaɛ* f. *ṣalɛa* pl. *ṣəlᵊɛ.* He has a bald head. *raaso ˀaṣlaɛ.* — He has a bald spot. *fii qərne ṣalɛa b-raaso.*

bale - *baale* pl. *-aat.*

Balkan - *l-balqaan.* The Balkan states. *duwal ᵊl-balqaan.*

ball - 1. *ṭaabe* pl. *-aat.* They played ball all afternoon. *ləɛbu bᵊṭ-ṭaabe ṭuul baɛd ᵊḍ-ḍəhᵊr.* 2. *kabkuube* pl. *kabakiib, karra* pl. *-aat.* I'd like a ball of white wool. *bəddi kabkuubet ṣuuf ˀabyaḍ.* 3. *kabkuube* pl. *kabakiib.* Shape the meat into little balls and place them in the frying pan. *kabkeb ᵊl-laḥme kabakiib ᵊzğaar w-ḥəṭṭon bᵊl-məqlaaye.*

balled up - *mxarbaṭ.* He was all balled up. *kaan kəllo mxarbaṭ.*

ball - *ḥafle* (pl. *-aat*) *raaqṣa, baal* pl. *-aat.* Have you been invited to the ball? *nɛazamᵊt ləl-ḥafle r-raaqṣa?*

**We had a real ball at the party. *waḷḷa nḅaṣaṭna ktiir bᵊl-ḥafle.*

ball bearing - *ruulma* pl. *ruulmanaat, kərsi biili* pl. *karaasi biiliyye.*

ballet - *baléa.*

balloon - *ḅaaḷoon* pl. *-aat.*

ballot - *warqetˇ* (pl. *wraaqˇ*) *ˀəntixaab.* Have all the ballots been counted? *šuu kəll ᵊwraaq ᵊl-ˀəntixaab ᵊnɛaddu?*

secret ballot - *ˀəqtiraaɛ sərri.*

to cast a ballot - *ṣawwaṭ.* How many ballots were cast for their candidate? *kam waaḥed ṣawwaṭu la-mraššḥon?* or **kam ṣooṭ ˀaxad ᵊmraššḥon?*

ball-point pen - *qalam* (pl. *qlaam*) *stiilo.*

ballroom - *ṣaalyetˇ* (pl. *-aatˇ*) *ḥaflaat.*

Baltic Sea - *ḅaḥrˇ ᵊl-ḅalṭiiq.*

balm - *balasaan, balsam.*

balsam - *balasaan, balsam.*

balsam tree - *šažaretˇ* (pl. *šažarˇ*) *balasaan.*

banana - *mooze* coll. *mooz* pl. *-aat.*

band - 1. *žooqa* pl. *-aat* and *žwaaq.* The band played dances all evening. *ž-žooqa daqqet ˀalḥaan raaqṣa ṭuul ᵊl-masa.* 2. *šriiṭ* pl. *šaraayeṭ.* I need a new band for this hat. *laazəmni šriiṭ ᵊždiid la-hal-bərneeṭa.*

bandage - *ḍmaaḍ* pl. *-aat.* Don't take off the bandage. *laa tqiim ᵊḍ-ḍmaaḍ.*

to bandage - *ḍammaḍ.* You'd better bandage the cut at once. *ʔaḥsán-lak ᵊḍḍammeḍ ᵊž-žərᵊḥ ɛal-ḥaarek.*

bandit - *qaṭṭaaɛ˜* (pl. *qəṭṭaaɛ˜*) *ṭariiq.*

band leader - *raʔiis˜* (pl. *rəʔasa˜*) *žooqa.*

bandoleer - *znaad˜* (pl. *-aat˜*) *fašak.*

bang - *xabṭa* pl. *-aat.* She was startled by the loud bang. *šahqet mən ᵊl-xabṭa l-qawiyye.*

to bang - *xabaṭ (o xabᵊṭ//nxabaṭ).* He banged the book down on the table. *xabaṭ l-ᵊktaab ɛaṭ-ṭaawle.*— Who's that banging on the door? *miin ɛam yəxboṭ ɛal-baab?*

banister - *darabziin* pl. *-aat.*

bank - *ḍaffe* pl. *ḍfaaf.* After the heavy rains, the river overflowed its banks. *baɛd ᵊl-maṭar ᵊl-qawiyye ṇ-ṇahᵊṛ ṭaff ɛala ḍaffteeno.*

bank - *ḅaṇk* pl. *bnuuk(e).* I keep my money in the bank. *bxalli maṣariyyi bᵊl-ḅaṇk.*

to bank on - *ttakal ɛala.* You can bank on that. *fiik təttékel ɛala haš-šii.*

bank book - *daftar˜* (pl. *dafaater˜*) *šakkaat.*

banker - *bankyeer* pl. *-iyye.*

bank note - *waraqa naqdiyye* pl. *wraaq naqdiyye, ḅaṇknoot* pl. *-aat.*

bankrupt - *mfalles, məfles.* He's bankrupt. *huwwe mfalles.*

to go bankrupt - *fallas.* The company went bankrupt during the depression. *š-šərke fallaset ʔiyyaam ᵊl-kasaad.*

bankruptcy - *ʔəflaas, tafliise.* The firm had to go into bankruptcy. *š-šərke nǎabret təɛlen ʔəflaasa.*

banner - *raaye* pl. *-aat.*

banquet - *waliime* pl. *walaayem.*

baptism - *ɛmaad.*

to **baptize** - *ɛammad//tɛammad.* When is the baby going to be baptized? *ʔeemta laḥa yətɛammad ᵊl-beebée?*

bar - **1.** *looḥ* pl. *lwaaḥ, qaaleb* pl. *qawaaleb.* Here's a bar of soap. *hayy looḥ ṣaabuun.* -- He bought a bar of chocolate. *štara qaaleb šakaleeṭa.* **2.** *qaḍiib* pl. *qəḍbaan.* He barricaded the door with an iron bar. *darbas ᵊl-baab ᵊb-qaḍiib ḥadiid.* **3.** *ḅaar* pl. *-aat.* Let's meet in the bar in an hour. *mnəštémeɛ bᵊl-ḅaar baɛᵊd saaɛa.* — Let's have a drink at the bar. *xalliina naaxod qadaḥ ɛal-ḅaar.* **4.** *maqṭaɛ* pl. *maqaaṭeɛ.* He played a few bars of my favorite waltz. *daqq-álli kam maqṭaɛ mən ʔaḥabb ᵊl-vaalsaat la-qalbi.* **5.** *nağaabet˜* (pl. *-aat˜*) *muḥaamiin.* When were you admitted to the bar? *ʔeemta nqabalt ᵊb-nağaabet ᵊl-muḥaamiin?*

behind bars - *bᵊš-šabake, ɛand xaalto.* We heard he's behind bars. *sməɛna ʔənno bᵊš-šabake.*

to bar - **1.** *darbas//ddarbas.* He forgot to bar the gate. *nəsi ydarbes ᵊl-bawwaabe.* **2.** *sadd (ə sadd//nsadd).* A fallen tree barred our way. *fii šažara waaqɛa saddét-ᵊlna ṭariiqna.* **3.** *manaɛ (a manᵊɛ//mmanaɛ).* They barred him from joining the club. *manaɛúu yənḍamm lən-naadi.*

Barada River - *ṇahᵊṛ˜ barada.*

barbarian - **1.** (n.) *waḥᵊš* pl. *wḥuuš, barbari* pl. *baraabra.* **2.** (adj.) *mətwaḥḥeš, barbari*.*

barbaric - *barbari*, waḥši*.*

barbarism - *barbariyye, waḥšiyye, tawaḥḥoš.*

barbed wire - *ʔaslaak šaaʔike* (pl.).

barber - *ḥallaaq* pl. *-iin* and *-a.* Is there a good barber in town? *fii šii ḥallaaq ᵊmniiḥ bᵊl-balad?*

barber shop - *(dəkkaanet˜) ḥallaaq* pl. *(dakakiin˜) ḥallaaqiin.*

bare - **1.** *makšuuf.* The nights are too chilly now to go out with bare arms. *l-layaali ktiir baarde hallaq la-təmši fiiha w-ʔideek makšuufe.* **2.** *ɛaryaan, ɛaari.* The trees are still bare. *š-šažar ləssaato ɛaryaan.* **3.** *ʔažrad* f. *žarda* pl. *žərᵊd.* The walls look so bare. *l-ḥiiṭaan ᵊmbayyne ktiir žarda.* **4.** *mžarrad.* These are the bare facts. *hayy ᵊl-ḥaqaayeq l-ᵊmžarrade.*

**She strangled him with her bare hands. *b-ʔideeha xdanqəto.*

**You shouldn't run around in your bare feet! *l-mafruuḍ maa təmši ḥaafi.*

to bare - *kašaf (e/o kašᵊf) ɛan.* Bare your left arm for the vaccination please. *kšeef ɛan ʔiidak ᵊš-šmaal lət-taṭɛiim baḷḷa.*

barefoot - *ḥaafi* pl. *-yiin* and *ḥawaafa.* Children, don't run around barefoot! *ya wlaad, laa təmšu ḥawaafa!*

bareheaded - *raaso makšuuf.* Don't walk bareheaded in the glaring sun. *laa təmši w-raasak makšuuf* (or ***bala šii ɛala raasak*) *bᵊš-šams ᵊl-məḥᵊrqa.*

barely - **1.** *doob-* + pron. suff., *bᵊl-kaad.* He's barely ten. *doobo ɛəmro ɛašr ᵊsniin.* -- I can barely meet my expenses. *(yaa-)doobi quum ᵊb-maṣariifi.* **2.** *bᵊz-zoor.* She barely managed it. *bᵊz-zoor dabbarəta.* -- We barely got by. *bᵊz-zoor nafadna.*

bargain - **1.** *ʔəttifaaq* pl. *-aat.* According to our bargain you were to pay half. *ḥasab ʔəttifaaqna kaan ɛaleek tədfaɛ ᵊn-nəṣṣ.* **2.** *ṣafqa* pl. *-aat, šarwe* pl. *-aat.* After much haggling, they struck a bargain. *baɛᵊd ʔaxᵊd w-radd ṭawiil ᵊttafaqu ɛaṣ-ṣafqa.* **3.** *laqṭa* pl. *-aat.* This book was a bargain. *hal-ᵊktaab kaan laqṭa.*

**All right, it's a bargain! *ṭayyeb, ttafaqna baqa!*

**That's just part of the bargain. *halli byaakol ḥəlwə́ta byaakol mərrə́ta.*

into the bargain - **1.** *bᵊl-beeɛa, bᵊl-koome.* Throw that bracelet into the bargain, and you've got a deal. *ḥəṭṭ has-swaara bᵊl-beeɛa wᵊš-šarwe xalṣet.* **2.** *fooq haad(a).* I lost all my money and got bawled out into the bargain. *xṣərᵊt kəll maṣariyyi w-fooq haada ʔakalᵊt bahdale.*

to strike a bargain - *ttafaq ɛal-beeɛa, ttafaq ɛaṣ-ṣafqa.* Did you strike a bargain? *ttafaqtu ɛal-beeɛa?*

to bargain - *faaṣal, kaasar, saawam.* I tried to bargain with him. *ḥaawalᵊt faaṣlo.*

**We got more trouble than we bargained for. *ʔəžətna mašaakel ʔaktar məmma kaan bᵊl-ḥəsbaan.*

bark - *qəšᵊr.* Birch trees have a thin bark. *šažar ᵊl-batuula qəšro rqiiq.*

to **bark** - **1.** *ɛawwa.* The dog barked at me. *l-kalᵊb ɛawwa ɛaliyyi.* **2.** *ɛayyaṭ, ṣarax (a ṣarᵊx, ṣraax).* The foreman barked at everybody today. *l-ᵊmnaaẓer kaan ɛam yɛayyeṭ ɛala* (or *yəṣrax b-*) *kəll ᵊl-ɛaalam ᵊl-yoom.*

**You're barking up the wrong tree. *ɛam ᵊddəqq ɛal-baab ᵊl-ġalaṭ.*

barley - *šɛiir.*

barn - *baayke* pl. *bawaayek.*

barnyard - *ḥooš* pl. *ḥwaaš.*

barometer - *baarometr* pl. *-aat.*

barrack(s) - *qəšle* pl. *qəšal, sakane* pl. *-aat.* Our barracks were built of concrete. *qəšlətna kaanet ᵊmɛammara bᵊl-beetoṇ.* -- The refugees were housed in barracks. *sakkanu l-laažʔiin ᵊb-sakanaat.*

barrel - **1.** *barmiil* pl. *baramiil.* The oil well yields one thousand barrels a day. *biir-ᵊz-zeet ɛam yaɛṭi ʔalᵊf barmiil bᵊl-yoom.* **2.** *maasuura* pl. *mawasiir.* I have to clean and oil the barrel of this rifle. *laazem naḍḍef w-zayyet maasuurᵊt hal-baaruude.*

barrier - *ḥaažez* pl. *ḥawaažez.*

base - *ğaaɛde* pl. *ğawaaɛed.* The base of the statue is still standing. *ğaaɛədt ᵊt-təmsaal ləssaaha waaqfe.* — The country maintains a naval and an air base on the island. *d-dawle ʔəlha ğaaɛde baḥriyye w-ğaaɛde žawwiyye bᵊž-žaziire.*

to base - *bana (i ə // nbana).* On what do you base your figures? *ɛala ʔanu ʔasaas ɛam təbni ʔarğaamak?* — His argument is based on the assumption that ... *ḥəžžto mabniyye ɛala farᵊḍ ʔənno ...*

baseless - *bala ʔasaas.* The newspapers ran a completely baseless story about her. *ž-žaraayed katbet qəṣṣa ɛanha kəlla bala ʔasaas.*

basement - *qabu* pl. *ʔəqᵊbye.*

bashful - *xažuul.* She's bashful in company. *hiyye xažuule lamma bətkuun maɛ ᵊn-naas.*

**Don't be bashful, go right to it. *maa bədda ḥaya, mədd ʔiidak!*

basic - *ʔasaasi*.*

basically - *bᵊl-ʔasaas, ʔasaasan.*

basil - *riiḥaan.*

basin - **1.** *maġsale* pl. *maġaasel.* You can wash the baby's clothes in the basin. *btəqᵊdri təġᵊsli ʔawaaɛi l-beebée bᵊl-maġsale.* **2.** *ḥooḍ* pl. *ḥwaaḍ.* The basin is surrounded by trees on three sides. *l-ḥooḍ ɛala tlətt žihaato fii šažar.*

basis - *ʔasaas* pl. *ʔəsos.* We can't continue on this basis. *maa mnəqder nəstmerr ɛala hal-ʔasaas.* -- This concept constitutes the basis of his entire theory. *hal-fəkra hiyye ʔasaas kəll naẓariito.*

on the basis of - *binaaʔan ɛala.* On the basis of their agreement, the two countries pledge mutual assistance in case of aggression. *binaaʔan ɛala ttifaaqiiton ᵊd-dawᵊlteen byətɛahhadu yɛaawnu baɛḍon ᵊb-ḥaalet ʔəɛtidaaʔ.*

basket – (large, two or one-handled, made of cane) *salle* pl. *-aat* and *səlal;* (shallow, made of bast or rush) *sabat* pl. *-aat* and *sbuute;* (soft, two-handled, of varying size) *qəffe* pl. *-aat* and *qəfaf.*
basketball – *kəret˜ ᵊs-salle.*
Basra – *l-baṣra.*
to **baste** – *sarraž//tsarraž.* It's better to baste the hem first. *ʔaḥsan ᵊtsarrež l-ᵊkfaafe bᵊl-ʔawwal.*
to **baste** – *balbal.* Don't forget to baste the meat every 15 minutes. *laa tənsi tbalᵊbli l-laḥme kəll rəbᵊε saaεa.*
bat – *waṭwaaṭ* pl. *waṭawiiṭ.* I'm afraid of bats. *bxaaf mən ᵊl-waṭawiiṭ.*
bat – *maḍrab* pl. *maḍaareb.* He hit the ball so hard that the bat broke. *ḍarab ᵊṭ-ṭaabe b-quwwe la-daraže ʔənno nkasar ᵊl-maḍrab.*
  to bat – *ḍarab (o ḍarᵊb//nḍarab).* He batted the ball over the fence. *ḍarab ᵊṭ-ṭaabe la-fooq ᵊs-syaaž.*
  **He really went to bat for me. *bᵊl-ḥaqiiqa saanadni sande mniiḥa.*
  **He told his story without batting an eye. *ḥaka qəṣṣto biduun-ma trəff εeeno.*
batch – **1.** *rəsme* pl. *rəsam.* What happened to the batch of papers on my desk? *šuu ṣaar ᵊb-rəsmet ᵊl-waraq yalli kaanet εala ṭaawəlti?* **2.** *εažne* pl. *-aat, xabze* pl. *-aat.* That's the second batch of bread we baked today. *hayy taani εažne xabaznaaha l-yoom.* **3.** *sərbe* pl. *sərab.* The patrol returned with a batch of prisoners. *d-dooriyye rəžεet w-maεa sərbet ʔəsara.*
bath – **1.** *ḥammaam* pl. *-aat.* I'd like a hot bath. *bəddi ʔaaxod ḥammaam ṣəxᵊn.* **2.** *ḥammaam* pl. *-aat* and *ḥamamiim.* Have you a room with a bath? *fii εandkon ʔuuḍa b-ḥammaam?*
  to take a bath – *tḥammam, ʔaxad ḥammaam.* I took a bath before going to bed. *tḥammamᵊt qabᵊl-ma rəḥᵊt εal-farše.*
to **bathe** – **1.** *sabaḥ (a sbaaḥa).* We went bathing almost every day. *rəḥna sabaḥna ʔaktar ᵊl-ʔiyyaam.* **2.** *ḥammam, ġassal.* Bathe the baby in lukewarm water. *ḥammᵊmi l-beebe b-mayy faatre.*
bathhouse – *kabiin* pl. *-aat.* Go and change in the bathhouse. *ruuḥ ġayyer bᵊl-kabiin.*
bathing cap – *ṭaqiiṭ˜* (pl. *ṭawaaqi˜*) *sbaaḥa.*
bathing suit – *maayóo* pl. *maayohaat, ṭaqm˜* (pl. *ṭquumt˜*) *ᵊsbaaḥa.*
bathing trunks – *kalsoon˜* (pl. *-aat˜*) *ᵊsbaaḥa.*
bathrobe – *bərnoṣ˜* (pl. *baraaneṣ˜*) *ḥammaam.*
bathroom – *ḥammaam* pl. *-aat* and *ḥamamiim.*
bath towel – *manšafe* pl. *manaašef.*
bathtub – *baanyo* pl. *baanyoyaat.*
battalion – (infantry) *foož* pl. *fwaaž;* (motorized, armored) *katiibe* pl. *kataayeb.*
batter – *εažiine* pl. *-aat.* Let the batter stand for fifteen minutes. *xalli l-εažiine təstriiḥ rəbᵊε saaεa.*
  to batter down (or **in**) – *kassar.* They battered down the door. *kassaru l-baab.*
battered – *mharmaš.* He owns a battered old jalopy. *εando ṭəmbor ᵊmharmaš mən εahᵊd žədd žəddo.*
battery – *baṭṭaariyye* pl. *-aat.* My car has to have a new battery. *sayyaarti laazəma baṭṭaariyye ždiide.* — The ship came within range of the shore batteries. *s-safiine ṣaaret taḥᵊt marma baṭṭaariyyaat ᵊs-saaḥel.*
battle – *maεrake* pl. *maεaarek.*
battlefield – *saaḥet˜ (-aat˜) maεrake.*
battleship – *baarže* pl. *bawaarež.*
Bavaria – *bavaarya.*
Bavarian – *bavaari*.*
to **bawl** – *ṣarax (a ṣarᵊx, ṣraax), εayyaṭ (εyaaṭ).* The child's been bawling for an hour. *l-beebe ṣar-lo saaεa εam yəṣrax.*
  to bawl out – *bahdal, šaršaḥ.* Why did he bawl you out? *leeš bahdalak?*
bay – *xaliiž* pl. *xəlžaan.* We went swimming in the bay. *rəḥna sabaḥna bᵊl-xaliiž.*
bayonet – *sənge* pl. *-aat* and *sənag, ḥarbe* pl. *-aat,* and *ḥraab.*
bazaar – *suuq* pl. *swaaq, baazaar* pl. *-aat.*
to **be** – *kaan (u koon).* **1.** after auxiliaries: It can't be so. *muu məmken ᵊtkuun heek.* — It must be close to five o'clock already. *laazem ykuun ṣaar qariib ᵊs-saaεa xamse.* — That was probably the mailman. *bižuuz kaan ᵊl-boosṭaži.* **2.** in past tense: Was he there too? *kaan huwwe kamaan ᵊhniik?* — Where have you been all this time? *ween kənᵊt kəll hal-waqᵊt?* — It was raining when we left the house. *kaanet εam tənzel maṭar lamma ṭləεna mn ᵊl-beet.* **3.** future tense: He'll be here tomorrow. *bikuun hoon bəkra.* **4.** optative: If only he were here! *yaa reeto kaan hoon!* or *bass law kaan hoon!* **5.** in conditional clauses: If I were you, I'd stay (at) home. *law kənt ᵊb-maḥallak (kənt) bəbqa bᵊl-beet.* **6.** To state a general axiom: Concussion of the brain is often dangerous. *ʔəhtizaaz ᵊl-məxx marraat ᵊktiire bikuun xəṭer.*
  **I've been here since yesterday. *ṣar-li hoon ᵊmn ᵊmbaareḥ.*
  **How long have you been in this country? *qaddeeš ṣar-lak ᵊb-hal-ᵊblaad?*
  **How are you? *kiif ḥaalak?* or *šloonak?*
  **How is his father? *kiif ḥaal ʔabúu?* or *šloon ʔabúu?*
  **How much will that be? *qaddeeš byəṭlaε ḥaqqo?*
  **How much is that watch? *qaddeeš ḥaqq has-saaεa* or *b-qaddeeš has-saaεa?*
  **Here is the book you wanted. *hayy l-ᵊktaab yalli kaan bəddak-yáa.*
  **Here are the paper clips he has been asking for. *hayy šakkaalaat ᵊl-waraq yalli kaan εam yəṭlə́bon.*
  **There you are! What are we going to do now? *šəft ᵊn-natiiže!? šuu bəddna nsaawi hallaq?*
  **Oh, there you are! I've been looking for you all over. *haa, leekak hoon! maa xalleet εaleek qərne.*
  **Be that as it may! *mahma kaan ykuun!* or *šuu-ma kaan ᵊl-ʔamr ykuun.*
  **You're coming along, aren't you? *ʔənte žaaye maεi, muu heek?* (or *wəlla la??*)
  **He's your cousin, isn't he? *huwwe ʔəbᵊn εammak, muu heek?* (or *wəlla la??*)
  **It's all right with me. *maa fii maaneε εandi.*
  **What's it about? *šuu l-qəṣṣa?*
  **The book is about politics. *l-ᵊktaab εan ᵊs-siyaase.*
  **What is this sponge for? *la-šuu has-sfənže?*
  **He is to go tomorrow. *l-mafruuḍ yruuḥ bəkra.*
  there is, there are – *fii.* There are some people like that. *fii baεᵊḍ naas mən haš-šəkᵊl.* — There is only one book on the table. *fii ktaab waaḥed bass εaṭ-ṭaawle.*
  **There's nothing to that story. *hal-qəṣṣa maa-la ʔasaas.*
beach – *blaaž* pl. *-aat.* We built a fire on the beach. *šaεalna naar bᵊl-ᵊblaaž.*
bead – **1.** *ḥabbe* pl. *-aat.* This rosary has 33 beads. *hal-masbaḥa fiiha tlaatáa w-tlaatiin ḥabbe.* **2.** *nəqṭa* pl. *nəqaṭ.* Tiny beads of sweat formed on his forehead. *fii nəqaṭ ᵊzġiire mn ᵊl-εaraq baanet εala žbiino.* **3.** *niišaan.* The bead of this rifle seems to be out of line. *niišaan hal-baaruude mbayyen εaláe muu ṯaabeṭ.*
beam – **1.** *žəsᵊr* pl. *žsuura.* The roof is supported by strong beams. *s-saqᵊf mərtə́kez εala žsuura qawiyye.* **2.** *šεaaε* pl. *-aat* and *ʔašiεεa.* A beam of light came through the window. *fii šεaaε ḍaww faat ᵊmn ᵊš-šəbbaak.* **3.** *ʔišaara* pl. *-aat.* The station emits a strong directional beam. *l-ᵊmḥaṭṭa bətbəss ʔišaara mwažžha qawiyye.*
  to beam – *šaqraq.* She beams every time he talks to her. *bətšaqrə́q-lo kəll-ma biḥaakiiha.*
bean – **1.** (kidney bean) *faaṣuuliyye.* **2.** (black-eye bean) *luubye.* **3.** (broad bean) *fuul.*
bear – *dəbb* pl. *dbab.*
to **bear** – **1.** *tḥammal.* I can't bear the heat any longer. *maa εaad fiyyi ʔətḥammal ᵊš-šoob.* **2.** *ḥamal (e ḥamᵊl//nḥamal), tḥammal.* He has to bear the whole burden himself. *εaláe yəḥmel kəll ᵊl-ḥəmᵊl la-ḥaalo.* **3.** *žaabet (i žayabaan).* She bore him three sons. *žaabə́t-lo tlətt ṣəbyaan.*
  **The coin bears the date 1125. *l-εəmle εaleeha taariix sənᵊt ʔalf w-miyye w-xamsáa εəšriin.*
  **Bear to your left when you come to the crossroads. *xalliik εala šmaalak waqt ᵊbtəṣal la-maqṭaε ᵊṭ-ṭəroq.*
  **He brought considerable pressure to bear on him. *ḍaġaṭ εaláe ktiir.*
  to bear on – *tεallaq b-.* Give me all the facts that bear on this case. *εaṭiini kəll ᵊl-ḥaqaayeq yalli btətεallaq ᵊb-hal-qaḍiyye.*
  to bear out – *daεam (a/i daεᵊm//ndaεam).* The present development bears out what he had been claiming all the time. *t-taṭawwor ᵊl-ḥaali byədεem kəll šii kaan yəddᵊεii εala ṭuul.*
  to bear up under – *tḥammal.* How is she bearing up under it all? *kiif εam tətḥammal kəll haš-šii?*
  to bear with – *tḥammal, ḥaḍam (o ḥaḍᵊm).* I guess

we'll have to bear with him another week. *šaayéf-lak mašbuuriin nəthammalo* (or *nəh°dmo*) *žəmᶜa taanye.*

bearable – *mahmuul, (šii) byəntaaq.* The heat is still bearable. *š-šoob ləssaato mahmuul* (or *ləssaato byəntaaq*).

beard – *daq°n* (f.) pl. *dquun(e), ləhye* pl. *ləha.* I'm growing a beard. *ᶜam rabbi daq°n.*

bearing – **1.** *kərsi* pl. *karaasi.* This motor needs new bearings. *hal-motoor bəddo karaasi ždiide.* **2.** *ᶜalaaqa.* What bearing does that have on what we're doing? *šuu ?əlo haš-šii ᶜalaaqa b-halli ᶜam naᶜ°mlo?*

to get one's bearings – *tbayyan tariiqo.* Let's first get our bearings. *?awwal šii xalliina nətbayyan tariiqna.*

to lose one's bearings – *taah (u tawahaan).* The plane lost its bearings and crashed in the desert. *t-tayyaara taahet fa-thattamet b°l-barriyye.*

beast – *wah°š* pl. *whuuš(e).*

beast of burden – *daabbe* pl. *dawaabb.*

beat – **1.** *daqqa* pl. *-aat, darbe* pl. *-aat.* The beat of his pulse is rather feeble. *daqqaat nabdo šwayye dᶜiife.* **2.** *wazn (°l-muusiiqa).* He tapped the beat with a pencil. *taabaᶜ wazn °l-muusiiqa b-daqdaqaat qalamo.* **3.** *doora* pl. *-aat.* This policeman has been on this beat for twenty-five years. *haš-šərti şar-lo b-had-doora xamsda ᶜəšriin səne.*

to beat – **1.** *ġalab (e/o ġal°b//nġalab).* We beat them in today's game. *ġalabnaahon °b-ləᶜbet °l-yoom.* **2.** *xafaq (e/o xaf°q//nxafaq).* Don't forget to beat the egg whites. *laa tənsa maa təxfeq bayaad °l-beed.* **3.** *naffad.* Did you beat the carpets? *šuu naffadt °s-səžžaad?* **4.** *daqq (ə daqq).* Tell the boy to stop beating that drum. *quul ləl-walad haažto ydəqq hat-tab°l.* **5.** *xafaq (e/o xafaqaan).* His heart beat wildly when he saw her. *qalbo xafaq °ktiir waq°t šaafha.* **6.** *taqtaq.* The rain was beating on the roof. *l-matar kaanet ᶜam °ttaqteq ᶜal-?əstuuh.*

**Stop beating around the bush! *haaštak doora w-laffe!* or *haaštak °thuum hawaali l-mawduuᶜ.*

**That beats everything! *w-°hyaat ?alla, taff °l-keel!* or *wallaahi haada biġatti kəll šii!*

**Beat it! *nqəleᶜ mən hoon!*

**Let's beat it! *yalla, xalliina nəfróka!*

to beat someone to – *sabaq (e/o sab°q) hada la-.* He beat me to it. *sabaqni ?əlha.*

to beat someone up – *darab (o ə) hada qatle, taᶜma hada qatle.* They beat him up. *taᶜmúu qatle.*

beautiful – *həlu, žamiil.* What a beautiful day! *šuu hap-nhaar °l-həlu!*

beautifully – *b-šək°l həlu.* He writes beautifully. *byəktob °b-šək°l həlu.*

beauty – **1.** *žamaal, halaawe.* It takes a poet to describe the beauty of an evening in the desert. *maa fii ġeer šaaᶜer byəqder yuuşef žamaal °l-masawiyye b°ş-şahra.* **2.** *həlwe* pl. *-aat.* She's really a beauty. *hiyye mən haqa həlwe.*

beauty parlor – *şaalon˜* (pl. *-aat˜*) *tažmiil.*

because – *la?ənn-* + pron. suff. He didn't come because he was sick. *maa ?əža la?ənno kaan °dᶜiif.*

because of – **1.** *b-sabab˜.* The excursion was canceled because of rain. *l-məšwaar bəţel °b-sabab °l-matar.* **2.** *mənšaan, la-?až°l˜.* I was late because of you. *t?axxar°t mənšaanak* (or *la-?ažlak*). — I did it because of her. *ᶜməlta la-?ažla.* — I don't want you to do it just because of me. *maa bəddi-yaak taᶜmέla bass mənšaani* (or ***mənšaan xaatri*).

to become – *şaar (i şayaraan).* He became famous overnight. *şaar mašhuur °b-leele w-dəhaaha.* — What became of them? *šuu şaar fiihon?* — What has become of my purse? *šuu şaar °b-žəzdaani?*

becoming – **1.** *laabeq.* That hat is very becoming. *hal-bərneeta ktiir laabqa.* **2.** *laabeq, raayeh, žaaye.* That color is very becoming to you. *hal-loon °ktiir laabέq-lak* (or *raayέh-lak* or *žaaye ᶜaleek*).

bed – **1.** *tax°t* pl. *txuute.* I want a room with two beds. *bəddi ?uuda b-taxteen.* — When's the maid going to make our beds? *?eemta l-xaadme laha tsaawi txuutətna?* **2.** *farše* pl. *-aat.* He still has to stay in bed. *ləssa laazem ytamm b°l-farše.* **3.** *hood* pl. *hwaad.* Don't forget to water the flower beds. *laa tənsa maa təsqi hwaad °z-zhuur.* **4.** *?ardiyye, ?ar°d* (f.). The bed of this wadi is dry almost all year. *?ardiit hal-waadi naašfe ?aktar ?iyyaam °s-səne.*

**He got up on the wrong side of the bed today. *mətşabbeh b°š-šeetaan °l-yoom.*

to go to bed – **1.** *naam (a ə).* I went to bed late last night. *nəm°t mət?axxer °mbaareh.* **2.** *raah ᶜal-farše.* The doctor thinks I had better go to bed. *d-doktoor biquul ?ənno ?ahsán-li ruuh ᶜal-farše.*

to put to bed – *nayyam.* I have to put the kids to bed. *laazem ruuh nayyem l-°wlaad.*

bedbug – *baqqa* coll. *baqq* pl. *-aat.*

bedding: Air the bedding today. *hawwi t-txuute l-yoom.* -- She changes the bedding every two weeks. *bətġayyer °š-šaraašef kəll žəm°ᶜteen.*

Bedouin – *badawi** pl. *badu.*

bedroom – *?uudet˜ (?uwad˜) noom.*

bedspread – *ġata˜* (pl. *?əġ°tyet˜*) *tax°t.*

bee – *nahle* coll. *nah°l* pl. *-aat.*

**She's busy as a bee. *hiyye mət°l ?əmm °l-ᶜaruus, maa btəqᶜod ?abadan.*

beech (tree) – *(šažaret˜) zaan.*

beef – *lah°m baqar.*

beefsteak – *bəfteek* pl. *-aat.*

beehive – *kwaara* pl. *-aat.*

beer – *biira.*

Beersheba – *biir sab°ᶜ.*

beet – *raas˜ šawandar* coll. *šawandar* pl. *ruus˜ šawandar.*

beetle – *xən°fse* pl. *xanaafes.* The beetles have eaten all the leaves. *l-xanaafes ?akalu kəll °l-waraq.*

before – **1.** *mən qab°l.* It never happened before. *maa şaar haš-šii ?abadan mən ?ab°l.* **2.** *qab°l.* The telegram should be here before evening. *t-təllaġraaf laazem ykuun hoon qabl °l-masa.* -- I'll be there before two. *bkuun °hniik qabl °t-tənteen.* -- Come at five, not before. *taaᶜa s-saaᶜa xamse, muu qab°l.* -- Business (comes) before pleasure. *š-šəġ°l byəži qabl °l-baş°t.* **3.** *qab°l-ma.* Call me up before you go. *talfén-li qab°l-ma truuh.* **4.** *qəddaam.* He's to appear before the judge next week. *laazem yəhdar qəddaam °l-qaadi ž-žəmᶜa ž-žaaye.* **5.** *qəddaam, tah°t ?iid˜.* The case before the court has turned out more complicated than was expected. *l-qadiyye yalli tah°t ?iid °l-mahkame bayyanet °mᶜaqqade ?aktar məmma ftakaru.*

before long – *ᶜan qariib.* Before long he'll be able to help you. *ᶜan qariib bişiir bisaaᶜdak.*

the day before – *qabl °b-yoom.* It had rained the day before. *kaanet naazle matar qabl °b-yoom.*

the day before yesterday – *?awwal(t) °mbaareh.* He was here the day before yesterday. *kaan hoon ?awwalt °mbaareh.*

to put something before something else – *faddal* or *qaddam šii ᶜala šii taani.* He puts his career before his family. *bifaddel məh°nto ᶜala ᶜeelto.*

beforehand – **1.** *mən qab°l, salaf.* I knew it beforehand. *ᶜrəfto mən qab°l.* **2.** *qabl °b-waq°t.* You should have told me beforehand. *kaan laazem °tqəl-li qabl °b-waq°t.*

to beg – **1.** *talab (o talab).* The children begged for pennies. *l-°wlaad talabu frangaat.* **2.** *tražža.* They begged us to help them. *tražžuuna nᶜaawénon.* **3.** *šahad (a šhaade).* We'll pay you back, even if we have to beg. *mənražžéᶜ-lak °l-maşaari hatta w-law kənna bəddna nəšhad.*

**I beg your pardon! *l-ᶜafu!* or *bala mwaaxaze!*

**I beg your pardon, you can't possibly mean that! *mən baᶜ°d ?amrak, bət?ammal ?ənnak °tkuun maa ᶜam təᶜni haš-šii!*

**I beg your pardon? *naᶜam?*

beggar – *šahhaad* pl. *-iin.* There's a beggar at the door. *fii šahhaad ᶜal-baab.* — Beggars can't be choosers. *š-šahhaadiin maa bišaartu.*

to begin – *bada (a bdaaye), ballaš.* The performance begins at half-past eight. *l-hafle btəbda s-saaᶜa tmaane w-nəşş.* — It's beginning to rain. *ᶜam °tballeš °tšatti.* — Let's begin with the housing problem. *xalliina nəbda b-məšk°lt °l-masaaken.*

**The supply doesn't begin to meet our needs. *l-kammiyye maa-la ᶜam °tkaffi haažətna w-laa ᶜala wažh °t-taqriib.*

**To begin with, we haven't enough money. *?awwal ši, maa ᶜanna maşaari kfaaye.*

beginner – *məbtédi* pl. *-yiin, məstažədd* pl. *-iin.*

beginning – *bdaaye.* This is only the beginning. *hayy muu ?aktar mən l-°bdaaye ləssa.*

beginnings – *?awaayel* (pl.), *bdaaye.* The beginnings of Arabic poetry are unknown. *?awaayel °š-šəᶜr °l-ᶜarabi muu maᶜruufe.*

to begrudge – *hasad (e/o has°d).* I begrudge him his luck. *bəh°sdo ᶜala baxto.*

not to begrudge – *tmanna la-, raad (i ə) la-, safat (o saf°t) la-.* I don't begrudge it to you. *bətmannda-lak-yda* or *brəd-lak-yda* or *bəsfét-lak-yda.*

in **behalf** - 1. *difaaƐan Ɛan.* Let me say a few words in behalf of my country's policy. *smaḥúu-li ʔəḥki kəlᵊmteen difaaƐan Ɛan ᵊsyaaset ᵊblaadi.* 2. *mənšaan, la-maṣlaḥet˜* ... His friends intervened in his behalf. *ʔaṣḥaabo ddaxxalu mənšaano* (or *la-maṣlaḥto*).

on behalf of - *bᵊn-nyaabe Ɛan, b-ʔəsᵊm˜* ... I want to thank you on behalf of our organization. *btəsma-ḥúu-li ʔəškərkon bᵊn-nyaabe Ɛan* (or *b-ʔəsm*) *ᵊmnaẓẓamətna.*

to **behave** - 1. *dabbar ḥaalo, tṣarraf.* Nobody knows how he'll behave in a time of crisis. *maa ḥada byaƐref kiif bəddo ydabber ḥaalo waqt ᵊl-ʔazme.* 2. *salak (o sluuk).* He doesn't know how to behave. *maa byaƐref yəslok (maƐ ᵊn-naas).*

**Behave yourself! *tʔaddab baqa!*

behavior - 1. (conduct, reaction) *taṣarrof* or *taṣarrufaat* (pl.). 2. (manners) *sluuk.*

behind - 1. *(b-)qafa˜, wara˜, xalf˜.* There's a garage behind the house. *fii karaaž qafa l-beet.* 2. *wara˜, (b-)qafa˜.* Who's behind that scheme? *miin wara had-dasiise?* -- What's behind it all? *šuu wara haš-šii kəllo?* 3. *wara, bᵊl-qafa.* Watch out for the car behind! *ʔoƐa s-sayyaara yalli wara!* 4. *wara.* He was attacked from behind. *haažamúu mən wara.*

to be behind - 1. *ʔaxxar, qaṣṣar.* My watch is always ten minutes behind. *saaƐti daayman bətʔaxxer Ɛašᵊr daqaayeq.* 2. *tʔaxxar, qaṣṣar.* I'm somewhat behind in my monthly payments. *ʔana šwayye mətʔaxxer ᵊb-dafƐaati š-šahriyye.*

**He's always behind the times. *huwwe muu mmaaši waqto.*

to fall behind - *qaṣṣar.* He has fallen behind in his work. *ṣaar ᵊmqaṣṣer ᵊb-šəġlo.*

to leave behind - *tarak (o/e tarᵊk//ntarak).* We had to leave everything behind. *nžabarna nətrok kəll šii.*

to stay behind - *bəqi (a ə).* Why did he have to stay behind? *leeš ᵊḍṭarr yəbqa?*

being - 1. *kyaan.* Kindness and generosity are the essence of his being. *l-ləṭᵊf wᵊl-karam hənne žoohar ᵊkyaano.* 2. *kaaʔen* pl. *-aat, maxluuq* pl. *-aat.* God, the Creator of all beings. *ʔaḷḷa, xallaaq kəll ᵊl-kaaʔinaat.*

to bring into being - *ʔawžad, xalaq (o/e xalᵊq).* Our industrial age has brought a new type of man into being. *Ɛaṣᵊrna ṣ-ṣinaaƐi ʔawžad ʔənsaan ᵊždiid.*

to come into being - *naša? (a nšuuʔ).* How has the world come into being? *kiif našaʔ ᵊl-Ɛaalam?*

Beirut - 1. He lives in Beirut. *saaken ᵊb-beeruut.* 2. *beeruuti˜* pl. *bayaarte* and *bawaarte.* The Beirut businessmen. *t-təžžaar ᵊl-bayaarte.*

to **belch** - *tbaƐƐaž, ddašša.*

Belgian - *balžiiki*.*

Belgium - *balžiika.*

Belgrade - *bəlᵊgraad.*

belief - *ʔəƐtiqaad, ʔiimaan.* My belief in him was seriously shaken. *ʔəƐtiqaadi fii dəaƐaƐ tamaam.* — It is my firm belief that ... *b-ʔəƐtiqaadi l-ʔakiid ʔənno ...* or ***ʔana məqtəneƐ tamaam ʔənno ...*

to **believe** - 1. *Ɛtaqad, ftakar, ẓann (ə ẓann).* I don't believe he did it. *maa bəƐtəqed ʔənno huwwe saawaaha.* 2. *saddaq.* I don't believe a word he says. *maa bsaddeq w-laa kəlme biquula.* 3. *ʔaaman, Ɛtaqad.* Do you believe in his sincerity? *bətʔaamen ᵊb-ʔəxlaaṣo?*

to **belittle** - *qallal qiimet˜* ... He keeps belittling everything I do. *biḍall biqallel qiimet kəll šii baƐᵊmlo.*

bell - 1. *žaraṣ* pl. *žraaṣ.* Ring the bell twice if you want something. *dəqq ᵊž-žaraṣ marrteen ʔiza bəddak šii.* 2. *naaquus* pl. *nawaqiis.* You can see the bells in the tower. *bətšuuf ᵊn-nawaqiis bᵊl-bərᵊž.*

belladonna - *sətt ᵊl-ḥəsᵊn, balladonna.*

bellboy - *farraaš* pl. *-e.*

bellows - *mənfaax* pl. *manafiix.*

belly - *baṭᵊn* pl. *bṭuune.*

to **belong** - 1. *(kaan) tabaƐ˜, (kaan) la-.* Does this book belong to you? *šuu hal-ᵊktaab tabaƐak?* or *šuu hal-ᵊktaab ʔəlak?* 2. *ntasab.* He too belongs to our club. *huwwe kamaan byəntəseb la-naadiina.*

**This book doesn't belong here. *hal-ᵊktaab maḥallo muu hoon.*

**This card belongs in the other file. *hal-karᵊt maḥallo b-ġeer hal-ᵊmṣannaf.*

belongings - *ġraaḍ* (pl.), *ʔamtiƐa* (pl.). He had to leave all his belongings behind. *nžabar yətrok kəll ᵊġraaḍo* (or *ʔamtəƐto*).

below - 1. *taḥᵊt˜.* The temperature here seldom gets below zero. *l-ḥaraara hoon qəllet-ma btənzel taḥt ᵊṣ-ṣəfᵊr.* 2. *taḥᵊt.* From the window they could watch the parade below. *mn ᵊš-šəbbaak qədru yətfarražu Ɛal-ʔəstəƐraaḍ taḥᵊt.*

belt - 1. *qšaaṭ* pl. *qəšᵊṭ, zənnaar* pl. *zananiir.* Do you wear a belt? *bətḥəṭṭ ᵊqšaaṭ?* 2. *qšaaṭ* pl. *qəšᵊṭ.* The belt has come off the fan. *l-ᵊqšaaṭ faltaan bᵊl-marwaḥa.*

**He's got a few under his belt. *šarbə́n-lo kam qadaḥ ᵊmnaaḥ.*

**That's hitting below the belt! *hayy laʔəmane!* or *hayy waṭaawe!*

**Shut up, or I'll belt you one! *xraas, wəlla bkasser raasak!*

bench - *maqƐad* pl. *maqaaƐed.* The benches were only recently painted. *l-maqaaƐed maa ṣar-lon zamaan madhuuniin.*

bend - *ḥanye* pl. *-aat, Ɛawže* pl. *-aat.* Our house is just beyond the bend in the road. *beetna ḥaakem raʔsan baƐᵊd ḥanyet ᵊṭ-ṭariiq.*

to bend - 1. *Ɛawaž (e/o Ɛawž//nƐawaž).* He bent the wire. *Ɛawaž ᵊš-šriiṭ.* 2. *tana (i tani//ntana).* I can't bend my wrist. *maa-li Ɛam ʔəqder ʔətni mafṣal ʔiidi.* 3. *ntana, nḥana.* The tree bends when the wind blows. *š-šažara btəntə́na waqt ᵊbyəṭlaƐ ᵊl-hawa.*

**We must bend every effort. *laazem naƐmel kəll žahᵊdna.*

to bend down or **over** - *ḥana (i ḥani) ḥaalo, nḥana.* Bend down so I can talk to you better. *ʔəḥni ḥaalak šwayye ḥatta təfham šuu Ɛam quul.*

beneath - *taḥᵊt˜.* He was buried beneath the tree. *dafanúu taḥt ᵊš-šažara.* -- I put it beneath all the other papers. *ḥaṭṭeeta taḥᵊt kəll l-ᵊwraaq ᵊt-taanye.*

**That's beneath him. *haada muu mən qiimto* or *haada ʔawṭa mən məstawda.*

beneficial - *mufiid, naafeƐ.*

beneficiary - *məntəfeƐ* pl. *-iin.*

benefit - *manfaƐa* pl. *manaafeƐ, faayde* pl. *fawaayed.* I don't expect to get any benefit out of it. *maa-li məntə́ẓer mənha ʔayy manfaƐa* or ***maa-li məntə́ẓer ʔəstfiid mən haš-šaġle ʔabadan.*

to be a benefit - *nafaƐ (a nafᵊƐ), faad (i ʔifaade).* The trip wasn't of much benefit to us. *s-safra maa nafƐətna šii ktiir.*

to benefit - 1. *stafaad.* We hope we'll eventually benefit from this development. *nšaaḷḷa bᵊn-nihaaye mnəstfiid mən hat-taṭawwor.* 2. *nafaƐ (a nafᵊƐ), faad (i ʔifaade).* The trip abroad has benefited her greatly. *s-safra bᵊl-xaareǧ nafƐə́ta ktiir.*

bent - 1. *məḥni*.* He's bent with age. *ḍahro məḥni mən kəbr ᵊs-sənn.* 2. *maƐwuuž, məlwi*.* The nail is bent. *l-bəsmaar maƐwuuž.* 3. *qaatel ḥaalo, mayyet (la-).* She's bent on going to Europe this summer. *qaatle ḥaala* (or *mayyte*) *la- truuḥ la-ʔurubba haṣ-ṣeefiyye.*

bent out of shape - *maṭƐuuž.* The cover is bent out of shape. *l-ᵊġlaaf (kəllo) maṭƐuuž.*

Berber - *barbari** coll. *barbar* pl. *baraabra.*

Berlin - *barliin.*

beside - *žamb˜, mšaqqiit˜.* Please put this trunk beside the other one. *mən faḍlak ḥəṭṭ has-sanduuq žamb ᵊt-taani.* -- Who's that standing beside your father? *miin haada yalli waaqef ᵊmšaqqiit ʔabuuk?*

**That's beside the point. *haada barraat ᵊl-baḥᵊs.*

beside oneself - *ṭaaleƐ diino.* She was beside herself with rage. *kaan ṭaaleƐ diina mn ᵊl-ġaḍab.*

besides - 1. *fooq haada, ʔəla zaalek.* He's a good worker, and besides, everybody likes him. *huwwe šaġġiil ᵊmniiḥ, w-fooq haada kəll ᵊn-naas bətḥəbbo.* 2. *fooq˜, zyaade Ɛala, Ɛilaawe Ɛala.* Besides his wages he gets tips. *fooq maƐaašo* (or *zyaade Ɛala maƐaašo*) *byaaxod baxašiiš.*

best - 1. *ʔaḥsan˜, ʔafḍal˜.* That's the best thing you can do under the circumstances. *haada ʔaḥsan šii məmken taƐᵊmlo b-heek ḥaale.* — That's the best coffee I've had in a long time. *hayy ʔaḥsan qahwe šrəbta mən zamaan.* — He's my best friend. *huwwe ʔafḍal ṣaaḥeb ʔəli.* 2. *xeer.* We want only your best. *kəll halli bəddna-yə́a huwwe xeerak.* — Perhaps it's all for the best. *məmken kəll šii la-xeer.*

3. *ʔaḥsan šii.* I like it best this way. *heek ḥabbə́ba ʔaḥsan šii.* -- I work best in the morning. *bəštə́ġel ʔaḥsan šii bᵊṣ-ṣabaaḥ.*

at best - *b-ʔaḥsan ᵊl-ʔəḥtimaalaat.* At best this is a poor substitute. *b-ʔaḥsan ᵊl-ʔəḥtimaalaat haada*

badal muu naafeɛ.
the best part of - 1. *ʔaktar˜.* I was away the best part of the week. *maa kənᵊt hoon ʔaktar ᵊl-ʔəsbuuɛ.* **2.** *ʔaḥsan šii.* The best part of the play was the second act. *ʔaḥsan šii bᵊt-tamsiiliyye kaan ᵊl-faṣl ᵊt-taani.*
to do one's best - *ɛəmel žahdo.* I'll do my best to help you. *baɛmel žahdi saaɛdak.*
to get the best of - 1. *ləɛeb (a ə) ɛala.* We have to be careful that he doesn't get the best of us. *laazem naɛṭi baalna ḥatta maa yəlɛab ɛaleena.* **2.** *tmallak, tġallab ɛala, tṣallaṭ ɛala.* Jealousy got the best of him and he slapped her. *tmallakə́to (or tġallabet ɛalée) l-ġiire fa-qaam w-laṭdša kaff.*
to make the best of something - *mašša ḥaalo b-šii.* We don't like our new apartment, but we'll have to make the best of it. *maa-lna ḥaabbiin šaqqətna ž-ždiide, bass laazem ᵊnmašši ḥaalna fiiha.*
bet - *šarᵊṭ* pl. *šruuṭa.* When are you going to pay up the bet? *ʔeemta laḥa tədfaɛ ᵊš-šarᵊṭ?*
**That's your best bet. *hayy ʔaḥsan fərṣa ʔəlak.*
to bet - 1. *raahan, šaaraṭ.* I bet you he missed the train. *braahnak ʔənno faato t-treen.* -- Want to bet? *bətraahen?* or ***bətruuḥ šarᵊṭ?* **2.** *ləɛeb (a ləɛᵊb).* I bet five dollars on the black horse. *lɛəbᵊt xamᵊs dolaaraat ɛal-ᵊḥṣaan ᵊl-ʔaswad.*
**You can bet your life on that! *bqəṣṣ ʔiidi ʔiza maa bikuun heek.*
Bethlehem - *beet˜ laḥᵊm.*
to **betray** - **1.** *xaan (u xyaane), ġadar (e/o ġadᵊr) b-.* He betrayed his best friend. *xaan ʔaɛazz ṣaaḥeb ʔəlo (or ġadar ᵊb-ʔaɛazz ṣaaḥeb ʔəlo).* **2.** *xayyab.* She's betrayed my confidence. *xayyabet siqati fiiha.* **3.** *warža.* Her answer betrays her ignorance. *žawaaba biwarži žahla.*
better - 1. *ʔaḥsan, ʔafḍal.* Don't you have a better room? *maa ɛandak ʔuuḍa ʔaḥsan?* -- How long are we supposed to stay? The longer the better. *qaddeeš mafruuḍ fiina nəbqa? kəll-ma ṭawwalna ʔaḥsan.* -- When do you want me to come? The sooner the better. *ʔeemta bəddak-yaani ʔəži? kəll-ma ɛažžalᵊt ʔaḥsan.* -- They did it better after a little practice. *ɛəmlúuha ʔaḥsan baɛᵊd šwayyet tamriin.* -- We'd better go before it rains. *ʔafḍál-lna nruuḥ qabᵊl-ma tšatti.* -- You'd better go. *ʔaḥsán-lak ᵊtruuḥ.* **2.** *ʔaḥsan.* Do you feel better? *šloon, šaayef ḥaalak ʔaḥsan?* -- We'll be better off if we move. *ḥaalətna bətkuun ʔaḥsan ʔiza ntaqalna.*
the better part of - *məɛẓam˜.* I spent the better part of the morning in bed. *maḍḍeet məɛẓam qabl ᵊḍ-ḍəhᵊr bᵊt-taxᵊt.*
to get the better of someone - 1. *ləɛeb (a ləɛᵊb) ɛala ḥada.* He'll try to get the better of you. *laḥa yḥaawel yəlɛab ɛaleek.* **2.** *tṣallaṭ ɛala ḥada.* Curiosity got the better of her. *l-ᵊfḍuuliyye tṣallaṭet ɛaleeha.*
between - *been.* We'll meet between six and seven. *mnəžtə́meɛ been ᵊs-sətte wᵊs-sabɛa.* -- Put the lamp between the two chairs. *ḥəṭṭ ᵊḍ-ḍaww been ᵊl-kərsiyyeen.*
between you and me - *beeni w-beenak, beenaatna.* Between you and me, it's his own fault. *beeni w-beenak, xaržo.*
few and far between - *qalaayel* (pl.), *naadriin* (pl.). Honest people are few and far between. *n-naas ᵊl-ʔawaadem qalaayel ᵊktiir.*
in between - 1. *b-hal-ʔasna.* We had lunch in between. *tġaddeena b-hal-ʔasna.* **2.** *beenaathon, been(aat)˜ ᵊt-tneen.* Her two brothers sat on either side of the couch and she sat in between. *ʔəxwaata t-tneen qaɛad kəll waaḥed mənhon ɛala ṭaraf ᵊl-kanabe w-hiyye qaɛdet beenaathon.*
beverage - 1. (alcoholic) *mašruub* pl. *-aat.* **2.** (non-alcoholic) *šaraab* pl. *-aat.*
beware - *ʔoɛa* f. *ʔoɛi* pl. *ʔoɛu, ʔəṣḥa* f. *ʔəṣḥi* pl. *ʔəṣḥu.* Beware of him! *ʔoɛa mənno!*
bewildered - *mətḥayyer.* I am completely bewildered by his behavior. *ʔana tamaam mətḥayyer mən taṣarrfo.*
beyond - 1. *qaaṭeɛ.* The house is beyond the river. *l-beet qaaṭeɛ ᵊn-nahᵊr.* **2.** *baɛᵊd.* The house is right beyond the hospital. *l-beet raʔsan baɛd ᵊl-məstašfa.* **3.** *biduun.* He's guilty beyond a reasonable doubt. *huwwe məzneb biduun ʔadna šakk.* **4.** *fooq.* She's living beyond her means. *ɛaayše fooq ʔəmkaaniyyaata.*
**He is beyond help. *huwwe maa fii mənno ʔamal.*
**I wouldn't put it beyond him. *maa bəstəbɛə́da ɛanno.*

Bhamdoun - *bḥamduun.*
biannual - *nəṣᵊf sanawi*.* They're holding their biannual convention. *məžtəmɛiin ᵊb-ʔəžtimaaɛon ᵊn-nəṣf ᵊs-sanawi.*
biased - *mətḥayyez.*
Bible - *l-ᵊktaab l-ᵊmqaddas, l-ʔənžiil.*
bibliography - *(qaaʔimet˜) ᵊl-maraažeɛ.* Read the bibliography at the end of the book carefully. *ʔəqra l-maraažeɛ ᵊb-ʔaaxer l-ᵊktaab ᵊb-ʔəntibaah.*
bicarbonate of soda - *karbonaat˜ ṣooda.*
bicycle - *bəsᵊkleet* (f.) pl. *-aat.* My bicycle needs fixing. *bəsᵊkleetti bədda taṣliiḥ.*
to bicycle - *rəkeb (a rkuub) ɛal-bəsᵊkleet.* We went bicycling last Sunday. *rəḥna rkəbna ɛal-bəsᵊkleet yoom ᵊl-ʔaḥad ᵊl-maaḍi.*
bid - *ɛarᵊḍ* pl. *ɛruuḍ(a).* All bids for the new building must be in by the fifteenth. *kəll l-ᵊɛruuḍa mənšaan ᵊl-binaaye ž-ždiide laazem tətqaddam qabᵊl xamᵊṣṭaɛš ᵊš-šahᵊr.*
to bid - *zaawad, zaayad.* He bid ten dollars for the rug. *zaawad bᵊs-səžžaade ɛašᵊr dolaaraat.*
to **bide one's time** - *tʔanna.* I'm biding my time until I get a chance to speak up. *ɛam ʔətʔanna ḥatta təžiini fərṣa ʔəḥki yalli b-qalbi.*
big - 1. *kbiir* pl. *kbaar.* They live in a big house. *saakniin ᵊb-beet ᵊkbiir.* -- Her father is a big lawyer. *ʔabuuha muḥaami kbiir.* -- He has a big office in that building. *ɛando maktab ᵊkbiir ᵊb-hal-binaaye.* -- We don't carry such big sizes. *maa ɛanna qyaasaat ᵊkbiire hal-qadd.* **2.** *ṭawiil* pl. *ṭwaal.* He's a big fellow for his age. *huwwe ṭawiil bᵊn-nəsbe la-ɛəmro.*
**He's a big shot now. *ṣaar ʔakaaber hallaq.*
**He talks big. *byətbažžaḥ ᵊktiir* or *kalaamo ʔakbar mənno.*
**He has a big heart. *ṣədro raḥᵊb.*
bigger - 1. *ʔakbar.* Their house is bigger than ours. *beeton ʔakbar mən beetna.* -- We're moving into bigger offices next month. *mnəntə́qel la-makaateb ʔakbar bᵊš-šahr ᵊž-žaay.* -- She wears a bigger size. *btəlbes ᵊqyaas ʔakbar.* **2.** *ʔaḍxam.* He's bigger than his brother. *huwwe ʔaḍxam mən ʔaxúu.*
bigmouth - *mwažhan* pl. *-iin.* Why didn't you hit that bigmouth? *leeš maa ḍarabᵊt hal-ᵊmwažhan?*
bilateral - *sunaaʔi*.* This is based on a bilateral agreement. *haada mabni ɛala ʔəttifaaqiyye sunaaʔiyye.*
bilingual - *b-luġateen.* What you need is a bilingual dictionary. *halli laazmak qaamuus ᵊb-luġateen.*
**He's completely bilingual. *byəḥki luġateen mətl ᵊl-mayy.*
bill - *mənqaar* pl. *manaqiir.* Storks have long bills. *l-ḥažž laglag mənqaaro ṭawiil.*
bill - 1. *faatuura* pl. *fawatiir.* We have to pay this bill today. *laazem nədfaɛ hal-faatuura l-yoom.* **2.** *ḥsaab* pl. *-aat.* Waiter, the bill, please! *garsoon, haat l-ᵊḥsaab mən faḍlak.* **3.** *banknoot* pl. *-aat.* Give me some small bills, please. *ɛaṭiini kam banknoot ᵊzġiir ʔiza bəddak.* **4.** *mašruuɛ˜ qaanuun* pl. *mašariiɛ˜ qawaniin.* The bill was passed in the Lower House. *mašruuɛ ᵊl-qaanuun ᵊtsaadaq ɛalée b-mažles ᵊn-nuwwaab.* **5.** *ʔəɛlaan* pl. *-aat.* You're not allowed to post any bills here. *mamnuuɛ ɛaleek ᵊtlazzeq ʔəɛlaanaat hoon.*
bill of lading - *boliišet˜* (pl. *bawaaleṣ˜*) *šaḥᵊn.*
bill of sale - *ɛaqd˜* (pl. *ɛquud˜*) *ᵊl-beeɛ.*
to foot the bill - *tḥammal* or *dafaɛ (a dafᵊɛ) ᵊl-maṣariif.* Who's going to foot the bill for all this? *miin bəddo yətḥammal maṣariif kəll haš-šii?*
to bill - 1. *qayyad.* Bill me for that. *qayyə́da ɛaliyyi.* **2.** *baɛat (a baɛᵊt) faatuura.* We'll bill you later. *mnəbɛát-lak faatuura baɛdeen.*
billboard - *looḥet˜* (pl. *-aat˜*) *ʔəɛlaanaat.*
billfold - *žəzdaan* pl. *žazadiin.*
billiards - *bəlyaardo.* Let's play a game of billiards! *xalliina nəlɛab bəlyaardo.*
billion - *bəlyoon* pl. *balayiin.* That runs into billions. *hayy btəbloġ balayiin.*
billy goat - *tees* pl. *tyuus(e).*
bimonthly: It's a bimonthly magazine. *l-mažalle btəṭlaɛ kəll šahreen marra.* -- Have you read the bimonthly report? *qareet ᵊt-taqriir yalli byəṭlaɛ kəll šahreen marra?*
to **bind - 1.** *žallad.* Do you know of anyone who can bind these magazines for me? *btaɛrə́f-li ḥada yžallə́d-li hal-mažallaat?* **2.** *ʔalzam.* The contract binds him to finish the job within a year. *l-kontráa btəlᵊzmo ʔənno yxalleṣ ᵊš-šaġle b-səne.*
binding - *məlzem.* This agreement is binding. *hal-*

ʔəttifaaq məlzem.

binder - **1.** *mžalled* pl. *-iin.* The newspapers are at the binder's. *ž-žaraayed Ɛand l-ᵊmžalled.* **2.** *malaff* pl. *-aat, mṣannaf* pl. *-aat.* Put these papers in a separate binder. *ḥəṭṭ hal-ᵊwraaq ᵊb-malaff la-ḥaalo.*

bindery - *maḥall˜* (pl. *-aat˜*) *tažliid.*

binding - *žəlde* pl. *-aat.* The binding is damaged. *ž-žəlde manzuuƐa.*

binoculars - *naaḍuur* pl. *nawaḍiir.*

birch - *(šažaret˜) batuula.*

biographer - *mʔarrex˜* (pl. *-iin˜*) *siire* and *siyar.*

biography - *siire* pl. *siyar, taariix˜* (pl. *tawariix˜*) *ḥayaat.*

biologic(al) - *biyolooži*.*

biologist - *Ɛaalem˜* (pl. *Ɛəlamaaʔ˜*) *biyoloožya.*

biology - *biyoloožya.*

bird - (small) *Ɛaṣfuur* pl. *Ɛaṣafiir,* (large) *ṭeer* pl. *ṭyuur.* What kind of bird is this? *šuu žənᵊs hal-Ɛaṣfuur?* -- A bird in the hand is worth two in the bush. *Ɛaṣfuur bᵊl-ʔiid ʔaḥsan mən Ɛašara Ɛaš-šažara.* -- He killed two birds with one stone. *ḍarab Ɛaṣfuureen ᵊb-ḥažar (waaḥed).*

birth - *wlaade* pl. *-aat.* They announced the birth of their child. *ʔaƐlanu wlaadet ṭəflon.*

by birth - *b-mawled.* Are you American by birth? *ʔənte ʔameerki b-mawled?*

birthday - *Ɛiid˜* (pl. *Ɛyaad˜*) *miilaad.* When is your birthday? *ʔeemta Ɛiid miilaadak?*

birthplace - *maḥall˜* (pl. *-aat˜*) *ᵊwlaade.*

birth rate - *nəsbet˜* (pl. *nəsab˜*) *mawaliid.*

bishop - **1.** *ʔəsqof* pl. *ʔasaaqifa.* His uncle is a bishop. *Ɛammo ʔəsqof.* **2.** *fiil* pl. *fyaal.* You've already lost one bishop and a knight. *ṣaar mayyə́t-lak fiil w-faras.*

bit - *šakiime* pl. *šakaayem.* This bridle doesn't have a bit. *hal-ližaam maa-lo šakiime.*

bit - *ẓġiir.* He only has a bit part but he carries it off well. *dooro ẓġiir laaken taaqno.*

**Why does he always have to add his two bits' worth? *leeš daayman bikatter ġalabe bala ṭaƐme?*

a bit - *šwayye.* The tea is a bit too strong. *š-šaay šwayye tqiil.* -- Can't you wait a bit more? *maa fiik tənṭəẓə́r-lak kamaan šwayye?* -- That's going a bit too far. *haš-šii Ɛam yəṭlaƐ Ɛan ḥaddo šwayye.*

a bit of - *šwayyet˜.* There was a bit of sarcasm in his words. *kaan fii šwayyet tahakkom ᵊb-kalaamo.*

bit by bit - *nətfe nətfe.* We learned the story bit by bit. *Ɛrəfna l-qəṣṣa nətfe nətfe.*

not a bit - **1.** *(w-laa) nətfet˜.* There isn't a bit of bread in the house. *maa fii w-laa nətfet xəbᵊz bᵊl-beet.* **2.** *maa ... ʔabadan.* That doesn't surprise me a bit! *maa bəstaġreb haš-šii ʔabadan!* -- That doesn't make a bit of difference. *maa btəfreq ʔabadan.*

to smash to bits - *ṭarbaš.* In his rage he smashed everything to bits. *mən ġeeẓo ṭarbaš kəll šii.*

bite - **1.** *ləqme* pl. *ləqam.* We haven't a bite left. *muu baqyaan Ɛanna w-laa ləqme.* -- I haven't had a bite to eat all day. *ṭuul ᵊn-nhaar maa ʔakalᵊt w-laa ləqme.* -- Won't you have a bite with us? *maa btaakə́l-lak ləqme maƐna?* **2.** *qarṣa* pl. *-aat.* The bite itches. *l-qarṣa bətḥəkk.*

to bite - **1.** *Ɛaḍḍ (a Ɛaḍḍ//nƐaḍḍ).* Will the dog bite? *šuu l-kalb biƐaḍḍ?* -- He bit into the apple. *Ɛaḍḍ ᵊt-təffaaḥa.* **2.** *qaraṣ (o qarᵊṣ//nqaraṣ).* A mosquito must have bitten me. *laazem ᵊtkuun naamuuse qarṣətni.*

**The fish are biting well today. *s-samak Ɛam yəži Ɛaṭ-ṭəƐᵊm ᵊl-yoom.*

**I tried twice but he didn't bite. *žarrabᵊt Ɛallqo marrteen bass maa Ɛəleq.*

biting - **1.** *qaareṣ.* It's a biting wind. *hal-hawa qaareṣ.* **2.** *laadeƐ.* She made some very biting remarks about him. *qaalet Ɛanno šwayyet ᵊmlaaḥaẓaat ᵊktiir laadƐa.*

bitter - **1.** *mərr.* That tastes bitter. *ṭaƐmə́ta mərra.* **2.** *qaareṣ.* It was bitter cold. *kaan barᵊd qaareṣ.* **3.** *qaasi.* He has had some bitter experiences. *maraq ᵊb-tažaareb qaasye.* **4.** *laduud.* They're bitter enemies. *hənne ʔaƐdaaʔ laduudiin.*

**They fought to the bitter end. *ḥaarabu la-ʔaaxer daqiiqa.*

bitterly - *b-maraara.* He complained to me bitterly. *štakáa-li b-maraara.*

bitterness - *maraara.*

biweekly - **1.** *nəṣᵊf šahri*.* That's the biweekly publication I told you about. *hayye n-našra n-nəṣf ᵊš-šahriyye yalli qəlt-ə́llak Ɛaleeha.* **2.** *mažalle* (pl. *-aat*) *nəṣᵊf šahriyye.* The society publishes a biweekly. *ž-žamƐiyye btənšor mažalle nəṣᵊf šahriyye.*

black - **1.** *ʔaswad* f. *sooda* pl. *suud.* His hair is black. *šaƐro ʔaswad.* -- His leg is all black and blue from his fall. *rəžlo kəlla zarqa w sooda mən waqᵊƐto.* **2.** *qaatem.* Her future looks pretty black. *məstaqbə́la mbayyen Ɛalée qaatem.*

to black out - *ġaṭṭ (ə ə) Ɛala qalbo.* She blacked out for a moment. *ġaṭṭ Ɛala qalba laḥẓa.*

blackbird - *šaḥruur* pl. *šaḥariir.*

blackboard - *looḥ* pl. *lwaaḥ.* Write it on the blackboard. *ktə́ba Ɛal-looḥ.*

black list - *laayḥa* (pl. *lawaayeḥ*) *sooda, qaayme* (pl. *qawaayem*) *sooda.* His name is said to be on the black list. *biquulu ʔəsmo Ɛal-laayḥa s-sooda.*

blackmail - *balᵊṣ.* When everything else failed he tried blackmail. *waqᵊt kəll ḥiyalo fəšlet ḥaawal ᵊl-balᵊṣ.*

to blackmail - **1.** *balaṣ (o balᵊṣ//mbalaṣ).* He had been blackmailing her for years. *kaan Ɛam yəblə́ṣa la-sniin.* **2.** *haddad.* You can't blackmail me into doing that. *maa fiik ᵊthaddədni la-saawi haš-šaġle.*

black market - *s-suuq ᵊs-sooda.*

blackout - *ʔəṭfaaʔ˜ ʔanwaar.* During the war, we had a blackout almost every night. *ʔasnaaʔ ᵊl-ḥarᵊb taqriiban kəll leele kaan yṣiir Ɛanna ʔəṭfaaʔ ʔanwaar.*

Black Sea - *l-baḥr ᵊl-ʔaswad.*

black sheep - *balluuƐa* pl. *balaliiƐ.* He's the black sheep of the family. *huwwe balluuƐet ᵊl-Ɛeele.*

blacksmith - *ḥaddaad* pl. *-iin* and *-e.*

bladder - *masaane* pl. *-aat.*

blade - **1.** *naṣle* pl. *-aat.* I need a knife with two blades. *laazə́mni səkkiine b-naṣᵊlteen.* **2.** *šafra* pl. *-aat.* These blades don't fit my razor. *haš-šafraat maa byərkabu Ɛala ʔaalet ᵊḥlaaqti.* **3.** *waraqa* pl. *wraaq.* He chewed on a blade of grass. *Ɛalak waraqet ḥašiiš.*

blame - **1.** *malaame.* He took the blame for their mistake. *tḥammal malaamet ġalṭə́ton.* **2.** *loom.* Don't put the blame on me! *laa tḥəṭṭ ᵊl-loom Ɛaliyyi!* or ***laa tluumni ʔana!*

to blame - *laam (u loom, malaame//nlaam).* Don't blame me! *laa tluumni ʔana!* -- Under those circumstances I could hardly blame her. *taḥᵊt haẓ-ẓuruuf ṣəƐeb Ɛaliyyi luuma.* -- He blamed us for the accident. *laamna nəḥna Ɛal-ḥaades.* -- I don't blame you for going. *maa bluumak Ɛala rooḥtak.* -- We're not blaming you for anything. *maa Ɛam ᵊnluumak Ɛala šii.* -- He blames everything on me. *Ɛam yluumni Ɛala kəll šii ṣaar.*

**Who's to blame for that? *ġalṭet miin haš-šii?*

blank - **1.** *ʔəstimaara* pl. *-aat.* Would you help me to fill out this blank? *bətsaaƐə́dni b-təƐbaayet hal-ʔəstimaara?* **2.** *faraaġ* pl. *-aat.* Fill in all the blanks. *Ɛabbi kəll ᵊl-faraaġaat.* **3.** *ʔabyaḍ* f. *beeḍa* pl. *biiḍ, faaḍi.* The envelope contained only a blank sheet of paper. *ẓ-ẓarᵊf kaan fii bass waraqa beeḍa.* **4.** *faaḍi.* She gave me a blank stare. *ṭallaƐet Ɛaliyyi taṭliiƐa faaḍye.*

**My mind is a complete blank today. *ʔaḷḷa mṭammes Ɛala Ɛaqli l-yoom.*

blanket - *ḥraam* pl. *-aat.* Take another blanket and you won't be cold. *xəd-lak ᵊḥraam taani ḥatta maa təbrod.*

to blanket - *ġaṭṭa.* A thick fog blanketed the airfield. *ḍabaab ʔaswad ġaṭṭa l-maṭaar.*

blasphemy - *kəfᵊr.*

blast - *ʔənfižaar* pl. *-aat.* You could hear the blast for miles. *kaan fiik təsmaƐ ᵊl-ʔənfižaar Ɛala bəƐᵊd ʔamyaal.*

full blast - *b-kəll quwwe.* The plant is going full blast. *l-maƐmal Ɛam yəštə́ġel ᵊb-kəll quwwto.*

to blast - *fažžar.* They're blasting a tunnel. *Ɛam yfažžru tuneel.*

blast furnace - *maṣhar* pl. *maṣaaher, fərᵊn Ɛaali* pl. *fraan Ɛaalye.*

blaze - *ḥariiq* pl. *ḥaraayeq.* The blaze destroyed a whole block. *l-ḥariiq xarrab ḥaara kaamle.*

blazing - **1.** *mətwahhež.* The blazing fire cast eerie shadows on the opposite wall. *n-naar ᵊl-mətwahhže Ɛakset xyaalaat mawᵊḥše Ɛal-ḥeeṭ l-ᵊmqaabel.* **2.** *məḥreq.* We had to stand for half an hour in the blazing sun. *nžabarna nwaqqef nəṣṣ saaƐa bᵊš-šams ᵊl-məḥᵊrqa.*

bleach - *bayaaḍ.* Buy some bleach on your way home. *štrii-lak šwayyet bayaaḍ ᵊb-ṭariiqak Ɛal-beet.*

to bleach – **1.** *byaḍḍ.* The wash is bleaching in the sun. *l-ġasiil ɛam byəbyaḍḍ bᵊš-šamᵊs.* **2.** *bayyaḍ.* Does she really bleach her hair? *ɛan ḥaqa bətbayyeḍ šaɛra?*
to **bleat** – *maɛɛa.*
to **bleed** – **1.** *nezel (e ø) menno damm.* My nose is bleeding. *mənxaari ɛam yənzel mənno damm.* **2.** *nazaf (e naziif).* He was bleeding heavily. *kaan ɛam yənzef ᵊktiir.*
**She nearly bled to death. *taqriiban ṣafi damma.*
**My heart bleeds for you. *qalbi ɛam yətqaṭṭaɛ ɛaleek.*
blend – *maziiž.* The color is a perfect blend of red and yellow. *l-loon maziiž raakez mən ʔaḥmar w-ʔaṣfar.*
**I smoke my own blend. *bdaxxen təbġi l-xaaṣṣ.*
to blend – **1.** *nmazaž.* These colors don't blend. *hal-ʔalwaan maa btənməžež (maɛ baɛḍa).* **2.** *mazaž (e mazᵊž//nmazaž).* They blend several kinds of tobacco for this cigarette. *byəmᵊzžu ɛəddet ʔanwaaɛ mən ᵊt-təbġ ᵊb-ṣanᵊɛ has-sigaaraat.*
to **bless** – **1.** *baarak.* The priest turned around and blessed them. *l-xuuri ltafat w-baarákon.* **2.** *razaq (e/o rəzᵊq), mann ɛala.* God has blessed him with many children. *ʔaḷḷa razaqo wlaad ᵊktiir* or *ʔaḷḷa mann ɛaléé b-ᵊwlaad ᵊktiir.*
blessing – **1.** *raḥme* pl. *-aat, nəɛme* pl. *nəɛam.* It was really a blessing that she came. *bᵊl-ḥaqiiqa žayyéta kaanet raḥme.* **2.** *barake* pl. *-aat.* The bishop gave them his blessing. *l-ʔəsq̈of mandḥon barᵊkto.*
**You have my blessing. *ʔaḷḷa ywaffqak.*
blind – **1.** *ʔabažoor* pl. *-aat.* Shall I pull up the blinds? *ʔərfaɛ ᵊl-ʔabažooraat?* 2. *ʔaɛma* f. *ɛamya* pl. *ɛəmyaan.* A blind beggar knocked on our door. *fii šaḥḥaad ʔaɛma daqq ɛala baabna.* -- He's blind in one eye. *huwwe ʔaɛma b-ɛeen waaḥde.* -- I'm not blind to her faults. *ʔana maa-li ʔaɛma ɛan ʔaxṭaaʔa.* -- He's filled with a blind hatred for cats. *kəllo kərᵊh ʔaɛma ləl-qaṭṭaat.* **3.** *ɛal-ɛəmyaani.* She had to make a blind decision. *nžabret ᵊtqarrer ɛal-ɛəmyaani.* -- We had to drive almost blind in the fog. *ḍṭarreena nsuuq taqriiban ɛal-ɛəmyaani bᵊḍ-ḍabaab ᵊl-ʔaswad.*
to go blind – *ɛəmi (a ɛama).* I hope he's not going blind. *nšaaḷḷa maa ykuun ɛam yəɛma.*
to blind – *ɛama (i ɛama//nɛama).* The sun is blinding me. *š-šamᵊs ɛam təɛmiini.*
blind alley – *ḥaara* (pl. *-aat*) *masduude.* There is a blind alley between the two buildings. *fii ḥaara masduude been ᵊl-binaayteen.*
**That's just leading up a blind alley. *haš-šaġle maa-lha ʔaaxra.*
blindness – *ɛama.*
to **blink** – *rafraf.* He blinked his eyes. *rafraf ɛyuuno.*
blister – *faqfuule* pl. *faqafiil.* He has a blister on his foot. *fii faqfuule b-rəžlo.*
bloc – *kətle* pl. *kətal.*
block – **1.** *blook* pl. *-aat.* What do you plan to do with these blocks? *šuu naawi taɛmel ᵊb-hal-blookaat?* **2.** *ḥaara* pl. *-aat.* The fire destroyed a whole block. *l-ḥariiq xarrab ḥaara kaamle.* **3.** *šaareɛ* pl. *šawaareɛ.* Walk three blocks and then turn right. *ʔəmši tlatt šawaareɛ w-baɛdeen ᵊlfeet ɛala yamiinak.*
block and tackle – *bakara mrakkabe.*
to block – **1.** *sadd (ə sadd//nsadd).* A big truck blocked the road. *fii kamyoon ᵊkbiir sadd ᵊṭ-ṭariiq.* **2.** *kawa (i kawi//nkawa).* I have to have my old hat blocked. *bərneeṭṭi l-qadiime laazem tənkawa.*
blockade – *ḥṣaar* pl. *-aat.* The boat got caught running the blockade. *l-markab ᵊnkamaš w-huwwe ɛam yḥaawel yəxreq l-ᵊḥṣaar.*
blond – *ʔašqar* f. *šaqra* pl. *šəqᵊr.* She has blond hair. *šaɛra ʔašqar.*
blonde – *šaqra* pl. *šəqᵊr.* Who's that good-looking blonde over there? *miin haš-šaqra l-ḥəlwe hniike?*
blood – *damm* pl. *ʔədᵊmye.* He's lost a lot of blood. *ḍawwaɛ damm ᵊktiir.* -- Blood is thicker than water. *d-damm biḥənn* or *d-damm maa bişiir mayy.*
**They murdered him in cold blood. *qatalúu mən-ġeer-ma tənraff-ɛllon ɛeen.*
blood group – *zəmret~* (pl. *zəmar~*) *damm.*
bloodless: The government was overthrown in a bloodless revolution. *l-ᵊḥkuume nqalbet ᵊb-sawra biduun-ma tənhəder nəqṭet damm.*
blood money – *diyye* pl. *-aat.*
blood poisoning – *tasammom~ damm.*
blood pressure – *ḍaġᵊṭ~ damm.* He has high blood pressure. *ḍaġᵊṭ dammo* (or **ḍaġṭo) *ɛaali.*
bloodshed – *safᵊk~ damm.* All that bloodshed wasn't necessary. *kəll safk ᵊd-damm haada maa kan-lo lzuum.*
bloodshot – *məḥmarr.* His eyes are bloodshot from lack of sleep. *ɛyuuno məḥmarra mən qəllet ᵊn-noom.*
bloodstain – *bəqɛet~* (pl. *bəqaɛ~*) *damm.*
bloodthirsty – *mətɛaṭṭeš ləd-damm.* I don't think he's so bloodthirsty as he talks. *maa bəɛtəqed ʔənno mətɛaṭṭeš ləd-damm qadd-ma ɛam yəḥki.*
blood vessel – *ɛərᵊq~* (pl. *ɛruuq~*) *damm.*
bloody – **1.** *malyaan damm.* His handkerchief was all bloody. *maḥramto kaanet malyaane damm.* **2.** *damawi**. The bloody battle lasted for hours. *l-maɛrake d-damawiyye bəqyet saaɛaat.*
**He came out of the fight with a bloody nose, that's all. *ṭəleɛ mən l-ᵊxnaaqa b-mənxaar ɛam yənzel menno damm, muu ʔaktar.*
in **bloom** – *mʔazher.* The apricots are in bloom now. *l-məšmoš ᵊmʔazher hallaq.*
**The apple trees are in full bloom. *zahr ᵊt-təffaaḥ ᵊb-ɛəzzo.*
to bloom – *ʔazhar (biʔazher ø).* The roses bloomed all summer. *l-ᵊwruud ʔazharu kəll ᵊṣ-ṣeef.*
blossom – *zahra* coll. *zahᵊr* pl. *-aat* and *zhuur.* The blossoms are falling off the trees. *z-zahᵊr ɛam yhərr mən ɛaš-šažar.*
to blossom – *ʔazhar (biʔazher ø), fattaḥ.* The lilacs will probably start blossoming next week. *l-leelak bižuuz yʔazher ᵊž-žəmɛa ž-žaaye.*
to blossom out – *ḥəlyet (a ø) ɛal-kabar.* My, she's certainly blossomed out the last few years. *maa-šaaḷḷa, šuu ḥəlyet ɛal-kabar ᵊb-hal-kam səne!*
blot – **1.** *ləṭɛet~* (pl. *ləṭaɛ~*) *ḥəbᵊr, bəqɛet~* (pl. *bəqaɛ~*) *ḥəbᵊr.* The page is full of blots. *ṣ-ṣafḥa malaane ləṭaɛ ḥəbᵊr.* **2.** *laṭxa* pl. *-aat, waṣme* pl. *-aat.* Nothing can wipe out the blot on his record. *maa fii šii yəmḥi hal-laṭxa mən ṣiiṭo.*
to blot – *naššaf.* Blot the signature before you fold the letter. *naššef ᵊl-ʔəmḍa qabᵊl-ma təṭwi l-maktuub.*
to blot out – **1.** *sadd (ə sadd//nsadd).* The trees blot out the view. *š-šažaraat ɛam ysəddu l-manẓar.* **2.** *maḥa (i maḥi//mmaḥa).* He can't blot out the memory of the accident. *maa ɛam yəqder yəmḥi l-ḥaades mən zaakərto.*
to blot up – *naššaf.* Take a blotter and blot up the ink. *xəd-lak naššaafe w-naššef ᵊl-ḥəbᵊr.*
blotter – *naššaafe* pl. *-aat.* Quick, give me a blotter! *qawaam, ɛaṭiini naššaafe!*
Bloudane – *bluudaan.*
blouse – *bluuz* pl. *-aat.* I'd like to put on a fresh blouse. *žaay ɛala baali ʔəlbəs-li bluuz ᵊždiid.*
blow – **1.** *ḍarbe* pl. *-aat, xabṭa* pl. *-aat.* He killed her with a blow on the head. *qatála b-ḍarbe ɛala raasa.* **2.** *ḍarbe* pl. *-aat, mṣiibe* pl. *maṣaayeb.* Grandfather's death was a hard blow. *mootet žəddi kaanet ḍarbe qaasye.* **3.** *nafxa* pl. *-aat.* At the blow of a horn, the workers scattered in all directions. *ɛala nafxet ᵊl-boraẓaan ᵊš-šaġġiile tfarṭaɛu b-kəll ᵊž-žihaat.*
**That blow struck home. *hal-ḥaki xaraq ləl-ɛaḍᵊm.*
to blow – **1.** *ṭəleɛ (a ṭluuɛ).* A strong wind was blowing. *kaan ṭaaleɛ hawa qawi.* **2.** *nasaf (o nasᵊf).* The sand was blowing across the road. *r-ramᵊl kaan ɛam yənsof ɛaṭ-ṭariiq nasᵊf.* **3.** *ṣaffar.* When the whistle blows, it's time to knock off. *waqᵊt bətṣaffer ᵊṣ-ṣaffeera bişiir waqᵊt nəxloṣ ᵊš-šəġᵊl.* **4.** *ḥtaraq.* One of the fuses must have blown. *laazem ykuun waaḥed mən ᵊl-baašoonaat ᵊḥtaraq.*
**A whistle blew in the distance. *sməɛna ṣəffeera mən ɛala masaafe.*
**When do they blow taps? *ʔeemta byəḍᵊrbu ʔaaxer boraẓaan?*
**He blows hot one moment and cold the next. *mət-qalleb, maa-lo qaraar.*
**Blow the horn three times. *zammer tlatt marraat.*
**I have to blow my nose. *laazem nəff manaxiiri.*
**She'll blow her top if we're late. *biṭiir ɛaqᵊlha ʔiza tʔaxxarna.*
**The policeman blew his whistle. *š-šərṭi ṣaffar.*
to blow away – **1.** *ṭaar (i ø).* The paper blew away. *l-waraqa ṭaaret.* **2.** *ṭayyar.* The wind blew the dead leaves away. *l-hawa ṭayyar waraq ᵊš-šažar ᵊl-haarer.*
to blow out – **1.** *ṭafa (i ṭafi//nṭafa).* Blow out the candle. *ʔəṭfi š-šamɛa.* **2.** *nfaxat.* The old tire blew out. *l-kawšuuk ᵊl-ɛatiiq ᵊnfaxat.*

to blow over - *hədi (a ə).* The storm will blow over soon. *l-ɛaaṣfe raḥa təhda ɛan qariib.*
to blow up - 1. *nfažar.* The powder plant blew up. *maṣnaɛ ᵊl-baaruud ᵊnfažar.* 2. *ṭaar (i ṭayaraan) ɛaqlo, nfažar.* He blew up when he heard the news. *ṭaar ɛaqlo lamma səmeɛ ᵊl-xabar.* 3. *nasaf (e/o nasᵊf//ntasaf).* The enemy has blown up all the bridges. *l-ɛaduww nasaf kəll ᵊž-žsuura.* 4. *nafax (o nafᵊx//ntafax).* The kid wants you to blow up his balloon for him. *l-walad bəddo-yaak tənfəx-lo ḅaaḷoono.*

blowout - *ṭaqqet˜ kawšuuk.* A blowout at high speed is very dangerous. *ṭaqqet ᵊl-kawšuuk ɛas-sərɛa l-qawiyye maa fii ʔaxṭar mənha.*
**We had a blowout on the way home. *ṭaqq maɛna l-kawšuuk ᵊb-ṭariiqna ɛal-beet.*

blowtorch - *baaboor˜ (pl. bawabiir˜) ᵊlḥaam.*

blowup - *takbiir.* It's a blowup of a picture I took a year ago. *hayy takbiir la-ṣuura ʔaxádta mən səne.*

blue - 1. *ʔazraq f. zarqa pl. zərᵊq.* She has beautiful blue eyes. *ɛaleeha ɛyuun zərᵊq ḥəlwiin.* 2. *maqmuuṭ.* She looks blue this morning. *mbayyen ɛaleeha maqmuuṭa l-yoom.*
**He arrived out of the blue. *maa šəfnáa ʔəlla b-wəššna* or *wəṣel bala ɛəlᵊm w-laa xabar.*
**The news came like a bolt out of the blue. *nəzel ɛaleena l-xabar mətl ᵊṣ-ṣaaɛiq̈a.*
**I get the blues when it rains. *byəqmoṭ qalbi lamma bətmaṭṭer.*

blueprint - *xariiṭa pl. xaraayeṭ.*

bluff - 1. *balfe pl. -aat.* That's only a bluff. *hayy muu ʔaktar mən balfe.* 2. *balᵊf.* I'd call his bluff if I were you. *bwarži balfo law kənt ᵊb-maḥallak.*
to bluff - *balaf (e/o balᵊf).* He's only bluffing. *(huwwe) bass ɛam yəblef.*

bluing - *niile.*

blunder - *ġalṭa pl. -aat.* I made an awful blunder. *ɛməlᵊt ġalṭa faẓiiɛa.*

blunt - 1. *muu ḥadd.* You can't cut meat with a blunt knife. *maa btəqder təqṭaɛ laḥme b-səkkiine muu ḥadde.* 2. *žəfeṣ.* She can be very blunt at times. *ʔaḥyaanan fiiha tkuun žəfṣa ktiir.*

bluntly - *b-žafaaṣa.* He told me the truth very bluntly. *qal-li l-ḥaqiiqa b-kəll žafaaṣa.*

to **blush** - *ḥmarr.* She blushes easily. *btəḥmarr qawaam.*

board - 1. *looḥ xašab pl. lwaaḥ xašab.* We need some large boards. *laazəmna šii lwaaḥ xašab ᵊkbiire.* 2. *looḥ pl. lwaaḥ.* Write it on the board. *ktə́ba ɛal-looḥ.* 3. *mažles pl. mažaales.* The board meets twice a month. *l-mažles byəžtə́meɛ marrteen bᵊš-šahᵊr.*
board of directors - *mažles˜ (pl. mažaales˜) ʔidaara.*
board of health - *mudiiriit˜ ṣaḥḥa.*
above board - *maa fii ləɛbe.* Is this transaction really above board? *hal-ᵊmɛaamale bᵊl-ḥaqiiqa maa fiiha ləɛbe?*
on board - *raakeb.* Is everybody on board? *šuu raakbiin ᵊl-kəll?*
room and board - *ʔakᵊl w-noom.* How much do you pay for room and board? *qaddeeš ᵊbtədfaɛ ʔakᵊl w-noom?*
to board - 1. *rəkeb (a rkuub).* We boarded the train in Homs. *rkəbna t-treen ᵊb-ḥəmᵊṣ.* 2. *nəzel (e nzuul).* She's boarding with us. *naazle ɛanna.*

boardinghouse - *ḅanṣyoon pl. -aat, nazᵊl pl. nəzol.* Do you know of a nice boardinghouse? *btaɛrə́f-li šii ḅanṣyoon ᵊmniiḥ?*

boast - *tafaaxor.* He made good his boast that he would marry the prettiest girl in town. *ḥaqqaq tafaaxro b-ᵊžwaazo ʔaḥla bənᵊt bᵊl-balad.*
to boast - *tbažžaḥ, tbaaha, nafax (o ə) ḥaalo.* Stop boasting! *ḥaaže tətbažžaḥ* or *ḥaaže tənfox ḥaalak!*

boat - 1. *šaxtuura pl. šaxatiir.* We went fishing in his boat. *rəḥna nəṣṭaaḍ samak ᵊb-šaxtuurto.* 2. *baaxra pl. bawaaxer.* This boat goes to Australia. *hal-baaxra bətruuḥ la-ʔostraalya.*
**We're all in the same boat. *kəllna bᵊl-hawa sawa.*
boat trip - *safra (pl. -aat) bᵊl-baḥᵊr.* The boat trip will take five days. *s-safra bᵊl-baḥᵊr btaaxod xamᵊst iyyaam.*

bobby pin - *malqaṭ˜ (pl. malaaqeṭ˜) šaɛᵊr.*

body - 1. *žəsᵊm pl. ʔažsaam.* He has a rash on his body. *ṭaalə́ɛ-lo ḥaraara b-kəll žəsmo.* -- There are solid, liquid, and gaseous bodies. *fii ʔažsaam ṣəlbe w-maayɛa w-ġaaziyye.* 2. *žəsse pl. žəsas.* The body was found in a dark alley. *wažadu ž-žəsse b-ḥaara ɛətme.* 3. *šaasii pl. šaasiyyaat.* The body of the car needs complete overhauling. *šaasii s-sayyaara laazmo šadwade kaamle.* 4. *hayʔa pl. -aat.* He addressed the legislative body. *xaṭab qəddaam ᵊl-hayʔa t-tašriiɛiyye.* 5. *ṣəlᵊb.* Such an item shouldn't be in the body of the dictionary. *heek maadde laazem maa tkuun ᵊb-ṣəlb ᵊl-q̈aamuus.* 6. *mažmuuɛa pl. -aat.* The volumn contains a body of laws on immigration. *l-ᵊmžallad byəḥtə́wi ɛala mažmuuɛet q̈awaniin mətɛallqa bᵊl-həžra.*
**They barely manage to keep body and soul together. *bᵊl-kaad yṭaalɛu ləqmə́ton.*
in a body - *dafɛa waaḥde.* They left the hall in a body. *ṭəlɛu mn ᵊl-qaaɛa dafɛa waaḥde.*

bodyguard - *ḥaares šaxṣi coll. ḥaras šaxṣi pl. ḥərraas šaxṣiyyiin.*

to **bog down** - *ġarraz.* The car bogged down in the mud. *s-sayyaara ġarrazet bᵊṭ-ṭiin.*
**He's bogged down with work. *ġarqaan bᵊš-šəġᵊl la-qaraqiiṭ ʔadanée.*

boil - *dəmmale pl. damaamel.* He has a boil on his neck. *ṭaalə́ɛ-lo dəmmale b-raqᵊbto.*
to boil - 1. *ġali (i ġalayaan).* The water is boiling. *l-mayy ɛam təġli.* 2. *ġala (i ġali// nġala).* Have you boiled the milk yet? *ġaleeti l-ḥaliib?* 3. *salaq (e salᵊq//nsalaq).* I want my eggs boiled. *bəddi l-beeḍ masluuq.* 4. *faar (u fawaraan).* They were boiling with rage. *kaanu ɛam yfuuru mən kətr ᵊl-ġeeẓ.*

boiler - 1. (steam engine) *qaaẓaan pl. -aat.* 2. (small) *ṭanžara pl. ṭanaažer.*

bold - 1. *žarii?.* That was a bold statement. *kaan taṣriiḥ žarii?.* 2. *žasuur.* She's not bold enough to ask for permission. *maa-la žasuura kfaaye təṭlob ʔəzᵊn.*

boldness - *žərʔa, žasaara.*

bolt - 1. *bərġi pl. baraaġi.* This nut doesn't fit the bolt. *hal-ɛazqa muu la-hal-bərġi.* 2. *toob pl. twaab.* There are only ten yards of material left in this bolt. *baqyaan bass ɛašᵊr yardaat ᵊqmaaš ᵊb-hat-toob.* 3. *dəqᵊr pl. dquura.* Did you push the bolt shut? *sakkart ᵊd-dəqᵊr?*
**That news came like a bolt out of the blue. *nəzel ɛaleena l-xabar mətl ᵊṣ-ṣaaɛiq̈a.*
to bolt - 1. *daqqar.* You forgot to bolt the garage door. *nsiit ᵊddaqqer baab ᵊl-karaaž.* 2. *šarad (o šruud).* Suddenly the horse shied and bolted. *ɛala ġafle l-ᵊḥṣaan žəfel w-šarad.*

bomb - *qəmble pl. qanaabel, gəlle pl. gəlal.* The whole district has been destroyed by bombs. *kəll ᵊl-manṭiqa xarrabə́ta l-qanaabel.*
to bomb - *ḍarab (o ḍarᵊb//nḍarab).* The planes bombed the factory again during the night. *ṭ-ṭayyaaraat rəžɛet w-ḍarbet ᵊl-maɛmal ʔasnaaʔ ᵊl-leel.*

bomber - *q̈aazəft˜ (pl. q̈aazifaat˜) qanaabel.*

bond - 1. *sanad pl. -aat.* He invested all his money in bonds. *waẓẓaf kəll maṣarii b-sanadaat.* 2. *ṣila pl. -aat.* There's a firm bond between the two friends. *fii ṣila qawiyye been ᵊr-rfiiqeen.*

bone - 1. *ɛaḍme coll. ɛaḍᵊm pl. -aat and ɛḍaam.* Give the dog a bone. *ɛaṭi l-kalb ɛaḍme.* -- I feel chilled to the bone. *ḥaases ᵊl-barᵊd xaareq b-ᵊɛḍaami.* -- He's nothing but skin and bones. *kəllo žəld w-ɛaḍᵊm.* 2. *ḥasake coll. ḥasak pl. -aat.* This fish has an awful lot of bones. *has-samake fiiha ḥasak ᵊktiir.*
**I feel it in my bones that it's going to rain. *ḥaases ʔana bədda tmaṭṭer.*
**He made no bones about his intentions. *maa xalla šii mxabba ɛan nawayda.*
**I have a bone to pick with you. *ʔəli ḥsaab ṣaffii maɛak.*

bonus - *ʔəkraamiyye pl. -aat.*

book - 1. *ktaab pl. kətᵊb.* Did you like the book? *ɛažabak l-ᵊktaab?* -- That's one for the books. *hayy qəṣṣa btənzel bᵊl-kətᵊb* or ***hayy qəṣṣa maa btəntasa.* 2. *ɛəlbet˜ (ɛəlab˜) kəbriit.* Hand me that book of matches please. *naawəlni hal-ɛəlbet ᵊl-kəbriit mən faḍlak.*
**He goes by the book in everything he does. *bisaawi kəll šii ḥasab ᵊl-q̈aaɛde ɛaš-šaɛra.*
to keep books - *məsek (e masᵊk) dafaater.* Did he keep books for you? *məsə́k-lak dafaatrak?*
to book - 1. *ḥažaz (e/o ḥažᵊz//nḥažaz).* Have you already booked air passage? *sabaq w-ḥažazᵊt bᵊṭ-ṭayyaara?* 2. *waqqaf.* They booked him for vagrancy. *waqqafúu b-təhmet tašarrod.*

bookbindery – *maḥall˜* (pl. *-aat˜*) *tažliid.*
bookbinding – *tažliid.*
bookcase – *xzaanet˜* (pl. *xazaayen˜*) *kətᵊb.* Close the bookcase. *sakker ᵊxzaanet ᵊl-kətᵊb.*
(open) bookcase – *raff˜* (pl. *rfuuf˜*) *kətᵊb.* Did you dust the bookcase? *masaḥᵊt ġabret raff ᵊl-kətᵊb?*
book end – *sannaadet˜* (pl. *-aat˜*) *kətᵊb.*
bookkeeper – *mḥaaseb* pl. *-iin.*
bookkeeping – *mḥaasabe, mask˜ dafaater.*
booklet – *karraase* pl. *-aat.*
bookshelf – *raff˜* (pl. *rfuuf˜*) *kətᵊb.*
bookstore – *maktabe* pl. *-aat* and *makaateb.*
bookworm: He's a regular bookworm. *ḥaaṭeṭ raaso daayman bᵊl-ᵊktaab.* — I've never seen a bookworm like her in all my life. *b-ḥayaati maa šəfᵊt ḥada mətla ḥaaṭeṭ raaso bᵊl-kətᵊb.*
boom – **1.** *laεlaεa.* You could hear the boom of the cannon. *kənᵊt təsmaε laεlaεt ᵊl-madaafeε.* **2.** *rawaaž.* He made all his money in the boom. *εəmel kəll sarᵊwto ʔiyyaam ᵊr-rawaaž.* **3.** *ʔənεaaš.* How do you explain this sudden boom? *kiif bətfasser hal-ʔənεaaš ᵊl-fužaaʔi?*
to boom – **1.** *laεlaε.* He has a booming voice. *ṣooṭo bilaεleε.* **2.** *raayež.* Our business is booming now. *šəġᵊlna raayež hallaq.*
to **boost** – *εalla.* The drought has boosted the prices of corn. *l-qaḥᵊṭ εalla ʔasεaar ᵊd-dəra.*
boot – *žazme* pl. *-aat.* When I go fishing I wear high boots. *waqt ᵊbruuḥ εala ṣeeḍ ᵊs-samak bəlbes žazme εaalye.*
bootblack – *booyaži* pl. *iyye.*
booth – **1.** *kəšᵊk* pl. *kšaak.* There were many booths at the fair. *kaan fii kšaak ᵊktiire bᵊl-maεraḍ.* **2.** *talifoon ᵊεmuumi.* I'm calling from a booth. *εam bəḥki mən talifoon ᵊεmuumi.*
border – **1.** *ḥduud* (pl.). When do we reach the border? *ʔeemta laḥa nəṣal εal-ᵊḥduud?* **2.** *ḥaffe* pl. *-aat.* The border of this rug is getting frayed. *ḥaffet ᵊs-səžžaade badet tnassel.*
to border on: Syria borders on Jordan in the south. *suuriyya biḥədda mn ᵊž-žanuub ᵊl-ʔərdon.* — That borders on the ridiculous. *haš-šii qariib mən ᵊl-mahzale.*
bore – *εyaar* pl. *-aat.* We need pipes of a larger bore. *laazəmna ʔanabiib εyaaron ʔakbar.*
**She's an awful bore. *damma tqiil ᵊktiir.*
to bore – **1.** *ḥafar (e ḥafᵊr//nḥafar).* We'll have to bore a hole through the wall. *laazem nəḥfer bəxᵊš bᵊl-ḥeeṭ.* **2.** *mallal.* His speech bored me. *xṭaabo mallalni* (or ***xallaani məll*).
boring – *mməll.* We spent a boring evening at their house. *maḍḍeena sahra mməlle b-beeton.*
to be bored – *mall (ə malal).* Weren't you bored to death? *maa ṭaqqeet mən ᵊl-malal?*
boredom – *malal.*
boric acid – *boriik.*
born: He's a born liar. *(huwwe) kazzaab mən waqᵊt-ma xəleq.*
to be born – **1.** *wəled* (*-yəlad* and *-yuulad wlaade*). Where were you born? *meen wlədᵊt?* — My great-grandfather was born in Boston. *ʔabu žəddi wəled b-boosṭən.* **2.** *xəleq (a ə), wəled.* She was born blind. *xəlqet εamya.*
to **borrow** – **1.** *stεaar.* She borrowed the book from him. *stεaaret l-ᵊktaab mənno.* **2.** *ʔaxad//ttaaxad.* The word is borrowed from French. *hal-kəlme məttaaxde mn ᵊl-frənsaawi.* **3.** *ddayyan.* She borrowed ten pounds from me. *ddayyanet εašᵊr leeraat mənni.*
Bosrah – *bəṣra ʔaski šaam.*
boss – **1.** *raʔiis* pl. *rəʔasa.* Do you know my boss? *btaεref raʔiisi?* **2.** *siid* pl. *ʔasyaad.* Who wouldn't want to be his own boss! *miin maa byətmanna ykuun siid ḥaalo!*
to boss (around) – *tʔammar εala.* Who gave him the right to boss me around? *miin wakkalo yətʔammar εaliyyi?*
botanical – *nabaati*.*
botanist – *εaalem˜* (pl. *εəlama˜*) *nabaat.*
botany – *εəlm˜ ᵊn-nabaat.*
both – *tneenaat-* + pron. suff. Both brothers are in the navy. *l-ʔaxxeen tneenaaton bᵊl-baḥriyye.* — We both visited him. *tneenaatna zərnâ.*
both ... and – *b-nafs ᵊl-waqᵊt.* He's both intelligent and hard working. *huwwe zaki w-šaġġiil ᵊb-nafs ᵊl-waqᵊt.*
both (things) – *t-tneen, tneenaaton.* Would you want to be rich or famous? — I'd like to be both. *bəṭḥəbb ᵊtkuun ġani walla mašhuur?* — *bfaḍḍel kuun ᵊt-tneen.*
bother – *ġalabe, səqle.* It's no bother at all. *maa fii ġalabe ʔabadan.*
**Please don't go to any bother on my account. *daxiilak laa tġalleb ḥaalak mənšaani.*
**He's only a bother. *ḥəṭṭo ləl-ʔəzεaaž bass.*
**His constant questions are getting to be a bother. *ʔasʔəlto l-mətkarrᵊra badet ᵊddaayeq ᵊn-naas.*
to bother – **1.** *daayaq//ddaayaq, zaεaž (e ʔəzεaaž// nzaεaž).* Please don't bother me! *bətražžaak laa təzεəžni!* — I really hate to bother you. *bᵊl-ḥaqiiqa bəkrah ʔəzᵊεžak.* — What's bothering you? *šuu mdaayqak?* — Does the smoke bother you? *d-dəxxaan εam ydaayqak?* **2.** *ʔannab.* His conscience bothered him. *ḍamiiro ʔannabo.* **3.** *htamm.* I can't bother with that. *maa bəqder ʔəhtamm ᵊb-haš-šii.* **4.** *ġallab ḥaalo.* Please don't bother. *bətražžaak laa tġalleb ḥaalak.*
bottle – *qanniine* pl. *qanaani.* Shall I get a few bottles of beer? *ruuḥ žiib kam qanniinet biira?* — I'd like a bottle of ink. *laazəmni qanniinet ḥəbᵊr.*
to bottle – *εabba bᵊl-qanaani.* Do they bottle the milk there on the farm? *biεabbu l-ḥaliib bᵊl-qanaani hniik bᵊl-mazraεa?*
bottleneck – *maʔzaq̈* pl. *maʔaazeq̈.*
bottom – **1.** *səfᵊl.* He found it at the bottom of the trunk. *laqaaha b-səfl ᵊs-sanduuq.* — We've reached bottom! Things can't get worse. *wṣəlna ləs-səfᵊl! l-ḥaale muu maεquul tᵊltəεen ʔaktar* (or ***wṣəlna la-ʔasfal ᵊs-saafiliin!* ...) **2.** *qaaε.* The water is so clear you can see the bottom of the lake. *l-mayye raayqa la-daraže fiik ᵊtšuuf qaaε ᵊl-buḥayra.* **3.** *ṣəlᵊb, žoohar.* We have to get to the bottom of this affair. *laazem nədxol la-ṣəlb hal-masʔale.* **4.** *taḥtaani*, səflaani*.* Your shirts are in the bottom drawer. *qəmṣaanak bᵊd-dərž ᵊt-taḥtaani.*
**I thank you from the bottom of my heart. *bəšᵊkrak mən ṣamiim qalbi.*
from top to bottom – *mən fooq la-taḥᵊt.* The house was searched from top to bottom. *l-beet ᵊtfattaš mən fooq la-taḥᵊt.*
to be at the bottom of – *(kaan) wara˜ ..., (kaan) ʔasaas˜ ....* I'd like to know what's at the bottom of all this. *yaa-tara šuu wara kəll haš-šii.*
boulder – *ṣaxra* pl. *-aat* and *ṣxuur(a).*
to **bounce** – **1.** *ṭažž (e ṭažž), ṭažṭaž.* This ball doesn't bounce. *haṭ-ṭaabe maa bəṭṭežž.* — Stop bouncing that ball. *ḥaaže ṭṭažṭež haṭ-ṭaabe.* **2.** *raqqaṣ.* She likes to bounce the baby on her knee. *bəṭḥəbb ᵊtraqqeṣ ᵊl-beebée εala rəkᵊba.* **3.** *qallaε//tqallaε.* He was bounced yesterday. *tqallaε ᵊmbaareḥ.*
bound – **1.** *mažbuur, məḍṭarr.* We're bound by friendship to help them out. *mažbuuriin ᵊnsaaεədon ᵊb-ḥəkm ᵊs-sadaaqa.* **2.** *mžallad.* The book isn't bound properly. *l-ᵊktaab maa-lo mžallad ᵊmniiḥ.* **3.** *məžhet˜ ...* That boat is bound for America. *hal-baaxra məžhəta ʔameerka.* **4.** *laa bədd (mən).* It was bound to happen sooner or later. *kaan laa bədd mən ᵊḥṣuulha εaažilan ʔaw ʔaažilan.* **5.** *mən kəll bədd.* She's bound to be late. *mən kəll bədd laḥa tətʔaxxar.*
bound up with – *mətwaqqef εala.* The success of this operation is bound up with utmost precision. *nažaaḥ hal-εamaliyye mətwaqqef εala dəqqa mətnaahye.*
boundary – *ḥduud* (pl.).
boundless – *maa-lo ḥadd.* He has boundless self-confidence. *siq̈ato b-nafso maa-la ḥadd.*
bounds – *ḥduud* (pl.). His pride knows no bounds. *kəbriyaaʔo maa-la ḥduud.*
out of bounds – **1.** *mən fooq ᵊl-ʔaṣaṭiiḥ.* The price he's asking is way out of bounds. *s-səεᵊr yalli εam yəṭᵊlbo mən fooq ᵊl-ʔaṣaṭiiḥ.* **2.** *barraat l-ᵊḥduud.* The boys got completely out of bounds. *l-ᵊwlaad ṭəlεu barraat l-ᵊḥduud εal-ʔaxiir.* — Military police picked up the soldier out of bounds. *š-šərṭa l-εaskariyye kamšet ᵊl-εaskari barraat l-ᵊḥduud.*
within the bounds of – *ḍəmn ᵊḥduud˜ ...* You should try to live within the bounds of your salary. *laazem ᵊtḥaawel ᵊtεiiš ḍəmn ᵊḥduud maεaašak.*
bouquet – *baaqa* pl. *-aat.* Where did you get that beautiful bouquet of roses? *mneen žəbᵊt baaqet hal-ward ᵊl-ḥəlu?*
bow – **1.** *muq̈addame* pl. *-aat.* I like to stand at the bow of the ship. *bḥəbb waqqef εand muq̈addamt ᵊs-safiine.* **2.** *ḥanye* pl. *-aat, ʔənḥinaaʔa* pl. *-aat.* His low bow seemed a little ridiculous. *ḥənito*

ləl-ʔarᵊḍ ẓahret lən-naas saxiife šwayye.

to bow - 1. *nḥana.* He bowed and left the stage. *nḥana w-tarak ᵊl-masraḥ* -- He always bows to his father's wishes. *daayman byənḥəni la-rəġbaat ʔabúu.* **2.** *ḥana (i ḥani//nḥana).* They bowed their heads in silent prayer. *ḥanu ruuson ᵊb-ṣalda ṣaamṭa.*

bow - 1. *qooṣ* pl. *qwaaṣ.* Boys like to play with bows and arrows. *l-ᵊwlaad biḥəbbu yəlεabu bᵊl-qooṣ wᵊn-naššaab.* **2.** *εəqde* pl. *εəqad.* She had a pretty bow in her hair. *kaanet ḥaaṭṭa εəqde ḥəlwe εala šaεra.*

bowl - 1. *zəbdiyye* pl. *zabaadi.* Put these apples into a bowl. *ḥəṭṭ hat-təffaaḥaat ᵊb-zəbdiyye.* **2.** *ṭaase* pl. *-aat.* The beggar held out his bowl. *š-šaḥḥaad madd ṭaasto.*

to bowl over - *ṭayyar εaql˜ ...* The news nearly bowled me over. *l-xabar kaan raḥa yṭayyér-li εaqli.*

bowlegged - *ʔafṣaε* f. *faṣεa* pl. *fəṣᵊε.*

box - 1. *εəlbe* pl. *εəlab.* Shall I put the shoes in a box? *ḥəṭṭ ᵊṣ-ṣabbaaṭ ᵊb-εəlbe?* -- I have another box of cigars. *εandi εəlbet siigaar taanye.* **2.** *sanduuq* pl. *sanadiiq.* Would you drop this letter in the box for me? *btəlḥə́š-li hal-maktuub bᵊs-sanduuq?* **3.** *loož* pl. *lwaaž.* All boxes are sold out for the premiere. *kəll ᵊl-lwaaž ᵊttaaxadet ləl-ḥafle l-ʔəftitaaḥiyye.*

to box - 1. *laakam, ləεeb (a ləεᵊb) boks.* Do you like to box? *bəthəbb ᵊtlaakem?* or *bəthəbb təlεab boks?* **2.** *ḥaṭṭ ᵊb-sanadiiq.* We have to box her things and send them to her. *laazem ᵊnḥəṭṭ-ə́lha ġraaḍa b-sanadiiq w-nəbεə́t-la-yáahon.*

boxer - *mlaakem* pl. *-iin.* He was a pretty good boxer in college. *kaan ᵊmlaakem maa bo šii bᵊž-žaamεa.*

boxing - *mlaakame.* He likes boxing and wrestling. *biḥəbb l-ᵊmlaakame wl-ᵊmṣaaraεa.*

box office - *giišée* (f.) pl. *giišeeyaat, šəbbaak˜* (pl. *šababiik˜*) *tazaaker.* The box office is open from ten to four. *l-giišée faatḥa mn ᵊl-εašara ləl-ʔarbεa.*

boy - 1. *ʔəbᵊn* pl. *ṣəbyaan.* How old is your boy? *qaddeeš εəmᵊr ʔəbnak?* **2.** *ṣabi* pl. *ṣəbyaan, walad* pl. *wlaad.* The boy is not older than seven years. *ṣ-ṣabi εəmro muu ʔaktar mən sabε ᵊsniin.*

**Boy, oh boy, what a night! *ya laṭiif məlla leele!*

boycott - *mqaaṭaεa.* The boycott was lifted. *l-ᵊmqaa-ṭaεa rtafεet.*

to boycott - *qaaṭaε.* For some reason or other, they're boycotting that store. *la-sabab mən ᵊl-ʔasbaab, εam yqaaṭεu hal-maxzan.*

boy scout - *kaššaaf* pl. *-e.*

brace - 1. *ḥammaale* pl. *-aat.* The motor is held in place by four braces. *l-motoor ᵊmrakkaz εala ʔarbaε ḥammaalaat.* **2.** *kammaaše* pl. *-aat.* The braces that hold the scaffolding together are loose. *l-kammaašaat yalli maaskiin ᵊs-sqaale raxwiin.* **3.** *mšadd ḥadiid* pl. *-aat ḥadiid.* He's still wearing a brace on his left leg. *ləssáa laabes ᵊmšadd ḥadiid ᵊb-rəžlo š-šmaal.*

to brace oneself - 1. *laqa (i laqi) kətfo.* They both braced themselves against the door. *tneenaaton laqu ktaafon εal-baab.* **2.** *šadd (ə šadd) ḥaalo* (or *ḥeelo*). Brace yourself. I've got bad news. *šədd ḥaalak. εandi ʔaxbaar εaaṭle.*

to brace up - 1. *farfaš, našnaš.* I need a whiskey to brace me up. *laazəmni kaas wiski yfarfəšni.* **2.** *šadd (ə šadd) ḥeelo.* Brace up! *šədd ḥeelak!*

bracelet - *swaara* pl. *-aat* and *ʔasaawer.* I've lost my bracelet. *ḍaawaεt ᵊswaarti.*

bracket - 1. *sannaade* pl. *-aat.* He used two brackets to hold up the shelf. *ḥaṭṭ sannaadteen yəḥᵊmlu r-raff.* **2.** *fiʔa* pl. *-aat.* He's still in a rather low income bracket. *ləssaato b-fiʔa daxla waaṭi.* **3.** *məεtərḍa* pl. *-aat.* I don't understand the word in brackets. *maa fhəmt ᵊl-kəlme halli been məεtərᵊḍteen.*

to brag - *tbažžaḥ, tfašwar, tbaaha.* Does he always brag that way? *heek εaadto byətbažžaḥ?* -- Don't brag so much! *haaše tətfašwar!*

braid - 1. *ḍfiire* pl. *ḍafaayer.* I admire her blond braids. *(ʔana) məεžab ᵊktiir ᵊb-ḍafaayə́ra š-šəqᵊr.* **2.** *šriiṭ* pl. *šaraayeṭ.* With all that braid, the doorman looks almost like an admiral. *b-kəll haš-šaraayeṭ ᵊl-bawwaab ṭaaleε mətᵊl ʔamiiraal.*

to braid - *ḍafar (o ḍafar//nḍafar).* Ask mother to braid your hair. *ṭləbi mən ʔəmmek təḍfə́r-lek šaεrek.*

brain - *məxx* pl. *mxaax, dmaaġ* pl. *ʔadmiġa.* The bullet had penetrated his brain. *r-rṣaaṣa xarqet ᵊb-məxxo.* -- He hasn't a brain in his head. *huwwe maa fii məxx (ᵊb-raaso)* or ***huwwe mmaxxex.*

**She's a real brain. *hiyye bᵊl-ḥaqiiqa zakiyye ktiir.*

brains - *εaqlaat* (pl.). She hasn't got much brains. *εaqlaata šwayye maḥduude.*

to rack one's brain(s) - *kassar raaso.* There's no use racking your brains over that problem. *muu məḥᵊrze tkasser raasak ᵊb-hal-məšᵊkle.*

to brain someone - *kassar raas˜ ḥada.* If you do that again I'll brain you. *ʔiza εməlᵊt haš-šii marra taanye bkasser raasak.*

brake - *fraam* pl. *-aat.* The brake doesn't work. *l-ᵊfraam maa-lo εam yəštə́ġel.* -- I tried to put on the brakes, but it was already too late. *žarrabᵊt ʔəḍrob ᵊfraam, laaken sabaq ᵊs-seef ᵊl-εazal.*

branch - 1. *ġəṣᵊn* pl. *ġṣaan, εərᵊq* pl. *εruuqa.* The wind broke off several branches. *l-hawa kassar kam ġəṣᵊn.* **2.** *farᵊε* pl. *fruuε(a).* What branch of the service are you in? *b-ʔanu farᵊε bᵊž-žeeš ʔənte?* **3.** *šəεbe* pl. *šəεab, farᵊε* pl. *fruuε(a).* The bank has two branches in town. *l-bank ʔəlo šəεᵊbteen bᵊl-balad.*

to branch off - *tfarraε.* The road branches off here. *ṭ-ṭariiq byətfarraε mən hoon.*

to branch out - 1. *farraε.* If the tree keeps branching out that way it will block our view entirely. *ʔiza š-šažara bədda ḍḍall ᵊtfarreε heek bətsədd ᵊl-manẓar kəllo.* **2.** *fataḥ (a fatᵊḥ) šəεbe* or *šəεab.* Our company is going to branch out before long. *šərkətna bədda təftaḥ šəεab εan qariib.*

brand - *ṣənᵊf* pl. *ṣnaaf, maarka* pl. *-aat.* What brand do you smoke? *šuu ṣ-ṣənᵊf yalli bəddaxxno?* -- What brand of coffee do you prefer? *šuu maarket ᵊl-qahwe yalli bətfaḍḍə́la?*

to brand - 1. *waṣam (e waṣᵊm//ttaṣam).* He was branded as a traitor. *waṣamúu bᵊl-ᵊxyaane.* **2.** *wasam (wašam)(e wasᵊm, wašᵊm), damaġ (a damᵊġ// ndamaġ).* Have the new horses been branded yet? *l-xeel ᵊž-žədad sabaq w-wasamuuhon?*

brand-new - *ždiid mən ʔəmm-* + pron. suff., *ždiid ᵊxlanž* (invar.). The wrecked car was brand-new. *s-sayyaara l-ᵊmṭaḥbaše kaanet ᵊždiide mən ʔəmma.*

brass - 1. *nḥaas ʔaṣfar.* Brass is an alloy of copper and zinc. *n-nḥaas ᵊl-ʔaṣfar xaliiṭ mən ᵊnḥaas w-tuutye.* -- Where did you buy this beautiful brass tray? *mneen ᵊštareet haṣ-ṣaniyye l-ḥəlwe nḥaas ʔaṣfar?* **2.** *kibaar˜ ḍəbbaaṭ* (pl.). The President was accompanied by the top Army brass. *r-raʔiis kaan ᵊb-ṣəḥᵊbto kibaar ḍəbbaaṭ ᵊž-žeeš.*

brassière - *sutyaan* pl. *-aat.*

brat - *mažquum, madluuε, maayeε.* He's an insolent brat. *huwwe mažquum wəqeḥ.*

brave - *šəžaaε* pl. *šəžεaan, žasuur.* She's a brave girl. *waḷḷa bənᵊt šəžaaεa.*

to brave - *maa nṭašš b-.* Let's brave the heat and go for a walk. *xalliina maa nənṭašš bᵊš-šoob w-nəṭlaε naεmel məšwaar.*

bravely - *b-šažaaεa.* They bravely withstood the attack. *b-šažaaεa ṣamadu ləl-ᵊhžuum.*

bravery - *šažaaεa, žasaara.* He was commended for his bravery. *ʔasnu εaléе la-šažaaεto.*

brawl - *xnaaqa* pl. *-aat* and *xanaayeq.* He got mixed up in a brawl last night. *twarraṭ b-ᵊxnaaqa leelt ᵊmbaareḥ.*

to brawl - *εarbad.* Brawling sailors roamed the streets. *kaan fii baḥḥaara mεarᵊbdiin daaru bᵊš-šawaareε.*

to **bray** - *šanhaq.*

Brazil - *l-baraziil.*

breach - 1. *xarᵊq.* This constitutes a flagrant breach of contract. *haada bišakkel xarᵊq faaḍeḥ ləl-kontraat.* **2.** *qaṭiiεa.* This eventually led to a breach between the two countries. *bᵊl-ʔaaxiir haš-šii ʔadda la-qaṭiiεa been ᵊd-dawᵊlteen.* **3.** *səġra* pl. *-aat* and *səġar.* The counterattack created a breach on the left flank. *l-ᵊhžuum l-ᵊmεaakes fataḥ səġra bᵊl-maysara.*

bread - *xəbᵊz.* Please slice the bread. *baḷḷa qaṭṭeε ᵊl-xəbᵊz.*

**How does he earn his bread? *kiif byəsḥab maεiišto?*

loaf of bread - *rġiif˜* (pl. *ʔərᵊġfet˜*) *xəbᵊz.* We need two loaves of bread. *laazəmna rġiifeen xəbᵊz.*

piece or slice of bread - *šaqfet˜* (pl. *šəqaf˜*)

xəb°z, xəbze pl. *-aat.*

break - 1. *kas°r.* He suffered a bad break of the shinbone. *nṣaab °b-kas°r malEuun °b-qaṣbet rəžlo.* **2.** *qaṭiiEa.* A break between the two countries can no longer be avoided. *maa Eaad məmken tafaadi l-qaṭiiEa been °d-daw°lteen.* **3.** *ʔəstiraaḥa.* We need a break before we go on to the next job. *laazəmna ʔəstiraaḥa qab°l-ma nəbda b°š-šaġle t-taanye.* **4.** *fərṣa.* Let's give him a break. *xalliina naEṭii fərṣa.*

**Let's take a break now. *xalliina nəstrəḥ-°lna šwayye hallaq.*

bad (or tough) break - *ḥaẓẓ Eaaṭel.* He's had a lot of bad breaks in his life. *ḥakamo ḥaẓẓ Eaaṭel °ktiir °b-ḥayaato.* — That's a tough break. *faẓaaEa Eala hal-ḥaẓẓ °l-Eaaṭel!*

lucky break - *fərṣa maa btəttamman.* Meeting him was a lucky break for me. *ʔəžtimaaEi fii kaan fərṣa maa btəttamman ʔəli.*

to break - 1. *kasar (e kas°r//nkasar).* Who broke the dish? *miin kasar °ṣ-ṣaḥ°n?* — The boys have broken the window. *l-°wlaad kasaru š-šəbbaak.* — This is the second time he broke the world record. *hayy °l-marra t-taanye halli byəkser fiiha r-raqam °l-qiyaasi l-Eaalami.* **2.** *qaṭaE (a qaṭ°E//nqaṭaE).* He broke the string. *qaṭaE °l-xeeṭ.* **3.** *xaffaf, kasar ḥəddet~* ... The awning broke his fall from the third-floor window. *l-xeeme xaffafet* (or *kasret ḥəddet~*) *waq°Eto mən šəbbaak °ṭ-ṭaabeq °t-taalet.* **4.** *xaalaf.* He has broken the law. *xaalaf °l-qaanuun.* **5.** *fasax (a fas°x//nfasax).* She broke her engagement. *fasxet xəṭbə́ta.* **6.** *rəžeE (e ržuuE) Ean* and *b-.* He won't break his word. *maa byəržaE Ean kəl°mto.* **7.** *ballaġ.* We'll have to break the news to him gently. *laazəm °nballġo l-xabar Eala mah°lna w-°b-laṭaafe.* **8.** *nkasar.* The window broke when she slammed the door. *š-šəbbaak °nkasar waq°t tarset °l-baab.* **9.** *nkasret ḥədd°to.* This hot spell should break soon. *moožet °l-ḥarr laa bədd tənkə́ser ḥəddə́ta Ean qariib.* **10.** *nqaṭaE.* The string broke. *nqaṭaE °l-xeeṭ.* **11.** *ražaf (e ražafaan).* His voice broke with emotion. *ṣooṭo ražaf mən šəddet ʔənfiEaalo.* **12.** *Etaraf, qarr.* After long interrogation he finally broke. *baE°d ʔəstəžwaab ṭawiil qarr b°l-ʔaaxiir.*

**I broke my leg. *nkasret rəžli.*

to break down - 1. *Eəṭel (a Eəṭ°l).* The machine broke down this morning. *l-maakiina Eəṭlet °l-yoom Eala bəkra.* **2.** *nhaar.* He broke down when he heard the news. *nhaar lamma səmeE °l-xabar.* **3.** *kassar.* The police broke down the door. *š-šərṭa kassaret °l-baab.* **4.** *faraz (e/o far°z//nfaraz).* Let's break down these figures into income and expenses. *xalliina nəfrez hal-ʔarqaam la-mən w-la-ʔila.*

to break in - 1. *marran.* I'll have to break in another beginner. *laazəm marren məstažədd taani.* **2.** *rawwaḍ//trawwaḍ.* The horse hasn't been broken in yet. *l-°ḥṣaan ləssa maa trawwaḍ.* **3.** *ʔaalaš// tʔaalaš.* Who's going to break in the new car? *miin bəddo yʔaaleš °s-sayyaara ž-ždiide?*

to break into - *faat (u foote).* Last night thieves broke into our neighbor's house. *leelt °mbaareḥ faatu ḥaramiyye b-beet žaarna.*

to break off - 1. *qaṭaE (a qaṭ°E//nqaṭaE).* They broke off relations. *qaṭaEu l-Ealaaqaat beenáton.* **2.** *qasam (e/o qasme//nqasam).* Break off a piece for me, please. *qsə́m-li šaqfe mən faḍlak.* **3.** *nkasar.* Then the branch broke off. *w-baEdeen °l-Eərq °nkasar.* **4.** *waqqaf.* He suddenly broke off in the middle of the sentence. *b-nəṣṣ °ž-žəmle Eala ġafle waqqaf.*

to break out - 1. *harab (o harab).* He broke out of prison. *harab mən °l-ḥab°s.* **2.** *bada (a ø).* The fire broke out toward midnight. *l-ḥariiq bada ḥawaali nəṣṣ °l-leel.* **3.** *ẓahar (a ẓhuur).* A cholera epidemic has broken out in the city. *wabaaʔ °l-koleera ẓahar b°l-madiine.* **4.** *habb.* She broke out with the measles. *habbet fiiha l-°ḥmeera.* **5.** *kadd.* He always breaks out in a sweat when he's nervous. *daayman bikəddo l-Earaq lamma binarvez.*

to break up - 1. *ḥall (ə ḥall//nḥall).* The police broke up the meeting. *š-šərṭa ḥallu l-ʔəžtimaaE.* **2.** *šattat.* The opposition tried to break up the meeting. *l-°mEaaraḍa ḥaawalet °tšattet °l-ʔəžtimaaE.* **3.** *daab (u dawabaan).* The ice will break up soon. *ž-žaliid Ean qariib biduub.*

**Break it up! *fəḍḍuuha!*

to break someone of something - *baṭṭal ḥada Eaadet~ šii.* I'll break him of biting his fingernails. *laḥa baṭṭlo Eaadet ʔak°l ʔaḍafiiro.*

breakdown - 1. *fašal.* We must avoid a breakdown in the negotiations at all costs. *mahma kallaf °l-ʔam°r laazem nətfaada fašal l-°mfaawaḍaat.* **2.** *Eəṭ°l.* The breakdown of the machine caused a lot of delay. *Eəṭl °l-makana sabbab taʔxiir °ktiir.* **3.** *ʔənhiyaar* pl. *-aat.* She had a nervous breakdown. *kaan maEa ʔənhiyaar Eaṣabi.*

breakfast - *kas°r~ ṣəfra, tarwiiqa.* I always have an egg for breakfast. *daayman baakol beeḍa Eala kasr °ṣ-ṣəfra.*

to have breakfast - *kasar (e kasr) °ṣ-ṣəfra, trawwaq.* Have you had breakfast yet? *sabaq w-kasart °ṣ-ṣəfra?*

breast - 1. *ṣəḍ°r* pl. *ṣḍuur(a).* She clutched the baby to her breast. *ḍammet °l-beebée la-ṣədra.* **2.** *bəzz* pl. *bzaaz.* One of her breasts had to be removed. *nžabaru yqiimúu-la bəzz mən °bzaaza.*

**Make a clean breast of it. *fəšš qalbak.*

breath - *nafas.* Hold your breath. *ḥbees nafas.* — I'm completely out of breath. *maqṭuuE nafasi Eal-ʔaaxiir.*

**Don't mention the two of us in the same breath. *laa təžməlna maE baE°ḍna.*

**Save your breath. *bala ḥaki.*

breath of air - *nasmet~* (pl. *-aat~*) *hawa.* There isn't a breath of air today. *maa fii w-laa nasmet hawa l-yoom.*

**Let's go out and get a breath of fresh air. *xalliina nəṭlaE °nšəmm šwayyet hawa.*

under one's breath - *b-ṣooṭ waaṭi.* She said the words under her breath. *qaalet °l-kalaam °b-ṣooṭ waaṭi.*

to catch one's breath - *rtaaḥ šwayye.* I have to catch my breath first. *ʔawwal šii laazem ʔərtaḥ-li šwayye.*

to **breathe - 1.** *tnaffas.* He's breathing regularly. *Eam yətnaffas °b-ʔəntiẓaam.* **2.** *laqaṭ (o laq°ṭ) nafas.* Give me a minute to breathe. *Eaṭiini daqiiqa la-ʔəlqoṭ nafas.*

**Don't breathe a word of this to anyone. *laa təḥki kəlme la-ḥada Ean haš-šii.*

**I'll breathe again when I'm done with this job. *maa byəhda baali la-xalleṣ haš-šaġle.*

to breathe one's last - *naazaE.* He is breathing his last. *Eam ynaazeE.*

breed - *žən°s* pl. *ʔažnaas.* What breed of dog is it? *šuu žən°s hal-kal°b?*

to breed - *rabba.* My uncle breeds horses. *Eammi birabbi xeel.*

breeding - *tərbaaye.* Breeding horses is his hobby. *suusto tərbaayt °l-xeel.* — You can tell a man's breeding by the way he talks. *fiik taEref tərbaayet °l-ʔənsaan mən ṭariiqet ḥakyo.*

breeze - *nasmet~ hawa, nasiim.* At night we got a cool breeze from the lake. *b°l-leel °ʔžaana nasmet hawa rəṭbe mn °l-buḥayra.*

to **brew - 1.** *xammar.* We brew our own beer. *mənxammer biirətna la-ḥaalna.* **2.** *Eass (ə Easiis).* You can always tell when trouble is brewing at the office. *fiik daayman təḥser waq°t fii mašaakel Eam °tEəss b°l-maktab.*

brewery - *maṣnaE~* (pl. *maṣaaneE~*) *biira.*

bribe - *rašwe* pl. *-aat, barṭiil* pl. *baraṭiil.* He was caught accepting a bribe. *nkamaš w-huwwe Eam yaaxod rašwe.*

to bribe - *barṭal//tbarṭal, raša (i rašu//rtaša).* You can't bribe him. *maa fiik °tbar°ṭlo.* — They bribed him to lie at the hearing. *rašúu la-ykazzeb b°l-°mḥaakame.*

bribery - *barṭale, rašwe.*

brick - *ʔaažərra* coll. *ʔaažərr* pl. *-aat.* Their house is built of red brick. *beeton mabni mən ʔaažərr ʔaḥmar.* — A brick wall encloses the garden. *suur mən ʔaažərr °mḥaaweṭ °ž-žneene.*

bricklayer - *məEmaari* pl. *-iyye.*

bricklaying - *Eamaar.*

bridal bouquet - *buukée~* (pl. *buukeeyaat~*) *l-Earuus.*

bridal money - *naq°d, mah°r.*

bride - *Earuus* pl. *Earaayes.*

bridegroom - *Eariis* pl. *Eərsaan.*

bridge - 1. *žəs°r* pl. *žsuura.* There's a bridge across the river a mile from here. *fii žəsr °byəqṭaE °n-nah°r Eala masaafet miil mən hoon.* — The dentist is making a new bridge for me. *ḥakiim l-°snaan Eam yaEməl-li žəsr °ždiid la-snaani.* **2.** *ġərfet~ qiyaade.* Look, there is the captain on the bridge. *leek °l-qəbṭaan °b-ġərfet °l-qiyaade.* **3.** *ḥṣaan.*

The bridge of my violin is broken. *ḥsaan ᵊl-kamanža tabaᶜi maksuur.* **4.** *bridž.* Do you play bridge? *btaᶜref taləᶜab bridž?*
**He burned his bridges behind him. *qaṭaᶜ ᶜala ḥaalo xṭuuṭ ᵊr-ražᶜa.*

bridle - *lžaam* pl. *-aat.* Look at that beautiful silver-plated bridle. *šuuf hal-lžaam ᵊl-ḥəlu l-ᵊmraṣṣaᶜ ᵊb-fəḍḍa.*
to bridle - **1.** *lažam (e/o lažᵊm//ltažam).* Ask the stableboy to bridle the horse for me. *quul ləs-saayes yəlžəm-li l-ᵊḥṣaan.* **2.** *ḥafaẓ (a ḥafᵊẓ).* He should learn to bridle his tongue. *laazem yətᶜallam yəḥfaẓ kalaamo.*

brief - **1.** *məxtáṣar, qaṣiir.* He left a brief message. *tarak risaale məxtaṣara.* **2.** *məxtaṣar, muužaz.* Let me give you a brief outline of what I have in mind. *xalliini ʔaᶜṭiik šarᵊḥ məxtaṣar ᶜan halli b-baali.* **3.** *qaṣiir.* Unfortunately, my stay in Cairo was very brief. *la-suuʔ ᵊl-ḥaẓẓ ʔiqaamti bᵊl-qaahira kaanet qaṣiire ktiir.* **4.** *mzakkra* pl. *-aat.* He spent all night drafting that brief. *madda l-leel kəllo ᶜam ynaẓẓem hal-ᵊmzakkra.*
**Please be brief. *mən faḍlak ᵊb-ʔəxtiṣaar.*
in brief - *b-ʔəxtiṣaar, b-kəlᵊmteen.* In brief, our plan is this. *b-ʔəxtiṣaar, hayy xəṭṭətna.*
to brief - *laxxaṣ la-.* Let me brief you on the situation. *xalliini laxxəṣ-lak ᵊl-waḍᵊᶜ.*

briefcase - *šantaaye* pl. *šanaati.*

briefly - **1.** *šwayye.* He paused briefly before he advanced his most important argument. *waqqaf šwayye qabᵊl-ma yqaddem ʔahamm ḥəžže ᶜando.* **2.** *b-kəlᵊmteen, b-ʔiižaaz, b-ʔəxtiṣaar.* Let me tell you briefly what I've found out so far. *xalliini qəl-lak ᵊb-kəlᵊmteen šuu ktašafᵊt la-hallaq.*

brigade - *liwaaʔ* pl. *ʔalwiye.*

brigadier - *liwaaʔ* pl. *ʔalwiye.*

bright - **1.** *mšaᶜšeᶜ.* I like a bright fire. *bḥəbb naar ᵊmšaᶜᵊšᶜa.* **2.** *faateḥ.* She likes to wear bright colors. *bətḥəbb təlbes ʔalwaaᶜi loona faateḥ.* **3.** *zaki** pl. *ʔazkiya, fəteḥ* pl. *fətᵊḥ.* He's a bright boy. *huwwe walad zaki.* **4.** *ᶜaẓiim.* That was a bright idea! *hayy kaanet fəkra ᶜaẓiime.* **5.** *mfarfeš.* She's always bright and cheerful. *hiyye daayman ᵊmfarᵊfše mabṣuuṭa.* **6.** *laameᶜ.* His future doesn't look so bright. *məstaqbalo mbayyen ᶜalée muu laameᶜ kəll hal-qadd.*
**We have to start out bright and early. *laazem nətḥarrak mən ᶜala bəkret ᵊṣ-ṣəbᵊḥ.*

brilliant - **1.** *zaahi.* You can tell his paintings by the brilliant colors. *fiik taᶜref ṣəwaro mən ʔalwaana z-zaahye.* **2.** *baaher.* He's a brilliant speaker. *huwwe xaṭiib baaher.* **3.** *laameᶜ.* He's the most brilliant man I know. *huwwe ʔalmaᶜ šaxᵊṣ baᶜᵊrfo.*

brim - **1.** *šəffe* pl. *šəfaf.* The glass is filled to the brim. *l-kaase malaane ləš-šəffe.* **2.** *kanaar* pl. *-aat.* He pulled the brim of his hat over his eyes. *nazzal kanaar bərneeṭto fooq ᵊᶜyuuno.*

to **bring** - *žaab (i žayabaan//nžaab).* Bring me a glass of water, please. *žəb-li kaaset mayy mən faḍlak.* -- He brought the children a present. *žaab ləl-ᵊwlaad ᵊhdiyye* -- May I bring a friend with me? *məmken žiib maᶜi rfiiq ʔəli?* -- The car should bring a good price. *s-sayyaara maᶜquul džiib səᶜr ᵊmniiḥ.*
to bring about - *sabbab.* The depression brought about a change in living standards. *l-kasaad sabbab taġyiir ᵊb-məstáwa l-maᶜiiše.*
to bring along - *žaab (i žayabaan) maᶜo.* Bring your children along! *žiib ᵊwlaadak maᶜak!*
to bring back - **1.** *ražžaᶜ.* Please bring the book back. *mən faḍlak ražžeᶜ l-ᵊktaab.* -- He's dead, all the money in the world won't bring him back now. *maat w-kəll maal ᵊd-dənye maa biražžᶜo.* **2.** *ḥaya (i ʔəḥyaaʔ).* This trip has brought back many memories. *has-safra ḥayet zəkriyyaat ᵊktiire.*
to bring down - *nazzal.* I also brought down the big box. *nazzalᵊt kamaan ᵊṣ-ṣanduuq l-ᵊkbiir.* -- That should bring him down a peg. *haš-šii məntáẓar ynazzlo ᶜan saržo.*
**Her song brought down the house. *ġənniita qayyamet ᵊl-ḥaaḍriin w-qaᶜdéton.*
to bring home - *barhan.* He brought home his argument in a fiery speech. *b-xəṭbe ḥamasiyye barhan ləl-kəll ḥəžžto.*
to bring in - *žaab (i žayabaan//nžaab).* The dance brought in a hundred dollars. *l-ḥafle r-raaqṣa žaabet miit dolaar.* -- The police brought him in in handcuffs. *š-šərṭa žaabto mkalbaš.*
to bring out - **1.** *ṭaalaᶜ la-barra.* Can't you bring the ball out? *maa fiik ᵊṭṭaaleᶜ ᵊṭ-ṭaabe la-barra?* **2.** *ṭaalaᶜ.* They're bringing out a new edition of my book. *ᶜam yṭaalᶜu ṭabᶜa ždiide mn ᵊktaabi.* **3.** *qaddam.* He brought out his point convincingly. *qaddam wəžhet naẓaro b-ṣuura məqᵊnᶜa.*
to bring round - *qanaᶜ (e ʔəqnaaᶜ//nqanaᶜ).* I hope I can bring him round to our point of view. *nšaaḷḷa ʔəqder ʔəqᵊnᶜo b-wəžhet naẓarna.*
to bring to - *ṣaḥḥa.* Cold water will bring him to. *l-mayy ᵊl-baarde bətṣaḥḥii.*
to bring to bear - *staᶜmal.* He brought all his influence to bear. *staᶜmal kəll nufuuzo.*
to bring to terms - *qabbal.* You just wait. I'll bring him to terms yet. *ṣboor, ləssa bqabblo.*
to bring up - **1.** *ṭaalaᶜ la-fooq.* Stay there. I'll bring the suitcase up. *xalliik ᵊb-maḥallak. ʔana bṭaaleᶜ ᵊš-šanṭa la-fooq.* **2.** *rabba.* Her mother died, so her aunt brought her up. *ʔəmma maatet, qaamet xaalə́ta rabbə́ta.* **3.** *zakar (o zəkᵊr//nzakar).* I'll bring it up at the next meeting. *bəzkə́ra bᵊl-ʔəžtimaaᶜ ᵊž-žaaye.*

brisk - *raayež.* He's doing a brisk business with old manuscripts. *tižaarto raayže bᵊl-maxṭuuṭaat ᵊl-qadiime* or **maašye ḥaalo ktiir bᵊl-maxṭuuṭaat ᵊl-qadiime.*

Britain - *briṭaanya.*

British - *briṭaani**.

Briton - *briṭaani** pl. *-iyyiin.*

broad - **1.** *ᶜariiḍ* pl. *ᶜraaḍ.* He has broad shoulders. *ktaafo ᶜraaḍ.* **2.** *waaḍeḥ.* She gave us a broad hint. *lammaḥə́t-ᵊlna talmiiḥa waaḍḥa.* **3.** *šaamel.* That's a pretty broad statement you're making. *haada kalaam šaamel šwayye mən ṭarafak.* **4.** *waaseᶜ.* And I want you to understand it in the broadest meaning of the word. *w-bəddi-yaak təfham hal-kəlme b-ʔawsaᶜ maᶜaaniiha.*
**The crate is as broad as it's long. *s-saḥḥaara ᶜarḍa qadd ṭuula.*
**It happened in broad daylight. *ḥaṣlet ᵊb-nəṣṣ ᵊn-nhaar.*

broadcast - *ʔizaaᶜa* pl. *-aat.* Did you listen to the broadcast? *smə́ᶜt ᵊl-ʔizaaᶜa?* -- Do you receive the Arabic broadcasts of the Voice of America here? *byəṣalkon hoon ᵊl-ʔizaaᶜa l-ᶜarabiyye tabaᶜ ṣooṭ ʔameerka?*
to broadcast - **1.** *zaaᶜ (i ʔizaaᶜa//nzaaᶜ).* They broadcast directly from London. *biziiᶜu raʔsan mən london.* -- The station broadcasts symphonic music three nights a week. *l-ᵊmḥaṭṭa bədziiᶜ muusiiqa səmfooniyye tlatt layaali bᵊž-žəmᶜa.* **2.** *našar (o našᵊr).* If you tell her she'll broadcast it all over the neighborhood. *ʔiza qəlt-əla laḥa tənšor ᵊl-xabar been ᵊž-žiire kəlla.*
**I wouldn't broadcast it, if I were you. *law kənt ᵊb-maḥallak maa bṭabbel w-laa bzammer fiiha.*

broad-minded - *raḥb˜ ᵊṣ-ṣədᵊr.* She's a very broad-minded person. *hiyye raḥbet ᵊṣ-ṣədr ᵊktiir* or **ṣədra raḥb ᵊktiir.*

broad-mindedness - *raḥaabet˜ ṣədᵊr.* His broad-mindedness is well known. *raḥaabet ṣədro maᶜruufe.*

brocade - *brookaar.*

to **broil** - *šawa (i šawi//nšawa).*

broke - *mfalles, maksuur.* I'm broke again. *šaᶜni mfalles taani marra.*
to go broke - *fallas, nkasar.* He nearly went broke. *kaan laḥa yfalles.*

broken - **1.** *manzuuᶜ.* My watch is broken. *saaᶜti manzuuᶜa.* **2.** *mkassar.* He speaks broken Arabic. *byəḥki ᶜarabi mkassar* or **bilaṭṭeš bᵊl-ᶜarabi talṭiiš.* **3.** *maksuur.* She virtually died of a broken heart. *bᵊl-waaqeᶜ maatet mən qalba l-maksuur.*

broker - *səmsaar* pl. *samaasra.*

brokerage - **1.** *maktab˜* (pl. *makaateb˜*) *kəməsyoon.* He has a respected brokerage in Beirut. *ᶜando maktab kəməsyoon məᶜtabar ᵊb-beeruut.* **2.** *ᶜmuule, kəməsyoon.* How much brokerage did you pay? *qaddeeš dafaᶜt ᵊᶜmuule?*

bronze - *broonz.* Bronze is an alloy of copper and tin. *broonz xaliiṭ mən ᵊnḥaas w-ʔaẓdiir.* -- He collects bronze statues. *byəžmaᶜ tamasiil broonz.*

brook - *saaqye* pl. *sawaaqi.* The brook dries up in summer. *s-saaqye btənšaf bᵊṣ-ṣeef.*

broom - *mqašše* pl. *-aat.*

brother - **1.** *ʔaxx (ʔaxuu- + pron. suff., ʔax(u)˜,* my ~ *ʔaxi)* pl. *ʔəxwe* and *ʔəxwaat,* fig. and com. *ʔəxwaan.* Have you a brother? *ʔəlak ʔaxx?* -- He's my (half) brother. *huwwe ʔaxi mən ʔabi* (or *ʔəmmi* respectively). — He's a bookkeeper at Khouri

Brothers'. *byəšt̊ǵel ᵊmḥaaseb ɛand xuuri ʔəxwaan.*
brotherhood – 1. *ʔuxuwwe.* The meetings were conducted in a spirit of brotherhood and friendship. *l-ʔəǰtimaaɛaat ǰaret ᵊb-rooḥ ᵊl-ʔuxuwwe wᵊṣ-ṣadaaqa.* 2. *ʔəxwaan* (pl.). He's a member of the Muslim Brotherhood. *huwwe ɛəḍu b-ǰamɛiit ᵊl-ʔəxwaan ᵊl-məsᵊlmiin.*
brother-in-law – 1. (sister's husband) *ṣəhᵊr* pl. *ʔəṣᵊhra.* 2. (wife's brother) *ʔəbᵊn˜ ʔəḥma* pl. *wlaad˜ ʔəḥma.* 3. (wife's sister's husband) *ɛadiil* pl. *ɛədala.*
brotherly – *ʔaxawi*.*
brow – 1. *ǰbiin.* He wiped the sweat off his brow. *masaḥ ᵊl-ɛaraq mən ɛala ǰbiino.* 2. *ḥaaǰeb* pl. *ḥawaaǰeb.* He raised his brows in astonishment. *rafaɛ ḥawaaǰbo b-dahše.*
to **browbeat** – *haddad.* They browbeat him into saying yes. *haddadúu la-ḥatta qəbel.*
brown – 1. (chestnut) *kastanaawi*.* 2. (dark brown) *bənni*.* 3. (honey-colored) *ɛasali*.* 4. (complexion) *ʔasmar* f. *samra* pl. *səmᵊr.* Her hair and eyes are brown. *šaɛra w-ᵊɛyuuna loonon kastanaawi.*
 to brown – 1. *tḥammar.* Put the chicken in the oven to brown. *ḥəṭṭ ᵊǰ-ǰaaǰe bᵊl-wəǰaaq la-təṭḥammar.* 2. *ḥammar.* Brown the meat well. *ḥammer ᵊl-laḥme mniiḥ.*
to **browse** – 1. *tṣaffaḥ.* I was just browsing through the book. *kənᵊt bass ɛam ʔətṣaffaḥ bᵊl-ᵊktaab.* 2. *tfarraǰ.* I don't want to buy anything, just browse. *maa bəddi ʔəštə́ri šii, bass ɛam ʔətfarraǰ.*
bruise – *raḍḍa* pl. *-aat* and *rḍuuḍa.* He had a bruise on his left foot. *kaan fii raḍḍa b-ʔəǰro š-šmaal.*
 to bruise – *raḍḍ (ə raḍḍ//nraḍḍ).* The boy bruised his knee. *l-walad raḍḍ rəkᵊbto.*
brunette – *samra* pl. *səmᵊr.*
brush – 1. *fəršaaye* pl. *faraaši.* You can use this brush for your shoes. *fiik təstaɛmel hal-fəršaaye la-ṣabbaaṭak.* — Who left the brush in the paint? *miin tarak ᵊl-fəršaaye bᵊd-dhaan?* 2. *syaaǰ.* The police searched the brush for the missing child. *š-šərṭa dawwaret bᵊs-syaaǰ ɛal-walad ᵊl-mafquud.* 3. *mnaawaše.* I had a brush with the law yesterday. *ṣaaret ᵊmnaawaše beeni w-been ᵊš-šərṭa mbaarəḥ.*
 to brush – 1. *farša//tfarša.* I brush my hair every evening. *bfarši šaɛri kəll leele.* — I have to brush my teeth. *laazem farši snaani.* 2. *daqar (ə/o daqᵊr//ndaqar).* The car didn't hit the cat, it just brushed it. *s-sayyaara maa daɛset ᵊl-qaṭṭa, daqrə́ta bass.* — Be careful not to brush against the wet paint. *ʔəṣḥa tədqor bᵊd-dhaan, ləssa maa nəšef.*
 **She brushed by without saying a word. *faǰxet mən qəddaami bala w-laa kəlme.*
 to brush aside – *maa ntaššš la-.* He brushed my protests aside. *maa ntaššš la-ʔəḥtiǰaaǰaati.*
 to brush off – *farša.* Brush off your overcoat. *farši manṭook.*
 to brush up on – *marran.* I'm brushing up on my German. *ɛam marren ʔalmaaniiti.*
brush-off: They gave him the brush-off. *maa ltakašu fii.*
Brussels – *brukseel.*
brutal – *waḥši*.*
brutality – *waḥšiyye, tawaḥḥoš.*
brute – *waḥᵊš* pl. *wḥuuš(e).*
bubble – *fəqqeeɛa* pl. *faqaqiiɛ.* You can see the bubbles rise to the surface. *fiik ᵊtšuuf ᵊl-faqaqiiɛ ɛam təṭlaɛ ɛala wəšš ᵊl-mayy.*
 **One day the whole business is going to burst like a bubble. *šii yoom ləssa kəll haš-šaġle laḥa təfqaɛ farᵊd faqɛa.*
 to bubble – *faar (u fawaraan).* The water is beginning to bubble. *l-mayy badet ᵊtfuur.*
buck – *dakar* pl. *dkuura.* The herd consists of one buck and five does. *l-qaṭiiɛ fii waaḥed dakar w-xamse ʔanaati.*
 to pass the buck – *ḥaṭṭ ᵊl-loom.* Don't try to pass the buck to me. *laa tḥaawel ᵊtḥəṭṭ ᵊl-loom ɛaliyyi.*
 to buck – *ɛaakas, ɛaanad.* He keeps bucking every order. *biḍall yɛaakes kəll ʔamᵊr.*
 **Buck up! Things are bound to get better. *šədd ḥeelak! l-ʔawḍaaɛ laa bədd təṭḥassan.*
bucket – 1. *saṭᵊl* pl. *sṭuul(e).* 2. (in a well) *dalu* pl. *ʔədᵊlwe.*
buckle – *bakle* pl. *-aat.* I lost the buckle of my leather belt. *ḍawwaɛᵊt baklet ᵊqšaaṭi ǰ-ǰəlᵊd.*
 to buckle – 1. *bakkal.* I can't buckle my belt. *maa-li ɛam bəqder bakkel ᵊqšaaṭi.* 2. *qawwaṣ.* The linoleum buckled from the heat. *l-linoolyom qawwaṣ mən ᵊl-ḥaraara.* 3. *qaṣaf (ə/o qaṣᵊf).* His knees buckled under him. *qaṣfet rəkabo taḥt ᵊmmənno.*
 to buckle down to – *rakaz (ə/o rakze) ɛala.* It's about time we buckled down to work. *ḥal-lna baqa nərkoz ɛaš-šəġᵊl.*
bud – *bərɛom* pl. *baraaɛem.* The frost killed all the buds. *s-sqiiɛ mawwat kəll ᵊl-baraaɛem.*
 **The uprising was nipped in the bud. *qamaɛu s-sawra b-mahda.*
Buddha – *buuza.*
Buddhism – *l-buuziyye.*
Buddhist – *buuzi*.*
budding – *naaše?.* He's a budding author. *huwwe mʔallef naaše?.*
budget – *miizaaniyye* pl. *-aat.* The Cabinet today discussed the budget for the coming fiscal year. *l-wazaara l-yoom baḥset miizaaniit ᵊs-səne l-maaliyye ǰ-ǰaaye.* — Our budget doesn't allow that. *miizaaniitna maa btəsmə́ḥ-ᵊlna b-haš-šii.*
 to budget – *qassam.* You'll have to learn to budget your salary. *laazem tətɛallam ᵊtqassem maɛaašak.*
buffalo – *ǰaamuus* pl. *ǰawamiis.*
buffet – *buufée* pl. *buufeeyaat.* The dishes are in the buffet. *ṣ-ṣḥuun bᵊl-buufée.*
bug – 1. *ḥašara* pl. *-aat.* The leaves were covered with bugs. *waraq ᵊš-šaǰar kaan malaan ḥašaraat.* 2. *ɛeeb* pl. *ɛyuub.* Of course, there are still a few bugs to be ironed out. *ṭabɛan ləssa fii šwayyet ᵊɛyuub bədda taṣliiḥ.* 3. *makroob* pl. *-aat.* I've come down with some kind of bug. *laqaṭᵊt šii makroob w-šaɛni bᵊl-farše.*
 **He's bugs. *maxluuɛ huwwe.*
 (bed) bug – *baqqa* coll. *baqq* pl. *-aat.* The mattress was full of bugs. *l-farše kaanet malaane baqq.*
bugle – *boraṣaan* pl. *-aat.*
to **build** – *ɛammar//tɛammar, bana (i bina//nbana).* Our neighbor is building a new house. *ǰaarna ɛam yɛammer beet ᵊǰdiid.*
 to build in – *rakkab//trakkab.* I'm going to build in some bookcases here. *raḥa rakkeb hoon kam ᵊxzaane ləl-kətᵊb.*
 to build up – 1. *bana (i bina//nbana).* He built up the business. *huwwe yalli bana š-šəġᵊl.* 2. *rafaɛ (a rafᵊɛ//nrafaɛ).* The program is designed to build up the morale of the troops. *l-bərnaameǰ ᵊmsaawa la-ḥatta yərfaɛ maɛnawiyyaat ᵊǰ-ǰeeš.*
building – *binaaye* pl. *-aat, ɛamaara* pl. *-aat.* Both offices are in one building. *l-maktabeen ᵊb-binaaye waaḥde.*
bulb – 1. *lampa* pl. *-aat, balloora* pl. *-aat.* This bulb is burnt out. *hal-lampa ḥtarqet.* 2. *baṣale* coll. *baṣal* pl. *-aat.* When are you going to plant the tulip bulbs? *ʔeemta laḥa təzraɛ baṣalaat ᵊt-tuuliib?*
Bulgaria – *bəlġaarya.*
Bulgarian – *bəlġaari*.*
bulge – *ɛabɛabe.* What's that bulge in your pocket? *šuu hal-ɛabɛabe b-ǰeebtak?*
 to bulge – 1. *ntafax.* His briefcase is bulging with all kinds of papers. *šanətto məntə́fxa b-ʔawraaq mən kəll ʔanwaaɛ.* 2. *baḥlaq.* Her eyes bulged with surprise. *baḥlaqet ᵊɛyuuna b-dahše.*
bulk – *məɛẓam.* The bulk of my salary goes for rent and food. *məɛẓam maɛaaši biruuḥ ʔəǰret beet w-ʔakᵊl.*
bulky – *ḍaxᵊm.* I can't carry this package, it's too bulky. *maa fiini ʔəḥmel hal-baakeet, ḍaxm ᵊktiir.*
bull – *toor* pl. *twaar.* The ranch is famous for the excellent bulls it raises. *l-mazraɛa mašhuura b-tərbaayet ᵊtwaar məmtaaze.*
bulldozer – *ǰarraara* pl. *-aat, traktoor* pl. *-aat.*
bullet – *rṣaaṣa* coll. *rṣaaṣ* pl. *-aat.* The bullet lodged in his shoulder. *r-rṣaaṣa ḍallet ᵊb-kətfo.*
bulletin – 1. *našra* pl. *-aat.* The society issues a monthly bulletin. *ǰ-ǰamɛiyye bəṭṭaaleɛ našra šahriyye.* 2. *ǰariide* (pl. *ǰaraayed*) *rasmiyye.* I read it in the government bulletin. *qareeta bᵊǰ-ǰariide r-rasmiyye tabaɛ l-ᵊḥkuume.*
bulletin board – *looḥet˜* (pl. *-aat˜*) *ʔəɛlaanaat.*
bullfight – *mṣaaraɛᵊt˜* (pl. *-aat˜*) *siiraan.*
bullfighter – *mṣaareɛ˜* (pl. *-iin˜*) *siiraan.*
bully – *looḥ* pl. *lwaaḥ.* The big bully thought he could scare me. *hal-looḥ l-ᵊkbiir ḥassab fii yxawwefni.*
 to bully – *tmahtar b-.* Stop bullying that little boy. *haaǰtak tətmahtar ᵊb-haṭ-ṭəfᵊl.*
bum – 1. *sarsari* pl. *-iyye.* A bum came to our door.

(waaḥed) sarsari daqq ʕala baabna. 2. *ʕawaaṭli* pl. *-iyye.* He'll be a bum all his life. *laḥa yḍall ʕawaaṭli ṭuul ʕəmro.*

bump - 1. *nəbbeera* pl. *-aat.* Where did you get that bump on your head? *mən ʔeeš ṭaalʔət-əllak han-nəbbeera b-raasak?* 2. *ṭalʕa* pl. *-aat.* The car went over a bump. *s-sayyaara marqet fooq ṭalʕa (bᵊṭ-ṭariiq).*

to bump into - 1. *ṣaadaf.* Guess who I bumped into yesterday. *ḥzeer miin ṣaadaft ᵊmbaareḥ.* 2. *ṭaraq (o ṭarᵊq).* He bumped into the chair in the dark. *ṭaraq ᵊl-kərsi bᵊl-ʕətme.*

bumper - *ṭabboon* pl. *-aat.* Only the bumper was slightly damaged. *bass ᵊṭ-ṭabboon ᵊthaššam šwayye.*

**They had a bumper crop of cotton this year. *maḥṣuul qəṭnon kaan ṭəḥfe has-səne.*

bumpy - *waʕer.* We drove for an hour over a bumpy road. *səqna saaʕa ʕala ṭariiq waʕer.*

bunch - 1. *žərze* pl. *žərəz.* Let me have a bunch of radishes, please. *ʕaṭiini žərzet fəžᵊl mən faḍlak.* 2. *baaqa* pl. *-aat, buukée* pl. *buukeeyaat.* Go out in the garden and pick yourself a nice bunch of flowers. *ṭlaaʕ ʕaž-žneene w-ᵊqṭaaʕ la-ḥaalak šii baaqet warᵊd.* 3. *qərṭa.* What's this bunch of people doing here? *hal-qərṭet ᵊn-naas šuu ʕam taʕmel hoon?* — You're a fine bunch! *məlla qərṭa məḥtarame!*

bundle - 1. *ḥəzme* pl. *ḥəzam, rəzme* pl. *rəzam.* Is that bundle too heavy for you? *hal-ḥəzme tqiile ʕaleek ᵊktiir?* 2. *kətle* pl. *kətal.* She's just a bundle of nerves. *hiyye kətlet ʔaʕṣaab.*

buoy - *ʕawwaame* pl. *-aat.* Don't swim beyond that buoy over there. *laa təsbaḥ barraat ᵊḥduud ᵊl-ʕawwaame hniik.*

burden - 1. *ḥəmᵊl, ʕəbᵊʔ.* I don't want to be a burden to you. *maa bəddi kuun ḥəmᵊl ʕaleek.* 2. *ʕəbᵊʔ* pl. *ʔaʕbaaʔ.* They have to bear the burden of the expenses. *ʕaleehon yətḥammalu ʕəbʔ ᵊl-maṣariif.* — The burden of proof rests with the presecutor. *ʕəbʔ ᵊl-ʔəsbaat matruuk lən-naaʔeb ᵊl-ʕaamm.*

to burden - 1. *taqqal ʕala, ġallab.* I don't want to burden you with that. *maa bəddi taqqel ʕaleek ᵊb-haš-šii* (or *ġallbak ᵊb-haš-šii*). 2. *ḥammal.* She's burdened with a lot of responsibility. *hiyye mḥammale masʔuuliyye kbiire.*

bureau - *biirо́o* pl. *biirooyaat.* The bottom drawer of the bureau is stuck. *dərž ᵊl-biiro̗o t-taḥtaani ʕaṣyaan.*

bureaucracy - *biiruq̈raaṭiyye.*

bureaucrat - *biiruq̈raaṭi* pl. *-iyyiin.*

bureaucratic - *biiruq̈raaṭi*.*

burglar - *ḥaraami* pl. *-iyye.*

to **burglarize** - *ṣaṭa (i ṣaṭu//nṣaṭa) ʕala.* The bank was burglarized last night. *l-ḅaṇk ᵊnṣaṭa ʕalée mbaareḥ bᵊl-leel.*

burglary - *ṣaṭu.*

burial - *dafᵊn.*

Burma - *bərma.*

burn - *ḥarᵊq* pl. *ḥruuq(a).* This is a serious burn. *haada ḥarᵊq xəṭer.*

to burn - 1. *ḥtaraq.* This wood burns well. *hal-ḥaṭab byəḥtə́req ᵊmniiḥ.* 2. *ḥaraq (e/o ḥarᵊq//nḥaraq).* They burned their old papers. *ḥaraqu wraaqon ᵊl-ʕatiiqa.* — Watch out, these peppers will burn your tongue. *ʔəṣḥa l-ᵊfleefle btəḥrə́q-lak ᵊlsaanak.* — I burned my mouth with steaming coffee. *ḥaraqᵊt təmmi bᵊl-qahwe l-ġalyaane.* — I've burned my fingers once already. *sabaq w-ḥaraqᵊt ʔaṣabiiʕi marra.*

**He has money to burn. *maʕo maṣaari maa btaakə́la n-niiran.*

**He's burnt his bridges behind him. *qaṭaʕ ʕala ḥaalo xaṭṭ ᵊr-rabʕa.*

**I'm burning with curiosity. *ṭaaqeq ʕala ma ʔaʕref.*

burnt - *maḥruuq.* The meat is burnt to a crisp. *l-laḥme maḥruuqa ʕal-ʔaaxiir.* — The rice tastes burnt. *r-rəzz ṭaʕᵊmto maḥruuqa.*

to burn down - 1. *ḥtaraq kəllo.* The building has burned down. *l-binaaye ḥtarqet kəlla.* 2. *ḥaraq (e/o ḥarᵊq//nḥaraq).* They burnt down the shack. *ḥaraqu l-kuux.*

to burn out - *ḥtaraq.* This bulb is burned out. *ḥtarqet hal-balloora.*

to burn up - *ḥtaraq.* His books burned up in the fire. *kətbo ḥtarqu bᵊl-ḥariiqa.*

**He's burnt up because he can't come along. *maḥruuq qalbo laʔənno maa fii yəži maʕna.*

burp - *tədšaaye* pl. *-aat.*

to burp - *ddašša.*

to **burst** - 1. *ṭaqq (ə ə), nfažar, nfaxat.* The water pipe burst. *buuri l-ṃayy ṭaqq.* 2. *nfažar, nhadd.* Last year the dam burst. *s-səne l-ṃaadye nfažar ᵊs-sadd.* 3. *ṭaff.* Her closet is bursting with clothes. *xzaanə́ta ṭaaffe bᵊl-ʔawaaʕi.*

**She's bursting with joy. *laḥa ṭṭiir mən kətret faraḥha.*

to burst into - 1. *faat (u ə) ᵊb-zaʕže ʕala.* She burst into the room. *faatet ʕal-ʔuuḍa b-zaʕže.* 2. *nfažar b-.* She burst into tears. *nfažret bᵊl-bəke.* 3. *fəlet (a falataan).* He burst into loud laughter. *fəlet bᵊḍ-ḍəḥk ᵊb-ṣooṭ ʕaali.*

to burst out - *nfažar b-.* She burst out crying. *nfažret bᵊl-bəke.*

to **bury** - 1. *dafan (e/o dafᵊn//ndafan), qabar (e/o qabᵊr//nqabar).* She was buried yesterday. *dafanuuha mbaareḥ.* 2. *ṭamar (o ṭamᵊr//nṭamar).* He buried the gun in the garden. *ṭamar ᵊl-farᵊd bᵊž-žneene.* — My passport got buried under the other papers. *žawaaz safari nṭamar taḥᵊt l-ᵊwraaq ᵊt-taanyaat.*

to bury oneself in - *ġaṭaṣ (o ġaṭᵊṣ) b-.* He keeps burying himself in his books. *biḍall ġaaṭeṣ ᵊb-kətbo.*

to bury the hatchet - *xaza (i ə) š-šeeṭaan.* Why don't you two bury the hatchet? *leeš maa btəxzu š-šeeṭaan ʔəntu t-tneen?*

bus - *baaṣ* pl. *-aat, baṣṣ* pl. *-aat.* Would you rather go by bus? *bətfaḍḍel ᵊtruuḥ bᵊl-baaṣ?*

bush - *syaaž.* He hid behind the bush. *txabba wara s-syaaž.*

to beat about (or **around**) **the bush** - *ḥaam (u ḥawamaan) ḥawaali l-mawḍuuʕ.* Stop beating about the bush! *ḥaaže baqa tḥuum ḥawaali l-mawḍuuʕ!*

busily - *b-ʕažqa.* He was busily packing his bags. *kaan ʕam yḍəbb šanaṭíi b-ʕažqa.*

business - 1. *maḥall* pl. *-aat, šəġᵊl* pl. *ʔašġaal.* They're selling their business. *ʕam ybiiʕu maḥallon.* 2. *šəġᵊl* pl. *ʔašġaal.* What business is he in? *šuu šəġlo?* or ***šuu byəštə́ġel?* — He knows his business. *fahmaan šəġlo.* — Business before pleasure. *š-šəġᵊl qabl ᵊl-basᵊṭ.* — Business is good. *l-ʔašġaal maašye mniiḥ.* — Don't meddle in other people's business. *laa təddaaxal ᵊb-šəġᵊl ġeerak.* — Mind your own business! *ʕaleek mən šəġlak!* — That's none of your business! *haada muu šəġlak!* or ***haada maa bixəṣṣak!* — He had no business asking such questions. *maa kaan šəġlo yəsʔal heek ʔasʔile.* 3. *šaġle* pl. *-aat, masʔale* pl. *masaaʔel.* Let's settle this business right away. *xalliina hallaq ᵊnfəḍḍ haš-šaġle.* — I won't have anything to do with that kind of business. *maa bəddaaxal ᵊb-heek šaġle.*

**When he drew that gun I knew he meant business. *waqᵊt saḥab hal-fard ᵊfhəmᵊt ʔənno ʕaaniiha.*

on business - *b-šəġᵊl.* I have to see him on business. *laazem šuufo b-šəġᵊl.* — The boss is out on business. *r-raʔiis ġaayeb ᵊb-šəġᵊl.*

to do business with - *tʕaamal maʕ.* I can't do business with a man like that. *maa bəqder ʔətʕaamal maʕ heek waaḥed.* — I used to do a lot of business with them. *ʔana wiyyaahon kənna nətʕaamal maʕ baʕᵊḍna.*

to go into business - *fataḥ (a fatᵊḥ) šəġᵊl.* She has gone into business for herself. *fatḥet šəġᵊl la-ḥaala.*

businessman - *ražol˜* (pl. *rižaal˜*) *ʔaʕmaal.*

bust - 1. *təmsaal nəṣfi* pl. *tamasiil nəṣfiyye.* A sculptor is doing a bust of him. *waaḥed naḥḥaat ʕam yaʕməl-lo təmsaal nəṣfi.* 2. *ṣədᵊr* pl. *ṣḍuur(a).* That blouse is a little too tight across the bust. *hal-ᵊbluuz dayyeq šwayye naaḥ ᵊṣ-ṣədᵊr.*

to **bustle** - *ʕažaq (e ʕažqa) ḥaalo.* Why does she always have to bustle around like that? *leeš daayman ᵊbtəʕžeq ḥaala heek?*

busy - 1. *mašġuul.* We're very busy at the office. *mašġuuliin nəḥna ktiir bᵊl-maktab.* — The line's busy! *l-xaṭṭ mašġuul!* — I'm even too busy to read the paper. *mašġuul la-daraže ḥatta ʔənni maa maʕi waqᵊt ʔəqra ž-žariide.* 2. *maʕžuuq.* They live on a busy street. *hənne saakniin ᵊb-šaareʕ maʕžuuq.*

**He leads a busy life. *ḥayaato kəlla rakᵊḍ.*

to keep busy - *šaġal (e šəġᵊl).* This will keep you busy until I get back. *haš-šii byəšᵊġlak la-ḥatta ʔəržaʕ.*

busybody - *ktiir˜* (f. *ktiiret˜* pl. *ktaar˜*) *ġalabe.* I've never seen such a busybody in all my life. *b-ḥayaati maa šəft ᵊktiir ġalabe mətᵊl haad.*

but - 1. *bass, laaken.* We can go with you, but we'll

have to come back early. *mnəqder ᵊnruuḥ maƐkon bass laazem nəržaƐ bakkiir.* -- I didn't mean you but your friend. *maa Ɛaneetak ʔənte bass Ɛaneet ᵊrfiiqak.* -- The suit is expensive, but then it fits well. *l-badle ġaalye laaken raakze.* **2.** *bass.* I saw him but a minute ago. *šəfto mən daqiiqa bass.* **3.** *ʔəlla, ġeer˜-.* Nobody was there but me. *maa kaan fii ḥada hniik ʔəlla ʔana* (or ... *hniik ġeeri*). **4.** *mən Ɛada, ʔəlla.* All but one were saved. *naǧu kəllon mən Ɛada waaḥed.*

**He was so nervous that he all but wrecked the machine. *mən kətᵊr narvazto maa ṡafi beeno w-been kasr ᵊl-maakiina ʔəlla šaƐra.*

**She all but succeeded. *maa kaanet beenha w-been ᵊn-nažaaḥ ʔəlla šaƐra.*

**It's all but decided. *maa bəqi ʔəlla yəṭlaƐ ᵊl-qaraar.*

**I was anything but pleased with it. *ʔabadan maa kənᵊt raḍyaan Ɛan haš-šaġle.*

**She's anything but bright. *maa fiiha w-laa nəqṭet zaka.*

**Nothing but lies! *kəllo kəzᵊb!*

**It never rains but it pours. *l-maṣaayeb maa btəži ʔəlla dafƐa waaḥde.*

butcher - *laḥḥaam* pl. *-e* and *-iin.* I always buy my meat at the same butcher's. *daayman bəštəri laḥᵊmti mən Ɛand nafs ᵊl-laḥḥaam.*

butcher shop - *(dəkkaanet˜) laḥḥaam* pl. *(dakakiin˜) laḥḥaame.* Try that butcher shop. *žarreb hal-laḥḥaam.* -- They opened a new butcher shop on the corner. *fataḥu dəkkaanet laḥḥaam ᵊždiid Ɛas-suuke.*

to butcher - *dabaḥ (a dabᵊḥ//ndabaḥ).* They butcher up to two hundred head of sheep a day. *byədbaḥu la-ḥadd miiteen raas ġanam bᵊl-yoom.*

butt - **1.** *qabḍa* pl. *-aat, maske* pl. *-aat.* Take the gun by the butt. *mseek ᵊl-farᵊd mən qabᵊṭṭo.* **2.** *Ɛaqᵊb˜ sigaara* pl. *Ɛqaab˜ sagaayer.* The ash tray is full of butts. *ṣaḥn ᵊs-sigaara malaan ᵊƐqaab sagaayer.* **3.** *məḥwar, markaz.* Doesn't he realize that he's the butt of their jokes? *šuu maa ḥass ʔənno huwwe məḥwar tankiiton?*

to butt - *naṭaḥ (a naṭᵊḥ).* The goat kept butting its head against the fence. *l-maƐzaaye ḍallet tənṭaḥ ᵊl-xəṣṣ ᵊb-raasa.*

to butt in - **1.** *ddaaxal.* This is none of your business, so don't butt in! *haada muu šəġlak fa-laa təddaaxal!* **2.** *qaaṭaƐ.* Every time we talk, her little brother butts in with a question. *kəll-ma mnəḥki sawa ʔaxuuha ẓ-ẓġiir biqaaṭəƐna b-šii suʔaal.*

butter - (fresh) *zəbde,* (clarified) *samne.* Let me have a pound of butter, please. *Ɛaṭiini mən faḍlak nəṣṣ kiilo zəbde.*

to butter - *ḥaṭṭ zəbde Ɛala.* Shall I butter your toast? *ḥəṭṭ zəbde Ɛala xəbᵊztak l-ᵊmqammara?*

**He knows on which side his bread is buttered. *byaƐref ween byəmši suuqo.*

butterfly - *farraaše* pl. *-aat.*

button - *zərr* pl. *zraar.* She sewed the button on for me. *qaṭbət-li z-zərr.*

to button (up) - *zarrar.* Button up your overcoat. *zarrer manṭook.*

buttonhole - *Ɛərwe* pl. *Ɛaraawi.* He's wearing a flower in his buttonhole. *ḥaaṭeṭ warde b-Ɛərᵊwto.*

to buttonhole - *tƐarbaš b-.* He buttonholed me on my way out. *tƐarbaš fiyyi w-ʔana ṭaaleƐ.*

buy - *šarwe* pl. *-aat.* That's a good buy. *hayy šarwe mniiḥa.*

to buy - **1.** *štara* (verbal noun *šəre//nšara*). What did you buy? *šuu štareet?* — Who did you buy it from? *mən miin ᵊštareeta?* -- Buy me a bus ticket, too. *štrii-li tazkart baṣṣ ʔəli kamaan.* **2.** *qəbel (a qbuul//nqabal).* I don't buy that suggestion. *maa bəqbal hal-ʔəqtiraaḥ.*

to buy back - **1.** *rəžeƐ štara.* By the way, I bought the car back. *b-hal-ᵊmnaasabe ržəƐt ᵊštareet ᵊs-sayyaara.* **2.** *staǧlab marra taanye.* You can't buy him back with flattery and promises. *maa fiik təstažᵊlbo marra taanye bᵊl-madᵊḥ wᵊl-ᵊwƐuud.*

to buy out - *štara ḥəṣṣet˜* ... He finally bought his partner out. *bᵊl-ʔaaxiir štara ḥəṣṣet ᵊšriiko.*

to buy up - *štara.* All the trucks have been bought up by the government. *l-ᵊḥkuume štaret kəll ᵊl-kamyoonaat.*

buzz - *wazwaze.* The buzz of a mosquito kept me awake. *wazwazt ᵊn-naamuuse maa xallə́tni naam.*

to buzz - *wazwaz.* The fly buzzed around my ear. *d-dəbbaane wazwazet ḥawaali ʔədni.*

**The air was buzzing with excitement. *ž-žaww kaan bisuudo hayažaan.*

buzzer - *žaraṣ* pl. *žraaṣ.*

by - **1.** *žanᵊb˜, mšaqqiit˜.* The house stands alone by the river. *l-beet qaaƐed waḥdo žanb ᵊn-nahᵊr.* **2.** *qariib la-.* His family lives over by us. *Ɛeelto saakne qariib la-beetna.* **3.** *b-.* I'll send it to you by mail. *bəbƐat-lak-yáa bᵊl-boosṭa.* -- We came by car. *ʔžiina bᵊs-sayyaara.* -- We went swimming by moonlight. *sabaḥna b-ḍaww ᵊl-qamar.* -- I don't see how he can work by day and live it up by night. *maa-li Ɛarfaan kiif byəqder yəštəġel bᵊn-nhaar w-yəshar bᵊl-leel.* -- That horse won by a length. *hal-ᵊḥṣaan rəbeḥ ᵊb-ṭuul.* -- The apples are sold by the kilo. *t-təffaaḥ byənbaaƐ bᵊl-kiilo.* -- The boats are rented by the hour. *š-šaxatiir ᵊbtətʔažžar bᵊs-saaƐa.* -- The table is four feet by six. *ṭ-ṭaawle ʔarbaƐ ᵊqdaam ᵊb-sətte.* -- The night club was closed by order of the police. *l-kabarée tsakkaret ᵊb-ʔamr ᵊš-šərṭa.* **4.** *qərᵊb˜.* He'll be back by five o'clock. *byəržaƐ qərb ᵊs-saaƐa xamse.* **5.** *Ɛala.* She can't work by artificial light. *maa fiiha təštəġel Ɛala ḍaww ʔəṣṭinaaƐi.*

**Her typing improves day by day. *ṭabƐa Ɛal-ʔaale l-kaatbe Ɛam yətḥassan yoom Ɛan yoom.*

**Step by step he fought his way through the crowd. *xaṭwe xaṭwe fataḥ ṭariiqo been ᵊl-Ɛaalam.*

**One by one they left the room. *ṭəlƐu mn ᵊl-ʔuuḍa waaḥed waaḥed.*

**This book was written by a Frenchman. *hal-ᵊktaab taʔliif waaḥed fransaawi.*

by and by - **1.** *šwayye šwayye.* You'll get used to it by and by. *btətƐawwad Ɛaleeha šwayye šwayye.* **2.** *baƐd ᵊšwayye.* They'll be here by and by. *bikuunu hoon baƐd ᵊšwayye.*

by and large - *Ɛal-ᵊƐmuum, Ɛmuuman.* By and large, the results were satisfactory. *Ɛal-ᵊƐmuum ᵊn-nataayež kaanet mərḍiyye.*

by far - *b-ᵊktiir.* This is by far the best hotel in town. *hal-ʔoteel ʔaḥsan b-ᵊktiir mən ġeer ʔoteelaat ᵊl-balad.*

by oneself - *waḥdo, la-ḥaalo.* I did that by myself. *Ɛməlᵊt haš-šii waḥdi.*

by the way - *b-hal-ᵊmnaasabe.* By the way, I met a friend of yours yesterday. *b-hal-ᵊmnaasabe ṣaadafᵊt waaḥed mən ᵊṣḥaabak ᵊmbaareḥ.*

bygone - *maaḍi.* He keeps referring to those bygone events. *biḍall yəḥki Ɛan hal-ḥawaades ᵊl-maaḍye.*

**Let bygones be bygones. *yalli faat maat or yalli maḍa maḍa.*

to **bypass** - *tḥaaša.* We bypassed the major cities on our trip. *tḥaašeena l-mədn ᵊr-raʔiisiyye b-safrətna.*

byproduct - *mantuuž saanawi* pl. *mantuužaat saanawiyye.*

bylaw - *niẓaam* pl. *ʔanẓime.*

C

cab - *taksi* pl. *taksiyyaat.* You can get a cab at that corner any time of the day. *fiik ᵊtlaaqi taksi Ɛala haz-zaawye ṭuul ᵊn-nhaar.*

cabbage - *yaxana, malfuuf.*

cabin - *kabiin* pl. *-aat.* We have a cabin in the mountains. *fii Ɛanna kabiin bᵊž-žabal.* -- Where is my cabin, steward? *ween ᵊl-kabiin tabaƐi yaa sayyed?*

cabinet - **1.** *xzaane* pl. *xazaayen.* We keep our good dishes in the small cabinet. *mənḥəṭṭ ᵊṣḥuunna l-ᵊmniiḥa bᵊl-ᵊxzaane ẓ-ẓġiire.* **2.** *wazaara* pl. *-aat.* The cabinet met with the President yesterday. *l-wazaara žtamƐet ᵊb-raʔiis ᵊž-žamhuuriyye mbaareḥ.*

cable - **1.** *kaabel* pl. *-aat.* The bridge is supported by cables. *ž-žəsr ᵊmƐallaq ᵊb-kaablaat.* -- Can the cable be laid within ten days? *byənmadd ᵊl-kaabel ᵊb-Ɛašᵊrt iyyaam?* **2.** *tallaġraaf* pl. *-aat, barqiyye* pl. *-aat.* I want to send a cable to New York. *bəddi ʔəbƐat tallaġraaf la-niyoork.*

to cable - *baƐat (a baƐᵊt) tallaġraaf, ʔabraq.*

Cable immediately when you arrive! *bεaat tallaġraaf ḥaalan waqt ᵊbtə́ṣal.*
café - *qahwe* pl. *qahaawi.*
caftan - *q̈əfṭaan* pl. *q̈afaṭiin.*
cage - *qafaṣ* pl. *qfaaṣ.* The room is just like a cage! *l-ʔuuḍa mətl ᵊl-qafaṣ!*
in **cahoots** - *mətwaaṭeʔ.* He's in cahoots with him. *huwwe mətwaaṭeʔ maεo* or ***daafniin ᵊš-šeex zangi sawa.*
Cairo - *l-q̈aahra.*
cake - *gaato* pl. *gaatoyaat.* I'd like cake with my coffee. *bḥəbb ʔaaxod gaato maε qahᵊwti.*
cake of soap - *looḥ˜* (pl. *lwaaḥ˜*) *ṣaabuun.* Can I have a towel and a cake of soap? *baḷḷa εaṭiini baškiir w-looḥ ṣaabuun.*
calamity - *faažεa* pl. *fawaažeε, kaarse* pl. *kawaares, nakbe* pl. *-aat.*
calcium - *kalᵊs, kalsyoom.*
to **calculate** - *ḥasab (e/o ḥasᵊb//nḥasab).* It was difficult to calculate the costs. *kaan ṣaεᵊb ḥasb ᵊt-takaliif.*
calculating machine - *ʔaale* (pl. *-aat*) *ḥaasbe.*
calculation - *ḥsaab.* According to my calculations we'll be there by tomorrow morning. *εala hawa ḥsaabi mənkuun ᵊhniik bəkra εala bəkra.*
calculus - *ḥsaab.* Have you studied differential and integral calculus in school? *darasᵊt šii ḥsaab ᵊt-tafaaḍol wᵊt-takaamol bᵊl-madrase?*
calendar - **1.** *rəznaama* pl. *-aat, taq̈wiim* pl. *taq̈awiim.* Do you have a calendar for the coming year? *fii εandak rəznaama ləs-səne ž-žaaye?* **2.** *taq̈wiim.* Can you show me how to figure out a date of the Muslim calendar in terms of the Christian calendar? *fiik ᵊtwaržiini kiif laaqi taariix mən ᵊt-taq̈wiim ᵊl-həžri mqaabel ᵊt-taq̈wiim ᵊl-miilaadi?* **3.** *bərnaameǯ* pl. *baraameǯ.* What events are on the calendar this month? *šuu fii mnaasabaat ᵊb-bərnaameǯ haš-šahᵊr?*
calf - **1.** *εəžᵊl* pl. *εžuul(e).* Cows and calves were grazing in the field. *l-baqaraat wᵊl-ᵊεžuule kaanu εam yərεu bᵊl-ḥaqle.* **2.** *žəlᵊd˜ εəžᵊl.* That bag is made of genuine calf. *haš-šanta maεmuule mən žəlᵊd εəžᵊl ʔaṣli.* **3.** *baṭṭet˜* (pl. *-aat˜*) *rəžᵊl.* The bullet hit him in the calf. *r-rṣaaṣa ṣaabto b-baṭṭet rəžlo.*
caliph - *xaliife* pl. *xəlafa.*
call - **1.** *talifoon* pl. *-aat.* Were there any calls for me? *ʔəžaani šii talifoon?* **2.** *daεwe.* He was among the first who followed the call to arms. *huwwe kaan mən ʔawwal halli labbu d-daεwe la-ḥaml ᵊs-silaaḥ.* **3.** *zaqzaqa.* The call of a bird woke me at dawn. *zaqzaqet šii εaṣfuur fayyaqə́tni ṣ-ṣəbᵊḥ.*
**I thought I heard a call for help. *tṣawwarᵊt ʔənno kaan fii ḥada εam yəstanžed.*
**That was a close call! *l-xalaaṣ kaan εəžbe waḷḷa!*
to pay a call - *zaar (u zyaara//nzaar).* We went to pay a call on them but they weren't at home. *rəḥna nzuuron bass maa kaanu bᵊl-beet.*
to call - **1.** *naada, ṣarax (a ə) la-.* I called him but he didn't hear me. *naadeeto bass maa səməεni.* **2.** *naada la-, ṣarax la-, baεat (a baεᵊt) wara˜, ṭalab (o ṭalab).* Shall I call a cab? *naadi la-taksi?* -- Call a doctor! *bεaat wara doktoor!* **3.** *samma.* What do you call this in Arabic? *šuu bətsammi haada bᵊl-εarabi?* **4.** *ʔaεlan.* The conductor calls all stops. *l-kondaktoor byaεlen lᵊ-ᵊmḥaṭṭaat kəlla.* **5.** *daεa (i daεwe//ndaεa) ləl-ʔəžtimaaε.* The conference was called for the fourth. *l-məʔtámar ᵊndaεa ləl-ʔəžtimaaε ᵊb-ʔarbεa š-šahᵊr.* **6.** *εayyan, ḥaddad.* The director called a rehearsal for four o'clock. *l-mudiir εayyan broova s-saaεa ʔarbεa.* **7.** *naada.* Has my name been called yet? *naadu ʔəsmi šii?* or ***ṭaleε ʔəsmi šii?*
to call attention to - *nabbah la-, lafat (e lafᵊt) ᵊn-naẓar la-.* I called his attention to his mistake. *nabbahto* (or *lafatt naẓaro*) *la-ġalᵊṭṭo.* -- May I call your attention to the fact that ... *btəsmáḥ-li ʔəlfet naẓarak ʔənno ..*
to call away - *stadεa.* He was called away unexpectedly. *stadεúu εala ġafle.*
to call back - **1.** *ttaṣal b-.* I'll call you back later. *bəttəṣel fiik baεᵊd ᵊšwayye.* **2.** *nadah (a nadᵊh).* He called back something I couldn't understand. *nadah ᵊb-šii maa fhəmto.* **3.** *stadεa.* The ambassador was called back for consultation. *stadεu s-safiir ləl-ᵊmšaawara.* **4.** *ṣarax (a ṣarᵊx) la-, nadah la-.* Call him back; he just left a minute ago. *ṣrax-lo; maa ṣar-lo raayeḥ daqiiqa.*
to call down - *ʔannab, bahdal.* I was late and got called down for it. *tʔaxxarᵊt w-qaamu ʔannabuuni.*
to call for - **1.** *ʔəža ʔaxad.* Will you call for me at the hotel? *btəži taaxədni mn ᵊl-ʔoteel?* **2.** *raaḥ žaab.* I have to call for my laundry. *laazem ruuḥ žiib ġasiili.* **3.** *stawžab, staḥaqq.* That calls for a celebration. *haada məstawžeb ʔəḥtifaal* or ***hayy bədda ḥafle.*
to call for help - *stanžad, ṭalab (o ṭalab) ᵊn-nažde.* I'll call for help if you don't go away. *bəstanžed ʔiza maa bətruuḥ mən hoon.*
to call in - **1.** *fawwat.* Call them in. *fawwə́ton.* **2.** *saḥab (a saḥᵊb//nsaḥab).* All the old currency is being called in. *εam yəsḥabu kəll ᵊl-εəmle l-qadiime.* **3.** *stašaar.* We had to call in a specialist. *ḍṭarreena nəstašiir ʔəxtiṣaaṣi.*
to call off - **1.** *laġa (i ʔəlġaaʔ//ltaġa).* The broadcast was called off for technical reasons. *l-ʔizaaεa ltaġet la-ʔasbaab fanniyye.* **2.** *naada.* Stand up when he calls off your name. *waqqef εala ḥeelak waqᵊt binaadi ʔəsmak.*
to call on - **1.** *zaar (u zyaara//nzaar).* We'll call on you next Sunday. *mənzuurak ᵊl-ʔaḥad ᵊž-žaaye.* **2.** *maraq (o ə) εala.* Our agent will call on you tomorrow. *wakiilna byəmroq εaleek bəkra.* **3.** *ṭalab (o ṭalab) mən.* You can call on him for help. *fiik təṭlob mənno maεuune.*
to call out - **1.** *ṣarax (a ṣarᵊx) la-, naada.* The fire department had to be called out. *ḍṭarru yəṣraxu ləl-ʔəṭfaaʔiyye.* **2.** *naada.* The professor calls out the students' names at the beginning of each class. *l-ʔəstaaz binaadi ʔasmaaʔ ᵊṭ-ṭəllaab ᵊb-ʔawwal kəll ḥəṣṣa.* **3.** *nadah (a nadᵊh).* ''Watch your step!'', he called out to me. *nadah "ʔoεak!".*
to call to account - *ḥaasab.* I'll call him to account. *laḥa ḥaasbo.*
to call together - *žamaε (a žamᵊε//nžamaε) sawa.* He called all of us together. *žamaεna kəllna sawa.*
to call (up) - **1.** *talfan la-, ttaṣal b-.* I'll call you up tomorrow. *btalfə́n-lak bəkra* or *bəttəṣel fiik bəkra.* **2.** *naada la-.* They called me up to the stage. *naadúu-li εal-masraḥ.* 3. *ṭalab (o ṭalab// nṭalab), stadεa.* He has been called up for military duty. *ṭalabúu ləl-xədme l-εaskariyye.*
caller - *zaayer* pl. *zəwwaar.* Have we had many callers today? *ʔəžaana zəwwaar ᵊktiir ᵊl-yoom?*
calligrapher - *xaṭṭaaṭ* pl. *-iin.*
calligraphy - *ḥəsn˜ ᵊl-xaṭṭ, εəlm˜ ᵊl-xaṭṭ.*
calling card - *biṭaaq̈et˜* (pl. *-aat˜*) *zyaara, kart* pl. *kruut(e).*
callous - **1.** *mdammel.* His callous hands show that he's done manual labor all his life. *ʔidée l-ᵊmdammle bəddəll εala ʔənno štaġal ᵊb-ʔidée ṭuul εəmro.* **2.** *bala ḥəss.* You have to be very callous if you're not moved by this sight. *laazem ᵊtkuun bala ḥəss ʔiza maa kənt ᵊbtətʔassar ᵊb-hal-manẓar.*
callus - *dmaal.* I got calluses on my hands from digging. *ʔidayyi malaane dmaal mən ᵊl-ḥafᵊr.*
calm - **1.** *raayeq, haadi.* The sea is calm today. *l-baḥᵊr raayeq ᵊl-yoom.* **2.** *haadi.* Ordinarily, he's a calm and rather aloof person. *εaadatan huwwe šaxᵊṣ haadi w-mənzə́wi.*
to keep calm - *hədi (a hduww).* Keep calm, everybody! *ʔəhdu kəllkon.*
to calm - *hadda.* We tried to calm the frightened animals. *žarrabna nhaddi l-ḥaywaanaat ᵊl-marεuube.*
to calm down - **1.** *hadda, rawwaq.* Try to calm him down! *εmeel žahdak ᵊthaddíi!* **2.** *hədi (a hduww).* It took her some time to calm down. *staḥmalet maεa mədde la-hədyet.*-- The wind has calmed down. *hədi l-hawa.* **3.** *ṭawwal baalo, hadda baalo, hədi.* Calm down, everything's going to be all right. *ṭawwel baalak, kəll šii raḥa yəmḍa εala xeer.*
calmly - *b-rawaaq, b-ᵊhduww.* She took the news calmly. *ʔaxdet ᵊl-xabar ᵊb-rawaaq.*
camel - *žamal* pl. *žmaal.*
camel driver - *žammaal* pl. *-e.*
camel litter - *hoodaž* pl. *hawaadež.*
camelia - *kameelya.*
camera - *ʔaalet˜* (pl. *-aat˜*) *taṣwiir, kámeera* pl. *-aat.*
camouflage - *tamwiih.* You could barely make out the guns under the camouflage. *bᵊl-kaad kaan fiik ᵊtšuuf ᵊl-madaafeε mən ᵊt-tamwiih.*
to camouflage - *mawwah.* The crew camouflaged the tank with branches and netting. *s-sadane mawwahu d-dabbaabe b-šabak w-ᵊġṣuun.*
camp - **1.** *mxayyam* pl. *-aat.* Did you see that large refugee camp a few miles out of town? *šəft ᵊmxayyam ᵊl-laažʔiin l-ᵊkbiir yalli εala bəεᵊd kam miil mən*

ᵊl-balad? **2.** *žaaneb, ṭaraf.* You never quite know what camp he is in. *b-ḥayaatak maa fiik taᶜref maᶜ ˀanu žaaneb huwwe.*

to camp – *xayyam.* We camped in the desert. *xayyamna bᵊṣ-ṣaḥra.*

campaign – *ḥamle* pl. *-aat.* He took part in the African campaign. *štarak bᵊl-ḥamle b-ˀafriiqya.* -- The election campaign begins in late August. *l-ḥamle l-ˀəntixaabiyye btəbda b-ˀawaaxer ˀaab.* -- That's part of our big advertising campaign. *haada žəzᵊˀ mən ḥamlet ᵊd-diᶜaaye l-waasᶜa tabaᶜna.*

to campaign – *qaam (u qyaam) ᵊb-ḥamle.* She's campaigning for equal rights for women. *qaayme hiyye b-ḥamle la-msaawaat ᵊḥquuq ᵊl-marˀa bᵊr-ražol.*

camphor – *kaafuur.*

can – *ᶜəlbe* pl. *ᶜəlab.* Give me a can of peas. *ᶜaṭiini ᶜəlbet bazaalya.*

can opener – *fattaaḥet˜* (pl. *-aat˜*) *ᶜəlab.*

to can – *kabas (e kabᵊs//nkabas).* Every summer my mother cans vegetables. *kəll ṣeef ˀəmmi btəkbes xəḍar.*

canned – *mᶜallab.* We carry no canned meat. *maa ᶜanna laḥm ᵊmᶜallab* (or ***laḥᵊm˜ ᶜəlab).*

canned goods – *mᶜallabaat* (pl.). We've already used up our canned goods. *stahlakna kəll l-ᵊmᶜallabaat yalli b-muunᵊtna.*

can – **1.** *ᶜəref (-yaᶜref ə).* Can you speak English? *btaᶜref təḥki ˀəngliizi?* **2.** *qəder (e ə), ġəḍer (e ə), ḥəsen (e ə), məmken* (invar.); *fii-* + pron. suff. Can you call me up at three o'clock? *btəqder* (or *btəḥsen* or *məmken* or *fiik*) *təttəṣel fiyyi s-saaᶜa tlaate?* -- You can't go swimming in this lake. *maa btəqder* (or *maa btəḥsen* or *muu məmken* or *maa fiik*) *təsbaḥ ᵊb-hal-buḥayra.* -- He could be first in class if he wanted to. *kaan byəqder* (or *byəḥsen* or *məmken* or *fii* or ***byəṭlaᶜ ᵊb-ˀiido* or ***b-ˀəmkaano*) *ykuun ˀawwal waaḥed bᵊṣ-ṣaff law raad.* -- Could I look at it, please? *məmken* (or *bəḥsen* or *fiyyi* or *bəqder* or ***btəsmaḥ-li*) *ˀəṭṭallaᶜ ᶜalée, mən faḍlak?* 3. *bižuuz* (invar.), *žaayez* (invar.), *məmken* (invar.). He could have said that. *bižuuz ykuun qaal haš-šii.* -- It could be. *bižuuz* or *žaayez* or *məmken.*

**He did everything he could. *ᶜəmel kəll halli byəṭlaᶜ ᵊb-ˀiido* (or ... *halli b-ˀəmkaano*).

**Are you leaving next week? – I can't say yet. *bəddak ᵊtsaafer ᵊž-žəmᶜa ž-žaaye? – ləssa maa baᶜref.*

Canada – *kanada.*

Canadian – *kanadi*.*

canal – **1.** *qanaaye* pl. *ˀəqᵊnye, tərᶜa* pl. *təraᶜ.* The canal dried out and finally was covered up. *l-qanaaye nəšfet qaamu bᵊl-ˀaaxiir ṭammuuha.* **2.** *ġanaat* pl. *ˀaġniye, ġanaal.* I read in the paper that they plan to deepen the Suez Canal. *qareet bᵊž-žariide ˀənno ᶜam yfakkru yġammqu ġanaat ᵊs-swees.*

canary – *qanaayra* pl. *-aat.*

Canary Islands – *žəzor˜ ᵊl-kanaari.*

to cancel – **1.** *laġa* and *ˀalġa (i ˀəlġaa//nlaġa* and *ltaġa).* This order has been canceled. *haṭ-ṭalabiyye nlaġet.* (In a restaurant, etc.) *haṭ-ṭalab ᵊnlaġa.* -- I'd like to cancel my room reservation. *bəddi ˀəlġi ḥažᵊz ˀuuḍṭi.* -- The meeting was canceled. *l-ˀəžtimaaᶜ ᵊltaġa.* -- I had to cancel my doctor's appointment. *nᵊžabarᵊt ˀəlġi mawᶜᵊdi maᶜ ᵊd-doktoor.* **2.** *baṭṭal//bəṭel (a ə).* These postage stamps are canceled. *haṭ-ṭawaabeᶜ ᵊmbaṭṭaliin* (or *baṭlaane*). **3.** *ˀabṭal.* These new developments cancel our previous agreement. *hat-taṭawwuraat ᵊl-ˀaxiire btəbṭel ˀəttifaaqna s-saabeq.*

**He canceled the rest of my debt. *saamaḥni b-baqiit deeni.*

cancer – *ṣaraṭaan, ṣalaṭaan.* They discovered too late that he had cancer. *baᶜᵊd-ma faat ᵊl-waqt ᵊktašafu ˀənno maᶜo ṣaraṭaan.*

candelabrum – *šamᶜadaan* pl. *-aat.*

candid – *ṣariiḥ.* A candid reply is all I want. *kəll yalli bəddi-yđa žawaab ṣariiḥ.*

candidacy – *taršiiḥ.*

candidate – *mraššaḥ* pl. *-iin.* We have three candidates for the position. *fii ᶜanna tlett ᵊmraššaḥiin ləl-manṣeb.*

to put up as a candidate – *raššaḥ.* Our party isn't putting anyone up as a candidate. *ḥəzᵊbna muu mraššeḥ ḥada.*

candied – *msakkar.* This candied fruit really looks delicious. *hal-faakye l-ᵊmsakkara ḥaqiiqatan manẓdra bišahhi.*

candle – *šamᶜa* pl. *-aat.* We had to light a candle. *nžabarna nəšᶜel šamᶜa.*

candlestick – *šamᶜadaan* pl. *-aat.*

candy – *sakaaker* (pl.).

cane – **1.** *ᶜəkkaaze* pl. *ᶜakakiiz.* After he broke his leg, he had to walk with a cane for many weeks. *baᶜᵊd-ma nkasret rəžlo nžabar yəmši ᶜal-ᶜəkkaaze la-ᶜəddet ˀasabiiᶜ.* **2.** *basṭoon* pl. *-aat.* You seldom see him take a walk without a cane. *naader ᵊtšuufo ᶜam yətmašša bala basṭoon.* **3.** *xeerazaan, xeezaraan.* This is the best cane for weaving baskets and furniture. *haada ˀaḥsan xeerazaan la-ᶜamal ᵊs-səlal wᵊl-mubiilya.*

cane sugar – *səkkar˜ qaṣab.*

cannibal – *ˀaakel˜* (pl. *ˀaakliin˜*) *luḥuum ᵊl-bašar.*

cannibalism – *ˀakᵊl˜ luḥuum ᵊl-bašar.*

cannon – *madfaᶜ* pl. *madaafeᶜ.*

canoe – *kaanúu* pl. *kaanuyaat.*

cantaloupe – *qaaquune* coll. *qaaquun* pl. *-aat.*

canteen – *maṭara* pl. *-aat.* Did you fill up your canteen? *ᶜabbeet maṭᵊrtak?*

canvas – *kəttaan.* My gym shoes are made of canvas. *ṣabbaaṭ ᵊr-ryaaḍa tabaᶜi maᶜmuul mən kəttaan.*

cap – **1.** *ṭaaqiyye* pl. *ṭawaaqi.* He's wearing a cap. *huwwe laabes ṭaaqiyye.* **2.** *ġaṭa* pl. *ˀəġᵊṭye.* I've lost the cap of my fountain pen. *ḍawwaᶜᵊt ġaṭa s-stiilo tabaᶜi.* -- Put the cap back on the bottle. *ržaaᶜ ḥəṭṭ ᵊl-ġaṭa ᶜal-qanniine.* **3.** *talbiis.* That tooth needs a cap. *has-sənn laazmo talbiis.*

capability – *maqᵊdra, qədra.*

capable – *qaader, məqtéder.* She's a very capable person. *hiyye waaḥde qaadra ktiir.*

capable of – *qaader ᶜala.* He's capable of handling the situation. *huwwe qaader ᶜala mᶜaalažt ᵊl-waḍᵊᶜ.*

capacity – **1.** *siᶜa.* The tank has a capacity of one hundred gallons. *l-xazzaan siᶜəto miit gaaloon.* -- The auditorium has a limited capacity. *l-ᵊmdarraž siᶜəto maḥduude.* **2.** *quwwe.* What's the capacity of this generator? *qaddeeš quwwet hal-ᵊmwalled?* **3.** *ṣifa.* I'm here in my capacity as guardian. *ˀana hoon ᵊb-ṣifati waṣi.* **4.** *waẓiife.* What's his capacity? What does he do? *šuu waẓiifto?* (or ***šuu maḥallo bᵊl-ˀᵊᶜraab?*) *šuu byaᶜmel?*

filled to capacity – *malaan ᶜal-ˀaaxiir.* After the heavy rains, the reservoir is filled to capacity. *baᶜd ᵊl-ˀamṭaar ᵊl-qawiyye l-xazzaan bişaffi malaan ᶜal-ˀaaxiir.*

cape – **1.** *kaab* pl. *-aat.* Where did you buy that lovely cape? *mneen ᵊštareeti hal-kaab ᵊl-ḥəlu?* **2.** *raˀᵊs* pl. *ruˀuus.* The tanker should now be off the Cape of Good Hope. *naaqəlt ᵊz-zeet laazem ᵊtkuun hallaq ᵊqbaal raˀs ᵊr-ražaaˀ ᵊṣ-ṣaaleḥ.*

capital – **1.** *ᶜaaṣme* pl. *ᶜawaaṣem.* Have you ever been in the capital? *ṣərt ᵊb-ḥayaatak šii l-ᶜaaṣme?* **2.** *rəsmaal* pl. *rasamiil.* How much capital do you need to start your business? *qaddeeš laazmak rəsmaal ḥatta təbda šəġlak?* -- His capital is invested abroad. *rəsmaalo mwaẓẓaf bᵊl-xaarež.* **3.** *ˀaṣḥaab˜ ruˀuus˜ ᵊl-ˀamwaal* (pl.). Relations between capital and labor have improved in the last few years. *l-ᶜalaaqaat been ˀaṣḥaab ruˀuus ᵊl-ˀamwaal wᵊl-ᶜəmmaal ᵊtḥassanet bᵊs-sniin ᵊl-ˀaxiire.* **4.** *raaˀeᶜ, ᶜaẓiim.* That's a capital idea! *hayy fəkra raaˀiᶜa!*

capital city – *ᶜaaṣme* pl. *ᶜawaaṣem.*

capital offense – *žinaaye* pl. *-aat.*

capital punishment – *ᶜuquubet˜ ˀəᶜdaam.*

capitalism – *raˀᵊsmaaliyye.*

capitalist – *raˀᵊsmaali* pl. *-iyyiin.*

capitalistic – *raˀᵊsmaali*.*

to capitalize on – *staġall, stasmar.* They capitalized on his mistakes. *staġallu ġalṭaato.*

capricious – *sweeᶜaati*.* She can be very capricious at times. *fiiha tkuun sweeᶜaatiyye ktiir baᶜḍ ᵊl-ˀawqaat.*

capsule – **1.** *bəršaane* pl. *-aat.* Take one capsule after every meal. *xood bəršaane baᶜᵊd kəll waqᶜa.* **2.** *kabsuul* pl. *-aat.* They're designing an entirely new space capsule. *ᶜam yṣammᵊmu kabsuul faḍaaˀi məbtákar.*

captain – **1.** *ġəbṭaan* pl. *ġabaaṭne.* The captain was the last to leave the sinking ship. *l-ġəbṭaan kaan ˀaaxer waaḥed tarak ᵊl-baaxra l-ġarqaane.* **2.** *raˀiis* pl. *rəˀasa.* The captain was taken prisoner with his entire company. *r-raˀiis ᵊnˀasar maᶜ kəll sariito.* -- Who's the captain of the team? *miin raˀiis ᵊl-fariiq?*

caption – *šarᵊḥ.* What does the caption under the picture say? *šuu biquul ᵊš-šarᵊḥ taḥt ᵊṣ-ṣuura?*

captive – *ˀasiir* pl. *ˀəsara.* They herded the captives

into the stockade. *lahašu l-ˀasara bᵊz-zariibe.* -- He's the captive of his passions. *huwwe ˀasiir šahawaato.*
captivity - *ˀasᵊr.*
to **capture** - 1. *ˀasar (e ˀasᵊr//nˀasar).* They captured a general and his entire staff. *ˀasaru ženeraal w-kəll ˀarkaan ḥarbo.* 2. *ˀaxad (-yaaxod ˀaxᵊd//ttaaxad).* The town was captured without a shot. *l-balad ttaaxadet mən ġeer-ma tənḍə́reb w-laa rṣaaṣa.* 3. *ṣawwar.* The poem captures the unforgettable beauty of a desert evening. *l-qaṣiide ɛam ᵊtṣawwer žamaal masawiyye bᵊṣ-ṣaḥra maa byəntə́sa.*
car - 1. *sayyaara* pl. *-aat, ˀotombiil* pl. *-aat.* I have to put the car into the garage. *laazem ḥəṭṭ ᵊs-sayyaara bᵊl-garaaž.* 2. *fargoon* pl. *-aat* and *faragiin.* The last three cars were derailed in the collision. *l-fargoonaat ᵊt-tlaate l-ˀaaxraaniyye ṭəlɛu ɛan ᵊs-səkke mn ᵊl-ˀəṣṭidaam.*
carat - *qiiraaṭ* pl. *qarariiṭ.*
caravan - *qaafle* pl. *qawaafel.*
caravansary - *xaan* pl. *-aat.*
caraway - *karaawya.*
carbine - *bənduqiyye* pl. *banaadeq.*
carbon paper - *waraq˜ karboon.*
sheet of carbon paper - *warqet˜* (pl. *-aat˜* and *wraaq˜*) *karboon.*
carburetor - *karbaratoor* pl. *-aat.*
card - 1. *warqet˜ šadde* coll. *šadde* pl. *wraaq˜ šadde.* They played cards all evening. *ləɛbu šadde ṭuul ᵊl-leel.* 2. *kart* pl. *kruut(e).* Did you get my card? *stalamᵊt karti?* 3. *kart* pl. *kruut(e), biṭaaqa* pl. *-aat.* Here's my card. Call me when you need me. *hayy karti. ttə́ṣel fiyyi lamma bəddak-yḍani.*
**He's quite a card! *ḥaqiiqatan huwwe nahfe!*
to card - *nadaf (o nadᵊf//ntadaf).* After shearing, they clean and card the wool. *baɛᵊd-ma biqəṣṣu ṣ-ṣuuf binaḍḍfúu w-byənᵊdfúu.*
cardamom - *heel.*
cardboard - *kartoon.* The box isn't very sturdy, it's just cardboard. *s-sanduuq maa-lo qawi ktiir, maɛmuul mən kartoon bass.*
piece of cardboard - *kartoone* pl. *-aat.* Put a piece of cardboard in between. *ḥəṭṭ kartoone beenaaton.*
cardinal - 1. *kardinaal* pl. *-iyye* and *karaadle.* The Pope received the three cardinals in private audience. *l-baaba staqbal ᵊl-kardinaaliyye t-tlaate b-ᵊmqaabale xaaṣṣa.* 2. *ˀaṣli*.* The cardinal points are north, south, east, and west. *ž-žihaat ᵊl-ˀaṣliyye l-ˀarbɛa hənne š-šmaal wᵊž-žnuub wᵊš-šarᵊq wᵊl-ġarᵊb.* -- In French, you use the cardinal number with the date. *bᵊl-frənsaawi btəstaɛmel ᵊl-ˀaɛdaad ᵊl-ˀaṣliyye bᵊt-taariix.*
care - 1. *ɛnaaye, ˀəɛtə́na.* Regular care of the teeth is important. *l-ᵊɛnaaye ɛala ṭuul bᵊs-snaan šii mhəmm.* -- I put a lot of care into that. *ṣaraft ᵊɛnaaye kbiire b-haš-šaġle* or **ɛtaneet ᵊb-haš-šaġle ktiir.* 2. *mɛaalaže.* He's under the doctor's care. *huwwe taḥt ᵊmɛaalažt ᵊd-doktoor.* 3. *ˀamaane, wdaaɛa.* May I leave my jewels in your care? *fiini xalli ṣiiġti b-ˀamaantak?*
care of - *b-waaṣəṭṭ˜.* Send me the letter care of my brother. *bɛat-li l-maktuub ᵊb-waaṣəṭṭ ˀaxi.*
to take care not to ... - *ṭḥaaša.* I took care not to mention anything. *ṭḥaašeet ˀəzkor šii.*
to take care of - 1. *ɛtana b-, daar (i ø) baalo ɛala.* Don't worry, I'll take care of your children. *laa ykən-lak fəkᵊr, bəɛtə́ni b-ᵊwlaadak* (or *bdiir baali ɛala wlaadak*). -- He takes good care of his clothes. *byəɛtə́ni ktiir ᵊb-ˀawaaɛii.* 2. *xallaṣ, dabbar.* I still have a few things to take care of. *ləssa fii ɛaliyyi kam šaġle bəddi xallə́ṣa.* 3. *dabbar.* We'll take care of everything. *nəḥna mədabber kəll šii.* 4. *ḥafaẓ (a ḥəfᵊẓ//nḥafaẓ).* Take care of my money for me. *ḥfaẓ-li maṣariyyi (ɛandak).*
**That takes care of that! *xalaṣna baqa wᵊs-salaam.*
to take care of oneself - *ɛtana b-ḥaalo, daar (i ø) baalo ɛala ḥaalo.* You have to take better care of yourself. *laazem təɛtə́ni b-ḥaalak ˀaktar.*
**Good-by. Take care of yourself! *b-ˀamaan ˀaḷḷa, maɛ ᵊs-salaame!*
to care - 1. *ˀəža ɛala baal-* + pron. suff. of subj. I don't care to go to the movies. *muu žaaye ɛala baali ruuḥ ɛas-siinama.* 2. *hamm (ə ø) ḥada.* I don't care what he thinks. *maa bihəmmni šuu byəɛtə́qed huwwe* or **maa bətɛalleq ɛala rəžli šuu byəɛtə́qed huwwe.* -- What do I care! *šuu bihəmmni!* -- Who cares? *šuu bihəmm?*
**Do you care if he comes along? *fii ɛandak maaneɛ yəži maɛna?*
**I don't care about anything. *bᵊn-nəsbe ˀəli kəll šii matᵊl baɛḍo.*
**For all I care, you can go. *bᵊn-nəsbe ˀəli btəqder ᵊtruuḥ.*
**I couldn't care less! *maa bətɛalleq ɛala rəžli!*
to care for - 1. *daar (i ø) baalo ɛala, ɛtana b-.* My sister is caring for the children today. *ˀəxti bəddiir baala ɛal-ᵊwlaad ᵊl-yoom.* 2. *ɛtana b-.* This garden is well cared for. *haž-žneene məɛtə́na fiiha mniiḥ.* 3. *ḥabb.* Do you care for gravy on your meat? *bətḥəbb šii maraqa ɛal-laḥme tabaɛak?* -- Do you care for her? *šuu bətḥəbba šii?*
career - 1. *maslak mihani* pl. *masaalek mihaniyye.* Her career is more important to her than her marriage. *maslə́ka l-mihani ˀahamm ɛanda mən ziižə́ta.* 2. *məhne* pl. *məhan.* He made forensic medicine his career. *ttaxaz ᵊṭ-ṭəbb ᵊš-šarɛi məhne ˀəlo.* -- He's had a brilliant career. *tqaddam ᵊb-məhᵊnto taqaddom ɛažiib.* 3. *šaġle.* He seems to make a career out of insulting people. *byəẓhar ɛalée ˀənno ɛaamel ˀihaanet ᵊn-naas šaġᵊlto.*
carefree - *hani*.* He leads a carefree life. *ɛaayeš ɛiiše haniyye.*
careful - 1. *ḥəzer.* He's a very careful person. *huwwe waaḥed ḥəzer ᵊktiir.* 2. *daqiiq.* He made a careful report. *ɛəmel taqriir daqiiq (ɛan ᵊl-mawḍuuɛ).* -- A careful analysis revealed that ... *mn ᵊt-taḥliil ᵊd-daqiiq ᵊtbayyan ˀənno ...*
to be careful - 1. *ntabah, ɛaṭa baalo.* Be careful to put his name on the guest list. *ntə́beh ᵊtḥəṭṭ ˀəsmo b-liistet ᵊl-maɛzuumiin.* -- Be careful! There is a car coming. *ntə́beh, fii sayyaara žaaye!* or **ˀoɛa (or ˀəṣḥa) s-sayyaara!* 2. *htamm b-.* She's awfully careful about her reputation. *btəhtamm ᵊktiir ᵊb-səmɛə́ta.*
to be careful not to ... - *ṭḥaaša.* I was careful not to mention anything. *ṭḥaašeet ˀəzkor šii.*
carefully - 1. *b-rəfᵊq, b-ḥazar.* They lifted the stretcher carefully. *rafaɛu l-ḥammaale b-rəfᵊq.* 2. *b-ˀəntibaah, b-dəqqa, b-ᵊɛnaaye.* Check the figures carefully. *fḥaaṣ ᵊl-ˀarqaam ᵊb-ˀəntibaah.*
careless - 1. *məhmel, məthaamel.* She's become careless lately. *ṣaaret məhᵊmle b-hal-ˀiyyaam.* 2. *ṭaayeš.* He's careless with his money. *huwwe ṭaayeš ᵊb-maṣaarii.* 3. *saxiif.* One careless mistake can ruin everything. *ġalṭa saxiife waaḥde btəxreb kəll šii.*
carelessly - *b-ˀəhmaal, b-tahaamol.* She's been doing her work rather carelessly these days. *ɛam təštə́ġel šəġla b-šwayyet ˀəhmaal hal-ˀiyyaam.*
cargo - *šaḥᵊn* pl. *-aat.*
Caribbean - *kariibi*.*
caricature - *karikatuur* pl. *-aat, rasᵊm hazli* pl. *rsuum(e) hazliyye.*
carnation - *qərənfle* coll. *qərənfol* pl. *-aat.*
carnival - *karnavaal, ɛiid˜ ᵊl-maraafeɛ.*
carpenter - *nažžaar* pl. *-iin.*
carpet - *səžžaade* coll. *səžžaad* pl. *-aat.* This is a nice carpet. *hayy səžžaade ḥəlwe waḷḷa.*
to have someone on the carpet - *wabbax ḥada.* The boss had him on the carpet again this morning. *r-raˀiis rəžeɛ w-wabbaxo l-yoom ɛala bəkra.*
to carpet - *ġaṭṭa//tġaṭṭa* (or *faraš o farᵊš// nfaraš*) *bᵊs-səžžaad.* All the stairs are being carpeted this week. *kəll ᵊd-draaž ɛam yġaṭṭuuhon bᵊs-səžžaad haž-žəmɛa.*
carriage - 1. *qaame.* Despite her age, her carriage is still very graceful. *bᵊr-raġᵊm ɛan taqaddom sənna ləssaata qaamə́ta ktiir ẓariife.* 2. *ɛarabiyye* pl. *-aat, ɛarabaaye* pl. *-aat.* You can hire a carriage near the railroad station. *btəstaˀžə́r-lak ɛarabiyye qərᵊb l-ᵊmḥaṭṭa.*
carrot - *žazara* coll. *žazar* pl. *-aat.*
to **carry** - 1. *ḥamal (e ḥamᵊl//nḥamal).* He'll carry your bags for you. *byəḥmə́l-lak šanaatiik.* 2. *naqal (o naqᵊl//ntaqal).* Mosquitoes carry swamp fever. *n-naamuus byənqol ᵊl-malaarya.* 3. *faaz (u fooz) b-, rəbeḥ (a rəbᵊḥ).* He carried the election with an overwhelming majority. *faaz bᵊl-ˀəntixaabaat ᵊb-ˀaġlabiyye saaḥiqa.* 4. *baaɛ (i beeɛ).* Do you carry men's shirts? *bətbiiɛu qəmṣaan rəžžaaliyye?* or **ɛandkon qəmṣaan rəžžaaliyye?* 5. *ˀawžab.* That carries the death penalty. *haada byuužeb ɛuquubt ᵊl-ˀəɛdaam.*
**His opinion carries great weight. *raˀyo ˀəlo wazn ᵊkbiir.*

**Sound carries well at night. *ṣ-ṣoot byənsə́meε ᵊmniiḥ bᵊl-leel* or *ṣ-ṣoot biwaṣṣel la-bεiid bᵊl-leel.*
**The motion was carried. *l-ʔəq̈tiraaḥ ᵊnqabal.*
**That's carrying things a little too far. *hallaq zaadet šwayye εan ḥadda.*
to carry away - *ʔaxad ᵊb-mašaaεer~ ..., hazz (ə hazz).* The crowd was carried away by the speech. *l-xiṭaab ʔaxad ᵊb-mašaaεer ᵊž-žamhuur* or *l-xiṭaab hazz ᵊž-žamhuur hazz.*
to carry on - *waaṣal, baqqa.* His son carries on the business. *ʔəbno biwaaṣel šəġlo.*
**Don't carry on so. *xalaṣna baqa, staṭεem!*
**Carry on! *kammel!*
to carry out - **1.** *naffaz.* We'll try to carry out your plan. *mənḥaawel ᵊnnaffez mašruuεak.* **2.** *ḥaṭṭ barra.* Carry out the garbage before you go to school. *ḥəṭṭ ᵊz-zbaale barra qabᵊl-ma truuḥ εal-madrase.*
cart - *ṭəmbor* pl. *ṭanaaber.* A cart will be enough for moving your things. *ṭəmbor bikaffi la-naqlet ᵊġraaḍak.*
to cart away - *raḥḥal//traḥḥal.* The sand has to be carted away. *r-ramᵊl laazem yətraḥḥal mən hoon.*
carton - *εəlbet~* (pl. *εəlab~*) *kartoon;* (of cigarettes) *krooz* pl. *-aat.*
cartoon - *karikatuur* pl. *-aat, rasᵊm hazli* pl. *rsuum(e) hazliyye.*
cartridge - *fašake* coll. *fašak* pl. *-aat.*
to carve - **1.** *ḥafar (e/o ḥafᵊr//nḥafar).* They specialize in carving little animals. *ʔəxtiṣaaṣon ḥafᵊr tamasiil ḥaywaanaat ᵊẓġiire.* -- He carved his name in the bark of the tree. *ḥafar ʔəsmo b-qəšret ᵊs-sažara.* **2.** *šarraḥ.* Will you carve the turkey? *bətšarreḥ ʔənte d-diik ᵊl-ḥabaš?*
carving knife - *səkkiinet~* (pl. *sakakiin~*) *laḥme.*
Casablanca - *d-daar ᵊl-beeḍa.*
case - **1.** *sanduuq* pl. *sanadiiq.* Leave the bottles in the case. *xalli l-qanaani bᵊs-sanduuq.* **2.** *beet* pl. *byuut.* I need a case for my glasses. *laazəmni beet mənšaan kəzᵊlki.*
case - **1.** *ʔiṣaabe* pl. *-aat.* There were five new cases of malaria. *ṣaar xamᵊs ʔiṣaabaat malaarya ždad.* **2.** *qaḍiyye* pl. *qaḍaaya.* I read about the case in the newspaper. *qareet εan ᵊl-qaḍiyye bᵊž-žariide.* -- He presented his case well. *εaraḍ qaḍiito εarḍ ᵊmniiḥ.* **3.** *daεwa* pl. *daεaawi, qaḍiyye* pl. *qaḍaaya.* He's lost his case. *xəser daεᵊwto* (or *daεwə́a*). **4.** *ḥaale* pl. *-aat.* In that case, forget what I told you. *b-hal-ḥaale ʔənsa halli qəlt-əllak-yə́a.* -- That being the case, I think we should give up the project. *ṭaala-ma l-ḥaale heek ᵊl-ʔafḍal εandi ʔənno nətrok ᵊl-mašruuε.*
**The doctor is out on a case. *l-ḥakiim ṭaleε yšuuf mariiḍ.*
in any case - *εala kəll ḥaal, mahma kaanet ᵊl-ḥaale.* I'll call in any case. *bəttə́ṣel fiik εala kəll ḥaal* or *mahma kaanet ᵊl-ḥaale bəttə́ṣel fiik.*
in case - *ʔiza.* Wait for me in case I'm late. *nṭəẓərni ʔiza ṣaar w-tʔaxxarᵊt ʔana.* -- In case you have any objection say so. *ʔiza fii εandak ʔəεtiraaḍ haato.*
in case of - *b-ḥaalet~ ...* In case of fire, use the emergency exit. *b-ḥaalet (ᵊḥduus) ḥariiqa staεmel maxraž ᵊn-nažaat.* -- In case of illness, please notify my family. *b-ḥaalet (ᵊḥduus) maraḍ ᵊεmeel maεruuf xabber εeelti.*
cash - **1.** *maṣaari* (pl.). I have no cash with me. *maa-li ḥaamel maεi maṣaari.* **2.** *naqdi.* I'll pay cash. *bədfaε naqdi.* -- We sell only for cash. *mənbiiε naqdi bass.*
to cash - *ṣaraf (o/e ṣarᵊf//nṣaraf).* Can you cash a check for me? *btəqder təṣrə́f-li šakk?*
cashier: - Pay the cashier, please. *dfaaε ləs-sanduuq mən faḍlak.*
cashmere - *kašmiir.* Where did you buy this lovely cashmere sweater? *mneen ᵊštareet hal-kanze l-kašmiir ᵊl-ḥəlwe?*
casket - *taabuut* pl. *tawabiit.*
cast - *mmassliin* (pl.). The new play has an excellent cast. *t-tamsiiliyye ž-ždiide fiiha mmassliin məmtaaziin.*
(plaster) cast - *žabṣiin.* How long will you have to wear the cast? *qaddeeš bəddak ᵊtxalli ž-žabṣiin?*
to cast - *sabak (e sabᵊk//nsabak).* The statue will be cast in bronze. *t-təmsaal byənsə́bek bᵊl-broonz.*
**She cast a furtive glance at him. *ṭṭallaεet εalée taṭliiεa xaaṭfe.*
**The die is cast. *q̈uḍiya l-ʔamᵊr.*
to cast a ballot - *ṣawwat.* How many ballots were cast for their candidate? *kaam waaḥed ṣawwat la-mraššə́ḥon?*
to cast anchor - *rasa (i rasu).* We cast anchor at daybreak. *raseena εand ᵊl-fažᵊr.*
castle - **1.** *qaṣᵊr* pl. *qṣuur(a),* (fortified) *qalεa* pl. *qlaaε.* Did you see the old castle? *šəft ᵊl-qaṣr ᵊl-εatiiq?* **2.** *rəxx* pl. *rxaax.* I'm taking the pawn with the castle. *laḥa ʔaakol ᵊl-beedaq bᵊr-rəxx.*
to castle - *bayyat.* You should have castled in the seventh move. *kaan laazem ᵊtbayyet bᵊl-ḥarake s-saabεa.*
castor oil - *zeet~ xarwaε.*
casual - **1.** *εal-maaši* (invar.). It was just a casual remark. *kaanet ᵊmlaaḥaẓa εal-maaši, muu ʔaktar.* **2.** *εaraḍi*.* It was a casual meeting, but it had great consequences. *kaan ʔəžtimaaε εaraḍi, bass ṣar-lo εawaaqeb xaṭiira.* -- He's only a casual acquaintance. *maεrəfti fii εaraḍiyye bass.* **3.** *mfarraε.* The party's quite informal, so come in casual clothes. *l-ḥafle muu mrassame ʔabadan, taεa w-ʔənte laabes ᵊmfarraε.*
to be casual about - *stahwan, staxaff b-.* I wish I could be as casual about it as he is. *yaa-reet yəṭlaε ᵊb-ʔiidi ʔəstahwen haš-šaġle qadd-ma byəstahwə́na huwwe.*
casually - **1.** *εal-maaši.* He said it to me quite casually. *qal-li-yə́aha εal-maaši.* **2.** *bᵊl-εaraḍ.* I know him casually. *baεᵊrfo bᵊl-εaraḍ.*
casualties - **1.** *ḍaḥaaya* (pl.). The number of traffic casualties is increasing year after year. *εadad ḍaḥaaya s-seer εam yəzdaad səne baεᵊd səne.* **2.** *xaṣaayer* (pl.). Our casualties in Africa were relatively small. *xaṣaayərna b-ʔafriiq̈ya kaanet baṣiiṭa nəsbiyyan.*
cat - *qaṭṭ* f. *qaṭṭa* pl. *qaṭaaṭ.* Don't forget to let out the cat before you go to bed. *laa tənsa maa ṭṭaaleε ᵊl-qaṭṭ la-barra qabᵊl-ma tnaam.* -- When the cat's away, the mice will play. *lamma biġiibu l-qaṭaaṭ, byərdaḥu l-fiiraan.*
**Who let the cat out of the bag? *miin faša s-sərr?*
catalogue - *kataloog* pl. *-aat.*
catastrophe - *kaarse* pl. *kawaares, nakbe* pl. *-aat, mṣiibe* pl. *maṣaayeb.*
catch - **1.** *qəfᵊl* pl. *qfaal.* The catch on the camera is broken. *qəfl ᵊl-kámeera manzuuε.* **2.** *εəlle* pl. *εəlal.* There must be a catch to it some place. *laazem ykən-la εəlle b-šii qərne.* **3.** *ṣeeḍ.* Ten fish is a good catch. *εašᵊr samakaat ṣeeḍ ᵊmniiḥ.* **4.** *laqṭa* pl. *-aat.* She's a good catch. *hiyye laqṭa mniiḥa.*
to play catch - *ləεeb (a ləεᵊb) ṭəmmeeme.* Do you want to play catch? *bəddak təlεab ṭəmmeeme?*
to catch - **1.** *laqaṭ (o laqᵊṭ), ṣṭaaḍ, kamaš (e kamᵊš).* We caught a lot of fish. *laqaṭna samak ᵊktiir.* **2.** *snaawal, kamaš, laqaṭ.* Here, catch this! *xood, snaawə́la!* **3.** *laqaṭ, kamaš.* I caught him at it. *laqaṭṭo fiiha.* -- He was caught red-handed. *kamašúu bᵊž-žərm ᵊl-mašhuud.* **4.** *laqaṭ, fəhem (a fəhᵊm).* I didn't catch his name. *maa laqaṭṭ ʔəsmo.* **5.** *laḥḥaq.* I have to catch the five-o'clock train. *laazem laḥḥeq treen ᵊs-saaεa xamse.* **6.** *nεada (a εadwe) b-.* I caught the measles from him. *nεadeet bᵊl-ᵊḥmeera mənno.* **7.** *εəleq (a e).* A fishbone caught in my throat. *fii ḥasake εəlqet ᵊb-zoozet ḥalqi.* -- I caught my coat on a nail. *manṭooyi εəleq ᵊb-bəsmaar.* **8.** *qaraṭ (o qarᵊṭ//nqaraṭ).* I've caught my finger. *qaraṭṭ ʔəṣbaεti.* **9.** *daqqar.* The lock doesn't catch well any more. *l-qəfᵊl maa εaad ydaqqer maẓbuuṭ.*
**I caught a glimpse of the house through the trees. *lamaḥᵊt ᵊl-beet mən been ᵊs-sažar.*
to catch cold - *ʔaxad barᵊd.* You'll catch cold if you don't put on a scarf. *btaaxod barᵊd ʔiza maa bətḥəṭṭ laḥše.*
to catch fire - *štaεal.* The wood is so dry that it will catch fire easily. *l-xašab naašef la-daraže byəštə́εel fiiha b-ᵊshuule.*
to catch hold - *masak (e masᵊk).* Catch hold of the other end. *mseek ᵊṭ-ṭaraf ᵊt-taani.*
to catch on - *fəhem (a fəhᵊm).* He catches on quickly. *byəfham ᵊb-sərεa* or ***huwwe fəteḥ.* -- She immediately caught on to the idea. *fəhmet ᵊl-fəkra ḥaalan.*
**That tune caught on, you might say, overnight. *han-naġme matᵊl-ma tquul daržet bayna εašiyyatin w-ḍuḥaaha.*

to catch someone's eye - *lafat (e laf°t) naẓar˜ hada.* The neckties in the window caught my eye. *l-krafataat b°l-waažha lafatu naẓari.*

to catch up - **1.** *šahhal.* Try to catch up in your work. *ḥaawel °tšahhel °b-šeġlak.* **2.** *Ꜥawwaḍ.* I have to catch up on my sleep. *laazem Ꜥawweḍ °n-noom °l-maksuur Ꜥaliyyi.* **3.** *ləḥeq (a luḥaqaan).* Go ahead! I'll catch up with you! *sbəqni! bəlḥaqak!* **4.** *masak (e mas°k).* We caught him up on his previous assertions. *masaknda b-ʔəddiꜤaaʔaato s-saabqa.*

**Lack of sleep will catch up with you sooner or later. *bəthəss °b-qəllet °n-noom Ꜥaažilan ʔaw ʔaažilan.*

to get caught - *Ꜥəleq (a ø).* I got caught in the rain on my way home. *Ꜥləq°t b°l-maṭar °b-ṭariiqi Ꜥal-beet.* -- The candy got caught in my throat. *s-səkkara Ꜥəlqet °b-ḥalqi.* -- My foot got caught in the stirrup. *ʔəžri Ꜥəlqet b°r-rakkaabe.*

**Don't get caught by the police. *laa txalli š-šərṭa tək°mšak.*

catching - *məꜤdi**. Measles are catching. *l-°ḥmeera məꜤdiyye.*

categorical - *qaaṭeꜤ, baatt.* The government issued a categorical denial. *l-°ḥkuume ṭaalaꜤet takziib qaaṭeꜤ.*

categorically - *b-ṣuura qaaṭꜤa, b-ṣuura baatte.*

category - *ṣən°f* pl. *ʔaṣnaaf.*

caterpillar - *duudet˜ rabiiꜤ* coll. *duud˜ rabiiꜤ* pl. *-aat˜ rabiiꜤ.* We have to spray the trees against caterpillars. *laazem °nrəšš °š-šažar ḍədd duud °r-rabiiꜤ.*

cathedral - *katədraaʔiyye* pl. *-aat.*

Catholic - *katuliiki** pl. *katuliik* and *kawaatle.*

Catholicism - *katlake, mazhab˜ °l-katuliik.*

cattle - *baqar.* They raise fine cattle in this part of the country. *birabbu baqar məmtaaz °b-hal-qərne mən l-°blaad.*

cauliflower - *qarnabiiṭ, zahra.*

cause - **1.** *sabab* pl. *ʔasbaab.* What is the cause of the delay? *šuu sabab °t-taʔxiir?* **2.** *qaḍiyye* pl. *qaḍaaya.* He died for a noble cause. *maat fii sabiil qaḍiyye nabiile.*

to cause - **1.** *sabbab.* What caused the accident? *šuu yalli sabbab °l-ḥaadse?* -- The storm caused great havoc. *l-Ꜥaaṣfe sabbabet xaraab haaʔel.* -- He causes her a lot of grief. *Ꜥam ysabbəb-la ḥəzn °ktiir.* **2.** *ʔasaar, sabbab.* His answer caused surprise. *žawaabo ʔasaar dahše* or ***žawaabo dahaš °n-naas.*

caution - *ḥazar.* We stress caution in this kind of operation. *mənṣərr Ꜥal-ḥazar °b-heek Ꜥamaliyye.* -- He moved along the edge of the gorge with caution. *məši Ꜥala kanaar °l-haawye b-ḥazar.*

to caution - *ḥazzar, nabbah.* She cautioned me against it. *ḥazzarətni mən haš-šaġle.*

cautious - **1.** *mətḥazzer, məḥtəres.* You don't have to be so cautious with me. *maa fii lzuum °tkuun hal-qadd mətḥazzer maꜤi.* **2.** *ḥəzer, ḥariis.* My uncle is a very cautious man. *Ꜥammi ražžaal ḥəzer °ktiir.*

cautiously - *b-ḥazar, b-ʔəḥtiraas.* He felt his way cautiously toward the door. *tḥassas ṭariiqo naaḥ °l-baab °b-ḥazar.*

cavalry - *xayyaale* (pl.).

cavalryman - *xayyaal* pl. *-e.*

cave - *mġaara* pl. *-aat* and *maġaayer, kah°f* pl. *khuuf.* We hid in a cave. *txabbeena b-°mġaara.*

to cave in - *habaṭ (o hbuuṭ).* I'm afraid the house is going to cave in. *xaayəf-lak °l-beet bəddo yəhboṭ.*

caviar - *kavyaar.*

cavity - *suus (b°s-snaan).* I didn't have a cavity until I was 14 years old. *maa ballaš °s-suus b-°snaani ʔəlla ḥatta ṣaar Ꜥəmri ʔarbaṭaꜤ°š.*

cease-fire - *waq̈°f˜ ʔəṭlaaq̈˜ °n-naar.* The cease-fire will begin at midnight. *waq̈°f ʔəṭlaaq̈ °n-naar byəbda nəṣṣ °l-leel.*

cedar - *ʔarze* coll. *ʔar°z* pl. *-aat.*

ceiling - **1.** *saq°f* pl. *ʔəs°qfe* and *squuf.* The ceiling is painted white. *s-saq°f madhuun ʔabyaḍ.* **2.** *l-ḥadd °l-ʔaq̈ṣa.* The government has lowered the ceiling on farm prices. *l-°ḥkuume nazzalet °l-ḥadd °l-ʔaq̈ṣa tabaꜤ ʔasꜤaar °l-maḥṣuulaat °z-ziraaꜤiyye.*

to **celebrate** - *ḥtafal b-.* We're celebrating his birthday tomorrow. *bəddna nəḥtəfel °b-Ꜥiid miilaado bəkra.*

celebration - *ʔəḥtifaal* pl. *-aat, ḥafle* pl. *-aat.* The celebration took place yesterday. *l-ʔəḥtifaal ṣaar °mbaarḥa.*

celebrity - *šax°ṣ šahiir* pl. *ʔašxaaṣ šahiiriin.* He's quite a celebrity in academic circles. *huwwe šax°ṣ šahiir b°l-ḥalaq̈aat °ž-žaamꜤiyye.*

celery - *karaf°s.*

cell - **1.** *zənzaane* pl. *-aat.* Take the prisoner to his cell. *xood °l-maḥbuus la-zənzaanto.* **2.** *ṣoomaꜤa* pl. *ṣawaameꜤ.* After midnight mass, the monks returned to their cells. *baꜤ°d qəddaas nəṣṣ °l-leel rəžꜤu r-rəhbaan la-ṣawaaməꜤon.* **3.** *xaliyye* pl. *xalaaya.* You can see the individual cells under the microscope. *fiik °tšuuf °l-xalaaya kəll waaḥde la-ḥaala taḥt °l-məkrəskoob.*

cellar - *qabu* pl. *ʔəq°bye.*

celluloid - *saluloyd.*

cement - *šmeento, ʔəsmant.* Mix more sand with the cement. *xlooṭ ram°l ʔaktar maꜤ °š-šmeento.*

to cement - **1.** *ṭala (i ø) b°š-šmeento.* The cellar has just been cemented. *l-qabu hallaq ṭalúu b°š-šmeento.* **2.** *lazzaq//tlazzaq.* Will you be able to cement the vase? *fiik °tlazzeq °l-mazhariyye?*

cemetery - *maqbara* pl. *maqaaber, tərbe* pl. *tərab.*

censer - *mabxara* pl. *mabaaxer.*

censor - *mraaqeb* pl. *-iin.*

censorship - *mraaqabe.* The censorship has been lifted *rafaꜤu l-°mraaqabe.*

census - *ʔəḥṣaaʔ˜* (pl. *-aat˜*) *səkkaan, təꜤdaad˜ səkkaan.*

cent - **1.** *sant* pl. *-aat.* There are a hundred cents in a dollar. *fii miit sant b°d-dolaar.* **2.** *qər°š, nḥaase.* I haven't a cent in change. *maa maꜤi w-laa qərš °fraaṭa.* -- He doesn't have a cent. *maa Ꜥando w-laa nḥaase.* **3.** *qər°š.* I'm almost down to my last cent. *ʔana taqriiban °mfalles, muu baqyaan maꜤi ʔəlla kam qər°š.* -- I wouldn't give a cent for it. *walla maa bədfaꜤ fii w-laa qər°š.*

**Do you have to put in your two cents' worth? *ḍaruuri təṭlaꜤ °b-hal-ʔafkaar °s-saxiife?*

center - **1.** *nəṣṣ, waṣ°ṭ.* The table is standing in the center of the room. *ṭ-ṭaawle maḥṭuuṭa b-nəṣṣ °l-ʔuuḍa.* -- He lives in the center of the town. *huwwe saaken °b-nəṣṣ °l-balad.* **2.** *markaz* pl. *maraakez.* A line from the center to the circumference of a circle is called the radius. *l-xaṭṭ mən markaz °d-daaʔire la-muḥiiṭa ʔəsmo nəṣ°f q̈əṭ°r.* -- The city is the political and cultural center of the north. *l-madiine hiyye l-markaz °s-siyaasi w°s-saq̈aafi ləš-šamaal.* -- Have you ever visited the French Cultural Center? *šuu zər°t šii l-markaz °s-saq̈aafi l-fərnsaawi?* -- Where's the center of the storm located? *ween markaz °l-Ꜥaaṣfe?* -- The center of gravity. *markaz °s-səq̈°l.* **3.** *maḥaṭṭ.* She's the center of attention. *hiyye maḥaṭṭ °l-ʔanẓaar.*

to be centered on - *trakkaz Ꜥala.* All his thoughts were centered on her. *kəll tafkiiro kaan mətrakkez Ꜥaleeha.*

centigrade - *santiġraad* (invar.). The temperature here can go up as high as 50 degrees centigrade. *l-ḥaraara hoon ʔaḥyaanan °btəṣal la-xamsiin santiġraad.*

centimeter - *ṣanṭimətr* pl. *-aat, ṣanṭi* (invar.).

centipede - *ʔəmm ʔarbꜤa w-ʔar°bꜤiin.*

central - **1.** *markazi**. The central station is located 50 km from here. *l-°mḥaṭṭa l-markaziyye mawžuude Ꜥala masaafet xamsiin kiiloəmtr mən hoon.* -- Many people believe the central government has too much power. *fii naas °ktiir byəꜤtəqdu ʔənno l-°ḥkuume l-markaziyye ʔəlha ṣəlṭaat ʔaktar °mn °l-laazem.* **2.** *raʔiisi*, žawhari**. That's the central idea of his treatise. *hayye l-fəkra r-raʔiisiyye b-maq̈aalto.*

Central Europe - *ʔawrəbba l-wuṣṭa.*

century - *q̈ar°n* pl. *q̈ruun.*

ceremony - **1.** *ʔəḥtifaal* pl. *-aat.* The ceremony was held yesterday afternoon. *l-ʔəḥtifaal ṣaar °mbaareḥ baꜤd °d-dəh°r.* **2.** *kəlfe, takliif, rasmiyyaat* (pl.). Don't stand so much on ceremony. *maa bəddak kəll hal-kəlfe.*

certain - **1.** *baꜤ°ḍ˜ ...* There are certain things we have to discuss. *fii baꜤḍ °l-ʔašya laazem nəbḥəsa.* — Certain people, whom I'd rather not name... *fii baꜤ°ḍ naas °l-ʔaḥsan maa ʔəzkor ʔasmaahon ...* **2.** *mꜤayyan.* Certain events brought about the resignation of the minister. *fii ḥawaades °mꜤayyane ʔaddet la-ʔəstiq̈aalt °l-waziir.* **3.** *mqarrar.* The time is certain, but we haven't decided on the place yet. *l-waqt °mqarrar, laaken ləssa maa Ꜥtamadna Ꜥal-maḥall.* **4.** *mətʔakked.* I'm certain she forgot all about it. *ʔana mətʔakked ʔənna nəsyet kəll* *haš-šağle.* **5.** *ʔakiid, mən kəll bədd.* It's certain to rain before we leave. *ʔakiid laḥa tšatti qabᵊl-ma nruuḥ.* **6.** *ʔakiid mənno.* One thing is certain... *fii šii waaḥed ʔakiid mənno...*

certainly - 1. *ʔakiid.* She's certainly right. *ʔakiid maεa ḥaqq.* **2.** *ʔakiid, rasman.* Now I certainly won't do it. *hallaq baqa ʔakiid maa raḥa saawiiha.* **3.** *εal-mazbuuṭ.* He certainly gave it to him! *laṭašo-yḍaha b-wəššo εal-mazbuuṭ* or ***walla laṭašo-yḍaha b-wəššo.*

**Why certainly! *maεluum!*

certificate - 1. *šahaade* pl. *-aat.* You'll have to show us some kind of certificate. *laazem ᵊtwaržiina šii šahaade.* **2.** *taqriir* pl. *taqariir.* He needs a doctor's certificate. *laazmo taqriir ᵊmn ᵊṭ-ṭabiib.*

to **certify - 1.** *sabbat, šəhed (a šahaade) b-.* He'll certify that there were no witnesses present. *laḥa ysabbet* (or *yəšhad*) *ʔənno maa kaan fii šhuud mawžuudiin.* **2.** *saddaq εala, saadaq εala.* A notary public has to certify the signature. *laazem kaateb ᵊl-εadl ysaddeq εal-ʔəmḍa.*

certified - 1. *q̈aanuuni**. He's a certified public accountant. *huwwe mḥaaseb q̈aanuuni.* **2.** *msaddaq.* This is a certified copy of the original document. *hayy ṣuura msaddaqa εan ᵊl-wasiiq̈a l-ʔaṣliyye.*

chain - 1. *sənᵊsle* pl. *sanaasel, səlᵊsle* pl. *salaasel.* She wears a golden chain. *btəlbes sənᵊsle dahab.* **2.** *səlᵊsle.* This led to a whole chain of events. *haada ʔadda la-səlᵊslet ḥawaades εan ṣaḥiiḥ.* **3.** *zanžiir* pl. *zanažiir, žanziir* pl. *žanaziir.* The roads are icy. You'd better put the chains on the tires. *ṭ-ṭəroq ᵊmžallde. l-ʔaḥsan ᵊtḥəṭṭ ᵊz-zanažiir εad-dawaliib.* -- The chain broke when they tried to hoist the wrecked car from the river. *z-zanžiir ᵊnqaṭaε lamma ḥaawalu yərfaεu s-sayyaara l-ᵊmhawwra mn ᵊn-nahᵊr.* **4.** *šabake* pl. *-aat.* The company operates a chain of filling stations all over the country. *š-šərke bəddiir šabaket ᵊmḥaṭṭaat banziin ᵊb-kəll ᵊblaadna.*

chain reaction - *radd~ fəεl ᵊmsalsal.*

chain smoker - *mdaxxen rasmi* pl. *mdaxxniin rasmiyyiin, mdaxxen mədmen, mədmen* (pl. *-iin*) *εat-tadxiin.*

to chain - 1. *rabaṭ (o rabᵊṭ//nrabaṭ) (ᵊb-zanžiir).* Have you chained the dog? *šuu rabaṭṭ ᵊl-kalb (ᵊb-zanžiir)?* **2.** *zanžar, žanzar.* They chained the prisoner to the post. *zanžaru l-maḥbuus bᵊl-εaamuud.*

chair - 1. *kərsi* pl. *karaasi.* Please sit down in this chair. *tfaḍḍal εood εala hal-kərsi.* -- He holds a chair in philosophy at the Syrian University. *byəšğel kərsi b-farε ᵊl-falsafe bᵊž-žaamεa s-suuriyye.* -- The murderer was sent to the electric chair. *l-qaatel ḥakamu εaléε bᵊl-ʔəεdaam bᵊl-kərsi l-kahrabaaʔi.* **2.** *raʔiis.* The chair asks for a vote. *r-raʔiis εam yəṭlob yḥəṭṭu l-masʔale εat-taṣwiit.*

easy chair - *kərsi məryeḥ* pl. *karaasi mərᵊyḥa.* Sit in the easy chair. *εood εal-kərsi l-məryeḥ.*

to chair - *traʔʔas.* Who chaired the meeting? *miin yalli traʔʔas ᵊl-ʔəžtimaaε?*

chairman - *raʔiis* pl. *rəʔasa.*

chairmanship - *raʔaase.*

chalk - *ṭabašiir* (pl.), (a piece of chalk) *ṭabšuura.* Do you have any colored chalk? *fii εandkon ṭabašiir ᵊmlawwane?*

to chalk: He usually chalks the figures on the board. *εaadatan biḥəṭṭ* (or *byəktob*) *ᵊl-ʔarq̈aam εal-looḥ.* -- Chalk that up to experience. *sažžəla taḥᵊt baab ᵊl-xəbra.*

challenge - *taḥaddi* pl. *-iyyaat.* Our team accepted their challenge. *fariiqna qəbel taḥaddiihon* or ***fariiqna qəbel ynaazəlon.* -- I chose this field because I thought it would be a real challenge. *naqqeet hal-ḥaqᵊl laʔənno ẓanneet fii taḥaddi εan ṣaḥiiḥ la-mada ʔəmkaaniyyaati.*

to challenge - 1. *tḥadda.* I challenge the winner! *bətḥadda r-rabḥaan!* -- I challenge anybody else to do that! *bətḥadda miin-ma kaan yaεmel haš-šii.* **2.** *ṭaεan (a ṭaεᵊn) b-.* We challenge his theory because we feel it lacks the proper scientific foundations. *mnəṭεan ᵊb-naẓariito laʔənno mənšuuf ʔənna naaqṣa ᵊl-ʔəsos ᵊl-εəlmiyye l-laazme.*

Chamber of Commerce - *ğərfet~* (pl. *ğəraf~*) *tižaara.*

Chamber of Deputies - *mažles~* (pl. *mažaales~*) *ᵊn-nuwwaab.*

chamber pot - *mabwale* pl. *mabaawel.*

champagne - *šampanya.*

champion - 1. *baṭal* pl. *ʔabṭaal.* He's the present world champion. *huwwe l-baṭal ᵊl-ḥaali bᵊl-εaalam.* **2.** *mdaafeε* (pl. *-iin*) *εan.* The deputy is a champion of economic reform. *n-naaʔeb huwwe mdaafeε εan ᵊl-ʔəṣlaaḥ ᵊl-ʔəq̈tiṣaadi.*

championship - *buṭuule, buṭuuliyye.* They're fighting for the championship. *εam yətbaarazu mənšaan ᵊl-buṭuule.*

chance - 1. *fərṣa* pl. *fəraṣ.* Give me a chance. *εaṭiini fərṣa.* -- I had a chance to go to California. *ṣar-li fərṣa ruuḥ la-kalifoornya.* **2.** *ṣədfe, šans.* You shouldn't rely on mere chance. *bəddak raʔyi? laa təεtəmed εaṣ-ṣədfe bass.* **3.** *ʔəḥtimaal* pl. *-aat.* Is there any chance of catching the train? *fii ʔəḥtimaal w-law ḍaʔiil laḥḥeq ᵊt-treen?* **4.** *warqet~* (pl. *wraaq~*) *yaa-naṣiib.* Won't you buy a chance? *maa bəddak təštəri warqet yaa-naṣiib?* **5.** *bᵊṣ-ṣədfe.* A chance meeting changed their whole life. *ʔəžtimaaε bᵊṣ-ṣədfe ğayyár-lon kəll mažra ḥayaaton.*

**Not a chance! *məstaḥiil!*

**Chances are he won't get the job. *l-ʔağlab maa laḥa yəḥṣal εaš-šağle.*

**I'm afraid you don't stand a chance of getting the job. *xaayəf-lak maa εandak w-laa bṣiiṣ ʔamal la-taaxod haš-šağle.*

by chance - *bᵊṣ-ṣədfe.* I met him by chance. *šəfto bᵊṣ-ṣədfe* or ***ṣaadafto mṣaadafe.*

to take a chance - *žarrab ḥaẓẓo, žaazaf, xaaṭar.* Shall we take a chance? *nžarreb ḥaẓẓna?* -- I'll take the chance. *bəddi žaazef.* -- Let's take a chance on him. *xalliina nžarreb ḥaẓẓna w-ᵊnžarrbo.*

to chance - *žaazaf.* He'll get mad if you tell him. - I'll chance it! *ʔiza qəlt-əllo laḥa yəzεal ᵊktiir. - maεleeši bžaazef!*

chancellor - *məstašaar* pl. *-iin.*

chandelier - *trayya* pl. *-aat.*

change - 1. *tabdiil* pl. *-aat, tağyiir* pl. *-aat.* Have there been any changes in my absence? *ṣaar fii šii tabdiilaat b-ᵊğyaabi?* -- I'm for a change in the administration. *ʔana mən raʔyi tabdiil bᵊl-ʔidaara.* -- This requires a change in our plans. *haada byəstalzem tağyiir ᵊb-xəṭaṭna.* **2.** *tağyiir~ šəkᵊl.* You need a change. *laazmak tağyiir šəkᵊl.* **3.** *fraaṭa.* Have you any change? *maεak fraaṭa šii?* **4.** *ṣraafe.* Can you give me change for five pounds? *balla maεak ᵊṣraafet xamᵊs leeraat?* or ***balla ṣrəf-li* (or *fəkk-əlli*) *xamᵊs leeraat.* **5.** *kmaale.* That'll be 4,50 out of five pounds, don't forget your change. *haada ḥaqqo ʔarbεa w-nəṣṣ mən xamᵊs leeraat, laa tənsa l-ᵊkmaale.* -- Keep the change. *l-ᵊkmaale ʔəlak (baxšiiš).*

for a change - *tağyiir~ šəkᵊl.* For a change I'd like to go to the movies tonight. *bəddi ruuḥ εas-siinama l-leele tağyiir šəkᵊl.*

to change - 1. *ṣaraf (e ṣarᵊf), fakk (ə fakk).* Can you change a ten-pound bill for me? *fiik təṣrəf-li* (or *ᵊtfəkk-əlli*) *εašᵊr leeraat?* **2.** *baddal, ḥawwal.* I'd like to change American dollars into pounds. *raayed baddel dolaaraat ʔameerkiyye b-leeraat* or *raayed ḥawwel dolaaraat ʔameerkiyye la-leeraat.* **3.** *ğayyar, baddal.* We may have to change our plans. *məḥtəmal nəḍṭarr ᵊnğayyer xəṭaṭna.* -- The maid changes the beds every Monday. *ṣ-ṣaanεa bətbaddel bayaaḍ ᵊt-txuut kəll taneen.* -- You'll have half an hour to change buses in Damascus. *maεak nəṣṣ saaεa la-tğayyer fiiha l-baaṣ bᵊš-šaam.* -- I'd like to change clothes before dinner. *žaaye εala baali ğayyer ʔawaaεiyyi qabl ᵊl-εaša.* -- It will take her five minutes to change. *btaaxəda xamᵊs daqaayeq la-tğayyer.* -- You'll have to change your tone if you want to talk to me. *laazem ᵊtğayyer laḥᵊžtak ʔiza bəddak təḥki maεi.* -- I've changed my mind. *ğayyarᵊt fəkri.* -- Change places with me so you can see better. *ğayyer maḥallaat maεi la-ḥatta tšuuf ʔaḥsan.* **4.** *tğayyar, tbaddal.* The weather is going to change. *ṭ-ṭaqᵊṣ laḥa yətğayyar.* -- You'll be surprised how he's changed. *btəstağreb kiif ᵊtğayyar.* -- Did you see her face change when she heard the news? *šəfᵊt kiif ᵊtbaddal wəšša lamma səmεet ᵊl-xabar?* -- Nothing has changed. *maa fii šii tğayyar.* **5.** *naqal (o ə), ğayyar, baddal.* We have to change at the next station. *laazem mənqol bᵊl-ᵊmḥaṭṭa ž-žaaye.*

to change hands - *ntaqal mən ʔiid la-ʔiid.* This hotel has changed hands several times. *hal-ʔoteel ᵊntaqal mən ʔiid la-ʔiid εəddet marraat.*

changeable - *mətqalleb, mətğayyer.* The weather is very changeable around here. *ṭ-ṭaqᵊṣ mətqalleb ᵊktiir ᵊb-han-nawaaḥi.* -- She has a changeable disposition. *ṭabεa mətqalleb.*

channel - 1. *mažra* pl. *mažaari*. The two lakes are joined by a narrow channel. *l-buḥayᵊrteen mattaṣliin ᵊb-mažra dayyeq*. 2. *mḥaṭṭa* pl. *-aat*. What channel is the program on? *Eala ʔani mḥaṭṭa l-barnaamež?*
**The application will have to go through proper channels. *l-ʔastimaara laazem taaxod mažraaha ṭ-ṭabiiEi*.
the (English) Channel - *baḥr˜ ᵊl-maanš*.
to channel - 1. *xaṣṣaṣ*. The agency channels most of the funds into irrigation. *l-ʔidaara batxaṣṣeṣ ʔaktar ʔamwaala lar-rayy*. 2. *waššah la-, ṣaraf (o ṣarᵊf) b-*. Why don't you channel your efforts in another field? *leeš maa batwaššeh ᵊžhuudak la-mažaal taani?*
to chant - 1. *ʔaddan*. At our house you can hear the muezzin chant the call to prayer. *man beetna fiik tasmaE l-ᵊmʔadden Eam yʔadden ᵊl-ʔadaan*. 2. *rattal*. The imam chanted a passage from the Koran. *l-ʔimaam rattal žazʔ ᵊmn ᵊl-q̈urʔaan*.
chaos - *fawḍa*.
chaotic - *fawḍawi**.
chapel - *kniise* pl. *kanaayes*.
chaperone - *šaabaroon* pl. *-aat, naaṭuur* f. *naaṭuura* pl. *nawaṭiir*.
chapped - *mšaqqeq, mqaššeb*. My lips are chapped. *šafafi mšaqqᵊqiin*.
chapter - 1. *faṣᵊl* pl. *fṣuul*. Did you read the last chapter of this book? *qareet ᵊl-faṣl ᵊl-ʔaxiir man hal-ᵊktaab?* 2. *ṣuura* pl. *ṣawar*. The Koran is divided into 114 chapters. *l-q̈urʔaan ᵊmqassam la-miyye w-ʔarbᵊEṭaašar ṣuura*. 3. *žazᵊʔ* pl. *ʔažzaaʔ*. That's a closed chapter in my life. *haada žazᵊʔ man ḥayaati maḍa w-raaḥ*.
character - 1. *ṭabᵊE* pl. *ʔaṭbaaE, xalᵊq* pl. *ʔaxlaaq*. I've misjudged his character. *kanᵊt ġalṭaan ᵊb-ḥakmi Eala ṭabEo*. 2. *šaxṣiyye* pl. *-aat*. How many characters are there in the play? *kam šaxṣiyye fii bᵊt-tamsiiliyye?* 3. *ramᵊz* pl. *rmuuz*. I wish I could read these Chinese characters. *yaa-reet ʔaqder ʔaqra har-rmuuz ᵊṣ-ṣiiniyye*. 4. *ṣuura* pl. *ṣawar*. That man is a familiar character here. *har-raššaal ṣuura maʔluufe hoon*. 5. *tarkiibe, nahfe*. He's quite a character! *Ean ṣaḥiiḥ huwwe tarkiibe!*
**That boy has character! *hal-walad dagri!*
characteristic - 1. *xaaṣṣ b-*. That's characteristic of our time. *haš-šii xaaṣṣ ᵊb-Eaṣᵊrna* or **haš-šii man mumayyizaat Eaṣᵊrna*. 2. *xanṭaq manṭaq Ean* (invar.). That's a characteristic reaction of his. *haada radd faEᵊl xanṭaq manṭaq Eanno*. — That attitude is characteristic of her. *hal-mawqef tabaEa xanṭaq manṭaq Eanna*. 3. *ṣifa* pl. *-aat*. They're trying to improve the heat-resisting characteristics of this fiber. *Eam yžarrbu taḥsiin ṣifet taḥammol ᵊl-ḥaraara b-hal-liif*. 4. *miize* pl. *-aat*. They always mention that characteristic in her first. *daayman byazᵊkru hal-miize fiiha ʔawwal šii*.
charades - *laEbet˜ ᵊš-šaaraat*. Toward the end of the party we all played charades. *naaḥ ʔaaxer ᵊl-ḥafle lEabna kalliyyaatna laEbet ᵊš-šaaraat*.
charcoal - *faḥᵊm*.
charcoal brazier - *manqal* pl. *manaaqel*.
chard - *salᵊq*.
charge - 1. *ḥašwe* pl. *-aat, dakke* pl. *-aat*. The charge is big enough to blow all of us up. *l-ḥašwe kafiile b-ʔanno tṭayyarna kallna*. 2. *kalfe* pl. *kalaf, rasᵊm* pl. *rsuum(e)* and *rsuumaat*. There's no charge for delivery. *maa fii kalfe Eat-tawṣiil*. 3. *tahme* pl. *taham*. What are the charges against this man? *šuu ᵊt-taham ḍadd har-raššaal?* 4. *Eahde*. I leave the children in your charge. *batrok l-ᵊwlaad ᵊb-Eahᵊdtak*.
free of charge - *bᵊl-mažaan, mažaanan, biiduun kalfe, b-balaaš*. We'll mail it to you free of charge. *mnabEat-lak-ydaha bᵊl-bosṭa bᵊl-mažaan*.
in charge of - *masʔuul Ean, matkaffel b-*. Who's in charge of this section? *miin masʔuul Ean hal-qasᵊm?*
to take charge - 1. *twalla, ʔaxad masʔuuliit˜*... He's taking charge of the new branch. *laḥa yatwalla l-farE ᵊž-ždiid* or *laḥa yaaxod masʔuuliit ᵊl-farE ᵊž-ždiid*. 2. *twalla zimaam˜*... He took charge of the situation. *twalla zimaam ᵊl-waḍᵊE*.
to charge - 1. *ṭalab (o ṭalab)*. What do you charge for these shoes? *qaddeeš ᵊbtaṭlob ᵊb-haṣ-ṣabbaaṭ?* or **qaddeeš Eam taaxod ḥaqq haṣ-ṣabbaaṭ?* 2. *qayyad*. Charge this to my account. *qayyéda Eala ḥsaabi*. 3. *Eabba*. We'll ask him to charge the battery for us. *mnaṭlob manno yEabbii-lna l-baṭṭaariyye*. 4. *taham (o/e tahᵊm* and *ʔatthaam// ntaham)*. They charged him with grand larceny. *tahamúu b-sarqa žinaaʔiyye*.
**You've charged me too much! *kattarᵊt Ealiyyi ktiir!*
charitable - 1. *maḥsen*. She's a charitable old lady. *hiyye satt ᵊxtyaara maḥᵊsne*. 2. *xayri**. She spends her free time working for a charitable organization. *btaštáġel ᵊb-waqᵊt faraaġa la-mnaẓẓame xayriyye*.
charity - 1. *ʔaḥsaan*. Charity is one of the noblest virtues. *l-ʔaḥsaan man ʔanbal ᵊl-faḍaaʔel*. 2. *ṣadaqa*. She's too proud to accept charity. *btatraffaE Ean ᵊqbuul ᵊṣ-ṣadaqa man katᵊr Eazzet nafsa*. 3. *l-barr wᵊl-ʔaḥsaan*. He gives all his money to charity. *byaṣrof kall maṣarii b-sabiil ᵊl-barr wᵊl-ʔaḥsaan*. 4. *žamEiyye* (pl. *-aat*) *xayriyye*. He left his entire estate to his favorite charity. *xallaf kall tarᵊkto la-ʔafḍal žamEiyye xayriyye Eando*.
charm - 1. *taEwiize* pl. *-aat*. Her grandmother taught her the charm as a little girl. *satta Eallamáta t-taEwiize man ẓaġára*. — That's a pretty charm you have on your bracelet. *hayy taEwiize ḥalwe b-ʔaswaartek*. — Some people nail a horseshoe to the door as a lucky charm. *fii naas biḥaṭṭu ḥadwet faras Eal-baab ka-taEwiize la-žalb ᵊl-ḥaẓẓ*. 2. *fatne, saḥᵊr*. She used all her charms to get what she wanted. *staEmalet kall fatnáta la-taḥṣal Eala yalli badda-yáa*.
**She has a lot of charm. *hiyye fattaane ktiir*.
to charm - *fatan (e a//nfatan), saḥar (e saḥᵊr// nsaḥar)*. He charms everybody with his smile. *byaften kall ᵊn-naas ᵊb-ᵊbtisaamto*.
charming - *saaḥer, fattaan*. His sister is a very charming person. *ʔaxto saaḥra ktiir*.
charter - *miisaaq̈* pl. *mawasiiq̈*. Both countries signed the U.N. Charter. *d-doolteen ᵊt-tanteen maḍu miisaaq̈ ᵊl-ʔamam ᵊl-mattaḥide*.
to charter - *staʔžar*. You can charter a plane to go to Palmyra. *fiik tastaʔžer ṭayyaara (škaarsa) la-truuḥ la-tadmor*.
chase - *mṭaarade*. The police caught the car thief after a wild chase. *š-šarṭa kamšet saareq ᵊs-sayyaara baEd ᵊmṭaarade faẓiiEa*.
**He led us a merry chase. *ḍaḥek Eala daqᵊnna*.
to chase - 1. *qallaE, ṭarad (o ṭarᵊd//nṭarad)*. I chased the dog out of the house. *qallaEt ᵊl-kalᵊb la-barraat ᵊl-beet*. — Chase the beggar away. *qalleE ᵊš-šaḥḥaad*. 2. *laheq (a laḥaqaan)*. I've been chasing you all morning. *ṣar-li kall qabl ᵊḍ-ḍahᵊr Eam ʔálḥaqak (man qarne la-qarne)*.
chassis - *šaasíi* pl. *-iyyaat*.
chaste - *Eafiif, ṭaaher*.
chastity - *Eaffe, ṭahaara*.
chat - *msaamara* pl. *-aat*. We had a nice chat. *žara beenaatna msaamara ẓariife*.
to chat - *tsaamar*. We chatted all evening. *tsaamarna kall ᵊs-sahra*.
chatter - *sarsara*. Stop that foolish chatter! *ḥaaštak sarsara bala ṭaEme!*
to chatter - 1. *sarsar*. They chatter incessantly. *bisarᵊsru bala waqfe*. 2. *ṭaqṭaq, ražaf (e ražafaan)*. My teeth are chattering. *snaani Eam yṭaqᵊṭqu*.
chatterbox - *sarsaar* pl. *-iin*.
chauffeur - *šofoor* pl. *-iyye*.
cheap - 1. *rxiiṣ* pl. *rxaaṣ*. Fruit is very cheap here. *l-faakye ktiir ᵊrxiiṣa hoon*. — He offered me the car cheap. *Earaḍ Ealiyyi s-sayyaara rxiiṣa*. 2. *waaṭi*. That's cheap stuff. *haš-šii waaṭi*. — He played a cheap trick on me. *laEeb Ealiyyi laEbe waaṭye*. 3. *mbahdal, mšaršaḥ*. She looked cheap in those clothes. *ṭalEet ᵊmbahdale b-hal-ʔawaaEi*.
**His kindness made me feel cheap. *laṭaafto xaššalatni*.
cheat - *ġaššaaš* pl. *-iin, matlaaEeb* pl. *-iin*. They all know he's a cheat. *l-kall byaEᵊrfu ʔanno ġaššaaš*.
to cheat - 1. *ġašš (a ġašš//nġašš), laEeb (a laEbe) Eala*. Be careful they don't cheat you! *ʔoEak yġaššuuk!* or *ʔaṣha yalEabu Ealeek!* — He cheated him out of all his money. *ġaššo (or laEeb Ealée) w-ʔaxad kall maṣarii*. 2. *ġašš*. He's always cheating at exams. *daayman huwwe biġašš bᵊl-ᵊfḥuuṣa*. 3. *zoogal*. I don't like to play tricktrack with a man who cheats. *maa bḥabb ʔalEab ṭaawle maE zalame bizoogel*.
check - 1. *šakk* pl. *-aat, šeek* pl. *-aat*. I'll send you a check tomorrow. *babEát-lak šakk bakra*. 2. *waṣᵊl* pl. *wṣuulaat*. Give your baggage check to the porter. *Eaṭi l-ḥammaal waṣᵊl Eafšak*. — Here's the check for your hat, sir. *hayy waṣᵊl barneeṭṭak*

ya sayyed. 3. *ḥsaab.* Waiter, the check please! *garsoon, mən faḍlak l-ᵊḥsaab!* 4. *ɛalaame* pl. *-aat.* If he's not present put a check before his name. *ʔiza maa kaan ḥaaḍer ḥəṭṭ ɛalaame qəddaam ʔəsmo.* 5. *taṭliiɛa.* Make a quick check to see if the mail has arrived. *ɛməl-lak taṭliiɛa b-sərɛa w-šuuf ʔiza ʔəžet ᵊl-boosṭa.*

**I can't keep a check on everyone. *maa fiini xalli ɛeeni ɛala kəll ᵊn-naas.*

**You can't move the rook, you're in check. *maa btəqder ᵊtḥarrek ᵊr-rəxx, ʔənte makšuuš.*

to keep (or **hold**) **in check** – *waqqaf, ḥažaz (o ḥažᵊz//nḥažaz).* I'm no longer able to hold him in check. *maa ɛaad fiini waqqfo.*

to check – 1. *wadaɛ (-yuudaɛ wadᵊɛ//nwadaɛ).* Check your hat and coat here. *wdaaɛ bərneeṭṭak w-manṭook hoon.* 2. *baɛat (a baɛᵊt//nbaɛat, šaḥan (a šaḥᵊn// nšaḥan).* I want this baggage checked through to Cairo. *bəddi hal-ᵊġraaḍ yənbəɛtu ləl-q̈aahira.* 3. *ɛallam ɛala, ʔaššar ɛala.* Check the items you want. *ɛallem ɛal-ᵊġraaḍ yalli bəddak-yáaha.* -- Did you check these items off the list? *ɛallamᵊt ɛala han-nafdaat bᵊl-liista?* 4. *faḥaṣ (a faḥᵊṣ//nfaḥaṣ).* Please check the oil. *mən faḍlak ᵊfḥaṣ-li z-zeet.* 5. *fattaš, šaaf (u šoofe), ṭṭallaɛ ɛala.* Our passports will be checked at the border. *žawaazaatna bifattšuuhon ɛal-ᵊḥduud.* 6. *ḍabaṭ (o ḍabᵊṭ).* She checked her impulse to slap the child. *ḍabṭet ḥaala ḥatta maa təlṭoš ᵊl-walad kaff.* 7. *kašš (ə kašš// nkašš).* If you make this move I'll check you. *ʔiza ɛməlᵊt hal-ḥarake bkəššak.* 8. *ṭaabaqu baɛḍon, twaafaqu.* The two statements don't check. *hat-taṣriiḥeen maa biṭaabqu baɛḍon.* 9. *ṭaabaq, twaafaq.* That checks with what he told me. *haada biṭaabeq maɛ halli qal-li-yda.*

to check out – 1. *ġaadar.* We have to check out of the hotel by noon. *laazem ᵊnġaader ᵊl-ʔoteel nawaaḥi ḍ-ḍəhᵊr.* 2. *staɛaar.* May I check this book out overnight? *məmken ʔəstaɛiir hal-ᵊktaab la-bəkra?* 3. *tsabbat mən, tʔakkad mən, tḥaqqaq mən.* You'd better check out his story. *ʔaḥsán-lak tətsabbat mən qəṣṣto.*

to check up on – 1. *tsabbat mən, tʔakkad mən, tḥaqqaq mən.* We have to check up on his statements. *laazem nətsabbat mən ʔaq̈waalo.* 2. *staɛlam ɛan, saʔal (a ə) ɛan, tḥaqqaq mən.* Did you check up on him? *staɛlamᵊt ɛanno?*

checkbook – *daftar˜* (pl. *dafaater˜*) *šakkaat.*

checkers – *ḍaama.* Let's play a game of checkers! *xalliina nəlɛáb-ᵊlna daqq ḍaama!*

checkmate – *š-šaah maat.*

to checkmate – *mawwat ᵊš-šaah.* With the pieces you have you can't checkmate me. *b-hal-qəṭaɛ yalli maɛak maa fiik ᵊtmawwát-li šaahi.*

cheek – *xadd* pl. *xduud(e).* My cheek is all swollen. *xaddi kəllo warmaan.*

**He said that with his tongue in his cheek. *qaal haš-šii nəṣṣ ɛan mazᵊḥ w-nəṣṣ ɛan žadd.*

cheer – *htaaf* pl. *-aat.* We could hear the cheers from quite a distance. *kaan fiina nəsmaɛ l-ᵊhtaafaat mən ɛala masaafe.*

**They gave him a cheer. *hatafúu-lo.*

to cheer – *hataf (e htaaf) la-.* The crowd cheered the speaker. *ž-žamhuur hataf ləl-xaṭiib.*

to cheer up – 1. *farfaš, baṣaṭ (e/o baṣᵊṭ).* We visit her often to cheer her up. *mənzuura marraat ᵊktiir ḥatta nfarfə́ša.* 2. *farfaš, nbaṣaṭ.* Cheer up, he'll be back soon. *farfə́š-lak šwayye, byəržaɛ ɛan qariib.*

cheerful – 1. *mšaqreq, farḥaan, mabṣuuṭ.* He's very cheerful today. *huwwe mšaqreq ᵊktiir ᵊl-yoom.* 2. *mfarfeḥ, mzahzeh.* Isn't this a cheerful room? *hal-ʔuuḍa mfarᵊfḥa, muu heek?*

cheerfulness – *šaqraqa, farfaḥa, bašaaše.*

cheese – *žəbne, žəbᵊn.* What kind of cheese do you have? *šuu nooɛ ᵊž-žəbne yalli ɛandak?*

cheetah – *fahᵊd* pl. *fhuud(e).*

chef – *raʔiis˜ (rəʔasaaʔ˜) ṭabbaaxiin.*

chemical – *kiimaawi*, kiimaaʔi*.* He's working in a chemical laboratory. *ɛam yəštə́ġel ᵊb-maxbar kiimaawi.*

chemist – *kiimaawi* and *kiimaaʔi* pl. *-iyyiin.*

chemistry – *kiimya.*

cherry – *karaze* coll. *karaz* pl. *-aat.*

chess – *šaṭranž, saṭranž.* Do you play chess? *btəlɛab šaṭranž?*

chess set – *šaṭranž* and *saṭranž* pl. *-aat.*

chest – 1. *ṣədᵊr* pl. *ṣduura.* He has a broad chest. *ṣədro ɛariiḍ.* 2. *sanduuq* pl. *sanadiiq.* Put the tools in the chest. *ḥəṭṭ ᵊl-ɛədde bᵊs-sanduuq.*

**That's a load off my chest! *hallaq ᵊrtaaḥ baali!*

chest of drawers – *biirə́o* pl. *biiroyaat.* She bought a beautiful chest of drawers. *štaret biirə́o ẓariif.*

chestnut – 1. *kastanaaye* coll. *kastana* pl. *kastanaayaat.* Let's buy some roasted chestnuts. *xalliina naštrii-lna šwayyet kastana məšwiyye.* 2. *kastanaawi*.* Her hair is a beautiful chestnut color. *šaɛᵊrha loono kastanaawi ḥəlu.*

**I'm always expected to pull the chestnuts out of the fire for other people. *daayman mafruuḍ fiyyi ʔəṣreq ḥaali la-ʔažᵊl ġeeri.*

chestnut tree – *šažaret˜* (coll. *šažar˜* pl. *-aat˜* and *ʔaššaar˜*) *kastana.*

to **chew** – *ɛalak (e/o ɛalᵊk), maḍaġ (a maḍᵊġ).* Chew your food well. *ɛleek ʔaklak ᵊmniiḥ.*

chewing gum – *məstke, ɛəlke.*

chicken – *žaaže* coll. *žaaž* pl. *-aat.* We're having chicken for dinner. *ṭaabxiin nəḥna žaaž ɛal-ɛaša.* -- They raise a few chickens. *birabbu kam žaaže.*

chicken farm – *madžaže* pl. *madaažež.*

chicken pox – *žədri˜ mayy.*

chick pea – *ḥəmṣa* and *ḥəmṣaaye* coll. *ḥəmmoṣ* pl. *ḥəmṣaat* and *ḥəmṣaayaat.*

chief – 1. *raʔiis* pl. *rəʔasa.* Who's the chief of this division? *miin raʔiis hal-qəsᵊm?* 2. *raʔiisi*.* What are the chief exports of Germany? *šuu hiyye ṣaadraat ʔalmaanya r-raʔiisiyye?* 3. *ʔawwal.* He's the chief adviser to the prime minister. *huwwe l-məstašaar ᵊl-ʔawwal tabaɛ raʔiis ᵊl-wəzara.*

chief clerk – *baaškaateb* pl. *baaškəttaab, raʔiis˜* (pl. *rəʔasaaʔ˜*) *kəttaab.*

chief engineer – *raʔiis˜* (pl. *rəʔasaaʔ˜*) *ᵊmhandsiin.*

chief inspector – *raʔiis˜* (pl. *rəʔasaaʔ˜*) *ᵊmfattšiin.*

chief justice – *q̈aaḍi˜ l-q̈uḍaat.*

chief of police – *mudiir˜* (pl. *mədaraat˜*) *ᵊš-šərṭa.*

chief of protocol – *mudiir˜* (pl. *mədaraaʔ˜*) *tašriifaat.*

chief of staff – *raʔiis˜* (pl. *rəʔasaaʔ˜*) *ʔarkaan.*

child – *ṭəfᵊl* f. *ṭəfle* pl. *ʔaṭfaal.* They took the child along on the trip. *ʔaxadu ṭ-ṭəfᵊl maɛon bᵊs-safra.* -- I've been used to it ever since I was a child. *ʔana mətɛawwed ɛalée mən waqᵊt-ma kənᵊt ṭəfᵊl* (or ***... mən ṣaġari).* -- I'm interested in child welfare. *ʔana məhtamm ᵊb-riɛaayet ᵊṭ-ṭəfᵊl.*

**Don't be such a child! *ḥaaštak waldane!*

to act (or **behave**) **like a child** – *twaldan.*

childhood – *ṭfuule, ṣaġar.* I spent part of my childhood in the country. *maḍḍeet mədde mn ᵊṭfuulti bᵊr-riif.* -- They were childhood friends. *kaanu ṣḥaab ᵊṭ-ṭfuule.*

childish – *mwaldan.* I've never seen such a childish person in my life. *b-ḥayaati maa šəfᵊt waaḥed ᵊmwaldan heek.*

**That was a childish thing to say! *hal-ḥaki mənnak kaan waldane ɛan ṣaḥiiḥ!*

**Don't be so childish! *ḥaaštak waldane baqa!*

Chile – *š-šiili.*

Chilean – *šiili*.*

chill – *qašɛariire.* I've got a chill. *maɛi qašɛariire.* -- Suddenly I felt a chill. *ɛala ġafle ḥasseet ᵊb-qašɛariire.*

to chill – 1. *barrad.* Chill the glasses before serving the cocktail. *barred ᵊl-kaasaat qabᵊl-ma tqaddem fiihon ᵊl-kokteel.* -- The rain chilled me to the bone. *l-maṭar barradətni ləl-ɛaḍᵊm.* 2. *barad (o ə).* Put the watermelon in the cellar to chill. *ḥəṭṭ ᵊl-baṭṭiixa bᵊl-qabu la-təbrod.*

chilly – 1. *baared.* We were given a chilly reception. *staqbaluuna ʔəstəqbaal baared.* 2. *šwayye bardaan.* I feel chilly. *ʔana šwayye bardaan.*

**It's chilly outside. *d-dənye šwayyet barᵊd barra.*

chimney – 1. *madxane* pl. *madaaxen.* The chimney is being repaired. *ɛam yṣallḥu l-madxane.* 2. *balloora* pl. *-aat.* Where's the chimney for the lamp? *ween ᵊl-balloora tabaɛ ᵊl-kaaz?*

chimpanzee – *šambanzi* (invar.).

chin – *daqᵊn* (f.) pl. *dquun.* He has a protruding chin. *daqno baarze.*

**Chin up! *šədd ḥeelak baqa!*

China – *ṣ-ṣiin.*

china – 1. *maalqi, boorṣalaan, (Chinese) ṣiini*.* The cup is made of the finest china you can buy. *l-fənžaan maɛmuul mən ʔaḥsan maalqi fiik ᵊtlaaqii* *b*ᵊ*s-suuq.* **2.** *ṭaqᵊm˜* (pl. *ṭquumet˜*) *maalqi.* Are you going to use the good china for the dinner tonight? *laḥa tḥaṭṭi ṭaqm* ᵊ*l-maalqi l-*ᵊ*mniiḥ* *ɛal-ɛaša l-yoom?*

Chinese – **1.** *ṣiini**. There are several Chinese restaurants in town. *fii ɛeddet maṭaaɛem ṣiiniyye b*ᵊ*l-balad.* **2.** *ṣiini** pl. *-iyyiin* and *-iyye*, coll. pl. *ṣiin.* I know a number of Chinese students. *baɛref ɛadad* ᵊ*mn* ᵊ*ṭ-ṭəllaab* ᵊ*ṣ-ṣiiniyyiin.* **2.** *ṣiiniyye* pl. *-aat.* Those women are Chinese, not Japanese. *han-nəswaan ṣiiniyyaat, muu yaabaaniyyaat.* **3.** *ṣiini* (invar.). She studied Chinese for about a year. *darset (*ᵊ*ṣ-)ṣiini ḥawaali səne.*

chip – **1.** *šəqfet˜* ᵊ*nšaara* pl. *nšaara.* He hacked away at the log and chips were flying in all directions. *šaffa qərmiit* ᵊ*l-xašab w-qaamet* ᵊ*n-nšaara ṣaaret* ᵊ*ṭṭiir* ᵊ*b-kəll* ᵊ*š-šihaat.* **2.** *fiiše* coll. *fiiš* pl. *fiyaš.* Give me five blue and ten red chips. *ɛaṭiini xamᵊs fiyaš zərᵊq w-ɛašara ḥəmᵊr.*
**He's a chip of the old block. *ṭaaleɛ la-ʔabúu.*
**He always seems to have a chip on his shoulder. *mbayyen ɛaléé daayman naquuz.*

to **chirp** – *zaqzaq.*

chisel – *zmiil* pl. *ʔazamiil.*

chocolate – **1.** *šokolaaṭa, šakaleeṭa.* Is this chocolate sweet or bitter? *haš-šokolaaṭa ḥəlwe wəlla mərra?* — I want to buy a box of chocolates. *bəddi ʔəštə́ri ɛəlbet šokolaaṭa.* **2.** *kaakaaw.* I'd like a cup of (hot) chocolate. *šaaye ɛala baali fənšaan kaakaaw.*

choice – **1.** *tənqaaye.* You made a good choice in (picking) that man. *ɛməlᵊt ṭayyeb* ᵊ*b-tənqaaytak la-har-rəžžaal.* **2.** *ʔəxtiyaar, xiyaar.* If I had the choice I'd go by plane. *law kan-li l-ʔəxtiyaar la-kənᵊt rəḥᵊt b*ᵊ*ṭ-ṭayyaara.* — That doesn't leave us very much of a choice. *haada maa byətrə́k-*ᵊ*lna mažaal* ᵊ*ktiir ləl-ʔəxtiyaar.* **3.** *taškiile* pl. *-aat.* The store has a wide choice of fabrics. *l-maxzan fii taškiile kbiire mn* ᵊ*l-mansuužaat.* **4.** *məmtaaz.* These are choice cuts of meat. *hayy šarḥaat laḥᵊm məmtaaze.*
**I had no other choice. *maa ṭələɛ* ᵊ*b-ʔiidi ġeer heek.*

choir – *žooqa* pl. *-aat, kooras.* He sings in the choir. *biġanni maɛ* ᵊ*ž-žooqa.*

choirboy – *mrattel* pl. *-iin.*

choke – *šarraaqa* pl. *-aat.* Something's wrong with the choke. *fii šii xarbaan b*ᵊ*š-šarraaqa.*
to choke – **1.** *xanaq (o xanᵊq//xtanaq).* You're choking me. *ɛam təxnəqni.* — The collar is choking me. *l-qabbe ɛam təxnəqni.* **2.** *xtanaq.* I nearly choked on that fishbone. *kənᵊt laḥa ʔəxtə́neq mən hal-ḥasake.*
**I could choke you for that remark. *biqəl-li ɛaqli ʔə́dbaḥak ɛala hal-kalaam.*
to choke back – *šaraq (o šarᵊq).* She choked back the tears. *šarqet* ᵊ*dmuuɛa.*
choked up – *masṭuum.* The stovepipe was all choked up. *buuri ṣ-ṣooba kaan kəllo masṭuum.*

cholera – *koleera.*

to **choose** – *naqqa, xtaar, ntaxab.* You'll have to choose between the two. *laazem* ᵊ*tnaqqi waaḥed* ᵊ*mn* ᵊ*t-tneen.* — I chose the books carefully. *naqqeet* ᵊ*l-kətᵊb b-kəll ʔəntibaah.*

choosy – *mwanwan.* Don't be so choosy. *laa tkuun hal-qadd* ᵊ*mwanwan.*

chop – *kastaleeta* pl. *-aat.* We're having chops for dinner. *ɛanna kastaleeta ɛal-ɛaša.*
**The dog licked his chops. *l-kalᵊb laḥas buuzo.*
to chop – *qaṭaɛ (a qaṭᵊɛ//nqaṭaɛ).* Did you chop some wood? *qaṭaɛt* ᵊ*šwayyet ḥaṭab?*
to chop down – *qaṭaɛ (a qaṭᵊɛ//nqaṭaɛ).* They chopped the dead tree down. *qaṭaɛu š-šažara l-mayyte.*
to chop off – *qaṭaɛ (a qaṭᵊɛ//nqaṭaɛ).* Be careful you don't chop your finger off. *ʔoɛa təqṭaɛ ʔəṣbaɛtak.*
to chop up – *qaṭṭaɛ.* Have you chopped up the wood already? *šuu qaṭṭaɛt* ᵊ*l-ḥaṭab?* — Did the butcher chop up the meat for you? *qaṭṭə́ɛ-lak* ᵊ*l-laḥme l-laḥḥaam?*

Christ – *(s-sayyed)* ᵊ*l-masiiḥ.*

to **christen** – **1.** *ɛammad w-samma.* They christened their son John. *ɛammadu ʔəbnon w-sammúu žoon.* **2.** *daššan.* We christened the boat yesterday. *daššanna l-markab* ᵊ*mbaareḥ.*

Christian – *masiiḥi*, nəṣraani** pl. *naṣaara.* He's a member of the Young Men's Christian Association. *huwwe ɛəḍu b-žamɛiiyet* ᵊ*š-šəbbaan* ᵊ*l-masiiḥiyyiin.*

Christianity – **1.** (religion) *(d-dayaane) l-masiiḥiyye.* **2.** (Christendom) *l-ɛaalam* ᵊ*l-masiiḥi, n-naṣaara.*

Christmas – *ɛiid˜* ᵊ*l-miilaad.* Christmas comes on a Wednesday this year. *ɛiid* ᵊ*l-miilaad byəhkom yoom* ᵊ*l-ʔarbaɛa has-səne.* — We've put the Christmas presents under the tree. *ḥaṭṭeena hadaaya ɛiid* ᵊ*l-miilaad taḥt* ᵊ*š-šažara.*

chromium – *kroom.*

chronic – *məzmen.* He has a chronic disease. *maɛo maraḍ məzmen.* — He's a chronic complainer. *huwwe mədzammer məzmen* or ***maa bətšuufo ʔəlla ɛam yədzammar.*

Chtaura – *štuura.*

to **chuckle** – *tkarkar.* He chuckled whenever he thought of it. *kəll-ma kaan yfakker fiiha kaan yətkarkar.*

chum – *rfiiq* pl. *rəfaqa* and *rfaaq.*

chummy – **1.** *ʔaniis.* You'll like him, he's chummy and easy to get along with. *byəɛᵊžbak, huwwe ʔaniis w-dammo xafiif.* **2.** *xooš booš* (invar.). We're not that chummy, you know. *nəḥna maa-lna kəll hal-qadd xooš booš, laahazᵊt kiif.*

church – **1.** *kniise* pl. *kanaayes.* Is there a Catholic church around here? *fii kniise katuliikiyye b-han-nawaaḥi?* **2.** *ṭaayfe* pl. *ṭawaayef.* What church does he belong to? *mən ʔani ṭaayfe huwwe?*

cider – *ɛaṣiir˜ təffaaḥ.*

cigar – *siigaar* pl. *-aat.*
cigar store – *dəkkaanet˜* (pl. *dakakiin˜*) *beeɛ˜ dəxxaan, bayyaaɛ˜* (pl. *-iin˜*) *dəxxaan.*

cigarette – *sigaara* pl. *-aat* and *sagaayer, sikaara* pl. *-aat* and *sawakiir.* Have a cigarette! *tfaḍḍal sigaara!*
cigarette case – *ɛəlbet˜* (pl. *ɛəlab˜*) *sigaara.*
cigarette lighter – *qaddaaḥa* pl. *-aat, wallaaɛa* pl. *-aat.*

cinch – *ḥzaam* pl. *-aat.* This saddle needs a new cinch. *has-sarᵊž laazmo ḥzaam* ᵊ*ždiid.*
**That job's a cinch! *haš-šaġle bətṣiir ɛal-ɛəmyaani.*

cinnamon – *qərfe.*

circle – **1.** *daaʔire* pl. *dawaaʔer.* This circle is too small, draw another one. *had-daaʔire zġiire ktiir, rsoom waaḥde ġeera.* **2.** *ḥalaqa* pl. *-aat.* He has a wide circle of friends. *ɛando ḥalaqa kbiire mn* ᵊ*ṣ-ṣḥaab.* **3.** (pl. only) *ʔawsaaṭ.* It is said in diplomatic circles that ... *biquulu b*ᵊ*l-ʔawsaaṭ* ᵊ*d-diblomaasiyye ʔənno ...*
**This job has him going in circles. *haš-šaġle mlabbəkto ktiir.*
**He's so slow I can run circles around him. *huwwe baṭiiʔ la-daraže fiini laḥḥqo w-ʔana ɛam ʔəzḥaf.*
to circle – *ḥaam (u ø).* The airplane is circling over the town. *ṭ-ṭayyaara ɛam* ᵊ*tḥuum fooq* ᵊ*l-balad.*

circular – **1.** *mdawwar, məstadiir.* There's a circular walk around the garden. *fii manša mdawwar ḥawaali ž-žneene.* **2.** *manšuur* pl. *-aat* and *manašiir.* Our advertising department sends out circulars every month. *qəsm* ᵊ*d-diɛaaye ɛanna biṭaaleɛ manašiir kəll šahᵊr.*

to **circulate** – **1.** *daar (u dawaraan).* This causes the blood to circulate faster. *haada bixalli d-damm yduur ʔasraɛ.* **2.** *daar ɛala ʔalson˜* ᵊ*n-naas.* There's a strange rumor circulating. *fii ʔišaaɛa ġariibe daayre ɛala ʔalson* ᵊ*n-naas.*

circulation – **1.** *dawra damawiyye.* She has poor circulation. *dawrə́ta d-damawiyye ḍɛiife.* **2.** *ʔəntišaar.* Our paper has a circulation of a hundred-fifty thousand. *žariidətna ʔəntišaara miyye w-xamsiin ʔalᵊf ɛadad.*
to put into circulation – *nazzal lət-tadaawol.* The government has put new currency into circulation. *l-*ᵊ*ḥkuume nazzalet ɛəmle ždiide lət-tadaawol.*

circumference – *muḥiiṭ* pl. *-aat, madaar* pl. *-aat.*

circumstances – **1.** *ẓruuf* (pl.), *ʔaḥwaal* (pl.). Under those circumstances I could hardly blame her. *b-haẓ-ẓruuf kiif kaan fiini luuma.* — We still don't know all the circumstances surrounding the event. *ləssaana maa mnaɛref kəll* ᵊ*ẓ-ẓruuf* ᵊ*l-muḥiiṭa b*ᵊ*l-ḥaades.* **2.** *ʔaḥwaal* (pl.). He's in very good circumstances. *ʔaḥwaalo ktiir* ᵊ*mniiḥa.*

circumstantial – *ẓarfi**. He was convicted on circumstantial evidence. *žarramúu ɛala ʔasaas bayyine ẓarfiyye.*

circus – *sərᵊk* pl. *-aat* and *sruuke.*

cistern – *ṣahriiž* pl. *ṣahariiž.*

to **cite** – *stašhad b-.* He cited well-known authors in his speech. *stašhad* ᵊ*b-kəttaab mašhuuriin b-*ᵊ*xṭaabo.*

citified – *mdamšaq.* I can't stand his citified ways. *maa fiini ʔətḥammal ḥarakaato l-*ᵊ*mdamšaqa.*

citizen – *mwaaṭen* pl. *-iin.* He addressed the leading

citizens of his town. *xaṭab b-ᵊkbaar l-ᵊmwaaṭniin ᵊb-balado.*
**I'm an American citizen. *žənsiiti ʔameerkiyye.*

citizenship – *žənsiyye* pl. *-aat.* We applied for citizenship last month. *ṭalabna ž-žənsiyye š-šahr ᵊl-maaḍi.*

city – **1.** *madiine* pl. *mədon, balad* pl. *blaad.* How far is the nearest city? *qaddeeš ᵊbtəbᶜed ʔaqrab madiine?* -- The addresses of all residents may be found in the city directory. *ᶜanawiin kəll ᵊl-ʔahaali bətlaaqiiha b-daliil ᵊl-ᶜanawiin tabaᶜ ᵊl-balad.* **2.** *madiine.* She's not accustomed to city life. *maa-la mətᶜawwde ᶜala ḥayaat ᵊl-madiine.* **3.** *baladiyye.* She is in the city hospital. *hiyye b-məstašfa l-baladiyye.*
city hall – *(daar˜) ᵊl-baladiyye.*

civil – **1.** *mʔaddab.* At least he was civil to us. *ᶜal-qaliili kaan ᵊmʔaddab maᶜna.* **2.** *laayeq.* That was the only civil thing for him to do. *haada kaan ᵊš-šii l-laayeq ᵊl-waḥiid halli kaan laazem yaᶜᵊmlo.* **3.** *madani*.* This concerns the civil authorities. *haada mən ʔəxtiṣaaṣ ᵊṣ-ṣəlṭaat ᵊl-madaniyye.* -- Civil Code. *l-qaanuun ᵊl-madani.*
civil servant – *mwaẓẓaf˜* (pl. *-iin˜*) *ᵊḥkuume.*
civil service – *xədme ḥkuumiyye.*

civilian – **1.** *madani** pl. *-iyyiin.* There were civilians and soldiers in the crowd. *kaan fii madaniyyiin w-ᶜaskariyyiin bᵊl-ḥašᵊd.* **2.** *madani*.* Was he wearing civilian clothes? *kaan laabes ʔawaaᶜi madaniyye?* or *kaan laabes madani?*

civilization – *ḥaḍaara* pl. *-aat.*

civilized – *mmaddan.* If they were really civilized, they'd settle the matter peacefully. *law kaanu ḥaqiiqatan ᵊmmaddaniin kaanu yḥəllu l-məšᵊkle b-salaam.*

claim – *mṭaalabe* pl. *-aat, ʔəddiᶜaaʔ* pl. *-aat.* His claim to the land is no longer valid. *mṭaalabto bᵊl-ʔarᵊḍ maa ᶜaadet ṣaḥiiḥa.*
to lay claim to – *ddaᶜa b-, ṭaalab b-.* I lay no claim to that. *maa bəddəᶜi b-haš-šii.*
to claim – **1.** *ṭaalab b-, ddaᶜa b-.* I claim my share. *bṭaaleb ᵊb-ḥəṣṣti.* **2.** *ddaᶜa, zaᶜam (o zaᶜᵊm).* She claims to know the man. *btəddəᶜi ʔənno btaᶜref ᵊr-rəžžaal.*
**Where do I claim my baggage? *mneen bəqder ʔaaxod ᶜafši?*

clamp – *mšadd* pl. *-aat, kammaaše* pl. *-aat.* Leave the clamp on while the glue dries. *xalli l-ᵊmšadd la-been-ma yənšaf ᵊl-ġəre.*
to clamp – *šadd (ə šadd//nšadd).* Clamp the two boards together. *šədd ᵊl-looḥeen ᶜala baᶜḍon.*

to **clap** – *saffaq.* The audience clapped when he finished his speech. *l-ḥaaḍriin saffaqu lamma ntaha mən xiṭaabo.* -- He clapped his hands for the waiter. *saffaq ləl-ġarṣoon.*

to **clarify** – *waḍḍaḥ, fassar.* Can you clarify this passage for me? *fiik ᵊtwaḍḍəḥ-li hal-maqṭaᶜ?*

clash – *ʔəṣṭidaam* pl. *-aat, ʔəštibaak* pl. *-aat.* There have been no border clashes since the truce. *maa ᶜaad ṣaar ʔəṣṭidaamaat ᶜal-ᵊḥduud mən waqt ᵊl-hədne.*
to clash – **1.** *ḍḍaarabu maᶜ baᶜḍon.* Those two colors clash. *hal-looneen byəḍḍaarabu maᶜ baᶜḍon.* **2.** *ṣṭadam, tšaabak.* Demonstrators clashed with the police early this morning. *fii mədẓaahriin ᵊṣṭadamu maᶜ ᵊš-šərṭa l-yoom qabl ᵊḍ-ḍəhᵊr.*

clasp – *qəfᵊl* pl. *qfuule* and *qfaal, bakle* pl. *-aat.* The clasp on my bracelet is broken. *qəfl ᵊswaarti manzuuᶜ.*
to clasp – **1.** *šadd (ə šadd) ᶜala.* She clasped my hand in both of hers. *šaddet ᶜala ʔiidi b-ʔiideeha.* **2.** *ḍamm (ə ḍamm), ḥaḍan (o ḥaḍᵊn).* She clasped the baby to her breast. *ḍammet ᵊl-walad la-ṣədra.*

class – **1.** *darᵊs* pl. *druus(e).* My first class starts at eight-thirty. *ʔawwal darᵊs ᶜandi byəbda s-saaᶜa tmaane w-nəṣṣ.* -- Classes begin in September. *d-druus ᵊbtəbda b-ʔeeluul.* **2.** *darᵊs* pl. *druus(e), maadde* pl. *mawaadd.* How many classes did you have the first semester? *kam darᵊs kaan ᶜandak bᵊl-faṣl ᵊl-ʔawwal?* **3.** *ṣaff* pl. *ṣfuuf(e).* I'll meet you in class. *bšuufak bᵊṣ-ṣaff.* **4.** *mətxarržiin* (pl.). Most of last year's class have good positions now. *məᶜẓam ᵊl-mətxarržiin tabaᶜ ᵊs-səne l-maaḍye ṣar-lon maraakez ᵊmniiḥa hallaq.* **5.** *mawaliid* (pl.). The classes of 1924 and 1925 were called up. *mawaliid sənᵊt ʔarᵊbᶜa w-ᶜəšriin w-xamsa w-ᶜəšriin ṭalabuuhon ləl-xədme.* **6.** *ṭabaqa* pl. *-aat.* The educated class in our country is growing rapidly. *ṭ-ṭabaqa l-mətᶜallme b-blaadna ᶜam təzdaad ᵊb-sərᶜa.* **7.** *nooᶜ* pl. *nwaaᶜ, ṣənᵊf* pl. *ʔaṣnaaf.* This class of books is suitable for children only. *han-nooᶜ ᵊmn ᵊl-kətᵊb xarž ᵊwlaad bass.* **8.** *daraže* pl. *-aat.* I'm traveling second-class this time. *msaafer hal-marra bᵊd-daraže t-taanye* or **msaafer hal-marra bᵊs-səkondo.*
**This car has class! *has-sayyaara mqaddara məmtaaze.*

classical – **1.** *klaasiiki*.* I prefer to listen to classical music. *bfaḍḍel ʔəsmaᶜ muusiiqa klaasiikiyye.* **2.** *faṣiiḥ,* (f. only) *fəṣḥa.* He delivered his speech in classical Arabic. *ʔalqa xiṭaabo bᵊl-ᶜarabi l-faṣiiḥ* (or *bᵊl-ᶜarabiyye l-fəṣḥa*).

classification – *taṣniif.* What classification do these plants belong in? *šuu taṣniif han-nabataat?*

to **classify** – *ṣannaf, bawwab.* Will you help me classify these books? *bətsaaᶜədni ṣannef hal-kətᵊb?*
classified – **1.** *sərri*.* Don't give out any classified information. *laa tbuuḥ ᵊb-ʔayy maᶜluumaat sərriyye.* **2.** *mbawwab.* I'd like to put a classified ad in tomorrow's paper. *bəddi ḥəṭṭ ʔəᶜlaan ᵊmbawwab ᵊb-žariidet bəkra.*

classroom – *ṣaff* pl. *ṣfuuf(e).* The teacher is still in the classroom. *l-ʔəstaaz ləssᶜa bᵊṣ-ṣaff.*

clatter – *qarqaᶜa, ṭarṭaqa.* We heard the clatter of dishes in the kitchen. *sməᶜna qarqaᶜt ᵊṣ-ṣḥuun bᵊl-maṭbax.*

clause – **1.** *banᵊd* pl. *bnuud(e), šarᵊṭ* pl. *šruuṭ.* Our lease should contain a clause covering property damage. *ᶜaqd ᵊl-ʔiižaar tabaᶜna b-raʔyi laazem yəḍḍamman banᵊd yġaṭṭi ʔayy ᶜəṭl ᵊw-ḍarar bᵊl-məlᵊk.* **2.** *žəmle* pl. *žəmal.* In Arabic, we use a circumstantial clause in this case. *bᵊl-ᶜarabi mnəstaᶜmel žəmle ḥaaliyye b-heek ḥaale.*

claw – **1.** *maxlab* pl. *maxaaleb.* The hawk had a mouse in its claws. *ṣ-ṣaqᵊr kaan ḥaamel faara b-maxaalbo.* **2.** *ḍəfᵊr* pl. *ʔaḍafiir, maxlab* pl. *maxaaleb.* That cat sure has sharp claws! *hal-qaṭṭa ʔaḍafiira ḥadde ᶜan ḥaqa!*
to claw – *xarmaš.* Watch out, that cat'll claw you! *ʔoᶜa l-qaṭṭa laḥa txarᵊmšak!*

clay – *ṭiin.* Is this clay good for pottery? *haṭ-ṭiin ᵊmniiḥ la-msaawaat ᵊl-fəxxaar?* -- The huts are built of clay. *l-ᵊkwaax mabniyye mən ṭiin.*
**You'll find your hero has feet of clay. *bətšuuf ṣaaḥbak bᵊl-wəšš ᵊrxaam w-bᵊl-qafa ṣxaam.*

clean – **1.** *ndiif* pl. *ndaaf.* This plate is not clean. *haṣ-ṣaḥᵊn muu ndiif.* **2.** *basiiṭ.* The new building has very clean lines. *l-binaaye ž-ždiide taṣmiima basiiṭ ᵊktiir.*
**Scrub the floor clean. *naḍḍef ᵊl-ʔarḍ ᵊmniiḥ.*
**Here's a clean draft of my thesis. *hayy məbyaḍḍa mən ʔəṭruuḥti.*
**The thieves got clean away. *l-ḥaramiyye maa ᶜaad ban-lon ʔasar.*
**A new broom sweeps clean. *s-səkkiine ž-ždiide daayman btəbqa ṭayybe.*
to clean – **1.** *naḍḍaf.* Has the maid cleaned the room yet? *l-xaadme naḍḍafet ᵊl-ʔuuḍa wəlla ləssa?* -- Please clean the chicken for me. *mən faḍlak naḍḍəf-li ž-žaaže.* -- Where can I have my clothes cleaned? *ween fiini ʔəbᶜat ʔawaaᶜiyyi lət-tanḍiif?* **2.** *farša, naḍḍaf.* I have to clean my teeth. *laazem farši snaani.*
to clean house – *ᶜazzal ᵊl-beet.* We're cleaning house. *ᶜam ᵊnᶜazzel ᵊl-beet.*
**The new administration will have to clean house. *l-ᵊḥkuume ž-ždiide laazem ᵊtnaḍḍef ᵊž-žihaaz l-ᵊḥkuumi.*
to clean out – *faḍḍa.* She's going to clean out the desk before she leaves. *laḥa tfaḍḍi ṭ-ṭaawle qabᵊl-ma twaddeᶜ.*
**They cleaned me out all right. *šannaṭuuni la-ʔaaxer qərᵊš maᶜi.*
to clean up – **1.** *ġassal, xassal.* I'd like to clean up before dinner. *žaaye ᶜala baali ġassel qabl ᵊl-ᶜaša.* **2.** *naḍḍaf.* When are you going to clean up the mess in your room? *ʔeemta laḥa tnaḍḍef ᵊl-karkabe b-ʔuuḍtak?*

cleaner – **1.** *mnaḍḍef* pl. *-aat.* This cleaner will remove all the spots. *hal-ᵊmnaḍḍef biziil kəll ᵊl-bəqaᶜ.* **2.** *maṣbaġa* pl. *maṣaabeġ, maḥall˜* (pl. *-aat˜*) *tanḍiifaat, kawwa* pl. *kawwaaye.* Do you know of a good cleaner around here? *btaᶜrəf-li šii maṣbaġa mniiḥa b-han-nawaaḥi?* -- Most of my dresses are at the cleaner's. *ʔaktar ʔawaaᶜiyyi bᵊl-maṣbaġa* (or *b-maḥall ᵊt-tanḍiifaat* or *ᶜand ᵊl-kawwa*). -- Please take this suit to the cleaner. *mən faḍlak xəd-li hal-badle ᶜal-maṣbaġa* (or *ᶜat-tanḍiifaat* or *la-ƐEand ˀl-kamwa).*

cleaning - *tandiif.* The house needs a good cleaning. *l-beet laazmo tandiif maaken.*

cleaning plant - *mahall˜ (pl. -aat˜) tandiifaat.*

cleaning woman - *ṣaanƐa* pl. *-aat* and *ṣənnaaƐ, xaadme* pl. *-aat.*

cleanser - *mnaddef* pl. *-aat.*

clear - **1.** *ṣaafi, raayeq.* The water is deep and clear. *l-mayy ğamiiqa w-ṣaafye.* -- We have had clear weather all week. *ṭ-ṭaqˀṣ kaan raayeq kəll ˀš-šəmƐa l-maadye.* -- Try to keep a clear head. *ḥaawel ˀtxalli tafkiirak ṣaafi.* **2.** *waadeḥ.* His voice was very clear over the radio. *ṣooṭo Ɛar-raadyo kaan waadeḥ ˀktiir.* -- It is clear from the letter that he isn't satisfied. *waadeḥ ˀmn ˀl-maktuub ˀənno maa-lo radyaan.* **3.** *saalek.* Is the road clear up ahead? *ṭ-ṭariiq saalek qəddaam?* **4.** *mərtaaḥ.* Don't look at me! My conscience is clear. *laa tbaḥleq fiyyi! damiiri mərtaaḥ.*

**Did I make myself clear on that point? *nšaaḷḷa kuun fahhamtak han-nəqṭa b-wuduuḥ.*

**The news came out of a clear sky. *l-xabar nəzel mətl ˀs-saaƐiğa.*

**They found the culprit so you're in the clear now. *baƐˀd-ma laqu l-məzneb ˀənte hallaq ˀtbarreet.*

to clear - **1.** *naḍḍam.* Did you clear the table? *naḍḍamti ṭ-ṭaawle?* **2.** *barra.* The hearing cleared him completely. *l-ˀmḥaakame barrto tamaam.* **3.** *txallaṣ mən.* My bags haven't cleared customs yet. *šanatiyyi ləssa maa txallaṣu mn ˀl-gəmrok.* **4.** *xallaṣ Ɛala.* We can't give you any money until we clear your check. *maa mnəqder naƐṭiik maṣaari qabˀl-ma nxalleṣ Ɛala šakkak.* **5.** *txallaṣ Ɛala* + pron. suff. of subject. The checks haven't cleared yet. *š-šakkaat ləssa maa txallaṣ Ɛaleehon.* **6.** *ṣəḥi (a ṣaḥu).* The sky is clearing at last. *s-sama ˀaxiiran Ɛam təṣḥa.*

**The horse cleared the wall easily. *l-ˀḥṣaan naṭṭ fooq ˀl-ḥeeṭ b-ˀshuule.*

**The truck will clear the underpass easily. *l-kamyoon byəmroq bˀn-nafaq b-ˀshuule.*

to clear away - *qaam (i qayamaan//nqaam).* Ask her to clear away the dishes. *qəl-la tqiim ˀṣ-ṣḥuun.*

to clear off - *qaam (i qayamaan//nqaam).* Clear this stuff off your table! *qiim hal-ˀğraad mən Ɛala ṭaawəltak!*

to clear one's throat - *tnaḥnaḥ.* The speaker cleared his throat. *l-xaṭiib ˀtnaḥnaḥ.*

to clear out - **1.** *fadda.* Please clear out this closet. *mən fadlak faddi hal-ˀxzaane.* **2.** *šammaƐ ˀl-xeeṭ, fardk(h)a.* He cleared out in the middle of the night. *šammaƐ ˀl-xeeṭ ˀb-sawaad ˀl-leel.* -- Clear out, and fast! *frəka qawaam!*

to clear up - **1.** *ḥall (ə ḥall//nḥall), dabbar// ddabbar.* We'll have to clear up this problem before we go on to the next one. *laazem ˀnḥəll hal-masˀale qabˀl-ma nəntəqel lət-taanye.* **2.** *ṣəḥi (a ṣaḥu).* The weather has cleared up. *ṭ-ṭaqˀṣ ṣəḥi.*

clearance - **1.** *mažaal, wasƐa.* The truck has plenty of clearance on that side. *l-kamyoon ˀəlo mažaal waafer ˀb-hal-ṭaraf.* **2.** *mwaafaqa rasmiyye.* You'll need a clearance to work here. *laazmak ˀmwaafaqa rasmiyye la-təštəğel hoon.*

clearly - *b-wuduuḥ.* Please speak clearly! *Ɛmeel maƐruuf ˀəḥki b-wuduuḥ!*

clergy - *ˀəkliiros.*

clergyman - *qəssiis* pl. *qasaawse.*

clerical - *ktaabi*.* She's looking for clerical work. *Ɛam ˀddawwer Ɛala šağle ktaabiyye.*

clerk - **1.** *kaateb* pl. *kəttaab* and *katabe.* He's a clerk in a big office. *huwwe kaateb ˀb-maktab ˀkbiir.* **2.** *bayyaaƐ* pl. *-iin.* I can't find a clerk to wait on me. *maa-li Ɛam laaqi bayyaaƐ yšuuf šuu bəddi.*

clever - **1.** *zaki** pl. *ˀazkiya, fəteḥ, fəṭen, šaaṭer.* He's a clever fellow. *huwwe zalame zaki.* **2.** *šaaṭer, maaher.* This tailor is very clever at altering suits. *hal-xayyaaṭ šaaṭer ˀktiir ˀb-taṣliiḥ ˀl-badlaat.* **3.** *fahmaan.* This situation calls for a clever businessman. *hal-wadˀƐ byəṭṭallab ražol ˀaƐmaal fahmaan.* **4.** *ḥədeq.* She's always saying clever things. *daayman bətquul šağlaat ḥədqa.*

click - *ṭaqqa* pl. *-aat.* I heard the click of the lock. *sməƐˀt ṭaqqet ˀl-qəfˀl.*

to click - **1.** *ṭaqṭaq.* I think I heard the lock click. *kaˀənni sməƐt ˀl-qəfˀl Ɛam yṭaqṭeq.* **2.** *məši (i maši).* Everything clicked beautifully. *kəll šii məši Ɛala maa yuraam.*

**The show clicked the first night. *t-tamsiiliyye mən ˀawwal leele ṣar-la rawaaž.*

to click shut - *ntaras, nṭabaq.* The door clicked shut. *l-baab ˀntaras.*

client - *zbuun* pl. *zabaayen.* He sent some of his clients to another lawyer. *baƐat baƐˀḍ zabaayno la-muḥaami taani.*

climate - **1.** *manaax* pl. *-aat.* The climate here is colder than I expected. *l-manaax hoon ˀabrad məmma kənt ˀmḥasseb.* **2.** *žaww.* The political climate in that country is just right for a revolution. *ž-žaww ˀs-siyaasi b-hal-ˀblaad xəṣeb tamaam la-šii sawra.*

climax - *zarwe.*

climb - *ṭalƐa* pl. *-aat.* You'll find the climb steep and difficult. *laḥa tlaaqi ṭ-ṭalƐa waaqfe w-ṣaƐbe.*

to climb - **1.** *tƐarbaš (Ɛala).* The boys climbed the tree. *l-ˀwlaad ˀtƐarbašu Ɛaš-šažara.* -- He climbed over the fence. *tƐarbaš mən fooq ˀl-xəṣṣ.* **2.** *tsallaq.* I haven't yet climbed the mountain. *ləssa maa tsallaqt ˀž-žabal.* **3.** *ṭəleƐ (a ṭluuƐ, ṭalƐa) Ɛala.* I don't like to climb stairs. *maa bḥəbb ˀəṭlaƐ Ɛad-daraž.* **4.** *Ɛalla.* The plane began to climb rapidly. *ṭ-ṭayyaara badet ˀtƐalli b-sərƐa.*

to climb down - *nəzel (e nzuul).* The boy climbed down the ladder. *l-walad nəzel Ɛas-səllom.*

to climb up - *ṭəleƐ (a ṭluuƐ, ṭalƐa) Ɛala.* Can you climb up a ladder? *btəqder təṭlaƐ Ɛala šii səllom?*

to clinch - **1.** *baššam.* The nail can't hold if you don't clinch it. *l-bəsmaar maa biƐalleq ˀiza maa bətbaššmo.* **2.** *sabbat.* Have you clinched the deal at last? *sabbatt ˀṣ-ṣafqa ˀaxiiran?*

to cling - **1.** *tƐallaq.* The child is clinging to its mother. *ṭ-ṭəfˀl mətƐalleq ˀb-ˀəmmo.* **2.** *lazzaq.* Your clothes cling to you in this humid weather. *ˀawaƐiik bətlazzeq fiik ˀb-heek ṭaqˀṣ rəṭeb.*

clinic - *Ɛyaade* pl. *-aat.* You can get free treatment at the clinic. *fiik təṭṭabbab ˀb-balaaš bˀl-ˀƐyaade.*

clip - **1.** *šakle* pl. *-aat.* She wore a golden clip on her dress. *kaanet ḥaaṭṭa šakle dahab Ɛala rooba.* **2.** *məšˀṭ* pl. *mšaaṭ.* He put a new clip in the rifle and continued firing. *ḥaṭṭ məšṭ ˀždiid bˀl-bənduğiyye w-taabaƐ l-ˀqwaaṣ.*

paper clip - *šakkaalet˜ (pl. -aat˜) waraq.* Please give me a box of paper clips. *mən fadlak Ɛaṭiini Ɛəlbet šakkaalaat waraq.*

to clip - **1.** *qaṣṣ (ə qaṣṣ//nqaṣṣ).* Don't clip my hair too short! *laa tqəṣṣ-əlli šaƐri qaṣiir ˀktiir.* -- The gardener clipped the hedge. *ž-žneenaati qaṣṣ ˀs-syaaž.* -- I clipped this article out of a magazine. *qaṣṣeet hal-mağaale mən mažalle.* **2.** *šakal (o šakˀl), šakkal.* Clip this sheet to the others and put them aside. *škool hal-waraqa maƐ ˀl-baqiyye w-ḥəṭṭon Ɛala žanab.* -- Clip these papers together. *šakkel hal-ˀwraaq maƐ baƐdon.*

clippers - *maakiint˜ (pl. -aat˜) ˀḥlaaqa.*

clipping - *qṣaaṣa* pl. *-aat.* He sent me a newspaper clipping about the election. *baƐdt-li qṣaaṣet žariide Ɛan ˀl-ˀəntixaabaat.*

cloakroom - *maḥall˜ (pl. -aat˜) manaaṭi.*

clock - *saaƐa* pl. *-aat.* We always set our clock by the radio. *daayman ˀmnəẓboṭ saaƐətna Ɛar-raadyo.*

alarm clock - *saaƐa mnabbeh.* pl. *saaƐaat ˀmnabbeh.* I was late for work because my alarm clock didn't ring. *tˀaxxarˀt Ɛaš-šəğˀl laˀənno saaƐti l-ˀmnabbeh maa ṭannet.*

to clock - *Ɛayyar ˀl-waqˀt Ɛala.* Will you clock him in this race? *bətƐayyer Ɛalée l-waqt ˀb-has-sabaq?*

clockwise - *maƐ Ɛaqaareb˜ ˀs-saaƐa.* Just turn that handle clockwise. *bass dawwer hal-maske maƐ Ɛaqaareb ˀs-saaƐa.*

clockwork: Their business runs like clockwork. *šəğlon maaši mətl ˀs-saaƐa.*

clog - *bqaab* pl. *qabaqiib.* It looks like I need a new pair of shower clogs. *mbayyen laazəmni žooz qabaqiib ḥammaam ždad.*

to clog (up) - **1.** *ṣaṭam (o ṣaṭˀm//nṣaṭam).* Something clogged the drain. *fii šii ṣaṭam ˀl-balluuƐa.* **2.** *nṣaṭam.* The drains clog up whenever it rains. *l-mazariib ˀbtənṣəṭem lamma bətmaṭṭer.*

close - **1.** *ˀəntihaaˀ, ˀaaxer.* I'll see you at the close of the meeting. *mnəltəqi sawa baƐˀd ˀəntihaaˀ (or b-ˀaaxer) ˀl-ˀəžtimaaƐ.* **2.** *ḥamiim.* He's a close friend of mine. *huwwe ṣaaḥeb ḥamiim ˀəli.* **3.** *qariib* pl. *qraab.* That plan is pretty close to what we want. *hal-xəṭṭa qariibe nooƐan maa la-halli b-baalna.* -- We sat close together. *qaƐadna qraab la-baƐˀdna.* -- The hotel is close to the station. *l-ˀoteel qariib Ɛal-ˀmḥaṭṭa.* **4.** *maḥṣuur.* The air is very close in this room. *l-hawa mahsuur ᵊktiir ᵊb-hal-ʔuuda.* **5.** *daqiiq.* Close scrutiny revealed a number of errors in this report. *t-tadqiiq ᵊd-daqiiq ᵊb-taqriiro ʔaghar Ɛeddet ʔaglaat.*

**He won by a close vote. *rəbeh ᵊb-farᵊq daʔiil bᵊl-ʔaswaat.*

**Pay close attention! *ntəbeh ᵊmniih!*

**That was a close call! *wallaahi kaan ᵊl-xalaas Ɛəžbe!*

close by - *bᵊl-qərᵊb.* Is there a restaurant close by? *fii matƐam bᵊl-qərᵊb?*

from close up - *Ɛan qariib, mən qariib.* From close up it looks entirely different. *Ɛan qariib baayne tamaam ġeer šəkᵊl.*

to close - **1.** *sakkar//tsakkar.* Please close the door! *Ɛmeel maƐruuf sakker ᵊl-baab!* -- The stores close at six. *l-maxaazen bətsakker ᵊs-saaƐa sətte.* -- The road is closed for repairs. *t-tariiq ᵊmsakkar lət-taƐbiid.* **2.** *tsakkar.* The door closed quietly. *l-baab ᵊtsakkar biduun soot.* **3.** *Ɛaqad (o Ɛaqᵊd//nƐaqad).* We closed the deal this morning. *Ɛaqadna s-safqa l-yoom Ɛala bəkra.* **4.** *xatam (o xatᵊm//nxatam).* They closed the conference in an atmosphere of toleration and understanding. *xatamu l-məʔtdmar ᵊb-žaww kəllo tasaamoh w-tafaahom.*

**Don't close your eyes to the facts! *laa tətġaada Ɛan ᵊl-waaqeƐ!*

closely - *b-dəqqa.* Look at it closely. *ttallaƐ Ɛaleeha b-dəqqa* or ***daqqeq ᵊn-nazar fiiha.*

closet - *xzaane* pl. *-aat* and *xazaayen.* Her closet is full of new clothes. *xzaanə́ta malaane ʔawaaƐi ždiide.*

cloth - **1.** *qmaaš* pl. *ʔaqmiše.* Do you have this cloth in a better quality? *fii Ɛandkon hal-ᵊqmaaš ᵊb-žənᵊs ʔahsan?* **2.** *xərqa* pl. *xəraq, qmaaše* pl. *-aat* and *qamaayeš, šartuuta* pl. *šaratiit.* Use a clean cloth for dusting. *staƐᵊmli xərqa ndiife la-mash ᵊl-ġabra.*

**He made the story up out of whole cloth. *fabrak ᵊl-qəssa mən ʔawwdla la-ʔaaxə́ra.*

cloth binding - *žəldet˜ (pl. žluud˜) ᵊqmaaš.* The book has a cloth binding. *žəldet l-ᵊktaab ᵊqmaaš.*

to **clothe** - *kasa (i kəswe//nkasa).* Who's going to feed and clothe all those poor children? *miin laha ytaƐmi w-yəksi kəll hal-ʔatfaal ᵊl-fəqara?*

clothes - *ʔawaaƐi* (pl.), *tyaab* (pl.), *malaabes* (pl.). She wants to buy some new clothes. *bədda təštə́ri ʔawaaƐi ždad.*

**Clothes make the man. *l-ʔənsaan nəsso xə́rqa w-nəsso xəlqa.*

clothes closet - *xzaanet˜* (pl. *-aat˜* and *xazaayen˜*) *ʔawaaƐi.*

clothes hanger - *Ɛəlleeqet˜* (pl. *-aat˜*) *ʔawaaƐi.*

clothes hook - *Ɛəlleeqet˜* (pl. *-aat˜*) *ʔawaaƐi.*

clothes rack - *Ɛəlleeqet˜* (pl. *-aat˜*) *ʔawaaƐi.*

clothes tree - *taƐliiqa* pl. *taƐaliiq.*

clothesline - *habᵊl˜* (pl. *hbaal˜*) *ġasiil.*

clothespin - *malqat˜* (pl. *malaaqet˜*) *ġasiil, šakkaalet˜* (pl. *-aat˜*) *ġasiil.*

clothing - *ʔawaaƐi* (pl.), *tyaab* (pl.), *malaabes* (pl.).

cloud - *ġeeme* coll. *ġeem* pl. *-aat* and *ġyuum.* The sun has disappeared behind the clouds. *š-šams ᵊxtafet wara l-ġeem.*

**The car disappeared in a cloud of dust. *s-sayyaara maa Ɛaadet baanet mən ᵊƐžiiž l-ᵊġbaar.*

**My friend always has his head in the clouds. *saahbi daayman Ɛaqlo saabeh bᵊl-xayaal.*

to cloud - *labbad.* This recent development has clouded the political situation. *hat-tatawwor ᵊl-ʔaxiir labbad ᵊl-wadƐ ᵊs-siyaasi.*

to cloud up - *ġayyam.* Just after we started on our way the sky clouded up. *haalan baƐᵊd-ma mšiina b-tariiqna s-sama ġayyamet.*

cloudy - **1.** *mġayyem.* Better take an umbrella; it's rather cloudy today. *ʔahsán-lak taaxə́d-lak šamsiyye maƐak; haakem ᵊd-dənye mġayyme l-yoom.* **2.** *ġaamed, məbham.* That was pretty cloudy reasoning if you ask me. *ʔiza bəddak raʔyi haada kaan taƐliil šwayye ġaamed.*

clover - *barsiim.*

club - **1.** *Ɛasaaye* pl. *-aat* and *Ɛəsi.* The policeman had to use his club. *š-šərti nžabar yəstaƐmel Ɛasaayto.* **2.** *naadi* pl. *nawaadi* and *ʔandiye.* Are you a member of the club? *ʔənte Ɛədu bᵊn-naadi?* **3.** *sbaati* (invar.). I bid one club. *bsammi waahed sbaati.*

clue - **1.** *ʔasar* pl. *ʔaasaar.* This clue may help us find the murderer. *hal-ʔasar bižuus ysaaƐedna nlaaqi l-qaatel.* **2.** *ʔišaara* pl. *-aat, talmiiha* pl. *-aat.* Can you give me a clue? *btəqder taƐtiini šii ʔišaara?*

clumsy - **1.** *malxuum, səmež.* Don't be so clumsy! *laa tkuun hal-qadd malxuum!* **2.** *ġaliiz* pl. *ġlaaz.* He's as clumsy as a bear. *huwwe ġaliiz mətl ᵊd-dəbb.* **3.** *baayex.* That's a pretty clumsy excuse. *haada Ɛəzᵊr baayex šwayye.*

clutch - *dəbᵊryaaž.* Take your foot off the clutch! *qiim rəžlak Ɛan ᵊd-dəbᵊryaaž!*

**He had him in his clutches. *kaan maasko mən xawaniiqo.*

to clutch - *tkammaš b-.* The child clutched my hand. *t-təfl ᵊtkammaš ᵊb-ʔiidi.*

to clutch at - *madd (ə madd) ʔiido la-.* He clutched at the rope but missed it. *madd ʔiido la-yəmsek ᵊl-habᵊl bass maa lahhaq.*

coach - **1.** *fargoon* pl. *-aat* and *faragiin.* In the train crash one of the coaches fell down the embankment. *b-tahwiiret ᵊt-treen waahed ᵊmn ᵊl-faragiin wəqeƐ mən Ɛala kətf ᵊt-tariiq.* **2.** *mdarreb* pl. *-iin.* He's the best coach the team ever had. *huwwe ʔahsan ᵊmdarreb ʔəža ləl-fariiq.*

to coach - *darrab.* He coached him for the examination. *darrabo mənšaan ᵊl-fahᵊs.*

coal - **1.** *fahᵊm* pl. *fhuum.* We have to order coal. *laazem ᵊnwassi Ɛala fahᵊm.* **2.** *žamra* coll. *žamᵊr* pl. *-aat.* Set the pot on the coals. *hətti t-tanžara Ɛaž-žamᵊr.*

**They really raked him over the coals for such a stupid mistake. *haraqu diino Ɛan sahiih mənšaan ġalta saxiife mətᵊl hayy.*

coal bin - *tanaket˜ (-aat˜) fahᵊm.*

coal mine - *manžam˜* (pl. *manaažem˜*) *fahᵊm.*

coalition - **1.** *ʔəʔtilaaf* pl. *-aat.* The coalition lasted only six months. *l-ʔəʔtilaaf daam bass sətt əšhor.* **2.** *ʔəʔtilaafi**. A coalition government may bring stability to the country. *hkuume ʔəʔtilaafiyye məmken təžleb ᵊl-ʔəstəqraar la-hal-ᵊblaad.*

coarse - **1.** *xəšen.* They covered the chairs with very coarse material. *ġattu l-karaasi b-ᵊqmaaš xəšen ᵊktiir.* **2.** *ġaliiz, tqiil.* His manners are coarse. *tasarrufaato ġaliiza.*

coast - *saahel* pl. *sawaahel, šatt* pl. *štuut* and *šawaati.* We approached the coast at night. *qarrabna Ɛas-saahel bᵊl-leel.*

**The coast is clear. *ž-žaww xaali.*

Coast Guard - *haras˜ ᵊš-šawaateʔ.*

to coast - *karr (ə karr).* The automobile coasted to a stop. *s-sayyaara dallet ᵊtkərr hatta waqqafet.* -- They coasted down the hill on their bicycles. *karru bᵊn-nazle Ɛala bəsᵊkleetaaton.*

**We've done enough work; we can coast now. *štaġalna kfaaye, fiina nəmši Ɛala mahᵊlna hallaq.*

coat - **1.** *manto* pl. *mantoyaat* and *mantohaat* and *manaati, kabbuud* pl. *kababiid, balto* pl. *baltoyaat.* You can't go without a coat in this weather. *haraam Ɛaleek ᵊtruuh bala manto b-heek taqᵊs.* **2.** *žaakeet* pl. *-aat* and *žawakiit.* The pants and vest fit, but the coat is too small. *l-bantaroon wᵊs-sədriyye žaayiin ᵊmnaah laaken ᵊž-žaakeet ᵊzġiir ᵊktiir.* **3.** *šaƐᵊr.* The foal has a beautiful coat. *l-məhᵊr šaƐro həlu.* **4.** *wəšš* pl. *wšuuh.* This door needs another coat of paint. *hal-baab laazmo wəšš ᵊdhaan taani.*

coat hanger - *Ɛəlleeqet˜* (pl. *-aat˜*) *ʔawaaƐi.*

coated - *mġatta.* The car was coated with mud. *s-sayyaara kaanet ᵊmġattaaye bᵊt-tiin.*

**Your tongue is coated. *lsaanak wəsex* (or *ʔabyad*).

cobbler - *skaafi* pl. *-iyye.*

cobweb - *Ɛəšš˜* (pl. *Ɛšaaš˜*) *Ɛankabuut.* There's a huge cobweb in that corner. *fii Ɛəšš Ɛankabuut ᵊkbiir ᵊb-hal-qərne.*

cockroach - *sarsuur* pl. *sarasiir.*

cocoa - *kaakaaw.*

coconut - *žooset˜* (coll. *žoos˜* pl. *-aat˜*) *hənᵊd.*

C.O.D. - *t-tasliim Ɛand ᵊd-dafᵊƐ.* I'll mail the package to you C.O.D. *bəbƐə́t-lak ᵊt-tard, ᵊt-tasliim Ɛand ᵊd-dafᵊƐ.*

code - **1.** *qawaaƐed* (pl.). He has a very strict code of ethics. *huwwe maaši Ɛala qawaaƐed ʔaxlaaqiyye ktiir saarme.* **2.** *šiifra* pl. *-aat.* We've broken the enemy's code. *fakkeena šiifret ᵊl-Ɛaduww.*

cod-liver oil - *zeet˜ samak.*

coexistence - *taƐaayoš.* He wrote an article about peaceful coexistence. *katab maqaale Ɛan ᵊt-taƐaayoš ᵊs-səlmi.*

coffee - **1.** *bənn.* The coffee is freshly roasted.

l-bənn ᵊmhammaṣ taaza. **2.** *qahwe.* Would you like a cup of coffee? *bəddak fənžaan qahwe?*
coffee grinder – *ṭaahuunet˜* (pl. *ṭawahiin˜*) *bənn.*
coffee grounds – *ṭəhᵊl qahwe.* Empty the coffee grounds in the garbage pail. *kəbb ṭəhl ᵊl-qahwe b-tanaket ᵊz-zbaale.*
coffee shop – *qahwe* pl. *qahaawi.*
coffeehouse – *qahwe* pl. *qahaawi.*
coffeehouse owner – *qahwaati* pl. *-iyye, qahwaži* pl. *-iyye.*
coffeepot – *ʔəbriiq˜* (pl. *ʔabariiq˜*) *qahwe,* (with long handle) *doole* pl. *-aat.*
coffin – *taabuut* pl. *tawabiit.*
cognac – *konyaak.*
coil – *laffe* pl. *-aat.* You'll have to buy a coil of wire. *laazem təštəri laffet ᵊšriiṭ.*
to coil up – **1.** *laff (ə laff//nlaff, ltaff).* He coiled up the wire. *laff ᵊš-šriiṭ.* **2.** *ltaff ƹala baƹḍo.* The snake was lying there all coiled up. *l-ḥayye qaaƹde hniik məltaffe ƹala baƹḍa.*
coin – **1.** *qəṭƹet˜* (pl. *qəṭaƹ˜*) *ƹəmle.* He collects coins. *byəžmaƹ qəṭaƹ ƹəmle.* **2.** *frank* pl. *-aat.* Let's toss a coin to see who goes. *xalliina nəlḥoš ᵊfrank la-nšuuf miin biruuḥ.*
to coin – **1.** *sakk (ə sakk//nsakk).* When did they coin this money? *ʔeemta sakku hal-ƹəmle?* **2.** *ṣaaġ (i ṣ).* He loves to coin new expressions. *ktiir biḥəbb yṣiiġ taƹabiir ᵊždiide.*
to coincide – *ṣaadaf.* His coming coincided with my leaving. *žayyto ṣaadafet maƹ rooḥti.*
coincidence – *ṣədfe* pl. *ṣədaf.* What a strange coincidence! *məlla ṣədfe ġariibe!*
coke – *faḥᵊm˜ kook.* We heat with coke. *məndaffi b-faḥᵊm kook.*
cold – **1.** *barᵊd.* I can't stand the cold up here in the mountains. *maa fiini ʔətḥammal ᵊl-barᵊd hoon bᵊž-žabal.* **2.** *rašᵊḥ, zkaam.* He has a bad cold. *maƹo rašḥ ᵊtqiil.* **3.** *baared.* I'd like a glass of cold water. *žaaye ƹala baali kaaset mayy baarde.* -- The nights are cold in the desert. *l-layaali baarde bᵊṣ-ṣaḥra.* — Their welcome was rather cold. *ʔəstəqbaalon kaan šwayye baared.* **4.** *bardaan.* I'm awfully cold. *faqaaƹa šuu bardaan (ʔana).*
**The blow knocked him cold. *l-lakme ḍayyaƹə́t-lo ṣawaabo.*
**He murdered her in cold blood. *qatə́la biduun-ma trəff ƹeeno* or *qatə́la mən-ġeer-ma tənraff-ə́llo ƹeen.*
**He's a cold, unscrupulous person. *huwwe zalame bala ḥəss w-laa ḍamiir.*
cold war – *ḥarᵊb baarde.* With the coming of the space age, the cold war has taken on new aspects. *maƹ bidaayet ƹaṣr ᵊl-faḍaaʔ ᵊl-ḥarb ᵊl-baarde ʔaaxde ʔawžoh ᵊždiide.*
to catch (or **take**) **cold** – *raššaḥ, ʔaxad barᵊd.* I caught cold yesterday. *raššaḥt ᵊmbaareḥ.*
**You'll catch your death of cold. *ləssa bətmuut ᵊmn ᵊl-barᵊd.*
cold-blooded: The frog is a cold-blooded animal. *ḍ-ḍəfḍaƹa mən zawaat ᵊd-damm ᵊl-baared.* -- How can you be so cold-blooded at a time like this? *kiif fiik ᵊtkuun dammak baared kəll hal-qadd ᵊb-heek waqᵊt?*
coldly – *b-ᵊbruud(e).* They greeted him coldly. *sallamu ƹalée b-ᵊbruud.*
to **collaborate** – **1.** *tƹaawan.* Who's collaborating with you on the book? *miin ƹam yətƹaawan maƹak ᵊb-taʔliif l-ᵊktaab?* **2.** *maalaʔ.* He was shot because he collaborated with the enemy. *qawwaṣúu laʔənno maalaʔ ᵊl-ƹaduww.*
collaboration – **1.** *taƹaawon (maƹ).* **2.** *mmaalaʔa* (cf. collaborate).
collaborator – **1.** *zamiil* pl. *zəmala.* **2.** *mmaaleʔ* pl. *-iin* (cf. collaborate).
collapse – *ʔənhiyaar.* Exhaustion caused his collapse. *l-ʔəžhaad sabbab ʔənhiyaaro.*
to collapse – **1.** *nhaar, nhadam.* The bridge suddenly collapsed. *ž-žəsᵊr ƹala ġafle nhaar.* **2.** *nhaar.* He collapsed in the middle of the street. *nhaar ᵊb-nəṣṣ ᵊš-šaareƹ.*
collar – *qabbe* pl. *-aat.* He accidentally tore his collar. *ƹaraḍan šaraṭ qabbto.*
collar bone – *(ƹaẓᵊm˜) tərqʷawa.*
to collar – *ƹabaṭ (o ƹabᵊṭ).* The police collared him as he left the building. *š-šərṭa ƹabəṭṭo w-huwwe ṭaaleƹ ᵊmn ᵊl-binaaye.*
colleague – *zamiil* pl. *zəmala.*
to **collect** – **1.** *žamaƹ (a žamᵊƹ//nžamaƹ).* Her son collects stamps. *ʔəbna byəžmaƹ ṭawaabeƹ.* **2.** *žamaƹ, lamm (ə lamm//ltamm).* How much money has the society collected so far? *qaddeeš žamƹet ᵊž-žamƹiyye maṣaari la-ḥadd hallaq?* -- When is the mail collected here? *ʔeemta byəžmaƹu l-bariid hoon?* **3.** *žammaƹ, žamaƹ, lamm.* Did you collect all the notebooks? *žammaƹᵊt kəll ᵊd-dafaater?* **4.** *stažmaƹ.* Give me a chance to collect my thoughts. *ƹaṭiini fərṣa la-ʔəstažmeƹ ʔafkaari.* **5.** *qabaḍ (a qabᵊḍ//nqabaḍ).* When can I collect my money? *ʔeemta fiini ʔəqbaḍ maṣariyyi?* **6.** *ḥtašad, džammaƹ.* A crowd collected in the square. *fii žamƹ ᵊḥtašad bᵊs-saaḥa.*
collected – *raabeṭ˜ ᵊž-žaʔᵊš.* In spite of the danger, she remained calm and collected. *ƹar-raġᵊm ᵊmn ᵊl-xaṭar bəqyet haadye w-raabṭet ᵊž-žaʔᵊš.*
collection – **1.** *mažmuuƹa* pl. *-aat.* The library has a famous collection of books on America. *l-maktabe fiiha mažmuuƹet kətᵊb mašhuura ƹan ʔameerka.* **2.** *lamme* pl. *-aat.* When is the last collection? *ʔeemta ʔaaxer lamme?* -- They took up a collection after the concert. *ƹəmlu lamme baƹd ᵊl-ḥafle l-muusiiqiyye.*
collective – **1.** *žamaaƹi*.* It's a collective undertaking. *haada ƹamal žamaaƹi.* **2.** *ʔəžmaali*, žamaaƹi*.* They imposed a collective penalty of 10,000 pounds on the village. *faraḍu ġaraame ʔəžmaaliyye ƹašᵊrt aalaaf leera ƹal-qʷarye.* **3.** *ʔəsᵊm˜ žənᵊs.* Does this noun have a collective? *hal-ʔəsᵊm ʔəlo ʔəsᵊm žənᵊs?*
college – **1.** *kəlliyye* pl. *-aat.* He's studying at the College of Arts and Sciences. *ƹam yədros ᵊb-kəlliyyet ᵊl-ʔaadaab wᵊl-ᵊƹluum.* **2.** *žaamƹa* pl. *-aat.* His son wants to go to college. *ʔəbno bəddo yruuḥ ƹaž-žaamƹa.*
to **collide** – *tṣaadam (maƹ).* Two cars collided in the fog. *fii sayyaarteen ᵊtṣaadamu bᵊḍ-ḍabaab.*
collision – *taṣaadom* pl. *-aat.*
colloquial – *ƹaammi*, daarež.* He spoke to the class in colloquial Arabic. *ḥaka bᵊṣ-ṣaff bᵊl-ƹarabi l-ƹaammi.*
Cologne – *koloonya.*
colon – *nəqᵊṭṭeen* (dual). Use a comma instead of a colon. *ktoob faaṣle ƹawaaḍ nəqᵊṭṭeen.*
colonel – *ƹamiid* pl. *ƹəmada, koloneel* pl. *-iyye.*
colonial – *ʔəstəƹmaari*.* Their colonial policy has changed a lot in the last few years. *siyaasə́ton ᵊl-ʔəstəƹmaariyye tġayyaret ᵊktiir bᵊs-sniin ᵊl-ʔaxiire.*
colonialism – *ʔəstəƹmaar.*
colonist – *məstaƹmer* pl. *-iin.*
to **colonize** – *staƹmar.* They colonized the country during the 18th and 19th centuries. *staƹmaru l-ᵊblaad been ᵊl-qʷarn ᵊt-taamen wᵊt-taaseƹ ƹašar.*
colony – **1.** *məstaƹmara* pl. *-aat.* **2.** (of aliens) *žaalye* pl. *žawaali.*
color – *loon* pl. *ʔalwaan.* I don't like these colors. *maa btəƹžəbni hal-ʔalwaan.* -- His color is bad. *loono muu ƹala baƹḍo.*
**He finally showed his true colors. *bᵊl-ʔaaxiir warža ḥaalo ƹala ḥaqiiqto.*
**He passed the exam with flying colors. *nažaḥ bᵊl-faḥᵊṣ ᵊb-tafawwoq baaher.*
to color – **1.** *lawwan.* The children had to color the map of the Middle East. *l-ᵊwlaad kaan ƹaleehon ylawwnu xariiṭet ᵊš-šarq ᵊl-ʔawṣaṭ.* **2.** *ṣabaġ (o ṣabᵊġ//nṣabaġ).* That paper usually colors its presentation of the news. *haž-žariide ƹaadə́ta btəṣboġ ᵊl-ʔaxbaar ᵊb-ṣəbġa xaaṣṣa fiiha.* **3.** *ḥmarr.* She colored when they complimented her. *ḥmarret lamma madaḥuuha.*
colored – *mlawwan.* Have you any colored handkerchiefs? *ƹandkon šii mahaarem ᵊmlawwane?*
colored man – *zənži* pl. *znuuž, ƹabᵊd* pl. *ƹabiid.* He has always been a friend of the colored man. *daayman kaan byəššor maƹ ᵊz-znuuž.*
color-blind – *ʔaƹma˜ l-ʔalwaan* f. *ƹamya˜ l-ʔalwaan* pl. *ƹəmyaan˜ ᵊl-ʔalwaan.*
colorful – **1.** *zaahi.* Her garden is colorful this time of year. *žneenə́ta bətkuun zaahye b-hal-waqᵊt ᵊmn ᵊs-səne.* **2.** *mzahzeh.* He told us a very colorful story. *ḥakə́-lna qəṣṣa mzahᵊzha ktiir.*
colt – *məhᵊr* pl. *mhuura.*
column – **1.** *ƹaamuud* pl. *ƹawamiid.* You can recognize the house by its white columns. *fiik ᵊtmayyez ᵊl-beet mən ƹawamiido l-biiḍ.* -- Where is that column of smoke coming from? *mneen žaaye ƹaamuud ᵊd-dəxxaan haada?* -- The article is in the third column on the first page. *l-maqʷaale bᵊl-ƹaamuud ᵊt-taalet ᵊmn ᵊṣ-ṣafḥa l-ʔuula.* **2.** *ƹaamuud* pl. *ƹawamiid, xaane* pl. *-aat.* Write your name in the right-hand column. *ktoob ʔəsmak bᵊl-ƹaamuud yalli*

Eal-yamiin. **3.** *zaawye* pl. *zawaaya.* He writes a weekly column for the daily newspaper. *ʔəlo zaawye ʔəsbuEiyye bᵊš-šariide.* **4.** *ratiil* pl. *rataaʔel.* The bombers attacked a column of enemy tanks on the road. *l-ǧaazifaat haašamu ratiil mən dabbaabaat ᵊl-Eaduww Eaṭ-ṭariiq.*

comb – *məšᵊṭ* pl. *mšaaṭ.* Where can I buy a comb? *mneen fiini ʔəštəri məšᵊṭ?*

to comb – **1.** *ṣarraḥ, maššaṭ.* Did Mother comb your hair? *ʔəmmek ṣarraḥə́t-lek šaErek?* **2.** *fattaš.* The police combed the whole city. *š-šərṭa fattašu l-balad mən ʔawwəla la-ʔaaxə́ra.*

combat – *ǧitaal.* The troops are trained and ready for combat. *š-šunuud xalaṣu tamriin w-ṣaaru ʔahᵊl ləl-ǧitaal.* -- Troops in full combat gear were moved into the capital. *nazzalu ləl-Eaaṣme šyuuš b-ᵊmEəddaat kaamle ləl-ǧitaal.*

to see combat – *ḥaarab.* Half of these soldiers have never seen combat before. *nəṣṣ haš-šunuud ᵊb-ḥayaaton maa ḥaarabu mən qabᵊl.*

to combat – *kaafaḥ.* We must make every effort to combat disease. *laazem naEmel ʔaǧṣa šahᵊdna la-mkaafaḥt ᵊl-ʔamraaḍ.*

combination – **1.** *šamᵊE been ... w-.* How do you like the combination of red and gray? *šuu raʔyak ᵊb-haš-šamᵊE been ᵊl-ʔaḥmar w-ᵊrṣaaṣi?* **2.** *sərr˜* (pl. *ʔasraar˜*) *fatᵊḥ˜ ...* We are the only ones who know the combination to this safe. *nəḥna l-waḥiidiin yalli mnaEref sərr fatᵊḥ has-sanduuq ᵊl-ḥadiid.*

to **combine** – **1.** *šamaE (a šamᵊE//nšamaE).* So far, no one knows how to combine the two chemical elements. *la-ḥadd hallaq maa ḥada byaEref kiif yəšmaE ᵊl-Eənᵊṣreen ᵊl-kiimaawiyyiin.* **2.** *waḥḥad, šamaE.* If we combine our efforts we'll be able to do it. *ʔiza waḥḥadna šhuudna fiina naEmə́la.* **3.** *məšyu (i ø) maE baEḍon.* Will these ingredients combine all right? *hal-ḥašakiil byəmšu maE baEḍon ᵊmniiḥ?*

to **come** – **1.** *ʔəša (-yəši šayye,* ap. *šaaye,* impv. *taEa* f. *taEi* pl. *taEu).* How often does he come to town? *kəll qaddeeš byəši Eal-balad?* -- They're coming to visit us this evening. *šaayiin yzuuruuna l-yoom Eašiyye.* -- This cloth comes only in two colors. *hal-ᵊqmaaš byəši bass ᵊb-looneen.* -- I don't know whether I'm coming or going! *maa-li Earfaan ḥaali raayeḥ wəlla šaaye!* -- Come here, son! *taEa la-hoon ya ʔəbni!* **2.** *ṭəleE (a ø), ʔəša.* Nothing came of it. *maa ṭəleE mənna šii.* **3.** *ḥall (ə ḥluul), ḥaan (i ø), ṣaar (i ø), ʔəša.* The time has come to take action. *ḥall ᵊl-waqᵊt la-naEmel šii.* **4.** *ṣaar (i ø), ḥaṣal (a ḥṣuul), wəqeE (-yəqaE wquuE).* The revolution won't come for several weeks yet. *s-sawra maa laḥa tṣiir qabᵊl Eəddet ʔasabiiE.* **5.** *ḥakam (o ø).* That holiday comes on a Monday. *hal-Eiid byəḥkom yoom ᵊt-taneen.*

**He comes from a very rich family. *huwwe mən Eeele ǧaniyye ktiir.*

**He comes from Aleppo. *huwwe mən ḥalab.*

**Where I come from it often rains for weeks. *b-baladi ʔaḥyaanan ᵊbtənzel ᵊl-maṭar la-məddet ʔasabiiE mətwaalye.*

**Business comes before pleasure. *š-šəǧᵊl qabl ᵊl-basᵊṭ.*

**Come now, you don't really mean that! *xalaṣna baqa, ʔənte maa btəqṣə́da!*

**Dancing comes natural to her. *r-raqᵊṣ xalqaan maEa* or *r-raqṣ ᵊb-damma.*

**How did you come to think of that? *kiif haš-šii xaṭar ᵊb-baalak?*

**How did you come to buy that old car? *kiif ṣaar ḥatta štareet has-sayyaara l-Eatiiqa?*

to come about – *ḥaṣal (a ḥṣuul), ḥadas (o ḥduus), ṣaar (i ø).* How did all this come about? *kəll haš-šii kiif ḥaṣal?*

to come across – *ṣaadaf.* He's the most intelligent fellow I've ever come across. *huwwe ʔaska zalame ṣaadafto b-ḥayaati.* -- I came across my friend's name in this book. *ṣaadafᵊt ʔəsᵊm ṣaaḥbi b-hal-ᵊktaab.*

**When is he going to come across with the money? *ʔeemta laḥa yšiib ᵊl-maṣaari?*

to come after – **1.** *ʔəša yaaxod ...* I've come after my passport. *ʔšiit ʔaaxod basboori.* **2.** *ʔəša baEd˜ ...* Her name comes after mine on the list. *ʔəsma byəši baEᵊd ʔəsmi bᵊl-liista.*

to come again – *rəšeE (a rašEa), ʔəša taani marra.* You'll see, he'll come again. *bətšuuf, ləssa byəršaE.*

**Come again? I didn't quite get you the first time. *naEam? maa fhəmᵊt Ealeek ʔawwal marra.*

**Do come again! We were so happy to see you. *šarrə́fna kamaan! nbaṣaṭna ktiir ᵊb-šooftak.*

to come along – **1.** *raaḥ maE˜ ..., ʔəša maE˜ ...* Do you want to come along? *bəddak ᵊtruuḥ maEi?* -- Come along with me. *taEa maEi.* **2.** *məši (i maši).* Everything's coming along fine, thanks. *šəkran, kəll šii maaši Eala maa yuraam.* -- How's your work coming along? *kiif maaši šəǧlak?*

to come apart – *faraṭ (o farᵊṭ).* The chair came apart when he sat on it. *faraṭ ᵊl-kərsi lamma qaEad Ealée.*

to come around – **1.** *wəEi (-yuuEa ø), ṣəḥi (a ø).* Throw some water on him if he doesn't come around soon. *rəššo b-mayy ʔiza maa wəEi baEd ᵊšwayye.* **2.** *ʔəsEan la-.* He should come around to our way of thinking before long. *laa bədd-ma yəsEen la-raʔᵊyna Ean qariib.*

**Why don't you come around some evening? *leeš maa btəši dzuurna* (or *btəši ḥawaleena*) *b-šii masawiyye?*

to come back – *rəšeE (a ršuuE, rašEa).* I told him to come back next week. *qəlt-ə́llo yəršaE ᵊš-šəmEa š-šaaye.*

**She came back at them with a sharp reply. *raddet Ealeehon ᵊb-šawaab laazeE.*

**The whole incident came back to her when they mentioned my name. *dzakkaret kəll ᵊl-ḥaades lamma zakaru ʔəsmi.*

**It's all coming back to me now. *hallaq Eam bədzakkar.*

to come by – **1.** *maraq (o ø), marr (ə ø).* He's coming by here this afternoon. *byəmroq la-hoon ᵊl-yoom baEd ᵊḍ-ḍəhᵊr.* **2.** *ḥaṣṣal Eala.* How did he come by all that money? *kiif ḥaṣṣal Eala kəll hal-maṣaari?*

to come down – **1.** *nəzel (e nazle).* Can you come down for a moment? *fiik tənzel šii daqiiqa?* **2.** *nazzal.* We can't come down a penny on this price. *maa mnəqder ᵊnnazzel w-laa qərᵊš mən has-səEᵊr.*

to come down with – *qaEad (o ø) bᵊl-farše b-sabab˜ ...* He came down with a bad cold. *qaEad bᵊl-farše b-sabab rašᵊḥ qawi.*

to come for – *ʔəša yaaxod ...* He came for his books yesterday. *ʔəša yaaxod kətbo mbaarḥa.*

to come forward – *tqaddam.* When volunteers were called for, six men came forward. *waqᵊt ṭalabu məṭṭawwEiin sətt ᵊršaal ᵊtqaddamu.*

to come in – **1.** *faat (u foote).* Please come in. *tfaḍḍal fuut* or **tfaḍḍal šarref.* **2.** *warrad, ʔəša.* The money due is coming in slowly. *l-maṣaari l-məstḥaqqa Eam ᵊtwarred šwayye šwayye.*

**Come in! *tfaḍḍal!* or *šarref!*

**He doesn't have enough sense to come in out of the rain. *maa byaEref kuuEo mən buuEo.*

to come in handy – *faad (i ø), nafaE (a ø).* English will come in very handy to you later. *ləssa l-ʔəngliizi bifiidak bᵊl-məstaqbal.*

to come off – **1.** *salat (o ø), nxalaE.* One leg of the table has come off. *rəšᵊl mən rəšleen ᵊṭ-ṭaawle saltet.* **2.** *nqaṭaE.* The button has come off. *z-zərr ᵊnqaṭaE.* **3.** *ḥall (ə ø).* The color comes off these gloves. *loon hal-ᵊkfuuf biḥəll.* **4.** *ṭəleE (a ø).* His joke didn't come off very well. *nəkᵊtto muu ṭaaləEt-ə́lla ktiir.*

**Come off it! Can't you see you've hurt his feelings? *ṣṭaṭEem baqa! maa-lak šaayef ʔənnak šaraḥᵊt Eawaaṭfo.*

to come on – **1.** *laqa (-ylaaqi).* I came on the missing documents quite unexpectedly. *laqeet ᵊl-wasaaʔeǧ ᵊḍ-ḍaayEa b-ṭariiq ᵊṣ-ṣədfe.* **2.** *bada (a ø).* The newscast comes on at four o'clock. *našret ᵊl-ʔaxbaar ᵊbtəbda s-saaEa ʔarbEa.*

**Come on or we'll miss the train. *yaḷḷa, hallaq bifuutna t-treen.*

to come out – **1.** *ṭəleE (a ṭalEa).* Please come out here. *mən faḍlak ᵊṭlaaE la-hoon.* -- Why don't you come out to the farm with us? *leeš maa btəṭlaE maEna Eal-mazraEa?* -- The stain won't come out. *l-bəqEa maa laḥa təṭlaE.* -- Who came out on top in the fight? *miin ṭəleE ᵊl-ǧaaleb bᵊl-ᵊmqaatale?* -- Come right out with it! *ṭlaaE fiiha Eal-ḥaarek!* **2.** *ṭəleE, ṣadar (o ṣduur).* My book came out last month. *l-ᵊktaab tabaEi ṭəleE ᵊš-šahr ᵊl-maaḍi.* **3.** *baan (a ø), tbayyan.* Now it comes out that I was right. *hallaq baan ʔənno kaan ᵊl-ḥaqq maEi.*

**The President has come out against the change. *r-raʔiis ṣarraḥ ʔənno ḍəḍḍ ᵊt-taǧyiir.*

to come over - *ʔəža*. Can you come over for a moment? *fiik təži (la-hoon) šii lahẓa?* -- Some friends are coming over to see us this evening. *baɛd əṣhaabna žaayiin yzuuruuna l-yoom ɛašiyye.*

**What's come over you? *šuu ṣaayər-lak?*

to come through - 1. *maraq (o ə), marr (ə ə)*. You can't come through that door. *maa fiik təmroq mən hal-baab.* -- Does the bus come through here? *l-baaṣ byəmroq mən hoon?* -- He came through the operation nicely. *marr bəl-ɛamaliyye b-nažaah.* 2. *wəṣel (-yəṣal and -yuuṣal ə)*. Have your immigration papers come through yet? *wəṣlu wraaq əl-həžra tabaɛaatak?*

to come to - 1. *ṭəleɛ (a ə)*. The bill comes to two pounds. *l-faatuura ṭaalɛa leerteen.* 2. *wəṣel (-yəṣal and -yuuṣal ə) la-*. His property doesn't quite come to the river. *məlko muu waaṣel tamaam la-ḥadd ən-nahər.* 3. *wəɛi (-yuuɛa waɛi), ṣəḥi (a ə)*. After a few minutes she came to. *baɛəd kam daqiiqa wəɛyet.* 4. *ʔadda la-*. Who knows what all this will come to? *maa ḥada byaɛref la-šuu haš-šii biʔaddi.*

to come to pieces - *faraṭ (o farəṭ)*. It will come to pieces if you touch it. *ʔiza daqarət fiiha btəfroṭ.*

to come true - *tḥaqqaq*. Her dream came true. *ḥəlma tḥaqqaq.*

to come up - 1. *ṭəleɛ (a ṭalɛa)*. Won't you come up for a cup of coffee? *maa btəṭlaɛ taaxə́d-lak fənžaan qahwe?* -- A thunderstorm is coming up. *fii ɛaaṣfe ṭaalɛa.* 2. *nabbaz, nabaz (o nabəz)*. The wheat is beginning to come up. *l-qaməḥ ɛam yəbda ynabbez.* 3. *ṣaar (i ə), ḥadas (o ḥduus)*. This problem comes up every day. *hal-masʔale bətṣiir kəll yoom.* -- Something new has come up. *ḥadas šii ždiid.*

**When will the bill come up for a vote? *ʔeemta laha yəṭraḥu mašruuɛ əl-q̈aanuun ɛat-taṣwiit?*

to come up to - 1. *ṭəleɛ (a ə) qadd˜* ... It doesn't come up to our expectations. *muu ṭaalɛa qadd-ma tʔammalna.* 2. *ṭəleɛ la-, wəṣel (-yəṣal and -yuuṣal ə) la-*. She only comes up to my shoulder. *ṭaalɛa bass la-ktaafi.*

to come upon - *laqa (-ylaaqi), wažad (-yuužed ə)*. I came upon the solution by accident. *laqeet əl-ḥall əb-ṭariiq əṣ-ṣədfe.*

to come under - *daxal (o dxuul) taḥət˜* ... What regulation does this come under? *taḥət ʔayy niẓaam haš-šağle btədxol?*

comedown - *tuuṭaaye*. His new job is a real comedown for him. *šağəlto ž-ždiide tuuṭaaye ʔəlo ɛan ḥaqa.*

comedy - 1. *komiidya* pl. *-aat, riwaaye* (pl. *-aat*) *hazliyye*. Did you like the comedy? *ɛažəbtak əl-komiidya?* 2. *masxara*. Cut the comedy. *ḥaaže masxara baqa.*

comfort - 1. *raaḥa*. She is only concerned about her own comfort. *muu haamə́ma ʔəlla raaḥə́ta.* 2. *mwaasda, ɛaza*. That's no comfort to me! *haada muu mwaasda ʔəli!*

comforts - *wasaaʔel˜ raaḥa* (pl.). Here we have all the comforts we could hope for. *hoon fii kəll wasaaʔel ər-raaḥa halli mnətmannaaha.*

to comfort - *waasa, ɛazza*. This news will comfort you. *hal-xabar laha ywaasiik.*

comforting - *mɛazzi, mwaasi*. That's a comforting thought. *hayy fəkra mɛazzye.*

comfortable - 1. *məryeḥ*. This chair isn't very comfortable. *hal-kərsi muu məryeḥ əktiir.* 2. *kbiir, waaseɛ*. He won the election by a comfortable margin. *rəbeḥ əl-ʔəntixaabaat əb-farq əkbiir.*

**They never feel comfortable around strangers. *ʔabaden maa byaaxdu raaḥə́ton* (or *ḥərriiton*) *qəddaam əl-ğəraba.*

**Make yourself comfortable! *tfaḍḍal əstriiḥ!*

comical - *məḍḥek, hazli**.

comma - *faaṣle* pl. *fawaaṣel*.

command - 1. *ʔamər* pl. *ʔawaamer*. Why didn't they carry out his command? *leeš maa naffazúu-lo ʔamro?* 2. *tamakkon*. Everyone admires her excellent command of the language. *kəll ən-naas məɛžabiin əb-tamakkə́na l-ɛaẓiim əmn əl-luğa.* 3. *q̈iyaade*. He was transferred to a new command. *ntaqal la-taḥət q̈iyaade ždiide.*

to be in command of - *ṣayṭar ɛala*. Are they really in command of the situation now? *ɛan ḥaqa hənne hallaq əmṣayṭriin ɛal-waḍəɛ?*

**Who's in command here? *miin ṣaaḥeb əl-ʔamər hoon?* or *miin əl-masʔuul hoon?*

to have a command of - *tmakkan mən, taqan (e ʔətqaan)*. Does he have a good command of English? *mətmakken huwwe tamaam əmn əl-ʔəngliizi?*

to command - *ʔamar (o ʔamər)*. She thinks she can command them to do whatever she wishes. *mḥassbe ʔənno fiiha təʔmə́ron ysaawu šuu-ma bətḥəbb.*

commander - 1. *q̈aaʔed* pl. *q̈aada* and *q̈uwwaad*. He's the new commander of the Third Army. *huwwe l-q̈aaʔed əž-ždiid tabaɛ əž-žeeš ət-taalet.* 2. *mq̈addam (baḥri)* pl. *mq̈addamiin (baḥriyyiin)*. My brother is a commander in the Navy. *ʔaxi rətəbto mq̈addam bəl-baḥriyye.*

commandos - *mağawiir* (pl.), *komandos* (pl.).

to **commend** - 1. *ʔasna ɛala*. They commended him for his good behavior. *ʔasnu ɛalée la-ḥəsən taṣarrfo.* 2. *ḥaṭṭ (e ḥaṭaṭ)*. She commended the children to my care. *ḥaṭṭet l-əwlaad taḥt ərɛaayti.*

comment - *taɛliiq̈* pl. *-aat* and *taɛaliiq̈*. The comments in the foreword of the book are very helpful. *t-taɛaliiq̈ b-əmqaddamt l-əktaab əmfiide ktiir.* -- No one listened to her comments about the film. *maa ḥada ntabah la-taɛliiq̈aata ɛal-fələm.* -- What do you think of her new clothes? — No comment! *šuu raʔyak əb-ʔawaɛiiha ž-ždiide?* -- *bala taɛliiq̈!*

to comment on - *ɛallaq̈ ɛala*. She commented on the many changes in the town. *ɛallaq̈et ɛat-tağyiiraat l-əktiire bəl-balad.*

commentary - *taɛliiq̈* pl. *-aat* and *taɛaliiq̈*. His news commentary was brief but clear. *taɛliiq̈o ɛal-ʔaxbaar kaan məxtaṣar laaken waaḍeḥ.*

commentator - *mɛalleq̈* pl. *-iin*.

commerce - *tižaara*. The cabinet took measures to step up commerce with other nations. *mažles əl-wəzara ʔaxad tadabiir la-tanšiiṭ ət-tižaara maɛ ğeer duwal.*

commercial - 1. *tižaari**. He's well known in commercial circles. *huwwe maɛruuf əktiir bəl-ʔawsaaṭ ət-tižaariyye.* -- Commercial treaty. *mɛaahade tižaariyye.* 2. *diɛaaye* pl. *-aat*. The program continued after a short commercial. *kammalu l-bərnaamež baɛəd diɛaaye qaṣiire.*

commission - 1. *ləžne* pl. *ližaan*. The commission has promised to investigate the matter. *l-ləžne waɛdet ətḥaqqeq bəl-qaḍiyye.* 2. *ɛmuule* pl. *-aat*, *kəməsyoon* pl. *-aat*. I don't get any commission for what I sell here. *maa baaxod ʔayy əɛmuule ɛala halli bbiiɛo hoon.* 3. *baraaʔa* pl. *-aat*. He got his commission as second lieutenant in July. *wəṣəlto baraaʔto b-taɛyiino mlaazem əb-tammuuz.*

out of commission - *mɛaṭṭal*. My car's out of commission right now. *sayyaarti hallaq əmɛaṭṭale.*

commissioner - *məɛtamad* pl. *-iin*, *mfawwaḍ* pl. *-iin*.

to **commit** - 1. *rtakab, q̈taraf*. Who committed the crime? *miin ərtakab əž-žariime?* 2. *ɛahad (o ɛahəd), wakkal*. He committed his sister to my care.. *ɛahad ʔəli* (or *wakkalni*) *b-ərɛaayet ʔəxto.* 3. *ʔalzam, rabaṭ (o rabəṭ)*. I'm sorry, I can't commit myself just yet. *mətʔassef maa fiini ʔəlzem ḥaali b-hal-waqət.* 4. *ḥaṭṭ (ə ḥaṭaṭ//nḥaṭṭ)*. She had to be committed to an asylum. *nžabaru yḥəṭṭuuha b-məstašfa mažaniin.*

**He committed suicide. *ntaḥar.*

committee - *ləžne* pl. *ližaan*.

common - 1. *ɛaamm*. He has the common good at heart. *byəhtamm bəṣ-ṣaaleḥ əl-ɛaamm.* 2. *məštárak*. That's our common duty. *haada waažəbna l-məštárak.* 3. *žaari*. Is that a common practice? *šuu haš-šii ɛaade žaarye?* 4. *ɛaadi**. This is said to be the century of the common man. *biquulu ʔənno hal-q̈arən huwwe q̈arn ər-ražol əl-ɛaadi.* 5. *ɛaammi**. She's rather common. *hiyye šwayye ɛaammiyye.*

**It is common knowledge that he lies. *šii maɛruuf ʔənno byəkzeb.*

in common - *šaraake*. The three sisters own the house in common. *l-ʔəxwaat ət-tlaate byəməlku l-beet šaraake.*

**She and I have nothing in common. *ʔana wiyyaaha maa fii šii beenaatna məštárak.*

**The two countries have many problems in common. *d-dawəlteen fii ɛandon mašaakel əktiir məštarake beenaaton.*

commotion - *ʔəḍṭiraab, haraž w-maraž, hayažaan*. There was a terrific commotion in the street. *kaan fii ʔəḍṭiraab faẓiiɛ bəš-šaareɛ.*

communicable - *saari*. The government is trying to stamp out communicable diseases. *l-əḥkuume ɛam ətḥaawel təqḍi ɛal-ʔamraaḍ əs-saarye.*

communication - 1. *mwaaṣalaat* (pl.). The committee will study problems of communication in that country. *l-ləžne laha tədros mašaakel l-əmwaaṣalaat əb-hal-əblaad.* 2. *ʔəttiṣaal*. We're not in communication with them. *maa-lna ɛala ʔəttiṣaal* *maʕon.*

communion – *qərbaan.* Their daughter had her first communion last Sunday. *bənton ᵊtnaawalet ʔawwal qərbaana yoom ᵊl-ʔaḥad ᵊl-maaḍi.*

communiqué – *bayaan rasmi* pl. *-aat rasmiyye, balaaġ rasmi* pl. *-aat rasmiyye.*

communism – *šuyuuʕiyye.*

communist – *šuyuuʕi** pl. *-iyyiin* and *-iyye.*

community – *balde* pl. *blaad.* How many families are living in this community? *kaam ʕeele saakniin ᵊb-hal-balde?*

compact – **1.** *ʕəlbet˜* (pl. *ʕəlab˜*) *boodra.* There was nothing but a compact and a comb in her bag. *maa kaan fii ʔəlla ʕəlbet boodra w-məšṭ ᵊb-šantaayə́ta.* **2.** *madbuuk, maḥšuuk.* That's a very compact package. *haada ṭard ᵊktiir madbuuk.*

companion – *rfiiq* pl. *rəfaqa, ṣaaḥeb* pl. *ṣḥaab.* Children need companions their own age. *l-ᵊwlaad byəḥtaažu rəfaqa mən žiilon hənne.*

companionable – *maʕᵊšraani**.

company – **1.** *sariyye* pl. *saraaya.* I served in his company during the last war. *xadamt ᵊb-sariito ʔasna l-ḥarb ᵊl-maaḍye.* **2.** *šərke* pl. *-aat.* What company do you represent? *šuu š-šərke yalli bətmassə́la?* **3.** *zuwwaar* (pl.), *ḍyuuf* (pl.). Are you expecting company this evening? *žaayiinkon zuwwaar ᵊl-leele?* **4.** *ṣəḥbe.* I find him very good company. *šaayef ṣəḥᵊbto ẓariife ktiir.*

**Keep me company for a while. *xalliik maʕi šwayye.*

**A man is known by the company he keeps. *luu tasʔal ʕan il-marʔ bal sal ʕan qariinih.*

comparable to – *mmaasel la-, mʕaadel la-.* This project is comparable to the one they undertook last year. *hal-mašruuʕ ᵊmmaasel la-halli ʕəmlúu s-səne l-maaḍye.*

comparative – **1.** *nəsbi**. They live in comparative comfort. *ʕaayšiin ᵊb-rafaaha nəsbiyye.* **2.** *muqaaren.* The university offers a course in comparative literature. *ž-žaamʕa btaʕṭi maadde bᵊl-ʔadab ᵊl-muqaaren..* **3.** *tafḍiil.* Use the comparative form of the adjective. *staʕmel ṣiiġet ᵊt-tafḍiil la-haṣ-ṣifa.*

comparatively – *nəsbatan, nəsbiyyan, bᵊn-nəsbe.* The lesson was comparatively easy. *d-darᵊs kaan hayyen nəsbatan.*

to **compare** – **1.** *qaaran//tqaaran.* We compared the two methods. *qaaranna ṭ-ṭariiqteen.* **2.** *tqaaran.* This hotel doesn't compare with the other hotels here. *hal-ʔoteel maa byətqaaran maʕ baqiit ᵊl-ʔoteelaat hoon.*

**I can't compare with you. *maa-li qaddak ʔana* or *maa fiini ʔəṭlaʕ qaddak.*

comparison – *mqaarane* pl. *-aat.* A comparison of the two political parties will show you that ... *l-ᵊmqaarane been ᵊl-ḥəzbeen ᵊs-siyaasiyyiin bətwaržiik ʔənno ...* -- That's a lame comparison. *hal-ᵊmqaarane ḍʕiife.*

compartment – **1.** *ġərfe* pl. *ġəraf.* All compartments in this car are crowded. *kəll ᵊl-ġəraf ᵊb-hal-fargoon maʕžuuqa.* **2.** *beet* pl. *byuut.* The document was hidden in a secret compartment of the safe. *l-wasiiqa kaanet ᵊmxabbaaye b-beet sərri b-sanduuq ᵊl-ḥadiid.*

compass – **1.** *boosḷa* and *boosḷaaye* pl. *boosḷayaat.* Without the compass we would have been lost. *law-laa l-boosḷa kənna ḍəʕna.* **2.** *biikaar* pl. *-aat.* I can draw a circle without a compass. *fiini ʔərsom daayre biduun biikaar.*

compatible – *mətmaaši, mətwaafeq.* Their actions are not compatible with the welfare of the country. *ʔaʕmaalon muu mətmaašye maʕ maṣlaḥet l-ᵊblaad.*

to **compel** – *žabar (e/o žabᵊr//nžabar), ḍṭarr, ġaṣab (o ġaṣᵊb//nġaṣab).* You compel me to take this step. *ʕam təžbərni ʔəttə́xez hal-xaṭwe.*

to **compensate** – *ʕawwaḍ.* His success compensated for all the sacrifices he had made. *nažaaḥo ʕawwaḍ (ʕalée) ʕan kəll ᵊt-taḍḥiyaat yalli kaan ʕəmə́la.*

compensation – *taʕwiiḍ* pl. *-aat.* I demand full compensation. *bəṭlob taʕwiiḍ kaamel.*

to **compete** – **1.** *nəzel (e nzuul).* Are you competing in the contest? *ʔənte naazel bᵊl-ᵊmbaarḍa?* **2.** *zaaḥam, naafas.* Of course, I can't compete with you. *ṭabʕan maa fiini zaaḥmak* (or *naafsak* or ***ʔəṭlaʕ qaddak*).

competence – *ʔahliyye, žadaara.* His competence in the field is well known. *ʔahliito b-hal-ḥaqᵊl maʕruufe mniiḥ.*

competent – **1.** *qadiir, məqtə́der, ʔahᵊl* (invar.). Everyone considers him a competent scholar. *l-kəll ᵊbyəʕtəbrúu ʕallaame qadiir.* **2.** *məxtaṣṣ.* The competent authorities. *ṣ-ṣəlṭaat ᵊl-məxtaṣṣa.*

competition – **1.** *mzaaḥame, mnaafase,* (business) *mḍaarabe.* He can't stand competition. *maa byətḥammal l-ᵊmzaaḥame.* **2.** *mbaarḍa* pl. *mbaarayaat.* The competition this afternoon will attract a large crowd. *l-ᵊmbaarḍa l-yoom baʕd ᵊḍ-ḍəhᵊr laḥa təžleb žamʕ ᵊkbiir.*

to be in competition with – *zaaḥam, naafas,* (business) *ḍaarab.* They're in competition with each other. *ʕam yzaaḥmu baʕḍon ᵊl-baʕᵊḍ.*

competitive: We'll pick the winner on a competitive basis. *mənnaqqi l-faaʔez ʕala ʔasaas ᵊt-tanaafos.*-- Everything's done on a competitive basis. *kəll šii biṣiir ʕala ʔasaas ᵊt-tanaafos* (in business: *ʕala ʔasaas l-ᵊmḍaarabe).*

competitor – *mḍaareb* pl. *-iin.* My competitor went bankrupt. *mḍaarbi fallas.*

to **compile** – *ʔallaf.* They're compiling a colloquial dictionary. *ʕam yʔallfu qaamuus ʕaammi.*

to **complain** – **1.** *šaka (i šakwa), štaka (šakwa).* She complains of severe pains. *ʕam təški mən ʔawžaaʕ šadiide.* **2.** *štaka, tšakka.* We complained to the manager about the noise. *štakeena ləl-mudiir mənšaan ᵊḍ-ḍoože.* -- Stop complaining! *ḥaaštak tətšakka!*

complaint – **1.** *šakwa* pl. *šakaawi.* Your complaint is unjustified. *šakwaak maa-la mbarrer.* -- Do you have any complaints? *fii ʕandak šii šakaawi?* **2.** *daʕwa* pl. *daʕaawi, šakwa* pl. *šakaawi.* He filed a complaint in court. *rafaʕ daʕwa bᵊl-maḥkame.*

complaint department – *daaʔərt˜* (pl. *dawaaʔer˜*) *ᵊš-šakaawi.* Where is the complaint department? *ween daaʔərt ᵊš-šakaawi?*

complete – **1.** *kaamel.* My collection is complete now. *mažmuuʕti kaamle ṣaaret hallaq.* **2.** *tamaam* (invar.). He's a complete fool. *huwwe mahbuul tamaam.*

**All arrangements are complete. *kəll ᵊt-taḥḍiiraat tammet.*

to complete – *tammam//ttammam.* Did you complete your work? *šuu tammamᵊt šəġlak?*

completely – *tamaam, tamaaman.* He convinced me completely. *qanaʕni tamaam.* -- I admit that I was completely wrong about him. *bəʕtə́ref ʔənno ḥəkmi ʕalée kaan ġalaṭ tamaam.* -- He's completely out of his mind. *huwwe mažnuun tamaaman.*

complex – **1.** *mʕaqqad, mšarbak, ʕawiiṣ.* We need time to study this complex problem. *laazəmna waqᵊt la-nədros hal-məšᵊkle l-ᵊmʕaqqade.* **2.** *mrakkab* pl. *-aat, ʕəqde* pl. *ʕəqad.* People say he has an inferiority complex. *biquulu ʔənno fii ʕando mrakkab naqᵊṣ.*

complexion – *bašra.* He has a very dark complexion. *loon bašᵊrto ʔasmar ᵊktiir.*

to **complicate** – *ʕaqqad, šarbak.* Don't complicate matters any more than they are. *laa tʕaqqed ᵊl-ʔumuur ʔaktar məmma hiyye mʕaqqade hallaq.*

complicated – **1.** *mʕaqqad, ʕawiiṣ, mšarbak.* That's a complicated question. *hayy masʔale mʕaqqade.* **2.** *mʕaqqad.* He's a complicated personality. *šaxṣiito mʕaqqade.*

complication – **1.** *taʕqiid* pl. *-aat.* If there are any more complications, we'll have to give up the project. *ʔiza fii taʕqiidaat kamaan laazem ᵊnbaṭṭel kəll ᵊl-mašruuʕ.* **2.** *mḍaaʕafaat* (pl.). Complications after the operation caused his death. *l-ᵊmḍaaʕafaat baʕd ᵊl-ʕamaliyye sabbabet mooto.*

compliment – **1.** *kombliṃaan* pl. *-aat.* Thanks for the compliment! *šəkran ʕal-kombliṃaan tabaʕak!* -- She's just fishing for compliments. *ʕam ᵊddawwer ʕala šii kombliṃaan.* **2.** *taḥiyye* pl. *-aat.* They sent him the tickets with the compliments of the management. *baʕatúu-lo t-tazaaker maʕ taḥiyyaat ᵊl-ʔidaara..*

to compliment – *madaḥ (a madᵊḥ, madiiḥ//mmadaḥ).* He complimented me on my cooking. *madaḥni ʕala ṭabxi.*

to **comply** – *labba.* We are very sorry, but we cannot comply with your request. *mətʔassfiin ᵊktiir bass maa fiina nlabbi ṭalabak.*

to **compose** – **1.** *ʔallaf.* He composed that symphony during the war. *ʔallaf has-səmfoniyye waqt ᵊl-ḥarᵊb.* **2.** *naẓam (o naẓᵊm).* He composed a beautiful poem in memory of the event. *naẓam qaṣiide ḥəlwe təzkaaran ləl-ḥaadse.*

composed – *raziin.* He remained composed during the whole trial. *bəqi raziin ṭuul l-ᵊmḥaakame.*

composed of – *mʔallaf mən.* This fabric is composed of wool and rayon. *hal-ᵊqmaaš ᵊmʔallaf mən* *ṣuuf w-ḥariir ʔəṣṭinaaƐi.*

to compose oneself - *hadda baalo, hadda ḥaalo.* Try to compose yourself. *ḥaawel ᵊthaddi baalak.*

composer - *mlaḥḥen* pl. *-iin, mʔallef˜* (pl. *-iin˜*) *muusiiqa.*

composition - 1. *laḥᵊn* pl. *ʔalḥaan.* The orchestra is going to play his compositions tonight. *l-ʔorkeestra laḥa təƐzef šii mən ʔalḥaano l-leele.* 2. *ʔənšaaye* pl. *-aat.* Have you done your English composition? *Ɛməlᵊt ʔənšaayet ᵊl-ʔəngliizi tabaƐak?* 3. *ʔənša.* I'm taking a course in Arabic composition next fall. *laḥa ʔaaxod darᵊs ʔənša Ɛarabi b-faṣl ᵊl-xariif ᵊž-žaaye.* 4. *tarkiib.* Exactly what is the chemical composition of this product? *qəl-li šuu t-tarkiib ᵊl-kiimaawi bᵊt-tafṣiil la-hal-ᵊbḍaaƐa?* 5. *tartiib.* The composition of that painting is excellent. *tartiib hal-looḥa məmtaaz.*

composure - *razaane, rbaaṭet˜ ᵊž-žaʔᵊš.* I admire his composure in difficult situations. *ʔana ktiir məƐžab b-razaanto* (or *b-ᵊrbaaṭet žaʔšo*) *bᵊl-ḥaalaat ᵊṣ-ṣaƐbe.*

to **comprehend** - *fəhem (a fəhᵊm).* Does he ever comprehend what you say? *b-Ɛəmro byəfham Ɛaleek šuu Ɛam ᵊtquul?*

comprehension - *fəhᵊm.* My comprehension of the subject is rather limited. *fəhmi ləl-mawḍuuƐ maḥduud šwayye.*

comprehensive - 1. *šaamel, šaameƐ.* His statement was fairly comprehensive. *taṣriiḥo kaan nooƐan maa šaamel.* 2. *faḥᵊṣ˜* (pl. *fḥuuṣet˜*) *taxarrož.* When will he take his comprehensive? *ʔeemta bətfuut faḥṣ ᵊt-taxarrož?*

compress - *šaašiyye* pl. *šawaaši.* A cold compress will relieve the pain. *šaašiyye baarde bətxaffef ᵊl-wažaƐ.*

to compress - *ḍaġaṭ (a ḍaġᵊṭ//nḍaġaṭ).* The air is compressed by a pump. *l-hawa btəḍġaṭo ṭrəmbe.*

compromise - 1. *ḥall* (pl. *ḥluul*) *waṣaṭ.* It's only a compromise. *hayye Ɛibaaratan Ɛan ḥall waṣaṭ.* 2. *tanaazol Ɛan.* If you ask me, that's a compromise of your principles. *ʔiza bəddak raʔyi haada tanaazol Ɛan mabaadʔak.*

to compromise - 1. *ttafaq Ɛala ḥall waṣaṭ.* Did the parties finally compromise? *ṭ-ṭarafeen ᵊttafaqu Ɛala ḥall waṣaṭ?* 2. *tnaazal Ɛan.* Don't compromise anything that is important to you. *laa tətnaazal Ɛan ʔayy šii ʔəlo ʔahammiyye Ɛandak.*

compulsory - *ʔəžbaari*, ʔəlzaami*.* Secondary education is compulsory in that country. *t-taƐliim ᵊs-saanawi ʔəžbaari b-hal-ᵊblaad.*

comrade - 1. *rfiiq* pl. *rəfaqa.* He asked his comrades to wait for him. *ṭalab mən rəfaqaato yəstannu.* 2. *rafiiq̈* pl. *rifaaq̈.* Members of some leftist parties call each other "comrade." *ʔaƐḍaaʔ baƐḍ ᵊl-ʔaḥzaab ᵊl-yasaariyye bixaaṭbu baƐḍon ᵊb-laq̈ab rafiiq̈.*

to **conceal** - 1. *xabba, xafa (i ø), katam (o kətmaan).* Are you concealing something from me? *Ɛam ᵊtxabbi Ɛanni šii?* -- He could barely conceal his joy. *bᵊz-zoor kaan Ɛam yəxfi farᵊḥto.* 2. *xabba, xafa.* They concealed the money in the wall. *xabbu l-maṣaari bᵊl-ḥeeṭ.*

conceited - *maġruur.* He's a conceited fool. *huwwe maḥbuul maġruur.*

conceivable - *maƐquul.* But it isn't conceivable that he'd leave without us. *laaken muu maƐquul yruuḥ huwwe balaana.*

to **conceive** - 1. *dabbar.* They conceived a clever plan. *dabbaru xəṭṭa kəlla makᵊr.* 2. *tṣawwar.* She couldn't conceive that they would lie to her. *maa qədret tətṣawwar ʔənno byəkᵊzbu Ɛaleeha.* -- I can't conceive of her doing such a thing. *maa fiini ʔətṣawwar ʔənno hiyye btaƐmel heek šii.*

to **concentrate** - 1. *rakkaz//trakkaz.* We'll have to concentrate on the first part. *laazem ᵊnrakkez Ɛal-qəsm ᵊl-ʔawwal.* 2. *žammaƐ//džammaƐ, rakkaz// trakkaz.* The most important industries are concentrated in the North. *ʔahamm ᵊṣ-ṣinaaƐaat mədžammƐa bᵊš-šamaal.* 3. *stažmaƐ ʔafkaaro.* Concentrate a little harder! *stažmeƐ ʔafkaarak ʔaktar mən heek šwayye.*

concentration - 1. *ḥaṣr˜ ᵊdmaaġ.* This problem requires a lot of concentration. *hal-məšᵊkle bədda ktiir ḥaṣr ᵊdmaaġ.* 2. *tažammoƐ.* The concentration of population in one area raises many difficulties. *tažammoƐ ᵊs-səkkaan ᵊb-manṭiqa waaḥde biʔaddi la-Ɛəddet ᵊṣƐuubaat.*

concept - *fəkra* pl. *ʔafkaar, mafhuum* pl. *mafahiim.* He can't get this concept straight. *maa fii yəfham hal-fəkra Ɛala ḥaqiiqə́ta.*

conception - *fəkra* pl. *ʔafkaar.* He has no conception of what we're doing. *maa Ɛando fəkra šuu Ɛam naƐmel* or ***maa-lo Ɛam yəqder yətṣawwar ᵊš-šii yalli Ɛam naƐᵊmlo.*

concern - 1. *mʔassase* (pl. *-aat*) *ṣinaaƐiyye.* How long have you been with this concern? *qaddeeš ṣar-lak ᵊb-hal-ᵊmʔassase ṣ-ṣinaaƐiyye?* 2. *ʔəhtimaam.* His concern for their safety was not necessary. *ʔəhtimaamo b-salaamə́ton maa kaan ḍaruuri.* 3. *qalaq, šəġᵊl˜ baal.* There's no reason for concern. *maa fii daaƐi ləl-qalaq* (or *la-šəġl ᵊl-baal*). 4. *šəġᵊl.* She said it was no concern of mine. *qaalet ʔənno haš-šii muu šəġli ʔana* (or ***... haš-šii maa bixəṣṣni*).

to show concern - *htamm.* She showed great concern for their welfare. *htammet ᵊktiir ᵊb-maṣlaḥə́ton.*

to concern - *xaṣṣ (ə ø).* This concerns you! *haada bixəṣṣak ʔənte!*

concerning - *b-ᵊxṣuuṣ˜ ...* He said nothing concerning vacation. *maa nawwah šii b-ᵊxṣuuṣ ᵊl-Ɛəṭle.* -- I have a question concerning my tickets. *Ɛandi suʔaal b-ᵊxṣuuṣ ᵊt-tazaaker tabaƐi.*

as far as I'm concerned, etc. - *bᵊn-nəsbe ʔəli, mən žəhti.* As far as he's concerned it's all right. *bᵊn-nəsbe ʔəlo maa fii maaneƐ.* -- As far as I'm concerned you can do as you like. *mən žəhti fiik taƐmel halli bəddak-yda.*

to be concerned about - *qəleq (a qalaq) Ɛala.* We're concerned about their safety. *nəḥna qalqaaniin Ɛala salaamə́ton.*

to be concerned with - *Ɛtana b-.* I'm not concerned with the details. *ʔana maa bəƐtə́ni bᵊt-tafaṣiil* or ***t-tafaṣiil muu šəġli ʔana.*

concert - *ḥafle* (pl. *-aat*) *muusiiqiyye, konseer* pl. *-aat.* How did you like the concert? *kiif šəft ᵊl-ḥafle l-muusiiqiyye?*

concerted - *mwaḥḥad.* Concerted efforts will improve our relations with them. *mažhuudaatna l-ᵊmwaḥḥade raḥa tḥassen Ɛalaaqaatna maƐon.*

conciliation - *msaalame, mṣaalaḥa.*

conciliatory - *msaalem.* In spite of his conciliatory attitude they couldn't come to terms. *bᵊr-raġᵊm mən mawᵊqfo l-ᵊmsaalem maa twaṣṣalu la-ʔəttifaaq.*

concise - *muužaz, məxtḍṣar.* He sent a concise report to his employer. *baƐat taq̈riir muužaz la-raʔiiso.*

to **conclude** - 1. *Ɛaq̈ad (o Ɛaq̈ᵊd//nƐaq̈ad).* They concluded the treaty only two years ago. *Ɛaq̈adu l-ᵊmƐaahade mən sənteen bass.* 2. *stantaž, stadall, zdall.* What do you conclude from his remark? *šuu btəstəntež mən kalaamo?* 3. *xtatam, xatam (o xitaam //nxatam).* They concluded the meeting on a happy note. *xtatamu l-ʔəžtimaaƐ ᵊb-žaww baṣṭ w-suruur.*

conclusion - 1. *xitaam, ʔəxtitaam.* Everyone applauded at the conclusion of his speech. *kəll ᵊn-naas saffaqu waqᵊt xitaam kəlᵊmto.* 2. *xitaam.* In conclusion, I should like to state that ... *bᵊl-xitaam ᵊbḥəbb quul ʔənno ...* 3. *ʔəstəntaaž* pl. *-aat.* His conclusions were not at all accurate. *ʔəstəntaažaato maa kaanet daqiiqa ʔabadan.*

to draw conclusions from - *stantaž mən.* What conclusions am I to draw from that? *šuu l-mafruuḍ fiyyi ʔəstantež mən haš-šii?*

concrete - 1. *baaṭoon.* The bridge is built of concrete. *ž-žəsᵊr mabni mən baaṭoon.* -- They built a concrete walk around the garden. *banu mamša baaṭoon dawaayer ᵊž-žneene.* 2. *ḥaqiiqi*, Ɛamali*.* Give me a concrete example. *Ɛaṭiini misaal ḥaqiiqi.*

to **concur** - *waafaq.* If the members of the committee concur, we shall begin the new project at once. *ʔiza ʔaƐḍaaʔ ᵊl-ləžne waafaqu mnəbda l-mašruuƐ ᵊž-ždiid Ɛal-ḥaarek.*

concurrence - *mwaafaqa.* We do not need his concurrence. *maa mnəḥtaaž la-mwaafaqto.*

concussion - *ʔəhtizaaz.* Concussion of the brain is often serious. *ʔəhtizaaz ᵊl-məxx marraat ᵊktiire bikuun xəṭer.*

to **condemn** - *ḥakam (o ḥəkᵊm//nḥakam) Ɛala.* The court condemned him to death. *l-maḥkame ḥakmet Ɛalée bᵊl-ʔəƐdaam.*

**A committee has condemned this building. *fii ləžne ʔamret ᵊb-tahbiiṭ ᵊl-binaaye.*

condition - 1. *šarᵊṭ* pl. *šruuṭ.* The conditions of the treaty are very clear. *šruuṭ l-ᵊmƐaahade waaḍḥa ktiir.* -- I'll accept the offer on one condition. *bəqbal ᵊl-Ɛarᵊḍ Ɛala šarᵊṭ waaḥed.* 2. *ḥaale.* The house was in poor condition. *l-beet kaan ᵊb-ḥaale taƐbaane.* -- You're in no condition to leave the house. *ḥaaltak maa bətsaaƐdak təṭlaƐ ᵊmn ᵊl-beet.*

**He keeps his things in good condition. *byəƐtə́ni*

b-ᵊġraaḍo ktiir ᵊmniiḥ.

on (or under) any condition - *b-ʔayy ḥaal ᵊmn ᵊl-ʔaḥwaal.* I won't go on any condition. *maa bruuḥ ᵊb-ʔayy ḥaal ᵊmn ᵊl-ʔaḥwaal.*

conditional - 1. *mašruuṭ, mq̈ayyad ᵊb-šarᵊṭ.* His promise to help us was only conditional. *waεdo ʔəlna bᵊl-ᵊmsaaεade maa kaan ʔəlla mašruuṭ.* 2. *šarṭi*.* That's a conditional clause with "ʔən". *hayy žəmle šarṭiyye b-"ʔən".*

conduct - *sluuk.* Your conduct is disgraceful. *sluukak məxzi.*

to conduct - 1. *qaad (u qyaade//nqaad).* Who's conducting the orchestra tonight? *miin εam yquud ᵊl-ʔorkeestra l-yoom εašiyye?* 2. *dabbar.* He conducts his father's business rather well. *εam ydabber šəġᵊl ʔabúu tadbiir laa baʔsa bihi.* 3. *naqal (o naqᵊl//ntaqal).* Metal conducts heat better than wood. *l-maεaaden ᵊbtənqol ᵊl-ḥaraara ʔaḥsan ᵊmn ᵊl-xašab.*

to conduct oneself - 1. *tṣarraf.* She conducts herself like a lady. *btətṣarraf taṣarrof ᵊl-xaanmaat.* 2. *tḥabbak.* He conducted himself well during the cross-examination. *tḥabbak ᵊmniiḥ ʔasna ʔəstənṭaaqo.*

conductor - 1. *kəmᵊsyaari* pl. *-iyye.* Did the conductor punch your ticket? *l-kəmᵊsyaari baxáš-lak tazkartak?* 2. *q̈aaʔed* pl. *q̈uwaad.* Who's the conductor of the orchestra? *miin q̈aaʔed ᵊl-ʔorkeestra?*

to **confer** - 1. *mann (ə mann) b-,ʔanεam b-.* They conferred special honors on him. *mannu εalée b-karaamaat xaaṣṣa.* 2. *tḥaadas.* The President conferred with the Prime Minister yesterday. *r-raʔiis ᵊtḥaadas maε raʔiis ᵊl-wazara mbaareḥ.*

conference - 1. *məʔtámar* pl. *-aat.* The conference lasted three days. *l-məʔtámar daam tlətt iyyaam.* 2. *ʔəžtimaaε* pl. *-aat, mqaabale* pl. *-aat.* He had a conference with the Mayor. *kaan εando ʔəžtimaaε maε raʔiis ᵊl-baladiyye.*

to **confess** - *εtaraf (b-).* I have to confess that I haven't read it yet. *laazem ʔəεtéref ʔənni ləssa maa qareeta.* — The defendant confessed. *l-məddaεa εalée εtaraf.*

confession - *ʔəεtiraaf* pl. *-aat.* The criminal made a full confession. *l-məžrem ᵊεtaraf ʔəεtiraaf kaamel.* — When did you last go to confession? *ʔeemta kaan ʔaaxer marra rəḥᵊt fiiha ləl-ʔəεtiraaf?* or ***ʔeemta ʔaaxer marra εtarafᵊt?*

to **confide** - 1. *ʔtaman, wasaq (-yuusaq ø) b-.* Can I confide in you? *fiini ʔəʔtəmnak?* (or *ʔuusaq fiik?*) 2. *sarr (ə ø).* She confided all kinds of secrets to me. *sarrə́t-li ʔasraar mən žamiiε ᵊl-ʔažnaas.* 3. *wadaε (-yuudaε wadᵊε, wdaaεa//nwadaε).* They confided their valuables to my care. *wadaεu ġraaḍon ᵊs-samiine maεi.*

confidence - 1. *ʔəṭməʔnaan.* His air of confidence fooled us. *εalaamaat ᵊl-ʔəṭməʔnaan εala wəššo xadεətna.* 2. *siq̈a (b-), ʔəεtimaad (εala).* We don't want to destroy his confidence in us. *maa bəddna nṭayyer siq̈ato fiina.*

**He told me that in confidence. *qal-li haš-šii beeni w-beeno.*

to have confidence in - *εtamad εala, wasaq (-yuusaq siq̈a) b-.* I have confidence in him. *bəεtə́med εalée.*

confident - *məṭmaʔənn, waaseq, εala siq̈a.* I'm confident that everything will turn out all right. *ʔana məṭmaʔənn ʔənno kəll šii laḥa yəmši mniiḥ.*

confidential - *maktuum, sərri*.* This letter is confidential. *hal-maktuub maktuum.*

confidentially: He told it to you confidentially? *qal-lak-yáaha beeno w-beenak?* — Confidentially, I don't like that proposal. *beeni w-beenak* (or *l-ḥaki b-sərrak*) *hal-ʔəq̈tiraaḥ muu εaažəbni.*

to **confine** - 1. *qaεεad.* A severe cold has confined him to bed all week. *rašᵊḥ qawi qaεεado bᵊl-farše ṭuul ᵊž-žəmεa.* 2. *xtaṣar.* Please confine your talk to the facts. *mən faḍlak ᵊxtəṣer kalaamak εal-waq̈aayeε.*

to **confirm** - 1. *saadaq εala.* Have they confirmed his appointment yet? *saadaqu εala taεyiino wəlla ləssa?* 2. *sabbat//tsabbat.* That only confirms my faith in him. *w-haada kamaan bisabbet ʔiimaani fii.* — She was confirmed at St. Mary's. *tsabbatet bᵊl-ᵊkniise l-məryamiyye.*

confirmation - 1. *taʔkiid.* We are waiting for a confirmation of this report. *mənṭəẓriin taʔkiid hal-xabar.* 2. *msaadaqa εala.* The confirmation of his appointment is still outstanding. *ləssa laazə́mto l-ᵊmsaadaqa εala taεyiino.* 3. *tasbiit.* Confirmation will take place in the cathedral next Sunday. *t-tasbiit biṣiir bᵊl-katədraaʔiyye yoom ᵊl-ʔaḥad ᵊž-žaaye.*

to **confiscate** - *ṣaadar.* The stolen goods were confiscated by the police. *š-šərṭa ṣaadaret l-ᵊġraaḍ ᵊl-masruuqa.*

conflict - 1. *taḍaarob, tanaaq̈oḍ.* There seems to be a conflict of interests here. *ẓ-ẓaaher ʔənno fii taḍaarob bᵊl-maṣaaleḥ ᵊb-hal-ḥaale.* 2. *tanaazoε, taṣaaroε.* It's the eternal conflict between good and evil. *maa huwwe ʔəlla t-tanaazoε ᵊl-ʔazali been ᵊl-xeer wᵊš-šarr.* 3. *xilaaf* pl. *-aat.* This conflict was bound to break out sooner or later. *hal-xilaaf kaan laa bədd mənno εaažilan ʔaw ʔaažilan.*

to conflict - *tnaaq̈aḍ.* If the two reports conflict, don't believe either of them. *ʔiza t-taq̈riireen byətnaaq̈aḍu laa tsaddeq laa haad w-laa haad.*

to **conform** - *ttabaε.* He doesn't want to conform to local customs. *maa biḥəbb yəttə́beε ᵊl-εaadaat ᵊl-maḥalliyye.*

in **conformity with** - *wəfqan la-, ḥasab~ ...* She acted in conformity with my wishes. *εəmlet wəfqan la-rəġᵊbti.*

to **confuse** - *xarbaṭ, laxbaṭ.* His talk confused me. *kalaamo xarbaṭni.* — He must have confused me with someone else. *laazem ykuun xarbaṭ beeni w-been waaḥed taani.*

confusion - 1. *xarbaṭa, laxbaṭa.* That will cause a lot of confusion. *haš-šaġle laḥa tsabbeb xarbaṭa ktiire.* 2. *haraž w-maraž.* He escaped in the confusion. *fəlet bᵊl-haraž wᵊl-maraž.*

congestion - 1. *ʔəḥtiq̈aan.* The doctor says he has a congestion in his lungs. *d-doktoor qaal ʔənno maεo ʔəḥtiq̈aan bᵊr-riʔa.* 2. *ʔəzdiḥaam.* Traffic congestion makes him very nervous. *ʔəzdiḥaam ᵊl-muruur bixallíi ktiir ᵊmnarvez.*

Congo - *l-konġo.*

to **congratulate** - *hanna.* We congratulated him on his success. *hanneenḍa εala nažaaḥo.* — May I congratulate you on your birthday? *bhanniik ᵊb-εiid miilaadak.*

congratulations - *tahaani* (pl.). Our heartiest congratulations! *ʔaḥarr tahaaniina!*

**Congratulations! *bhanniik!*

to **congregate** - *ḥtašad.* A crowd congregated in the square. *fii žamε ᵊḥtašad bᵊs-saaḥa.*

congregation - *ṭaayfe* pl. *ṭawaayef.* Our congregation has a new pastor. *ṭaayfətna ʔəžaaha xuuri ždiid.*

congress - *məʔtámar.* He got up to address the congress. *waqqaf yəxṭob bᵊl-məʔtámar.*

to **conjugate** - *ṣarraf.* Did she conjugate the verb correctly? *ṣarrafet ᵊl-fəεᵊl maẓbuuṭ?*

conjugation - *taṣriif* pl. *-aat* and *taṣariif.* He hasn't learned all the conjugations yet. *ləssa maa tεallam ᵊt-taṣriif kəllo.*

conjunction - *ḥarᵊf~* (pl. *ḥruuf~*) *εaṭᵊf.* Name some conjunctions for me. *sammíi-li kam ḥarᵊf εaṭᵊf.*

to **connect** - 1. *waṣal (-yuuṣel waṣᵊl//nwaṣal) b-.* Operator, please connect me with the main office. *santraal, wṣəlni mən faḍlak bᵊl-maktab ᵊr-raʔiisi.* — Connect these wires to the battery. *wṣeel haš-šaraayeṭ bᵊl-baṭṭaariyya.* 2. *rakkab, waṣal.* Did they connect your telephone yet? *rakkabúu-lak* (or *waṣalúu-lak*) *ᵊt-talifoon wəlla ləssa?* 3. *qaaran been~.* It's funny, but I never connected the two in my mind. *εažiib, ᵊb-ḥayaati maa qaaranᵊt been ᵊt-tneen.*

connecting rod - *byeel* pl. *-aat.*

connection - 1. *mwaaṣale* pl. *-aat.* Telephone connections with that town are very poor. *l-ᵊmwaaṣalaat ᵊt-talifooniyye maε hal-balad ᵊktiir ᵊḍεiife.* 2. *εalaaqa* pl. *-aat, waaṣṭa* pl. *waṣaayeṭ.* He has very good connections. *ʔəlo εalaaqaat ᵊktiir ᵊmniiḥa.* 3. *waṣle* pl. *-aat.* A faulty connection caused the short circuit. *waṣle εaaṭle (bᵊš-šaraayeṭ) sabbabet ᵊl-kontaak.*

**In what connection did he mention it? *b-ᵊxṣuuṣ ʔeeš* (or *b-ᵊmnaasabᵊt ʔeeš*) *zakára?*

**I missed my connection in Aleppo. *raaḥ εaliyyi* (or *faatni*) *t-treen* (or *raaḥet εaliyyi, faatə́tni ṭ-ṭayyaara,* etc.) *b-ḥalab.*

to make connections - 1. *ġayyar ᵊt-treen* (or *ᵊl-baaṣ,* etc.). You make connections at the next station. *bətġayyer ᵊt-treen bᵊl-ᵊmḥaṭṭa ž-žaaye.* 2. *ləḥeq (a laḥaqaan), laḥḥaq.* I hope I can still make connections with the afternoon train. *nšaaḷḷa byəṭlaε ᵊb-ʔiidi ʔəlḥaq treen baεd ᵊḍ-ḍəhᵊr.*

to **conquer** - *stawla εala.* He wanted to conquer the

whole world. *raad yəstawli Ɛal-Ɛaalam kəllo.*
conqueror - *faateḥ* pl. *-iin, ġaazi* pl. *ġəzaat.*
conscience - *ḍamiir.* I have a clear conscience. *ḍamiiri məṛtaaḥ.* -- Now his conscience is bothering him. *ḍamiiro Ɛam yƐazzbo hallaq.* -- He has no conscience in these matters. *maa-lo ḍamiir w-laa wəždaan ᵊb-haš-šaġlaat.*
in all conscience - *b-kəll taᵓkiid.* In all conscience, I cannot give him my approval. *b-kəll taᵓkiid maa bəqder waafqo Ɛala haš-šaġle.*
conscientious - *ṣaaḥeb˜ zəmme* f. *ṣaaḥbet˜ zəmme* pl. *ṣḥaab˜ zəmme.* He's a conscientious worker. *huwwe šaġġiil ṣaaḥeb zəmme.*
conscious - **1.** *daryaan (b-), šaaƐer (b-), ḥaases (b-).* I wasn't conscious of my mistake. *maa kənᵊt daryaan ᵊb-ġalᵊṭṭi.* **2.** *waƐyaan.* Doctor, is he conscious? *daxlak ya doktoor, huwwe waƐyaan?*
consciousness - *waƐi, šuƐuur.*
consecutive - **1.** *mətwaali, məttaabeƐ.* He forgot his umbrella on three consecutive days. *nəsi šamsiito tlətt iyyaam mətwaalye.* **2.** *mutalaaḥeq, mutataabeƐ.* He's very good at consecutive interpreting. *huwwe ktiir ᵊmniiḥ bᵊt-taržame l-mutalaaḥiqa.*
consent - *mwaafaqa (Ɛala), msaadaqa (Ɛala).* This was done without my consent. *haš-šii ṣaar biduun ᵊmwaafaqti.*
to consent - *waafaq Ɛala.* He consented to stay. *waafaq (Ɛala ᵓənno) yəbqa.*
consequence - *Ɛaaqbe* pl. *Ɛawaaqeb.* I'm afraid of the consequences. *ᵓana xaayef ᵊmn ᵊl-Ɛawaaqeb.*
**That's of no consequence. *haš-šii maa-lo ᵓahammiyye ᵓabadan* or *haš-šii muu zaat baal ᵓabadan.*
as a consequence - *bᵊn-natiiže, li-zaalek, mənšaan heek.* The car had a flat tire and as a consequence we were late for the meeting. *s-sayyaara duulaab mən dawaliiba banšar w-bᵊn-natiiže tᵓaxxarna Ɛan ᵊl-ᵓəžtimaaƐ.*
consequently - *bᵊn-natiiže, li-zaalek, mənšaan heek.*
conservation - *mḥaafaẓa Ɛala.* The government is concerned with the conservation of natural resources. *l-ᵊḥkuume məhtamme bᵊl-ᵊmḥaafaẓa Ɛas-sarwaat ᵊṭ-ṭabiiƐiyye.*
conservatism - *mḥaafaẓa.*
conservative - **1.** *mḥaafeẓ.* He's too conservative. *huwwe mḥaafeẓ ᵓaktar ᵊmn ᵊl-laazem.* **2.** *mətḥaffeẓ, məƐtədel.* That's a fairly conservative estimate. *haada taqdiir mətḥaffeẓ la-daraže.*
to **consider** - **1.** *baḥas (a baḥᵊs//nbaḥas), Ɛtabar.* We have to consider the problem from every angle. *laazem nəbḥas ᵊl-qaḍiyye mən kəll nawaaḥiiha.* **2.** *ftakar b-.* I'll consider it. *bəftəker fiiha.* **3.** *Ɛtabar, ḥasab (e/o ø).* I consider him an able chemist. *bəƐtəbro kiimaawi fahmaan.* **4.** *ᵓaxad ᵊb-Ɛeen ᵊl-ᵓəƐtibaar.* We have to consider his age. *laazem naaxod Ɛəmro b-Ɛeen ᵊl-ᵓəƐtibaar.* **5.** *raaƐa, ḥasab ᵊḥsaab la-.* He never considers the feelings of others. *maa biraaƐi ᵓabadan šuƐuur ᵊl-ġeer* (or *maa byəḥsob ᵓabadan ᵊḥsaab la-šuƐuur ᵊl-ġeer*).
considerable - *məḥtáram, laa baᵓᵊs fii.* That's a considerable sum. *haada mablaġ məḥtáram* (or ... *mablaġ laa baᵓᵊs fii*). -- Solving the problem took considerable effort. *ḥall ᵊl-masᵓale ṭṭallab ᵊžhuud laa baᵓᵊs fiiha.*
considerate: My boss is very considerate. *raᵓiisi biraaƐi ᵓumuur ġeero ktiir.* -- That was very considerate of you. *haada kaan kəllo taqdiir mənnak.*
consideration - **1.** *baḥᵊs, tafkiir.* This requires careful consideration. *haš-šii bəddo baḥᵊs daqiiq.* **2.** *ᵓəƐtibaar* pl. *-aat.* There are three considerations which we should not overlook. *fii tlətt ᵓəƐtibaaraat laazem maa nədžaahálon.*
under consideration - *taḥt ᵊn-naẓar, taḥt ᵊd-diraase.* Three plans are under consideration. *fii tlətt mašariiƐ taḥt ᵊn-naẓar.*
to have (or **show**) **consideration** - *raaƐa šuƐuur˜ ..., Ɛtabar, tqaḷḷan.* He had no consideration for anybody. *maa kaan yraaƐi šuƐuur ḥada* or *maa kaan yəƐtəber* (or *yətqaḷḷan*) *ḥada.*
to take into consideration - *ᵓaxad ᵊb-Ɛeen ᵊl-ᵓəƐtibaar, fakkar b-, ftakar b-.* We have to take several things into consideration. *fii Ɛəddet ᵓašya laazem naaxə́da b-Ɛeen ᵊl-ᵓəƐtibaar* (or ... *laazem ᵊnfakker, nəftə́ker fiiha*).
on **consignment** - *b-rasm ᵊl-ᵓamaane.* He took the goods on consignment. *ᵓaxad l-ᵊbḍaaƐa b-rasm ᵊl-ᵓamaane.*
to **consist of** - *(kaan) mᵓallaf mən.* The meal consisted of fish, vegetables, and coffee. *l-wažbe kaanet ᵊmᵓallafe mən samak w-xəḍar w-qahwe.*
to consist in - *(kaan) Ɛibaara Ɛan.* His entertainment consists in laughing at the mistakes of others. *təslaayto Ɛibaara Ɛan ᵊḍ-ḍəḥᵊk Ɛala ġalṭaat ġeero.*
consistent - **1.** *manṭiqi*.* He's not very consistent in his work. *huwwe muu manṭiqi hal-qadd ᵊb-šəġlo.* **2.** *məttə́feq (maƐ), mətmaaši (maƐ).* His attitude is not consistent with our policy. *mawᵊqfo muu məttə́feq maƐ siyaasətna* or **mawᵊqfo maa byəttə́feq (or byətmaaša) maƐ siyaasətna.*
to **console** - *Ɛazza.* No one can console her over the loss of her father. *maa fii ḥada yƐazziiha Ɛan fəqdaana la-ᵓabuuha.*
to **consolidate** - **1.** *qawwa//tqawwa.* He is trying to consolidate his power so that he can win the election. *Ɛam yḥaawel yqawwi nufuuzo ḥatta yərbaḥ bᵊl-ᵓəntixaab.* **2.** *damaž (o damᵊž//ndamaž), ḍamm (ə ḍamm//nḍamm), žammaƐ//džammaƐ.* The government consolidated the railroad companies under one head. *l-ᵊḥkuume damžet šərkaat səkak ᵊl-ḥadiid taḥᵊt ᵓidaara waaḥde.* **3.** *ndamažu (maƐ baƐḍon), nḍammu maƐ baƐḍon.* The two firms consolidated last month. *š-šərᵊkteen ᵊndamažu maƐ baƐḍon bᵊš-šahr ᵊl-maaḍi.*
conspiracy - *mᵓaamara* pl. *-aat.*
conspirator - *mətᵓaamer* pl. *-iin.*
to **conspire** - *tᵓaamar (maƐ).* They conspired to overthrow the government. *tᵓaamaru yəqᵊlbu l-ᵊḥkuume* (or ... *Ɛala qalb l-ᵊḥkuume*).
constant - **1.** *məstmərr, bala waqfe, biduun ᵓənqiṭaaƐ.* The constant noise is getting on my nerves. *haḍ-ḍoože l-məstmərra Ɛam ᵊthədd-ə́lli ᵓaƐṣaabi.* **2.** *daaᵓem, məstadiim.* He's in constant danger. *huwwe b-xaṭar daaᵓem.* **3.** *saabet.* His attitude remained constant despite their arguments. *mawᵊqfo bəqi saabet bᵊr-raġᵊm Ɛan xanaayə́qon.*
constantly - *Ɛala ṭuul, bala waqfe, biduun ᵓənqiṭaaƐ.* The phone has been ringing constantly. *t-talifoon ṣar-lo mədde Ɛam ydəqq Ɛala ṭuul* or **t-talifoon ṣar-lo mədde Ɛam ydəqq maa fatar.*
to **constitute** - *šakkal.* Proper housing constitutes the major problem in their city. *masᵓalet ᵊl-masaaken ᵊṣ-ṣaalḥa bətšakkel ᵓahamm məšᵊkle b-baládon.*
constitution - **1.** *dastuur* pl. *dasatiir.* The Constitution of the United States went into effect in 1789. *dastuur ᵊl-wilaayaat ᵊl-məttəḥde bada l-Ɛamal fii sənᵊt ᵓalf w-sabᵊƐ miyye w-təsƐda w-tmaaniin.* **2.** *bənye.* He has a very strong constitution. *bənᵊyto ktiir qawiyye.*
constitutional - *dastuuri*.* They want to pass a constitutional amendment. *bəddon ysənnu taƐdiil dastuuri.*
to **construct** - *Ɛammar//tƐammar, bana (i binaaᵓ//nbana).* Our company plans to construct a new hotel on this site. *šərkətna niyyə́ta tƐammer ᵓoteel ᵊždiid ᵊb-han-nəqṭa.*
construction - **1.** *binaaye* pl. *-aat, Ɛamaara* pl. *-aat.* They're going to tear down every construction in this quarter. *raḥa yəhᵊdmu kəll ᵊl-binaayaat ᵊb-hal-ḥayy.* **2.** *taƐmiir, Ɛamaar, binaaᵓ.* Construction of the new house will start next month. *taƐmiir ᵊl-beet ᵊž-ždiid byəbda bᵊš-šahr ᵊž-žaaye.*
under construction - *taḥt ᵊt-taƐmiir.* The bridge is still under construction. *ž-žəsᵊr ləssáa taḥt ᵊt-taƐmiir* or **ž-žəsᵊr ləssda Ɛam yənbə́na.*
consul - *qənṣol* pl. *qanaaṣel.*
consulate - *qənṣliyye* pl. *-aat.* Were you at the American consulate? *kənᵊt bᵊl-qənṣliyye l-ᵓameerkiyye?*
to **consult** - *stašaar.* You should have consulted us. *kaan ᵓaḥsán-lak təstašiirna.*
consultation - *mšaawara* pl. *-aat.* My consultation with the doctor won't take long. *mšaawarti maƐ ᵊl-ḥakiim maa raḥa ṭṭuul.*
to **consume** - **1.** *ᵓakal (-yaakol ᵓakᵊl), stahlak.* My car consumes a lot of gas. *sayyaarti btaakol banziin ᵓakᵊl.* -- I've never seen anyone consume so much bread. *b-ḥayaati maa šəfᵊt ḥada byaakol xəbᵊz hal-qadd.* **2.** *xarrab//txarrab, ḥaraq (e ḥarᵊq//nḥaraq).* The fire consumed three public buildings. *l-ḥariiqa xarrabet tlətt binaayaat ᵊƐmuumiyye.*
consumer - *məstahlek* pl. *-iin.*
consumption - **1.** *ᵓəstəhlaak.* Consumption has gone up fifty per cent. *l-ᵓəstəhlaak zaad bᵊl-miyye xamsiin.* **2.** *səll.* He died of consumption. *maat bᵊs-səll.*
contact - **1.** *ᵓəttiṣaal* pl. *-aat.* Contact with them gave him a new perspective. *ᵓəttiṣaalo fiihon xallda yšuuf ᵊl-ᵓumuur ġeer šəkᵊl* (or *fatáḥ-lo ᵓəfq ᵊždiid*). -- I made several new business contacts on

that trip. *εməlᵊt εəddet ʔəttiṣaalaat tižaariyye ždiide b-has-safra.* **2.** *waaṣṭa* pl. *waṣaayeṭ.* Our contact in the capital informs us of the latest developments. *waaṣəṭṭna bᵊl-εaaṣme bixabbərna εan ʔaaxer ᵊt-taṭawwuraat.*

to come into contact - *qaabal, tεarraf εala.* He's never come into contact with foreigners. *b-ḥayaato maa qaabal ʔažaaneb.*

to contact - *ttaṣal b-.* I'll contact you as soon as I arrive. *bəttṣ́əl fiik saaεet-ma bəṣal.*

contagious - *məεdi*.* Preventive medicine is lowering the rate of contagious diseases. *ṭ-ṭəbb ᵊl-wiqaaʔi εam yxaffeḍ nəsbet ᵊl-ʔamraaḍ ᵊl-məεdiyye.*

to **contain** - **1.** *ḥtawa εala.* That trunk contains clothing. *has-sanduuq byəḥtə́wi εala ʔawaaεi* or ***has-sanduuq fii ʔawaaεi.* **2.** *ḍḍamman.* The contract seems to contain a number of unusual stipulations. *hal-ᵊmqaawale byəẓhar ʔənno btəḍḍamman* (or ***fiiha*) *εəddet ᵊšruuṭ šaazze.* **3.** *ẓabaṭ (o ẓabᵊṭ).* She couldn't contain her joy any longer. *maa εaad ṭəleε ᵊb-ʔiidha təẓboṭ farḥa.*

container - *waaεa* pl. *-aat.*

to **contemplate** - *fakkar.* We're contemplating a trip to the mountains. *εam ᵊnfakker ᵊb-rəḥle ləž-žbaal.* -- He said he wanted to be alone to contemplate. *qaal ʔənno bəddo yəbqa waḥdo la-yfakker.*

contemporary - **1.** *mεaaṣer, ḥaali*.* I find contemporary politics very confusing. *šaayə́f-lak ᵊs-siyaase l-ᵊmεaaṣra bətḥayyer ᵊktiir.* **2.** *mžaayel, mεaaṣer.* They were contemporaries of his father. *kaanu mžaayliin ʔabúu.*

contempt - **1.** *ʔəzdiraaʔ, ʔəḥtiqaar.* He couldn't hide his contempt for them. *maa qəder yxabbi ʔəzdiraaʔo ʔəlhon.* **2.** *taḥqiir, ʔihaane.* They fined him for contempt of court. *ḥaṭṭu εalée ġaraame b-sabab taḥqiir ᵊl-maḥkame.*

contemptible - *məḥtáqar, ḥaqiir, xasiis.* That was a contemptible lie! *hayy kaanet kəzbe məḥtáqara!*

content - **1.** *məḥtáwa* pl. *məḥtawayaat.* The alcoholic content of this wine is negligible. *məḥtáwa l-kuḥuul ᵊb-han-nbiid ṭafiif.* **2.** *məḥtawayaat* (pl.). The content of the course is excellent. *məḥtawayaat ᵊd-darᵊs məmtaaze.*

contents - *məḥtawayaat* (pl.), *mawḍuudaat* (pl.). Dissolve the contents of this package in one glass of water. *dawweb məḥtawayaat hal-baakeet ᵊb-kaaset mayy.* -- The contents of your trunk have to be examined. *məḥtawayaat sanduuqak laazem tətfattaš.*

table of contents - *fahras* pl. *fahaares, fahras˜ ᵊl-məḥtawayaat.*

content - *məktə́fi, raḍyaan, qanεaan.* He was content with what we offered him. *kaan məktə́fi b-halli εaraḍnda εalée.*

contentment - *qanaaεa, ʔəktífa.*

contest - *mbaaraze* pl. *-aat.* Who won the contest? *miin rəbeḥ l-ᵊmbaaraze?*

to contest - *ṭaεan (a ṭaεᵊn//nṭaεan) b-.* They're contesting the will. *εam yəṭεanu bᵊl-waṣiyye.*

context - *siyaaq˜ ᵊl-ḥadiis.* The meaning of that word depends on its context. *maεnaat hal-kəlme byətwaqqaf εala siyaaq ᵊl-ḥadiis yalli žaaye fíi.*

**Please give this word in context. *mən faḍlak εaṭiini hal-kəlme kiif-ma btəži bᵊl-ḥaki.*

**Can you give me that statement in context? *fiik taεṭiini n-naṣṣ ᵊl-kaamel yalli ʔəža hat-taṣriiḥ fii?*

continent - *qaarra* pl. *-aat.* He has traveled to every continent. *saafar la-kəll ᵊl-qaarraat.*

continual - *məst(a)mərr, bala waqfe, biduun ʔənqiṭaaε.* The continual noise is getting on my nerves. *haḍ-ḍoože l-məstmərra εam ᵊtḥədd-ə́lli ʔaεṣaabi.*

continually - *b-ʔəstəmraar, bala waqfe, biduun ʔənqiṭaaε, εala ṭuul.* The line is continually busy. *b-ʔəstəmraar ᵊl-xaṭṭ mašġuul.*

continuation - *ʔəstəmraar, mwaaṣale, mwaaẓabe.*

to **continue** - **1.** *waaṣal.* They continued the talks for three days. *waaṣalu l-ᵊmḥaadasaat tlətt iyyaam.* **2.** *kammal, waaṣal.* We'll continue our discussion tomorrow. *mənkammel baḥᵊsna bəkra.* **3.** *waaṣal, taabaε.* Let's continue with our work. *xalliina nwaaṣel šəġᵊlna.* **4.** *kammal.* They continued the fence on out to the road. *kammalu l-xəṣṣ la-barra εand ᵊṭ-ṭariiq.* -- Continue, I'm listening. *kammel, εam bəsmə́ε-lak.* **5.** *stamarr.* The heat is continuing. *š-šoob məstmərr.* **6.** *twaaṣal.* The performance continued after a short intermission. *l-εarḍ ᵊtwaaṣal baεᵊd ʔəstiraaḥa qaṣiire.*

to continue on - *kammal.* I want to continue on to Aleppo. *bəddi kammel la-ḥalab.*

continuous - *məstmərr, mətwaaṣel.* Where does that continuous noise come from? *mneen žaaye haḍ-ḍoože l-məstmərra?*

continuously - *bala waqfe, biduun ʔənqiṭaaε, b-ʔəstəmraar, εala ṭuul.* The phone has been ringing continuously. *t-talifoon ṣar-lo mədde εam ydəqq bala waqfe.*

contract - *mqaawale* pl. *-aat, kontraat* pl. *-aat.* I refuse to sign that contract. *bərfoḍ ʔəmḍi hal-ᵊmqaawale.*

to contract - **1.** *qallaṣ.* Heat expands, cold contracts. *l-ḥaraara bətmadded wᵊl-buruude bətqalleṣ.* **2.** *tqallaṣ.* The metal must have contracted. *l-maεdan laazem ykuun ᵊtqallaṣ.* **3.** *tεahhad.* They've contracted to put up the building in five months. *tεahhadu yəbnu l-binaaye b-xamᵊst əšhor.* **4.** *laqaṭ (o laqᵊṭ).* I contracted pneumonia. *laqaṭṭ zaat ᵊr-riʔa.*

contractor - *mqaawel* pl. *-iin, mətεahhed* pl. *-iin.*

to **contradict** - **1.** *naaqaḍ, kazzab.* He wrote an article to contradict what they had said. *katab maqaale ḥatta ynaaqeḍ fiiha ʔaqwaalon.* **2.** *naaqaḍ.* This contradicts every known theory. *haada binaaqeḍ kəll naẓariyye maεruufe.* -- Don't contradict me! *laa tnaaqəḍni!*

contradiction - *mnaaqaḍa* pl. *-aat, tanaaqoḍ.* His thesis is full of contradictions. *ʔəṭruuḥto malaane mnaaqaḍaat* or *ʔəṭruuḥto kəlla tanaaqoḍ.*

contradictory - *mətnaaqeḍ.* We heard several contradictory reports on it. *sməεna εəddet ʔaxbaar mətnaaqḍa εanha.*

contraption - *makana* (pl. *-aat*) *ġariibe.* What kind of contraption is that? *šuu hal-makana l-ġariibe?*

contrary - *εaniid.* She's very contrary. *hiyye εaniide ktiir.*

contrary to - **1.** *εakᵊs˜ ..., b-εakᵊs˜ ...* Contrary to all expectations he passed the exam. *εakᵊs kəll halli twaqqaεnda nažaḥ bᵊl-faḥᵊṣ.* **2.** *εakᵊs˜ ..., b-εakᵊs˜ ..., mxaalef˜ ..., mεaakes˜ ..., ḍəḍḍ˜ ...* That's contrary to our agreement. *haada εakᵊs ʔəttifaaqna.*

on the contrary - *bᵊl-εakᵊs, εal-εakᵊs.* On the contrary, nothing could be worse. *bᵊl-εakᵊs, maa fii šii bikuun ʔaεṭal mən heek.* -- On the contrary, that's what he wants. *bᵊl-εakᵊs, haada halli bəddo-yáa.*

contrast - *tabaayon, ʔəxtilaaf.* There's a big contrast between the two brothers. *fii tabaayon ᵊkbiir been ᵊl-ʔaxxeen.*

to contrast - *qaaran, waazan.* He contrasted the programs of the two parties. *qaaran ᵊl-bərnaamžeen tabaε ᵊl-ḥəzbeen.* -- She contrasted his poem with one she had read in the magazine. *qaaranet qaṣiidto b-qaṣiide qará́ta bᵊl-mažalle.*

**These red flowers contrast well with the dark background. *hal-ᵊwruud ᵊl-ḥəmᵊr ṭaalεiin ḥəlwiin maε ᵊl-ʔaswad yalli waraahon.*

to **contribute** - **1.** *tbarraε b-.* Have you contributed anything to the fund? *tbarraεt ᵊb-šii ləs-sanduuq?* **2.** *zaad (i zyaade) εala.* This noise just contributes to the confusion. *haḍ-ḍoože bədziid kamaan εal-balbale.* **3.** *saaham b-.* She contributed a fine article to the magazine. *saahamet ᵊb-maqaale ẓariife ləl-mažalle.*

**He contributes to the local paper. *byənšor mən mədde la-mədde bᵊž-žariide l-maḥalliyye.*

contribution - *tabarroε* pl. *-aat.* We received your contribution with thanks. *tsallamna tabarruεaatak maε ᵊš-šəkᵊr.*

**Contributions to the magazine are welcome. *mənraḥḥeb ᵊb-ʔayy ᵊmsaahame ʔadabiyye ləl-mažalle.*

control - *ṣayṭara.* He lost control of the car. *fəqed ᵊṣ-ṣayṭara εala sayyaarto.* -- The conservatives won control of the Senate. *l-ᵊmḥaafẓiin rəbḥu ṣ-ṣayṭara εala mažles ᵊš-šiyuux.* -- The children are getting beyond my control. *l-ᵊwlaad εam yəṭlaεu εan ṣayṭarti.*

**Is everything under control? *kəll šii maaši maẓbuuṭ?*

controls - *qyaade.* The co-pilot took over the controls. *ṭ-ṭayyaar l-ᵊmεaawen ᵊstalam l-ᵊqyaade.*

to have control of - **1.** *malak (e ∅) zimaam˜ ...* He seems to have control of the situation. *byəẓhar εalée maalek zimaam ᵊl-waḍᵊε.* **2.** *ṣayṭar εala.* The Liberals have control of the House of Representatives. *l-ʔaḥraar ᵊmṣayṭriin εala mažles ᵊn-nuwwaab.*

to have under control - *ẓabaṭ (o ẓabᵊṭ).* He always has himself under control. *daayman byəẓboṭ ḥaalo.*

to control - 1. *ṣayṭar εala.* He controls sixty percent of the business. *bišayṭer εala səttiin bəl-miyye mn əš-šərke.* 2. *ẓabaṭ (o ẓabəṭ), ḍabaṭ (o ḍabəṭ).* He tried to control his temper, but he simply couldn't. *ḥaawal yəẓboṭ ʔaεṣaabo, bass maa qəder.* -- You have to learn to control yourself. *laazem tətεallam təẓboṭ ḥaalak.*

**Who controls the House of Representatives? *šuu ʔaqwa ḥəzəb b-mažles ən-nuwwaab?*

controversial - *məxtdlaf fii.* He loves to talk about controversial subjects. *biḥəbb yəḥki εan mawaḍiiε məxtdlaf fiiha.*

controversy - *xilaaf* pl. *-aat.* The newspaper published both sides of the controversy. *ž-žariide našret wəžəhteen ən- naẓar ət-tənteen tabaε əl-xilaaf.*

convenience - *ʔasbaab~ ər-rafaahiyye* (pl.). Our new apartment has every modern convenience. *l-ʔabarṭmaan əž-ždiid tabaεna fii kəll ʔasbaab ər-rafaahiyye l-ḥadiise.*

**Call me at your earliest convenience. *talfə́n-li b-ʔaqrab waqət binaasbak.*

convenient - *mwaafeq, mnaaseb.* The bus service here is very convenient. *mwaaṣalaat əl-baaṣ hoon əktiir əmwaafqa.* -- The apartment is convenient to my work. *l-ʔabarṭmaan əmnaaseb la-šəġli.*

conveniently - *b-əshuule, b-raaḥa.* You can do it conveniently while you're in town. *btəqder taεmə́la b-əshuule w-ʔənte bəl-balad.*

**The hotel is conveniently located. *l-ʔoteel waaqeε əb-markaz əmnaaseb.*

convent - *deer~* (pl. *dyuuret~*) *raahbaat.*

convention - 1. *mahražaan* pl. *-aat.* Were you at last year's convention? *kənət b-əl-mahražaan tabaε εaamnawwal?* 2. *l-εərf wəl-εaade.* She does everything according to convention. *btaεmel kəll šii ḥasab əl-εərf wəl-εaade.*

conventional - *ʔəεtiyaadi*, εaadi*.* I prefer the conventional method. *bfaḍḍel əl-mənhaaž əl-ʔəεtiyaadi.*

**They're awfully conventional. *maa byəmšu ʔəlla ḥasab əl-εərf wəl-εaade.*

conversation - 1. *ḥadiis* pl. *ʔaḥadiis.* The conversation at lunch was rather dull. *l-ḥadiis waqt əl-ġada kaan əšwayye mməll.* 2. *mḥaadase* pl. *-aat.* The conversations between the representatives of the two countries were very fruitful. *l-əmḥaadasaat been manduubiin əd-doolteen kaanet məsəmra ktiir.*

to have a conversation - *tḥaadas.* I had a long conversation with the boss. *tḥaadasət maε ər-raʔiis waqət ṭawiil.*

to **convert** - 1. *qanaε (e ʔəqnaaε//qtanaε).* Can't I convert you to my way of thinking? *maa bəqder ʔəqənεak əb-wəžhet naẓari?* 2. *ḥawwal, baddal, ġayyar.* I'd like to convert these dollars into pounds. *ḥaabeb ḥawwel had-dolaaraat la-leeraat.*

convict - *masžuun* pl. *masažiin.* Three convicts escaped. *fii tlatt masažiin harabu.*

to convict - *žarram//džarram.* They convicted him of murder. *žarramúu bəl-qatəl.*

conviction - 1. *qanaaεa.* Nothing can shake his conviction. *maa fii šii yzaḥzeḥ qanaaεto.* 2. *ʔidaane.* His conviction is a foregone conclusion. *ʔidaanto laa bədd mənha.*

to **convince** - *qanaε (e ʔəqnaaε//qtanaε).* You can't convince me. *maa btəqder təqnəεni.* -- That's not a convincing argument. *hayy maa-lha ḥəžže məqənεa* or *hayy ḥəžže maa btəqneε.*

cook - *ṭabbaax* pl. *-iin,* f. *ṭabbaaxa* pl. *-aat.* She's the best cook we ever had. *hiyye ʔaḥsan ṭabbaaxa ʔəžet la-εanna.* -- Too many cooks spoil the broth. *kətret əṭ-ṭabbaaxiin əbtəḥreq əṭ-ṭaεaam.*

to cook - 1. *ṭabax (o ṭabəx//nṭabax).* We don't have time to cook tonight. *maa fii εanna waqət nəṭbox əl-leele.* 2. *stawa.* Give the meat time to cook well. *xalli l-laḥme εan-naar la-təstə́wi mniiḥ.*

**What's cooking these days? *šuu ṣaayer bəd-dənye hal-ʔiyyaam?*

**What did they cook up now? *šuu ṭaaleε əb-raason hallaq?*

**If he's late again, we'll really cook his goose! *ʔiza tʔaxxar taani marra mnəḥəlko εan ṣaḥiiḥ!*

cookie - *baskoote* coll. *baskoot* pl. *-aat.* I brought you some cookies. *žəbt-ə́llak šwayyet baskoot.*

cooking - *ṭabəx.* Her cooking is wonderful! *ṭabxa εaẓiim!*

cool - 1. *baared.* The nights are rather cool here. *l-layaali hoon baarde šwayye.* -- Keep it in a cool place. *hfḍa b-maḥall baared.* -- Their welcome was very cool. *ʔəstəqbaalon kaan əktiir baared.* 2. *xafiif.* Wait until I get into something cool! *stanna la-ḥəṭṭ εaliyyi šii xafiif.*

**He's made a cool million. *rəbeḥ malyoon εala baared əl-maaʔ.*

to get cool - *barad (o ø).* It gets pretty cool here towards evening. *d-dənye btəbrod əktiir hoon naaḥ əl-masa.*

to keep cool - 1. *ḍall haadi.* I tried to keep cool when he insulted me. *ḥaawalət ḍall haadi lamma bahdalni* or **ḥaawalət ʔaaxod bahdalto b-bruude.* 2. *boorad.* It's impossible to keep cool in this weather. *məstaḥiil əl-waaḥed yboored əb-haṭ-ṭaqəṣ.*

to cool - *barad (o ø).* Don't let this soup cool too long. *laa txalli haš-šooraba təbrod əktiir.*

to cool off - 1. *barad (o ø).* Stop the engine and let it cool off. *ʔəṭfi l-mootoor w-xalli yəbrod.* 2. *barad (o ø) xəlqo.* That'll give her time to cool off. *haada byaεṭiiha waqət yəbrod xəlqa.*

cooling system - *žihaaz~* (pl. *ʔažhizet~*) *tabriid.* The cooling system is clogged with rust. *žihaaz ət-tabriid masṭuum bəṣ-ṣəde.*

coop - *qənn* pl. *qnaan.* Clean out the chicken coop. *naḍḍef qənn əž-žaažaat.*

cooped up - *maḥbuus.* I can't keep the children cooped up in the house all day long. *maa fiini xalli l-əwlaad maḥbuusiin ṭuul ən-nhaar bəl-beet.*

to **co-operate** - *tεaawan.* He promised to co-operate with the police in the search for the killer. *waεad ʔənno yətεaawan maε əš-šərṭa bət-taftiiš εal-qaatel.*

co-operation - *taεaawon.* Can we count on your co-operation? *mnəqder nəεtə́med εala taεaawnak maεna?*

co-ordination - *tansiiq.* We can reach our goal only through a real co-ordination of efforts. *maa mnəqder nəṣal la-hadafna ʔəlla b-tansiiq ḥaqiiqi la-žhuudna.*

copper - *nḥaas.*

Copt - *qəbṭi** coll. *qəbṭ* pl. *ʔaqbaaṭ.*

Coptic - *qəbṭi** pl. *ʔaqbaaṭ.*

copy - 1. *nəsxa* pl. *nəsax.* Send me a copy of his book. *bεat-li nəsxa mn əktaabo.* 2. *ṣuura* pl. *ṣuwar, nəsxa* pl. *nəsax.* I made a copy of the letter. *εmələt ṣuura εan əl-maktuub.* 3. *εadad* pl. *ʔaεdaad, nəsxa* pl. *nəsax.* Do you have a copy of this morning's paper? *fii εandak εadad mən žariidt haṣ-ṣabaaḥ?*

to copy - 1. *naqal (o naqəl), nasax (a nasəx).* Copy this letter exactly. *nqool hal-maktuub bəl-ḥarəf.* 2. *naqal, qallad.* She copies the clothes she sees in the movies. *btənqol əl-mooḍaat halli bətšuufon bəs-siinama.*

cord - 1. *xeeṭ* pl. *xiiṭaan.* I haven't enough cord to tie up the package. *maa εandi xiiṭaan əkfaaye ḥatta ʔərboṭ əl-baakeet.* 2. *šriiṭ* pl. *šaraayeṭ.* We'll have to get a new cord for the iron. *laazə́m-əlna šriiṭ əždiid mənšaan əl-məkwaaye.*

cordial - 1. *likəər.* We have a wide selection of cordials. *εanna taškiile kbiire mn əl-likəər.* 2. *wəddi*.* His greeting was extremely cordial. *salaamo kaan əktiir wəddi.*

coriander - *kəzbara.*

cork - 1. *falliin, fanniin.* Our country exports a lot of cork. *blaadna bətṣadder falliin əktiir.* 2. *falliine* pl. *-aat, fanniine* pl. *-aat.* The cork fell into the bottle. *l-falliine saltet bəl-qanniine.*

to cork - *sadd (ə sadd//nsadd).* Don't forget to cork the bottle. *laa tənsa maa tsədd əl-qanniine.*

corkscrew - *fattaaḥet~* (pl. *-aat~*) *qanaani.*

corn - 1. *dəra.* They grow a lot of corn in Syria. *byəzraεu dəra ktiir əb-suuriyya.* 2. *bəsmaar (~ ər-rəžəl)* pl. *basamiir (~ ər-rəžəl).* He stepped on my corn. *daεə́s-li εala bəsmaar rəžli.*

corner - 1. *suuke* pl. *suwak, zaawye* pl. *zawaaya.* They live right around the corner. *hənne saakniin raʔsan wara s-suuke.* 2. *qərne* pl. *qəran, zaawye* pl. *zawaaya.* The man you want is sitting in that corner. *z-zalame yalli bəddak-yda qaaεed əb-haadiik əl-qərne.* -- He turned down the corner of the page. *tana zaawiit əṣ-ṣafḥa.* 3. *naaḥye* pl. *nawaaḥi.* People came from the four corners of the earth. *n-naas ʔəžet mən kəll nawaaḥi l-maεmuura.* 4. *qərne.* They have him in a corner now. *hallaq zaanqiino bəl-qərne.*

to have a corner on - *ḥtakar.* That company has a corner on the wheat market. *haš-šərke məḥtəkra suuq əl-qaməḥ.*

to corner - 1. *zanaq (o zanəq//nzanaq) bəl-qərne.* They cornered her into saying she would go. *zanaquuha bəl-qərne ḥatta rəḍyet ətruuḥ* or

**sakkaru Ɛaleeha kəll ᵊṭ-ṭəroq ḥatta qəblet ᵊtruuḥ. 2. ḥtakar. As a matter of fact, they've cornered the market. l-ḥaqiiqa hiyye ʔənno hənne məḥtəkriin ᵊs-suuq.

cornerstone - ḥažar ʔasaasi pl. ḥžaar ʔasaasiyye.

corporal - Ɛariif pl. Ɛərafa. The corporal is on guard duty. l-Ɛariif waaqef ᵊb-noobet ᵊḥraase.

corporal punishment - Ɛuquube žəsmaaniyye.

corporation - šərke pl. -aat. The corporation has large oil interests. š-šərke ʔəlha ʔiid ᵊkbiire b-ṣinaaƐt ᵊz-zeet.

corpse - žəsse pl. žəsas.

correct - 1. maẓbuuṭ. Is this the correct address? šuu haada l-Ɛənwaan ᵊl-maẓbuuṭ? -- He always does the correct thing. byaƐmel daayman ᵊš-šii l-maẓbuuṭ (or **ᵊš-šii mətᵊl-muu laazem). 2. mlaayem, laayeq, mnaaseb, mwaafeq. She always wears the correct clothes for every occasion. daayman ᵊbtəlbes ᵊl-ʔawaaƐi l-ᵊmlaayme la-kəll ᵊmnaasabe.

to correct - 1. ṣaḥḥaḥ. Please correct the mistakes in my French. mən faḍlak ṣaḥḥéḥ-li ġalṭaati bᵊl-frənsaawi tabaƐi. 2. ṣallaḥ. You oughtn't to correct him all the time in front of other people. ʔafḍál-lak maa tṣallḥo daayman b-ᵊḥḍuur ᵊn-naas. -- Correct me if I'm wrong. ṣalléḥni ʔiza kənᵊt ġalṭaan.

**I stand corrected. bəƐtéref ᵊb-xaṭaʔi.

correction - taṣḥiiḥ pl. -aat. Please make the necessary corrections. Ɛmeel maƐruuf saawi t-taṣḥiiḥaat ᵊl-laazme.

**Correction! We were only there for two days. ġalaṭ! (or Ɛandak!) nəḥna bqiina hniik yoomeen bass.

to **correspond** - 1. twaafaq, ṭaabaq. The translation does not correspond to the original. t-taržame maa btətwaafaq maƐ ᵊl-ʔaṣᵊl (or maa bəṭṭaabeq ᵊl-ʔaṣᵊl). 2. raasal, traasal (maƐ), kaatab, tkaatab (maƐ). We've been corresponding with each other for six years. ṣar-ᵊlna sətt ᵊsniin Ɛam ᵊnraasel baƐᵊḍna (or Ɛam nətraasal (maƐ baƐᵊḍna)).

correspondence - 1. mraasalaat (pl.). My job is to take care of the correspondence. šaġᵊlti ʔəhtamm bᵊl-ᵊmraasalaat. -- His correspondence is large and varied. mraasalaato waasƐa w-mətnawwƐa. 2. mraasale pl. -aat, mkaatabe pl. -aat. My correspondence with him was interrupted when the war broke out. mraasalti maƐo nqaṭƐet waqᵊt bada l-ḥarᵊb. 3. taṭaaboq. Observe the exact correspondence of the two terms. laaḥeẓ ᵊt-taṭaaboq ᵊl-kaamel been ᵊl-kəlᵊmteen.

correspondent - mraasel pl. -iin, mkaateb pl. -iin. He's a correspondent for our newspaper. huwwe mraasel la-žariidətna.

corridor - koridoor pl. -aat, mamša pl. mamaaši.

corrupt - faased. He's utterly corrupt, both morally and professionally. huwwe faased la-ʔaaxer ḥadd, muu b-ʔaxlaaqo bass, kamaan ᵊb-ʔašġaalo. -- They discovered the company's corrupt business transactions. ktašafu ʔaƐmaal ᵊš-šərke l-faasde.

to corrupt - fasad (e fasaad//nfasad). That type of literature may corrupt the morals of young people. han-nooƐ ᵊmn ᵊl-manšuuraat məmken yəfsed ʔaxlaaq ᵊš-šabaab.

corruption - fasaad. They're trying to eliminate corruption in the government. Ɛam yžarrbu yəstaʔᵊṣlu l-fasaad bᵊl-ᵊḥkuume.

cosmetics - ʔadawaat˜ ġandara (pl.), ʔadawaat˜ tažmiil. What brand of cosmetics does she use? ʔayy nooƐ mən ʔadawaat ᵊl-ġandara btəstaƐmel?

cost - 1. kəlfe, takaliif (pl.). The cost of building that house was not high. kəlfet Ɛamaar hal-beet maa kaanet Ɛaalye. 2. kəlfe. He was forced to sell everything at less than cost. nžabar ybiiƐ kəll šii b-ʔaqall mən kəlᵊfto.

at all costs - mahma kallaf ᵊl-ʔamᵊr, b-ʔayy taman. He wants it at all costs. bəddo-yáaha mahma kallaf ᵊl-ʔamᵊr.

at any cost - mahma kallaf ᵊl-ʔamᵊr, b-ʔayy taman. He's trying to get ahead at any cost. Ɛam yḥaawel yətqaddam mahma kallaf ᵊl-ʔamᵊr.

cost of living - kəlfet˜ ᵊl-maƐiiše, takaliif˜ ᵊl-maƐiiše. The cost of living is rising. kəlfet ᵊl-maƐiiše Ɛam tərtéfeƐ.

to cost - kallaf. How much did your car cost? qaddeeš kallafétak sayyaartak? -- That mistake will cost him dearly. hal-ġalṭa bətkallfo ġaali.

costly - tamiin, ġaali. She wears costly clothes. btəlbes ʔawaaƐi tamiine.

costume - 1. ʔawaaƐi tanakkuriyye (pl.). Are you going to wear a costume to the party? laḥa təlbes ʔawaaƐi tanakkuriyye bᵊl-ḥafle? or **laḥa tətnakkar bᵊl-ḥafle? 2. ṭaqᵊm pl. ṭquume. She needs shoes to complete her new fall costume. laazəmha kəndra la-tkammel ṭaqᵊmha l-xariifi ž-ždiid. 3. taqliid. I bought some costume jewelry for this dress. štareet šwayyet maṣaaġ taqliid mənšan har-roob. 4. tanakkuri*. We're going to a costume party this evening. laḥa nruuḥ la-ḥafle ṭanakkuriyye l-leele.

cottage - kuux pl. kwaax. They have a small cottage on the lake. Ɛandon kuux ᵊẓġiir Ɛal-buḥayra.

cotton - 1. qəṭᵊn. These socks are made of cotton. haž-žraabaat maƐmuule mən qəṭᵊn. -- You'll find some cotton in the medicine chest. bətlaaqi qəṭᵊn b-ᵊxzaanet ᵊl-ʔədᵊwye. 2. qəṭni*, qəṭᵊn. She bought a new cotton dress. štaret fəṣṭaan qəṭni ždiid.

cotton gin - ḥallaažet˜ (pl. -aat˜) qəṭᵊn, maḥlažet˜ (pl. maḥaalež˜) qəṭᵊn. The five farmers jointly bought a new cotton gin. l-xams ᵊmzaarƐiin ᵊštaru šərke ḥallaažet qəṭn ᵊždiide.

couch - kanabe pl. -aat. She sat on the couch to rest for a minute. qaƐdet Ɛal-kanabe la-təstréḥ-la šwayye.

cough - saƐle, sƐaal. Do you have something that's good for a cough? fii Ɛandak šii ləs-saƐle?

to cough - saƐal (o saƐle). The baby has been coughing all night. l-beebée ṣar-lo Ɛam yəsƐol ṭuul ᵊl-leel.

council - mažles pl. mažaales. The council met to discuss the problem. žtamaƐ ᵊl-mažles la-yəbḥas ᵊl-mawḍuuƐ.

councilman - Ɛəḍu˜ (pl. ʔaƐḍaaʔ˜) mažles ᵊl-baladiyye.

counsel - 1. mašwara pl. -aat. They followed our counsel. Ɛəmlu b-mašwarətna. 2. muḥaami pl. -iin and -iyye. They could afford the best counsel. kaan fiihon ywakklu ʔaḥsan muḥaami.

count - koont pl. -aat and knuute. She married a count. dzawwažet koont.

count - 1. taƐdaad, ʔəḥṣa pl. ʔəḥṣaʔaat. The recent count was completely inaccurate. t-taƐdaad ᵊl-ʔaaxiir kaan maġluuṭ kəllo. 2. təhme pl. təham. He was found guilty on three counts. ʔadaanúu Ɛala ʔasaas tlatt təham.

to count - 1. Ɛadd (ə Ɛadd//nƐadd). Her little boy can count from one to fifteen. ʔəbᵊnha ẓ-ẓġiir byəqder yƐədd mən waaḥed la-xamᵊṣṭaƐᵊš. -- Please count your change. mən faḍlak Ɛədd l-ᵊkmaale tabaƐak. 2. Ɛtabar, Ɛadd. I count that as another reason for his dismissal. bəƐtéber haada sabab taani la-ṣarfo mn ᵊl-xədme. -- You can count yourself lucky. fiik təƐtéber ḥaalak maḥẓuuẓ. 3. nḥasab, nƐadd. That doesn't count. haš-šii maa byənḥéseb.

**Every minute counts! kəll daqiiqa ʔəlha qiiméta!

**Count me in. ʔana maƐkon.

**You can count me out. btəqder ᵊtxalliini barra.

**Counting the children there are fifteen of us. maƐ l-ᵊwlaad nəḥna xamᵊṣṭaƐšar waaḥed.

to count on - 1. Ɛtamad Ɛala. We're counting on you. məƐtəmdiin Ɛaleek. 2. Ɛtamad Ɛala, ttakal Ɛala. You can count on me. fiik təƐtəmed Ɛaliyyi.

counter - 1. ṭaawle pl. -aat. We must ask you to stay on that side of the counter. mnətražžak təbqa Ɛaṭ-ṭaraf ᵊt-taani mn ᵊṭ-ṭaawle. 2. baar. Let's have a cup of coffee at the counter. xalliina naaxod fənžaan qahwe Ɛal-baar.

to **counteract** - rawwaḥ, xaffaf. He drank some coffee to counteract the effect of the alcohol. šəreb šwayyet qahwe la-yrawweḥ mafƐuul ᵊl-xamᵊr.

counterfeit - mzayyaf. That's counterfeit money. hayy maṣaari mzayyafe.

to counterfeit - zayyaf. He admitted he had counterfeited some money a few years ago. Ɛtaraf ʔənno kaan Ɛam yzayyef maṣaari qabᵊl kam səne.

countess - koontees pl. -aat.

countless - maa byənƐadd. I've been to that place countless times. rəḥᵊt la-hal-maḥall marraat maa btənƐadd (or **Ɛala Ɛadad šaƐᵊr raasi).

country - 1. blaad (pl., used for sg. and pl.) pl. also bəldaan. I've visited many countries. zərt ᵊblaad ᵊktiire. -- In my country it often rains for weeks. b-ᵊblaadi bətmaṭṭer ʔaḥyaanan məddet ʔasabiiƐ Ɛat-tawaali. -- That's beautiful country around there. l-ᵊblaad ḥəlwe b-haadiik ᵊn-nawaaḥi. -- I've never been out of the country. b-ḥayaati maa ṭləƐᵊt barraat l-ᵊblaad. 2. riif, ḍeeƐa. They want to move to the country. bəddon yəntəqlu lər-riif. 3. fala, barriyye. I spent the afternoon out in the country. *maḍḍeet baʿd ᵊḍ-ḍahᵊr bᵊl-fala.* 4. *riifi*.* The country roads are in bad shape. *ṭ-ṭəroq ᵊr-riifiyye b-ḥaale ʿaaṭle.*

countryman – *mwaaṭen* pl. *-iin.* He met several of his countrymen on the train. *ṣaadaf ʿəddet ᵊmwaaṭniin mən balado bᵊt-treen.*

couple: I'm living with an elderly couple. *ʾana saaken ᵊb-beet rəžžaal w-marto mətqaddmiin bᵊs-sənn.* -- We invited four couples. *ʿazamna ʾarbaʿ ᵊržaal w-nəswaanon.*

a couple of – 1. *tneen* f. *tənteen* + pl., or simple dual, or *žooz* + pl. I have a couple of kids to take care of. *ʿandi tneen ᵊwlaad* (or *waladeen* or *žooz ᵊwlaad*) *quum fiihon.* 2. *kam˜ ...* Wait here a couple of minutes. *xalliik hoon kam daqiiqa* (or ****daqiiqteen tlaate*).

coupon – *kuupoon* and *kuuboon* pl. *-aat.*

courage – *žərʾa, žaraaʾa, šažaaʿa, žaraaʿa.* It takes courage to do that. *haš-šaġle bədda žərʾa.* -- He has the courage of his convictions. *ʿando ž-žərʾa l-kaafye la-ysaawi halli byəʿtəqed fii.*

**Don't loose courage. *laa tšabbet ʿazaaymak.*

courageous – *šəžaaʿ.*

course – 1. *ʾəttižaah* pl. *-aat.* The plane is holding a straight course. *ṭ-ṭayyaara mḥaafẓa ʿala ʾəttižaah məstaqiim.* 2. *ṣaḥᵊn* pl. *ṣḥuun.* The dinner had four courses. *l-ʿaša kaan ᵊmʾallaf mən ʾarbaʿ ṣḥuun.* 3. *maadde* pl. *mawaadd.* What courses did you take this year? *šuu l-mawaadd yalli ʾaxádta has-səne?* 4. *mažra.* The river has changed its course. *n-nahᵊr ġayyar mažráa.* -- The sickness has run its course. *l-maraḍ ʾaxad mažráa.* 5. *malʿab* pl. *malaaʿeb.* He went out to the golf course early this morning. *l-yoom ᵊṣ-ṣəbᵊḥ raaḥ la-malʿab ᵊl-golf.*

**The year has almost run its course. *s-səne taqriiban xalṣet.*

as a matter of course – *b-ṭabiiʿet ᵊl-ḥaal.* I did it as a matter of course. *ʿməlta b-ṭabiiʿet ᵊl-ḥaal.*

during the course of – *ʾasnaaʾ˜, xilaal˜, b-baḥr˜.* He'll call you sometime during the course of the day. *laḥa ytalfə́n-lak ᵊb-šii waqᵊt ʾasnaaʾ ᵊn-nhaar.*

in due course – *b-waqta.* We will notify you in due course. *mənxabbrak ᵊb-waqta.*

in the course of – *ʾasnaaʾ˜, xilaal˜, b-baḥr˜.* I heard from him twice in the course of the year. *sməʿᵊt mənno marrteen ʾasnaaʾ ᵊs-səne.*

of course – 1. *ṭabʿan, bᵊṭ-ṭabᵊʿ.* Of course I know what you mean! *ṭabʿan baʿref šuu ʿam təʿni!* 2. *mbala.* You don't know him then? — Of course I do! *lakaan maa btaʿᵊrfo? — mbala baʿᵊrfo!* 3. *ḥatman, maʿluum.* Why, of course! *ʾee, ḥatman!*

court – 1. *saaḥa* pl. *-aat.* We have two rooms facing the court. *ʿanna ʾuudṭeen biṭəllu ʿas-saaḥa.* 2. *balaaṭ* pl. *-aat.* The ambassador has not yet been received at court. *ləssa maa staqbalu s-safiir bᵊl-balaaṭ.* 3. *malʿab* pl. *malaaʿeb.* The court is still too wet for a game. *l-malʿab ləssáa mabluul la-yənlə́ʿeb ʿalée.* 4. *maḥkame* pl. *maḥaakem.* We took the matter to court. *ʾaxadna l-qaḍiyye ʿal-maḥkame.*

to court – *tḥabbab la-.* He's been courting her for quite some time. *ṣar-lo mədde ṭawiile ʿam yətḥabbáb-la.*

**You're courting trouble if you go there alone. *bətkuun ʿam ᵊdžarr ᵊš-šarr ᵊb-ʾideek ʾiza bətruuḥ la-hniik la-ḥaalak.*

courteous – *laṭiif* pl. *ləṭafa, mhazzab.* He could at least have been courteous. *ʿal-qaliili kaan laazem ykuun laṭiif.*

to be courteous to – *žaamal, laaṭaf.* Children should learn very soon to be courteous to older people. *l-ᵊwlaad ʿala bakkiir laazem yətʿallamu yžaamlu yalli ʾakbar mənnon.*

courtesy – 1. *mžaamale.* I have to go out of courtesy. *laazem ruuḥ ᵊb-sabiil l-ᵊmžaamale.* 2. *maʿruuf.* I'll do it as a courtesy. *baʿmə́la ka-maʿruuf.* 3. *ləṭᵊf.* We appreciate the many courtesies you have extended to us. *mənqadder kəll ᵊl-ləṭᵊf halli waržeetna-yaá.*

courthouse – *maḥkame* pl. *maḥaakem.*

courtroom – *maḥkame* pl. *maḥaakem.*

cousin – 1. (paternal uncle's son) *ʾəbᵊn˜* (pl. *wlaad˜*) *ʿamm.* 2. (paternal uncle's daughter) *bənᵊt˜* (pl. *banaat˜*) *ʿamm.* 3. (maternal uncle's son) *ʾəbᵊn˜* (pl. *wlaad˜*) *xaal.* 4. (maternal uncle's daughter) *bənᵊt˜* (pl. *banaat˜*) *xaal.*

cover – 1. *ġaṭa* pl. *ʾəġᵊṭye.* The covers on the armchairs and sofa are dirty. *ʾəġṭiit ᵊl-kalaaṭeq wᵊl-kanabe wəsxiin.* -- Where are the covers for these boxes? *ween ᵊl-ʾəġᵊṭye la-hal-ʿəlab?* 2. *žəlde* pl. *-aat.* Who's torn off the covers of this book? *miin nazaʿ žəldet hal-ᵊktaab?* 3. *lḥaaf* pl. *ləḥᵊf, ḥraam* pl. *-aat.* I didn't have enough covers last night. *maa kaan ʿandi ləḥᵊf ᵊkfaaye leelt ᵊmbaareḥ.* 4. *maʾwa, maxbaʾ.* They ran for cover when they saw the enemy. *ltažu la-maʾwa lamma šaafu l-ʿaduww.*

**I read this book from cover to cover. *qareet hal-ᵊktaab mən ʾawwalo la-ʾaaxro.*

to take cover – *txabba.* The soldiers took cover when the planes flew overhead. *l-ʿaskar ᵊtxabbu lamma ṣaaret ᵊṭ-ṭayyaaraat fooq raason.* -- Take cover! It's going to rain. *txabba! laḥa tənzel maṭar.*

to cover – 1. *ġaṭṭa//tġaṭṭa.* Snow covered everything in the area. *t-talᵊž ġaṭṭa kəll šii bᵊl-manṭiqa.* -- The table was just covered with dust. *ṭ-ṭaawle kaanet ᵊmġaṭṭaaye kəlla ġabra.* -- This blanket won't cover the bed. *hal-ᵊḥraam maa bikaffi yġaṭṭi t-taxᵊt.* -- I believe this amount of money covers everything. *b-raʾyi hal-mablaġ biġaṭṭi kəll šii.* -- This check is covered. *haš-šakk ᵊmġaṭṭa.* 2. *ġaṭṭa, xabba.* Do you think we can cover the stains with some paint? *bədẓənn fiina nġaṭṭi hal-ləṭaʿ ᵊb-šii dhaan?* 3. *labbas, naǧǧad.* We covered the sofa with cretonne. *labbasna l-kanabe kreetoon* or *naǧǧadna l-kanabe b-kreetoon.* 4. *ʾamman.* This insurance covers the house against fire and theft. *has-sookarta bətʾammen ᵊl-beet ḍədd ᵊl-ḥariiq wᵊs-sərqa.* 5. *štamal ʿala.* His book covers the political history of three countries. *ktaabo byəštə́mel ʿat-taariix ᵊs-siyaasi tabaʿ tlətt duwal.* 6. *htamm b-.* Who's going to cover the local news while he's not here? *miin halli laḥa yəhtamm bᵊl-ʾaxbaar ᵊl-maḥalliyye b-ᵊġyaabo?* 7. *qaṭaʿ (a qaṭᵊʿ//nqaṭaʿ).* We covered the distance in three hours. *qaṭaʿna l-masaafe b-ᵊtlətt saaʿaat.*

**Is your house covered by insurance? *beetak ᵊmsookar* (or *ᵊmʾamman*)?

to cover up – 1. *ġaṭṭa.* Cover me up. *ġaṭṭini.* 2. *xafa (i ø), xabba, ġaṭṭa.* He tried to cover up his mistake. *ḥaawal yəxfi ġalᵊṭṭo.*

coverage – 1. *taqdiim.* The news coverage in that magazine is excellent. *taqdiim ᵊl-ʾaxbaar ᵊb-hal-mažalle ʿaẓiim.* 2. *taʾmiin, sookarta.* Do you have any coverage against theft? *fii ʿandak šii taʾmiin ḍədd ᵊs-sərqa?*

cow – *baqara* pl. *-aat.* They milk the cows at six. *byəḥᵊlbu l-baqaraat ᵊs-saaʿa sətte.*

to cow – *xawwaf.* Don't let them cow you! *laa txalliihon yxawwfuuk!*

coward – *žabaan* pl. *žəbana, nadᵊl* pl. *ʾandaal, nazᵊl* pl. *ʾanzaal.* Don't be such a coward. *laa tkuun hal-qadd žabaan!*

cowardice – *žəbᵊn, nadaale, nazaale.*

cowardly – *žabaan* pl. *žəbana, nadᵊl* pl. *ʾandaal, nazᵊl* pl. *ʾanzaal.* Only a cowardly person like him would do such a thing. *maa ḥada bisaawi heek šii ġeer waaḥed žabaan mətlo.*

**That was a cowardly thing to do. *haada kaan ʿamal kəllo žəbᵊn w-nadaale.*

cozy – *mkankan.* This room is very cozy in the winter. *hal-ʾuuḍa ktiir ᵊmkankane bᵊš-šəte.*

crab – *səlṭʿaan* pl. *ṣalaaṭʿiin.* Have you ever eaten crabs? *b-ḥayaatak ʾakalᵊt ṣalaaṭʿiin?*

**He's an old crab. *maa byəḍḥák-lo sənn.*

to crab – *tʾafʾaf (ʾafʾafe).* Stop crabbing! *ḥaažtak ʾafʾafe!*

crabby – *ʿaabes, mnarvez.* He was crabby at the office today. *kaan ʿaabes ᵊl-yoom bᵊl-maktab.*

crack – 1. *šaqq* pl. *šquuq(a).* Water is leaking through a crack in the dam. *l-mayy ʿam təzrob mən šaqq bᵊs-sadd.* -- I could see it through a crack in the fence. *qdərᵊt šuufa mən šaqq bᵊl-xəṣṣ.* -- The cracks in the wall have to be repaired. *šquuqet ᵊl-ḥeeṭ laazə́ma taṣliiḥ.* 2. *šaʿᵊr* pl. *šʿuura.* There's a crack in the glass. *fii šaʿᵊr bᵊl-ᵊqzaaz* or ***l-ᵊqzaaz mašʿuur.* 3. *ṭaqṭaqa.* I thought I heard the crack of a rifle. *ka-ʾənni sməʿᵊt ṭaqṭaqet bənduqiyye.* 4. *lahše* pl. *-aat.* I wonder what he meant by that crack. *ʾəbṣar šuu qaṣad ᵊb-hal-lahše.* 5. *ḍarbe* pl. *-aat, laṭše* pl. *-aat.* He gave him a crack across the mouth. *ḍarabo ḍarbe* (or *laṭašo laṭše*) *ʿala təmmo.*

**Let me have a crack at it! *xalliini ʾana žarreb ḥaẓẓi!*

at the crack of dawn – *ʿand šaqqet ᵊḍ-ḍaww.* We got up at the crack of dawn. *fəqna ʿand šaqqet ᵊḍ-ḍaww.*

to crack - **1.** *kassar.* I'll crack the nuts. *ʔana bkasser ᵊž-žooz.* **2.** *šaɛar (e ø//nšaɛar).* I've cracked the crystal of my watch. *šaɛarᵊt ballooret saaɛti.* **3.** *nšaɛar.* The glass cracked when I poured the hot water in. *l-kaase nšaɛret lamma ṣabbeet fiiha l-mayy ᵊṣ-ṣəxne.* **4.** *šaḥḥaṭ.* The singer's voice cracked. *ṣooṭ l-ᵊmġanni šaḥḥaṭ.*

**He didn't crack a smile. *maa nšaqq təmmo w-laa b-ʔəbtisaame.*

**He's always cracking jokes. *daayman byəṭlaɛ ᵊb-nəkat.*

to crack down - *šaddad l-ᵊxnaaq.* The government is cracking down on smuggling. *l-ᵊḥkuume ɛam ᵊtšadded l-ᵊxnaaq ɛat-tahriib.*

to crack up - **1.** *tḥaṭṭam.* The authorities want to know why the plane cracked up. *ṣ-ṣəlṭaat bədda taɛref leeš ᵊṭ-ṭayyaara tḥaṭṭamet.* **2.** *nhaar.* He cracked up under the strain. *nhaar mən kətret ᵊl-ʔəžhaad.*

**The movie isn't all it's cracked up to be. *l-fəlᵊm muu mətᵊl-ma ṭabbalu w-zammaru fii.*

cracked - **1.** *mašɛuur.* The cup is cracked. *l-fənžaan mašɛuur.* **2.** *maqṭuuɛ.* The old man spoke in a cracked voice. *l-ᵊxtyaar ḥaka b-ṣooṭ maqṭuuɛ.* **3.** *mažnuun.* He's completely cracked. *huwwe mažnuun ɛan-ṣaḥiiḥ.*

cradle - **1.** *sriir* pl. *saraayer.* **2.** (fig.) *mahᵊd.*

crafty - *maaker, makkaar.* He's a crafty business-man. *huwwe taažer maaker.*

to **cram** - **1.** *ḍabb (ə ḍabb//nḍabb).* He crammed everything into one trunk. *ḍabb kəll šii b-sanduuq waaḥed.* **2.** *nahat (a nahᵊt).* He's cramming for the exam. *naazel nahᵊt mənšaan ᵊl-faḥᵊṣ.*

cramp - **1.** *tašannož.* I can't swim anymore; I have a cramp in my leg. *maa ɛaad fiini ʔəsbaḥ, ṣaayér-li tašannož ᵊb-rəžli.* **2.** *mġiiṣ, maġᵊṣ.* He has bad stomach cramps. *žaayíi mġiiṣ qawi b-məɛᵊdto.*

crane - **1.** *wənᵊš* pl. *-aat* and *wnuuše, raafɛa* pl. *rawaafeɛ.* They need a crane to lift that. *laazə́mon wənᵊš la-yərfaɛu haš-šii.* **2.** *kərki* pl. *karaaki, ġərniiq* pl. *ġaraaneq.* Our zoo is going to receive two cranes before long. *žneenet ᵊl-ḥaywaanaat tabaɛna laḥa yəžiiha kərkiyyeen ɛan qariib.*

to crane - *madd (ə madd).* We craned our necks to see him. *maddeena ruusna ḥatta nšuufo.*

crank - **1.** *manaweel* pl. *-aat.* The crank is under the seat. *l-manaweel taḥt ᵊl-maqɛad.* **2.** *maṣruuɛ* pl. *maṣariiɛ.* Some crank must have sent these letters. *šii maṣruuɛ laazem ykuun baɛat hal-makatiib.*

crankshaft - *wilbrəkd* pl. *wilbrəkayaat, graank* pl. *-aat.*

crash - **1.** *qarqaɛa.* The tray fell down with a loud crash. *ṣ-ṣeeniyye wəqɛet ᵊb-qarqaɛa qawiyye.* **2.** *ʔəṣṭiḍaam* pl. *-aat.* Was anyone hurt in the crash? *ḥada nžaraḥ bᵊl-ʔəṣṭiḍaam?* **3.** *ʔənhiyaar.* He lost all his money in the stock-market crash of 1929. *xəṣer kəll maṣaríi b-ʔənhiyaar suuq ᵊl-ʔashom sənᵊt təsɛda w-ɛəšriin.*

to crash - **1.** *tḥaṭṭam.* Their plane crashed into the water. *ṭayyaarə́ton ᵊtḥaṭṭamet ɛal-mayy.* **2.** *hawwar.* He was driving extremely fast when he crashed. *kaan ɛam ysuuq ᵊb-sərɛa faẓiiɛa lamma hawwar.*

crate - *saḥḥaara* pl. *-aat* and *saḥahiir, sanduuq* pl. *sanadiiq.* A crate full of books has come. *ʔəža saḥḥaara malaane kətᵊb.*

to **crave** - *ṭəmeɛ (a ṭamaɛ) b-.* Those children crave affection. *hal-ᵊwlaad byəṭmaɛu bᵊl-ᵊḥnuun.*

craving - *ṭamaɛ* pl. *ʔaṭmaaɛ.* He can't satisfy his craving for power. *maa byəqder yəšbeɛ ʔaṭmaaɛo bᵊt-taḥakkom.*

to **crawl** - **1.** *zaḥaf (a zaḥᵊf).* The baby crawled under the table. *l-beebée zaḥaf taḥt ᵊṭ-ṭaawle.* **2.** *zabaq (o zabᵊq).* The dog crawled under the fence and got away. *l-kalᵊb zabaq mən taḥt ᵊl-xəṣṣ w-harab.* **3.** *naġal (o naġᵊl).* The place was crawling with ants. *l-maḥall kaan ɛam yənġol bᵊn-namᵊl naġᵊl.*

crayon - *qalam˜* (pl. *qlaam˜*) *talwiin.*

crazy - *mažnuun* pl. *mažaniin.* Are you crazy? *šuu mažnuun ʔənte?*

**That's a crazy idea. *hayy fəkra kəlla žnaan.*

to be crazy about - *žann (ə žnuun, žnaan) ɛala, maat (u ø) ɛala.* I'm crazy about bananas. *ʔana bžənn ɛal-mooz.*

to drive crazy - *žannan.* You'll drive me crazy yet. *ləssa bədžannənni.*

to **creak** - *zaqzaq.* The door creaks terribly. *l-baab ɛam yzaqzeq zaqzaqa faẓiiɛa.*

cream - **1.** *kreem(a).* Do you take cream with your coffee? *btaaxod kreem ᵊb-qahᵊwtak?* **2.** *kreem* pl. *-aat.* That cream is rather dry for my skin. *hal-ᵊkreem naašef šwayye ɛala žəldi.* **3.** *kreem* (invar.), *beež faateḥ.* The walls are cream. *l-ḥiiṭaan (loonon) kreem.* **4.** *zəbde, nəxbe, xiire.* This tobacco is the cream of the crop. *hat-təbᵊġ (huwwe) zəbdet ᵊl-maḥṣuul.* -- These five students are the cream of the crop. *hal-xamᵊs talamiiz hənne nəxbet ᵊṣ-ṣaff.*

to **create** - **1.** *xalaq (e xalᵊq//nxalaq).* God created the universe. *ʔaḷḷa xalaq ᵊl-koon.* **2.** *ʔawžad, xalaq.* We have to create a position for him. *laazem nuužə́d-lo waẓiife.* **3.** *ʔabdaɛ, xalaq.* That artist has created another masterpiece. *hal-fannaan ʔabdaɛ kamaan təḥfe ždiide.* **4.** *sabbab, ʔasaar.* The incident created a lot of excitement. *l-ḥaades sabbab hayažaan ᵊktiir.*

creation - **1.** *xalᵊq, takwiin.* There are a number of theories about the creation of the world. *fii ɛəddet naẓariyyaat bətɛaalež xalq ᵊl-ɛaalam.* **2.** *ʔiižaad, xalᵊq, ʔəḥdaas.* The creation of new jobs will help the economy. *ʔiižaad waẓaayef ᵊždiide bisaaɛed ᵊl-ḥayaat ᵊl-ʔəq̈tiṣaadiyye.* **3.** *ɛaalam, dənye, koon.* She's the prettiest thing in all creation. *hiyye ʔaḥla waaḥde bᵊl-ɛaalam* or ***ʔaḥla mənna ʔaḷḷa maa xalaq.* **4.** *məbtákar˜* (pl. *-aat˜*) *mooḍa.* She's wearing one of his latest creations. *hiyye laabse mən ʔaḥdas məbtakaraat ᵊl-mooḍa tabaɛo.*

creature - *maxluuq* pl. *-aat,* (pl. only) *kaaʔinaat.* The fire frightened all the creatures in the forest. *l-ḥariiqa raɛɛabet kəll ᵊl-maxluuqaat bᵊl-ġaabe.*

**The poor creatures are hungry. *hal-masakiin žuuɛaaniin.*

credentials - **1.** *wraaq subuutiyye* (pl.). They let him in when they saw his credentials. *samaḥúu-lo yfuut baɛᵊd-ma šaafu wraaqo s-subuutiyye.* **2.** *wraaq˜ ʔəɛtimaad* (pl.). The ambassador hasn't presented his credentials yet. *s-safiir ləssa maa qaddam wraaq ʔəɛtimaado.*

credible - *maɛquul.* His story sounded very credible. *qəṣṣto ẓahret maɛquule tamaam.*

credit - **1.** *faḍᵊl* pl. *ʔafḍaal.* He likes to take credit for what somebody else has done. *biḥəbb yəddə́ɛi l-faḍᵊl la-ʔašya msaawiiha ġeero.* **2.** *madᵊḥ, madiiḥ.* I did the work and he got the credit. *ʔana ɛməlt ᵊš-šəġᵊl w-huwwe ḥaṣal ɛal-madᵊḥ.*

**Do you have any credit at this store? *bidayy-nuuk šii b-hal-maxzan?*

**We do not extend credit here. *maa məndayyen hoon.*

**His credit is good. *ʔəmdə́a mniiḥ.*

**He's a credit to his profession. *bišarref ṣanᵊɛto.*

**Did you mention him in the credits in your book? *zakarto maɛ halli kan-lon ᵊl-faḍᵊl ɛala ktaabak?*

**His name appeared in the credits at the beginning of the film. *ʔəsmo ẓahar maɛ yalli kan-lon ᵊl-faḍl ᵊb-ʔawwal ᵊl-fəlᵊm.*

**He has five successful movies to his credit. *ɛando xamᵊs ʔaflaam naažḥa taḥᵊt ʔəsmo.*

credit slip - *waṣᵊl* (pl. *wṣuule*) *bᵊl-mablaġ.* Did you get a credit slip when you returned the shoes? *ʔaxadt waṣᵊl bᵊl-mablaġ lamma ražžaɛt ᵊṣ-ṣabbaaṭ?*

letter of credit - *ʔəɛtimaad* pl. *-aat.*

on credit - **1.** *bᵊd-deen.* Can I have this dress on credit? I'll pay you next week. *məmken ʔaaxod hal-fəṣṭaan bᵊd-deen? bədfáɛ-lak ᵊž-žəmɛa ž-žaaye.* **2.** *bᵊt-taqsiiṭ.* We can buy the furniture on credit, with twelve months to pay. *fiina nəštə́ri l-farᵊš bᵊt-taqsiiṭ ɛala tnaɛšar šahᵊr.*

to give someone credit for - *šəhed (a ø) la-ḥada b-.* There's one thing you've got to give him credit for. *fii šii waaḥed laazem təšhə́d-lo fii.*

**I gave him credit for more sense than that. *ẓanneeto ʔaɛqal mən heek.*

to credit - **1.** *saddaq.* You can't credit those reports. *maa fii l-waaḥed ysaddeq hal-ʔaxbaar.* **2.** *qayyad la-ḥsaab˜ ...* We'll credit you with this amount. *mənqayyə́d-lak hal-mablaġ la-ḥsaabak.* **3.** *ɛaṭa l-faḍᵊl (b-).* The newspapers credited him with rescuing the baby from the fire. *ž-žaraayed ɛaṭəto l-faḍᵊl ᵊb-ʔənq̈aaz ᵊṭ-ṭəfl ᵊmn ᵊl-ḥariiqa.*

creditor - *daaʔen* pl. *-iin, dayyaan* pl. *-iin, ṣaaḥeb˜* (pl. *ṣḥaab˜*) *ᵊd-deen.*

to **creep** - *maši (i maši), zaḥaf (a zaḥᵊf).* There's a bug creeping along the wall. *fii baqqa maašye ɛal-ḥeeṭ.*

crescent - *hlaal* pl. *-aat*. Her new earrings are shaped like crescents. *ḥalqaata ž-žədad hee?ə́ton mətᵊl l-ᵊhlaal*. -- The Fertile Crescent. *l-ᵊhlaal ᵊl-xaṣiib*.

crew - **1.** (of a ship, airplane, etc.) *baḥḥaara* (pl.), *mallaaḥiin* (pl.). The entire crew was saved when the ship sank. *l-baḥḥaara kəllon ᵊtxallaṣu waqᵊt ġərqet ᵊs-safiine*. **2.** (of a tank, machine gun, etc.) *sadane* (pl.). The tank has a crew of five. *d-dabbaabe ?əla sadane ɛaddon xamse*.

crime - **1.** *l-?əžraam*. They're doing their best to combat crime in the big cities. *ɛam yaɛᵊmlu žahdon ykaafḥu l-?əžraam bᵊl-mədon l-ᵊkbiire*. **2.** *žariime* pl. *žaraayem*. What crime do they accuse him of? *šuu ž-žariime yalli taahmiino fiiha?*
 **It would be a crime to throw that food away. *ḥaraam ᵊtkəbb hal-?akᵊl*.

criminal - **1.** *məžrem* pl. *-iin*. The criminal escaped from prison. *l-məžrem harab ᵊmn ᵊs-səžᵊn*. **2.** *?əžraami**. That's criminal negligence! *haada tahaamol ?əžraami!*
 criminal court - *maḥkamet˜* (pl. *maḥaakem˜*) *ᵊž-žinaayaat*.

to **cringe** - *qanfad, kašš*. The child cringes when anyone yells at him. *l-walad biqanfed lamma ḥada biɛayyeṭ ɛaléé*.

cripple - *mkarsaḥ* pl. *-iin*. The cripple can't carry that big suitcase. *l-ᵊmkarsaḥ maa fii yəḥmel haš-šanta l-ᵊkbiire*. -- He'll be a cripple for life. *laḥa yḍall ᵊmkarsaḥ ṭuul ḥayaato*.
 to cripple - **1.** *karsaḥ*. The accident crippled him permanently. *l-ḥaades karsaḥo mada ḥayaato*. **2.** *šall (ə šalal//nšall)*. The air raid crippled their defense operations. *l-ġaara ž-žawwiyye šallet ɛamaliyyaaton ᵊd-difaaɛiyye*.

crisis - **1.** *kriiz(a), ḥaddet˜ ᵊl-maraḍ*. Doctor, has he passed the crisis? *daxlak ya doktoor, nšaaḷḷa ətaaz l-ᵊkriiza?* **2.** *?azme* pl. *-aat*. The resignation of the finance minister has lead to a cabinet crisis. *?əstiqaalet waziir ᵊl-maaliyye sabbabet ?azme wazaariyye*.

crisp - **1.** *mqarmaš*. The cookies are fresh and crisp. *l-baskoot taaza w-ᵊmqarmaš*. **2.** *taaza* (invar.). Use crisp lettuce in the salad. *ḥəṭṭi xass taaza bᵊṣ-ṣalaṭa*. **3.** *mənɛeš*. The air is a bit crisp tonight. *l-hawa mənɛeš ᵊšwayye l-leele*.

critic - *naqqaad* pl. *-iin, məntaqed* pl. *-iin*.

critical - **1.** *mdaqqeq*. He's an extremely critical scholar. *huwwe ɛallaame mdaqqeq ləl-ġaaye*. **2.** *daqiiq*. The latest note is undergoing a critical study by the Foreign Ministry. *l-ᵊmzakkra l-?axiire ɛam yəžri ɛaleeha diraase daqiiqa b-wazaart ᵊl-xaaržiyye*. **3.** *faaṣel, ḥaasem*. This is a critical period in his training. *hayy marḥalę faaṣle b-tamriino*. **4.** *xəṭer, məxṭer, m?axṭer*. His condition is critical. *ḥaalto ṣ-ṣəḥḥiyye xəṭra*. **5.** *m?axṭer*. He's still on the critical list. *ləssḍa b-liistet l-ᵊm?axᵊṭriin*.

criticism - *?əntiqaad*. He can't stand criticism. *maa fii yətḥammal ᵊl-?əntiqaad*. -- She had nothing to offer but criticism. *maa kaanet šaaṭra b-šii ġeer ᵊl-?əntiqaad*.

to **criticize** - *naqqad, ntaqad, naddad b-*. He severely criticized their work. *naqqad šəġlon ᵊb-šədde*.

to **crochet** - *ɛəmel šəġl ᵊkroošé*.

crocodile - *təmsaaḥ* pl. *tamasiiḥ*.

crook - *məḥtaal* pl. *-iin, ġaššaaš* pl. *-iin*. That crook took most of their money. *hal-məḥtaal ?axad ?aktar maṣariihon*.

crooked - **1.** *maṭɛuuž*. This pin is crooked. *had-dabbuus maṭɛuuž*. **2.** *məḥtaal, ġaššaaš*. Don't deal with them; they're all crooked. *laa tɛaaməlon, hənne kəllon məḥtaaliin*.

crop - *maḥṣuul* pl. *-aat* and *maḥaṣiil, ġalle* pl. *ġlaal*. The farmers expect a good crop this year. *l-ᵊmzaarɛiin mət?ammliin ᵊb-maḥṣuul ᵊmniiḥ has-sane*.
 to crop up - *ẓahar (a ẓhuur), ṭəleɛ (a ṭluuɛ)*. Many new problems are sure to crop up. *mən kəll bədd fii ktiir mašaakel ᵊždiide laḥa təẓhar*.

cross - **1.** *ṣaliib* pl. *ṣəlbaan*. Do you see the church with the big cross on the steeple? *šaayef l-ᵊkniise halli fii ɛala bərža ṣaliib ᵊkbiir?* -- The central office of the International Red Cross is in Geneva. *l-maqarr ᵊr-ra?iisi tabaɛ ᵊṣ-ṣaliib ᵊl-?aḥmar ᵊd-duwali b-žəneef*. **2.** *məḥne* pl. *məḥan*. I'm afraid we'll have to bear this cross. *xaayə́f-lak la-nənžəber nətḥammal hal-məḥne*. **3.** *ɛaabes*. He's cross today. *ɛaabes huwwe l-yoom*.
 **The mule is a cross between a horse and a donkey. *l-baġᵊl nəṣṣ ᵊḥṣaan w-nəṣṣ ᵊḥmaar*.
 **They're working at cross purposes most of the time. *?aɛmaalon məḍḍaarbe b-?aktar ᵊl-?awqaat*.
 cross section - *maqṭaɛ ɛarḍi*. That's a cross section of the house. *haada maqṭaɛ ɛarḍi ləl-beet*.
 to cross - **1.** *qaṭaɛ (a qaṭᵊɛ//nqaṭaɛ)*. Cross the street at the green signal. *qṭaaɛ ᵊš-šaareɛ ɛal-?išaara l-xaḍra*. -- When do we cross the border? *?eemta laḥa nəqṭaɛ l-ᵊḥduud?* **2.** *tqaaṭaɛ*. The two principal avenues cross over there. *š-šaarɛeen ᵊr-ra?iisiyye byətqaaṭaɛu hniik*.
 **Cross your heart! *b-šarafak?*
 **I'll keep my fingers crossed. *bḍall ?ədɛíi-lak*.
 to cross one's mind - *xaṭar (o/e ə) ɛala baal˜ ḥada, ?əža ɛala baal˜ ḥada*. It never crossed my mind that he would object. *?abadan maa xaṭar ɛala baali ?ənno laḥa yəɛtə́reḍ*.
 to cross out - *šaxaṭ (o šaxᵊṭ//nšaxaṭ) ɛala, šaṭab (o šaṭᵊb//nšaṭab) ɛala*. Cross out the items that you don't want. *šxooṭ ɛal-?ašya yalli maa bəddak-yḍaha*.

cross-eyed - *?aḥwal* f. *ḥoola* pl. *ḥuul*.

crossing - **1.** *mṣallabe* pl. *-aat*. There's no traffic light at this crossing. *maa fii ?išaaret muruur ɛala hal-ᵊmṣallabe*. **2.** *safra* pl. *-aat*. Did you have a good crossing? *nšaaḷḷa safᵊrtak kaanet ᵊmwaffaqa?*

crossword puzzle - *ləɛbet˜* (pl. *ləɛab˜*) *ᵊl-kəlmaat ᵊl-mətqaaṭɛa*.

crow - *qaaq* pl. *qiiqaan*. There was a crow sitting in the tree. *kaan fii qaaq qaaɛed ɛaš-šažara*.
 **It's only eight kilometers as the crow flies. *muu ?aktar mən ᵊtmən kilomətraat qaaduumiyye* (or *ᵊmqaaṭaɛa*).
 to crow - **1.** *kaaka, ṣaaḥ (i ṣyaaḥ)*. I woke up when the cock crowed. *fəqᵊt ɛala mkaakaat ᵊd-diik*. **2.** *tbažžaḥ*. He crowed over his success. *tbažžaḥ ᵊb-nažaaḥo*.

crowbar - *ɛatale* pl. *-aat*.

crowd - **1.** *žamᵊɛ* pl. *žmuuɛa*. Have you seen the crowd in front of the theater? *šəft ᵊž-žamᵊɛ qəddaam ᵊl-masraḥ?* **2.** *ɛažqa, zaḥme*. I lost him in the crowd. *ḍawwaɛto bᵊl-ɛažqa*. **3.** *žamaaɛa* pl. *-aat, ?ərṭa* pl. *-aat*. I don't like the crowd he hangs around with. *maa btəɛžəbni ž-žamaaɛa halli bišaakə́lon*.
 to crowd - **1.** *nḥašak*. We all crowded into the bus. *kəllna nḥašakna bᵊl-baaṣ*. **2.** *daffaš, zaaḥam*. Quit crowding! *ḥaaže ddaffeš*. **3.** *ḥašak (o ḥašᵊk//nḥašak)*. The police crowded the prisoners into a small room. *š-šərṭa ḥašket ᵊl-maḥabiis ᵊb-?uuḍa ẓġiire*.
 crowded - *maɛžuuq*. The train was terribly crowded, as usual. *t-treen kaan ᵊktiir maɛžuuq, mətl ᵊl-ɛaade*.
 crowded to capacity - *malaan ɛal-?aaxiir, malaan la-diino*. The hall was crowded to capacity. *l-qaaɛa kaanet malaane ɛal-?aaxiir* (or *malaane la-diina*).

crown - *taaž* pl. *tiižaan*.

crucial - *ḥaasem, faaṣel*. He avoided the crucial question. *džannab ᵊl-masᵊ?ale l-ḥaasme*.

crude - **1.** *dəbež, fažž*. He's a rather crude person. *huwwe šaxᵊṣ dəbež ᵊšwayye*. **2.** *fažž*. That was a crude remark. *hayy kaanet ᵊmlaaḥaẓa fažža*. **3.** *xaam* (invar.). We ship many barrels of crude oil to the refineries every day. *kəll yoom ᵊmnəbɛat ᵊktiir baramiil zeet xaam ləl-maṣaafi*.

cruel - *qaasi*. How can he be so cruel? *kiif fii ykuun qaasi kəll hal-qadd?*

cruelty - *qasaawe*.

crumb - *fatfuute* pl. *fatafiit*. The birds ate the crumbs of bread. *l-ɛaṣafiir ?aklet fatafiit ᵊl-xəbᵊz*.

to **crush** - **1.** *faɛas (a faɛᵊs//nfaɛas)*. He crushed my hat when he sat on it. *faɛas bərneeṭṭi lamma qaɛad ɛaleeha*. **2.** *kassar//tkassar*. Careful, you'll crush the eggs. *?əṣḥa tkasser ᵊl-beeḍ*. **3.** *maɛas (a maɛᵊs//mmaɛas)*. We were nearly crushed in the crowd. *kənna laḥa nəmmə́ɛes bᵊz-zaḥme*. **4.** *ḥaṭṭam//tḥaṭṭam*. He was crushed by the news. *ḥaṭṭamo l-xabar*.

crust - **1.** *qəšre* coll. *qəšᵊr* pl. *qšuura*. The crust of this bread is burned. *qəšret hal-xəbᵊz maḥruuqa*. **2.** *waqaaḥa*. He has a lot of crust, asking you to do that for him! *laa šakk ɛando waqaaḥa ktiir la-yəṭlob mənnak taɛməl-lo haš-šaġle*.

crutch - *ɛəkkaaze* pl. *ɛakakiiz*. He has to walk on crutches. *laazem yəmši ɛala ɛakakiiz*.

cry - **1.** *ṣarxa* pl. *-aat*. Then we heard a loud cry. *baɛdeen ᵊsməɛna ṣarxa ɛaalye*. **2.** *ṣoot* pl. *?aṣwaat*.

The cry of the bird woke us up. *ṣooṭ ᵊṭ-ṭeer fayyaqna.* **3.** *mnaadda.* The cry for reform is getting stronger. *l-ᵊmnaadda bᵊl-ʔəṣlaaḥ ɛam təqwa.*
**You'll feel better if you have a good cry. *btəthassan ḥaaltak ʔiza btəflat bᵊl-bəke.*
a far cry from – *bɛiid ᵊktiir ɛan.* That's a far cry from the truth. *haada bɛiid ᵊktiir ɛan ᵊl-ḥaqiiqa.*
to cry – *bəki (i bəke).* She cried when she heard the news. *bəkyet waqᵊt səmɛet ᵊl-xabar.* -- The baby cried all night. *l-beebée bəki ṭuul ᵊl-leel.*
**She cried her eyes out. *baqqet ᵊɛyuuna mn ᵊl-bəke.*
to cry out – **1.** *ɛayyaṭ (ɛayaaṭ), ṣarax (a ṣraax, ṣarxa).* The old man cried out in pain. *l-ʔəxtyaar ɛayyaṭ mən kətr ᵊl-wažaɛ.* **2.** *naada ɛala.* The peddler cried out his wares. *l-bayyaaɛ naada ɛala bḍaaɛto.*
**For crying out loud! *daxiil ɛərḍak!*
cube – *kaɛᵊb* pl. *kɛaab.*
cucumber – *xyaara* coll. *xyaar* pl. *-aat.* We raised some cucumbers last year. *zaraɛna šwayyet ᵊxyaar ɛaamnawwal.*
**He's as cool as a cucumber. *qalbo baared maa fii šii bihəzzo.*
to **cuddle** – *ḥaḍan (e ḥaḍᵊn), ḥtaḍan.* She cuddled the baby in her arms. *ḥaḍnet ᵊl-beebée b-ʔideeha.*
to cuddle up – *tkaɛwak.* The children cuddled up in their blankets. *l-ᵊwlaad ᵊtkaɛwaku b-ʔḥraamaaton.*
cue – **1.** *ʔišaara* pl. *-aat.* I'll give you the cue when to start. *baɛṭiik ʔišaara ʔeemta təbda.* **2.** *ɛaṣaayet˜ (pl. ɛəṣi˜) bəlyaar.* This cue is too heavy for me. *ɛaṣaayet ᵊl-bəlyaar hayye tqiile ktiir ɛaliyyi.*
to take a cue from – *məši (i maši) ɛala xaaṭer˜ ...* I took my cue from her. *mšiit ɛala xaaṭəra.*
cuff – **1.** *qabbet˜ kəmm* pl. *qabbaat˜ ᵊkmaam, maqlab˜ kəmm* pl. *maqaaleb˜ ᵊkmaam.* The cuffs of his shirt were torn. *qabbaat ᵊkmaam qamiiṣo kaanet mašruuṭa.* **2.** *qalbe* pl. *-aat.* I could only get trousers without cuffs. *maa kaan fiini laaqi ʔəlla banṭaroon bala qalbaat.*
on the cuff – *ɛal-ᵊḥsaab, bᵊd-deen.* Will you give me a beer on the cuff? *btaɛṭiini waaḥed biira ɛal-ᵊḥsaab?*
cuff link – *zərr˜ (pl. zraar˜) ᵊkmaam.* I lost one of my cuff links. *ḍawwaɛᵊt farde mn ᵊzraar ᵊkmaami.*
culprit – *məzneb* pl. *-iin.*
to **cultivate** – **1.** *kasar (e kasᵊr), ḥarat (o ḥarᵊt).* As soon as the snow is gone in spring, the farmers begin to cultivate the land around here. *ʔawwal-ma biruuḥ ᵊt-talᵊž bᵊr-rabiiɛ ᵊl-fallaaḥiin byəbdu yəkᵊsru l-ʔarᵊḍ nawaaḥi hoon.* **2.** *rabba.* He cultivates roses for his own pleasure. *birabbi wruud la-basṭo.* **3.** *hazzab.* She's cultivating a taste for classical music. *ɛam ᵊthazzeb zooqa bᵊl-muusiiqa l-klaasikiyye.*
cultivation – *tahziib, tasqiif.* Real cultivation of the mind takes time and application. *tahziib ᵊl-ɛaql ᵊṣ-ṣaḥiiḥ bəddo waqᵊt w-ʔəžtihaad.*
cultural – *saqaafi**.
culture – **1.** *saqaafe.* The ancient Greeks attained a high degree of culture. *l-yuunaaniyyiin ᵊl-qədama twaṣṣalu la-daraže ɛaalye mn ᵊs-saqaafe.* **2.** *ḥaḍaara* pl. *-aat.* He is studying about the development of various Eastern cultures. *ɛam yədros ɛan taṭawwor baɛḍ ᵊl-ḥaḍaaraat ᵊš-šarqiyye.*
cultured – **1.** *msaqqaf, mhazzab.* She's a cultured woman. *hiyye sətt ᵊmsaqqafe.* **2.** *zarᵊɛ* (invar.). She's wearing cultured pearls. *laabse luulu zarᵊɛ.*
cunning – **1.** *maaker, qərᵊḥ.* He's a cunning old fox. *huwwe waaḥed maaker ɛatiiq.* **2.** *mahḍuum, ẓariif.* They have a cunning little girl. *ɛandon bənt ᵊẓġiire mahḍuume.*
cup – **1.** *fənžaan* pl. *fanažiin.* Will you have a cup of coffee? *btəšrab-lak fənžaan qahwe?* **2.** *keele* pl. *-aat.* Shall I take a cup along? *ʔaaxod maɛi keele?* **3.** *kaʔᵊs* pl. *kʔuuse.* Who won the cup? *miin rəbeḥ ᵊl-kaʔᵊs?*
cupboard – *namliyye* pl. *namaali.*
curb – *rṣiif* pl. *ʔərᵊṣfe.* He didn't park the car close enough to the curb. *maa ṣaff ᵊs-sayyaara qariib ᵊkfaaye lər-rṣiif.*
**The government put a curb on extraordinary expenditures. *l-ᵊḥkuume šaddadet ɛal-maṣariif halli zaayde ɛan ᵊl-lzuum.*
to curb – *ẓabaṭ (o ẓabᵊṭ).* You'll have to learn to curb your temper. *laazem tətɛallam təẓboṭ ʔaɛṣaabak.*
to **curdle** – **1.** *ḥammaḍ.* The milk curdled overnight. *l-ḥaliib ḥammaḍ ʔasnaaʔ ᵊl-leel.* **2.** *džammad.* His story will make your blood curdle. *qəṣṣto bətxalli dammak yədžammad.*
cure – *dawa* pl. *ʔadᵊwye.* There is no cure for cancer. *maa fii dawa ləs-saraṭaan.*
to cure – **1.** *šafa (i šifa//šəfi a šifa), ṭayyab.* This medicine will cure you if you take it regularly. *had-dawa byəšfiik ʔiza ʔaxadto b-ʔəntiẓaam.* **2.** *qooram.* We have to cure enough meat to last us for the winter. *laazem ᵊnqoorem laḥme kfaaye tʔaddiina kəll ᵊš-šəte.*
**That should cure him of meddling in other people's business. *haš-šii laḥa yɛallmo ʔənno maa yəddaaxal ᵊb-ʔumuur ᵊn-naas.*
to be cured – *ṭaab (i ṭayabaan), šəfi (a šifa).* He's completely cured. *ṭaab ɛal-ʔaaxiir.*
curfew – *ɛadam˜ ᵊt-tažawwol.* The commanding officer set an eight-o'clock curfew for the civilian population. *ḍ-ḍaabeṭ ᵊl-masʔuul ɛayyan ᵊs-saaɛa tmaane la-bədᵊʔ ɛadam ᵊt-tažawwol ləl-madaniyyin.*
curiosity – *fuḍuuliyye, kətret˜ ġalabe.* The noise aroused my curiosity. *ḍ-ḍoože nabbahᵊt-li fuḍuuliiti.*
curious – **1.** *fuḍuuli*, ktiir˜ ġalabe* pl. *ktaar˜ ġalabe.* Don't be so curious; this isn't any of your business. *laa tkuun hal-qadd fuḍuuli, haš-šii maa bixəṣṣak.* **2.** *mətšawweq.* I'm curious to know what the answer will be. *ʔana mətšawweq ʔaɛref šuu ž-žawaab laḥa ykuun.* **3.** *ġariib, ɛažiib.* This is a curious piece of furniture. *hayy qətɛet moobiilya ġariibe.* -- What a curious looking person! *qaddeeš heeʔet hal-ʔənsaan ġariibe!*
curl – *šaɛde* pl. *-aat.*
**She has natural curls. *šaɛra mšaɛɛad ᵊb-ṭabiiɛto.*
to curl – **1.** *džaɛɛad.* Her hair curls naturally. *šaɛra byədžaɛɛad ᵊb-ṭabiiɛto.* **2.** *šaɛɛad.* She wants to curl your hair for you. *bədda džaɛɛəd-lek šaɛrek.*
to curl up – *tkaɛwak, kaɛwak ḥaalo.* The dog curled up and went to sleep. *l-kalb ᵊtkaɛwak w-naam.*
curler – *buugadiin* (invar.). You can't run around like that with curlers in your hair! *ɛeeb təmši heek wᵊl-buugadiin ᵊb-šaɛrek!*
curly – *mšaɛɛad.* Her little boy has curly hair. *walda ẓ-ẓġiir šaɛro mšaɛɛad.*
current – **1.** *tayyaar* pl. *-aat.* He got caught in the strong current and drowned. *žarafo t-tayyaar ᵊl-qawi w-ġəreq.* -- The electric current has been turned off. *t-tayyaar ᵊl-kahrabaaʔi nqaṭaɛ.* **2.** *žaari.* The bill for the current month is enclosed. *faatuuret ᵊš-šahr ᵊž-žaari bᵊd-daaxel.* **3.** *ḥaali*, žaari, ʔaaxer˜ ...* I read that in the current issue of the magazine. *qareeto bᵊl-ɛadad ᵊl-ḥaali (or b-ʔaaxer ɛadad) tabaɛ ᵊl-mažalle.* **4.** *daarež.* What's the current usage of that term? *šuu l-ʔəstəɛmaal ᵊd-daarež la-hal-ʔəṣṭilaaḥ?*
curriculum – *bərnaamež˜ (pl. baraameež˜) diraase.* Your curriculum for this year will be rather difficult. *bərnaamež diraastak la-has-səne laḥa ykuun šwayye ṣaɛᵊb ɛaleek.*
curse – **1.** *laɛne* pl. *-aat.* He muttered a curse under his breath. *tamtam ᵊb-laɛne.* **2.** *laɛne, mṣiibe, məḥne, balwe.* His promotion is more of a curse than a blessing. *tarfiiɛo laɛne ʔaktar mənno nəɛme.*
to curse – *laɛan (a laɛᵊn), sabb (ə sabb).* He curses constantly. *byəlɛan ɛala ṭuul.* -- Why did he curse you? *leeš sabbak?*
to **curtail** – *qattar, naqqaṣ.* The government will have to curtail its spending for the next six months. *l-ᵊḥkuume laḥa tənžəber ᵊtqatter maṣariifa bᵊs-sətt əšhor ᵊž-žaaye.*
curtain – *bərdaaye* pl. *baraadi.* I want curtains for all the windows. *bəddi baraadi ləš-šababiik kəllon.*
curtain rod – *qədde* pl. *qədad.*
curve – *kuuɛ* pl. *kwaaɛ.* Slow down before you reach the curve. *xaffef seerak qabᵊl-ma təṣal ləl-kuuɛ.*
to curve – *tɛarwaž.* The road curves badly for the next mile. *ṭ-ṭariiq byətɛarwaž ᵊktiir ɛala masaafet miil mən hoon.*
cushion – *mxadde* pl. *-aat, sannaade* pl. *-aat, ṭərraaḥa* pl. *ṭarariiḥ.* We need some cushions for the sofa. *laazəmna kam ᵊmxadde mənšaan ᵊl-kanabe.*
cuspidor – *mabzaqa* pl. *mabaazeq.*
custody – **1.** *ḥiḍaane.* The child is in the custody of his aunt. *l-walad taḥᵊt ḥiḍaanet ɛammto.* **2.** *ḥabᵊs.* He was taken into custody. *ʔaxaduu ɛal-ḥabᵊs.*
custom – **1.** *ɛaade* pl. *-aat.* That custom died out a long time ago. *hal-ɛaade raaḥet mən zamaan.* -- That's not the custom here. *l-ɛaade hoon muu heek.* **2.** *tafṣiil.* He only wears custom clothes. *maa*

byəlbes ʔəlla ʔawaaƐi tafṣiil.
customs – *gəmrok* pl. *gamaarek, žəmrok* pl. *žamaarek.* Do we have to pay customs on this? *laazem nədfaƐ gəmrok Ɛala haš-šii?*
customs inspection – *taftiiš gəmᵊrki, taftiiš˜ gamaarek.* When do we pass the customs inspection? *ʔeemta mnəmroq bᵊt-taftiiš ᵊl-gəmᵊrki?*

customary – *Ɛaadi*.* It's not customary here to leave calling cards. *muu šii Ɛaadi hoon tətrok biṭaaqaat ᵊzyaara.*

customer – *zbuun* pl. *zabaayen.* There weren't very many customers today. *maa kaan fii zabaayen ᵊktiir ᵊl-yoom.*
**He's a pretty sharp customer! *huwwe zalame Ɛal-maẓbuṭ!*

cut – **1.** *qaṭᵊƐ* pl. *qṭuuƐa, žərᵊḥ* pl. *žruuḥa.* The cut is nearly healed. *l-qaṭᵊƐ taqriiban ṭaab.* **2.** *šarḥa* pl. *-aat.* The butcher gave me a good cut of meat last time. *l-laḥḥaam Ɛaṭaani šarḥet laḥm ᵊmniiḥa ʔaaxer marra.* **3.** *kasᵊm, tafṣiil.* I like the cut of that suit. *ḥaabeb ʔana kasᵊm hal-badle.* **4.** *taxfiiḍ.* He has been expecting a cut in salary for some time. *ṣar-lo mədde Ɛam yətwaqqaƐ taxfiiḍ ᵊb-maƐaašo.*
short cut – *ṭariiq˜* (pl. *ṭəroq˜*) *ᵊmqaaṭaƐa.* You can take a short cut here. *fiik taaxod ṭariiq ᵊmqaaṭaƐa mən hoon.*
to cut – **1.** *qaṭaƐ (a qaṭᵊƐ).* This is the only knife that cuts well. *hayy ᵊs-səkkiine l-waḥiide yalli btəqṭaƐ ᵊmniiḥ.* -- I cut my finger. *qaṭaƐᵊt ʔəṣbaƐti.* -- Who cuts the cards this time? *miin byəqṭaƐ ᵊš-šadde hal-marra?* **2.** *qaṭaƐ, qaṭṭaƐ.* Will you cut the bread, please. *ləṭfan ᵊqṭaaƐ ᵊl-xəbᵊz.* **3.** *qaṣṣ (ə qaṣṣ//nqaṣṣ), qaṭaƐ.* The gardener will cut the grass tomorrow. *ž-žneenaati biqəṣṣ ᵊl-ḥašiiš bəkra.* **4.** *xaffaḍ, nazzal.* The company cut the salaries of four employees. *š-šərke xaffaḍet maƐaašaat ʔarbaƐ məstaxdamiin.* -- These prices will be cut next month. *hal-ʔasƐaar ᵊbtətxaffaḍ ᵊš-šahr ᵊž-žaaye.* **5.** *qaṣṣar//tqaṣṣar.* The movie had to be cut in several places. *l-fəlᵊm nžabaru yqaṣṣrúu b-Ɛəddet maḥallaat.* **6.** *nqaṭaƐ.* This cake doesn't cut easily. *hal-gaato maa byənqə́ṭeƐ b-ᵊshuule.*
**During the whole term he cut only two classes. *b-kəll ᵊl-faṣᵊl fardka bass marrteen ᵊmn ᵊṣ-ṣaff.*
**The baby is cutting its first tooth. *l-beebe Ɛam yəṭlə́Ɛ-lo ʔawwal sənn.*
**He cuts quite a figure in his new suit. *ṭaalƐət-əllo ḥəlwe l-badle ž-ždiide.*
**Your remark cut her to the quick. *kalaamak ʔassar fiiha ktiir.*
to cut across – *məši (i maši) mqaaṭaƐa.* He cut across the field. *məši mqaaṭaƐa bᵊl-ḥaqle.*
to cut corners – *šaffa.* Maybe we can get by on a smaller budget by cutting a few corners. *yəmken fiina nmašši l-ḥaal ᵊb-miizaaniyye ʔaẓġar ʔiza šaffeenda-lna šii šwayye.*
to cut down – **1.** *qaṭaƐ (a qaṭᵊƐ//nqaṭaƐ).* They have to cut down some trees in order to build a house. *laazem yəqṭaƐu kam šažara ḥatta yəbnu beet.* **2.** *xtaṣar.* We'll have to cut our expenses down. *laazem nəxtə́ṣer maṣariifna.*
to cut in – *qaaṭaƐ.* She always cuts in when I'm talking. *daayman bətqaaṭəƐni waqᵊt bəḥki.*
to cut loose – *ṣaar harᵊž w-marᵊž.* They cut loose the minute the teacher steps out of the room. *b-daqiiqet-ma byəṭlaƐ ᵊl-ʔəstaaz ᵊmn ᵊṣ-ṣaff biṣiiru harᵊž w-marᵊž.*
to cut off – **1.** *qaṭaƐ (a qaṭᵊƐ//nqaṭaƐ)* Cut it off at the end. *qṭaaƐo b-ʔaaxro.* -- He cut them off without a cent. *qaṭáƐon w-xallaahon bala nḥaase.* **2.** *qaṭaƐ Ɛala.* Operator, I've been cut off! *ṣantraal, ᵊnqaṭaƐ Ɛaliyyi l-xaṭṭ!*
to cut open – *fataḥ (a fatᵊḥ//nfataḥ).* We'll have to cut the blister open. *laazem nəftaḥ ᵊl-faqfuule.*
to cut out – *qaṣṣ (ə qaṣṣ//nqaṣṣ).* I cut the picture out of a magazine. *qaṣṣeet ᵊṣ-ṣuura mən mažalle.*
**Cut it out! *ḥaaže baqa!*
cut out – *maxluuq.* He's not cut out to be a teacher. *huwwe muu maxluuq ykuun ᵊmƐallem.*
to cut short – **1.** *qaṣṣar.* We had to cut our trip short. *nžabarna nqaṣṣer safrətna.* **2.** *qaaṭaƐ.* He cut me short. *qaaṭaƐni.*
to cut through – **1.** *qaṣṣ (ə qaṣṣ).* You've cut through the lining. *qaṣṣeet l-ᵊbṭaane.* **2.** *məši (i maši) mqaaṭaƐa.* We cut through the park on our way home. *mšiina mqaaṭaƐa bᵊl-ḥadiiqa b-ṭariiqna Ɛal-beet.*
to cut up – **1.** *qaṭṭaƐ, qassam.* Cut it up in four pieces. *qaṭṭƐo ʔarbaƐ šəqaf.* **2.** *warža ḥaalo.* Their little girl loves to cut up when we're around. *bənton ᵊẓ-ẓġiire bətḥəbb ᵊtwarži ḥaala b-ᵊḥḍuurna.*

cute – *maḥḍuum, ẓariif.* She's a cute little girl. *hiyye bənt ᵊẓġiire maḥḍuume.*
cutlet – *kastaleeta* pl. *-aat.* I like my cutlet well done. *bḥəbb ᵊl-kastaleeta tabaƐi tkuun məstwiyye mniiḥ.*
cutting – **1.** *ṭəƐᵊm* pl. *ṭƐuume.* I'll plant these cuttings over there. *laḥa ʔəzraƐ haṭ-ṭƐuume hniike.* **2.** *ḥaadd, laazeƐ.* That was a cutting remark. *hayy kaanet ᵊmlaaḥaẓa ḥaadde.*
cylinder – *silandar* pl. *silandraat.*
cynic – *məthakkem* pl. *-iin.*
cynical – **1.** (remark, etc.) *tahakkumi*.* **2.** (person) *məthakkem.*
cynicism – *tahakkom.*
Cypriote – *qəbᵊrṣi** pl. *qabaarṣe.*
Cyprus – *qəbroṣ.*
Czech – *tšiiki** pl. *-iyyiin.*
Czechoslovakia – *tšekoslovaakya.*
Czechoslovakian – *tšekoslovaaki*.*

D

dad(dy) – *baaba* (invar.), *ʔabb* (*ʔabuu-* + pron. suff., *ʔab(u)˜*, my ~ *ʔabi*) pl. *ʔabbaat.* Is your dad home? *(l-)baaba bᵊl-beet?* or *ʔabuuk bᵊl-beet?*
daffodil – *naržes ʔaṣfar.*
dagger – *xanžar* pl. *xanaažer.*
dahlia – *daalya.*
daily – **1.** *bᵊl-yoom, yoomiyyan.* The mail is delivered twice daily. *l-bariid byətwazzaƐ marrteen bᵊl-yoom.* **2.** *yoomi*.* The daily rate is only three dollars. *t-taƐriife l-yoomiyye bass tlətt dolaaraat.* **3.** *žariide* (pl. *žaraayed*). In the morning, on my way to the office, I usually buy one of the dailies. *bᵊṣ-ṣəbᵊḥ, w-ʔana raayeḥ Ɛala šəġli bəštə́ri Ɛaadatan žariide mn ᵊž-žaraayed.*
**That's a daily occurrence around here. *haš-šii byəḥdos hoon kəll yoom.*
dairy – *maƐmal˜* (pl. *maƐaamel˜*) *ʔalbaan.* I bought the eggs at the dairy. *štareet ᵊl-beeḍaat mən maƐmal ᵊl-ʔalbaan.*
daisy – *ʔaqḥawaane* coll. *ʔaqḥawaan* pl. *-aat.*
dam – *sadd* pl. *sduud.* The dam is broken. *s-sadd maksuur.*
to dam – *sadd (ə sadd/nsadd).* When are they going to dam the river? *ʔeemta raḥa ysəddu n-nahᵊr?*
damage – *ḍarar* pl. *ʔaḍraar.* How much damage did the fire cause? *qaddeeš ᵊḍ-ḍarar yalli sabbabə́to l-ḥariiqa?*
damages – *taƐwiiḍ, taƐwiiḍaat* (pl.). He had to pay damages. *nžabar yədfaƐ taƐwiiḍ.*
to damage – *Ɛawwar//tƐawwar, ʔaza (i ʔaẓi//nʔaza).* The storm damaged the roof. *l-Ɛaaṣfe Ɛawwaret ᵊl-ʔəṣṭuuḥ.*

Damascene – *šaami** pl. *šwaam, dimašqi** pl. *-iyyiin* and *damaašqa.*
Damascus – *š-šaam, dimašq.*
damask – *damaasko.* This tablecloth is of the finest damask. *hal-ġaṭa ṭ-ṭaawle maƐmuul mən ʔafxar damaasko.*
damn – *malƐuun.* Throw that damn cat out! *lḥooš hal-qaṭṭa l-malƐuune la-barra!*
**I don't give a damn what he says. *Ɛala rəžli maa biƐalleq šuu biquul.*
to damn – **1.** *qaddar Ɛala.* He believes some souls are damned to everlasting punishment. *biʔaamen ʔənno fii baƐḍ ᵊl-ʔarwaaḥ ᵊmqaddar Ɛaleeha l-Ɛazaab ᵊl-ʔazali.* **2.** *laƐan (a laƐᵊn//ltaƐan).* Damn that nail, I tore my coat again! *yaḷḷa yəlƐan hal-bəsmaar, šaraṭ-li žaakeeti taani marra!* -- Go ahead, do it and be damned! *yaḷḷa ruuḥ saawiiha w-ᵊltə́Ɛen!*
**Damn (it)! *yəfḍaḥ ḥariima!* or *yəxreb beeta!* or

yəhreq diina! or *yəlɛan ʔabuuha!*
**I'll be damned if I do it! *bkuun ɛarṣa* (or *dayyuus*) *ʔiza saaweeta!*
damp – *mnaddi, rəṭeb.* Everything gets damp in the cellar. *kəll šii bişiir ᵊmnaddi bᵊl-qabu.*
to **dampen** – **1.** *nadda, raṭṭab.* Have you dampened the clothes yet? *naddeeti l-ʔawaaɛi wəlla ləssa?*
2. *hammad, xammad.* His remark dampened our spirits. *mlaaḥaẓto hammadet həmmətna.*
dampness – *rṭuube.*
damson – *xooxa* coll. *xoox* pl. *-aat.*
dance – **1.** *baal* pl. *-aat, ḥafle* (pl. *-aat*) *raaqṣa.* Are you going to the dance? *laḥa truuḥ ɛal-baal?*
2. *raqṣa* pl. *-aat.* The next dance will be a waltz. *r-raqṣa ž-žaaye bədda tkuun vaals.* — May I have the next dance? *btəsmaḥíi-li bᵊr-raqṣa ž-žaaye?*
to dance – *raqaṣ (o raqᵊṣ).* They danced until midnight. *raqaṣu la-nəṣṣ ᵊl-leel.* — We danced to radio music. *raqaṣna ɛala muusiiqa r-raadyo.*
dancer – *raqqaaṣ* pl. *-iin,* f. *raqqaaṣa* pl. *-aat, ʔartiist* pl. *-aat.* There is a new dancer at the night club now. *fii raqqaaṣa ždiide bᵊl-kabarée hallaq.*
**She's a good dancer. *hiyye btərqoṣ ᵊmniiḥ.*
dandruff – *qəšret˜ raas.* How do I get rid of my dandruff? *kiif məmken ʔəxloṣ mən qəšret ᵊr-raas tabaɛi?*
dandy – **1.** *ġanduur* pl. *ġanaadra.* He's always been something of a dandy. *daayman kaan nooɛan-ma ġanduur.* **2.** *ɛaal* (invar.). That's just dandy! *waḷḷa šii ɛaal!*
Dane – *danimarki** pl. *-iyyiin.*
danger – *xaṭar* pl. *ʔaxṭaar.* The doctor says she is out of danger now. *d-doktoor ɛam yquul ʔənno zaal ᵊl-xaṭar ɛanha hallaq.* — He's in danger of losing his job. *fii xaṭar ʔənno yəxṣar waẓiifto.*
dangerous – *xəṭer, məxṭer.* Is it dangerous to swim here? *s-sbaaḥa hoon xəṭra?* — Some of the animals around here are pretty dangerous. *baɛḍ ᵊl-ḥaywaanaat ᵊb-hal-qaraani məxᵊṭra ktiir.*
Danish – *danimarki**.
Danube – *(nahr˜) ᵊd-daanuub.*
dare – *taḥaddi* pl. *-yaat.* Are you going to take his dare? *laḥa təqbal taḥaddiyaato?*
to dare – **1.** *starža, džaasar.* I didn't dare leave the baby alone. *maa staržeet ʔətrok ᵊl-beebée la-ḥaalo.* **2.** *džarraʔ, džaasar, starža.* I don't dare tell him. *maa bədžarraʔ xabbro.* — How dare you open my mail? *kiif btədžaasar təftaḥ makatiibi?*
**Don't you dare! *starži!*
**Don't you dare take it! *starži w-xəda!*
dark – **1.** *ɛətme, ẓalaam.* The road is hard to find in the dark. *ṣaɛb ᵊmlaaqaat ᵊṭ-ṭariiq bᵊl-ɛətme.*
2. *məẓlem.* I don't want to walk through these dark alleys. *maa bəddi ʔəmši b-hal-ḥaaraat ᵊl-məẓᵊlme.* — The future seems pretty dark to him right now. *l-məstaqbal byəẓhar ɛalée ktiir məẓlem bᵊn-nəsbe ʔəlo bᵊl-waqt ᵊl-ḥaaḍer.* **3.** *ġaameq.* She looks nice in dark colors. *btəṭlaɛ ẓariife bᵊl-ʔalwaan ᵊl-ġaamqa.* **4.** *ʔasmar* f. *samra* pl. *səmᵊr.* He has a dark complexion, just like his father. *bəšᵊrto samra, tamaam mətᵊl ʔabúu.*
**Don't keep me in the dark! *laa təxfi ɛanni!*
to get dark – *ɛattam.* In summer it gets dark late. *bᵊṣ-ṣeef btəɛattem mətʔaxxra.*
darling – **1.** *ḥabiib* pl. *ḥabaayeb,* f. *ḥabiibe* pl. *-aat.* You look tired tonight, darling. *mbayyen ɛaleek taɛbaan, ya ḥabiibi, ᵊl-leele.* — My darling children picked these flowers for me. *ḥabiibaati l-ᵊwlaad (ʔaḷḷa yərḍa ɛaleehon) qaṭafúu-li hal-wardaat.*
2. *maḥbuub* pl. *-iin.* He's his mother's darling. *huwwe maḥbuub ʔəmmo* or **huwwe bəbbu ɛeen ʔəmmo.*
3. *maḥḍuum.* She wears darling clothes. *btəlbes ʔawaaɛi maḥḍuume.*
to **darn** – *rata (i rati//rtata).* Did you darn my socks? *rateetíi-li žraabaati?*
**Darn it! Where's my tie? *yəxreb beeta! ween kraafti?*
**He knew darn little about it. *ɛəref fiiha qadd ᵊl-qašše.*
**I don't give a darn about it! *maa bətɛalleq ɛala rəžli!*
**I'll be darned if that isn't my old school teacher! *daxiil ɛərḍak! hayy ᵊmɛallmi l-qadiim!*
dash – **1.** *rašše* pl. *-aat.* All it needs is a dash of salt. *kəll šii laazəma raššet məlᵊḥ.* **2.** *xeeṭ˜, nəqṭet˜, šwayyet˜.* Could I have my coffee with a dash of brandy? *məmken žəb-li qahᵊwti w-fiiha xeeṭ konyaak?* **3.** *šaxṭa* pl. *-aat.* Put a dash after the first word. *həṭṭ šaxṭa baɛᵊd ʔawwal kəlme.*
4. *rakde* pl. *-aat.* Who won the hundred-meter dash? *miin rəbeḥ rakdet ᵊl-miit mətᵊr?*
to make a dash – *qafaz (e qafᵊz), naṭṭ (ə naṭṭ).* He grabbed his hat and made a dash for the door. *xaṭaf bərneeṭṭo w-qafaz naaḥ ᵊl-baab.*
to dash – **1.** *rašš (ə rašš//nrašš).* He came right to when I dashed some water in his face. *ṣəḥi waqᵊt-ma rašše̋et-éllo šwayyet mayy ɛala wəššo.*
2. *naṭṭ (ə naṭṭ), rakad (o rakᵊd).* He likes to dash from one place to another. *biḥəbb ynəṭṭ mən qərne la-qərne.*
to dash off – **1.** *fardk(h)a mətl ᵊl-barq.* Before I could answer, he dashed off. *qabᵊl-ma qdərt žaawbo fardka mətl ᵊl-barq.* **2.** *laḥaš (e/o laḥᵊš).* I have to dash off a few lines to my brother. *laazem ʔəlḥəš-li šii saṭreen la-ʔaxi.*
dashboard – *taablóo* pl. *tabloyaat.*
data – *maɛluumaat* (pl.). He compiled the data during his trip. *žamaɛ ᵊl-maɛluumaat ʔasna rəḥᵊlto.*
date – (fresh) *balaḥa* coll. *balaḥ* pl. *-aat,* (dried) *tamra* coll. *tamᵊr* pl. *-aat,* (pressed) *ɛažwe.* Give me a kilo of dates. *ɛaṭiini kiilo balaḥ.*
date palm – *naxle* pl. *-aat.*
date – **1.** *taariix* pl. *tawariix.* What's the date today? *šuu t-taariix ᵊl-yoom?* **2.** *mawɛed* pl. *mawaɛiid, waqᵊt* pl. *ʔawqaat, taariix* pl. *tawariix.* You set the date. *ʔənte btəɛayyen ᵊl-mawɛed.* **3.** *miiɛaad* pl. *mawaɛiid, mawɛed* pl. *mawaɛiid.* I have a date for lunch today. *ɛandi miiɛaad ɛal-ġada l-yoom.*
**Who's your date tonight? *maɛ miin ṭaaleɛ ᵊl-yoom ɛašiyye?*
**Don't keep your date waiting. (approx.:) *laa txalli ṣaaḥbek yənṭéẓer.*
**These machines are out of date. *hal-maakiinaat bəṭel ʔəstəɛmaala.*
up-to-date – *ɛala ʔaaxer mooḍa.* Her clothes are always up-to-date. *tyaaba daayman ɛala ʔaaxer mooḍa.*
**I'm not up-to-date on this matter. *ʔana maa-li məṭṭéleɛ ɛala ʔaaxer taṭawwuraat hal-qaḍiyye.*
up to date – *la-ḥadd hallaq, la-has-saaɛa.* Up to date we haven't heard from him. *la-ḥadd hallaq maa ʔəžaana mənno šii.*
to date – **1.** *ʔarrax, tarrax.* He forgot to date the letter. *nəsi yʔarrex ᵊl-maktuub.* **2.** *ṭeleɛ (a ṭalɛa) maɛ.* He dates her regularly. *byəṭlaɛ maɛa ɛala ṭuul.*
**The oldest house in town dates from the 17th century. *ʔaqdam beet bᵊl-balad byəržaɛ taariixo ləl-qarn ᵊs-saabeɛ ɛašar.*
daughter – *bənᵊt* pl. *banaat.*
daughter-in-law – *kənne* pl. *kanaayen.* She's his daughter-in-law, not his sister-in-law. *hiyye kənnto — žooзet ʔəbno — muu kənnto žoozet ʔaxúu.*
davenport – *kanabe* pl. *-aat, kanabaaye* pl. *-aat.* Don't let the children sit on the davenport. *laa txalli l-ᵊwlaad yəqᵊɛdu ɛal-kanabe.*
dawn – *fažᵊr.* We had to get up at dawn. *nžabarna nfəzz maɛ ᵊl-fažᵊr.*
to dawn on – *laaḥ (u ø) la-, tfattaḥ la-.* It finally dawned on me what he meant. *ʔaxiiran laḥ-li šuu kaan ɛam yəɛni.*
day – **1.** *nhaar* pl. *-aat.* He's been sleeping all day. *ṣar-lo naayem ṭuul ᵊn-nhaar.* — I've been working day and night. *ɛam ʔəštéġel leel ᵊnhaar.* **2.** *yoom* pl. *ʔiyyaam.* He spent five days in Paris. *maḍḍa xamᵊst iyyaam b-baariiz.* — I see his brother every day. *bšuuf ʔaxúu kəll yoom.* — Tuesday is my day off. *t-talaata yoom ɛəṭᵊlti.* — He's seen better days. *šaaf ʔiyyaam ʔaḥsan.* — He's had his day. *kan-lo ʔiyyaam* or **kan-lo zamaan.*
**He was quite an athlete in his day. *kaan ryaaḍi maaken b-zamaano.*
**Let's call it a day! *ḥaažətna l-yoom!*
a day – *bᵊl-yoom, yoomiyyan.* Take these pills three times a day. *xood hal-ḥabbaat tlətt marraat bᵊl-yoom.* — He earns eight dollars a day. *biṭaaleɛ tmən dolaaraat bᵊl-yoom.*
any day – *b-hal-kam yoom.* They'll be coming to visit us any day now. *raḥa yəžu ysuuruuna b-hal-kam yoom.*
by the day – **1.** *yoom baɛᵊd yoom, yoom ɛan yoom.* He gets richer by the day. *ɛam yəġna yoom baɛᵊd yoom.* **2.** *bᵊl-yoom, bᵊl-yoomiyye.* You can rent this room by the day. *fiik təstaʔžer hal-ʔuuḍa bᵊl-yoom.*
day after day – *yoom baɛᵊd yoom, yoom ɛan yoom.* Day after day he tells us the same old story. *yoom*

baεᵊd yoom biεə́d-ᵊlna nafs ᵊl-qəṣṣa.
day by day - *yoom baεᵊd yoom, yoom εan yoom.* Day by day his condition is improving. *yoom baεᵊd yoom ḥaalto εam təthassan.*
day in, day out - *kəll yoom, yoom baεᵊd yoom.* We eat the same old thing day in, day out. *mnaakol nafs ᵊš-šii kəll yoom.*
every other day - *yoom ʔee yoom laʔ.* I only work every other day. *bass bəštə́ġel yoom ʔee yoom laʔ.*
from day to day - *mn ᵊl-yoom lət-taani, mən yoom la-yoom, yoom baεᵊd yoom, yoom εan yoom.* His condition is getting worse from day to day. *ḥaalto εam təltə́εen ᵊmn ᵊl-yoom lət-taani.*
one of these days - 1. *b-hal-kam yoom.* I'll drop by your house one of these days. *bəmroq εaleek bᵊl-beet ᵊb-hal-kam yoom.* 2. *ləssa byəži yoom.* One of these days you'll be sorry you didn't study. *ləssa byəži yoom bəddak təndam laʔənnak maa darast.*
the day after tomorrow - *baεᵊd bəkra.* He's leaving the day after tomorrow. *laḥa ysaafer baεᵊd bəkra.*
the other day - *muu mən zamaan, maa-l-* + pron. suff. *zamaan, qabᵊl mədde.* I saw him the other day. *muu mən zamaan* (or *maa-li zamaan*) *šəfto.*
these days - *(b-)hal-ʔiyyaam.* Prices are very high these days. *l-ʔasεaar ġalyaane ktiir hal-ʔiyyaam.*

daybreak - *fažᵊr.*

to **daydream** - *ḍarab (o ø) ʔaxmaas ᵊb-ʔasdaas.* You aren't being paid to daydream. *maa-lak εam taaxod maεaaš mənšaan təḍrob ʔaxmaas ᵊb-ʔasdaas.*

daylight - *ḍaww˜ ᵊnhaaṛ.*

to **daze** - *bahar (a bahᵊr//nbahar).* The bright light dazed him for a moment. *ḍ-ḍaww ᵊṣ-ṣaaṭeε baharo laḥẓa.*
dazed - *maxbuul, mḥayyar.* He seemed completely dazed. *baan εalée kaan maxbuul tamaam.*

dead - 1. *mayyet* pl. *mawta.* They buried their dead. *kaanu ydᵊfnu mawtaahon.* 2. *mayyet* pl. *-iin* and *ʔamwaat.* His father is dead. *ʔabúu mayyet* or ***ʔabúu maat.* -- I'm dead tired. *ʔana mayyet ᵊmn ᵊt-taεab.* 3. *baared, baayex.* The meeting was pretty dead. *l-ʔəžtimaaε kaan baared ᵊktiir.*
**He brought the car to a dead stop. *waqqaf ᵊs-sayyaara εal-ʔaaxiir.*
**I'm dead broke. *ʔana mfalles εal-ʔaaxiir* (or *tamaam*).
**He must be dead drunk. *laazem ykuun sakraan la-ʔabu mooze.*
**I'm dead certain I put it there. *ʔana mətʔakked tamaam ʔənni ḥaṭṭeeta hniik.*
**I'm in dead earnest about it. *ʔana žaaded mən kəll qalbi b-haš-šaġle.*
**It happened in the dead of night. *ḥadset ᵊb-sawaad ᵊl-leel.*
**That's been dead and buried (for) a long time. *haš-šii maḍa w-ᵊntasa mən zamaanaat.*
**The fire is dead. *n-naaṛ ᵊnṭafet.*
**They stopped dead in their tracks. *waqqafu εala ġafle mətᵊl l-ᵊmbasmariin.*
**He's dead set on it. *mayyet huwwe εaleeha* or *qaatel ḥaalo εaleeha.*
Dead Sea - *l-baḥr ᵊl-mayyet, baḥᵊr˜ luuṭ.*

dead-end (street) - *ṭariiq* (pl. *ṭəroq*) *sadd.* You'll have to turn left to avoid the dead-end. *laazem ᵊdduur εala šmaalak la-tətfaada ṭ-ṭariiq ᵊs-sadd.*

deadline: I don't think we can meet the deadline. *maa bẓənn fiina nəxloṣ bᵊl-waqt l-ᵊmḥaddad.* -- The deadline for this job is tomorrow noon. *ʔaaxer waqᵊt la-haš-šaġle bəkra ḍ-ḍəhᵊṛ.*

deadlock: The negotiations ended in a deadlock. *l-ᵊmfaawaḍaat ᵊntahet ᵊb-maʔzaq̈ maa-lo maxraž.* -- I don't see how either side can break the deadlock. *maa-li εarfaan kiif ʔayy waaḥed mn ᵊṭ-ṭarafeen byəqder yḥəll hal-εəqde.*

deadly - *mumiit, qattaal, qaatuuli*.* That snake's bite is deadly. *εaḍḍet hal-ḥayye mumiite.*

deaf - *ʔaṭraš* f. *ṭarša* pl. *ṭərᵊš* and *ṭaršaan.* He's completely deaf. *huwwe ʔaṭraš tamaam.*
**He's deaf to all requests. *maa byəsmaε w-laa ʔayy ṭalab.*
**When he wants something he can talk you deaf, dumb, and blind! *lamma bəddo šii mənnak ᵊlsaano maa byəftor.*
deaf and dumb - *ʔaṭraš ʔaxras* f. *ṭarša xarsa* pl. *ṭərᵊš xərᵊs* and *ṭaršaan xərsaan.* He was born deaf and dumb. *xəleq ʔaṭraš ʔaxras.*

to **deafen** - *ṭarraš.* The explosion deafened him permanently. *l-ʔənfižaar ṭarrašo ṭuul ḥayaato.* — The noise is deafening. *l-qarwaše bəṭṭarreš.*

deal - 1. *ṣafqa* pl. *-aat, beeεa* pl. *-aat.* He made a lot of money on that deal. *ṭaalaε maṣaari ktiir ᵊb-haṣ-ṣafqa.* 2. *šarwe* pl. *-aat.* I got a real good deal on this rug. *ḥṣəlᵊt εala šarwe ktiir ᵊmniiḥa b-has-səžžaade.* 3. *fatt.* Whose deal is it? *fatt miin?*
**All I want is a square deal. *kəll halli ṭaalbo mεaamale mənᵊṣfe.*
**He got a raw deal. *tεaamal ᵊmεaamale waaṭye.*
a good deal - 1. *ktiir, šii ktiir.* He smokes a good deal. *bidaxxen ᵊktiir.* 2. *b-ᵊktiir.* It's a good deal larger than I thought. *ʔawsaε b-ᵊktiir məmma ftakart.*
a great deal - *šii ktiir.* We still have a great deal to do. *ləssa εaleena šii ktiir naεᵊmlo.*
to deal - 1. *ḍarab (o ḍarᵊb//nḍarab).* He dealt him a terrible blow on the head. *ḍarbo ḍarbe faẓiiεa εala raaso.* 2. *fatt (ə fatt//nfatt).* Who dealt the cards last time? *miin fatt ᵊš-šadde ʔaaxer marra?* 3. *taažar.* They deal exclusively in leather goods. *bitaažru bass bᵊl-baḍaayeε ᵊž-žəldiyye.*
to deal with - 1. *εaamal.* He dealt fairly with me. *εaamalni b-ʔənṣaaf.* 2. *tεaamal maε.* He deals directly with the company. *byətεaamal raʔsan maε ᵊš-šərke.* 3. *εaalaž.* The book deals with labor problems. *l-ᵊktaab biεaaləž mašaakel ᵊl-εəmmaal.*

dealer - 1. *wakiil* pl. *wəkala.* Did you buy the car from a dealer or from a private person? *štareet ᵊs-sayyaara mn ᵊl-wakiil wəlla mən šii šaxᵊṣ?* 2. *taažer* pl. *təžžaar.* I got a good bargain from a secondhand furniture dealer. *ṣaḥḥə́t-li šarwe mniiḥa mən taažer moobiilya məstaεmale.*

dear - *εaziiz* pl. *-iin* and *ʔaεəzza.* Dear friend, you're wrong again. *yaa ʔaxi l-εaziiz, hayy ʔənte ġalṭaan taani marra.* -- His sister is very dear to him. *ʔəxto ktiir εaziize εalée.*
**Are you tired, dear? *šú bak taεbaan, yaa ruuḥi?*
**My dear father is very sick. *ʔabi — ʔaḷḷa yṭawwə́l-ᵊlna εəmro — ḍaεfaan ᵊktiir.*
**Oh dear, we'll be late again! *yaa salaam, laḥa nətʔaxxar marra taanye.*

dearly - 1. *ġaali.* He had to pay dearly for his mistake. *kallafə́to ġalᵊṭṭo ġaali.* 2. *mən kəll ᵊl-qalb.* She would dearly love to go with us but she doesn't have the time. *mən kəll qalba bətḥəbb ᵊtruuḥ maεna bass maa εanda waqᵊt.*

death - 1. *moot, wafaat* pl. *wafayaat.* We read about his death in the newspapers. *qareena xabar mooto bᵊž-žaraayed.* 2. *moote* pl. *-aat.* His death was rather mysterious. *mootto kaanet nawεan maa ġariibe.*
**You'll catch your death of cold. *bətmuut ᵊmn ᵊl-bard.*
**He'll be the death of me yet. *ləssa bimawwə́tni.*
**Don't work yourself to death. *laa təhlek ḥaalak bᵊš-šəġᵊl.*
death penalty - *ʔəεdaam.* That crime carries the death penalty. *haž-žariime εq̈aaba l-ʔəεdaam.*
to put to death - *ʔaεdam* and *εadam (e ʔəεdaam// nεadam).* The murderer was put to death this morning. *ʔaεdamu l-qaatel ᵊl-yoom εala bəkra.*

debate - *mnaaq̈aše* pl. *-aat.* The debate went on for hours. *l-ᵊmnaaq̈aše stamarret saaεaat w-saaεaat.*
to debate - *naaq̈aš.* We debated the question for a long time. *naaq̈ašna l-masʔale mədde ṭawiile.*
to debate with oneself - *zaan(h)a (i ø) b-εaqlo.* I debated with myself whether or not to go. *zənta b-εaqli ʔiza bruuḥ wəlla laʔ.*

debt - *deen* pl. *dyuun.* This payment settles your debt. *had-dafεa bətsadded deenak.* -- He's up to his ears in debts. *ġaaṭeṣ bᵊd-dyuun la-qaraqiiṭ ʔadaano.*
in debt - *madyuun.* Is he still in debt? *ləssda madyuun?*

debtor - *madyuun* pl. *-iin, madiin* pl. *-iin.*

decadence - *ʔənḥiṭaaṭ, tadahwor.*

decadent - *mənḥaṭṭ, məddahwer.*

decay - 1. *tafassox.* Decay set in rapidly. *t-tafassox ballaš ᵊb-sərεa.* 2. *tasawwos.* Tooth decay is caused by certain deficiencies in the diet. *tasawwos ᵊs-snaan byəži b-sabab εadam ᵊkfaayet baεḍ ᵊl-mawaadd bᵊl-ʔakᵊl.*
to decay - 1. *tfassax.* The cadaver had already begun to decay. *ž-žəsse mən mədde badet tətfassax.* 2. *sawwas.* The root of my wisdom tooth seems to be decayed. *šərᵊš dərs ᵊl-εaqᵊl tabaεi mbayyen εalée msawwes.* -- Too much sugar will decay your teeth. *ʔakl ᵊs-səkkar ᵊktiir bisawwə́s-lak ᵊsnaanak.*

deceit - *ġašš, xidaaε, makᵊr.*

deceitful - *ġaššaaš, xaddaaε, maaker.*

to **deceive** - *ġašš (ə ġašš//nġašš), xadaε (a xadᵊε//nxadaε)*. Appearances are deceiving. *l-maẓaaher bətġəšš*. -- His polite words deceived us at first. *kalaamo l-ᵊmhazzab bᵊl-ʔawwal ġaššna*. -- You're deceiving yourself if you believe that ... *bətkuun εam təxdaε haalak ʔiza btəεtəqed ʔənno ...*

December - *kaanuun ᵊl-ʔawwal*.

decent - **1.** *ʔaadami** pl. *ʔawaadem*. He's a decent fellow. *huwwe šaxᵊṣ ʔaadami* or ***huwwe zalame εala salaamto*. **2.** *məḥtdram*. He makes a decent living. *εando daxᵊl məḥtdram*.

to **decide** - **1.** *εtamad, q̈arrar*. I decided to stay. *εtamadt ʔəbqa*. -- Let him decide. *xallii huwwe yq̈arrer* or ***xalli l-q̈araar ʔəlo*. -- What did you decide on? *εala šuu εtamadt?* **2.** *batt (ə batt//nbatt) b-, faṣal (e faṣᵊl//nfaṣal) b-*. It isn't easy to decide that question. *muu hayyen ᵊl-batt ᵊb-hal-masʔale*.

decided - *mḥaqqaq*. It was a decided victory for our side. *kaan naṣr ᵊmḥaqqaq la-ṭarafna*.

decidedly - *ḥatman*. He's decidedly taller than they are. *ḥatman huwwe ʔaṭwal mənhon*.

decision - *q̈araar* pl. *-aat*. At last he's come to a decision. *bᵊl-ʔaaxiir wəṣel la-q̈araar*. -- We have never regretted our decision. *b-ḥayaatna maa ndəmna εala q̈araarna*.

decisive - *faaṣel, ḥaasem*.

deck - *ḍahᵊr* pl. *ḍhuur(a)*. Is he in his cabin or on the deck? *bᵊl-kabiin tabaεo huwwe walla εaḍ-ḍahᵊr?*

deck of cards - *šadde* pl. *-aat*. Let's take a new deck of cards. *xalliina nəstaεmel šadde ždiide*.

declaration - **1.** *bayaan* pl. *-aat, taṣriiḥ* pl. *-aat*. He read the declaration to the assembly. *qara l-bayaan εal-mažles*. **2.** *bayaan* pl. *-aat, taṣriiḥ* pl. *-aat* and *taṣariiḥ*. He handed a declaration of his goods to the customs inspector. *sallam bayaan ᵊġraaḍo la-mfatteš ᵊl-gəmrok*.

to **declare** - **1.** *ʔaεlan* and *εalan (e ʔəεlaan//nεalan)*. They declared war on us. *ʔaεlanu l-ḥarb εaleena*. **2.** *ṣarraḥ εan, bayyan εan*. Do I have to declare the tobacco at the customs? *laazem ṣarreḥ šii εan ᵊt-təbᵊġ bᵊl-gəmrok?* **3.** *ṣarraḥ*. He declared he would never consent to such a thing. *ṣarraḥ ʔənno b-ḥayaato maa biwaafeq εala heek šii*.

decline - *tadahwor*. The newspapers reported a decline in the nation's economy. *ž-žaraayed ḥaket εan tadahwor ʔəq̈tiṣaad l-ᵊblaad*.

to be on the decline - **1.** *zaal (u zawaal)*. The epidemic is on the decline. *l-wabaaʔ εam yzuul*. **2.** *ddahwar, nḥaṭṭ, ddaaεa*. His health is on the decline. *ṣaḥḥto εam təddahwar*.

to decline - **1.** *ddaaεa, ddahwar, nḥaṭṭ, habaṭ (o hbuuṭ)*. His strength is declining rapidly. *quwwto εam təddaaεa b-sərεa*. **2.** *rafaḍ (o rafᵊḍ//nrafaḍ)*. I declined his offer. *rafaḍt εarḍo*. **3.** *εtazar εan*. They had to decline his invitation. *ḍṭarru yəεtəzru εan εaziimto*.

décolleté - *deekoltée* pl. *deekoltaat*.

to **decorate** - *zayyan, zawwaq*. She decorated the house very nicely for her daughter's wedding. *zayyanet ᵊl-beet ᵊktiir ḥəlu εala εərs bənta*.

**The president himself will decorate him for his bravery. *r-raʔiis nafso laḥa yεalləq-lo wisaam la-šažaaεto*.

decoration - **1.** *ziine* pl. *ziyan*. The decorations are in very bad taste. *z-ziine maa fiiha zooq ʔabadan*. **2.** *niišaan* pl. *nayašiin, wisaam* pl. *ʔawsime*. What did he get the decoration for? *mənšaan ʔeeš ʔaxad ᵊn-niišaan?*

decrease - *tanaaq̈oṣ, hbuuṭ*. Statistics show a decrease in the death rate in the last few years. *l-ʔəḥṣaaʔaat bətwarži tanaaq̈oṣ ᵊb-nəsbet ᵊl-wafayaat bᵊs-sniin ᵊl-ʔaxiire*.

to decrease - **1.** *xaff (ə ø), qall (ə ø)*. The pain should decrease by tomorrow. *l-ʔamal ʔənno l-wažaε bixəff la-bəkra*. **2.** *xaffaḍ, nazzal, qallal*. The main office decreased his travel allowance. *l-maktab ᵊr-raʔiisi xaffaḍ badal safaro*.

decree - *marsuum* pl. *marasiim*. The decree goes into effect tomorrow. *l-marsuum laḥa yənεəmel fii mən bəkra*.

to decree - *q̈arrar*. The government decreed a holiday. *l-ᵊḥkuume q̈arraret εəṭle*.

to **dedicate** - **1.** *karras, waqaf (-yuuqef ø)*. He dedicated his life to medicine. *karras ḥayaato ləṭ-ṭəbb*. **2.** *hada*, also *ʔahda (i ʔəhdaaʔ//nhada)*. He dedicated his latest book to his sister. *hada ktaabo l-ʔaxiir la-ʔəxto*.

dedication - **1.** *tadšiin*. Many people were present for the dedication of the new school. *fii ktiir naas kaanu ḥaaḍriin ᵊb-ḥaflet tadšiin ᵊl-madrase ž-ždiide*. **2.** *ʔəxlaaṣ*. Everybody admires his dedication to science. *l-kəll məεžab ᵊb-ʔəxlaaṣo ləl-εəlᵊm*.

to **deduct** - *xaṣam (o xaṣᵊm//nxaṣam), ḥasam (o ḥasᵊm//nḥasam), nazzal//tnazzal*. The merchant deducted ten percent from the price. *t-taažer xaṣam εašara bᵊl-miyye mn ᵊs-səεᵊr*.

deductible: Will these expenses be deductible? *hal-maṣariif ᵊbtənxəṣem (or btətnazzal)?* -- You have a deductible amount of 600 dollars a year. *fii εandak sətt miit dolaar muu maḥsuube (or btətnazzal) bᵊs-səne*.

deed - **1.** *sanad˜* (pl. *-aat˜*) *ṭaabo, sanad˜ tamliik*. It won't take long to transfer the deed to you. *maa bədda waqt ᵊktiir la-nḥawwəl-lak sanad ᵊṭ-ṭaabo (b-ʔəsmak)*. **2.** *maʔsara* pl. *maʔaaser, fəεᵊl* pl. *ʔafεaal*. Everyone will remember his noble deeds. *kəll waaḥed biḍall yədzakkar maʔasro n-nabiile*.

to deed - *ṭawwab, faraġ (o faraaġ//nfaraġ)*. My father has deeded the house to me. *ʔabi ṭawwəb-li l-beet*.

deep - **1.** *ġamiiq* pl. *ġmaaq*. The river is very deep at this point. *n-nahᵊr ġamiiq ᵊktiir hoon*. -- The thieves hid in a deep cave. *l-ḥaraamiyye txabbu b-ᵊmġaara ġamiiqa*. **2.** *εamiiq̈*. That subject is too deep for me. *hal-mawḍuuε εamiiq̈ εaliyyi ktiir*. **3.** *ṭxiin* pl. *ṭxaan*. A man with a deep voice answered the phone. *fii zalame ṣooṭo ṭxiin radd εat-talifoon*. **4.** *baaleġ*. He expressed deep concern for their safety. *warža ʔəhtimaam baaleġ ᵊb-salaaməton*.

**The lake is a hundred feet deep. *l-buḥayra ġəmqa miit qadam*.

**He was deep in thought when I entered his room. *kaan ġarqaan bᵊt-tafkiir lamma fətt εala ʔuuḍṭo*.

defamation - *wšaaye, ʔəftiraa(ʔ)*.

defeat - *haziime* pl. *hazaayem*. The enemy suffered a crushing defeat. *l-εaduww εaana haziime saaḥq̈a*.

to defeat - **1.** *hazam (e haziime//nhazam), ġalab (e ġalbe//nġalab)*. He's been defeated twice in the elections. *nhazam marrteen bᵊl-ʔəntixaabaat*. -- We defeated their team at soccer. *ġalabna fariiq̈on bᵊl-futbool*. **2.** *rafaḍ (o rafᵊḍ//nrafaḍ* and *rtafaḍ)*.

defect - *εeeb* pl. *εyuub, εəlle* pl. *εəlal, xalal*. There must be a defect in the motor. *laazem ykuun fii εeeb bᵊl-mootoor*.

to defect - *harab (o harab)*. A good soldier would never defect to the enemy's side. *l-εaskari l-ᵊmniiḥ ᵊb-ḥayaato maa byəhrob ləl-εaduww*.

to **defend** - *daafaε εan*. They decided not to defend the town. *qarraru maa ydaafεu εan ᵊl-balad*. -- It'll take a good lawyer to defend him. *laazem muḥaami qaader ydaafeε εanno*.

defense - **1.** *difaaε*. The defense of their country rests in the hands of a very small army. *d-difaaε εan ᵊblaadon ᵊb-ʔiid žeeš ᵊktiir ᵊṣġiir*. -- Who is going to argue for the defense? *miin raḥa yquum bᵊd-difaaε?* **2.** *quwwet˜ difaaε*. Their entire defense is at the bottom of that hill. *kəll quwwet difaaεon ᵊmrakkaze b-səfᵊl hat-talle*.

**I'm not going to come to your defense this time. *hal-marra maa laḥa ḥaami εannak*.

to **define** - **1.** *εarraf*. Can you define the word "democracy?" *fiik ᵊtεarref kəlmet "ᵊd-dimu-q̈raaṭiyye"?* **2.** *ḥaddad, εayyan*. This black line defines our border exactly. *hal-xaṭṭ ᵊl-ʔaswad biḥadded ᵊḥduudna tamaam*. **3.** *waḍḍaḥ*. Would you please define your statement for the press? *btaεmel maεruuf ᵊtwaḍḍeḥ taṣriiḥak ləṣ-ṣaḥaafe?*

definite - *mεayyan, mḥaddad*. Do you have any definite plans? *fii εandak šii mašariiε ᵊmεayyane?* -- Let's set aside a definite period for recreation. *xalliina nxaṣṣeṣ mədde mεayyane lət-tarfiih*.

definite article - *laam˜ ᵊt-taεriif, ʔadaat˜ ᵊt-taεriif*.

definitely - *ḥatman, q̈aṭεan, mən kəll bədd*.

to **defy** - **1.** *naawaʔ*. Defying our orders will get you nowhere. *mnaawaʔet ʔawaamərna maa laḥa tfiidak*. **2.** *naaqaḍ*. Their acrobatics seem to defy the law of gravity. *bahlawaaniiton bətnaaqeḍ εala maa yəẓhar q̈aanuun ᵊž-žaazbiyye*. **3.** *tḥadda*. I defy you to answer my question. *bətḥaddaak ᵊdžaaweb εala suʔaali*.

**His stupidity defies description. *ḥamranto maa btənwəṣef*.

degree - **1.** *daraže* pl. *-aat*. Last night the temperature dropped ten degrees. *l-leele l-maaḍye nazlet ᵊl-ḥaraara εašᵊr daražaat*. -- The ship changed course by thirty degrees. *s-safiine ġayyaret* *mažraaha tlaatiin daraže.* **2.** *šahaade* pl. *-aat, dəblooma* pl. *-aat.* My father has a degree in English. *ʔabi maεo šahaade bᵊl-ʔəngliizi.*

a degree of – *nooε mən.* I noticed a degree of humor in his voice. *laaḥaẓᵊt nooε ᵊmn ᵊl-mazᵊḥ ᵊb-ṣooṭo.*

by degrees – *šwayye šwayye, bᵊt-tadriiž, tadriižiyyan.* You have to get accustomed to the climate by degrees. *laazem tətεawwad εal-manaax bᵊt-tadriiž.*

to a certain degree – *la-daraže, la-ḥadd.* To a certain degree he himself is responsible for it. *la-daraže huwwe b-zaato masʔuul εanna.*

Deir-ez-Zor – *deer˜ ᵊz-zoor.*

delay – *taʔxiir, εooqa.* Bad weather caused all this delay. *ṭ-ṭaqṣ ᵊl-εaaṭel sabbab kəll hat-taʔxiir.* -- The building contractor will be held responsible for any delay in the work. *l-ᵊmqaawel bikuun masʔuul εan ʔayy taʔxiir bᵊš-šəġᵊl.*

**The letter arrived with some delay. *l-maktuub wəṣel mətʔaxxer šwayye.*

without delay – *bala taʔxiir, εal-ḥaarek, εal-foor.* Do it without delay. *saawiiha bala taʔxiir.*

to delay – **1.** *ʔaxxar//tʔaxxar.* I was delayed on the way. *tʔaxxarᵊt bᵊṭ-ṭariiq.* **2.** *ʔaxxar//tʔaxxar, ʔažžal//tʔažžal.* We're going to delay the trip for a week. *baddna nʔaxxer ᵊr-rəḥle žəmεa.* **3.** *tʔaxxar.* Don't delay on your way home from school. *laa tətʔaxxar ᵊb-ṭariiqak εal-beet ᵊmn ᵊl-madrase.*

delegate – **1.** *manduub* pl. *-iin.* The delegates to the convention will arrive in the course of today and tomorrow. *l-manduubiin ləl-mahražaan laḥa yəṣalu xilaal ᵊl-yoom w-bəkra.* **2.** *naaʔeb* pl. *nəwwaab.* A delegate from my district will make a speech this evening. *naaʔeb mən manṭəqᵊtna bəddu yəlqi xiṭaab ᵊl-yoom εašiyye.*

to delegate – **1.** *ʔawfad.* We'll have to delegate one of our employees to meet our guests at the station. *laazem nuufed ḥada mn ᵊmwaẓẓafiinna la-yəstaqbel ᵊḍ-ḍyuuf bᵊl-ᵊmḥaṭṭa.* **2.** *wakkal b-.* He always delegates his work to me. *daayman biwakkəlni b-šəġlo.* **3.** *ḥammal.* Try to delegate more responsibility to your employees. *ḥaawel ᵊtḥammel ᵊmwaẓẓafiinak masʔuuliyyaat ʔaktar mən heek.*

delegation – *wafᵊd* pl. *wfuud.* Our delegation will return home tomorrow. *wafᵊdna laḥa yəržaε bəkra.*

deliberate – *maqṣuud, mətεammed.* We caught him in a deliberate lie. *laqaṭnda b-kəzbe maqṣuuda.*

to deliberate – *ddaawal b-.* The jury is deliberating his case now. *l-ᵊmḥallafiin εam yəddaawalu b-qaḍiito hallaq.*

deliberately – *εan qaṣᵊd, εan εamᵊd, qaṣdan, εamdan.* Did you deliberately hit her? *ḍarabta εan qaṣᵊd?*

delicate – **1.** *ḥassaas.* A camera is a very delicate instrument. *l-kameera ʔaale ktiir ḥassaase.* **2.** *daqiiq.* Our shop is noted for its delicate glassware. *maḥallna mašhuur ᵊb-badaayεo ᵊl-ballooriyye d-daqiiqa.* **3.** *daqiiq, naazek, šaaʔek.* That's a delicate subject. *haada mawḍuuε daqiiq.* **4.** *naazek.* She is in very delicate health. *ṣaḥḥə́ta ktiir naazke.*

delicious – *laziiz, ktiir ṭayyeb.* She served a delicious meal. *qaddamet ʔakle laziize.*

delight – *lazze* pl. *-aat, bahže* pl. *-aat.* Her performance was a delight to see. *kaanet lazze l-fərže εala tamsiila.*

to delight – *bahaž (e bahᵊž//nbahaž).* He delighted us with his vast knowledge. *bahažna b-maεrəfto l-waasεa.*

**I'm delighted to meet you. *tšarraft ᵊb-maεrəftak.*

delightful – *bahiiž, laziiz.* We spent a delightful evening at their house. *maḍḍeena sahra bahiiže b-beeton.*

to deliver – **1.** *sallam//tsallam.* We'll deliver your order within ten days. *mənsallmak ṭalabiitak ᵊb-εašᵊrt iyyaam.* **2.** *waṣṣal//twaṣṣal.* Please deliver these packages at my hotel. *mən faḍlak waṣṣə́l-li hal-baakeetaat εal-ʔoteel tabaεi.* **3.** *wazzaε//twazzaε.* How often is the mail delivered here? *kəll qaddeeš biwazzεu l-bariid hoon?*

delivery – **1.** *tasliim.* I'll pay you on delivery. *bədfaε-lak εand ᵊt-tasliim.* **2.** *tawziiε.* The letter came in the second delivery. *l-maktuub ʔəža bᵊt-tawziiε ᵊt-taani.*

**We cannot make a delivery on Sundays and holidays. *maa fiina nwaṣṣel l-ᵊġraaḍ ʔiyyaam ᵊl-ʔaḥad wᵊl-εəṭal.*

cash on delivery, c.o.d. – *d-dafᵊε εand ᵊt-tasliim.* I'll mail the package to you c.o.d. *bəbεə́t-lak ᵊṭ-ṭard wᵊd-dafᵊε εand ᵊt-tasliim.*

demand – **1.** *ṭalab, ʔəqbaal.* There's a big demand for television sets right now. *fii ṭalab faẓiiε εat-televəzyoonaat hal-ʔiyyaam.* -- The library can't supply the demand for books. *l-maktabe maa fiiha džaabeh kətret ᵊṭ-ṭalab εal-kətᵊb.* **2.** *ṭalab.* It's simply a question of supply and demand. *l-masʔale kəlla masʔalt εarḍ w-ṭalab.* **3.** *maṭlab* pl. *maṭaliib, ṭalab* pl. *-aat.* He makes no demands whatsoever. *maa-lo maṭaliib ʔabadan.*

**They make many demands on our time. *byaaxdu mən waqᵊtna šii ktiir.*

in demand – **1.** *marġuub.* He was in great demand as a speaker. *kaan marġuub ᵊktiir ka-mḥaaḍer huwwe.* **2.** *maṭluub, raayež.* Pure silk is very much in demand. *l-ḥariir ᵊl-ʔaṣli maṭluub ᵊktiir* (or ***εaléε ʔəqbaal ᵊktiir*).

on demand – *εand ᵊṭ-ṭalab.* You must show your identity card on demand. *laazem ᵊtwarži hawiitak εand ᵊṭ-ṭalab.*

**The film will be held over on demand. *naẓaran ləl-ʔəqbaal ᵊš-šadiid laḥa yətmaddad ᵊl-fəlᵊm.*

to demand – **1.** *ṭalab (o ṭalab//nṭalab), ṭaalab b-.* He's demanding more money. *εam yəṭlob maṣaari ʔaktar.* **2.** *ṭṭallab, ḥtaaž.* This job demands a thorough knowledge of two languages. *haš-šəġle btəṭṭallab maεᵊrfe waasεa b-luġateen.*

dementi – *takziib* pl. *-aat.* The government immediately issued a dementi. *l-ᵊḥkuume bᵊl-ḥaal ṭaalaεet takziib.*

democracy – *dimuqraaṭiyye.*

democrat – *dimuqraaṭi** pl. *-iyyiin.*

democratic – *dimuqraaṭi*.*

to **demonstrate** – **1.** *warža//twarža, farža//tfarža.* I'll now demonstrate how the machine works. *hallaq bwaržiikon kiif ᵊl-maakiina btəštə́ġel.* **2.** *dẓaahar.* The prisoners demonstrated for better medical care. *l-maḥabiis dẓaaharu mənšaan ᵊεnaaye ṭəbbiyye ʔaḥsan.*

**I'd like someone to demonstrate the washing machine to me. *bəddi ḥada ywaržiini kiif btəštə́ġel ᵊl-ġassaale.*

demonstration – **1.** *mẓaahara* pl. *-aat.* A political demonstration was held in the square yesterday. *qaamet ᵊmẓaahara syaasiyye mbaareḥ bᵊs-saaḥa.* **2.** *εarḍ* pl. *εruuḍ.* I enjoyed the wrestling demonstration this afternoon. *mbaṣaṭṭ ᵊktiir ᵊl-yoom baεᵊd ᵊḍ-ḍəhᵊr b-εarḍ l-ᵊmṣaaraεa.*

demonstrative pronoun – *ʔəsᵊm˜* (pl. *ʔasmaaʔ˜*) *ʔišaara.*

denial – *ʔənkaar* pl. *-aat.* That amounts to a denial of everything you believed in before. *haada b-masaabet ʔənkaar la-kəll šii kənt ᵊtʔaamen fii mən qabᵊl.*

Denmark – *d-danimark.*

to **denounce** – *naddad b-.* A government spokesman denounced the border incident as another case of flagrant aggression. *fii naaṭeq ᵊb-ʔəsᵊm l-ᵊḥkuume naddad ᵊb-ḥaades l-ᵊḥduud ka-daliil ʔaaxar εal-εədwaan ᵊs-saafer.*

dense – **1.** *kasiif.* We drove through (a) dense fog. *səqna b-ḍabaab kasiif* (or **ʔaswad*). **2.** *fəhmo tqiil.* She's awfully dense about some things. *faẓaaεa šuu fəhma tqiil ᵊb-baεḍ ᵊl-masaaʔel.*

**An area with such a dense population is, of course, very vulnerable in time of war. *ṭabεan manṭiqa hal-qadd məzdaḥme bᵊs-səkkaan bətkuun εarḍa ləl-ᵊhžuum waqt ᵊl-ḥarb.*

densely – *b-kasaafe, b-kətra.* Plants grow densely around the house. *n-nabaat byənbot ᵊb-kasaafe ḥawaali l-beet.*

**This area is densely populated. *hal-manṭiqa məzdaḥme bᵊs-səkkaan.*

density – *kasaafe.*

dent – *ṭaεže* pl. *-aat.* Have you noticed the dent in my front fender? *šəft ᵊṭ-ṭaεže halli b-rafraaf sayyaarti ᵊl-qəddaamaani?*

to dent – **1.** *ṭaεaž (a ṭaεᵊž//nṭaεaž).* I dented his rear door in the accident. *ṭaεažt-ə́llo baab sayyaarto l-warraani bᵊl-ḥaadse.* **2.** *nṭaεaž.* Be careful, this aluminum pot dents easily. *diir baalak, haṭ-ṭanžara l-ʔalumiinyoom ᵊbtənṭə́εež qawaam.*

dentist – *ḥakiim˜* (pl. *ḥəkama˜*) *snaan, ṭabiib˜* (pl. *ʔaṭəbba˜*) *snaan.*

denture – *ṭaqm˜* (pl. *ṭquumet˜*) *snaan, badlet˜* (pl. *-aat˜*) *snaan.*

to **deny** – **1.** *nakar (o/e nəkraan), kazzab//tkazzab.* He denied the whole thing. *nakar ᵊš-šii kəllo.*

2. *rafad (o rafᵊd//nrafad* and *rtafad), radd (ə radd //nradd* and *rtadd).* I couldn't deny him such a small favor. *maa tələE ᵊb-ʔiidi ʔərfəd-lo hal-maEruuf ᵊl-basiit.*
to deny oneself - *haram (e hərmaan) haalo.* She never denied herself anything. *b-hayaata maa harmet haala šii.*
to **depart** - **1.** *saafar, gaadar.* Our ship will depart in the morning. *baaxrətna bətsaafer ᵊs-səbᵊh.* **2.** *haad (i/u heed, hayadaan).* I have departed somewhat from the established theory. *hədt la-daraže Ean ᵊn-nazariyye l-maqbuule.*
department - **1.** *qəsᵊm* pl. *ʔaqsaam, farᵊE* pl. *fruuE(a), šəEbe* pl. *šəEab.* My father works in the clothing department. *ʔabi byəštəgel ᵊb-qəsm ᵊl-ʔawaaEi.* **2.** *wazaara* pl. *-aat.* This is a matter for the Department of State. *hayy masʔale mən ʔəxtisaas wazaart ᵊl-xaaržiyye.* **3.** *ʔəxtisaas* pl. *-aat.* That sort of thing isn't in my department. *heek šii muu mən ʔəxtisaasi.*
departure - *mawEed˜* (pl. *mawaEiid˜*) *safar.* The plane's departure is scheduled for three o'clock. *mawEed safar ᵊt-tayyaara mhaddad ᵊs-saaEa tlaate.*
to **depend on** - **1.** *Etamad Eala.* Can I depend on him? *fiini ʔəEtəmed Ealée?* — My family depends on me for their support. *Eeelti btəEtəmed Ealiyyi b-Eiišəta.* **2.** *twaqqaf Eala.* Our trip will depend on the weather. *safrətna btətwaqqaf Eat-taqᵊs.* -- Are you going to Beirut? - It depends. *raayeh Eala beeruut?* - *btətwaqqaf.*
dependent - **1.** *məEtəmed, məttəkel.* I'm financially dependent on him. *ʔana maaliyyan məEtəmed Ealée.* **2.** *Eaale* (invar.). I have four dependents. *fii Eandi ʔarbEa Eaale Ealiyyi.* — How many dependents do you have? *kam waahed fii Eaale Ealeek?* or ***kam waahed Eam ᵊtEiil?*
deplorable - *yursa lahu.* The economy of the country is in a deplorable state. *ʔəqtisaad l-ᵊblaad ᵊb-haale yursa laha.*
deposit - **1.** *wadiiEa* pl. *wadaayeE.* I still have to make a deposit at the bank. *ləssa Ealiyyi hətt wadiiEa bᵊl-bank.* **2.** *raEbuun* pl. *raEabiin.* If you leave a deposit, we'll lay it aside for you. *ʔiza bəthətt raEbuun mənxabbii-lak-yaaha Eala žanab.* **3.** *taʔmiin* pl. *-aat.* I had to pay five piasters deposit for the bottle. *nžabarᵊt hətt xams ᵊqruuš taʔmiin Eal-qanniine.* **4.** *maxzuun* pl. *-aat.* A deposit of gold was found here a year ago. *laqu maxzuun dahab Eaamnawwal hoon.* **5.** *rsuub* pl. *-aat.* A deposit has formed in the tea kettle. *saar fii rsuub ᵊb-səfᵊl ʔəbriiq ᵊš-šaay.*
to deposit - **1.** *wadaE (-yuudaE wadᵊE//nwadaE).* I'll have to deposit some money at the bank. *Ealiyyi ʔuudaE masaari bᵊl-bank.* **2.** *tarak (o/e tarᵊk) rawaaseb.* The river deposits tons of sand during each flood. *n-nahᵊr byətrok rawaaseb ʔatnaan w-ʔatnaan ᵊmn ᵊr-ramᵊl waqᵊt kəll fayadaan.* **3.** *hatt (ə hatat//nhatt).* Please deposit that paper in the waste basket. *balla hətt-ə́lli hal-waraqa b-sallet ᵊl-məhmalaat.*
to **depress** - **1.** *qammat (ᵊl-qalb).* His letters always depress me. *makatiibo daayman bətqamməṭ-li qalbi.* **2.** *kabas (e/o kabᵊs//nkabas).* Just depress this lever and the door will open. *bass ᵊkbees hal-maske wᵊl-baab byənfə́teh.*
depressed - *mfastek, magmuum, maqmuut.* He's been very depressed lately. *saayer ᵊmfastek ᵊktiir ᵊb-hal-ʔiyyaam.*
depression - **1.** *kasaad.* We lost all our money in the depression. *xsərna kəll masaariina bᵊl-kasaad.* **2.** *žuura* pl. *žuwar, həfra* pl. *həfar.* Water had collected in a depression in the rock. *l-mayy džammaEet ᵊb-žuura bᵊs-saxra.*
to **deprive** - **1.** *haram (e hərmaan//nharam), šallah.* I wouldn't want to deprive you of your cigarettes. *maa bəddi ʔəhᵊrmak (mən) sigaaraatak.* **2.** *haram.* He doesn't deprive himself of anything. *maa byəhrem haalo šii.* **3.** *žarrad//džarrad.* They were deprived of all their rights. *džarradu mən kəll ᵊhquuqon.*
**I won't be deprived of that pleasure. *maa laha rawweh Eala haali hal-basᵊt.*
depth - *gəmᵊq, Eəmᵊq.* The depth of this lake has never been measured. *gəmᵊq hal-buhayra b-hayaato maa nqaas.*
**The money was stolen in the depth of the night. *l-masaari nsarqet ᵊb-zalaam ᵊl-leel.*
deputy - *naaʔeb* pl. *nəwwaab.* The deputy of our district will address the assembly tomorrow. *naaʔeb mantəqᵊtna laha yəxtob bəkra bᵊl-mažles.*
Chamber of Deputies - *mažles˜ ᵊn-nəwwaab.*
Deraa - *darEa.*
to be **derailed** - *tələE (a tluuE) Ean ᵊl-xatt.* The train was derailed near Homs. *t-treen tələE Ean ᵊl-xatt qərᵊb həmᵊs.*
dervish - *darwiiš* pl. *darawiiš.*
to **descend** - **1.** *nəzel (e nzuul, nazle).* We descended quickly in the elevator. *nzəlna b-sərEa bᵊl-ʔasansoor.* **2.** *kafat (o kafᵊt).* All our relatives have descended upon us. *kəll qaraaybiinna kafatu Ealeena.*
to be descended - *ntasab.* He's descended from an old American family. *byəntəseb la-Eeele ʔameerkaaniyye qadiime.*
descendant - *saliil* pl. *-iin.*
to **describe** - *wasaf (-yuusef wasᵊf//nwasaf).* He described the man accurately. *wasaf ᵊr-rəžžaal ᵊb-dəqqa.*
**We described a circle around the town. *dərna doora kaamle hawaali l-balad.*
description - *wasᵊf* pl. *ʔawsaaf.* Can you give me a detailed description? *fiik taEtiini wasf ᵊmfassal?* -- The police checked, but the suspect didn't match the description. *l-booliis Eaayan ᵊl-ʔawsaaf, bass ᵊl-mašbuuh maa taabaq ᵊl-wasᵊf.*
desert - **1.** *sahra* pl. *sahaari, baadye* pl. *bawaadi.* They crossed the desert in twenty days. *qataEu s-sahra b-Eəšriin yoom.* **2.** *sahraawi*.* For a few miles we followed a desert trail. *Eala masaafet kam miil mšiina b-darᵊb sahraawi.*
to **desert** - **1.** *txalla Ean.* Don't desert me now! *laa tətxalla Eanni hallaq!* **2.** *hažar (o/e hažᵊr, həžraan).* He deserted his wife and children. *hažar marto w-wlaado.* **3.** *harab (o harab), farr (ə fraar).* The soldiers deserted in droves. *l-Easkar harabu žamaaEaat žamaaEaat.*
deserted - *mahžuur.* After a long march they came to a deserted village. *baEᵊd mašye tawiile wəslu la-deeEa mahžuura.*
deserter - *fraari** pl. *-iyye.*
to **deserve** - *st(a)haqq, staahal.* Such a good worker deserves better pay. *šaggiil ᵊb-hal-mənᵊh byəsthəqq raateb ʔaktar.*
**He deserves it! *xaržo!*
design - **1.** *tasmiim* pl. *-aat* and *tasamiim.* He's working on the design for a new refrigerator. *Eam yəštəgel Eala tasmiim barraade ždiide.* **2.** *rasme* pl. *-aat.* The tablecloth has a simple design. *gata t-taawle ʔəlo rasme basiita.*
**He's been making designs on my job. *haatet Eeeno Eala šagᵊlti.*
to design - **1.** *btakar moodet˜ ...* She designs her own clothes. *hiyye btəbtəker moodet ʔawaEiiha.* **2.** *Eəmel tasmiim˜ ...* Do you know who designed that bridge? *btaEref miin Eəmel tasmiim haž-žəsᵊr?*
**This chair is designed for comfort. *hal-kərsi maEmuul lər-raaha.*
desirable - **1.** *marguub (fii).* A change would be very desirable now. *t-tagyiir bikuun šii ktiir marguub (fii) hallaq.* **2.** *mwaafeq, mnaaseb.* This is a very desirable neighborhood for a hotel. *hayy mantiqa ktiir ᵊmwaafqa la-ʔoteel* or ***hayy mantiqa hafr w-tanziil la-ʔoteel.*
desire - **1.** *rəgbe* pl. *-aat.* My desires are easily satisfied. *rəgbaati mətwaadEa w-b-ᵊshuule btənqada.* **2.** *šarah.* He has an abnormal desire for money. *Eando šarah muu maEquul ləl-masaari.*
desk - **1.** *taawle* pl. *-aat.* This desk is too small for me. *hat-taawle zgiire Ealiyyi ktiir.* **2.** *maktab* pl. *makaateb.* Leave your key at the desk, please. *treek məftaahak bᵊl-maktab, mən fadlak.* -- Ask at the information desk over there. *sʔaal ᵊb-maktab ᵊl-ʔəstəElaamaat ᵊhniik.*
desolate - **1.** *muuheš, məqfer.* This must be a desolate place in winter. *hal-mahall laazem ykuun ᵊktiir muuheš bᵊš-šəte.* **2.** *wahdaani*.* His death has left her quite desolate. *mooto xallaaha wahdaaniyye.*
to desolate - *dammar.* A storm desolated the village. *fii Eaasfe dammaret ᵊd-deeEa.*
despair - **1.** *yaʔᵊs.* In despair, a man will grasp at any straw. *b-haalet yaʔᵊs ᵊl-ʔənsaan byətEallaq ᵊb-qəšše.* **2.** *sabab˜ yaʔᵊs.* He's the despair of his parents. *huwwe sabab yaʔᵊs ʔabúu w-ʔəmmo.*
to despair - *yəʔes (-yiiʔas yaʔᵊs).* Don't despair! *laa tiiʔas!* -- I despaired of his ever returning. *yʔəst mən ražᵊEto.*
desperate - **1.** *mayʔuus mən* + pron. suff., *yaáʔes.* She's in a desperate situation. *hiyye b-haale*

mayʔuus mənha. 2. *yaaʔes, yaʔsaan.* He seemed to be very desperate when he first arrived. *kaan ᵊmbayyen εalée ktiir yaaʔes lamma wəṣel la-hoon.* 3. *yaaʔes.* The driver made a desperate move to avoid the accident. *s-saaʔeq̈ εəmel ᵊmḥaawale yaaʔse la-yətfaada l-ʔaksiḍaan.*

to become desperate for – *staqtal εala.* The population became desperate for food. *n-naas ᵊstaqtalu εal-ʔakᵊl.*

to **despise** – *zdara, ḥtaqar.* I despise the way he acts. *bəzdéri taṣarrufaato.* -- He despises every-one who is not his social equal. *byəzdéri kəll waaḥed muu mən maq̈aamo l-ʔəžtimaaεi.*

dessert – (sweets) *ḥəlu,* (fruit) *fawaaki, froot̩to.* May I have my dessert now? *məmken ʔaaxod ᵊl-ḥəlu hallaq?*

destination: When do we reach our destination? *ʔeemta laḥa nəṣal?* -- What's the cargo's desti-nation? *la-ween raayḥa l-ᵊbḍaaεa?*

destined – 1. *mqarrar.* We were destined to arrive this morning. *kaan l-ᵊmqarrar nəṣal ᵊl-yoom εala bəkra.* 2. *mqaddar.* He seems destined to get involved in all kinds of trouble. *εala maa yəẓhar ᵊmqaddar εalée yəqaε ᵊb-mašaakel ᵊktiire.* 3. *məttəžeh.* Their plane is destined for Rome. *ṭayyaarə́ton məttəžha la-rooma.*

to **destroy** – 1. *ʔatlaf (e talaf//təlef a).* All my papers were destroyed in the fire. *kəll ᵊwraaqi təlfet bᵊl-ḥariiqa.* 2. *xarrab//txarrab, dammar//ddammar, hadam (e hadᵊm//nhadam).* The earth-quake destroyed a third of the town. *z-zalzale xarrabet təlt ᵊl-balad.* 3. *xayyab//xaab (i xeebe).* This development has destroyed our hopes for an early settlement. *hat-taṭawwor xayyáb-ᵊlna ʔaamaalna b-taswiye qariibe.*

destroyer – (ship) *mdammra* pl. *-aat.*

destruction – 1. *xaraab, damaar.* The fire caused a lot of destruction. *l-ḥariiqa sabbabet xaraab mahuul.* 2. *hadᵊm, hadd.* My company is in charge of the destruction of this building. *šərkətna mətεahhde b-hadᵊm hal-binaaye.*

to **detach** – *faṣal (e faṣᵊl//nfaṣal).* Shall I detach the stub? *ʔəfṣel ᵊl-ʔaruume šii?*

to detach oneself from – *nεazal εan.* I detached myself from the crowd. *nεazalᵊt εan ᵊl-ʔərṭa.*

detachment – *mafraze* pl. *mafaarez.* An army detach-ment seized the presidential palace at daybreak. *mafraze mn ᵊž-žeeš ᵊḥtallet qaṣr ᵊr-raʔaase εand ᵊl-fažᵊr.*

detail – 1. *tafṣiil* pl. *-aat* and *tafaṣiil.* Details of the robbery are in today's paper. *tafaṣiil ᵊn-nahᵊb bətšuufa b-žariidt ᵊl-yoom.* 2. *warše* pl. *-aat.* Who is in charge of this detail? *miin ᵊl-masʔuul εan hal-warše?*

in detail – *bᵊt-tafṣiil, mfaṣṣalan.* He described the incident in detail. *waṣaf ᵊl-ḥaadse bᵊt-tafṣiil.*

to go into detail(s) – *ḥaka (i ḥaki) εan tafarruεaat.* I don't want to go into details. *maa bəddi ʔəḥki εan tafarruεaat.*

to detail – 1. *kallaf.* I have to detail someone to mow the lawn. *laazem kallef ḥada yqəṣṣ ᵊl-ḥašiiš.* 2. *fannad, faṣṣal.* Detail your expenses. *fanned maṣariifak.*

detailed – *mfaṣṣal.* A detailed report of the survey will soon be published. *εan qariib laḥa yəṭlaε taq̈riir ᵊmfaṣṣal εan ᵊl-kašᵊf.* -- A detailed drawing of the house is in my office. *fii rasm ᵊmfaṣṣal ləl-beet ᵊb-maktabi.*

detective – *taḥarri* pl. *-iyye.*

detergent – *mnaḍḍef* pl. *-aat.*

determination – *εaziime, εazᵊm.* He showed great deter-mination. *ʔaẓhar εaziime baalġa.*

to **determine** – *ḥaddad.* Wages – among other factors – determine the prices. *l-ʔužuur – maε ġeer εawaamel -- bətḥadded ᵊl-ʔasεaar.*

determined – 1. *mṣammem, εaazem.* She's determined to have her way. *hiyye mṣammᵊme taεmel halli bədda-yáa.* 2. *ḥaazem.* He asked for a raise in a determined voice. *ṭalab zyaadet maεaaš ᵊb-lahže ḥaazme.*

**My father is a very determined man. *ʔabi ṣaaḥeb εaziime qawiyye.*

detour – *barme* pl. *-aat, laffe* pl. *-aat, doora* pl. *-aat.* We made a long detour to see the lake. *εməlna barme ṭawiile la-nətfarraž εal-buḥayra.*

to detour – 1. *ḥawwal//tḥawwal.* Traffic was detoured because of the automobile accident. *s-seer ᵊtḥawwal ᵊb-sabab ḥaades ᵊs-sayyaara.* 2. *baram (o/e barme), laff (e laffe), daar (u doora).* I detoured off the highway to avoid him. *baramᵊt εan ᵊṭ-ṭariiq la-ʔətḥaašáa.*

deuce – *žweeze* pl. *-aat.* I held three deuces and two kings. *kaan ᵊb-ʔiidi tlətt ᵊžweezaat w-tneen ʔəxṭyaariyye.*

**What the deuce do you mean? *ḥəll εan diini baqa, šuu btəqṣoḍ ᵊb-hal-kalaam?*

to **develop** – *ḥammaḍ.* Would you develop this film for me? *balla bətḥammə́ḍ li hal-fəlᵊm?*

**My son is developing into a man. *ʔəbni εam yṣiir rəžžaal.*

**It developed that we had been wrong. *tbayyan ʔənno kənna ġalṭaaniin.*

**I developed an interest in history. *ṣar-li maraaq bᵊt-taariix.*

development – 1. *taṭawwor* pl. *-aat.* Do you know any-thing about the latest developments? *εarfaan šii εan ᵊt-taṭawwuraat ᵊl-ʔaxiire?* 2. *numuww.* Discipline is essential to a boy's development. *n-niẓaam ᵊktiir ᵊmhəmm la-numuww l-ᵊwlaad.*

device – *žihaaz* pl. *ʔažhize.* This device should help speed production. *haž-žihaaz laazem ykuun ysaaεed εat-tasriiε bᵊl-ʔəntaaž.*

devil – *šeeṭaan* pl. *šayaṭiin, εəfriit* pl. *εafariit.*

to **devote** – 1. *karras, xaṣṣaṣ.* He devoted all his spare time to his studies. *karras kəll waqᵊt faraaġo ləd-diraase.* 2. *xaṣṣaṣ.* The first chapter is devoted to his childhood. *l-faṣl ᵊl-ʔawwal ᵊmxaṣṣaṣ la-ʔiyyaam ṭufuulto.*

devoted – *məxleṣ.* He's very devoted to his mother. *huwwe ktiir məxleṣ la-ʔəmmo.*

dew – *nəde.*

diabetes – *maraḍ˜ ᵊs-səkkar(i).*

to **diagnose** – *šaxxaṣ.* None of the doctors was able to diagnose the disease. *w-laa waaḥed ᵊmn ᵊd-dakaatra qəder yšaxxeṣ ᵊl-maraḍ.*

diagnosis – *tašxiiṣ* pl. *-aat.*

diagonal – 1. *qəṭᵊr* pl. *ʔaqṭaar.* Now draw the two diagonals of this rectangle. *rsoom hallaq ᵊl-qəṭreen la-hal-məstaṭiil.* 2. *mawruub.* The crack forms a diagonal line from one end of the wall to the other. *š-šaqq ʔaaxed kasᵊm xaṭṭ mawruub mən ʔawwal ᵊl-ḥeeṭ la-ʔaaxro.* 3. *warᵊb.* We walked across the field in a diagonal. *qaṭaεna l-ḥaqle bᵊl-warᵊb.*

diagonally – *bᵊl-warᵊb.* Cut it diagonally. *qṭáεa bᵊl-warᵊb.*

diagram – *xaṭṭ bayaani* pl. *xṭuuṭ bayaaniyye.*

dial – 1. *qərᵊṣ* pl. *qraaṣ.* My telephone dial is white. *qərṣ talifooni ʔabyaḍ.* 2. *miina* pl. *-aat.* The dial on my watch is dirty. *miinet saaεti wəsxa.*

to dial – *daqq (ə daqq//ndaqq).* She dialed the wrong number. *daqqet ᵊn-nəmre ġalaṭ.*

dialect – *lahže* pl. *-aat.*

diameter – *qəṭᵊr* pl. *ʔaqṭaar.* How much is the diameter of the pipe? *qaddeeš qəṭᵊr hal-buuri?*

diamond – 1. *ʔalmaase* coll. *ʔalmaas* pl. *-aat* and *ʔalamiis.* He put her diamonds in the safe. *ḥaṭṭ ʔalmaasaata b-ṣanduuq ᵊl-ḥadiid.* 2. *mεayyan* pl. *-aat.* The tray has the shape of a diamond. *kasm ᵊṣ-ṣaniyye mətl l-ᵊmεayyan.* 3. *diinaari* (invar.). Did you bid two diamonds? *sammeet šii tneen diinaari?*

diaper – *xərqa* pl. *xruuq.*

diarrhea – *shaal.*

diary – *daftar˜* (pl. *dafaater˜*) *ᵊmzakkaraat.* His diaries were found after his death. *dafaater ᵊmzakkaraato wažaduuha baεᵊd mooto.* — I've kept a diary ever since I was twenty years old. *ʔana maasek daftar ᵊmzakkaraat mən waqᵊt-ma kaan εəmri εəšriin.*

dice – *zahᵊr* (coll., one dice *zahra* or *fardet˜ zahᵊr* pl. *zahraat* or *fardaat˜ zahᵊr*). Let's play dice. *xalliina nəlεab bᵊz-zahᵊr.*

to dice – *qaṭṭaε ... raas ᵊl- εaṣfuur.* Dice the meat before browning it. *qaṭṭeε ᵊl-laḥme raas ᵊl-εaṣfuur qabᵊl-ma tḥammə́ra.*

to **dictate** – 1. *naqqal//tnaqqal, ʔamla.* He's dicta-ting a letter. *εam ynaqqel maktuub.* — Dictate the letter to my secretary. *naqqel sekᵊrteerti l-maktuub* or *ʔəmli l-maktuub εala sekᵊrteerti.* 2. *sayyar.* Her children dictate her whole life. *wlaada msayyríin-la kəll ḥayaata.*

dictation – *ʔəmla.* I give my students a dictation exercise once every week. *baεṭi ṭəllaabi tamriin ʔəmla bᵊž-žəmεa marra.*

**Will you please take some dictation? *məmken ʔəmli εaleeki šii maktuub?*

**I can't type from dictation. *maa bəqder ʔəktob εal-maakiina w-ykuun ḥada εam yəmli εaliyyi.*

dictator – *dəktatoor* pl. *-aat.*

dictatorship – *dəktatooriyye.*

dictionary – *q̈aamuus* pl. *q̈awamiis, məεžam* pl. *maεaažem.*

die – 1. *zahra* pl. *-aat, fardet~* (pl. *-aat~*) *zah°r.* The other die rolled under the sofa. *z-zahra t-taanye ddahražet taht °l-kanabe.* **2.** *qaaleb* pl. *qawaaleb.* This die is used to make aluminum pans. *hal-qaaleb byəstaE°mlúu la-msaawaat tanaažer ʔalumiinyoom.*

**The die is cast. *ğudiya l-ʔamr.*

to **die** – *maat (u moot, moote).* He died this morning at two o'clock. *maat °l-yoom sabaahan °s-saaEa tənteen.* -- I just about died laughing when I heard that. *kənt laha muut °mn °d-dəh°k lamma sməEt haš-šii.* -- I'm dying from this cough. *Eam muut mən has-saEle.* -- I'm dying to find out what he said. *raha muut Eala-ma ʔaEref šuu qaal.* -- The tree is dying. *š-šažara Eam °tmuut.* -- Old customs die hard. *l-Eaadaat °l-Eatiiqa bətmuut °b-suEuube.*

**The motor died. *l-motoor ntafa.*

to die away – *tlaaša.* The noise of the train died away in the distance. *soot °t-treen °tlaaša Eal-baE°d.*

to die down – 1. *xəmed (a ø).* We let the fire die down. *xalleena n-naar təxmad.* **2.** *həmed (a ø).* The excitement will die down in a few days. *l-hayažaan laha yəhmad baE°d kam yoom.*

to die off – *nqarad.* The old inhabitants are dying off. *s-səkkaan °l-qədama Eam yənqərdu.*

to die out – *nqarad.* This old custom is gradually dying out. *hal-Eaade l-qadiime Eam tənqəred šwayye šwayye.*

diet – 1. *həmye* pl. *-aat, režiim.* I have to keep a strict diet. *laazem ʔəmši Eala həmye šadiide.* -- I'm on a diet. *ʔana Eala režiim* or ***ʔana məhmi.* **2.** *ʔak°l.* For weeks our diet consisted of nothing but fish. *la-məddet ʔasabiiE maa kaan ʔak°lna ʔəlla samak.*

to diet – *htama, kaan Eala režiim.* I've been dieting for a month, but I still haven't lost any weight. *sar-li šah°r w-ʔana məhtəmi* (or *sar-li šah°r Ear-režiim*) *bass maa xsər°t šii.*

to **differ** – *xtalaf.* Various authorities differ on this subject. *fii maraažeE mətEadd°de btəxtəlef Eala hal-mawduuE.* -- They're brothers, but their appearances differ a great deal. *hənne ʔəxwaat bass heeʔəton btəxtəlef °ktiir.* -- Opinions differ here. *l-ʔaaraaʔ məxtəlfe hoon* or ***l-ʔaaraaʔ mətšaEEbe hoon.* -- I beg to differ with you. *btəsməh-li ʔəxtəlef maEak.*

difference – 1. *far°q* pl. *fruuq(a).* Can you explain the difference to me? *fiik °tfassər-li l-far°q?* **2.** *ʔəxtilaaf* pl. *-aat, xilaaf* pl. *-aat.* They reached an agreement in spite of certain differences of opinion. *twassalu la-ʔəttifaaq b°r-rağ°m Ean ʔəxtilaaf °l-ʔaaraaʔ nooEan maa.* **3.** *far°q, rasiid.* You can send us the difference later. *fiik təbEət-°lna l-far°q baEdeen.*

**Does it make any difference if I write in pencil? *btəfreq šii ʔiza katabt °b-qalam °rsaas?*

**It makes no difference when you come. *maa btəfreq ʔeemta-ma bəddak təži.*

**Oh, what's the difference! *xalləsna baqa, šuu btəfreq!*

different – 1. *məxtəlef.* I lived in three different houses last year. *sakan°t b-°tlətt °byuut məxtəlfe Eaamnawwal.* **2.** *ğeer~ ..., taani.* Can you show me a different color? *fiik °twaržiini ğeer loon* (or *... loon ğeer haad* or *... loon taani*)? -- That's a different matter. *haada ğeer šii* (or *... šii taani*). **3.** *ğeer~ šək°l.* That's quite different. *haada ğeer šək°l tamaam.*

**I like her because she's a little different. *ʔana haabəba laʔənna šwayye ğeer šək°l Ean °n-naas.*

to be different – *xtalaf.* These photographs are very different from each other. *haş-şuwar btəxtəlef °ktiir Ean baEda.*

differential – *dəfraansyeel* pl. *-aat.* The differential of my car isn't working properly. *d-dəfraansyeel tabaE sayyaarti maa Eam yəštəğel mazbuut.*

differential calculus – *hsaab tafaaduli.*

differently – *ğeer~ heek, ğeer~ šək°l.* I think differently about it. *bəEtəbəra ğeer heek.* -- You told me differently. *qəlt-əlli ğeer heek.* -- You'll have to spell that differently. *laazem thažžiiha ğeer šək°l.*

difficult – 1. *saE°b.* It's difficult to understand what he means. *saEb °l-waahed yəfham šuu byəqsod.* -- We have a difficult assignment in math. *Ealeena waziife saEbe b°r-riyaadiyyaat.* **2.** *Eawiis, saE°b.* That's a difficult subject. *haada mawduuE Eawiis.*

**Why do you have to be so difficult? *leeš ʔənte hal-qadd saEb °t-tafaahom maEak?*

difficulty – 1. *suube* pl. *-aat,* (pl. only) *masaaEeb.* He overcame all difficulties. *tğallab Eala kəll °s-suEuubaat.* **2.** *Eət°l, məš°kle.* There seems to be a difficulty in the wiring. *byəzhar fii Eət°l b°š-šaraayet.*

dig – *mlaahaza* pl. *-aat.* That was a dirty dig. *hayy kaanet °mlaahaza waatye.*

to dig – 1. *hafar (e/o haf°r//nhafar).* Dig the hole a little deeper. *hfeer °ž-žuura ʔağmaq šwayye.* **2.** *bahaš (a bah°š) Eala.* The whole family is out in the field digging potatoes. *l-Eeele kəlla b°l-haqle Eam təbhaš Eal-bataata.*

to dig in – 1. *ʔakal (-yaakol ʔak°l) malaat batno.* If you're hungry, just dig in! *ʔiza žuuEaan kool malaat batnak!* **2.** *hafar (e/o haf°r) la-haalo hafra.* Our company dug in under heavy artillery fire. *sariyyətna hafret la-haala həfar tah°t naar madfaEiyye haamye.*

to dig up – 1. *qalaE (a qal°E//nqalaE).* We'll have to dig up the rose bush. *laazem nəqlaE °l-warde.* **2.** *nabaš (e/o nab°š//ntabaš).* I don't know why he dug up that old story. *maa-li fahmaan leeš nabaš hal-qəssa l-qadiime.*

digest – *məxtaaraat* (pl.). He's preparing a digest of every major article on the topic. *Eam yhadder məxtaaraat mən kəll maqaale mhəmme b-hal-mawduuE.*

to digest – 1. *hadam (o had°m//nhadam).* Nuts are hard to digest. *ž-žooz saE°b hadmo.* **2.** *saddaq, hadam.* Her stories are a bit hard to digest. *qəsdsa saEb °šwayye tasdiiqa.*

digestion – *had°m.*

dignified – *žaliil* pl. *-iin* and *ʔažəllaaʔ, waquur.* His father was a dignified old gentleman. *ʔabúu kaan rəžžaal °msənn žaliil.*

dignity – *karaame, waqaar.*

dilemma – *maʔzaq* pl. *maʔaazeq.* That's the dilemma of our generation. *haada l-maʔzaq halli waaqeE fii žiilna.* -- I'm in a real dilemma. *ʔana b-maʔzaq Eal-mazbuut.*

diligence – *ʔəžtihaad, kadd.*

diligent – *məžtəhed.*

dim – 1. *naayes, məEtem.* I couldn't see anything in that dim light. *maa hsən°t šuuf šii b-had-daww °n-naayes.* **2.** *dEiif.* Your voice sounded very dim on the telephone. *sootak kaan °ktiir °dEiif Eat-talifoon.* **3.** *ʔaswad* f. *sooda.* He takes a pretty dim view of the future. *nazərto sooda ləl-məstaqbal.*

to dim – 1. *watta//twatta.* Why didn't you dim your headlights? *leeš maa watteet ʔədwiitak?* **2.** *daEef (a ø).* My grandfather's memory is dimming. *zaakərt žəddi Eam tədEaf.*

dimple – *ğammaaze* pl. *-aat.*

dinar – *diinaar* pl. *dananiir.*

to **dine** – *tEašša.* They're dining with the Ambassador tonight. *raha yətEaššu maE °s-safiir °l-yoom Eašiyye.* -- We always dine out on Sundays. *daayman yoom °l-ʔahad mnətEašša barra.*

dining car – *Earabet~* (pl. *-aat~*) *ʔak°l, fargoon~* (pl. *faragiin~*) *ʔak°l.* This train has no dining car. *hat-treen maa fii Earabet ʔak°l.*

dining room – *ʔuudet~* (pl. *ʔuwad~*) *ʔak°l, ʔuudet~ səfra.* Bring another chair into the dining room. *žəb-lak kərsi taani la-ʔuudet °l-ʔak°l.*

dinner – *Eaša* pl. *ʔəEšye.* We're giving a dinner in his honor. *Eaamliin-lo Eaša Eala šarafo.* -- Dinner's ready! *l-Eaša haader!*

to have dinner – *tEašša.* On Sundays we have dinner at six o'clock. *yoom °l-ʔahad mnətEašša s-saaEa sətte.*

diocese – *ʔəbəršiyye* pl. *-aat.*

dip – 1. *ğatse* pl. *-aat, ğatta* pl. *-aat.* I think I'll take a dip before breakfast. *žaaye Eala baali ʔəğtəs-li ğatse qabl °t-tarwiiqa.* **2.** *nazle* pl. *-aat.* There's a dip in the road ahead. *fii nazle b°t-tariiq qəddaam.* **3.** *taabe* pl. *-aat.* Give me a dip of ice cream, please. *Eatiini taabet buuza mən fadlak.*

to dip – 1. *watta, nazzal.* They dipped the flag in salute. *wattu l-Ealam la-ʔadaaʔ °t-tahiyye.* **2.** *ğattas.* I dipped my finger into the water. *ğattas°t ʔəsbaEi b°l-mayy.* **3.** *ğaraf (e/o ğar°f).* Let me dip you a bowl of soup. *xalliini ʔəğrəf-lak kəbšaayet šooraba.* **4.** *nhadar, nəzel (e nzuul).* This path dips into the woods a mile from here. *hat-taaruuq byənhəder ləl-ğaabe Eala masaafet miil mən hoon.*

**I have to dip into my savings now. *mažbuur ʔana hallaq ʔəndaar la-halli mwaffro.*

diphtheria - *dəftərya, xaanuuq.*
diploma - *dəbloom(a)* pl. *-aat, šahaade* pl. *-aat.*
diplomacy - *dəblomaasiyye.*
diplomat - *dəblomaasi** pl. *-iyyiin.*
diplomatic - *dəblomaasi**. The entire diplomatic corps attended the celebration. *kəll ᵊs-səlk ᵊd-dəblomaasi ḥaḍer ᵊl-ʔəḥtifaal.*
direct - **1.** *mbaašar, ḍəḡri* (invar.). There is no direct route. *maa fii ṭariiq ᵊmbaašar.* **2.** *mbaašar.* He claims to be a direct descendant of the Prophet. *byəddáᶜi ʔənno saliil ᵊmbaašar lən-nabi.* -- I prefer the direct approach to the problem. *ʔana bfaḍḍel ᵊl-ʔəq̄daam l-ᵊmbaašar ᶜala hal-məšᵊkle.* **3.** *ḍəḡri* (invar.). I like his direct manner. *byəᶜžəbni ṭabᶜo ḍ-ḍəḡri.*
**It's the direct opposite of what we expected. *haada ᶜakᵊs-ma nṭaẓarna tamaam.*
direct current - *tayyaar məṭṭə́red, tayyaar ᵊmbaašar.*
to direct - **1.** *ᶜaṭa (i ø) ... taᶜliimaat//ʔəža taᶜliimaat.* We were directed to follow the old regulations. *ʔəžaana taᶜliimaat nəmši ᶜal-ʔanẓime l-qadiime.* -- The main office directed us to do exactly that. *l-ʔidaara l-markaziyye ᶜaṭətna taᶜliimaat naᶜmel haad tamaam w-bass.* **2.** *maššā, waššah, daar (i ʔidaara).* A policeman is directing the traffic on that corner. *fii šərṭi ᶜam ymašši s-seer ᶜala has-suuke.* **3.** *daar (i ʔidaara).* Who's directing the play? *miin ᶜam ydiir ᵊt-tamsiiliyye?* **4.** *dall (ə ø//ndall).* Can you direct me to the post office? *fiik ᵊddəllni ᶜal-boosṭa?* **5.** *waššah.* I directed my lecture to the students. *waššaht ᵊmḥaaḍarti lət-ṭəllaab.*
direction - **1.** *ʔəttižaah* pl. *-aat.* In which direction did he go? *b-ʔayy ʔəttižaah raaḥ?* **2.** *žiha* pl. *-aat.* Sparks were flying in all directions. *š-šaraar ᵊṭṭaayar la-kəll ᵊž-žihaat.* -- They attacked us from all directions. *haažamuuna mən kəll ᵊž-žihaat.* **3.** *ʔidaara, ʔəšraaf.* They've made great progress under his direction. *tqaddamu taqaddom ᶜaẓiim taḥᵊt ʔidaarto.* -- The concert will be under the direction of our music teacher. *l-konseer bikuun taḥᵊt ʔəšraaf ᵊmᶜallem ᵊl-muusiiqa tabaᶜna.*
directions - **1.** *keefiyyet~ ʔəstəᶜmaal.* Follow the enclosed directions! *ttə́beᶜ keefiyyet ᵊl-ʔəstəᶜmaal ᵊl-mərfaqa.* **2.** *taᶜliimaat* (pl.). His directions are clear. *taᶜliimaato waaḍḥa.*
directly - *ḍəḡri, raʔsan, mbaašə́ratan.* Let's go directly to the hotel. *xalliina nruuḥ ḍəḡri ᶜal-ʔoteel.* -- Our house is directly opposite the store. *beetna raʔsan ᵊmwaažeh ᵊl-maxzan.*
director - *mudiir* pl. *mədara.*
directory - **1.** *daliil* pl. *dalaayel.* Look for his address in the telephone directory. *šuuf ᶜənwaano b-daliil ᵊt-talifoon.* **2.** *daliil* pl. *dalaayel, tablóo~* (pl. *tabloyaat~*) *ʔasaami.* The building directory is on the wall at the end of the hall. *daliil ᵊl-binaaye ᶜal-ḥeeṭ ᵊb-ʔaaxer ᵊl-mamša.*
dirt - **1.** *ṭraab* pl. *ṭaraayeb.* Dig up the dirt around the trees! *ḥfeer ᵊṭ-ṭraab ḥawaali š-šažaraat!* **2.** *ṭiin, waḥᵊl.* My gloves fell in the dirt. *kfuufi waqᶜu bᵊṭ-ṭiin.* **3.** *waṣax* pl. *ʔawṣaax.* I cleaned the dirt out of your drawers today. *naḍḍaft ᵊdruužak ᵊmn ᵊl-waṣax ᵊl-yoom.*
**She spreads dirt on people she doesn't even know. *bətšaršeḥ ᵊn-naas ḥatta halli maa btaᶜrə́fon.*
dirt road - *ṭariiq riifi* pl. *ṭərqaat riifiyye.*
dirt-cheap - *ʔarxaṣ ᵊmn ᵊṭ-ṭraab, ʔarxaṣ ᵊmn ᵊl-fəžᵊl.* I got it dirt-cheap. *ʔaxadta ʔarxaṣ ᵊmn ᵊṭ-ṭraab.*
dirty - **1.** *wəsex.* The floor is dirty. *l-ʔarᵊḍ wəsxa.* **2.** *malᶜuun, ᶜaaṭel.* We've had some real dirty weather this week. *kaan ᶜanna ṭaqᵊs malᶜuun ᶜan ḥaqa haž-žəmᶜa.* **3.** *waaṭi.* He gave us a dirty look. *ṭṭalaᶜ ᶜaleena taṭliiᶜa waaṭye* (or ** ... *taṭliiᶜa kəlla ləʔᵊm*). -- That's a dirty lie. *hayy kəzbe waaṭye.* — He played a dirty trick on us. *ləᶜeb ᶜaleena ləᶜbe waaṭye.* **4.** *raziil.* Most of his stories are pretty dirty. *ʔaktar qə́ṣaṣo raziile ktiir* or **ʔ*aktar qəṣaṣo mən taḥt ᵊz-zənnaar w-naazel.*
**That's a dirty shame! *ᶜeeb, šii biqarref!*
to dirty - *waṣṣax.* Don't dirty your shoes. *laa twaṣṣex ṣabbaaṭak.*
disadvantage - *(masaaʔa)* pl. *masaaweʔ, sayyiʔa* (pl. *-aat*). The disadvantages of this plan are quite obvious. *masaaweʔ hal-xəṭṭa waaḍḥa.*
**I'm at a disadvantage when I try to deal with my boss. *markazi ᶜaadatan ᵊḍᶜiif kəll-ma bḥaawel ʔətᶜaamal maᶜ raʔiisi.*

to **disagree** - **1.** *xtalaf.* I disagree with you. *ʔana bəxtə́lef maᶜak.* **2.** *tnaaqar.* Those two disagree all day long. *hat-tneen byətnaaqaru ᶜala ṭuul.* **3.** *maa waafaq.* I disagree with the method. *ʔana maa-li mwaafeq ᶜal-ʔəsluub.* **4.** *maa waata, maa waafaq.* Strawberries disagree with me. *l-ᵊfreez maa biwaatiini.*
disagreement - **1.** *xilaaf* pl. *-aat, ʔəxtilaaf* pl. *-aat.* What was your disagreement about? *ᶜala šuu kaan xilaafkon?* **2.** *ᶜadam~ ᵊmwaafaqa.* We sent them a note indicating our disagreement. *baᶜatnə́a-lon maktuub ᵊb-ᶜadam ᵊmwaafaqətna.*
to **disappear** - *xtafa.* He disappeared in the crowd. *xtafa bᵊl-ḥašᵊd.* -- My pencil has disappeared. *qalam ᵊr-rṣaaṣ tabaᶜi xtafa.*
to **disappoint** - *xayyab ʔamal~ ..., xayyab ẓann~ ...* Your conduct disappointed me. *taṣarrfak xayyab ʔamali.*
disappointment - *xeebet~* (pl. *-aat~*) *ʔamal.* It was a great disappointment to cancel our trip. *tabṭiil rəḥlə́tna kaan xeebet ʔamal faẓiiᶜa.*
**He is a disappointment to his family. *xayyab ʔamal ʔahlo.*
to **disapprove** - **1.** *maa staḥsan, maa waafaq.* He disapproves of our plans. *maa byəstaḥsen xəṭaṭna* or *maa biwaafeq ᶜala xəṭaṭna.* **2.** *rafaḍ (o rafᵊḍ// nrafaḍ* and *rtafaḍ).* The bank disapproved my request for a loan. *l-bank rafaḍ ṭalabi b-q̄arḍ.*
to **disarm** - **1.** *nazaᶜ (a nazᵊᶜ) silaaḥ~ ...* They disarmed the prisoners quickly. *nazaᶜu silaaḥ ᵊl-masažiin ᵊb-sərᶜa.* **2.** *kasar (e ø) ᵊš-šarr ᶜand.* His smile disarmed everyone present. *ʔəbtisaamto kasret ᵊš-šarr ᶜand kəll ᵊn-naas ᵊl-ḥaaḍriin.*
disarmament - *nazᵊᶜ~ silaaḥ.* The disarmament talks are to be resumed next month. *laḥa yəstaʔᵊnfu mbaaḥasaat nazᶜ ᵊs-silaaḥ ᵊš-šahr ᵊž-žaaye.*
disaster - *kaarse* pl. *kawaares, faažᶜa* pl. *fawaažeᶜ, nakbe* pl. *-aat.*
disastrous - *məfžeᶜ.*
discharge - **1.** *tasriiḥ* pl. *-aat.* I got my discharge in November. *ḥṣəlᵊt ᶜala tasriiḥi b-šahᵊr təšriin ᵊt-taani.* **2.** *ṭaqṭaqa* pl. *-aat.* The gun's discharge was very loud. *ṭaqṭə́qet ᵊl-baaruude kaanet ᶜaalye ktiir.* **3.** *ʔəfraaz* pl. *-aat.* You should see the doctor about that discharge from your eye. *ʔaḥsə́n-lak ᵊtšuuf ᵊd-doktoor mənšaan hal-ʔəfraaz ᵊmn ᵊᶜyuunak.*
to discharge - **1.** *ṭaalaᶜ.* Who discharged this man from the hospital? *miin ṭaalaᶜ har-rəžžaal ᵊmn ᵊl-məstašfa?* **2.** *sarraḥ.* The army discharged my brother a week ago. *ž-žeeš sarraḥ ʔaxi mən žəmᶜa.* **3.** *qaam (u qyaam) b-.* He discharged his duties promptly. *qaam ᵊb-waažbaato biduun taʔxiir.* **4.** *faḍḍa.* The battery in my car keeps discharging. *baṭṭaariit sayyaarti bəḍḍall ᵊtfaḍḍi.*
discipline - **1.** *niẓaam.* He insists on strict discipline. *bišərr ᶜala niẓaam šadiid.* **2.** *tərbaaye, taʔdiib.* I sent him to his room for discipline. *baᶜatto la-ʔuuḍto tərbaaye.*
to discipline - *žaaza//džaaza, qaaṣaṣ//tqaaṣaṣ.* The sergeant disciplined four soldiers for failure to salute an officer. *r-raqiib žaaza ʔarbaᶜ ᶜasaaker laʔənnon maa ʔəddu s-salaam la-waaḥed ẓaabeṭ.*
to **disconnect** - *qaṭaᶜ (a qaṭᵊᶜ//nqaṭaᶜ).* If you don't pay your bill we'll have to disconnect your line. *ʔiza maa btədfaᶜ faatuurtak mnənžə́ber nəqṭaᶜ xaṭṭak.* -- Operator, I got disconnected. *ṣanṭraal, nqaṭaᶜ ᶜaliyyi l-xaṭṭ.*
discontented - *məḍḍažžer, mətʔaffef.*
discount - *xaṣᵊm, ḥasᵊm.* Can you get a discount on these books? *fiik taaxod xaṣᵊm ᶜala hal-kətᵊb?*
to discount - **1.** *xaṣam (o xaṣᵊm//nxaṣam), ḥasam (e ḥasᵊm//nḥasam).* They'll discount ten percent of the price if you're a regular customer. *byaxᵊṣ-mú-lak ᶜašara bᵊl-miyye mn ᵊs-səᶜᵊr ʔiza ʔənte zbuun daayem.* **2.** *xaṣam, ḥazaf (e ḥazᵊf// nḥazaf).* You can generally discount half of what he says. *ᶜal-ᵊᶜmuum fiik təxṣom nəṣṣ halli byəḥkii.*
to **discourage** - **1.** *habbaṭ ᶜazᵊm~ ..., xammad ᶜaziimet~ ....* It discouraged me completely. *habbaṭə́t-li ᶜazmi ᶜal-ʔaaxiir.* **2.** *manaᶜ (a manᵊᶜ).* He did everything to discourage me from going. *ᶜəmel kəll žahdo la-yəmnaᶜni ruuḥ.* **3.** *habaṭ (o ø) ᶜazmo, xamdet (o ø) ᶜaziimto.* He discourages easily. *qawaam byəhboṭ ᶜazmo.*
**The results are very discouraging. *n-nataayež maa bətšažžeᶜ ʔabadan.*
to **discover** - **1.** *ktašaf.* Columbus discovered America in 1492. *kolombo ktašaf ʔameerka sənᵊt ʔalf w-ʔarbaᶜ miyye w-ᵊtneen w-təsᶜiin.* **2.** *wažad*

(-yuužed ø). We discovered that we had been wrong. *wažadna (ḥaalna) ʔənno kənna ǧalṭaaniin.*
discovery - *ʔəktišaaf* pl. *-aat.*
to **discuss** - *baḥas (a baḥᵊs//nbaḥas).* We discussed the question at length. *baḥasna l-masʔale b-ʔəshaab.* -- Discuss the matter with him. *bḥaas ᵊš-šaġle maʕo.*
discussion - *mnaaqaše* pl. *-aat, mḥaawara* pl. *-aat.*
disease - *maraḍ* pl. *ʔamraaḍ, daaʔ* pl. *-aat.*
to **disfigure** - *šawwah.* The scar disfigures his face. *š-šaṭᵊb bišawwəh-lo wəššo.*
disgrace - *ʕaar.* The way she behaves is a disgrace. *maslə́ka ʕaar.* -- He's a disgrace to his profession. *huwwe ʕaar la-məhᵊnto.*
to disgrace - *bahdal, šaršaḥ qiimet˜* ... You really disgraced yourself last night. *ḥaqiiqatan bahdalᵊt ḥaalak* (or *šaršaḥᵊt qiimtak) leelt ᵊmbaareḥ.*
disguise - *tanakkor.* I didn't recognize him in his disguise. *maa ʕrəfto b-tanakkro* or ***maa ʕrəfto w-huwwe mətnakker.*
to disguise - **1.** *xafa* and *ʔaxfa (i ʔəxfaaʔ// nxafa).* He disguised his handwriting. *ʔaxfa xaṭṭo.* -- He tried to disguise his embarrassment. *ḥaawal yəxfi ʔərtibaako.* **2.** *ġayyar//tġayyar.* He disguised his voice. *ġayyar ṣooṭo.*
to disguise oneself - *tnakkar, txaffa.* She disguised herself as a countrywoman. *tnakkaret ᵊb-zayy fallaaḥa.*
disgust - *qaraf, ʔəšməʔzaaz.* He turned away in disgust. *daar ḍahro b-qaraf.* -- They sensed our disgust and left. *ḥassu b-ʔəšməʔzaazna fa-raaḥu.*
to disgust - *qarraf, naffar.* His conduct disgusts me. *maslako biqarrəfni.* -- How disgusting! *šii biqarref!*
to be (or **feel**) **disgusted** - *qəref (a qaraf), šmaʔazz.* I'm disgusted with everything. *ʔana qarfaan mən kəll šii* or *ʔana məšmaʔəzz mən kəll šii.*
dish - **1.** (large, shallow or deep, for serving food) *žaaṭ* pl. *-aat;* (small, for butter, olives, cheese, etc.) *ṣaḥᵊn* pl. *ṣḥuun(e);* (bowl-like) *zəbdiyye* pl. *zabaadi.* He dropped the dish. *waqqaʕ ᵊž-žaaṭ.* **2.** *ṭabxa* pl. *-aat, ʔakle* pl. *-aat.* I have a recipe for a new dish. *ʕandi waṣfe la-ṭabxa ždiide.* **3.** *ṣaḥᵊn* pl. *ṣḥuun(e).* Give us each a dish of ice cream. *ʕaṭi kəll waaḥed mənna ṣaḥᵊn buuẓa.*
dishes - *ṣḥuun* (pl.). We'll have to buy dishes. *laazem nəštə́ri ṣḥuun.* -- Who's going to do the dishes tonight? *miin bəddo yəšli ṣ-ṣḥuun ᵊl-leele?*
dishcloth - *məšlaaye* pl. *-aat.*
dishwasher - *šalla˜* (pl. *šallayiin˜) ṣḥuun.* He works as a dishwasher in a nearby restaurant. *byəštə́ġel šalla ṣḥuun ᵊb-maṭxam qariib.*
dishwashing machine - *šallaayet˜* (pl. *-aat˜) ᵊṣḥuun.*
to **disinfect** - *ṭahhar//ṭṭahhar.* Did you disinfect the wound? *ṭahhart ᵊž-žərᵊḥ?*
disinfectant - *mṭahher* pl. *-aat.*
to **disinherit** - *ḥaram (e/o ḥərmaan//nḥaram) ᵊmn ᵊl-ʔərs.* His father threatened to disinherit him. *ʔabúu haddado ʔənno (b)yəḥᵊrmo (mn ᵊl-ʔərs).*
dislike - *kərᵊh.* I couldn't conceal my dislike for him. *maa qdərᵊt xabbi kərhi ʔəlo.*
to dislike - *kəreh (a kərᵊh//nkarah).* I dislike that fellow. *bəkrah haz-zalame.*
to **dislocate** - *xalaʕ (a xalᵊʕ//nxalaʕ).* How did you dislocate your shoulder? *kiif xalaʕᵊt kətfak?*
dismal - **1.** *məkreb, mġəmm.* It's a dismal day today. *l-yoom yoom məkreb.* **2.** *ḍʕiif, ḍaʔiil.* The chances of an early settlement appear dismal. *ẓ-ẓaaher ᵊl-ʔamal bᵊl-ᵊwṣuul la-taswiye qariibe ḍʕiif.*
to **dismiss** - **1.** *sarraḥ//tsarraḥ, ʕazal (e ʕazᵊl// nʕazal).* She was dismissed after two weeks. *tsarraḥet baʕᵊd žəmᵊʕteen.* **2.** *radd (ə radd/rtadd).* The court dismissed the complaint. *l-maḥkame raddet ᵊd-daʕwa.* **3.** *qaam (i ø) ... mən baalo, ṭannaš.* He dismissed the matter with a shrug of the shoulder. *qaam ᵊl-qaḍiyye mən baalo b-hazzet kətᵊf.* **4.** *ṣaraf (e ṣarᵊf//nṣaraf).* Our teacher dismissed us early today. *ʔəstaazna ṣarafna l-yoom bakkiir.*
to **disobey** - *ʕaṣa (i ʕəṣyaan//nʕaṣa).* He was court-martialed for disobeying an order. *ʔaḥaalúu ʕal-mažles ᵊl-ʕərfi la-ʔənno ʕaṣa ʔamᵊr.* -- Why did you disobey your mother? *leeš ʕaṣeet ʔəmmak?*
display - *maʕruuḍ* pl. *-aat.* Have you seen the beautiful displays in his shop window? *šəft ᵊl-maʕruuḍaat ᵊl-ḥəlwe halli b-waažəhto?*
on display - *maʕruuḍ.* The paintings are on display at the museum. *l-looḥaat maʕruuḍiin bᵊl-matḥaf.*
to make a display of - *tbaaha b-, tbažžaḥ b-.* Whenever she has a chance she makes a display of her patriotism. *kəll-ma biṣəḥḥ-ə́lla btətbaaha b-waṭaniita.*
to display - **1.** *ʔaẓhar, warža, ʔarža.* He displayed great courage. *ʔaẓhar šažaaʕa faayqa.* **2.** *tbažžaḥ b-.* You needn't display your ignorance. *maa fii lzuum tətbažžaḥ ᵊb-žahlak.* **3.** *ʕaraḍ (e/o ʕarḍ//nʕaraḍ).* The exhibitors displayed an assortment of rugs. *l-ʕaarḍiin ʕaraḍu taškiilet səžžaad.* **4.** *rafaʕ (a rafᵊʕ//rtafaʕ).* All the houses displayed flags. *kəll l-ᵊbyuut rafaʕu ʔaʕlaam.*
disposal - *taṣarrof.* I don't have the necessary funds at my disposal. *maa ʕandi l-ʔamwaal ᵊl-laazme taḥᵊt taṣarrfi* (or ***taḥᵊt ʔiidi).*
**I'm at your disposal. *taḥᵊt ʔamrak.*
to **dispose** - *txallaṣ mən, ṣarraf.* They will leave as soon as they dispose of their furniture. *byətᵊrku saaʕet-ma yətxallaṣu mən ʕafšon.* -- Because of the gasoline shortage, we had to dispose of our car. *b-sabab qəllet ᵊl-banziin ᵊnžabarna nṣarref sayyaarətna.* -- Where can I dispose of this? *ween fiini ʔətxallaṣ mən hayy?*
disposition - *ṭabᵊʕ, mizaaž.* She appears to have a very nice disposition. *byəẓhar ʕaleeha ʔəla ṭabʕ ᵊktiir ḥəlu.*
dispute - *xilaaf* pl. *-aat, nizaaʕ* pl. *-aat.* The border dispute has been going on for years. *l-xilaaf ḥawl l-ᵊḥduud ṣar-lo sniin w-sniin.*
disregard - *ʕadam˜ ʔəktiraas.* He seems to have an absolute disregard for authority. *byəẓhar ʕando ʕadam ʔəktiraas məṭlaq ləṣ-ṣəlṭa.*
to disregard - **1.** *maa ktaras b-, maa htamm b-.* If I were you, I'd simply disregard the letter. *law kənt ᵊb-maḥallak kənt maa ktarasᵊt bᵊl-maktuub.* **2.** *tġaaḍa ʕan, ġaḍḍ (ə ġaḍḍ//nġaḍḍ) ᵊn-naẓar ʕan, ʔahmal.* We can't disregard his objections. *maa fiina nətġaaḍa ʕan ʔəʕtiraaḍaato.*
dissatisfied - *muu raḍyaan.* You look dissatisfied. *mbayyen ʕaleek muu raḍyaan.*
to **dissipate** - **1.** *baʕzaq, baddad.* He dissipated his entire fortune. *baʕzaq kəll sarᵊwto.* **2.** *tbaddad.* The fog is dissipating. *ḍ-ḍabaab ʕam yətbaddad.* **3.** *tʕattar.* If he continues to dissipate at this rate, he won't last long. *ʔiza bəddo ytamm ʕam yətʕattar ʕala hal-ᵊmʕaddal muu raḥa yṭawwel.*
dissipated - *mʕattar.* He leads a dissipated life. *huwwe ʕaayeš ḥayaat ᵊmʕattara* (or ***ḥayaat taʕtiir).*
**He has a terribly dissipated look. *faẓaaʕa šuu ʕaléé laaḥet ᵊl-faarṭiin.*
to **dissolve** - **1.** *dawwab.* Dissolve the tablet in a glass of water. *dawweb ᵊl-ḥabbe b-kaaset mayy.* **2.** *ḥall (e ḥall//nḥall), fasax (a fasᵊx//nfasax).* We dissolved our partnership for several reasons. *ḥalleena šaraakətna la-ʕəddet ʔasbaab.* **3.** *ḥall (e ḥall/nḥall).* The President has threatened to dissolve Parliament. *r-raʔiis haddad ᵊb-ḥall ᵊl-mažles.* **4.** *faḍḍ (ə faḍḍ//nfaḍḍ).* I hope they dissolve this meeting soon. *nšaaḷḷa yfəḍḍu hal-ʔəžtimaaʕ qawaam.* **5.** *daab (u dawabaan).* The pill dissolves in water. *l-ḥabbe bədduub bᵊl-mayy.*
distance - *masaafe* pl. *-aat.* The distance between Damascus and Beirut is a hundred and ten kilometers. *l-masaafe been ᵊš-šaam w-beeruut miyye w-ʕašᵊr kiilomətraat.* -- We can cover the distance in three hours. *fiina nəqṭaʕ ᵊl-masaafe b-ᵊtlətt saaʕaat.*
**He knows how to keep his distance. *byaʕref kiif yəḥfaẓ maqaamo.*
from a distance - *mən (ʕala) masaafe, mən (ʕala) bəʕᵊd, mn ᵊbʕiid.* You can see the tower from a distance. *fiik ᵊtšuuf ᵊl-bərᵊž mən (ʕala) masaafe.*
in the distance - *ʕala masaafe, ʕala bəʕᵊd.* We saw the village in the distance. *šəfna ḍ-ḍeeʕa ʕala masaafe.*
distant - *bʕiid.* She's a distant relative of mine. *btəqrəbni qərbe bʕiide.* -- They say he left for a distant country. *biquulu saafar la-blaad ᵊbʕiide.*
to **distill** - *qaṭṭar//tqaṭṭar.* Arrack is distilled from grapes. *l-ʕaraq biqaṭṭrúu mn ᵊl-ʕəneb.*
distillation - *taqṭiir.*
distillery - *maqṭara* pl. *maqaaṭer, maʕmal˜* (pl. *maʕaamel˜) taqṭiir.*
distinct - *waaḍeḥ.* There's a distinct difference between the two. *fii farᵊq waaḍeḥ been ᵊt-tneen.* -- I heard a very distinct noise in that room. *sməʕᵊt ḥəss ᵊktiir waaḍeḥ ᵊb-hal-ʔuuḍa.*
distinctive - *mmayyez.* It's a distinctive feature of that particular area. *hiyye ẓaahra mmayyze la-hal-manṭiqa.*
distinctly - *b-ᵊwḍuuḥ.* I told him distinctly not to come. *qəlt-ə́llo b-(kəll)ᵊwḍuuḥ maa yəži.*

**Would you please speak more distinctly. *Ƹmeel maƸruuf ʔəḥki b-ṣooṭ mafhuum ʔaktar.*
to **distinguish** - *mayyaz been, farraq been.* I can't distinguish the colors. *maa fiini mayyez been ᵊl-ʔalwaan.* -- I could hardly distinguish one twin from the other. *bᵊl-kaad farraqᵊt been fardet ᵊt-toom ᵊl-waaḥde, mn ᵊt-taanye.*
to distinguish oneself - *tmayyaz, mtaaz.* He distinguished himself by his courage. *tmayyaz ᵊb-šažaaƸto.*
distress - **1.** *šədde.* The Red Cross did everything to relieve the distress. *ṣ-ṣaliib ᵊl-ʔaḥmar Ƹəmel kəll žahdo la-yxaffef mən waṭʔet ᵊš-šədde.* **2.** *ḥaalet˜ yaʔᵊs.* The ship was in distress. *l-baaxra kaanet ᵊb-ḥaalet yaʔᵊs.* **3.** *hamm* pl. *hmuum, ġamm* pl. *ġmuum, karᵊb.* He caused his mother much distress. *sabbab la-ʔəmmo hamm w-ġamm.*
distress signal - *ʔišaaret˜* (pl. *-aat˜*) *ʔəstiraase, ʔišaaret˜ ʔəstənžaad.*
to distress - *daayaq.* My stomach's been distressing me. *ṣar-li mədde məƸᵊdti Ƹam ᵊddaayəqni.*
to **distribute** - *wazzaƸ//twazzaƸ.* The Red Crescent is distributing food to the population of the stricken area. *l-ᵊhlaal ᵊl-ʔaḥmar Ƹam ywazzeƸ ʔaġziye Ƹala ʔahaali l-manṭiqa l-muṣaabe.* -- The profits were evenly distributed. *l-ʔarbaaḥ ᵊtwazzaƸet bᵊt-tasaawi.*
district - **1.** *manṭiqa* pl. *manaaṭeq.* This is a very poor district. *hayy manṭiqa ktiir faqiire.* **2.** *manṭiqa* pl. *manaaṭeq, ḥayy* pl. *ʔaḥyaaʔ.* The city is divided into ten districts. *l-madiine maqsuume la-Ƹašᵊr manaaṭeq.* **3.** *qadaaʔ* pl. *ʔaqdiye.* Syria is divided into ten departments which, in turn, are subdivided into districts. *suuriyya mqassame la-Ƹašr ᵊmḥaafazaat w-haadool ᵊb-dooron ᵊmqassamiin la-ʔaqdiye.*
district attorney - see **public prosecutor.**
distrust - *suuʔ˜ ẓann, Ƹadam˜ siqa.* He's full of distrust for everyone and everything. *huwwe kəllo suuʔ ẓann bᵊd-dənye kəlla.*
to distrust - *maa wasaq (-yəsaq siqa) b-.* I distrust him. *maa bəsaq fii.*
to **disturb** - **1.** *zaƸaž (e ʔəzƸaaž//nzaƸaž).* Don't disturb the others! *laa təzƸež ᵊl-ġeer!* -- I'll just disturb you for a minute with this problem. *maa laḥa ʔəzᵊƸžak ʔaktar mən takke b-haš-šaġle.* -- I'm disturbed at that news. *ʔana mazƸuuž Ƹala hal-xabar.* **2.** *xarbaṭ//txarbaṭ.* Don't disturb these papers please. *laa txarbeṭ hal-ᵊwraaq mən fadlak.*
ditch - *xandaq* pl. *xanaadeq, ṭaaruuq* pl. *ṭawariiq.* The car got stuck in the ditch. *s-sayyaara Ƹəlqet bᵊl-xandaq.*
divan - *diiwaan* pl. *dawawiin, kanabe* pl. *-aat.*
dive - *ġaṭṣa* pl. *-aat.* Show me some more of your dives. *waržiini kam ġaṭṣa kamaan mən ġaṭṣaatak.*
to dive - **1.** *ġaṭaṣ (o ġaṭᵊṣ).* Don't be afraid to dive here. *laa txaaf təġṭoṣ hoon.* **2.** *ġaaṣ (u ġooṣ).* We'll be able to watch the submarine dive in about an hour. *baƸᵊd ḥawaali saaƸa fiina nətfarraž Ƹal-ġawwaaṣa w-hiyye Ƹam ᵊtġuuṣ.*
diver - **1.** *ġaṭṭaaṣ* pl. *-iin.* He's a diver on the Lebanese Olympic team. *huwwe ġaṭṭaaṣ bᵊl-fariiq ᵊl-ʔoləmbi l-ləbnaani.* **2.** *ġawwaaṣ* pl. *-iin.* Divers are searching for the drowned girl. *fii ġawwaaṣiin Ƹam ydawwru Ƹal-bənt ᵊl-ġarqaane.*
to **divide** - **1.** *tqaasam, qassam.* My partner and I divided the profits. *ʔana w-ᵊšriiki tqaasamna l-ʔarbaaḥ.* **2.** *qasam (e qəsme//nqasam), qassam.* Divide the total by four. *qseem ᵊl-mažmuuƸ Ƹala ʔarbƸa.* **3.** *qasam, qassam, žazzaʔ.* The book is divided into two parts. *l-ᵊktaab maqsuum la-qəsmeen* or *l-ᵊktaab ᵊmžazzaʔ žəzʔeen.* **4.** *wazzaƸ//twazzaƸ, farraq//tfarraq, qassam//tqassam.* The king divided the land among the peasants. *l-malek wazzaƸ ᵊl-ʔaraadi Ƹal-fallaaḥiin.* **5.** *tfarraƸ, nqasam.* At the end of the village the road divides. *b-ʔaaxer ᵊd-deeƸa ṭ-ṭariiq byətfarraƸ.* **6.** *tšaƸƸab, xtalaf.* Opinions are divided on that question. *l-ʔaaraaʔ mətšaƸƸbe b-hal-mawduuƸ.*
dividend - **1.** *maqsuum.* Multiply the dividend by four and divide the product by one hundred. *droob ᵊl-maqsuum ᵊb-ʔarbƸa w-ᵊqseem ᵊl-ḥaaṣel Ƹala miyye.* **2.** *faayde* pl. *fawaayed.* The company is paying high dividends. *š-šərke Ƹam tədfaƸ fawaayed Ƹaalye.*
divine - *ʔilaahi*.*
division - **1.** *qəsme* pl. *-aat, taqsiim* pl. *-aat.* A division of her estate will begin tomorrow. *qəsmet tərkə́ta btəbda bəkra.* **2.** *qəsme.* When are you going to take up division? *ʔeemta laḥa təbda tətƸallam ᵊl-qəsme?* **3.** *qəsᵊm* pl. *ʔaqsaam.* He works in another division. *byəštə́ġel ᵊb-qəsᵊm taani.* **4.** *fərqa* pl. *fəraq.* Ten divisions were destroyed. *fii Ƹašᵊr fəraq ᵊnsaḥqet.*
divisor - *l-maqsuum Ƹalée, qaasem.*
divorce - *ṭalaaq* pl. *-aat.* She's suing for divorce. *qaayme daƸwa ṭalaaq.*
to divorce - *ṭallaq//ṭṭallaq.* He divorced his wife several years ago. *ṭallaq marto mən kam səne.* -- She is divorced. *hiyye mṭallaqa.*
dizzy - *daayex.* I feel dizzy. *ḥaases ḥaali daayex.*
to **do** - **1.** *Ƹəmel (-yaƸmel Ƹamal//nƸamal), saawa// tsaawa.* Let him do it by himself. *xallíi yaƸməla la-ḥaalo.* -- What are you doing this afternoon? *šuu Ƹam ᵊtsaawi l-yoom baƸd ᵊd-dəhᵊr?* -- Do it for my sake. *Ƹməl-li-ydaha mənšaan xaaṭri.* -- What am I going to do with you? *šuu bəddi ʔaƸmel fiik?* -- They can't do a thing to him. *maa fiihon yaƸᵊmlúu-lo šii.* -- He does his duty. *byaƸmel waažbo.* -- I can't do more than forty miles an hour. *maa fiini ʔaƸmel ʔaktar mən ʔarbƸiin miil bᵊs-saaƸa.* **2.** *saawa// tsaawa.* My room hasn't been done yet. *ʔuuḍti ləssa maa tsaawet.* -- It takes her an hour to do her hair. *btaaxə́da saaƸa la-tsaawi šaƸra.* **3.** *kaffa, kafa (i kfaaye).* This roast will have to do for four people. *har-roosto laazem ykaffi ʔarbaƸt ənfos.* -- We'll have to make the money do. *laazem nxalli l-maṣaari tkaffi.* -- That'll do for now. *haada bikaffi bᵊl-waqt ᵊl-ḥaader.* -- This won't do, my friend! *haada maa bikaffi, yaa ṣaaḥbi.* -- Thank you, that will do nicely. *šəkran, byəkfi heek.* **4.** as auxiliary and pro-verb not to be translated: He doesn't work there any more. *maa Ƹaad Ƹam yəštə́ġel ᵊhniik.* -- Did you read today's paper? *qareet žariidt ᵊl-yoom?* -- Don't you want to come along? *maa bəddak təži maƸna?* -- But I did want to do it! *bass kaan bəddi saawiiha!* -- You do like it, don't you? *btəƸᵊžbak, muu heek?* -- He drinks whisky the way I do water. *byəšrab wəski metᵊl-ʔana-ma bəšrab mayy.*
**Let me introduce my friend Ali. — How do you do? *smaḥ-li qaddə́m-lak ṣaaḥbi Ƹali. — tšarrafna!*
**How do you do? I haven't seen you in a long time. *salaamaat! ṣaar zamaan maa šəftak.*
**What can I do for you? *šuu btəʔmor?* or *ʔamᵊr?* or *fii xədme?*
**That has nothing to do with the question. *maa-la Ƹalaaqa bᵊl-masʔale.*
**What has that to do with us? *šuu Ƹalaaqet haš-šii fiina?*
**That does it! I've had enough of his insolence. *hayy kasret ᵊž-žarra! ḥaažti baqa mən waqaaḥto.*
**That does it! Now we can turn to the next problem. *xalaṣna mənha! hallaq fiina nəndaar Ƹal-məšᵊkle t-taanye.*
**That did it, I fired him. *hayy kammalə́ta, w-qallaƸto.*
**We could do with a little more help. *maa mənquul šii ʔiza bišəḥḥ-ə́lna šwayyet ᵊmsaaƸade.*
do I, do you, etc., **don't I, don't you,** etc., **did(n't) I, did(n't) you,** etc. (= isn't that so?) - *muu heek?* He doesn't go, does he? *maa biruuḥ, muu heek?* -- You believe me, don't you? *Ƹam ᵊtsaddəqni, muu heek?* -- She wrote the letter, didn't she? *hiyye katbet ᵊl-maktuub, muu heek?*
to do away with - *ʔalġa//ltaġa.* They plan to do away with most of the requirements. *niyyə́ton yəlġu ʔaktar ᵊl-məṭṭallabaat.*
to do good - *faad (i ʔifaade), nafaƸ (a nafᵊƸ).* It won't do you much good to complain. *š-šakwa maa bətfiidak šii.* -- A vacation will do you lots of good. *šii fərṣa bətfiidak šii ktiir.*
to do harm - *ḍarr (ə ḍarar).* Will it do any harm if I leave it out? *biḍarr šii ʔiza ʔahmalta?* -- It did us more harm than good. *ḍarrətna ʔaktar maa nafƸətna.*
to do one's best - *Ƹəmel (-yaƸmel ø) žahdo.* I'll do my best to have it ready on time. *baƸmel žahdi ḥaddə́r-lak-ydaha Ƹal-waqᵊt.*
to do out of - *šallaḥ (mən).* He did me out of all my money. *šallaḥni (mən) kəll maṣariyyi.*
to do well - *ʔaqbal (-yʔaqbel ʔəqbaal).* The corn's doing well this year. *d-dəra mʔaqᵊble (mniiḥ) has-səne.*
**My sister is doing well. *ʔəxti maaši ḥaala l-ḥamdəlla.*
to do without - *staġna Ƹan, qaƸad (o ø) bala.* Can you do without this pencil for a while? *fiik*

təstağni *ɛan hal-qalam šwayye?* or *fiik təqɛod bala hal-qalam šwayye?*

dock - 1. *ḥooḍ* pl. *ʔaḥwaaḍ.* The ship has been in dry dock for the past two months. *s-safiine ṣar-la šahreen bᵊl-ḥooḍ ᵊž-žaaff.* **2.** *rṣiif* pl. *ʔarṣife.* I nearly fell off the dock. *kənt laḥa ʔəqaɛ mən ɛar-rṣiif.* **3.** *qaṭᵊɛ.* I had to take a dock in salary. *nžabarᵊt ʔəqbal qaṭɛ ᵊb-raatbi.*

to dock - 1. *rabaṭ (o rabᵊṭ), rasa (i rasu).* Where does the boat dock? *ween ᵊbtərboṭ ᵊl-baaxra?* **2.** *qaṭaɛ (a qaṭᵊɛ//nqaṭaɛ) ɛala.* I was fifteen minutes late, but they docked me for a whole hour. *tʔaxxarᵊt rəbᵊɛ saaɛa, qaamu qaṭaɛu ɛaliyyi saaɛa kaamle.*

doctor - 1. *doktoor* pl. *dakaatra, ḥakiim* pl. *ḥəkama, ṭabiib* pl. *ʔaṭəbba.* Please send for a doctor. *mən faḍlak ᵊṣraax la-doktoor.* 2. *doktoor* pl. *dakaatra.* He's a Doctor of Philosophy. *huwwe doktoor falsafe.*

to doctor up - *rootaš.* Do you think you can doctor up the text so no one will notice the mistakes right away? *bədḍənn fiik ᵊtrooteš ᵊn-naṣṣ ḥatta maa ḥada yšuuf ᵊl-ʔağlaaṭ la-ʔawwal wahle?*

doctorate - *doktoorḍa* (invar.).

document - *sanad* pl. *-aat, wasiiqa* pl. *wasaayeq.*

dodge - *barbuuke* pl. *barabiik.* What sort of dodge has he thought up now? *šuu l-barbuuke halli ṭəleɛ fiiha hallaq?*

to dodge - 1. *qaṣaɛ (a qaṣᵊɛ).* If I hadn't dodged, he would have hit me. *law-la maa qaṣaɛᵊt kaan ṣaabni.* **2.** *tmallaṣ mən.* He tried to dodge the question. *ḥaawal yətmallaṣ ᵊmn ᵊs-suʔaal.*

dog - *kalb* pl. *klaab.* Please take the dog out for a walk. *mən faḍlak xood ᵊl-kalb məšwaar.*

**He's going to the dogs. *ɛam yəfroṭ.*

dog tired - *halkaan (ᵊmn ᵊt-taɛab).* They were dog tired after the excursion. *kaanu halkaaniin ᵊmn ᵊl-məšwaar.*

to dog - *ləḥeq (a ləḥqaan).* He's been dogging my footsteps all day. *ṣar-lo laaḥəqni ɛad-daɛse ṭuul ᵊn-nhaar.*

doing - *ɛamal* pl. *ʔaɛmaal.* That must be his doing. *laazem ykuun haš-šii ɛamalo.*

doll - *ləɛbe* pl. *ləɛab.* She likes to play with dolls. *bətḥəbb təlɛab bᵊl-ləɛab.*

dollar - *dolaar* pl. *-aat, ryaal* pl. *-aat.*

dolled up - *maṭquum.* Where are you going all dolled up like that? *ween raayeḥ la-ḥatta maṭquum kəll haṭ-ṭaqme?*

dome - *qəbbe* pl. *qəbab.*

domestic - 1. *waṭani*.* Those are all domestic products. *hayy kəlla mantuužaat waṭaniyye.* **2.** *ɛaaʔili*.* Leave me out of your domestic problems. *laa ddaxxəlni b-mašaaklak ᵊl-ɛaaʔiliyye.* **3.** *ʔahli*, ʔaliif.* Of all the domestic animals I like the horse best. *mən kəll ᵊl-ḥaywaanaat ᵊl-ʔahliyye bḥəbb ʔaktar šii l-ᵊḥṣaan.*

**She's always been very domestic. *ṭuul ɛəmra beeta maɛbuuda* or *ṭuul ɛəmra ʔaḷḷa fooq w-beeta taḥᵊt.*

dominant - *saaʔed.*

domineering - *mətqamber, mətʔammer.*

to **donate** - *tbarraɛ b-.* I donated a dollar. *tbarraɛᵊt ᵊb-dolaar.*

donation - *tbarraɛ b-.* I donated a dollar. *tbarraɛᵊt mənraḥḥeb bᵊt-tabarruɛaat.*

to be **done - 1.** *xalaṣ (o ø).* All my lessons are done. *kəll ᵊdruusi xalaṣu.* -- Are you done with the ironing? *xalaṣti kawi?* **2.** *stawa.* In ten minutes the meat will be done. *baɛᵊd ɛašᵊr daqaayeq ᵊl-laḥme btəstəwi.*

to be done for - *raaḥet ɛala* + pron. suff. of subj. These tires are done for. *hal-kawašiik raaḥet ɛaleehon.* -- If the boss finds out about this I'm done for. *ʔiza dəri r-raʔiis ᵊb-haš-šağle raaḥet ɛaliyyi.*

done in - *manhuuk, halkaan.* I'm done in from working in this heat. *ʔana manhuuk ᵊmn ᵊš-šəğl ᵊb-haš-šoob.*

well-done - *məstəwi* mniiḥ.* I want the meat well-done. *bəddi l-laḥme məstwiyye mniiḥ.*

donkey - *ḥmaar* pl. *ḥamiir,* (female) *ḥmaara* pl. *ḥamiir,* (young one) *žaḥᵊš* f. *žaḥše* pl. *žḥaaš.*

door - *baab* pl. *bwaab.* Please open the door. *mən faḍlak ᵊftaaḥ ᵊl-baab.* -- Don't just stand in the door, come on in! *laa twaqqef ɛal-baab, fuut!*

**They live three doors from here. *saakniin taalet beet mən hoon.*

next door - *žamb˜* ... There's a laundry next door to us. *fii maṣbağa žambna.* -- Our next-door neighbor is a university professor. *žaarna (yalli) žambna ʔəstaaz žaamɛa.*

out of doors - *taḥt ᵊs-sama, barra.* Did you ever sleep out of doors? *b-ḥayaatak nəmᵊt taḥt ᵊs-sama?*

to show someone the door - *qallaɛ ḥada//tqallaɛ.* If he becomes insulting, show him the door. *ʔiza biṭawwel ᵊlsaano qallɛo.*

doorbell - *žaraṣ˜* (pl. *žraaṣ˜*) *baab.*

doorknob - *ṭaabet˜* (pl. *-aat˜*) *baab, masket˜* (pl. *-aat˜*) *baab.*

doorman - *bawwaab* pl. *-iin.*

door mat - *massaaḥa* pl. *-aat.*

dope - 1. *mxadder* pl. *-aat.* They were arrested for smuggling dope into the country. *waqqafuuhon la-ʔənnon ɛam yharrbu mxaddraat ləl-ᵊblaad.* **2.** *ḥmaar* pl. *ḥamiir.* That boy is a dope in school. *hal-walad ᵊḥmaar bᵊl-madrase.*

to dope - *bannaž.* They're saying he doped his horse for this race. *biquulu ʔənno bannaž ᵊḥṣaano la-has-sbaaq.*

dose - *žarɛa* pl. *-aat.* That's too big a dose for a child. *hayy žarɛa kbiire la-ṭəfᵊl.* -- Take it in small doses. *xədo ɛala žarɛaat ᵊẓğiire.*

dossier - *doosyée* pl. *doosyaat, malaff* pl. *-aat.*

dot - *nəqṭa* pl. *nəqaṭ.* Wear your dress with the blue dots. *lbəsi roobek ʔabu n-nəqaṭ ᵊz-zərᵊq.* -- Put three dots above the line. *ḥəṭṭ ᵊtlətt nəqaṭ fooq ᵊl-xaṭṭ.*

on the dot - *ɛat-takke, tamaam.* I'll see you at three on the dot. *bšuufak ᵊs-saaɛa tlaate ɛat-takke.*

right on the dot - *ɛad-daqiiqa.* He came right on the dot. *ʔəža ɛad-daqiiqa.*

dotted - *mnaqqaṭ.* Where did you buy that dotted scarf? *mneen štareet hal-ʔešarb l-ᵊmnaqqaṭ?*

double - 1. *məzwež, məžwez.* I can rent you a double room for ten pounds. *fiini ʔažžrak ʔuuḍa məzᵊwže b-ɛašᵊr leeraat.* **2.** *duubᵊl* (invar.). May I have a double portion of ice cream? *baḷḷa žəb-li ṣaḥᵊn buuẓa duubᵊl.* -- They charge double prices during the tourist season. *bidaffɛu ʔasɛaar duubᵊl b-muusem ᵊs-syaaḥa.* -- They pay double for overtime. *byədfaɛu duubᵊl barraat saaɛaat ᵊd-dawaam.* **3.** *ṭaaqeen, ɛala ṭaaqeen.* Fold the blanket double. *ʔəṭwi l-ᵊḥraam ṭaaqeen.* -- Sew it with a double thread. *xayyṭiiha b-xeeṭ ṭaaqeen.* **4.** *qadd˜ ... (b-)marrteen.* Your kitchen is double the size of mine. *maṭbaxak qadd maṭbaxi marrteen.* -- He makes double my salary. *biṭaaleɛ qadd maɛaaši marrteen.*

**He could be your double! *kaʔənno ṣuura ṭəbq ᵊl-ʔaṣᵊl ɛannak!*

doubles - *žooz žooz.* Let's play doubles. *xalliina nəlɛab žooz žooz.*

on the double - *rkiid.* Tell him to get here on the double. *qəl-lo yəži la-hoon rkiid.*

to double - 1. *ḍaaɛaf, doobal.* He's doubled his capital in two years. *ḍaɛaf rəsmaalo b-sənteen.* **2.** *dabal (o/e dabᵊl//ndabal).* He doubled my bid. *dabalni.*

to double up - *ṭaɛaž (a ṭaɛᵊž) šaqᵊfteen, tkaɛwak.* He doubled up with pain. *ṭaɛaž šaqᵊfteen mn ᵊl-wažaɛ.*

**We had to double up because there weren't enough beds to go around. *nžabarna nnaam məžᵊwziin laʔənno maa kaan fii txuut ᵊkfaaye.*

double-breasted - *b-ṣaffeen ᵊzraar.* He wore a double-breasted suit. *kaan laabes badle b-ṣaffeen ᵊzraar.*

doubt - *šakk* pl. *škuuk, reeb, riibe.* Do you have any doubts? *fii ɛandak ʔayy šakk?* -- There's no doubt about it. *maa fiiha šakk.*

in doubt - 1. *maškuuk fii.* The result is still in doubt. *n-natiiže ləssaaha maškuuk fiiha.* **2.** *šaakek, mšakkek.* If you're in doubt, ask your brother. *ʔiza kənᵊt šaakek, sʔaal ʔaxuuk.*

no doubt - *biduun šakk, bala šakk, maa fii šakk.* No doubt the train will be late. *biduun šakk ᵊt-treen laḥa yətʔaxxar.*

without a doubt - *biduun ʔayy šakk, bala šakk, maa fii šakk.* Without a doubt he's the best man for the job. *biduun ʔayy šakk huwwe ʔaṣlaḥ waaḥed ləš-šağle.*

to doubt - *šakk (ə šakk) b-.* I doubt if the story is true. *bšəkk ʔiza kaanet ᵊl-qəṣṣa ṣaḥiiḥa.* -- I don't doubt it in the least. *maa bšəkk fiiha məṭlaqan.*

doubtful - 1. *šaakek, mšakkek.* I'm still doubtful about being able to go. *ləssaani šaakek ʔiza b-ʔəmkaani ruuḥ.* **2.** *muriib.* He told us a pretty doubtful story to explain his absenc . *xabbarna qəṣṣa muriibe šwayye ɛan ʔasbaab ğyaabo.*

**It's doubtful if he'll get well. *fii šakk ʔiza biṭiib.*
doubtless – *biduun šakk, bala šakk, maa fii šakk.*
dough – 1. *ɛažiin(e)* pl. *-aat,* (bread ~) *ɛažne* pl. *-aat.* The dough has to be allowed to rise first. *l-ɛažiin bəl-ʔawwal laazmo waqət la-yənfoš.* 2. *ɛəmle.* Think of all the dough we can make in this deal. *ftəker qaddeeš fiina nsaawi ɛəmle b-haš-šaġle.*
dove – *ḥamaame* coll. *ḥamaam* pl. *-aat.*
down – *zaġab.* This pillow is filled with down. *hal-əmxadde məḥšiyye zaġab.*
down – 1. *taḥət.* Do you see the house down at the foot of the hill? *šaayef əl-beet yalli taḥət b-səfl ət-talle?* -- Did you look down there? *ṭṭallaɛət taḥt əhniik?* -- Who's that down there? *miin haada yalli taḥət?* 2. *naazel.* The prices are down now. *l-ʔasɛaar naazle hallaq.*
**The sun is down. *ġarbet əš-šaməs.*
**Wait till the wind is down a little. *stanna ḥatta yəhda l-hawa šwayye.*
**They live just two houses down the hill. *saakniin baɛəd beeteen bass bən-naazel.*
**The ring disappeared down the drain. *l-xaatem raaḥ bəl-balluuɛa.*
**Down with imperialism! *fal-yasqoṭ əl-ʔəstəɛmaar!*
**Why is he so down in the mouth? *šəbo hal-qadd xaayre ɛazaaymo?*
**They are down and out now. *kan-lon ʔiyyaam ɛəzz əmžaah.*
from ... on down – *mən ... w-naazel.* The whole government is corrupt from the President on down. *l-əḥkuume kəlla faasde mn ər-raʔiis w-naazel.*
up and down – 1. *sərri mərri.* He was walking up and down the room. *kaan maaši sərri mərri bəl-ʔuuḍa.* 2. *ṭaaleɛ naazel.* Stop running up and down those stairs! *ḥaaštak ṭaaleɛ naazel ɛala had-daraž!* -- When the plane hit the storm it began to dance up and down. *lamma ṭ-ṭayyaara waažahet əl-ɛaaṣfe ṣaaret təlɛab ṭaalɛa naazle.* -- The man kept moving the lantern up and down. *z-zalame tamm ylawweḥ bəl-faanuus ṭaaleɛ naazel.* 3. *mən fooq la-taḥət.* He looked her up and down. *ṭṭallaɛ ɛaleeha mən fooq la-taḥət.*
to down – 1. *karwaɛ.* He downed his beer and ran outside. *karwaɛ biirto w-ṭəleɛ ərkiid.* 2. *nazzal.* Our squadron downed three airplanes in this afternoon's battle. *sərəbna nazzal tlətt ṭayyaaraat b-maɛrakt əl-yoom baɛd əḍ-ḍəhər.*
downgrade – *nazle* pl. *-aat.* The road has a steep downgrade. *ṭ-ṭariiq ʔəlo nazle qawiyye.*
to be on the downgrade – *ddahwar.* Their company's business appears to be on the downgrade. *ẓ-ẓaaher ʔənno ʔašġaal šərkəton ɛam təddahwar.*
to downgrade – *nazzal//tnazzal.* He would rather resign than be downgraded. *bifaḍḍel yəstaqiil ɛan ʔənno yətnazzal.* -- They've downgraded the project from "high priority" to routine business. *nazzalu l-mašruuɛ mən "muhəmm žəddan" la-šii ɛaadi.*
downhearted – *xaayer~ əl-ɛazaayem.* He looks downhearted. *mbayyen ɛalée xaayer əl-ɛazaayem* (or *xaayre ɛazaaymo*).
downhill – *bən-nzuul.* Don't shift into neutral going downhill. *laa tboomer bən-nzuul.*
down payment – *raɛbuun* pl. *raɛabiin.*
downpour – *zaxxa* pl. *-aat.* We were caught in the downpour. *ɛləqna taḥt əz-zaxxa.*
downstairs – 1. *taḥət.* I'll be waiting downstairs. *laḥa ʔəstanna taḥət.* 2. *la-taḥət.* Go downstairs and get it. *nzeel la-taḥət w-žiiba.* 3. *mən ɛad-daraž.* He tripped and fell downstairs. *tfarkaš w-wəqeɛ mən ɛad-daraž.* 4. *taḥtaani*.* The downstairs apartment is vacant. *l-ʔabarṭmaan ət-taḥtaani faaḍi.*
downtown – 1. *ɛal-əmdiine, ɛal-balad.* Let's go downtown. *xalliina nruuḥ* (or *nənzel*) *ɛal-əmdiine.* 2. *bəl-balad.* He's downtown right now. *huwwe bəl-balad hallaq.*
**The downtown section is very crowded in the late afternoon. *qalb əl-balad bikuun əktiir maɛžuuq baɛd əl-ɛaṣr.*
doze – *ġafwe* pl. *-aat, sahwe* pl. *-aat.* I think I'll take a little doze. *fəkri ʔaaxéd-li šii ġafwe ẓġiire.*
to doze – *səhi (a sahwe).* I've just been dozing. *kənt sahyaan bass.*
to doze off – *kaba (i kabi).* He dozed off after supper. *kaba baɛd əl-ɛaša.*
dozen – *dazziine* pl. *-aat.*
draft – 1. *kurandeer* pl. *-aat.* I can't stand the draft in this room. *maa fiini ʔəthammal əl-kurandeer b-hal-ʔuuḍa.* 2. *mažra~ hawa, kurandeer.* The fire went out because there wasn't enough draft. *ṇ-ṇaaṛ ənṭafet laʔənno maa kaan fii mažra hawa kfaaye.* 3. *maṣraf~* (pl. *maṣaaref~*) *hawa.* Did you open the draft of the furnace? *fataḥət maṣraf əl-hawa tabaɛ l-əwžaaq?* 4. *məswadde* pl. *-aat.* The first draft is ready. *ʔawwal məswadde ḥaaḍra.* 5. *ḥawaale* pl. *-aat, taḥwiil* pl. *taḥawiil.* Our bank wrote us a draft for the balance. *ḅankna katəb-əlna ḥawaale bər-raṣiid.* 6. *taǰniid.* I'm no longer eligible for the draft. *maa ɛədt ṣaaleḥ lət-taǰniid.*
drafting board – *looḥ~* (pl. *lwaaḥ~*) *rasəm.*
to draft – 1. *daɛa (i daɛwe//ndaɛa) ləl-xədme.* The army intends to draft 5,000 men next month. *ž-žeeš naawi yədɛi ləl-xədme xaməst aalaaf nafar bəš-šahr əl-qaadem.* 2. *sawwad//tsawwad.* I'm going to help you draft the letter. *bəddi saaɛdak b-taswiid əl-maktuub.* 3. *xaṭṭaṭ, rasam (o rasəm// nrasam).* The architect is drafting a new floor plan. *l-əmhandes ɛam yxaṭṭeṭ xariiṭa ždiide ləl-bina.*
draftboard – *mažles~* (pl. *mažaales~*) *ǰərɛa.*
draftsman – *rassaam* pl. *-e* and *-iin.*
drafty – *məhwi.* It's a drafty place. *l-maḥall məhwi.*
to drag – 1. *šaḥaṭ (a šaḥəṭ//nšaḥaṭ).* I had to drag the trunk into the house myself. *nžabarət ʔəšḥaṭ əs-sanduuq la-žuwwaat əl-beet la-ḥaali.* 2. *žarr (ə žarr//nžarr).* Everytime I want to go somewhere, I have to drag my little brother along. *kəll-ma bəddi ruuḥ la-šii maḥall bənžəber žərr ʔaxi ẓ-ẓġiir maɛi.* 3. *žaržar.* He could hardly drag himself to work. *bəz-zoor qəder yžaržer ḥaalo ləš-šəġəl.* -- Your coat is dragging on the floor. *kabbuudak ɛam yžaržer ɛal-ʔarḍ.* 4. *maṭmaṭ.* Time drags when you don't have anything to do. *l-waqət bimaṭmeṭ lamma maa bikuun fii ɛandak šii tsaawi.*
**They dragged the river for the body. *fattašu ṇ-ṇahṛ bəš-šabakaat ɛaž-žəsse.*
to drag on – *maṭṭ (ə maṭṭ).* The meeting dragged on for three hours. *l-ʔəžtimaaɛ maṭṭ tlətt saaɛaat.*
**The days just dragged on. *l-ʔiyyaam žaržaret baɛḍa l-baɛḍ.*
drain – 1. *balluuɛa* pl. *balaliiɛ.* The drain is stopped up again. *l-balluuɛa nṣaṭmet taani marra.* 2. *ʔəstənzaaf.* It means a terrible drain on our natural resources. *haada maɛnaato ʔəstənzaaf faẓiiɛ la-mawaarədna ṭ-ṭabiiɛiyye.*
to drain – 1. *faḍḍa.* They drained the swimming pool only yesterday. *bass əmbaareḥ faḍḍu baḥret əs-sbaaḥa.* 2. *stanzaf.* The Government's wild spending has drained the Treasury of its capital reserves. *maṣariif l-əḥkuume l-haaʔile stanzafet əl-ʔamwaal əl-ʔəḥtiyaaṭiyye b-əxzaanet əd-doole.* 3. *nazz (ə nazz).* This wound hasn't been draining properly. *haž-žərəḥ maa ɛam ynəzz əmniiḥ.* 4. *ṣarraf.* The water drains into the reservoir. *l-ṃayy bətṣarref ləl-ḥaawuuẓ.*
to drain off – *ṣarraf.* The water doesn't drain off. *l-ṃayy maa-la ɛam ətṣarref.*
drainage – *taṣriif.*
drama – *draama* pl. *-aat.*
dramatic – *draamatiiki*.*
drastic – *ṣaarem, šadiid.* Only drastic measures can put an end to that. *bass tadabiir ṣaarme məmken twaqqef haš-šii.*
draw – *taɛaadol.* The wrestling match ended in a draw. *mbaaraat l-əmṣaaraɛa ntahet bət-taɛaadol* (or **ntahet kiit*).
to draw – 1. *rasam (o/e rasəm//nrasam).* He draws best with crayons. *byərsom ʔaḥsan šii b-əqlaam talwiin.* 2. *saḥab (a saḥəb//nsaḥab).* He drew a winning number. *saḥab nəmre raabḥa.* -- Draw a deep breath. *sḥaab nafas ġamiiq.* 3. *žalab (e žaləb// nžalab), žazab (o žazəb//nžazab).* The concert is sure to draw a big crowd. *l-konseer ʔakiid laḥa yəžleb žamɛ əkbiir.* 4. *ṭaalaɛ, saḥab, qabaḍ (a qabəḍ).* They draw good wages. *biṭaalɛu ʔžuuraat məḥtárame.* 5. *ṭaalaɛ.* My investments draw five percent interest. *tawẓiif maṣariyyi biṭaaləɛ-li xamse bəl-miyye (faayde).*
**You have to draw the line somewhere. *haš-šii laazem yənwəḍəɛ-lo ḥadd.*
**Draw your own conclusions from that! *stantež halli bəddak-yáa mən haš-šii!*
**The meeting is drawing to a close. *l-ʔəžtimaaɛ qarrab yəxloṣ.*

to draw into - 1. *faat (u foote) la-* and *Eala.* The train is just drawing into the station. *t-treen hallaq Eam yfuut Eal-ᵊmḥaṭṭa.* 2. *žarr (ə žarr// nžarr) la-, warraṭ//twarraṭ b-.* I've been drawn into this argument against my will. *nžarreet la-hal-ᵊmžaadale ġaṣban Eanni.*

to draw out - 1. *saḥab (a saḥᵊb//nsaḥab).* I'll have to draw out fifty dollars from the bank. *laazem ʔəsḥab xamsiin dolaar mn ᵊl-bank.* 2. *stadraž, stazlaq, ḥakka.* See if you can draw him out. *šuuf ʔiza fiik təstadᵊržo.*

to draw up - 1. *rasam (o/e rasᵊm//nrasam).* Who drew up the plan? *miin rasam ᵊl-xəṭṭa?* 2. *naẓẓam// tnaẓẓam, rattab//trattab, ḥaḍḍar//tḥaḍḍar, hayyaʔ// thayyaʔ.* I'll draw up the report. *ʔana bnaẓẓem ᵊt-taqriir.*

drawer - *dərž* pl. *druuž(e).* My passport is in the top drawer. *l-basboor tabaEi bᵊd-dərž ᵊl-fooqaani.*

drawers - *kalsoon* pl. *-aat, lbaas* pl. *-aat.*

drawing - *rasme* pl. *-aat.*

drawn - *saalet.* His face looked drawn. *wəššo mbayyen Ealée saalet.*

dread - *xoof.* I have a dread of doctors. *ḥaakəmni xoof mn ᵊd-dakaatra.*

to dread - *xaaf (a xoof//nxaaf) mən.* I dread the dark. *bxaaf mn ᵊl-Eatme.*

dreadful - 1. *faẓiiE, mərEeb.* Have you heard the dreadful news? *smeEt ᵊl-xabar ᵊl-faẓiiE?* 2. *faẓiiE, məzri*, mhargal.* She wears dreadful clothes. *btəlbes ʔawaaEi faẓiiEa.*

dream - *manaam* pl. *-aat, ḥəlᵊm* pl. *ʔaḥlaam.* I had a funny dream last night. *šəfᵊt manaam ġariib leelt ᵊmbaareḥ.* -- None of my childhood dreams has come true. *w-laa ḥəlᵊm mən ʔaḥlaam ᵊṭfuulti tḥaqqaq.*

to dream - *ḥəlem (a ḥəlᵊm).* Last night I dreamed that I was home. *mbaarḥa ḥləmᵊt ʔənni kənt maE ʔahli.* -- I wouldn't dream of doing it. *maa bəḥlam b-ᵊmsaawaata.* -- I've been dreaming of this for a long time. *ṣar-li bəḥlam b-haš-šii mən zamaanaat.*

to dream up - *ṭəleE (a ø) b-.* I wonder what he's going to dream up next. *maa-li Earfaan yaa-tara b-ʔeeš laḥa yəṭlaE ᵊl-marra ž-žaaye.*

dreary - 1. *kaʔiib.* It was an awfully dreary day. *kaan nhaar ᵊktiir kaʔiib.* 2. *mġəmm.* We went to a real dreary movie. *kənna b-fəlᵊm ktiir ᵊmġəmm.*

dress - 1. *roob* pl. *rwaab, fəṣṭaan* pl. *faṣaṭiin.* She wants to buy a new dress. *bədda təštəri roob ᵊždiid.* 2. *libaas, ʔálbise* (pl.). We have to be in full military dress for the dinner. *laazem ᵊnkuun b-libaas Easkari rasmi mənšaan ᵊl-Eaša.*

to dress - 1. *labbas//tlabbas.* Mother is just dressing the baby. *maama Eam ᵊtlabbes ᵊl-beebée.* 2. *ləbes (e ləbᵊs).* I'll dress quickly. *laḥa ʔəlbes ᵊb-Eažale.* -- His wife dresses in good taste. *marto btəlbes ᵊb-zooq ᵊktiir.* 3. *rattab//trattab.* They dress the store windows in the evening. *birattbu l-waažhaat ᵊl-masa.* 4. *ḍammad//ḍḍammad.* Did you dress the wound? *ḍámmadṭ ᵊž-žərᵊḥ?*

to dress up - *ṭaqam (o ṭaqᵊm) ḥaalo, nṭaqam, handam ḥaalo, thandam.* Look at him, all dressed up! *šuufo qaddeeš maṭquum!*

dresser - *biiro* pl. *biiroyaat, dreswaar* pl. *-aat.* The new handkerchiefs are on the dresser. *l-maḥaarem ᵊž-ždiide Eal-biiro.*

dressing - 1. *ḥašwe* pl. *-aat.* They served roast duck with a dressing of chestnuts and apples. *qaddamu baṭṭ ᵊmḥammar maE ḥašwet kastana w-təffaaḥ.* 2. *ḍmaaḍ* pl. *-aat.* The nurse changes his dressing every morning. *l-ᵊmmarrḍa bətġayyér-lo ḍmaaḍo kəll yoom Eala bəkra.* 3. *ṣalṣa* pl. *-aat.* Do we have a choice of dressings for our salad? *fiina naxtaar mən taškiilet ṣalṣaat ləṣ-ṣalaṭa tabaEna?*

dressing gown - *roob-də-šaambᵊr* pl. *rwaab-də-šaambᵊr.*

dressing table - *twaleet* pl. *-aat.*

dressmaker - *xayyaaṭa* pl. *-aat.*

dress rehearsal - *broova* (pl. *-aat*) *nihaaʔiyye.*

dress suit - *badle* (pl. *-aat*) *rasmiyye.*

drier - *ʔaalet˜* (pl. *-aat˜*) *tanšiif.* Put the clothes in the drier. *ḥəṭṭ ᵊl-ġasiil b-ʔaalet ᵊt-tanšiif.*

drift - 1. *maġza* pl. *maġaazi, marma* pl. *maraami, ʔəttižaah* pl. *-aat.* I couldn't get the drift of his speech. *maa fhəmᵊt maġza xiṭaabo.* 2. *mansaf* pl. *manaasef.* His shoe came off in a drift of sand. *fardet ṣabbaaṭo nšalḥet ᵊb-mansaf ramᵊl.*

to drift - 1. *nsaaq bᵊt-tayyaar.* They drifted in the open sea for days. *nsaaqu bᵊt-tayyaar ᵊb-Earḍ ᵊl-baḥᵊr ʔiyyaam w-ʔiyyaam.* 2. *məši (i məši) maE ᵊt-tayyaar.* They haven't got any clear-cut policy, they're just drifting along. *maa fii Eandon syaase marsuume, maašyiin maE ᵊt-tayyaar w-bass.*

**People have been drifting in and out of my office all day. *ṣar-lon ᵊn-naas Eam yfuuto w-yəṭlaEu mən maktabi ṭuul ᵊn-nhaar.*

drill - 1. *madqab* pl. *madaaqeb.* The mechanic needs another drill. *l-miikaniiki laazmo madqab taani.* 2. *tamriin* pl. *-aat* and *tamariin.* She is going to give us a drill in Arabic verb forms today. *laḥa taEṭiina tamriin bᵊl-ʔafEaal ᵊl-Earabiyye l-yoom.* 3. *tadriib* pl. *-aat* and *tadariib.* His platoon is having a drill this afternoon. *faṣiilto fii Eanda tadriib ᵊl-yoom baEd ᵊḍ-ḍəhᵊr.*

to drill - 1. *naqqab.* They're drilling for oil in that area. *Eam ynaqqbu Eaz-zeet b-hal-manṭiqa.* 2. *ḥafar (e ḥafᵊr//nḥafar).* The dentist has to drill this tooth. *ḥakiim l-ᵊsnaan laazem yəḥfer has-sənn.* 3. *marran.* Our teacher drilled us in arithmetic. *ʔəstaazna marranna bᵊl-ᵊḥsaab.* 4. *ddarrab, tmarran.* The soldiers drill every day. *l-Easkar byəddarrabu kəll yoom.*

to drill a hole in - *baxaš (o/e baxᵊš//nbaxaš).* Drill a hole in the board. *bxooš ᵊl-looḥ ᵊl-xašab.*

drink - 1. *šərbe* pl. *-aat.* May I have a drink of water? *məmken taEṭiini šərbet mayy?* 2. *mašruub* pl. *-aat.* What kind of drinks have you? *šuu l-mašruubaat halli Eandak?* 3. *qadaḥ* pl. *qdaaḥ.* I only had three drinks. *šrəbᵊt tlətt ᵊqdaaḥ bass.* -- May I offer you a drink? *btaaxə́d-lak qadaḥ?* 4. *šərᵊb, səkᵊr.* Drink has ruined his health. *š-šərᵊb xarə́b-lo ṣaḥḥto.*

to drink - *šəreb (a šərᵊb//nšarab).* Drink plenty of water! *šraab mayy ᵊktiir!* -- He drinks a lot more than he did a year ago. *hallaq Eam yəšrab ʔaktar b-ᵊktiir mən Eaamnawwal.* -- Let's drink to your return! *xalliina nəšrab la-ražᵊEtak bᵊs-salaame!* -- I drink to your health. *bəšrab naxᵊb ṣaḥḥtak* or *bəšrab Eala ṣaḥḥtak.*

drip - *tanqiiṭ.* The plumber is supposed to fix that drip in the faucet. *l-ḥaddaad mafruuḍ fii yṣalleḥ hat-tanqiiṭ bᵊl-ḥanafiyye.*

to drip - 1. *naqqaṭ.* The faucet is dripping. *l-ḥanafiyye Eam ᵊtnaqqeṭ.* 2. *dalaf (o dalᵊf), naqqaṭ.* Water dripped from the roof for an hour. *l-mayy dalfet mn ᵊl-ʔəṣṭuuḥ saaEa.*

**When he got home, he was dripping wet. *waqᵊt wəṣel Eal-beet kaanet ᵊl-mayy Eam ᵊdzarzeb mən dyaalo.*

drive - 1. *məšwaar* (pl. *mašaawiir*) *bᵊs-sayyaara.* We took a nice drive. *Eməlna məšwaar bᵊs-sayyaara ḥəlu.* 2. *ḥamle* pl. *-aat.* In the last drive we raised five hundred dollars. *bᵊl-ḥamle l-ʔaaxraaniyye žamaEna xamᵊs miit dolaar.* 3. *traksyoon.* Our car has front-wheel drive. *sayyaarətna ʔəla traksyoon qəddaamaani.*

to drive - 1. *saaq (u swaaqa//nsaaq).* Can you drive a truck? *btaEref tsuuq kamyoon?* -- He drove very carefully. *saaq ᵊb-taʔanni.* -- Drive the horses over to the left. *suuq ᵊl-ʔəḥᵊṣne naaḥ ᵊš-šmaal.* 2. *raaḥ (u rooḥa) bᵊs-sayyaara.* We're going to drive out there next Sunday. *laḥa nruuḥ bᵊs-sayyaara la-hniik ᵊl-ʔaḥad ᵊž-žaaye.* 3. *waṣṣal ... bᵊs-sayyaara.* I'll drive you there. *bwaṣṣlak la-hniik bᵊs-sayyaara.* 4. *dafaE (a dafᵊE//ndafaE) la-.* Hunger drove him to stealing. *ž-žuuE dafaEo ləs-sərqa.* 5. *ḥass (e ḥass//nḥass).* The foreman drives his workers continually. *l-ᵊmnaaẓer biḥəss Eəmmaalo Eala ṭuul.* 6. *fawwat//tfawwat.* Drive the nail into the wall. *fawwet ᵊl-bəsmaar bᵊl-ḥeeṭ.* 7. *ḥaraf (e ḥarᵊf//nḥaraf).* The boat was driven off its course. *l-markab ᵊnḥaraf Ean mažṛa.*

**Let's drive out into the country. *xalliina naEməl-lna məšwaar bᵊs-sayyaara bᵊl-fala.*

**What are you driving at? *šuu Eam təqṣoḍ?*

**You'll drive me crazy yet. *ləssa bədžannənni.*

to drive around - *daar (u doora) bᵊs-sayyaara.* We just drove around in town. *bass dərna bᵊl-balad bᵊs-sayyaara.*

to drive away - *qallaE//tqallaE.* Drive the dog away. *qalleE ᵊl-kalb.*

**I shouted, but he drove away. *Eayyaṭᵊt bass saaq w-məši.*

to drive back - 1. *radd (ə radd//rtadd).* We drove the enemy back across the river. *raddeena l-Eaduww la-wara n-nahᵊr.* 2. *ražžaE... bᵊs-sayyaara.* Can you drive me back to town? *fiik ᵊtražžəEni Eal-balad bᵊs-sayyaara?*

driver - 1. *sawwaaq* pl. *-iin, sawwiiq* pl. *-iin.* He's a good driver. *huwwe sawwaaq šaaṭer.* 2. *šofoor* pl. *šoferiyye.* The cab driver charged us too much.

šofoor ᵊt-taksi daffaᶓna ktiir ᵊktiir. **3.** *ᶓarbaži* pl. *-iyye.* The driver lost control of the horses. *l-ᶓarbaži fəltet mənno l-ʔəḥᵊṣne.*

driver's license - *šahaadet˜* (pl. *-aat˜*) *swaaqa.*

drive shaft - *transməsyoon* pl. *-aat, ᶓaamuud˜* (pl. *ᶓawamiid˜*) *tašġiil.*

drizzle - *baxxa* pl. *-aat.* I've been standing in this drizzle for an hour. *ṣar-li waaqef taḥt hal-baxxa saaᶓa.*

to drizzle - *baxx (ə baxx), baxbax.* It's been drizzling all day. *ṣar-la ᶓam ᵊtbəxx ṭuul ᵊn-nhaar.*

to **drool** - *šattet (ə ø) ryaalto.* The dog's drooling all over the rug. *l-kalb ᶓam ᵊtšətt ryaalto ᶓas-səžžaade kəlla.*

to **droop** - **1.** *dəbel (a dabalaan).* The flowers are beginning to droop. *l-ᵊwruud ᶓam yəbdu yədbalu.* -- We rested under the drooping branches of a willow. *strəḥna taḥᵊt ʔaġṣaan ṣəfṣaaf ᵊd-dablaane.* **2.** *salat (o ø).* He has drooping shoulders. *ktaafo saalte.*

drop - **1.** *nəqṭa* pl. *nəqaṭ.* Take three drops in a glass of water. *xood tlətt nəqaṭ ᵊb-kaaset mayy.* **2.** *hbuuṭ.* We've had a drop in enrollment this year. *kaan fii ᶓanna hbuuṭ b-nəsbet ᵊl-ʔəntisaab has-səne.* **3.** *nazle.* There is a drop of fifteen feet to the ground. *fii nazle ġəmqa xamᵊṣṭaᶓšar qadam ləl-ʔarḍ.*

**He'll give you a lecture at the drop of a hat. *byaᶓməl-lak ᵊmḥaaḍara ᶓala daqra.*

to drop - **1.** *waqeᶓ (-yəqaᶓ wquuᶓ).* The box dropped out of the window. *l-ᶓəlbe waqᶓet mn ᵊš-šəbbaak la-barra.* **2.** *nəzel (e nzuul), habaṭ (o hbuuṭ).* The temperature dropped very rapidly. *l-ḥaraara nəzlet b-sərᶓa faẓiiᶓa.* **3.** *nhaar, waqeᶓ ᶓal-ʔarḍ.* Some of them dropped from exhaustion. *baᶓḍon nhaaru mən šəddet ᵊt-taᶓab.* **4.** *waqqaᶓ.* You dropped something. *waqqaᶓᵊt šii* or ***waqeᶓ mənnak šii.* **5.** *rama (i rami//nrama).* The planes dropped supplies behind our lines. *ṭ-ṭayyaaraat ramet ᵊmᶓəddaat wara xṭuuṭna.* -- Please drop this card in the (letter) box. *mən faḍlak ᵊrmii-li hal-kart bosṭaal ᵊb-sanduuq ᵊl-boosṭa.* **6.** *tarak (e/o tarᵊk//ntarak), daššar//ddaššar.* Let's drop the subject! *xalliina nətrek ᵊl-mawḍuuᶓ!* **7.** *nazzal.* Please drop me at the corner. *mən faḍlak nazzəlni ᶓas-suuke.* **8.** *faṣal (e faṣᵊl//nfaṣal).* I'll be dropped from the club. *laḥa ʔənfəṣel mən ᵊn-naadi.*

to drop in (at) - *maraq (o ø) ᶓala, marr (ə ø) ᶓala.* Drop in to see me tomorrow. *mrooq ᶓaliyyi bəkra.*

to drop off - *laḥaš (o laḥᵊš//nlaḥaš).* Can you drop this off at the tailor's for me? *fiik təlḥəš-li-ydaha ᶓand ᵊl-xayyaaṭ?*

**I dropped off to sleep immediately. *nəmᵊt b-laḥẓəta.*

to drop a hint - *lammaḥ.* She dropped a hint that she wanted to go. *lammaḥet ʔənno bədda truuḥ.*

to drop a line - *katab (o ø) kəlᵊmteen.* If possible, drop me a line. *ʔiza məmken ktəb-li kəlᵊmteen.*

to drop to one's knees - *naxx (ə naxx) ᶓala rəkabo.* She dropped to her knees to pick it up. *naxxet ᶓala rəkᵊba la-tqiima.*

dropper - *qaṭṭaara* pl. *-aat.*

drought - *maḥᵊl, žafaaf.* The drought was bad for the wheat crop. *l-maḥᵊl ḍarr maḥṣuul ᵊl-qamᵊḥ.*

drove - *sərbe* pl. *sərab.* People came in droves. *n-naas ʔəžu sərab sərab.*

to **drown** - **1.** *ġəreq (a ġaraq).* He drowned in the river. *ġəreq bᵊn-nahᵊr.* **2.** *ġarraq.* I couldn't drown the kittens. *maa ḥsənᵊt ġarreq ᵊl-qaṭaaṭ ᵊẓ-ẓġaar.*

to drown out - *ṭaġa (i ṭaġi) ᶓala.* The noise drowned out his words. *ḍ-ḍooše ṭaġet ᶓala kalaamo.*

drowsiness - *nᶓaas.*

drowsy - *naᶓsaan.* I feel drowsy in the afternoon. *bḥəss ḥaali naᶓsaan baᶓd ᵊḍ-ḍəhᵊr.*

to get drowsy - *nəᶓes (a naᶓas).* I'm getting drowsy. *ᶓam ʔənᶓas.*

to make drowsy - *naᶓᶓas.* A heavy dinner always makes me drowsy. *daayman ᵊl-ᶓaša t-tqiil binaᶓᶓəsni.*

drug - **1.** *dawa* pl. *ʔədᵊwye.* This drug is sold only on prescription. *had-dawa maa byənbaaᶓ ʔəlla b-raažeeta.* **2.** *mxadder* pl. *-aat.* He became addicted to drugs. *ṣaar mədmen ᶓal-ᵊmxaddraat.*

to drug - *xaddar//txaddar, bannaž//tbannaž.* The doctor drugged him to ease the pain. *d-doktoor xaddaro la-yxaffef ᵊl-wažaᶓ.*

drugstore - see **pharmacy.**

drum - **1.** *ṭabᵊl* pl. *ṭbuul(e),* (elongated, open at one end) *dərbakke* pl. *-aat.* Can you hear the drums? *saameᶓ ᵊṭ-ṭbuule?* -- They were beating the drums all night. *kaanu ᶓam ydəqqu ṭ-ṭbuule ṭuul ᵊl-leel.* **2.** *barmiil* pl. *baramiil.* They unloaded six drums of gasoline. *nazzalu təsᵊᶓ baramiil banziin.*

to drum - **1.** *ṭaqṭaq.* Please stop drumming on the table! *ḥaaštak ᵊṭṭaqṭeq ᶓaṭ-ṭaawle baḷḷa!* **2.** *basmar//tbasmar (b-).* These rules have been drummed into me. *hal-qawaaᶓed tbasmaret fiyyi.*

to drum up - *lamlam.* He's trying to drum up votes. *ᶓam yḥaawel ylamlem ʔaṣwaaṭ.*

drumbeat - *daqq˜ ᵊṭbuul.*

drummer - *daqqiiq˜ ṭabᵊl* pl. *daqqiiqet˜ ṭbuul.*

drunk - *sakraan* pl. *-iin.* Was that drunk annoying you? *has-sakraan kaan ᶓam ydaayqak šii?* -- Is he drunk again? *šuu sakraan taani marra huwwe?*

**He looks as if he's been out on a drunk. *heeʔto kaʔənno kaan ᶓam yduur yəskar.*

to get drunk - *səker (a səkᵊr).* He got drunk at the birthday party. *səker ᵊb-ḥaflet ᶓiid ᵊl-miilaad.*

drunkard - *sakkiir* pl. *-iin, səkarži* pl. *-iyye, xammiir* pl. *-iyye, xamərži* pl. *-iyye.*

Druze - *dərzi* pl. *druuz.*

dry - **1.** *naašef, našfaan.* The wash isn't dry yet. *l-ġasiil ləssa muu naašef* (or **...*ləssa maa nəšef*). -- My throat is dry. *ḥalqi naašef.* -- The well is dry. *l-biir našfaan.* **2.** *naašef.* The lecture was so dry, I walked out. *l-ᵊmḥaaḍara kaanet naašfe la-daraže ʔənni ḥamalt ḥaali w-ᵊmšiit.* **3.** *žaaff.* It's been a dry summer. *kaanet ṣeefiyye žaaffe.* **4.** *yaabes.* Let's gather some dry wood. *xalliina nəžməᶓ-ᵊlna šwayyet ḥaṭab yaabes.* **5.** *seek* (invar). I'd like a good dry wine. *bəddi nbiid seek ᵊmniiḥ.*

dry cleaner - *maḥall˜* (pl. *-aat˜*) *tanḍiif(aat).* Do you know of a good dry cleaner around here? *btaᶓrəf-li šii maḥall tanḍiifaat ᵊmniiḥ b-han-nawaaḥi?*

**I sent your gray suit to the dry cleaner. *baᶓatt-əllak badᵊltak ᵊr-rṣaaṣi lət-tanḍiif.*

dry land - *l-yaabse.* It's good to be on dry land again. *maa ʔaḥlaaha ᵊr-ražᶓa ᶓal-yaabse.*

to go dry - *nəšef (a našafaan˜) ḥaliiba.* Our cow has gone dry. *baqrətna nəšef ḥaliiba.*

**My mind has gone dry lately. *naḍbet ʔafkaari b-hal-mədde.*

to run dry - *nəšef (a našafaan).* The well ran dry last summer. *l-biir nəšef ᵊṣ-ṣeef ᵊl-maaḍi.*

to dry - **1.** *nəšef (a našafaan).* The paint dries in five hours. *d-dhaan byənšaf b-xamᵊs saaᶓaat.* **2.** *naššaf//tnaššaf.* Who's going to dry the dishes? *miin laḥa ynaššef ᵊṣ-ṣḥuun?* -- Dry yourself well. *naššef ḥaalak ᵊmniiḥ.* **3.** *žaffaf//džaffaf.* They are going to dry some fruit for us. *bəddon yžaffᵊfú-lna šwayyet fawaaki.* **4.** *yabbas//tyabbas.* We dry most of the mint in our garden. *mənyabbes ʔaktar ᵊn-naᶓnaᶓ b-ᵊžneenətna.*

dried - *mžaffaf.* Buy me a kilo of dried apricots. *štrii-li kiilo məšmoš ᵊmžaffaf.*

dried dates - *tamᵊr.*

to dry out - **1.** *nəšef (a našafaan).* Hang the wash in the sun so it'll dry out. *nšoor ᵊl-ġasiil bᵊš-šamᵊs la-yənšaf.* **2.** *žaffaf//džaffaf.* They have to dry out that swamp before they can build the road. *laazem yžaffᵊfu hal-məstanqaᶓ qabᵊl-ma yəbnu ṭ-ṭariiq.*

to dry up - **1.** *nəšef (a našafaan).* Every summer this stream dries up. *kəll ṣeefiyye has-saaqye btənšaf.* **2.** *yəbes (-yəbas yabaas).* Due to the long drought, the grass and the plants are drying up. *b-sabab ᵊž-žafaaf ᵊṭ-ṭawiil, l-ḥašiiš wᵊz-zarᵊᶓ ᶓam yəbasu.*

dual - **1.** *msanna.* What's the dual of "mažra"? *šuu msanna "mažra"?* **2.** *məzdəwež.* A mile from here begins the dual highway. *baᶓᵊd miil mən hoon byəbda ṭ-ṭariiq ᵊl-məzdəwež.*

**It serves a dual purpose. *btəqḍi ġaraḍeen.*

duchess - *duuqa* pl. *-aat.*

duck - *baṭṭa* coll. *baṭṭ* pl. *-aat.* We're having roast duck for dinner. *ᶓaamliin baṭṭ ᵊmḥammar ᶓal-ᶓaša.*

to duck - **1.** *ṭaxxa.* He ducked his head. *ṭaxxa raaso.* **2.** *ġaṭṭaṣ.* Duck your head under the water. *ġaṭṭeṣ raasak bᵊl-mayy.* -- They ducked him in the lake. *ġaṭṭaṣú bᵊl-buḥayra.* **3.** *zaqq (ə ø).* Let's duck into the alley so they don't see us. *xalliina nzəqq ləl-ḥaara ḥatta maa yšuufuuna.*

due – *ḥaqq*. Let everyone have his due. *ɛaṭi kəll waaḥed ḥaqqo.*
dues – *ʔəštiraak*. I pay my dues every month. *bədfaɛ ʔəštiraaki kəll šahᵊr.*
**With all due respect to your learning, I disagree. *maɛ kəll ʔəḥtiraami la-ɛəlmak, ʔana maa bwaafeq maɛak.*
**They live in a town due north of here. *ɛaayšiin b-balad raʔsan šmaal mən hoon.*
**In due time you'll see my point. *ləssa byəži waqᵊt btəfham wažhet naẓari.*
due to – *b-natiižet˜...*, *b-sabab˜...* Due to an oversight, she wasn't invited. *b-natiižet sahu maa nɛazmet.*
to be due – *staḥaqq*. The rent is due next Monday. *l-ʔiižaar byəstḥəqq ᵊt-taneen ᵊž-žaaye.*
to be due to – **1.** *kaan natiižet˜...* That's due to a mistake. *haada natiižet ġalaṭ.* **2.** *kaan mənṭḍər ...* He's due to arrive at ten. *mənṭḍər yəži ᵊs-saaɛa ɛašara.*
duel – *mbaaraze* pl. *-aat.*
duke – *duuq̌* pl. *-aat.*
dull – **1.** *mtallam.* This knife is dull. *has-səkkiine mtallame.* **2.** *baayex, tqiil, mməll.* After dinner we had to listen to a dull speech from our boss. *baɛd ᵊl-ɛaša ḍṭarreena nəsmaɛ kəlme baayxa mən raʔiisna.* **3.** *mməll.* It's been a real dull day around here. *kaan yoom mməll ɛan ḥaqa hoon.* **4.** *kaamed, baahet.* She likes dull colors. *bətḥəbb ᵊl-ʔalwaan ᵊl-kaamde.* **5.** *baliid* pl. *bəlada.* I have seen dull students before, but none like him. *šəfᵊt talamiiz bəlada b-ḥayaati laaken maa šəfᵊt ʔablad mən heek.*
**He's terribly dull. *faẓaaɛa qaddeeš bimallel.*
to dull – *tallam//ttallam.* You'll dull the blade doing that. *ʔiza bəḍḍall taɛmel heek bəttallem ᵊš-šafra.*
dumb – **1.** *mahbuul, maždууb.* Boy, that guy is dumb! *yaa ʔaḷḷa, qaddeeš haz-zalame mahbuul!* **2.** *ʔaxras* f. *xarsa* pl. *xərᵊs* and *xərsaan.* He's been deaf and dumb from birth. *mən waqᵊt-ma wəled huwwe ʔaṭraš w-ʔaxras.* -- Can't you speak? You're not dumb, are you? *leeš maa ɛam təḥki? ʔənte maa-lak ʔaxras!*
**That was dumb of you! *hayy kaanet hablane mənnak!*
to strike dumb – *balkam//tbalkam.* His insolence struck me dumb. *waqaaḥto balkamətni.* -- We were struck dumb by the news. *tbalkamna mn ᵊl-xabar.*
to be **dum(b)founded** – *tbalkam, xəres (a xaras).* I was completely dumbfounded when I heard it. *tbalkamᵊt fard marra lamma sməɛt ᵊl-xabar* or **l-xabar ʔəžaani mətl ᵊḍ-ḍarbe ɛar-raas.*
dump – **1.** *mazbale* pl. *mazaabel.* That empty lot is used as a dump. *hal-fasḥa məstaɛmale mazbale.* **2.** *xaan* pl. *-aat.* Their house is an awful dump. *faẓaaɛa beeton šuu mətl ᵊl-xaan.*
**I've been down in the dumps all day. *mizaaži məltəɛen ṭuul ᵊn-nhaar.*
to dump – **1.** *farraġ//tfarraġ.* They dumped the coal in front of the basement. *farraġu l-faḥᵊm qəddaam ᵊl-qabu.* -- Please don't dump the coffee grounds in the sink! *baḷḷa laa tfarreġ ṭəḥl ᵊl-qahwe bᵊl-mažla.* **2.** *laḥaš (o laḥᵊš//ltaḥaš).* He simply dumped all his packages on the table. *laḥaš kəll bakeetaato ɛaṭ-ṭaawle w-xalaṣ.*
dumpy – *mdaɛbal.* She has a dumpy figure. *kasma mdaɛbal.*
dune – *kasiib* pl. *kəsbaan.* The dunes extend for miles. *l-kəsbaan btəmtadd la-ʔamyaal w-ʔamyaal.*
dung – *zəbᵊl.*
duplicate – *nəsxa* (pl. *nəsax*) *ṭəbq ᵊl-ʔaṣᵊl.* Is this the original or a duplicate? *hayy ᵊl-ʔaṣᵊl walla nəsxa ṭəbq ᵊl-ʔaṣᵊl?*
to duplicate **1.** *nasax (a nasᵊx//ntasax).* Our machine will duplicate 75 copies a minute. *ʔaalətna btənsax xamsḍa w-sabɛiin nəsxa bᵊd-daqiiqa.* **2.** *karrar//tkarrar.* I wonder if he can duplicate the record. *yaa-tara fii ykarrer ᵊr-raq̌am ᵊl-q̌iyaasi?*
durable – *ḍayaan* (invar.), *matiin.* It's a durable material. *huwwe qmaaš ḍayaan.*
for the **duration of** – *məddet˜...* We'll be out of town for the duration of the summer. *laḥa nkuun barraat ᵊl-balad məddet ᵊṣ-ṣeefiyye.*
during – **1.** *ʔasna˜ ...*, *ʔasnaaʔ˜...*, *waqt˜ ...*, *məddet˜...* I met him during the war. *tɛarraft ɛalée ʔasna l-ḥarb.* **2.** *ʔasna˜ ...*, *ʔasnaaʔ˜ ...* She got up and left during the movie. *ḥamlet ḥaala w-məšyet ʔasna l-fəlᵊm.*
dust – *ġabra.* There's a heavy layer of dust on the table. *fii ṭabqet ġabra smiike ɛaṭ-ṭaawle.*
dust cloth – *naffaaḍa* pl. *-aat.*
to dust – *masaḥ (a masᵊḥ//mmasḥet) ġabret˜ ...* Please dust my desk. *baḷḷa msaḥli-li ġabret ṭaawəlti.*
dusty – *məġber.* The roads are very dusty this time of the year. *ṭ-ṭəroq bətkuun məġᵊbra ktiir b-heek waqt ᵊmn ᵊs-səne.*
Dutch – *holandi**.
Dutchman – *holandi** pl. *-iyyiin.*
duty – **1.** *waažeb* pl. *-aat,* (moral or religious) *farḍ* pl. *fruuḍ.* It was his duty to support his parents. *kaan waažbo* (or *farḍ ɛalée*) *yɛiil ʔəmmo w-ʔabúu.* **2.** *waažeb* pl. *-aat, waẓiife* pl. *waẓaayef.* Answering the phone is one of my duties. *r-radd ɛat-talifoon ʔaḥad waažbaati.* **3.** *gəmrok* pl. *gamaarek.* How much duty is there on this tobacco? *qaddeeš ᵊl-gəmrok ɛala had-dəxxaan?*
duty free – *xaaleṣ mn ᵊl-gəmrok.* Apples imported from Lebanon are duty free. *t-təffaaḥ ᵊl-məstawrad mən ləbnaan xaaleṣ mn ᵊl-gəmrok.*
off duty – *barraat ᵊl-waẓiife.* The policeman was off duty when he arrested the man. *š-šərṭi kaan barraat ᵊl-waẓiife lamma waqqaf ᵊr-rəžžaal.*
**I'm off duty after five-thirty. *waqᵊt dawaami byəxloṣ ᵊs-saaɛa xamse w-nəṣṣ.*
on duty – *mnaaweb.* Talk to the officer on duty. *ʔəḥki maɛ ᵊẓ-ẓaabeṭ l-ᵊmnaaweb.*
**I'm on duty all night. *ɛandi waẓiife ṭuul ᵊl-leel.*
dwarf – *q̌əzᵊm* pl. *ʔaq̌zaam.*
to **dwell on** – *ṭawwal ᵊl-ḥaki ɛan.* There's no point in dwelling on this subject any longer. *maa fii faayde nṭawwel ᵊl-ḥaki ɛan hal-mawḍuuɛ ʔaktar mən heek.*
dye – *ṣbaaġ* pl. *-aat.* Please get me a package of blue dye. *žəb-li baḷḷa ɛəlbet ᵊṣbaaġ ʔazraq.*
to dye – *ṣabaġ (e/o ṣbaaġ//nṣabaġ).* I dyed my blue dress black. *ṣabaġᵊt roobi l-ʔazraq ʔaswad.* -- Is she dying her hair? *ɛam təṣbeġ šaɛra?*
dynamite – *diinamiit.*
dynamo – *dinamo* pl. *dinamoyaat.*
dynasty – *ʔəsra* pl. *ʔəsar.*
dysentery – *ẓənṭaariyye.*

E

each – **1.** *kəll˜.* He comes here each week. *byəži la-hoon kəll žəmɛa.* **2.** *kəll˜ waaḥed.* Each of us received a pack of cigarettes. *kəll waaḥed mənna ʔaxad baakeet sigaara.* -- We each went to a different movie. *kəll waaḥed mənna raaḥ la-siinama məxtəlfe.* -- These apples are a piaster each. *hat-təffaaḥaat kəll waaḥde b-qərᵊš.*
each and every one – *kəll˜ waaḥed.* You can count on each and every one of us. *fiik təɛtə́med ɛala kəll waaḥed mənna.*
each one – *kəll˜ waaḥed.* Each one has to contribute his full share. *kəll waaḥed laazem yqaddem ḥəṣṣto t-taamme.*
each other – *baɛḍ-* + pron. suff. pl. (*ᵊl-baɛᵊḍ*). You see each other every day? *bətšuufu baɛᵊḍkon* (*ᵊl-baɛᵊḍ*) *kəll yoom?* — We have to help each other. *laazem nətsaaɛed baɛᵊḍna* (*l-baɛᵊḍ*). -- They have nothing to do with each other. *maa fii ɛalaaqa been baɛḍon* (*ᵊl-baɛᵊḍ*).
eager – **1.** *mətšawweq.* I'm eager to meet your friend. *ʔana mətšawweq la-ʔətɛarraf ɛala ṣaaḥbak.* **2.** *maḥruuq (ɛala), mayyet (ɛala).* He's eager to get started. *huwwe maḥruuq ɛala-ma yəbda.* **3.** *ṭamuuḥ.* She's an eager student. *hiyye təlmiize ṭamuuḥa.*
eagle – *nəsᵊr* pl. *nsuur(a), ɛəq̌aab* pl. *ɛəq̌baan.*
ear – *ʔədᵊn* f. (dual *ʔədᵊnteen*) pl. *ʔadaan* and *ʔadaneen.* His ear was cut off in the accident.

ʔədno nqaṭεet bᵊl-ʔaksidaan. -- She is deaf in her right ear. *hiyye ṭarša b-ʔədna l-yamiin.* -- I have no ear for music. *maa εandi ʔədᵊn muusiiqiyye.* -- He's up to his ears in debt. *ġaateṣ bᵊd-deen la-qaraqiiṭ ʔadaano.* -- Walls have ears. *l-ḥiiṭaan ʔəla ʔadaan.* -- It goes in one ear and out the other. *bətfuut mən ʔədᵊn btəṭlaε ᵊmn ᵊt-taanye.* -- When I heard that I pricked up my ears. *lamma sməεᵊt haš-šii fattaḥᵊt ʔadaani.* -- Go on with your story, I'm all ears. *kamməl qəṣṣtak, ʔana kəlli ʔadaan.* -- Unfortunately, he turned a deaf ear to my request. *maε ᵊl-ʔasaf sakkar ʔadanée la-ṭalabi.*

**He has his ear to the ground. *maa bətfuuto laa šaarde w-laa waarde.*

ear lobe - *šaḥmet~ ʔədᵊn* pl. *šaḥmaat~ ʔadaan.*

ear of corn - *εarnuus~* (pl. *εaraniis~*) *dəra.*

ear of wheat - *sabalet~* (coll. *sabal~* pl. *-aat~*) *qamᵊḥ.*

eardrum - *ṭablet~ ʔədᵊn* pl. *ṭablaat~ ʔadaan.*

early - 1. *bakkiir.* Please wake me early. *balla fayyəqni bakkiir.* -- I have to get up early in the morning. *laazem fiiq εala bəkra bakkiir.* -- Please come as early as possible. *mən faḍlak taεa qadd-ma fiik bakkiir.* -- We were early at the party. *ʔžiina bakkiir εal-ḥafle* or ***kənna mbakkriin εal-ḥafle.* 2. *εala bakkiir, bakkiir.* School will end early this year. *l-madrase laḥa təxloṣ εala bakkiir has-səne.* -- Easter comes early this year. *εiid ᵊl-fəṣᵊḥ has-səne žaaye εala bakkiir.* 3. *ʔawwal~..., εala bakkiir.* We usually leave early in the season. *εaadatan ᵊmnətrek ᵊb-ʔawwal ᵊl-muusem* (or ... *εala bakkiir bᵊl-muusem).* 4. *ʔawaaʔel~ ...* The author was born in the early twentieth century. *l-ᵊmʔallef wəled ᵊb-ʔawaaʔel ᵊl-qarn ᵊl-εəšriin.* 5. *bakkiiri* f. *bakkiire, mbakker.* You can already find early fruit on the market. *fiik ᵊtlaaqi hallaq fawaaki bakkiire bᵊs-suuq.* 6. *qariib, mbakker, sariiε.* We expect an early reply. *mnətwaqqaε žawaab qariib.* 7. *ʔawwali**. I heard the early election returns on the late news. *sməεᵊt nataayež ᵊl-ʔəntixaabaat ᵊl-ʔawwaliyye b-ʔaaxer našret ᵊl-ʔaxbaar.*

**Tell me something about the early days of your life. *ḥkīi-li šii εan ʔiyyaam ᵊṭfuultak* (or *ʔiyyaam ṣibaak*).

**The early bird catches the worm. *yalli byəsboq byaaxod fəstoq.*

to **earn** - 1. *ṭaalaε, εəmel (-yaεmel ə).* How much do you earn a week? *qaddeeš bəṭṭaaleε bᵊž-žəmεa?* 2. *kəseb (a kasᵊb//nkasab), ktasab.* He earned his reputation the hard way. *kəseb šəhᵊrto b-žadd w-kadᵊḥ.* 3. *kassab.* His conduct earned him universal respect. *sluuko kassabo ʔəḥtiraam ᵊž-žamiiε.*

**She earns her living as a dressmaker. *εaayše mən wara l-ᵊxyaaṭa.*

earphone - *sammaaεa* pl. *-aat.*

earring - *ḥalaqa* and *fardet~ ḥalaq* coll. *ḥalaq* pl. *ḥalaqaat.*

earth - 1. *ʔarḍ.* The distance between the earth and the moon is 380,000 kilometers. *l-masaafe been ᵊl-ʔarḍ wᵊl-qamar tlaat miyye w-ᵊtmaaniin ʔalf kiiloməṭᵊr.* 2. *dənye, εaalam.* Nothing on earth can save him. *maa fii šii bᵊd-dənye bixallṣo.* 3. *ṭraab.* This ditch has to be filled with earth. *hal-xandaq laazem yənṭəmer bᵊṭ-ṭraab.*

**Now let's get back to earth! *hallaq xalliina nəržaε ləl-waaqeε.*

**He has a down-to-earth attitude toward sex. *mawᵊqfo mn ᵊl-masaaʔel ž-žənsiyye mawqef waaqεi.*

earthquake - *zalzale* pl. *zalaazel, zəlzaal* pl. *zalaazel.*

ease - *shuule.* Did you notice the ease with which he does things? *laaḥaẓᵊt qaddeeš ᵊs-shuule yalli bidabber fiiha l-ʔašyaaʔ?*

at ease - *mərtaaḥ.* I never feel quite at ease when I'm with her. *εəmri maa bəšεor ᵊb-ḥaali mərtaaḥ εal-maẓbuuṭ waqᵊt kuun maεa.*

to set at ease - *ṭamman, rayyaḥ baal~ ...* His smile set me at ease. *ʔəbtisaamto ṭammanətni* (or *rayyaḥə́t-li baali).*

to stand at ease - *st(a)raaḥ.* The sergeant told his soldiers to stand at ease. *r-raqiib ʔamar εasaakro yəstriiḥu.*

**He always puts his guests completely at ease. *daayman bixalli ḍyuufo yəšᵊεru kaʔənnon ᵊb-beeton.*

to ease - 1. *xaffaf//txaffaf.* This medicine will ease the pain. *had-dawa bixaffef ᵊl-wažaε.* 2. *sahhal//tsahhal, hayyan//thawwan.* Another secretary would help ease my work. *law fii səkrəteera taanye bətsahhel šəġli (εaliyyi).* 3. *marraq// tmarraq.* I watched them ease the big box through the narrow door. *šəfton εam ymarrqu s-sanduuq l-ᵊkbiir ᵊmn ᵊl-baab ᵊd-dayyeq.*

to ease up - *ḥalḥal.* The pressure is beginning to ease up. *ḍ-ḍaġᵊṭ εam yəbda yḥalḥel.*

easily - 1. *b-ᵊshuule.* You can easily get there in one hour. *b-ᵊshuule fiik təṣal la-hniik ᵊb-saaεa.* 2. *biduun šakk, bala šakk, laa šakk.* That's easily the best solution. *biduun šakk haada ʔaḥsan ḥall.*

**I can easily believe that. *ṭabεan ᵊbsaddeq haš-šii.*

east - 1. *šarᵊq.* The wind's coming from the east. *l-hawa žaaye mn ᵊš-šarᵊq.* 2. *naaḥ ᵊš-šarᵊq.* The arrow points east. *s-sahᵊm bidəll naaḥ ᵊš-šarᵊq.* 3. *εaš-šarᵊq.* They moved east. *ntaqalu εaš-šarᵊq.* 4. *šarqi**. In the afternoon we usually get an east wind. *εaadatan baεd ᵊḍ-ḍahᵊr byəžiina hawa šarqi.*

east of - *b-šarq~* ... Our house is east of the railroad tracks. *beetna b-šarq ᵊs-səkke l-ḥadiid.*

Easter - *εiid~ ᵊl-fəṣᵊḥ,* (Christian usage:) *εiid~ l-ᵊkbiir.*

eastern - *šarqi**. I know the eastern part pretty well. *baεref ᵊl-manṭiqa š-šarqiyye mniiḥ.*

easy - *sahᵊl, hayyen.* That was an easy question. *haada kaan suʔaal sahᵊl.* -- English would be easy for you. *l-ʔəngliizi bikuun hayyen εaleek.*

**It's easy for you to talk! *šuu εala baalak wᵊl-qaaḍi xaalak?*

**He got off easy at that. *txallaṣ mən haš-šaġle b-ᵊshuule.*

**He's now living on Easy Street. *εaayeš hallaq ḥayaat naaεme raaġde.*

**Take it easy! Why get excited? *haddi baalak! maa bədda narvaze.*

**Take it easy! Tomorrow's another day! *εala mahlak! l-ʔiyyaam žaaye!*

**I'm taking it easy today. *ʔana mrayyeḥ ḥaali l-yoom.*

**He's an easy-going fellow. *huwwe zalame maa biḥammə́la.*

easy chair - *qəlṭoq* pl. *qalaaṭeq, kəlṭoq* pl. *kalaaṭeq.*

to **eat** - *ʔakal (-yaakol ʔakᵊl//ttaakal).* I haven't eaten a thing in two days. *maa ʔakalt šii mən yoomeen.* -- Let's eat out tonight. *xalliina naakol barra hal-masa.* -- We watched the acid eat into the metal. *šəfna l-ḥaamoḍ εam yaakol ᵊl-maεdan.* -- She's eating her heart out. *l-ḥasra εam taakol qalba.*

**He walked in just as we sat down to eat. *faat w-naḥna εam nəqεod εaṣ-ṣəfra.*

to eat away - 1. *žaraf (e žarᵊf//nžaraf).* The rains have eaten away a lot of the topsoil. *l-ʔamṭaar žarfet ᵊktiir mən wəšš ᵊt-tərbe.* 2. *ʔakal (-yaakol ʔakᵊl//ttaakal).* The salt is eating away the metal on the underside of my car. *l-məlᵊḥ εam yaakol ᵊl-maεdan ᵊb-səfᵊl sayyaarti.*

to eat up - 1. *ʔakal (-yaakol ʔakᵊl//ttaakal).* The expenses are gradually eating up our profits. *l-maṣariif εam taakol ʔarbaaḥna bᵊt-tadriiž.* 2. *ʔakal kəll~* ... She's eaten up the chocolate. *ʔaklet kəll ᵊš-šokolaata.*

eau de Cologne - *koloonya.*

ebb - *jazᵊr.*

ebony - *(xašab) ʔabanuus.*

eccentric - 1. *šaazz~ ᵊṭ-ṭabᵊε, ġariib~ ᵊl-ʔaṭwaar.* He's something of an eccentric. *huwwe nooεan maa šaazz ᵊṭ-ṭabᵊε* or ***ṭabεo nooεan maa šaazz.* 2. *šaazz, ġariib.* Everybody is talking about her eccentric behavior. *kəll ᵊn-naas εam yəḥku εala taṣarrə́fa š-šaazz.*

echo - *ṣada.* If you listen you can hear the echo. *ʔiza btaεṭi ʔədnak ᵊbtəsmaε ᵊṣ-ṣada.*

to echo - 1. *dawa (i dwiyy).* The sound of the shot echoed through the hills. *ṣooṭ ᵊṭ-ṭalqa dawa bᵊl-hadabaat.* 2. *raddad.* Stop echoing every word he says. *haaže tradded kəll kəlme biqüula.*

economic - *ʔəqtiṣaadi**. Their economic condition is bad because of the drought. *ḥaalə́ton ᵊl-ʔəqtiṣaadiyye εaaṭle b-sabab ᵊl-maḥᵊl.*

economical - 1. *məqtə́ṣed, mdabber.* She's a very economical housewife. *hiyye sətt beet ᵊktiir məqtəṣda.* 2. *mwaffer.* This type of heating is very economical. *han-nooε ᵊmn ᵊt-tədfaaye mwaffer ᵊmniiḥ.*

economics - *(εᵊlm~ ᵊl-) ʔəqtiṣaad.*

economist - *ʔəqtiṣaadi** pl. *-iyyiin.*

to **economize** - *qtaṣad.* We're really going to have to economize. *mən ḥaqa laazem nəqtə́ṣed.*

economy - *ʔəqtiṣaad, ʔəqtiṣaadiyyaat* (pl.). The

economy of the country is not healthy. *ʔəq̈tiṣaad l-ᵊblaad muu saliim.*

eczema – *ʔakzima.*

edge – **1.** *ṭaraf* pl. *ʔaṭraaf.* He lives at the edge of (the) town. *saaken ᵊb-ṭaraf ᵊl-balad.* **2.** *ḥaffe* pl. *-aat, ṭaraf* pl. *ʔaṭraaf.* Don't put the glass so close to the edge. *laa tḥəṭṭ ᵊl-kaase hal-qadd qariib ᵊmn ᵊl-ḥaffe.* **3.** *ḥarᵊf* pl. *ḥruuf, ṭaraf* pl. *ʔaṭraaf.* Tilt the crate on its edge to get it through the door. *qleeb ᵊs-saḥḥaara ɛala ḥarfa ḥatta təmroq bᵊl-baab.* **4.** *ḥadd.* The edge of this knife is dull. *ḥadd has-səkkiin ᵊmtallam.*

**You have the edge on me. *kafftak raažḥa ɛala kaffti.*

on edge – *mnarvez.* She's on edge today. *hiyye mnarᵊvze l-yoom.*

to edge (one's way) – *zabbaq ḥaalo.* I could hardly edge my way through the crowd. *bᵊz-zoor zabbaqᵊt ḥaali bᵊl-ɛažqa.*

to be **edible** – *ttaakal.* Is the fruit of this tree edible? *samar haš-šažara byəttaakal?*

edition – *ṭabɛa* pl. *-aat.* Have you seen the new edition of his works? *šəft ᵊt-ṭabɛa ž-ždiide la-mᵊallafaato?*

editor – *mḥarrer* pl. *-iin.* My brother has just become editor of our local newspaper. *ʔaxi hallaq ṣaar ᵊmḥarrer ᵊb-žariidətna l-maḥalliyye.*

**Who is the editor of this collection of contemporary Egyptian stories? *miin ṭaalaɛ hal-mažmuuɛa mn ᵊl-qəṣaṣ l-ᵊmɛaaṣra l-məṣriyye?*

editorial – *maq̈aale* (pl. *-aat*) *ʔəftitaaḥiyye.* Did you read the editorial? *qareet šii l-maq̈aale l-ʔəftitaḥiyye?*

to **educate** – *ɛallam.* We have to educate our children to tolerance. *laazem ᵊnɛallem ᵊwlaadna ᵊt-tasaamoḥ.*

educated – *msaq̈q̈af, mətɛallem, mɛallam.* He's an educated person. *huwwe zalame msaq̈q̈af.*

education – **1.** *saq̈aafe.* What kind of education have you had? *šuu nooɛ ᵊs-saq̈aafe yalli ḥsəlᵊt ɛaleeha?* **2.** *tarbiye.* He wants to go into education when he finishes college. *bəddo yədxol ᵊb-miidaan ᵊt-tarbiye baɛᵊd-ma yxalleṣ ᵊž-žaamɛa.* **3.** *taɛliim.* Her education has been neglected. *ʔahmalu taɛliima.*

eel – *ḥankliis.*

effect – *taʔsiir* pl. *-aat.* His appeal produced the desired effect. *nidaaʔo kan-lo t-taʔsiir ᵊl-maṭluub.*

**He just does it for effect. *ɛam yaɛməla bass la-ywarži ḥaalo.*

to have an effect on – *ʔassar b-.* Scolding has no effect on him. *l-bahdale maa bətʔasser fii.*

to go into effect – *tnaffaz, ṭṭabbaq, sara (i sarayaan) mafɛuulo.* That law will go into effect next month. *hal-q̈aanuun byətnaffaz* (or *yəsri mafɛuulo*) *ᵊš-šahr ᵊž-žaaye.*

to put into effect – *waḍaɛ (-yuuḍaɛ waḍᵊɛ˜// nwaḍaɛ) mawḍeɛ ᵊt-tanfiiz.* The new ruling was just put into effect. *n-niẓaam ᵊž-ždiid bass hallaq nwaḍaɛ mawḍeɛ ᵊt-tanfiiz.*

to take effect – *ɛaṭa (-yaɛṭi ə) taʔsiir.* The injection is beginning to take effect. *l-ʔəbre ɛam təbda taɛṭi taʔsiira.*

to effect – *ɛəmel (-yaɛmel ə//nɛamal), saawa// tsaawq.* He effected the change without difficulty. *ɛəmel ᵊt-taġyiir biduun ᵊṣɛuube.*

effective – **1.** *faɛɛaal.* This is an effective remedy against headache. *haada dawa faɛɛaal ḍədd wažaɛ ᵊr-raas.* **2.** *naafez.* The raise will be effective the first of the month. *z-zyaade bətkuun naafze mən ʔawwal ᵊš-šahᵊr.*

to become effective – *tnaffaz, ṭṭabbaq, sara (i sarayaan) mafɛuulo.* The order becomes effective tomorrow. *l-ʔamᵊr byətnaffaz* (or *byəsri mafɛuulo*) *mən bəkra.*

efficiency – **1.** *taqaane, šaṭaara, kafaaʔa.* We all admire his efficiency. *kəllna məɛžabiin ᵊb-taqaanto.* **2.** *taqaane.* This new method combines efficiency with economy. *hal-ʔəsluub ᵊž-ždiid byəžmaɛ been ᵊt-taqaane wᵊl-ʔəq̈tiṣaad.*

efficient – *mətqan, šaaṭer, kafuuʔ.* He's efficient in everything he does. *huwwe mətqan ᵊb-kəll šii byaɛᵊmlo.*

**Their company is noted for its efficient offices. *šərkə́ton maɛruufe b-kafaaʔet dawaayə́ra.*

effort – **1.** *žahᵊd* pl. *žhuud, mažhuud* pl. *-aat.* All his efforts were in vain. *kəll ᵊžhuudo raaḥet suda.* -- Did he really make an effort? *saawa šii mažhuud ɛan ḥaqa?* **2.** *žahᵊd* pl. *žhuud.* That's a waste of effort. *haada ḍyaaɛet žahᵊd.* **3.** *taɛab.* That isn't worth the effort. *maa byəḥrez ᵊt-taɛab.*

egg – *beeḍa* coll. *beeḍ* pl. *-aat.* How much is a dozen eggs? *b-qaddeeš dazziinet ᵊl-beeḍ?*

**Don't put all your eggs in one basket! *laa džaazef ᵊb-kəll šii halli maɛak ᵊb-ḍarbe waaḥde!*

egg beater – *xaffaaqet˜* (pl. *-aat˜*) *beeḍ.*

egg whisk – *xaffaaqet˜* (pl. *-aat˜*) *beeḍ.*

to egg on – *ḥarraḍ.* His friends egged him on. *ṣḥaabo ḥarraḍúu.*

eggplant – *beetənžaane* coll. *beetənžaan* pl. *-aat.*

egg whisk – *xaffaaqet˜* (pl. *-aat˜*) *beeḍ.*

egoism – *ʔanaaniyye.*

egoistic – *ʔanaani**.

Egypt – *maṣᵊr.*

Lower Egypt – *l-wažh ᵊl-baḥri.*

Upper Egypt – *l-wažh ᵊl-q̈əbli, ṣ-ṣaɛiid.*

Egyptian – *maṣri** and *məṣri** pl. *-iyyiin* and *maṣaarwe.*

eight – **1.** *tmən(t).* I lived there for eight months. *sakant ᵊhniik tmənt əšhor.* -- We are eight students in class. *nəḥna tmən talamiiz bᵊṣ-ṣaff.* **2.** *tmaanye.* There were eight of us at the party. *kənna tmaane bᵊl-ḥafle.* -- Bring us eight coffees. *žəb-ᵊlna tmaane qahwe.* -- She's eight now. *ɛəmra tmaane hallaq.* **3.** *s-saaɛa tmaane.* The bus leaves at eight. *l-baaṣ byəmši s-saaɛa tmaane.* -- It's already eight. *ṣaaret ᵊs-saaɛa tmaane.*

eighteen – **1.** *tmənṭaɛšar.* I spent eighteen pounds on it. *ṣaraft ᵊtmənṭaɛšar leera ɛaleeha.* **2.** *tmənṭaɛš.* There are eighteen of us in class. *nəḥna tmənṭaɛᵊš bᵊṣ-ṣaff.*

eighteenth – **1.** *t-taamen ɛašar.* That was in the Eighteenth Century. *haš-šii ṣaar bᵊl-q̈arn ᵊt-taamen ɛašar.* **2.** *t-tmənṭaɛš* (invar.), *t-taamen ɛašar.* It's the eighteenth house from here. *huwwe l-beet ᵊt-tmənṭaɛᵊš mən hoon.* **3.** *tmənṭaɛš.* He left on the eighteenth of August. *saafar b-ᵊtmənṭaɛᵊš ʔaab.* -- I think the eighteenth comes on a Friday. *bəɛtə́qed (yoom) ᵊt-tmənṭaɛᵊš byəḥkom yoom žəmɛa.*

one eighteenth – *waaḥed mən tmənṭaɛš.* The initial payment is one eighteenth of the bill. *ʔawwal dafɛa waaḥed mən tmənṭaɛš ᵊmn ᵊl-faatuura.* -- Two eighteenths equal one ninth. *tneen mən tmənṭaɛᵊš bisaawu təsᵊɛ.*

eighth – **1.** *taamen.* That's his eighth book. *haada ktaabo t-taamen* (or *taamen kətbo* or *taamen ᵊktaab ʔəlo*). **2.** *tmaane, tmaanye.* He left on the eighth of February. *saafar b-ᵊtmaane šbaaṭ.* -- I think the eighth comes on a Monday. *bəɛtə́qed (yoom) ᵊt-tmaane byəḥkom yoom taneen.*

one eighth – *təmᵊn* pl. *tmaan.* That is one eighth of my salary. *haada təmᵊn maɛaaši.*

eightieth – *t-tmaaniin.* It's his eightieth birthday. *haada ɛiid miilaado t-tmaaniin.*

one eightieth – *waaḥed mən tmaaniin.*

eighty – *tmaaniin.* My grandfather came to Damascus eighty years ago. *žəddi ʔəža lə-š-šaam mən tmaaniin səne.*

eighties – *t-tmaaniin.* He must be in his eighties by now. *laazem ykuun bᵊt-tmaaniin hallaq.*

**My grandmother is in her late eighties. *sətti b-ḥiiṭaan ᵊt-təsɛiin.*

either – **1.** *waaḥed mən* + dual. Does either of these roads lead to Aleppo? *fii waaḥed mən haṭ-ṭariiqeen biwaddi la-ḥalab šii?* -- Does either of these two students speak French? *fii waaḥed ᵊmn ᵊt-təlmiizeen byəḥki frənsaawi šii?* **2.** *ʔayy waaḥed mən* + dual. Either (one) is correct. *ʔayy waaḥed ᵊmn ᵊt-tneen maẓbuuṭ.* -- Either dictionary will serve its purpose. *ʔayy waaḥed ᵊmn ᵊl-q̈aamuuseen byuufi bᵊl-ġaraḍ ᵊl-maṭluub.* **3.** *kamaan.* He doesn't know it either. *huwwe kamaan maa byaɛrə́fa.* -- My brother can't understand it either. *ʔaxi kamaan muu fahmaana.*

**There were trees on either side of the road. *kaan fii šažar ɛala ṭarafeen ᵊṭ-ṭariiq.*

either ... or – *yaa ... yaa.* I leave either tonight or tomorrow morning. *bsaafer yaa l-leele yaa bəkra ɛala bəkra.* -- Either I go or he does! *yaa ʔana bruuḥ yaa huwwe!*

elaborate – *mfaṣṣal, mṭawwal.* He gave us an elaborate description of the trip. *waṣáf-ᵊlna s-safra waṣf ᵊmfaṣṣal.*

**We ate a very elaborate dinner with them. *tɛaššeena maɛon ɛaša fii ʔalwaan ᵊktiir.*

to elaborate (up)on – *faṣṣal.* Can you elaborate upon your statement? *fiik ᵊtfaṣṣel taṣriiḥak?*

elastic – **1.** *maṭṭaaṭ* pl. *-aat.* Do you need any elastic for the blouse? *laazmek šii maṭṭaaṭ ləl-ᵊbluuz?* **2.** *maṭṭaaṭ, lastiiki**. An elastic girdle is better than a corset. *ž-žaartyeer* *ᵊl-maṭṭaaṭ ʔaḥsan ᵊmn ᵊl-korsée.* 3. *maṭṭaaṭ.* They've taken a real elastic stand on that issue. *ttaxazu mawqef mən ḥaqa maṭṭaaṭ ᵊb-hal-qaḍiyye.* 4. *ṭari*.* I need a very elastic ruler for this work. *laazəmni maṣṭara ṭariyye ktiir la-haš-šaġle.*

elbow – *kuuɛ* pl. *kwaaɛ.* I banged my elbow. *ṭaraqᵊt kuuɛi.*

elderly – *msənn.* He's an elderly gentleman. *huwwe sayyed ᵊmsənn.*

to **elect** – *ntaxab.* Whom are they going to elect president this time? *miin laḥa yəntəxbúu raʔiis has-səne?*

election – *ʔəntixaab* pl. *-aat.*

electric – 1. *kahrabaaʔi*.* Don't touch that electric wire. *laa tədqor ᵊb-haš-šriiṭ ᵊl-kahrabaaʔi.* — He died on the electric chair. *maat bᵊl-kərsi l-kahrabaaʔi.* 2. *kahrabaaʔi*, kahraba* (invar.). All the electric lights went out. *kəll ᵊl-ʔəḍᵊwye l-kahrabaaʔiyye* (or *ᵊl-ʔəḍᵊwye l-kahraba*) *nṭafet.* 3. *ɛal-kahraba.* I bought an electric iron. *štareet məkwaaye ɛal-kahraba.* — Have you seen my electric razor? *šəft maakiinet l-ᵊḥlaaqa ɛal-kahraba tabaɛi?*

**There was a bad electric storm here last night. *ṭalɛet ɛaaṣfe malɛuune fiiha barᵊq w-raɛᵊd leelt ᵊmbaareḥ.*

electric bulb – *lamba* pl. *-aat, ballooret˜* (pl. *-aat˜*) *kahraba.*

electrical – *kahrabaaʔi*.* They sell mostly electrical appliances. *bibiiɛu ʔaktar šii ʔadawaat kahrabaaʔiyye.*

electrician – *kahrabži* pl. *-iyye.*

electricity – *kahraba.*

electrification – *kahrabe.* The electrification of the area is almost finished. *kahrabt ᵊl-manṭiqa ɛala wašak təxloṣ.*

to **electrify** – *kahrab//tkahrab.* They electrified the Helwan line not too long ago. *kahrabu xaṭṭ ḥəlwaan mən mədde muu bɛiide.*

electromagnet – *maġnaṭiis kahrabaaʔi* pl. *-aat kahrabaaʔiyye.*

electromagnetic – *kahraṭiisi*.*

electromotor – *mootoor* (pl. *-aat*) *kahraba.*

electron – *ʔalaktroon* pl. *-aat.*

electronic – *ʔalaktrooni*.*

electrotherapy – *mdaawda ɛal-kahraba.*

elegance – *ʔanaaqa.*

elegant – *ʔaniiq.*

element – 1. *ɛənṣor* pl. *ɛanaaṣer.* How many chemical elements do you know? *kam ɛənṣor kiimaawi btaɛref?* — There is a strong Kurdish element in that area. *fii ɛənṣor kərdi qawi b-hal-manṭiqa.* 2. *žoohar* pl. *žawaaher, ɛənṣor* pl. *ɛanaaṣer.* The ancients knew four elements: fire, water, earth, and air. *l-qədama ɛərfu ʔarbaɛ žawaaher hənne n-naar wᵊl-maaʔ wᵊl-ʔarḍ wᵊl-hawa.*

**There's an element of truth in what he says. *fii šii mn ᵊṣ-ṣəḥḥa b-kalaamo.*

elements – 1. *ʔawwaliyyaat* (pl.), *mabaadi* (pl.). The children are taught the elements of geometry in elementary school. *l-ᵊwlaad ɛam yətɛallamu ʔawwaliyyaat ᵊl-handase bᵊl-madrase l-ʔəbtidaaʔiyye.* 2. *ɛanaaṣer ṭabiiɛiyye* (pl.) Long exposure to the elements has made these people a hardy lot. *ṭuul taɛarroḍ hal-qoom ləl-ɛanaaṣer ᵊṭ-ṭabiiɛiyye žaɛdlon yətḥallu bᵊl-ᵊxšuune.*

elementary – *ʔawwali*.*

elementary school – *madrase* (pl. *madaares*) *ʔəbtidaaʔiyye, madrase ʔawwaliyye.*

elephant – *fiil* pl. *fyaal.*

to **elevate** – *rafaɛ* (*a rafᵊɛ//rtafaɛ* and *nrafaɛ*). Their excellent art department has elevated the name of the school. *l-qəsm ᵊl-fanni l-məmtaaz tabaɛ ᵊl-madrase rafaɛ ʔəsᵊmha ɛaali.*

elevator – *ʔaṣanṣoor* pl. *-aat.*

eleven – 1. *ʔidaɛšar.* I've visited the Middle East eleven times. *zərt ᵊš-šarq ᵊl-ʔawṣaṭ ʔidaɛšar marra.* 2. *ʔidaɛš.* There're eleven of us in class. *nəḥna ʔidaɛᵊš bᵊṣ-ṣaff.* — I counted eleven Arabs at that party. *ɛaddeet ʔidaɛᵊš ɛarab ᵊb-hal-ḥafle.* 3. *s-saaɛa ʔidaɛš.* It's already eleven. *ṣaar ᵊs-saaɛa ʔidaɛš.*

eleventh – 1. *l-ḥaadi ɛašar.* He ruled in the early eleventh century. *ḥakam ᵊb-ʔawaaʔel ᵊl-qarn ᵊl-ḥaadi ɛašar.* 2. *l-ʔidaɛš* (invar.), *l-ḥaadi ɛašar.* It's the eleventh time he's called today. *hayy ᵊl-marra l-ʔidaɛš* (or *l-marra l-ḥaadye ɛašar*) *yalli bitalfen fiiha l-yoom.* 3. *ʔidaɛš.* He arrived on the eleventh of March. *wəṣel ᵊb-ʔidaɛᵊš ʔaadaar.* — I think the eleventh comes on a Thursday. *bəɛtəqed (yoom) ᵊl-ʔidaɛᵊš byəḥkom yoom xamiis.*

one eleventh – *waaḥed mən ʔidaɛš.* One eleventh of the road is finished. *waaḥed mən ʔidaɛš ᵊmn ᵊṭ-ṭariiq xalaṣ.*

El Haseke – *l-ḥasake,* (locally) *l-ᵊḥsətše.*

eligible – *ṣaaleḥ.* He's the most eligible man for that job. *huwwe ʔaṣlaḥ waaḥed la-haš-šaġle.*

**My brother just became eligible for the draft. *ʔaxi hallaq ʔəžet qarᵊɛto.*

to **eliminate** – 1. *ʔazaal.* We can easily eliminate these difficulties. *b-kəll ᵊshuule fiina nəziil haṣ-ṣɛuubaat.* 2. *ʔaṣqaṭ.* He was eliminated in the third race. *ʔaṣqaṭúu bᵊš-šooṭ ᵊt-taalet.* 3. *laġa* (*i ʔəlġa//ltaġa*). We're going to eliminate that course next year. *bəddna nəlġi had-dars ᵊs-səne ž-žaaye.*

elite – *nəxbe, xiire, zəbde.*

El Karak – *l-karak.*

elliptic – *beeḍawi*.*

elm – (*šažaret˜*) *dardaar.*

else – 1. *kamaan.* Who else will be there? *miin kamaan bəddo ykuun ᵊhniik?* — What else can we do this afternoon? *šuu mnaɛmel kamaan ᵊl-yoom baɛd ᵊḍ-ḍəhᵊr?* 2. *ġeer heek.* Tell me, what else could I do under the circumstances? *qəl-li b-heek ᵊẓruuf šuu kaan byəṭlaɛ ᵊb-ʔiidi ʔaɛmel ġeer heek?* — Why else would he do a thing like that? *leeš ġeer heek bəddo yaɛmel mətᵊl haš-šii?* 3. *ġeer ᵊhniik* (or *ġeer hoon* respectively). Where else can he be at this time of the day? *ween məmken ykuun ġeer ᵊhniik ᵊb-hal-waqt ᵊmn ᵊn-nhaar?*

**Where else can she be but at home? *ween məmken ᵊtkuun ġeer bᵊl-beet?*

anybody (or **somebody**) **else** – *ḥada taani, ḥada ġeer-* + pron. suff. Is anybody else here? *fii ḥada taani hoon?* or *fii ḥada ġeerna* (or *ġeerak, ġeero* etc., depending on context) *hoon?*

anyone (or **someone**) **else** – *ḥada taani.* Will someone else go with us? *fii ḥada taani raayeḥ maɛna?*

anything (or **something**) **else** – *šii taani, ġeer šii, šii ġeero.* Do you have anything else? *fii ɛandak šii taani?*

anywhere (or **somewhere**) **else** – 1. *b-maḥall taani, b-ġeer maḥall, b-maḥall ġeero.* Can't we meet anywhere else? *šuu maa fiina nəltəqi b-maḥall taani?* 2. *la-maḥall taani, la-ġeer maḥall, la-maḥall ġeero.* Why don't we go somewhere else? *leeš maa mənruuḥ la-maḥall taani?*

everybody (or **everyone**) **else** – *l-baqiyye.* Everybody else has gone. *l-baqiyye raaḥu.*

everything else – *l-baqiyye.* I'll take everything else. *ʔana baaxod ᵊl-baqiyye.*

or else – *wəlla.* Hurry, or (else) we'll be late! *staɛžel wəlla mnətʔaxxar!* — You do it, or else ...! *saawiiha wəlla ...!*

elsewhere – 1. *b-maḥall taani, b-ġeer maḥall, b-maḥall ġeero.* We'll have to look around elsewhere. *mažbuuriin ᵊndawwer ᵊb-maḥall taani.* 2. *la-maḥall taani, la-ġeer maḥall, la-maḥall ġeero.* If you don't like it here, we'll go elsewhere. *ʔiza muu ɛaažbak hoon mənruuḥ la-maḥall taani.*

embargo – *ḥaṣᵊr.* They're pressuring the government to lift the embargo on goods from that country. *ɛam yəḍġaṭu ɛal-ᵊḥkuume tərfaɛ ᵊl-ḥaṣᵊr ɛal-baḍaayeɛ mən hadiik l-ᵊblaad.*

to **embarrass** – *ḥaraž* (*e ʔəḥraaž//nḥaraž*). That child is always embarrassing me with his questions. *hal-walad ɛala ṭuul byəḥrəžni b-suʔaalaato.* — It was an embarrassing situation. *kaanet ḥaale məḥᵊrže.*

to be embarrassed – *ddaayaq, xəžel* (*a xažal*). I was terribly embarrassed when he asked me that question. *ddaayaqt ᵊktiir lamma saʔalni has-suʔaal.*

embassy – *safaara* pl. *-aat.*

ember – *žamra* coll. *žamᵊr* pl. *-aat.*

emblem – *šiɛaar* pl. *-aat.*

to **embrace** – 1. *ɛaanaq.* He embraced his father at the train station. *ɛaanaq ʔabúu bᵊl-ᵊmḥaṭṭa.* 2. *šamal* (*o š*), *štamal ɛala.* His work embraces several fields. *ɛamalo byəšmol ɛəddet ḥuquul.*

to **embroider** – *ṭarraz.* I'm going to embroider this tablecloth later on. *bəddi ṭarrez ġaṭa haṭ-ṭaawle baɛdeen.*

embroidery – *taṭriiz.* Look at the beautiful embroidery. *šuuf hat-taṭriiz ᵊl-ḥəlu.*

emerald – *zmərrde* coll. *zmərrod* pl. *-aat.*

emergency – 1. *ḥaalet˜* (pl. *-aat˜*) *ṭawaareʔ.* Do you think he could act quickly in an emergency? *fii yaa-tdra yətṣarraf ᵊb-sərɛa b-ḥaalet ṭawaareʔ?* 2. *ḍaruura, lzuum.* It'll do in an emergency.

byəmši ḥaala ɛand ᵊḍ-ḍaruura. -- In case of emergency call the doctor. ɛand ᵊḍ-ḍaruura ṣraax ləl-ḥakiim.

emergency brake - (of an automobile) fraam˜ (pl. -aat˜) ʔiid, (of a train) fraam˜ ṭawaareʔ.

emergency exit - maxraž˜ (pl. maxaarež˜) nažaat.

emigrant - mhaažer pl. -iin.

to **emigrate** - haažar. In recent years many people have emigrated from Europe. b-has-sniin ᵊl-ʔaxiire fii ktiir naas haažaru mən ʔawrəbba.

emir - ʔamiir pl. ʔəmara.

emirate - ʔamaara pl. -aat.

emotion - ʔənfiɛaal, taʔassor. He couldn't hide his emotion. maa qəder yəktom ʔənfiɛaalo.

emperor - ʔambaraṭoor pl. ʔabaaṭira.

to **emphasize** - šaddad. He emphasized that the main problem was disarmament. šaddad ʔənno l-masʔale r-raʔiisiyye hiyye masʔalet nazɛ ᵊs-silaaḥ.

emphatically - bataatan. I'll have to deny that emphatically. ʔana məḍṭarr kazzeb haš-šii bataatan.

empire - ʔambaraṭooriyye pl. -aat.

to **employ** - staxdam, šaġġal. This factory employs a thousand workers. hal-fabriika btəstaxdem ʔalf ɛaamel.

employed - məstaxdam. Where are you employed? ween məstaxdam ʔənte?

employee - məstaxdam pl. -iin, (white collar) mwaẓẓaf pl. -iin.

employer - məstaxdem pl. -iin.

employment - šaġle, (white collar) waẓiife. What kind of employment did you finally get? šuu š-šaġle yalli laqeeta bᵊl-ʔaaxiir?

employment agency - maktab˜ (pl. makaateb˜) ʔəstəxdaam. He got his job through an employment agency. laqa šaġᵊlto b-waaṣəṭṭ maktab ʔəstəxdaam.

empress - ʔambaraṭoora pl. -aat.

empty - 1. faarġa pl. fawaareġ. I'll get my deposit back when I return the empties. bəstaržeɛ ᵊt-taʔmiin tabaɛi lamma bražžeɛ ᵊl-fawaareġ. 2. faaḍi. Do you have an empty box? fii ɛandak sanduuq faaḍi? -- I wouldn't drink on an empty stomach if I were you. b-maḥallak maa bəšrab ɛala məɛde faaḍye. 3. faafuuši*. He made empty threats. haddad tahdiidaat faafuušiyye.

to empty - 1. faḍḍa, farraġ. Please empty this drawer. baḷḷa faḍḍi had-dərᵊž. 2. fəḍi (a ə). The hall emptied in five minutes. ṣ-ṣaala fəḍyet ᵊb-xamᵊs daqaayeq. 3. ṣabb (ə ṣabb). The river empties into the ocean. ṇ-ṇahᵊr bişəbb bᵊl-muḥiiṭ.

empty-handed - (w-)ʔidée faaḍye. She returned empty-handed. rəžɛet w-ʔideeha faaḍye.

to **enable** - makkan. This experience should enable you to get a good position. xəbra mən han-nooɛ bət-makknak taaxod šaġle mniiḥa.

enamel - miina.

to **encourage** - šažžaɛ. He encouraged me to stick it out. šažžaɛni ṣaaber. -- Our school doesn't encourage sports. madrasətna maa bətšažžeɛ ᵊr-riyaaḍa.

to **encroach (up)on** - tɛadda ɛala, džaawaz ɛala. That would be encroaching upon his rights. haada bikuun taɛaddi ɛala ḥquuqo. --Don't encroach on my territory! laa tətɛadda ɛala ḥduudi!

encyclopedia - daaʔərt˜ (pl. dawaaʔer˜) maɛaaref.

end - 1. ʔaaxer, n(i)haaye. I'll pay you the balance at the end of the month. bədfdɛ-lak ᵊr-raṣiid ᵊb-ʔaaxer ᵊš-šahᵊr. -- They live at the end of this street. saakniin ᵊb-ʔaaxer haš-šaareɛ. 2. nihaaye. The soldiers fought bravely to the very end. ž-žunuud ḥaarabu b-šažaaɛa lən-nihaaye (or **ləl-ʔaaxiir). 3. ʔawaaxer (pl.) The author was born at the end of the Nineteenth Century. l-ᵊmʔallef wəled ᵊb-ʔawaaxer ᵊl-qarn ᵊt-taaseɛ ɛašar. 4. ṭaraf pl. ʔaṭraaf. Tie the two ends of the rope together. rbooṭ ṭarafeen ᵊl-ḥabᵊl maɛ baɛḍon. 5. ġaaye pl. -aat. He believes that the end justifies the means. byəɛtəqed ʔənno l-ġaaye bətbarrer ᵊl-waaṣṭa.

**Except for a few loose ends, everything is done. maa ɛada kam šaġle ṭafiife kəll šii xalaṣ.

**He scolded a bit and that was the end of it. xaanaq ᵊšwayye w-xalṣet ᵊl-qəṣṣa.

**You can't go to the movies, and that's the end of it! ʔənte muu laḥa truuḥ ɛas-siinama wᵊs-salaam!

in the end - bᵊl-ʔaaxiir, bᵊn-nihaaye. He'll consent in the end. ləssa biwaafeq bᵊl-ʔaaxiir.

no end of - maa-lo ʔaaxer, maa-lo nhaaye. We had no end of trouble on the trip. ṣaarət-ᵊlna mašaakel maa-la ʔaaxer bᵊs-safra. -- He gave us no end of trouble. sabbdb-ᵊlna wažaɛ raas maa-lo ʔaaxer.

odds and ends - ḥaraṭiiq (pl.) Our cellar is full of odds and ends. l-qabu tabaɛna malaan ḥaraṭiiq.

**I still have some odds and ends to take care of. ləssa ɛaliyyi kam šaġle hoon w-ᵊhniik bəddi xallṣon.

on end - bala waqfe, biduun ʔənqiṭaaɛ. It's been raining now for five days on end. ṣar-la naazle l-maṭar xamᵊst iyyaam bala waqfe.

to come to an end - ntaha, xalaṣ (o xalaaṣ). Those good times have come to an end now. hadiik ᵊl-ʔawqaat ᵊl-ḥəlwe ntahet hallaq.

to make (both) ends meet - žaab (i žayabaan˜) r-raaseen sawa. He hardly earns enough to make both ends meet. bᵊl-kaad daxlo ykaffii yžiib ᵊr-raaseen sawa.

to put an end to - waḍaɛ (-yuuḍaɛ waḍᵊɛ˜//nwaḍaɛ) ḥadd la-, ḥaṭṭ nihaaye la. Can't you put an end to this arguing? maa fiikon baqa tuuḍaɛu ḥadd la-hal-ʔaxᵊd wᵊr-radd?

to end - 1. xatam (o xatᵊm//nxatam), ʔanha. He ended his speech with a quotation from the Koran. xatam xiṭaabo b-šaahed ᵊmn ᵊl-qərʔaan. -- That rain ended a long dry spell. hal-maṭar ʔanhet mədde ṭawiile mn ᵊž-žafaaf. 2. qaḍa (i qaḍa//nqaḍa) ɛala. An airplane crash ended her life. ḥaadəst ṭayyaara qaḍet ɛala ḥayaata. 3. xalaṣ (o xalaaṣ), ntaha. When did the show end? ʔeemta xalas ᵊl-ɛarḍ? -- Won't this gossip ever end? šuu muu laḥa yəxloṣ hal-ḥaki ɛan-naas ʔabadan? -- This road ends two miles south of Damascus. haṭ-ṭariiq byəxloṣ miileen b-ᵊžnuub ᵊš-šaam.

**That won't end well. hal-qəṣṣa maa-la ʔaaxra ṭayybe.

**All's well that ends well. l-ʔaaxra ya faaxra.

endless - maa-lo ʔaaxer, maa-lo nhaaye, bala nhaaye. Her story was endless. kaanet qəṣṣəta maa-la ʔaaxer. -- I'm getting a little tired of your endless complaints. ɛam ʔəsʔam mən tašakkiyaatak yalli maa-la ʔaaxer.

to **endorse** - 1. žayyar. You forgot to endorse this check, sir. nsiit ᵊdžayyer haš-šakk yaa sayyed. 2. ʔayyad. All major parties endorse this policy. kəll ᵊl-ʔaḥzaab ᵊr-raʔiisiyye biʔayydu has-syaase.

endurance - žalad, msaabara.

to **endure** - tḥammal, kaabad, ɛaana. They had to endure no end of hardships. nžabaru yətḥammalu mataaɛeb maa-la ʔaaxer.

enema - ḥəqne pl. ḥəqan.

enemy - ɛaduww pl. ʔaɛdaaʔ. Even his enemies respected him. ḥatta ʔaɛdaaʔo ḥtaramúu.

energy - 1. našaaṭ. He's full of energy. kəllo našaaṭ. 2. quwwe. Playing football requires a lot of energy. ləɛb ᵊl-futbool bəddo quwwe ktiir. 3. ṭaaqa. She is doing research in atomic energy. ɛam taɛmel ᵊbḥuus ᵊb-miidaan ᵊṭ-ṭaaqa z-zarriyye.

to **enforce** - naffaz//tnaffaz, ṭabbaq//ṭṭabbaq. The police are really enforcing the speed ordinance around schools. l-booliis ɛam ynaffzu b-ṣaraame niẓaam taḥdiid ᵊs-sərɛa naaḥ ᵊl-madaares. -- This law has never been strictly enforced. hal-qaanuun ᵊb-ḥayaato maa ṭṭabbaq ᵊb-ḥazafiiro.

to **engage** - 1. staxdam. We've just engaged a new maid. mən kam yoom staxdamna (or **žebna) ṣaanɛa ždiide. 2. tɛaaqad maɛ. We engaged him for two concerts. tɛaaqadna maɛo mənšaan tneen konseer. 3. daxalu (o dxuul) maɛ baɛḍon, tšaabaku. These two gears engage only when the engine is started. hal-ᵊmsannaneen byədᵊxlu maɛ baɛḍon bass waqᵊt bikuun ᵊl-mootoor maaši. 4. ddaaxal, tɛaaṭa. I don't engage in politics. ʔana maa bəddaaxal bᵊs-syaase.

engaging - žazzaab. He has a very engaging manner. ʔaṭbaaɛo žazzaabe ktiir.

engaged - 1. xaaṭeb f. maxṭuube. How long have they been engaged? qaddeeš ṣar-lon xaaṭbiin? 2. mašġuul. He's engaged in a conference right now. huwwe mašġuul hallaq ᵊb-ʔəžtimaaɛ.

engagement - 1. mawɛed pl. mawaɛiid. I have an engagement this evening. ɛandi mawɛed ᵊl-masa. 2. xəṭbe, xṭuube pl. -aat. She announced her engagement. ʔaɛlanet xəṭbəta.

engine - 1. mootoor and motoor pl. -aat, mḥarrek pl. -aat. You left the engine running. xalleet ᵊl-mootoor maaši. 2. maakiina pl. -aat, qaaṭira pl. -aat. This train has two engines. hat-treen ʔəlo maakiinteen. 3. sayyaaret˜ (pl. -aat˜) ʔəṭfaaʔiyye. I counted no less than seven engines at the site of the fire. halli ɛaddeeton muu ʔaqall mən sabᵊɛ sayyaaraat ʔəṭfaaʔiyye b-makaan ᵊl-ḥariiq.

engineer - 1. mhandes pl. -iin. I've asked the engineer to draw a new set of plans. ṭalabᵊt mən l-ᵊmhandes yərsom ṭaqᵊm xaraayeṭ ᵊždiid. 2. məkanᵊsyaan pl. -iyye. The engineer and the fireman were the only two people to get hurt in the train crash. *l-məkan°syaan w°l-ɛaṭaṭši waḥdon halli nžaraḥu b-ḥaadəst °l-°əṣṭidaam.*

engineers - *fərqet~ °l-handase.* He served with the Forty-Second Engineers. *xadam °b-fərqet °l-handase nəmra tneen w-°ar°bɛiin.*

(stationary) engineer - *mekanist* pl. *-iyye.* The engineer says there's something wrong with the boiler. *l-mekanist ɛam yquul °anno fii ɛəṭ°l b°l-qaazaan.*

to engineer - *dabbar.* Wasn't that cleverly engineered? *šaayef qaddeeš kaanet °mdabbara b-ɛayaaqa?*

England - *°əngəltra.*

English - **1.** *°əngliizi.* He speaks a very good English. *byəḥki °əngliizi ktiir °mniiḥ.* **2.** *°əngliizi*.* That's an old English custom. *hayy ɛaade °əngliiziyye qadiime.* **3.** *°əngliizi* pl. *°əngliiz.* He's English. *huwwe °əngliizi.* -- We have three English students in class. *fii ɛanna tlətt ṭəllaab °əngliiz °b-ṣaffna.* -- I wasn't born yet when the English were in this country. *ləssa maa kənt °wlədt waq°t kaanu l-°əngliiz °b-hal-°blaad.*

Englishman - *°əngliizi* coll. pl. *°əngliiz.* I met three Englishmen in the first two days already. *tɛarraf°t ɛala tlaate °əngliiz °b-hal-yoomeen.*

Englishwoman - *°əngliiziyye* pl. *-aat.*

to **enjoy** - **1.** *tmattaɛ b-.* He's enjoying an active life. *ɛam yətmattaɛ °b-ḥayaat kəlla našaaṭ.* -- He's enjoying excellent health. *ɛam yətmattaɛ °b-ṣaḥḥa məmtaaze.* **2.** *nbaṣaṭ b-.* Did you enjoy the swim? *nbaṣaṭṭ b°s-sbaaḥa?* -- He doesn't enjoy life any more. *maa ɛaad yənbəṣeṭ °b-ḥayaato.*

**How did you enjoy the picture? *kiif ɛažabak °l-fəl°m?*

to enjoy oneself - *nbaṣaṭ.* Did you enjoy yourself at the dance? *nbaṣaṭṭ šii b°l-baal?*

enjoyable - *saarr, məmteɛ.* That was a very enjoyable evening. *kaanet leele ktiir saarra.*

to **enlarge** - *kabbar//tkabbar.* I'll enlarge these pictures for you. *bkabbər-lak haṣ-ṣuwar.*

to **enlist** - *ṭṭawwaɛ.* He enlisted in the navy two days ago. *ṭṭawwaɛ b°l-baḥriyye mən yoomeen.*

enormous - *mahuul, haa°el, ḍax°m.* That's an enormous project. *haada mašruuɛ mahuul.* -- But think of the enormous costs! *bass xood baalak °mn °t-takaliif °ḍ-ḍaxme!*

**It takes an enormous amount of time to read that book. *qraayet hal-°ktaab bədda waq°t ṭawiil °ktiir.*

enormously - *b-ṣuura haa°ile.* The need for raw materials has grown enormously. *l-ḥaaže ləl-mawaadd °l-°awwaliyye zdaadet °b-ṣuura haa°ile.*

enough - *kfaaye* (invar.), *kaafi.* Do you have enough money? *maɛak maṣaari kfaaye?* -- Have you had enough to eat? *kaan ɛandak °akl °kfaaye?*

**I've had enough of that talk. *ḥaašti mən hal-ḥaki!*

**Enough of these idle speculations! *ḥaašətna mən hal-°ḥsaabaat °l-baaṭle!*

**Would you be kind enough to open the window? *btaɛmel maɛruuf təftaḥ °š-šəbbaak?*

**Would you be good enough to hand me the paper? *btaɛmel maɛruuf °tnaawəlni ž-žariide?*

**He seemed glad enough to do it. *kaan °mbayyen ɛalée °ənno bəddo yaɛməla ɛan ṭiibet xaaṭer.*

to be enough - *kaffa, kafa (i kfaaye).* Will that be enough? *haada bikaffi?* -- Will a hundred pounds be enough for you? *miit leera bətkaffiik?* -- Your answer isn't enough for me. *žawaabak muu kaafi °əli.*

to **enroll** - **1.** *saǧǧal, qayyad.* I'm going to enroll my son in first grade. *bəddi saǧǧel °əbni b°ṣ-ṣaff °l-°awwal.* **2.** *saǧǧal ḥaalo, qayyad ḥaalo.* I am going to enroll in night school. *bəddi saǧǧel ḥaali b°l-madrase l-masaa°iyye.*

to **ensure** - *ḍəmen (a ḍamaan//nḍaman), kəfel (a ə // nkafal).* There's nothing that can positively ensure the success of such a project. *maa fii šii byəḍman b°l-miyye miyye nažaaḥ heek mašruuɛ.*

to **enter** - **1.** *daxal (o dxuul), faat (u foote).* Everyone rose when the guest of honor entered. *l-kəll qaam lamma ḍeef °š-šaraf daxal.* -- Do you think we can enter through this door? *btəɛtəqed fiina nfuut mən hal-baab?* **2.** *daxal.* Does money enter into the motive for the crime? *l-maṣaari daaxle b-dawaaɛi ž-žariime?* **3.** *daxxal, qayyad, saǧǧal.* Enter these names in the list. *daxxel hal-°asaami b°l-liista.* -- Did you enter the last bill? *qayyadt °aaxer faatuura šii?*

enterprise - *mašruuɛ* pl. *-aat* and *mašariiɛ.* Who is going to finance this enterprise? *miin bəddo ymawwel hal-mašruuɛ?*

to **entertain** **1.** *ṭarab (o ṭarab//nṭarab).* He entertained the guests with his amusing stories. *ṭarab °ḍyuufo b-ḥakayda ṭ-ṭariife.*

**They entertain a great deal. *ḍ-ḍyuuf maa byəṭlaɛu mən beeton.*

**I've been entertaining a notion to go home this afternoon. *ṣar-li ɛam luuka b-ɛaqli mədde ruuḥ °l-yoom bakkiir baɛd °ḍ-ḍəh°r ɛal-beet.*

entertainment - **1.** *ɛəddet~ °ṭ-ṭarab.* Who's going to provide the entertainment? *miin laḥa yžiib ɛəddet °ṭ-ṭarab?* **2.** *təslaaye, tasliye.* What do you do for entertainment around here? *šuu btaɛmel hoon məšaan təslaaye?*

enthusiasm - *ḥamaas(e), taḥammos.* He didn't show any enthusiasm for my suggestion. *maa warža °ayy ḥamaase la-°əqtiraaḥi.*

enthusiastic - *mətḥammes.* I'm real enthusiastic about going to the dance this weekend. *°ana mətḥammes °ktiir ruuḥ ɛal-baal b-°aaxer hal-°əsbuuɛ.*

entire - **1.** *kaamel.* For an entire year he was laid up in a hospital. *bəqi səne kaamle b°l-məstašfa.* **2.** *kəll °l-, kəll-* + pron. suff., *b-kaamel-* + pron. suff. Our entire day was spent shopping for clothes. *kəll °nhaarna* (or *nhaarna kəllo* or *nhaarna b-kaamlo*) *ṣarafnda ɛam nətsawwaq °awaaɛi.* -- The entire village was flooded last winter. *kəll °ḍ-ḍeeɛa* (or *ḍ-ḍeeɛa kəlla* or *ḍ-ḍeeɛa b-kaaməla*) *ṭaafet °š-šətwiyye l-maaḍye.* -- The entire amount has to be paid in cash. *l-mablaġ b-kaamlo laazem yəndəfeɛ naqdan.*

entirely - **1.** *ɛat-tamaam, tamaaman, kəlliyyan.* You're entirely right. *maɛak ḥaqq ɛat-tamaam.* -- The two are entirely different. *t-tneen byəxtəlfu tamaaman.* **2.** *°akiid, ḥatman.* He charged you entirely too much for that suit. *°akiid baaɛak hal-badle b-°aktar mən ḥaqqa b-°ktiir.*

to be **entitled to** - *st(a)ḥaqq.* He's entitled to a pension. *huwwe məst(a)ḥəqq raateb taqaaɛod.*

entrance - **1.** *madxal* pl. *madaaxel.* Where is the entrance? *ween °l-madxal?* **2.** *dxuul.* Were you accepted for entrance into school? *waafaqu ɛala dxuulak ləl-madrase?*

to **entrust** - *°amman//t°amman ɛala.* He entrusted the car to me. *°ammanni ɛas-sayyaara.*

**I entrust it to your care. *bxallii b-ɛəh°dtak.*

entry - **1.** *nafde* pl. *-aat.* The last entry was five dollars. *°aaxer nafde kaanet xam°s dolaaraat.* **2.** *dxuul.* He was sentenced to one year for unlawful entry into Jordan. *ḥakamúu səne la-dxuulo l-°ərdon dxuul ġeer šarɛi.*

to **enumerate** - *ɛaddad//tɛaddad, sarad (o sar°d//nsarad).* He enumerated all the factors that would speak against the plan. *ɛaddad kəll °l-ɛawaamel halli ḍəḍḍ °l-mašruuɛ.*

envelope - *ẓar°f* pl. *ẓruuf(e), mġallaf* pl. *-aat.* I need an envelope for this letter. *laazəmni ẓar°f məšaan hal-maktuub.*

envious - **1.** *ḥasuud, ġayyuur.* He's just envious, that's all. *huwwe ḥasuud muu °aktar.* **2.** *maḥsuud, ġayyuur.* He's envious of your success. *huwwe maḥsuud mən nažaaḥak.*

environment - *bii°a* pl. *-aat, muḥiiṭ* pl. *-aat, wasaṭ* pl. *°awsaaṭ.* What sort of environment did he grow up in? *šuu l-bii°a halli naša° fiiha?*

envoy - *manduub* pl. *-iin.*

envy - **1.** *ḥasad, ġiire.* He was green with envy. *kaan ɛam yəġli mn °l-ḥasad (w°l-ġiire).* **2.** *mawḍeɛ~ ḥasad.* You'll be the envy of all your friends. *laḥa tkuun mawḍeɛ ḥasad kəll °ṣḥaabak* or ***kəll °ṣḥaabak laḥa yəḥ°sduuk.*

to envy - *ḥasad (o/e ḥasad//nḥasad), ġaar (a ġiire) mən.* I envy you! *bəḥ°sdak!* or *bġaar mənnak!* -- They envied him his success. *ḥasadúu ɛala nažaaḥo.*

epidemic - **1.** *wabaa°* pl. *°awbi°a.* An epidemic has broken out among the cattle. *tfašša wabaa° b°l-baqar.* **2.** *wabaa°i*.* Many epidemic diseases have disappeared completely. *fii °amraaḍ wabaa°iyye ktiir zaalet tamaaman.*

epilepsy - *ṣar°ɛ, ṣarɛa.*

epileptic: She's an epileptic. *mṣaabe b°ṣ-ṣar°ɛ.* -- He had an epileptic fit. *°əžəto noobet ṣar°ɛ.*

episode - *ḥaadse* pl. *ḥawaades.*

Epsom salts - *məl°ḥ °əngliizi.*

equal - *mətsaawi, mɛaadel.* I'll give each of you an equal amount to start with. *baɛṭi kəll waaḥed mablaġ mətsaawi la-təbdu fii.* -- Cut this bread into two equal parts. *qṭaaɛ har-rġiif la-šaq°fteen mətsaawyiin.* -- We are equals as far as our rights and duties are concerned. *nəḥna mətsaawyiin mən naaḥiit l-°ḥquuq w°l-waažbaat.*

**You have to treat him as your equal. *laazem °tɛaamlo ka-waaḥed naẓiirak* (or *masiilak* or *mətlak*).

to be equal to (something) - *kaan qadd˜ (šii).* I don't think I'm equal to that job. *ma bəftəker ʔənni qadd haš-šağle.*
to equal - **1.** *saawa, tsaawa maɛ, ɛaadal, tɛaadal maɛ.* The gains will never equal the losses. *l-ʔarbaaḥ maa bətsaawi ʔabadan ᵊl-xaṣaayer.* **2.** *saawa.* Five times fourteen equals seventy. *ʔarbaṭaɛš ᵊb-xamse bisaawu sabɛiin.* **3.** *wəṣel (-yəṣal and -yuuṣal ø) la-.* It will be hard to equal his accuracy. *bikuun ṣaɛb ᵊl-waaḥed yəṣal ləd-dəqqa tabaɛo.*
equality - *msaawda(t).*
equally: The two books are equally important. *l-ᵊktaabeen mətsaawyiin bᵊl-ʔahammiyye.* -- The two armies are equally well equipped. *ž-žeešeen mətsaawyiin bᵊt-tažhiizaat ᵊl-məmtaaze.* -- I liked his first play equally well. *ḥabbeet tamsiiliito l-ʔuula qadd-ma ḥabbeet hayy.*
equation - *mɛaadale* pl. *-aat.*
equator - *xaṭṭ˜ ᵊl-ʔəstiwaaʔ.*
equatorial - *ʔəstiwaaʔi*.*
equilibrium - *tawaazon.*
to **equip** - *žahhaz//džahhaz.* Our planes are equipped with the latest instruments. *ṭayyaaraatna mžahhaze b-ʔaḥdas ᵊl-ʔaalaat.* -- We equipped ourselves with plenty of food and water for the trip across the desert. *žahhazna ḥaalna b-ʔakl w-mayy ᵊkfaaye məšaan ᵊs-safra qaaṭeɛ ᵊṣ-ṣaḥra.*
equipment - *tažhiizaat* (pl.), *muɛəddaat* (pl.).
equivalent - **1.** *mɛaadel, mwaazi, msaawi.* The decision has to be approved by the undersecretary or by an officer of equivalent rank. *l-q̈araar laazem yətsaddaq mən q̈əbal ᵊl-ʔamiin ᵊl-ɛaamm ʔaw mən ᵊmwaẓẓaf kbiir b-rətbe mɛaadle.* **2.** *mɛaadel, mqaabel.* The fee is 100 pounds or its equivalent in American currency. *r-rasm miit leera ʔaw mɛaadlo* (or ***ʔaw maa yuɛaadəla*) *bᵊl-ɛəmle l-ʔameerkaaniyye.* **3.** *maqabiil* (invar.). That word has no equivalent in English. *hal-kəlme maa-la maqabiil bᵊl-ʔəngliizi.*
era - *ɛaṣᵊr* pl. *ɛṣuur.*
to **erase** - **1.** *maḥa (i maḥi//mmaḥa).* He erased the signature. *maḥa l-ʔəmḍa.* **2.** *masaḥ (a masᵊḥ// mmasaḥ).* Will you please erase the board? *baḷḷa msaaḥ ᵊl-looḥ.* **3.** *maḥa, masaḥ.* Who erased the sentence on the board? *miin maḥa ž-žəmle yalli kaanet ɛal-looḥ?* **4.** *ṭamaṣ (o ṭamᵊṣ//nṭamaṣ).* All signs of their camp had been carefully erased. *kəll ɛalaamaat maxyəmon ᵊnṭamṣet b-ḥazaaqa.*
eraser - *maḥḥaaye* pl. *-aat.* I bought two pencils and an eraser. *štareet qalameen w-maḥḥaaye.* -- We need some chalk and an eraser. *laazəmna ṭabašiir w-maḥḥaaye.* -- Shall I wet the eraser? *bəll ᵊl-maḥḥaaye šii?*
erect - *šaales, waaqef.* He would look much better if he would walk erect. *kaanet šoofto bətkuun ᵊktiir ʔaḥla law yəmši šaales.*
**The guards stood very erect at the door. *l-ḥaras kaanu waaqfiin mətl ᵊl-ʔalef ɛal-baab.*
to erect - **1.** *qaam (i ʔiq̈aame).* We plan to erect a monument in his honor. *b-niyyətna nqiim naṣᵊb taxliid ʔəlo.* **2.** *bana (i bina//mbana).* They're erecting the new museum near my home. *ɛam yəbnu l-matḥaf ᵊž-ždiid qərᵊb beetna.*
errand - *məšwaar* pl. *mašawiir.* I have a few errands to do. *ɛaliyyi kam məšwaar ʔəq̈diihon.* -- I have no time to run errands for you. *maa maɛi waqᵊt la-qəm-lak b-mašawiirak.*
error - *ġalṭa* pl. *-aat.* There must be some error. *laazem ykuun fii šii ġalṭa.* -- Did I make an error? *ɛməlt šii ġalṭa ʔana?* or ***ġləṭṭ šii?*
escape - *harab, fraar.* The prisoners' escape was cleverly planned. *harab ᵊl-maḥabiis kaan ᵊmdabbar b-kəll ḥazaaqa.*
**We had a narrow escape. *nafadna b-ʔəɛžuube.*
to escape - **1.** *harab (o harab), farr (ə fraar).* Two prisoners have escaped from the penitentiary. *fii tneen maḥabiis harabu mn ᵊs-səžᵊn.* **2.** *nafad (o nafde), fəlet (a falataan).* The thief escaped. *l-ḥaraami nafad.* **3.** *fəlet, malaṣ (o malᵊṣ).* We escaped to France. *flətna la-fransa.* **4.** *faat (u ø).* Her face is familiar but her name escapes me. *wəšša muu ġariib ɛaliyyi laaken ʔəsma ɛam yfuutni.* -- Nothing escapes her. *maa fii šii bifuuta.* **5.** *naffad.* Gas is escaping through a crack in the pipe. *l-ġaaz ɛam ynaffed mən šaqq bᵊl-buuri.*
Eskimo - *ʔəskimo* (invar.).
especially - *b-ṣuura xaaṣṣa, xaaṣṣatan, xṣuuṣan.* She's especially interested in sports. *hiyye ʔəla maraaq b-ṣuura xaaṣṣa bᵊs-spoor.* -- The poor, especially, had to suffer a lot. *l-fəqara xaaṣṣatan tɛazzabu ktiir.*
espionage - *žaasuusiyye, tažassos.* He was found guilty of espionage. *žarramúu bᵊž-žaasuusiyye.*
essence - *ləbb, žawhar, xulaaṣa.* That, in short, is the essence of his theory. *haada, bᵊl-ʔəxtiṣaar, huwwe ləbb naẓariito.*
in essence - *bᵊl-xulaaṣa, bᵊl-ʔasaas, ʔasaasiyyan.* In essence, it's an economic question. *bᵊl-xulaaṣa ᵊl-masʔale masʔale ʔəq̈tiṣaadiyye.*
essential - **1.** *ʔasaasi*.* Fresh vegetables are essential to good health. *l-xəḍar ᵊt-taaza šii ʔasaasi ləṣ-ṣaḥḥa.* **2.** *žawhari*, ʔasaasi*.* This is an essential point. *hayy nəqṭa žawhariyye.*
essentials - *ʔasaasiyyaat* (pl.). You can learn the essentials in an hour. *fiik tətɛallam ᵊl-ʔasaasiyyaat ᵊb-saaɛa.*
essentially - *ʔasaasiyyan, bᵊl-ʔasaas, bᵊl-xulaaṣa.* It's essentially a political question. *ʔasaasiyyan hayy masʔale syaasiyye.* -- These assumptions are essentially correct although I would question some of the details. *hal-ʔəftiraaḍaat ʔasaasiyyan maẓbuuṭiin maɛ ʔənni bətsaaʔal ɛan baɛḍ ᵊt-tafarruɛaat.*
to **establish** - **1.** *ʔassas//tʔassas.* This firm was established in 1905. *haš-šərke tʔassaset sənt ʔalf w-təsɛa miyye w-xamse.* **2.** *bana (i bina//mbana).* He's established quite a reputation as an author. *bana šəhra laa baʔᵊs fiiha ka-mʔallef.* **3.** *saššal.* He established a new record. *saššal raq̈am q̈iyaasi ždiid.* **4.** *ḥaddad.* The police still haven't established the motive. *š-šərṭa ləssa maa ḥaddadet ᵊd-dawaafeɛ.*
estate - **1.** *məlᵊk* pl. *ʔamlaak.* He has a beautiful estate in the Bekaa Valley. *ɛando məlᵊk faaxer b-sahᵊl l-ᵊbqaaɛ.* **2.** *tərke* pl. *-aat* and *tərak.* His entire estate went to his oldest son. *tərᵊkto kəlla ṭəlɛet la-ʔəbno l-ᵊkbiir.*
estimate - **1.** *taxmiin* pl. *-aat, taqdiir* pl. *-aat.* My estimate was pretty accurate. *taxmiini kaan la-daraže maẓbuuṭ.* **2.** *taqdiiraat* (pl.), *taxmiinaat* (pl.). The painter made us an estimate. *d-dahhaan ɛəməl-lna taqdiiraat.* **3.** *raʔi.* These prices are way too high, in my estimate. *hal-ʔasɛaar ɛaalye ktiir ᵊktiir b-raʔyi.*
to estimate - *qaddar, xamman.* The commission estimated the flood damage at a million dollars. *l-ləžne qaddaret ʔaḍraar ᵊl-fayaḍaan b-malyoon dolaar.*
et cetera - *ʔila ʔaaxirihi, w-ɛala hal-mənwaal, w-ġeer heek, w-ġeero.*
eternal - *ʔazali*, ʔabadi*.*
eternity - *ʔazaliyye.*
ether - *ʔasiir, rooḥ˜ ləqmaan.*
ethical - *ʔaxlaaqi*.*
ethics - **1.** *ɛəlm˜ ᵊl-ʔaxlaaq, falsafe ʔaxlaaqiyye.* I took two courses in ethics. *ʔaxadt darseen b-ɛəlm ᵊl-ʔaxlaaq.* **2.** *waažbaat ʔadabiyye* (pl.). It's a question of professional ethics. *hayy masʔalet waažbaat ᵊl-məhne l-ʔadabiyye.*
Ethiopia - *l-ḥabaše.*
Ethiopian - **1.** *ḥabaši*.* He studied Ethiopian languages. *daras ᵊl-luġaat ᵊl-ḥabašiyye.* **2.** *ḥabaši** coll. *ḥabaš* pl. *ʔaḥbaaš.* There were three Ethiopians with us on the boat. *kaan fii tlatt ʔaḥbaaš* (or *tlaate ḥabaš*) *maɛna bᵊl-baaxra.*
eucalyptus tree - *šažaret˜* (coll. *šažar˜* pl. *-aat˜*) *kaafuur.*
eunuch - *məxṣi* pl. *-iyyiin, ṭawaaši* pl. *-iyye.*
Euphrates - *(nahr˜) ᵊl-furaat.*
Europe - *ʔawrəbba, ʔoorəbba.*
European - *ʔawrəbbi*.*
to **evacuate** - **1.** *ʔaxla, faḍḍa.* The government evacuated the town. *l-ᵊḥkuume ʔaxlet ᵊl-balad.* **2.** *ʔažla.* They had to evacuate the local population. *nžabaru yažlu ʔahaali l-manṭiqa.*
evacuation - *ʔəxlaaʔ, ʔəžlaaʔ.*
to **evaporate** - *tbaxxar.* The alcohol has all evaporated. *s-sbeetro kəllo tbaxxar.*
evaporated milk - *ḥaliib ᵊmkassaf.*
Eve - *ḥawwa.*
even - **1.** *məžwez.* Two, four, and six are even numbers. *tneen w-ʔarbɛa w-satte ʔaɛdaad məžᵊwze.* **2.** *məttəzen, məɛtədel.* He has an even disposition. *ʔəlo ṭabᵊɛ məttəzen.* **3.** *ḍəgri* (invar.), *məstəwi.* A billiard table must have an even surface. *ṭaawəlt ᵊl-bəlyaardo laazem ykuun ṣaṭḥa ḍəgri.* **4.** *kiit* (invar.). Now we are even. *nəḥna hallaq kiit.* **5.** *ɛal-maẓbuuṭ, bᵊẓ-ẓabᵊṭ.* I have an even dozen left. *ṣafyaan ɛandi dazziine waaḥde ɛal-maẓbuuṭ.* **6.** *ḥatta.* Even a layman can understand that. *ḥatta*

r-ražol əl-εaadi byəfham haš-šii. -- That's even better. *haada ḥatta ʔaḥsan.* -- Even now I can't convince him. *ḥatta hallaq maa-li qadraan ʔaqənεo.* -- I couldn't even see him. *maa qdərət šuufo ḥatta.*-- Not even he knows the truth. *ḥatta huwwe muu εarfaan əl-ḥaqiiqa.*

even so - *maε haada, maε (kəll) ṣaalek, bər-raġəm mən heek.* Even so I can't agree with you. *maε haada maa fiini waafeq maεak.*

even though - *maε ʔənno, bər-raġəm ʔənno.* Even though he succeeds in everything he's not satisfied. *maε ʔənno huwwe naažeḥ əb-kəll šii muu məktəfi.*

to break even - *žaab (i žayabaan~) ər-raaseen sawa.* He's just breaking even. *yaḷḷa yžiib ər-raaseen sawa.*

to get even - *ntaqam, stadd.* Just wait, I'll get even with you! *stanna, ləssa bəntəqem mənnak!*

to even (up) - **1.** *εaddal, saawa ḍəgri.* Would you even up this hem for me? *btaεəmli maεruuf tεaddlli-li had-daayer?* **2.** *εaadal.* We need just one more point to even the score. *bass laazəmna kamaan bənṭ la-nεaadel ən-nataayež.*

evening - *masa* pl. *masawaat.* The evenings here are cold. *l-masa hoon barəd.* -- It's been raining three evenings in a row. *ṣar-la εam tənzel maṭar tlatt masawaat mətwaalye.* -- We take a walk every evening. *mnaεmel məšwaar kəll masa.* -- Good evening! *masa l-xeer!* answer: *masa l-xeeraat!* or *miit masa!*

evenings - *l-masa, εašiyye, bəl-leel.* Is this restaurant open evenings? *hal-maṭεam byəftaḥ əl-masa?*

in the evening - *(εand) əl-masa, (εand) εašiyye.* She usually calls in the evening. *εaadatan bəttalfen εand əl-masa.*

this evening - *l-masa, εašiyye.* Are they coming this evening? *žaayiin əl-masa?*

evenly - **1.** *εala swiyye waaḥde, bət-tasaawi.* The paint isn't spread evenly. *d-dhaan muu mwazzaε εala swiyye waaḥde.* **2.** *εala swiyye waaḥde.* Are these curtains hanging evenly? *hal-baraadi mεallaqiin εala swiyye waaḥde?* **3.** *bət-tasaawi.* Divide these apples evenly among you. *tqaasamu hat-təffaaḥaat beenaatkon bət-tasaawi.*

event - **1.** *ḥaades* pl. *ḥawaades.* The subsequent course of events proved how right he was. *mažra l-ḥawaades əl-mətεaaqbe barhanet qaddeeš kaan maεo ḥaqq.* **2.** *mnaasabe* pl. *-aat.* Her party was the most important social event of the year. *ḥafləta kaanet ʔahamm mnaasabe ʔəžtimaaεiyye ṣaaret has-səne.*

in any event - *εala kəll ḥaal, εala kullin, mahma ṣaar.* I'll be there in any event. *bkuun əhniik εala kəll ḥaal.*

in that event - *b-hal-ḥaale, b-heek ḥaale.* In that event, I will not go. *b-hal-ḥaale maa bruuḥ.*

in the event of - *b-ḥaalet~...* In the event of an accident, notify the police. *b-ḥaalet wḍuuε ḥaades xabber əl-booliis.*

eventually - *bəl-ʔaaxiir.* He'll give in eventually. *bəl-ʔaaxiir bisallem.*

ever - **1.** *b-ḥayaat-* or *b-εəmr-* + pron. suff. of subject. Have you ever been in the United States? *b-ḥayaatak rəḥət la-ʔameerka?* -- Who ever heard of such a thing! *miin əb-εəmro səmeε heek šii?* **2.** *daayman, εala ṭuul.* We are ever willing to assist you. *nəḥna daayman məstεəddiin nsaaεdak.*

**Thank you ever so much. *šəkran žaziilan.*

**She is seldom, if ever, absent from school. *bən-naader-ma tətġayyab εan əl-madrase, haada ʔiza tġayyabet.*

ever since - **1.** *mən waqət~ ...* Ever since that accident I've had pains in my leg. *mən waqət hal-ʔaksiḍaan ṣar-li wažaε əb-rəžli.* **2.** *mən waqət-ma.* Ever since she got out of the hospital, she stayed pretty much by herself. *mən waqət-ma ṭəlεet mn əl-məstašfa ṣaaret təbtəεed εan ən-naas.*

hardly ever - *naader-ma, qəllet-ma.* I hardly ever have a headache. *naader-ma yəžiini wažaε raas.*

more than ever - *ʔaktar mən kəll waqət qable.* I loathe this job more than ever. *bəkrah haš-šaġle ʔaktar mən kəll waqət qable.*

not ... ever - *maa ... ʔabadan, maa ... b-ḥayaat-* (or *b-εəmr-*) + pron. suff. of subject. Haven't you ever been there? *maa rəḥət la-hniik ʔabadan?* or *b-ḥayaatak maa rəḥət la-hniik?*

every - *kəll~.* He comes here every week. *byəži la-hoon kəll žəmεa.* -- Give every child one apple. *εaṭi kəll walad təffaaḥa.* -- Every one of us received a pack of cigarettes. *kəll waaḥed mənna ʔəžda baakeet sigaara.*

every now and then - *mən waqət la-waqət, been mədde w-mədde.* We go to a movie every now and then. *mənruuḥ εas-siinama mən waqət la-waqət.*

every once in a while - *mən waqət la-waqət, been mədde w-mədde.* He takes a drink every once in a while. *byaaxəd-lo qadaḥ mən waqət la-waqət.*

every other day - *yoom ʔee yoom laʔ, kəll yoomeen.* They have meat for dinner every other day. *byətεaššu laḥme yoom ʔee yoom laʔ.*

every other month - *šahər ʔee šahər laʔ, kəll šahreen.* He comes to us about every other month. *byəži la-εanna yaεni šahər ʔee šahər laʔ.*

every other week - *žəmεa ʔee žəmεa laʔ, kəll žəmεteen.* I see him every other week. *bšuufo žəmεa ʔee žəmεa laʔ.*

every time - *kəll-ma.* It rains every time we want to go out. *kəll-ma mənḥəbb nəṭlaε la-barra btənzel maṭar.*

each and every one - *kəll waaḥed.* You can count on each and every one of us. *fiik təεtəmed εala kəll waaḥed mənna.*

everybody - **1.** *kəll waaḥed.* Everybody has to do his duty. *kəll waaḥed laazem yquum əb-waažbo.* **2.** *l-kəll.* I told it to everybody. *ḥakeeta ləl-kəll.* -- Everybody laughed. *l-kəll ḍəḥku.*

everybody else - *l-baqiyye.* It's all right with me if it's all right with everybody else. *maa fii εandi maaneε ʔiza l-baqiyye maa εandon maaneε.*

everyone - see **everybody**.

everything - *kəll šii.* He's mixed up everything. *xarbaṭ kəll šii.* -- I'll do everything (that's) necessary. *baεmel kəll šii laazem.*

everything else - *l-baaqi.* Everything else is simple. *l-baaqi basiiṭ.*

everywhere - *b-kəll qərne, b-kəll maḥall.* I've looked everywhere for that book. *dawwart əb-kəll qərne εala hal-əktaab.*

evidence - **1.** *daliil* pl. *ʔadəlle, bayyine* pl. *-aat.* He was convicted on false evidence. *žarramuu binaaʔan εala ʔadəlle kaazbe.* -- He was acquitted for lack of evidence. *tbarra li-εadam wžuud əl-ʔadəlle.* **2.** *ʔasar* pl. *ʔaasaar.* The rain washed away all evidence of their camp. *l-maṭar žarfet kəll ʔaasaar maxyəmon.*

evident - *mbayyen, ẓaaher, waaḍeḥ.* It was quite evident that she was sick. *kaan əmbayyen tamaam ʔənna mariiḍa.*

evidently - *εala-ma yəẓhar.* Evidently he flunked the exam. *εala-ma yəẓhar ṣaqaṭ bəl-faḥəṣ.*

evil - **1.** *šarr* pl. *šruur.* He chose the lesser evil. *xtaar ʔahwan əš-šarreen.* **2.** *šərriir.* She is a very evil woman. *hiyye mara šərriire ktiir.*

evil eye - *l-εeen.* That woman has the evil eye. *hal-mara bətṣiib bəl-εeen.*

ewe - *ġaname* pl. *-aat.*

ex- - *saabeq.* He's an ex-general. *huwwe ženeraal saabeq.*

exact - **1.** *maẓbuuṭ.* Make those measurements just as exact as possible. *εmeel hal-maqayiis maẓbuuṭa qadd-muu bəl-ʔəmkaan.* -- I can't tell you the exact number right now. *maa fiini qəl-lak əl-εadad əl-maẓbuuṭ b-had-daqiiqa.* **2.** *daqiiq, maẓbuuṭ.* He's very exact in his work. *huwwe daqiiq əktiir əb-šəġlo.*

**You've done the exact opposite of what I said. *εmələt tamaam εaks halli qəlt-əllak-yda.*

exact copy - *nəsxa* (pl. *nəsax*) *ṭəbq əl-ʔaṣəl.*

exactly - **1.** *εat-tamaam, εal-maẓbuuṭ, tamaam.* That's exactly the same. *haada nafs əš-šii εat-tamaam.* -- It's exactly five o'clock. *s-saaεa xamse tamaam.* **2.** *b-εeen-* + pron. suff., *b-ẓaat-* + pron. suff. That's exactly the point I'm trying to make. *hayy əl-ḥəžže b-εeena halli εam ḥaawel ʔəsbəta.* **3.** *maẓbuuṭ, tamaam.* Exactly! That's what I told her, too. *maẓbuuṭ! haada halli qəlt-əlla-yda kamaan.*

**That wasn't exactly nice of you. *bəddak əṣ-ṣaraaḥa? haada maa kaan ḥəlu mənnak.*

exactness - *dəqqa.* What we expect is exactness. *halli mnətwaqqaεo d-dəqqa.*

to **exaggerate** - *baalaġ.* You're exaggerating as usual. *εam ətbaaleġ mətl əl-εaade.*

exam - *faḥəṣ* pl. *fḥuuṣ(a), ʔəmtiḥaan* pl. *-aat.* The exam was easy. *l-faḥəṣ kaan hayyen.*

examination - **1.** *faḥəṣ* pl. *fḥuuṣ(a), ʔəmtiḥaan* pl. *-aat.* We had an examination in history class this morning. *kaan εanna faḥṣ əb-dars ət-taariix əl-yoom εala bəkra.* **2.** *faḥəṣ* pl. *fḥuuṣ(a).* What did the hospital's examination show? *šuu ṭaleᶜ mən faḥṣ ᵊl-məstašfa?* 3. *ʔəstənṭaaq.* The examination of the witnesses lasted two hours. *ʔəstənṭaaq ᵊš-šhuud stamarr saaᶜteen.*

to **examine** - 1. *faḥaṣ (a faḥᵊṣ//nfaḥaṣ).* The doctor examined me thoroughly. *l-ḥakiim faḥaṣni b-kəll dəqqa.* 2. *stanṭaq.* The witnesses haven't been examined yet. *š-šhuud ləssa maa stanṭaquuhon.* 3. *raažaᶜ.* I'm here to examine the books. *ʔana ʔžiit la-hoon la-raažeᶜ ᵊd-dafaater.*

example - 1. *matal* pl. *ʔamtaal.* Could you give me an example? *fiik taᶜṭiini matal?* 2. *qədwe, ʔəmsuule.* You should set a good example for the others. *laazem ᵊtkuun qədwe ḥasane lən-naas.* 3. *ᶜəbra (lən-naas).* We must make an example of this man. *laazem nəžᶜal mən har-rəžžaal ᶜəbra lən-naas.*

for example - *masalan, matalan.* Let's take Russia, for example ... *xood ruusya masalan ...*

to follow the example of - *qtada b-* We all followed his example. *kəllna qtadeena fii.*

to **excavate** - *naqqab b-, ḥafar (e/o ḥafᵊr//nḥafar) b-.* French archeologists excavated this town. *fii ᶜəlama ʔaasaar fransaawiyyiin naqqabu b-hal-balad.*

excavations - *ḥafriyyaat* (pl.).

to **exceed** - *džaawaz.* Their profits should exceed fifteen thousand pounds this year. *l-məntdᵊar ʔənno ʔarbaaḥon has-səne tədžaawaz xamasṭaᶜšar ʔalf leera.*

exceedingly - *ləl-ġaaye.* She's an exceedingly beautiful woman. *hiyye ḥəlwe ləl-ġaaye.*

excellent - 1. *məmtaaz, baareᶜ, mətfawweq.* He's an excellent tennis player. *huwwe laᶜᶜiib tanes məmtaaz.* 2. *məmtaaz.* That's an excellent idea! *hayy fəkra məmtaaze!* 3. *ᶜaal* (invar.). Excellent! That's just what we wanted. *ᶜaal! haada halli kaan bəddna-yda.*

except - *ʔəlla, maa ᶜada.* Everybody believed it except him. *kəllon saddaquuha ʔəlla huwwe* (or *maa ᶜadda*).

except for - *maa ᶜada, ʔəlla.* I like the book except for one chapter. *ḥaabeb l-ᵊktaab maa ᶜada faṣᵊl waaḥed.*

to except - *stasna.* I except, of course, all those present. *ṭabiiᶜi ʔana bəstasni kəll ᵊl-ḥaadriin.*

exception - *ʔəstəsna* pl. *ʔəstəsnaaʔaat.* This law is enforced without exception. *hal-qaanuun byəṭṭabbaq biduun ʔəstəsna.* -- We make no exceptions. *maa fii ᶜanna ʔəstəsnaaʔaat.*

**Every rule has its exceptions. *kəll qaaᶜde ʔəla šuzuuz.*

with the exception of - *b-ʔəstəsnaaʔ~ ..., maa ᶜada~ ...* With the exception of a few minor flaws it's a good dictionary. *b-ʔəstəsnaaʔ šwayyet ᵊᶜyuub ṭafiife l-qaamuus ᵊmniiḥ.*

excerpt - *ʔəqtibaas* pl. *-aat, məqtdbas* pl. *-aat.*

excess - 1. *zaayed.* Pour off the excess fat. *qiimi d-dəhne z-zaayde.* 2. *zyaade.* I drink sometimes, but not to excess. *baᶜḍ ᵊl-ʔawqaat bəšrab, bass muu b-ᵊzyaade.*

in excess of - *fooq~ ..., halli biziid ᶜan ...* The insurance company will pay for anything in excess of 500 pounds. *šərket ᵊt-taʔmiin btədfaᶜ kəll šii fooq ᵊl-xamᵊs miit leera* (or *kəll šii halli biziid ᶜan ᵊl-xamᵊs miit leera*).

excessive - *zaayed, b-ʔəfraaṭ.* Excessive smoking can cause lung cancer. *t-tadxiin ᵊz-zaayed* (or *t-tadxiin ᵊb-ʔəfraaṭ*) *məmken ysabbeb ṣaraṭaan ᵊr-riʔa.*

exchange - *tabaadol.* The Red Cross arranges for the exchange of prisoners. *ṣ-ṣaliib ᵊl-ʔaḥmar ᶜam ydabber tabaadol ᵊl-ʔasra.*

**We had an exchange of words, that's all. *tlaasanna b-kam kəlme w-bass.*

rate of exchange - *səᶜr~* (pl. *ʔasᶜaar~*) *ᵊl-ᶜəmle.* What's the rate of exchange today? *šuu səᶜr ᵊl-ᶜəmle l-yoom?*

in exchange for - *ᶜawaaḍ~ ...* I gave him a cigarette case in exchange for his lighter. *ᶜaṭeeto ᶜəlbet sigaaraat ᶜawaaḍ qaddaaḥto.*

to exchange - 1. *tbaadal.* I was exchanging ideas with your friend. *kənt ᶜam ʔətbaadal ʔaaraaʔ maᶜ ṣaaḥbak.* 2. *baddal, badaal.* I want to exchange this book for another one. *bəddi baddel hal-ᵊktaab b-waaḥed ġeero.*

excited - 1. *məthayyež.* Why are you so excited? *leeš ʔənte hal-qadd məthayyež?* 2. *mətḥammes.* I'm not too excited about the whole idea. *ʔana maa-li mətḥammes ᵊktiir la-kəll hal-fəkra.*

to get excited - *saar (u sawaraan), thayyaž.* She got very excited when she heard the news. *saaret ᵊktiir lamma səmᶜet ᵊl-xabar.* -- Don't get excited! *ʔəhda, laa tsuur!*

excitement - *hayažaan.* What is all the excitement down at the corner about? *la-šuu kəll hal-hayažaan ᵊhniik ᶜas-suuke?*

exciting - *musiir.* That was an exciting story. *kaanet qəṣṣa musiira.*

exclamation point - *ʔišaaret~* (pl. *-aat~*) *taᶜažžob.*

excuse - *ᶜəzᵊr* pl. *ʔaᶜzaar.* That's no excuse for not going to school. *haada muu ᶜəzᵊr ʔənnak maa truuḥ ᶜal-madrase.* -- He's never at a loss for an excuse. *ᶜəzro b-kəmmo muu ᶜand ʔəmmo.*

to excuse - 1. *ġaḍḍ (ə ġaḍḍ) ᵊn-naẓar ᶜan.* Please excuse my bad Arabic. *bətražžaak ᵊtġəḍḍ ᵊn-naẓar ᶜan ᶜarabiiti l-ᵊmkassara.* 2. *ᶜaṭa (ḥada) ʔəzᵊn.* The manager excused her for the afternoon because of a headache. *l-mudiir ᶜaṭaaha ʔəzᵊn tənṣəref baᶜd ᵊḍ-ḍəhᵊr b-sabab wažaᶜ raasa.*

**Excuse me, please! *ᶜafwan!* or *ᶜan ʔəznak!*

**You may be excused now. *fiik ᵊtruuḥ hallaq.*

to excuse oneself - *staʔzan, ᶜtazar.* He suddenly excused himself and left the room. *fažʔatan ᵊstaʔzan w-tarak ᵊl-ʔuuḍa.* -- I'd like to excuse myself; it's getting late. *bəddi ʔəstaʔzen, tʔaxxaret ᵊd-dənye.*

to **execute** - 1. *ᶜadam (o/e ʔəᶜdaam//nᶜadam).* The murderer was executed this morning. *l-qaatel ᵊnᶜadam ᵊl-yoom ṣabaaḥan.* 2. *naffaz//tnaffaz.* I want you to execute my orders to the letter. *bəddi-yaak ᵊtnaffəz-li ʔawaamri bᵊl-ḥarf.*

executioner - *žallaad* pl. *-iin.*

to **exempt** - *ᶜafa (i ʔəᶜfa//nᶜafa).* I've been exempted from the exam. *nᶜafeet mn ᵊl-faḥᵊṣ.*

exequatur - *baraaʔet~ qənṣol.*

exercise - 1. *tamriin* pl. *tamariin.* Exercise ten is difficult. *t-tamriin ᵊl-ᶜaašer ṣaᶜᵊb.* 2. *ḥarake.* I need more exercise. *laazəmni ḥarake ʔaktar.*

to exercise - 1. *ᶜəmel tamariin ryaaḍiyye.* You have to exercise every morning. *laazem taᶜməl-lak tamariin ryaaḍiyye kəll yoom ᶜala bəkra.* 2. *ṭabbaq.* He exercises his authority very wisely. *biṭabbeq ṣəlᵊṭṭo b-kəll ḥəkme.*

to **exhaust** - 1. *stanfaz.* I've exhausted all possibilities. *stanfazᵊt kəll ᵊl-ʔəmkaaniyyaat.* 2. *stahlak.* I've exhausted every last bit of money that was in my savings account. *stahlakᵊt ʔaaxer qərš b-ᵊḥsaab ᵊt-taṣmiid tabaᶜi.* 3. *ʔanhak.* The long illness has exhausted him more than I had expected. *maraḍo ṭ-ṭawiil ʔanhako ʔaktar məm-ma kənᵊt mətwaqqeᶜ.*

exhausted - *manhuuk, halkaan mn ᵊt-taᶜab.* I was completely exhausted after that long trip. *kənᵊt manhuuk tamaam mən has-safra ṭ-ṭawiile.*

exhaust pipe - *ʔəšᵊtmaan* pl. *-aat.*

exhibit - 1. *maᶜraḍ* pl. *maᶜaareḍ.* Have you seen the agricultural exhibit? *šəft ᵊl-maᶜraḍ ᵊz-ziraaᶜi?* 2. pl. only: *maᶜruuḍaat.* Some of the exhibits were in very poor taste. *baᶜḍ ᵊl-maᶜruuḍaat maa kaan fiihon zooq ʔabadan.*

to exhibit - 1. *ᶜaraḍ (o/e ᶜarᵊḍ//nᶜaraḍ).* He's at present exhibiting some of his paintings at the National Museum. *bᵊl-waqt ᵊl-ḥaaḍer ᶜam yəᶜroḍ baᶜᵊḍ ṣuwaro bᵊl-matḥaf ᵊl-waṭani.* 2. *tbaaha b-.* His wife loves to exhibit her jewelry. *marto bətḥəbb tətbaaha b-maṣaaġa.*

exhibition - *maᶜraḍ* pl. *maᶜaareḍ.*

exile - *manfa* pl. *manaafi.* The king is now in exile on an island. *l-malek hallaq b-manfa b-šii žaziire.*

to **exist** - 1. *kaan mawžuud.* That exists only in your imagination. *haš-šii mawžuud bass b-ᵊmxayyəltak.* -- Such a thing doesn't exist. *heek šii muu mawžuud bᵊd-dənye.* 2. *ᶜaaš (i ᶜiiše).* How does he manage to exist on so little? *kiif qadraan yᶜiiš b-hal-qəlle?*

**He doesn't exist, as far as I'm concerned. *huwwe muu bᵊl-ᵊwžuud bᵊn-nəsbe ʔəli.*

existence - 1. *ḥayaat, ᶜiiše.* He's leading a miserable existence. *ᶜaayeš ḥayaat taᶜiise.* 2. *wžuud.* He's not even aware of my existence. *huwwe muu ᶜarfaan ḥatta b-ᵊwžuudi.*

in existence - *mawžuud.* This company has been in existence for fifty years. *haš-šərke ṣar-la mawžuude xamsiin səne.*

existentialism - *l-mazhab ᵊl-wužuudi, l-wužuudiyye.*

existentialist - *wužuudi** pl. *-iyyiin.*

exit - 1. *maxraž* pl. *maxaarež.* The exit is at the end of the hall. *l-maxraž b-ʔaaxer ᵊl-mamraq.* 2. *ṭalᶜa* pl. *-aat.* He made a hasty exit. *ṭəleᶜ*

ṭalεa b-εažale.
to **expand** – 1. *wassaε.* Russia has expanded her network of communications enormously. *ruusya wassaεet šabaket l-ᵊmwaaṣalaat tabdεa b-ṣuura mədᵊhše.* -- We're going to expand our business next year. *laḥa nwasseε ʔašġaalna s-səne ž-žaaye.* 2. *tmaddad.* Be careful, that glass will expand as you heat it. *ʔočak, hal-balloor byətmaddad taḥt ᵊl-ḥaraara.* 3. *twassaε.* Can you expand on this topic a little more? *fiik tətwassaε šwayye b-hal-mawḍuuε?*
expansion – 1. *tawassoε.* The steady expansion of the country is a matter of grave concern to its neighbors. *tawassoε l-ᵊblaad ᵊl-məṭṭəred εam ysiir ǧalaǧ ᵊž-žiiraan.* 2. *tamaddod.* We discussed the law of expansion of gases in school today. *baḥasna ǧaanuun tamaddod ᵊl-ġaazaat bᵊl-madrase l-yoom.*
to **expect** – 1. *nṭaẓar.* I expect him at three o'clock. *ʔana mənṭəẓro s-saaεa tlaate.* -- Does he expect a tip? *šuu εam yənṭəẓer baxšiiš?* 2. *twaqqaε.* No one expected this turn of events. *maa ḥada twaqqaε taṭawwor hal-ḥawaades.* -- You can't expect that of him. *muu maεquul tətwaqqaε haada mənno.*
expectation – *ʔamal* pl. *ʔaamaal.* He came here with little money and great expectations. *ʔəža la-hoon w-maεo maṣaari qaliile w-ʔaamaal ᵊkbiire.*
**Contrary to my expectation, the experiment turned out well. *b-εakᵊs-ma twaqqaεt ᵊt-tažrube nažḥet.*
expense – *maṣruuf* pl. *-aat* and *maṣariif.* I can't afford the expense. *muu b-qədᵊrti hal-maṣruuf.* -- Did you have any expenses? *dafaεᵊt šii maṣariif?* -- Please don't go to any expense on my account. *bətražžaak laa tḥammel ḥaalak maṣariif mənšaani.* -- This will put me to considerable expense. *haada bikalləfni maṣariif baahẓa.*
at the expense of – *εala ḥsaab˜ ...* He made the trip at his company's expense. *saawa s-safra εala ḥsaab šərᵊkto.*
expensive – 1. *ġaali.* This apartment is too expensive. *haš-šaqqa ktiir ġaalye.* 2. *tamiin, ġaali.* She wears expensive clothes. *btəlbes ʔawaaεi tamiine.*
experience – 1. *xəbra.* Have you any experience in such matters? *fii εandak ʔayy xəbra b-heek ᵊʔmuur?* -- I know from experience it won't work. *baεref bᵊl-xəbra ʔənna maa raḥa təmši.* 2. *ḥaadse* pl. *ḥawaades, qəṣṣa* pl. *qəṣaṣ.* I had a strange experience last night. *ṣar-li ḥaadse ġariibe leelt ᵊmbaareḥ.*
to experience – *ṣaar maε* + pron. suff. of subject. I've never experienced anything like it before. *b-ḥayaati maa ṣaar maεi heek šii mən qabᵊl.*
experienced – *mḥannak, ʔəlo xəbra ṭawiile.* He's an experienced driver. *huwwe šofoor ᵊmḥannak.*
experiment – *tažrube* pl. *tažaareb* and *tažaarob.* The experiment was successful. *t-tažrube kaanet naažḥa.*
to experiment – *žarrab, xtabar.* I experimented with the new colors. *žarrabᵊt bᵊl-ʔalwaan ᵊž-ždiide.*
expert – *xabiir* pl. *xəbara.* The experts declared the document to be a forgery. *l-xəbara ǧarraru ʔənno l-wasiiǧa mzayyafe.* -- We need an expert mechanic for this job. *laazəmna miikaniiki xabiir la-haš-šaġle.* -- I need some expert advice. *laazəmni naṣiiḥet xabiir.*
to **expire** – *xalṣet (o ə) məddet* – + pron. suff. of subject. My passport has expired. *l-basboor tabaεi xalṣet məddᵊto.*
to **explain** – 1. *šaraḥ (a šarᵊḥ//nšaraḥ), fassar// tfassar.* Can you explain this sentence to me? *fiik təšrəḥ-li haž-žəmle?* 2. *šaraḥ, waḍḍaḥ, bayyan.* Our guide explained the importance of the Middle East. *d-daliil tabaεna šarəḥ-ᵊlna ʔahammiit ᵊš-šarǧ ᵊl-ʔawṣaṭ.* 3. *fassar, barrar.* How are you going to explain losing your money? *kiif bəddak ᵊtfasser xṣaaret maṣariik?*
explanation – 1. *šarᵊḥ* pl. *šruuḥ, tafsiir* pl. *tafasiir.* The explanation of chapter five lasted an hour. *šarḥ ᵊl-faṣl ᵊl-xaames ʔaxad saaεa.* 2. *εəzᵊr* pl. *ʔaεzaar.* I hope you've got a good explanation for where you've been all day. *nšaaḷḷa ykuun εandak εəzᵊr maεquul la-ġeebtak ṭuul ᵊn-nhaar.*
to **explode** – 1. *fažžar.* They plan to explode another bomb next week. *niyyəton yfažžru qəmble taanye ž-žəmεa ž-žaaye.* 2. *nfažar.* The shell hit the house but didn't explode. *l-ǧaziife ṣaabet ᵊl-beet bass maa nfažret.*
exploit – *maržale* pl. *maraažel.* He never stops talking about his exploits. *maa byəhda lahẓa yəḥki εan maraažlo.*
to exploit – *st(a)ġall.* He exploits his employees shamelessly. *byəst(a)ġəll məstaxdamiino biduun ḥaya.* -- He did his best to exploit the situation. *εəmel žahdo yəst(a)ġəll ᵊl-waḍᵊε.*
to **explore** – 1. *stakšaf.* When was that island first explored? *ʔeemta stakšafu haž-žaziire ʔawwal marra?* 2. *baḥas (a baḥᵊs//nbaḥas).* We explored all the possibilities. *baḥasna kəll ᵊl-ʔəmkaaniyyaat.*
explosion – *ʔənfižaar* pl. *-aat.* You could hear the explosion for miles. *kaan fiik təsmaε ᵊl-ʔənfižaar εala masaafet ʔamyaal w-ʔamyaal.*
explosive – *maadde mətfažžra* pl. *mətfažžraat.*
export – *taṣdiir* pl. *-aat.* The government has stopped the export of coal. *l-ᵊḥkuume waqqafet taṣdiir ᵊl-faḥᵊm.*
exports – *ṣaadraat* (pl.). The country's exports stayed far below its imports this past year. *ṣaadraat l-ᵊblaad bəqyet ʔaqall mən waardaata b-ᵊktiir has-səne l-maadye.*
to export – *ṣaddar.* Germany exports optical lenses. *ʔalmaanya bətṣadder εadasaat ləl-baṣar.*
exporter – *mṣadder* pl. *-iin.*
to **expose** – 1. *εarraḍ.* That kind of work exposes you to constant danger. *han-nooε mn ᵊl-εamal biεarrḍak la-xaṭar məstmərr.* -- How long did you expose the shot? *qaddeeš εarraḍṭ ᵊṣ-ṣuura?* 2. *faḍaḥ (a faḍᵊḥ//nfaḍaḥ).* He was exposed as a spy. *nfaḍaḥ ka-žaasuus.*
exposition – *maεraḍ* pl. *maεaareḍ.*
exposure meter – *boosoomətᵊr* pl. *-aat.*
express – 1. *ʔəksᵊbrees* pl. *-aat.* Is the next train an express? *t-treen ᵊž-žaaye ʔəksᵊbrees?* 2. *ṣariiḥ.* It was his express wish. *kaanet hayy rəġᵊbto ṣ-ṣariiḥa.* -- We came with the express intention of staying just an hour. *ʔžiina b-niyye ṣariiḥa ʔənno nəbqa bass saaεa.*
(by) express – *bᵊl-ʔəksᵊbrees.* We're sending your trunk by express. *mnəbεə̄t-lak ᵊs-sanduuq tabaεak bᵊl-ʔəksᵊbrees.*
to express – *εabbar εan.* You can express your opinion freely. *fiik ᵊtεabber εan raʔyak ᵊb-ḥərriyye.* -- You haven't expressed yourself clearly. *maa εabbarᵊt εan nafsak b-ᵊwḍuuḥ.*
expression – 1. *taεbiir* pl. *-aat* and *taεaabiir.* There's no better expression for it. *maa fii ʔaḥsan mən heek taεbiir ʔəla.* -- That's an old-fashioned expression. *haada taεbiir mən sənt žədd žəddi.* 2. *taεaabiir* (pl.). I can tell by the expression on your face that you don't like it. *šaayef mən taεaabiir wəššak ʔənnak maa-lak ḥaabə̄ba.*
to **extend** – 1. *mtadd.* The dunes extended for miles. *kəsbaan ᵊr-ramᵊl kaanet məmtadde la-ʔamyaal w-ʔamyaal.* 2. *maddad, žaddad.* I'd like to get this visa extended. *ḥaabeb madded hal-viiza.* 3. *qaddam.* May we extend (to you) our hearty congratulations? *mənqaddə̄m-lak tahaaniina l-qalbiyye?*
extension – 1. *məhle* pl. *məhal.* He gave me another week's extension. *εaṭaani məhle žəmεa taanye.* 2. *tamdiid* pl. *-aat.* He's asked for an extension of his leave. *ṭalab tamdiid ʔižaazto.* 3. *xaṭṭ farεi* pl. *xṭuuṭ farεiyye.* I'll take his call on the extension in my office. *baaxod talifoono bᵊl-xaṭṭ ᵊl-farεi halli b-maktabi.*
extension cord – *šriiṭ* (pl. *šaraayeṭ) waṣle, waṣle* pl. *-aat.* We need an extension cord for this lamp. *laazəmna šriiṭ waṣle la-haḷ-ḷamḅa.*
extension piece – *waṣle* pl. *-aat.* I can't find the second extension piece for the dining-room table. *maa-li εam laaqi l-waṣle t-taanye tabaε ṭaawəlt ᵊl-ʔakᵊl.*
extensive – *šaamel, waaseε.* He's currently conducting an extensive study of rural life in Turkey. *bᵊl-waqt ᵊl-ḥaaḍer εam yquum b-diraase šaamle la-ḥayaat ᵊr-riif ᵊb-tərkiyya.*
extent – *mada.* The extent of the catastrophe is still unknown. *mada l-kaarse ləssaato muu maεruuf.*
**I'll try to give you the full extent of my information on him. *bḥaawel ʔaεṭiik kaamel maεluumaati εanno.*
to a certain extent – *la-daraže.* To a certain extent he is responsible for the disaster. *la-daraže huwwe masʔuul εan ᵊl-kaarse.*
to that extent – *la-hal-ḥadd.* I agree with you to that extent. *la-hal-ḥadd ʔana məttə̄feq maεak.*
external – *xaarži*, barraani*.*
extra – 1. *zyaade* (invar.). Do you have a few extra pencils? *fii εandak kam qalam zyaade?* 2. *zyaade, ʔiḍaafi*.* I'm getting extra pay for working nights. *εam ʔaaxod raateb zyaade laʔənni εam ʔəštə̄ġel bᵊl-leel.* -- Make an extra copy for the main file.

Emeel nəsxa ʔiḍaafiyye ləd-doosyée l-Eaamme.
extraordinary - *fooq ᵊl-Eaade* (invar.). Only an extraordinary woman could accomplish all that. *bass mara fooq ᵊl-Eaade byəṭlaE b-ʔiida taEməl kəll haš-šii.*
extravagant - *məthawwer.* They're an extravagant lot. *hənne ʔərṭa məthawwra.* -- She has an extravagant taste in clothes. *ʔəla zooq məthawwer bᵊt-tyaab.*
extreme - *ʔaqṣa* f. *qəṣwa.* Their house is at the extreme end of the island. *beeton bᵊṭ-ṭaraf ᵊl-ʔaqṣa bᵊš-šaziire.* -- We had to resort to extreme measures. *nšabarna nəttéxez tadabiir qəṣwa* (or *ʔaqṣa˜ tadabiir).*
extremely - *ləl-ġaaye, la-ʔaqṣa ḥadd.* This news is extremely sad. *l-xabar məḥzen ləl-ġaaye.* -- I'll be extremely surprised if he does it. *bətEaššab la-ʔaqṣa ḥadd ʔiza saawaaha.*
eye - **1.** *Eeen* (f., dual *Eeenteen*) pl. *Eyuun.* On a clear day you can see the town from here with the naked eye. *b-ᵊnhaar ṣaaḥi fiik ᵊtšuuf ᵊl-balad mən hoon bᵊl-Eeen l-ᵊmšarrade.* -- I've had my eye on that for a long time. *ṣar-li zamaan ḥaaṭeṭ Eeeni Eala haš-šii.* **2.** *səqᵊb* pl. *sqaab, bəxᵊš* pl. *bxaaš.* The eye of this needle is too small. *səqᵊb hal-ʔəbre ktiir ᵊzġiir.*
**I never laid eyes on him. *b-ḥayaati maa šəfto.*
**We just don't see eye to eye. *mnəxtélef ᵊb-wəžhaat ᵊn-naẓar w-bass.*
evil eye - *l-Eeen.* That woman has the evil eye. *hal-mara bətṣiib bᵊl-Eeen.*
hook and eye - *kəbšaaye* pl. *-aat.* Zippers are more practical than hooks and eyes. *s-saḥḥaab Eamali ʔaktar mn ᵊl-kəbšaayaat.*
in the eyes of - *b-naẓar˜* ... In my eyes, he's a genius. *b-naẓari huwwe Eabqari.*
to catch somebody's eye - *lafat (e/o laftet˜) naẓar˜ ḥada.* I've been trying to catch your eye for the last half hour. *ṣar-li nəṣṣ saaEa Eam ḥaawel ʔəlfet naẓarak.*
to keep an eye on - *xalla Eeeno Eala, daar (i ə) baalo Eala.* Keep an eye on the children while I'm out. *xalli Eeenak Eal-ᵊwlaad b-ġeebti.*
to make eyes at - *baṣbaṣ Eala.* Stop making eyes at that woman! *ḥaaštak ᵊtbaṣbeṣ Eala hal-mara!*
to eye - *baḥlaq b-.* He eyed the chocolate longingly. *baḥlaq bᵊš-šokolaata məšthiiha.*
eyeball - *bəbbu˜ Eeen* pl. *bəbbuyaat˜ Eyuun.*
eyebrow - *ḥaažeb* pl. *ḥawaažeb.*
eyeglasses - *kəzlok* pl. *kazaalek, Eweenaat* (pl.).
eyelashes - *həd ᵊb* pl. *hdaab, rəmᵊš* pl. *rmuuš, riif˜ ᵊl-Eeen.*
eyelid - *šəfᵊn* pl. *šfuun(e).*
eyesight - *baṣar, naẓar.* My eyesight is letting up. *baṣari Eam yəḍEaf.*
eyewitness - *šaahed˜* (pl. *šhuud˜*) *Eayaan.*

F

fable - *xuraafe* pl. *-aat, ʔəṣṭuura* pl. *ʔaṣaṭiir.*
fabric - *qmaaš* pl. *ʔaqᵊmše, nasiiž, mansuuž* pl. *-aat.*
piece of fabric - *qmaaše* pl. *-aat* and *qamaayeš.*
façade - *waašha* pl. *-aat.*
face - **1.** *wəšš* pl. *wšuuh.* I'd tell him that right to his face. *kənt ᵊbqəl-lo haš-šii b-wəššo.* -- She slammed the door in my face. *ṭarqet ᵊl-baab ᵊb-wəšši.* -- Stop staring people in the face. *ḥaaše tbaḥleq ᵊb-wəšš ᵊn-naas.* -- He doesn't dare show his face around here again. *maa byəstarži ywarži wəššo hoon marra taanye.* -- There I was - face to face with my rival. *hayy ʔana - wəšš la-wəšš qəddaam l-ᵊmzaaḥem tabaEi.* -- They finally had to agree with us to save face. *bᵊl-ʔaaxiir ᵊḍṭarru yəttəfqu maEna ḥatta maa yəṭlaEu b-sawaad ᵊl-wəšš.* **2.** *waašha* pl. *-aat.* Do you see that sign on the face of the building? *šaayef hal-looḥa Eala waašhet ᵊl-binaaye?*
face value - *qiime ᵊəsmiyye.* These bonds can be cashed at face value in ten years. *has-sanadaat məmken qabḍa baEᵊd Eašr ᵊsniin ᵊb-qiiméta l-ʔəsmiyye.*
**She takes everything at face value. *btaaxod kəll šii Eala ḥabbto.*
in the face of - *ʔamaam˜* ... The police evacuated the town in the face of the storm. *š-šərṭa ʔaxlet ᵊl-madiine ʔamaam ᵊl-Eaaṣfe.*
on the face of it - *bᵊẓ-ẓaaher, ḥasab ᵊẓ-ẓaaher.* On the face of it, it looks like a good proposition. *bᵊẓ-ẓaaher ᵊl-ʔəqtiraaḥ ᵊmbayyen ᵊmniiḥ.*
to make faces - *laawaq.* Stop making faces. *ḥaaštak ᵊtlaaweq.*
to face - **1.** *waašah.* I can't face him. *maa bəqder waašho.* **2.** *šaabah, waašah.* Let's face the facts! *xalliina nšaabeh ᵊl-ḥaqaayeq!* **3.** *ṭall (ə ə) Eala* or *naaḥ.* Our windows face south. *šababiikna bəṭṭəll Eaš-šanuub.* -- Our room faces on the street. *ʔuuḍətna bəṭṭəll Eaš-šaareE.*
**My room faces the front. *ʔuuḍṭi qəddaamaaniyye.*
**Face the wall. *diir wəššak Eal-ḥeeṭ.*
**The building is faced with red brick. *l-binaaye wəšša ʔaažərr.*
facing - *mwaažeh, mqaabel, qəddaam.* He lives in the house facing the theater. *huwwe saaken bᵊl-beet yalli mwaažeh ᵊl-masraḥ.*
to **facilitate** - *sahhal, hawwan.* This method will facilitate our work greatly. *haṭ-ṭariiqa raḥa tsahhel šəġᵊlna ktiir.*
fact - *ḥaqiiqa* pl. *ḥaqaayeq.* That's a well-known fact. *hayy ḥaqiiqa maEruufe.*
facts - *waqaaʔeE* (pl.). What are the facts of the case? *šuu waqaaʔeE ᵊl-qaḍiyye?* -- Her story doesn't correspond to the facts. *qəṣṣə́ta maa btəṭṭaabaq maE ᵊl-waqaaʔeE.* -- Let's stick to the facts. *xalliina maa nəxroš Ean ᵊl-waqaaʔeE.*
**Please stick to facts. *bətraššaak xalliik ḍəmn ᵊl-ḥaqaayeq.*
as a matter of fact - *bᵊl-ḥaqiiqa, bᵊl-waaqeE.* As a matter of fact, I wasn't even there. *bᵊl-ḥaqiiqa ḥatta ʔənni maa kənt ᵊhniik.*
factor - *Eaaməl* pl. *Eawaaməl.* That's a factor I hadn't thought of. *haada Eaaməl maa ftakart fii.*
factory - *fabriika* pl. *fabaarek, maṣnaE* pl. *maṣaaneE, maEmal* pl. *maEaaməl.*
factual - *waaqEi.* His reports are always factual. *taqariiro daayman waaqEiyye.*
faculty - **1.** *quwwe* pl. *qəwa.* Her mental faculties seem to be slightly impaired. *qəwaaha l-Eaqliyye byəẓhar ʔənna šwayye xarbaane.* **2.** *heeʔet˜* (pl. *-aat˜*) *ʔasaadze.* Is he a member of the faculty? *huwwe mən heeʔet ᵊl-ʔasaadze?*
to **fade** - **1.** *baax (u bawaxaan).* My socks faded in the wash. *šraabaati baaxu bᵊl-ġasiil.* -- The wallpaper is all faded. *waraq ᵊl-ḥiiṭaan kəlla baayxa.* **2.** *dəbel (a dabalaan).* These roses faded very quickly. *hal-ᵊwruud dəblu b-sərEa.* **3.** *tlaaša.* The music faded in the distance. *l-muusiiqa tlaašet bᵊl-bəEᵊd.*
to **fail** - **1.** *fəšel (a fašal).* His experiment failed. *tašrəbto fəšlet.* -- All our efforts failed. *kəll ᵊšhuudna fəšlet.* **2.** *ṣaqaṭ (o ṣquuṭ).* Five students failed in geometry. *fii xamᵊs talamiiz ṣaqaṭu bᵊl-handase.* **3.** *ṣaqaṭ b-.* Ten students failed the exam. *fii Eašᵊr talamiiz ṣaqaṭu bᵊl-faḥᵊṣ.* **4.** *ḍəEef (a ḍaEafaan), xaff (ə xafafaan).* His eyesight is failing. *baṣaro Eam yəḍEaf.* **5.** *baar (u bawaraan).* The crops failed last year. *l-muusəm baar Eaamnawwal.* **6.** *txalla Ean.* I won't fail you. *maa bətxalla Eannak.* **7.** *xaan (u ə).* If my eyes don't fail me, it's he. *ʔiza Eyuuni maa-la Eam ᵊtxuunni laazem ykuun haada huwwe.*
**Don't fail to see the new movie at the "Metropol." *ʔəṣḥa maa tšuuf ᵊl-fəlm ᵊš-šdiid b-siinama mətropool.*
**Don't fail to wake me at six. *ʔəṣḥa maa tfayyəqni s-saaEa sətte.*
**He never fails to spoil our fun. *maa biṣiir ʔəlla-ma yxarbeṭ keefna.*
**Don't you fail to do it. *mən kəll bədd saawiiha.*
**It never fails to rain when we want to go somewhere. *maa biṣiir ʔəlla-ma tənzel maṭar waqᵊt mənḥəbb naEməl šii məšwaar.*
without fail - *mən kəll bədd, ḥatman.* I'll be there without fail. *mən kəll bədd bkuun ᵊhniik.*
failure - **1.** *fašal.* The failure of the operation was to be expected. *fašal ᵊl-Eamaliyye kaan bᵊl-ḥəsbaan.* **2.** *ṣquuṭ.* My sister is upset because of her failure in the exam. *ʔəxti masEuuše b-sabab ᵊṣquuṭa bᵊl-faḥᵊṣ.*
**As a businessman he was a complete failure.

ka-ražol ʔaεmaal kaan faašel εal-mazbuuṭ.

heart failure - *sakte qalbiyye.* He died of heart failure. *maat ᵊb-sakte qalbiyye.*

faint - 1. *daayex.* I feel faint from all this smoke. *ḥaases ḥaali daayex mən kətᵊr had-dəxxaan.* — I'm faint with hunger. *ʔana daayex mn ᵊž-žuuε.* 2. *ḍaʔiil, ḍεiif.* There's only a faint hope left. *maa ṣafi ʔəlla ʔamal ḍaʔiil.* 3. *qaliil.* We haven't the faintest idea of what you mean. *maa εanna ʔaqall fəkra εan halli εam təqᵊṣḍo.* 4. *xafiif, xaafet.* I heard a faint noise. *sməεᵊt ḥəss xafiif.*

**She lay in a dead faint. *kaanet ᵊmṣaṭṭaḥa məġma εaleeha.*

to faint - *ġaṭṭ (ə ø) εala qalb-* + pron. suff. of subject, *ġəmi (a ø) εala* + pron. suff. of subject. She fainted with fright. *ġaṭṭ εala qalba mn ᵊl-xoof.*

fair - *maεraḍ* pl. *maεaareḍ.* Were you ever at the Damascus Fair? *b-ḥayaatak zərᵊt maεraḍ dimašq?*

fair - 1. *mənṣef, εaadel.* You're not being fair with him. *maa-lak mənṣef maεo.* 2. *mwaafeq.* That's a fair price. *haada səεr ᵊmwaafeq.* 3. *ṣaaḥi.* The weather's supposed to be fair all weekend. *ṭ-ṭaqᵊṣ mənṭazar ykuun ṣaaḥi kəll ʔaaxer ᵊl-ʔəsbuuε.* 4. *ʔašqar* f. *šaqra* pl. *šəqᵊr.* She has blue eyes and fair hair. *εyuuna zərᵊq w-šaεra ʔašqar.* 5. *wasaṭ* (invar.), *nəṣṣ εala nəṣṣ* (invar.), *nəṣṣ waaḥde* (invar.). The work is only fair. *š-šəġᵊl bass wasaṭ.*

**It wouldn't be fair to take just one of them with us. *maa bikuun ʔənṣaaf naaxod bass waaḥed mənnon maεna.*

**It's only fair that I warn you. *l-ḥaqq ʔənni nabbhak.*

to play fair - *ʔanṣaf.* He wasn't playing fair with me. *maa kaan εam yənṣəfni* (or *yənṣef maεi*).

fairly - 1. *b-ʔənṣaaf, b-εadaale, b-ḥaqq.* I don't think they dealt very fairly with us at all. *maa bəftəker ʔənno εaamaluuna b-ʔənṣaaf ʔabadan.* 2. *la-daraže.* I know him fairly well. *baεᵊrfo mniiḥ la-daraže.* -- It was a fairly enjoyable party. *kaanet ḥafle məbᵊhže la-daraže.*

fairy tale - *xuraafe* pl. *-aat.* That sounds like a fairy tale. *haš-šii kaʔənno xuraafe.*

faith - 1. *diin* pl. *ʔadyaan.* I don't know what his faith is. *maa baεref šuu diino.* 2. *ʔiimaan.* Nothing can shake her faith in her husband's genius. *maa fii šii yzaεzeε ʔiimaana b-εabqariit žooza.* 3. *siqa.* I lost faith in him. *ḍaaεet siqati fii.*

in good faith - *b-ḥəsn˜ niyye.* We acted in good faith. *tṣarrafna b-ḥəsn niyye.*

in bad faith - *b-suuʔ˜ niyye.*

faithful - 1. *məxleṣ.* He's always been faithful to his wife. *daayman kaan məxleṣ la-marto.* 2. *ʔamiin.* His faithful dog stayed with him in the hour of danger. *kalbo l-ʔamiin laazamo b-saaεet ᵊl-xaṭar.*

fake - 1. *taqliid* (invar.). That picture is a fake. *haṣ-ṣuura taqliid.* 2. *məḥtaal* pl. *-iin.* He's not a real doctor, he's a fake. *huwwe muu ṭabiib ḥaqiiqi, huwwe məḥtaal.*

to fake - 1. *zawwar, zayyaf.* The documents were faked. *l-wasaayeq ᵊmzawwara.* 2. *loofak.* I think you're just faking. *bəẓənn ʔənnak εam ᵊtloofek.*

falcon - *baaz* pl. *-aat, ṣaqᵊr* pl. *ṣquura.*

fall - 1. *waqεa* pl. *-aat.* He hasn't recovered from his fall yet. *ləssa maa ṭaab mən waqᵊεto.* 2. *ṣquuṭ, ʔənxifaaḍ.* We had quite a fall in temperature last night. *leelt ᵊmbaareḥ ṣaar fii ṣquuṭ ᵊmniiḥ bᵊl-ḥaraara.* 3. *ṣquuṭ, ʔənhiyaar.* The invading Mongols finally brought about the fall of the Abbasid Empire. *l-maġuul ᵊl-ġəzaat ʔaxiiran sabbabu ṣquuṭ ᵊd-doole l-εabbaasiyye.* 4. *xariif.* I'll be back next fall. *bəržaε bᵊl-xariif ᵊž-žaaye.* 5. *xariifi*ᵊ. We had the most beautiful fall weather last year. *kaan ᵊṭ-ṭaqṣ ᵊl-xariifi s-səne l-maaḍye mən ʔažmal-ma ykuun.*

falls - *šallaal* pl. *-aat.* The falls are a few kilometers south of the town. *š-šallaal εala masaafet kam kiilomətᵊr žnuub ᵊl-balad.*

to fall - 1. *wəqeε (-yəqaε* and *-yuuqaε wquuε, waqεa), waqaε (-yuuqaε wquuε, waqεa).* He fell from the ladder. *wəqeε mən εas-səllom.* -- Did she hurt herself when she fell? *ʔaset ḥaala lamma waqεet?* -- I stumbled and fell flat on my face. *tšarkalᵊt w-waqaεt εala wəšši.* 2. *nəzel (e nzuul), ṣaqaṭ (o ṣquuṭ), nxafaḍ.* The temperature fell almost 15 degrees last night. *l-ḥaraara nəzlet taqriiban xamᵊṣṭaεšar daraže leelt ᵊmbaareḥ.* — Prices have been falling ever since. *l-ʔasεaar ṣaaret tənzel mən waqta.* 3. *nəzel.* Snow started falling while we were at the movie. *bada t-talᵊž yənzel lamma kənna bᵊs-siinama.* 4. *ṣaqaṭ (šahiid).* My brother fell in the battle of Tobrouk. *ʔaxi ṣaqaṭ šahiid b-maεraket ṭəbroq.* 5. *wəqeε, waqaε, ḥakam (o ø).* Christmas falls on a Wednesday this year. *εiid ᵊl-miilaad byəqaε yoom ʔarbεa has-səne.*

**I fell asleep in the warm sun. *ʔaxadni n-noom b-dafa š-šamᵊs.*

**His jokes always fall flat. *nəkato daayman btəṭlaε baayxa.*

to fall apart - 1. *faraṭ (o ø).* The old house is falling apart. *l-beet ᵊl-εatiiq εam yəfroṭ.* 2. *tšattat.* The organization seems to be falling apart. *εala-ma yəẓhar l-ᵊmnaẓẓame εam tətšattat.*

to fall back - 1. *wəqeε (-yəqaε* and *-yuuqaε wquuε, waqεa) la-wara.* Don't be afraid, let yourself fall back. *laa txaaf xalliik təqaε la-wara.* 2. *nsaḥab, traažaε.* The enemy began to fall back across the river. *l-εaduww bada yənsəḥeb qaaṭeε ᵊn-nahᵊr.*

to fall back on - *ltaža la-.* We can always fall back on our savings. *daayman fiina nəltəži ləl-mablaġ halli mṣammdiino.*

to fall behind - *tʔaxxar.* We fell behind in the rent. *tʔaxxarna bᵊl-ʔiižaar.*

to fall down - *wəqeε (-yəqaε* and *-yuuqaε wquuε, waqεa), waqaε (-yuuqaε wquuε, waqεa).* Be careful, don't fall down. *diir baalak, ʔoεa təqaε.*

**I hope he won't fall down on the job. *nšaaḷḷa yəṭlaε qadda.*

to fall for - 1. *nxadaε b-.* I fell for his sob story. *nxadaεt ᵊb-qəṣṣet maskanto.* 2. *wəqeε (-yəqaε* and *-yuuqaε ø) b-ġaraam˜* ... Do you think she's going to fall for him? *btəεtəqed raḥa təqaε ᵊb-ġaraamo?*

to fall in - *habaṭ (o hbuuṭ), ṣaqaṭ (o ṣquuṭ), wəqeε (-yəqaε* and *-yuuqaε wquuε), waqaε (-yuuqaε wquuε).* Before long, the roof is going to fall in. *εan qariib ᵊs-saqᵊf byəhboṭ.*

to fall off - 1. *salat (o ø).* The lid fell off. *l-ġaṭa salat.* 2. *qall (ə ø), xaff (ə ø).* Receipts have been falling off lately. *l-maʔxuudaat εam ᵊtqəll hal-ʔiyyaam.*

to fall out - *harr (ə hararaan), ṣaqaṭ (o ṣquuṭ).* All his hair fell out. *kəll šaεro harr.*

**They had a falling out. *ftaraqu εan baεḍon.*

to fall short of - 1. *qaṣṣar εan.* The collection fell short of what we had expected. *l-lamme qaṣṣaret εan halli kənna mətwaqqεiino.* 2. *maa waṣṣal.* The arrow fell short of its mark. *s-sahᵊm maa waṣṣal ᵊl-hadaf.*

to fall through - *tfarkaš.* The plans for the picnic fell through. *mašruuε ᵊs-seeraan ᵊtfarkaš.*

to fall to - *ṭəleε (a ø) εala.* It fell to me to tell him the bad news. *ṭəleε εaliyyi ʔana ʔənno qəl-lo l-xabar ᵊl-εaaṭel.*

to fall to pieces - *faraṭ (o farᵊṭ), nəzel (e ø) šaqfe šaqfe.* That old book is falling to pieces. *hal-ᵊktaab ᵊl-εatiiq εam yəfroṭ.*

to fall under - *daxal (o dxuul) ḍəmᵊn, wəqeε (-yəqaε* and *-yuuqaε wquuε) taḥt.* That falls under tax-free income. *haš-šii byədxol ḍəmn ᵊd-daxl ᵊl-məεfa.*

false - 1. *kaazeb.* The excuse he gave us was obviously false. *l-εəzᵊr halli εaṭaana-yда kaan εala-ma yəẓhar kaazeb.* 2. *εiire* (invar.). My father has had false teeth since he was twenty-five. *ʔabi ʔəlo snaan εiire mən waqᵊt kaan εəmro xamsda w-εəšriin səne.* 3. *ġalaṭ* (invar.). Is this true or false? *haada ṣaḥiiḥ wəlla ġalaṭ?* 4. *baaṭel.* It was a false alarm. *kaan ʔənzaar baaṭel.* 5. *wažhane* (invar.). Come on, no false modesty please. *haaštak baqa, bala tawaaḍoε wažhane.*

fame - *ṣiiṭ, šəhra.* His fame has spread far. *ṣiiṭo ṭayyar ᵊl-ʔaafaaq.*

familiar - 1. *məṭṭələε εala.* I'm not familiar with that book. *maa-li məṭṭələε εala hal-ᵊktaab.* 2. *maʔluuf.* Soldiers are a familiar sight these days. *l-εaskar ṣaaru ṣuwar maʔluufe b-hal-ʔiyyaam.*

**It's good to see a familiar face. *mniiḥ ᵊl-waaḥed yšuuf wəšš byaεᵊrfo.*

**Don't get too familiar. *xalliik ḍəmn ᵊr-rasmiyyaat.*

family - 1. *ʔahᵊl, εeele* pl. *-aat* and *εiyal.* Did you notify his family? *xabbarᵊt ʔahlo?* 2. *εeele* pl. *-aat* and *εiyal.* She comes from a wealthy family. *hiyye mən εeele ġaniyye.* -- Who's your family doctor? *miin ṭabiib ᵊl-εeele tabaεkon?*

famine - *mažaaεa* pl. *-aat.* Many people died during the famine. *fii naas ᵊktiir həlku bᵊl-mažaaεa.*

famous - *mašhuur, šahiir.* She's a famous dressmaker. *hiyye xayyaaṭa mašhuura.* -- The place is famous for its excellent cuisine. *l-maḥall mašhuur ᵊb-ṭabxo l-mašhuur.*
to become famous - *štahar.* The university became famous for its outstanding research in nuclear physics. *š-šaamεa štahret ᵊb-ʔabḥaasa l-mətfawwqa bᵊl-fiizya n-nawawiyye.*
to make famous - *šahar (e ø//nšahar* and *štahar).* His book made him famous. *ktaabo šaharo.*

fan - **1.** *marwaḥa* pl. *maraaweḥ.* Turn on the fan. *šaġġel ᵊl-marwaḥa.* -- Where did you buy this beautiful Japanese fan? *mneen ᵊštareeti hal-marwaḥa l-yaabaaniyye l-ḥəlwe?* **2.** *haawi* pl. *huwaat.* We're both soccer fans. *nəḥna t-tneen mən huwaat ᵊl-futbool.*
to fan - *hawwa.* Would you fan the fire while I get some more wood. *baḷḷa hawwi n-naar been-ma šiib šwayyet ḥaṭab kamaan.*
to fan out - *ntašar.* The soldiers fanned out across the field. *š-šnuud ᵊntašaru b-kəll šihaat ᵊl-ḥaqᵊl.*

fanatic - *mətεaṣṣeb* pl. *-iin.* He's a religious fanatic. *huwwe mətεaṣṣeb bᵊd-diin.*

fanatical - *mətεaṣṣeb.* They belong to a fanatical sect. *byəntə́mu la-ṭaayfe mətεaṣṣbe.*

fanaticism - *taεaṣṣob.*

fancy - **1.** *nazwe* pl. *-aat.* It's just a passing fancy with her. *hayy muu ʔaktar mən nazwe bətruuḥ w-ᵊbtəši maεa.* **2.** *mzaxraf, mzarkaš, mzayyan.* She doesn't like fancy clothes. *maa bətḥəbb ᵊl-ʔawaaεi l-ᵊmzaxrafe.* **3.** *luuks* (invar.). The chocolates came in a fancy package. *ḥabbaat ᵊš-šəkalaaṭa kaanet ᵊmεabbaaye b-baakeet luuks.* -- Have you ever been in his fancy office? *b-ḥayaatak šəfᵊt šii maktabo l-luuks?* **4.** *šiik* (invar.). You look very fancy in that new dress. *ṭaalεa šiik ᵊktiir ᵊb-hal-fəsṭaan ᵊš-šdiid.* **5.** *xaareq.* I'll bet they get a fancy price for that. *braahnak bəddo yəšiihon səεᵊr xaareq b-haš-šii.*
to fancy - *tṣawwar.* Fancy me in tails! *tṣawwarni laabes ᵊl-fraak!* -- I fancy he'll want it. *bətṣawwaro bəddo-yə́daha.*

fantastic - **1.** *mahuul, xaareq.* A fantastic number of people were in line to buy theater tickets. *kaan fii εadad mahuul mn ᵊn-naas waaqfiin bᵊl-xaṭṭ la-yəštə́ru tkuute ləl-masraḥ.* **2.** *xaareq.* Those kids tell the most fantastic lies I've ever heard. *hal-ᵊwlaad byəṭlaεu b-kəzbaat xaarqa b-ḥayaati maa smeεᵊt mətla.* **3.** *εaẓiim, faaxer, xaareq.* I guess they had a fantastic trip to Europe. *bẓənn-ə́llak safrə́ton la-ʔawrəbba kaanet εaẓiime.*

far - **1.** *bεiid* pl. *bεaad.* Is it far? *bεiid ᵊl-maḥall?* -- People came from far and near. *n-naas ʔəšu mən qariib w-ᵊbεiid* (or ***mən sadd w-ġamiiq*). -- Don't go far. *laa truuḥ (la-)bεiid.* -- That's not far wrong. *haada muu bεiid εan ᵊṣ-ṣawaab.* **2.** *ktiir.* I'm far behind in my work. *ʔana mqaṣṣer ᵊktiir ᵊb-šəġli.* -- She's far ahead of the rest of the class. *hiyye mətqaddme ktiir εan baqiit ᵊṣ-ṣaff.* **3.** *b-ᵊktiir.* It's far better than I had expected. *ʔaḥsan b-ᵊktiir məmma twaqqaεᵊt.*
**Far be it from me to criticize you! *ḥaaša ləllaah ʔəntəqdak!*
**That young fellow will go far. *hal-walad ʔəlo məstaqbal baaher.*
**This joke has gone far enough. *hal-mazᵊḥ wəṣel la-ḥaddo.*
**That's going too far! *l-masʔale ṭəlεet εan ᵊḥduuda!*
**His latest book is a far cry from his earlier works. *faṣaaεa qaddeeš fii boon šaaseε been ᵊktaabo l-ʔaxiir w-ᵊmʔallafaato s-saabqa!*
**You shouldn't carry things too far. *l-ʔawla maa twaṣṣel l-ᵊʔmuur la-ḥduuda.*
**He is by far the most famous man in town. *maa fii ḥada ʔašhar mənno bᵊl-balad laa qariib w-laa bεiid.*
**Honest people are few and far between. *n-naas ᵊš-šərafa naadriin* (or *qlaal*) or *n-naas ᵊš-šərafa btəqder ᵊddawwer εaleehon bᵊs-sraaž wᵊl-ᵊftiile.*
far away - *bεiid.* Is the airport far away? *l-maṭaar ᵊbεiid?*
far from - **1.** *bεiid mən.* Is the bus terminal far from here? *mḥaṭṭet ᵊl-baaṣaat ᵊbεiide mən hoon?* -- How far is it from here to Homs? *qaddeeš ᵊbεiid mən hoon la-ḥəmᵊṣ* or ***qaddeeš ᵊl-bəεᵊd mən hoon la-ḥəmᵊṣ?* **2.** *maa ... ʔabadan.* It's far from perfect, but it will do. *muu kaamle ʔabadan bass bətmašši l-ḥaal.* -- He's far from satisfied. *maa-lo raḍyaan ʔabadan.*
far off - *bεiid.* The wedding is not far off. *l-εərᵊs muu bεiid.* -- The post office isn't far off. *l-boosṭa muu bεiide.* -- Clouds were forming far off to the east. *l-ġeem kaan εam yədšammaε ᵊbεiid naaḥ ᵊš-šarᵊq.*
as far as - **1.** *la-ḥadd˜ ...* We walked together as far as the gate. *mšiina sawa la-ḥadd ᵊl-bawwaabe.* -- The idea is good, as far as it goes. *l-fəkra mniiḥa la-ḥadd hallaq.* **2.** *ḥasab-ma.* As far as I know everything is all right. *ḥasab-ma baεref kəll šii maaši mniiḥ.*
**As far as you could see, everything was covered with snow. *εala mada n-naẓar kəll šii kaan ᵊmġaṭṭa bᵊt-talᵊš.*
as far as I'm concerned, etc. - *bᵊn-nəsbe ʔəli,* etc., *mən šihati,* etc., *mən naaḥi,* etc. As far as he's concerned it's all right. *bᵊn-nəsbe ʔəlo maa fii maaneε.* -- As far as I'm concerned you can do as you like. *bᵊn-nəsbe ʔəli fiik taεmel halli bəddak-yə́da.*
on the far side of - *qaaṭeε˜ ..., bᵊš-šiha t-taanye mən.* Our house is on the far side of the river. *beetna qaaṭeε ᵊn-nahᵊr.*
so far - *la-ḥadd˜ hallaq, la-hallaq.* So far you've been pretty lucky. *la-ḥadd hallaq ʔənte maḥẓuuẓ.* -- I haven't had any news so far. *la-hallaq maa ʔəšaani ʔaxbaar.* -- He hasn't shown up so far. *la-hallaq maa ʔəša.* -- So far, so good. *la-hallaq mniiḥ.* -- How are things? -- So far so good. *kiif ᵊl-ʔaḥwaal? - la-hallaq* (or ***la-hoon*) *l-ḥamdəlla kəll šii maaši mniiḥ.*
so far as - *ḥasab-ma.* So far as I know he is still in Australia. *ḥasab-ma baεref ləssə́a b-ʔostraalya.*
to go too far in - *tmaada b-.* I think you've gone too far in your criticism. *šaayə́f-lak ᵊtmaadeet (ᵊktiir) ᵊb-ʔəntiqaadak.*

farce - *mahzale* pl. *mahaazel, maṣxara* pl. *maṣaaxer.* That election was nothing but a farce. *hal-ʔəntixaabaat maa kaanet ʔəlla mahzale.*

fare - **1.** *taεriifet˜* (pl. *taεariif˜*) *rəkbe, ʔəšret˜* (pl. *ʔšuur˜* and *ʔəšrawaat˜*) *rəkbe, nawloon˜* (pl. *-aat˜*) *rəkbe.* The fare is fifty piastres. *taεriifet ᵊr-rəkbe xamsiin qərᵊš.* **2.** *taεriifet˜ safar, ʔəšret˜ safar, nawloon˜ safar.* A number of airlines have raised their fares. *fii εəddet šərkaat ṭayaraan rafaεu taεriifet ᵊs-safar.* **3.** *nawloon, taεriife, ʔəšra.* Have your fares ready! *ḥaḍḍru n-nawloon!* **4.** *raakeb* pl. *rəkkaab.* How many fares did you have today? *kam raakeb kaan fii εandak ᵊl-yoom?* **5.** *ʔakᵊl.* They have very good fare for the price. *ʔaklon ᵊktiir ṭayyeb bᵊn-nəsbe ləl-ʔasεaar.*

Far East - *š-šarq ᵊl-ʔaqṣa.*

farewell - *wadaaε.* The embassy held a farewell party for him. *s-safaara saawə́t-lo ḥaflet wadaaε.*

farm - *mazraεa* pl. *mazaareε.* The two farms are far from each other. *l-mazraεteen ᵊbεaad εan baεḍon.*
farm hand - *ʔšiir* pl. *ʔəšara.*
chicken farm - *madšaže* pl. *madaašež, mazraεet˜* (pl. *mazaareε˜*) *žaaž.* My brother just started working on a chicken farm. *ʔaxi ballaš yəštə́ġel b-madšaže.*
to farm - *zaraε (a zarᵊε//nzaraε).* The field hasn't been farmed in years. *l-ḥaqle ṣar-la sniin maa nzarεet.*

farmer - *mzaareε* pl. *-iin.* Most farmers have already harvested their crops. *ʔaktar l-ᵊmzaarεiin ḥaṣadu maḥaṣiilon.*

farming - *flaaḥa, ziraaεa.* There isn't much farming in this region. *maa fii flaaḥa ktiir ᵊb-hal-manṭiqa.*

farther - *ʔabεad.* You'll have to walk a little farther. *laazem təmšii-lak ʔabεad šwayye.* -- Nothing is farther from my mind. *maa fii šii ʔabεad mən heek ᵊb-xaaṭri.*

farthest - *ʔabεad-ma ykuun.* Which of the three places is farthest from here? *ʔanu maḥall mn ᵊt-tlaate ʔabεad-ma ykuun la-hoon?* -- They wanted to see who could throw (the) farthest. *ḥabbu yšuufu miin fii yərmi la-ʔabεad-ma ykuun.*

to **fascinate** - *saḥar (e səḥᵊr//nsaḥar), fatan (e ø// nfatan).* The entire audience was fascinated by his story. *kəll ᵊs-saamεiin nsaḥaru b-qəṣṣto.*
fascinating - **1.** *mšawweq.* This is a fascinating book. *haada ktaab ᵊmšawweq.* **2.** *faaten.* She's a fascinating woman. *hiyye sətt faatne.*

fashion - *mooḍa* pl. *-aat.* Is that the latest fashion? *haada ʔaaxer mooḍa?* -- Green has gone out of fashion. *l-ʔaxḍar bəṭlet mooḍṭo.*
after a fashion - *nooεan maa, la-daraže.* She keeps house, after a fashion. *bəddabber ᵊl-manzel nooεan*

maa.

fashionable - 1. *xlanž* (invar.), *šiik* (invar.), *ʔaniiq̈*. They live in a fashionable district. *saakniin ᵊb-manṭiqa xlanž.* -- She's famous for her fashionable parties. *hiyye mašhuura b-ḥaflaata l-ʔaniiq̈a.* 2. *mooḍa* (invar.). Drinking vodka is no longer considered fashionable in those circles. *šərb ᵊl-voodka maa Ɛaad məƐtdbar mooḍa b-hal-ʔawṣaaṭ.*

fast - *ṣoom, ṣyaam.* When does the fast begin? *ʔeemta ṣ-ṣoom byəbda?*

to fast - *ṣaam (u ṣoom, ṣyaam).* Yes, I'm fasting. *naƐam, ʔana ṣaayem.*

fast - 1. *sariiƐ.* He's a fast worker. *huwwe šaġġiil sariiƐ.* -- If you get a fast train, you can get here in two hours. *ʔiza btərkab treen sariiƐ btəṣal la-hoon b-saaƐteen.* -- Can't you walk a little faster? *maa fiik təmši ʔasraƐ (b-)šwayye?* 2. *mqaddem, msabbeq.* My watch is ten minutes fast. *saaƐti mqaddme Ɛašᵊr daqaayeq.* 3. *mƐattar.* He travels in a real fast crowd. *byəmši maƐ ʔərṭa mƐattara Ɛal-maẓbuuṭ.* 4. *saabet.* Are these colors fast? *hal-ʔalwaan saabte?* 5. *b-sərƐa, b-Ɛažale.* Why do you drive so fast? *leeš saayeq ᵊb-has-sərƐa?* -- Don't talk so fast. *laa təḥki b-has-sərƐa.*

**I didn't hear a thing, I was fast asleep. *maa sməƐᵊt šii, kənt ġarqaan bᵊn-noom.*

**The boat was stuck fast in the mud. *š-šaxtuura kaanet Ɛalqaane bᵊṭ-ṭiin.*

as fast as - *b-ʔasraƐ-ma.* Come back as fast as you can. *ržaaƐ b-ʔasraƐ-ma b-ʔəmkaanak.*

hard and fast - *saabet, ṣaarem.* In this case you can't make hard and fast rules. *b-heek ḥaale maa fiik ᵊtḥəṭṭ q̈awaaƐed saabte.*

to make fast - *rabaṭ (o rabᵊṭ//rtabaṭ* and *nrabaṭ).* Make the boat fast. *rbooṭ ᵊš-šaxtuura.*

to fasten - 1. *rabaṭ (o rabᵊṭ//rtabaṭ* and *nrabaṭ).* Where can I fasten the string? *ween bəqder ʔərboṭ ᵊš-šriiṭ?* 2. *daqqar.* Fasten the door when you come in. *daqqer ᵊl-baab baƐᵊd-ma tfuut.*

fat - 1. *dəhᵊn,* (suet) *šaḥᵊm.* This meat has too much fat. *hal-laḥᵊm fii dəhn ᵊktiir.* 2. *dəhne, dəhᵊn.* Brown the meat in fat, not in butter. *ḥammri l-laḥme bᵊd-dəhne, muu bᵊs-samne.* 3. *mədhen.* The meat is too fat. *l-laḥme ktiir mədᵊhne.* 4. *smiin* pl. *smaan.* Who's that fat woman over there? *miin hal-mara s-smiine hniik?* 5. *q̈axᵊm.* He draws a fat salary without really working. *Ɛam yṭaaleƐ maƐaaš q̈axᵊm biduun-ma yəštəġel.* 6. *xəṣeb, ġani*, ṭayyeb.* Anything grows in this fat soil. *ḥayaḷḷa šii byəṭlaƐ ᵊb-hal-ʔarḍ ᵊl-xəṣbe.*

to get fat - *səmen (a səmᵊn).* He's gotten fat these days. *səmen ᵊb-hal-ʔiyyaam.*

to make fat - *samman.* Watch out, this food will make you fat. *diir baalak, hal-ʔakᵊl bisammnak.*

fatal - 1. *q̈aaḍi, mumiit.* The blow was fatal. *ḍ-ḍarbe kaanet q̈aaḍye.* 2. *manḥuus.* That was a fatal mistake. *kaanet xaṭiiʔa manḥuuse.*

fatalism - *ʔəƐtiq̈aad bᵊl-q̈aḍaaʔ wᵊl-q̈adar.*

fatalistic - *msallem.* Don't be so fatalistic, get up and do something. *laa tkuun hal-qadd ᵊmsallem, ḥrək-lak šwayye w-saawi šii.*

fatally: He was fatally injured in the accident. *nžaraḥ žarᵊḥ mumiit bᵊl-ḥaades.* -- He was fatally stabbed in the chest. *ntaƐan ᵊb-ṣədro ṭaƐne mumiite.*

fate - 1. *naṣiib, qəsme.* His fate is to be poor all his life. *qəsᵊmto w-naṣiibo yəbqa faqiir ṭuul Ɛəmro* or ***mqaddar Ɛaléə yəbqa ...* 2. *maṣiir.* The fate of our country now seems to be in the hands of the scientists. *byəẓhar ʔənno maṣiir ᵊblaadna hallaq ᵊb-yad ᵊl-Ɛəlamaaʔ.* 3. *l-q̈aḍaaʔ wᵊl-q̈adar.* She believes blindly in fate. *bətʔaamen Ɛal-Ɛamya bᵊl-q̈aḍaaʔ wᵊl-q̈adar.*

**Well, we've done all we can, the rest is up to fate. *hallaq ᵊƐməlna kəll halli byəṭlaƐ ᵊb-ʔiidna, l-baaqi Ɛala ʔaḷḷa.*

father - 1. *ʔabb (ʔabb˜* and *ʔabu˜,* with pron. suff. *ʔabuu˜-,* my father *ʔabi)* pl. *ʔabbaat* and *ʔabbahaat* and *ʔabawaat, waaled* (no pl.). How is your father? *ʔabuuk kiif ṣaḥḥto?* 2. *waaled.* Write name and address of father here. *ḥəṭṭ hoon ʔəsm ᵊl-waaled w-Ɛənwaano.* 3. *ʔabb* pl. *ʔaabaaʔ.* Father Michael was a good preacher. *l-ʔabb miixaʔiil* (or *ʔabuuna miixaʔiil) kaan waaʔeẓ ᵊmniiḥ.* 4. *ʔaab.* In the name of the Father, of the Son, and of the Holy Ghost. Amen. *b-əsm ᵊl-ʔaab wᵊl-ʔəbᵊn wᵊr-rooḥ ᵊl-q̈ədᵊs. ʔaamiin.*

reverend father - (as a religious title and form of address) *ʔabuuna.*

fatherhood - *ʔubuwwe.*

father-in-law - *Ɛamm* pl. *Ɛmuum(e)* and *Ɛmaam, ʔabu l-mara.*

fatherland - *waṭan* pl. *ʔawṭaan.*

fatigue - *taƐab.*

Fatimid - *faaṭimi*.*

to fatten - *samman.* That kind of food fattens terribly. *faẓaaƐa šuu bisammen han-nooƐ mn ᵊl-ʔakᵊl.* --We're fattening this sheep for the holidays. *Ɛam ᵊnsammen hal-xaaruuf ləl-Ɛiid.*

fatty - *dəhni*.* Avoid all fatty substances for a while. *tḥaaša ᵊl-mawaadd ᵊd-dəhniyye la-mədde.*

faucet - *ḥanafiyye* pl. *-aat.* The faucet is dripping. *l-ḥanafiyye Ɛam ᵊtnaqqeṭ.*

fault - 1. *naaqṣa* pl. *nawaaqeṣ.* We all have our faults. *maa ḥada xaali mn ᵊn-nawaaqeṣ ġeer ʔaḷḷa.* 2. *xaṭiiʔa* pl. *-aat* and *xaṭaaya.* It's not his fault. *hayy muu xaṭiiʔto.*

to find fault - *nakwaš Ɛala Ɛəlal.* You're always finding fault. *daayman Ɛam ᵊtnakweš Ɛala Ɛəlal.*

faulty - *manzuuƐ.* The short circuit was caused by a faulty connection. *l-kəntaak tsabbab Ɛan waṣle manzuuƐa.*

favor - 1. *maƐruuf, žamiile.* I want to ask you a favor. *laḥa ʔəṭlob mənnak maƐruuf.* -- He's done me many favors. *Ɛəməl-li maƐruuf marraat ᵊktiire.* -- You don't have to do me any favors! *maa fii lzuum taƐmel maƐi ʔayy maƐruuf!* 2. *maƐruuf.* Do me a favor and hand me that book over there. *Ɛməl-li maƐruuf naawəlni hal-ᵊktaab ᵊhniik.*

in favor of - *la-saaleḥ˜ ..., la-maṣlaḥ(e)t˜ ....* The board of arbitration decided in favor of the employees. *mažles ᵊt-taḥkiim ḥakam la-ṣaaleḥ ᵊl-məstaxdamiin.* -- She spoke in my favor. *ḥaket la-ṣaalḥi.*

**That speaks in his favor. *hayy ḥasane ʔəlo.*

to be in favor of - *faḍḍal.* I'm in favor of leaving today. *ʔana bfaḍḍel ᵊr-rooḥa l-yoom.*

to curry favor with - *dzallaf la-, massaḥ žuux la-.* He's always trying to curry favor with the boss. *daayman Ɛam yḥaawel yədzallaf lər-raʔiis.*

to favor - *faḍḍal.* He favors the youngest child. *bifaḍḍel ʔaṣġar l-ᵊwlaad.*

favorable - 1. *mlaaʔem, mnaaseb.* He bought the house on very favorable terms. *štara l-beet b-ᵊšruuṭ ᵊktiir ᵊmlaaʔme.* 2. *saaneḥ, mnaaseb.* I'm only waiting for a favorable opportunity. *ʔana bass Ɛam ʔəntəẓer fərṣa saanḥa.* 3. *mniiḥ.* The tennis tournament will be held tomorrow if the weather is favorable. *mbaaraat ᵊt-tanes bətṣiir bəkra ʔiza ṭ-ṭaqṣ ᵊmniiḥ.*

favorite - *ʔafḍal˜ ...* Red is my favorite color. *l-ʔaḥmar ʔafḍal loon Ɛandi.* -- This is his favorite book. *haada ʔafḍal ᵊktaab Ɛando.* -- It was our favorite pastime. *kaanet ʔafḍal təslaaye Ɛanna.*

**This book is a great favorite with children. *hal-ᵊktaab ᵊktiir maḥbuub Ɛand ᵊl-ʔaṭfaal.*

fear - *xoof.* He doesn't know the meaning of fear. *maa byaƐref maƐna l-xoof.*

**He took a taxi for fear of missing the train. *xaaf yfuuto t-treen, qaam ʔaxad taksi.*

fears - *maxaawef* (pl.). Your fears are unfounded. *maxaawfak maa-la ʔasaas.*

to fear - *xaaf (a xoof//nxaaf) mən.* You have nothing to fear. *maa fii šii txaaf mənno.*

fearful - 1. *xaayef.* Mother is so fearful about my health. *ʔəmmi ktiir xaayfe Ɛala ṣaḥḥti.* 2. *muriiƐ.* We're facing a fearful problem. *Ɛam ᵊnwaažeh məšᵊkle muriiƐa.*

fearfully - *b-ṣuura muriiƐa.* I was fearfully seasick on the boat. *dəxᵊt bᵊl-baaboor ᵊb-ṣuura muriiƐa.*

feather - *riiše* coll. *riiš* pl. *-aat* and *riyaš.* The feathers are coming out of the pillow. *r-riiš Ɛam yəṭlaƐ mən l-ᵊmxadde.* -- This hat is as light as a feather. *hal-bərneeṭa xafiife mətl ᵊr-riiš.*

**Birds of a feather flock together. *ʔinna ṭ-ṭuyuura Ɛala ʔaškaaliha taq̈aƐu.*

feature - *miize* pl. *-aat.* It is the principal feature of this literary movement. *hiyye l-miize r-raʔiisiyye la-hal-ḥarake l-ʔadabiyye.*

features - *malaameḥ* (pl.). He has pleasant features. *malaamḥo žazzaabe.*

main feature - *fəlᵊm* pl. *ʔaflaam.* When does the main feature start? *ʔeemta l-fəlᵊm byəbda?*

featured - *raʔiisi*.* The featured work of the concert will be Beethoven's Ninth Symphony. *l-q̈əṭƐa r-raʔiisiyye bᵊl-konseer bətkuun s-sənfooniyye t-taasƐa tabaƐ beethooven.*

February - *šbaaṭ.*

feddan - *faddaan* pl. *fadadiin.*

federal - *ʔəttiḥaadi**, *fədəraali**.
federation - *ʔəttiḥaad*. He advocates federation of the Arab states. *biṭaaleb b-ʔəttiḥaad ᵊd-duwal ᵊl-ɛarabiyye.*
fee - **1.** *ʔəžra* pl. *ʔžuur* and *ʔəžrawaat*. The doctor's fee was one hundred dollars. *ʔəžret ᵊd-doktoor kaanet miit dolaar.* **2.** *rasᵊm* pl. *rsuum*. Did you pay the fees? *dafaɛt ᵊr-rsuum?*
feed - **1.** *ʔakᵊl*. Have you ordered the feed for the chickens? *waṣṣeet ɛala ʔakl ᵊž-žaažaat šii?* **2.** *ɛalaf*. The truck with the cattle feed has just arrived. *l-kamyoon halli fii l-ɛalaf tabaɛ ᵊl-baqar hallaq wəṣel.*
to feed - **1.** *ṭaɛma*. She's feeding the baby its breakfast. *ɛam ᵊṭṭaɛmi l-beebe kasr ᵊṣ-ṣəfra tabaɛo.* -- The new restaurant will feed five hundred people an hour. *l-maṭɛam ᵊž-ždiid biṭaɛmi xamᵊs miit šaxṣ ᵊb-saaɛa.* **2.** *marraq*. You'll have to feed this meat into the grinder slowly. *laazem ᵊtmarrqi hal-laḥme bᵊl-farraame šwayye šwayye.*
to be fed up with - *mall (ə malal) mən, səʔem (a saʔamaan and saʔaame) mən*. I'm fed up with this whole business. *ʔana maalel mən kəll haš-šagle.*
to **feel** - **1.** *dass (ə dass), žass (ə žass)*. The doctor felt my pulse. *d-doktoor dass-ᵊlli nabḍi.* **2.** *tḥassas, tlammas*. He felt his way to the window. *tḥassas ṭariiqo naaḥ ᵊš-šəbbaak.* **3.** *ḥass (ə ḥəss) b-, šaɛar (o šɛuur) b-*. You can feel the tumor right here under my armpit. *fiik ᵊtḥəss bᵊl-waram hoon taḥᵊt baaṭi.* -- All of a sudden I felt a sharp pain in my back. *ɛala ġafle šaɛart ᵊb-wažaɛ ḥaadd ᵊb-ḍahri.* -- You'll feel the salary cut in the months to come. *ləssa bətḥəss tanziil maɛaašak bᵊl-ʔəšhor ᵊž-žaaye.* **4.** *ḥass b-ḥaalo, šaɛar b-ḥaalo*. He doesn't feel well. *ḥaases ᵊb-ḥaalo muu ɛala baɛḍo.* -- She feels sick. *ḥaasse b-ḥaala ḍaɛfaane.* -- Sometimes I feel lonesome. *baɛḍ ᵊl-ʔaḥyaan bəšɛor ᵊb-ḥaali waḥdaani.* -- How do you feel today? *kiif ḥaases ᵊb-haalak ᵊl-yoom?*
**His head feels hot. *ḥaases raaso kaʔənno maɛo ṣxuune.*
**The stove still feels warm. *ṣ-ṣoobya ləssaaha ṣəxne.*
**I know just how you feel. *ʔana bəšɛor maɛak.*
**You don't know how it feels! *maa btaɛref qaddeeša ṣaɛbe!*
**How do you feel about this? *šuu raʔyak ᵊb-haš-šii?*
**He feels very strongly about women drinking. *huwwe bᵊl-miyye miyye ḍədd šərb ᵊn-nəswaan ᵊl-xamᵊr.*
**I feel like a fool. *šaayef ḥaali ḥmaar mən ḥaqa.*
**I don't feel up to it right now. *šaayef ḥaali muu qaddha hallaq.*
**I feel like taking a cold shower. *žaaye ɛala baali ʔaaxod duuš baared.*
**Do you feel like dancing? *žaaye ɛala baalak tərqoṣ?*
to feel for - *šəfeq (a šafaqaan) ɛala*. I really feel for you. *mən kəll qalbi bəšfaq ɛaleek.*
to feel out - *žass (ə žass˜) nabḍ˜ ..., xadd (ə xadd˜) baaṭen˜ ...* I'll feel him out and let you know. *bžəss nabḍo w-ᵊbqəl-lak.*
to get (used to) the feel of - *ʔaxad ʔahᵊd ɛala, tɛawwad ɛala*. I haven't got the feel of the car yet. *ləssaani maa ʔaxadt ʔahᵊd ɛas-sayyaara.* -- I can't get used to the feel of the racket. *maa-li ɛam ʔəḍder ʔətɛawwad ɛar-rakeet.*
feeling - **1.** *šɛuur* (no pl.). I really didn't mean to hurt your feelings. *ʔakiid maa qaṣadt ʔabadan ʔəžraḥ ᵊšɛuurak.* -- What a strange feeling! *yaa ʔaḷḷa ɛala haš-šɛuur ᵊl-ġariib!* **2.** *maraaq*. He has no feeling for music. *maa-lo maraaq bᵊl-muusiiqa.*
**He doesn't have a feeling for the language. *maa biɛiiš bᵊl-luġa.*
**I have no feeling in my right arm. *ʔiidi l-yamiin ᵊmnammle.*
**I have a feeling (that) he won't come. *qaayəl-li qalbi ʔənno muu raḥa yəži.*
fellow - *zalame* pl. *zəlᵊm*. He's a nice fellow. *huwwe zalame ɛala salaamto.*
**Poor fellow! *məskiin!*
fellow worker - *zamiil* pl. *zəmala*. How do you get along with your fellow workers? *kiif maaši ḥaalak maɛ zəmalaatak?*
felt - *ləbbaad*.
piece of felt - *ləbbaade* pl. *-aat, šaqfet˜* (pl. *šəqaf˜*) *ləbbaad*.
female - *ʔəntaaye* pl. *ʔanaati, ʔənsa*. Is this cat a male or a female? *hal-qaṭṭa dakar wəlla ʔəntaaye?*
female plug - *briiz* pl. *-aat*.
feminine - **1.** *mʔannas*. "*ʔarḍ*" is a feminine noun. "*ʔarḍ*" *ʔəsm ᵊmʔannas.* **2.** *nəswaani**. Her taste in such things is very feminine. *zooqa b-heek ʔašya ktiir nəswaani.*
feminist - *nisaaʔi**. She's the founder of the feminist movement in Egypt. *hiyye mʔassᵊset ᵊl-ḥarake n-nisaaʔiyye b-maṣᵊr.*
fence - *xəṣṣ* pl. *xṣaaṣ, ḥaažez* pl. *ḥawaažez*. There is a hole in the fence. *fii bəxᵊš bᵊl-xəṣṣ.*
to fence in - *ḥaṭṭ xəṣṣ ḥawaali˜ ...* We're going to fence in the backyard this spring. *mənḥəṭṭ xəṣṣ ḥawaali ž-žneene l-warraaniyye har-rabiiɛ.*
to **fence** - *ləɛeb (a ləɛᵊb) bᵊs-seef wᵊt-tərᵊs, baaraz*. Do you know how to fence? *btaɛref təlɛab bᵊs-seef wᵊt-tərᵊs?*
fencing - *mbaaraze*.
fender - *rafraaf* pl. *rafariif*.
to **ferment** - *txammar*. The wine is fermenting. *n-nbiit ɛam yətxammar.*
fermentation - *ʔəxtimaar, taxmiir*.
ferry - *mɛaddiyye* pl. *-aat*.
ferryboat - *mɛaddiyye* pl. *-aat*.
fertile - **1.** *xəṣeb, məxṣeb, xaṣiib*. The soil here is very fertile. *l-ʔarḍ hoon xəṣbe ktiir.* -- He has a very fertile imagination. *ɛando xayaal xəṣeb ᵊktiir.* **2.** *waluud*. Their women are said to be very fertile. *qaal nəswaanon waluudiin ᵊktiir.*
Fertile Crescent - *l-hilaal ᵊl-xaṣiib*.
fertility - *xaṣᵊb*.
fertilizer - *samaad* pl. *-aat* and *ʔasmide*.
to **fester** - *tqayyaḥ*. Is the wound still festering? *ləssɛa ž-žərᵊḥ mətqayyeḥ?*
festival - **1.** *ʔəḥtifaal* pl. *-aat*. The festival was canceled at the last minute. *ltaġa l-ʔəḥtifaal ᵊb-ʔaaxer daqiiqa.* **2.** *mahražaan* pl. *-aat*. The Baalbak festivals are world-famous. *mahražaanaat bɛalbak ʔalon šəhra ɛaalamiyye.*
festivity - *ʔəḥtifaal* pl. *-aat*.
to **fetch** - *žaab (i žayabaan)*. Could you fetch me a glass of water? *baḷḷa bədžəb-li kaaset mayy?*
feud - *ɛadaawe, ḍaġiine*. There is a long standing feud between the two families. *fii ɛadaawe mətʔaṣṣle been ᵊl-ɛeelteen.*
feudal - *ʔəqṭaaɛi**.
feudalism - *l-ʔəqṭaaɛiyye*.
fever - **1.** *ṣxuune, ḥaraara*. Both my brothers are in bed with a fever this morning. *ʔəxwaati t-tneen bᵊl-farše maɛon ᵊṣxuune l-yoom ɛala bəkra.* **2.** *ḥəmma*. He is in the hospital with typhoid fever. *huwwe bᵊl-məstašfa maɛo ḥəmma tiifoʔiid.*
**They were all in a fever of excitement. *kaanu kəllon b-ḥaalet hayažaan šadiid.*
feverish - **1.** *ṣaaxeb*. Why all the feverish activity over there? *šuu fii la-hal-ḥarake ṣ-ṣaaxbe hniik?* **2.** *ṣaxnaan*. He feels feverish. *ḥaases ḥaalo ṣaxnaan.*
few - *qaliil* pl. *qlaal*. Few people come to see us in summer. *fii naas qaliil bizuuruuna bᵊṣ-ṣeef.* -- Few students stay here to work over the summer. *fii ṭəllaab ᵊqlaal byəbqu hoon bᵊṣ-ṣeef la-yəštəġlu.*
**Honest people are few and far between. *n-naas ᵊš-šərafa naadriin* (or *qlaal*) or *n-naas ᵊš-šərafa btəqder ᵊddawwer ɛaleehon bᵊs-sraaž wᵊl-ᵊftiile.*
a few - *kam* (with foll. sg.). May I ask a few questions? *məmken ʔəsʔal kam suʔaal?* -- I have a few things to ask you. *fii kam šaġle bəddi ʔəsʔalak-ydaha.* -- I saw him only a few times. *šəfto bass kam marra.* -- I had a letter from him a few days ago. *ʔəžaani maktuub mənno mən kam yoom.*
every few - *kəll kam* (with foll. sg.). We go to see him every few days. *mənzuuro kəll kam yoom.* -- Tell him not to disturb me every few hours. *qəl-lo laa yəzɛəžni kəll kam saaɛa.*
quite a few - *ɛadad laa baʔᵊs fii mən*. Quite a few people were present. *kaan ḥaader ɛadad laa baʔᵊs fii mn ᵊn-naas.*
fez - *ṭarbuuš* pl. *ṭarabiiš*.
fiancé - *xaṭiib* pl. *-iin*. Give my regards to your fiancé. *sallmi-li ɛala xaṭiibek.*
fiancée - *xaṭiibe* pl. *-aat*. My fiancée writes every day. *xaṭiibti btəktəb-li kəll yoom.*
fiber - *liif* pl. *ʔalyaaf*.
fibrous - *liifi**.
fickle - *mətqalleb*. She's a very fickle person. *hiyye mətqallbe ktiir.*
fiddle - *kamanža* pl. *-aat*. Quit scratching that fiddle. *ḥaaže dzaqzeq b-hal-kamanža.*

**He won't play second fiddle to anyone. *b-ḥayaato maa byəlɛab door saanawi, yaa ʔawwal yaa bala.*

to fiddle - *ləɛeb (a ləɛəb).* Don't fiddle with the radio! *laa təlɛab bᵊr-raadyo!*

to fiddle away - *baɛzaq.* He fiddled away the whole day doing absolutely nothing. *baɛzaq ᵊn-nhaar kəllo biduun-ma ɛəməl šii.*

to **fidget** - *tharqaṣ.* Stop fidgeting. *haaže tətharqaṣ.*

field - **1.** *ḥaqᵊl* pl. *ḥ(u)quul.* We walked across the fields. *mšiina qaateɛ l-ᵊḥquul.* -- Saudi Arabia lives almost exclusively from its oil fields. *l-mamlake l-ɛarabiyye s-suɛuudiyye taqriiban ɛaayše bass ɛala ḥquul ᵊz-zeet tabdɛa.* **2.** *ḥaqᵊl* pl. *ḥuquul, miidaan* pl. *mayadiin, mədmaar* pl. *madamiir.* He's the best man in his field. *huwwe ʔaḥsan waaḥed bᵊl-ḥaqᵊl tabaɛo.* -- I have done some studies in that field. *ɛməlᵊt baɛᵊḍ diraasaat ᵊb-hal-miidaan.* **3.** *miidaan.* The enemy's field artillery opened fire. *madfaɛiit ᵊl-miidaan tabaɛ ᵊl-ɛaduww ʔaṭlaqet niiraana.* **4.** *malɛab* pl. *malaaɛeb.* The teams are coming onto the field. *l-fariiqeen žaayiin ɛal-malɛab.*

field glasses - *naaḍuur* pl. *nawaḍiir.*

fierce - **1.** *muxiif.* The heat's fierce today. *š-šoob ᵊl-yoom muxiif.* **2.** *ɛaniif, ḥaami, šadiid.* Many were killed in the fierce battle that followed. *fii ktiir qətlu bᵊl-maɛrake l-ɛaniife halli ṣaaret baɛdeen.*

**He gave me a fierce look. *ṭṭallaɛ ɛaliyyi taṭliiɛa kəlla ġaḍab.*

fiery - *ḥamaasi*.* The president made a fiery speech. *r-raʔiis ʔalqa xiṭaab ḥamaasi.*

fifteen - **1.** *xamᵊṣṭaɛšar.* The repair cost me fifteen pounds. *t-taṣliiḥ kallafni xamᵊṣṭaɛšar leera.* **2.** *xamᵊṣṭaɛš.* There are fifteen of us in the class. *nəḥna xamᵊṣṭaɛš bᵊṣ-ṣaff.*

fifteenth - **1.** *l-xaames ɛašar.* The city was almost completely destroyed by fire in the Fifteenth century. *l-madiine ddammaret taqriiban la-ʔaaxəra b-ḥariiq bᵊl-qarn ᵊl-xaames ɛašar.* **2.** *l-xamᵊṣṭaɛš, l-xaames ɛašar.* That's my fifteenth trip across the Mediterranean. *hayy safᵊrti l-xamᵊṣṭaɛš qaateɛ ᵊl-baḥr ᵊl-mətwaṣṣeṭ.* **3.** *xamᵊṣṭaɛš.* He's expected on May fifteenth. *məntaẓar yəži b-xamᵊṣṭaɛš ʔayyaar.*

one fifteenth - *waaḥed mən xamᵊṣṭaɛš.* We've only raised one fifteenth of the money we need. *lammeena bass waaḥed mən xamᵊṣṭaɛš mn ᵊl-maṣaari yalli məḥtaažiina.* -- Three fifteenths equal one fifth. *tlaate mən xamᵊṣṭaɛš bisaawu xəmᵊs.*

fifth - **1.** *xaames.* This is my fifth job in two years. *hayy waẓiifti l-xaamse* (or *xaames waẓiife bəšġəla*) *b-has-sənteen.* **2.** *xamse.* The next payment is due on the fifth of March. *d-dafɛa ž-žaaye btəstḥəqq ᵊb-xamse ʔaadaar.* — The fifth comes on a Sunday, I think. *bəɛtəqed (yoom) ᵊl-xamse byəḥkom yoom ʔaḥad.*

one fifth - *xəmᵊs* pl. *ʔaxmaas.* He got only one fifth of the estate; his older brother received three fifths. *ʔaxad bass xəms ᵊt-tərke w-ʔaxu l-ᵊkbiir tlətt ᵊxmaas.*

fifth column - *ṭaabuur xaames* pl. *ṭawabiir xaamse.*

fiftieth - *l-xamsiin.* It's his fiftieth birthday. *haada ɛiid miilaado l-xamsiin.*

one fiftieth - *waaḥed mən xamsiin.*

fifty - *xamsiin.* I gave him fifty dollars. *ɛaṭeeto xamsiin dolaar.*

fifties - **1.** *l-xamsiin.* He's in his fifties. *huwwe bᵊl-xamsiin.* **2.** *l-ɛaqᵊd ᵊl-xamsiin.* The company was founded in the late fifties. *š-šərke tʔassaset ᵊb-ʔawaaxer ᵊl-ɛaqᵊd ᵊl-xamsiin.*

**He's in his late fifties. *huwwe b-ḥiiṭaan ᵊs-səttiin.*

fifty-fifty - *bᵊn-nəṣṣ, mnaaṣafe.* I'll go fifty-fifty with you on the expenses. *bruuḥ maɛak bᵊn-nəṣṣ bᵊl-maṣariif.* — We'll go fifty-fifty on the profits. *mənruuḥ ᵊmnaaṣafe bᵊl-ʔarbaaḥ.*

fig - *tiine* coll. *tiin* pl. *-aat.*

fight - **1.** *mkaafaḥa, kifaaḥ (ḍədd).* He played an important part in the fight against tuberculosis. *ləɛeb door ᵊmhemm b-ᵊmkaafaḥt ᵊs-səll.* **2.** *maɛrake* pl. *maɛaarek, niḍaal.* It was a fight to the finish. *kaanet maɛrake yaa qaatel yaa maqtuul.* **3.** *mbaaraat~* (pl. *mbaarayaat~*) *ᵊmlaakame.* I watched the fight on television. *tfarražᵊt ɛala mbaaraat l-ᵊmlaakame bᵊt-televəzyoon.* **4.** *mḍaarabe* pl. *-aat, mqaatale* pl. *-aat.* When the police arrived the fight was already over. *lamma wəṣlet ᵊš-šərṭa kaanet l-ᵊmḍaarabe xalṣet.* **5.** *xnaaqa* pl. *-aat* and *xanaayeq.* He had a fight with his wife. *ṣaar fii xnaaqa beeno w-been marto.* **6.** *ɛaziimet~ ᵊmqaawame.* He hasn't any fight left in him. *maa ṣəfi fii ɛaziimet ᵊmqaawame.*

**The losing team put up a good fight. *l-fariiq ᵊl-xaaṣer kaafaḥ ᵊb-basaale.*

to fight - **1.** *ḥaarab.* The soldiers fought bravely. *ž-žnuud ḥaarabu b-basaale.* **2.** *kaafaḥ, qaawam.* You've got to fight that habit. *laazem ᵊtkaafeḥ hal-ɛaade.* **3.** *txaanaq, ḍḍaarab.* Have you been fighting again? *ržəɛtu tətxaanaqu?*

**He fought through the entire campaign. *štarak bᵊl-ḥamle mən ʔawwəla la-ʔaaxəra.*

**I'm going to fight this suit. *bəddi ʔəmši b-had-daɛwa la-ʔaaxəra.*

**We'll fight this thing out at the next meeting. *mnəxṣom haš-šağle bᵊl-ʔəžtimaaɛ ᵊž-žaaye - yaa nəḥna yaa hənne.*

**Let them fight it out by themselves. *xalliihon yəxᵊṣmuuha been baɛḍon.*

fighter plane - *ṭayyaara* (pl. *-aat*) *mṭaarde.*

figurative - *mažaazi*.* The word is used here in a figurative sense. *l-kəlme məstaɛmale hoon ᵊb-maɛna mažaazi.*

figuratively - *mažaazan.*

figure - **1.** *ɛadad* pl. *ʔaɛdaad, raqᵊm* pl. *ʔarqaam.* Add up these figures. *žmaaɛ hal-ʔaɛdaad.* **2.** *qawaam.* She has a nice figure. *qawaama ḥəlu.* **3.** *šakᵊl* pl. *ʔaškaal.* Figure seven shows the parts of the engine. *šakᵊl sabɛa biwarži qəṭaɛ ᵊl-motoor.* **4.** *šaxṣiyye* pl. *-aat.* He's a mighty important figure in this town. *huwwe šaxṣiyye kbiire ktiir ᵊktiir b-hal-balad.*

**Are you good at figures? *ʔənte mniiḥ bᵊl-ᵊḥsaab?*

to figure - **1.** *xamman, ẓann (ə ẓann), ftakar.* I figure it's about five-thirty. *bxammen s-saaɛa ḥawaali xamse w-nəṣṣ.* -- The way I figure, it will cost about twenty dollars. *ḥasab-ma bxammen bətkallef ḥawaali ɛəšriin dolaar.* **2.** *ḥassab.* We didn't figure on having company. *maa ḥassabna ʔənno raḥa yəžiina ḍyuuf.*

to figure out - **1.** *ḥall (ə ḥall//nḥall).* Can you figure out this problem? *fiik ᵊtḥəll hal-məšᵊkle?* **2.** *ḥasab (o ḥsaab), ɛəmel ᵊḥsaabo.* Figure out how much it will cost. *ḥsoob qaddeeš bətkallef.* **3.** *ḥazar (e ḥəzᵊr).* Can you figure out what he means? *fiik təḥzer šuu qaṣdo?*

**I can't figure him out. *huwwe baab ᵊmsakkar, maa-li ɛam ʔəfhamo.*

to figure up - **1.** *ḥasab (o ḥsaab), ɛəmel ᵊḥsaabo.* Figure up how much I owe you. *ḥsoob qaddeeš ʔəlak maɛi.* **2.** *žamaɛ (a žamᵊɛ//nžamaɛ).* Did you figure up the first column? *žamaɛᵊt ʔawwal xaane?* **3.** *wəṣel (-yəṣal* and *-yuuṣal ə), balaġ (o ə).* The bills figure up to a hundred dollars. *l-fawatiir btəṣal la-miit dolaar* (or *btəbloġ miit dolaar*).

file - **1.** *mabrad* pl. *mabaared.* You need a finer file for that. *laazmak mabrad ʔanɛam la-haš-šii.* **2.** *ʔəḍbaara* pl. *-aat* and *ʔaḍabiir, doosyée* pl. *doosyaat, malaff* pl. *-aat.* See if you can find it in the personnel files. *šuuf ʔiza məmken tlaaqiiha b-ʔaḍabiir ᵊl-məstaxdamiin.* **3.** *səžəll* pl. *-aat, mṣannaf* pl. *-aat.* I can't find that letter in the file. *maa-li ɛam laaqi hal-maktuub bᵊs-səžəll.* -- Isn't her address in the file? *ɛənwaana muu bᵊl-ᵊmṣannaf?* **4.** *ṣaff* pl. *ṣfuuf.* Line up in single file! *nṣaffu b-ṣaff waaḥed!*

card file - *sanduuq~* (pl. *sanadiiq~*) *kruute.*

on file - *bᵊl-ʔəḍbaaraat, bᵊs-səžəll.* Do we have his application on file? *ṭalabo ɛanna-yda bᵊl-ʔəḍbaaraat?*

to file - **1.** *barad (o barᵊd//nbarad)* I have to file my nails. *laazem ʔəbrod ʔaḍafiiri.* **2.** *ḥaṭṭ bᵊl-ᵊmṣannaf.* I told you to file these letters. *qəlt-əllak ᵊtḥəṭṭ hal-makatiib bᵊl-ᵊmṣannaf.* **3.** *qaddam.* I filed my application today. *qaddamᵊt ṭalabi l-yoom.*

filing cabinet - *xzaanet~* (pl. *xazaayen~*) *ᵊmṣannafaat.*

fill - *malaat~ ᵊl-baṭᵊn.* They never had enough to eat their fill. *b-ḥayaaton maa kaan ɛandon ʔakl ᵊkfaaye la-yaaklu malaat baṭnon.*

**I've had my fill of it! *wəṣlet maɛi la-manaxiiri mən haš-šağle!*

to fill - **1.** *ɛabba//tɛabba, malla//tmalla* and *nmala* and *ntala.* Fill this bottle with water. *ɛabbi hal-qanniine mayy.* -- Fill the glass only halfway. *malli l-kaase la-nəṣṣa bass.* -- We have many positions we can't fill for lack of qualified people. *fii ɛanna waẓaayef ᵊktiire maa-lna ɛam nəqder ᵊnɛabbiihon li-ɛadam wžuud ᵊṣ-ṣaaleḥ.* **2.** *ḥaša* *(i ḥašu//nḥaša), ḥašša//tḥašša.* This tooth will have to be filled. *has-sənn laazem yənḥdša.* 3. *ʔaxad (-yaaxod ø//ttaaxad).* The sofa just about fills half of the room. *ṣ-ṣoofa ʔaaxde taqriiban nəṣṣ ᵊl-ʔuuḍa.* 4. *qaam (u ø) b-.* My salary fills most of my needs. *maɛaaši biquum ᵊb-ʔaktar ḥaažaati.* 5. *tammam//ttammam.* The order hasn't been filled yet. *ṭ-ṭalabiyye ləssa maa ttammamet.*

filled – *malaan.* The hall was filled to capacity. *ṣ-ṣaaḷa kaanet malaane la-təmma.*

to fill in – 1. *ṭamaṛ (o ṭamᵊṛ//nṭamaṛ).* They're going to fill in this abandoned canal. *bəddon yəṭᵊmṛu hal-qanaaye l-matruuke.* 2. *ɛabba//tɛabba.* Fill your name in here. *ɛabbi ʔəsmak hoon.* -- Fill in all the blanks. *ɛabbi kəll ᵊl-faraaġaat.*

**I'm just filling in here. *ʔana bəštə́ġel hoon bᵊn-nyaabe bass.*

to fill out – 1. *ɛabba//tɛabba, malla//tmalla* and *nmala.* Fill out this blank. *ɛabbi hal-ʔəstimaara.* 2. *səmen (a səmᵊn).* Don't worry, you'll fill out as you get older. *laa txaaf, btəsman ɛal-kabar.*

to fill up – 1. *ɛabba (ləš-šəffe), malla (ləš-šəffe).* He filled up the glasses. *ɛabba l-kaaṣaat ləš-šəffe.* -- May I fill up your glass? *ɛabbii-lak kaasak?* -- Fill 'er up! *ɛabbi d-dabbo!* 2. *tɛabba, ntala.* The theater was slowly filling up. *l-masraḥ kaan ɛam yətɛabba* (or *yəntə́li*) *šwayye šwayye.*

filling – *ḥašwe* pl. *-aat.* I've lost a filling. *ḍaaɛet mənni ḥašwe.*

filling station – *mḥaṭṭet˜* (pl. *-aat˜*) *banziin.*

filly – *məhra* pl. *-aat.*

film – 1. *ṭabaqa* pl. *-aat.* A thin film of oil formed on the water. *fii ṭabaqa rqiiqa mn ᵊz-zeet tšak-kalet ɛal-mayy.* 2. *ġašaawe* pl. *-aat.* It's as if I had a film over my eyes. *kaʔənno fii ɛala ɛyuuni ġašaawe.* 3. *fəlᵊm* pl. *ʔaflaam.* I don't particularly like funny films. *maa-li maraaq ᵊktiir bᵊl-ʔaflaam ᵊl-hazliyye.* -- I have to get a new (roll of) film. *laazem žiib fəlm ᵊždiid.* 4. *siinamaaʔi*.* She's a famous film star. *hiyye nažme siinamaaʔiyye mašhuura.*

film industry – *ṣinaaɛet˜ ᵊs-siinama.*

to film – *ṣawwar.* They filmed the entire ceremony. *ṣawwaru l-ʔəḥtifaal ᵊb-kaamlo.*

filter – 1. *məṣfaaye* pl. *maṣaafi.* Where's the filter for the coffeepot? *ween ᵊl-məṣfaaye tabaɛ ᵊbriiq ᵊl-qahwe?* 2. *mraššḥa* pl. *-aat.* Please exchange the oil filter when you lubricate the car. *baḷḷa ġayyə́r-li mraššəḥt ᵊz-zeet lamma bətšaḥḥem ᵊs-sayyaara.* 3. *fəlter* pl. *fəltraat.* Use a yellow filter when you take pictures in snow. *ḥaṭṭ fəlter ʔaṣfar* (or *ṣafra*) *lamma btaaxod ṣuura bᵊt-talᵊž.* -- I've switched to cigarettes with filter lately. *baddalt ṣərt ʔəšrab sigaaraat fəlter.* 4. *mṣaffa.* I don't care for filter cigarettes. *maa bḥəbb ᵊs-sigaaraat l-ᵊmṣaffaaye.*

to filter – *ṣaffa.* You'd better filter the water before you drink it. *ʔaḥsə́n-lak ᵊtṣaffi l-mayy qabᵊl-ma təšrə́ba.*

filth – *waṣaaxa, waṣax, ḏazaaṛa.* I've never seen such filth in my life. *b-ḥayaati maa šəfᵊt heek waṣaaxa.*

**I don't see how you can read such filth. *maa baɛref kiif fiik təqra heek šii wəṣex raziil.*

filthy – 1. *wəṣex, ḏəzer.* You can't imagine how filthy that place is. *maa fiik tətṣawwaṛ qaddeeš wəṣex hal-maḥall.* 2. *raziil.* If it's another filthy story, don't tell it. *ʔiza qəṣṣa raziile mətᵊl hayye laa təḥkiiha.*

fin – *zaɛnafe* pl. *zaɛaanef.* The fish has a huge dorsal fin. *s-samake ʔəla zaɛnafe kbiire b-ḍahṛa.*

final – 1. *nihaaʔi*.* Is that your final decision? *haada ḏaraarak ᵊn-nihaaʔi?* 2. *ʔaxiir, ʔaaxraani*, nihaaʔi*, ʔaaxer˜* ... This is the final lecture. *hayy l-ᵊmḥaaḍara l-ʔaxiire* or *ḥayy ʔaaxer ᵊmḥaaḍara.* 3. *faḥᵊṣ nihaaʔi* pl. *fḥuuṣ(a) nihaaʔiyye, ʔəmtiḥaan nihaaʔi* pl. *ʔəmtiḥaanaat nihaaʔiyye.* How did you make out on your French final? *šuu n-natiiže bᵊl-faḥṣ ᵊl-frənsaawi n-nihaaʔi tabaɛak?*

**You can't go to the dance, and that's final! *maa fii rooḥa ɛal-baal wᵊs-salaam!*

finals – *mbaarda nihaaʔiyye.* The tennis finals are being played tomorrow. *l-ᵊmbaaraa n-nihaaʔiyye tabaɛ ᵊt-tanes byəlɛabuuha bəkra.*

finally – *ʔaxiiran, bᵊn-nihaaye, bᵊl-ʔaaxiir.* He finally admitted he was wrong. *ʔaxiiran ᵊɛtaraf ʔənno kaan məxṭeʔ.*

finance – *l-maaliyye.* The Minister of Finance resigned yesterday. *waziir ᵊl-maaliyye staɛfa ᵊmbaareḥ.*

to finance – *mawwal.* Who's going to finance the undertaking? *miin bəddo ymawwel ᵊl-mašruuɛ?*

financial – *maali*.* For financial reasons I must say no. *la-ʔasbaab maaliyye məḍṭarr ʔərfoḍ.*

find – *laqṭa.* This book is a real find. *hal-ᵊktaab laqṭa ɛan ḥaqa.*

to find – 1. *laqa (-ylaaqi mlaaqaat//ltaqa), wažad* (imperf. *-yuužed* very rare *ø//nwažad*). I found five pounds in the street. *laqeet xamᵊs leeraat bᵊṭ-ṭariiq.*--I found him at home. *wažadto bᵊl-beet.* -- I found the place very crowded. *laqeet ᵊl-maḥall ᵊktiir maɛžuuq.* 2. *šaaf (u ø).* I find her very nice. *šaayə́fa ktiir laṭiife.* 3. *zdall ɛala.* I looked for the place all over town but I couldn't find it. *dərt ᵊl-balad kəlla ɛam dawwer ɛala hal-maḥall bass maa zdalleet ɛalée.*

**The judge found him guilty of treason. *l-qaaḍi žarramo bᵊl-ᵊxyaane.*

**I never can find my way around here. *maa baɛref ruuḥ w-ʔəži b-hal-qərne.*

**You'll easily find your way from that corner on. *mən has-suuke fiik taɛref ṭariiqak b-ᵊshuule.*

to find out – 1. *laqa (-ylaaqi mlaaqaat//ltaqa), ɛəref (-yaɛref maɛᵊrfe//nɛaraf).* Can't you find out his address? *maa fiik ᵊtlaaqi ɛənwaano?* or *maa fiik taɛref šuu ɛənwaano?* 2. *ɛəref.* I'll find out what's behind it. *ləssa baɛref šuu fii waraaha.* — Try to find out where they moved. *ḥaawel taɛref la-ween ntaqalu.* — I found it out just yesterday. *ɛrəfᵊt ɛanha bass ᵊmbaareḥ.* -- I found him out long ago. *ɛrəfto mən zamaanaat šuu huwwe.*

fine – *ġaraame* pl. *-aat, žaza naqdi* pl. *žazaʔaat naqdiyye.* He had to pay a stiff fine. *nžabar yədfaɛ ġaraame ɛaalye.*

to fine – *ġarram.* The judge fined him ten dollars. *l-qaaḍi ġarramo ɛašᵊr dolaaraat.*

fine – 1. *rfiiɛ* pl. *rfaaɛ.* I'd like a pen with a fine point. *bəddi stiilo riišto rfiiɛa.* 2. *daqiiq.* It's an exceedingly fine lens. *hiyye ɛadase daqiiqa ləl-ġaaye.* -- That's what I call a fine distinction between the two. *haada halli bsammīi tafriiq daqiiq been ᵊt-tneen.* 3. *naaɛem.* You have to grind it down to a fine powder. *laazem təṭḥə́na ḥatta tṣiir boodra naaɛme.* -- You need a finer fabric than this one. *laazmak ᵊqmaaš ʔanɛam mən heek.* 4. *mniiḥ.* He's a fine boy. *huwwe walad ᵊmniiḥ.* -- He's getting the finest care that money can buy. *ɛam yəɛṭə́nu fii ʔaḥsan ɛinaaye bᵊd-dənye.* 5. *ɛaẓiim, faaxer.* That's a fine car you have! *ɛandak sayyaara ɛaẓiime waḷḷa!* -- Where did you get that fine material? *mneen ᵊštareet hal-ᵊqmaaše l-faaxra?* 6. *žamiil.* A lot of new paintings are at the fine arts center this week. *fii ṣuwaṛ ᵊždiide ktiir maɛruuḍa b-daar ᵊl-funuun ᵊž-žamiile haž-žəmɛa.*

**That's fine! *ɛaal!*

**That's a fine way to treat a friend! *ɛaal! lakaan heek bətɛaamel rəfaqaatak!*

**You're a fine one! *ɛeeb ɛaleek! maa btəstə́ḥi?*

**One fine day, he popped up again. *yoom mn ᵊl-ʔiyyaam rəžeɛ.*

**That was mighty fine of him. *haada kaan ləṭf ᵊktiir mənno.*

**Thanks, I'm feeling fine. *l-ḥamdəlla ʔana mabṣuuṭ.*

**I had a fine time last night. *nbaṣaṭṭ ᵊktiir leelt ᵊmbaareḥ.*

finger – *ʔəṣbaɛ,* also *ʔəṣbaɛa (ʔəṣbaɛet˜)* pl. *ʔaṣaabeɛ* and *ʔaṣabiiɛ.* Take care not to burn your finger. *ʔəṣḥa təḥreq ʔəṣbaɛtak.*

**He let the opportunity slip through his fingers. *xalla l-fərṣa təflat mən ʔiido.*

**Keep your fingers crossed! *dɛii-li bᵊt-tawfiiq!*

**He's got a finger in every pie. *kəll ɛərᵊs ʔəlo qərᵊṣ.*

**There's something wrong, but I can't put my finger on it. *fii šii muu maẓbuuṭ bass maa-li ɛarfaan ween.*

index finger – *šaahde, sabbaabe.*

middle finger – *l-ʔəṣbaɛa l-wəṣṭa.*

ring finger – *bənṣaṛ.*

little finger – *xənṣaṛ.*

to finger – *lamas (e lamᵊs//nlamas* and *ltamas).* If you don't intend to buy it, don't finger it. *ʔiza muu niitak təštriiha laa təlmə́sa.*

fingerprint – *baṣmet˜* (pl. *-aat˜*) *ʔaṣaabeɛ.*

finish – 1. *vərniiš, warniiš.* You're rubbing the

finish off the car. *Ɛam təqhaṭ vərniiš ᵊs-sayyaara.* 2. *bərdaax.* Your table has a nice finish. *ṭaawəltak bərdaaxa ktiir ḥəlu.*

**I read the book from start to finish in one day. *qareet l-ᵊktaab mən ʔawwalo la-ʔaaxro b-yoom waaḥed.*

**It was a fight to the finish. *kaanet maƐrake yaa qaatel yaa maqtuul.*

to finish - 1. *xalaṣ (o ə), xallaṣ.* Have you finished the job? *xalaṣt ᵊš-šaġle?* -- Let me finish eating. *xalliini ʔəxloṣ ʔakᵊl.* -- After you finish this letter come to my office. *baƐᵊd-ma təxloṣ hal-maktuub taƐa la-maktabi.* 2. *kammal, xalaṣ, xallaṣ.* I couldn't even finish my supper. *ḥatta maa qdərᵊt kammel Ɛašaayi.* -- I couldn't finish my coffee. *maa qdərᵊt kammel qahᵊwti.* -- He didn't even let me finish. *ḥatta maa xallaani kammel kalaami.*

to be finished - *xalaṣ (o ə).* When will the bridge be finished? *ʔeemta byəxloṣ ᵊž-žəsᵊr?* -- When you're finished, come over here a minute. *lamma btəxloṣ taƐa la-hoon šii daqiiqa.* -- Actually, the road was finished almost a year ahead of time. *bᵊl-ḥaqiiqa ṭ-ṭariiq xalaṣ qabᵊl waqto b-səne taqriiban.*

**If he does that once more, he'll be finished. *ʔiza Ɛəmel haš-šii taani marra bətruuḥ Ɛalée.*

fire - 1. *ṇaaṛ* (f) pl. *ṇiiraaṇ.* Has the fire gone out? *šuu ṇ-ṇaaṛ ᵊnṭafet?* -- If you're cold, I'll make a fire. *ʔiza bardaan bəšƐéᵊl-lak ṇaaṛ.* -- You're playing with fire if you do a thing like that. *ʔiza btaƐmel heek šii bətkuun Ɛam təlƐab bᵊṇ-ṇaaṛ.* -- We were under enemy fire all day. *kənna taḥᵊt ṇaaṛ ᵊl-Ɛaduww ṭuul ᵊṇ-ṇhaaṛ.* 2. *ḥariiq* and *ḥariiqa* pl. *ḥaraayeq.* We had a big fire in town last year. *ṣaar fii Ɛanna ḥariiqa kbiire bᵊl-balad ᵊs-səne l-maaḍye.*

to be on fire - *ḥtaraq.* The house is on fire. *l-beet Ɛam yəḥtəreq.*

to catch fire - *šaƐal (e ə).* The stable caught fire. *l-yaaxor šaƐal.*

to set fire to - *ḥaraq (e/o ḥarᵊq//nḥaraq).* The soldiers set fire to the bridge. *l-Ɛaskar ḥaraqu ž-žəsᵊr.*

to set on fire - *ḥaraq (e/o ḥarᵊq//nḥaraq).* He set the house on fire. *ḥaraq ᵊl-beet.*

to fire - 1. *qawwaṣ.* The policeman fired a warning shot. *š-šərṭi qawwaṣ ᵊrṣaaṣa mətᵊl ʔənzaar.* -- And then I fired. *w-ḥiina qawwaṣᵊt.* -- We kept firing at the repeating enemy until we ran out of ammunition. *tamneena nqawweṣ Ɛal-Ɛaduww ᵊl-mətraažeƐ la-ʔaaxer rṣaaṣa maƐna.* -- I fired this gun only once. *qawwaṣt mən hal-fard ᵊrṣaaṣa waaḥde.* 2. *qallaƐ//tqallaƐ, Ɛazal (e/o Ɛazal//nƐazal).* Why did the boss fire him? *leeš ᵊr-raʔiis qallaƐo?*

**The shore batteries kept firing at the ship. *baṭṭaariyyaat ᵊs-sawaaḥel ḍallet təḍrob ᵊl-baaxra bᵊl-ġanaabel.*

**I'm all ears, fire away! *ʔana kəlli ʔadaan, ʔəḥki!*

firearm - *slaaḥ ṇaaṛi** pl. *ʔasliḥa naariyye.*

fire department - *maṣlaḥt ᵊl-ʔəṭfaaʔiyye.*

fire engine - *sayyaaret˜* (pl. *-aat˜*) *ʔəṭfaaʔiyye.*

fire escape - *səllom˜* (pl. *salaalem˜*) *nažaat.*

fire exit - *maxraž˜* (pl. *maxaarež˜*) *nažaat.*

fire extinguisher - *ṭaffaayet˜* (pl. *-aat˜*) *ḥariiq.* There's a fire extinguisher on every floor. *fii ṭaffaayet ḥariiq ᵊb-kəll ṭaabeq.*

fire insurance - *taʔmiin ḍədd ᵊl-ḥariiq, sookarta ḍədd ᵊl-ḥariiq.*

fireman - 1. (sg. rare: *ražol˜ ʔəṭfaaʔiyye*) pl. *ržaal˜ ʔəṭfaaʔiyye.* One fireman was seriously injured. *fii waaḥed mən ᵊržaal ᵊl-ʔəṭfaaʔiyye nžaraḥ žərᵊḥ qawi.* 2. *ƐaṭaṭŠi* pl. *-iyye.* Both the engineer and the fireman escaped unhurt. *tneenaaton ᵊl-məkanᵊsyaan wᵊl-Ɛaṭaṭši nafadu saalmiin.*

firewood - *ḥaṭab.*

fireworks - *šənneek.*

firm - 1. *šərke* pl. *-aat.* What firm do you represent? *šuu š-šərke yalli bətmassə́la?* 2. *ṣəlᵊb.* The ground is firm once you get out of this swampy area. *l-ʔarḍ bətṣiir ṣəlbe baƐᵊd-ma təṭlaƐ mən hal-manṭiqa l-məstanqaƐ.* 3. *ḥaasem.* That country won't take a firm stand on any of these important issues. *had-doole maa laḥa təttáxez mawqef ḥaasem ᵊb-ʔayy qaḍiyye mən hal-qaḍaaya l-ᵊmhəmme.*

first - 1. *ʔawwal˜ ..., ʔawwal* f. *ʔuula, ʔawwalaani*.* It's the first house around the corner. *huwwe ʔawwal beet* (or *l-beet ᵊl-ʔawwal* or *l-beet ᵊl-ʔawwalaani*) *wara s-suuke.* -- They live on the first floor. *saakniin bᵊṭ-ṭaabeq ᵊl-ʔawwal* (or *ᵊb-ʔawwal ṭaabeq* or *bᵊṭ-ṭaabeq ᵊl-ʔawwalaani*). -- Is this his first offense? *hayy ʔawwal ᵊmxaalafe ʔəlo?* or *hayy ᵊmxaalafto l-ʔuula* (or *l-ʔawwalaaniyye*)? -- Is this the first time you were here? *hayy ʔawwal marra* (or *l-marra l-ʔuula yalli* or *l-marra l-ʔawwalaaniyye yalli*) *btəži fiiha la-hoon?* -- It was love at first sight. *waqaƐ ᵊl-ḥəbb beenaaton mən ʔawwal naẓra* (or *mn ᵊn-naẓra l-ʔuula* or *l-ʔawwalaaniyye*). -- He's always the first one to complain. *huwwe daayman ʔawwal waaḥed byətšakka* or *huwwe daayman ᵊl-ʔawwal* (or *ᵊl-ʔawwalaani*) *yalli byətšakka.* 2. *waaḥed, ʔawwal.* They'll arrive on the first of August. *byəṣalu b-waaḥed ʔaab.* -- I get paid on the first of every month. *bəqbaḍ maƐaaši bᵊl-waaḥed* (or *bᵊl-ʔawwal* or ***b-ʔawwal yoom*) *mən kəll šahᵊr.* 3. *bᵊl-ʔawwal, ʔawwal˜ šii, ʔawwalan.* First let me ask you a question. *bᵊl-ʔawwal xalliini ʔəsʔalak suʔaal.*

**I'll do it the first thing in the morning. *baƐmə́la Ɛal-ḥaarek ṣabaaḥan.*

**He doesn't know the first thing about tennis. *maa byaƐref badiihiyyaat ᵊt-tanes.*

first aid - *ʔəsƐaaf ʔawwali.* Do you know anything about first aid? *btaƐref šii Ɛan ᵊl-ʔəsƐaaf ᵊl-ʔawwali?*

first-class - *daraže ʔuula, briimo.* It's a first-class job you've done. *Ɛməlᵊt šəġᵊl daraže ʔuula.* -- I always travel first-class. *daayman bsaafer daraže ʔuula* (or *bᵊd-daraže l-ʔuula*).

first lieutenant - *mlaazem ʔawwal* pl. *mlaazmiin ʔawwaliin.*

first name - *ʔəsᵊm ʔawwalaani.* What is your first name? *šuu ʔəsmak ᵊl-ʔawwalaani?*

first-rate - *daraže ʔuula.* He's a first-rate tennis player. *huwwe laƐƐiib tanes daraže ʔuula* (or *mn ᵊd-daraže l-ʔuula*).

at first - *bᵊl-ʔawwal.* I wouldn't believe it at first. *maa saddaqta bᵊl-ʔawwal.*

first of all - 1. *ʔawwalan.* First of all, you misunderstood me. *ʔawwalan ᵊfhəmᵊtni ġalaṭ.* 2. *bᵊl-ʔawwal, ʔawwal˜ (kəll) šii, qabᵊl kəll šii.* First of all, I'd like to give you the facts. *bᵊl-ʔawwal bəddi qəl-lak ᵊl-ḥaqaayeq.*

in the first place - *ʔawwalan, ʔawwal˜ šii.* In the first place I have no money, and besides ... *ʔawwalan maa Ɛandi maṣaari w-fooq haada ...*

first things first - *l-ʔawwal bᵊl-ʔawwal, ʔawwal b-ʔawwal.* Wait a minute! Let's start with first things first. *Ɛala mahlak! xalliina nəbda l-ʔawwal bᵊl-ʔawwal.*

fiscal - *maali*.*

fish - *samake* coll. *samak* pl. *ʔasmaak,* with numbers from 3 to 10 *samakaat.* The kids brought home three fish for supper. *l-ᵊwlaad žaabu tlətt samakaat ləl-Ɛaša.* -- Do you like fish? *bətḥəbb ᵊs-samak šii?*

**He drinks like a fish. *byəšrab mən kaƐb ᵊṣ-ṣərmaaye.*

**That's a pretty kettle of fish! *hayy xarbaṭa məḥtárame waḷḷa!*

to fish - 1. *ṣṭaad samak.* Do you want to go fishing? *bətḥəbb ᵊtruuḥ təṣṭaad samak?* 2. *ṣṭaad.* He's always fishing in troubled waters. *daayman Ɛam yəṣṭaad bᵊl-maaʔ ᵊl-Ɛəker.*

**I'm trying to fish the cork out of the bottle. *Ɛam ḥaawel ṭaaleƐ ᵊl-fanniine mn ᵊl-qanniine.*

**He fished through his pockets for his keys. *ḥaṭṭ ʔiido b-žiyabo Ɛam ydawwer Ɛala mafatiiḥo.*

**She's just fishing for compliments. *bass Ɛam ᵊddawwer Ɛala šii kombliṃaan.*

fishbone - *ḥasake* coll. *ḥasak* pl. *-aat.* A fishbone caught in his throat. *Ɛəlqet ḥasake b-žoozet ḥalqo.*

fisherman - *ṣayyaad˜* (pl. *-iin˜*) *samak.*

fishhook - *sənnaara* pl. *sananiir.*

fishing industry - *ṣinaaƐet˜ ṣeed˜ samak.*

fishing tackle - *Ɛəddet˜ ṣeed˜ samak.*

fist - *qabḍet˜* (pl. *-aat˜*) *ʔiid.* Did he hit you with his fist? *ḍarabak ᵊb-qabḍet ʔiido?*

fit - *noobe* pl. *-aat.* We had to call the doctor because the old man had a violent fit. *nžabarna nəṣrax ləd-doktoor laʔənno l-ʔəxtyaar ʔəžəto noobe šadiide.*

**Every time I mention it he has a fit. *kəll maa bžiib səkra biṭiir Ɛaqlo.*

**This suit isn't a good fit. *hal-badle muu raakze.*

**He doesn't feel fit today. *šaaƐer ᵊb-ḥaalo muu Ɛala baƐḍo l-yoom.*

to be fit - *ṣəleḥ (a ṣalaaḥ).* What sort of work is he fit for? *šuu nooε ᵊl-εamal halli byəṣlaḥ-lo?* — This meat isn't fit to eat. *hal-laḥme maa btəṣlaḥ ləl-ʔakᵊl* or ***hal-laḥme maa btəttaakal.* — The wine isn't fit to drink. *n-nbiit maa byəṣlaḥ ləš-šərᵊb* or ***n-nbiit maa byənšə́reb.*

**Wait until your father hears about that! He'll be fit to be tied. *stanna ḥatta yəsmaε fiiha ʔabuuk! biṭiir εaqlo.*

to fit - **1.** *ʔəža εala.* These shoes don't fit me. *haṣ-ṣabbaaṭ muu žaaye εaliyyi.* — The coat fits perfectly. *l-manṭo žaaye ḥafr w-tanziil.* **2.** *rəkeb (a ø).* This screw doesn't fit. *hal-bərġi maa εam yərkab.* — These parts don't fit together. *hal-qəṭaε maa-la εam tərkab εala baεḍa.*

**I'm busy, but I'll try to fit you in somewhere. *ʔana mašġuul bass bḥaawel dabbə́r-lak šii kam daqiiqa.*

**He couldn't fit another thing into his suitcase. *maa qəder ywasseε la-šii taani b-šantaayto.*

fitting - **1.** *broova* pl. *-aat.* When will the suit be ready for a fitting? *ʔeemta l-badle bətkuun ḥaaḍra ləl-ᵊbroova?* **2.** *mnaaseb.* Let's wait for a fitting occasion. *xalliina nəstanna la-waqt ᵊmnaaseb.*

five - **1.** *xamᵊs(t).* We stayed there for five months. *bqiina hniik xamᵊst əšhor.* — They have five children. *εandon xams ᵊwlaad.* **2.** *xamse.* There were five of us at the party. *kənna xamse bᵊl-ḥafle.* — Bring us five coffees. *žəb-ᵊlna xamse qahwe.* — The boy is five. *ṣ-ṣabi εəmro xamse.* **3.** *s-saaεa xamse.* It's already five. *ṣaaret ᵊs-saaεa xamse.* — The plane leaves at five. *ṭ-ṭayyaara bətsaafer ᵊs-saaεa xamse.*

fix - *warṭa, maʔzaq.* He's in a terrible fix. *huwwe waaqeε ᵊb-warṭa malεuune.*

to fix - **1.** *ḥaddad//tḥaddad.* The price was fixed at one hundred dollars. *s-səεr ᵊtḥaddad ᵊb-miit dolaar.* **2.** *ẓabbaṭ.* Fix your tie. *ẓabbeṭ ᵊkraaftak.* **3.** *ṣallaḥ.* Can you fix the typewriter for me? *fiik ᵊtṣallə́ḥ-li maakiint l-ᵊktaabe?* **4.** *ḥaḍḍar.* I have to fix supper now. *laazem ḥaḍḍer ᵊl-εaša hallaq.* **5.** *dabbar.* I will fix that swindler. *ləssa bdabber hal-məḥtaal.* — Don't worry, I'll fix it somehow so that you can have a talk with him. *laa ykən-lak fəkᵊr ʔana bdabbərha ʔənnak təḥki maεo.*

fixed - *mᵊεannan.* He has a fixed salary. *ʔəlo maεaaš ᵊmᵊεannan.*

fixed star - *saabte* pl. *sawaabet.*

to fix up - *rattab//trattab.* Everything is fixed up again. *kəll šii rəžeε w-ᵊtrattab mətᵊl εaadto.*

flabby - **1.** *mərxi*.* My muscles are all flabby after this long illness. *εaḍalaati kəlla mərxiyye baεᵊd haḍ-ḍaεfe ṭ-ṭawiile.* **2.** *mhalheṭ.* She'd be very nice looking if she weren't so flabby. *kaanet bətkuun ᵊktiir ḥəlwe law maa kaanet ᵊmhalᵊhṭa hal-qadd.*

flag - *beeraq* pl. *bayaareq, εalam* pl. *ʔaεlaam.*

flag pole - *εaamuud˜ beeraq* (or *εalam*) pl. *εawamiid˜ bayaareq (ʔaεlaam).*

flake - **1.** *nadfe* pl. *nadaf.* The snow is falling in big flakes. *t-talᵊž εam yənzel ᵊb-nadaf ᵊkbaar.* **2.** *qəšra* pl. *qšuur.* The paint is coming off the walls in big flakes. *d-dhaan εam yəṭlaε mn ᵊl-ḥiiṭaan b-ᵊqšuur ᵊkbiire.*

flame - *lahiib* (sg. and pl.). The flames were from five to ten feet high. *l-lahiib kaan ḍaareb b-ᵊεluww mən xamse la-εašᵊr ᵊqdaam.*

**She's an old flame of mine. *kənt yoom mn ᵊl-ʔiyyaam ṭaabes fiiha.*

flame thrower - *qaazifet˜* (pl. *-aat˜*) *lahiib.*

to be in flames - *ltahab.* Soon the whole house was in flames. *waqᵊtha l-beet kaan εam yəltə́heb.*

to flame - *ltahab.* The oil was flaming brightly. *z-zeet kaan εam yəltə́heb ʔəltihaab qawi.*

flamingo - *bašruuš.*

flannel - *faneella.*

flap - **1.** *ġaṭa* pl. *ʔəġᵊṭye, qalbe* pl. *-aat.* Do you want your pockets with or without flaps? *bəddak žiyabak b-ġaṭa wəlla bala ġaṭa?* **2.** *qalbe* pl. *-aat.* Hand me an envelope with a bigger flap. *naawəlni šii ẓarᵊf qalᵊbto ʔakbar mən heek.*

to flap - **1.** *trafraf.* The flags were flapping in the breeze. *l-ʔaεlaam kaanet εam ᵊtrafref bᵊn-nasiim.* **2.** *rafraf, xaffaq.* The bird kept flapping its wings but couldn't get off the ground. *l-εaṣfuur ḍall yrafref b-ᵊžnaaḥaato bass maa qəder yṭiir mən εal-ʔarḍ.*

flash - **1.** *lamḥet˜ baṣar.* It was all over in a flash. *xalṣet ᵊb-lamḥet baṣar* or ***xalṣet εala-ma tquul ʔee.* **2.** *barᵊq.* He answered quick as a flash. *žaawab b-sərεa mətl ᵊl-barᵊq.*

flash of lightning - *barᵊq.* Did you see the flash of lightning? *šəft ᵊl-barᵊq?*

to flash - **1.** *ḍawa (i ḍaww).* I saw a light flash on and off. *šəfᵊt ḍaww εam yəḍwi w-yəṭfi.* **2.** *žaal (u ø).* Many thoughts flashed through my mind. *žaalet ᵊb-xaaṭri ʔafkaar ᵊktiire.* **3.** *tlaala bᵊš-šarar.* His eyes flashed with anger. *εyuuno tlaalet bᵊš-šarar mən kəṭᵊr ġaḍabo.*

**He flashed the light right in my face. *ṣawwab ᵊḍ-ḍaww εala wəšši.*

flashing light - *ḍaww mətqaṭṭeε.*

flashlight - *biil* pl. *byaal.* Can you lend me your flashlight? *fiik ᵊtεiirni l-biil tabaεak?*

flat - **1.** *šaqqa* pl. *šəqaq, ṭaabeq* pl. *ṭawaabeq, ʔabartmaan* pl. *-aat.* I just moved into a new flat. *maa ṣar-li zamaan ntaqalᵊt la-šaqqa ždiide.* **2.** *msaṭṭaḥ.* His house has a flat roof. *beeto ʔəlo ʔəṣṭuuḥ ᵊmsaṭṭaḥ.* — Let him lie flat on the ground until we can get a doctor. *xallii msaṭṭaḥ εal-ʔarḍ la-nžiib ḥakiim.* **3.** *sahᵊl* (invar.). The country is flat around there. *l-ʔarḍ sahᵊl b-han-nawaaḥi.* **4.** *ʔafṭaṣ* f. *faṭṣa* pl. *fəṭᵊṣ.* He has a flat nose. *mənxaaro ʔafṭaṣ.* **5.** *ʔabṭaš* f. *baṭša* pl. *bəṭᵊš.* The army won't take him because of his flat feet. *ž-žeeš maa byəqbalo mənšaan rəžlée ᵊl-bəṭᵊš.* **6.** *baayex, baared.* His jokes always fall flat. *daayman nəkato btəṭlaε baayxa.*

**On the way back we had a flat. *b-ražεətna fii waaḥed kawšuuk banšar.*

**The food tastes flat. *l-ʔakle maa-la ṭaεme.*

**I made it to the station in five minutes flat. *rəḥᵊt εal-ᵊmḥaṭṭa b-xamᵊs daqaayeq εat-takke.*

**His answer was a flat "no". *žawaabo kaan ᵊb-kəlme waaḥde "laʔ".*

(flat)iron - *məkwaaye* pl. *makaawi.*

to **flatter** - *koolak, massaḥ žuux la-.* He tried to flatter me. *ḥaawal ykooləkni* (or *ḥaawal ymassə́ḥ-li žuux*).

**I read a very flattering article about him. *qareet maqaalc kəlla madiiḥ εanno.*

**That's a very flattering dress you're wearing. *waḷḷa har-roob žaaye εaleeki bədaε.*

to flatter oneself - *ẓann (ə ø) ḥaalo, ftakar ḥaalo.* He flatters himself to be a good judge of character. *biẓənn ḥaalo ʔənno εando baṣiira ḥaaẓqa b-ʔaṭbaaε ᵊn-naas.*

to feel flattered - *ntafaš.* She felt flattered by his remarks. *ntafšet b-ᵊmlaaḥaẓaato.*

flattery - *koolake, tamsiiḥ˜ žuux.*

flavor - *ṭaεme.* The coffee has lost all its flavor. *l-bənn raaḥet ṭaεᵊmto kəlla.*

to flavor - *ṭaεεam.* We use cinnamon to flavor the candy. *mnəstaεmel qərfe la-nṭaεεem ᵊs-sakaaker.*

flax - (raw) *qənneb,* (teased) *kəttaan, qəšᵊr qənneb.*

flea - *barġuut* pl. *baraġiit.*

to **flee** - *harab (o harab), farr (ə fraar).* The population fled to the country. *s-səkkaan harabu ləd-ḍiyaε.*

fleet - *ʔəṣṭool* pl. *ʔaṣaṭiil.* Part of the enemy fleet was destroyed. *fii qəsᵊm mən ʔəṣṭool ᵊl-εaduww ᵊddammar.*

flesh - *laḥᵊm.* The flesh around the wound became discolored after two days. *l-laḥᵊm ḥawaali ž-žərᵊḥ ᵊzraqq baεᵊd yoomeen.* — He's my own flesh and blood. *huwwe dammi w-laḥmi.*

**That's the way of all flesh. *haada maṣiir kəll ḥayy.*

flexibility - *muruune, luyuune.*

flexible - *maren, layyen.* They should adopt a flexible policy. *laazem yətbannu syaase marine.*

to **flicker** - **1.** *ražaf (e ražᵊf).* The light is flickering. *ḍ-ḍaww εam yəržef.* **2.** *lahlab.* Little flames were flickering here and there. *fii lahbaat ᵊẓġiire kaanet εam tətlahleb hoon w-ᵊhniik.*

flight - **1.** *harab, fraar.* The reporters questioned him about his flight from behind the Iron Curtain. *məxᵊbriin ᵊṣ-ṣəḥof saʔalúu εan harabo mən wara s-sitaar ᵊl-ḥadiidi.* **2.** *raḥle* pl. *-aat.* All flights were canceled on account of the storm. *kəll ᵊr-raḥlaat ᵊltaġet b-sabab ᵊl-εaaṣfe.* **3.** *daraž* pl. *draaž.* How many more flights do we have to climb? *kam daraž ləssa laazem nəṭlaε?*

to put to flight - *harrab.* We put them to flight. *harrabnaahon.*

to **fling** - *laḥaš (o laḥᵊš//nlaḥaš* and *ltaḥaš).* He flung his coat on the chair and rushed to the telephone. *laḥaš kabbuudo εal-kərsi w-naṭṭ εat-talifoon.*

to fling about or **around** - *laḥwaš.* I wish you wouldn't fling your things around like that.

ya-reetak maa tlaḥweš ᵊġraadak heek hoon w-hoon.

to have a fling at – *žarrab.* Let me have a fling at it. *xalliini ʔana žarrᵊba.*

flint – 1. *ḥažar* pl. *ḥžaar(a).* All the lighter needs is a new flint. *l-qaddaaḥa maa bədda ʔəlla ḥažar.* 2. *ḥažar ṣawwaan.* Here's a piece of flint I found over there. *hayy šaqfet ḥažar ṣawwaan laqeeta hniik.*

flirt – *mġaazale, mnaaġaše.* A little flirt won't do any harm. *mġaazale baṣiiṭa maa bəḍḍərr.*

to flirt – 1. *ġaazal, naaġaš.* She flirts with every man she meets. *bətġaazel kəll rəžžaal bətšuufo.* 2. *laak (u ø), laaš (u ø).* I've been flirting with the idea of going to South America for a long time now. *ṣar-li zamaan ʕam luuka b-fəkri rooḥet ʔameerka ž-žanuubiyye.*

float – 1. *ʕawwaame* pl. *-aat.* Let's swim out to the float. *xalliina nəsbaḥ ləl-ʕawwaame.* 2. *fawwaaše* pl. *-aat.* That's the first time I'm fishing with this float. *hayy ʔawwal marra bəṣṭaad fiiha b-hal-fawwaaše.*

to float – 1. *faaš (u fawašaan), ʕaam (u ʕoom).* A big iceberg was floating in the water. *kaan fii žabal talž ᵊkbiir faayeš ʕala saṭḥ ᵊl-mayy.* — He swam for a while and then floated. *sabaḥ šwayye w-baʕdeen faaš.* 2. *fawwaš//tfawwaš, ʕawwam//tʕawwam.* Later on they float the logs down the river. *baʕdeen bifawwšu ž-žzuuʕa bᵊn-naazel mn ᵊn-nahᵊr.* — They managed to float the ship within an hour. *qədru yfawwšu s-safiine b-məddet saaʕa.*

flock – 1. *qaṭiiʕ* pl. *qəṭʕaan, sərbe* pl. *sərab.* They followed him like a flock of sheep. *məšyu warḍa mətᵊl qaṭiiʕ ġanam.* 2. *sərbe* pl. *sərab.* We saw a flock of birds flying south. *šəfna sərbet ᵊṭyuur ṭaayra naaḥ ᵊž-žanuub.*

to flock – 1. *ddaffaq.* The children flocked into the circus. *l-ᵊwlaad ᵊddaffaqu la-žuwwaat ᵊs-sərk.* 2. *ḥtašad.* People came flocking to hear her. *n-naas ᵊḥtašadu ḥatta yəsmaʕuuha.*

flood – *fayaḍaan* pl. *-aat.* Many perished in the flood. *fii ktiir həlku bᵊl-fayaḍaan.*

to flood – 1. *ġamar (o ġamᵊr//nġamar) bᵊl-mayy, faaḍ (i fayaḍaan).* The river flooded the entire eastern section of the town. *n-nahᵊr ġamar kəll ᵊl-qəsm ᵊš-šarqi ləl-balad bᵊl-mayy.* 2. *faaḍ (i fayaḍaan).* The river floods every year. *n-nahᵊr bifiiḍ kəll səne.*

floor – 1. *ʔarḍ.* My glasses fell on the floor. *kəzᵊlki waqaʕ ʕal-ʔarḍ.* 2. *ṭaabeq* pl. *ṭawaabeq.* We live on the first floor. *nəḥna saakniin bᵊṭ-ṭaabeq ᵊl-ʔarḍi.* — I live on the second floor. *ʔana saaken bᵊṭ-ṭaabeq ᵊl-ʔawwal* (for some speakers also *ᵊṭ-ṭaani*).

**May I have the floor? *məmken ʔaaxod ḥaqq ᵊl-kalaam?*

floor plan – *mxaṭṭaṭ* pl. *-aat.*

flop: The play was a flop. *t-tamsiiliyye fəšlet.* — As a teacher he's a complete flop. *ka-mʕallem huwwe faašel ʕal-ʔaaxiir.*

to flop – 1. *rama (i ø) ḥaalo.* She flopped into a chair. *ramet ḥaala ʕala kərsi.* 2. *fəšel (a fašal).* Her second book flopped miserably. *ktaaba t-taani fəšel fašal zariiʕ.*

florist – *zhuuraati* pl. *-iyye.* Her brother is a florist. *ʔaxuuha zhuuraati.* — Is there a florist in the neighborhood? *fii zhuuraati b-han-nawaaḥi?*

flour – *ṭḥiin.* I want a sack of flour. *bəddi kiis ᵊṭḥiin.*

to **flourish** – *zdahar.* After a few bad years their business flourishes again. *baʕᵊd kam səne ʕaaṭle ʕaad šəġlon w-ᵊzdahar taani marra.*

flow – *tadaffoq.* The flow of refugees has increased over the past few days. *tadaffoq ᵊl-laažᵊiin ᵊzdaad b-hal-kam yoom ᵊl-ʔaaxraaniyyaat.* — As a result, the flow of foreign aid into the country was stopped all of a sudden. *b-natiižet zaalek, tadaffoq l-ᵊmsaaʕadaat ᵊl-xaaržiyye ʕal-ᵊblaad nqaṭaʕ ʕala ġafle.*

to flow – 1. *saal (i sayalaan), ddaffaq.* Tears were flowing down her cheeks. *d-dmuuʕ kaanet ʕam ᵊtsiil mən ᵊʕyuuna ʕala xduuda.* 2. *saal, žara (i žarayaan).* The river flows south from here on. *n-nahᵊr bisiil mən hoon naaḥ ᵊž-žanuub.* 3. *ddaffaq.* Millions in foreign capital flow into the country every year. *fii malayiin mn ᵊr-rasamiil ᵊl-ʔažnabiyye ʕam təddaffaq ʕal-ᵊblaad kəll səne.* 4. *ṣabb (ə ṣabb).* The Danube flows into the Black Sea. *nahr ᵊd-daanuub biṣəbb bᵊl-baḥr ᵊl-ʔaswad.*

flowing – *faḍfaaḍ.* She wore a flowing gown. *kaanet laabse roob faḍfaaḍ.*

flower – *zahra* coll. *zahᵊr* pl. *-aat* and *zhuur, warde* coll. *ward* pl. *-aat* and *wruud.* What beautiful flowers you have in your garden! *maa ʔaḥla z-zhuur halli b-ᵊžneentak!*

flower shop – *dəkkaanet˜* (pl. *dakakiin˜*) *ᵊzhuur, zhuuraati* pl. *-iyye.* There's a flower shop at the next corner. *fii dəkkaanet ᵊzhuur ʕas-suuke ž-žaaye.*

flowerpot – *šaqfet˜* (pl. *šəqaf˜*) *ᵊzriiʕa.*

flu – *ʔənfluwanza, səʕᵊr.* Our whole family had the flu. *kəll ʕeelətna ṣar-lon ʔənfluwanza.*

to **fluctuate** – *tqallab.* Prices fluctuate. *l-ʔasʕaar ʕam tətqallab.*

fluency – *ṭalaaqa.*

fluently – *b-ṭalaaqa.* He speaks German fluently. *byəḥki ʔalmaani b-ṭalaaqa* or **byəḥki ʔalmaani mətl ᵊl-mayy.*

fluid – 1. *saaʔel* pl. *sawaaʔel, maaʔeʕ* pl. *mawaaʔeʕ.* The fluid has evaporated. *s-saaʔel ᵊtbaxxar.* 2. *saaʔel, maaʔeʕ.* I watched them pour the fluid metal into a mold. *tfarražᵊt ʕaleehon w-hənne ʕam yṣəbbu l-maʕdan ᵊs-saaʔel ᵊb-qaaleb.*

lighter fluid – *banziin ləl-qaddaaḥa.*

transmission fluid – *zeet˜ ᵊt-transməsyoon.*

flurry – *habbe* pl. *-aat.* The radio predicted snow flurries for tomorrow. *r-raadyo qaal ʔənno bəkra bəddo yṣiir kam habbet talž.*

to **flush** – *ḥmarr.* He flushed with anger. *ḥmarr mən kətr ᵊl-ġaḍab.* 2. *šadd (ə šadd) siifoon˜ ...* Don't forget to flush the toilet. *laa tənsa maa tšədd siifoon beet ᵊl-mayy.*

to **be flush with** – *kaan ʕala sawiyye waaḥde w-.* The track is flush with the ground. *l-xaṭṭ ᵊl-ḥadiidi ʕala sawiyye waaḥde wᵊ l-ʔarḍ.*

flush box – *siifoon* pl. *-aat.*

fly – *dəbbaane* coll. *dəbbaan* pl. *-aat.* The flies around here are terrible! *d-dəbbaan hoon məzʕež ᵊktiir!*

to fly – 1. *ṭaar (i ṭayaraan).* The birds are flying south. *ṭ-ṭyuur ṭaayriin naaḥ ᵊž-žanuub.* 2. *saafar bᵊṭ-ṭayyaara.* We're flying to Paris tomorrow. *laḥa nsaafer bᵊṭ-ṭayyaara bəkra la-baariiz.* — Are you going to fly or go by boat? *laḥa tsaafer bᵊṭ-ṭayyaara wəlla bᵊl-baaxra?* or **laḥa tsaafer bᵊž-žaww wəlla bᵊl-baḥᵊr?* 3. *naqal (o naqᵊl// ntaqal) bᵊṭ-ṭayyaara.* The child was flown to a hospital. *ṭ-ṭəfᵊl naqaluu bᵊṭ-ṭayyaara ʕal-məstašfa.* 4. *saaq (u sooq, sawaqaan).* Can you fly a plane? *btaʕref ᵊtsuuq ṭayyaara?*

**The ship was flying the American flag. *l-baaxra kaanet maašye taḥt ᵊl-ʕalam ᵊl-ʔameerki.*

to fly into a rage (or **passion**) – *ṭaar (i ø) ʕaqlo.* My mother flew into a rage when I told her. *ʔəmmi lamma xabbarta ṭaar ʕaqla.*

flyer – *ṭayyaar* pl. *-iin.* He's a famous flyer. *huwwe ṭayyaar mašhuur.*

flying fish – *samake ṭayyaara* coll. *samak ṭayyaar* pl. *ʔasmaak ṭayyaara,* with numbers 3 to 10 *samakaat ṭayyaara.*

flying saucer – *ṭabaq ṭaaʔer* pl. *ʔaṭbaaq ṭaaʔira.*

flypaper – *waraqet˜* (coll. *waraq˜* pl. *wraaq˜*) *dəbbaan.*

flyspeck – *xara˜ dəbbaan.*

fly swatter – *qattaalet˜* (pl. *-aat˜*) *dəbbaan.*

flywheel – *ḥaddaafe* pl. *-aat.*

foal – *məhᵊr* pl. *mhuura.*

foam – *raġwe.* There's more foam than beer. *fii raġwe ʔaktar məmma ykuun fii biira.*

to foam – *raġa (i raġwe).* What can you do to keep the beer from foaming? *šuu fiik taʕmel ḥatta maa txalli l-biira tərġi?*

**He was foaming with rage. *kaan dammo ʕam yfuur mn ᵊl-ġaḍab.*

to **focus** – 1. *ẓabbaṭ.* Do you know how to focus the camera? *btaʕref ᵊdẓabbeṭ ᵊl-kdameera?* 2. *rakkaz.* He focused his attention on that one particular problem. *rakkaz ʔəntibaaho ʕala haš-šaġle l-waaḥde.*

fodder – *ʕalaf.*

fog – *ḍabaab, ġteeṭa.* A dense fog shut out the view. *kaan fii ḍabaab kasiif ḥažab ᵊl-manẓar.*

foggy – 1. *mḍabḍeb.* It was a foggy day. *kaan nhaar ᵊmḍabḍeb.* 2. *məbham.* He's full of foggy notions about this and that. *huwwe malaan ʔaaraaʔ məbhame ʕan kəll šii.*

**It's foggy outside. *fii ḍabaab barra.*

fold – *tanye* pl. *-aat, ṭaʕže* pl. *-aat.* The curtains are faded at the folds. *l-baraadi baayxiin ʕand ᵊt-tanyaat.*

to fold – 1. *ṭawa (i ṭawi, ṭawye//nṭawa).* Help me fold the blanket. *saaʕədni ʔəṭwi l-ᵊḥraam.* --

Fold the curtains and put them away. *ʔəṭwi l-baraadi w-xabbiihon.* 2. *tana (i tani, tanye//ntana).* Shall I fold the letter twice? *ʔətni l-maktuub tanᵊyteen?* 3. *laff (ə laff//nlaff).* Fold the gloves in tissue paper. *ləff l-ᵊkfuuf b-waraq šaffaaf.* 4. *kattaf.* He folded his arms. *kattaf saaƐdeeno.*

**Fold your hands. *šabbek ʔaṣabiiƐak.*

to fold in one's arms - *Ɛaanaq, ḍamm (ə ḍamm).* She folded the child in her arms. *Ɛaanaqet ᵊṭ-ṭəfᵊl.*

to fold up - 1. *sakkar.* That newspaper folded up last year. *haž-žariide sakkaret Ɛaamnawwal.* 2. *tkaƐwak, ṭaƐaž (a ṭaƐᵊž) šaqᵊfteen.* He folded up like a jacknife. *tkaƐwak mətl ᵊl-ḥayye.*

folder - 1. *mṣannaf* pl. *-aat, malaff* pl. *-aat, ʔəḍbaara* pl. *-aat* and *ʔaḍabiir.* The copies are in the blue folder. *n-nəsax bᵊl-ᵊmṣannaf ᵊl-ʔazraq.* 2. *karraase* pl. *-aat, brošuur* pl. *-aat.* I'll get you some folders from the travel agency. *bžəb-lak šwayyet karraasaat mən maktab ᵊs-syaaḥa.*

folding chair - *kərsi* (pl. *karaasi*) *bortatiif, kərsi byəṭṭabbaq.*

folklore - *folkloor.*

folk music - *muusiiqa šaƐbiyye.*

folks - 1. *ʔahᵊl.* How are your folks? *kiif (ḥaal˜) ʔahlak?* 2. *naas, Ɛaalam, žamaaƐa.* Let's go, folks. *yaḷḷa nəmši yaa naas.*

folk song - *ġənniyye* (pl. *ġanaani*) *šaƐbiyye.*

to **follow** - 1. *ləḥeq (a laḥaqaan).* Somebody's following us. *fii ḥada Ɛam yəlḥaqna.* — Follow me. *lḥaqni.* 2. *ttabaƐ, məši (i maši) Ɛala.* Follow these instructions exactly. *ttəbeƐ* (or *ʔəmši Ɛala) hat-taƐliimaat bᵊl-ḥarf.* — Let's follow this method. *xalliina nəmši Ɛala hat-ṭariiqa.* 3. *taabaƐ.* I couldn't follow his explanation. *maa qdərᵊt taabeƐ šarḥo.* — Have you been following the news lately? *Ɛam ᵊttaabeƐ ᵊl-ʔaxbaar b-hal-ʔiyyaam?* 4. *ttabaƐ, taabaƐ, məši Ɛala.* He's following in his father's footsteps. *Ɛam yəttəbeƐ xaṭwaat ʔabúu.* 5. *qtada b-.* I think I'll follow your example. *bẓənn bəqtədi fiik.* 6. *tbayyan.* From this it follows that ... *mən heek byətbayyan ʔənno ...* 7. *ʔeža baƐd ...* The hot weather was followed by heavy rains. *moožet ᵊl-ḥarr ʔəža baƐda ʔamṭaaṛ šadiide.*

**We'll follow later. *mnəži baƐdeen.*

**Her eyes followed him sadly. *naẓaraata məšyet maƐo b-ḥəzᵊn.*

**I don't follow you there. *maa-li Ɛam ʔəfham Ɛaleek hoon.*

to follow up - *ḥaqqaq.* We try to follow up every complaint. *Ɛam ᵊnḥaawel ᵊnḥaqqeq kəll šakwa.*

as follows - *kal-ʔaati, kat-taali, ka-ma yali.* The letter reads as follows ... *naṣṣ ᵊl-maktuub kal-ʔaati ...*

follower - *taabeƐ* pl. *ʔatbaaƐ.* He's one of his most faithful followers. *huwwe waaḥed mən ʔaxlaṣ ʔatbaaƐo.*

following - 1. *ʔatbaaƐ* (pl.), *mᵊʔayydiin* (pl.). He has a very large following. *ʔəlo ʔatbaaƐ ᵊktiir.* 2. *taani.* The following day it rained. *bᵊl-yoom ᵊt-taani nəzlet maṭaṛ.* 3. *taali.* I need the following items:... *laazəmni l-ᵊgraaḍ ᵊt-taalye:...*

fond - *Ɛaziiz.* I have only fond memories of that place. *maa Ɛandi ġeer zəkriyyaat Ɛaziize la-hal-maḥall.* — Her fondest wish came true. *ʔaƐazz ʔamaaniiha tḥaqqaq.*

to be fond of - *ḥabb (ə ḥəbb).* We're fond of music. *mənḥəbb ᵊl-muusiiqa* or ***nəḥna məġramiin bᵊl-muusiiqa.* — She's very fond of children. *bətḥəbb l-ᵊwlaad ᵊktiir.*

to become fond of - *ṣaar (i ṣ) yḥəbb.* We became very fond of the child. *ṣərna nḥəbb ᵊl-walad ᵊktiir.*

food - 1. *mawaadd ġizaaʔiyye* (pl.). Food is getting scarcer and scarcer. *l-mawaadd ᵊl-ġizaaʔiyye kəll-maa-la Ɛam ᵊtqəll.* 2. *ʔakᵊl, ṭaƐaam.* The food was plain but substantial. *l-ʔakᵊl kaan baṣiiṭ bass ᵊmġazzi.*

**This will give you food for thought. *haada biġazzíi-lak ʔafkaarak.*

foodstuff - *madde* (pl. *mawaadd*) *ġizaaʔiyye.*

fool - *mažnuun* pl. *mažaniin, mahbuul* pl. *mahabiil, ḥmaaṛ* pl. *ḥamiir, ġabi* pl. *ʔaġbiya.* He's a fool if he believes that story. *bikuun mažnuun ʔiza bisaddeq hal-qəṣṣa.* — He's nobody's fool. *huwwe muu ḥmaaṛ.*

**There's no fool like an old fool. *šaayeb w-Ɛaayeb.*

**They sent him on a fool's errand. *baƐatúu məšwaar mafxuut.*

to make a fool of oneself - *saawa ḥaalo masxaṛa.* If you want to make a fool of yourself, go ahead and do it. *ʔiza bəddak ᵊtsaawi ḥaalak masxaṛa maa ḥada maanƐak, ᵊƐməla.*

to fool - 1. *mazaḥ (a mazᵊḥ).* I was only fooling. *kənt Ɛam ʔəmzaḥ bass.* 2. *ḍḍaḥḥak//nḍaḥak Ɛala, ləƐeb (a ləƐᵊb//nlaƐab) Ɛala.* You can't fool me. *maa fiik təḍḍaḥḥak Ɛaliyyi.*

to fool around - 1. *ləƐeb (a ləƐᵊb), qaaraš.* Don't fool around with that radio while I'm gone. *laa təlƐab b-har-raadyo w-ʔana maa-li hoon* or *laa tqaareš har-raadyo ...* 2. *maġyaṣ.* He just fools around. *bass Ɛam ymaġyeṣ.*

to fool away - *maġyaṣ b-.* He fools his time away. *Ɛam ymaġyeṣ ᵊb-waqto.*

foolish - 1. *saxiif* pl. *səxafa, ʔahbal* f. *habla* pl. *həbᵊl.* She's just a foolish woman. *hiyye mara saxiife wᵊs-salaam.* — Don't be foolish! *laa tkuun saxiif!* or ***ḥaaštak saxaafe!* 2. *ṭaayeš, saxiif.* That was a foolish thing to do. *haada kaan Ɛamal ṭaayeš.*

foot - 1. *rəžᵊl* (f., dual *rəžᵊlteen*) pl. *rəžleen, ʔəžᵊr* (f., dual *ʔəžᵊrteen*) pl. *ʔəžreen, qadam* pl. *qdaam.* My foot feels numb. *rəžli maa-li Ɛam ḥəss fiiha.* — A good rest and he'll be back on his feet again. *baƐᵊd raaḥa mniiḥa byəržaƐ biquum Ɛala rəžlée.* 2. *qadam* pl. *qdaam.* She's about five foot two. *ṭuula ḥawaali xams ᵊqdaam w-ʔənšeen.* — He's over six feet tall. *ṭuulo ʔaktar mən sətt ᵊqdaam.* — He's always on his feet. *daayman Ɛala qadamo (maa byəqƐod).* 3. *səfᵊl, kaƐb.* The chest of drawers is at the foot of the bed. *l-biiro Ɛand səfl ᵊt-taxᵊt.* — We stopped for a short rest at the foot of the mountain. *twaqqafna la-nəstriiḥ šwayye Ɛand səfl ᵊž-žabal.* 4. *səfᵊl, ʔaaxer.* You find the sentence at the foot of the page. *bətlaaqi ž-žəmle b-səfl ᵊṣ-ṣafḥa.*

**He's old enough to stand on his own feet. *wəṣel la-sənn la-ydabber ḥaalo la-ḥaalo.*

**Things won't improve until you put your foot down. *l-ʔawḍaaƐ maa laḥa tətḥassan ʔəlla-ma tḥəṭṭ ʔiidak.*

**I really put my foot in it that time! *hal-marra mən ḥaqa ṭləƐt ᵊb-mafxuute faẓiiƐa!*

**I'm trying to put my best foot forward. *Ɛam ḥaawel qaddem ʔaḥsan maa Ɛandi.*

on foot - *Ɛal-maaši, maši, maaši* (inflected). We had to cover the rest of the way on foot. *nžabarna nəqṭaƐ ᵊkmaalet ᵊṭ-ṭariiq Ɛal-maaši* (or *maašyiin*).

**There must be something on foot. *laazem ykuun fii šii Ɛam yənṭəbex.*

to foot the bill for - *tḥammal maṣariif˜ ..., tkaffal maṣariif˜ ...* Who's going to foot the bill for all this? *miin bəddo yətḥammal maṣariif kəll haš-šii?*

foot-and-mouth disease - *həmma q̈ulaaƐiyye.*

football - (ball) *ṭaabet˜* (pl. *-aat˜*) *futbool,* (game = soccer) *futbool, kuret˜ q̈adam,* (= American) *futbool ʔameerkaani.*

footnote - *ḥaašye* pl. *ḥawaaši, mlaaḥaẓa* pl. *-aat.*

footpath - *ṭariiq* (pl. *ṭəroq*) *qaaduumiyye.*

footprint - *Ɛalaamet˜ qadam* pl. *Ɛalaamaat˜ ᵊqdaam, ʔasar˜ qadam* pl. *ʔaasaar˜ ᵊqdaam.* We followed the footprints. *lḥəqna Ɛalaamaat l-ᵊqdaam.*

footrest - *takkaayet˜* (pl. *-aat˜*) *rəžleen, sannaadet˜* (pl. *-aat˜*) *rəžleen.*

footsteps - 1. *mašye, xaṭwaat* (pl.). I think I heard footsteps in the hall. *kaʔənni sməƐᵊt mašyet ḥada bᵊl-kooridoor.* 2. *xaṭwaat* (pl.). He's following in his father's footsteps. *Ɛam yəttəbeƐ xaṭwaat ʔabúu.*

for - 1. *la-, lə-* (with pron. suff. *ʔəl-,* as an enclitic *-l-, -ll-*), *mənšaan, məšaan.* Is there anything I can do for him? *fii šii məmken ʔaƐməl-lo-yáa?* or *fii šii məmken ʔaƐᵊmlo mənšaano?* — Here's a telegram for the boss. *hayy taliġraaf lər-raʔiis.* — We need a new rug for the living room. *laazəmna səžžaade ždiide mənšaan ʔuḍṭ l-ᵊqƐuud.* — They have an extra man for keeping the books. *Ɛandon rəžžaal zyadde la-ḥəfẓ ᵊl-kətᵊb.* — The boy brought a package for my sister. *l-walad žaab-la baakeet la-ʔəxti.* — Aspirin is good for headaches. *l-ʔasbiiriin mniiḥ la-wažaƐ ᵊr-raas.* — What is it for? *la-šuu haš-šii?* — They're fighting for a good cause. *Ɛam yḥaarbu la-ġaraḍ nabiil.* — For you it's a small amount, but for him it's a lot of money. *ʔəlak ʔənte mablaġ baṣiiṭ laaken ʔəlo huwwe maṣaari ktiir.* 2. *la-.* Let's leave the rest for tomorrow. *xalliina nxalli l-baqiyye la-bəkra.* — Are there any letters for me? *fii ʔəli šii maktuub?* — Go open the door for her. *ruuḥ ftaḥ-la l-baab.* — Say hello to him for me. *salləm-li εalée.* — They left Damascus for Beirut. *taraku š-šaam la-beeruut.* — The train for Paris leaves in five minutes. *t-treen la-baariiz byəmši baεᵊd xamᵊs daqaayeq.* — For that very reason I turned down the offer. *la-has-sabab b-εeeno rafaḍt ᵊl-εarᵊḍ.* — He has no time for such nonsense. *maa εando waqᵊt la-hal-εalk.* — For miles around the roads were under water. *la-ʔamyaal mən kəll naaḥye ṭ-ṭəroq kaanet maǧmuura bᵊl-mayy.* — For miles he didn't speak a word. *la-ʔamyaal w-ʔamyaal maa ḥaka w-laa kəlme.* — What's that supposed to be good for? *ya-tára haš-šii la-šuu byənfaε?* — He married her for money, not for love. *džawwáza ləl-maṣaari, muu ləl-ḥəbb.* 3. *tabaε˜.* Show me your homework for tomorrow. *waržiini waẓiiftak tabaε bəkra.* — Have you seen the cord for the electric iron somewhere around here? *šəft ᵊš-šriiṭ tabaε ᵊl-məkwaaye b-šii qərne?* 4. *εala.* He deserves a medal for so much bravery. *byəstḥəqq niišaan εala heek šažaaεa.* — I'll spank him for that lie. *bəḍᵊrbo εala qaḍda εala hal-kəzbe.* — I could kill him for doing such a stupid thing. *ʔaax law ʔəqᵊlto εala heek εamal saxiif!* 5. *maε.* Are you for or against him? *ʔənte maεo wəlla ḍəḍḍo?* — Are you for the plan or against it? *ʔənte maε ᵊl-mašruuε wəlla ḍəḍḍo?* 6. *ka-, mə(n)šaan.* For a boy of five he's very tall. *ka-walad εəmro xams ᵊsniin huwwe ṭawiil ᵊktiir.* — For an American, he speaks Arabic well. *ka-waaḥed ʔameerkaani byəḥki εarabi mniiḥ.* 7. *ʔasna, xilaal, b-.* That should keep you busy for the next few weeks. *haada məntḍ̣ar yxalliik mašǧuul ʔasna hal-kam žəmεa ž-žaaye.* 8. *maε, bᵊr-raǧᵊm mən.* You don't convince me for all your clever arguments. *maa fiik təqnəεni maε kəll ḥəžažak ᵊl-ḥədqa.* — He's still very active for his age. *ləssaato ktiir našiiṭ maε kəbᵊr εəmro.* 9. *mqaabel, la-.* For every good teacher there are five bad ones. *mqaabel kəll ᵊmεallem mniiḥ fii xamse εaṭliin.* 10. *εawaaḍ˜, badaal˜, b-makaan˜, b-maḥall˜.* I'm just helping out for my brother who's ill. *bass εam ʔəštəǧel εawaaḍ ʔaxi halli mariiḍ.* 11. *εan, bᵊn-niyaabe εan.* Do you have the authority to sign this contract for him? *εandak ṣalṭa təmḍi hal-kontraat εanno?*

**I've been wearing this coat for three years. *ṣar-li bəlbes hal-manṭo tlatt ᵊsniin.*

**They haven't heard from him for a long time. *ṣar-lon zamaan maa-lon εam yəsmaεu mənno.*

**For five months he hasn't had any news from her. *ṣar-lo xamᵊst əšhor maa səmeε mənha.*

**We lived there for years. *sakanna hniik ᵊsniin.*

**So much for that. *ḥaažətna mən haš-šaǧle.*

**All he's left me is debts for me to pay. *kəll halli tarak-li-yáa dyuun εala raqᵊbti.*

**It's for you to take the responsibility. *εaleek ʔənte taaxod ᵊl-masʔuuliyye.*

**I'm all for it. *ʔana mwaafeq bᵊl-miyye miyye.*

**What do you use for fuel? *šuu btəstaεmel maḥruuqaat?*

**What do you eat for breakfast? *šuu btaakol kasr ṣəfra?*

**For all I know he's still in Europe. *kəll halli baεᵊrfo ləssaato b-ʔawrəbba.*

for my (your, his, etc.) own sake - *la-maṣlaḥti (-ak, -ek, -o, etc.), la-ṣaalḥi (-ak, -ek, -o, etc.).* Do it for your own sake. *εməla la-maṣlaḥtak.*

for the sake of - 1. *mə(n)šaan˜, kərmaal˜, mənšaan xaaṭer˜, la-ʔažl˜.* I don't want you to go to any trouble for her sake. *maa bəddi-yaak tǧalleb ḥaalak mənšaanha.* — They went back to each other for the children's sake. *rəžεu la-baεḍon kərmaal l-ᵊwlaad.* — He postponed his vacation for the boss's sake. *ʔažžal ʔaxᵊd fərᵊṣto mənšaan xaaṭer ᵊr-raʔiis.* **2.** *mənšaan˜, kərmaal˜, la-ʔažl˜.* I gave in for the sake of peace. *sallamᵊt mənšaan ᵊṣ-ṣəlᵊḥ.*

for heaven's sake - *mənšaan ʔaḷḷa baqa.* For heaven's sake, stop! *mənšaan ʔaḷḷa baqa, ḥaaže!*

as for - *bᵊn-nəsbe la-, ʔamma.* As for me, I'll wait here. *bᵊn-nəsbe ʔəli (or ʔamma ʔana) bəntəẓer hoon.*

but for - *law-laa.* But for his intervention I'd be out of a job today. *law-laa waṣaaṭto kənt ᵊbkuun daayer baṭṭaal εaṭṭaal.* — But for him I wouldn't be alive today. *law-láa maa kənt ᵊbkuun ṭayyeb hallaq.*

if it hadn't been for - *law-laa.* If it hadn't been for the money I would have gone. *law-laa ḥkaayet ᵊl-maṣaari kənt rəḥt.* — If it hadn't been for her I'd be a poor man today. *law-laaha kənt šaḥḥaad ᵊl-yoom ʔana.* — If it hadn't been for them we would be in Paris now. *law-laahon la-kənna mənkuun hallaq ᵊb-baariiz.*

if it weren't for - *law-laa.* If it weren't for the children he would have left his wife a long time ago. *law-laa l-ᵊwlaad la-kaan tarak marto mən zamaan.*

what for - 1. *leeš, la-šuu.* Why don't you write him a letter? - What for? *leeš maa btəktəb-lo maktuub? - leeš?* **2.** *la-šuu, mə(n)šaan šuu.* Get me a few nails. - What for? *žəb-li kam bəsmaar. - la-šuu?*

to **forbid** - *manaε (a manᵊε//nmanaε).* I forbid you to do such a thing. *bəmnaεak taεmel heek šii.*

God forbid - *ḥaaša ləllaah, maεaaza ḷḷaah, ʔaḷḷa laa yqadder.*

force - 1. *quwwe.* We had to use force. *nžabarna nəstaεmel ᵊl-quwwe.* — That's force of habit. *hayy quwwet ᵊl-εaade.* **2.** *quwwe, εənf.* Force won't get you anywhere. *l-quwwe maa bətwaṣṣlak la-šii.* **3.** *šədde, quwwe.* The storm hasn't reached it's full force yet. *l-εaaṣfe ləssa maa wəṣlet la-ʔaq̈ṣa šəddəta.*

by force - *bᵊl-quwwe, bᵊz-zoor.* They had to drag him away by force. *nžabaru yəsḥabúu bᵊl-quwwe.*

from force of habit - *taḥᵊt˜ taʔsiir˜ ᵊl-εaade.* She does it from force of habit. *btaεməla taḥᵊt taʔsiir ᵊl-εaade.*

in force - *naafez, saari l-mafεuul, maεmuul fii.* Are these laws still in force? *hal-q̈awaniin ləssaaha naafze (or saarye l-mafεuul or maεmuul fiiha)?*

in full force - *b-kaamel quwwto.* The police came out in full force. *š-šərṭa ṭəlεet ᵊb-kaamel quwwəta.*

**The family turned out in full force. *ʔəžet ᵊl-εeele - kbaara w-ᵊẓǧaara w-qaṭaaṭa.*

Air Force - *silaaḥ˜ ᵊṭ-ṭayaraan.*

Armed Forces - *q̈uwwaat ᵊmsallaḥa (pl.).*

police force - *ržaal˜ ᵊš-šərṭa (pl.).* How large is the police force? *qaddeeš εadad ᵊržaal ᵊš-šərṭa?*

force majeure - *sabab q̈aaher pl. ʔasbaab q̈aahra.*

to come into force - *nεamal fii, sara (i sarayaan) mafεuulo, tnaffaz, ṭṭabbaq.* When did these laws come into force? *ʔeemta hal-q̈awaniin nεamal fiihon (or sara mafεuulon or tnaffazu)?*

to force - 1. *žabar (e/o žabᵊr//nžabar), ʔažbar.* You can't force me. *maa fiik təžbərni.* — They forced him to sign the agreement. *ʔažbarúu yəmḍi l-ʔəttifaaq.* **2.** *xalaε (a xalᵊε//nxalaε).* Someone must have forced the door. *laazem ykuun fii ḥada xalaε ᵊl-baab.*

**We'll have to force our way in. *laazem nədxol bᵊl-quwwe.*

**You can't force things. *maa fiik tətεažžal bᵊl-ᵊʔmuur qabᵊl ʔawaana.*

to force back - *radd (ə radd//nradd).* Inch by inch they forced the enemy back. *raddu l-εaduww šəbᵊr šəbᵊr.*

forced labor - *ṣəxra.*

forced landing - *hbuuṭ ʔəḍṭiraari pl. habṭaat ʔəḍṭiraariyye.* The plane made a forced landing. *ṭ-ṭayyaara habṭet ᵊhbuuṭ ʔəḍṭiraari.*

forceful - *qawi*.*

forcibly - *bᵊl-quwwe, bᵊz-zoor.*

ford - *maxaaḍa pl. -aat.* There's a ford two miles up the river. *fii maxaaḍa miileen ṭaaleε mn ᵊṇ-ṇahᵊṛ.*

to ford - *xaaḍ (u xooḍ//nxaaḍ) b-.* You can't ford this river, the current is too strong. *maa fiik ᵊtxuuḍ b-han-nahᵊr, ᵊt-tayyaar qawi ktiir.*

forearm - *zənd pl. znuud.*

forecast - *tanabbo? pl. -aat.* His forecast turned out to be wrong. *tanabbᵊʔo ṭələε ǧalaṭ.*

to forecast - *tnabbaʔ b-.* They forecast cooler weather. *εam yətnabbaʔu b-ṭaqᵊṣ ʔabrad mən heek.*

forehead - *žbiin pl. -aat, žabha pl. -aat.*

foreign - 1. *ʔažnabi*.* You see a lot of foreign cars around here. *εam ᵊtšuuf sayyaaraat ʔažnabiyye ktiir ᵊb-han-nawaaḥi.* — Do you speak any foreign languages? *btəḥki šii luǧa ʔažnabiyye?* **2.** *xaarži*.* The country has received about a hundred million in foreign aid so far. *l-ᵊblaad ʔəžaaha la-ḥadd hallaq ḥawaali miit malyoon msaaεadaat xaaržiyye.*

foreign minister - *waziir˜ (pl. wəzaraaʔ˜) ᵊl-xaaržiyye.*

Foreign Ministry (or Office) - *wazaaret˜ ᵊl-xaaržiyye.*

foreigner - *ʔažnabi** pl. *ʔažaaneb, ġariib* pl. *ġəraba.* Before the war many foreigners came here. *qabl ᵊl-ḥarb fii naas ʔažaaneb ᵊktiir ʔəžu la-hoon.*
foreman - *mnaažer* pl. *-iin.*
in the **forenoon** - *qabl ᵊḍ-ḍəhᵊr.* What did you do in the forenoon? *šuu ʕməlᵊt qabl ᵊḍ-ḍəhᵊr?*
forest - *ġaabe* pl. *-aat.*
forever - **1.** *ləl-ʔabad, la-ʔabad˜ ᵊl-ʔaabidiin.* I'm afraid I'll be stuck in this place forever. *šaayéf-lak laḥa ʔəʕlaq hoon ləl-ʔabad.* **2.** *daayman, ʕala ṭuul.* He's forever telling that same old story. *daayman biʕiid w-byəftoq nafs ᵊl-qəṣṣa.*
foreword - *tawṭiʔa* pl. *-aat, muqaddime* pl. *-aat.* Who wrote the foreword to the book? *miin katab ᵊt-tawṭiʔa tabaʕ l-ᵊktaab?*
to **forge** - **1.** *ṣanaʕ (a ṣənᵊʕ//nṣanaʕ).* The natives forge their own crude weapons. *ʔahl l-ᵊblaad byəṣnaʕu ʔasləḥton ᵊl-bidaaʔiyye la-ḥaalon.* **2.** *zayyaf.* It looks as if someone had forged this passport. *byəẓhar fii ḥada zayyaf hal-baasboor.* **3.** *zawwar.* The signature was definitely forged. *ʔakiid hal-ʔəmḍa mzawwar.*
forgery - **1.** *tazyiif.* You have to admit it's a very clever forgery. *laazem təʕtéref ʔənno hat-tazyiif kəllo mahaara.* **2.** *tazwiir.* The signature is a clumsy piece of forgery. *l-ʔəmḍa mzawwar tazwiir baahet.*
to **forget** - *nəsi (a nəsyaan, nasu//ntasa).* She has forgotten everything. *nəsyet kəll šii.* — I forgot to call you (up). *nsiit ʔaʕmél-lak talifoon.* — Don't forget to leave a message for him at the desk. *laa tənsa maa tətrék-lo* (also: *laa tənsa tətrék-lo*) *kəlme bᵊl-maktab.*
to forget oneself - *ḍaaʕ (i ø) ṣawaabo.* I forgot myself for a moment. *ḍaaʕ ṣawaabi šii kam ləḥẓa.* — Shut up or I'll forget myself. *sakker niiʕak walla bidiiʕ ṣawaabi waḷḷa.*
forgetfulness - *nəsyaan.* My forgetfulness cost me dearly. *nəsyaani kallafni ġaali ktiir.*
to **forgive** - **1.** *saamaḥ//tsaamaḥ, ġafar (o ġəfraan//nġafar) la-* or *ʕan, samaḥ (a samaaḥ//nsamaḥ) ʕan.* He'll never forgive you for that. *b-ḥayaato maa bisaamḥak ʕaleeha* or *b-ḥayaato maa byəġfər-lak-yaaha* (or *byəġféra ʕannak*) or *b-ḥayaato maa byəsmaḥ ʕannak ʕaleeha.* **2.** *ġafar la-, samaḥ ʕan.* God will forgive you. *ʔaḷḷa byəġfér-lak* (or *byəsmaḥ ʕannak*).
**Forgive me, it was a mistake. *ʕafwan* (or *ʕafwak* or *laa tʔaaxəzni*) *kaanet ġalṭa.*
to ask someone to forgive - *stasmaḥ mən ḥada.* Ask him to forgive you. *stasmeḥ mənno.*
fork - *šooke* pl. *-aat* and *šuwak.* Could I have a knife and fork please? *məmken taʕṭiini šooke w-səkkiin?*
to fork - *tšaʕʕab.* The road forks beyond the village. *ṭ-ṭariiq byətšaʕʕab baʕd ᵊḍ-ḍeeʕa.*
form - **1.** *šəkᵊl* and *šakᵊl* pl. *ʔaškaal.* In the distance we could see the dim forms of mountains. *ʕala masaafe šəfna ʔaškaal ᵊmġabbše la-žbaal.* — The appeal was written in the form of an open letter to the editor. *n-nidaaʔ kaan ᵊb-šakl ᵊktaab maftuuḥ ləl-ᵊmḥarrer.* — The city's layout is in the form of a rectangle. *l-madiine ḥaakme b-šakᵊl məstaṭiil.* — The poem is flawless in form, but poor in content. *l-qaṣiide maa fiiha ʕeeb mən naaḥiit ᵊš-šakl, bass ᵊḍʕiife bᵊl-maġza.* **2.** *šakᵊl, ṭariiqa, ʔəsluub.* You can't handle the matter in this form. *maa fiik ᵊtʕaalež ᵊl-qaḍiyye b-haš-šakᵊl.* **3.** *baab* pl. *bwaab, nooʕ* pl. *ʔanwaaʕ.* These are the principal forms of poetic expression. *hayy l-ᵊbwaab ᵊr-raʔiisiyye lət-taʕbiir ᵊš-šəʕri.* **4.** *ṣiiġa* pl. *ṣiyaġ.* It's a very common verb form in Arabic. *hayy ṣiiġa fəʕliyye ktiir maʔluufe bᵊl-ʕarabi.* **5.** *ʔəstimaara* pl. *-aat.* You'll have to fill out this form. *laazem ᵊtʕabbi hal-ʔəstimaara.*
**I'm in good form today. *ʔaḷḷa faateḥ ʕaliyyi l-yoom.*
**He was in bad form that day. That's why he lost the game. *kaan ʔaḷḷa muu faateḥ ʕalée yoomə́ta, mən heek ᵊnġalab.*
matter of form - *masʔale* (pl. *masaaʔel*) *šakliyye.* It's only a matter of form, but you have to do it. *hayye masʔale šakliyye, bass laazem taʕmə́la.*
to form - **1.** *ʔallaf, šakkal.* He formed a new cabinet. *ʔallaf wazaara ždiide.* — Later on, they formed their own party. *baʕdeen šakkalu ḥəzbon la-waḥdon.* **2.** *šakkal.* They formed a circle around the flagpole. *šakkalu ḥalaqa ḥawaali ʕaamuud ᵊl-beeraq.* — This group of words forms the third category. *hal-mažmuuʕa mn ᵊl-kəlmaat bətšakkel ᵊṣ-ṣənf ᵊt-taalet.* **3.** *kawwan.* I haven't formed an opinion yet. *ləssa maa kawwanᵊt fəkra.* **4.** *saawa.* Can you form an imperative from this verb? *fiik ᵊtsaawi ṣiiġet ᵊl-ʔamᵊr mən hal-fəʕᵊl?*
**This noun doesn't form a plural. *hal-ʔəsᵊm maa-lo žamᵊʕ.*
**He formed that habit over the years. *ṣaaret maʕo hal-ʕaade maʕ ᵊs-sniin.*
formal - *rasmi**. You needn't be that formal. *muu laazem ᵊtkuun hal-qadd rasmi.* — He paid him a formal visit. *zaaro zyaara rasmiyye.* — She made a formal apology. *ʕtazret ʔəʕtizaar rasmi.*
formality - **1.** *šakliyyaat* (pl.). It's only a formality. *hayy bass šakliyyaat.* **2.** *rasmiyyaat* (pl.). I wish you wouldn't stand so much on formality. *ya-reetak maa tətmassak hal-qadd bᵊr-rasmiyyaat.*
formally - *rasmiyyan, b-ṣuura rasmiyye.* He has formally resigned. *staʕfa rasmiyyan.*
formation - **1.** *taʔliif, taškiil.* The formation of the new cabinet will be announced shortly. *taʔliif ᵊl-wazaara ž-ždiide laḥa yənʕəlen ʕan qariib.* **2.** *tarkiib* pl. *tarakiib.* The area shows interesting geological formations. *l-manṭiqa fiiha tarakiib žiyoloožiyye mhəmme.* **3.** *niẓaam.* The planes flew in close formation. *ṭ-ṭayyaaraat kaanet ṭaayra b-niẓaam məndamm.*
former - **1.** *saabeq.* The former owner has retired. *l-maalek ᵊs-saabeq ᵊtqaaʕad.* **2.** *ʔawwalaani**. I prefer the former suggestion. *bfaḍḍel ᵊl-ʔəqtiraaḥ ᵊl-ʔawwalaani.*
formerly - *bᵊs-saabeq, bᵊl-maaḍi, saabiqan.* This was formerly the business section. *haada kaan bᵊs-saabeq ᵊl-qəsm ᵊt-tižaari.*
fort - *ḥəṣᵊn* pl. *ḥṣuun, qalʕa* pl. *qlaaʕ.* There's an old fort on the hill. *fii ḥəṣᵊn ʕatiiq ʕala raas ᵊž-žabal.*
and so **forth** - *w-heek, w-ʕala heek, ʔila ʔaaxirihi.*
fortieth - *l-ʔarᵊbʕiin.* It's his fortieth birthday. *haada ʕiid miilaado l-ʔarᵊbʕiin.*
one fortieth - *waaḥed mən ʔarᵊbʕiin.*
fortifications - *taḥṣiinaat* (pl.).
to **fortify** - *ḥaṣṣan.* They hastily fortified the town. *ḥaṣṣanu l-madiine b-sərʕa.*
to fortify oneself - *qawwa ḥaalo.* I have to fortify myself first. *ʔawwal šii laazem qawwi ḥaali.*
fortnight - *žəmᵊʕteen, ʔəsbuuʕeen.* A fortnight ago I was in Paris. *mən žəmᵊʕteen kənt ᵊb-baariiz.*
fortress - *qalʕa* pl. *qlaaʕ.*
fortunate - **1.** *saʕiid.* That was a fortunate coincidence. *hayy kaanet ṣədfe saʕiide.* **2.** *maḥẓuuẓ.* He was fortunate. *kaan maḥẓuuẓ.*
fortunately - *mən ḥəsn˜ ᵊl-ḥaẓẓ.* Fortunately I met someone who spoke English. *mən ḥəsn ᵊl-ḥaẓẓ* (or *mən ḥəsᵊn ḥaẓẓi*) *tʕarrafᵊt ʕala waaḥed kaan yəḥki ʔəngliizi.*
fortune - *sarwe* pl. *-aat.* She inherited a large fortune. *wərtet sarwe ḍaxme.*
to tell someone's fortune - *naǧǧam la-ḥada.* I had my fortune told by an old gypsy woman. *fii waaḥde nawariyye ʔəxtyaara naǧǧamə́t-li.*
fortuneteller - *mnaǧǧem* pl. *-iin.*
fortunetelling - *tanǧiim.*
forty - *ʔarᵊbʕiin.* Can you lend me 40 pounds? *fiik ᵊddayyənni ʔarᵊbʕiin leera?*
forties - **1.** *l-ʔarᵊbʕiin.* She's in her forties. *hiyye bᵊl-ʔarᵊbʕiin.* **2.** *l-ʕaqd ᵊl-ʔarᵊbʕiin.* The family moved here during the forties. *l-ʕeele ntaqlet la-hoon bᵊl-ʕaqd ᵊl-ʔarᵊbʕiin.*
**He's in his late forties. *huwwe b-ḥiiṭaan l-xamsiin.*
forward - *la-qəddaam.* A pawn moves only forward or sideways, never backward. *l-beedaq byəmši bass la-qəddaam w-la-žanab, muu la-wara ʔabadan.*
to come or **step forward** - *tqaddam.* When volunteers were called for, six men came forward. *waqt ṭalabu məṭṭawwʕiin sətt ᵊržaal ᵊtqaddamu.*
to look forward to - *tšawwaq la-.* I'm looking forward to your visit. *ʔana mətšawweq la-zyaartak.* — We're all looking forward to seeing him again. *kəllna mətšawwqiin la-šoofto taani marra.*
to forward - *baʕat (a baʕᵊt, bəʕtaan//nbaʕat).* Shall I forward your mail to your new address? *ʔəbʕə́t-lak bariidak la-ʕənwaanak ᵊž-ždiid?*
foul - **1.** *fuul.* It was a foul! *kaanet fuul haḍ-ḍarbe!* **2.** *laʔiim, waaṭi.* That was a foul blow. *kaanet ḍarbe laʔiime hayy.* **3.** *kariih.* Where does that foul smell come from? *mneen žaaye har-riiḥa l-kariiha?*

to **found** - *ʔassas//tʔassas*. When was the club founded? *ʔeemta tʔassas ᵊn-naadi?*

foundation - **1.** *ʔasaas* pl. *-aat*. The storm shook the foundations of the building. *l-εaaṣfe hazzet ʔasaasaat ᵊl-binaaye*. — Your remarks are completely without foundation. *mlaaḥaẓaatak kəlla maa-la ʔasaas*. **2.** *mʔassase* pl. *-aat*. He works for the Ford Foundation. *byəštǵel b-ᵊmʔassaset foord*.

founder - *mʔasses* pl. *-iin*. He's one of the original founders. *huwwe waaḥed mən l-ᵊmʔassᵊsiin ᵊl-ʔaṣliyyiin*.

founder's shares - *ʔashom˜ taʔsiis*.

foundry - *masbak* pl. *masaabek*.

fountain - *baḥra* pl. *-aat*, (spouting) *fawwaaret˜* (pl. *-aat˜*) *ṃayy*, (drinking) *sabiil˜* (pl. *səbol˜*) *ṃayy*.

fountain pen - *stiilo* pl. *stiiloyaat*, *qalam˜* (pl. *qlaam˜*) *ḥəbᵊr*. I'll have to fill my fountain pen. *laazem εabbi s-stiilo tabaεi*.

four - **1.** *ʔarbaε(t)*. We stayed almost four months. *bqiina taqriiban ʔarbaεt əšhor*. — They have four children. *εandon ʔarbaε ᵊwlaad*. **2.** *ʔarᵊbεa*. There were only four of us at the party. *kənna bass ʔarᵊbεa bᵊl-εaziime*. — Waiter, bring us four teas. *garsoon, mən faḍlak ʔarᵊbεa šaay*. — The boy is four. *ṣ-ṣabi εəmro ʔarᵊbεa*. **3.** *s-saaεa ʔarᵊbεa*. It's already four. *ṣaaret ᵊs-saaεa ʔarᵊbεa*. — The train arrives at four. *t-treen byəṣal ᵊs-saaεa ʔarᵊbεa*.

to crawl on all fours - *zaḥaf (a zaḥᵊf) εal-ʔarᵊbεa*. We had to crawl on all fours through the tunnel. *nžabarna nəzḥaf εal-ʔarᵊbεa bᵊn-nafaq̈*.

fourteen - **1.** *ʔarbaṭaεšar*. I owe you fourteen pounds. *ʔəlak maεi ʔarbaṭaεšar leera*. **2.** *ʔarbaṭaεš*. There're fourteen of us in class. *nəḥna ʔarbaṭaεš bᵊṣ-ṣaff*.

fourteenth - **1.** *r-raabeε εašar*. The town is first mentioned in the Fourteenth Century. *l-balad ʔəža ʔəsma ʔawwal marra bᵊl-q̈arn ᵊr-raabeε εašar*. **2.** *l-ʔarbaṭaεš*, *r-raabeε εašar*. That was my fourteenth visit to Syria. *hayy kaanet safᵊrti l-ʔarbaṭaεš* (or *r-raabεa εašar*) *la-suuriyya*. **3.** *ʔarbaṭaεš*. He's expected on June fourteenth. *məntaẓar yəži b-ʔarbaṭaεš ᵊḥzeeraan*.

one fourteenth - *waaḥed mən ʔarbaṭaεš*. We've only raised one fourteenth of the money we need. *lammeena bass waaḥed mən ʔarbaṭaεš mn ᵊl-maṣaari halli məḥtaažiina*. — Two fourteenths equal one seventh. *tneen mən ʔarbaṭaεš bisaawu səbᵊε*.

fourth - **1.** *raabeε*. This is his fourth job in two years. *hayy waẓiifto r-raabεa* (or *raabeε waẓiife byəšǵəla*) *b-has-sənteen*. **2.** *ʔarᵊbεa*. He died on May fourth. *maat ᵊb-ʔarᵊbεa ʔayyaar*. — I'll be there on the fourth of the month. *bkuun ᵊhniik ᵊb-ʔarᵊbεa š-šahᵊr*. — The fourth comes on a Saturday. *(yoom) ᵊl-ʔarᵊbεa byəḥkom yoom sabᵊt*.

one fourth - *rəbᵊε* pl. *ʔarbaaε*. Only one fourth of the students were listening. *bass rəbε ᵊt-talamiiz kaanu εam yəstəmεu*.

fox - *taεlab* pl. *taεaaleb*.

fraction - **1.** *kasᵊr* pl. *ksuur*. Leave out the fractions and just give me the round numbers. *qiim l-ᵊksuur w-εaṭiini l-ʔaεdaad ᵊṣ-ṣaḥiiḥa*. **2.** *žəzᵊʔ* pl. *ʔažzaaʔ*, *q̈əsᵊm* pl. *ʔaq̈saam*. He got only a fraction of his father's fortune. *təlǝε-lo bass žəzᵊʔ mən sarwet ʔabúu*.

**He had to make the decision in a fraction of a second. *nžabar yaεmel ᵊl-q̈araar b-ʔaqall mən saanye*.

fracture - *kasᵊr* pl. *ksuura*. The fracture is healing slowly. *l-kasᵊr εam yṭiib εala mahlo*.

to fracture - *kasar (e/o kasᵊr//nkasar)*. He fell off the bicycle and fractured his arm. *wəqeε mən εal-bəsᵊkleet w-kasar ʔiido* (or ***nkasret ʔiido*).

fragile - *sariiε˜ ᵊl-εaṭab*.

fragrant - *məεṭer*, *εaaṭer*.

frame - **1.** *bərwaaẓ* pl. *barawiiẓ*. I'd like to have a frame for this picture. *laazəmni bərwaaẓ la-haṣ-ṣuura*. — I've broken the frame of my glasses. *kasart bərwaaẓ kəzᵊlki*. **2.** *heekal* pl. *hayaakel*. The frame of the house was finished in two days. *heekal ᵊl-beet xalaṣ b-yoomeen*. **3.** *bənye*. He has a heavy frame. *bə́nito qawiyye*.

frame of mind - *ḥaale nafsiyye*. In her present frame of mind she shouldn't be left alone. *b-ḥaalə́ta n-nafsiyye l-ḥaaḍra bikuun ʔaḥsan maa təntə́rek la-ḥaala*.

to frame - *barwaẓ*. I'd like to have this picture framed. *bəddi barweẓ haṣ-ṣuura*.

framework - *niṭaaq̈*. Within the framework of this program. *ḍəmᵊn niṭaaq̈ hal-barnaamež*.

franc - *frank* and *frang* pl. *-aat*.

France - *fraansa*.

Franciscan - *fransəskaani** pl. *fransəskaan*.

frank - *ṣariiḥ*. Is that your frank opinion? *haada raʔyak ᵊṣ-ṣariiḥ?* — Be frank with me! *xalliik ṣariiḥ maεi!*

to be frank - *b-kəll ṣaraaḥa, bəddak ᵊṣ-ṣaraaḥa?* To be frank, I don't know. *b-kəll ṣaraaḥa, ʔana maa baεref*.

frankly - **1.** *b-kəll ṣaraaḥa*. Why don't you tell me frankly what really happened? *leeš maa bətqə́l-li b-kəll ṣaraaḥa šuu ṣaar εan ṣaḥiiḥ?* **2.** *b-kəll ṣaraaḥa, bəddak ᵊṣ-ṣaraaḥa?* Frankly, I don't know. *b-kəll ṣaraaḥa, ʔana maa baεref*.

frantic - *yaaʔes*. He made frantic efforts to free himself. *εəmel mažhuudaat yaaʔse la-yxalleṣ ḥaalo*.

fraternal - *ʔaxawi**.

fraud - *ʔəḥtiyaal*.

fraudulent - *ʔəḥtiyaali**.

freckles - *namaš* (coll.).

free - **1.** *ḥərr* pl. *-iin* and *ʔaḥraar*. You're living in a free country. *ʔənte εaayeš bᵊ-blaad ḥərra*. — You're free to go at any time. *ʔənte ḥərr ᵊtruuḥ ʔeemta-ma bəddak*. — He's free with his money. *huwwe ḥərr ᵊb-maṣaarii*. **2.** *faaḍi*. Will you be free tomorrow? *ʔənte faaḍi bəkra?* **3.** *xaali*, *xaaleṣ*. Show me the man who's free from faults. *waržiini r-rəžžaal yalli xaali mn ᵊn-nawaaqeṣ*. **4.** *məεfa*. Charitable contributions are tax free. *t-tabarruεaat ᵊl-xeeriyye məεfaaye mn ᵊḍ-ḍaraayeb*. **5.** *b-balaaš*, *mažaanan*. Admission is free. *d-dxuuliyye b-balaaš*. — I got it free. *ʔaxadta b-balaaš*.

**Could you give me a free translation of the sentence? *fiik ᵊttaržə́m-li haž-žəmle taržame b-taṣarrof?*

**Will you give me a free hand in this matter? *btəṭleq̈ ʔiidi b-haš-šaǵle?*

**Did you do it of your own free will? *εməlta b-məṭlaq̈ ʔiraadtak?*

**The animals are grazing free all summer. *l-ḥaywaanaat εam tərεa ṭuul ᵊṣ-ṣeef bala ḥaažez w-laa bawwaab*.

free and easy - *biduun takliif*. He has a free and easy way about him. *ʔaṭbaaεo kəlla biduun takliif*.

free speech - *ḥərriyyet˜ ᵊl-kalaam*. Without free speech there is no real democracy. *biduun ḥərriyyet ᵊl-kalaam maa fii diimuqraaṭiyye ṣaḥiiḥa*.

to set free - *ʔaṭlaq̈ saraaḥ˜* ... Two hours later, they set the prisoners free. *baεᵊd saaεteen ʔaṭlaq̈u saraaḥ ᵊl-ʔasara*.

to free - *ḥarrar*. The First Army freed the town. *ž-žeeš ᵊl-ʔawwal ḥarrar ᵊl-balad*.

freedom - *ḥərriyye* pl. *-aat*.

free-for-all - *mlaaṭaše been ᵊl-kəll*. The game ended in a free-for-all. *l-ᵊmbaaráa xalṣet b-ᵊmlaaṭaše been ᵊl-kəll*.

freely - **1.** *b-(kəll) ṣaraaḥa*. He admitted freely that he took the money. *εtaraf ᵊb-kəll ṣaraaḥa ʔənno ʔaxad ᵊl-maṣaari*. — You can speak freely. *fiik təḥki b-ṣaraaḥa*. **2.** *b-saxaawe*. He spends his money freely. *byəṣref maṣaarii b-saxaawe*.

freemason - *maasooni* pl. *-iyye*.

freemasonry - *l-maasooniyye*.

to **freeze** - **1.** *səqeε (a sqiiε)*. We froze all winter long. *sqəεna ṭuul ᵊš-šəte*. — I'm freezing. *ʔana saqεaan*. — My feet are freezing. *rəžlayyi saqεaane*. **2.** *džammad*, *džallad*. The water in the pitcher froze during the night. *l-ṃayy bᵊl-ᵊbriiq džammadet bᵊl-leel*. — The (water) pipes are frozen. *ʔanabiib ᵊl-ṃayy džammad*. **3.** *žammad*. The government has frozen all foreign accounts. *l-ᵊḥkuume žammadet kəll l-ᵊḥsaabaat ᵊl-ʔažnabiyye*.

frozen - *mžammad*, *mədžammed*. They don't have frozen food in that store. *maa fii εandon ʔaǵziye mžammade b-hal-maḥall*.

to freeze off - *səqeε (a sqiiε)*. My ears nearly froze off in the icy wind. *ʔadanayyi kaanu laḥa yəsqaεu mn ᵊz-zamhariir*.

to freeze over - *džallad*. The pond is frozen over. *l-baḥra džalladet*.

to freeze to death - *maat (u moot) mn ᵊl-bard*. They froze to death. *maatu mn ᵊl-bard*.

freezing point - *daražet˜ ᵊt-tažammod*.

freight - *šaḥᵊn*. Including freight and insurance the car will cost ten thousand Syrian pounds. *bi-ma fii š-šaḥᵊn wᵊt-taʔmiin ᵊs-sayyaara bətkallef εašᵊrt aalaaf leera suuriyye*. — How much is the freight on this trunk? *qaddeeš šaḥᵊn has-sanduuq?* — I'll send the box by freight. *bəbεat has-sanduuq bᵊš-šaḥᵊn*.

freight car - *fargoon˜* (pl. *faragiin˜*) *šaḥᵊn*.

freight elevator - *ʔaṣanṣoor˜* (pl. *-aat˜*) *ᵊbḍaaƐa.*
freight train - *treen˜* (pl. *-aat˜*) *šaḥᵊn.*
freighter - *baaxərt˜* (pl. *bawaaxer˜*) *šaḥᵊn.*
French - **1.** *frənsaawi.* He speaks a very good French. *byəḥki frənsaawi mniiḥ.* **2.** *frənsaawi**. Do you like French wine? *bətḥəbb ᵊn-nbiit ᵊl-frənsaawi?*
Frenchman - *frənsaawi* pl. *-iyye* and *-iyyiin.*
Frenchwoman - *frənsaawiyye* pl. *-aat.*
frequent - *mətkarrer.* It's a frequent mistake that non-Arabs make. *hayy ġalṭa mətkarrᵊra bisaawuuha ġeer ᵊl-Ɛarab.*
**He's a frequent guest at our house. *huwwe ḍeef byətraddad ᵊktiir Ɛala beetna.*
frequently - *marraat ᵊktiire, miraaran w-təkraaran.* I see him frequently. *bšuufo marraat ᵊktiire.*
fresh - **1.** *taaza* (invar.). Are these eggs fresh? *hal-beeḍ taaza?* -- Eat a lot of fresh fruit. *kool fawaaki taaza ktiir.* **2.** *ṭaleq̈.* Let's go out for some fresh air. *xalliina nəṭlaƐ Ɛal-hawa ṭ-ṭaleq̈.* **3.** *baared.* A fresh wind was blowing. *kaan fii hawa baared Ɛam yənsof.* **4.** *ḥəlu.* After six days, they ran out of fresh water. *baƐᵊd sətt iyyaam xalṣet mən Ɛandon ᵊl-ṃayy ᵊl-ḥəlwe.* **5.** *ʔabu l-lsaan ᵊṭ-ṭawiil.* I can't stand that fresh kid. *maa-li Ɛam ʔəṭḥammal hal-walad ʔabu l-lsaan ᵊṭ-ṭawiil.*
friction - *ʔəḥtikaak.* They're testing a new method to reduce friction heat. *Ɛam yžarrbu ṭariiqa ždiide la-taxfiif ḥaraaret ᵊl-ʔəḥtikaak.*
**There's friction between the two. *daayman byətnaaqaru maƐ baƐḍon.*
friction tape - *twaal.*
Friday - *(yoom˜) ᵊž-žəmƐa.*
Good Friday - *ž-žəmƐa l-ḥaziine, žəmƐet˜ ᵊl-ʔaalaam.*
friend - **1.** *ṣaaḥeb* pl. *ṣḥaab, rfiiq* pl. *rəfaqa, sadiiq* pl. *sədaqa* and *ʔasdiq̈a.* He's a good friend of mine. *huwwe ṣaaḥeb Ɛaziiz Ɛaliyyi.* -- My son went hiking with his friends. *ʔəbni raaḥ maƐ rəfaqaato Ɛas-seeraan.* -- The two are close friends. *t-tneen ᵊṣḥaab ᵊktiir.* -- He makes friends easily. *byaƐmel ᵊṣḥaab la-ḥaalo b-ᵊshuule.* **2.** *ṣaaḥeb* pl. *ṣḥaab.* Are we friends again? *ržəƐna ṣḥaab?* **3.** *ṣadiiq̈a* pl. *-aat, rfiiqa* pl. *-aat.* She's an old friend of ours. *hiyye ṣadiiq̈a qadiime ʔəlna.*
friendly - **1.** *laṭiif.* She has a friendly smile for everybody. *Ɛala təmma ʔəbtisaame laṭiife la-kəll waaḥed.* **2.** *wəddi**. We came to a friendly agreement. *twaṣṣalna la-ʔəttifaaq wəddi.* -- The argument was settled in a friendly way. *n-nizaaƐ tsawwa b-ṣuura wəddiyye.*
friendship - *sadaaqa, ṣəḥbe.*
fright - *xoof.* I almost died with fright. *kənt laḥa muut mn ᵊl-xoof.*
**She looks a fright in the morning. *heeʔə́ta bətxawwef Ɛala bəkra.*
to **frighten** - **1.** *raƐab (e rəƐᵊb//rtaƐab), raƐƐab.* For a moment, you frightened me. *raƐabᵊtni mədde.* **2.** *xawwaf.* Don't let that frighten you. *laa txalli haš-šii yxawwfak.* -- You can't frighten me! *maa btəḥsen ᵊtxawwəfni.*
to be (or **get**) **frightened** - *rtaƐab.* Don't be frightened! *laa tərtə́Ɛeb!* -- I got terribly frightened. *rtaƐabᵊt tamaam.*
frightful - *mərƐeb.*
frog - *ḍəfḍaƐa* pl. *ḍafaadeƐ.*
from - **1.** *mən.* He just received a check from his father. *hallaq wəṣlo šakk mən ʔabúu.* -- I've just come from the rehearsal. *hallaq ᵊržəƐᵊt mn ᵊl-broova.* -- I saw it from the window. *šəfta mn ᵊš-šəbbaak.* -- He's from Aleppo. *huwwe mən ḥalab.* -- That's a quotation from Mutanabbi. *haada ʔəstəšhaad mn ᵊl-mətanabbi.* -- The chair slipped out from under him. *zaḥal ᵊl-kərsi mən taḥto.* -- From where I stand I can't see a thing. *mən maḥall-maa-li waaqef maa-li šaayef šii.* -- From now on I'll be on time. *mən hallaq w-raayeḥ bəži Ɛal-waqᵊt.* -- The situation changes from day to day. *l-waḍᵊƐ Ɛam yətġayyar mən yoom la-yoom* (or ***yoom baƐᵊd yoom).* -- Office hours are from eight to twelve. *saaƐaat ᵊd-dawaam mn ᵊt-tmaane lət-ṭnaƐᵊš.* -- The situation went from bad to worse. *l-waḍᵊƐ məši mən sayyeʔ la-ʔaswaʔ.* -- He kept me from making a big mistake. *xallaṣni mən Ɛamal ġalṭa kbiire.* -- He was tired and nervous from overwork. *kaan taƐbaan w-ᵊmnarvez mən kətr ᵊš-šəġᵊl.* **2.** *mən, Ɛan.* I live ten miles from the city. *ʔana saaken Ɛala bəƐᵊd Ɛašᵊr ʔamyaal mən ᵊl-madiine.* **3.** *Ɛan.* I backed away from the dog. *baƐƐadᵊt Ɛan ᵊl-kalb.* **4.** *mən Ɛand.* She was coming from the dentist's. *kaanet žaaye mən Ɛand ṭabiib ᵊs-snaan.* -- Would you fetch those things from the butcher's for me? *bədžə́b-li hal-ᵊġraaḍ mən Ɛand ᵊl-laḥḥaam?*
**From what he says she must be a very bright girl. *ḥasab qoolo laazem ᵊtkuun zakiyye ktiir.*
where ... from - *mneen.* Where are you from? *mneen ʔənte?* -- Where did you get this book from? *mneen žəbt hal-ᵊktaab?*
**Where I come from it often rains for weeks. *b-ᵊblaadna ʔaḥyaanan btənzel ᵊl-ṃaṭaṛ la-məddet ʔasabiiƐ.*
front - **1.** *waažha* pl. *-aat.* The front of the house is painted white. *waažəht ᵊl-binaaye madhuune b-ʔabyaḍ.* **2.** *žabha* pl. *-aat.* Were you at the Tunisian front? *ḥaarabᵊt bᵊž-žabha t-tuunsiyye?* **3.** *ʔawwal˜ ...* We had seats in the front row. *maḥallaatna kaanet ᵊb-ʔawwal ṣaff.* -- The table of contents is in the front (of the book). *l-fahras ᵊb-ʔawwal l-ᵊktaab.* **4.** *qəddaamaani**. In winter we shut off the front rooms. *bᵊš-šəte mənsakker ᵊl-ʔuwaḍ ᵊl-qəddaamaaniyye.*
front door - *baab˜ ᵊṣqaaq.* Someone left the front door open. *fii ḥada xalla baab ᵊṣ-ṣqaaq maftuuḥ.*
in front - *qəddaam.* He was marching in front. *kaan maaši qəddaam.*
in front of - *qəddaam˜ ...* Let's meet in front of the post office. *xalliina nəžtə́meƐ qəddaam ᵊl-booṣṭa.*
frost - **1.** *saqƐa, zmeeta.* We'll have (a) frost tomorrow. *bəkra bəddo yṣiir saqƐa.* **2.** *saqƐa.* There's frost on the trees. *fii saqƐa Ɛaš-šažar.*
frostbitten - *saqƐaan.* His ears were frostbitten. *ʔadaano kaanet saqƐaane.*
frown - *Ɛabse* pl. *-aat.* I don't like the frown on his face. *maa bḥəbb hal-Ɛabse Ɛala wəššo.*
to **frown** - *Ɛabas (o/e Ɛabᵊs).* Why is he frowning? *leeš Ɛaabes huwwe?* -- Why are you frowning at me like that? *leeš Ɛam təƐbes fiyyi heek?*
to frown on - *stahžan.* Her whole family frowned on the match. *kəll Ɛeelə́ta stahžanet ᵊž-žwaaze.*
fruit - **1.** *faakye, fawaaki* (pl.). Do you have any fresh fruit? *fii Ɛandkon faakye taaza?* -- This tree bears no fruit. *haš-šažara maa btəḥmel fawaaki.* -- We have a few fruit trees in our garden. *fii Ɛanna kam šažret fawaaki b-žneenətna.* **2.** *samara.* And what was the fruit of your long discussion? *w-šuu kaan samret ᵊmnaaqašətkon ᵊṭ-ṭawiile?*
to **fry** - *qala (i qali//nqala).* Shall I fry the fish? *ʔəqli ᵊs-samake?*
fried - *məqli**. We had fried chicken for dinner. *kaan Ɛanna žaaž məqli Ɛal-Ɛaša.* -- I'd like two fried eggs. *bəddi beeḍteen məqliyye.*
frying pan - *məqlaaye* pl. *-aat* and *maqaali.*
**He jumped - as you would say - out of the frying pan into the fire. *qaam - mətᵊl-ma bətquul - mən taḥt ᵊd-dalf la-taḥt ᵊl-məzraab.*
fuel - *maḥruuqaat* (pl.). Coal, wood, and oil are used here as fuels. *l-faḥᵊm wᵊl-ḥaṭab wᵊz-zeet məstaƐ-maliin hoon maḥruuqaat.*
**You're just adding fuel to the fire! *ʔənte bass Ɛam ᵊdziid ᵊṭ-ṭiin balle.*
to **fulfill** - *qaam (u qyaam) b-.* They try to fulfill every wish of the child. *biḥaawlu yquumu b-kəll rəġbe l-walad bəddo-yáaha.*
full - **1.** *malaan, malyaan.* Is the kettle full? *l-ʔəbriiq malaan?* -- The book is full of mistakes. *l-ᵊktaab malaan ġaḷaṭ.* **2.** *kaamel, taamm.* The papers carried a full account of the incident. *ž-žaraayed ʔəža fiiha sarᵊd kaamel ləl-ḥaades.* **3.** *kaamel˜ ..., b-kaamel-* + pron. suff. I paid the full amount. *dafaƐᵊt kaamel ᵊl-mablaġ* (or *ᵊl-mablaġ ᵊb-kaamlo).* **4.** *waaseƐ.* The dress has a very full skirt. *l-fəsṭaan ʔəlo tannuura waasƐa ktiir.* **5.** *šabƐaan.* I'm full. *ʔana šabƐaan.*
**He's always full of funny stories. *daayman taḥt ᵊlsaano fii nəkte.*
**Are you working full time now? *Ɛam təštə́ġel ṭuul ᵊl-waqᵊt hallaq?*
in full - *b-kaamel-* + pron. suff. I paid the bill in full. *dafaƐt ᵊl-faatuura b-kaamə́la.*
fully - **1.** *tamaam, bᵊt-tamaam, Ɛat-tamaam.* Are you fully aware of what is going on? *ʔənte Ɛarfaan tamaam šuu ṣaayer?* -- He described it fully. *waṣáfa bᵊt-tamaam.* -- I'm fully resolved to do it. *ʔana məƐtə́med Ɛat-tamaam saawiiha.* **2.** *Ɛal-qaliili.* There were fully two hundred people at the reception. *kaan fii Ɛal-qaliili miiteen zalame b-ḥaflet ᵊl-ʔəstəqbaal.*
fume - *ġaaz* pl. *-aat.* The escaping fumes were

poisonous. *l-ġaazaat ᵊṭ-ṭaalƐa kaanet ᵊmsamme.*
fun - 1. *təslaaye, tasliye.* Fishing is a lot of fun. *ṣeed ᵊs-samak təslaaye ktiir ḥəlwe.* — I just did it for fun. *Ɛməlta lət-təslaaye bass.* -- Let's try just for the fun of it. *xalliina nžarrəba la-mžarrad ᵊt-təslaaye* or ***xalliina nžarrəba w-nədrob ᵊṭ-ṭiine bᵊl-ḥeeṭ.* 2. *mazᵊḥ.* I only said it in fun. *qəlta Ɛala sabiil ᵊl-mazᵊḥ bass.* 3. *Ɛakra.* Now the fun begins! *hallaq ᵊl-Ɛakra btəbda!*
to have fun - *nbaṣaṭ, tsalla.* We had a lot of fun last night. *nbaṣaṭna šii ktiir leelt ᵊmbaareḥ.*
to make fun - *mazaḥ (a mazᵊḥ).* I was only making fun. *ʔana bass kənt Ɛam ʔəmzaḥ.*
to make fun of - 1. *qarraq Ɛala.* Are you making fun of me? *Ɛam ᵊtqarreq Ɛaliyyi?* 2. *stahza b-, tmaṣxar Ɛala.* You didn't have to make fun of him in front of all those people. *maa kaan laazem təstahzi fii qəddaam kəll han-naas.*
function - *waẓiife* pl. *waẓaayef.* What is his function in the office? *šuu waẓiifto bᵊl-maktab?*
in an official function - *b-ṣifa rasmiyye.* He attended the party in an official function. *ḥəḍer ᵊl-ḥafle b-ṣifa rasmiyye.*
to function - *štaġal (šəġᵊl), məši (i maši).* The radio doesn't function properly. *r-raadyo maa-lo Ɛam yəštəġel ᵊmniiḥ.*
fund - 1. *sanduuq* pl. *sanadiiq.* How much do you have in the fund now? *qaddeeš fii Ɛandak hallaq bᵊs-sanduuq?* 2. *zaxiire.* He has an inexhaustible fund of jokes. *fii Ɛando zaxiire maa btənfod mn ᵊn-nəkat.*
funds - *ʔamwaal* (pl.). Our funds are running low. *ʔamwaalna Ɛam ᵊtxəff.* -- He has misappropriated public funds. *xtalas ᵊl-ʔamwaal ᵊl-Ɛaamme.*
fundamental - *ʔasaasi**. That's a fundamental difference. *haada farᵊq ʔasaasi.*
fundamentals - *ʔasaasiyyaat* (pl.). They haven't learned the fundamentals of logic yet. *ləssa maa tƐallamu ʔasaasiyyaat ᵊl-manṭeq.*
funeral - (Muslim) *žnaaze* pl. *žanaayez,* (Christian) *žənnaaz* pl. *-aat* and *žananiiz.* I have to go to a funeral. *laazem ʔəṭlaƐ b-ᵊžnaaze.*
funnel - 1. *daaxuune* pl. *dawaxiin, madxane* pl. *madaaxen.* The steamer has three funnels. *l-baaxra ʔəla tlətt dawaxiin.* 2. *qəmᵊƐ* pl. *qmuuƐa,* also *qmaaƐ.* The funnel is too big for the bottle. *l-qəmƐ ᵊkbiir Ɛal-qanniine.*
funny - 1. *mədḥek.* That's a very funny story. *hayy qəṣṣa mədᵊḥke ktiir.* 2. *Ɛažiibe* (invar.), *ġariibe* (invar.). (That's) funny! Yesterday you said the exact opposite. *Ɛažiibe! mbaareḥ qəlt ᵊl-Ɛaks bᵊt-tamaam.* — Funny, I can't find my pen. *ġariibe, maa-li Ɛam laaqi qalami.* 3. *ġariib, Ɛažiib.* Funny things are going on around here. *fii masaayel ġariibe Ɛam ᵊtṣiir ᵊb-han-nawaaḥi.* -- That's a funny way of looking at the problem. *hayy ṭariiqa ġariibe bətƐaalež fiiha l-masʔale.*
fur - 1. *farwe* coll. *faru* pl. *-aat.* Most furs come from Canada and Russia. *ʔaktar ᵊl-faru byəži mən kanada w-ruusya.* 2. *šaƐᵊr.* Our cat has beautiful fur. *qaṭṭətna šaƐra ḥəlu.*
furious - *ġaḍbaan ᵊktiir.* My boss will be furious if I don't come. *raʔiisi bəddo ykuun ġaḍbaan ᵊktiir ʔiza maa ʔžiit.*
furnace - *mawqade* pl. *mawaaqed.* Who takes care of the furnace? *miin bidiir baalo Ɛal-mawqade?*
blast furnace - *fərᵊn Ɛaali* pl. *fraan Ɛaalye.*
to **furnish** - 1. *faraš (o farᵊš//nfaraš).* I haven't furnished my new apartment yet. *ləssa maa faraš**ᵊ**t šaqqti ž-ždiide.* -- We rented a furnished house. *staʔžarna beet mafruuš.* 2. *žahhaz, zawwad.* The management will furnish you with everything you need. *l-ʔidaara bədžahhzak ᵊb-kəll šii bəddak-yda.* 3. *žaab (i žayabaan).* Can you furnish proof? *fiik ᵊdžiib bərhaan?*
furniture - *mobiilya* pl. *-aat.* We still have to buy some furniture. *ləssa laazem nəštəri šwayyet mobiilya kamaan.*
furrier - *farra* pl. *farraaye* and *farraayiin.*
further - 1. *ʔiḍaafi**. Whom can I ask for further information? *miin bəqder ʔəsʔalo maƐluumaat ʔiḍaafiyye?* 2. *ʔabƐad.* The house is a little further down the street. *l-beet ʔabƐad mən hoon b-ᵊšwayye bᵊš-šaareƐ.* -- You'll have to walk a little further. *laazem təmši ʔabƐad b-ᵊšwayye.*
until further notice - *la-ʔəšƐaar ʔaaxar.* This store will be closed until further notice. *hal-maxzan bitamm msakker la-ʔəšƐaar ʔaaxar.*
furthermore - *bᵊl-ʔiḍaafe Ɛala zaalek, fooq zaalek.* Furthermore, I would like to say ... *bᵊl-ʔiḍaafe Ɛala zaalek bəddi quul ...*
fury - *ġeeẓ, ġaḍab.* She couldn't control her fury. *maa qədret təẓboṭ ġeeẓa.*
fuse - 1. *buušoon* and *baašoon* pl. *-aat.* The fuse blew out. *l-buušoon ᵊḥtaraq.* 2. *ftiile* pl. *fataayel.* He lit the fuse and ran (away) as fast as he could. *šaƐal l-ᵊftiile w-rakad qadd-ma yəqder.*
fuselage - *heekal* pl. *hayaakel.*
fuss - *ṭooše w-looše.* Don't make such a fuss over him! *ḥaažtak baqa ṭooše w-looše mənšaano!*
**Don't make so much fuss! *ḥaaže tkabbəra* or *ḥaaže ṭṭabbel w-ᵊdzammer.*
to fuss around - *faƐa (i faƐi).* She's been fussing around in the kitchen all morning. *ṣar-la Ɛam təfƐi bᵊl-maṭbax mən Ɛala bəkra ləḍ-ḍəhᵊr.*
to fuss with - *ləƐeb (a ləƐᵊb) b-.* He's always fussing with his tie. *Ɛala ṭuul byəlƐab b-ᵊgraafto.*
fussy - 1. *mʔannaf.* He's very fussy about food. *huwwe ktiir ᵊmʔannaf ᵊb-ʔaklo.* 2. *mwaswas.* He's very fussy about his clothes. *huwwe ktiir ᵊmwaswas ᵊb-ləbso.*
futile - *faašel.* He made a futile effort to retrieve his property. *Ɛəmel žahᵊd faašel la-yəstrədd məlko.*
futility - *Ɛadam~ žadwa.* After a while I realized the futility of what I was doing. *baƐd ᵊšwayye Ɛrəfᵊt Ɛadam žadwa ʔaƐmaali.*
future - 1. *məstaqbal.* The job has no future. *š-šaġle maa-la məstaqbal.* — In the future, come on time! *bᵊl-məstaqbal taƐa Ɛal-waqᵊt!* 2. *žaaye, qaadem.* He introduced his future son-in-law to us. *qaddəm-ᵊlna ṣəhro ž-žaaye.*
**Everyone says he'll be our future president. *kəll ᵊn-naas biquulu ʔənno biṣiir raʔiisna bᵊl-məstaqbal.*

G

gabardine - *gabardiin.*
gable - *žabaloone* pl. *-aat.* The house has three gables. *l-beet ʔəlo tlətt žabaloonaat.*
Gabriel - *žəbriil.*
gadfly - *dəbbaanet~* (coll. *dəbbaan~* pl. *-aat~*) *faraṣ.*
gag - 1. *kammaame* pl. *-aat.* Take the gag out of his mouth. *qiim ᵊl-kammaame mən təmmo.* 2. *nahfe* pl. *-aat.* There are a few good gags in the new show. *fii kam nahfe ḥəlwe bᵊl-ʔəstəƐraaḍ ᵊž-ždiid.*
to gag - 1. *kammam.* They tied him up and gagged him. *rabaṭúu w-kammamúu.* 2. *kamm (ə kamm~// nkammet) ʔafwaah~ ...* Time and again, the government's tried to gag the press. *marra baƐᵊd marra, l-ᵊḥkuume ḥaawalet ᵊtkəmm ʔafwaah ᵊṣ-ṣəḥof.* 3. *xtanaq.* I almost gagged on the fishbone. *kənt laḥa ʔəxtə́neq mn ᵊl-ḥasake.* -- The collar is gagging me. *l-qabbe Ɛam təxnəqni.*
to **gain** - 1. *stafaad.* What did you gain by that? *šuu stafədt mən haš-šii?* 2. *kəseb (a kasb), ktasab.* He's gained a lot of experience in that job. *kəseb xəbra ktiir ᵊb-haš-šaġle.* 3. *tƐaafa.* The patient is gaining rapidly. *l-mariiḍ Ɛam yətƐaafa b-sərƐa.*
**He's gained a lot (of weight) recently. *zaad wazno ktiir b-hal-madde l-ʔaaxraaniyye.*
**He has gained my confidence. *ʔaamant-ə́llo.*
**Can't you go faster? The car behind us is gaining on us. *maa fiik ᵊtƐažžel šwayye? s-sayyaara halli b-qafaana laḥa yḥaṣṣəlna.*
to gain a footing - *rakaz (o rakze).* He couldn't gain a footing anywhere. *maa qəder yərkoz w-laa b-maḥall.*
to gain ground - *šaaƐ (i šuyuuƐ), ntašar.* That theory has gained ground in recent years. *han-naẓariyye šaaƐet ᵊktiir b-has-sniin ᵊl-ʔaxiire.*
gait - *mašye, mašwe.*
gale - *zoobaƐa* pl. *zawaabeƐ.* The gale caused great

damage. *z-zoobaεa sabbabet xaṣaayer ᵊktiire.*
gall - *maraara.* He has trouble with his gall. *fii maεo šii b-maraarto.*
gall bladder - *maraara.*
gallery (art gallery) *matḥaf˜* (pl. *mataaḥef˜*) *ᵊl-funuun ᵊž-žamiile.*
galley - *məswadde* pl. *-aat.* The galleys have come back from the printer's. *l-məswaddaat rəžεu mən εand ᵊṭ-ṭabbaaε.*
gallon - *gaaloon* pl. *-aat.* One American gallon is not quite four liters. *l-gaaloon ᵊl-ʔameerki ʔaqall b-ᵊšwayye mən ʔarbaε liitraat.*
gallop - *ṭraad, mṭaarade.* The horse broke into a gallop. *l-ᵊḥṣaan bada yəmši ṭraad.*
to gallop - *ṭaarad.* The horse galloped in the direction of the stables. *l-ᵊḥṣaan ṭaarad naaḥ ᵊl-ʔəṣṭablaat.*
galosh - *ṣabb* pl. *-aat, gaalooš* pl. *gawaliiš.*
gamble - *muq̈aamara.* It was a pure gamble, but we had to risk it. *kaanet muq̈aamara maḥᵊḍ, bass ᵊḍṭarreena nžaazef.*
to gamble - **1.** *qaamar.* They were gambling for high stakes. *kaanu εam yqaamru εala rhuune εaalye.* **2.** *žaazaf, ġaamar, xaaṭar.* He's gambling with his life. *εam yžaazef ᵊb-ḥayaato.*
to gamble away - *xəṣer (a xaṣaara) ... bᵊl-ᵊqmaar.* He gambled his whole salary away. *xəṣer kəll maεaašo bᵊl-ᵊqmaar.*
gambling - *qmaar, mqaamara.* Gambling is forbidden in several countries. *l-ᵊqmaar mamnuuε ᵊb-εəddet ᵊblaad.*
game - **1.** *ləεbe* pl. *ləεab.* I saw through his game. *ktašafᵊt ləεᵊbto.* — They realized that their game was up. *εərfu ʔanno ləεbᵊton ᵊnfaḍḥet.* — Do you sell any games here? *bətbiiεu ləεab hoon?* **2.** *ləεᵊb* pl. *ʔalεaab.* The Olympic games are held every four years. *l-ʔalεaab ᵊl-ʔoolombiyye bətṣiir kəll ʔarbaε ᵊsniin.* **3.** *daqq* pl. *dquuq.* Would you like to play a game of chess? *bətḥəbb təlεab daqq šaṭranž?* **4.** (*ḥaywaanaat˜*) *ṣeeḍ.* There's a lot of game in this region. *fii ḥaywaanaat ṣeeḍ ᵊktiir ᵊb-hal-manṭiqa.* **5.** *ṣeeḍ.* The game laws are very strict. *q̈awaniin ᵊṣ-ṣeeḍ ᵊktiir ṣaarme.* **6.** *məstεədd.* I'm game for anything. *ʔana məstεədd la-kəll šii.*
**He's playing a good game today. *εam yəlεab ᵊmniiḥ ᵊl-yoom.*
**Their team put up a game fight. *fariiqon naaḍal ᵊb-basaale.*
gang - **1.** *εiṣaabe* pl. *-aat.* The head of the gang was a notorious criminal. *raʔiis ᵊl-ʔiṣaabe kaan məžrem maεruuf.* **2.** *ʔərṭa* pl. *-aat, zəmra* pl. *zəmar.* I can't stand the whole gang. *maa bṭiiq kəll hal-ʔərṭa.* **3.** *warše* pl. *-aat.* Who's the foreman of your gang? *miin ᵊmnaaẓer waršətkon?*
gangrene - *ġanġariina, ġarġariina.*
gangster - *šaq̈i* pl. *ʔašq̈iya.*
gap - **1.** *faraaġ* pl. *-aat.* The gap he's left has to be filled. *l-faraaġ yalli tarako laazem yətεabba.* **2.** *fažwe* pl. *-aat, faraaġ* pl. *-aat.* There's a gap in the row of houses. *fii fažwe b-ṣaff hal-ᵊbyuut.* — There's a gap between his front teeth. *fii fažwe b-ᵊsnaano l-qəddaamaaniyye.* **3.** *fažwe* pl. *-aat.* There are large gaps in his education. *fii fažwaat ᵊkbiire b-saq̈aafto.* **4.** *səġra* pl. *-aat* and *səġar.* Our infantry smashed a wide gap in the enemy's lines. *mušaatna fataḥu səġra kbiire b-ᵊxṭuuṭ ᵊl-εaduww.*
garage - *garaaž* and *karaaž* pl. *-aat.*
garbage - *zbaale* pl. *zabaayel.* Garbage is collected daily. *biqiimu z-zbaale kəll yoom.* — They forgot to empty the garbage cans today. *nəsyu yfaḍḍu tan(a)kaat ᵊz-zbaale l-yoom.*
garbage collector, garbage man - *zabbaal* pl. *-e* and *-iin.*
garden - *žneene* pl. *žanaayen, ḥadiiq̈a* pl. *ḥadaayeq̈.* These flowers are from our own garden. *haz-zhuur mn ᵊžneenətna.*
truck garden - *bəstaan* pl. *basatiin.*
gardener - *žneenaati* pl. *-iyye,* (truck gardener) *bəstaani* pl. *basaatne, bəstanži* pl. *-iyye.*
to **gargle** - *tġarġar, traġraġ.* Gargle every three hours. *tġarġar kəll tlətt saaεaat.*
garlic - *tuum.*
clove of garlic - *raas* (pl. *ruus*) *tuum.*
garment - **1.** *toob* pl. *tyaab.* The *εabbaaye* is a garment worn mostly by Bedouins. *l-εabbaaye toob byəlᵊbsúu bᵊl-ġaaleb ᵊl-badu.* **2.** *malbuusaat* (pl.), *ʔalbise.* Both brothers work in the garment industry. *l-ʔaxxeen ᵊt-tneen byəštəġlu b-ṣinaaεet ᵊl-malbuusaat.*
to **garnish** - *zawwaq.* Garnish the fish with parsley and lemon. *zawwqi s-samake b-baqduunes w-leemuun.*
garrison - *ḥaamye* pl. *-aat.* He was transferred to the Aleppo garrison. *naqalúu la-ḥaamiit ḥalab.*
garter - *žartyeer* pl. *-aat.*
gas - **1.** *gaaz, ġaaz.* Turn off the gas. *sakker ᵊl-gaaz.* -- We cook by gas. *mnəṭbox εal-gaaz.* **2.** *ġaaz* pl. *-aat.* Poison gases were used in the First World War. *l-ġaazaat ᵊs-saamme staεmaluuha bᵊl-ḥarb ᵊl-εaalamiyye l-ʔuula.* **3.** *banziin.* We have enough gas for ten miles. *fii εanna banziin ᵊkfaaye la-εašᵊr ʔamyaal.*
**Did the dentist give you gas? *ḥakiim ᵊl-ʔasnaan bannažak* (or *xaddarak*)*?*
gas mask - *kammaamet˜* (pl. *-aat˜*) *ġaaz.*
gas station - *mḥaṭṭet˜* (pl. *-aat˜*) *banziin.*
gaseous - *ġaazi*.*
gasoline - *banziin.*
gasoline station - *mḥaṭṭet˜* (pl. *-aat˜*) *banziin.*
to **gasp for breath** - *šahaq (a šahqa).*
gastric - *məεdi*.* Gastric juice. *εuṣaara məεdiyye.*
gastritis - *ʔəltihaab ᵊl-məεde.*
gate - **1.** *bawwaabe* pl. *-aat.* Drive right through the gate! *suuq w-ᵊmrooq bᵊl-bawwaabe.* -- The gates of the lock swung slowly open. *bawwaabaat ᵊl-hawiis nfatḥet šwayye šwayye.* **2.** *baab* pl. *bwaab.* Don't forget to lock the gate when you leave the garden. *laa tənsa maa təqfel ᵊl-baab waqt-ən btətrek ᵊž-žneene.* — The city gates were closed at sundown. *bwaab ᵊl-balad kaanet tətsakkar maε ᵊġruub ᵊš-šamᵊs.* — Ask the man at the gate when the train leaves. *sʔaal ᵊr-ražžaal yalli εand ᵊl-baab ʔeemta t-treen byəmši.* **3.** *ḥaažez* pl. *ḥawaažez.* The watchman forgot to lower the gates at the railroad crossing. *l-ḥaares nəsi ynazzel ᵊl-ḥažez εand maεbar səkket ᵊl-ḥadiid.*
**Why did you give him the gate? *leeš ṣarraftłi?*
to **gather** - **1.** *žamaε (a žamᵊε//nžamaε), lamm (ə lamm//ltamm), laqaṭ (o laqᵊṭ//ltaqaṭ).* The children gathered wood in the forest. *l-ᵊwlaad žamaεu ḥaṭab mn ᵊl-ḥərš.* **2.** *žamaε, žamaε šaml˜ ...* The shepherd gathered his flock. *r-raaεi žamaε (šaml) ᵊl-qaṭiiε tabaεo.* **3.** *žamaε.* The teacher gathered the students around him. *l-ᵊmεallem žamaε ᵊt-talamiiz ḥawalée.* **4.** *stažmaε.* I had to gather all my strength in order to open the door. *ḍṭarreet ᵊstažmeε kəll quwwti la-ḥatta ʔəftaḥ ᵊl-baab.* **5.** *žtamaε, džammaε, ḥtašad.* A large crowd gathered in front of the City Hall. *žtamaε ḥašd ᵊkbiir qəddaam ᵊl-baladiyye.* **6.** *staxlaṣ, stantaž.* I gather from what you say that you don't like him. *εam ʔəstaxləṣ, mən halli εam ᵊtquulo ʔənnak maa btəḥəbbo.*
gay - **1.** *raayeq.* We had a very gay party at our house last night. *kaan fii εanna sahra ktiir raayqa leelt ᵊmbaareḥ.* **2.** *mlawwan.* The street was decorated with gay flags. *š-šaareε kaan ᵊmzayyan b-bayaareq ᵊmlawwane.* **3.** *ẓariif* pl. *ẓraaf.* We spent the evening in gay company. *maḍḍeena l-maswiyye maε rəfaqa ẓraaf.*
gazelle - *ġazaal* pl. *ġəzlaan.*
gear - **1.** *msannan* pl. *-aat.* I had to put in two new gears. *nžabart ḥəṭṭ ᵊmsannaneen žədad.* **2.** *giir.* The car's in gear. *s-sayyaara bᵊl-giir.* — How do you shift gears on this car? *kiif bətġayyer ᵊl-giir b-has-sayyaara?* **3.** *fiitees* pl. *-aat, sərεa* pl. *-aat.* The car has four gears. *s-sayyaara ʔəlha ʔarbaε fiiteesaat.* **4.** *ġraaḍ* (pl.). Put the camping gear in the car. *ḥəṭṭ ᵊġraaḍ l-ᵊmxayyam bᵊs-sayyaara.* **5.** *žihaaz.* Something is wrong with the steering gear. *fii šii mansuuε ᵊb-žihaaz ᵊl-q̈iyaade.*
first gear - *brəmyeer, briimeer.* Put the car in first gear. *ḥəṭṭ ᵊs-sayyaara εal-brəmyeer.*
second gear - *doozyeem.* Shift into second gear. *ġayyer ləd-doozyeem.*
third gear - *tərwazyeem.* You have to drive in third gear in town. *laazem ᵊtsuuq εat-tərwazyeem bᵊl-balad.*
gearshift lever - *ʔiid˜ ᵊl-fiitees.*
gecko - *ʔabu breeṣ* pl. *ʔabu breeṣaat.*
gelatine - *žeelatiin.*
gem - **1.** *ḥažar kariim* pl. *ʔaḥžaar kariime.* The gems are invaluable. *l-ʔaḥžaar ᵊl-kariime maa btəttamman.* **2.** *žoohara.* Our cook is a gem. *ṭabbaaxna žoohara.*
general - **1.** *ženeraal* pl. *-iyye.* He's a general. *huwwe ženeraal.* **2.** *εaamm.* A general election is held every year. *bişiir ʔəntixaabaat εaamme kəll səne.* — He's a general practitioner. *huwwe ṭabiib εaamm.*
general delivery - *ʔidaart˜ ᵊl-bariid.* Write to me (in care of) general delivery. *ktəb-li b-waasəṭṭ*

ʔidaart ᵊl-bariid.
in general – *ɛal-ᵊɛmuum, b-ṣuura ɛaamme, ʔažmaalan.* In general, things are all right. *ɛal-ᵊɛmuum kəll šii maaši ɛala ma yuraam.*
generalization – *taɛmiim* pl. *-aat.* He likes to make sweeping generalizations. *biḥəbb ysaawi taɛmiimaat šaamle.*
to **generalize** – *ɛammam.* It's unfair to generalize like that. *muu ḥaqq ᵊtɛammem heek.*
generally – *ɛal-ᵊɛmuum, b-ṣuura ɛaamme, ʔažmaalan.* He's generally on time. *ɛal-ᵊɛmuum byəži ɛal-waqᵊt.*
**It's a generally known fact that ... *šii maɛruuf ʔənno ...*
generation – *žiil* pl. *ʔažyaal.* His family has been in America for four generations. *ɛeelto ṣar-la b-ʔameerka mən ʔarbaɛ ʔažyaal.*
generator – *diinamo* pl. *diinamoyaat.*
generosity – **1.** *karam, saxaawe* and *ṣaxaawe, saxaaʔ.* His generosity is almost proverbial among the poor. *karamo taqriiban byəndᵊreb fii l-masal ɛand ᵊl-fəqara.* **2.** *rahaabet˜ ṣadᵊr.* He handled the whole affair with a great deal of generosity. *ɛaalaž ᵊl-məšᵊkle b-kəll rahaabet ṣadᵊr.*
generous – **1.** *saxi** and *ṣaxi** pl. *ʔasxiya (ʔaṣxiya).* He's a very generous donor. *huwwe mətbarreɛ saxi ktiir.* — We couldn't do without her generous contributions. *maa kaan byəmši ḥaalna law-laa tabarruɛaata s-saxiyye.*
**He took a very generous attitude toward the whole thing. *ttaxaz mawqef kəllo rahaabet ṣadᵊr mn ᵊš-šaġle.*
to be generous – *tkaaram, tṣaaxa.* Don't be so generous with other people's money. *laa tətkaaram hal-qadd ᵊb-maṣaari ġeerak.*
Geneva – *žneef, žaneef.*
genial – *ʔaniis* pl. *-iin* and *ʔənasa.* He's a genial fellow. *huwwe zalame ʔaniis.*
genie – *žənni* coll. pl. *žənn.*
genitals – *ʔaɛḍaaʔ tanaasuliyye* (pl.).
genius – *naabġa* pl. *nawaabeġ, ɛabqari** pl. *ɛabaaqra.* Many people consider him a genius. *fii naas ᵊktiir byəɛtəbrúu naabġa.*
gentle – **1.** *ɛaliil.* There was a gentle breeze coming from the sea. *kaan ṭaaleɛ nasiim ɛaliil mn ᵊl-baḥᵊr.* **2.** *waadeɛ, naaɛem.* This horse is very gentle. *hal-ᵊḥṣaan ᵊktiir waadeɛ.* **3.** *wadiiɛ, naaɛem, laṭiif.* She's a gentle old lady. *hiyye sətt ᵊkbiire wadiiɛa.*
gentleman – **1.** *sayyid* pl. *saada* and *siyaad.* Who's the gentleman you were talking to a minute ago? *miin ᵊs-sayyed yalli kənt ɛam təḥki maɛo mən daqiiqa?* **2.** *sayyed* pl. *saada.* Ladies and gentlemen! *sayyidaati saadati!* or *sayyidaati ʔaanisaati saadati!*
**He's a perfect gentleman. *huwwe zalame məḥtdram ᵊb-kəll maɛna l-kəlme.*
gently – **1.** *b-naɛaame, b-laṭaafe.* He knocked gently on the door. *daqq ᵊl-baab b-naɛaame.* **2.** *b-rəqqa, b-laṭaafe.* You'll have to treat him gently. *laazem ᵊtɛaamlo b-rəqqa.* **3.** *b-ṣuura tadriižiyye, tadriižiyyan.* The terrain sweeps gently downward. *l-ʔarḍ ᵊbtənḥəder ᵊb-ṣuura tadriižiyye.*
genuine – *ʔaṣli**. That's genuine leather. *haada žəld ʔaṣli.*
geographer – *žəġraafi* pl. *-iyye* and *-iyyiin.*
geographic – *žəġraafi**.
geography – *žəġraafya.* The geography of the Middle East. *žəġraafiit ᵊš-šarq ᵊl-ʔawsaṭ.*
geological – *žiyolooži**.
geologist – *žiyolooži* pl. *-iyye* and *-iyyiin.*
geology – *žiyoloožya, ɛəlm˜ ṭabaqaat˜ ᵊl-ʔarḍ.*
geometrical – *handasi**.
geometry – *handase.*
geophysical – *žiyofiizyaaʔi**.
geophysics – *žiyofiizya.*
germ – **1.** *makroob* pl. *-aat, žarsuum(e)* pl. *žarasiim.* Don't cough and spread your germs all over the place. *laa tqəḥḥ w-tənšor makroobaatak hoon w-hoon.* **2.** *bəzre* coll. *bəzᵊr* pl. *bzuur.* Wheat germs contain a lot of vitamins. *bəzr ᵊl-qamᵊḥ fii ktiir viitamiinaat.* **3.** *nuwaat, manšaʔ, mambaʔ.* What he said may contain the germ of a new theory. *halli qaalo bižuuz yəḥtəwi ɛala nuwaat naẓariyye ždiide.*
germ cell – *xaliyye* (pl. *xalaaya*) *žərsuumiyye.*
German – **1.** *ʔalmaani* coll. pl. *ʔalmaan.* Are there many Germans here? *fii ʔalmaan ᵊktiir hoon?* **2.** *ʔalmaani**. He's of German stock. *ʔaṣlo ʔalmaani.* **3.** *ʔalmaani* (invar.). He speaks a good German. *byəḥki ʔalmaani mniiḥ.*
Germany – *ʔalmaanya.*
gestation – *ḥamᵊl.* How long is the period of gestation of a dog? *qaddeeš məddet ḥaml ᵊl-kalb?*
gesture – **1.** *ḥarake* pl. *-aat.* His gestures are very expressive. *ḥarakaato ktiir ᵊmɛabbra.* **2.** *mžaamale* pl. *-aat.* Her refusal was merely a polite gesture. *rafḍa maa kaan ʔəlla mžaamale laṭiife.*
to **get** – **1.** *stalam, ʔaxad (-yaaxod ʔaxᵊd//ttaaxad).* When did you get my letter? *ʔeemta stalamt maktuubi?* or **ʔeemta wəṣlak maktuubi? — When will they get the telegram? *ʔeemta bəddon yəstəlmu l-barqiyye?* or **ʔeemta btəṣálon ᵊl-barqiyye? **2.** *ʔaxad.* You can get the answer by Monday. *fiik taaxod ᵊž-žawaab yoom ᵊt-taneen.* — How much change did you get? *qaddeeš ʔaxadt ᵊfraaṭa?* **3.** *ḥəṣel (a ḥṣuul//nḥaṣal) ɛala.* How did you get my address? *kiif ᵊḥṣəlt ɛala ɛənwaani?* — That's hard to get now. *haada ṣaɛᵊb təḥṣal ɛalée hallaq.* — I got myself a radio. *ḥṣəlt-ə́lli ɛala raadyo.* — Where can I get a dictionary like that? *ween fiini ʔəḥṣal ɛala qaamuus mətᵊl haad?* — Where did you get that pretty dress? *mneen ḥṣəlti ɛala har-roob ᵊl-ḥəlu?* — Where else can you get a car that cheap? *mneen təḥṣal ɛala sayyaara b-har-rəxᵊṣ?* **4.** *žaab (i žayabaan//nžaab).* Can you get me another copy? *fiik ᵊdžəb-li nəsxa taanye?* — Get me a towel, quick! *žəb-li manšafe, qawaam!* — I have to get something for dinner. *laazem žiib šii ləl-ɛaša.* — Wait till I get my hat. *stanna la-žiib bərneeṭṭi.* — Can you get Arab stations on your radio? *btəḥsen ᵊdžiib ᵊmḥaṭṭaat ɛarabiyye b-raadyook?* **5.** *waṣṣal.* Can you get this message to him? *fiik ᵊtwaṣṣə́l-lo har-risaale?* — I'm trying to find a way of getting the furniture to Aleppo. *ɛam dawwer ɛala ṭariiqa waṣṣel fiiha l-ɛafᵊš la-ḥalab.* **6.** *waqqaɛ.* That'll get you into trouble sooner or later. *haada biwaqqɛak ᵊb-mašaakel ɛaažilan ʔaw ʔaažilan.* — You got me in a real bad fix. *waqqaɛᵊtni b-warṭa malɛuune.* **7.** *fawwat.* How did you manage to get everything into one room? *kiif dabbart ḥaalak w-fawwatt kəll šii b-ʔuuḍa waaḥde?* — Do you think we can get all the suitcases into the trunk? *btəɛtə́qed fiina nfawwet kəll ᵊš-šanaati bᵊs-sanduuq?* **8.** *kamaš (e kamᵊš//nkamaš), məsek (e ə//nmasak).* I hope the police will get them. *ya-reet ᵊl-booliis yəkᵊmšuuhon.* — They got the wrong man. *ġəlṭu w-kamašu ġeer halli kaanu ɛam ydawwru ɛalée.* **9.** *fəhem (a fahm//nfaham).* Do you get the idea? *fhəmt ᵊl-fəkra?* — You got me wrong. *fhəmtni ġalaṭ.* — I didn't get what he said. *maa fhəmt halli qaalo.* — I get it! *fhəmᵊt!* **10.** *ḥayyar.* That problem gets me. *hal-məšᵊkle ɛam ᵊtḥayyərni.* — Now you've got me! I don't know what to answer. *hallaq ḥayyartni! maa baɛref šuu žaaweb.* **11.** *narfaz.* His snoddy attitude gets me. *šoofet ḥaalo bətnarfəzni.* — So much noise in the office gets us. *kətr ᵊḍ-ḍažže bᵊl-maktab bətnarfəzna.* **12.** *xalla.* Can you get him to go there? *fiik ᵊtxallíi yruuḥ la-hniik?* — I don't think you can get him to pay that way. *maa bəɛtə́qed ʔənnak ᵊtxallíi yədfaɛ b-haṭ-ṭariiqa.* **13.** *wəṣel (-yəṣal* and *-yuuṣal wṣuul).* How can I get there? *kiif bəṣal la-hniik?* — I can get there in an hour. *bəṣal la-hniik ᵊb-saaɛa.* — How did you get here? *kiif ᵊwṣəlt la-hoon?* — Wait till we get to Beirut. *stanna la-nəṣal la-beeruut.* — I can't get at my luggage. *maa fiini ʔəṣal la-ɛafši.* — We'll have to get to the bottom of the matter. *laazem nətɛammaq bᵊl-qaḍiyye la-nəṣal la-žoohára.* **14.** *wəqeɛ (-yəqaɛ wquuɛ).* He got into bad company. *wəqeɛ ᵊb-šəllet baaḅa ḥasan.* — He got into trouble when he was 18 years old. *wəqeɛ ᵊb-mašaakel mən waqᵊt kaan ɛəmru ṭmanṭaɛš.* **15.** *faat (u foote).* How did you get into the house? *kiif fətt ɛal-beet?* — Then he got into the car and drove off. *baɛdeen faat ɛas-sayyaara w-məši.* — I got into the wrong room. *fətt ɛal-ʔuuḍa l-ġalaṭ.* — Did any water get into the cellar? *faatet šii mayy ɛal-qabu?* **16.** (with foll. adjective, look up under the latter:) He never gets tired. *b-ḥayaato maa byətɛab.* — I hope he doesn't get sick. *nšaaḷḷa maa yəmraḍ.* — He's getting old. *ɛam yxatyer.* — All of them got drunk. *kəllon səkru.* — It's getting late. *tʔaxxaret ᵊd-dənye.* — I got awfully hungry. *žəɛt ᵊktiir ᵊktiir.* — Will he get well again? *yaa-tara biṭiib?* — How did you get so dirty? *šloon ᵊtwaṣṣaxᵊt la-had-daraže?* — The soot from the factory gets everything dirty. *š-šaḥḥaar mn ᵊl-fabriika biwaṣṣex kəll šii.* — How long will it take you to get ready? *qaddeeš byaaxdak la-tḥadder ḥaalak?* — I have to get breakfast ready. *laazem ḥadder kasr ᵊṣ-ṣəfra.* — How can I get rid of him? *kiif bəqder ʔətxallaṣ mənno?* — I'll get even

with him some day. *ləssa bəstadd mənno yawman maa.* — I got my feet wet. *mballet rəžlayyi.* **17.** (in passive constructions, see respective verb:) I'll get fired if I'm late. *bənᶜə́zel ʔiza tʔaxxart.* — I got cheated on that car. *ngaššeet ᵊb-has-sayyaara.*

**What have you got in your hand? *šuu fii b-ʔiidak?*

**I've got it! *laqaṭṭa!* or *ʔəžet!*

**Get going! *frəka mən hoon!* or *ḥleeq mən hoon!* or *yaḷḷa ʔəmši!*

**Let's get going! *xalliina nballeš.*

**I can't seem to get going today. *ʔaḷḷa mṭammeṣ ᶜala qalbi l-yoom.*

**He ought to get to work on it right away. *ʔaḥsán-lo yəbda yəštə́ġel fiiha ḥaalan.*

**How did you get by the guard? *kiif nafadᵊt mən ᶜal-ḥaares?*

**He got there ahead of me. *sabaqni la-hniik.*

**You can't get through there. *maa fiik təmroq mən ᵊhniik.*

**That kind of music gets to me. *han-nooᶜ mn ᵊl-muusiiqa biʔasser ᶜaliyyi.*

**I got a haircut. *qaṣṣeet šaᶜri.*

**What does it get me? *šuu byəžiini mənna?*

**I just got a glimpse of him. *bass lamaḥto lamḥa.*

**He's gotten somewhere in life. *twaffaq ᵊb-ḥayaato mniiḥ.*

**He got the worst of it. *nḍarr ʔaktar waaḥed huwwe.*

**I couldn't get you on the phone. *talfant-ə́llak maa laqeetak.*

**I'll get at the real reason yet. *ləssa bəktə́šef ᵊs-sabab ᵊl-ḥaqiiqi.*

**Just let me get at him once! *xalliini ʔəᶜlaq fii šii marra bass!*

**Now don't get on your high horse again! *yaḷḷa baqa ḥaažtak ᶜažrafe!*

**He got five years in prison. *nḥakam xams ᵊsniin ḥabᵊs.*

I've got to, you've got to, etc. - *laazem* or *laa bədd-ma* (with foll. imperf. without *b-*). I've got to go. *laazem ruuḥ.* — You've got to do it for me. *laazem taᶜməl-li-yáaha* or *laa bədd-ma taᶜməl-li-yaaha.*

to get about - *baram (o barᵊm), džawwal.* He gets about a great deal. *byəbrom ᵊktiir.*

to get across - *fahham, waḍḍaḥ.* I wasn't able to get the idea across to him. *maa ḥsənᵊt fahhmo l-fəkra.*

to get along - 1. *məši (i ø), raaḥ (u ø).* I'll have to be getting along now. *laazem ʔəmši hallaq.* **2.** *məši ḥaalo.* How are you getting along in your work? *šloon maaši ḥaalak ᵊb-šəġlak?* **3.** *dabbar raaso, dabbar ḥaalo.* I'll get along somehow. *bdabber raasi kiif-ma kaan.* **4.** *nsažam, tfaaham.* I can't get along with him. *maa bəqder ʔənsə́žem maᶜo.* — We get along well with each other. *mnənsə́žem ᵊktiir maᶜ baᶜᵊdna.*

**He's getting along in years, too. *huwwe r-rəxᵊr ᶜam yxatyer.*

**How are you getting along? *kiif ᵊl-ḥaal?*

to get around - 1. *baram (o barᵊm), džawwal.* We got around a lot. *baramna ktiir.* **2.** *ntašar, nfaša.* The story got around quickly. *l-qəṣṣa ntašret qawaam.* **3.** *džaawaz.* You won't get around him. *maa fiik tədžaawazo.* **4.** *džannab, tḥaaša.* You can't get around taking the responsibility. *maa fiik tədžannab ʔaxd ᵊl-masʔuuliyye.*

**She gets around pretty well for her age. *hiyye ḥarake ktiir bᵊn-nəsbe la-ᶜəmra.*

to get away - 1. *falaṣ (o falṣ).* I'm sorry, but I couldn't get away. *ᶜadam mʔaaxaze, maa ḥsənt ʔəfloṣ.* **2.** *nafad (o nafde), ẓamaṭ (o ẓamṭa).* You won't get away with that. *maa fiik tənfod b-haš-šaġle.* **3.** *raḥal (a rḥiil).* I want to get away from the city. *raayed ʔərḥal mn ᵊl-madiine.* **4.** *xalaṣ (o xalaaṣ* and *xalaṣaan).* If you think you can get away from me, you're mistaken. *ʔiza ẓaanen ʔənnak fiik təxloṣ mənni ʔənte ġalṭaan ᵊktiir.* **5.** *baᶜᶜad.* I couldn't get her away from the window. *maa ḥsənᵊt baᶜᶜə́da mn ᵊš-šəbbaak.*

to get back - 1. *rəžeᶜ (a ržuuᶜ, ražᶜa).* When did you get back? *ʔeemta ržəᶜᵊt?* **2.** *staržaᶜ, st(a)radd.* Did he get his money back? *ᶜaad ᵊstaržaᶜ maṣarii?* — I want to get my money back! *bəddi stradd maṣariyyi.*

**I'll get back at him yet! *ləssa bdabbro!*

to get by - 1. *dabbar ḥaalo, dabbar raaso.* I don't have much money, but I think I'll get by. *maa maᶜi maṣaari ktiir, laaken bẓənn fiini dabber ḥaali.* **2.** *nafad (o nafde), ẓamaṭ (o ẓamṭa).* Do you think you'll get by with that excuse? *btəᶜtə́qed btənfod b-hal-ᶜəzᵊr?*

to get down - 1. *nəzel (e nzuul).* How do we get down again? *kiif fiina nənzel?* — Get down from that bike. *nzeel mən ᶜal(a) hal-bəsᵊkleet.* **2.** *ṣafan (o ṣafᵊn).* When you really get down to it the difference is insignificant. *waqt-ən btəṣfon fiiha ᶜal-maẓbuuṭ ᵊl-farᵊq maa-lo ʔahammiyye.*

to get in - 1. *faat (u foote).* How did he manage to get in? *kiif ġəḍer yfuut?* **2.** *wəṣel (-yəṣal* and *-yuuṣal wṣuul).* What time did the train get in? *ʔeemta wəṣel ᵊt-treen?* **3.** *fawwat, daxxal.* Please get the clothes in before it rains. *baḷḷa fawwə́t-li l-ʔawaaᶜi qabᵊl-ma tənzel ᵊl-maṭar.* — I'll get you in somehow. *bfawwtak ᵊb-šii ṭariiqa.*

**He doesn't let you get a word in edgewise. *maa bixalliik tətnaffas ᵊb-kəlme.*

to get off - 1. *nəzel (e nazle).* You have to get off in ten minutes. *laazem tənzel baᶜᵊd ᶜašᵊr daqaayeq.* **2.** *nafad (o nafde).* He got off with a light sentence. *nafad ᵊb-ḥəkᵊm basiiṭ.* **3.** *falaṣ (o falṣ), nafad.* This time you won't get off so easy. *hal-marra maa btəfloṣ ᵊb-has-shuule.* **4.** *šalaḥ (a šalᵊḥ//nšalaḥ).* I can't get my shoes off. *maa-li ḥasnaan ʔəšlaḥ ṣabbaaṭi.*

to get on - 1. *rəkeb (a rəkbe), ṭəleᶜ (a ṭalᶜa).* We got on in Chtaura. *rkəbna b-ᵊštuura.* **2.** *nsažam, tfaaham.* The three of us get on very well. *tlaatətna mnənsə́žem maᶜ baᶜᵊdna ktiir ᵊmniiḥ.* **3.** *məši (i ø) ḥaalo.* How are you getting on in your work? *kiif maaši ḥaalak ᵊb-šəġlak?*

**He's getting on in years, too. *huwwe r-rəxᵊr ᶜam yxatyer.*

**How are you getting on? *kiif ᵊl-ḥaal?*

to get on with - *kammal.* Now let's get on with the discussion. *hallaq xalliina nkammel ḥadiisna.*

to get out - 1. *ṭaalaᶜ.* I can't get the nail out. *maa ᶜam ʔəḥsen ṭaaleᶜ ᵊl-bəsmaar.* — How much did you get out of this deal? *qaddeeš ṭaalaᶜᵊt mən haṣ-ṣafqa?* — Get the dog out of the house! *ṭaaleᶜ ᵊl-kalb mn ᵊl-beet!* — They're getting out a new book. *ᶜam yṭaalᶜu ktaab ᵊždiid.* **2.** *qaam (i qayamaan//nqaam).* Get that out of your head. *qiim haš-šii mən baalak.* **3.** *staxlaṣ.* You won't get much out of him. *maa fiik təstaxleṣ mənno šii ktiir.* **4.** *šaaᶜ (i šayaᶜaan).* I don't know how the story got out. *maa baᶜref kiif šaaᶜet ᵊl-qəṣṣa.* — We mustn't let this news get out. *laazem maa nxalli hal-xabar yšiiᶜ.* **5.** *nəzel (e nzuul, nazle).* I'll have to get out at the next stop. *laazem ʔənzel bᵊl-ᵊmḥaṭṭa ž-žaaye.* **6.** *ṭəleᶜ (a ṭluuᶜ, ṭalᶜa), xaraž (o xruuž).* How do you get out of that room? *kiif ᵊbtəṭlaᶜ mən hal-ʔuuḍa?* — Get out of that car! *ṭlaaᶜ mən has-sayyaara!* — Get out (of here)! *ṭlaaᶜ (mən hoon)!* **7.** *baᶜᶜad.* Get out of my way! *baᶜᶜed mən ṭariiqi!* **8.** *ẓamaṭ (o ẓamṭa), nafad (o nafde).* How did you ever get out of that mess? *kiif ẓamaṭṭ mən hal-warṭa maa baᶜref!*

**Get out of his way when he's in a bad mood. *tḥaašáa waqt bətkuun ṭalᶜa soodto.*

**I was so frightened, I couldn't get a word out. *kənt xaayef la-daraže maa ṭəleᶜ maᶜi w-laa kəlme.*

to get over something - *səli (a ø) šii.* He certainly got over his wife's death quickly. *waḷḷa səli mootet marto qawaam.*

to get through - 1. *xalaṣ (o xluuṣ), xallaṣ.* What time do you get through at the office? *s-saaᶜa qaddeeš btəxloṣ mn ᵊl-maktab?* **2.** *wəṣel (-yəṣal* and *yuuṣal ø) la-.* I called him twice but I couldn't get through to him. *talfant-ə́llo marrteen bass maa ḥsənt ʔuuṣə́l-lo.*

**I tried hard to make him understand but I'm afraid I never got through to him. *ḥaawalt žahdi fahhmo, laaken šaayə́f-lak maa ḥarrakt fii šii.*

to get together - 1. *žtamaᶜ.* Let's get together tonight at my house. *xalliina nəžtə́meᶜ ᵊl-yoom ᶜašiyye b-beeti.* **2.** *ttafaq.* They never seem to get together on anything. *ᶜala-ma yəẓhar b-ḥayaaton maa byəttəfqu ᶜala šii.*

to get up - 1. *faaq (i feeqa), ṣəḥi (a ṣaḥwe).* I get up at six every morning. *bfiiq ᵊs-saaᶜa sətte kəll yoom ᵊṣ-ṣəbᵊḥ.* **2.** *waqqaf ᶜala ḥeelo, qaam (u ø) ᶜala ḥeelo, fazz (ə ø) ᶜala ḥeelo.* Get up when I talk to you! *waqqef ᶜala ḥeelak waqᵊt bəḥki maᶜak!* **3.** *ṭəleᶜ (a ṭluuᶜ).* I don't know how the cat got up on that shelf. *maa baᶜref kiif ṭəlᶜet ᵊl-qaṭṭa ᶜala har-raff.*

**How did the book get up there? *kiif waṣel l-ᵊktaab la-fooq?*

**It took me some time to get up enough courage to talk to him. *staḥmalᵊt madde ṭawiile la-ḥatta ṣaar Ɛandi žaraaʔa kaafye ʔaḥki maƐo.*

ghost - 1. *rooḥ* (f.) pl. *ʔarwaaḥ, šabᵊḥ* pl. *ʔašbaaḥ.* You can't make me believe in ghosts. *maa fiik ᵊtxalliini ʔaƐtəqed bᵊl-ʔarwaaḥ.* 2. *rooḥ.* On the third day, he gave up his ghost. *bᵊl-yoom ᵊt-taalet ʔaslam ᵊr-rooḥ* (or *ṭəlƐet rooḥo).*

**He hasn't a ghost of a chance of getting the job. *maa fii Ɛando w-laa bṣiiṣ ʔamal ʔənno yəḥṣal Ɛaš-šaġle.*

the Holy Ghost - *r-rooḥ ᵊl-qədᵊs.*

giant - 1. *Ɛəmlaaq* pl. *Ɛamaalqa.* Compared to me, he's a giant. *bᵊn-nəsbe ʔəli huwwe Ɛəmlaaq.* 2. *haaʔel, mahuul.* There was a giant crop of potatoes this year. *kaan fii maḥṣuul haaʔel mn ᵊl-baṭaaṭa has-səne.*

**He's no mental giant. *maa-lo hal-qadd fəteḥ.*

Gibraltar - *žabal˜ ṭaareq.*

gift - 1. *hdiyye* pl. *hadaaya.* Thank you for your beautiful gift. *bəšᵊkrak Ɛala hadiitak ᵊl-laṭiife.* 2. *mawhibe* pl. *mawaaheb.* He has a gift for drawing. *Ɛando mawhibe lər-rasᵊm.*

**Don't look a gift horse in the mouth. *Ɛəmrak laa tfalli hdiyye, xəda Ɛala Ɛəllaata.*

**I wouldn't take that as a gift! *maa baaxə́da w-law kaanet ᵊb-balaaš!*

gifted - *mawhuub.* He's a gifted boy. *huwwe ṣabi mawhuub.*

to **giggle** - *ṣṣahṣal.* The girls kept on giggling. *l-banaat ḍallu yəṣṣahṣalu.*

gill - *xayšuum* pl. *xayašiim.*

gimlet - *madqab* pl. *madaaqeb.*

ginger - *zanᵊzbiil, zanžabiil.*

gin - 1. *maḥlaže* pl. *maḥaalež.* The cotton is loaded on trucks and sent to the gin. *l-qəṭᵊn byəthammal Ɛal-kamyoonaat w-ᵊbyənbə́Ɛet ləl-maḥlaže.* 2. *ḥallaaže* pl. *-aat, maḥlaže* pl. *maḥaalež.* The new cotton gin broke down yesterday. *ḥallaažet ᵊl-qəṭn ᵊž-ždiide nkasret ᵊmbaarḥa.* 3. *žənn.* I don't care for gin very much. *maa bḥəbb ᵊž-žənn ᵊktiir.*

to gin - *ḥalaž* (*o ḥalž//nḥalaž).* The farmers have no facilities to gin their own cotton. *l-ᵊmzaarƐiin maa Ɛandon ʔadawaat la-yəḥᵊlžu qəṭnon la-ḥaalon.*

giraffe - *ziraafe* pl. *-aat.*

girder - *žəsᵊr* (pl. *žsuura*) *ḥadiid.*

girdle - *mšadd* pl. *-aat, korsée* pl. *korseeyaat.* She shouldn't go around without a girdle. *ʔaḥsán-la maa təṭlaƐ bala mšadd.*

girl - 1. *bənᵊt* (f.) pl. *banaat,* (contrasted with 'young man' and implying possession of all desirable qualities of young womanhood) *ṣabiyye* pl. *ṣabaaya.* Isn't she a pretty girl! *bəllaahi Ɛaleek muu bənᵊt ḥəlwe!* 2. *ṣaanƐa* pl. *ṣənnaaƐ, xaadme* pl. *-aat.* We pay our girl fifty pounds a month. *mnədfaƐ la-ṣaanƐətna xamsiin leera bᵊš-šahᵊr.*

gist - *ləbb, xulaaṣa, žoohar, beet˜ ᵊl-q̈aṣiid.* That's the gist of the matter. *haada ləbb ᵊl-qaḍiyye* or *haada beet ᵊl-q̈aṣiid bᵊl-qaḍiyye.*

to **give** - 1. *Ɛaṭa* (*-yaƐṭi Ɛəṭyaan//nƐaṭa*). Please give me the letter. *bətražžaak Ɛaṭiini l-maktuub.* — I'll give you five pounds for it. *baƐṭiik xamᵊs leeraat fii.* — What did he give you for your birthday? *šuu Ɛaṭaak* (or ***žab-lak*) *ᵊb-Ɛiid miilaadak?* — The teacher gave us a lot of homework. *l-ᵊmƐallem Ɛaṭaana waẓaayef ᵊktiire.* -- Can you give me another hour to finish? *btaƐṭiini saaƐa taanye la-xalleṣ?* — You'll have to give me more time. *laazem taƐṭiini waqᵊt ʔaktar.* — He gave me his word on it. *Ɛaṭaani qoolo b-haš-šii.* 2. *sallam, Ɛaṭa.* Give the letter to him personally. *sallmo l-maktuub ᵊb-ʔiido.* 3. *sabbab.* This noise gives me a headache. *haḍ-ḍooże Ɛam ᵊtsabbə́b-li waẓaƐ raas.* — That fellow gives me a lot of trouble. *haz-zalame Ɛam ysabbə́b-li mašaakel ᵊktiir.* 4. *zakar* (*o zəkᵊr// nzakar*). Did he give a reason? *zakár-lak šii sabab?* 5. *ʔalq̈a.* Who's giving the speech at the dinner? *miin laḥa yəlq̈i l-xiṭaab ᵊb-ḥaflet ᵊl-Ɛaša?* 6. *raxa* (*i raxi*). Does this material give? *hal-ᵊqmaaš byərxi?* — The shoes will give after you've worn them a while. *ṣ-ṣabbaaṭ ᵊbyərxi Ɛal-ləbᵊs.*

**Give him my regards. *sallə́m-li Ɛalée.*

**There's one thing you've got to give him credit for. *fii šii waaḥed laazem təšhə́d-lo fii.*

**My old coat still gives me good service. *kabbuudi l-Ɛatiiq ləssáa byəxdəmni mniiḥ.*

**I don't give a damn. *maa bətƐalleq Ɛala ṣərmaayti.*

**I don't give a hoot about that. *haš-šii maa biƐalleq Ɛala režli.*

**Nobody's going to give a hoot about that. *maa ḥada laḥa yənṭašš ᵊb-haš-šii.*

**We had to give him the air. *kaan laazem ᵊnqallƐo.*

**Why did you give him the gate? *leeš ṣarraftʼi?*

to give away - 1. *baxšaš.* I gave my old clothes away. *baxšašt ʔawaƐiyyi l-Ɛatiiqa.* 2. *faša* (*i faši//nfaša*), *baaḥ* (*u bawaḥaan//mbaaḥ*) *b-.* Don't give away my secret! *laa təfši sərri* or *laa tbuuḥ ᵊb-sərri.*

**Who gave away the bride? *miin kaan wakiil ᵊl-Ɛaruus?*

to give back - *raẓẓaƐ//traẓẓaƐ.* Please give me back my pen. *balḷa raẓẓə́Ɛ-li qalami.* — Give it back to him. *raẓẓəƐ-lo-yda.*

to give in - 1. *tsaahal.* You give in to the child too much. *Ɛam tətsaahal maƐ ᵊl-walad ᵊktiir ᵊktiir.* 2. *sallam.* For the sake of peace I gave in. *məšaan ᵊl-wifaaq̈ sallamᵊt.*

to give off - *ṭaalaƐ, Ɛaṭa* (*-yaƐṭi ø*). This flower gives off a strange odor. *haz-zahra bəṭṭaaleƐ riiḥa ġariibe.*

to give oneself up - *sallam ḥaalo.* They gave themselves up to the police. *sallamu ḥaalon ləl-booliis.*

to give out - 1. *farraq, wazzaƐ.* Who's giving out the candy? *miin Ɛam yfarreq ᵊs-sakaaker?* 2. *nafad* (*o nafaad*), *xalaṣ* (*o xluuṣ*). Our supply of ink is giving out. *ʔəḥtiyaaṭi l-ḥəbᵊr tabaƐna Ɛala wašak yənfod.*

to give up - 1. *tarak* (*e/o tarᵊk*). He gave up his job. *tarak šəġlo.* — I gave up the idea a long time ago. *tarakt ᵊl-fəkra mən zamaan.* 2. *tarak, baṭṭal.* I'm going to give up smoking. *laḥa ʔətrok ᵊt-tadxiin.* 3. *sallam, staslam.* I don't give up that easily. *maa bsallem ᵊb-has-shuule.*

to give way - *xafas* (*e/o xafᵊs*). The boards gave way under his weight. *l-lwaaḥ xafasu mən təqlo.* — The bridge gave way. *ž-žəsᵊr xafas.*

given - *mḥaddad, mƐayyan.* I have to finish in a given time. *laazem ʔəxloṣ ᵊb-waqt ᵊmḥaddad.*

glad - *mabṣuuṭ, masruur.* We're very glad about it. *nəḥna ktiir mabṣuuṭiin la-haš-šii.*

**Glad to meet you! *tšarrafna!*

**I'll be glad to do that for you. *b-kəll suruur baƐmə l-lak-yáaha.*

gladly - *b-kəll suruur.* Would you do me a favor? - Gladly. *btaƐmə́l-li maƐruuf? - b-kəll suruur* (answer: *ʔalḷa ytawwel Ɛəmrak!*).

glance - *lamḥa* pl. *-aat, naẓra* pl. *-aat.* I could tell at a glance that something was wrong. *b-lamḥa waaḥde Ərəfᵊt ʔənno fii šii ġalaṭ.*

to glance - *ṭṭallaƐ xaṭᵊf.* He glanced at his watch. *ṭṭallaƐ Ɛala saaƐto xaṭᵊf.*

gland - *ġədde* pl. *ġədad.*

glare - *wahᵊž.* The glare hurts my eyes. *l-wažᵊh Ɛam yəʔzii-li Ɛyuuni.*

to glare at - *nawwas ᵊƐyuuno b-.* Why are you glaring at me like that? *šəbak Ɛam ᵊtnawwes ᵊƐyuunak fiyyi heek?*

glaring - *wahhaaž.* How can you work in that glaring light? *kiif fiik təštəġel b-haḍ-ḍaww ᵊl-wahhaaž?*

glass - 1. *qzaaz, qžaaz, balloor.* The pitcher is made of glass. *l-ʔəbriiq maƐmuul mən ᵊqzaaz.* 2. *kaase* pl. *-aat, kəbbaaye* pl. *-aat.* May I have a glass of water? *məmken ʔaaxod kaaset mayy?* 3. *kaas* pl. *-aat.* We all had a glass of wine. *kəllna šrəbna kaas ᵊnbiit.*

glasses - *kəzlok* pl. *kazaalek, Ɛweenaat* (pl.), *naḍḍaaraat* (pl.). I can't read that without my glasses. *maa fiini ʔəqra haš-šii bala kəzᵊlki.*

hour glass - *saaƐa* (pl. *-aat*) *ramliyye, saaƐet˜ ramᵊl.*

magnifying glass - *mkabbra* pl. *-aat.* You can only see it with a magnifying glass. *maa fiik ᵊtšuufa ʔəlla b-ᵊmkabbra.*

piece of glass - *qžaaze* pl. *-aat, qzaaze* pl. *-aat, šaqfet˜* (pl. *šəqaf˜*) *ᵊqzaaz.* I cut myself on a piece of glass. *žaraḥt ḥaali b-ᵊqžaaze.*

glazier - *qəmarži* pl. *-iyye.*

gleam - *bṣiiṣ˜ ḍaww.* There was still a faint gleam in the sky. *kaan ləssa fii bṣiiṣ ḍaww bᵊs-sama.*

to gleam - *lamaƐ* (*a lamaƐaan*). His eyes were gleaming with excitement. *Ɛyuuno kaanet Ɛam təlmaƐ mən kətᵊr-ma kaan mənfə́Ɛel.*

glider - *ṭayyaara* (pl. *-aat*) *širaaƐiyye.*

to **glisten** - *baraq (o briiq), lamaɛ (a lamaɛaan).* The tower was glistening in the sun (light). *l-bərž kaan ɛam yəbroq b-ḍaww ᵊš-šamᵊs.*
to **glitter** - 1. *tlaʔlaʔ, lamaɛ (a lamaɛaan).* The snow glittered in the sun. *t-talᵊž kaan ɛam yətlaʔlaʔ ᵊb-ḍaww ᵊš-šamᵊs.* 2. *lamaɛ.* All is not gold that glitters. *muu kəll šii lamaɛ dahab.*
to **gloat over** - *šəmet (a šamaate) b- or la-.* He can't help gloating over his competitor's loss. *maa ɛam yəḥsen ʔəlla yəšmat b-ᵊxsaaret ᵊmzaaḥmo.*
globe - 1. *kura ʔarḍiyye, kuret˜ ᵊl-ʔarḍ.* The Soviet space capsule circled the globe twenty times. *safiinet ᵊl-faḍaaʔ ᵊs-sovyeetiyye daaret ḥawl ᵊl-kura l-ʔarḍiyye ɛəšriin marra.* — They're mounting a huge globe in the entrance hall. *ɛam yrakkbu kura ʔarḍiyye ḍaxme bᵊl-madxal.* 2. *gloob* pl. *-aat.* One of these days we should replace the globe in the bathroom. *šii yoom mn ᵊl-ʔiyyaam laazem ᵊnbaddel ᵊl-gloob bᵊl-ḥammaam.*
gloomy - 1. *mġəmm, məqmeṭ.* Yesterday was a very gloomy day. *mbaareḥ kaan ṇhaaṛ ᵊmġəmm ᵊktiir.* 2. *kaʔiib.* He always has a gloomy look on his face. *daayman fii naẓra kaʔiibe ɛala wəššo.*
glorious - *mažiid.*
glory - *mažd.*
glossy - *lammaaɛ.*
glove - *kaff* pl. *kfuuf.* I bought a pair of gloves yesterday. *štareet žooz ᵊkfuuf ᵊmbaareḥ.*
**They worked hand in glove. *štaġalu ʔiid ᵊb-ʔiid.*
**This suit fits like a glove. *hal-badle žaaye ɛaléé mətl ᵊl-xaatem.*
glow - *ʔažiiž.* The glow of the fire. *ʔažiiž ᵊṇ-ṇaaṛ.*
to glow - *thallal.* Her face glowed with joy. *wəšša kaan məthallel bᵊl-faraḥ.*
glue - 1. *ṣamᵊġ.* I bought a bottle of glue. *štareet qanniinet ṣamᵊġ.* 2. *ġəre.* I ran out of glue before I could finish the chair. *xalaṣ ᵊl-ġəre ɛandi qabᵊl-ma xalleṣ ᵊl-kərsi.*
**He stuck to me like glue. *ɛəleq fiyyi mətl ᵊt-tamᵊr-tiine.*
to glue - 1. *lazzaq.* I think I can glue the vase. *bẓənn fiini lazzeq ᵊl-mašrabiyye.* — The cover is only glued on. *ž-žəlde bass ᵊmlazzaqa talziiq.* — I glued the cup back together. *lazzaqt ᵊl-fənžaan maɛ baɛḍo.* 2. *ġarra.* Glue the board to the frame. *ġarri l-looḥ ɛal-bərwaaẓ.*
**He stood as if glued to the spot. *waqqaf kaʔənno mmasmar bᵊl-ʔarḍ.*
**He kept his eyes glued on her. *maa qaam naẓaro ɛanha.*
gluey - *ṣamġi*, ġarawi*.*
glutton(ous) - *ʔakkiil* pl. *-e.* Don't be such a glutton! *laa tkuun ʔakkiil hal-qadd!*
glycerine - *gliiseriin.*
to **gnash** - *kazz (ə kazz) ɛala.* He gnashed his teeth. *kazz ɛala snaano.*
gnat - *barġaše* coll. *barġaš* pl. *-aat.*
to **gnaw on** - *qarqaḍ.* The dog's been gnawing on that bone for almost an hour. *ṣar-lo hal-kalb ɛam yqarqeḍ ᵊl-ɛaḍme šii saaɛa.*
to **go** - 1. *raaḥ (u rooḥa, rawaḥaan).* I go to the movies once a week. *bruuḥ ɛas-siinama marra bᵊž-žəmɛa.* -- Where are you going? *ween raayeḥ?* -- Are you going there too? *raayeḥ ʔənte la-hniik kamaan?* -- This chair goes in the corner. *hal-kərsi biruuḥ ɛal-qərne.* — The vase went to pieces. *l-mašrabiyye raaḥet šəqaf šəqaf.* — The house went for a song. *l-beet raaḥ quul ᵊb-balaaš.* — I don't know whether I'm coming or going! *maa-li ɛarfaan ḥaali raayeḥ wəlla žaaye.* 2. *məši (i maši), raaḥ.* We have to go now. *laazem nəmši hallaq.* 3. *məši.* The train is going fast. *t-treen maaši b-sərɛa.* — This tie doesn't go with the suit. *hal-ᵊgraafe maa btəmši maɛ ᵊl-badle.* — He goes under an assumed name. *maaši taḥᵊt ʔəsᵊm mustaɛaar.* — I hope the incident will go unnoticed. *nšaḷḷa l-ḥaadse btəmši (or btəmroq) biduun-ma ḥada yəntəbéh-la.* — Whatever he says goes! *halli biquulo byəmši.* 4. *ṭələɛ (a ø).* The wine has gone to his head. *n-nbiit ṭələɛ la-raaso.* — The first prize went to an elderly gentleman. *ž-žaayze l-ʔuula ṭələɛet la-rəžžaal ᵊmsənn.* -- Our salesman is going on the road next week. *l-bayyaaɛ tabaɛna laḥa yəṭlaɛ ɛal-beeɛ barraat ᵊl-balad ᵊž-žəmɛa ž-žaaye.* — Is the whole cast going on the road? *l-fərqa kəlla laḥa təṭlaɛ tədžawwal?*
**One, two, three, go! *waaḥed, tneen, tlaate - rkədu!*
**That goes without saying. *haš-šii maa bəddo kalaam.*
**It goes without saying that you're invited. *badiihi ʔənnak ʔənte maɛzuum* or *maa bədda ḥaki ʔənte maɛzuum.*
**That's the way things go. *heek ḥaal ᵊd-dənye.*
**We'll let it go at that. *mənxalliiha ɛand hoon.*
**They went without food for three days. *bəqyu bala ʔakl ᵊtlətt iyyaam.*
**We didn't go hungry. *maa žəɛna.*
**I'm going crazy! *raḥa žənn!*
**Don't go to any trouble. *laa tġalleb ḥaalak.*
**He really went out of his way to make us feel at home. *waḷḷa ġallab ḥaalo ʔaktar mn ᵊl-laazem məšaan yʔammen raaḥətna.*
**Go to the devil. *nšəneq.*
**The trip and everything that went with it cost me a hundred dollars. *s-safra w-kəll šii fiiha kallafni miit dolaar.*
**That's going a little too far! *haš-šii ɛam yəṭlaɛ ɛan ḥaddo!*
**He's on the go day and night. *huwwe ɛala rəžlo leel w-ᵊṇhaaṛ.*
gone - *raayeḥ.* How long has he been gone? *qaddeeš ṣar-lo raayeḥ?*
**All our wine is gone. *kəll ᵊn-nbiit ɛanna xalaṣ.*
**The snow is all gone. *daab kəll ᵊt-talᵊž.*
**Everything is gone. *kəll šii ṃaḍa w-raaḥ.*
I am going to, you are going to, etc - *raḥa, laḥa, bəddi, bəddak,* etc. (with foll. verb in imperf. without *b-*). I'm going to bake a cake. *raḥa ʔəxbez gaato.* — We're going to leave today. *bəddna nsaafer ᵊl-yoom.* — The roof is going to fall in. *s-saqᵊf laḥa yəhboṭ.*
to go ahead - 1. *sabaq (e/o sabᵊq).* You go ahead. I'll follow later. *sbəqni w-ʔana bəlḥaqak baɛdeen.* 2. *kammal.* Just go ahead. Don't let me stop you! *kammel, laa txalliini waqqfak!* 3. *raaḥ (u ø).* Go ahead. Take it. *ruuḥ xədha.* — Go ahead. You tell him! *ruuḥ ʔənte qəl-lo!*
to go along: They're all going to Duma. Shall I go along? *kəllon raayḥiin la-duuma. ruuḥ maɛon?* -- I don't go along with that. *maa bwaafeq ɛala haš-šii.*
to go around - *daar (u doora), laff (ə ø).* Go around and make sure that all doors are locked. *duur bᵊl-beet w-ᵊtʔakkad ʔənno kəll baab ᵊmsakkar.*
**There's enough cake to go around. *fii gaato ykaffi l-kəll.*
to go at - 1. *ɛaalaž.* You're not going at it right. *ʔənte maa-laak ɛam ᵊtɛaaləžša maẓbuuṭ.* 2. *hažam (o hžuum) ɛala.* He went at him with a knife. *hažam ɛalée b-səkkiin.* — They went at the food like hungry wolves. *hažamu ɛal-ʔakᵊl mətl l-ᵊḍwaal.*
to go away - *raaḥ (u rooḥa), məši (i maši).* When did he go away? *ʔeemta raaḥ?* — Go away! *ʔəmši baqa!* or ***fréka mən hoon* or ***waržiina ɛarḍ ᵊktaafak!*
to go back - *rəžeɛ (a ržuuɛ, rašɛa).* When are you going back to Aleppo? *ʔeemta raažeɛ la-ḥalab?* — She went back into the house. *rəžɛet la-žuwwaat ᵊl-beet.*
to go back on - 1. *rəžeɛ (a ržuuɛ) b-.* I never go back on my word. *maa bəržaɛ ᵊb-kalaami ʔabadan.* 2. *txalla ɛan.* I don't go back on my friends. *maa bətxalla ɛan ᵊṣḥaabi.*
to go by - 1. *faat (u fawataan).* I wouldn't let that opportunity go by, if I were you. *law ʔana maa bxalli hal-fərṣa tfuutni.* 2. *maraq (o mruuq) b-žanb˜ ...* He went right by me without saying a word. *maraq ᵊb-žambi biduun-ma yəḥki w-laa kəlme.* 3. *ttabaɛ, məši (i maši) ɛala.* You can't always go by the rules. *maa fiik təttəbeɛ ᵊl-qaaɛde daayman.* — Don't go by what he says. *laa təmši ɛala qoolo.* 4. *tqayyad b-.* Don't go by me! *laa tətqayyad fiyyi.*
**He goes by an assumed name. *maaši taḥᵊt ʔəsᵊm mustaɛaar.*
**She goes by her maiden name. *məḥtəfẓa b-ʔəsᵊm ɛeeləta.*
to go down - 1. *nəzel (e nzuul), nxafaḍ.* Prices are going down. *l-ʔasɛaar ɛam tənzel.* 2. *nəzel.* The elevator is going down. *l-ʔaṣanṣoor ɛam yənzel.*
**Those weeks will go down in history as the turning point in our international relations. *hal-ʔasabiiɛ bədda tədxol ᵊb-səžəll ᵊt-taariix ka-nəqṭet ᵊt-taḥawwol ᵊb-ɛalaaqaatna d-duwaliyye.*
to go in - *faat (u foote).* She just went in. *hallaq faatet.*
to go in for - 1. *htamm b-.* Do you go in for

sports? *btəhtamm bᵊr-riyaaḍa?* or *******ʔəlak maraaq bᵊr-riyaaḍa?*

**I don't go in for that sort of thing. *maa bḥəṭṭ ʔəṣbaᶜti b-heek šaġle.*

to go in on – *šaarak b-.* Would you like to go in with me on this deal? *bətḥəbb ᵊtšaarəkni b-haš-šaġle?*

to go into – 1. *faat (u foote) ᶜala.* Let's go into the house. *xalliina nfuut ᶜal-beet.* 2. *baḥas (a baḥᵊs).* Let's not go into the matter now! *bala-ma nəbḥas ᵊl-masʔale hallaq.*

to go off – *žara (i žarayaan), məši (i maši).* The meeting went off without an incident. *l-ʔəžtimaaᶜ žara biduun ḥaades.*

**Be careful, the gun might go off! *ʔoᶜa, l-fard bižuuz yəṭlaᶜ mənno rṣaaṣa!*

to go on – 1. *tamm (a ø), bəqi (a ø), ḍall (a ø), stamarr.* He went on talking. *tamm yəḥki.* 2. *stamarr.* This can't go on any longer. *haš-šii muu məmken yəstamərr ʔaktar mən heek.* — The show must go on. *l-ᶜarḍ laazem yəstamərr.* 3. *kammal.* Please go on! *mən faḍlak kammel!*

**Go on! I don't believe that! *ḥaaže! maa bsaddeq haš-šii!*

**He went on to say that ... *w-baᶜdeen qaal ʔənno ...*

to go out – 1. *ṭəleᶜ (a ṭalᶜa).* He just went out. *hallaq ṭəleᶜ.* — Let's go out tonight. *xalliina nəṭlaᶜ ᶜala šii maḥall ᵊl-leele.* — Sometimes we go out to dinner. *ʔaḥyaanan ᵊmnəṭlaᶜ ᵊmnətᶜašša barra.* 2. *nṭafa.* Suddenly the lights went out. *fažʔatan ᵊnṭafet ᵊl-ʔəḍᵊwye.* — The fire's gone out. *nṭafet ᵊn-naar.*

to go over – 1. *ṣaar (i ø) rawaaž la-.* Do you think his play will go over? *btəᶜtəqed ʔənno tamsiiliito bəddo yṣər-la rawaaž?* 2. *staᶜraḍ.* Let's go over the details once more. *xalliina nəstaᶜreḍ ᵊt-tafaṣiil marra taanye.* 3. *raažaᶜ.* I've gone over all the figures, but I can't find the mistake. *raažaᶜᵊt kəll ᵊl-ʔarqaam bass maa laqeet ween ᵊl-ġalṭa.*

**I'm going over to his house for an hour. *raḥa ruuḥ la-ᶜando šii saaᶜet zamaan.*

to go through – 1. *məši (i ø).* Do you think my application will go through? *btəᶜtəqed ʔənno ṭalabi laḥa yəmši?* 2. *maraq (o marqa) mən.* You can't go through here. *maa btəḥsen təmroq mən hoon.* — On our way here we went through a number of deserted villages. *ᶜala ṭariiqna w-nəḥna žaayiin la-hoon maraqna ᶜala ᶜəddet ḍiyaᶜ mahžuura.* 3. *faat (u foote) mən.* That table will never go through the door. *haṭ-ṭaawle maa btəfuut mn ᵊl-baab ʔabadan.* 4. *məši (i maši) ḍədd.* He went through the red light. *məši ḍədd ᵊḍ-ḍaww ᵊl-ʔaḥmar.*

**The poor woman has gone through a lot. *məskiine hal-mara qaḍḍet ᵊktiir* (or *maraq ᶜala raasa šii ktiir*).

**They went through hard times after the war. *qaḍḍu ktiir baᶜd ᵊl-ḥarb.*

to go up – 1. *ṭəleᶜ (a ṭalᶜa).* Did you see him go up? *šəfto ṭəleᶜ šii?* 2. *rtafaᶜ.* Prices are going up. *ᶜam tərtəfeᶜ ᵊl-ʔasᶜaar.* — Meat has gone up. *l-laḥme rtafaᶜ səᶜra.*

to let go (of) – *fallat.* Let go of my hand! *fallet ʔiidi!*

to let oneself go – *fallat(h)a.* Lately she's let herself go terribly. *faṣaaᶜa šuu fallatəta ʔaaxer ᵊl-ḥəṣṣa.*

to let someone go – *ᶜafa (i ᶜafu) ᶜan ḥada.* This time we'll let you go. *hal-marra laḥa nəᶜfi ᶜannak.*

goal – 1. *hadaf* pl. *ʔahdaaf.* He has set himself a very high goal. *ḥaaṭeṭ la-nafso hadaf rafiiᶜ ᵊktiir.* 2. *gool* (invar.), *hadaf* pl. *ʔahdaaf.* Our team made three goals in the first half. *fariiqna fammat tlaate gool* (or *tlətt ʔahdaaf*) *bᵊš-šooṭ ᵊl-ʔawwal.*

goalkeeper – *goolaar* pl. *-iyye.*

goat – 1. *məᶜzaaye* coll. *məᶜze* pl. *maᶜaasi.* How old do goats live to be? *qaddeeš bətᶜiiš ᵊl-məᶜze?* 2. *kabš˜ ᵊl-fidaaʔ.* He's always the goat. *humme kabš ᵊl-fidaaʔ daaʔiman.*

**Don't let him get your goat. *laa txallii yʔarrəqa ᶜaleek.*

**She gets my goat. *bəṭṭaaleᶜ diini.*

goatherd – *maᶜᶜaaz* pl. *-iin.*

goblet – *qadaḥ* pl. *qdaaḥ.*

God – *ʔaḷḷa, ʔaḷḷaah.* God forbid! *maᶜaaz ʔaḷḷaah!* or *ḥaaša ləllaah!* — Thank God! *l-ḥamdu ləllaah!* or *l-ḥamdəlla!* — God bless you! (when someone sneezes) *yarḥámuka ḷḷaah!* (as an expression of gratitude) *katter xeerak!* or *ʔaḷḷa yəkter ᶜaleek ᵊl-xeer!* — God willing! *nšaaḷḷa!* or *n-šaaʔa ḷḷaah!* — For God's sake! *məšaan ʔaḷḷa!*

godchild – *falyuun* pl. *falayiin,* f. *falyuune* pl. *-aat.*

goddaughter – *falyuune* pl. *-aat.*

goddess – *ʔilaaha* pl. *-aat.*

godfather – *šbiin* pl. *šabaayen.*

godmother – *šbiine* pl. *-aat.*

godson – *falyuun* pl. *falayiin.*

gold – 1. *dahab.* Is that real gold? *haada dahab ʔaṣli?* — Many of those gold mines were abandoned in recent years. *fii ᶜadad mən hal-manaažem ᵊd-dahab ᵊntarket bᵊs-sniin ᵊl-ʔaxiire.* — Their business is a veritable gold mine. *tižaarəton ᶜan ḥaqa kənz mən dahab.* 2. *dahab, dahabi*.* I bought my wife a gold watch. *štareet la-marti saaᶜet dahab* (or *saaᶜa dahab* or *saaᶜa dahabiyye*).

gold brick – *sabiiket˜* (pl. *sabaayek˜*) *dahab.*

golden – *dahabi*.*

goldsmith – *ṣaayeġ* pl. *ṣummaaġ* and *ṣiyyaaġ,* coll. pl. *ṣaaġa.*

golf – *goolf.* Do you play golf? *ʔənte btəlᶜab goolf?*

gonorrhea – *taᶜqiibe, sayalaan.*

good – 1. *ṣaaleḥ, maṣlaḥa, xeer.* I'm only thinking of your good. *ʔana maa-li ᶜam ʔəftəker ʔəlla b-ṣaalḥak.* — He did it for the common good. *ᶜəməla ləṣ-ṣaaleḥ ᵊl-ᶜaamm.* 2. *mniiḥ* pl. *mnaaḥ.* He's a good student. *humme təlmiiz ᵊmniiḥ.* — He's very good at figures. *humme mniiḥ ᵊktiir bᵊl-ᵊḥsaab.* — It's a good stove. *hayy ṣooba mniiḥa.* — That's good. *mniiḥ!* 3. *ṭayyeb.* Good! Now go ahead and write him a letter. *ṭayyeb! yaḷḷa ktəb-lo maktuub hallaq.* 4. *ẓariif, ḥəlu.* That was a good joke. *kaanet nəkte ẓariife.* 5. *ṣaaleḥ.* The passport is good until the fifteenth. *ž-žawaaz ṣaaleḥ la-yoom xamᵊṣṭaᶜš.* 6. *wažiih.* They think they're fighting for a good cause. *məᶜtəqdiin ʔənnon ᶜam yḥaarbu la-sabab wažiih.* 7. *ᶜala salaamto.* They are good children. *hənne wlaad ᶜala salaamə́ton.*

**Good afternoon. *marḥaba,* answer: *marḥabteen* or *miit marḥaba* or *maraaḥeb.*

**Good morning. *ṣabaaḥ ᵊl-xeer,* answer: *ṣabaaḥ ᵊl-xeeraat* or *ṣabbḥak bᵊl-xeer,* answer: *ʔaḷḷa yṣabbḥak bᵊl-xeeraat.*

**Good evening. *masa l-xeer,* answer: *masa l-xeeraat* or *massiik bᵊl-xeer,* answer: *ʔaḷḷa ymassiik bᵊl-xeeraat.*

**Good night! (to the person leaving) *təṣbeḥ ᶜala xeer,* answer: *w-ʔənte mən ʔahlo.*

**Good heavens! *yaa ʔaḷḷa!* or *yaa salaam!*

**That's all to the good! *xeeriyye halli heek ṣaaret!*

**At the end of the game he was five dollars to the good. *b-ʔaaxer ᵊl-ləᶜbe ṭəleᶜ rabḥaan xamᵊs dolaaraat.*

**Would you be good enough to give it to him? *btaᶜmel maᶜruuf taᶜṭii-yáa?*

**Have a good time! *nbəṣəṭ!* or *rawweq!*

**He has a good head on his shoulders. *ᶜaléé məxx maa-lo ʔaxx.*

**The tires are good for another year. *l-kawašiik biḍaaynu səne taanye.*

**Make the tea good and strong! *taqqəl-li š-šaay ᵊmniiḥ!*

**I haven't seen him for a good while. *ṣar-li zamaan* (or *mədde*) *maa šəfto.*

**Be a good boy now! *ᶜood ᶜaaqel baqa!*

**Be a good girl now! *ᶜədi ᶜaaqle baqa.*

goods – *bḍaaᶜa* pl. *baḍaayeᶜ.* The goods were sent by freight. *l-ᵊbḍaaᶜa raaḥet šaḥᵊn.* — These goods are very much in demand now. *hal-baḍaayeᶜ maṭluube ktiir hal-ʔiyyaam.* — Cotton goods are comparatively expensive. *l-baḍaayeᶜ ᵊl-qəṭniyye ġaalye nəsbiyyan.*

good faith – *ḥəsᵊn˜ niyye.* I'm sure he acted in good faith. *ʔana mətʔakked ʔənno tṣarraf ᶜan ḥəsᵊn niyye.*

good turn – *maᶜruuf, ḥasane* pl. *-aat, žmiile.* He did me a real good turn yesterday. *ᶜəmel maᶜi maᶜruuf ᵊkbiir ᵊmbaareḥ.* — They've done us many good turns. *ᶜəmlu maᶜna ḥasanaat ᵊktiir.* — One good turn deserves another. *l-ḥasane btəstaahel ḥasane.*

a good deal of – *šii ktiir.* He spent a good deal of time on it. *ṣaraf ᶜaleeha waqᵊt šii ktiir.* — There's a good deal of truth in that. *fii šii ktiir ᵊmn ᵊṣ-ṣəḥḥa b-haš-šii.*

a good many – *ktiir* (invar.), *ktaar* (pl.). There

were a good many foreigners in the hotel. *kaan fii ʔažaaneb ᵊktiir bᵊl-ʔoteel.*

as good as - *kaʔənn-* + pron. suff. The radio is as good as new. *r-raadyo kaʔənno ždiid* or *******r-raadyo yuɛtábar ᵊždiid.* — The work is as good as done. *š-šəğᵊl kaʔənno xalaṣ* or *******š-šəğᵊl mnəḥᵊsbo xalaṣ.*

for good - *ɛala ṭuul.* I'm through with him for good. *qaṭaɛt ɛalaaqti maɛo ɛala ṭuul.*

too good - *ḥweenet-* + pron. suff. These shoes are too good for such weather. *haṣ-ṣabbaaṭ ḥweento b-heek ṭaqᵊṣ.* — She's too good for that job. *ḥweenə́ta b-haš-šağle.*

**It's too good to be true. *laa yaa, muu maɛquul!*

to be good for - *səwi (a ə).* He's good for ten thousand dollars. *byəswa ɛašᵊrt aalaaf dolaar.* -- Is this pencil good for sketching? *hal-qalam ᵊr-rṣaaṣ byəswa šii lər-rasᵊm?*

to do good - *nafaɛ (a nafᵊɛ).* The vacation has done him good. *l-ʔižaaze nafᵊɛto ktiir.* — What good will it do him? *šuu raḥa tənfaɛo?*

to make good - **1.** *twaffaq.* I'm sure he'll make good. *ʔana mətʔakked ʔənno raḥa yətwaffaq.* **2.** *ɛawwaḍ ɛan.* I'll make good the damage. *ʔana bɛawweḍ ɛan ᵊḍ-ḍarar.* **3.** *wafa (-yuufi wafaaʔ) b-.* He made good his promise. *wafa b-waɛdo.*

good-by - (said by the person leaving) *xaaṭrak (xaaṭrek, xaaṭərkon),* (said by the person staying behind) *maɛ ᵊs-salaame,* answer: *ʔaḷḷa ysallmak (ysallmek, ysalləmkon).* Good-by! Have a good trip! *maɛ ᵊs-salaame! nšaaḷḷa safra saɛiide!*

to say good-by to someone - **1.** *waddaɛ ḥada.* We're going to drive our neighbors to the airport and say good-by to them there. *bəddna naaxod žiiraanna bᵊs-sayyaara ɛal-maṭaar w-ᵊnwaddə́ɛon ᵊhniik.* -- Our neighbors are leaving tomorrow and we haven't said good-by to them yet. *žiiraanna msaafriin bəkra w-ləssa ma waddaɛnaahon.* **2.** *qaal (u ə) xaaṭrak,* etc., or *qaal maɛ ᵊs-salaame* (see above). Ziyad, did you say good-by to your uncle? *ya zyaad qəlt xaaṭərkon la-ɛammak?*

good-for-nothing: He's a good-for-nothing. *maa byəswa nḥaase* or *maa byəswa xabaro.* -- Their oldest son turned out a real good-for-nothing. *ʔəbnon l-ᵊkbiir ṭəleɛ maa byəswa nḥaase ɛan ḥaqa.*

Good Friday - *žəmɛet~ ᵊl-ʔaalaam, ž-žəmɛa l-ḥaziine.*

good-looking - *ḥleewa* (invar.). He's a good-looking man. *huwwe rəžžaal ᵊḥleewa.* — Who was that good-looking young man I saw you with last night? *miin haš-šabb l-ᵊḥleewa* (or *******haš-šbuubiyye) halli šəftek maɛo mbaaresḥ ᵊl-masa?*

good-natured - *wadiiɛ, ḥaliim.* He's a good-natured fellow. *huwwe zalame wadiiɛ.*

goodness - *nəbl~ ᵊl-qalb.* In her goodness, she left half of the estate to an orphanage. *mən nəbᵊl qalba tarket nəṣṣ ᵊt-tərke la-daar ʔaytaam.*

**Oh, my goodness! *daxiil ɛərḍak!*

**Goodness knows. I tried often enough! *ʔaḷḷa ɛaliim qaddeeš žarrabᵊt!*

for goodness' sake - **1.** *daxiil ɛərḍak.* For goodness' sake! Can you imagine that! *daxiil ɛərḍak! šii maa byətsaddaq!* **2.** *daxiil ʔaḷḷa w-ᵊmḥammad, mənšaan ʔaḷḷa.* For goodness' sake, stop that noise. *daxiil ʔaḷḷa w-ᵊmḥammad, ḥaaʐtak qarwaše baqa.*

goose - *wazze* coll. *wazz* pl. *-aat.* We had goose for dinner. *kaan ɛanna wazze ɛal-ɛaša.*

**I'll cook his goose! *waḷḷa la-ʔəhᵊlko!* or *waḷḷa ləssa bwaržii nžuum ᵊḍ-ḍəhᵊr!*

gorgeous - *faaxer, badiiɛ, baaher.*

gorilla - *ġorella* pl. *-aat.*

Gospel - *ʔənžiil* pl. *ʔanažiil.*

gossip - **1.** *ḥaki bᵊl-qafa.* I wouldn't believe that gossip. *law ᵊb-maḥallak maa bsaddeq hal-ḥaki bᵊl-qafa.* **2.** *ḥakka* (pl. *ḥakkayiin*) *bᵊl-qafa,* f. *ḥakkaaye* (pl. *-aat*) *bᵊl-qafa.* His wife is an old gossip. *marto ḥakkaaye bᵊl-qafa ɛatiiqa.*

to gossip - *ḥaka (i ḥaki) bᵊl-qafa.* She gossips too much. *btəḥki bᵊl-qafa ktiir ᵊktiir.*

gourd - *yaqṭiine* coll. *yaqṭiin* pl. *-aat,* also *yaqṭiile,* etc.

gourmet: He's a gourmet if I ever saw one. *ʔiza fii ḥada bᵊd-dənye byaɛref ṭaɛmet təmmo bikuun huwwe.* — They're regular gourmets. *byaɛᵊrfu ṭaɛmet təmmon ɛal-mazbuuṭ.*

to **govern** - *ḥakam (o ḥəkᵊm//nḥakam).* The British made an excellent job of governing that country. *l-ʔəngliiz waržu baraaɛa ɛaẓiime b-ḥəkᵊm hal-ᵊblaad.*

**All prepositions govern the genitive. *kəll ᵊḥruuf ᵊž-žarr bidžərr ᵊl-ʔəsᵊm.*

government - **1.** *ḥkuume* pl. *-aat.* The government should do something about that. *l-ᵊḥkuume laazem taɛmə́l-la šii b-haš-šağle.* **2.** *wazaara* pl. *-aat, ḥkuume* pl. *-aat.* Who heads the new government? *miin byərʔas l-wazaara ž-ždiide?* **3.** *ḥkuumi*.* All government agencies will be closed tomorrow. *kəll ᵊd-dawaayer l-ᵊḥkuumiyye msakkra bəkra.*

governmental - *ḥkuumi*.*

governor - **1.** *ḥaakem* pl. *ḥəkkaam.* Who's the present Governor of Michigan? *miin ḥaakem wilaayet mišigan ᵊl-ḥaali?* **2.** *mḥaafeẓ* pl. *-iin.* He was appointed governor of Aleppo province. *ɛayyanúu mḥaafeẓ ɛala mḥaafaẓt ḥalab.*

to **grab** - **1.** *kamaš (o kamᵊš//nkamaš).* He grabbed the thief by the collar. *kamaš ᵊl-ḥaraami mən qabbto.* **2.** *xaṭaf (o xaṭᵊf).* Don't grab, you'll get your share all right. *laa təxṭof, ḥəṣṣtak žaayiitak!* **3.** *ʔaxad (-yaaxod ʔaxᵊd).* I just want to grab a bite. *bass bəddi ʔaaxə́d-li ləqme.*

grace - *nəɛme.* By the grace of God. *b-nəɛmet ʔaḷḷa.*

**Let's say grace. *la-nṣalli.*

**He wants to get into her good graces. *ɛam yḥaawel yədzallə́f-la* or *ɛam yḥaawel ymassə́ḥ-la žuux.*

period of grace - *məhle* (pl. *məhal*) *q̈aanuuniyye.*

with good grace - *b-raḥaabet~ ṣədᵊr.* He accepted failure with good grace. *tqabbal fašalo b-raḥaabet ṣədᵊr.*

graceful - *rašiiq.* Her movements are very graceful. *ḥarakaata ktiir rašiiqa.*

gracious - *kariim, laṭiif.* She's a very gracious hostess. *hiyye mḍiife kariime ktiir.*

**My gracious! *ya salaam!* or *ya ʔaḷḷa!*

grade - **1.** *ɛalaame* pl. *-aat.* He received the highest grades in the class. *ʔaxad ʔaḥsan ɛalaamaat bᵊṣ-ṣaff.* **2.** *ṣaff* pl. *ṣfuuf.* In what grade is your boy? *b-ʔanu ṣaff ʔəbnak?* **3.** *žənᵊs* pl. *ʔažnaas, ṣənᵊf* pl. *ʔaṣnaaf, nooɛ* pl. *ʔanwaaɛ.* We buy the best grade of milk. *mnəštə́ri ʔaḥsan žənᵊs ḥaliib.*

**He'll never make the grade. *b-ḥayaato maa byənžaḥ.*

to grade - **1.** *ṣannaf//tṣannaf.* Oranges are graded according to size and quality. *l-bərdqaan byətṣannaf ḥasab l-ᵊqyaas wᵊṣ-ṣənᵊf.* **2.** *ṣallaḥ//tṣallaḥ.* I have to grade some papers tonight. *laazem ṣalleḥ kam waraqa l-leele.*

gradual - *tadriiži*, šwayye šwayye* (invar.). I noticed a gradual improvement. *laaḥaẓᵊt taḥasson tadriiži.*

gradually - *šwayye šwayye, bᵊt-tadriiž.* He's gradually getting better. *ṣaḥḥto šwayye šwayye ɛam təṭḥassan.*

graduate - *xərriiž* pl. *-iin, mətxarrež* pl. *-iin.* Most of our graduates have found good positions. *ʔaktar xərriižiinna* (or *ʔaktar ᵊl-mətxarržiin mən ɛanna*) *ḥəṣlu ɛala maraakez ᵊmniiḥa.*

to graduate - **1.** *darraž//ddarraž.* Taxes are graduated according to income. *ḍ-ḍaraayeb btəddarraž ḥasab ᵊd-daxᵊl.* **2.** *txarraž.* She graduated from American University. *txarražet mən ᵊž-žaamɛa l-ʔameerkiyye.*

graduation - *taxarrož.*

to **graft** - *ṭaɛɛam.* You should graft the shoots no later than November. *laazem ᵊṭṭaɛɛem ᵊl-ɛəqal muu ʔalqas mən təšriin ᵊt-taani.*

grain - **1.** *ḥbuub* (pl.). Canada exports meat and grain. *kanada bətṣadder ᵊlḥuum w-ᵊḥbuub.* **2.** *taɛriiq, taɛriiqa.* This wood has a beautiful grain. *hal-xašab ʔəlo taɛriiq ḥəlu.* **3.** *ṭabɛ.* That goes against my grain. *haada ḍəḍḍ ṭabɛi.* **4.** *zarra, ʔasar.* There isn't a grain of truth in the story. *maa fii w-laa zarra mn ᵊṣ-ṣəḥḥa bᵊl-qəṣṣa.*

**Take what he says with a grain of salt. *xood kalaamo b-šwayye mn ᵊt-taḥaffoẓ.*

grain elevator (or silo) - *məstawdaɛ~* (pl. *-aat~*) *ᵊḥbuub.*

gram - *ġraam* pl. *-aat, graam* pl. *-aat.*

grammar - **1.** *q̈awaaɛed~ ᵊl-luġa* (pl.), *q̈awaaɛed* (pl.), (specif., Arabic) *ṣarf w-naḥu.* I never really studied German grammar. *b-ḥayaati maa darast q̈awaaɛed ᵊl-luġa l-ʔalmaaniyye ɛan žadd.* **2.** *ktaab~* (pl. *kətᵊb~*) *q̈awaaɛed~ ᵊl-luġa, ktaab~ q̈awaaɛed,* (specif., of Arabic) *ktaab~ ṣarf w-naḥu.* Have you a good grammar for beginners? *fii ɛandak ᵊktaab ṣarf w-naḥu mniiḥ ləl-məbtadiʔiin?*

grammarian - *naḥawi* pl. *-iyyiin.*

grammatical - *naḥawi*.* That's a grammatical question. *hayy masʔale naḥawiyye.* — They don't speak grammatical Arabic, but they make themselves understood. *maa byəḥku ɛarabi naḥawi bass byənfə́hem ɛaleehon.*

gramophone - *sanduuq˜* (pl. *sanadiiq˜*) *samaε, gramofoon* pl. *-aat.*

Granada - *ġərnaaṭa.*

grand - **1.** *kbiir* pl. *kbaar.* The dance will be held in the grand ball-room. *l-baal bəddo yṣiir b-q̈aaεet ᵊl-ˀəḥtifaalaat l-ᵊkbiire.* **2.** *εaẓiim.* It was a grand idea. *kaanet fəkra εaẓiime.*

**He's living in grand style. *εaayeš mətᵊl l-ᵊmluuk.*

grand piano - *byaano (pl. byaanoyaat) ˀakəə.*

grand total - *mažmuuε εaamm, mažmuuε kəlli.*

grandchild - (son's son) *ˀəbᵊn˜* (pl. *wlaad˜*) *ˀəbᵊn,* (daughter's son) *bənᵊt˜* (pl. *wlaad˜*) *bənᵊt,* (son's daughter) *bənᵊt˜* (pl. *banaat˜*) *ˀəbᵊn,* (daughter's daughter) *bənᵊt˜* (pl. *banaat˜*) *bənᵊt.*

granddaughter - (son's daughter) *bənᵊt˜* (pl. *banaat˜*) *ˀəbᵊn,* (daughter's daughter) *bənᵊt˜* (pl. *banaat˜*) *bənᵊt.*

grandfather - *žədd* pl. *žduud* and *ždaad.*

grandmother - *sətt* pl. *-aat.*

grandson - (son's son) *ˀəbᵊn˜* (pl. *wlaad˜*) *ˀəbᵊn,* (daughter's son) *ˀəbᵊn˜* (pl. *wlaad˜*) *bənᵊt.*

granite - *graniit.*

to **grant** - **1.** *manaḥ (a manᵊḥ//mmanaḥ).* They granted us the entire amount. *manaḥuuna kaamel ᵊl-mablaġ.* — The Pope granted him a private audience. *l-baaba manaḥo mqaabale xaaṣṣa.* **2.** *εtaraf.* I grant that I was wrong. *bəεtəref ˀənni kənᵊt ġalṭaan.*

granted - **1.** *εala farḍ, law faraḍna, nəftəreḍ, frooḍ.* Granted that the statement is correct... *εala farᵊḍ (ˀənno) t-taṣriiḥ ṣaḥiiḥ...* **2.** *maẓbuuṭ, ṣaḥiiḥ.* Granted, I was wrong, but... *maẓbuuṭ, ᵊġləṭṭ, bass...*

to take something for granted - *εtabar šii mafruuġ mənno.* You take too much for granted. *btaεtəber ˀašyaaˀ ᵊktiire mafruuġ mənna.* — I took it for granted that he'd be there. *εtabarᵊt ˀamᵊr mafruuġ mənno ˀənno laḥa ykuun ᵊhniik.*

granulated sugar - *səkkar naaεem.*

grape - **1.** *εənbaaye* and *εənbe* coll. *εəneb* pl. *εənbaayaat, εənbaat, ḥabbet˜* (pl. *-aat˜*) *εəneb.* Pick up that grape before someone steps on it. *qiim hal-εənbaaye qabᵊl-ma ḥada yədεas εaleeha.* -- Mostly they grow grapes imported from France. *byəzraεu εal-ġaaleb εəneb məstawrad mən fransa.*

bunch of grapes - *εanquud˜* (pl. *εanaqiid˜*) *εəneb.*

green, unripe grape - *ḥəṣᵊrmaaye* and *ḥəṣᵊrme* coll. *ḥəṣrom* pl. *ḥəṣᵊrmaayaat, ḥəṣᵊrmaat.*

grapefruit - *greefoone* coll. *greefoon* pl. *-aat.*

grapevine - *karme* pl. *-aat,* (trellised) *daalye* pl. *dawaali.*

graphite - *grafiit.*

to **grasp** - **1.** *tkammaš b-.* She grasped the rope with both hands. *tkammašet bᵊl-ḥabl ᵊb-ˀidteena t-tənteen.* **2.** *fəhem (a fəhᵊm//nfaham).* I don't quite grasp what you mean by that. *maa-li εam ˀəfham εal-maẓbuuṭ šuu εam təεni b-haš-šii.*

to have a good grasp of - *kaan fahmaan tamaam b-.* He has a good grasp of the subject. *huwwe fahmaan tamaam bᵊl-mawḍuuε.*

grass - *ḥašiiš.* Did you cut the grass? *qaṣṣeet ᵊl-ḥašiiš?*

blade of grass - *ḥašiiše* pl. *-aat* and *ḥašaayeš.*

grasshopper - *qabbuuṭ* pl. *qababiiṭ.*

grassy - *məεšeb.*

grate - *manṣab* pl. *manaaṣeb.* The furnace needs a new grate. *l-fərᵊn laazmo manṣab ᵊždiid.*

to grate - *bašar (o bašᵊr//mbašar).* Grate some cheese. *bšoor šwayyet žəbne.*

**This noise grates on my nerves. *had-doože εam tədrob εala ˀaεṣaabi.*

grateful - *mamnuun.* I'm grateful to you for your help. *ˀana mamnuunak ᵊktiir la-maεuuntak.* — You should have seen how grateful he was! *ya-reetak kənt ᵊtšuuf qaddeešo kaan mamnuun!*

grater - *mabšara* pl. *mabaašer.*

to **gratify** - *ḥaqqaq, ˀamman.* He gratified her every wish. *ḥaqqáq-la* (or *ˀammál-la*) *kəll rəġbaata.*

gratifying - *msərr, məfreḥ.* The news is very gratifying. *l-xabar ᵊktiir ᵊmsərr.*

to be gratified by - *nsarr b-, fəreḥ (a faraḥ) b-.* I was gratified by the unexpected turn of events. *nsarreet ᵊb-taḥawwol ᵊl-ˀawḍaaε ᵊl-ġeer mənṭáẓar.*

gratis - *b-balaaš, maž(ž)aanan.* They send it to you gratis. *byəbyatúu-lak-yáaha b-balaaš.*

gratitude - *εərfaan bᵊž-žamiil.* His gratitude knows no bounds. *εərfaano bᵊž-žamiil maa-lo ḥadd.*

**That's gratitude for you! *hayy žaza l-maεruuf!*

grave - *qabᵊr* pl. *qbuúr(a).* The coffin was lowered into the grave. *t-taabuut ᵊnḥaṭṭ bᵊl-qabᵊr.* -- He looks as though he had one foot in the grave. *mbayyen εalée kaˀənno εala ḥaffet ᵊl-qabᵊr.*

**In this kind of job you always have one foot in the grave. *b-heek šaġle l-waaḥed εala ṭuul ḥaaṭeṭ rooḥo εala kaffo* (or *ḥaaṭeṭ rəžᵊl bᵊd-dənye w-rəžᵊl bᵊl-ˀaaxra).*

grave - **1.** *maxḍuuḍ.* His face was very grave. *wəššo kaan maxḍuuḍ ᵊktiir.* **2.** *mᵊaxṭer, məxṭer.* His condition is grave. *ḥaalto ṣ-ṣəḥḥiyye mᵊaxṭra.* **3.** *faẓiiε.* That's a grave mistake. *hayy ġalṭa faẓiiεa.*

gravel - *baḥᵊṣ, ḥaṣa, ḥaṣu.* The path is covered with gravel. *l-mamša mafruuš baḥᵊṣ.*

graveyard - *maqbara* pl. *maqaaber, žabbaane* pl. *-aat.*

gravitation - *žaazbiyye, quwwet tažaazob.*

gravity - **1.** *žaazbiyye.* The law of gravity. *q̈aanuun ᵊž-žaazbiyye.* **2.** *səq̈ᵊl.* The center of gravity. *markaz ᵊs-səq̈ᵊl.* -- Specific gravity. *s-səq̈l ᵊn-nooεi.* **3.** *xṭuura.* We're not underestimating the gravity of the situation. *maa-lna εam ᵊnqallel ᵊxṭuuret ᵊl-waḍᵊε.*

gravy - *maraqa.* Do you care for gravy on your meat? *bəddak maraqa εala laḥᵊmtak?*

gray - *rmaadi**, (light gray) *sənžaabi**, (lead-colored) *rṣaaṣi**, (charcoal-colored) *baaruudi**. Gray and red go together well. *r-rmaadi wᵊl-ˀaḥmar byəmšu maε baεḍon.* -- He always wears gray suits. *daayman byəlbes badlaat rmaadiyye* (or *rmaadi).*

to gray - *šaab (i šayabaan).* His hair is beginning to gray. *šaεro bada yšiib.*

to **graze** - **1.** *raεa (a raεu).* The cows are grazing in the fields. *l-baqaraat εam yərεu bᵊl-ᵊḥquul.* **2.** *šaṭab (o šaṭᵊb).* The bullet just grazed his shoulder. *r-rṣaaṣa šaṭbət-lo kətfo bass.*

grease - **1.** *šaḥᵊm, dəhne.* Don't leave the grease in the pan. *laa txalli š-šaḥᵊm bᵊl-məqlaaye.* **2.** *šaḥᵊm.* Did you put some grease in the transmission? *ḥaṭṭeet šwayyet šaḥᵊm bᵊt-transməsyoon?*

to grease - **1.** *ṭala (i ṭali)... bᵊs-samne.* Don't forget to grease the pan. *laa tənsa maa təṭli l-məqlaaye bᵊs-samne.* **2.** *šaḥḥam.* The car needs greasing. *s-sayyaara bədda tašḥiim.*

to grease somebody's palm - *barṭal//tbarṭal ḥada, raša (i rašwe//rtaša) ḥada.* They had to grease somebody's palm to get these seats. *nžabaru ybarᵊṭlu ḥada la-ḥatta yəḥṣalu εal-maḥallaat.*

greasy - **1.** *mədhen.* The dishes are still greasy. *ṣ-ṣḥuun ləssaahon mədᵊhniin.* — The soup is too greasy. *š-šooraba ktiir mədᵊhne.* **2.** *mšaḥḥem.* Tell the mechanic not to touch the seats with his greasy hands. *qel-lo ləl-miikaniiki laa yədqor ᵊl-maq̈aaεed w-ˀidée mšaḥḥmiin.* **3.** *zəfer.* You've had enough chicken, now wash your greasy hands. *ˀakalᵊt žaaž ᵊkfaaye, ruuḥ xassel ˀideek ᵊz-zəfre.*

great - **1.** *kbiir* pl. *kbaar.* It's a great risk you're taking. *ˀənte εam taεmel mžaazafe kbiire.* -- You'd be doing me a great favor. *bətkuun εam taεmᵊl-li maεruuf ᵊkbiir.* **2.** *εaẓiim* pl. *εəẓama.* She's the greatest singer of our time. *hiyye ˀaεẓam mġannye b-ˀiyyaamna.* -- He's great at telling stories. *huwwe εaẓiim b-ḥaki l-ḥakaaya.* — That's a great idea! *hayy fəkra εaẓiime!*

**He's a great man now and has forgotten his old friends. *ṣaar šaxṣiyye* (or *šii məḥtáram) hallaq w-maa yədzakkar ᵊṣḥaabo.*

**It's a great pity. *yaa xṣaara.*

**That's great! *šii εaal!*

a great many - *εadad ᵊkbiir mən, šii ᵊktiir mən.* A great many books have been written on that subject. *εadad ᵊkbiir mn ᵊl-kətb ᵊnkatbet ᵊb-hal-mawḍuuε.*

Great Britain - *briiṭaanya l-εəẓma.*

great-grandfather - (grandfather's father) *ˀabu˜ ž-žədd,* (grandmother's father) *ˀabu˜ s-sətt.*

great-grandmother - (grandfather's mother) *ˀəmm˜ ᵊž-žədd,* (grandmother's mother) *ˀəmm˜ ᵊs-sətt.*

greatly - *ktiir.* She exaggerated greatly. *baalaġet fiiha ktiir.*

Greece - *l-yuunaan.*

greed - *ṭamaε.* His greed knows no bounds. *ṭamaεo maa-lo ḥadd.*

greedy - *ṭammaaε.* Don't be so greedy. *laa tkuun hal-qadd ṭammaaε.*

Greek - **1.** *yuunaani* pl. *-iyyiin,* coll. pl. *yuunaan,* also *ruumi* coll. *ruum* pl. *ˀarwaam.* His father is a Greek. *ˀabúu yuunaani.* **2.** *yuunaaniyye* pl. *-aat,* coll. pl. *yuunaan, ruumiyye* coll. *ruum* pl. *-iyyaat.* She's a Greek. *hiyye yuunaaniyye.* **3.** *yuunaani**. Do you like Greek wines? *bətḥəbb l-ᵊnbiit* *ᵊl-yuunaani?* 4. *yuunaani* (invar.). He speaks Greek. *byəḥki yuunaani.*

**That's all Greek to me. *haada žaayiini mətl ᵊs-səryaani.*

Greek Orthodox Church - *kniiset˜ ᵊr-ruum ᵊl-ʔortodoks.*

**He's a member of the Greek Orthodox Church and his wife is a catholic. *huwwe ruum ʔortodoks w-marto (waaḥde) katuliik.*

green - 1. *ʔaxḍar* f. *xaḍra* pl. *xəḍᵊr,* (light green) *fəstqi*,* (dark green) *zeeti*.* Hand me that green envelope over there. *naawəlni haẓ-ẓarf ᵊl-ʔaxḍar mən ᵊhniik.* 2. *ʔaxḍar.* There were green meadows as far as the eye could see. *kaan fii mruuž xaḍra ɛala madd ᵊn-naẓar.* 3. *ʔaɛžar* f. *ɛažra* pl. *ɛəžᵊr.* (Eating) green apples will give you a stomach-ache. *ʔakl ᵊt-təffaaḥ ᵊl-ʔaɛžar bisaawii-lak wažaɛ məɛde.* 4. *baġu* (invar.), *ġašiim.* I'm still green at this job. *ləssaani baġu b-haš-šaġle.*

**She has a green thumb. *kəll šii btəzraɛo byəṭlaɛ.*

greens - *xəḍar* (pl.), *xəḍra* pl. *xəḍrawaat.* You should eat some greens every day. *laazem taakol šii xəḍar kəll yoom.*

to turn green - *xḍarr.* The trees are already turning green. *l-ʔašžaar ṣaaret təxḍarr.* — He turned green with envy. *xḍarr w-ᵊṣfarr mən kətr ᵊl-ḥasad.*

greengrocer - *xəḍari* pl. *-iyye, xəḍarži* pl. *-iyye.*

greenhouse - *beet˜* (pl. *byuut˜*) *qzaaz.*

to **greet** - 1. *ḥayya, raḥḥab b-.* They greeted her with applause. *ḥayyuuha bᵊt-tasfiiq.* — We greet you on behalf of ... *mənraḥḥeb fiikon bᵊn-niyaabe ɛan ...* 2. *sallam ɛala.* Who's that young lady you just greeted? *miin ᵊl-madᵊmwazeel halli hallaq sallamt ɛaleeha?*

greeting - 1. *tarḥiib, taʔhiil w-tashiil.* We never expected such a warm greeting. *b-ḥayaatna maa twaqqaɛna heek tarḥiib ḥaarr.* 2. *taḥiyye* pl. *-aat, salaam* pl. *-aat.* He didn't notice my greeting. *maa ntabah la-taḥiiti.* — They sent us greetings from Rome. *baɛatúu-lna taḥiyyaat mən rooma.*

greyhound - *kalb slaaqi* pl. *klaab ᵊslaaqiyye.*

grief - *ḥəzᵊn.* She couldn't conceal her grief. *maa ġədret təxfi ḥəzna.*

**Good grief! *daxiil ɛərdak!*

grill - *məšwaaye* pl. *-aat* and *mašaawi.* Broil the chops on the grill. *ʔəšwi l-kastaleetaat ɛal-məšwaaye.*

to grill - 1. *šawa i* (*šawi//nšawa*). Would you like your lamb chops grilled? *bətḥəbb ᵊl-kastaleetaat tabaɛak məšwiyye?* 2. *qarrar.* They grilled the prisoner for hours. *ḍallu yqarrᵊru l-masžuun saaɛaat ɛan ḥaqa.* 3. *məstaḥabb.* It was a grim decision we had to make. *kaan q̈araar muu məstaḥabb ᵊḍṭarreena nəttəxzo.*

grim - 1. *ɛaabes.* There was a grim look on his face. *kaan wəšžo ɛaabes.*

**He signed the letter with a grim smile. *maḍa l-maktuub w-ɛala wəššo ʔəbtisaamet ɛasᵊm w-taṣmiim.*

to **grimace** - *žaɛlak wəššo.* She grimaced when she saw the food. *žaɛlaket wəšša waqᵊt šaafet ᵊl-ʔakᵊl.*

grimy - *wəṣex, q̈əzer.*

grin - *ḍaḥke.* He had a broad grin on his face. *kaan ɛala wəššo ḍaḥke ɛariiḍa* (or *ḍaḥke waaṣle la-ʔadaano*).

to grin - *šannak.* He grinned from ear to ear. *šannak tašniike mn ᵊl-ʔədᵊn ləl-ʔədᵊn.*

**Grin and bear it! *tqabbála b-rooḥ mərḥa!*

grind - *mašaq̈q̈a* pl. *mašaaq̈q̈.* It was a terrible grind, but we made it. *kaan fii mašaaq̈q̈ faẓiiɛa, laaken məši l-ḥaal bᵊl-ʔaaxiir.*

**Get me a pound of coffee - fine grind. *žəb-li nəṣṣ kiilo bənn - naaɛəm.*

to grind - *ṭaḥan (a ṭaḥᵊn//nṭaḥan).* How do you want me to grind your coffee? *kiif bəddak-yaani ʔəṭḥán-lak ᵊl-qahwe?*

to grind out - *fabrak, bafrak.* He grinds out one novel after another. *bifabrek l-qəṣṣa wara t-taanye.*

to grind one's teeth - *kaskaz ɛala snaano, kazz (ə kazz) ɛala snaano.* She grinds her teeth in her sleep. *bətkazkez ɛala snaana w-hiyye naayme.*

grip - 1. *qabḍa, qabḍet˜ ᵊl-ʔiid, kamše(t˜ ᵊl-ʔiid).* He has a strong grip. *ʔəlo qabḍa qawiyye* or *qabḍet ʔiido qawiyye.* 2. *šanta* pl. *-aat* and *šənat, šantaaye* pl. *-aat* and *šanaati.* Where can I check my grip? *ween buudaɛ šanᵊtti?*

**Since his wife's death he's completely lost his grip. *mən waqᵊt-ma maatet marto thargal tamaam.*

to come to grips with - *ɛaalaž.* We'll have to come to grips with the problem sooner or later.

laazem ᵊnɛaalež ᵊl-məšᵊkle ʔawwalta ʔaw ʔaaxərta.

to **gripe** - *tʔafʔaf, tmalmal, tšakka.* Stop griping about everything! *ḥaaštak ᵊtʔafʔaf ᵊb-kəll šii!*

grippe - *griib.* Our whole family had the grippe. *l-beet kəllo kaan žaayiihon ᵊl-griib* or **kaan ᵊmgarreb.*

grit - *sabaat.* That boy has grit. *hal-walad ɛando sabaat.*

to grit one's teeth - *šadd (ə ə) ɛala snaano.* He gritted his teeth and set to work. *šadd ɛala snaano w-bada yəštéġel.*

groan - *ʔanne* pl. *-aat.* What was that groan for? *leeš hal-ʔanne?*

groans, groaning - *ʔaniin.* We heard his groans all night long. *sməɛna ʔaniino ṭuul ᵊl-leel.*

to groan - *ʔann (ə ʔaniin).* He groaned in his sleep. *ʔann ᵊb-noomo.*

grocer - *sammaan* pl. *-e, baqqaal* pl. *-e* and *-iin.* I got the cheese at the grocer's downstairs. *žəbt ᵊž-žəbne mən ɛand ᵊs-sammaan taḥᵊt.*

groceries - *smaane w-xəḍar.* Will you deliver these groceries to my house? *btaaxə́d-li has-smaane wᵊl-xəḍar ɛal-beet?*

grocery (store) - *baq̈q̈aaliyye* pl. *-aat.*

groove - *təlᵊm* pl. *tlaam.*

grooved - *mtallam.*

to **grope** - *tḥassas.* He groped for the switch in the dark. *tḥassas ɛam ydawwer ɛala məftaaḥ ᵊl-kahraba bᵊl-ɛətme.* — He groped his way to the door. *tḥassas ṭariiqo ləl-baab.*

gross - 1. *krooz* pl. *-aat.* How many dozens are in a gross? *kam dazziine fii bᵊl-krooz?* 2. *faẓiiɛ.* That was a gross mistake. *hayy kaanet ġalṭa faẓiiɛa.* 3. *ʔəžmaali*.* What was your gross income last year? *šuu kaan daxlak ᵊl-ʔəžmaali s-səne l-maaḍye?*

grotto - *mġaara* pl. *-aat.*

grouchy - *mbarṭem, mətnaašef.* Why is he so grouchy? *šəbo hal-qadd ᵊmbarṭem?*

ground - 1. *ʔarḍ* (f.) pl. *ʔaraaḍi.* The ground is still wet. *l-ʔarḍ ləssaata ṭariyye.* — Every inch of ground was stubbornly defended. *ṣaaru daafaɛu b-ɛənᵊd ɛan kəll šəbᵊr mn ᵊl-ʔarḍ.* — How much ground goes with the house? *qaddeeš masaaḥt ᵊl-ʔarḍ halli maɛ ᵊl-beet?* 2. *sabab* pl. *ʔasbaab, daaɛi* pl. *dawaaɛi.* I reject the whole thing on many grounds. *bərfoḍ kəll haš-šii la-ʔasbaab ᵊktiire.* 3. *ʔarḍi*.* Our apartment is on the ground floor. *šaqqətna bᵊt-taabeq ᵊl-ʔarḍi.* 4. *žawfi*.* They had to go down to a depth of a hundred meters before they hit ground water. *nžabaru yənzlu la-ɛəmᵊq miit mətᵊr la-wəṣlu ləl-miyaah ᵊž-žawfiyye.*

**The village was leveled to the ground. *ḍ-ḍeeɛa mmaḥet ɛan bəkret ʔabuuha.*

**He's lost a lot of political ground in recent years. *nəzlet ʔasᵊhmo s-siyaasiyye b-hal-kam səne l-ʔaaxraaniyye.*

grounds - 1. *ḥawaaši* (pl.). The house is very small, but the grounds are beautiful. *l-beet ᵊẓġiir ᵊktiir, laaken ḥawaašti ḥəlwe.* 2. *təḥᵊl.* Throw the grounds into the sink. *kəbb ᵊt-təḥᵊl bᵊl-balluuɛa.* 3. *muužeb.* That's no grounds for divorce. *haada muu muužeb ləṭ-ṭalaaq.*

from the ground up - *mən ʔasaas-* + pron. suff. He changed everything from the ground up. *ġayyar kəll šii mən ʔasaaso.*

to gain ground - *šaaɛ (i šayaɛaan, šyuuɛ).* The new method is rapidly gaining ground. *ṭ-ṭariiqa ž-ždiide ɛam ᵊtšiiɛ ᵊb-sərɛa.*

to hold (or stand) one's ground - *sabat (o sbuut), ṣamad (o ṣmuud).* I can stand my ground in any debate. *bəḥsen ʔəsbot ᵊb-ʔayy ᵊmnaaq̈aše.*

to ground - *waṣal (-yuuṣel waṣᵊl) ᵊl-baared b-.* Did you ground the radio? *waṣalt ᵊl-baared bᵊr-raadyo?*

groundless - *bala ʔasaas.* Her fears are groundless. *maxaawə́fa bala ʔasaas* (or ***maa-la ʔasaas*).

ground meat - *laḥme mafruume.*

group - 1. *fiʔa* pl. *-aat.* The class was divided into three groups. *ṣ-ṣaff ᵊmqassam la-tlatt fiʔaat.* 2. *žamaaɛa* pl. *-aat.* A group of people had gathered at the corner. *fii žamaaɛa mn ᵊn-naas ᵊḥtašadu ɛas-suuke.*

to group - *žammaɛ ... fiʔaat.* Group the men according to age. *žammeɛ ᵊr-ržaal fiʔaat ḥasab ʔaɛmaaron.*

to **grow** - 1. *kəber (a kəbᵊr).* Your boy has certainly grown a lot. *waḷḷa ʔəbnak kəber ᵊmniiḥ.* — She grows on you as you get to know her. *kəll-ma btaɛrəfha ʔaktar kəll-ma btəkbar ᵊb-ɛeenak.*

2. *zdaad, dzaayad, kəber.* The crowd grew rapidly. *l-ḥašd ᵊzdaad ᵊb-sərᶜa.* — The population grows at a fantastic rate. *ᶜadad ᵊs-səkkaan ᶜam yədzaayad ᵊb-sərᶜa mahuule.* 3. *nama (a nmuww), nabat (o ə).* Grass has begun to grow between the rails. *fii ḥašiiš ᶜam yənma been ᵊl-qəḍbaan ᵊl-ḥadiidiyye.* 4. *nama, kəber.* My, that tree behind the house is growing fast! *yaa ᵓaḷḷa qaddeeš haš-šažara wara l-beet ᶜam tənma!* 5. *ṣaar (i ṣayaraan).* The storm grew worse and worse. *l-ᶜaaṣfe ṣaaret ᵓafẓaᶜ w-ᵓafẓaᶜ.* 6. *zaraᶜ (a zarᵊᶜ//nzaraᶜ).* They grow a lot of grain in this area. *byəzraᶜu ḥbuub ᵊktiir ᵊb-hal-qərne.* 7. *rabba.* I grow roses. *brabbi wruud.* 8. *rabba, raxa (i raxi).* How long have you been growing a beard? *qaddeeš ṣar-lak ᶜam ᵊtrabbi daqᵊn?*

**She's grown old. *xatyaret.*

to grow away – *tbaaᶜad.* He has grown away from his family. *tbaaᶜad ᶜan ᶜeelto.*

to grow up – *kəber (a kəbᵊr).* The children are growing up fast. *l-ᵊwlaad ᶜam yəkbaru b-sərᶜa.* — We grew up together. *kbərna sawa.*

to **growl** – *hamhar.* The dog growled when he heard the noise. *l-kalb hamhar lamma səmeᶜ ᵊl-ḥəss.*

grown – *baaleġ raašed.* The girl must be a grown woman by now. *l-bənᵊt laazem ᵊtkuun hallaq ṣaaret baalġa raašde.*

grown-up – 1. *ṣabiyye* pl. *ṣabaaya.* She has a grown-up daughter. *ᶜanda bənt ṣabiyye.* 2. *šabb* pl. *šabaab.* She has a grown-up son. *ᶜanda ṣabi šabb.* 3. *šabaab w-ṣabaaya* (pl.). They have grown-up children. *ᶜandon ᵊwlaad šabaab w-ṣabaaya.* — Their children are already grown up. *wlaadon ṣaaru šabaab w-ṣabaaya.*

grownup – *kbiir* pl. *kbaar.* Children should keep quiet when grownups are talking. *l-ᵊwlaad laazem yəsᵊktu lamma l-ᵊkbaar byəḥku.*

growth – 1. *ᵓəzdiyaad, n(u)muww.* There has been a steady growth in the national product during the last ten years. *ṣaar fii ᵓəzdiyaad muṭṭarid bᵊl-maḥṣuul ᵊl-waṭani bᵊl-ᶜašr ᵊsniin ᵊl-ᵓaaxraaniyye.* 2. *zaayde, numuww, nutuuᵓ.* That growth on your finger will have to be removed. *haz-zaayde b-ᵓəṣbaᶜtak bəddo qaṭᵊᶜ.*

**He has a two days' growth of beard. *ṣar-lo yoomeen maa qaṣš daqno.*

grudge – *ḍaġiine.* I can't understand his grudge against her. *maa-li fahmaan leeš haḍ-ḍaġiine huwwe ḥaamə́la ᶜaleeha.*

to hold (or **bear**) **a grudge** – *tḥaamal.* I don't hold a grudge against him. *ᵓana maa bətḥaamal ᶜalée.*

grudgingly – *ġaṣban ᶜanno.* She gave in grudgingly. *sallamet ġaṣban ᶜanha.*

gruff – *ġaliiẓ.* He has a gruff voice. *ṣooṭo ġaliiẓ.*

to **grumble** – *dzammar, tnatwar, džaafaṣ.* He grumbles each time he's asked to help. *byədzammar kəll-ma ḥada byəṭlob mənno msaaᶜade.*

guarantee – *kafaale* pl. *-aat, ḍamaane* pl. *-aat.* You get a five-year guarantee on this watch. *btaaxod kafaale xams ᵊsniin la-has-saaᶜa.* — What guarantee do I have that he'll pay? *šuu d-ḍamaane ᵓəli ᵓənno laḥa yədfaᶜ?* or ***šuu byəḍmán-li ᵓənno laḥa yədfaᶜ?*

to guarantee – 1. *ḍəmen (a ḍamaan//nḍaman), kəfel (a kafaale//nkafal).* I can't guarantee that. *maa fiini ᵓəḍman haš-šii.* 2. *ᵓakkad.* I guarantee that you'll like that movie. *bᵓakkə́d-lak ᵓənnak bəddak ᵊtḥəbb ᵊl-fəlᵊm.*

guard – *ḥaares* pl. *ḥərraas,* coll. *ḥaras.* The guard didn't let me pass. *l-ḥaares maa xallaani ᵓəmroq.* — The guard is changed at two o'clock. *l-ḥaras byətġayyar ᵊs-saaᶜa tənteen.*

to be on (one's) guard – *ᵓaxad ḥazaro, tḥazzar.* You have to be on your guard with her. *laazem taaxod ḥazarak mənha.*

to put someone on his guard – *žaᶜal (a žaᶜᵊl) ḥada yətḥazzar.* That remark of his immediately put me on my guard. *hal-ᵊmlaaḥaẓa tabaᶜo b-daqiiqə́ta žaᶜlətni ᵓətḥazzar.*

to stand guard – *waqqaf ḥaares, qaam (u qyaam) bᵊl-ᵊḥraase.* Who's going to stand guard? *miin laḥa ywaqqef ḥaares?*

to guard – 1. *ḥaras (o ḥraase//nḥaras).* The building is guarded day and night. *l-binaaye maḥruuse leel w-ᵊnhaar.* 2. *ḥtaras.* You can't guard against everything. *maa fii l-waaḥed yəḥtə́res mən kəll šii.*

**He gave me a guarded answer. *kaan ḥəzer ᵊb-žawaabo.*

guardian – *waṣi* pl. *ᵓawṣiya.* He was appointed guardian of his nephew. *ᶜayyanúu waṣi ᶜala ᵓebᵊn ᵓaxúu.*

guardianship – *wiṣaaye.*

guerrilla warfare – *ḥarb˜ ᵊl-ᶜiṣaabaat.*

guess – *ḥəzᵊr* pl. *ḥzuura.* It was a good guess, though. *maᶜ zaalek kaan ḥəzr ᵊmniiḥ.* — It's only a guess. *muu ᵓaktar mən ḥəzᵊr.*

**I'll give you three guesses. *fiik təḥzer ᵓawwale w-taanye w-taalte.*

to guess – 1. *ḥazar (e/o ḥəzᵊr//nḥazar).* That isn't hard to guess. *haada muu ṣaᶜb ᵊl-waaḥed yəḥᵊzro.* 2. *ftakar b-.* Who would have guessed that! *miin kaan byəftə́ker ᵊb-heek šii!* 3. *ẓann (ə ẓann), ftakar, ᶜtaqad.* I guess he's sick. *bẓənno ḍᶜiif.*

guest – *ḍeef* pl. *ḍyuuf.* He's a welcome guest. *huwwe ḍeef ᵓahla w-sahla fii.* — I was a guest at his house. *kənᵊt ḍeef ᵊb-beeto.*

guidance – 1. *ᵓəršaad.* 2. (divine) *huda.*

guide – 1. *daliil* pl. *ᵓadəlla.* We took a guide. *ᵓaxadna daliil.* 2. *daliil* pl. *dalaayel.* All the theaters are listed in the guide. *kəll duur ᵊl-lahu mawžuude bᵊd-daliil.*

to guide – 1. *dall (ə ə//ndall).* Can you guide us there? *fiik ᵊddəllna la-hniik?* 2. *ᵓaršad.* He needs someone to guide him in his studies. *laazmo waaḥed yərᵊšdo b-diraasto.*

guidebook – *daliil* pl. *dalaayel.*

guidepost – *ᶜalaamet˜* (pl. *-aat˜*) *ṭariiq.*

guillotine – *maqṣale* pl. *maqaaṣel.*

guilt – *zamb* pl. *znuub.* Guilt is written all over his face. *z-zamb ẓaaher ᶜala wəššo tamaam.*

guilty – *məzneb.* Do you think he's guilty? *btəᶜtə́qed huwwe məzneb?*

**I have a guilty conscience. *ḍamiiri biᵓannəbni.*

guitar – *giitaar* pl. *-aat.*

gulf – 1. *xaliiž* pl. *xəlžaan.* The Persian Gulf. *l-xaliiž ᵊl-faarsi.* 2. *huwwe* pl. *-aat.* That only widened the gulf which separates them. *haš-šii bass wassaᶜ ᵊl-huwwe halli beenaaton.*

gull – *lawras˜* (pl. *lawaares˜*) *baḥᵊr.*

gum – 1. *ləsse.* My gum is sore here. *ləssti ᶜam tuužaᶜni hoon.* — My gums are very sensitive. *ləssti ḥassaase ktiir.* 2. *ṣamᵊġ.* Put a little gum on the flap of the envelope. *ḥəṭṭ šwayyet ṣamᵊġ ᶜala qalbet ᵊẓ-ẓarᵊf.*

chewing gum – *məstke, ᶜəlke.*

to gum – *ṣammaġ.* Did you gum the labels? *ṣammaġt ᵊl-ᵓeetikeetaat?*

gun – 1. *baaruude* pl. *bawariid.* Just lean the gun against the table. *bass waqqef ᵊl-baaruude ᶜala žamb ᵊṭ-ṭaawle.* 2. *farᵊd* pl. *fruude.* He always carries a gun in his pocket. *daayman byəḥmel fard ᵊb-žeebto.* 3. *madfaᶜ* pl. *madaafeᶜ.* The big guns could be heard for miles. *l-madaafeᶜ ᵊt-tqiile nsamᶜet mən ᵓamyaal w-ᵓamyaal.* — The ship fired a salute of twenty-one guns. *s-safiine ḍarbet waaḥed w-ᶜəšriin madfaᶜ taḥiyye.*

**Don't jump the gun! *laa tətsarraᶜ!*

**Stick to your guns! *xalliik saabet! laa tətraažaᶜ!*

**I wonder what he's up to now, the son of a gun. *yaa-tara šuu ṭaaleᶜ maᶜo hallaq hal-ᵓəbn ᵊl-kalb.*

**He's (out) gunning for you. *ḥaaṭeṭ kᶜaaro w-ᵊkᶜaarak* or *muu ḥaalel ᶜannak.*

gunpowder – *baaruud.*

gunsmith – *qərdaḥi* pl. *-iyye.*

to **gush** – *ddaffaq.* Blood was gushing from the torn artery. *d-damm kaan ᶜam yəddaffaq mən ᵊš-šəryaan ᵊl-mətmazzeq.*

gutter – 1. *ṭaaruuq* pl. *ṭawariiq.* You're going to end up in the gutter. *bəddak ᵊtṣaffi bᵊṭ-ṭawariiq.* 2. *məzraab* pl. *mazariib.* The gutters on our house need repairing. *l-mazariib tabaᶜ beetna bəddon taṣliiḥ.*

guttural – *ḥarf ḥalqi* pl. *ḥruuf ḥalqiyye.* It's very hard for an English speaker to pronounce the Arabic gutturals. *ṣaᶜb ᵊktiir ᶜala yalli byəḥku ᵓəngliizi lafᵊẓ l-ᵊḥruuf ᵊl-ḥalqiyye l-ᶜarabiyye.*

guy – *zalame* pl. *zəlᵊm.* He's a nice guy. *huwwe zalame laṭiif.*

gym – 1. *malᶜab šətwi* pl. *malaaᶜeb šətwiyye.* Our school has a large gym. *b-madrasətna fii malᶜab šətwi kbiir.* 2. *(dars˜) riyaaḍa.* We have gym three times a week. *fii ᶜanna dars riyaaḍa tlətt marraat bᵊž-žəmᶜa.*

gymnasium – *malᶜab šətwi* pl. *malaaᶜeb šətwiyye.*

gynecologist – *ṭabiib˜* (pl. *ᵓaṭəbba˜*) *ᵓamraaḍ nisaaᵓiyye.*

gypsum – *žabṣiin.*

gypsy - 1. *nawari* coll. pl. *nawar*. That man is a gypsy. *haz-zalame nawari*. 2. *nawariyye* pl. *-aat*, coll. pl. *nawar*. That woman is a gypsy. *hal-mara nawariyye*.

H

habit - *ɛaade* pl. *-aat*. That's a bad habit. *hayy ɛaade radiyye*. — I'm in the habit of sleeping late. *ʔana ɛaadti naam (la-)ḍahwe* or ***ʔana məɛtaad naam (la-)ḍahwe*. — I'm trying to break myself of the habit of smoking. *ɛam ʔaɛmel žahdi baṭṭel ɛaadet ət-tadxiin maɛi*.
to get in(to) the habit of - *ɛtaad ɛala, tɛawwad ɛala*. I got into the habit of smoking at college. *ɛtədt ɛat-tadxiin bəž-žaamɛa*.
habitat - *mawṭen* pl. *mawaaṭen*.
to **hack** - *qaṭṭaɛ*. The rabble literally hacked the corpse to pieces. *r-ruɛaaɛ qaṭṭaɛu ž-žəsse ɛan haqa šəqaf šəqaf*.
hackneyed - *məbtdzal*. Her style abounds in hackneyed phrases. *ʔəsluuba malaan ɛibaaraat məbtazale*.
haggard - *msaḥnek*. His face looks old and haggard. *wəššo mbayyen ɛalée mahruum w-əmsaḥnek*.
The **Hague** - *laahaay*.
to **haggle** - *faaṣal, saawam*. We had to haggle for hours until the dealer came down with the price. *nžabarna nfaaṣel saaɛaat ḥatta t-taažer nəzel šwayye bəs-səɛər*.
hail - *barad, ḥabb˜ ɛaziiz*. That's not rain, that's hail. *haada muu maṭar, hada barad*. — The hail almost destroyed the entire crop. *ḥabb əl-ɛaziiz kaan laḥa yətlef əl-muusem kəllo*.
to hail - *nəzel (e nzuul) barad* or *ḥabb˜ ɛaziiz*. It's hailing. *naazel barad*.
**Let's stay here until it stops hailing. *xalliina nəbqa hoon ḥatta yənqəṭeɛ ḥabb əl-ɛaziiz*.
to **hail** - 1. *ɛayyaṭ la-, ṣarax (a ə) la-, nadah (a ə) la-*. The doorman hailed a passing cab. *l-bawwaab ɛayyaṭ la-taksi maareq*. 2. *ʔasna ɛala*. The critics hailed it as the best play of the year. *n-nuqqaad ʔasnu ɛaleeha ʔənna ʔaḥsan masraḥiyye has-səne*. 3. *hataf (o htaaf) la-*. Crowds hail him everywhere. *ž-žamahiir byəhətfu-lo ween-ma biruuḥ*.
**His parents hail from California. *ʔahlo ʔaṣlo mən kalifoornya*.
hailstone - *ḥabbet˜ (pl. -aat˜) ɛaziiz, barade* pl. *-aat*.
hair - 1. *šaɛər*. What color is her hair? *šuu loon šaɛra?* — It takes her an hour to do her hair. *btaaxóda saaɛa la-tsaawi šaɛra*. — The tents are made of goat's hair. *l-xiyam msaawaaye mən šaɛər məɛze*. 2. *šaɛra* pl. *-aat*. There's a hair in the soup. *fii šaɛra bəš-šooraba*. — The stone missed me by a hair. *maa bəqi beeni w-been əl-ḥažar ʔəlla šaɛra*. — I missed the streetcar by a hair. *maa bəqi beeni w-been ət-trammaay ʔəlla šaɛra*. 3. *wabar*. Where did you buy this pretty camel's hair coat? *mneen əštareet hal-kabbuut əl-ḥəlu wabar əž-žamal?*
**They're always getting into each other's hair. *daayman binattfu šuwaš baɛdon*.
**That's splitting hairs! *hayy mmaaḥake bala ṭaɛme!*
hairbrush - *fəršaayet˜* (pl. *-aat˜* and *faraaši˜*) *šaɛər*.
haircut - *qaṣṣa* pl. *-aat, qaṣṣet˜ šaɛr*. Where'd you get that funny haircut? *mneen žəbt hal-qaṣṣa l-ġariibe?* — Haircut, please. *mən faḍlak qaṣṣet šaɛər*.
to get a haircut - *qaṣṣ (ə qaṣṣa) šaɛro*. I have to get a haircut. *laazəmni qaṣṣet šaɛər*. — When did you get your last haircut? *ʔeemta ʔaaxer marra qaṣṣeet fiiha šaɛrak?*
hair dresser - *ḥallaaq˜* (pl. *-iin˜*) *ləs-sayyidaat*.
hairpin - *malqaṭ˜* (pl. *malaaqeṭ˜*) *šaɛər*.
hair-raising: That was a hair-raising experience. *hayy kaanet ḥaadse bətwaqqef šaɛr ər-raas*. — He told us a hair-raising story. *hakáa-lna qəṣṣa bətwaqqef šaɛr ər-raas*.
hairsplitting - *mmaaḥake*.
half - *nəṣṣ* pl. *nṣaaṣ*. I'll give him half of my share. *baɛṭii nəṣṣ ḥəṣṣti*. — Give me half a kilo of butter. *ɛaṭiini nəṣṣ kiilo zəbde*. — Shall I cut the cake in half? *ʔəqṭaɛ əl-gaato bən-nəṣṣ (or nəṣṣeen)?* — I'll be back in half an hour. *bəržaɛ baɛəd nəṣṣ saaɛa*. — Mix the flour and the sugar half and half.. *xlooṭ əṭ-ṭhiin wəs-səkkar nəṣṣ əb-nəṣṣ*. — Give me one-and-a-half yards of this material. *ɛaṭiini yard w-nəṣṣ mən hal-əqmaaš*. — We'll be there at half past eight. *mənkuun əhniik əs-saaɛa tmaane w-nəṣṣ*. — I got it for half price at a sale. *štareeta b-nəṣṣ səɛər b-šii ʔokazyoon*. — Children pay half price on the bus. *l-əwlaad byədfaɛu nəṣṣ taɛriife bəl-baaṣ*. — They put him on half pay during his sick leave. *ḥaṭṭúu ɛala nəṣṣ maɛaaš məddet ʔižaazto l-maraḍiyye*. — Will you go halves with me? *bətruuḥ maɛi bən-nəṣṣ?* or ***bətruuḥ maɛi mnaaṣafe?* — This job is only half done. *haš-šaġle bass ṣaar la-nəṣṣa*. — The meat is only half done. *l-laḥme bass əstawet nəṣṣ ʔəstíwa*.
**I've been listening with only half an ear. *kənt ɛam ʔəsmaɛ ʔədən hoon w-ʔədn əhniik*.
**I've half a mind to go tomorrow. *ʔana mətxooṭer ruuḥ bəkra*.
**That isn't half bad. *haada muu baṭṭal ʔabadan*.
half-hour - *nəṣṣ˜ saaɛa*. I waited for him a good half-hour. *stanneeto nəṣṣ saaɛa w-ʔabaḥḥ*. — He held a half-hour conference at his office. *ɛaqad ʔəžtimaaɛ nəṣṣ saaɛa b-maktabo*.
halfhearted - *faater*. Halfhearted measures won't help at all. *t-tadabiir əl-faatre maa btənfaɛ ʔabadan*.
at **halfmast** - *mnakkas*. All flags are at halfmast today. *kəll əl-ʔaɛlaam əmnakkase l-yoom*.
halfway - *b-nəṣṣ˜ əṭ-ṭariiq*. We ran out of gas halfway to town. *nqaṭaɛna mn əl-banziin əb-nəṣṣ əṭ-ṭariiq* (or *əb-nəṣṣ ṭariiqna*) *ləl-balad*.
**Halfway measures will not suffice. *ʔanṣaaf əl-ḥuluul maa byəmši ḥaala*.
**I'm willing to meet him halfway. *məstɛədd ʔəqsem əl-beedar beeni w-beeno bən-nəṣṣ*.
halitosis - *riiḥ˜ ət-təmm*.
hall - 1. *kooridoor* pl. *-aat, mamarr* pl. *-aat, mamša* pl. *mamaaši*. He lives down the other end of the hall. *saaken əb-ʔaaxer əl-kooridoor*. 2. *madxal* pl. *madaaxel*. We need a new rug for our front hall. *laazəmna səžžaade ždiide ləl-madxal ər-raʔiisi*. 3. *qaaɛa* pl. *-aat*. The hall seats more than 500 people. *l-qaaɛa btəsaɛ ʔaktar mən xaməs miit zalame*.
city hall - *binaayet˜* (pl. *-aat˜*) *əl-baladiyye*, (of Damascus) *binaayet l-əmḥaafaẓa*. His office is in the City Hall. *maktabo b-binaayet əl-baladiyye*.
hallstand - *qənṣliyye* pl. *-aat*.
hallucination - *halwase* pl. *-aat*.
hallway - *kooridoor* pl. *-aat, mamarr* pl. *-aat*.
halo - *haale* pl. *-aat*.
halting - *mətqaṭṭeɛ*. He spoke in a halting voice. *ḥaka b-ṣooṭ mətqaṭṭeɛ*.
ham - *žamboon*. Would you like some ham for breakfast? *bətḥəbb žamboon maɛ kasr əṣ-ṣəfra?*
Hama - *ḥama*.
Hamitic - *ḥaami**.
hammer - 1. *šaakuuš* pl. *šawakiiš*. Please hand me the hammer. *mən faḍlak naawəlni š-šaakuuš*. 2. *diik* pl. *dyaak*. Watch out, the hammer of the pistol is cocked. *ntəbeh əd-diik tabaɛ əl-fard taḥt əḍ-ḍarb*.
to hammer - *daqdaq*. Our neighbor has been hammering all day long. *žaarna ṣar-lo ɛam ydaqdeq ṭuul ən-nhaar*.
**The rules have been hammered into me. *ɛallamuuni l-qawaaɛed tarəs*.
to hammer in - *daqq (ə daqq//ndaqq)*. He can't even hammer in a nail. *maa byəṭlaɛ ḥatta b-ʔiido ydəqq bəsmaar*.
hand - 1. *ʔiid* (f.) dual *ʔiidteen* pl. *ʔiideen* and *ʔayaadi* (my hands *ʔiidiyyi*, your hands *ʔiideek, ʔiideeki*, etc.). Where can I wash my hands?

ween fiini ġassel ʔiidiyyi? (as a euphemism:) *ween ᵊt-twaleet?* — He's very clever with his hands. *huwwe ktiir šaaṭer b-ᵊʔəstəƐmaal ʔiidée.* — Hands off! *šhaab ʔiideek!* — Hands up! *rfaaƐ ʔiideek!* — This job has to be done by hand. *haš-šaġle laazem tənƐəmel bᵊl-ʔiid.* — He must have had a hand in that. *laazem ykuun kan-lo ʔiid* or ***yad (or **ʔəṣbaƐ) ᵊb-haš-šaġle.* — I've got a lot of work on my hands. *fii šəġl ᵊktiir been ʔiidiyyi* or ***ʔana mašġuul ᵊktiir hallaq.* — They worked together hand in glove. *štaġalu ʔiid ᵊb-ʔiid.* 2. *yad* pl. *ʔayaadi.* We're all in the hands of God. *kəllna been ʔayaadi l-mawla.* 3. *Ɛaqrab* pl. *Ɛaqaareb.* The minute hand on my watch is broken. *Ɛaqrab ᵊd-daqaayeq tabaƐ saaƐti maksuur.* 4. *waraq* (coll. pl.). I had a very poor hand in the last game. *kaan maƐi waraq malƐuun l-fatte l-maadye.*

**I wash my hands of it. *maa Ɛaad ʔəli Ɛlaaqa b-haš-šaġle.*

**Keep your hands off that! *xalliik ᵊbƐiid Ɛan haš-šaġle!*

**The business has changed hands. *t-tižaara tġayyar mallaakiina.*

**He has the situation well in hand. *mṣayṭer Ɛal-mawqef.*

**From now on I'll take things into my own hands again. *mən hallaq w-raayeḥ ḥa-ʔərƐaƐ ʔana dabber ᵊl-ʔumuur.*

**I can't lay my hands on it right now. *maa fiini ḥadded ᵊb-Ɛəlle hallaq.*

**Can you take these tickets off my hands? *fiik ᵊtxalləṣni mən hat-tazaaker?*

**His students are getting out of hand. *talamiizo maa Ɛaadu yənḍabbu.*

**The matter is out of my hands. *maa Ɛaad fii ʔəli Ɛlaaqa bᵊl-qəṣṣa.*

**I don't want to show my hand too soon. *maa bəddi ʔəkšaf Ɛan xəṭaṭi qabl l-ᵊlzuum.*

**He's an old hand in the business. *huwwe Ɛatiiq bᵊl-maṣlaḥa.*

at first hand - *mən maṣdaro, mən manbaƐo, mən ʔasaaso.* I got this information at first hand. *ḥṣəlt Ɛala hal-maƐluumaat mən maṣdára.*

on hand - *mawžuud.* We haven't that size on hand. *muu mawžuud Ɛanna hal-ᵊqyaas.* — He's always on hand when I want him. *huwwe daayman mawžuud waqᵊt bəḥtaažo.*

on the one hand ... on the other hand - *mən žiha ... w-mən žiha (taanye).* On the one hand he wants it finished, on the other hand he doesn't give us the material. *mən žiha bəddo-yáaha təxloṣ w-mən žiha taanye maa byaƐṭiina l-mawaadd.*

to give a hand - *saaƐad, Ɛaawan.* Can you give me a hand with this box? *fiik ᵊtsaaƐədni b-has-sanduuq?*

to lend a hand - *saaƐad, Ɛaawan.* Would you lend me a hand? *məmken tsaaƐədni?*

to shake hands - 1. *tṣaafaḥ.* They shook hands. *tṣaafaḥu.* 2. *ṣaafaḥ.* The host shook hands with each guest. *ṣaaḥeb ᵊd-daƐwa ṣaafaḥ ᵊl-madƐuwwiin waaḥed waaḥed.*

to shake someone's hand - *ṣaafaḥ ḥada.* She shook my hand. *ṣaafaḥətni.*

to hand - *naawal.* Will you hand me that pencil? *məmken tnaawəlni hal-qalam?*

to hand back - *ražžaƐ.* Hand it back to me, will you? *ražžəƐ-li-yáaha baḷḷa.*

to hand in - *qaddam.* I'm going to hand in my application tomorrow. *ḥa-qaddem ᵊl-ʔəstədƐa tabaƐi bəkra.*

to hand out - *wazzaƐ, farraq.* Hand these tickets out! *wazzeƐ hat-tazaaker!*

to hand over - 1. *naawal.* Would you hand that book over, please? *məmken ᵊtnaawəlni hal-ᵊktaab mən faḍlak?* 2. *sallam.* They made us hand over all our money. *žabaruuna nsallem kəll maṣariina.*

handbag - *šanta* pl. *-aat, šantaaye* pl. *šanaati.*

handbook - *məxtáṣar* pl. *-aat.*

hand brake - *fraam˜* (pl. *-aat˜*) *ʔiid.*

handcuff - *kalabša* pl. *-aat.* Here every policeman carries a pair of handcuffs with him. *kəll booliis hoon ḥaamel maƐo kalabša.*

to handcuff - *kalbaš.* They handcuffed the prisoners. *kalbašu l-maḥabiis.*

hand drill - *madqab* pl. *madaaqeb.*

handful - *kamše* pl. *-aat.* He took a handful of nuts. *ʔaxad kamšet žooz.*

**Only a handful of people showed up. *maa ʔəža ʔəlla šwayyet naas.*

hand grenade - *ġəmble* (pl. *ġanaabel*) *yadawiyye, rəmmaane* pl. *-aat.*

to **handicap** - *Ɛarqal//tƐarqal, labbak//tlabbak.* He's been handicapped by poor eyesight all his life. *ṭuul Ɛəmro kaan ᵊmƐarqal ᵊb-ḍəƐᵊf naẓaro.*

handkerchief - *maḥrame* pl. *maḥaarem.*

handle - 1. *maske* pl. *-aat.* My suitcase needs a new handle. *šantaayet ʔawaaƐiyyi laazə́ma maske ždiide.* 2. *ʔədᵊn* (f.) pl. *ʔaadaan, maske* pl. *-aat.* The handle of this cup is broken off. *ʔədᵊn hal-fənžaan maksuura.*

**At the slightest occasion he flies off the handle. *la-ʔaqalla šaġle bižənn ᵊžnaano.*

to handle - 1. *Ɛaamal.* He knows how to handle people. *byaƐref kiif yƐaamel ᵊn-naas.* -- You have to handle him with kid gloves. *laazem ᵊtƐaamlo mətl ᵊṣ-ṣiini.* 2. *laƐwaṣ b-, baƐwaṣ b-.* Look at it all you want, but don't handle it. *ṭṭallaƐ Ɛaleeha qadd-ma bəddak bass laa tlaƐweṣ fiiha.* 3. *tƐaamal b-.* We don't handle that brand. *maa mnətƐaamal ᵊb-hal-marka.* 4. *qaam (u qyaam) b-.* I simply can't handle all the work by myself. *b-kəll basaaṭa maa fiini quum bᵊš-šəġᵊl kəllo waḥdi b-raasi.* 5. *staƐmal.* Can you handle a gun? *fiik təstaƐmel farᵊd?* -- Our washing machine is hard to handle. *ġassaalətna ṣaƐᵊb ʔəstəƐmaala.*

**This car is easy to handle. *has-sayyaara hayyne swaaqə́ta.*

**It's glass! Handle it with care! *haada qzaaz! bəddo Ɛnaaye bᵊl-ḥamᵊl!*

**I can't handle him any more. *maa Ɛaad fiini Ɛalée.*

handle bar(s) - *kidoon* pl. *-aat.*

handmade - *šəġᵊl˜ ʔiid* (invar.). I bought a beautiful handmade Japanese fan. *štareet marwaḥa yaabaaniyye šəġᵊl ʔiid ᵊktiir ḥalwe.*

handmill - *žaaruuše* pl. *žawariiš.*

handrail - *darabziin* pl. *-aat.*

handsome - 1. *ḥalu.* He's a handsome man. *huwwe rəžžaal ḥalu.* 2. *məḥtáram.* That's a handsome sum of money. *haada mablaġ məḥtáram.*

handwriting - *xaṭṭ.* His handwriting is illegible. *xaṭṭo maa byənqára.*

handy - 1. *hayyen ᵊl-ʔəstəƐmaal, sahl ᵊl-ʔəstəƐmaal.* This can opener is very handy. *hal-fattaaḥa ktiir hayyen ʔəstəƐmaala.* 2. *taḥt ʔiid-* + pron. suff. Have you got a pencil handy? *fii taḥt ʔiidak qalam?* or ***waaṣle ʔiidak qalam?*

**He's a handy fellow around the house. *bifəšš ᵊl-qalb bᵊl-beet.*

to come in handy - 1. *ʔəža b-waqto.* The extra money comes in very handy. *l-maṣaari z-zaayde žaaye b-waqta.* 2. *faad (i ʔifaade).* Typing will come in handy to you some day. *l-ᵊṭbaaƐa Ɛal-ʔaale l-kaatbe ləssa byəži yoom bətfiidak.*

to **hang** - 1. *šanaq (o šanᵊq//nšanaq).* They hanged him yesterday. *šanaqúu mbaareḥ.* 2. *Ɛallaq//tƐallaq.* Can't you hang the picture a little higher? *maa fiik ᵊtƐalleq ᵊṣ-ṣuura ʔaƐla b-šwayye?* -- Where can I hang my coat? *ween Ɛalleq kabbuudi?* -- The picture has hung here for quite a while. *ṣ-ṣuura ṣar-la mədde mƐallaqa hoon.* -- Is that your hat hanging there? *hayy bərneeṭṭak yalli mƐallaqa hniik?* -- His life hung by a thread. *ḥayaato kaanet ᵊmƐallaqa Ɛala šaƐra.* 3. *dandal//ddandal.* Why are you hanging your head? *leeš ᵊmdandel raasak?*

**Hang it all, I've mislaid my glasses again. *yəfḍaḥ ḥariimak, hayy kamaan maa baƐref ween ḥaṭṭeet kəzᵊlki.*

**I don't give a hang any more. *maa Ɛaadet ᵊtƐalleq Ɛala rəžli.*

**Now I'm getting the hang of it. *hallaq Ɛam ʔəbda ləmm ᵊb-haš-šaġle.*

to hang around - *tsakkaƐ b-.* He's always hanging around the tavern. *daayman byətsakkaƐ bᵊl-baar.* -- He's been hanging around the house for a week already. *ṣar-lo mətsakkeƐ žəmƐa bᵊl-beet.*

to hang on (to) - 1. *tƐamšaq (b-), tmassak (b-).* I hung on as tight as I could. *tƐamšaqᵊt qadd-ma kaan fiyyi.* 2. *ḥtafaẓ (b-), tmassak (b-), tƐamšaq (b-).* I'll hang on to the stock until it goes up again. *laḥa ʔəḥtə́feẓ bᵊl-ʔashom la-təṭlaƐ taani marra.* 3. *masak (e mask) (b-).* Hang on to my hat for a minute, will you? *msək-li b-bərneeṭṭi šii daqiiqa ʔiza bəddak.* 4. *xabba, ḥtafaẓ.* Hang on to this money for me. *xabbi-li hal-maṣaari maƐak.*

to hang out - 1. *našar (o našᵊr//ntašar).* Did you hang the wash out? *našart ᵊl-ġasiil?* 2. *ddandal.* Do you always have to hang out of that window? *laazem daayman təddandal mən ɛaš-šəbbaak?* **3.** *lafa (i lafi).* That's where he usually hangs out. *hayy ᵊl-qərne yalli ɛaadatan byəlfii-la.*

to hang up - 1. *ɛallaq//tɛallaq.* Hang up your hat and coat. *ɛalleq bərneṭṭak w-kabbuudak.* 2. *sakkar ᵊt-talifoon.* He got angry and hung up (on me). *zəɛel w-sakkar ᵊt-talifoon (ɛaliyyi).*

hangar - *hangaar* pl. *-aat.*

hanger - *ɛəlleeqa* pl. *-aat, taɛliiqa* pl. *-aat.* Put your coat on a hanger. *ɛalleq manṭook ᵊb-ɛəlleeqa.*

hangman - *žallaad* pl. *-iin* and *-e.*

hangnail - *daaḥuus, dooḥaas.*

to **happen** - **1.** *ṣaar (i ə), ḥadas (o ḥduus), ḥaṣal (a ḥṣuul), waqaɛ (-yuuqaɛ* and *-yəqaɛ wquuɛ).* When did that happen? *ʔeemta haš-šii ṣaar?* -- What happened to you? *šuu ṣar-lak?* -- Such things do happen. *heek ʔašya btəḥdos.* -- What happened to the typewriter? Did someone use it? *šuu ṣaar bᵊl-ʔaale l-kaatbe? fii ḥada staɛmála?* -- What happened to my typewriter? Did someone take it? *šuu ṣaar bᵊl-ʔaale l-kaatbe tabaɛi? fii ḥada ʔaxáda?* **2.** *ṣadaf* (invar.), *ḥakam* (invar.). I don't happen to agree with you. *ṣadaf ʔənno maa-li məttə́feq maɛak.* -- She happened to be present when he said that. *ṣadaf ʔənno kaanet ḥaadra lamma qaal haš-ši.* -- How did he happen to get the job? *kiif ḥakam w-ʔaxad haš-šaġle?* -- How did you happen to think of that? *kiif ḥakam w-ᵊftakart ᵊb-haš-šii?*

happiness - *saɛaade.* I wish you all the happiness in the world. *bətmannǻa-lak kəll ᵊs-saɛaade.*

happy - **1.** *saɛiid* pl. *-iin* and *səɛada.* That was his happiest day. *haada kaan ʔasɛad yoom ᵊb-ḥayaato.* 2. *mabṣuuṭ, məṛtaaḥ.* I don't feel at all happy about it. *maa-li mabṣuuṭ ʔabadan ᵊb-haš-šaġle.* -- He's not very happy in his new job. *maa-lo məṛtaaḥ ᵊb-šaġᵊlto ž-ždiide.*

**Happy New Year! *kəll səne* (or *kəll ɛaam*) *w-ʔənte saalem;* (answer: *w-ʔənte b-xeer).*

**Happy birthday! *kəll səne* (or *kəll ɛaam*) *w-ʔənte saalem;* (answer: *w-ʔənte b-xeer).*

harbor - *miina* pl. *mawaani, marfaʔ* pl. *maraafeʔ.*

hard - **1.** *qaasi.* I can't sleep on a hard mattress. *maa bəqder naam ɛala farše qaasye.* -- His death was a hard blow to us. *mooto kaan ḍarbe qaasye ɛaleena.* -- He's a hard man. *huwwe rəžžaal qaasi.* 2. *yaabes.* The bread is hard as a rock. *l-xəbᵊz yaabes mətl ᵊṣ-ṣaxᵊr.* **3.** *ṣaɛᵊb.* Those were hard times. *kaanet ʔiyyaam ṣaɛbe.* -- It's hard for me to climb stairs. *ṣaɛb ɛaliyyi ʔəṭlaɛ ɛad-draaž.* -- He's a hard man to get along with. *huwwe rəžžaal ṣaɛᵊb tətɛaamal maɛo.* **4.** *tqiil.* He's hard of hearing. *samaɛo tqiil.* **5.** *b-žədd.* He worked hard all day. *štaġal ᵊb-žədd ṭuul ᵊn-nhaar.*

**I had a hard time finding the place. *laqeet ᵊṣɛuube laaqi l-maḥall.*

**It was raining hard when he left. *kaanet ɛam bədəxx lamma raaḥ.*

**He's a hard worker. *huwwe šaġġiil.*

**The ground was frozen hard. *l-ʔarḍ kaanet ᵊmžammde tažmiid.*

hard and fast - *saabet.* In this case you can't make hard and fast rules. *b-hal-ḥaale maa fiik ᵊtḥəṭṭ ʔanẓime saabte.*

hard up for - *malḥuuq ɛala.* He's always hard up for money. *huwwe daayman malḥuuq ɛal-maṣaari.*

to try hard - *ɛəmel žahdo.* He tried hard to do it right. *ɛəmel žahdo yaɛmə́la maẓbuuṭ.*

hard-boiled - *masluuq.* All we got was some hard-boiled eggs. *kəll šii qaddamúu-lna beeḍ masluuq.*

**You can't expect a hard-boiled businessman like him to give you anything for free. *maa fiik tətʔammal mən taažer ʔaxu ʔəxto mətᵊl haad yaɛṭiik šii b-balaaš.*

hardly - **1.** *yaa-doob-* + pron. suff., *bᵊl-kaad, yaḷḷa.* He can hardly make himself understood. *yaa-doobo yəqder yɛabber ɛan nafso.* -- She could hardly read and write when she came to the city. *yaa-dooba kaanet taɛref təqra w-təktob lamma ʔəžet ɛal-balad.* **2.** *yaa-doob-, yaḷḷa, bᵊl-kaad, b-ᵊmžarrad-ma.* He had hardly opened his mouth to speak when ... *yaa-doobo kaan fataḥ təmmo lamma* ... -- We had hardly gotten outside the city when the car broke down. *yaa-doobna kənna ṭləɛna barraat ᵊl-balad lamma s-sayyaara xərbet.* **3.** *qəllet-ma.* I hardly know those people. *qəllet-ma baɛref haž-žamaaɛa.* -- I hardly ever go out. *qəllet-ma ʔəṭlaɛ ᵊmn ᵊl-beet.*

**I hardly think so. *maa bẓənn heek.*

**You can hardly expect me to believe that. *maa fiik təntə́ẓer mənni ʔənno saddeq haš-šii.*

hardship - *mašaqqa* (pl. *mašaaqq*). They had to endure many hardships. *ɛaanu mašaqqa ktiir.*

hardware - *lawaazem~ ᵊl-binaaʔ* (pl.), *ʔadawaat~ ᵊḥdaade* (pl.).

harem - *ḥariim.*

harm - **1.** *ḍarar.* You can never undo the harm you've done. *maa fiik ᵊdziil ᵊḍ-ḍarar halli ɛməlto.* 2. *ʔisaaʔa.* I meant no harm by it. *maa qaṣadt fiiha ʔayy ʔisaaʔa.*

**No harm done! *maɛleeš!*

**There's no harm if there are two. *maa ɛalée šii ʔiza kaanu tneen.*

to do harm to - *ḍarr (ə ḍarar//nḍarr).* A vacation wouldn't do you any harm. *ʔiza btaaxə́d-lak šii fərṣa maa biḍərrak.* -- This dry weather has done a lot of harm to the crop. *haṭ-ṭaqṣ ᵊn-naašef ḍarr ᵊl-mazruuɛaat ᵊktiir.*

to harm - *ʔaza (i ʔaza//nʔaza).* He wouldn't harm a fly. *maa byəʔzi namle.*

harmless: It's a harmless sleeping pill. *hayy ḥabbet noom maa biḍərr* (or *maa mənha ḍarar).* -- He's a harmless fool. *huwwe waaḥed mažduub maa mənno ḍarar.*

harmonica - *ʔarmuniika* pl. *-aat.*

harmony - *ʔəlfe.* There was a perfect harmony between the two. *kaan fii ʔəlfe taamme been ᵊt-tneen.*

to be in harmony - *twaafaq, ttafaq.* His plans are in complete harmony with mine. *xəṭaṭo btətwaafaq tamaam maɛ xəṭaṭi.*

harp - *haarb* pl. *-aat.* She plays the harp. *bədəqq ɛal-haarb.*

to harp on - *naqar (o naqᵊr) ɛala.* Stop harping on that same subject! *haaštak naqᵊr ɛala nafs ᵊl-mawḍuuɛ!*

harrow - *maslafe* pl. *masaalef.*

harsh - *ṣaarem, qaasi.* Those ar harsh terms. *hayye šruuṭ ṣaarme.*

**This soap contains no harsh ingredients. *haṣ-ṣaabuun maa fiiha ʔazzaayaat.*

harvest - *ġalle* pl. *ġlaal, ḥṣaad.* We had a good harvest this year. *has-səne kaanet ᵊl-ġalle mniiḥa.*

to harvest - *ḥaṣad (o ḥṣaad//nḥaṣad).* When do you harvest the wheat around here? *ʔeemta btəḥᵊṣdu l-qamḥ ᵊb-hal-qaraani?*

hassock - *buuf* pl. *-aat, ṭərraaḥa* pl. *ṭarariiḥ.*

haste - *ɛažale.* Haste makes waste. *l-ɛažale mn ᵊš-šeeṭaan* or *l-ɛažale fiiha nadaame.*

hastily - *b-ɛažale.* They took leave rather hastily. *waddaɛu w-raaḥu b-ɛažale šwayye.* -- The translation was hastily done and is full of mistakes. *t-taržame ṣaaret ᵊb-ɛažale w-malaane ʔaġlaaṭ.*

hasty: You shouldn't make hasty decisions. *ʔaḥsə́n-lak maa tətsarraɛ ᵊb-qaraaraatak.* -- I wouldn't be hasty about it. *b-maḥallak maa bətsarraɛ fiiha.*

hat - *bərneeṭa* pl. *baraniiṭ.*

to **hatch (out)** - *faqqas.* Three more chicks hatched today. *fii tlətt ṣiiṣaan faqqasu kamaan ᵊl-yoom.* -- Only seven of the eggs hatched out. *bass sabɛa mn ᵊl-beeḍaat faqqasu.*

to hatch up - *dabbar.* What did you hatch up this time? *hal-marra šuu dabbarᵊt?* or ***šuu ṭəleɛ maɛak hal-marra?*

hatchet - *balṭa* pl. *-aat.* You wouldn't have a hatchet handy, would you? *muu waaṣle ʔiidak la-balṭa, muu heek?*

**Come on, let's bury the hatchet and forget the whole thing! *yaḷḷa xalliina nədfon ᵊl-ɛadaawe w-nənsa l-maaḍi.*

hate - *bəġᵊḍ.* His feeling of dislike gradually turned into hate. *kərho šwayye šwayye tḥawwal la-bəġᵊḍ.*

to hate - *baġaḍ (o bəġᵊḍ//nbaġaḍ), kəreh (a kərh// nkarah).* I hate people who are selfish. *bəbġoḍ ᵊn-naas ᵊl-ʔanaaniyyiin.* -- God! How I hate getting up in the morning! *ya ʔaḷḷa! šuu bəkrah ᵊl-feeqa ɛala bəkra!*

**I hated to tell her that to her face. *ṣəɛeb ɛaliyyi qəl-lha haš-šii la-wəšša.*

hatred - *bəġᵊḍ.*

haughty - *mɛanṭaẓ, mɛažraf, šaayef ḥaalo.* You seldom meet a haughtier man than him. *qəllet-ma tšuuf waaḥed ʔaɛanṭaẓ mənno.*

**That's a rather haughty attitude you're taking. *haada mawqef šwayye fii ɛažrafe mən naaḥiitak.*

haul - *ṣeeḍ.* The fishermen had a good haul today. *ṣayyaadiin ᵊs-samak kaan ɛandon ṣeeḍ ᵊmniiḥ ᵊl-yoom.*

to haul - **1.** *žarr (ə žarr//nžarr).* The horses were unable to haul the heavy load. *l-ʔəḥᵊṣne maa qədru yžərru l-ḥəml ᵊt-tqiil.* -- They hauled me out of bed at six o'clock this morning. *žarruuni žarr* *mn ᵊl-farše s-saaɛa sətte ɛala bəkra.* 2. *naqal (o naqᵊl//ntaqal).* We hired a truck to haul the furniture to our new home. *staᵓžarna kamyoon la-nənqol ᵊl-ɛafᵊš la-beetna ž-ždiid.*

to haul down – *nazzal//tnazzal.* Has the flag been hauled down yet? *l-ɛalam ᵊtnazzal wəlla ləssa?*

to haul off – *rafaɛ (a rafᵊɛ) ᵓiido.* He hauled off as if he meant to hit me. *rafaɛ ᵓiido kaᵓənno bəddo yəḍrəbni*

to haul out – *žaab (i žayabaan//nžaab).* I wish the boy wouldn't haul out all his toys and spread them all over the house. *yaa-reet ᵊl-walad maa yžiib ləɛabo kəllon w-ybaḥtəron malaat ᵊl-beet.*

haunted – *maskuun.* People say the house is haunted. *qaal ᵓənno l-beet maskuun.*

to have – no verbal equivalent, paraphrased with prepositions: 1. *ɛand, maɛ.* I have two tickets for the theater. *ɛandi tazkarteen ləl-masraḥ.* -- Do you have a pencil you can lend me? *fii ɛandak qalam ᵊtɛiirni?* -- Who had the book last? *miin kaan ɛando l-ᵊktaab ᵓaaxer marra?* -- He has a heart disease. *maɛo maraḍ qalb.* -- I have a headache. *maɛi wažaɛ raas.* -- They have a lot of money. *ɛandon maṣaari ktiir.* -- Do you have the key? *maɛak ᵊl-məftaaḥ?* -- England had many colonies in the past. *ᵓəngəltra kaan ɛanda (or kan-la) məstaɛmaraat ᵊktiire bᵊl-maaḍi.* 2. *ɛand, la-.* They have three children. *ɛandon (or ᵓəlon) tlətt ᵊwlaad.* -- My grandfather had three houses. *žəddi kan-lo tlətt ᵊbyuut.* -- She has beautiful eyes. *ᵓəla ɛyuun ḥəlwe ktiir.* -- You have a talent for music. *ᵓəlak mawhibe ləl-muusiiqa.* 3. *la-.* The table has four legs. *ṭ-ṭaawle ᵓəla ᵓarbaɛ rəžleen.* -- The argument has no end. *l-ᵊmḥaažaže maa-la ᵓaaxer.* -- The streets have no sidewalks. *š-šawaareɛ maa-lon ᵓərᵊṣfe.* -- That university doesn't have a great name. *haž-žaamɛa maa-la šəhra.*

**Has he done his job well? *saawa šəġlo mniiḥ?*

**Has someone called while I was out? *fii ḥada talfan w-ᵓana barra?*

**How long have you been in Damascus? *qaddeeš ṣar-lak bᵊš-šaam?*

**How long have you been waiting for me? *qaddeeš ṣar-lak ɛam tənṭəṛni?*

**I've been standing here for two hours. *ṣar-li waaqef hoon saaɛteen.*

**I'm having my teeth fixed. *ɛam ṣalleḥ snaani.*

**I'm having the car greased. *ɛam šaḥḥem ᵊs-sayyaara.*

**We're having our house painted. *ɛam ᵊndahhen beetna.*

**I had my shoes soled. *ḥaṭṭeet naɛᵊl la-ṣabbaaṭi.*

**I'll have to have my appendix out. *laazem qiim ᵊz-zaayde.*

**Wouldn't it be better to have the tooth out right now? *muu ᵓaḥsan ᵊtqiim ᵊs-sənn hallaq?*

**She's going to have a baby soon. *laḥa yəžiiha walad ɛan qariib.*

**I haven't had a thing to eat today. *maa ᵓakalt šii l-yoom.*

**Good stockings are simply not to be had. *l-kalsaat l-ᵊmniiḥa maa btənwəžed w-bass.*

**Let's have the knife! *haat ᵊs-səkkiine!*

**Please have a seat. *tfaḍḍal ᵊstriiḥ.*

**Let's have a walk. *xalliina nəmšii-lna šwayye.*

**He has had his way. *maa ṣaar ᵓəlla-ma mašša halli bəddo-yda.*

**All right, have it your way. *ṭayyeb, mətᵊl-ma bəddak.*

**What did she have on? *šuu kaanet laabse?*

**He has it in for you. *haaṭeṭ ᵊkɛaaro b-ᵊkɛaarak* or *muu ḥaalel ɛannak.*

**Wouldn't it be better to have it out with him right now? *muu ᵓaḥsan nənhiiha maɛo ɛal-haarek?*

I had better, you had better, etc. – *ᵓaḥsán-li, ᵓaḥsán-lak, ᵓaḥsán-lek,* etc., *ᵓafḍál-li, ᵓafḍál-lak,* etc. You'd better do it right away. *ᵓaḥsán-lak taɛməla haalan.* -- She'd better be careful with him. *ᵓaḥsán-la tətwaɛɛa mənno.*

to have to – 1. (present and future) *laazem* (invar.) + verb in imperf. without *b-.* I have to leave early. *laazem ruuḥ bakkiir.* -- We'll have to throw a party for these people. *laazem ᵊnsaawi ḥafle la-haž-žamaaɛa.* 2. (past) *nžabar* or *ḍṭarr* + verb in imperf. without *b-.* We had to make a detour. *nžabarna nəṭlaɛ ɛan ᵊṭ-ṭariiq w-naɛməl laffe.* -- They had to fire him. *ḍṭarru yəṣᵊrfúu mn ᵊl-xədme.*

**You have to have new shoes. *laazmak ṣabbaaṭ ᵊždiid.*

not to have to – *muu ḍaruuri* (invar.) or *maa fii lzuum* + verb in imperf. without *b-.* You don't have to go. *muu ḍaruuri truuḥ.* -- You won't have to sign again. *maa fii lzuum təmḍi marra taanye.* -- You didn't have to shout like that. *maa kaan ḍaruuri* (or *maa kaan fii lzuum*) *ᵊtɛayyeṭ heek.*

hawk – *ṣaqᵊr* pl. *ṣquur.*

hawk nose – *mənxaar maɛkuuf* pl. *manaxiir maɛkuufe.*

hay – *ḥašiiš yaabes.* In winter they mostly feed hay. *bᵊš-šəte bᵊl-ġaaleb byəɛᵊlfu l-ḥayawaanaat ḥašiiš yaabes.*

**It's time to hit the hay. *ṣaar waqt ᵊnruuḥ ɛal-farše.*

**Make hay while the sun shines. *dəqq ᵊl-ḥadiid w-huwwe ḥaami.*

hay fever – *ḥəmma~ l-qašš.*

hazard – *mžaazafe* pl. *-aat, mxaaṭara* pl. *-aat.* That's a hazard we have to take into account. *hayy ᵊmžaazafe laazem nəḥsəb-la ḥsaaba.*

hazardous – *xəṭer, məxṭer.* The icy roads make driving very hazardous. *z-zmeeta ɛaṭ-ṭəroq bətsaawi s-swaaqa xəṭra ktiir.*

haze – *ɛbuuq.* There's always a thin haze over the mountains. *daayman fii ɛbuuq xafiif fooq ᵊž-žbaal.*

hazelnut – *bəndqa* coll. *bəndoq* pl. *-aat.*

he – *huwwe.*

head – 1. *raas* pl. *ruus.* My head hurts. *raasi ɛam yəžaɛni.* -- My head is spinning. *raasi daayex.* -- I need nails with larger heads. *laazəmni basamiir raason ᵓakkar mən heek.* -- Lettuce is ten piasters a head. *l-xass ᵊr-raas ᵊb-ɛašr ᵊqruuš.* -- He sold five head of cattle. *baaɛ xamᵊs ruus baqar.* -- Begin at the head of the page. *ᵓəbda b-raas ᵊṣ-ṣafḥa.* -- We were sitting at the head of the table. *kənna qaaɛdiin ᵊb-raas* (or ***b-ṣədr*) *ᵊṭ-ṭaawle.* -- The mayor rode at the head of the procession. *raᵓiis ᵊl-baladiyye kaan raakeb b-raas ᵊl-mawkeb.* 2. *raᵓiis* pl. *rəᵓasa.* He's the head of the gang. *huwwe raᵓiis ᵊl-ɛiṣaabe.* -- He's the head of the firm. *huwwe raᵓiis ᵊš-šərke.* 3. *rabb* pl. *ᵓarbaab.* He's the head of the family. *huwwe rabb ᵊl-ɛeele.* 4. *mudiir* pl. *mədara, raᵓiis* pl. *rəᵓasa.* Who is the new head of the school? *miin ᵊl-mudiir ᵊž-ždiid tabaɛ ᵊl-madrase?*

**That may cost him his head. *haada məmken ykallfo ḥayaato.*

**My friend is head over heels in love. *ṣaaḥbi ṭaabes la-qaraqiiṭ ᵓadanée.*

**He has a good head for arithmetic. *ɛando məxx ləl-ᵊḥsaab.*

**Heads or tails? *ṭərra yəmma naqᵊš?*

**I can't make heads or tails of the story. *maa-li fahmaan ᵊl-qəṣṣa ᵓawwalta mən ᵓaaxərta.*

**I can't keep everything in my head. *maa fiini ᵓədzakkar kəll šii.*

**That's over my head. *məstaḥiil ɛaliyyi ᵓəfham haš-šii.*

**I don't want to go over his head. *maa bəddi ᵓətṣarraf biduun-ma šaawro.*

**You hit the nail on the head. *žəbta ḥafr w-tanziil.*

out of one's head – *mažnuun* pl. *mažaniin.* The man is positively out of his head. *laa šakk ᵊr-rəžžaal mažnuun.*

to come to a head – *balaġ (o bluuġ) ḥaddo.* Things had to come to a head sooner or later. *kaan laa bədd ᵓəlla l-ᵓumuur təbloġ ḥadda.*

to go to someone's head – *kabbar raas~ ḥada.* Success has gone to his head. *n-nažaaḥ kabbar raaso.*

to keep one's head – *ḥafaẓ (a ḥəfᵊẓ) ɛala ṣawaabo.* Fortunately, everyone kept his head. *mən ḥəsn ᵊl-ḥaẓẓ l-kəll ḥafaẓu ɛala ṣawaabon.*

to lose one's head – *ḍawwaɛ ṣawaabo.* The most important thing is not to lose your head. *ᵓahamm šii ᵓənno maa ḍḍawweɛ ṣawaabak.*

to put heads together – *tšaawaru maɛ baɛḍon.* I'm sure that if you put your heads together, you'll find a solution. *ᵓana mətᵓakked ᵓiza btətšaawaru maɛ baɛḍkon bətlaaqu ḥall.*

to take (or get) into one's head – *ḥaṭṭ ᵊb-ɛaqlo.* He just took it into his head that nobody likes him. *ḥaṭṭ ᵊb-ɛaqlo ᵓənno maa ḥada biḥəbbo.*

to head – 1. *traᵓᵓas.* He hopes to head his department some day. *byətᵓammal ᵓənno laḥa yətraᵓᵓas šii yoom ᵊl-qəsᵊm halli huwwe fii.* 2. *ttažah, twažžah.* You're heading in the wrong direction. *ᵓənte məttéžeh b-ᵓəttižaah ġalaṭ.* -- They're heading for California. *hənne mətwažžhiin ɛala kaalifoornya.*

-- We headed straight for the coast. *twažžahna ḍəġri ləs-saaḥel.* -- Where are you headed? *la-ween məttážžeh?* or ***ween raayeḥ?*
**His name heads the list of candidates. *ʔəsmo b-raas* (or *b-ṣədᵊr*) *ḍaaʔəmt l-ᵊmraššaḥiin.*
**My boy heads his class at school. *ʔəbni ʔawwal waaḥed* (or *l-ᵊbrənži*) *b-ṣaffo bᵊl-madrase.*
to head back - *ražeɛ (a ržuuɛ).* Let's head back to town before it gets dark. *xalliina nəržaɛ ɛal-balad qabᵊl-ma tɛattem ᵊd-dənye.*
headache - *wažaɛ˜ raas.* I've a bad headache. *maɛi wažaɛ raas qawi.* -- The problem gave us a lot of headache. *l-masʔale sabbabət-lna wažaɛ raas ᵊktiir.*
heading - *ɛənwaan* pl. *ɛanawiin.*
head lettuce - *xass.*
headlight - *ḍaww qəddaamaani* pl. *ʔəḍᵊwye qəddaamaaniyye.*
headline - *maanšeet* pl. *-aat.*
headlong - *rawwaasi* (invar.). He plunged headlong into the river. *šakk rawwaasi bᵊn-nahṛ.*
headquarters - **1.** *l-qiyaade l-ɛaamme.* This officer was attached to headquarters. *haḍ-ḍaabeṭ ʔalḥaʔúu bᵊl-qiyaade l-ɛaamme.* **2.** *markaz* pl. *maraakez.* For further information, apply to party headquarters. *ʔiza bəddak maɛluumaat ʔaktar raažeɛ markaz ᵊl-ḥəzᵊb.*
police headquarters - *daaʔərt˜ ᵊš-šərṭa.* He was taken to police headquarters. *ʔaxadúu la-daaʔərt ᵊš-šərṭa.*
headwaiter - *raʔiis˜* (pl. *rəʔasa˜*) *l-garaasne.*
to make **headway** - *tqaddam.* We made only slow headway in the deep snow. *maa tqaddamna ʔəlla b-bəṭᵊʔ mən kətr ᵊt-tuluuž.*
head wind - *riiḥ bᵊl-wəšš.* We had a strong head wind all the way. *ḥakamna riiḥ qawi b-wəššna ṭuul ᵊṭ-ṭariiq.*
to **heal** - *ṭaab (i ṭayabaan), laḥam (o lḥaam).* The wound isn't healing properly. *ž-žərᵊḥ maa ɛam yṭiib ka-ma yažeb.*
health - *ṣaḥḥa.* How's his health? *kiif ṣaḥḥto?* -- He's been in poor health lately. *ṣaḥḥto mətʔaxxra b-hal-ʔiyyaam.* -- (Here's) to your health! *b-ṣaḥḥtak!* -- We drank to our friend's health. *šrəbna la-ṣaḥḥet ṣaaḥəbna* or ***šrəbna naxᵊb ṣaaḥəbna.*
healthy - **1.** *ṣəḥḥi**. This isn't a healthy climate. *haada muu manaax ṣəḥḥi.* **2.** *qawi**, *məḥtáram.* They have a healthy respect for him. *byəḥtərmúu ʔəḥtiraam qawi.* -- I worked up a healthy appetite in the garden. *mən šəġli bᵊž-žneene ṣaar ɛandi šahiyye məḥtárame.*
**He's a healthy boy. *huwwe walad ṣaḥḥto qawiyye.*
**She looks very healthy. *mbayyen ɛaleeha ṣaḥḥə́ta ktiir ᵊmniiḥa.*
to **hear** - *səmeɛ (a samaɛ//nsamaɛ).* I didn't hear anything. *maa sməɛt šii.* -- I won't hear of it! *maa bəddi ʔəsmaɛ ɛan haš-šaġle.* -- I've never heard of him. *b-ḥayaati maa sməɛt fii.* -- I hear someone coming. *samɛaan fii ḥada žaaye.* -- You can't hear yourself in this noise. *l-waaḥed maa fii byəsmaɛ ḥaalo b-haḍ-ḍooše.*
**Well then, I'll expect to hear from you. *ṭayyeb ʔana mənṭə́ẓer ʔaxbaarak.*
**We haven't heard from her for more than a year. *ṣar-ᵊlna ʔaktar mən səne maa ʔəžaana ʔaxbaar mənha.*
hearing - **1.** *samaɛ.* His hearing is very poor. *samaɛo ḍɛiif ᵊktiir.* -- My aunt is hard of hearing. *ɛammti samə́ɛa tqiil.* -- When did he lose his hearing? *ʔeemta faqad samaɛo?* **2.** *ʔəstəžwaab* pl. *-aat.* The hearing was set for June sixth. *l-ʔəstəžwaab ᵊtḥaddad yoom sətte ḥzeeraan.*
from **hearsay** - *qiil ɛan qaal.* I know it only from hearsay. *bass baɛrə́fa qiil ɛan qaal.*
hearse - *ɛarabiyyet˜* (pl. *-aat˜*) *dafn ᵊl-mawta.*
heart - *qalb* pl. *qluub.* He has a weak heart. *qalbo ḍɛiif.* -- I haven't got the heart to do it. *maa-li qalb saawiiha.* -- It breaks my heart to see him suffer like that. *šoofto ɛam yətɛazzab btəksə́r-li qalbi.* -- His heart isn't in it. *muu ḥaaṭet qalbo fiiha.* -- The business section is in the heart of town. *l-manṭiqa t-tižaariyye b-qalb ᵊl-balad.*
**He's a man after my own heart. *huwwe rəžžaal žaaye ɛala zooqi.*
**Cross my heart! I didn't do it! *b-šarafi! maa ɛməlta!*
**Don't lose heart. *laa tiiʔas.*
hearts - *kubba* (invar.). Hearts are trumps. *l-kubba ʔatúu.* -- Why didn't you play the two hearts right away? *leeš maa lɛəbt ᵊl-warᵊqteen kubba ḍəġri?*
at heart - *qalbiyyan.* At heart he's really a good fellow. *qalbiyyan huwwe zalame ɛala salaamto.*
by heart - *ɛan ẓahr˜ ᵊl-qalb, ɛan ġeeb.* I learned the poem by heart. *ḥafaẓt ᵊl-qaṣiide ɛan ẓahr qalbi.*
heart and soul - *qalban w-qaaliban.* She's in this work heart and soul. *hiyye ḥaabbe haš-šaġle qalban w-qaaliban.*
to get to the heart of - *daxal (o dxuul) la ṣəlb˜ ...* I intend to get to the heart of this matter. *niiti ʔədxol la-ṣəlb ᵊl-mawḍuuɛ.*
to take to heart - **1.** *ʔaxad ᵊb-žədd.* He took my words very much to heart. *ʔaxad kalaami b-kəll žədd.* **2.** *zəɛel (a zaɛal) ɛala.* She's taking her cat's death very much to heart. *zaɛlaane ktiir ɛala mootet qaṭṭə́ta.*
heart attack - *noobe* (pl. *-aat*) *qalbiyye.*
heartbeat - *xafaqaan˜ qalb.*
heartburn - *ḥarqa bᵊl-məɛde.* I've a heartburn. *maɛi ḥarqa bᵊl-məɛde.*
heartily - **1.** *b-šahiyye.* We ate heartily. *ʔakalna b-šahiyye.* **2.** *mən kəll ᵊl-qalb.* We laughed heartily. *ḍḥəkna mən kəll qalbna.*
hearty - **1.** *šabbaaɛi**. We had a hearty meal. *ʔakalna ʔakle šabbaaɛiyye.* **2.** *qalbi**. They send you hearty greetings. *biballġuuk taḥiyyaaton ᵊl-qalbiyye.*
**He's a hearty eater. *byaakol mən qalbo.*
hale and hearty - *ḥərek.* He's hale and hearty in spite of his age. *huwwe ḥərek raġᵊm taqaddmo bᵊs-sənn.*
heat - **1.** *šoob.* I can't stand the heat. *maa fiini ʔəṭḥammal ᵊš-šoob.* **2.** *ḥarr.* The radio has predicted a heat wave. *r-raadyo ɛam yətnabba moožet ḥarr.* **3.** *šofaaž.* Turn on the heat! *šɛel ᵊš-šofaaž!*
**The stove doesn't give enough heat. *ṣ-ṣooba maa ɛam ydaffi kfaaye.*
**The dog's in heat again. *l-kalbe bᵊl-miiɛaad taani marra.*
to heat - *daffa.* We don't heat these rooms in winter. *maa məndaffi hal-ʔuwaḍ bᵊš-šəte.*
to heat (up) - **1.** *ṣaxxan//tṣaxxan.* I'll have to heat up some water first. *bᵊl-ʔawwal laazem ṣaxxen šwayyet mayy.* **2.** *ḥəmi (a ḥamaawe).* The living-room radiator doesn't heat up. *r-raadyatoor tabaɛ ʔuuḍet l-ᵊqɛuud maa ɛam yəḥma.* -- It'll be five minutes before the iron heats up. *bədda xamᵊs daqaayeq ᵊl-məkwaaye la-təḥma.*
heating pad - *mxaddet˜* (pl. *-aat˜*) *kahraba.*
heat-resistant - *mqaawem ləl-ḥaraara, ḍədd ᵊl-ḥaraara* (invar.) Is that glass heat-resistant? *hal-ᵊqzaaz ᵊmqaawem ləl-ḥaraara?*
heaven - **1.** *samaaʔ* pl. *samawaat.* Our Father which art in heaven... *ʔabaana llazii fi s-samawaat...* **2.** *žanne.* His mother-in-law - God bless her soul - is in heaven now. *ḥamaato - ʔaḷḷa yərḥamha - bᵊž-žanne hallaq.*
**She was in seventh heaven. *kaanet ᵊb-ʔoož ᵊs-saɛaade.*
**For heaven's sake, stop that noise! *mənšaan ʔaḷḷa baqa haaštak qarwaše!*
**Heaven knows, I've tried often enough. *ʔaḷḷa byəɛlam qaddeeš žarrabᵊt!*
heavy - **1.** *tqiil* pl. *tqaal.* Is that box too heavy for you? *has-sanduuq ᵊtqiil ɛaleek ᵊktiir?* -- They brought up heavy artillery during the night. *žaabu madfaɛiyye tqiile ʔəsna l-leel.* -- I can't take heavy food. *l-ʔakl ᵊt-tqiil maa biwaafəqni.* -- This tobacco is very heavy. *had-dəxxaan ᵊktiir ᵊtqiil.* -- He had to pay a heavy fine. *nžabar yədfaɛ ġaraame tqiile.* -- She took a heavy dose of sleeping pills. *ʔaxdet ᵊɛyaar ᵊtqiil mən ᵊḥbuub ᵊn-noom.* **2.** *qawi**, *šadiid.* We can't leave in that heavy rain. *maa fiina nəmši b-hal-maṭar ᵊl-qawiyye.* -- A heavy storm devastated the area. *fii ɛaaṣfe qawiyye dammaret w-xarrabet ᵊl-manṭiqa.* **3.** *ġaliiẓ* pl. *ġlaaẓ.* He has rather heavy features. *malaamḥo ġaliiẓa šwayye.* -- The author writes a heavy style. *l-ᵊmʔallef byəktob ʔəsluub ġaliiẓ.* **4.** *xaṭiir, žasiim.* That's a heavy responsibility. *hayy masʔuuliyye xaṭiira.* **5.** *rahiib, ɛamiiq.* A heavy silence followed his words. *ṣaar baɛᵊd kalaamo skuut rahiib.* **6.** *faadeḥ, žasiim.* The enemy suffered heavy losses. *l-ɛaduww ᵊtkabbad xaṣaayer faadḥa.* **7.** *maaken.* He's a heavy drinker. *huwwe šarriib maaken.*
heavyweight - *l-wazn ᵊs-saqiil.* He won the heavyweight championship last year. *faaz b-ᵊbṭuuliyyet ᵊl-wazn ᵊs-saqiil ᵊs-səne l-maaḍye.*

Hebrew - *Eəbraani**.
hedge - *syaaž* pl. *-aat*. The two gardens are divided by a hedge. *ž-žneenteen fii beenaaton ᵊsyaaž.*
hedgehog - *qənfod* pl. *qanaafed*.
heel - **1.** *kaEᵊb* pl. *kEaab*. I have a blister on my heel. *ṭaalžE-li faqfuule b-kaEbi.* -- Careful, you're stepping on my heels! *ʔoEa, Eam tədEas Eala kEaabi!* **2.** *kEaabiyye* pl. *-aat*. These shoes need new heels. *haṣ-ṣabbaaṭ laazmo kEaabiyyaat.* **3.** *danab* pl. *dnaab*. Save the heel of the bread for me. *xallii-li danab ᵊr-rġiif ʔəli.* **4.** *ʔəbᵊn ḥaraam.* That guy's a real heel! *haz-zalame Ean ḥaqa ʔəbᵊn ḥaraam.*
down at the heel(s) - *Eaž-žanṭ*. He looks down at the heels. *mbayyen Ealée Eaž-žanṭ.*
height - **1.** *ʔərtifaaE*. How do you determine the height of a triangle? *kiif bətEayyen ʔərtifaaE ᵊl-musallas?* **2.** *ʔərtifaaE, Eluww, Eəlu.* The building, due to its height, dominates the entire city. *l-binaaye la-ʔərtifaaEa mhayᵊmne Eal-balad kəlla.* **3.** *ʔoož, zarwe, sumuww.* He was then at the height of his power. *b-waqta kaan ᵊb-ʔoož quwwto.*
**That's the height of stupidity. *hayy ġabaawe maa baEda ġabaawe.*
heir - *wariis* pl. *wərasa, waares* pl. *warase.* He's the sole heir. *huwwe l-wariis ᵊl-waḥiid.*
heiress - *wariise* pl. *wərasa, waarse* pl. *warase.*
Hejira - *l-həžra.*
helicopter - *hilikopter* (invar.).
hell - *žhannam* (f.), *n-naar* (f.). Heaven, Hell and Purgatory. *ž-žanne wᵊž-žhannam wᵊl-maṭhar.* -- Go to hell! *w-ᵊžhannam taaxdak!*
**They are in a hell of a fix. *waaqEiin ᵊb-warṭa malEuune waḷḷa!*
**It's the hell of a place to live in. *haada maḥall malEuun l-waaḥed yEiiš fii.*
Hellenic - *halliini**.
hello - **1.** *ʔalóo.* Hello, operator! You've cut me off! *ʔalóo ṣanṭraal! qaṭaEti (l-ᵊmxaabara) Ealiyyi!* **2.** *marḥaba.* Hello, how are you? *marḥaba, kiif ḥaalak?*
helmet - *xuude* pl. *xuwad, xuuze* pl. *xuwaz.*
help - **1.** *msaaEade, mEaawane, maEuune.* Do you need any help? *bəddak šii msaaEade?* **2.** *xadam.* It's difficult to get help these days. *b-hal-ʔiyyaam ṣaEb ᵊl-waaḥed ylaaqi xadam.* **3.** *nažde.* He called for help, but nobody heard him. *ṭalab ᵊn-nažde* (or ***stanžad*) *bass maa ḥada səmEo.*
**Help! Help! *yaa žamaaEa! yaa naas! yaahóo!*
to help - *saaEad, Eaawan.* Please help me. *baḷḷa saaEədni.* -- I helped him as well as I could. *Eaawanto qadd-ma qdərt.* -- Could you help me with this translation? *fiik ᵊtsaaEədni b-hat-taržame?*
**I can't help it, but that's my opinion. *maE ᵊl-ʔasaf, haada raʔyi.*
**I couldn't help but see it. *maa ṭaleE ᵊb-ʔiidi ʔəlla šuufa.*
**I couldn't help laughing. *maa ṭaleE ᵊb-ʔiidi ʔəlla ʔəḍḥak.*
**Can I help you? *ʔamᵊr xədme?*
**I can't help it. *šuu byəṭlaE ᵊb-ʔiidi?*
**Sorry, that can't be helped. *maE ᵊl-ʔasaf, maa fii bᵊl-yad ḥiile.*
to help oneself - *madd (ə ə) ʔiido.* Please help yourself! *tfaḍḍal mədd ʔiidak!*
to help out - *saaEad.* Can I help you out with a few pounds? *fiini saaEdak* (or ***ʔəqḍii-lak ġaraḍak*) *ᵊb-kam leera?* -- She helps out in a restaurant on Sunday. *bətsaaEed ᵊb-šii maṭEam yoom ᵊl-ʔaḥad.*
to help to - *qaddam.* Can I help you to something? *fiini qaddém-lak šii?*
helper - *msaaEed* pl. *-iin, mEaawen* pl. *-iin.*
helpful - *mufiid.* You've given me a very helpful hint. *lammaḥt-əlli talmiiḥa mufiide ktiir.*
**I was only trying to be helpful. *kəll ġaayti kaanet ʔənni saaEed.*
**She's always very helpful. *daayman ʔəla lahfe.*
helping: May I have another helping of the vegetables? *məmken ʔəskob marra taanye l-xəḍar?* -- I've already had two helpings. *sakabt marrteen.*
helpless - *Eaažez.* I feel completely helpless in this situation. *šaaEer ᵊb-ḥaali Eaažez tamaam ᵊb-hal-waḍᵊE.*
**He stared at the broken vase with a helpless expression on his face. *baḥlaq bᵊl-vaaz ᵊl-maksuur w-Eala wəššo taṭliiEet waaḥed muu ṭaaleE ᵊb-ʔiido šii.*
hem - *daayer* pl. *dawaayer.* I'll have to let out the hem. *laazem nazzel ᵊd-daayer.*
to hem in - *zarak (o zark//nzarak, daḥaš (a daḥᵊš //ndaḥaš).* The house is hemmed in between two tall buildings. *l-beet mazruuk been binaayteen Eaalyiin.*
to **hem and haw** - *ḥamham w-tnaḥnaḥ.* Stop hemming and hawing, give me a straight answer. *ḥaaže thamhem w-tətnaḥnaḥ, Eaṭiini žawaab ṣaafi.*
hemisphere - *nəṣf˜* (pl. *ʔanṣaaf˜*) *kəra.*
hemorrhage - *naziif.*
hemorrhoid - *baasuur* pl. *bawasiir.*
hemp - *qənneb.*
hen - *žaaže* pl. *-aat.*
hence - *mənšaan heek, la-heek, li-zaalek.*
henna - *ḥanne.*
her - *-ha, -a.* She broke her arm. *kasret ʔiid(h)a.* -- Here comes my wife, ask her. *hayy marti žaaye, ʔəsʔəl(h)a.*
herb - *ḥašiiše* pl. *ḥašaayeš.* Herbs are still widely used as home remedies. *l-ḥašaayeš ləssaahon məstaEmale ʔədᵊwye beetiyye.*
herd - *qaṭiiE* pl. *qəṭEaan.* Who owns this herd? *miin ṣaaḥeb hal-qaṭiiE?*
to herd - *zarab (o zarᵊb//nzarab).* They herded us all into a small room. *zarabuuna kəllna b-ʔuuḍa zġiire.*
here - **1.** *hoon, hoone.* We can't stay here. *maa fiina nəbqa hoon.* -- The papers here say nothing about the accident. *ž-žaraayed hoon maa Eam yəḥku šii Ean ᵊl-ḥaades.* **2.** *la-hoon.* Come here! *taEa la-hoon!* **3.** *hayy, leek, šaE-* + pron. suff. Here's the book. *hayy l-ᵊktaab* or *leek l-ᵊktaab* or *leeko l-ᵊktaab* or *šaEo l-ᵊktaab.* -- Here's your money. *hayy maṣariik* or *leek maṣariik* or *leekon maṣariik* or *šaEon maṣariik.*
**Here's how! *b-ṣaḥḥtak!*
**I wish I could change this film. - Here's how. *yaa-reetni ʔəqder ġayyer hal-fəlᵊm. - šuuf kiif.*
**Here's to you! *b-ṣaḥḥtak!*
here and there - **1.** *ʔaḥyaanan, been mədde w-mədde.* Here and there you can still see horse cabs. *ʔaḥyaanan ləssa bətšəf-lak Earabiyyaat.* **2.** *hoon w-hoon, hoon w-ᵊhniik.* You'll find a few mistakes here and there. *bətlaaqi kam ġalṭa hoon w-hoon.*
hereafter - **1.** *mən hallaq w-raayeḥ.* Hereafter I'll be more careful. *mən hallaq w-raayeḥ bdiir baali ʔaktar.* **2.** *l-ʔaax(i)ra.* Do you believe in the hereafter? *bətʔaamen bᵊl-ʔaaxra?*
hereditary - *wiraasi**.
heredity - *wiraase.*
heresy - *harṭaqa.*
heretic - *harṭuuqi* pl. *haraaṭqa.*
heretical - *harṭuuqi**.
heritage - *miiraas.*
hermit - *naasek* pl. *nəssaak.*
hermitage - *ṣoomaEa* pl. *-aat* and *ṣawaameE.*
hernia - *ftaaq* pl. *-aat, fətᵊq* pl. *ftuuqa.*
hero - *baṭal* pl. *ʔabṭaal.*
heroic - *buṭuuli**, *baasel.*
heroine - *baṭale* pl. *-aat.*
heroism - *buṭuule, basaale.*
hers - *tabdE(h)a.* The book is hers. *l-ᵊktaab tabdEa.*
**My hat is bigger than hers. *bərneeṭṭi ʔakbar mən bərneeṭəta.*
**A friend of hers told it to me. *ṣaaḥeb ʔəla xabbarni-yđaha.*
herself - **1.** *b-zaat(h)a, nafs(h)a.* She did it herself. *hiyye b-zaata Eaamlə́ta.* **2.** *ḥaal(h)a, nafs(h)a.* She cut herself with the knife. *žarḥet ḥaala bᵊs-səkkiin.* -- She fell on the stairs and hurt herself. *waqEet Ead-daraž w-ʔaazet ḥaala* (or ***tʔaazet*).
**She's not herself today. *hiyye muu Eala baEḍa l-yoom.*
**She was beside herself with grief. *kaan ṭaayer ṣawaaba mən kətr ᵊl-ḥəzᵊn.*
by herself - *la-ḥaala, (la-)waḥda.* She made the dress all by herself. *xayyaṭet ᵊr-roob kəllo la-ḥaala.* -- She doesn't like to be in the house all by herself. *maa bətḥəbb təqEod waḥda bᵊl-beet.*
to **hesitate** - *traddad.* He hesitated a moment before he answered. *traddad šwayye qabᵊl-ma žaawab.* -- I'm still hesitating whether I should do it or not. *ləssaani mətradded yaa-tə́ra ʔaEmə́la ʔaw laʔ.* -- Don't hesitate to call if you need me. *laa tətraddad tnaadii-li ʔiza ḥtəžtni.*
hesitation - *taraddod.* He answered without hesitation. *žaawab biduun ʔayy taraddod.*
hey - *hee.* Hey, what's the big idea? *hee, šuu*

maεnaata? -- Hey you! Come over here! *hee ʔənte! taεa la-hoon.*

hiccup - *ḥasqa* pl. *-aat.* I have the hiccups again. *rəžεət-li l-ḥasqa.*

hide - *žəld* pl. *žluud(e).* These hides still have to be tanned. *hal-ᵊžluud ləssa laazəma ṣbaaġa.* -- I'll tan your hide if you do that again. *bəhri žəldak ʔiza taεməla taani marra.*

to hide - **1.** *xabba//txabba.* He hid the money in the drawer. *xabba l-maṣaari bᵊd-dərᵊž.* **2.** *xafa (i ʔəxfaaʔ//nxafa).* He tried to hide his embarrassment. *ḥaawal yəxfi ʔərtibaako.* **3.** *ḥažab (o ḥažᵊb//nḥažab). ġaṭṭa.* The trees hide the view. *š-šažar εam təḥžob ᵊl-manẓar.* **4.** *txabba.* Let's hide in the garage. *xalliina nətxabba bᵊl-garaaž.*

hide-and-seek - *ṭəmmeeme.* The children played hide-and-seek in the courtyard. *l-ᵊwlaad ləεbu ṭəmmeeme bᵊd-dyaar.*

hieroglyphs - *kitaabe hiiruġliifiyye.*

high - **1.** *εaali.* There's a high mountain right behind the village. *fii žabal εaali raʔsan wara ḍ-ḍeeεa.* -- The high altitude doesn't suit my health. *l-ʔərtifaaε ᵊl-εaali maa biwaafeq ṣaḥḥti.* -- The table is a little high for the boy. *ṭ-ṭaawle šwayye εaalye εaṣ-ṣabi.* -- The river's very high today. *n-nahᵊr εaali ktiir ᵊl-yoom.* -- Watch out! This is a high-tension wire. *ʔoεak! haada šriiṭ voltaaž εaali.* **2.** *εaali, mərtəfeε.* A high percentage of the population are still illiterate. *fii nəsbe εaalye mn ᵊs-səkkaan ləssaaha ʔəmmiyye.* -- Everybody's complaining about the high prices. *kəll ᵊn-naas εam tətšakka mn ᵊl-ʔasεaar ᵊl-mərtəfεa* (or ***mən ʔərtifaaε ᵊl-ʔasεaar).* **3.** *εaali, rafiiε.* He holds a high position in the Foreign Ministry. *ʔəlo markaz εaali b-wazaart ᵊl-xaaržiyye.* **4.** *qawi*.* The car hit the tree at high speed. *s-sayyaara ḍarbet ᵊš-šažara b-sərεa qawiyye.* -- We played for high stakes. *ləεəbna ləεbe qawiyye.*

**That building is eight stories high. *hal-binaaye εəlwa tmən ṭawaabeq.*

**Prices have reached a new high. *l-ʔasεaar ᵊrtafεet la-daraže maa wəṣlət-la mən qabᵊl.*

**Now shift into high. *hallaq ḥəṭṭ ᵊl-katriyeem.*

**I have a high opinion of him. *ʔəlo qiime εandi kbiire.*

**It's high time we do something about it. *ʔaan ᵊl-ʔawaan baqa nsaawi šii b-haš-šaġle.*

**Most people at the party were a little high. *ʔaktar ᵊl-ḥaaḍriin bᵊl-ḥafle kaanet daayre l-ḥašiiše šwayye maεon.*

**We searched for it high and low. *maa xalleena εaleeha maṭraḥ.*

High Command - *l-qiyaade l-εəlya.*

High Commissioner - *mfawwaḍ saami* pl. *mfawwaḍiin saamyiin, manduub saami* pl. *manduubiin saamyiin.*

high school - *madrase* (pl. *madaares*) *saanawiyye.*

high tide - *madd.* Let's wait till high tide. *xalliina nəstanna l-madd.*

high treason - *xyaane εəẓma.*

in high spirits - *mšaqreq.* He's in high spirits today. *(huwwe) mšaqreq ᵊl-yoom.*

high and dry - *ʔiid mən wara w-ʔiid mən qəddaam, laa mən hoon w-laa mən hoon.* There I was, left high and dry. *maa šəft ḥaali ʔəlla ʔiid mən wara w-ʔiid mən qəddaam.*

highly - *žəddan, ktiir.* He seemed highly pleased. *kaan ᵊmbayyen εalee mabṣuuṭ žəddan.*

to speak highly of - *madaḥ (a madᵊḥ), ʔasna εala.* He spoke very highly of him. *madaḥo ktiir.*

to think highly of - *εtabar.* They think very highly of you. *byəεtəbruuk ᵊktiir.*

highness - *sumuww.*

His Royal Highness - *ṣaaḥeb˜ ᵊs-sumuww ᵊl-malaki.*

highway - *ṭariiq* pl. *ṭərəq.*

hill - *tall* pl. *tlaal, ḥadabe* pl. *-aat.* What's on the other side of the hill? *šuu fii b-qafa hat-tall?*

hilt - *maske* pl. *-aat, qabḍa* pl. *-aat, kamše* pl. *-aat.* The dagger's hilt is inlaid with silver. *masket ᵊl-xanžar ᵊmraṣṣaεa b-fəḍḍa.*

**She played her role to the hilt. *ləεbet doora la-ʔaaxro.*

himself - **1.** *b-zaato, nafso.* Did he do it himself? *εaaməla b-zaato?* **2.** *ḥaalo, nafso.* He cut himself with the razor. *žaraḥ ḥaalo bᵊl-muus.* -- He hurt himself badly. *ʔaza ḥaalo* (or ***tʔaaza) b-ṣuura malεuune.*

**He's not himself today. *muu εala baεḍo l-yoom.*

**He is beside himself with rage. *ṭaayer ṣawaabo mən kətr ᵊl-ġaḍab.*

by himself - *la-ḥaalo, (la-)waḥdo.* Did he make it all by himself or did you help him? *εaaməla la-ḥaalo wəlla saaεadto?* -- He shouldn't walk in the streets all by himself at night. *laazem maa yəmši bᵊš-šawaareε waḥdo bᵊl-leel.*

Hindi - *həndi.*

Hindu - *həndoosi* coll. pl. *həndoos.*

Hinduism - *l-həndoosiyye.*

hinge - *mfaṣṣale* pl. *-aat.* One of the hinges of the trunk broke off. *fii mfaṣṣale mn ᵊmfaṣṣalaat ᵊṣ-ṣanduuq ᵊnqaləεet.*

to hinge on - **1.** *twaqqaf εala.* Everything hinges on his decision. *kəll šii byətwaqqaf εala qaraaro.* **2.** *daar (u ə) ḥawl* and *εala.* The whole argument hinges on that point. *l-ᵊmḥaažaže kəlla εam ᵊdduur ḥawl han-nəqṭa.*

hint - *talmiiḥa* pl. *-aat, ʔišaara* pl. *-aat.* Can't you give me a hint? *maa fiik taεṭiini šii talmiiḥa?*

to hint - *lammaḥ.* He hinted that something was up. *lammaḥ (b-)ʔənno fii šii laḥa yṣiir.* -- What are you hinting at? *εan ʔeeš εam ᵊtlammeḥ?*

hip - *wərᵊk* pl. *wraak.*

hipbone - *εaḍmet˜* (pl. *εḍaam˜*) *wərᵊk, εaḍm˜ ᵊl-hərqufe.*

hip pocket - *žeebe* (pl. *žyuub* and *žiyab*) *warraaniyye.*

hippopotamus - *faras˜* (pl. *fraas˜*) *ᵊl-baḥᵊr.*

hire - *ʔiižaar, ʔəžra.* They have boats for hire there. *εandon šaxatiir ləl-ʔiižaar ᵊb-hal-maḥall.*

to hire - **1.** *staʔžar.* We hired the boat for the whole day. *staʔžarna š-šaxtuura ṭuul ᵊn-nhaar.* **2.** *staxdam,* (for white-collar work) *waẓẓaf.* We have to hire more people. *laazem nəstaxdem naas ʔaktar.*

his - **1.** *-o.* Have you got his address? *btaεref εənwaano?* -- God answered his prayer. *ʔaḷḷa stažaab duεa.* -- My car is older than his. *sayyaarti ʔaεtaq mən sayyaarto.* -- I met a friend of his. *tεarraft εala waaḥed mən ᵊṣḥaabo* (or ***εala ṣaaḥeb ʔəlo).* **2.** *ʔəlo, tabaεo.* The book is his. *l-ᵊktaab ʔəlo.*

to hiss - **1.** *nafax (o nafᵊx).* The snake hissed menacingly. *l-ḥayye kaanet εam tənfox bədda təqroṣ.* **2.** *hayyaṣ.* Every time he mentioned her name the audience hissed. *kəll-ma zakar ʔəsma l-ḥaaḍriin hayyaṣu-la.* -- He was hissed everywhere. *hayyaṣu-lo ween-ma raaḥ.* **3.** *tanfiis.* First I heard a hissing sound like that of escaping steam. *ʔawwal šii smeεᵊt ṣooṭ tanfiis mətᵊl tanfiis ᵊl-buxaar.*

historian - *mᵊʔarrex* pl. *-iin.*

historic - **1.** *taariixi*.* We visited most of the historic monuments. *zərna ʔaktar ᵊl-ʔaasaar ᵊt-taariixiyye.* **2.** *xaaled.* It was a truly historic moment. *kaanet laḥẓa εan ḥaqa xaalde.*

historical - *taariixi*.* I just can't remember historical details. *maa fiini ʔədsakkar ᵊt-tafaṣiil ᵊt-taariixiyye.*

history - *taariix.* Have you studied European history? *darast ᵊt-taariix ᵊl-ʔawrəbbi?* -- That picture has quite a history. *haṣ-ṣuura ʔəla taariix.*

hit - *ʔiṣaabe* pl. *-aat.* He scored four hits. *sažžal ʔarbaε ʔiṣaabaat.*

**His song became a hit over night. *ʔəġniito ṣaaret mooḍa been ᵊl-leele w-ḍuḥaaha.*

to hit - **1.** *ḍarab (o ḍarᵊb//nḍarab).* The ball hit the wall. *ṭ-ṭaabe ḍarbet ᵊl-ḥeeṭ.* -- Who hit you? *miin ḍarabak?* **2.** *ṭaraq (o ṭarᵊq//nṭaraq).* I hit my knee against the door. *ṭaraqᵊt rəkᵊbti bᵊl-baab.*

**The news hit me very hard. *l-xabariyye ʔassaret εaliyyi ktiir.*

to hit it off - *ẓabṭet (o ə) maεon.* How did the two hit it off? *šloon ẓabṭet maεon tneenaaton?*

to hit (up)on - *hədi (a hədu) εala.* How did you hit on that? *kiif ᵊhdiit εala haš-šaġle?*

hitch - **1.** *xaazuuq, xoozaaq.* I'm sure there's a hitch somewhere. *ʔana mətʔakked fii xaazuuq b-šii qərne.*

**Everything came off without a hitch. *kəll šii məši mətl ᵊl-ḥalaawe.*

to hitch - *rabaṭ (o rabᵊṭ//nrabaṭ).* Hitch your horse to the post. *rbooṭ ᵊḥṣaanak bᵊl-εaamuud.* -- Did you hitch the horses to the wagon yet? *rabaṭṭ ᵊl-ʔəḥᵊṣne bᵊl-εarabiyye šii wəlla ləssa?*

**That's where the hitch comes in! *hoone byəži ḍ-ḍarb l-ᵊmxoozeq.*

hives - *šəre.*

to hoard - *xazzan.* They're hoarding sugar. *εam yxazznu səkar.*

hoarse - *mabḥuuḥ.* I'm hoarse from talking. *ʔana mabḥuuḥ mən kətr ᵊl-ḥaki.*

**His voice always sounds a little hoarse. *ṣooṭo daayman kaʔanno fii šwayyet baḥḥa.*

hoax – *saḥbe* pl. *-aat.* The story was only a hoax. *l-qəṣṣa kaanet ᵊmžarrad saḥbe.*

hobby – *hiwaaye* pl. *-aat.* His latest hobby is collecting stamps. *ʔaaxer hiwaaye ʔəlo žamɛ ᵊṭ-ṭawaabeɛ.*

hockey – *hooki* (invar.)

hodgepodge – *xaliiṭ w-bliiṭ.*

hoe – *mažrafe* pl. *mažaaref, žaaruuf* pl. *žawariif.*

hog – *xanziir* pl. *xanaziir.* He raises hogs. *birabbi xanaziir.*

**Don't be such a hog! *laa tkuun šəreh la-had-daraže!*

to **hold** – **1.** *məsek (e masᵊk//mmasak), kamaš (e kamᵊš//nkamaš).* Hold him! *msəko!* -- Kindly hold this package a minute. *balla kməš-li hal-baakeet šii daqiiqa.* **2.** *ḥafaẓ (a ḥafᵊẓ).* Do you think this old bucket will hold water? *btəftəker has-saṭl ᵊl-ɛatiiq byəḥfaẓ ᵊl-mayy?* **3.** *ḥamal (e ḥamᵊl//nḥamal).* She held the baby in her arms. *ḥamlet ᵊl-beebée been ʔiideeha.* **4.** *faṭan (e ø//nfaṭan).* That speaker knows how to hold his audience. *hal-xaṭiib byaɛref kiif yəften ᵊs-saamɛiin.* **5.** *tṣarraf b-.* They hold the land under a ten-year lease. *ɛam yətṣarrafu bᵊl-ʔarḍ ᵊb-muužeb ɛaq̃ᵊd ʔiižaar ɛašr ᵊsniin.* **6.** *wəseɛ (-yəsaɛ ø).* The room holds twenty people. *l-ʔuuḍa btəsaɛ ɛəšriin zalame.* **7.** *ɛaq̃ad (e ɛaq̃ᵊd// nɛaq̃ad).* The meetings are held once a week. *l-ʔəžtimaaɛaat btənɛəq̃ed kəll žəmɛa marra.* **8.** *ʔažra, saawa.* Are they going to hold new elections? *laḥa yəžru ʔəntixaabaat ᵊždiide?* **9.** *məsek (e ø), ɛəleq (a ø).* That knot won't hold. *hal-ɛəqde maa-la ɛam təmsek.* **10.** *ṭṭabbaq, məši (i ø).* This rule doesn't hold in every case. *hal-q̃aaɛide maa btəṭṭabbaq ᵊb-kəll ḥaale.*

**Hold the wire so I can ask my husband. *xalliik ɛal-xaṭṭ la-ʔəsʔal žoozi.*

**He holds a high position. *ʔəlo markaz marmuuq̃.*

**You can't hold me responsible for that! *maa fiik ᵊtḥammələni ʔana l-masʔuuliyye ɛan haš-šaġle!*

**He held office for a long time. *bəqi b-markazo mədde ṭawiile.*

**Hold your tongue! *sədd təmmak!*

to hold back – **1.** *ʔaxxar//tʔaxxar.* I wanted to go, but he held me back. *kaan bəddi ruuḥ bass ʔaxxarni.* **2.** *waqqaf//twaqqaf.* When he gets in a rage there's no holding him back. *waqt biẑənn ᵊžnaano maa fii ḥada ywaqqfo.*

to hold down – *rakaz (o/e rakz) b-.* He's never been able to hold down a job for more than six months. *b-ḥayaato maa qəder yərkoz ᵊb-šaġle ʔaktar mən sətt əšhor.*

to hold off – *maaṭal.* Try to hold him off for a while until I've talked to the boss. *ḥaawel ᵊtmaaṭlo la-been-ma ʔəḥki maɛ ᵊr-raʔiis.*

to hold on – *stanna.* Can you hold on for a minute? I have to check the number again. *fiik təstanna* (or **ᵊ*txalliik ɛal-xaṭṭ*) *šii daqiiqa? bəddi raažeɛ ᵊn-nəmra marra taanye.*

to hold on to – **1.** *tmassak b-.* Hold on to me. *tmassak fiyyi.* -- Can you hold on to that job just a little longer? *fiik tətmassak ᵊb-haš-šaġle la-mədde ʔaṭwal šwayye?* **2.** *ḥtafaẓ b-.* Hold on to the money for a few days. *ḥtəfeẓ bᵊl-maṣaari šii kam yoom.*

to hold one's own – *ṭəleɛ (a ø) qadd ᵊl-qadd.* Don't worry, he's perfectly able to hold his own in debate. *laa ykən-lak fəkre, byəṭlaɛ qadd ᵊl-qadd w-ᵊzyaade bᵊl-ᵊmnaaq̃aše.*

to hold out – *ḍaayan.* We would have held out for months, if we'd had enough food. *kənna ḍaayanna ʔəšhor law kaan ɛanna ʔakᵊl kaafi.*

to hold over – *maddad//tmaddad.* The movie was held over for another week. *l-fəlm ᵊtmaddad žəmɛa taanye.*

to hold true – *ṣaḥḥ (ə ø).* That doesn't hold true in our case. *haš-šii maa biṣəḥḥ ᵊb-waḍᵊɛna.*

to hold up – **1.** *ʔaxxar//tʔaxxar.* You're holding me up. *ɛam ᵊtʔaxxərni.* -- What's holding things up? *šuu halli msabbeb ᵊt-taʔxiir?* **2.** *šallaḥ// tšallaḥ.* He was held up by two men last night. *fii tneen šallaḥuu leelt ᵊmbaareḥ.* **3.** *ḍaayan.* Will these shoes hold up? *haṣ-ṣabbaaṭ biḍaayen?* **4.** *rafaɛ (a rafᵊɛ).* When people find out he won't be able to hold up his head again. *lamma n-naas byədru maa biɛuud fii yərfaɛ raaso.*

to hold up under – *tḥammal.* How is he holding up under the strain? *kiif ɛam yətḥammal ᵊl-ʔəžhaad?*

to get hold of – *ttaṣal b-.* Where can I get hold of him? *ween bəqder ʔəttəṣel fii?*

**Wait till I get hold of him! I'll give him a piece of my mind then. *stanna la-yəɛlaq been ʔidayyi. bwaržii nžuum ᵊḍ-ḍəhᵊr.*

to lose one's hold – *fəltet (a falataan~) ʔiido.* He lost his hold and fell from the roof. *fəltet ʔiido w-wəqeɛ mən ɛaṣ-ṣṭuuḥ.*

to take hold of – *tmassak b-.* Take hold of my arm. *tmassak ᵊb-ʔiidi.*

to take a hold of – *tmallak zimaam~...* You'll have to take a firm hold of things. *laazem tətmallak zimaam l-ᵊʔmuur ᵊb-kəll ḥazᵊm.*

holder – **1.** *ɛallaaqa* pl. *-aat.* Put your toothbrush back in the holder when you're finished with it. *ražžeɛ fəršaayet ᵊsnaanak bᵊl-ɛallaaqa lamma btəxloṣ.* **2.** *ḥaamel* pl. *-iin.* The holder of the passport is entitled to... *ḥaamel ᵊž-žawaaz ʔəlo ḥaqq* ... -- The holder of several academic degrees. *ḥaamel ɛəddet šahaadaat žaamɛiyye.*

holdup – *tašliiḥa* pl. *-aat.* He had nothing to do with the holdup. *maa kan-lo ʔayy ɛalaaqa bᵊt-tašliiḥa.*

hole – **1.** *bəxᵊš* pl. *bxaaš, bəxwaaš* pl. *baxawiiš.* We have to drill a hole in the board first. *ʔawwal šii laazem nəbxoš bəxᵊš bᵊl-looḥ.* **2.** *bəxᵊš* pl. *bxaaš, šaqq* pl. *šquuq, xərᵊq* pl. *xruuq.* You have a hole in your pants. *fii bəxx ᵊb-banṭaloonak.* -- All of a sudden the snake disappeared in a hole in the wall. *fažʔatan l-ḥayye xtafet ᵊb-bəxᵊš bᵊl-ḥeeṭ.* **3.** *žuura* pl. *žuwar, ḥəfra* pl. *ḥəfar.* Drive slowly. The road is full of holes. *suuq ɛala mahlak. ṭ-ṭariiq malaan žuwar.* -- So far the house is no more than a big hole in the ground. *la-ḥadd hallaq ᵊl-beet muu ʔaktar mən žuura kbiire bᵊl-ʔarḍ.* **4.** *səġra* pl. *-aat, bəxᵊš* pl. *bxaaš.* The trip made a big hole in my pocketbook. *s-safra fatḥət-li səġra kbiire b-žeebti* or *s-safra baxšət-li bəxš ᵊkbiir ᵊb-žeebti.*

**He lives in a dingy hole. *(huwwe) ɛaayeš ᵊb-qabᵊr.*

**I'm five pounds in the hole. *ʔana maksuur ɛala xams ᵊwraaq.*

holiday – *ɛəṭle* pl. *ɛəṭal, fərṣa* pl. *fəraṣ.* Is today a holiday? *l-yoom ɛəṭle?* -- Where are you going to spend the Christmas holidays? *ween bəddak ᵊtmaḍḍi ɛəṭlet ɛiid ᵊl-miilaad?*

holiness – *q̃adaase.* His Holiness the Pope. *q̃adaaset ᵊl-baaba.*

Holland – *hoolanda.*

hollow – **1.** *mžawwaf.* The dish is covered by a hollow lid. *z-zəbdiyye mġaṭṭaaye b-ġaṭa mžawwaf.* **2.** *faaḍi.* These walls seem to be hollow. *hal-ḥiiṭaan mbayyen ɛaleeha faaḍye.*

**Her cheeks have become hollow after the long illness. *xduuda tfaxxatu baɛd ᵊl-marḍa ṭ-ṭawiile.*

to hollow out – **1.** *žawwaf//džawwaf, ḥafar (o ḥafᵊr//nḥafar).* We hollowed out half of the pumpkin. *žawwafna nəṣṣ ᵊl-yaqṭiine.* **2.** *ḥafar.* In some places, the long rains have hollowed out the road. *b-baɛḍ ᵊl-maḥallaat ᵊl-ʔamṭaar ᵊl-məstmərra ḥafret ᵊṭ-ṭariiq.*

holy – *mqaddas.* Are you going to visit the Holy Land? *laḥa dzuur ᵊl-ʔarḍ l-ᵊmqaddase?*

Holy Communion – *s-sərr l-ᵊmqaddas.*

Holy Ghost – *r-rooḥ ᵊl-q̃ədᵊs.*

Holy Saturday – *sabt~ ᵊn-nuur.*

Holy Thursday – **1.** (=Maundy Thursday) *xamiis~ ᵊl-ɛahᵊd, xamiis~ ᵊl-ġəsᵊl.* **2.** (=Ascension Day) *xamiis~ ᵊṣ-ṣuɛuud.*

Holy Week – *žəmɛet~ ᵊl-ʔaalaam.*

home – **1.** *beet* pl. *byuut.* There's no place like home. *maa fii šii mətᵊl beeto l-ʔənsaan.* -- The war has driven many people out of house and home. *l-ḥarb šarradet ɛaalam ᵊktiir mən ᵊbyuuta.* **2.** *maʔwa* pl. *maʔaawi.* Have you seen the new home for the aged? *šəft maʔwa l-ɛažaze ž-ždiid?* **3.** *daar* pl. *duur.* He spent his early childhood in a children's home. *maḍḍa ʔiyyaam ṣaġᵊrto b-daar ləl-ʔaytaam.* **4.** *waṭan* pl. *ʔawṭaan.* Palestine was my home once, but my family lives in Beirut now. *falasṭiin kaanet waṭani bass ɛeelti ɛaayše b-beeruut hallaq.* -- Do you have any news from home? *ɛandak ʔaxbaar šii ɛan ᵊl-waṭan?* **5.** *bᵊl-beet.* I'll be home all afternoon. *ʔana bᵊl-beet kəll baɛḍ ᵊḍ-ḍəhᵊr.* **6.** *ɛal-beet.* I have to go home a little earlier today. *laazem ruuḥ ɛal-beet ɛala bakkiir šwayye l-yoom.*

**My home is in California. *ʔana ʔaṣli mən kalifoornya.*

**Where is your home? *mən ween ʔənte?*
**He's longing for a home. *ḥaanen qalbo ʕala-ma yədžawwaz w-yətrakkan.*
**We're trying to find a nice home for the kittens. *ʕam ᵊndawwer ʕala beet yaaxdu hal-qaṭaaṭ.*
**He's gone home to America. *rəžeʕ ʕala blaado ʔameerka.*
at home – **1.** *bᵊl-beet.* I was at home all day yesterday. *kənt qaaʕed bᵊl-beet ṭuul ᵊn-nhaar ᵊmbaareḥ.* **2.** *bᵊd-daaxel.* At home and abroad ... *bᵊd-daaxel wᵊl-xaarež ...*
**At home it never rains at this time of the year. *b-ᵊblaadna maa btəmṭer ʔabadan ᵊb-hal-waqt ᵊmn ᵊs-səne.*
**Make yourself at home. *xood raaḥtak.*
away from home – *bᵊl-ġərbe.* Most of her life she lived away from home. *ʔaktar ḥayaata ʕaašet bᵊl-ġərbe.*
to drive something home to someone – *rassax šii b-ʕaqᵊl˜ ḥada.* If I could only drive it home to you that you have to be on time. *ya-reet ʔəḥsen rassə́xa b-ʕaqlak ʔənno laazem təži ʕal-waqᵊt.*

home economics – *tadbiir˜ ᵊl-manzel.*
homeless – *bala maʔwa* (invar.), *mətšarred.* Thousands were made homeless by the flood. *ʔaalaaf ᵊn-naas ṣaaru bala maʔwa* (or *ṣaaru mətšarrdiin* or ***tšarradu*) *b-sabab ᵊl-fayaḍaan.*
homemade – *beeti**. There's nothing like homemade food. *maa fii mətl ᵊl-ʔakl ᵊl-beeti.*
to be **homesick** – *stawḥaš ləl-waṭan, ḥann (ə ḥaniin) ləl-waṭan.* Are you never homesick? *maa btəstawḥeš ləl-waṭan ʔabadan?*
homesickness – *ḥaniin ləl-waṭan.*
home town – *masqaṭ˜ ᵊr-raas.* He wants to be buried in his home town. *bəddo ʔənno yədᵊfnúu b-masqaṭ raaso.*
**He's from my home town. *huwwe ʔəbᵊn baladi.*
homework – *waẓiife* pl. *waẓaayef.* Have you done all your homework? *saaweet kəll waẓiiftak* (or, of several courses, *kəll waẓaayfak*)?
homosexual – *luuṭi* pl. *-iyye.*
homosexuality – *liwaaṭa.*
Homs – *ḥəmᵊṣ.*
honest – *ʔamiin* pl. *-iin* and *ʔəmana.* Do you think he's honest? *btəʕtə́qed ʔənno ʔamiin?*
**He has an honest face. *wəššo bəddəll ʕal-ʔamaane.*
honestly – **1.** *ṣədq̃an.* I was honestly surprised. *ṣədq̃an ʔənni ndahašt.* **2.** *bᵊs-sədᵊq.* Tell me honestly ... *qəl-li bᵊs-sədᵊq ...* **3.** *b-kəll ṣaraaḥa, saddeq.* Honestly, I don't know what to do with you. *b-kəll ṣaraaḥa* (or *bəddak ṣaraaḥa*) *maa-li fahmaan šuu bəddi ʔaʕmel fiik.*
honesty – **1.** *ʔamaane.* There's no question about his honesty. *ʔamaanto maa ʕaleeha ḥaki.* **2.** *ʔəstiq̃aame.* Honesty is the best policy. *fi l-ʔəstiq̃aame s-salaame.*
honey – *ʕasal.*
honeycomb – *qərṣ˜* (pl. *qraaṣ˜*) *šahᵊd.*
honeymoon – *šahr˜ ᵊl-ʕasal.*
to **honk** – *ṭawwat (b-).* Honk the horn three times, and I'll come down. *ṭawweṭ bᵊz-zammuur tlətt marraat w-bənzə́l-lak.*
honor – *šaraf.* I have the honor to present ... *ʔəli š-šaraf qaddem ...* -- It's a great honor to be admitted to that club. *šaraf ᵊkbiir ʔənno l-waaḥed yənqə́bel ᵊb-han-naadi.* -- On my honor! *b-šarafi!* -- We gave a banquet in his honor. *saaweena maʔdube ʕala šarafo.* -- He's a man of honor. *huwwe ražol ṣaaḥeb šaraf* (or ***ražol šariif*). -- I give you my word of honor! *bqəl-lak kalaam šaraf!*
**Will you do me the honor to be my guest tonight? *bətšarrfúu-lna l-yoom bətkuunu ḍyuufna l-yoom?*
maid of honor – *waṣiifet˜* (pl. *-aat˜*) *šaraf.*
to do the honors – *waqqaf.* Will you do the honors at the party tonight? *bətwaqqef b-ḥaflet ᵊl-leele?*
with honors – *b-daražet˜ šaraf.* He passed with honors. *nažaḥ ᵊb-daražet šaraf.*
to honor – **1.** *karram.* The City will honor the returning hero at a banquet tonight. *l-ᵊmḥaafaẓa raḥa tkarrem ᵊl-baṭal ᵊl-ʕaaʔed ᵊb-maʔdube l-yoom ʕašiyye.* **2.** *qəbel (a ə//nqabal).* We can't honor this check. *maa fiina nəqbal haš-šakk.*
honorable – *šariif* pl. *šərafa, wažiih* pl. *wəžaha.*
honorary – *faxri**. He has an honorary doctorate. *maʕo doktorda faxriyye.*
**Is he an honorary member? *huwwe ʕəḍu šaraf?*
hood – **1.** *kaakuuliyye* pl. *-aat.* Next time I'm going to buy a coat with a hood. *l-marra ž-žaaye bəddi ʔəštə́ri kabbuut ᵊb-kaakuuliyye.* **2.** *ġaṭa* pl. *ʔəġᵊṭye.* Why don't you raise the hood and see what's wrong with the engine? *leeš maa btərfaʕ ᵊl-ġaṭa w-ᵊtšuuf ᵊl-mootoor šə́ bo.*
hoof – *ḥaafer* pl. *ḥawaafer,* (of a camel) *xəff* pl. *xfaaf.*
hook – **1.** *šangal* pl. *šanaagel.* Hang your coat on the hook. *ʕalleq kabbuutak ʕaš-šangal.* **2.** *ṣənnaara* pl. *ṣananiir.* Take the bait off the hook. *qiim ᵊṭ-ṭəʕᵊm mn ᵊṣ-ṣənnaara.* **3.** *kallaabe* pl. *-aat.* Now secure the hook to the bumper. *hallaq ʕalleq ᵊl-kallaabe bᵊṭ-ṭabboon.*
hook and eye – *kəbšaaye* pl. *-aat.* Shall I put on a zipper or hooks and eyes? *ḥəṭṭ-ə́llek saḥḥaab wəlla kəbšaayaat?*
by hook or by crook – *bᵊl-ḥaraam ʔaw bᵊl-ḥalaal, bᵊl-maʕruuf ʔaw bᵊl-matluuf.* He intends to get rich by hook or by crook. *naawi yṣiir ġani bᵊl-ḥaraam ʔaw bᵊl-ḥalaal.*
on one's own hook – *mən ḥaalo, mən ʕaqlo.* He did it on his own hook. *ʕəmə́la mən ḥaalo.*
to hook – **1.** *kamaš (e kamᵊš//nkamaš).* How many fish did you hook? *kam samake kamašt?* **2.** *ʕallaq.* She finally hooked him. *bᵊl-ʔaaxiir ʕallaqə́to.* **3.** *šabbak.* Help me hook this chain. *saaʕədni šabbek haž-žanziir.*
to hook up – *waṣṣal.* I haven't hooked up the new radio yet. *ləssa maa waṣṣalt ᵊr-raadyo ž-ždiid.*
hop – *naṭṭa* pl. *-aat, fašxa* pl. *-aat.* It's just a short hop by plane. *hiyye muu ʔaktar mən naṭṭa bᵊṭ-ṭayyaara.*
to hop – *naṭwaṭ.* She hopped with joy. *naṭwaṭet mən kətr ᵊl-faraḥ.*
to hop around – *naṭṭ (ə naṭṭ).* He was hopping around on one leg. *ʕam ynəṭṭ ʕala rəžᵊl waaḥde.*
hope – *ʔamal* pl. *ʔaamaal.* There's still hope. *ləssa fii ʔamal.* -- Don't give up hope! *laa təqṭaʕ ᵊl-ʔamal!* or ***laa tiiʔas!*
to hope – *tᵊʔammal.* She had hoped to see you. *kaanet mətʔammle tšuufak.* -- Let's hope for the best. *xalliina nətʔammal ᵊl-xeer.*
I hope (so), we hope (so) – *nšaaḷḷa.* I hope you didn't catch cold. *nšaaḷḷa tkuun maa ʔaxadt bard.*-- Will you be back by tomorrow night? - I hope so. *btəržaʕ la-ḥadd bəkra ʕašiyye? - nšaaḷḷa.* -- We hope he can come. *nšaaḷḷa yəqder yəži.*
let's hope – *nšaaḷḷa, xalliina nədʕi.* Let's hope this weather keeps up. *nšaaḷḷa haṭ-ṭaqᵊṣ ydaawem heek.*
hopeless – *mayʔuus mənno.* The situation is completely hopeless. *l-ḥaale mayʔuus mənha tamaam.*
hops – *ḥašiišt˜ ᵊd-diinaar.* Beer is made from hops and malt. *l-biira btənʕə́mel mən ḥašiišt ᵊd-diinaar wᵊš-šʕiir.*
horizon – *ʔəfoq̃* pl. *ʔaafaaq̃.*
horizontal – *ʔəfq̃i**.
hormone – *hormoon* pl. *-aat.*
horn – **1.** *qarᵊn* pl. *qruun(e).* They breed a kind of cattle with very long horns. *birabbu baqar qruunon ṭawiile ktiir.* -- The hilt of the knife is made of horn. *qabḍet ᵊl-muus maʕmuule mən qarᵊn.* **2.** *booraẓaan* pl. *-aat.* He plays the horn in the orchestra. *bidəqq booraẓaan bᵊl-ʔorkeestra.* **3.** *zammuur* pl. *zamamiir.* Blow the horn twice. *dəqq ᵊz-zammuur marrteen.*
hornet – *dabbuur* pl. *dababiir.*
horrible – *muriiʕ, mərʕeb, faẓiiʕ.* It was a horrible sight. *kaan manẓar muriiʕ.*
horrid – *šaniiʕ.* What a horrid picture! *qaddeeš ṣuura šaniiʕa!*
horror – *rəʕᵊb.* She stared at him with an expression of horror on her face. *baḥlaqet fii w-ʕala wəšša ʕalaamaat ᵊr-rəʕᵊb.*
horrors – *ʔahwaal* (pl.). The horrors of the war are indescribable. *ʔahwaal ᵊl-ḥarb fooq ḥadd ᵊl-waṣᵊf.*
horse – **1.** *ḥṣaan* pl. *ʔəḥᵊṣne.* Suddenly the horse shied. *fašʔatan l-ᵊḥṣaan žəfel.* **2.** (coll.) *xeel.* Let's go to the horse races. *xalliina nruuḥ ʕala sbaaq ᵊl-xeel.*
**A team of (wild) horses couldn't drag me there. *quwwet ʔaḷḷa maa btaaxədni la-hniik.*
**Now don't get on your high horse! *yaḷḷa baqa, ḥaažtak ʕažrafe!*
**You shouldn't look a gift horse in the mouth. *ʕəmrak laa tfalli hdiyye, xəda ʕala ʕəllaata.*
**That's a horse of different color. *haada šii taani.*
horse bean – *fuule* coll. *fuul* pl. *-aat.*

horsefly - *dəbbaanet~* (coll. *dəbbaan~* pl. *-aat~*) *faraṣ*.
horselaugh - *qahqaha*.
horseman - *xayyaal* pl. *-e*.
horse power - *ḥṣaan* pl. *ʔəḥəṣne*. The car has a 100 h.p. engine. *s-sayyaara fiiha motoor miit əḥṣaan.*
horseshoe - *ḥadwe* pl. *-aat*.
hortensia - *ʔərṭaaṣya*.
horticulture - *bastane*.
hose - **1.** *barbiiš* pl. *barabiiš*. The hose is still in the garden. *l-barbiiš ləssato bəž-žneene.* **2.** *žraabaat* (pl.), *kalsaat* (pl.). We just got a new shipment of hose. *hallaq ʔəžətna šaḥnet žraabaat əždiide.*
hosiery - *žraabaat* (pl.), *kalsaat* (pl.).
hospitable - *muḍiif, məḍyaaf*.
hospital - *məstašfa* pl. *məstašfayaat, xastaxaane* pl. *-aat*. When did you get home from the hospital? *ʔeemta ṭləεət mn əl-məstašfa?*
hospital attendant - *mmarreḍ* pl. *-iin*.
hospitality - *ḍyaafe*.
host - **1.** *muḍiif* pl. *-iin*. He's a wonderful host. *huwwe muḍiif maa-lo masiil.* **2.** *ṣaaḥeb~* (pl. *ṣḥaab~*) *əd-daεwe*. Have you been introduced to the host? *tεarrafət εala ṣaaḥeb əd-daεwe?*
hostage - *rahiine* pl. *rahaayen*.
hostess - **1.** *muḍiife* pl. *-aat*. She's a charming hostess. *hiyye muḍiife žazzaabe.* -- She works as a hostess with Air Liban. *btəštəġel muḍiife bəl-əxṭuuṭ əž-žawwiyye l-ləbnaaniyye.* **2.** *ṣaaḥəbt~* (pl. *-aat~*) *əd-daεwe*. Have you been introduced to our hostess? *tεarrafət εala ṣaaḥəbt əd-daεwe šii?*
hostile - *εadaaʔi**. I don't know why you take such a hostile attitude. *maa-li εarfaan leeš εam taaxod mawqef heek εadaaʔi.*
hostility - *εadaawe*. His hostility is quite obvious. *εadaawto baayne ləl-εayaan.*
hostilities - *ʔaεmaal εədwaaniyye* (pl.). Hostilities between the two countries ceased at midnight. *l-ʔaεmaal əl-εədwaaniyye been əl-baladeen waqqafet b-nəṣṣ əl-leele.*
hot - **1.** *ṣəxən, səxən*. Do you have hot water? *fii εandkon mayy ṣaxne?* -- I haven't had a hot meal in three days. *ṣar-li tlatt iyyaam maa ʔakalt ʔakle ṣəxne.* **2.** *šoob* (invar.). It's very hot here in summer. *ktiir šoob hoon bəṣ-ṣeef.* **3.** *məšweb, šoob* (invar.), *ḥaarr*. I can stand the hot weather pretty well. *bətḥammal əṭ-ṭaqṣ əl-məšweb b-raaḥa.* **4.** *mšawweb*. Aren't you hot in these clothes? *maa-lak əmšawweb əb-hal-ʔawaaεi?* **5.** *ḥadd, ḥaami*. He has a hot temper. *ṭabεo ḥadd.* -- This mustard sure is hot. *hal-xardal bala šakk ḥaami.* **6.** *taaza* (invar.). The scent is still hot. *riiḥet əl-ʔasar ləssaaha taaza.*
**The police were hot on his trail. *š-šərṭa kaanu laaḥqiino εad-daεse.*
**I made it hot for him. *ḥaraqət diino.*
hotel - *ʔoteel* pl. *-aat*. I'm looking for a cheap hotel. *εam ədawwer εala ʔoteel ərxiiṣ.*
hot plate - *ṣaxxaane* pl. *-aat*.
hour - *saaεa* pl. *-aat*. I'll be back in an hour. *bəržaε baεəd saaεa.* -- Wait a quarter of an hour. *stanna rəbəε saaεa.* -- She practices piano for hours. *btətmarran εal-byaano saaεaat εan ḥaqa.* -- I worked five hours overtime. *štaġalət xaməs saaεat əzyaade.* -- What are your working hours? *ʔeemta saaεaat dawaamak?*
**This place stays open till all hours. *hal-maḥall biḍall faateḥ la-εand əl-fažər.*
hour hand - *εaqrab~* (pl. *εaqaareb~*) *saaεaat*.
after hours - *baεd əš-šəġəl*. See me after hours. *šuufni baεd əš-šəġəl.*
at all hours - *b-ʔayy waqət, b-ʔayy waqten kaan.* I can be reached at all hours. *məmken əl-ʔəttiṣaal fiyyi b-ʔayy waqten kaan.*
**He comes home to lunch at all hours. *byəži εal-ġada ʔeemta-ma bəddo.*
hourglass - *saaεa* (pl. *-aat*) *ramliyye, saaεet~ raməl*.
house - **1.** *beet* pl. *byuut*. I want to rent a house. *bəddi ʔəstaʔžer beet.* -- I have searched the whole house. *fattašt əl-beet kəllo.* -- She keeps house for her uncle. *bəddiir beet εamma.* -- The war has driven many people out of house and home. *l-ḥarb šarradet εaalam əktiir mən əbyuuta.* **2.** *mažles* pl. *mažaales*. Both houses will meet in joint session tomorrow. *l-mažəlseen laḥa yəžtəmεu b-žalse məštarake bəkra.*
**The house is sold out. *t-tazaaker mənbaaεa kəlla.*
**The drinks are on the house. *l-mašruubaat εala ḥsaab əl-maḥall.*
to house - *ʔaawa//tʔaawa*. Where are they going to house the visitors? *ween bəddon yʔaawu ḍ-ḍyuuf?*
household - **1.** *manzel* pl. *manaazel*. I don't know how she can manage that big household all by herself. *maa-li εarfaan kiif εam əddabber la-ḥaala hal-manzel əb-kəbro.* **2.** *manzili**. Look in the section for household goods. *ṭṭallaε bəl-qsəm yalli bibiiεu fii ʔadawaat manziliyye.*
housemaid - *ṣaanεa* pl. *-aat* and *ṣənnaaε*.
housewife - *sətt~ beet* pl. *səttaat~ əbyuut.*
housework - *šəġəl manzili, šəġəl~ beet*. She simply hates housework. *hiyye btəkrah əš-šəġl əl-manzili.*
housing - *sakan*. Adequate housing is hard to find these days. *ṣaεb əl-waaḥed ylaaqi sakan əmnaaseb hal-ʔiyyaam.* -- The housing problem grows worse every year. *məškəlt əs-sakan εam təṣεab sane baεəd sane.*
how - **1.** *kiif, šloon*. How shall I do it? *kiif bəddi saawiiha?* -- How do you feel today? *šloonak əl-yoom?* -- I don't know how he got in. *maa baεref kiif faat.* **2.** *šuu, qaddeeš*. How nice! *šuu laṭiif!* -- How kind of you! *šuu ləṭəf mənnak!* -- How ugly she is! *qaddeeš bəšεa hiyye!* -- How long is the table? *qaddeeš ṭuul əṭ-ṭaawle?* -- How old are you? *qaddeeš εəmrak?*
how come - *šloon, kiif, leeš*. How come you're still here? *šloon ləssaatak hoon?*
how do you do - **1.** *marḥaba*. I just wanted to say "How do you do?" *bass ḥabbeet qəl-lak "marḥaba."* --How do you do? Haven't we met before? *marḥaba. ḥaṣəl-li š-šaraf w-tεarrafna mən qabəl?* **2.** *tšarrafna, ʔahla w-sahla*. I want you to meet my friend Ahmad. - How do you do! *bḥəbb qaddəm-lak sadiiqi ʔaḥmad. - tšarrafna!*
**That's a fine how-do-you-do! *hayy warṭa malεuune!*
how is it - *kiif, šloon, leeš*. How is it you didn't go to the party? *kiif maa rəḥət εal-ḥafle?*
how long - *qaddeeš*. How long shall we wait? *qaddeeš bəddna nəstanna?*
how many - *kam* (with foll. sg.). How many oranges shall I take? *kam bərdqaane ʔaaxod?* -- How many times do I have to tell you? *kam marra bəddi qəl-lak?*
how much - *qaddeeš*. How much did you pay for it? *qaddeeš dafaεət ḥaqqa?*
however - **1.** *bass, laaken*. I'd like to do it, however I have no time. *bḥəbb ʔənno saawiiha bass maa εandi waqət.* **2.** *kiif-ma, šloon-ma*. However you tackle the problem, the solution won't be easy. *kiif-ma εaalašt əl-masʔale bətlaaqi ʔənno l-ḥall muu hayyen.*
howl - *təεwaaye, εuwaaʔ*. I thought I heard the howl of a wolf. *kaʔənni smaεət təεwaayet diib.*
**He's a howl. *huwwe tarkiibe.*
to howl - **1.** *εawa* (*i εuwaaʔ*), *εawwa*. The dog has been howling all night. *l-kalb ṣar-lo εam yəεwi ṭuul əl-leel.* **2.** *ṣarrax*. The audience howled with laughter. *ž-žamhuur ṣaar yṣarrex mən əḍ-ḍəḥək.*
hub cap - *ṭaase* pl. *-aat, ṭaaset~ duulaab* pl. *ṭaasaat~ dawaliib*.
to **huddle** - *zdaḥam*. They huddled in a corner. *zdaḥamu b-zaawye.* -- The sheep huddled close together. *l-ġanam zdaḥmet εala baεḍa l-baεəḍ.*
to be in a huddle - *ḥaṭṭu raason maε baεḍon əl-baεəḍ*. Those two are always in a huddle. *hat-tneen daayman ḥaaṭṭiin raason maε baεḍon əl-baεəḍ.*
hug - *εabṭa* pl. *-aat*. She gave him a big hug. *εabəṭṭo εabṭa maakne.*
to hug - *εabaṭ* (*o εabəṭ//nεabaṭ*). She hugged her mother tightly. *εabṭet ʔəmma εabṭa qawiyye.*
**Our boats hugged the coast line all the way. *šaxatiirna tammet maašye b-əmḥaazaat əš-šaṭṭ ṭuul əṭ-ṭariiq.*
huge - **1.** *ḍaxəm, ḍəxem*. They're building a huge dam upriver. *εam yεammru sadd ḍaxəm εan-nahər mən fooq.* **2.** *haaʔel*. A huge explosion rocked the town. *ṣaar ʔənfižaar haaʔel hazz əl-balad hazz.*
hum - *wanne* pl. *-aat*. What's that peculiar hum? *šuu hal-wanne l-ġariibe?*
to hum - *hamham* (*b-*), *wann* (*ə wann*)(*b-*). What's that tune you're humming? *šuu han-naġme yalli εam əthamhem fiiha?*
**Things are always humming at this corner. *hal-qərne maa btəhda.*

**With the arrival of the new boss, things are humming at the office again. *maƐ žayyet ᵊr-raʔiis ᵊž-ždiid ṣaar fii rakde bᵊd-daayre taani marra.*

human – **1.** *bašari**. Overpopulation presents a serious threat to the human race. *tadaxxom ᵊs-səkkaan bikawwen tahdiid xaṭiir ləl-žəns ᵊl-bašari.* **2.** *ʔənsaani**. It's a common human weakness. *haada ḍəƐᵊf ʔənsaani maʔluuf.*

**I'm only human. *ʔana bašar kamaan.*

**It's only human to make mistakes. *maa ḥada maƐṣuum Ɛan ᵊl-xaṭaʔ ġeer ʔaḷḷa.*

human being – *ʔənsaan* pl. *bašar, bašar* (sg. and pl.). Don't forget he's a human being. *laa tənsa ʔənno ʔənsaan huwwe* (or *ʔənno huwwe bašar*).

**He treats us like human beings. *biƐaaməlna mətl ᵊl-Ɛaalam wᵊn-naas.*

humane – *ʔənsaani**.

humanities – *l-ʔaadaab.*

humanity – *l-bašariyye, l-ʔənsaaniyye.*

humble – *mətwaaḍeƐ.* He grew up in very humble circumstances. *rəbi b-waṣaṭ mətwaaḍeƐ.* -- She's always so humble. *hiyye daayman mətwaaḍƐa.*

to act humble – *twaaḍaƐ.* In the beginning he acted very humble. *bᵊl-ʔawwal twaaḍaƐ* or ***bᵊl-ʔawwal daarha waaṭye.*

humid – *rəṭeb.*

humidity – *rṭuube.*

to **humiliate** – *baxaƐ (a baxᵊƐ), bahdal, šaršaḥ.* You didn't have to humiliate him in front of those people. *maa kaan ḍaruuri təbxaƐo qəddaam ᵊn-naas.*

humility – *tawaaḍoƐ, xuḍuuƐ.*

humor – **1.** *mazaaž.* Are you in a good humor today? *mazaažak raayeq ᵊl-yoom?* -- What humor is he in today? *kiif mazaažo l-yoom?* **2.** *mazᵊḥ, mizaaḥ.* I don't like this kind of humor. *maa bḥəbb han-nooƐ ᵊmn ᵊl-mazᵊḥ.*

**He doesn't see the humor of it all. *maa Ɛam yšuuf ᵊž-žiha l-məḍᵊḥke fiiha.*

sense of humor – *rooḥ˜ ᵊn-nəkte.* He has no sense of humor. *maa Ɛando rooḥ ᵊn-nəkte.*

to humor – *saayar.* Why don't you just humor him this time? *leeš maa bətsaayro hal-marra?*

humorous – *hazli*, məḍḥek.* A collection of humorous stories. *mažmuuƐet qəṣaṣ hazliyye.*

hump – *ḥadbe* pl. *-aat.*

hunch: I have a hunch that something is wrong there. *qalbi qaayə́l-li ʔənno fii šii muu maẓbuuṭ ᵊhniik.*-- I just followed a hunch. *saaweet mətᵊl-ma qal-li qalbi.*

hunchback – **1.** *ḥadbe* pl. *-aat.* One had a hunchback. *waaḥed mənnon kan-lo ḥadbe.* **2.** *ʔaḥdab* f. *ḥadba* pl. *ḥədᵊb* and *ḥədbaan.* I mean the hunchback over there. *bəƐni l-ʔaḥdab ᵊhniik.*

hunchbacked – *ʔaḥdab* f. *ḥadba* pl. *ḥədᵊb* and *ḥədbaan.* You'll get hunchbacked sitting that way. *bətṣiir ʔaḥdab* (or ***btəṭlə́Ɛ-lak ḥadbe*) *ʔiza bəttamm təqƐod heek.*

hunched up – *məḥni*.* Your back hurts because you're sitting hunched up. *Ɛam yuužaƐak ḍahrak laʔənnak qaaƐed məḥni.*

hundred – *miyye* pl. *miʔaat.* How much is it by the hundred? *qaddeeš ḥaqqa bᵊl-miyye?* -- About a hundred people were present. *kaan ḥawaali miit zalame ḥaaḍer.* -- Hundreds of people were made homeless by the flood. *miʔaat ᵊn-naas ṣaaru bala maʔwa b-sabab ᵊl-fayaḍaan.* -- The repair alone cost me four hundred pounds. *t-taṣliiḥ waḥdo kallafni ʔarbaƐ miit leera.*

hundredth – *məʔawi*.* It's the company's hundredth anniversary. *huwwe Ɛiid ᵊš-šərke l-məʔawi.*

one hundredth – *žəzᵊʔ məʔawi* pl. *ʔažzaaʔ məʔawiyye.* One hundredth of an inch. *žəzᵊʔ məʔawi mn ᵊl-ʔənš.*

Hungarian – **1.** *həngaari* pl. *-iyye.* I met a Hungarian yesterday. *tƐarrafᵊt Ɛala waaḥed həngaari mbaareḥ.* **2.** *həngaariyye* pl. *-aat.* She's a Hungarian. *hiyye həngaariyye.* **3.** *həngaari* (invar.). He speaks a good Hungarian. *byəḥki həngaari mniiḥ.* **4.** *həngaari** The restaurant's specialty is Hungarian food. *l-maṭƐam məxtaṣṣ bᵊl-ʔaklaat ᵊl-həngaariyye.*

Hungary – *həngaarya, blaad˜ ᵊl-mažar.*

hunger – *žuuƐ.* I nearly died of hunger. *kənt laḥa muut mn ᵊž-žuuƐ.*

hungry – *žuuƐaan.* He has to feed ten hungry mouths. *laazem yṭaƐmi Ɛašᵊrt ənfos žuuƐaaniin.* -- I'm hungry. *ʔana žuuƐaan.*

to go hungry – *žaaƐ (u žuuƐ).* We didn't go hungry. *maa žəƐna.*

hunt – *ṣeed.* The duck hunt was called off. *ṣeed ᵊl-baṭṭ ᵊlṭaġa.*

to hunt – *ṣṭaad, ṣaad (i ṣeed//nṣaad), tṣayyad.* They're hunting rabbits. *Ɛam yəṣṭaadu ʔaraaneb.* -- We're going hunting tomorrow. *bəkra raayḥiin nətṣayyad.*

to hunt for – *dawwar Ɛala, fattaš Ɛala.* We are hunting for an apartment. *Ɛam ᵊndawwer Ɛala beet.*

to hunt up – *lamm (ə lamm), žammaƐ.* How many helpers did you hunt up? *kam waaḥed lammeet yalli ysaaƐduuk?*

hunter – *ṣayyaaḍ* pl. *-iin.*

hunting license – *rəxṣet˜* (pl. *rəxaṣ˜*) *ṣeed, ʔižaazet˜* (pl. *-aat˜*) *ṣeed.*

hurdle – *ḥaažez* pl. *ḥawaažez.*

hurricane – *zoobaƐa* pl. *zawaabeƐ.*

hurry – *Ɛažale.* There's no hurry. *maa fii Ɛažale.* -- What's the hurry? *leeš hal-Ɛažale?*

in a hurry – **1.** *məstaƐžel.* I'm in a big hurry. *ʔana məstaƐžel ᵊktiir.* **2.** *b-sərƐa, b-Ɛažale.* I read it in a great hurry. *qareeta b-sərƐa ktiir.*

**He wasn't in too big a hurry when he did that job. *mbayyen Ɛalée kaan ʔaaxed raaḥto b-haš-šaġle.*

to hurry – **1.** *staƐžal.* Don't hurry! *laa təstaƐžel!* or ***maa bədda Ɛažale!* -- Hurry! The bus is due any minute. *yaḷḷa staƐžel* (or ***xəffa*) *l-baaṣ laḥa yəži.* **2.** *Ɛažžal, staƐžal.* Don't hurry me. *laa tƐažželni.*

to hurry up – *staƐžal.* Hurry up! I haven't got all day. *yaḷḷa staƐžel!* (or ***xəffa!*) *ʔana maa-li waqᵊf Ɛaleek.*

to **hurt** – **1.** *wəžeƐ (-yuužaƐ* and *-yəžaƐ wažaƐ).* My arm hurts. *ʔiidi Ɛam tuužaƐni.* **2.** *ʔaza (i ʔaza// nʔaza).* He hurt himself badly when he fell down the stairs. *ʔaza ḥaalo Ɛan ḥaqa lamma wəqeƐ mən Ɛad-daraž.* **3.** *žaraḥ (a žarᵊḥ//nžaraḥ).* She hurt herself with a razor blade. *žarḥet ḥaala b-šafra.*-- I didn't want to hurt your feelings. *maa kaan niiti ʔəžraḥ Ɛawaaṭfak.* **4.** *mass (ə mass//mmass).* I didn't mean to hurt you with this remark. *maa kaan qaṣdi məssak ᵊb-hal-ᵊmlaaḥaẓa.* **5.** *ḍarr (ə ḍarr//nḍarr)* This will hurt business. *haada biḍərr ᵊt-tižaara.* -- Will it hurt if I'm late? *biḍərr šii ʔiza tʔaxxarᵊt?*

husband – *zoož* pl. *ʔazwaaž, žooz* pl. *žwaaz, ražžaal* pl. *ržaal.*

hush – *həṣṣ!* Hush! I can't hear a word. *həṣṣ! maa-li Ɛam ʔəsmaƐ šii.*

to hush up – *ṭamar (o ṭamᵊr//nṭamar).* The scandal was quickly hushed up. *ž-žərṣa nṭamret ᵊb-sərƐa.*

husky – **1.** *ḍaxm ᵊž-žəsse.* He's such a husky fellow! *qaddeešo ḍaxm ᵊž-žəsse!* **2.** *xəšen.* He has a husky voice. *ṣooṭo xəšen.*

hut – *kuux* pl. *kwaax.*

hydraulic brake – *fraam* (pl. *-aat*) *Ɛaz-zeet.*

hydrogen – **1.** *hədrožeen.* Oxygen and hydrogen. *l-ʔoksižeen wᵊl-hədrožeen.* **2.** *hədrožeeni*.* The hydrogen bomb. *l-qəmble l-hədrožeeniyye.*

hyena – *ḍabᵊƐ* pl. *ḍbaaƐ.*

hyphen – *waṣle* pl. *-aat.*

hypnosis – *tanwiim maġnaṭiisi.*

hypochondriac – *mwaswas* pl. *-iin.*

hypocrisy – *nifaaq.*

hypocrite – *mnaafeq* pl. *-iin.*

hypothesis – *faraḍiyye* pl. *-aat.*

hypothetical – *ʔəftiraaḍi*, faraḍi**

hysteria – *həstərya.*

hysterical – **1.** *mhaster.* I think she's a little hysterical. *bẓənna šwayye mhastra.* **2.** *həstiiri* mhaster.* She burst into hysterical laughter. *nfažret ᵊb-ḍəḥke həstiiriyye.*

to get hysterical – *hastar.* Don't get so hysterical about the whole thing. *laa thaster mənšaan haš-šaġle.*

I

I - *ʔana.*
ice - 1. *žaliid, smeeta.* There was ice on the road in the morning. *ʕaṭ-ṭariiq ṣ-ṣəbəḥ kaan fii žaliid.* 2. *žaliid.* Is the ice thick enough for skating? *ž-žaliid qaasi kfaaye ləs-sahlaqa?* 3. *buuẓ.* Put some ice in the glasses. *ḥəṭṭ šwayyet buuẓ bəl-kaasaat.*
ice cube - *šaqfet˜* (pl. *šəqaf˜*) *buuẓ.* Put three ice cubes in each glass. *b-kəll kaase ḥəṭṭ ətlətt šəqaf buuẓ.*
to ice - *zammaq, ḥaṭṭ əkreem (ʕal-gaato).* Ice the cake as soon as it's cool. *zammqi l-gaato lamma byəbrod.*
iced - *mtallaž.* I'd like some iced coffee. *bəddi kaaset qahwe mtallaže.*
iceberg - *žaliidiyye* pl. *-aat.*
icebox - *tallaaže* pl. *-aat,* (electric refrigerator) *barraad(e)* pl. *-aat.*
ice cream - *buuẓa, qeemaq.*
Iceland - *ʔəslanda.*
Icelandic - *ʔəslandi*.*
icing - *naaṭef.*
icy - 1. *baared mətl ət-talž, baared əktiir.* The water's icy. *l-mayye baarde mətl ət-talž.* 2. *msaqqeʕ.* There's an icy wind blowing from the mountains. *fii hawa msaqqeʕ žaaye mən naaḥ ž-žbaal.* 3. *mžalled.* Be careful, the streets are icy. *ntəbeh əš-šawaareʕ əmžallde.*
idea - *fəkra* pl. *ʔafkaar.* That's a good idea! *hayy fəkra mniiḥa.* — She has big ideas. *ʕanda ʔafkaar ʔakbar mənna* or *ʕanda ʔafkaar mən fooq əl-ʔaṣaṭiih.* — I haven't the faintest idea what he wants. *maa ʕandi ʔayy fəkra šuu bəddo.*— Of all the ideas! *ʔasxaf fəkra mən heek ʔaḷḷa maa xalaq!* -- What gives you that idea? *mneen ʔəžətak hal-fəkra?* or *mneen žəbət hal-fəkra?*
**I couldn't get used to the idea. *maa qdərət ʔətʕawwad ʕala haš-šii.*
**That's the idea! *hallaq žəbta!*
**The idea! *laa saamaḥa ḷḷaah!*
ideal - 1. *masal ʔaʕla* pl. *məsol ʕəlya.* Our ideals are freedom and independence. *məsəlna l-ʕəlya l-ḥərriyye wəl-ʔəstiqlaal.* 2. *qədwe, masal ʔaʕla.* He's my ideal. *huwwe qədwe ʔəli.* 3. *misaali*.* That's an ideal solution. *haada ḥall misaali.*
**This is an ideal place for swimming. *hal-maḥall təḥfe ləs-sbaaḥa.*
idealism - *misaaliyye.*
idealist - *misaali* pl. *-iyyiin.*
idealistic - *misaali*.*
identical - *mətəl baʕḍon.* The two copies are identical. *n-nəsəxteen mətəl baʕḍon.* — The two girls are wearing identical dresses. *l-benteen laabsiin fasaṭiin mətəl baʕḍon.*
identification - 1. *taḥqiiq əb-hawiyyet˜* ... Identification of the crash victims is still going on. *t-taḥqiiq əb-hawiyyet ḍaḥaaya l-ḥaades ləssáa žaari.* 2. *hawiyye* pl. *-aat.* Do you have any identification? *fii ʕandak šii yəsbet hawiitak?*
identification card - *biṭaaqet˜* (pl. *-aat˜*) *hawiyye, taskart˜* (pl. *tasaaker˜*) *hawiyye, hawiyye* pl. *-aat.* Your identification card, please. *biṭaaqet hawiitak ʕmeel maʕruuf.*
to identify - *tḥaqqaq əmn əl-hawiyye.* The police identified him by his fingerprints. *š-šərṭa tḥaqqaqet mən hawiito mən baṣmaat ʔaṣaabʕo.*
to identify oneself - *ʔasbat hawiito.* Can you identify yourself? *btəqder təsbet hawiitak?*
identity - *hawiyye.* The police still do not know the identity of the thief. *š-šərṭa ləssaata maa btaʕref hawiyyet əl-ḥaraami.*
ideology - *ʔədyoloožya.*
idiocy - *hablane, žadbane, ḥamrane.*
idiot - *mahbuul* pl. *mahabiil, mažduub* pl. *mažadiib.* Their second son was born an idiot. *ʔəbnon ət-taani wəled mahbuul.*
**What an idiot! *məlla ḥmaar!*
idiotic - *saxiif.* Look at this idiotic letter. *šuuf hal-maktuub əs-saxiif.* — This was an idiotic thing to do. *kaan ʕamal saxiif waḷḷa.*
**He stared at me with an idiotic smile. *baḥlaq fiyyi w-ʕala wəššo ʔəbtisaamet hablane.*
idle - 1. *bala šəgəl* (invar.), *ʕaaṭel ʕan əl-ʕamal, (qaaʕed) baṭṭaal.* He's been idle for some time. *ṣar-lo mədde bala šəgəl.* 2. *kaslaan.* He is an idle fellow. *huwwe waaḥed kaslaan.* 3. *faaḍi.* That's just idle talk. *haada kalaam faaḍi, muu ʔaktar.* 4. *mətʕaṭṭel, əmʕaṭṭal, waaqef.* The factory has been lying idle for years. *l-maṣnaʕ ṣar-lo sniin mətʕaṭṭel.*
**Her hands are never idle. *ʔideeha maa byəfətru.*
to idle - *štaġal ʕal-faaḍi.* The motor is idling. *l-motoor ʕam yəštəġel ʕal-faaḍi.*
Idlib - *ʔədleb.*
idol - 1. *ṣanam* pl. *ʔaṣnaam.* The natives of the island still worship idols. *səkkaan əž-žaziire ləssaaton ʕam yəʕəbdu ʔaṣnaam.* 2. *maʕbuud* pl. *-iin.* He's the people's idol. *huwwe maʕbuud əš-šaʕəb.*
if - 1. *ʔiza, ʔən* (enclitically *n-*) with foll. perfect. If anyone asks for me tell him I'll be right back. *ʔiza ḥada byəsʔal ʕanni qəl-lo bəržaʕ baʕd əšwayye.* — If you come with me I'll give you a pound. *n-əʔžiit maʕi baʕṭiik leera.* 2. *ʔiza kaan.* See if there's any mail for me. *šuuf ʔiza kaan fii ʔəli šii makatiib.* — I don't know if he'll come or not. *maa baʕref ʔiza kaan laḥa yəži ʔaw laʔ.* 3. *law.* If he had told me so I would have acted differently. *law (kaan) qal-li heek kənt əʕməlt ġeer heek.*
if ... only - *ya-reet, ʕala waah.* If I could only get there! *ya-reet ʔəqder ʔəṣal la-hniik!*
as if - *kaʔənn-* + pron. suff. He talks as if he had been there. *ʕam yəḥki kaʔənno kaan əhniik.* — They act as if they don't know anything about it. *ʕam yətṣarrafu kaʔənnon maa byaʕərfu šii ʕan əš-šaġle.*
even if - *w-law, ḥatta law* (both with foll. perf.). I'll go even if it rains. *bruuḥ əw-law kaanet əl-maṭar naazle.* — Even if he gave me 100 pounds I wouldn't do it. *ḥatta law ʕaṭaani miit leera maa bsaawiiha.*
to ignite - 1. *šaʕʕal.* We ignited the kerosene. *šaʕʕalna zeet əl-kaas.* 2. *štaʕal, ltahab.* The gasoline ignited when the car hit the tree. *l-banziin əštaʕal lamma s-sayyaara ḍarbet əš-šažara.*
ignition - *kontaak.* Leave the key in the ignition. *treek əl-məftaaḥ bəl-kontaak.*
ignorance - *žahəl.* I've never seen such ignorance. *b-ḥayaati maa šəfət mətl haž-žahəl.* — Ignorance of the law is no excuse. *ž-žahəl bəl-qaanuun muu ʕəzər.*
ignorant - *žaahel* pl. *-iin* and *žahale.* I've never met such an ignorant person before. *b-ḥayaati maa šəfət šaxəṣ žaahel mətəl heek.*
to ignore - 1. *tġaaḍa ʕan.* I would ignore the insult. *law əb-maḥallak kənət bətġaaḍa ʕan əl-bahdale.* 2. *džaahal.* I ignored him. *džaahalto.*
ill - *mariiḍ* pl. *mərada, ḍʕiif* pl. *ḍəʕafa.* He was very ill. *kaan mariiḍ əktiir.*
**He can ill afford to quit his job now. *muu taaleʕ əb-ʔiido yətrok šəġlo b-hal-ʔiyyaam.*
**He's ill at ease in such company. *maa byaaxod ḥərriito maʕ heek žamaaʕa.*
illegal - *ġeer qaanuuni*, ġeer šarʕi*.* This illegal action cost him dearly. *hal-ʕamal ġeer əl-qaanuuni* (or *l-ġeer qaanuuni*) *kallafo ġaali.*
illegitimate - *ġeer šarʕi*.* He is an illegitimate child. *huwwe ṭəfl ġeer šarʕi* (or ***ʔəbən ḥaraam*).
illiteracy - *ʔəmmiyye.*
illiterate - *ʔəmmi*.*
illness - *maraḍ* pl. *ʔamraaḍ.*
illogical - *muu manṭiqi.*
illusion - *wahəm* pl. *ʔawhaam.*
to illustrate - 1. *ṣawwar//tṣawwar.* The author commissioned one of the most famous artists to illustrate his latest book. *l-əmʔallef kallaf waaḥed mən ʔašhar əl-fannaaniin*

la-yṣawwə́r-lo ktaabo l-ʔaxiir. — This is an illustrated magazine. *hayy mažalle mṣawwara.* 2. *waḍḍaḥ, bayyan.* Let me illustrate this by an example. *xalliini waḍḍə́ḥ-lak haš-šii b-masal.*

illustration - 1. *ṣuura* pl. *ṣuwar.* The catalogue has many illustrations. *l-kataloog fii ṣuwar ᵊktiire.* 2. *misaal.* Here we have a beautiful illustration of what I'm trying to say. *haada misaal ḥayy la-halli ʕam ḥaawel quulo.*

ill will - *ʕadaawe* pl. *-aat, ḍaġiine* pl. *ḍaġaayen.* His insults caused a lot of ill will. *msabbaato sabbabet ʕadaawe ktiir.*

image - *ṣuura* pl. *ṣuwar.* The image I have of him is that of an old man. *ṣuurto b-ʕaqli ṣuuret waaḥed ʔəxṭyaaṛ.*

**She's the very image of her mother. *btəšbah ʔəmma tamaam* or *hiyye ṣuura ṭəbq ᵊl-ʔaṣᵊl la-ʔəmma.*

imaginable - *məmken taṣawwuro, maʕquul taṣawwuro.* He tried everything imaginable. *ḥaawal kəll šii məmken taṣawwuro.*

**It's hardly imaginable that he'll increase your salary. *muu maʕquule ʔənno huwwe yziid maʕaašak.*

imaginary - *xayaali**. Children often live in an imaginary world. *l-ʔaṭfaaḷ ʔaḥyaanan biʕiišu b-ʕaalam xayaali.*

imagination - 1. *xayaal* pl. *-aat, taxayyol* pl. *-aat, taṣawwor* pl. *-aat.* That's pure imagination. *haada kəllo xayaal.* 2. *mxayyile, xayaal.* She has a lively imagination. *ʕandha mxayyile xəṣbe.*

to **imagine** - 1. *tṣawwar.* I can't imagine what you mean. *maa fiini ʔətṣawwar šuu ʕam təʕni.* -- I imagine so. *bətṣawwar heek.* 2. *txayyal.* He's just imagining it. *huwwe bass ʕam yətxayyal haš-šii.*

**You're only imagining things. *hayye bass taxayyulaatak.*

**I can imagine. *bsaddeq!*

imam - *ʔimaam* pl. *ʔaʔəmme.*

to **imitate** - *qallad//tqallad.* He can imitate my voice. *fii yqalled ṣooṭi.*

imitation - 1. *taqliid.* That's a poor imitation. *haada taqliid ᵊḍʕiif.* 2. *taqliid, muu ʔaṣli**. This pocketbook is made of imitation leather. *haš-šantaaye maʕmuule mən žəlᵊd taqliid.*

immature - *muu naaḍež.* I think his behavior is completely immature. *bəʕtə́qed taṣarrfo taṣarrof muu naaḍež tamaam.*

immediate - 1. *mubaašar.* He is my immediate superior. *huwwe raʔiisi l-mubaašar.* 2. *ḥaali**, *ʔaani**. This check will take care of your immediate needs. *haš-šakk byəkfi ḥaažaatak ᵊl-ḥaaliyye.*

**There's no school in the immediate neighborhood. *maa fii madrase qariibe b-han-nawaaḥi.*

immediately - *raʔsan, ḥaalan, mbaašaratan.* Immediately afterwards I heard a scream. *w-baʕda raʔsan sməʕᵊt ṣarxa.* 2. *ḥaalan, ʕal-ḥaarek, ʕal-foor.* I'll go there immediately. *ḥaalan laḥa ruuḥ la-hniik.*

immense - 1. *waaseʕ ktiir.* They have an immense living room. *fii ʕandon ʔuuḍet ᵊqʕuud waasʕa ktiir.* 2. *ḍaxᵊm, haaʔel.* Immense quantities of meat are imported every month. *byəstawᵊrdu kammiyyaat ḍaxme mn ᵊl-lḥuum kəll šahᵊr.*

immigrant - *mhaažer* pl. *-iin.* About one thousand immigrants enter the country every year. *ḥawaali ʔalf ᵊmhaažer byədᵊxlu l-ᵊblaad kəll səne.*

to **immigrate** - *haažar.* Her grandfather immigrated to this country. *žədda haažar la-hal-ᵊblaad.*

immigration - *həžra, mhaažara.* He works in the immigration office. *byəštə́ġel b-daaʔərt ᵊl-həžra.*

immoral - 1. (of an act) *faased, ḥaraam* (invar.), *mxəll (bᵊl-ʔaadaab).* 2. (of a person) *bala ʔaxlaaq* (invar), *raziil* pl. *rəzala* and *ʔarzaal.*

immortal - 1. *xaaled.* Mutanabbi is considered one of the immortal poets of the Arabs. *l-mutanabbi yuʕtábar mn ᵊš-šəʕara l-ʕarab ᵊl-xaaldiin.* 2. *ʔazali**. Every human being is endowed with an immortal soul. *kəll ʔənsaan ʔəlo rooḥ ʔazaliyye.*

immortality - *ʔazaliyye.* Christians believe in the immortality of the soul. *l-masiiḥiyyiin byəʕtəqdu b-ʔazaliyyet ᵊn-nafs.*

immunity - 1. *ḥaṣaane.* His diplomatic immunity was revoked. *ḥaṣaanto d-diblomaasiyye ltaġet.* 2. *manaaʕa.* His immunity to all kinds of diseases is amazing. *šii mədheš manaaʕto ḍədd kəll šii fii ʔamraaḍ.*

impartial - *ġeer* (or *muu*) *mətḥayyez, mḥaayed.* I'll try to be impartial. *bḥaawel kuun ġeer mətḥayyez.*-- He took an impartial attitude. *ʔaxad mawqef ᵊmḥaayed.*

impartiality - *ʕadam˜ taḥayyoz.*

impatience - *ʕadam˜ ṣabᵊr.* His impatience can be very annoying at times. *ʕadam ṣabro bixalli l-waaḥed ynarvez ᵊktiir b-baʕḍ ᵊl-ʔaḥyaan.*

impatient - *bala ṣabᵊr* (invar.). I hate impatient customers. *bəkrah ᵊz-zabaayen halli bala ṣabᵊr.*

**He is very impatient. *maa ʕando ṣabᵊr ʔabadan.*

**Don't be so impatient! *laa tkuun baṣᵊltak maḥruuqa!*

impatiently - *b-faareġ˜ ᵊṣ-ṣabᵊr.* He was waiting impatiently when I arrived. *kaan ʕam yənṭə́ẓer b-faareġ ᵊṣ-ṣabᵊr lamma wṣəlt.*

imperative - 1. *(ṣiiġet˜ ᵊl-)ʔamᵊr.* What is the imperative of "katab"? *šuu ṣiiġt ᵊl-ʔamᵊr mən "katab"?* 2. *waažeb.* It is imperative for all students to attend the meeting. *waažeb ʕala kəll ᵊṭ-ṭəllaab ʔənno yəḥḍaru l-ʔəžtimaaʕ.*

imperialism - *ʔəstəʕmaar.*

imperialist - *mustaʕmer* pl. *-iin.*

imperialistic - *ʔəstəʕmaari**.

impersonal - 1. *ġeer* (or *muu*) *šaxṣi**. My question to you was strictly impersonal. *suʔaali ʔəlak kaan ġeer šaxṣi tamaam.* 2. *rasmi**. The negotiations were conducted in a cold, impersonal atmosphere. *l-ᵊmfaawaḍaat žaret ᵊb-žaww baared w-rasmi.*

impertinence - *waqaaḥa.* His impertinence is becoming unbearable. *waqaaḥto maa ʕaadet tənḥə́mel.*

impertinent - *wəqeḥ.* He's the most impertinent fellow I ever met. *huwwe ʔawqaḥ šaxᵊṣ šəfto b-ḥayaati.* -- She was very offended by his impertinent remark. *zəʕlet ᵊktiir mn ᵊmlaaḥaẓto l-wəqḥa.*

to **imply** - 1. *dall (ə ə) ʕala, waḥa (-yuuḥi ə).* His answer implied that he was in favor of the plan. *žawaabo dall ʕala taʔyiido ləl-xəṭṭa.* 2. *qaṣad (o qaṣᵊd//nqaṣad).* Are you implying that I'm a liar? *ʕam təqṣod šii ʔənni kazzaab?*

to **implore** - *twassal la-.* She implored him not to leave her. *twassalə́t-lo ʔənno maa yətrə́ka.*

impolite - *qaliil˜ ʔadab* pl. *qlaal˜ ʔadab.* She is very impolite. *hiyye qaliilet ʔadab ᵊktiir.*

**That was very impolite of him. *haada kaan ᵊktiir qəllet ʔadab mənno.*

**Why are you so impolite? *šuu hal-qəllet ᵊl-ʔadab?*

import - *ʔəstiiraad.* The government encouraged the import of raw materials. *l-ᵊḥkuume šažžaʕet ʔəstiiraad ᵊl-mawaadd ᵊl-ʔawwaliyye.*

to import - *stawrad.* Many countries import French wines. *fii blaad ᵊktiir btəstawred ᵊnbiit ᵊfrənsaawi.*

importance - *ʔahammiyye.* You attach too much importance to it. *ʔənte bətʕalleq ʕaleeha ʔahammiyye ktiir.* -- That's of no importance. *haš-šii maa-lo ʔahammiyye.*

important - *mhəmm, haamm.* I want to see you about an important matter. *bəddi šuufak b-masʔale mhəmme.*-- He was the most important man in town. *kaan huwwe ʔahamm rəžžaal bᵊl-balad.*

to **impose on** - 1. *staġall.* He's imposing on your good nature. *ʕam yəstġəll ṭiibet nafsak.* 2. *staḍʕaf, staġall.* Don't let them impose on you. *la txalliihon yəstaḍᵊʕfuuk.*

imposing - *faxᵊm.* What do they call that imposing monument? *šuu bisammu han-naṣb ᵊl-faxᵊm?*

imposition - *taqaale.* That's an imposition. *hayy taqaale.*

impossibility - *ʕadam˜ ʔəmkaaniyye, ʔəstiḥaale.* Now I'm beginning to realize the impossibility of your plan. *hallaq badeet ʔəšʕor b-ʕadam ʔəmkaaniyyet xəṭṭᵊtak.*

impossible - 1. *muu məmken.* Why is it impossible? *leeš muu məmken?* 2. *məstaḥiil.* All of a sudden, we found ourselves in an impossible situation. *mən qalb ᵊd-dənye wažadna ḥaalna b-waḍᵊʕ məstaḥiil.*

**That man is absolutely impossible! *haz-zalame maa byənṭaaq.*

impostor - *naṣṣaab* pl. *-iin, dažžaal* pl. *-iin, ʕawanṭaži* pl. *-iyye.*

impotent - 1. *ʕaažez.* 2. (sexually) *mahluul.*

to **impress** - *bahar (e ə//nbahar).* That doesn't impress me at all. *haš-šii maa byəbharni ʔabadan.*

**He impressed me as a very capable man. *ʕabba ʕeeni ka-ražol kəfᵊʔ.*

impression - *ʔənṭibaaʕ* pl. *-aat.* He made a good impression on me. *tarak ʔənṭibaaʕ ᵊmniiḥ ʕandi.* -- My impression of her was favorable. *ʔənṭibaaʕaati ʕanha kaanet ᵊmniiḥa.*

**I was under the impression that he isn't honest.

kənt ᵊmḥasseb ʔənno maa-lo ʔamiin.

to give the impression - *ʔawḥa.* He gives the impression of being a decent fellow. *byuuḥi ʔənno rəžžaal ʔaadami.*

to **imprison** - *ḥabas (e ḥabᵊs//nḥabas), sažan (o sažᵊn//nsažan).* The men were imprisoned for two months. *r-ržaal ᵊnḥabasu la-məddet šahreen.*

improbable - *muu məḥtámal, bᶜiid ᶜan ᵊl-ʔəḥtimaal.* It is improbable that she will go alone. *muu məḥtamal truuḥ la-ḥaala.*

to **improve** - **1.** *ḥassan.* I don't know how you can improve it. *maa baᶜref kiif bəddak tḥassno.* **2.** *tḥassan.* His condition has improved. *ḥaalto tḥassanet.* **3.** *tqaddam.* Ahmad is improving in school. *ʔaḥmad ᶜam yətqaddam bᵊl-madrase.*

improvement - **1.** *taḥsiin, taḥasson.* I don't see any improvement in her condition. *maa-li šaayef ʔayy taḥsiin b-ḥaaléta.* **2.** *taqaddom.* That's no improvement over what went before. *haada muu taqaddom ᶜala halli sabaq.*

improvisation - *ʔərtižaal.* The whole thing was an improvisation. *š-šaġle kəlla kaanet ʔərtižaal.*

to **improvise** - *rtažal.* He's good at improvising little speeches. *ᶜando maqdira laa baʔsa biha ᶜala ʔərtižaal xəṭab ᵊẓġiire.*

imprudence - *ᶜadamᵕ tabaṣṣor, ṭeeš.* It was her imprudence that caused the accident. *kaan ᶜadam tabaṣṣóra halli sabbab ᵊl-ḥaades.*

imprudent - *ṭaayeš.* I think he made a very imprudent decision. *bəᶜtéqed ᶜəmel ǵaraar ᵊktiir ṭaayeš.* -- That was very imprudent of you. *kaan ᶜamal ᵊktiir ṭaayeš mənnak.*

impudence - *waqaaḥa.*

impudent - *wəqeḥ.*

impulsive - *məndéfeᶜ.* She is a very impulsive person. *hiyye waaḥde məndəfᶜa ktiir.*

in - **1.** *b-* (with pron. suff. *fii-*). There's no stove in my room. *maa fii ṣooba b-ʔuuḍṭi.* -- He's in Aleppo now. *huwwe b-ḥalab hallaq.* -- My family lives in the country. *ᶜeelti saakne bᵊr-riif.* -- If I were in your place I would go. *law kənt ᵊb-maḥallak kənt ᵊbruuḥ.* -- Say it in English. *quula bᵊl-ʔəngliizi.* -- Write in ink. *ktoob bᵊl-ḥəbᵊr.* -- I can finish it in a week. *bxalléṣa b-žəmᶜa.* -- Did it happen in the daytime or at night? *ḥaṣlet bᵊṇ-nhaaṛ wəlla bᵊl-leel?* -- In other words ... *b-ᶜibaara ʔəxra ...* -- In my opinion ... *b-raʔyi ʔana ...* **2.** *baᶜᵊd.* I'll be back in three days. *bəržaᶜ baᶜd ᵊtlətt iyyaam.* -- I'll pay you in two weeks. *bədfdᶜ-lak baᶜᵊd žəmᵊᶜteen.* **3.** *hoon* (invar.), *mawžuud.* She's not in. *hiyye muu hoon* or *hiyye muu mawžuude.* -- He's at home today, but he'll be in tomorrow. *l-yoom bᵊl-beet bass bəkra bikuun hoon* (or *mawžuud hoon*).

**I'll see you in the morning. *bšuufak ᶜala bəkra* (or *ᵊṣ-ṣəbᵊḥ* or *ṣabaaḥan*).

**Where were you in the evening? *ween kənt ᵊl-masa?*

**We're three months behind in the rent. *nəḥna mətʔaxxriin ᶜan dafᶜ ᵊl-ʔəžra tlətt əšhor.*

**The boat is on its way in. *l-baaxra žaaye ᶜaṭ-ṭariiq.*

**Now we're in for it! *hallaq raḥa naakéla mərra!*

**Are you in on it, too? *btəmši maᶜna b-hal-masʔale ʔənte kamaan?*

**He has it in for you. *ᶜeeno ḥamra ᶜaleek.*

**He's in good with the boss. *ᶜalaaqaato mniiḥa maᶜ ᵊr-raʔiis.*

**He knows all the ins and outs. *byaᶜref ᵊš-šaarde wᵊl-waarde.*

all in - *halkaan mn ᵊt-taᶜab.* I'm all in today. *ʔana l-yoom halkaan mn ᵊt-taᶜab.*

inaccurate - *muu maẓbuuṭ.* This is an inaccurate estimate. *haada taqdiir muu maẓbuuṭ.*

inadequate - *muu kaafi.* That's an inadequate solution. *hal-ḥall muu kaafi.*

incense - *baxxuur.*

inch - *ʔənš* pl. *-aat, buuṣa* or *booṣa* pl. *-aat.* This ruler is 15 inches long. *hal-maṣṭara ṭuula xamaṣṭaᶜšar ʔənš.*

**He came within an inch of being run over. *maa ṣəfi beeno w-been ʔənno yəndáᶜes ʔəlla šaᶜra.*

**He's every inch a soldier. *huwwe žəndi b-laḥmo w-dammo* or *huwwe žəndi b-kəll maᶜna l-kəlme.*

**I used up every inch of the cloth. *staᶜmalt l-ᵊqmaaše la-ʔaaxer šaqfe fiiha.*

incident - *ḥaades* and *ḥaadse* pl. *ḥawaades.*

incidentally - **1.** *mən ġeer qaṣᵊd, bᵊl-ᶜaraḍ, ᶜaraḍan.* He just said it incidentally. *qaalha mən ġeer qaṣᵊd bass.* **2.** *b-hal-ᵊmnaasabe, bᵊl-ᵊmnaasabe.* Incidentally, I saw our friend Ali the other day. *b-hal-ᵊmnaasabe, šəfᵊt ṣaaḥəbna ᶜali mən yoomeen tlaate.*

to **include** - **1.** *ḥtawa ᶜala, ḍḍamman, štamal.* The dictionary doesn't include technical expressions. *l-ǵaamuus ma byəḥtəwi ᶜala ʔəṣṭilaaḥaat fanniyye.* **2.** *ḍaaf (i ʔəḍaafe //nḍaaf), ḍamm (ə ḍamm//nḍamm)* Include this in my bill. *ḍiif haada ᶜala ḥsaabi.*

**Gas and electricity are included in the rent. *l-ġaaz wᵊl-kəhraba daaxliin bᵊl-ʔəžra* or *ḍəmn ᵊl-ʔəžra.*

included - *bi-maa fii...* The room is five pounds, service included. *l-ʔuuḍa b-xamᵊs leeraat bi-maa fii l-xədme.*

including - *bi-maa fii...* He earns thirty dollars, including tips. *biṭaaleᶜ tlaatiin doolaar bi-maa fii l-baxšiiš.*

incognito - *mətxaffi.* He attended the ball incognito. *ḥəḍeṛ ᵊl-baal mətxaffi.*

income - *daxᵊl, waared* pl. *-aat.* How much of an income does he have? *qaddeeš daxlo?* or *qaddeeš waardo* (or *waardaato*)? -- He can manage pretty well on the income from his business. *mmašši ḥaalo mniiḥ mən waardaat tižaarto.*

income tax - *ḍariibetᵕ* (pl. *ḍaraayebᵕ*) *daxᵊl.*

incompetence - *ᶜadamᵕ kafaaʔa.* They fired him for incompetence and neglect. *qallaᶜúu la-ᶜadam kafaaʔto w-ʔəhmaalo.*

incomplete - *muu kaamel, muu taamm.* The details of your report are incomplete. *tafaṣiil taǵriirak muu kaamle.*

inconvenience - *ġalabe, təqle, səqle.* The trip entailed a lot of inconvenience for all of us. *s-safra sabbabət-ᵊlna ġalabe ktiir.*

to inconvenience - *ġallab, taqqal ᶜala.* I don't want to inconvenience you. *maa bəddi ġallbak* or *maa bəddi taqqel ᶜaleek.*

inconvenient - *muu mnaaseb.* He chose a very inconvenient time. *xtaar waqᵊt muu mnaaseb ʔabadan.* -- It will be inconvenient for us to go to the market today. *muu mnaaseb nruuḥ ᶜas-suuq ᵊl-yoom.*

incorrect - *muu maẓbuuṭ.* Some of what he said was incorrect. *fii šii b-kalaamo kaan muu maẓbuuṭ.*

increase - *tazaayod, ʔəzdiyaad, zyaade.* Statistics show a considerable increase in population. *l-ʔəḥṣaaʔaat bətwarži tazaayod malḥuuẓ bᵊs-səkkaan.*

to be on the increase - *zdaad, zaad (i zyaade).* The birth rate is on the increase. *nəsbet ᵊl-wilaade ᶜam təzdaad.*

to increase - **1.** *zaad (i zyaade//nzaad).* You have to increase your output. *laazem ᵊdziid ʔəntaažak.* **2.** *zdaad, zaad (i zyaade).* The population increased tremendously. *ᶜadad ᵊs-səkkaan ᵊzdaad zyaade haaʔile.*

incredible - *maa byətsaddaq.* She told us an incredible story. *ḥakét-ᵊlna qəṣṣa maa btətsaddaq.*

indecent - **1.** *ᶜeeb.* That's an indecent thing to say. *haada šii ᶜeeb yənḥáka.* **2.** *məṇṭaṛ.* She was picked up by the police for wearing indecent clothing. *kamdša l-booliis la-ʔənna kaanet laabse ʔawaaᶜi məṇṭaṛa.*

indecision - *taraddod.* Indecision is one of his worst qualities. *mən ʔalᶜan ᵊxṣaalo ᵊt-taraddod.*

indeed - *bᵊl-fəᶜᵊl, bᵊl-waaqeᶜ, ḥaqiiqatan, laa šakk.* That's very good indeed! *bᵊl-fəᶜᵊl haada ktiir ᵊmniiḥ.*

**Yes, indeed! *ʔée naᶜam!*

**Indeed? *ṣaḥiiḥ?* or *ᶜan ḥaqa?*

indefinite - **1.** *muu mᶜayyan, muu mḥaddad.* For an indefinite period. *la-məddе muu mᶜayyane.* **2.** *nakira* (invar.). This is an indefinite noun. *haada ʔəsᵊm nakira.*

independence - **1.** *ʔəstəqlaal.* In these days, all African colonies demand independence. *hal-ʔiyyaam kəll ᵊl-məstaᶜmaraat ᵊl-ʔafriiǵiyye ᶜam ᵊṭṭaaleb b-ʔəstəqlaala.* **2.** *ḥərriyye.* He insists on complete independence in his work. *ᶜam yṣərr ᶜala ḥərriyye taamme b-šəġlo.*

independent - *məstaǵəll, məstǵəll.* Lebanon is an independent state. *ləbnaan doole məstaǵəlle.* -- She's completely independent of her family. *hiyye məstǵəlle tamaam ᶜan ʔahla.*

**He's been independent ever since he was sixteen. *ṣar-lo məᶜtəmed ᶜala ḥaalo mən waqᵊt-ma kaan ᶜəmro səṭṭaᶜš.*

index - *fahras* pl. *fahaares.* Look for the name in the index. *dawwer ᶜal-ʔəsᵊm bᵊl-fahras.*

index finger - *šaahde, sabbaabe.*

India - *l-hənd.*

Indian - 1. *hendi* pl. *hnuud*. Not all Indians are Hindus. *muu kell l-ᵊhnuud handoos*. 2. *hendi ʔaḥmar* pl. *hnuud ḥemᵊr*. When I was a boy I used to read lots of stories about Indians and cowboys. *waqᵊt-ma kent ᵊẓġiir kent ʔeqra qeṣaṣ ᵊktiir ʕan l-ᵊhnuud ᵊl-ḥemᵊr wᵊl-kaawbooy*. 3. *hendi*ᵊ pl. *hnuud*. The Indian Ocean. *l-muḥiiṭ ᵊl-hendi*.

to **indicate** - *dall (e e) ʕala, bayyan*. His remark indicates that he's serious about it. *mlaaḥaẓto beddell ʕala ʔenno šaaded fiiha*.

indifferent - *muu mbaali, muu mehtamm*. Don't be so indifferent. *laa tkuun kell hal-qadd muu mbaali*. **I can't understand his indifferent attitude. *maa fiini ʔefham ʕadam mbaalaato*.

indigestion - *suuʔ~ haḍᵊm, taxme*. I have indigestion. *maʕi suuʔ haḍᵊm* or *maʕi taxme*.

indirect - *ġeer ᵊmbaašar*. The indirect route is more pleasant. *ṭ-ṭariiq ᵊl-ġeer ᵊmbaašar ʔasla*. **I wish you'd stop asking indirect questions. *ya-reet ᵊtwaqqef tesʔal suʔaalaat men taḥt la-taḥᵊt*.

indirectly - *b-ṣuura ġeer ᵊmbaašara*. She asked indirectly to be transferred. *ṭalbet b-ṣuura ġeer ᵊmbaašara ʔenna tentéqel*.

indispensable - 1. *laa bedd men*. A lot of experience is indispensable for this kind of work. *l-xebra laa bedd menha la-han-nooʕ mn ᵊš-šeġᵊl*. 2. *laa yustaġna ʕanno*. She thinks she is indispensable. *mḥassbe ʔenno laa yustaġna ʕanna*.

individual - 1. *fard* pl. *ʔafraad, šaxᵊṣ* pl. *ʔašxaaṣ*. The individual can do nothing. *l-fard la-ḥaalo maa byeqder yaʕmel šii* or **ʔiid waaḥde maa betsaffeq*. 2. *zalame* pl. *zelᵊm, šaxᵊṣ* pl. *ʔašxaaṣ, waaḥed*. He's a peculiar individual. *huwwe zalame ġariib* or *huwwe waaḥed ġariib*. 3. *xaaṣṣ*. We each have our individual taste. *kell waaḥed menna ʔelo zooqo l-xaaṣṣ*.

individually - *waaḥed waaḥed*. I wish to speak to the students individually. *ḥaabeb ʔeḥki maʕ ᵊṭ-ṭellaab waaḥed waaḥed*. -- The girls came individually to the station. *l-banaat ʔešu ʕal-ᵊmḥaṭṭa waaḥde waaḥde*.

Indo-China - *l-hend ᵊṣ-ṣiiniyye*.

indoors - 1. *šuwwaat~ ᵊl-beet, daaxel~ ᵊl-beet*. You'd better stay indoors today. *ʔaḥsán-lak teqʕod šuwwaat ᵊl-beet ᵊl-yoom*. 2. *šuwwa, bᵊd-daaxel*. If it rains the concert will be held indoors. *ʔiza laḥa tšatti l-ḥafle l-muusiiqiyye betṣiir šuwwa* (or *bᵊd-daaxel*).

industrial - *ṣinaaʕi*ᵊ. They are setting up industrial centers all over Syria. *ʕam yʔassᵊsu maraakez ṣinaaʕiyye ᵊb-suuriyya kella*.

industrialist - *ṣinaaʕi* pl. *-iyyiin*.

industrialization - *taṣniiʕ*. The industrialization of Egypt is making considerable progress. *taṣniiʕ maṣᵊr ʕam yetqaddam taqaddom maḥsuus*.

industry - 1. *ṣinaaʕa* pl. *-aat*. Many industries were developed after the war. *fii ʕeddet ṣinaaʕaat ᵊṭṭawwaret baʕd ᵊl-ḥarb*. 2. *šadd w-ʔeštihaad*. He solves his problems with thought and industry. *biḥell mašaaklo bi-šadd w-ʔeštihaad*.

inevitable - *laa bedd menno, laa mafarr menno*. An argument with him is inevitable now. *xnaaqa maʕo laa bedd* (or *laa mafarr*) *menna hallaq*. -- This was an inevitable conclusion. *haada kaan ʔestentaaš laa bedd menno*.

inevitably - *ḥatman*. Inevitably it had to come to this. *ḥatman maa kaan memken yṣiir ġeer halli ṣaar*.

inexperience - *ġašmane, ʕadam~ xebra*. We should take his inexperience into account. *laazem neḥsob ᵊḥsaab la-ġašmanto*.

inexperienced - *ġašiim* pl. *ġešᵊm* and *ġešama*. It's hard to work with inexperienced people. *ṣaʕb ᵊš-šeġᵊl maʕ naas ġešᵊm*.

infantile paralysis - *šalal~ ʔaṭfaal*.

infantry - *mušaat (f.)*.

infection - 1. (contagion) *ʕadwa*. 2. (inflammation) *ʔeltihaab*.

infectious - *meʕdi*ᵊ.

inferior - 1. *waaṭi*. How can you tell that it's an inferior quality? *šloon btaʕref ʔenno šenso waaṭi?* 2. *ʔawṭa*. This method is inferior to that. *hal-ᵊqmaaš ʔawṭa men hadaak*. 3. *ḍʕiif*. He is doing inferior work. *ʕam yenteš šeġl ᵊḍʕiif*.

inferiority - *waṭaawe*. The inferiority of the material is evident. *waṭaawet l-ᵊqmaaš baayne*.

inferiority complex - *murakkab~ naqᵊṣ, ʕeqdet~ naqᵊṣ*.

infidel - *kaafer* pl. *keffaar*.

infinite - *maa-lo nhaaye, bala nhaaye, bala ḥadd*. She has infinite patience with him. *ṣabra ʕaléе maa-lo nhaaye*. -- Whatever it is he does it with infinite care. *šuu-ma kaan byaʕmęla b-ᵊʕnaaye maa-la nhaaye*.

inflamed - *meltéheb*. My eye is inflamed. *ʕeeni meltéhbe*.

inflammable - *ḏaabel lel-ʔeltihaab*. The tank truck carried highly inflammable chemicals. *s-siiteern kaan ᵊmʕabba mawaadd kiimaawiyye ḏaable ktiir lel-ʔeltihaab*.

inflammation - *ʔeltihaab*.

inflation - *taḍaxxom maali*. He lost his fortune during the Inflation. *ṭaaret sarᵊwto ʔasna t-taḍaxxom ᵊl-maali*.

influence - 1. *taʔsiir*. You have always been a good influence on him. *daayman kan-lak taʔsiir ᵊmniiḥ ʕaléе*. 2. *nufuuz*. Both powers regard the area as their sphere of influence. *d-dawᵊlteen byeʕtebru l-manṭiqa manṭiqet nufuuzon*. **He has no influence whatsoever here. *maa-lo ʔayy kelme hoon*. **He was driving under the influence of alcohol. *kaan ʕam ysuuq w-huwwe sakraan*.

to influence - *ʔassar ʕala* or *b-*. I'm not trying to influence you. *ʔana maa-li ʕam ḥaawel ʔasser ʕaleek*. **He is trying to influence her in his favor. *ʕam yḥaawel yestmiila* (or *yestašlęba*) *ʔelo*.

influential - *ʔelo nufuuz*. He seems to be protected by an influential friend. *ẓ-ẓaaher ʔenno meḥmi men ṣadiiq ʔelo nufuuz*. -- He is an influential man in this town. *huwwe šaxᵊṣ ʔelo nufuuz b-hal-balad* or ** *kelᵊmto masmuuʕa b-hal-balad*.

influenza - *ʔenfluwanza*.

to **inform** - *xabbar//txabbar*. Nobody informed me in time. *maa ḥada xabbarni bᵊl-waqt ᵊl-laazem*.

to inform oneself - *ṭṭalaʕ*. First I'd like to inform myself about the climatic conditions of the country. *ʔawwal kell šii bḥebb ʔeṭṭéleʕ ʕal-ʔaḥwaal ᵊl-manaaxiyye b-hal-ᵊblaad*.

well informed - *meṭṭéleʕ, ʕarfaan*. He's unusually well informed. *huwwe ʕala ġeer ʕaade meṭṭéleʕ*.

informal - *ġeer rasmi*ᵊ. Did you attend the informal dinner at the end of the meeting? *ḥḍert ᵊl-ʕaša l-ġeer rasmi b-ʔaaxer ᵊl-ʔeštimaaʕ?*

information - 1. *maʕluumaat* (pl.) I can't give you any information about that. *maa beqder ʔaʕṭiik ʔayy maʕluumaat ʕan haš-šii*. 2. *ʔesteʕlaamaat* (pl.) Hello, is this Information? *ʔallo ʔesteʕlaamaat?*

to get information - *staʕlam, staxbar, ʔaxad maʕluumaat*. Where can I get some information about that? *mneen beqder ʔestaʕlem ʕan haš-šii?*

infraction - *mxaalafe* pl. *-aat*. Any infraction of these regulations will be severely punished. *ʔayy ᵊmxaalafe la-hal-ᵊʔnęẓime ʕaleeha ʕuḏuube šadiide*.

ingredient - 1. *ḥašuule* pl. *ḥašakiil*. Tell me all the ingredients you need for *kebbe*. *qel-li kell ᵊl-ḥašakiil halli btelzam lel-kebbe*. 2. *ʕenṣor* pl. *ʕanaaṣer*. The story has all the ingredients of slapstick comedy. *l-qeṣṣa fiiha kell ʕanaaṣer ᵊl-mahzale r-rxiiṣa*.

to **inhabit** - *sakan (o sekne//nsakan) b-*. The Ruala tribe inhabits the northern portion of the Arabian peninsula. *ʕašiiret ᵊr-rwala saakne b-ᵊšmaal šaziiret ᵊl-ʕarab*. -- This area was not inhabited until two years ago. *hal-manṭiqa maa nsaknet* (or *maa nsakan fiiha*) *ʔella men senteen w-šaaye*.

inhabitant - *saaken* pl. *sekkaan*, pl. only *ʔahᵊl* or *ʔahaali* (pl.). In 1950 Damascus had about 380,000 inhabitants. *kaan ʕadad sekkaan ᵊš-šaam sent ʔalf w-tesʕa miyye w-xamsiin ḥawaali tlaat miyye w-tmaaniin ʔalf*. -- All the inhabitants of the island are fishermen. *ʔahᵊl hal-šaziire kellon ṣayyaadiin samak*.

to **inherit** - *weret (-yrat* and *-yuurat wraate// nwarat)*. I inherited the ring from my mother. *wrett ᵊl-xaatem men ʔemmi*.

inheritance - *werte, wraate, miiraat*. My uncle left me a small inheritance. *ʕammi xallá-li werte ẓġiire*.

initial - 1. *ʔawwal ḥarf* pl. *ḥruuf ʔuula*. What are your initials? *šuu l-ᵊḥruuf ᵊl-ʔuula b-ʔesmak?* 2. *ʔawwali*ᵊ. The program is still in its initial stage. *l-bernaameš lessaato b-marḥalto l-ʔawwaliyye*.

to initial - *maḍa (i ʔemḍa) bᵊl-ᵊḥruuf ᵊl-ʔuula*. Initial all copies. *ʔemḍi kell ᵊn-nesax b-ᵊḥruuf ʔesmak ᵊl-ʔuula*.

injection - *ʔebre* pl. *ʔebar*. Are you getting injec-

tions? *ɛam taaxod ˀəbar?*
to **injure** - *žarah (a žarᵊh//nžarah)*. How many people were injured in the accident? *kam waahed ᵊnžarah bᵊl-haades?*
injury - *žərᵊh* pl. *žruuh(a)*.
ink - *həbᵊr*. I need ink for my fountain pen. *laazəmni həbᵊr la-stiilooyi.*
to ink - *hatt həbᵊr ɛala*. Don't ink the pad too heavily. *laa thətt həbr ᵊzyaade ɛaṣ-ṣṭampa.*
inlaid - **1.** *mfaṣṣaṣ*. Where did you get this beautiful inlaid table? *mneen žəbᵊt hat-taawle l-ᵊmfaṣṣaṣa l-həlwe?* **2.** *mnazzal*. They make lovely copper trays inlaid with silver. *byaɛᵊmlu ṣawaani nhaas həlwe mnazzdl-la fədda.*
inn - see **hotel** and **restaurant**.
inner - *žuwwaani**, *daaxli**. The inner door is locked. *l-baab ᵊž-žuwwaani maqfuul.*
innocence - *baraaˀa*. How did he prove his innocence? *kiif ˀasbat baraaˀto?*
innocent - *bariiˀ* pl. *-iin* and *ˀabriyaaˀ*. He's innocent of the charge. *huwwe bariiˀ mn ᵊt-təhme.* -- It was just an innocent remark. *hayy kaanet ᵊmlaahaẓa bariiˀa bass.* -- He put on an innocent face. *dẓaahar ˀənno bariiˀ.*
innovation - **1.** *bədɛa* pl. *bədaɛ*. **2.** (invention) *ˀəxtiraaɛ* pl. *-aat*. **3.** (new thing or idea) *šii ždiid* pl. *ˀašya ždiide*, *fəkra* (pl. *ˀafkaar*) *ždiide*.
to **inquire** - *stafham, staxbar, staɛlam*. I'll inquire about it. *raha ˀəstafhem ɛanha.* -- You'd better inquire first whether the job is still open. *ˀahsdn-lak ˀawwal təstaxber ˀiza kaan ᵊl-waẓiife ləssaaha šaaġra.*
inquiry - **1.** *ˀəstəɛlaam* pl. *-aat*, *ˀəstəfhaam* pl. *-aat*. We had a number of inquiries about this ad. *ˀəžaana ɛadad mn ᵊl-ˀəstəɛlaamaat b-ᵊxṣuuṣ hal-ˀəɛlaan.* **2.** *tahqiiq* pl. *-aat*. The inquiry revealed that he had secretly left the country. *t-tahqiiq kašaf ˀənno tarak l-ᵊblaad bᵊl-məxfi.*
inquisitive - *ktiir˜* (pl. *ktaar˜*) *ġalabe*, *kattaar˜ ġalabe*. Don't be so inquisitive! *laa tkuun ᵊktiir ġalabe!*
insane - *mažnuun* pl. *mažaniin*.
insane asylum - *məstašfa˜* (pl. *məstašfayaat˜*) *mažaniin*.
inscription - *ktaabe* pl. *-aat*. This inscription seems rather old. *hal-ᵊktaabe mbayyen ɛaleeha qadiime.*
insect - *hašara* pl. *-aat*.
insecticide - *mubiid˜* (pl. *-aat˜*) *hašaraat*.
inseparable - *muu məmken faṣlo, maa byənfəṣel*. The two questions are inseparable. *s-suˀaaleen muu məmken faṣlon* (or *maa byənfəṣlu ɛan baɛdon*).
**They've been inseparable since they were children. *ṣar-lon mən waqten kaanu ẓġaar maɛ baɛdon mətᵊl tiiẓeen b-ᵊlbaas.*
to **insert** - *daxxal, dahaš (a dahᵊš//ndahaš.)* Insert this sentence after the first paragraph. *daxxel haž-žəmle baɛd ᵊl-faqara l-ˀuula.*
inside - **1.** *daaxel, žuwwaat*. May I see the inside of the house? *məmken šuuf daaxel* (or *žuwwaat*) *ᵊl-beet?* **2.** *žuwwa*. He left it inside. *tarako žuwwa.* **3.** *la-žuwwa*. Why don't you come inside? *leeš maa bətfuut la-žuwwa?* **4.** *b-ẓarf˜*. Inside of five minutes the whole theater was empty. *b-ẓarf xamᵊs daqaayeq maa ṣəfi hada bᵊl-masrah.*
inside out - *ɛal-maqluub*. He has his sweater on inside out. *laabes kanᵊzto ɛal-maqluub.*
**He knows his business inside out. *byaɛref šaġᵊlto mətᵊl kaffo* (or *ɛat-taayer*)
**I know that guy inside out. *baɛref haz-zalame mətᵊl kaffi.*
**She knows the book inside out. *btaɛref l-ᵊktaab kəlme kəlme.*
**We know that town inside out. *mnaɛref hal-balad mətᵊl kaffna* (or ***qərne qərne*).
to turn inside out - **1.** *qalab (e/o qalb//nqalab)*. Somebody turned the sleeve of my coat inside out. *fii hada qaldb-li kəmm žaakeeti.* **2.** *qallab fooqaani tahtaani*. The police turned the place inside out, but they couldn't find anything. *š-šərta qallabu l-mahall fooqaani tahtaani bass maa laqu šii.*
insight - *ˀədraak, tafahhom*. The author shows profound insight into the political situation. *l-kaateb ɛam yəẓher ˀədraak ɛamiiq ləl-waḍɛ ᵊs-siyaasi.*
**That's how I got an insight into his character. *mən heek ṣərt ˀaɛref ˀatbaaɛo.*
insignia - *šaara* pl. *-aat*, *ɛalaame* pl. *-aat*. The insignia of his rank were hidden by his rain coat. *šaaraat rətᵊbto kaanet mxabbaaye tahᵊt tranškooto.*
insignificance - *ɛadam˜ ˀahammiyye, tafaaha*. I realize the insignificance of this matter. *ˀana šaayef ɛadam ˀahammiyyet haš-šaġle.*
to **insist** - *ˀaṣarr*. Why do you insist on going? *leeš ɛam bətṣərr ᵊtruuh?* or *leeš ɛam bətṣərr ɛar-rooha?*
insistent - *mṣərr*. Don't be so insistent! *laa tkuun ᵊmṣərr kəll hal-qadd!*
insomnia - *qalaq*. I'm suffering from insomnia these days. *ṣaayer maɛi qalaq hal-ˀiyyaam.*
to **inspect** - **1.** *fattaš*. They inspected the baggage carefully. *fattašu š-šanaati b-dəqqa.* **2.** *tfaqqad*. The official wishes to inspect the school today. *l-ᵊmwaẓẓaf raayed yətfaqqad l-madrase l-yoom.*
inspection - *taftiiš*. We lost more than one hour on account of the customs inspection. *ḍawwaɛna ˀaktar mən saaɛa b-sabab taftiiš ᵊl-gəmrok.*
inspector - *mfatteš* pl. *-iin*.
inspiration - *ˀəlhaam*.
to **inspire** - *ˀalham*. It was French art that inspired his finest works. *l-fann ᵊl-frənsaawi huwwe halli ˀalhamo yətlaɛ ᵊb-ˀahsan ˀəntaažo.*
to **install** - *rakkab (//trakkab), hatt (ə hatat//nhatt)*. The telephone will be installed tomorrow. *t-talifoon laha yətrakkab bəkra.*
installation - *tarkiib, hatat, waḍᵊɛ*. Telephone installation costs 15 pounds. *tarkiib ᵊt-talifoon bikallef xamᵊṣtaɛšar leera.*
installations - *mənšaˀaat* (pl.), *mˀassasaat* (pl.). Military and industrial installations. *mənšaˀaat ɛaskariyye w-ṣinaaɛiyye.*
installment - **1.** *qəṣᵊṭ* pl. *qṣaaṭ* and *qṣuuṭa*, *dafɛa* pl. *-aat*. You can pay it in five installments. *fiik tədfdɛa ɛala xams ᵊqṣaaṭ.* **2.** *marhale* pl. *maraahel*. The novel is appearing in installments. *l-qəṣṣa ɛam təṣdor ɛala maraahel.*
on installments - *bᵊt-taqṣiiṭ*. We bought the furniture on installments. *štareena l-mafruušaat bᵊt-taqṣiiṭ.*
instance - **1.** *masal* pl. *ˀdmsile*. This is another instance of his carelessness. *haada masal taani ɛala ɛadam ˀəntibaaho.* **2.** *haale* pl. *-aat*. In this instance you're wrong. *b-hal-haale ˀənte ġaltaan.*
for instance - *masalan, matalan*. There are quite a few possibilities, for instance... *fii ɛəddet ˀəmkaaniyyaat, masalan...*
instant - *lamhet˜ (-aat˜) baṣar, lahẓa* pl. *-aat*. He was gone in an instant. *xtafa b-lamhet baṣar.*
**Let me know the instant he arrives. *xabbərni ˀawwal-ma byəṣal.*
**The play was an instant success. *t-tamsiiliyye ɛal-haarek laqet nažaah.*
instantly - *ɛal-haarek, haalan, b-lahẓa, b-lamhet˜ baṣar.*
instead - *badaal-* + pron. suff., *ɛawaaḍ-* + pron. suff. What do you want instead? *šuu bəddak badaalo?*
instead of - **1.** *badaal˜, ɛawaaḍ˜*. He gave me tangerines instead of oranges. *ɛaṭaani yuusef ˀafandi badaal bərdqaan.* -- Couldn't you go instead of me? *maa fiik ᵊtruuh ɛawaaḍi?* **2.** *ɛawaaḍ-ma, badaal-ma*. Why don't you do something instead of complaining all the time? *leeš maa btaɛməl-lak šii ɛawaaḍ-ma təqɛod ṭuul ᵊl-waqt tətšakka?*
to **instigate** - *harrak, sabbab*. He instigated the whole thing. *huwwe harrak kəll haš-šii.*
instinct - *ġariize* pl. *ġaraayez*.
instinctive - **1.** *laa-šuɛuuri**. It was this instinctive movement that saved his life. *hal-harake l-laa-šuɛuuriyye hiyye halli ˀanqaẓət-lo hayaato.* **2.** *ġariizi*, ṭabiiɛi*, fəṭri**. A mother's love for her child is instinctive. *mhabbet ᵊl-ˀəmm la-ṭəfla ġariiziyye.*
institute - *maɛhad* pl. *maɛaahed*. He graduated from the Institute of Modern Languages. *txarraž mən maɛhad ᵊl-luġaat ᵊl-ɛaṣriyye.*
institution - *mˀassase* pl. *-aat*. That's a well-known institution in the Middle East. *hayy ᵊmˀassase maɛruufe ktiir bᵊš-šarq ᵊl-ˀawṣaṭ.*
to **instruct** - **1.** *darrab*. He instructed them in how to handle the fire extinguisher. *darrdbon kiif byəstaɛᵊmlu ṭaffaayt ᵊl-hariiqa.* **2.** *waṣṣa*. She instructed the children to be very careful on their way home. *waṣṣet l-ᵊwlaad ˀənno yəntəbhu mniih ᵊb-ṭariiqon ɛal-beet.*
instruction - *taɛliim, tadriis*. His method of instruction requires a thorough knowledge of the foreign language. *ṭariiqet taɛliimo btəṭṭallab maɛᵊrfe waasɛa bᵊl-luġa l-ˀažnabiyye.*
instructions - *taɛliimaat* (pl.), *ˀəršaadaat* (pl.).

The head nurse will give you instructions. *ra?iiset l-ᵊmmarrḍaat raḥa taᵋṭiik taᵋliimaat.*

instructions (for use) - *keefiyyet˜ ?əstəᵋmaal, ṭariiqet˜ ?əstəᵋmaal.* Read the instructions carefully! *?əqra keefiyyet ᵊl-?əstəᵋmaal b-dəqqa!*

instructive - *msaqqef, mufiid.* The lecture was very instructive. *l-ᵊmḥaaḍara kaanet ᵊmsaqqfe ktiir.*

instructor - 1. *mdarres* pl. *-iin, mᵋallem* pl. *-iin.* He was hired as an instructor at the University. *twaẓẓaf ᵊmdarres bᵊž-žaamᵋa.* 2. *mdarreb* pl. *-iin.* How do you like your new driving instructor? *kiif ᵊmlaaqi mdarreb ᵊs-swaaqa tabaᵋak ᵊž-ždiid?*

instrument - 1. *?aale* (pl. *-aat*) *muusiiqiyye.* Do you play an instrument? *btaᵋref ᵊddəqq ᵋala šii ?aale muusiiqiyye?* 2. *?adaat* pl. *?adawaat, ?aale* pl. *?awaayel.* Lay out the instruments for the operation. *ḥaḍḍer ᵊl-?adawaat ləl-ᵋamaliyye.*

to **insulate** - 1. *ḥaṭṭ (ə ḥaṭaṭ) twaal ᵋala.* You have to insulate this wire. *laazem ᵊtḥəṭṭ twaal ᵋala haš-šriiṭ.* 2. *ᵋazal (e ᵋazᵊl//nᵋazal)* The metal has to be insulated against heat. *l-maᵋdan laazem yənᵋézel ᵋan ᵊl-ḥaraara.*

insulated - *mlabbas.* Is this wire properly insulated? *haš-šriiṭ ᵊmlabbas mazbuuṭ?*

insulating tape - *twaal, šriiṭ ᵋaazel* pl. *šaraayeṭ ᵋaazle.*

insulator - *ᵋaazel* pl. *ᵋawaazel.*

insult - *?ihaane* pl. *-aat, bahdale* pl. *-aat.* I consider that an insult. *bəᵋtéber haš-šii ?ihaane.*

to insult - *bahdal//tbahdal, ḥaqqar//tḥaqqar, haan (i ?ihaane//nhaan).* You've insulted him. *bahdalto.*

insurance - *ta?miin, sookarta.* Do you have any insurance on the car? *ᵋaamel ta?miin ᵋas-sayyaara?*-- Can you recommend a good insurance company? *fiik ᵊtwaṣṣiini b-šərket ta?miin ᵊmniiḥa?*

to **insure** - *sookar, soogar, ?amman.* I have insured my house for 50,000 pounds. *sookart beeti ᵋala xamsiin ?alf leera.*

insurrection - *sawra* pl. *-aat, tamarrod* pl. *-aat.*

integrity - *nazaaha, ?əstiqaame.* His integrity has never been doubted. *nazaahto b-ḥayaato maa nšakk fiiha.*

intellectual - 1. *msaqqaf* pl. *-iin.* That magazine is read by many intellectuals. *hal-mažalle byəqruuha ᵋadad ᵊkbiir mən l-ᵊmsaqqafiin.* 2. *fəkri** There's an intellectual bond between them. *fii raabṭa fəkriyye beenaaton.*

intelligence - *zaka.* I'm not underestimating your intelligence. *?ana maa-li ᵋam ?əstxəff ᵊb-zakaak.*

intelligence work - *?aᵋmaal žaasuusiyye* (pl.).

intelligent - *zaki** pl. *?azkiya.* She's very intelligent. *hiyye zakiyye ktiir.*

**His answers are usually very intelligent. *žawaabaato ᵋaadatan kəlla zaka.*

intelligible - *waaḍeḥ, mafhuum.* I wish you'd start writing an intelligible style. *ya-reet təbda təktob b-?əsluub waaḍeḥ.*

to be intelligible - *nfaham.* His speech was barely intelligible. *xiṭaabo bᵊl-kaad ᵊnfaham.*

to **intend** - *nawa (i niyye), qaṣad (o qaṣᵊd).* What do you intend to do? *šuu naawi taᵋmel?* -- I intend to take her with me. *qaṣadᵊt ?aaxéda maᵋi.*

**That remark was intended for him. *hal-ᵊmlaaḥaẓa kaan huwwe l-maqṣuuḍ fiiha.*

**This merchandise is intended for Spain. *hal-ᵊbḍaaᵋa bədda truuḥ la-?əsbaanya.*

intense - *qawi*, zaayed.* I couldn't stand the intense heat. *maa ḍaayant ᵋaš-šoob ᵊl-qawi.*

to **intensify** - *zaad (i zyaade//nzaad).* You have to intensify your efforts. *laazem ᵊdziid ᵊžhuudak.*

intensity - *šədde.*

intensive - *mrakkaz.* This course requires intensive work. *hal-maadde btəstalzem diraase mrakkaze.*

intention - *maqṣaḍ* pl. *maqaaṣeḍ, niyye* pl. *-aat, qaṣᵊḍ.* Was that really your intention? *ᵋan ṣaḥiiḥ kaan haada maqṣadak?*

intently - *b-tamaᵋᵋon, b-?əntibaah.* They listened intently. *stamaᵋu b-tamaᵋᵋon.*

intercourse - 1. (social) *mᵋaašara, mxaalaṭa.* 2. (sexual) *žimaaᵋ, ᵋalaaqa žənsiyye.*

interest - 1. *?əhtimaam.* He takes an active interest in it. *byəhtamm ᵊb-hal-mas?ale ?əhtimaam faᵋᵋaal.* 2. *maraaq.* He has many interests. *?əlo maraaq b-?ašya ktiire.* 3. *faayde* and *faa?ide* pl. *fawaayed, faayez* pl. *fawaayez.* How much interest does the bank pay? *qaddeeš ᵊl-bank byədfaᵋ faayde?* -- I got my money back with interest. *staržaᵋᵊt maṣaariyyi maᵋ faayde.* 4. *ḥəṣṣa.* Do you have an interest in the business? *?əlak šii ḥəṣṣa b-hat-tižaara?* 5. *maṣlaḥa, ṣaaleḥ.* This is in your own interest. *haada la-maṣlaḥtak ?ənte.*

**We discussed all questions of interest. *baḥasna kəll ᵊl-mawaḍiiᵋ yalli bətxəṣṣna.*

**He said the whole thing was of no interest to him. *qaal ?ənno š-šii kəllo mən ?awwalo la-?aaxro maa bihəmmo.*

to interest - 1. *hamm (ə ø), xaṣṣ (ə ø).* This does not interest me at all. *haada maa bihəmmni ?abadan.* 2. *hamm.* Does this stuff really interest you? *ᵋan ḥaqa haš-šii bihəmmak?* 3. *žalab (ə ø), stažlab, stamaal.* Can't you interest him in that? *maa btəqder təžᵊlbo la-haš-šaġle?*

interesting - 1. *mufiid, mhəmm.* I read an interesting article about it. *qareet maqaale mufiide ᵋanha.* 2. *mhəmm.* The museum is full of interesting manuscripts. *l-matḥaf malyaan maxṭuuṭaat ᵊmhəmme.* 3. *məmteᵋ.* I don't think American football is very interesting. *maa bə?téqed ᵊl-futbool ᵊl-?amriikaanii məmteᵋ ᵊktiir.* 4. *ẓariif.* I find her a lot more interesting than him. *blaaqiiha ?aẓraf mənno b-ᵊktiir.*

**That's interesting! What else did he say? *šii ḥəlu! šuu qaal kamaan?*

**That sounds interesting! Tell me more about it. *šii ᵋaal! faṣṣél-li ᵋanna šwayye.*

to be interested in - *htamm b-.* I'm interested in sports. *bəhtamm bᵊs-sboor.* -- He's only interested in her money. *huwwe muu məhtamm ?əlla b-maṣariiha.*

to **interfere** - 1. *ddaaxal b-, ddaxxal b-.* Don't interfere in other people's affairs! *laa təddaaxal b-ᵊš?uun ġeerak!* 2. *ᵋawwaq, ᵋaṭṭal.* You're interfering with my work. *ᵋam ᵊtᵋawwéqni b-šəġli* or *ᵋam ᵊtᵋaṭṭəlni ᵋan šəġli.* 3. *ṣaar (i ø) maaneᵋ, ḥaṣal (a ø) maaneᵋ.* He'll leave on Sunday if nothing interferes. *bisaafer yoom ᵊl-?aḥad ?iza maa ṣaar maaneᵋ.*

interior - 1. *daaxel, žuwwaat.* The interior of the house is very beautiful. *daaxel ᵊl-beet ktiir ḥəlu.* 2. *daaxli*, žuwwaani*.* The interior walls are covered with cracks. *l-ḥiiṭaan ᵊž-žuwwaaniyye malaaniin ᵊšquuq.*

ministry of the interior - *wazaart˜ ᵊd-daaxliyye.*

intermission - *?əstiraaḥa* pl. *-aat.* I was in the foyer during the intermission. *kənᵊt bᵊṣ-ṣaaloon ?asnaa? ᵊl-?əstiraaḥa.*

internal - 1. *daaxli*.* The internal affairs of the country. *š?uun l-ᵊblaad ᵊd-daaxliyye.* 2. *baaṭni*, daaxli*.* He died of internal injuries. *maat ᵋala ?asar ᵊžruuḥ baaṭniyye.*

internal revenue service - *daa?ərt˜ ᵊḍ-ḍaraayeb.*

international - *duwali*, ?əmami*, ᵋaalami*.*

to **interpret** - 1. *fassar//tfassar.* He interpreted my words as an insult. *fassar kalaami ?ihaane.* -- It can be interpreted this way, too. *məmken tafsiira b-haṣ-ṣuura hayye kamaan.* 2. *taržam.* For years he interpreted for the prime minister. *bəqi sniin ytaržem la-ra?iis ᵊl-wəzara.*

interpretation - *tafsiir.* The interpretation of this poem is rather difficult. *tafsiir haš-šəᵋᵊr ṣaᵋb ᵊšwayye.*

interpreter - *mtaržem* pl. *-iin, təržmaan* pl. *taraažme.* I acted as interpreter. *ᵋmᵊlt təržmaan beenaathon.*

interrogation mark - *ᵋalaamet˜* (pl. *-aat˜*) *?əstəfhaam.*

interrogative pronoun - *?əsᵊm˜* (pl. *?asmaa?˜*) *?əstəfhaam.*

to **interrupt** - 1. *qaaṭaᵋ//tqaaṭaᵋ.* Don't interrupt me all the time! *laa tqaaṭəᵋni ᵋaṭ-ṭaalᵋa w-ᵋan-naazle.* 2. *zaᵋaž (e ?əzᵋaaž//nzaᵋaž).* Am I interrupting? *ᵋam bəzᵊᵋžak šii?*

interruption - 1. *?ənqiṭaaᵋ* pl. *-aat, tawaqqof* pl. *-aat.* I've been working without interruption since 10 o'clock in the morning. *ṣar-li ᵋam ?əštéġel biduun ?ənqiṭaaᵋ mn ᵊs-saaᵋa ᵋašara ᵋala bəkra.* 2. *?əzᵋaaž.* Pardon this interruption. *ᵋafwan ᵋala hal-?əzᵋaaž.*

interval - 1. *fatra* pl. *-aat.* After a short interval we continued on our trip. *baᵋᵊd fatra qaṣiire kammalna safrətna.* 2. *masaafe* pl. *-aat.* The trees are set at close intervals. *š-šažaraat mazruuᵋa ᵋala masaafe qariibe mən baᵋḍa.*

interview - *mqaabale* pl. *-aat.* The minister granted him a special interview. *l-waziir manaḥo mqaabale xaaṣṣa.*

to interview - *stažwab.* He interviewed him about his political opinions. *stažwabo b-ᵊxṣuuṣ ?aaraa?o s-siyaasiyye.*

intimate - *ḥamiim, məxleṣ.* We're intimate friends. *nəḥna ṣḥaab ḥamiimiin.*

to **intimidate** - *xawwaf//txawwaf.* He tried to

intimidate them first. *ʔawwal šii ḥaawal yxawwéfon.*
into - 1. *b-, žuwwaat˜.* Put it into the box. *ḥəṭṭo bəs-sanduuq* or (with emphasis on "into") *ḥəṭṭo žuwwaat əs-sanduuq.* 2. *ɛala.* Get into the car. *fuut ɛas-sayyaara.* -- He just went into the house next door. *hallaq faat ɛal-beet yalli žanbna.* 3. *la-.* Can you translate this into English? *fiik əttaržem hayy ləl-ʔəngliizi?*
intolerance - *ɛadam˜ tasaamoḥ, ɛadam˜ tasaahol, taɛaṣṣob.*
intolerant - 1. *muu samuuḥ, ġeer mətsaameḥ.* She's not only conceited, she's also intolerant. *hiyye muu bass šaayfe ḥaala, maa-la samuuḥa kamaan.* 2. *mətɛaṣṣeb.* The adherents of that sect are especially intolerant. *ʔatbaaɛ haṭ-ṭaayfe b-ṣuura xaaṣṣa mətɛaṣṣbiin.*
intoxicated - 1. (by liquor) *sakraan.* 2. (by hasheesh) *mḥaššeš.*
intoxicating - *məsker.* The sale of intoxicating beverages to children is prohibited. *mamnuuɛ beeɛ əl-mašruubaat əl-məskra ləl-əwlaad.*
to **introduce** - 1. *ɛarraf//tɛarraf.* I'd like to introduce you to my father. *bḥəbb ɛarrfak ɛala ʔabi.* 2. *daxxal.* He introduced a number of changes in his government's policy. *daxxal ɛəddet taɛdiilaat ɛala siyaaset əḥkuumto.* 3. *qaddam.* They introduced new proposals. *qaddamu ʔəq̈tiraaḥaat əždiide.*
introduction - 1. *muq̈addame* pl. *-aat.* It's mentioned in the introduction. *mazkuur bəl-muq̈addame.* 2. *taɛarrof.* After their mutual introduction they shook hands. *baɛəd taɛarréfon ɛala baɛdon tṣaafaḥu.*
intuition - *ḥadəs.*
to **invade** - *ġaza (i ġazu//nġaza).* Didn't Napoleon try to invade England? *maa ḥaawal nabolyoon yəġzi ʔəngəltra?*
invalid - 1. *baaṭel.* A will without a signature is invalid. *wṣiyye bala ʔəmḍa bətkuun baaṭle.* 2. *ɛaažez* pl. *ɛažaze.* He's been an invalid ever since. *ṣar-lo ɛaažez mən waqta.*
invasion - *ġazwe* pl. *-aat.*
to **invent** - 1. *xtaraɛ.* There's something new invented every day. *kəll yoom byəxtərɛu šii ždiid.* 2. *xtalaq, fabrak.* Did you invent that story? *ʔənte yalli xtalaqət hal-qəṣṣa?*
invention - *ʔəxtiraaɛ* pl. *-aat.*
inventor - *məxtéreɛ* pl. *-iin.*
to **invest** - *šaġġal, waṣṣaf, stasmar.* He invested his money in real estate. *šaġġal ʔamwaalo bəl-ɛaq̈aaraat.*
to **investigate** - *ḥaq̈q̈aq̈ b-.* The case is being investigated. *l-qaḍiyye rahn ət-taḥq̈iiq̈.*
investigation - *taḥq̈iiq̈* pl. *-aat.* An investigation has been ordered by the court. *l-maḥkame ʔamret əb-fatəḥ taḥq̈iiq̈.*
invisible - 1. *muu mbayyen.* The enemy tank was almost invisible. *dabbaabt əl-ɛaduww taqriiban maa kaanet əmbayyne.* 2. *sərri*.* The spy carried a letter written in invisible ink. *ž-žaasuus kaan maɛo risaale maktuube b-ḥəbər sərri.*
**She remained invisible for the rest of the evening. *maa ɛaadet bayyanet əb-baqiit əl-leele.*
invitation - *ɛaziime* pl. *ɛazaayem, daɛwe* pl. *-aat.* Many thanks for your kind invitation. *ʔalf šəkər ɛala ɛaziimtak əl-kariime.*
to **invite** - *ɛazam (e ɛaziime//nɛazam), daɛa (i daɛwe//ndaɛa).* Who did you invite to the party? *miin ɛazamto ɛal-ḥafle?* -- We're invited tonight. *nəḥna madɛuwwiin əl-leele.*
inviting - *mšahhi, məġri.* The food looks very inviting. *l-ʔakl əktiir əmšahhi.*
invoice - *faatuura* pl. *fawatiir.*
to **involve** - 1. *warraṭ//twarraṭ, šabak (e šabək// štabak).* He was involved in it, too. *huwwe kamaan twarraṭ fiiha.* 2. *hawa (i ø) ɛala.* The trip involved a lot of expense. *s-safra ḥawet ɛala nafaqaat əkbiire.* 3. *štamal ɛala, ḍḍamman.* The action involves a certain amount of risk. *l-ɛamal byəštémel ɛala šii mən l-əmžaazafe.*
involved - *mɛaqqad, mšarbak.* That's a very involved process. *hayye ɛamaliyye ktiir əmɛaqqade.*
to get involved - *twarraṭ.* I couldn't help getting involved in this. *twarraṭṭ əb-haš-šaġle ġaṣban ɛanni.* -- I don't want to get involved in this. *ma bəddi ʔətwarraṭ b-haš-šaġle.*
iodine - *yood.*
Iran - *ʔiiraan, blaad˜ əl-fərs.*
Iranian - *ʔiiraani*.*
Iraq - *l-əɛraaq, l-ɛiraaq̈.*
Iraqi - *ɛiraaq̈i*.*
Irbid - *ʔərbed.*
Ireland - *ʔiirlanda.*
iris - 1. (flower) *suusaane* coll. pl. *suusaan.* 2. (of the eye) *q̈uzaḥiyye(t˜ əl-ɛeen).*
Irish - *ʔərlandi*.*
irksome - *məḍni*, mətɛeb.* He still has to cope with many irksome problems. *ləssa ɛaléé ywaažeh ɛəddet mašaakel məḍniyye.*
iron - 1. *ḥadiid.* You have to be made of iron to stand all that. *laazem ətkuun ḥadiid la-ḥatta ḍḍaayen ɛala haš-šii.* -- Strike while the iron is hot. *dəqq əl-ḥadiid w-huwwe ḥaami.* 2. *məkwaaye* pl. *makaawi.* Is the iron still hot? *l-məkwaaye ləssaaha ḥaamye?* 3. *mən ḥadiid, ḥadiid.* An iron door knocker. *ṣaqqaaṭa mən ḥadiid* or *ṣaqqaaṭa ḥadiid* or *ṣaqqaaṭet˜ ḥadiid.* 4. *mən ḥadiid, ḥadiidi*.* He has an iron will. *ɛando ʔiraade mən ḥadiid* (or ***mətl əl-ḥadiid*). 5. *ḥadiidi*.* The Iron Curtain. *s-sitaar əl-ḥadiidi.*
piece, fixture, etc., **of iron** - *ḥadiide* pl. *ḥadaayed.*
to iron - *kawa (i kawi//nkawa).* Did you iron my shirt? *kaweetti-li qamiiṣi?*
to iron out - *sawwa.* There are still a few things to be ironed out. *ləssa fii baɛəḍ naqaṭ bədda taswiye.*
ironical - *haazeq.* He looked at me with an ironical smile. *ṭṭallaɛ ɛaliyyi w-ɛala wəššo ʔəbtisaame haazʔa.*
**It's ironical! Now that we have the money we don't need it any more. *d-dənye bəl-maqluub! hallaq əʔžətna l-maṣaari maa ɛaadet laazəmətna.*
ironing board - *ṭaawlet˜* (pl. *-aat˜*) *kawi.*
ironworks - *maṣnaɛ˜* (pl. *maṣaaneɛ˜*) *ḥadiid.*
irrational - 1. *ʔaṣamm* f. *ṣammaaʔ.* All of these are irrational numbers. *kəll hal-ʔaɛdaad ṣammaaʔ.* 2. *bala ɛaqəl* (invar.). You're acting like an irrational child. *ɛam tətṣarraf mətəl ṭəfəl bala ɛaqəl.* 3. *muu maɛquul.* Your behavior is irrational. *taṣarrfak muu maɛquul.*
irregular - 1. (not uniform) *ġeer* (or *muu*) *məntḍ̣əm.* 2. (troops, etc.) *ġeer niẓaami.* 3. (not normal) *šaazz.*
irregularity - 1. (lack of uniformity, method, or order) *ɛadam˜ ʔəntiẓaam, ɛadam niẓaam.* 2. (inconsistency) *ʔəxtilaal.* 3. (abnormality) *šuzuuz.*
irrelevant - *b-ġeer maḥall-* or *muu b-maḥall-* + pron. suff. His remarks were completely irrelevant. *mlaaḥaẓaato kaanet ʔabadan əb-ġeer maḥalla* or *mlaaḥaẓaato kaanet ʔabadan muu b-mḥalla.*
irresistable - *maa byətqaawam.* She thinks her charm is irresistable. *mḥassbe səḥra maa byətqaawam.*
irresponsible - *ɛadiim˜ əl-masʔuuliyye.* He's an irresponsible person. *huwwe šaxəṣ ɛadiim əl-masʔuuliyye* (or ***maa ɛando masʔuuliyye*).
**That was very irresponsible of you. *haada kaan ɛadam masʔuuliyye ktiir mənnak.*
to **irrigate** - *ṣaqa (i ṣaqi* and *ṣqaaye//nṣaqa), rawa (i rwaaye* and *rayy//rtawa).* Do you have to irrigate these fields? *laazem šii təṣqu hal-əḥquul?*
irrigation - *ṣqaaye, rayy.*
irritable - *məḥtadd, mənféɛel.* He was very irritable this morning. *kaan əktiir məḥtadd ɛala bəkra.*
to **irritate** - 1. *zaɛaž (e ʔəzɛaaž//nzaɛaž), narvaz// tnarvaz.* His remark irritated me. *kalaamo zaɛážni.* 2. *xarraš.* This soap doesn't irritate the skin. *haṣ-ṣaabuun maa bətxarreš əl-bəšra ʔabadan.*
Islam - *l-ʔəslaam.*
Islamic - *ʔəslaami*.*
island - *žaziire* pl. *žəzor* and *žazaayer.*
to **isolate** - *ɛazal (e ɛazəl//nɛazal).* The sick children were isolated. *l-əwlaad əl-məraḍa ɛazaluuhon (la-waḥdon).*
isolated - *maɛzuul, mənɛézel.*
isolation - *ɛəzle.* He lived in complete isolation for some time. *ɛaaš la-mədde b-ɛəzle taamme.*
Israel - *ʔəsraʔiil.*
Israeli - *ʔəsraʔiili*.*
issue - 1. *ɛadad* pl. *ʔaɛdaad.* I haven't read the last issue of the periodical. *maa qreet ɛadad əl-mažalle l-ʔaxiir.* 2. *q̈aḍiyye* pl. *q̈aḍaaya, masʔale* pl. *masaaʔel, məškle* pl. *mašaakel.* I don't want to make an issue of it. *maa bəddi ʔaɛmel mən hal-qəṣṣa q̈aḍiyye kbiire.* 3. *mawḍuuɛ* pl *mawaḍiiɛ.* That's not the issue. *muu haada l-mawḍuuɛ* or ***muu haada madaar əl-baḥs.* -- You're trying to avoid the issue. *ɛam bətḥaawel tətḥaaša* (or *tfaada*) *l-mawḍuuɛ.*
to issue - *ṭaalaɛ, ʔaṣdar.* Where do they issue

the passports? *ween biṭaalɛu l-basbooraat?*

to be issued - *ṣadar (o ṣuduur), ṭəleɛ (a ṭluuɛ).* The passport was issued by the Syrian consulate in Rome. *l-basboor ṣadar mn ᵊl-qənṣliyye s-suuriyye b-rooma.*

it - **1.** *huwwe, hiyye.* Which is my book? Oh, that's it. *ʔanu ktaabi? haa, haada huwwe.* -- Where is my hat? Here it is! *ween bərneeṭṭi? hayy hiyye!* or ***leekha hoon!* or ***šaḥḥaake!* **2.** *-o, -ha.* I can't do it. *maa bəqder saawiiha.* -- I can't give you the money today, I forgot it. *maa bəqder ʔaɛṭiik ᵊl-maṣaari l-yoom, nsiitha.* --I like that watch. I'll take it. *ɛažbə́tni has-saaɛa. laḥa ʔaaxə́da.* -- Forget it! *nsaaha!* or ***laa təhtamm!* or ***maa bihəmm!* -- He's had it! *ʔakdla!* -- Guess what's in it! *ḥzeer šuu fiiha* (or *šuu fii žuwwaata*).

**It's lovely today. *ṭ-ṭaqᵊṣ ḥəlu l-yoom.*

**It's cold outside. *d-dənye bard barra.*

**It's raining. *ɛam tənzel maṭar* or *ɛam ᵊtšatti.*

**Where is my hat? - I have it. *ween bərneeṭṭi? - maɛi.*

That's it! **1. (that's right) *hallaq žəbta!* or *mazbuuṭ!* **2.** (it's finished) *xalaṣ!* or *xalaṣna!*

**I knew it! *ɛrəft!*

**That's all there is to it. *hayy ᵊl-masʔale kəlla, šəft qaddeeš baṣiiṭa?* or *hayy kəll ᵊl-qəṣṣa.*

**There is nothing to it! *baṣiiṭa! maa fii ʔahyan mən heek.*

Italian - *ṭəlyaani** coll. pl. *ṭəlyaan.*

Italy - *ʔiṭaalya.*

to itch - *ʔakal (-yaakol ʔakalaan), raɛa (a raɛayaan), ḥakk (ə ḥkaak).* The wound itches. *ž-žərᵊḥ ɛam yaakəlni.* -- I itch all over. *žəsmi kəllo ɛam ᵊyḥəkkni.*

**I'm itching to get started. *maa-li msaddeq ʔeemta ʔəbda* or *ʔana mayyet la-ʔəbda.*

item - **1.** *ṣənf* pl. *ʔaṣnaaf.* We don't carry that item. *maa ɛanna haṣ-ṣənᵊf.* **2.** *xabar* pl. *ʔaxbaar.* Did you see the item in the paper? *šəft ᵊl-xabar bᵊž-žariide?* **3.** *nafde* pl. *-aat.* How many items are on that bill? *kam nafde fii ɛala hal-faatuura?*

to itemize - *fannad, ɛaddad, xaṣṣaṣ.* Itemize all your expenses. *fanned kəll maṣariifak.*

itself - **1.** *ḥaalo (ḥaalha), nafso (nafsa).* The child hurt itself. *ṭ-ṭəfᵊl ʔaza ḥaalo.* **2.** *zaato (zaatha).* The car itself is in good condition. *s-sayyaara zaatha b-ḥaale mniiḥa.* **3.** *la-waḥdo (la-waḥda), la-ḥaalo (la-ḥaala).* The house itself is worth that. *l-beet la-waḥdo byəswa hal-qiime.*

**That speaks for itself. *haš-šii maa bəddo tafsiir.*

by itself - *la-ḥaalo (la-ḥaalha), la-waḥdo (la-waḥda).* You can't use this expression by itself. *hat-taɛbiir maa fiik təstaɛᵊmlo la-ḥaalo.* -- This door closes by itself. *hal-baab bisakker la-ḥaalo.*

in itself - *b-ḥadd zaato (zaatha).* The plan in itself is good. *l-xəṭṭa b-ḥadd zaatha mniiḥa.*

ivory - *ɛaaž.*

ivy - *ɛaašeq˜ š-šažar.*

J

jack - **1.** *kriiko* pl. *kriikoyaat.* I left the jack in the garage. *tarakᵊt l-ᵊkriiko bᵊl-garaaž.* **2.** *šabb* pl. *šabaab, walad* pl. *wlaad.* He took the trick with the jack. *rəbeḥ ᵊd-daqq bᵊš-šabb yalli maɛo.*

**He's a jack-of-all-trades. *mətl ᵊz-zəbdiyye ṣ-ṣiini mneen-ma daqqeeta bətrənn.*

**You look as if you had hit the jack pot. *mbayyen ɛaleek kaʔənno ṭəleɛ ɛala wəššak kənz.*

to jack up - **1.** *rafaɛ (a rafᵊɛ//nrafaɛ) bᵊl-kriiko.* You'll have to jack up the car. *laazem tərfaɛ ᵊs-sayyaara.* **2.** *rafaɛ.* They've jacked up the price again. *rafaɛu s-səɛᵊr marra taanye.*

jackal - *ʔəbᵊn ʔaawa* pl. *banaat ʔaawa, waawi* pl. *waawiyaat.*

jackass - *ḥmaar* pl. *ḥamiir, mġaffal* pl. *-iin.* What a jackass! *qaddeešo ḥmaar!*

jackdaw - *zaaġ* pl. *ziiġaan.*

jacket - **1.** *žaakeet* pl. *-aat* and *žawakiit.* You can wear that jacket with flannel slacks. *haž-žaakeet biruuḥ maɛ banṭaloon faneella.* **2.** *qəšre* coll. *qəšᵊr* pl. *qšuur.* I boiled the potatoes in their jackets. *salaqt ᵊl-baṭaaṭa b-qəšra.* **3.** *ġilaaf* pl. *-aat.* The jacket of the book is all torn. *ġilaaf l-ᵊktaab kəllo mšaqqaq.*

jagged - *msannan.*

jail - *ḥabᵊs* pl. *ḥbuus, səžᵊn* pl. *sužuun.* He was sentenced to six months in jail. *ḥakamu ɛalée sətt əšhor ḥabᵊs.*

to jail - *ḥabas (e ḥabᵊs//nḥabas), sažan (o sažn //nsažan).* He was jailed for theft. *nḥabas mənšaan sərqa.*

jalopy - *(sayyaara) ṭəmbor* pl. *(sayyaaraat) ṭanaaber.*

jam - **1.** *mrabba* pl. *mrabbayaat, maɛquud* pl. *mɛaqqadaat.* I prefer homemade jam. *bfaḍḍel mrabba šəġl ᵊl-beet.* **2.** *warṭa* pl. *-aat.* I'm in an awful jam. *ʔana waaqeɛ b-warṭa ʔaḷḷa laa yuriik.* **3.** *ɛažqa* pl. *-aat, zaḥme* pl. *-aat.* On the way home we got caught in a traffic jam. *b-ṭariiqna ɛal-beet ᵊɛləqna b-ɛažqet seer.*

to jam - **1.** *šawwaš ɛala.* Somebody is jamming our broadcast. *fii ḥada ɛam yšawweš ɛala ʔizaaɛətna.* **2.** *qaraṭ (o qarᵊṭ//nqaraṭ), ɛaṣar (o ɛaṣᵊr//nɛaṣar).* He jammed his finger in the door. *qaraṭ ʔəṣbaɛto bᵊl-baab.*

jammed - **1.** *mɛalleq, ɛalqaan.* The gears are jammed. *l-viitees ᵊmɛalleq.* -- The drawer is jammed. *d-dərᵊž ɛalqaan.* **2.** *məzdə́ḥem.* The elevator was jammed with people. *l-ʔaṣanṣoor kaan məzdə́ḥem bᵊn-naas.*

to jangle - *xašxaš.* Her bracelets jangled as she ran. *lamma rakdet ʔasaawə́ra xašxašet.*

janitor - *bawwaab* pl. *-iin.*

January - *kaanun ᵊt-taani.*

Japan - *l-yaabaan.*

Japanese - **1.** *yaabaani**. Japanese goods are flooding the market. *l-baḍaayeɛ ᵊl-yaabaaniyye ɛam ᵊtġarreq ᵊs-suuq.* **2.** *yaabaani* (invar.). Do you know of anyone who speaks Japanese? *btaɛref ḥada byəḥki yaabaani?* **3.** *yaabaani** coll. pl. *yaabaan.* We have quite a number of Japanese students. *fii ɛanna ṭəllaab yaabaan ɛadad ᵊmniiḥ.*

jar - *marṭabaan* and *maṭrabaan* pl. *-aat.* I want a jar of jam. *bəddi marṭabaan ᵊmrabba.*

to jar - *hazz (ə hazz//nhazz).* Don't jar the table when you sit down. *laa thəzz ᵊṭ-ṭaawle lamma btəqɛod.*

jasmine - *yaasmiine* coll. *yaasmiin* pl. *-aat.*

jaundice - *yaraqaan, rayaqaan.*

Java - *žaawa.*

Javanese - *žaawi**.

jaw - *fakk* pl. *fkaak* and *fkuuk, ḥanak* pl. *ḥnuuk* and *ḥnaak.*

jawbone - *ɛaḍmet˜ (pl. -aat˜) fakk.*

jazz - *žaaz.*

jealous - **1.** *ġayyuur.* Her husband is very jealous. *žooza ġayyuur ᵊktiir.* **2.** *ġayraan.* She's jealous because you have a new fur coat. *hiyye ġayraane laʔənno ɛandek kabbuut faru ždiid.*

jealousy - *ġiire.* He's dying of jealousy. *huwwe mayyet ᵊmn ᵊl-ġiire.*

jeep - *(sayyaaret˜) žiip* pl. *sayyaaraat˜ žiip.*

jeer - *ṣarxa (pl. -aat) ḍədd˜.* The jeers of the crowd were still ringing in his ears. *ṣarxaat ᵊž-žamahiir ḍəddo ləssaaha kaanet ɛam tədwi b-ʔadanée.*

to jeer - *ṣarax (a ṣraax) ḍədd˜.* The audience jeered the singer. *l-ḥaaḍriin ṣaraxu ḍədd l-ᵊmġanni.*

jelly - *želatiin.*

to **jeopardize** - *ɛarraḍ ləl-xaṭar.* The incident jeopardized his whole career. *l-ḥaadse ɛarraḍet kəll məstaqbalo l-maslaki ləl-xaṭar.*

jeopardy - *xaṭar.* He put his own life in jeopardy. *ɛarraḍ ḥayaato ləl-xaṭar.*

jerboa - *yarbuuɛ* pl. *yarabiiɛ.*

Jericho - *ʔariiḥa.*

jerk - **1.** *ražže* pl. *-aat, hazze* pl. *-aat.* The train stopped with a jerk. *t-treen waqqaf b-ražže.* **2.** *ɛakruut* pl. *ɛakariit* and *ɛakaarte.* I'll fix him, the jerk! *ləssa bwaržli hal-ɛakruut!*

to jerk - *xaṭaf (o xaṭᵊf//nxaṭaf), nataš (o natᵊš//ntataš).* She jerked the book out of his hand. *xaṭfet l-ᵊktaab mən ʔiido.*

jerky - *mətqaṭṭeɛ.*

jersey - *žərsée.*

Jerusalem – *l-qədᵊs.*
jest – *nəkte* pl. *nəkat, masḥa* pl. *-aat.*
Jesuit – *yasuuεi* pl. *-iyyiin* and *-iyye.*
Jesus – (Christian usage) *yasuuε,* (Muslim usage) *εiisa.*
jet – *ṭayyaara* (pl. *-aat*) *naffaase, ṭayyaaret˜ žeet.* Did you fly by jet? *rkəbᵊt ṭayyaara naffaase?*
Jew – *yahuudi** coll. pl. *yahuud.*
jewel – **1.** *mžawhara* and *mžoohara* pl. *-aat.* A very valuable jewel is reported stolen from the museum. *εam yquulu ʔənno nsarqet ᵊmžawhara samiine ktiir ᵊmn ᵊl-matḥaf.* **2.** *ḥažar* pl. *ḥžaar.* My watch has seventeen jewels. *saaεti b-sabaεṭaažar ḥažar.*
  jewels – *ṣiiġa, maṣaaġ, mžawharaat* (pl.). She had to pawn her jewels. *nžabret tərhen ṣiiġəta.*
jeweler – *žawharži* and *žoohardži* pl. *-iyye, ṣaayeġ* pl. *ṣiyyaaġ.*
jewelry – *ṣiiġa, maṣaaġ, mžawharaat* (pl.).
Jewess – *yahuudiyye* pl. *-aat.*
Jewish – *yahuudi** coll. pl. *yahuud.*
to **jibe** – *ṭaabaq, nṭabaq εala.* This doesn't jibe with what I saw. *haš-šii maa biṭaabeq yalli šəfto.* -- The sentence doesn't jibe with the English translation. *haž-žəmle maa btənṭəbeq εat-taržame l-ʔəngliiziyye.*
Jidda – *žədde.*
jiffy – *laḥẓa, takke.* It'll only take a jiffy. *maa btaaxod ʔaktar mən laḥẓa.*
  in a jiffy – **1.** *baεᵊd laḥẓa, baεᵊd takke, b-ġamḍet˜ εeen.* I'll be back in a jiffy. *bəržaε baεᵊd laḥẓa.* **2.** *εala lamḥ˜ ᵊl-baṣar.* He was ready in a jiffy. *kaan ḥaaḍer εala lamḥ ᵊl-baṣar.*
to **jiggle** – **1.** *hazhaz, xaḍḍ (ə xaḍḍ).* You have to jiggle the handle a little. *laazem ᵊthazhez ᵊl-maske šwayye.* **2.** *xaḍxaḍ.* Pack the things well so they won't jiggle. *ḍəbb l-ᵊġraaḍ ᵊmniiḥ ḥatta maa yxaḍᵊxḍu.*
to **jilt** – *baaε (i ə//mbaaε), kabb (ə kabb//nkabb).* To everybody's surprise his fiancee jilted him and married his best friend. *la-dahšet ᵊž-žamiiε xaṭiibto baaεto w-džawwazet ʔaεazz ʔasdiǧaaʔo.*
jingoism – *naεra ǧawmiyye.*
jitters: Why do you have the jitters? *leeš marεuub?* -- I get the jitters every time I have to speak in public. *bərtəheb kəll-ma bəddi ʔəḥki qəddaam ᵊl-εaalam.* -- Exams invariably give me the jitters. *l-ʔəmtiḥaanaat εam tərεəbni kəll marra.*
job – **1.** *šaġle* pl. *-aat, waẓiife* pl. *waẓaayef.* I'm looking for a job. *εam dawwer εala šii šaġle.* -- He's afraid to lose his job. *xaayef yrawweḥ waẓiifto mən ʔiido.* **2.** *šaġle* pl. *-aat.* I have several jobs to do today. *εaliyyi εəddet šaġlaat ᵊl-yoom.* **3.** *šəġᵊl, šaġle, waẓiife.* It isn't my job to tell him that. *muu šəġli ʔana qəl-lo haš-šii.* **4.** *šaġle, εamal.* It wasn't an easy job to convince her. *maa kaanet šaġle hayyne la-ʔaqnəεa.*
  **It was a put-up job. *kaanet ṭabxa maṭbuuxa mən zamaan.*
  **You've done a very good job on that translation. *twaffaqᵊt tamaam ᵊb-hat-taržame.*
jockey – *žooki* pl. *-iyye.*
to **join** – **1.** *daxal (o dxuul) b-, ndamm la-.* When did he join the party? *ʔeemta daxal bᵊl-ḥəzᵊb?* -- He wants to join our club. *biriid yənḍamm lən-naadi tabaεna.* **2.** *ltaḥaq b-, daxal b-.* I'm joining the Army. *naawi ʔəltəḥeq bᵊž-žeeš.* — He joined the Navy a year ago. *ltaḥaq bᵊl-baḥriyye mən səne.* **3.** *waṣal (-yuuṣel waṣl//nwaṣal).* How do you join these two parts? *kiif laḥa tuuṣel haš-šaqᵊfteen?* **4.** *ltaqa maε.* Where does this road join the main highway? *ween haṭ-ṭariiq byəltaqa maε ᵊṭ-ṭariiq ᵊl-εaamm?* **5.** *tfaḍḍal maε.* Would you like to join us? *bətḥəbb tətfaḍḍal maεna?* **6.** *šaarak.* Won't you join us at the table? *tfaḍḍal šaarəkna bᵊṭ-ṭaawle.* -- Everybody joined in the singing. *kəll waaḥed šaarak bᵊl-ġəne.* **7.** *tlaaqa, ltaqa.* Where do these roads join? *ween haṭ-ṭəroq btətlaaqa?*
  **Everybody join in the chorus! *kəllna b-ṣooṭ waaḥed!*
  **Let's join forces. *xalliina kəllna ʔiid waaḥde.*
joint – **1.** *mafṣal* pl. *mafaaṣel.* All my joints ache. *kəll mafaaṣli εam təžaεni.* **2.** *məštarak.* The land is their joint property. *l-ʔarḍ məlk məštarak beenon.*
  to throw out of joint – *xalaε (a xalᵊε//nxalaε).* I threw my arm out of joint. *xalaεᵊt ʔiidi* or *nxalεet ʔiidi.*
joke – **1.** *nəkte* pl. *nəkat, masḥa* pl. *-aat.* I've heard that joke before. *smaεᵊt han-nəkte mən qabᵊl.* **2.** *mazᵊḥ.* That's carrying the joke too far. *εam tətmaada ktiir bᵊl-mazᵊḥ.* -- He can't take a joke. *maa byəlqa mazᵊḥ.* -- He tried to make a joke of the whole thing. *ḥaawal ydiir kəll ᵊš-šəġle mazᵊḥ.* **3.** *ləεbe.* I played a joke on him. *lεəbᵊt εaléε ləεbe.*
  to tell jokes – *rama (i rami) nəkat, nakkat.* He's always telling jokes. *daayman byərmi nəkat.*
  to joke – *mazaḥ (a mazᵊḥ).* This time I'm not joking. *hal-marra maa εam ʔəmzaḥ.* -- I was only joking. *kənᵊt εam ʔəmzaḥ bass.* -- All joking aside! *bala mazᵊḥ!*
jolly – **1.** *zəhraawi**. He's a jolly fellow. *huwwe šaxᵊṣ zəhraawi.* **2.** *ẓariif, laṭiif, saarr.* That was a jolly trip yesterday. *kaanet safra ẓariife mbaarḥa.*
jolt – *hazze* pl. *-aat, xaḍḍa* pl. *-aat, ražže* pl. *-aat.* The car stopped with a sudden jolt. *s-sayyaara waqqafet b-hazze εaniife.*
  to jolt – *hazz (ə hazz//nhazz), ražž (ə ražž//nražž).* The explosion jolted the whole house. *l-ʔənfižaar hazz ᵊl-beet kəllo hazz.* -- The news really jolted him. *l-xabar hazzo εan ḥaqa.*
Jordan – *l-ʔərdon.* He spent six months in Jordan. *maḍa sətt əšhor bᵊl-ʔərdon.* -- The Jordan river. *nahṛ ᵊl-ʔərdon* or ***nahṛ ᵊš-šariiεa.*
  **The Hashemite Kingdom of Jordan. *l-mamlake l-ʔərduniyye l-haašimiyye.*
Jordanian – *ʔərduni**.
to **jostle** – *dafaš (o dafᵊš//ndafaš).* He jostled me as he went by. *dafašni w-huwwe maareq.*
to **jot down** – *katab (o ə//nkatab), qayyad//tqayyad.* I managed to jot down his license number. *ḥsənᵊt ʔəktob nəmret sayyaarto.*
journal – **1.** (diary) *yawmiyyaat* (pl.) **2.** (in bookkeeping) *žərnaal* pl. *-aat.* **3.** (periodical) *mažalle* pl. *-aat.*
journalism – *ṣaḥaafe.* She studied journalism. *darset ṣaḥaafe.*
journalist – *ṣaḥaafi* pl. *-iyye* and *-iyyiin,* (woman) *ṣaḥaafiyye* pl. *-aat.*
journey – *raḥle* pl. *-aat.*
jovial – *bašuuš, ḍaḥuuk.* There is a jovial fellow! *yaa heek waaḥed bašuuš wəlla bala!*
joy – *faraḥ.* She was beaming with joy. *kaanet ᵊmšaεᵊšεa faraḥ.*
joyful – *məfreḥ, msərr.* It was a joyful occasion. *kaanet ᵊmnaasabe məfᵊrḥa.*
Judaism – *l-yahuudiyye, diin˜ ᵊl-yahuud* or *d-diin ᵊl-yahuudi.*
judge – **1.** *ǧaaḍi* pl. *ǧəḍaat, ḥaakem* pl. *ḥəkkaam.* When is the judge going to pass sentence? *ʔeemta l-ǧaaḍi raḥ yəṣder ᵊl-ḥəkᵊm?* **2.** *ḥakam* pl. *ḥəkkaam.* The judge says it's a net ball. *l-ḥakam εam yquul ʔənna šabake.* -- You be the judge of that! *ʔənte kuun ᵊl-ḥakam b-hal-masʔale!* **3.** *mḥakkem* pl. *-iin.* The judges awarded his picture the first prize. *l-ᵊmḥakkmiin εaṭu ṣuurto ž-žaayze l-ʔuula.*
  **She's not a good judge of human nature. *maa εanda faraase b-ʔaṭbaaε ᵊn-naas.*
  to judge – **1.** *ḥakam (o ḥəkᵊm//nḥakam) εala.* Don't judge him too harshly. *laa təḥkom εaléε b-qasaawe zaayde.* -- I can't judge that. *maa fiini ʔəḥkom εala haš-šii.* **2.** *qaas (i qyaas//nqaas).* Never judge others by yourself. *ʔabadan laa tqiis ᵊn-naas εala haalak.*
  **To judge by his face he isn't very enthusiastic. *mbayyen εala wəššo ʔənno muu mətḥammes ᵊktiir.*
judgment – **1.** *ḥəkᵊm, taqdiir.* You can rely on his judgment. *fiik təεtəmed εala ḥəkmo.* **2.** *ḥəkᵊm* pl. *ʔaḥkaam.* The president of the court will hand down his judgment today. *raʔiis ᵊl-maḥkame byəṣdor ḥəkmo l-yoom.* -- Don't make snap judgments. *laa tətsarraε ᵊb-ḥəkmak.* **3.** *raʔi.* In my judgment, you're making a mistake. *(ʔana) b-raʔyi ʔənte ġalṭaan.* -- He shows good judgment. *huwwe ṣaaḥeb raʔi mniiḥ.*
judicial – **1.** *ǧaanuuni**. Judicial procedures are very involved. *l-ʔəžraaʔaat ᵊl-ǧaanuuniyye ktiir ᵊmεaqqade.* **2.** *ǧaḍaaʔi**. The judicial system of the country. *n-niẓaam ᵊl-ǧaḍaaʔi tabaε l-ᵊblaad.*
judicious – *ḥakiim* pl. *ḥəkama.* He made a judicious selection. *kaan ḥakiim b-ʔəxtiyaaro.*
judiciously – *b-ḥəkme.* He went about the whole affair very judiciously. *dabbar ᵊl-ʔamᵊr b-kəll ḥəkme.*
jug – **1.** *ʔəbriiq* pl. *ʔabariiq.* **2.** (large, made of pottery, with two handles) *ḥəqq* pl. *ḥqaaq.*
juice – **1.** *εaṣiir.* I'd like a glass of grape juice, please. *ḅalla žəb-li kaaset εaṣiir εəneb.* **2.** *mayy.* These oranges give very little juice. *hal-*

bərdqaanaat maa fiihon ṃayy ᵊktiir or maa byə́Ɛᵊṣru ṃayy ᵊktiir.
juicy - **1.** *maawi*˜, *malaan ṃayy*. These lemons are very juicy. *hal-leemuunaat maawiyyaat ᵊktiir* (or *malaaniin ṃayy*). **2.** *mfalfal*. He's full of juicy stories. *ḥakaayḏa l-ᵊmfalfale maa btəxloṣ*.
July - *tammuuz*.
jumbled - *mlaxbaṭ, mxarbaṭ*.
jump - **1.** *naṭṭa* pl. *-aat*. With one jump he was over the hedge. *b-naṭṭa waaḥde ṣaar wara s-syaaž*. **2.** *qavze* pl. *-aat*. His jump broke the national record. *qavᵊzto ḏarbet ᵊr-raqam ᵊl-ʔahli*.
**You don't want him to get the jump on you, do you? *ʔakiid maa bəddak-yḏa yə́sᵊbqak, muu heek?*
to jump - **1.** *naṭṭ (ə naṭṭ), qafaz (e/o qafᵊz, qavze)*. How high can you jump? *šuu ʔaƐla šii btəqder ᵊtnəṭṭ?* -- He jumped off the streetcar. *naṭṭ mn ᵊt-tramwaay*. **2.** *ʔaġfal (e ʔəġfaal)*. We jumped pages seven to twelve. *ʔaġfalna ṣ-ṣafḥaat mn ᵊs-sabƐa ləṭ-ṭnaƐš*. **3.** *naqaz (o naqᵊz, naqze)*. He jumped when he heard the noise. *naqaz lamma səmeƐ ᵊṣ-ṣooṭ*.
**The train jumped the track. *t-treen ṭaleƐ Ɛan ᵊl-xaṭṭ*.
**He jumped at the offer. *ltaham ᵊl-Ɛarḍ ʔəltihaam*.
**Don't jump to conclusions. *laa tətsarraƐ bᵊl-ʔəstəntaaž*.
**It's enough to make you jump out of your skin. *haš-šii bišayyeb šaƐr ᵊr-raas*.
**He can go jump in the lake! *yruuḥ yəḍrob raaso bᵊl-ḥeeṭ!*
to jump around - *naṭwaṭ*. Stop jumping around. *ḥaaže tnaṭweṭ!* or *ḥaaštak naṭwaṭa!*
junction - *mafraq*˜ (pl. *mafaareq*˜) *ṭəroq*.
June - *ḥzeeraan*.
jungle - *ġaabaat* (pl.), *ʔadġaal* (pl.).
junk - **1.** *karakiib* (pl.). We'll have to clean the junk out of the garage. *laazem nṭaaleƐ hal-karakiib mn ᵊl-garaaž*. **2.** *xərḏa*. Where did you get that junk? *mneen žəbᵊt hal-xərḏa?*
**It's all junk. *kəll haš-šii ləl-kabb*.
to junk - *zatt (ə zatt//nzatt), kabb (ə kabb//nkabb)*. I'm afraid we'll have to junk our car soon. *šaayə́f-lak laazem ᵊnzətt sayyaarətna Ɛan qariib*.
Jupiter - **1.** (god) *žuubiteer*. **2.** (planet) *l-məštári*.
jurisdiction - **1.** *ṣəlṭa ḏaḏaaʔiyye, ḏaḏaaʔ*. The jurisdiction of a justice of the peace. *ṣ-ṣəlṭa l-ḏaḏaaʔiyye tabaƐ ḥaakem ᵊṣ-ṣəlᵊḥ*. **2.** *ṣalaaḥiyye, ʔəxtiṣaaṣ*. I have no jurisdiction in the matter. *maa-li ṣalaaḥiyye b-hal-ʔamᵊr*. -- That's outside my jurisdiction. *haada muu mən ʔəxtiṣaaṣi*.
jurist - *ḥuḏuuḏi* pl. *-iyyiin*.
jury - *mḥallafiin* (pl.). The jury hasn't brought in a verdict yet. *l-ᵊmḥallafiin ləssa maa ṭaalaƐu ḏaraaron*.
juryman - *mḥallaf* pl. *-iin*.
just - *Ɛaadel, mənṣef*. That's a just punishment. *haada žaza Ɛaadel*. -- He is a just man. *huwwe rəžžaal mənṣef*.
**He sleeps the sleep of the just. *naayem noom malaat Ɛyuuno*.
just - **1.** *hallaq*. I just arrived. *hallaq wṣəlṭ*. **2.** *tamaaman, Ɛaynan*. He's just like his father. *huwwe mətᵊl ʔabúu tamaaman* or *byəšbah ʔabúu. tamaaman*. -- He's just as lazy as his brother. *kaslaan tamaaman mətᵊl ʔaxúu*. **3.** *tamaam, tamaaman, Ɛat-tamaam*. The water's just right for swimming. *l-mayy ᵊmnaasbe tamaam ləs-sbaaḥa*. -- No more sugar, thank you, my coffee is just right. *maa bəddi səkkar, šəkran, qahᵊwti raakze tamaam*. **4.** *b-zaat-* or *b-Ɛeen* - + pron. suff. That's just what I wanted. *haada maṭluubi b-zaato*. -- That's just the word I meant. *hayye l-kəlme b-zaata yalli Ɛaneeta*. **5.** *bass*. He's just a little boy. *huwwe ṣabi zġiir bass*. **6.** *bᵊz-zoor*. We just made it to the station. *bəz-zoor laḥaqna lḥuuq ləl-ᵊmḥaṭṭa*.
**Just what do you mean? *fahhəmni šuu btaqṣoḏ*.
**I'm just dead tired. *ʔana mayyet ᵊmn ᵊt-taƐab*.
**It was just the other way around. *l-Ɛakᵊs halli ṣaar*.
**That's just the way it is! *haada l-ḥaaḏer!*
**There's just nothing you can do about it. *tráka la-ʔaḷḷa, maa byəṭlaƐ ᵊb-ʔiidak taƐmel šii*.
**Just don't worry! *w-laa yhəmmak!*
**Just imagine! *tṣawwar baqa!*
**The table was just covered with dust. *ṭ-ṭaawle kaanet malaane ġabra*.
**That takes just as long. *haš-šaġle btaaxod nafs ᵊl-waqᵊt*.
**Just for that I won't do it. *xṣuuṣi la-has-sabab maa baƐmə́la*.
justice - *Ɛadaale, Ɛadᵊl, ʔənṣaaf*. Don't expect justice from him. *laa təntə́zer ʔayy Ɛadaale mənno*.
justice of the peace - *ḥaakem*˜ (pl. *ḥəkkaam*˜) *ṣəlᵊḥ, ḏaaḏi*˜ (pl. *ḏəḏaat*˜) *ṣəlᵊḥ*.
ministry of justice - *wazaart*˜ *ᵊl-Ɛadliyye, wazaart*˜ *ᵊl-Ɛadᵊl*.
to do justice - *naṣaf* or *ʔanṣaf (e ʔənṣaaf)*. You're not doing him justice. *ʔənte maa-lak Ɛam tənᵊṣfo* (or *tənṣef maƐo*).
**The picture doesn't do you justice. *ʔənte muu ṭaaleƐ mniiḥ b-haṣ-ṣuura*.
justifiable - *ʔəlo mbarriraato*. I think this expenditure is justifiable. *bəənn hal-maṣruuf ʔəlo mbarriraato*. -- It's a justifiable step under the circumstances. *hiyye xaṭwe ʔəla mbarriraata b-haẓ-ẓuruuf*.
to justify - *barrar//tbarrar*. She tried to justify her actions. *ḥaawalet ᵊtbarrer ʔaƐmaala*.
justified - *mḥəqq*. I think you were perfectly justified in doing that. *bəənn kənt ᵊmḥəqq tamaaman b-hal-Ɛamal*. -- You're perfectly justified in asking for more money. *ʔənte mḥəqq tamaam ʔənnak təṭlob maṣaari ʔaktar*.
juvenile delinquency - *žaraaʔem*˜ *ᵊl-ʔaḥdaas* (pl.).

K

Kaaba - *l-kaƐbe*.
Kabul - *kaabuul*.
Karachi - *karaatši*.
karat - *qiiraaṭ* pl. *qarariiṭ*.
keen - *ḥadd*. He has a keen mind. *Ɛando zaka ḥadd*.
**I'm not so keen on that. *maa-li məstaqtel Ɛala haš-šaġle*.
to keep - **1.** *ḥtafaẓ b-*. May I keep this picture? *məmken ʔəḥtə́feẓ b-haṣ-ṣuura?* **2.** *ḥafaẓ (a ḥəfᵊẓ//nḥafaẓ), ḥtafaẓ b-*. Please keep this for me! *mən faḏlak ḥfaẓ-li-yaaha Ɛandak!* (or ... *ḥtə́fə́ẓ-li fiiha* ...). -- Where do they keep the money? *ween byəḥfaẓu l-maṣaari?* **3.** *ḥaafaẓ Ɛala*. Keep your temper! *ḥaafeẓ Ɛala ʔaƐṣaabak!* **4.** *wafa (-yuufi wafa//nwafa) b-, ḥaafaẓ Ɛala*. I relie on you to keep your word. *ʔana məƐtə́med Ɛaleek tuufi b-waƐdak*. **5.** *Ɛaṭṭal*. I won't keep you very long. *maa laḥa Ɛaṭṭlak ᵊktiir*. **6.** *katam (o kətmaan//nkatam), ḥafaẓ*. Can you keep a secret? *fiik təktom sərr?* **7.** *xabba*. Are you keeping something from me? *Ɛam ᵊtxabbi šii Ɛaliyyi?* **8.** *masek (e mask//mmasak)*. He keeps my books. *huwwe maasə́k-li ḥsaabaati*. **9.** *dabbar*. She keeps house for her brother. *bəddabber šuʔuun beet ʔaxuuha*. **10.** *manaƐ (a manᵊƐ//mmanaƐ)*. Nobody can keep you from going there. *maa ḥada byəqder yəmnaƐak truuḥ la-hniik* (or *Ɛan ᵊr-rooḥa la-hniik*). **11.** *ḏaayan*. This milk won't keep till tomorrow. *hal-ḥaliib maa bidaayen la-bəkra*. -- Will the meat keep in this weather? *l-laḥme bəddaayen ᵊb-heek ṭaqᵊṣ?* **12.** *mtanaƐ*. He can't keep from biting his fingernails. *maa byəqder yəmtə́neƐ Ɛan ʔakᵊl ʔaḏafiiro*. **13.** *ḏall (a ø), tamm (a ø)*. He kept talking all the time. *ḏall yəḥki ṭuul ᵊl-waqᵊt*. -- The policeman told us to keep moving. *š-šərṭi qal-lna nḏall maašyiin*. -- We sent him away, but he kept coming back. *ṣarafnḏa bass ḏall yəržaƐ Ɛaleena*. **14.** *xalla*. Sorry to have kept you waiting. *mətʔassef xalleetak tənṭə́zer*. -- Keep trying! *xalliik Ɛam ᵊtḥaawel!* -- Keep to the right. *xalliik Ɛal-yamiin*. -- Keep to the right, pass on the left! *xalliik Ɛal-yamiin w-ḏaawaz Ɛaš-šmaal*. -- Let's keep that in mind! *xalliina nxalli haš-šaġle b-baalna*. -- Shall I keep your dinner warm? *xallẓi-lak Ɛašaak ṣaxen?* -- Keep me posted. *xalliini Ɛala Ɛəlᵊm*.

Does your watch keep good time? *btəmši saaʕtak maẓbuuṭ ʕal-waqᵊt?*

**Keep track of the number of hours you've worked. *xalli b-baalak ᵊs-saaʕaat halli štaġalton.*

**Keep off the grass! *baʕʕed ʕan ᵊl-ḥašiiš!*

**Can't you keep quiet? *maa btəḥsen təskot?*

**Keep calm! *haddi ḥaalak!*

**Keep your powder dry. *xalliik ʕala ḥadar!*

**Keep your hands off that! *laa tədqor ᵊb-haš-šii.* (fig.) *laa tḥəṭṭ ʔəṣbaʕtak ᵊb-haš-šii.*

**Where have you been keeping yourself all this time? *ween kənᵊt ġaaṭeṣ kəll hal-ġeebe?*

**He kept his real intentions secret from me for quite a while. *xabba ʕanni maqaaṣdo l-ḥaqiiqiyye mədde.* -- Why don't you keep me company tonight? *leeš maa bəttamm maʕi l-leele?*

to keep away - *baʕʕad.* We have to do something to keep away the flies. *laazem naʕməl-lna šii šaġle la-nbaʕʕed ᵊd-dəbbaanaat.* -- You should keep the child away from the matches. *laazem ᵊtbaʕʕed ᵊl-walad ʕan ᵊl-kəbriit.* -- Keep away from that radio! *baʕʕed ʕan har-raadyo!*

to keep on - *ḍall (a ə), tamm (a ə), stamarr.* He kept on talking. *ḍall ʕam yəḥki.*

to keep out - **1.** *manaʕ (a manᵊʕ//mmanaʕ).* Ordinary glass keeps out ultraviolet rays. *l-ᵊqzaaz ᵊl-ʕaadi byəmnaʕ ᵊl-ʔašiʕʕa fooq ᵊl-banafsažiyye.* **2.** *baʕʕad.* Keep him out of my way! *baʕʕdo mən wəšši.* -- I'll try to keep you out of trouble. *baʕmel žahdi baʕʕdak ʕan ᵊl-mašaakel.* **3.** *tamm (a ə) ᵊbʕiid.* It's his affair. You'd better keep out of it. *haada šəġlo. ʔaḥsán-lak ᵊttamm ᵊbʕiid ʕanno.*

**Keep out of his way. *džannabo!*

**Keep him out of here. *laa txallii yqarreb la-hoon.*

to keep up - **1.** *waaẓab ʕala, stamarr b-.* Keep up the good work. *waaẓeb ʕala šəġlak ᵊl-maẓbuuṭ.* **2.** *taabaʕ.* Keep it up and see where it gets you. *xalliik ᵊmtaabeʕ heek w-šuuf šuu bişiir maʕak.* **3.** *laḥḥaq.* It's hard for me to keep up with the other students. *ṣaʕᵊb ʕaliyyi laḥḥeq ᵊt-ṭəllaab ᵊt-taanyiin bᵊd-diraase.* -- I can't keep up with you when you dictate so fast. *maa bəqder laḥḥqak lamma bətnaqqəlni b-has-sərʕa.* -- I can't keep up with my work. *maa-li ʕam laḥḥeq šəġli.*

**How much does it cost you per month to keep up your car? *qaddeeš bətkallfak sayyaartak bᵊš-šahr?*

keepsake - *təzkaar* pl. *-aat.*

kerosene - *zeet kaas.*

kettle - *ʔəbriiq* pl. *ʔabariiq,* (large, hung over open fire) *ḥalle* pl. *-aat* and *ḥəlal.* Take the kettle from the stove. *qiim ᵊl-ʔəbriiq mən ʕaṭ-ṭabbaax.*

**That's a pretty kettle of fish! *ʔamma xarbaṭa ʕan ṣaḥiiḥ!*

kettledrum - *ṭabᵊl* pl. *ṭbuul.*

key - *məftaaḥ* pl. *mafatiiḥ.* I've lost the key to my room. *ḍayyaʕᵊt məftaaḥ ʔuudṭi.* -- That was the key to the mystery. *haada kaan məftaaḥ ᵊs-sərr.* -- One of the keys on my typewriter gets stuck. *fii məftaaḥ biʕalleq bᵊl-ʔaale l-kaatbe tabaʕi.*

**Who's singing off key? *miin yalli ʕam yġanni barraat ᵊn-nooṭa?*

key hole - *bəxš˜* (pl. *bxaaš˜*) *ᵊl-ġaal.*

key position - *markaz ḥassaas* (or *raʔiisi*) pl. *maraakez ḥassaase* (or *raʔiisiyye*). He holds a key position in the government. *ʔəlo markaz ḥassaas bᵊl-ḥukuume.*

key ring - *ḥammaalet˜* (pl. *-aat˜*) *mafatiiḥ.*

khaki - *xaaki* (invar.).

kick - **1.** *rafse* pl. *-aat, labṭa* pl. *-aat.* The horse nearly gave me a kick. *l-ᵊḥṣaan kaan raḥa yərfəsni rafse* (or *yəlbəṭni labṭa*). -- I felt like giving him a good hard kick. *ʔəža ʕala baali ʔərᵊfso rafse maakne.* **2.** *naṭra* pl. *-aat.* The kick of a rifle can break your collar bone. *naṭret ᵊl-baaruude yəmken təksér-lak kətfak.*

**He gets a big kick out of sports. *ktiir byənṭəreb ᵊmn ᵊl-ʔalʕaab ᵊr-riyaaḍiyye.*

to kick - **1.** *ḍarab (o ḍarᵊb, ḍarbe) b-rəžlo.* Kick the ball! *ḍroob ᵊṭ-ṭaabe (b-rəžlak)!* or ***šuuṭ ᵊṭ-ṭaabe!* **2.** *rafas (e/o rafᵊs), raffas.* I hope this horse doesn't kick. *nšaḷḷa hal-ᵊḥṣaan maa byərfos.* **3.** *nakrab.* He kicks about everything. *daayman binakreb ʕala kəll šii.*

*He's kicking over the traces again. *ʕam yədžaawaz ḥduudo mətl ᵊl-ʕaade.*

to kick out - *qallaʕ, ṭarad (o ṭarᵊd).* I nearly kicked him out. *kənt ʕala wašᵊk qallʕo.*

kid - **1.** *žədi* pl. *žədyaan.* The goat had two kids. *l-məʕzaaye kan-la žədiyyeen.* **2.** *walad* pl. *wlaad, ṣabi* pl. *ṣəbyaan,* (girl) *bənt* pl. *banaat.* We'll feed the kids first. *mənṭaʕmi l-ᵊwlaad bᵊl-ʔawwal.*

**Don't act like a kid! *ḥaaže waldane!*

kid glove - *kaff* (pl. *kfuuf*) *žəld.* How much is a pair of kid gloves? *qaddeeš ḥaqq žooz ᵊkfuuf žəld?*

**You have to handle her with kid gloves. *laazem ᵊtʕaamə́la b-ʔiideen mən ḥariir.*

to kid - *mazaḥ (a mazᵊḥ).* I'm only kidding. *ʕam ʔəmzaḥ bass.*

to **kidnap** - *xaṭaf (o xaṭᵊf//nxaṭaf), xṭaṭaf.* They arrested him on the charge of kidnaping the girl. *waqqafúu b-təhmet ʔənno xaṭaf ᵊl-bənᵊt.*

kidney - *kəlwe* and *kəlye* pl. *kalaawi, kəle* pl. *kəlwaat.*

to **kill** - **1.** *qatal (e/o qatᵊl//nqatal* and *qətel a).* Did he really kill her? *ʕan ḥaqa qatə́la?* -- I was so mad, I could have killed him. *qaffaʕet maʕi kənt raayeḥ bəqᵊtlo.* -- He was killed in a traffic accident. *qətel b-ḥaades sayyaara.* -- We played cards to kill the time. *lʕəbna šadde la-nəqtel ᵊl-waqt.* -- Her son was killed in action. *ʔəbᵊnha nqatal* (or ***stašhad) bᵊl-maʕrake.* **2.** *mawwat.* This work is killing me. *haš-šəġᵊl ʕam ymawwətni.* -- The sting of a scorpion can kill a man. *qarṣet ᵊl-ʕaqrab bižuuz ᵊtmawwet.*

**We killed two birds with one stone. *ḍarabna ʕaṣfuureen ᵊb-ḥažar.*

**I'll give you something to kill the pain. *baʕṭiik šii ysakkə́n-lak ᵊl-wažaʕ.*

**The bill was killed in committee. *mašruuʕ ᵊl-qaanuun maat bᵊl-ləžne.*

**Be careful, or you will kill the engine. *ntəbeh raḥa təṭfi l-motoor.*

killer - *qaatel* pl. *-iin.*

kilocycle - *kiloosiikᵊl* pl. *-aat.*

kilogram - *kiilo* pl. *kiiloyaat.*

kilometer - *kiilomətr* pl. *-aat.*

kilowatt - *kiloowaaṭ* pl. *-aat.*

kin - *qaraaybiin* (pl.). They are all my kin. *kəllon qaraaybiini.*

kind - **1.** *nooʕ* pl. *ʔanwaaʕ.* This building is the only one of its kind. *hal-binaaye hiyye l-waḥiide mən nooʕa.* **2.** *žəns* pl. *ʔažnaas, šəkᵊl* pl. *ʔaškaal, ṣənf* pl. *ʔaṣnaaf, nooʕ* pl. *ʔanwaaʕ.* We have only two kinds of coffee. *fii ʕanna žənseen qahwe bass.* -- The shoes are made of two kinds of leather. *ṣ-ṣabbaaṭ maʕmuul mən nooʕeen žəld.* **3.** *nooʕ* pl. *ʔanwaaʕ.* What kind of house is that? *šuu nooʕ hal-beet?* -- What kind of person is he? *šuu nooʕo mn ᵊr-ržaal?*

kind of - *šwayye.* I felt kind of sorry for him. *qalbi ḥəzen ʕalée šwayye.*

all kinds of - *ʔaškaal ʔaškaal, ʔaškaal w-ʔalwaan.* There were all kinds of books on the table. *kaan fii kətᵊb ʔaškaal ʔaškaal ʕaṭ-ṭaawle.* -- You meet all kinds of people there. *bətšuuf naas ʔaškaal ʔaškaal ᵊhniik.*

in kind - *ʕaynan.* The farmers pay their workers in kind. *l-ᵊmzaarʕiin byədfaʕu ʔəžret fəllaaḥiinon ʕaynan.*

of the kind - *heek, mətᵊl heek.* I didn't say anything of the kind. *maa qəlt heek šii* (or *šii mətᵊl heek*) *ʔabadan.*

kind - **1.** *laṭiif* pl. *ləṭafa, ḥabbaab.* She's a very kind lady. *hiyye sətt laṭiife ktiir.* **2.** *laṭiif.* That was a kind thing to do. *haada kaan ʕamal laṭiif.* -- Children should be taught to be kind to animals. *l-ᵊwlaad laazem yətʕallamu ykuunu ləṭafa maʕ ᵊl-ḥaywaanaat* (or ***yətraʔʔafu bᵊl-ḥaywaanaat*). **3.** *ʕaṭuuf, laṭiif.* They were very kind to me while I was ill. *kaanu ktiir ʕaṭuufiin ʕaliyyi* (or *ləṭafa maʕi*) *məddet maraḍi.*

**That's very kind of you. *haada ktiir ləṭᵊf mənnak* or *haada mən ləṭfak.*

**Would you be so kind as to mail this letter for me? *btaʕmel maʕruuf tḥəṭṭ-ə́lli hal-maktuub bᵊl-boosṭa?*

kindergarten - *rawḍet˜* (pl. *ryaaḍ˜*) *ʔaṭfaal.*

kindly - **1.** *laṭiif* pl. *ləṭafa.* Her grandmother is a kindly old lady. *sətta ʔəxtyaara laṭiife.* **2.** *b-ləṭᵊf.* She received us most kindly. *staqbalətna b-kəll ləṭᵊf.* **3.** *baḷḷa, mən faḍlak, ʕmeel maʕruuf.* Kindly tell him to call me back. *baḷḷa qəl-lo ytalfə́n-li.* **4.** *ʔaržuuk* (f. *ʔaržuuki* pl. *ʔaržuukon*). Kindly mind your own business! *ʔaržuuk laa təddaaxal b-ᵊšʔuun ᵊl-ġeer.*

kindness - *ləṭᵊf, laṭaafe.* I appreciate your kindness. *ʔana bqadder laṭaaftak.* -- He showed me much kindness. *waršaani ləṭf ᵊktiir.*

king – **1.** (monarch) *malek* pl. *mluuk.* **2.** (chess) *šaah* pl. *-aat.* **3.** (cards) *ʔəxtyaar* pl. *-iyye.*

kingdom – *mamlake* pl. *mamaalek.*

kink – *fatle* pl. *-aat.* There's a kink in the rope. *fii fatle bᵊl-ḥable.*

**His argument has a few kinks. *ḥəššto fiiha kam lafte w-doora.*

kinky – *mkaʒber.* All his boys have kinky hair. *kəll ᵊwlaado šaʕron ᵊmkaʒber.*

kinship – *qaraabe.* The ties of kinship are strong in this society. *rawaabeṭ ᵊl-qaraabe b-hal-məʒtámaʕ qawiyye ktiir.*

kiosk – *bəṣṭa* pl. *-aat.*

kiss – *boose* pl. *-aat.* Give me a kiss. *ʕaṭiini boose.*

to kiss – **1.** *baas (u boos//mbaas).* He kissed him on both cheeks. *baaso mn ᵊl-xaddeen.* **2.** *bawwas.* He kissed her a good ten minutes. *tamm ybawwə́sa ʕašᵊr daqaayeq.* -- I could kiss you for this! *bbawwsak mən ʕyuunak!* **3.** *tbaawas.* Why don't you two kiss and make up. *yaḷḷa tbaawasu w-ᵊfrəṭuuha baqa.*

kitchen – *maṭbax* pl. *maṭaabex.* Do you mind if we eat in the kitchen? *fii ʕandak maaneʕ ʔiza ʔakalna bᵊl-maṭbax?*

kitchen stove – *wǧaaq* pl. *-aat, ṭabbaax* pl. *-aat.*

kitten – *qaṭṭa ẓġiire* pl. *qaṭaaṭ ᵊẓġaar, bəsse* pl. *-aat, bseene* pl. *-aat.*

knack – *mawhibe.* He's got a knack at fixing all kinds of things. *ʕando mawhibe b-taṣliiḥ kəll šii.* -- He has a knack for photography. *ʕando mawhibe bᵊt-taṣwiir.*

**Now I've got the knack of it. *hallaq msəkt raas ᵊš-šamuuṭ!* or *hallaq laqáṭṭa!* (or *kamášta!*).

to **knead** – *ʕaǧan (e/o ʕaǧᵊn//nʕaǧan).* You have to knead the dough thoroughly. *laazem təʕᵊǧni l-ʕaǧiine ʕal-maẓbuuṭ.*

knee – *rəkbe* pl. *rəkab.*

to **kneel** – **1.** *rakaʕ (a rkuuʕ).* She knelt on the floor. *rakʕet ʕal-ʔarḍ.* **2.** *naxx (ə naxx).* Camels kneel while they are being loaded. *l-ᵊǧmaal bətnəxx waqᵊt btətḥammal.*

to make kneel – *naxxax, barrak.* Make the camel kneel. *naxxex ᵊǧ-ǧamal.*

knife – (with a rigid blade) *səkkiin* and *səkkiine* pl. *sakakiin,* (with movable blade) *muus* pl. *mwaas.* Hand me your knife a minute. *naawəlni səkkiintak lаḥẓa.*

knight – **1.** (nobleman) *faares* pl. *fərsaan.* **2.** (chess) *faraṣ* pl. *fraaṣ.*

to **knit** – **1.** *štaġal (ṣuuf).* Did you knit these gloves yourself? *štaġalti hal-ᵊkfuuf la-ḥaalek?* **2.** *ltaḥam.* It took a long time for the bones to knit. *l-ᵊʕḍaam ʔaxadu mədde ṭawiile ḥatta ltaḥamu.*

knitting needle – *ʔəbret˜* (pl. *ʔəbar˜*) *ḥyaake.*

knob – *ṭaabe* pl. *-aat.*

knock – **1.** *daqqa* pl. *-aat, ṭarqa* pl. *-aat.* Did you hear the knock at the door? *sməʕt ᵊd-daqqa ʕal-baab?* **2.** *ṭaqṭaqa* pl. *-aat, daqdaqa* pl. *-aat.* Can you hear the knock in the engine? *saameʕ ṭaqṭaqet ᵊl-motoor?*

to knock – **1.** *daqq (ə daqq), ṭaraq (o ṭarᵊq).* Someone knocked at the door. *fii ḥada daqq ʕal-baab.* -- Please knock before you come in. *mən faḍlak dəqq qabᵊl-ma tfuut.* **2.** *xabaṭ (o xabᵊṭ).* Don't knock against the table. *laa təxboṭ bᵊṭ-ṭaawle.* **3.** *xabbaṭ, daqdaq.* Uphill the engine sometimes knocks. *bᵊṭ-ṭluuʕ ᵊl-motoor ʔaḥyaanan bixabbeṭ.*

**He knocked the knife out of his hand. *ṭayyár-lo s-səkkiine mən ʔiido.*

**He's knocked around all over the world. *maa xalla qərne bᵊd-dənye maa šaafa.*

**She's been knocked around a lot. *šəqyet ᵊktiir ᵊb-ḥayaata.*

to knock down – *saṭṭaḥ.* He knocked him down with one blow. *saṭṭaḥo b-lakme waaḥde.* **2.** *waqqaʕ.* Be careful not to knock anything down. *ʔəṣḥa twaqqeʕ šii.*

to knock off – **1.** *ṭayyar.* He nearly knocked my hat off. *kaan raḥa yṭayyə́r-li bərneeṭṭi (mən ʕala raasi).* **2.** *xaṣam (o xaṣᵊm//nxaṣam), nazzal// tnazzal.* He knocked off ten pounds from the bill. *xaṣam ʕašᵊr leeraat mən l-ᵊḥsaab.* **3.** *xalaṣ (o xalaaṣ) mən šəġlo.* We knocked off at 6 o'clock. *xalaṣna mən šəġᵊlna s-saaʕa sətte.*

**Let's knock off for today. *ḥaaže! xalliina nwaqqef ᵊl-yoom.*

to knock out – *ṭarah (a ṭarᵊḥ//nṭaraḥ).* He was knocked out in the tenth round. *nṭaraḥ bᵊš-šawle l-ʕaašra.*

to knock over – **1.** *qalab (o/e qalb//nqalab).* Who knocked the pail over? *miin qalab ᵊṣ-ṣaṭᵊl?* **2.** *waqqaʕ.* You almost knocked me over. *kənt laḥa twaqqəʕni.*

knocker – *ṣaqqaaṭa* pl. *-aat.*

knot – **1.** *ʕəqde* pl. *ʕəqad.* Can you untie this knot? *btəqder ᵊtfəkk hal-ʕəqde?* -- The board is full of knots. *hal-looḥ malaan ʕəqad.* **2.** *ʕəqde* pl. *ʕəqad, miil baḥri* pl. *ʔamyaal baḥriyye.* The ship can make fifteen knots an hour. *s-safiine btaʕmel xamsṭaʕšar ʕəqde bᵊs-saaʕa.*

to knot – *ʕaqad (o/e ʕaqᵊd//nʕaqad).* Shall I knot the string? *ʔəʕqod ᵊl-xeeṭ?* -- You have to knot the two ends. *laazem təʕqod ᵊṭ-ṭarafeen maʕ baʕḍon.*

knotted – *mʕaqqad.* The string is all knotted. *l-xeeṭ kəllo mʕaqqad* or ***kəllo ʕəqad.*

knotty – *mʕaqqad, mšarbak.* That's a knotty problem. *hayye məšᵊkle mʕaqqade.*

to **know** – *ʕəref (-yaʕref maʕᵊrfe//nʕaraf).* Do you know their address? *btaʕref ʕənwaanon?* -- I don't know any French at all. *maa baʕref frənsaawi ʔabadan.* -- I don't know how to drive a car. *maa baʕref suuq sayyaara.* -- I know he's ill. *ʕarfaan ʔənno mariiḍ.* -- I know her only by sight. *baʕrə́fa bass bᵊl-wəšš.* -- He became known as soon as he published the book. *ṣaar yənʕə́ref mən waqᵊt-ma ṭaalaʕ l-ᵊktaab.* -- I know it only from hearsay. *baʕrə́fa bass qiil ʕan qaal.* -- I knew it! *ʕrəft!* -- Do you know your way around here? *ʕarfaan ᵊl-madaaxel wᵊl-maxaareǧ hoon?* -- He knows what's what. *byaʕref šuu fii šuu maa fii.* -- Do you know anything about farming? *btaʕref šii ʕan ᵊz-ziraaʕa?* -- Do you know of a good restaurant around here? *btaʕref šii maṭʕam ᵊmniiḥ ᵊb-han-nawaaḥi?* -- He knew of my coming. *ʕəref ᵊb-ǧayyti.*

**What do you know? *ʔənte šúu bifahhmak?*

**What do you know! *laa tquula!* or *ʔaḷḷa ʔaʕlam!*

to let know – *xabbar, ʕarraf, ʕaṭa xabar.* I'll let you know tomorrow. *bxabbrak* (or *baʕṭiik xabar*) *bəkra.*

know-how – *ʕərᵊf.* He hasn't the kind of know-how that would qualify him for this job. *maa ʕando ʕərᵊf yʔahhlo la-haš-šaġle.*

knowingly – *ʕan ʕəlᵊm, ʕamdan, qaṣdan.* He wouldn't knowingly cheat us. *maa biġəššna ʕan ʕəlᵊm.*

**She looked at her brother knowingly. *ṭṭallaʕet bi-ʔaxuuha ṭaṭliiʕet waaḥde ʕarfaane.*

knowledge – *maʕᵊrfe* pl. *maʕaaref.* His knowledge of Arabic is poor. *maʕrəfto bᵊl-ʕarabi ḍʕiife.* -- He likes to display his knowledge. *biḥəbb yətbaaha b-maʕrə́fto.* -- I'll answer your questions to the best of my knowledge. *bǧaaweb suʔaalaatak ʕala qadd maʕrəfti* (or ***qadd-ma baʕref).*

to my knowledge, to your knowledge, etc. – *ʕala ʕəlmi, ʕala ʕəlmak (ʕəlmek),* etc. To my knowledge he's not there. *ʕala ʕəlmi huwwe muu hniik.* -- To our knowledge he's in Beirut. *ʕala ʕəlᵊmna huwwe b-beeruut.*

knowledgeable – *ʕarfaan, fahmaan, məṭṭəleʕ.* She seems quite knowledgeable in this field. *byəẓhar ʕaleeha ʕarfaane b-hal-mawḍuuʕ.*

Koran – *l-qərʔaan,* (copy) *məṣḥaf* pl. *maṣaaḥef.*

Koranic – *qərʔaani*.*

Korea – *kuuriyya.*

Korean – *kuuri*.*

Kurd – *kərdi* pl. *kraad* coll. pl. *l-kərd,* f. *kərdiyye* pl. *-aat* and *kraad.*

Kurdish – **1.** *kərdi*.* There is a number of Kurdish villages near Aleppo. *fii ʕəddet qəra kərdiyye qariibe mən ḥalab.* **2.** *kərdi* (invar.). I studied a little Kurdish in College. *darast kərdi šwayye bᵊǧ-ǧaamʕa.*

Kurdistan – *kərdəstaan.*

Kuwait – **1.** *l-ᵊkweet.* Have you ever been in Kuwait? *b-ḥayaatak rəḥt ʕal-ᵊkweet?* **2.** *kweeti*.* The Kuwait oil fields. *ḥuquul ᵊz-zeet l-ᵊkweetiyye.*

Kuwaiti – *kweeti* pl. *-iyye,* f. *kweetiyye* pl. *-aat.*

L

label - 1. *ʔetikeet* pl. *-aat.* There's no label on this bottle. *maa fii ʔetikeet ʕala hal-qanniine.* 2. *ʕalaame* pl. *-aat.* The label "mus." indicates a technical term of music. *ʕalaamet* "mus." *bəddəll ʕala ʔəṣṭilaaḥ fanni məxtaṣṣ bᵊl-muusiiqa.*

to label - 1. *ʕallam, marrak, ḥaṭṭ ʔetikeet ʕala.* Would you please label those jars for me. *baḷḷa ʕalləm-li* (or *ḥəṭṭ-ə́lli ʔetikeetaat*) *ʕala hal-maṭraḅaanaat.* 2. *waṣam (-yuuṣem waṣᵊm//nwaṣam).* He's been labeled a radical for many years. *nwaṣam bᵊt-taṭarrof mən zamaan.*

labor - 1. *šəǧᵊl, ʕamal.* This task involves a great deal of labor and perseverance. *hal-muhəmme bəddha šəǧᵊl w-muwaaẓabe ktiir.* 2. *maǧhuud, ǧhuud* (pl.), *mataaʕeb* (pl.). All our labor has been in vain. *kəll maǧhuudna raaḥ səda.* 3. *ʔəǧret˜* (pl. *ʔǧuur˜* or *ʔəǧrawaat˜*) *ᵊl-ʕəmmaal.* Labor alone will cost three hundred pounds. *ʔəǧret ᵊl-ʕəmmaal waḥda bətkallfak tlaat miit leera.* 4. *l-ʕəmmaal.* Labor will never agree to that proposal. *l-ʕəmmaal maa raḥa ywaafqu ʔabadan ʕala hal-ʔəqtiraaḥ.* -- Labor movement. *ḥaraket˜ ʕəmmaal* or ****ḥarake ʕəmmaaliyye.* -- The British Labor Party. *ḥəzb ᵊl-ʕəmmaal ᵊl-briiṭaani.* -- Labor union. *naqaabet˜* (pl. *-aat˜*) *ʕəmmaal.*

hard labor - *ʔašǧaal šaaqqa* (pl.). He was sentenced to five years at hard labor. *ḥakamúu bᵊl-ʔašǧaal ᵊš-šaaqqa xams ᵊsniin.*

to be in labor - *ṭəlqet (a ṭalq, ṭalqa).* She was in labor nine hours. *tammet ʕam təṭlaq təsᵊʕ saaʕaat* or *daam maʕha ṭ-ṭalᵊq təsᵊʕ saaʕaat.*

laboratory - *maxbar* pl. *maxaaber, məxtábar* pl. *-aat.*

laborer - *faaʕel* pl. *fʕaale, šaǧǧiil* pl. *-e.*

lace - 1. *dantella.* I'd like five meters of that lace. *qṭaʕ-li xams ᵊmtuura mən had-dantella.* 2. *šammaaṭa* pl. *-aat.* I need new laces for my shoes. *laazəmni šammaaṭaat ǧədad la-ṣabbaaṭi.*

to lace - *rabaṭ (o rabṭ//nrabaṭ) šammaaṭet˜* ... Wait till I lace my shoes. *stanna la-ʔərboṭ šammaaṭaat ṣabbaaṭi.*

lack - *ʔəftiqaar, naqᵊṣ, ʕaaze.* There's a lack of trained personnel. *fii ʔəftiqaar la-mwaẓẓafiin ᵊmmarraniin.*

for lack of - *la-ʕadam˜ wuǧuud˜* ..., *la-ʕadam˜ tawaffor˜* ... He was acquitted for lack of evidence. *barrúu la-ʕadam tawaffor ᵊl-ʔadəlle.*

**For lack of something better to do I went to the movies. *rəḥᵊt ʕas-siinama laʔənno maa kaan fii ʕandi šii ʔaḥsan saawíi.*

to lack - *nəqeṣ (a nəqṣaan).* There is something lacking in the meal. *fii šii naaqeṣ bᵊl-ʔakle.* -- I didn't lack anything there. *maa nəqəṣni šii hniik.*

lad - *ṣabi* pl. *ṣəbyaan, walad* pl. *wlaad.*

ladder - *səllom* pl. *salaalem.*

ladle - *kəbšaaye* pl. *-aat.*

lady - 1. *sətt* pl. *-aat, sayyide* pl. *-aat.* Is that lady his mother? *has-sətt ʔəmmo šii?* -- Ladies and Gentlemen! *sayyidaati, (ʔaanisaati), saadati!* -- Where's the ladies' room? *ween ᵊt-twaleet ləs-sayyidaat?* -- She didn't behave like a lady. *maa tṣarrafet taṣarrof sətt məḥtáram.* 2. *sətt* pl. *-aat, xaanom* pl. *-aat.* Let's join the ladies. *xalliina nəqʕod maʕ ᵊs-səttaat.*

to **lag behind** - *tʔaxxar ʕan, qaṣṣar ʕan.* He's always lagging behind the others. *huwwe daayman mətʔaxxer ʕan ᵊl-baqiyye.*

lake - *buḥayra* pl. *-aat.*

lamb - 1. *xaaruuf* pl. *xawariif* and *xərfaan.* 2. (meat) *laḥm˜ xaaruuf.*

lame - 1. *ʔaʕraǧ* f. *ʕarǧa* pl. *ʕərǧaan* and *ʕərᵊǧ.* He seems to be lame. *byəẓhar ʕaléi ʔaʕraǧ.* 2. *waahi, taʕbaan.* That's a lame excuse. *haada ʕəzr waahi.*

lament - *šakwa* pl. *-aat* and *šakaawi, ṣaʕawiiṭ* (pl.). The room was filled with her loud laments. *mallet ᵊd-dənye b-šakawiiha w-ṣaʕawiiṭa.*

to lament - *tḥassar ʕala, tʔammah ʕala.* There are some who lament the passing of colonialism. *fii naas btətḥassar ʕala ntihaaʔ ᵊl-ʔəstəʕmaar.*

lamp - *ḍaww* pl. *ʔəḍᵊwye, lampa* pl. *-aat.* We need a new lamp for this room. *laazəmna ḍaww ᵊǧdiid la-hal-ʔuuḍa.*

lamp shade - *ʔabaǧuur* pl. *-aat.* I'll buy a new lamp shade for the desk lamp. *raḥa ʔəštə́ri ʔabaǧuur ᵊǧdiid la-ḍaww ᵊṭ-ṭaawle.*

land - 1. *l-yaabse.* We were glad to see land again. *ḥamadna ʔaḷḷa yalli šəfna l-yaabse marra taanye.* 2. *barr.* They traveled by land and sea. *saafaru bᵊl-barr wᵊl-baḥᵊr.* 3. *ʔarḍ* (f.) pl. *ʔaraaḍi.* The land here is very fertile. *l-ʔarḍ* (or *l-ʔaraaḍi*) *hoon xəṣbe ktiir.*

to land - 1. *nəzel (e nazle, nzuul) b-, habaṭ (o hbuuṭ) b-.* He had to land his plane in a wheat field. *nǧabar yənzel b-ṭayyaarto b-ḥaqlet qamᵊḥ.* 2. *hadda, ḥaṭṭ (ə ḥaṭaṭaan), habaṭ (o hbuuṭ).* The plane landed smoothly. *ṭ-ṭayyaara haddet b-huduuʔ.* 3. *nəzel (e nzuul).* Enemy troops have landed at three points along the coast. *ǧyuuš ᵊl-ʕaduww nəzlet b-ᵊtlətt nəqaṭ ʕala ṭuul ᵊs-saaḥel.* 4. *nazzal//tnazzal.* America was forced to land troops in order to restore order. *ʔamriika nǧabret ᵊtnazzel ᵊǧyuuš la-ʔiʕaadet ᵊl-ʔamᵊn.* 5. *ṣaffa, ṣəfi (a ə).* We nearly landed in jail. *kənna raḥa nṣaffi bᵊl-ḥabᵊs.* 6. *ḥəṣel (a ḥṣuul) ʕala.* He managed to land a good job with a large oil company. *qəder yəḥṣal ʕala waẓiife məḥtárame b-šərket zeet ᵊkbiire.*

landlady - *ṣaaḥbet˜ beet* pl. *ṣaaḥbaat˜ ᵊbyuut.*

landlord - *ṣaaḥeb˜ beet* pl. *ṣḥaab˜ ᵊbyuut, ṣaaḥeb˜ məlᵊk* pl. *ṣḥaab˜ ʔamlaak.*

landmark - *ʕalam* pl. *maʕaalem.* The monument is a landmark of this area. *n-naṣᵊb ʕalam b-hal-manṭiqa.*

landowner - *mallaak* pl. *-iin.* The big landowners are by tradition conservatives. *l-mallaakiin l-ᵊkbaar mən ṭabiiʕə́ton ᵊmḥaafẓiin.*

lane - 1. *darb* pl. *druub.* Follow this lane to the main road. *xalliik ʕala had-darb la-təṣal ləṭ-ṭariiq ᵊl-ʕaamm.* 2. *xaṭṭ* pl. *xṭuuṭ.* Take the left lane at the next traffic light. *xood ᵊl-xaṭṭ ᵊš-šmaali ʕaḍ-ḍaww ᵊǧ-ǧaaye.*

language - 1. *luǧa* pl. *luǧaat, lsaan* pl. *ʔalson.* He knows several languages. *byaʕref ʕəddet luǧaat.* 2. *luǧa, kalaam.* He used strong language in dealing with them. *staʕmal luǧa qaasye maʕon.* 3. *luǧa.* The book is written in beautiful language. *luǧet l-ᵊktaab ᵊktiir ḥəlwe.*

lantern - *faanuus* pl. *fawaniis.*

lap - 1. *ḥəḍᵊn* pl. *ḥḍaan.* She held the baby in her lap. *ḥamlet ᵊṭ-ṭəfl ᵊb-ḥəḍna.* 2. *šooṭ* pl. *ʔašwaaṭ.* He was in the lead by five yards in the first lap. *kaan saabeq ᵊl-baqiyye b-xams yardaat b-ʔawwal šooṭ.*

to lap up - 1. *laḥas (a laḥᵊs).* The kitten lapped up the milk. *l-qaṭṭa ẓ-ẓǧiire laḥset ᵊl-ḥaliib.* 2. *ltaham.* His students lap up his every word. *ṭəllaabo byəltəhmu kəll kəlme mən kalaamo ᵊltihaam.*

lapse - *tawaqqof, ʔənqitaaʕ.* There was a sudden lapse in communication. *ḥadas ʕala ǧafla tawaqqof bᵊl-ᵊmxaabaraat.*

to lapse - *bəṭel (a bəṭlaan).* If I don't pay this premium my insurance policy will lapse. *ʔiza maa bədfaʕ hal-qəsᵊṭ booliiṣet ᵊt-taʔmiin tabaʕi btəbṭal.*

large - *kbiir* pl. *kbaar, ḍaxm, waaseʕ.* This room isn't large enough. *hal-ʔuuḍa muu waasʕa kfaaye.*

at large - 1. *faltaan.* The thief is still at large. *l-ḥaraami ləssaato faltaan.* 2. *muṭlaq˜ ᵊs-saraaḥ.* He's again at large. *huwwe muṭlaq ᵊs-saraaḥ mn ᵊǧdiid.* 3. *ʕal-ᵊʕmuum.* People at large won't understand your motives. *n-naas ʕal-ᵊʕmuum maa-lon raḥa yəfhamu bawaaʕsak.*

largely - *bᵊl-ʔaktariyye.* Our company is made up largely of volunteers. *sariyyə́tna mʔallafe bᵊl-ʔaktariyye mən məṭṭawwʕiin.*

large-scale - *waaseʕ˜ ᵊn-niṭaaq.* The city is considering a large-scale building program. *l-baladiyye ʕam tənẓor b-mašruuʕ binaaʔ waaseʕ ᵊn-niṭaaq.*

largesse - *saxaawe, karam.* He is remembered for his largesse toward the poor. *n-naas byədsakkarúu la-saxaawto w-karamo ʕal-fəqara.*

lark - *qəmbara* pl. *qanaaber.* The lark is my favorite bird. *l-qəmbara ʔaḥabb ʕaṣfuur ʕandi.*

**The picnic was quite a lark. *mbaṣaṭna ktiir ᵊktiir bᵊs-seeraan.*

last - **1.** *ʔaaxer, ʔaaxraani**. She spent her last cent on that dress. *ṣarfet ʔaaxer qərš maεha εala hal-fəṣṭaan.* -- Hand me the last book on the upper shelf. *naawəlni l-ᵊktaab ᵊl-ʔaaxraani (or ʔaaxer ktaab) mn ᵊr-raff ᵊl-fooqaani.* -- He came last. *huwwe ʔaaxer waaḥed ʔəža.* **2.** *maaḍi.* Last year I was in Europe. *s-səne l-maaḍye (or **s-səne yalli faatet) kənt ᵊb-ʔawrəbba.*

**Last but not least I'd like to mention the fact that... *ʔaxiiran wa-laysa ʔaaxiran briid šiir la-...*

**That's the last straw! *hallaq ṭafaḥ ᵊl-keel!*

last night - **1.** *leelet ᵊmbaarḥa.* Did you sleep well last night? *nəmt ᵊmniiḥ leelet ᵊmbaarḥa?* **2.** *mbaarḥa εašiyye.* Last night I went shopping. *mbaarḥa εašiyye rəḥᵊt tsawwaqᵊt.*

last year - *εaamnḍwwal, s-səne l-maaḍye.* Last year I spent the summer in Bloudane. *εaamnḍwwal ṣayyafᵊt b-ᵊbluudaan.*

at last - *ʔaxiiran, bᵊn-nihaaye.* Here we are at last! *ʔaxiiran wṣəlna!*

next to the last - *qabl ᵊl-ʔaaxraani**. You'll find it on the next to the last page. *bətlaaqiiha εaṣ-ṣafḥa qabl ᵊl-ʔaaxraaniyye.*

the last - *ʔaaxer waaḥed.* She was the last to leave. *hiyye ʔaaxer waaḥde tarket.*

to last - **1.** *daam (u dawaam), bəqi (a baqayaan), ḍall (a ø), tamm (a ø), stamarr.* The war lasted six years. *l-ḥarb daamet sətt ᵊsniin.* -- I'm afraid this good weather won't last long. *xaayə́f-lak haṭ-ṭaqṣ ᵊl-ḥəlu muu raḥa yəbqa ktiir.* **2.** *ḍaayan.* This suit didn't last at all. *hal-badle maa ḍaayanet ʔabadan.* -- I'm afraid he won't last much longer. *xaayə́f-lak ʔənno muu raḥa yḍaayen ʔaktar.* **3.** *ḍaayan, tḥammal.* Do you think you can last another mile? *šloon šaayef ḥaalak, btəqder ᵊḍḍaayen miil taani?* **4.** *kaffa, kafa (i kfaaye).* I don't think my money will last till the end of the month. *bəftə́ker maṣariyyi muu raḥa tkaffiini la-ʔaaxer ᵊš-šahr.*

lasting - *daayem.* Let us hope for a lasting peace. *xalliina nətʔammal mən ʔaḷḷa salaam daayem.*

Latakia - *l-laadqiyye.*

latch - **1.** (of a lock) *lsaan˜ (pl. -aat˜) ᵊl-ġaal.* **2.** (of a gate) *ṣaqqaaṭa* pl. *-aat.*

late - **1.** *l-marḥuum.* Your late father was a friend of mine. *l-marḥuum waaldak kaan ṣaaḥbi.* **2.** *mətʔaxxer, mətlaqqes.* I'll be home late in the afternoon. *bəši εal-beet mətʔaxxer baεd ᵊḍ-ḍəhr.* -- It was late when we finally left. *kaan ᵊl-waqᵊt mətʔaxxer lamma tarakna.* -- I usually get up late in the morning. *εaadatan bfiiq mətʔaxxer εala bəkra.* **3.** *b-saaεa mətʔaxxra.* She came late in the evening. *ʔəžet b-saaεa mətʔaxxra l-masa.* **4.** *b-ʔawaaxer˜ ...* He was born late in the 19th century. *wəled b-ʔawaaxer ᵊl-q̈arn ᵊt-taaseε εašᵊr.* **5.** *ʔaxiir, ʔaaxraani**. Have you heard the late news? *sməεt našret ᵊl-ʔaxbaar ᵊl-ʔaxiire?*

**He is in his late fifties. *huwwe b-ḥiiṭaan ᵊs-səttiin.*

**It was already too late. *sabaq ᵊs-seef ᵊl-εazal* or *kaan faat ᵊl-ʔawaan.*

to be late - *tʔaxxar.* You're late again! *tʔaxxarᵊt kamaan!* or *ʔžiit mətʔaxxer kamaan!* -- We'll be late for the last show. *laḥa nətʔaxxar εala ʔaaxer εarḍ.*

lately - *hal-ʔiyyaam, bᵊl-mədde l-ʔaxiire, muʔaxxaran.* I haven't been feeling so well lately. *hal-ʔiyyaam šaaεer b-ḥaali muu εala baεḍi.* -- I saw her lately. *šəfta muʔaxxaran.*

latent - *kaamen.* There are latent possibilities in the situation. *fii ʔəmkaaniyyaat kaamne b-hal-waḍᵊε.*

later - **1.** *baεdeen.* You'll find out later. *baεdeen bətšuuf.* **2.** *mətʔaxxer ʔaktar.* It's later than you think. *d-dənye mətʔaxxra ʔaktar məmma btəftə́ker.*

**One day later a letter came. *baεᵊd yoom ʔəža maktuub.*

latest - *ʔaaxer˜.* What's the latest news? *šuu ʔaaxer ᵊl-ʔaxbaar?* -- That's the latest style. *hayy ʔaaxer mooḍa.*

lather - *raġwe.* You missed a spot of lather behind your ear. *nsiit ᵊtqiim nəqṭet raġwe b-qafa ʔədnak.*

to lather - *raġa (i raġi).* This soap doesn't lather well. *haṣ-ṣaabuun maa btərġi mniiḥ.*

lattice - *taεriiše* pl. *-aat* and *taεariiš.*

laudable - *ḥamiid, maḥmuud.* The intention is laudable, but can it be realized? *n-niyye ḥamiide, bass məmken yaa-tara taḥqiiqa?*

laugh - *ḍəḥke* pl. *-aat.* What a dirty laugh! *šuu haḍ-ḍəḥke l-laʔiime!*

to laugh - *ḍəḥek (a ḍəḥᵊk).* Everybody laughed at him. *kəllon ḍəḥku εalée.* -- I had to laugh at him. *maa qdərt ʔəlla ʔəḍḥak εalée.* -- They laughed up their sleeve at his optimism. *ḍəḥku b-εəbbon εala tafaaʔlo.*

**He who laughs last laughs best. *l-ʔaaxra yaa faaxra.*

**That's no laughing matter. *hayy masʔale muu ḍəḥke.*

to laugh something off - *ʔaxad šii maṣxara.* He tried to laugh the whole thing off. *ḥaawal yaaxod ᵊl-q̈adiyye kəlla maṣxara.*

laughingstock - *ʔəḍḥuuke* pl. *ʔaḍaḥiik, maḍḥake* pl. *maḍaaḥek, maṣxara* pl. *maṣaaxer.* His gullibility made him the laughingstock of the whole town. *ġašmanto xallto ʔəḍḥuuke lən-naas kəllon.*

laughter - **1.** *ḍəḥke* pl. *-aat.* We heard loud laughter behind us. *sməεna ḍəḥke εaalye waraana.* **2.** *ḍəḥᵊk.* She shook with laughter. *maatet mn ᵊḍ-ḍəḥᵊk.*

to **launch** - **1.** *nazzal.* Another ship was launched on Monday. *nazzalu safiine ždiide yoom ᵊt-taneen.* **2.** *baεat (a baεᵊt), ʔarsal.* I hear they launched a new satellite. *sməεt ʔənnon baεatu ṣaaruux ᵊždiid.* **3.** *šann (ə šann//nšann).* The press launched a fierce attack on the Prime Minister. *ṣ-ṣaḥaafe šannet ḥamle εaniife εala raʔiis ᵊl-wazaara.* -- The presidential nominee will launch his campaign in a few weeks. *l-ᵊmraššaḥ lər-riyaase bəddo yaεmel ḥamᵊlto l-ʔəntixaabiyye baεᵊd kam žəmεa.* **4.** *baašar b-.* When do you expect to launch the project? *ʔeemta bədḍənn laḥa tbaašer b-hal-mašruuε?*

laundry - **1.** *maṣbaġa* pl. *maṣaabeġ.* Where's the nearest laundry? *ween ʔaqrab maṣbaġa?* **2.** *ġasiil.* My laundry just came back. *hallaq wəṣel ġasiili mən εand ᵊl-kawwa.* -- Do you know of someone to do my laundry? *btaεrə́f-li ḥada yġassə́l-li ġasiili?*

lavatory - *maṭhara* pl. *maṭaaher, beet mayy* pl. *byuut mayy* or *beet mayyaat.*

law - **1.** (secular) *q̈aanuun* pl. *qawaniin.* That's against the law. *haada ḍədd ᵊl-q̈aanuun.* **2.** (Islamic, canonical) *š-šariiεa, š-šarᵊε.* Canonical law provides that a woman's inheritance is half of that of a man. *š-šariiεa bətwarret ᵊl-mara nəṣṣ-ma byərat ᵊr-rəžžaal.* **3.** *sənne* pl. *sənan.* The law of nature. *sənnet ᵊṭ-ṭabiiεa.* **4.** *q̈aanuun* pl. *q̈awaniin, q̈aaεde* pl. *q̈awaaεed.* The law of gravity. *q̈aanuun ᵊž-žaazibiyye.* **5.** (unwritten) *εərf.* The law of the desert. *εərf ᵊl-badu* or *l-εərf bᵊṣ-ṣaḥra.* **6.** *ḥquuq* (pl.), *ḥuq̈uuq* (pl.). He's studying law. *byədros ᵊḥquuq.* -- She graduated from law school two years ago. *txarražet mən kəlliyyet ᵊl-ḥuq̈uuq mən sənteen.*

martial law - *ʔaḥkaam εərfiyye* (pl.). The city was placed under martial law. *waḍaεu l-madiine taḥt ᵊl-ʔaḥkaam ᵊl-εərfiyye.*

to practice law - *maaras ᵊl-muḥaamḍa.* Is he still practicing law? *ləssaato εam ymaares ᵊl-muḥaamḍa?*

lawsuit - *daεwa* pl. *daεaawi.* Did he win the lawsuit? *rəbeḥ ᵊd-daεwa?*

lawyer - *muḥaami* pl. *-yiin.*

lax - **1.** *raxu.* They have rather lax regulations in that school. *fii εandon ʔanẓime šwayye raxwe b-hal-madrase.* **2.** *mətraaxi.* He's a little lax in his work these days. *hal-ʔiyyaam šwayye mətraaxi b-šəġlo.* **2.** *mətraaxi, raxu, mətsaahel.* She's always been much too lax with her children. *kaanet daayman mətraaxye ktiir maε ᵊwlaada.*

laxative - *šarbe* pl. *-aat, məshel* pl. *-aat.*

to **lay** - **1.** *ḥaṭṭ (ə ḥaṭaṭ//nḥaṭṭ), waḍaε (-yuuḍaε waḍᵊε//nwaḍaε).* Lay the book on the table. *ḥəṭṭ l-ᵊktaab εaṭ-ṭaawle.* -- The workmen were laying tile on the groundfloor. *š-šaġġiile kaanu εam yḥaṭṭu blaaṭ bᵊṭ-ṭaabeq ᵊl-ʔarḍi.* -- He lays stress on correct grammar. *biḥəṭṭ ʔahammiyye kbiire εala ʔəstəεmaal q̈awaaεed ᵊn-naḥw wᵊṣ-ṣarf.* -- Don't lay the blame on me. *laa tḥəṭṭ ᵊl-ḥaqq εaliyyi.* **2.** *ḥaṭṭ, ḥaḍḍar.* Please have the maid lay the table. *baḷḷa xalli ṣ-ṣaanεa tḥəṭṭ ᵊṭ-ṭaawle.* **3.** *baaḍet (i ø).* Our hens are laying well. *žaažaatna εam ybiiḍu mniiḥ.* **4.** *raahan.* I'll lay ten to one that he does it. *braahnak εašara la-waaḥed ʔənno byaεməla.*

to lay aside - *ḥaṭṭ εala žanab.* He laid aside a pretty penny. *ḥaṭṭ εala žanab kam qərš ᵊnḍaaf.*

to lay claim to - *ṭaalab b-, ddaεa b-.* A distant relative laid claim to the estate. *fii qaraayeb ᵊbεiid ṭaalab bᵊl-wərte.*

to lay down - **1.** *ṣaṭṭaḥ.* Lay him down gently.

ṣaṭṭḥo b-rəfᵊq. 2. *wadaᶜ, rama (i rami).* They were ready to lay down their arms. *kaanu məstᶜəddiin yuudaᶜu ʔasləḥton.* 3. *wadaᶜ.* I lay down the rules here. *ʔana muu ġeeri buudaᶜ ᵊl-qawaaᶜed hoon.*

to lay for - *kaman (o ø) la-, traḅḅaṣ la-.* They laid for him at the corner. *kamanúu-lo ᶜas-suuke.*

to lay it on thick - *taxxána, kattára, taqqála.* He's certainly laying it on thick! *waḷḷaahi ᶜam ytaxxəna!*

to lay off - *ṣaraf (o/e ṣarᵊf//nṣaraf), txallaṣ mən.* We have to lay off some people. *laazem nəṣrof kam zalame.*

to lay out - 1. *ṣaraf (o/e ṣarᵊf).* How much did you lay out for me? *qaddeeš ṣaraft maṣaari mənšaani?* 2. *xaṭṭaṭ.* Lay out the foundations before you start digging. *xaṭṭᵊṭu l-ʔasaasaat qabᵊl-ma təḥᵊfru.* 3. *rasam (o rasᵊm).* The chairman laid out his plans for the future. *r-raʔiis rasam xəṭaṭo ləl-məstaqbal.* 4. *ᶜaraḍ (e/o ᶜarᵊḍ// nᶜaraḍ).* The street vendor was laying out his wares in front of him. *l-bayyaaᶜ kaan ᶜam yəᶜreḍ ᵊbḍaaᶜto qəddaamo.*

to lay up - *ḥaṭṭ ᶜala žanab, waffar.* He laid up a tidy sum over the years. *ḥaṭṭ ᶜala žanab mablaġ ᵊmniiḥ səne baᶜᵊd səne.*

to lay waste - *xarrab.* The whole region was laid waste by the storm. *l-ᶜaaṣfe xarrabet kəll ᵊl-manṭiqa.*

layer - *ṭabaqa* pl. *-aat.* Everything was covered with a heavy layer of sand. *kəll šii kaan ᵊmġaṭṭa b-ṭabaqa kasiife mn ᵊr-ramᵊl.* -- Put another layer of paper over it. *ḥəṭṭ ṭabaqa taanye waraq ᶜalée.*

layman - 1. *ᶜəlmaani* pl. *-iyyiin.* The committee consists of two members of the clergy and five laymen. *l-ləžne mᵊallafe mən ᶜədween mn ᵊl-xawaarne w-xamᵊs ᶜəlmaaniyyiin.* 2. *ʔəmmi* pl. *-iyyiin.* I'm a layman in this field. *ʔana ʔəmmi b-hal-mawḍuuᶜ.*

laziness - *kasal, kaslane.*

lazy - *kaslaan, kasuul.* Don't be so lazy! *laa tkuun hal-qadd kaslaan* or ****ḥaaže kaslane!* or ****šuu hal-kaslane!*

lead - *rṣaaṣ.* Is this made of lead? *haada maᶜmuul mən ᵊrṣaaṣ?*

lead - 1. *door raʔiisi.* Who's playing the lead? *miin ᶜam yəlᶜab ᵊd-door ᵊr-raʔiisi?* 2. *daliil* pl. *ʔadəlle.* The police had a number of leads on the case. *š-šərṭa kaan ᶜandon ᶜəddet ʔadəlle bᵊl-qaḍiyye.*

**Do you have any lead on finding a solution? *fii ᶜandak šii baab la-ḥall ᵊl-məšᵊkle?*

to be in the lead, to have a lead - *sabaq (o sabᵊq).* He was in the lead by five yards in the first lap. *kaan saabeq ġeero b-xamᵊs yardaat b-ʔawwal šooṭ.* -- She definitely has a lead over the others in getting this job. *hiyye saabqa ġeerha ḥatman ᵊb-ʔaxᵊd hal-waẓiife.*

to lead - 1. *qaad (u qyaade//nqaad).* Amr ibn As led the Arab armies into Egypt. *ᶜamr ᵊbn ᵊl-ᶜaaṣ qaad ᵊž-žyuuš ᵊl-ᶜarabiyye la-maṣr.* 2. *hada (i hdaaye//nhada).* The dog led the blind man along the street. *l-kalb hada l-ʔaᶜma ṭuul ᵊṭ-ṭariiq.* 3. *traʔʔas.* The mayor led the parade. *raʔiis ᵊl-baladiyye traʔʔas ᵊl-ʔəstəᶜraaḍ* (or ***kaan ᶜala raʔs ᵊl-ʔəstəᶜraaḍ*). 4. *dzaᶜᶜam ᶜala.* Who leads this group? *miin byədzaᶜᶜam ᶜala haž-žamaaᶜa?* 5. *sabaq (o sabᵊq).* He leads his class in arithmetic. *huwwe saabeq ṣaffo bᵊl-ᵊḥsaab.* 6. *waṣṣal, wadda.* Where will all this lead to? *la-ween biwaṣṣel kəll haš-šii?* -- That'll lead to nothing. *haš-šii maa biwaṣṣel la-ʔayy natiiže* or ***haš-šii maa-lo ʔaaxra.* -- Where does this road lead to? *la-ween biwaṣṣel haṭ-ṭariiq?* 7. *ʔadda.* The information you gave us lead to his arrest. *l-maᶜluumaat yalli ᶜaṭeetna-ydaha ʔaddet la-tawqiifo.*

**You'd better lead the child by the hand when you cross the street. *ʔaḥsán-lak təmsek ʔiid ᵊl-walad lamma btəqṭaᶜ ᵊṭ-ṭariiq.*

**I'll lead the way and you follow. *ʔana bəmši qəddaamak w-ʔənte btəlḥaqni.*

to lead up to - *qaṣad (o ø).* What do you think he was leading up to? *šuu btəftəkro kaan ᶜam yəqṣod?* -- That's just what I was leading up to. *haada b-ᶜeeno yalli qaṣadto.*

leader - *raʔiis* pl. *rəʔasa, zaᶜiim* pl. *zəᶜama.* The leaders of all parties were present. *rəʔasa l-ʔaḥzaab kəlla kaanu ḥaaḍriin.* -- Who is the leader of the group? *miin zaᶜiim ᵊž-žamaaᶜa?*

leading - *raʔiisi*.* Al Ahram is the leading newspaper of Cairo today. *"l-ʔahraam" hiyye ž-žariide r-raʔiisiyye bᵊl-qaahira l-yoom.*

leaf - 1. *waraqa* pl. *-aat* and *wraaq.* Tear off the leaves first. *qiim l-ᵊwraaq bᵊl-ʔawwal.* 2. *ṣafḥa* pl. *-aat, waraqa* pl. *-aat* and *wraaq.* Several leaves of the book are missing. *fii kam ṣafḥa mən l-ᵊktaab naaqṣiin.*

leaves - *waraq* (coll.). The leaves are beginning to turn yellow. *waraq ᵊš-šažar ᶜam yəṣfarr.*

to turn over a new leaf - *bada (a ø) ṣafḥa beeḍa.* He promised to turn over a new leaf. *waᶜad yəbda ṣafḥa beeḍa.*

to leaf through - *tṣaffaḥ, qallab.* I'm only leafing through the book. *ʔana ᶜam ʔətṣaffaḥ l-ᵊktaab bass.*

leaflet - *manšuur* pl. *-aat* and *manašiir.*

league - *žaamᶜa* pl. *-aat.* The Arab League. *žaamᶜet ᵊd-duwal ᵊl-ᶜarabiyye* or *ž-žaamᶜa l-ᶜarabiyye.*

leak - *bəxwaaš* pl. *baxawiiš, bəxᵊš* pl. *bxaaš.* There's a leak in the boat. *fii bəxwaaš bᵊš-šaxtuura.*

to leak - 1. *naffad mayy.* The boat is leaking. *š-šaxtuura ᶜam ᵊtnaffed mayy.* 2. *zarab (o zarᵊb).* This pot leaks. *haṭ-ṭanžara ᶜam təzrob.* 3. *šaršar, naznaz.* The faucet is leaking. *l-ḥanafiyye ᶜam ᵊtšaršer.*

to leak out - 1. *zarab (o zarb).* All the water is leaking out. *kəll ᵊl-mayy ᶜam təzrob.* 2. *tsarrab, faša (i faši).* The story leaked out somehow. *l-qəṣṣa tsarrabet maa baᶜref šloon.*

lean - 1. *naḥiif* pl. *nḥaaf* and *nəḥafa.* He's a lean man. *huwwe rəžžaal naḥiif.* 2. *məždeb.* It was a lean year for farmers. *kaanet səne məžᵊdbe* (or ***sənt qaḥᵊṭ*) *ləl-fallaaḥiin.*

lean meat - *habṛ.* Do you want fat meat or lean? *bəddak laḥᵊm mədhen wəlla habṛ* (or *laḥme mədᵊhne wəlla habṛa*)?

to lean - 1. *ddandal.* Don't lean out of the window. *laa təddandal ᵊmn ᵊš-šəbbaak.* 2. *maal (i meel).* He leans toward the right in politics. *bimiil naaḥ ᵊl-yamiin syaasiyyan.* 3. *nḥana.* She leaned over the railing. *nḥanet mən ᶜad-daraabziin.* -- If you lean forward you can see him. *ʔiza btənḥəni la-qəddaam məmken ᵊtšuufo.* 4. *ttaka, stanad.* There's nothing to lean against. *maa fii šii l-waaḥed yəttəki ᶜalée.* -- May I lean on your arm? *məmken ʔəttəki ᶜdla ʔiidak?* 5. *sanad (o/e sand// nsanad).* Don't lean your chair against the wall. *laa təsnod ᵊl-kərsi tabaᶜak ᶜal-ḥeeṭ.*

leap - *naṭṭa* pl. *-aat, qamze* pl. *-aat, qavze* pl. *-aat.* He cleared the ditch with one leap. *qaṭaᶜ ᵊl-xandaq b-naṭṭa waaḥde.*

leap year - *səne* (pl. *sniin*) *kabiise.*

to learn - 1. *tᶜallam.* He hasn't learned a thing. *maa tᶜallam šii.* 2. *ᶜəref (-yaᶜref ø).* He learned the truth too late. *ᶜəref ᵊl-ḥaqiiqa baᶜd fawaat ᵊl-ʔawaan.*

**I want to learn more about it. *bəddi maᶜluumaat ʔaktar ᶜanha.*

to learn by heart - *ḥafaẓ (a ḥəfᵊẓ) ᶜal-ġeeb.* She learned the poem by heart. *ḥavẓet ᵊl-qaṣiide ᶜal-ġeeb.*

lease - *ᶜaqᵊd˜* (pl. *ᶜquud˜*) *ʔiižaar.* We had to sign a lease for one year. *ḍṭarreena nəmḍi ᶜaqᵊd ʔiižaar la-səne.*

to lease - 1. *staʔžar.* Did you lease the apartment? *staʔžart ᵊl-beet?* -- They've leased the hotel for five years. *staʔžaru l-ʔoteel la-məddet xams ᵊsniin.* 2. *ʔažžar.* The landlord doesn't want to lease the apartment. *ṣaaḥeb ᵊl-beet maa bəddo yʔažžer ᵊl-beet.* -- We leased the hotel to them for five years. *ʔažžarnaahon ᵊl-ʔoteel la-məddet xams ᵊsniin.*

least - 1. *ʔaxaff˜.* That's the least of my worries. *haada ʔaxaff ᵊhmuumi.* 2. *ʔaqall˜.* He paid the least amount possible. *dafaᶜ ʔaqall mablaġ məmken.* -- The least thing upsets her. *ʔaqall šii binarvəza.*

**Least of all I'd have expected it from you. *ʔənte ʔaaxer waaḥed kənt bənṭəžer mənno haš-šii.*

**She deserves it least of all. *hiyye ʔaaxer waaḥde btəstᵊḥəqqo.*

at least - *ᶜal-ʔaqalli, bᵊl-maqalli, bᵊl-qaliili.* These shoes cost at least twenty pounds. *haṣ-ṣabbaaṭ ḥaqqo ᶜal-ʔaqalli ᶜəšriin leera.* -- At least you might have written to me. *bᵊl-maqalli kənt ᵊktəb-li.*

not in the least - *maa ... ʔabadan, maa ... mnoob.* It doesn't bother me in the least. *maa btəzᶜəžni ʔabadan.* -- It wouldn't surprise me in the least if ... *maa kənt bəndəheš ʔabadan ʔiza kaan ...*

the least - *ʔaqall šii.* That's the least you could do for him. *haada ʔaqall šii btəqder taᶜməl-*

lo-yda.

to say the least - *ʔaq̄all maa yuq̄aal.* He's a little touched in the head - to say the least. *ʔaq̄all maa yuq̄aal, fii šii b-ʕaqlo.*

leather - **1.** *žəld* pl. *žluud.* The meat is tough as leather. *l-laḥm qaasi mətl əž-žəld.* **2.** *žəld* (invar.). Do they have leather jackets in that store? *b-hal-maxzan fii ʕandon žawakiit žəld?*

piece of leather - *žəlde* pl. *-aat* and *žluud.*

leave - *ʔižaaze* pl. *-aat, fərṣa* pl. *fəraṣ.* He's taken a three months' leave. *ʔaxad ʔižaazt tlətt əšhor* (or *ʔižaaze tlətt əšhor*).

to leave - **1.** *raaḥ (u rooḥa).* I have to leave now. *laazem ruuḥ hallaq.* -- I'm leaving for good. *ʔana raayeḥ nihaaʔiyyan* or *ʔana raayeḥ rooḥa bala raždʕa.* **2.** *saafar (safar), məši (i ø), raaḥ.* The train leaves at two-thirty. *t-treen bisaafer əs-saaʕa tənteen w-nəṣṣ.* -- My father left yesterday for Europe. *ʔabi saafar əmbaarḥa la-ʔoorəbba.* **3.** *tarak (o/e tarək).* She left her husband after they were married two years. *tarket žooza baʕəd sənteen mn əžwaazon.* -- He left us in the lurch. *taraknа waqt əl-ḥazze w əl-lazze.* -- Leave me alone! *trəkni la-ḥaali!* or ******ʕiifni baqa!* **4.** *tarak, ṭəleʕ (a ṭluuʕ, ṭalʕa) mən.* I saw him leave the house. *šəfto w-huwwe ʕam yətrok əl-beet.* -- He left the room secretly. *ṭəleʕ əmn əl-ʔuuḍa b-əl-xəfye.* -- I'm leaving my job. *bəddi ʔəṭlaʕ mən šəġli.* **5.** *tarak, xalla.* He left a letter for you. *tarák-lak maktuub.* -- Didn't he leave any message for me? *maa xallá-li šii risaale?* -- He left word that he would be back soon. *tarak xabar ʔənno raaželʕ ʕan qariib.* -- He left his food on the plate. *tarak əl-ʔakl mətəl-ma huwwe b-ṣaḥno.* -- Don't leave your books lying around. *laa tətrok kətbak mlaḥwašiin hoon w-hoon.* -- When you copy it, don't leave anything out. *lamma btənsaxha laa tətrok šii barra.* -- Where did you leave your suitcase? *ween tarakt šantaaytak?* -- Leave it to me! *trək-li-yaaha!* -- He left the door open. *xalla l-baab maftuuḥ.* -- He left nothing undone. *maa xalla baab ʔəlla ṭaraqo* or *maa xalla ḥiile ʔəlla staʕmalha.* -- Leave some cake for me. *xallii-li šwayyet gaato.* **6.** *xallaf, tarak.* She left the house to her son. *xallafət-lo la-ʔəbənha l-beet.* **7.** *nəsi (a nəsyaan), tarak.* I must have left my briefcase somewhere. *laazem kuun nsiit šantaayti b-šii qərne.*

**Eight from fifteen leaves seven. *tmaane mən xaməṣṭaʕš byəbqa sabʕa.*

**Where does that leave me? *w-ween ṣfiit ʔana?*

**You'd better leave that alone! *ʔaḥsán-lak maa tqarreb ʕala haš-šii.*

**He was completely left out of the picture. *džaahalúu b-əl-marra.*

to be left - *bəqi (a ø), ṣəfi (a ø).* Are there any tickets left for tonight? *bəqi šii tasaaker la-ḥaflet əl-leel?* -- My brother got all the money, and I was left out in the cold. *ʔaxi ʔaxad kəll əl-maṣaari w-ṣfiit ʔana ʔiid mən wara w-ʔiid mən qəddaam.*

to be left back - *rasab (e/o rsuub).* He was left back in the third grade. *rasab b-əṣ-ṣaff ət-taalet.*

Lebanese - *ləbnaani*.*

Lebanon - *ləbnaan.*

lecture - *mḥaaḍara* pl. *-aat.* It was an interesting lecture. *kaanet əmḥaaḍara mufiide.* -- He's giving a lecture on international trade. *laḥa yəlqi mḥaaḍara ʕan ət-tižaara d-dawliyye.* -- She always gives us a lecture when we're late. *kəll-ma mnətʔaxxar btaʕmél-lna mḥaaḍara.*

to lecture - *ḥaaḍar.* He lectures on zoology at the university. *biḥaaḍer əb-ʕəlm əl-ḥaywaan b-əž-žaamʕa.*

**I'm sick and tired of your lecturing. *laʕet maʕi mn əmḥaaḍaraatak əli.*

lecturer - **1.** *ʔəstaaz mḥaaḍer* pl. *ʔasaadze mḥaaḍriin.* He's a lecturer in Arabic at the Syrian University. *huwwe ʔəstaaz əmḥaaḍer b-əl-ʕarabiyye b-əž-žaamʕa s-suuriyye.* **2.** *mḥaaḍer* pl. *-iin.* Tonight's lecturer is a famous historian. *mḥaaḍer əl-leele məʔarrex marmuuq̄.*

left - **1.** *šmaal* (invar.), *yasaar* (invar.). Take the other bag in your left hand. *xood əl-kiis ət-taani b-ʔiidak əš-šmaal.* **2.** *ʕaš-šmaal, ləš-šmaal, ʕal-yasaar, ləl-yasaar.* Turn left at the next corner. *lfeet ʕaš-šmaal* (or *ʕala šmaalak*) *b-əl-lafte ž-žaaye.*

at (or **to**) **the left of** - *ʕala šmaal˜ ..., ʕala yasaar˜ ...* We had seats at the left of the stage. *maḥallaatna kaanet ʕala šmaal əl-masraḥ.*

on the left - **1.** *ʕaš-šmaal, ʕal-yasaar.* You sit on the right, and I'll sit on the left. *ʔənte btəqʕod ʕal-yamiin w-ʔana bəqʕod ʕal-yasaar.* **2.** *ʕala šmaal˜ ..., ʕala yasaar˜ ...* I sat on the speaker's left. *qaʕadt ʕala šmaal əl-xaṭiib.*

left-handed - *ʕəsraawi** pl. *-iyye, yəsraawi** pl. *-iyye.* He's left-handed. *huwwe ʕəsraawi.*

**That was a left-handed compliment. *haada kaan madəḥ malġuum.*

leftist - **1.** *yasaari*.* All the leftist parties voted for him. *kəll əl-ʔaḥzaab əl-yasaariyye ṣawwatət-lo.* **2.** *yasaari* pl. *-iyyiin.* He always was a leftist. *ṭuul ʕəmro kaan yasaari.*

leg - **1.** *rəžəl* (f.) dual *rəžəlteen* pl. *ražleen, ʔəžər* (f.) dual *ʔəžərteen* pl. *ʔažreen.* I have a pain in my right leg. *ʕandi wažaʕ b-rəžli l-yamiin.* -- One leg of the chair is broken. *fii rəžəl b-əl-kərsi maksuura.* **2.** *saaq* (f.) pl. *siiqaan.* She has long legs. *siiqaana ṭwaal.* **3.** *faxəd* pl. *fxaad.* Can I have a small leg of lamb? *btaʕṭiini baḷḷa faxəd xaaruuf əzġiir.* 3. *marḥale* pl. *maraaḥel.* We're now on the last leg of the trip. *nəḥna hallaq əb-ʔaaxer marḥale mn əs-safra.*

**They say he's on his last legs. *ʕam yquulu wəṣel əl-məskiin la-ʔaaxer əṭ-ṭariiq* or *ʕam yquulu nhaayto qariibe l-məskiin.*

to pull someone's leg - *tmaqlas ʕala ḥada, qarraq ʕalée, tmasxar ʕalée, žaakar ḥada.* Stop pulling my leg. *ḥaaže tətmaqlas ʕaliyyi.*

legal - **1.** *q̄aanuuni*.* That's perfectly legal. *haada q̄aanuuni tamaaman.* **2.** *ḥuq̄uuq̄i*.* He's her legal adviser. *huwwe məstašaara l-ḥuq̄uuq̄i.*

legality - *q̄aanuuniyye, šarʕiyye.*

legend - **1.** *ʔəsṭuura* pl. *ʔasaṭiir.* The origin of the legend is unknown. *maṣdar hal-ʔəsṭuura mažhuul.* **2.** *ktaabe.* Can you tell me what the legend on the coin means? *fiik ətqəl-li šuu btəʕni l-əktaabe ʕala haḷ-ʕəmle?*

leggings - *ṭmaaq* pl. *-aat.*

legible - *maq̄ruuʔ.* His handwriting is hardly legible. *xaṭṭo b-əl-kaad ykuun maq̄ruuʔ* (or ****b-əl-kaad yənq̄ára*).

legion - **1.** *fərq̄a* pl. *fərad̄.* The Foreign Legion. *l-fərq̄a l-ʔažnabiyye.* **2.** *faylaq̄* pl. *fayaaleq̄.* The Arab Legion. *l-faylaq̄ əl-ʕarabi.*

**Those ideas are legion today. *hal-ʔafkaar b-hal-ʔiyyaam ktiire.*

legislation - *tašriiʕ.*

legitimate - **1.** *šarʕi*.* He is the legitimate heir. *huwwe l-waares əš-šarʕi.* **2.** *mašruuʕ.* They are perfectly legitimate conclusions. *hayy ʔəstəntaažaat mašruuʕa tamaaman.*

leisure - **1.** *waqət˜ faraaġ.* This job doesn't leave me much leisure. *haš-šaġle maa btətrók-li waqət faraaġ kaafi.* **2.** *raaḥa.* Do it at your leisure. *saawiiha ʕala raaḥtak.*

leisure time - *waqət˜ faraaġ, waqət˜ raaḥa.* I can do it in my leisure time. *fiiyi saawiiha b-waqət raaḥti.*

lemon - *leemuune* coll. *leemuun* pl. *-aat.*

lemonade - *leemunaaḍa.*

to **lend** - **1.** *ʕaar (i ʔiʕaara//nʕaar).* Can you lend me this book? *bətʕiirni hal-əktaab?* **2.** *dayyan, qaraḍ (o qarḍ).* Would you lend me ten pounds? *bəddayyənni* (or *btəqrəḍni*) *ʕašər waraqaat?*

**Lend me a hand, will you? *saaʕədni ʔiza bətriid.*

to lend itself - *naasab.* A play like this doesn't lend itself to translation. *tamsiiliyye mətəl hayy muu mnaasbe lət-taržame.*

length - *ṭuul.* Let's measure the length of the room! *xalliina nqiis ṭuul əl-ʔuuḍa.* -- He stretched full length on the bed. *tmaddad əb-kəll ṭuulo ʕat-taxət.*

at length - *b-ʔəshaab, b-ət-tafṣiil.* He discussed the plan at length. *ḥaka ʕan əl-xəṭṭa b-ʔəshaab.*

to **lengthen** - *ṭawwal.* These trousers have to be lengthened. *hal-banṭaloon bəddo taṭwiil.*

lengthwise - *b-əṭ-ṭuul.* Cut the material lengthwise. *qəṣṣ l-əqmaaš b-əṭ-ṭuul.*

lenient - *mətsaahel.* You're too lenient with him. *ʔənte ktiir mətsaahel maʕo.*

lens - *ʕadase* pl. *-aat, balloora* pl. *-aat.* Your camera has a good lens. *ʔaalet ət-taṣwiir tabaʕak ʔəla ʕadase mniiḥa.*

lentil - *ʕadase* coll. *ʕadas* pl. *-aat.* Add some lentils to the soup. *ḥəṭṭi šwayyet ʕadas b-əš-šooraba.*

leopard - *fahəd* pl. *fhuude.*

less - **1.** *ʔaqall, ʔanqaṣ.* I have less money with me than I thought. *maʕi maṣaari ʔaqall məm-ma kənt ʔəftəker.* -- He seems to know less than he thinks.

ž-žaaher ʔənno byəƐref ʔaqall məm-ma byəƐtəqed. -- I'm less convinced now than I was before. *qanaaƐti ṣaaret ʔaqall məm-ma kaanet Ɛaléе mən qabᵊl.* 2. *maa Ɛada, ʔəlla.* She will pay the amount less interest. *btədfaƐ ᵊl-mablaġ maa Ɛada l-faayde.*

more or less - *Ɛal-Ɛumuum, bᵊl-ʔəžmaal.* He's more or less right. *Ɛal-Ɛumuum Ɛando ḥaqq.*

lesson - 1. *dars* pl. *druus.* Translate Lesson Eleven for tomorrow. *taržem ᵊd-dars ʔidaƐš la-bəkra.* -- She gives Spanish lessons. *btaƐṭi druus bᵊl-ʔəsbaani.* 2. *waẓiife* pl. *waẓaayef, fariiḍa* pl. *faraayeḍ.* I'll have to do my lessons first. *laazem saawii waẓaayfi bᵊl-ʔawwal.* 3. *Ɛəbra* pl. *Ɛəbar, dars* pl. *druus.* Let that be a lesson to you. *xalli haš-šii ykə́n-lak Ɛəbra.* -- I hope you've learned your lesson. *nšaaḷḷa tkuun ʔaxadt Ɛəbra* or ***nšaaḷḷa tkuun Ɛtabart.*

lest - 1. *ḥatta maa, ʔaḥsan maa.* They went indoors lest they catch cold. *faatu la-žuwwa ḥatta maa yaaxdu barᵊd.* 2. *w-ʔəlla, ḥatta maa.* You'd better go now, lest you arrive late. *ʔaḥsə́n-lak truuḥ hallaq w-ʔəlla btətʔaxxar* (or *ḥatta maa tətʔaxxar*).

to let - 1. *ʔažžar (ʔiižaar, ʔižaar).* Have you rooms to let? *fii Ɛandak ʔuwaḍ ləl-ʔiižaar?* or *bətʔažžer ʔuwaḍ?* 2. *xalla.* He wouldn't let me do it. *maa xallaani saawiiha.* -- Will the customs officials let us pass? *mwaẓẓafiin ᵊl-gəmrok bixalluuna nəmroq?* -- Let's go home. *xalliina nruuḥ Ɛal-beet.*

let alone - *ʔaḷḷaahumma ḥatta.* He can't even understand German, let alone talk it. *ḥatta huwwe maa byəfham ʔalmaani, ʔaḷḷaahumma ḥatta yaƐref yəḥki.*

to let alone - *Ɛaaf (i ə), xalla waḥd-* + pron. suffix, *tarak (o/e tarᵊk) waḥd-* + pron. suffix. Can't you let me alone for five minutes? *maa btəqder tƐiifni šii xamᵊs daqaayeq Ɛal-qaliili?* or *maa btəqder txalliini waḥdi šii xamᵊs daqaayeq Ɛal-qaliili?*

to let down - 1. *nazzal.* Please let down the blinds. *ḅaḷḷa nazzə́l-li l-baraadi ž-žarraar.* 2. *xayyab ʔamal˜ ...* He let me down when I needed him most. *xayyab ʔamali waqᵊt kənt b-ʔašadd ᵊl-ḥaaže ʔəlo.* -- His son has let him down badly. *ʔəbno xayyə́b-lo ʔamalo ktiir ᵊktiir.* 3. *traaxa, ntaḥas.* He's beginning to let down in his work. *Ɛam yəbda yətraaxa b-šəġlo.*

to let go - 1. *tġaaḍa Ɛan.* This time I'll let it go. *hal-marra bətġaaḍa Ɛanha.* 2. *tarak (o/e ə).* First I wanted to do it, but then I let it go. *ʔawwal šii kənt bəddi ʔaƐmə́la, bass baƐdeen tarakta.*

to let go (of) - *tarak (o/e tark).* Don't let go of the rope. *laa tətrok ᵊl-ḥabᵊl.*

to let have - *Ɛaṭa (-yaƐṭi ə).* Please let me have the menu. *mən faḍlak Ɛaṭiini l-liista.* -- Can you let me have five pounds? *fiik taƐṭiini xamᵊs waraqaat?*

**I really let him have it! *maa xalleet Ɛaléе sətr ᵊmġaṭṭa!*

to let in - *fawwat.* Don't let anybody in. *laa tfawwet ḥada!*

to let in on - *xabbar b-.* Did you let him in on the secret, too? *xabbarto huwwe t-taani bᵊs-sərr?*

to let know - *Ɛaṭa (-yaƐṭi ə) xabar, xabbar.* Let me know right away. *Ɛaṭiini xabar ḥaalan.*

to let off - *nazzal.* Please let me off at the next stop. *ḅaḷḷa nazzə́lni* (or ***waqqə́f-li*) *bᵊl-ᵊmḥaṭṭa ž-žaaye.* -- Please let me off at the corner. *mən faḍlak nazzə́lni Ɛas-suuke.*

**I'll let you off easy this time. *hal-marra bənsaa-lak-yḍaha* or *hal-marra bxalliiha truuḥ heek.*

to let on - *ʔaẓhar Ɛala nafso.* She didn't let on that she knew anything about it. *maa ʔaẓharet Ɛala nafsa ʔənna Ɛarfaane ʔayy šii Ɛanha.*

to let out - 1. *xalla (ḥada* or *šii) yruuḥ* or *yəṭlaƐ* or (escape) *yəflat.* He wouldn't let me out. *maa xallaani ʔəṭlaƐ.* -- Let the water out of the sink. *xalli l-mayy truuḥ mn ᵊl-mažla.* 2. *fataḥ (a fatḥ), wassaƐ.* I told the tailor to let out the seams. *qəlt-ə́llo ləl-xayyaaṭ yəftaḥ ᵊl-xawaayeṭ.*

to let stand - *qəbel (a qbuul), waafaq Ɛala.* I can't let that objection stand. *maa bəqder ʔəqbal hal-ʔəƐtiraaḍ.*

to let up - 1. *ṭayyar.* They let up a balloon. *ṭayyaru baaḷoon.* 2. *hədi (a hadayaan).* The storm has let up. *l-Ɛaaṣfe hədyet.*

letdown - *xeebet˜ ʔamal.* The failure of our plans was a big letdown. *fašal xəṭaṭna kaan xeebet ʔamal ᵊkbiire.*

lethargy - *səbaat.*

letter - 1. *maktuub* pl. *makatiib, risaale* pl. *-aat.* Are there any letters for me? *fii šii ʔəli makatiib?* 2. *ḥarf* pl. *ḥruuf* and *ʔaḥruf.* The word has five letters. *l-kəlme mʔallafe mən xams ᵊḥruuf.* -- He sticks to the letter of the law. *byəttə́beƐ ᵊl-q̈aanuun ḥarf ḥarf.*

letter carrier - *bə́ośṭaži* pl. *-iyye.*

letter of credit - *ktaab˜* (pl. *kətᵊb˜*) *ʔəƐtimaad.*

letter of introduction - *ktaab˜* (pl. *kətᵊb˜*) *taƐriif, ktaab tawṣiye.*

lettuce - *xass.*

head of lettuce - *xasse* pl. *-aat, raas˜* (pl. *ruus˜*) *xass.*

letup - *tawaqqof, waqfe, ʔənq̈iṭaaƐ.* It's been raining without any letup for a week. *ṣar-la Ɛam tənzel ᵊl-maṭar žəmƐa biduun tawaqqof.*

level - 1. *məstə́wa.* His work isn't up to the usual level. *šəġlo ʔawṭa mən məstawa l-Ɛaadi.* - The water this year is at a very low level. *məstə́wa l-mayy has-səne ktiir waaṭi.* 2. *sahᵊl.* Is the country level or hilly? *l-ʔaraaḍi sahle ʔaw žabaliyye?* 3. *məstə́wi*.* This floor is not level. *ʔarḍ hal-ʔuuḍa muu məstwiyye.*

**He always keeps a level head. *Ɛaqlo maƐo Ɛala ṭuul.*

**He did his level best. *Ɛəmel kəll yalli b-ʔəstiṭaaƐto.*

**Is he on the level? *məmken l-waaḥed yəseq̈|fii?*

salary level - *|martabet˜* (pl. *maraateb˜*) *rawaateb.* There are five salary levels in our office. *fii xams maraateb lər-rawaateb b-daayərtna.*

sea level - *ṣaṭḥ˜ ᵊl-baḥr.* The Dead Sea is 1292 feet below sea level. *l-baḥr ᵊl-mayyet ʔawṭa mən ṣaṭḥ ᵊl-baḥr b-ʔalf w-miiteen w-tneen w-təsƐiin qadam.*

to be level with - *waaza ... bᵊl-ʔərtifaaƐ.* The bookcase is level with the table. *xzaanet ᵊl-kətᵊb bətwaazi ṭ-ṭaawle bᵊl-ʔərtifaaƐ.*

to level - *mahhad//tmahhad, samhad.* The ground has to be leveled. *l-ʔarḍ laazem tətmahhad* (or *bədda tamhiid*).

to level (to the ground) - *masaḥ (a masᵊḥ// mmasaḥ).* The artillery fire leveled the town. *l-madfaƐiyye mashet ᵊl-balad masᵊḥ* or ***l-madfaƐiyye maa xallet bᵊl-balad ḥažar Ɛala ḥažar.*

lever - 1. (in mechanics) *raafƐa* pl. *rawaafeƐ.* 2. (crowbar) *məxᵊl* pl. *mxaal, Ɛatale* pl. *Ɛatal.* 3. (e.g., gear-shift) *ʔiid* pl. *ʔiideen.*

liabilities - *dyuun* (pl.). His liabilities exceed by far his assets. *dyuuno ʔaktar mən mawžuudaato b-ᵊktiir.*

liable - *masʔuul Ɛan.* You will be liable for any damages. *ʔənte bətkuun masʔuul Ɛan kəll Ɛəṭᵊl w-ḍarar.*

**You're liable to catch cold if you're not careful. *btaaxod bard ʔiza maa btaƐṭi baalak.*

**He's liable to forget! *muu bƐiid Ɛaléе yənsa!*

liaison officer - *ḍaabeṭ˜* (pl. *ḍəbbaaṭ˜*) *ʔərtibaaṭ.*

liar - *kazzaab* pl. *-iin.*

liberal - 1. *ḥərr* pl. *ʔaḥraar.* He has very liberal views. *Ɛando ʔafkaar ḥərra ktiir.* -- The Liberal Party. *ḥəzb ᵊl-ʔaḥraar.* 2. *saxi** pl. *ʔasxiya, xayyer.* She's very liberal with her money. *hiyye ktiir saxiyye b-maṣariiha.*

to liberate - *ḥarrar.* We hope to liberate the captive nations. *mnətʔammal ᵊnḥarrer ᵊl-ʔəmam ᵊl-məstaƐbade.*

liberation - *taḥriir.*

liberty - 1. *ḥərriyye.* Liberty, equality, fraternity! *ḥərriyye, musaawa, ʔaxaaʔ!*

**You're at liberty to go at any time. *ʔənte ḥərr ᵊtruuḥ ʔeemta-ma bəddak.*

to take liberties - *ʔaxad ḥərriito, džarraʔ, džaawaz ḥaddo.* He takes too many liberties. *byaaxod ḥərriito ktiir* or *byədžarraʔ Ɛala ġeero ktiir* or *byədžaawaz ḥaddo ktiir.*

librarian - *maktabži* pl. *-iyye.*

library - *maktabe* pl. *-aat* and *makaateb, daar˜* (pl. *duur˜*) *kətᵊb.*

Libya - *liibya.*

Libyan - *liibi*.*

license - *rəxṣa* pl. *rəxaṣ, ʔižaaze* pl. *-aat.* You need a license to open a restaurant. *laazmak rəxṣa la-təftaḥ maṭƐam.*

(driver's) license - *rəxṣet˜* (pl. *rəxaṣ˜*) *ᵊswaaqa, šahaadet˜* (pl. *-aat˜*) *ᵊswaaqa.* You cannot drive without a license. *maa fiik ᵊtsuuq bala rəxṣet ᵊswaaqa.*

licensed - *q̈aanuuni*.* He's a licensed pharmacist. *huwwe ṣaydali q̈aanuuni.* 2. *ḥaamel rəxṣa.* He's a licensed electrician. *huwwe kahrabaži ḥaamel* *rəxṣa* (or ***kahrabaži mraxxdṣ-lo*).

license plate - *nəmra* pl. *nəmar, nəmret˜ ᵊs-sayyaara.*

to **lick** - **1.** *lahas (a lahᵊs), lahwas.* Just look at the cat licking her kittens. *šuuf ᵊl-bəsse ɛam ᵊtlahwes ᵊwlaadha.* **2.** *ṭaɛma ... qatle, ḍarab (o ḍarb).* I'm going to lick you if you don't stop. *bṭaɛmiik qatle ʔiza maa bətwaqqef ɛand ḥaddak.* **3.** *ġalab (o/e ġalb//nġalab), qəder (e ø) ɛala.* I bet I can lick you in checkers. *braahnak ʔənni bəġᵊlbak* (or *bəqder ɛaleek*) *bᵊḍ-ḍaama.*

lid - **1.** *ġaṭa* pl. *ʔəġᵊṭye.* Where's the lid for this pot? *ween ġaṭa haṭ-ṭanžara?* -- The lid of the suitcase is coming off. *ġaṭa š-šanta ɛam yənqəbeɛ.* **2.** *žəfᵊn* pl. *žfuun.* He has drooping lids. *žfuuno mṭabbqa.*

lie - *kəzbe* pl. *-aat, kəzb.* Everything he says is a lie! *kəll šii biquulo kəzb.* -- That's a big fat lie! *hayy kəzbe mən ḥaqa kbiire.*

to lie - *kazab (e kəzb), kazzab.* There's no doubt that he's lying. *maa fii šakk ʔənno ɛam yəkzeb.* -- He lied to me about his qualifications. *kazzab ɛaliyyi b-ᵊmʔahhlaato.*

**He lies like the devil. *huuwe ʔakzab mən ʔəbliis* or *ʔakzab mənno maa fii.*

to **lie** - **1.** *kaan mətlaqqeḥ, kaan mətṣaṭṭeḥ.* All day long he's lying on the couch reading cheap magazines. *ṭuul ᵊn-nhaar mətlaqqeḥ ɛal-kanabe ɛam yəqra mažallaat raxiiṣa.* **2.** *kaan maḥṭuuṭ.* The book was lying on the table only a minute ago. *mən daqiiqa kaan l-ᵊktaab maḥṭuuṭ ɛaṭ-ṭaawle.* **3.** *waqaɛ (-yəqaɛ ø).* Most of the town lies on the right bank of the river. *ʔaktar ᵊl-balad waaqɛa ɛaḍ-ḍaffe l-yamiin mn ᵊn-nahᵊr.*

**The factory has been lying idle for a year. *l-maṣnaɛ ṣar-lo mɛaṭṭal səne.*

to lie down - *tṣaṭṭaḥ, tlaqqaḥ.* I want to lie down for a few minutes. *bəddi ʔəṭṣaṭṭdḥ-li šwayye.*

**He's lying down on the job. *ɛam yətmaḷḷaṣ mn ᵊš-šəġᵊl.*

lieutenant - *mlaazem* pl. *-iin.*

life - **1.** *ḥayaat.* It was a matter of life or death. *kaanet masʔalet ḥayaat ʔaw moot.* -- Such is life! *heek ᵊl-ḥayaat!* -- Human lives don't count much in times of war. *ḥayaat ᵊl-bašar maa-la qiime ktiir ʔiyyaam l-ᵊḥruub.* -- He survived three attempts at his life. *naža mən tlatt ᵊmḥaawalaat ɛala ḥayaato.* **2.** *ɛəmr, ḥayaat.* In all my life I haven't seen a thing like this. *b-ɛəmri* (or *b-ḥayaati*) *maa šəft heek šii.* -- His life was all trouble and hardships. *ɛəmro kəllo kaan maṣaaɛeb w-mataaɛeb.* -- What a life! *šuu hal-ḥayaat!* **3.** *ɛiiše, ḥayaat.* He leads a quiet life. *ɛaayeš ɛiiše haadye.* **4.** *rooḥ* pl. *ʔarwaaḥ.* No lives were lost in the accident. *maa ṣaar xaṣaara bᵊl-ʔarwaaḥ bᵊl-ḥaades.* -- He was the life of the party. *kaan rooḥ ᵊl-ḥafle.* **5.** *našaaṭ, ḥayawiyye.* She's full of life. *hiyye malaane našaaṭ.* **6.** *taariix˜* (pl. *tawariix˜*) *ḥayaat, taržamet˜* (pl. *taraažem˜*) *ḥayaat.* He's writing a life of the President. *ɛam yəktob taariix ḥayaat ᵊr-raʔiis.*

**He lost his life in an accident. *maat b-ḥaades.*

**I can't for the life of me remember where I put it. *w-ᵊḥyaat ʔaḷḷa maa-li ɛam ʔədzakkar ween ḥaṭṭeeta.*

**There he stood as big as life. *w-kaan waaqef ᵊhniik ᵊb-laḥmo w-dammo.*

**You can bet your life on that. *fiik tətʔakkad mən haada bᵊl-miyye ʔalf.*

life belt - *ḥzaam˜* (pl. *-aat˜* and *ʔaḥzimet˜*) *nažaat.* Have your life belts ready! *ḥaḍḍru ʔaḥzimet ᵊn-nažaat tabaɛkon!*

life imprisonment - *səžn ᵊmʔabbad.* He was sentenced to life imprisonment. *ḥakamu ɛalée bᵊs-səžᵊn l-ᵊmʔabbad* or ***ḥakamu ɛalée mʔabbad.*

life insurance - *taʔmiin ɛal-ḥayaat.* How much life insurance do you have? *qaddeeš mablaġ ᵊt-taʔmiin ɛala ḥayaatak?*

lifeboat - *qaareb˜* (pl. *qawaareb˜*) *nažaat.*

lifeless - **1.** *bala ḥayaat, mayyet.* The Rub al Khali is lifeless desert. *r-rəbɛ ᵊl-xaali ʔarḍ ṣaḥrawiyye bala ḥayaat.* **2.** *baayex, mayyet.* It was a lifeless party we attended last night. *l-ḥafle yalli rəḥnda-la mbaareḥ kaanet baayxa.*

lifeline - *šəryaan˜* (pl. *šarayiin˜*) *ᵊl-ḥayaat.* The Suez Canal is the lifeline of traffic between three continents. *qanaat ᵊs-swees šəryaan ᵊl-ḥayaat ləl-muwaaṣalaat been tlatt qaarraat.*

lifetime - *ɛəmᵊr.* A thing like that happens only once in a lifetime. *šii heek maa byəḥṣal ʔəlla marra waaḥde bᵊl-ɛəmᵊr.* -- It would take a lifetime to finish such a huge project. *bədda l-ɛəmᵊr kəllo la-txalleṣ mašruuɛ ḍaxᵊm mətᵊl haad.*

lift - *rafɛa* pl. *-aat.* With one lift he heaved the sack on the table. *b-rafɛa waaḥde ḥaṭṭ ᵊl-kiis ɛaṭ-ṭaawle.*

**Can I give you a lift? *bəddak waṣṣlak?*

**Thanks, I have a lift. *šəkran, fii ḥada ywaṣṣəlni.*

**We got a lift from the knowledge that reinforcements were coming. *tnašnašna lamma ɛrəfna ʔənno fii naždaat žaaye.*

to lift - **1.** *rafaɛ (a rafᵊɛ//nrafaɛ* and *rtafaɛ).* It's too heavy to lift. *haada tqiil ᵊktiir maa byənrəfeɛ.* -- After two weeks, the ban was lifted. *baɛᵊd žəmᵊɛteen ᵊl-ḥaẓr ᵊrtafaɛ.* -- I won't lift a finger for him. *waḷḷa maa bərfdɛ-lo qašše.* **2.** *rtafaɛ.* Toward noon the fog lifted. *ḥawaali ḍ-ḍəhr ᵊrtafaɛ ᵊḍ-ḍabaab.*

ligament - *watar* pl. *wtaar.* I strained a ligament in my foot. *nfalaš watar ᵊb-ʔəžri.*

light - **1.** *ḍaww* pl. *ʔəḍᵊwye, nuur* pl. *ʔanwaar.* The light is too glaring. *ḍ-ḍaww ɛam yəbher ᵊktiir.* -- The lights of the town came on one by one. *ʔəḍwiit ᵊl-balad šaɛlet waaḥed waaḥed.*--That throws quite a different light on the matter. *haada byəlqi nuur ᵊždiid ɛal-qaḍiyye.* **2.** *nuur.* He's at last seen the light. *ʔaxiiran šaaf ᵊn-nuur.* **3.** *walɛa, šaɛle.* Do you have a light? *mən faḍlak walɛa.* **4.** *faateḥ.* She prefers light colors. *bətḥəbb ᵊl-ʔalwaan ᵊl-faatḥa.* -- I want a light blue hat. *bəddi bərneeṭa zarqa faatḥa* (or ***bərneeṭa loona samaawi*). **5.** *kaašef.* She has a light complexion. *loona kaašef.*

**It's staying light much longer. *n-nhaar ɛam yəṭwal.*

to bring to light - *kašaf (e kašf//nkašaf) ɛan, waḍḍaḥ//twaḍḍaḥ* and *ttaḍaḥ.* The investigation brought many new facts to light. *t-taḥqiiq kašaf ɛan ɛəddet ḥaqaayeq ᵊždiide.*

to come to light - *ẓahar (a ẓhuur), tbayyan, ttaḍaḥ.* A number of unexpected problems came to light during our research. *xilaal ʔabḥaasna ẓahdr-ᵊlna ɛəddet mašaakel ġeer mənṭdẓara.*

to light - **1.** *šaɛɛal, šaɛal (e šaɛl//nšaɛal).* Wait till I light the fire. *stanna la-šaɛɛel ᵊn-naar.* -- Light a match. *šɛeel kəbriite.* -- I want to light my pipe first. *bəddi ʔəšɛel ġalyuuni bᵊl-ʔawwal.* **2.** *ḍawwa, nawwar.* The street is poorly lighted. *š-šaareɛ muu mḍawwa mniiḥ.* -- The hall was brightly lighted. *l-qaaɛa kaanet ᵊmḍawwaaye mətl ᵊn-nhaar.*

**Is your cigarette still lit? *ləssaaha sigaartak šaaɛle?*

to light up - *baraq (o barᵊq).* The children's eyes lit up. *ɛyuun l-ᵊwlaad barqet barᵊq.*

light - *xafiif* pl. *xfaaf.* You take the light package and I take the heavy one. *ʔənte btəḥmel ᵊl-baakeet ᵊl-xafiif w-ʔana bəḥmel ᵊt-tqiil.* -- Why don't you take your light coat? *leeš maa btaaxod maɛak ᵊl-manṭo l-xafiif tabaɛak?* -- We had only a light meal. *ʔakalna ʔakle xafiife bass.*

**She's very light on her feet. *btərqoṣ b-ᵊshuule w-rašaaqa.*

lightbulb - *balloora* pl. *-aat, lamḅa* pl. *-aat.*

to **lighten** - *barqet (e barᵊq) ᵊd-dənye.* It's thundering and lightening. *(d-dənye) ɛam tərɛod w-təbreq.*

to **lighten** - *xaffaf.* Your help would certainly lighten his load. *msaaɛadtak ʔəlo ʔakiid bətxaffef ḥəmlo.*

lightheaded - *ṭaayeš.* He seems to be a lightheaded fellow. *byəẓhar ɛalée ṭaayeš šwayye.*

lighthouse - *manaara* pl. *-aat.*

lighting - *ʔiḍaaʔa, ʔəḍᵊwye* (pl.). The lighting is bad here. *l-ʔiḍaaʔa ktiir ᵊḍɛiife hoon.*

lightning - *barq,* (bolt of lightning) *ṣaaɛiqa* pl. *ṣawaaɛeq.* Lightning struck the church steeple. *ṣ-ṣaaɛiqa nəzlet ɛala bərž l-ᵊkniise.*

likable - *xafiif* (pl. *xfaaf*) *damm, xafiif˜ ᵊd-damm.* He's a likable fellow, don't you think? *huuwe xafiif damm, muu heek?* or ***dammo xafiif, muu heek?*

like - **1.** *mətᵊl˜.* You're just like my sister. *ʔənti tamaaman mətᵊl ʔəxti.* — He ran like mad. *rakad mətl ᵊl-mažaniin.* — There's nothing like traveling! *maa fii šii mətl ᵊs-safar!* **2.** *mmaasel, mšaabeh.* He will treat some matters of like importance. *bəddo yɛaalež kam mawḍuuɛ ʔəlhon ʔahammiyye mmaasle.* — She contributed a like sum. *tbarraɛet ᵊb-mablaġ mmaasel.* **3.** *mətᵊl-ma.* She's just like I pictured her. *hiyye tamaaman mət°l-ma tṣawwarṭa.* -- Was the party like I told you it would be? *kaanet °l-ḥafle mət°l-ma qelt-ǝllak laḥa tkuun?*

**It looks like rain. *mbayyen bədda tənzel maṭar* or *ẓ-ẓaaher bədda tšatti.*

**I don't feel like dancing. *muu žaaye ɛala baali ʔərqoṣ.*

**Like father, like son. *ʔəbn °l-wazz ɛawwaam.*

**That's just like him. *šuu l-mənṭdẓar mənno ġeer heek?*

**That's more like it! *hallaq qarrab°t!*

**They're as like as two peas in a pod. *hənne kaʔənnon toom.*

**I can't stand the likes of her. *maa fini ʔəṭḥammal °n-naas halli mətla.*

like this, like that - *heek.* It's not like that at all. *haada muu heek ʔabadan.* — Ordinarily, we do it like this. *ɛaadətna nsaawiiha heek.* — Why do you ask me a question like this? *leeš ɛam təsʔalni heek suʔaal* (or ***suʔaal mət°l haada*)? — I want something like this. *bəddi heek šii* (or ***šii mət°l haada*).

the like of it - *heek šii.* Did you ever see the like of it? *šəft heek šii b-ɛəmrak?*

what ... like - *kiif, šloon, šuu.* What's the weather like today? *kiif °ṭ-ṭaqṣ °l-yoom?*

**What's he like? *šuu huwwe mn °n-naas?* or *šuu nooɛo mn °r-ržaal?*

to like - 1. *ḥabb (ə ḥəbb).* I don't like cats. *maa bḥəbb °l-qaṭaaṭ.* — I like this kind of cake. *bḥəbb han-nooɛ mn °l-gaato.* — Do you like to dance? *bəthəbb °r-raq°ṣ?* — Would you like to dance now? *bətḥəbbi tər°qṣi?* — He never liked to do it. *b-ḥayaato maa ḥabb yaɛməla.* -- I like him. *bḥəbbo* or ***byəɛžəbni.* — If you don't like it, you can leave! *ʔiza maa bətḥəbb °l-haale* (or ***ʔiza muu ɛaažəbtak °l-ḥaale*) *btəqder °truuḥ.* **2.** *bədd-* + pron. suffix, *ḥabb.* Would you like another cup of coffee? *bəddak* (or *bətḥəbb*) *fənžaan qahwe taani?* — Would you like to go to a movie? *bəddak* (or *bətḥəbb*) *°truuḥ ɛas-siinama?* -- He would like to talk to you. *bəddo yəḥki maɛak.* **3.** *šaaf (u ə), ḥabb.* How do you like this town? *kiif šaayef hal-balad?* — How did you like the movie? *kiif šəft °l-fəl°m?*

**He's never liked it here. *b-ḥayaato maa kaan mabṣuuṭ hoon.*

likelihood - *ʔəḥtimaal, ʔəmkaaniyye.* There is a great likelihood that ... *fii ʔəḥtimaal °kbiir ʔənno ...*

in all likelihood - *ɛal-ʔaržaḥ.* In all likelihood he'll get the job. *ɛal-ʔaržaḥ byaaxod °š-šaġle.*

likely - *məḥtdmal, mražžaḥ.* It's not likely that he'll come any more. *muu məḥtdmal yəži mən hallaq w-raayeḥ.* — Do you think it's likely to rain? *btəɛtəqed ʔənno məḥtdmal °tmaṭṭer?* — This is a likely development we have to face. *haada taṭawwor məḥtdmal laazem °nwaažho.* — That's a more likely guess. *hal-ḥəz°r məḥtdmal ʔaktar.* — This is what is most likely going to happen. *məḥtdmal ʔaktar šii* (or ***l-ʔaržaḥ*) *haada yalli biṣiir.*

likeness - *tašaaboh.* There is a surprising likeness in their ideas. *fii tašaaboh mədheš °b-ʔafkaaron.*

**The picture is an excellent likeness of you. *ṣ-ṣuura ṭaalɛa ṭəbq °l-ʔaṣ°l mətlak.*

lily - *zambaqa* coll. *zambaq* pl. *-aat* and *zanaabeq.*

limb - *ṭaraf* pl. *ʔaṭraaf.* I couldn't move a limb. *maa qdər°t ḥarrek w-laa ṭaraf mən ʔaṭraafi.*

lime - *kəls.* The soil doesn't contain enough lime. *hat-tərbe maa fiiha kəls °kfaaye.*

limelight: He likes to be always in the limelight. *biḥəbb ḥaalo ykuun daayman maḥaṭṭ °l-ʔanẓaar.*

limit - 1. *ḥadd* pl. *ḥduud.* There's a limit to everything. *kəll šii ʔəlo ḥadd.* — As long as a person knows his limits it's all right. *ṭaala-ma l-ʔənsaan byaɛref °ḥduudo bikuun °mniiḥ.* **2.** *ʔaaxer.* I've reached the limit of my patience. *wəṣel ṣabri la-ʔaaxro.*

**That's the limit! *zaadet! la-hoon w-bass!*

speed limit - *ḥadd˜ °s-sərɛa.* The speed limit is thirty-five miles an hour. *ḥadd °s-sərɛa xamsaa w-tlaatiin miil b°s-saaɛa.*

to limit - *ḍtaṣar.* Please limit your talk to three minutes. *ḍtəṣer kalaamak bi-tlətt daqaayeq, mən faḍlak.*

limited - *maḥduud.* Our time is limited. *waq°tna maḥduud.*

limp - *mərxi*.* His arm hung limp in his sleeve. *ʔiido ddandalet mərxiyye mən kəmmo.*

to limp - *ɛaraž (o ɛar°ž).* He limps noticeably. *mbayyen ɛalée mniiḥ ʔənno byəɛrož.*

line - 1. *xaṭṭ* pl. *xṭuuṭ.* Draw a line between these two points. *rsoom xaṭṭ been han-nəq°ṭteen.* -- He can't draw a straight line. *maa byaɛref yərsom xaṭṭ ḍəġri.* — There are deep lines in his face. *fii xṭuuṭ ġamiiqa b-wəššo.* -- There's a long line of cars ahead of us. *fii xaṭṭ ṭawiil mn °s-sayyaaraat qəddaamna.* -- There's heavy traffic on that line. *hal-xaṭṭ mazḥuum °ktiir.* **2.** *ṣaff* pl. *ṣfuuf, xaṭṭ* pl. *xṭuuṭ.* There's a long line in front of the ticket office. *fii ṣaff ṭawiil qəddam °l-giišée.* — Keep in line! *xalliik b°ṣ-ṣaff!* — We had to stand in line for hours. *nžabarna nwaqqef b°ṣ-ṣaff saaɛaat.* **3.** *ṣaṭr* pl. *ṣṭuur(a)* and *ʔəṣṭor.* I still have a few lines to write. *ləssa fii ɛaliyyi kam ṣaṭr ʔəktóbon.* -- Drop me a line. *bɛat-li šii ṣaṭr ṣaṭreen.* **4.** *šəġ°l.* What line is he in? *šuu šəġlo?* **5.** *ʔəxtiṣaaṣ.* That's not in my line. *haada muu b-ʔəxtiṣaaṣi.* **6.** *taškiile.* They have a nice line of dresses. *fii ɛandon taškiilet faṣaṭiin ḥəlwe.* **7.** *ṣənf, maarka.* We don't carry that line. *maa ɛanna haṣ-ṣənf.* **8.** *ḥabl* pl. *ḥbaal.* The wash is still (hanging) on the line. *l-ġasiil ləssaato manšuur ɛal-ḥabl.*

**I can't keep my students in line any more. *maa ɛaad fiyyi dabber talamiizi.*

**It's along the line of what we discussed. *haada ḍəmn °l-mawḍuuɛ yalli ḥakeena fii.*

**Boy, does he have a smooth line! *yaa ʔaḷḷa, qaddeeš kalaamo ḥəlu žallaab!*

**You've got to draw the line somewhere. *laazem °tḥəṭṭ ḥadd faaṣel °b-šii qərne.*

(electric) line - *xaṭṭ˜ (kahraba)* pl. *xṭuuṭ˜ (kahraba), šriiṭ* pl. *šaraayeṭ.* There's a short circuit in the line. *fii kontaak b°l-xaṭṭ.*

(telephone) line - *xaṭṭ (°t-talifoon).* The line is still busy. *l-xaṭṭ ləssaa mašġuul.*

to form a line - *ṣṭaff.* Form a line double file. *ṣṭaffu žooz žooz.*

to line - 1. *baṭṭan.* The jacket is lined with rayon. *ž-žaakeet mbaṭṭan bṭaane ḥariir nabaati.* **2.** *ṭala (i ṭali//nṭala) ... žuwwa.* A copper goblet lined with silver. *ṭaaset °nḥaas məṭliyye žuwwa fəḍḍa.* **3.** *ṣṭaffu ɛala ʔaṭraaf˜ ...* People lined the streets to watch the parade. *n-naas ṣṭaffu ɛala ʔaṭraaf °š-šawaareɛ la-yətfarražu ɛal-ʔəstəɛraaḍ.*

to line up - *ṣṭaff.* Have the boys line up in the hall. *xalli ṣ-ṣəbyaan yəṣṭaffu b°l-qaaɛa.* — Everybody line up over here! *kəllkon ṣṭaffu hoon!*

lined up - *waaqef b°ṣ-ṣaff.* There are a lot of people lined up in front of the box office. *fii naas °ktiir waaqfiin b°ṣ-ṣaff qəddaam kuuwet °t-tazaaker.*

linen - 1. *kəttaan.* The tablecloth is made of linen. *ġaṭa ṭ-ṭaawle kəttaan.* **2.** *bayaaḍ.* I pay fifty pounds a month for my room, linen included. *bədfaɛ xamsiin leera ʔəžret °l-ʔuuḍa b°š-šah°r, bi-ma fiiha l-bayaaḍ.* **3.** *šaraašef* (pl.). The linen is changed every week. *biġayyru š-šaraašef marra b°ž-žəmɛa.*

linguist - *luġawi* pl. *-iyyiin.*

linguistics - *luġawiyyaat* (pl.).

lining - *bṭaane.* My coat needs a new lining. *l-manṭo tabaɛi laazmo bṭaane ždiide.*

link - *waṣle* pl. *-aat, ḥalaqa* pl. *-aat.* One link of my watch chain is broken. *fii waṣle maksuura b-səlsəlt saaɛti.* — One link in the chain is still missing. *fii ḥalaqa mən ḥalaqaat °s-səl°sle ləssaaha ḍaayɛa.*

to link - *šarbak//tšarbak, waṣal(-yuuṣel waṣl// nwaṣal).* You have to link the two ends of the chain. *laazem °tšarbek ṭarafeen °s-səl°sle.*

lint - *zaġbara.*

lion - *ʔasad* pl. *ʔsuud, sab°ɛ* pl. *sbaaɛ.*

lip - *šəffe* pl. *šəfaf.* My lips are all chapped from the wind. *šəfafi mṭaq°ṭqiin mn °l-hawa.*

**I'll have no lip from you! *ʔəsḥa trədd °b-wəšši!*

liquid - 1. *maayeɛ* pl. *mawaayeɛ, saayel* pl. *sawaayel.* He's only allowed liquids. *huwwe məḥmi ɛal-mawaayeɛ.* **2.** *saayel.* Do you have liquid soap? *fii ɛandak ṣaabuun saayle?*

to **liquidate - 1.** *ṣaffa//tṣaffa.* The company had to be liquidated to pay off its debts. *kaan laazem tətṣaffa š-šərke ḥatta yədfaɛu d-dyuun yalli ɛaleeha.* **2.** *zaal (i ʔizaale) mn °l-wužuud.* The government saw fit to have him liquidated. *l-ᵊḥkuume šaafet ḍaruuri ᵓənno dsiilo mn ᵊl-wužuud.*

liquor - *xamᵊr* pl. *xmuur, mašruubaat kuḥuuliyye* (pl.).

Lisbon - *ləšboona.*

to **lisp** - *qaraṭ (o qarᵊṭ) bᵊl-ḥaki.* Too bad (that) she lisps. *maᶜ ᵊl-ᵓasaf hiyye btəqroṭ bᵊl-ḥaki.*

list - *qaayme* pl. *qawaayem, žadwal* pl. *žadaawel, liista* pl. *-aat.* His name is not on the list. *ᵓəsmo muu bᵊl-qaayme.*

to list - *qayyad//tqayyad.* Why haven't you listed this item? *leeš maa qayyadᵊt han-nafde?*

to **listen** - 1. *ṣəġi (a ʹ), stamaᶜ.* They listened intently. *ṣəġyu b-ᵓəntibaah.* 2. *səməᶜ (a samᵊᶜ).* Listen! Somebody's coming. *smaaᶜ! fii ḥada žaaye.* 3. *ntabah, ᶜaṭa (-yaᶜṭi ʹ) baalo.* Listen for the sound of the bell. *ntəbeh la-ṣooṭ ᵊž-žaraṣ* or *ᶜaṭi baalak ᶜaž-žaraṣ.*

to listen in - *tsammaᶜ.* Somebody must be listening in. *bəənn fii ḥada ᶜam yətsammaᶜ (ᶜaleena).*

to listen to - 1. *səməᶜ, stamaᶜ la-.* I like to listen to classical music. *bḥəbb ᵓəsmaᶜ muusiiqa klaasikiyye.* — I can't listen to that any longer. *maa ᶜaad fiyyi ᵓəsmaᶜ hal-qəṣṣa.* 2. *ntabah la-, səməᶜ mən.* Why didn't you listen to me? *leeš maa ntabaht-əlli?* or *leeš maa sməᶜᵊt mənni?* 3. *səməᶜ mən, ṭaaᶜ (i ṭaaᶜa).* The child doesn't listen to me. *l-walad maa byəsmaᶜ mənni* (or *maa biṭiiᶜni*).

**She'll listen to reason. *btərḍax ləl-ᶜaqᵊl.*

listener - *məstəməᶜ* pl. *-iin.*

liter - *lətr* pl. *ltuura.*

literacy: What's the literacy rate in this country? *šuu nəsbet yalli byəqru w-ᵊbyəkᵊtbu b-hal-ᵊblaad?*

literal - *ḥarfi*.* Please make a literal translation of that. *mən faḍlak saawi taržame ḥarfiyye la-haad.*

literally - 1. *b-kəll maᶜna˜ l-kəlme.* She's literally penniless. *maa fii ᶜanda maṣaari b-kəll maᶜna l-kəlme.* 2. *kəlme kəlme, ḥarf ḥarf, ḥarfiyyan.* They translated the sentence literally. *taržamu ž-žəmle kəlme kəlme.*

**You mustn't take him too literally. *laa taaxod kalaamo ᶜala ḥabbto.*

literate: About 90% of the population are literate. *ḥawaali təsᶜiin bᵊl-miyye mn ᵊl-ᵓahaali byəqru w-ᵊbyəkᵊtbu.*

literature - 1. *ᵓadab* pl. *ᵓaadaab.* Have you read a great deal of Arabic literature? *qareet šii ktiir bᵊl-ᵓadab ᵊl-ᶜarabi?* 2. *mdawwanaat* (pl.). Please collect for me all the literature you can find on this subject. *ḍalla žmaᶜ-li kəll l-ᵊmdawwanaat yalli məmken tlaaqiiha b-hal-mawḍuuᶜ.* 3. *našraat* (pl.). The ministry has sent out a lot of literature on this topic. *l-wazaara ṭaalaᶜet našraat ᵊktiire ᶜan hal-mawḍuuᶜ.*

little - 1. *ṣġiir* pl. *ṣġaar.* She has a little girl. *ᶜandha bənt ᵊṣġiire.* 2. *qaliil, ḍaᵓiil.* That's of little value to me. *haš-šii qiimto qaliile bᵊn-nəsbe ᵓəli.* — It's of little importance. *ᵓahammiito qaliile.*

**He's little better than a thief. *maa fii farq ᵊkbiir beeno w-been ᵊl-ḥaraami.*

**This dictionary is little better than the other one. *maa fii farq ᵊkbiir been hal-qaamuus w-hadaak.*

little by little - *šwayye šwayye.* Little by little he calmed down. *šwayye šwayye huwwe hədi.*

a little - *šwayye.* I can speak a little French. *bəḥki šwayye(t) frənsaawi.*

in a little while - *baᶜd ᵊšwayye.* I'll come back in a little while. *bəržaᶜ baᶜd ᵊšwayye.*

little finger - *xənṣar* pl. *xanaaṣer.*

to **live** - 1. *ᶜaaš (i ᶜiiše).* He lived a happy life. *ᶜaaš ᶜiiše saᶜiide.* — He always worked hard and never really lived. *daayman kaan haaləkk ḥaalo bᵊš-šəġᵊl w-maa ᶜaaš ᶜiiše mᵊriḥa ᵓabadan.* — I couldn't live on so little. *maa bəqder ᶜiiš ᶜala haš-šii l-qaliil heek.* — He has barely enough to live on. *bᵊl-kaad ᶜando šii kfaaye yᶜiiš ᶜaleᶜ.* — Before the war I lived in France. *qabl ᵊl-ḥarb kənt ᶜaayeš b-ᵊfransa.* — Live and learn! *taala-ma ᶜaayeš kəll yoom btətᶜallam šii ždiid.* 2. *sakan (o səkna).* Does anyone live in this house? *fii ḥada saaken b-hal-beet?* — They live in the Rue de Bagdad. *saakniin ᵊb-šaareᶜ baġdaad.* 3. *ᶜaaš, ᶜtaaš, qtaat.* The people on this island live on nothing but fish. *səkkaan haž-žaziire biᶜiišu ᶜas-samak bass.*

**I don't know whether he's still living. *maa baᶜref ᵓiza kaan ləssda ṭayyeb.*

**Is your grandmother still living? *ləssaaha ṭayybe səttak?*

to live out - *kammal, ᶜaaš (i ʹ) la-ᵓaaxer˜ ...* She won't live out the winter. *yaḷḷa tkammel ᵊš-šətwiyye* or *yaḷḷa tᶜiiš la-ᵓaaxer ᵊš-šətwiyye.*

to live up to - 1. *ṭələᶜ (a ʹ) qadd˜ ...* He didn't live up to his reputation. *maa ṭələᶜ qadd halli kaan maᶜruuf ᶜanno.* — She didn't live up to my expectations. *maa ṭələᶜet qadd halli kənt məntəẓer mənna.* 2. *qaam (u qyaam) b-.* They didn't live up to the terms of the contract. *maa qaamu b-ᵊbnuud ᵊl-kontraato.*

live - 1. *ḥayy, ᶜaayeš.* I bought some live fish. *štareet kam samake ḥayye.* 2. *mbaašar.* Was the broadcast live or taped? *kaanet ᵊl-ᵓizaaᶜa mbaašara ᵓaw ᵊmsažžale?*

**Careful, that's a live wire. *ᵓəṣḥa haš-šriiṭ fii quwwe* (or *fii kooraan*).

live coals - *žamᵊr.* There are still live coals in the brazier. *ləssa fii žamᵊr bᵊl-manqal.*

livelihood - *maᶜiiše.* They gain their livelihood by hunting. *byəkᵊsbu maᶜiišəton bᵊṣ-ṣeed.*

lively - 1. *našiiṭ* pl. *-iin* and *nəšaṭa, malaan ḥayaat.* He's a lively boy. *huwwe walad našiiṭ.* 2. *ḥayy.* We had a lively conversation. *žaret beenaatna mḥaawara ḥayye.*

**Step lively! *ḥrook baqa! ᵓəmši!*

liver - *kəbᵊd* pl. *kbaad.*

liverwurst - *baaṭəe.*

livestock - *maašye* pl. *mawaaši.* We can't get enough feed for our livestock. *maa fiina nžiib ᶜaliif ᵊkfaaye la-mawašiina.*

living - 1. *ᶜiiše, maᶜiiše.* Living is awfully expensive here. *l-ᶜiiše hoon ġaalye ktiir.* — Living conditions are very bad. *ᵓaḥwaal ᵊl-ᶜiiše ktiir ᶜaaṭle.* 2. *maᶜaaš, quut, rəzᵊq.* He'll have to earn his own living. *laazem yərbaḥ maᶜaašo la-ḥaalo.* 3. *ḥayy.* German is a living language, Latin is not. *l-ᵓalmaani luġa ḥayye, laaken muu l-laatiini.*

**He's the living image of his father. *huwwe ṣuura ṭəbq ᵊl-ᵓaṣᵊl ᶜan ᵓabúu.*

to make a living - *saḥab (a saḥᵊb) rəzqo.* How can you make a living in that field? *kiif bəddak təsḥab rəzqak ᵊb-heek ᵓəxtiṣaaṣ?*

**His job's not very lucrative, but he makes a living. *šəġlo muu mdərr ᵊktiir, bass bimašši ḥaalo.*

living room - *ᵓuuḍet˜* (pl. *ᵓuwaḍ˜*) *qᶜuud.*

load - 1. *ḥəmᵊl* pl. *ḥmaal.* The load is too heavy for him. *l-ḥəml ᵊktiir ᵊtqiil ᶜaleᵉ.* 2. *šaḥne* pl. *-aat.* I ordered a load of coal. *waṣṣeet ᶜala šaḥnet faḥᵊm.*

**That takes a load off my mind. *haada ᶜam yrayyeḥ baali.*

**He has loads of money. *huwwe mtaqqal bᵊl-maṣaari.*

to load - 1. *ḥammal//tḥammal.* Load the cases on the truck. *ḥammel ᵊs-sanadiiq bᵊl-kamyoon.* — The cargo is just being loaded. *š-šaḥne ᶜam tətḥammal bᵊl-baaxra.* 2. *ᶜabba//tᶜabba, ḥaša (i ḥaši// nḥaša).* The gun was loaded. *l-fard kaan ᵊmᶜabba.* 3. *ᶜabba.* Do you know how to load the camera? *btaᶜref kiif ᵊtᶜabbi ᵓaalt ᵊt-taṣwiir?*

**We're loaded with work. *nəḥna ġaaṭṣiin bᵊš-šəġᵊl la-qaraqiiṭ ᵓadaanna.*

loaded down - *mḥammal.* She was loaded down with packages. *kaanet ᵊmḥammale baakeetaat.*

loaf - *rġiif* pl. *ᵓərᵊġfe.* Please give me three loaves of bread. *ᶜaṭiini tlətt ərᵊġfe-xəbᵊz.*

to loaf - *taqqal ᵓiido, tbaalad, mahyaṣ.* He was loafing on the job. *kaan ᶜam ytaqqel ᵓiido bᵊš-šəġᵊl.*

loan - 1. *qarḍ* pl. *qruuḍ.* I'd like to make a loan. *bəddi ᵓaᶜmel qarḍ.* 2. *deene* pl. *-aat.* Consider it a loan between friends. *ᶜtəber had-deene been ᵊṣḥaab.*

to loan - *qaraḍ (o/e qarᵊḍ), dayyan.* The bank loaned us 5,000 pounds. *l-bank qaraḍna xamᵊst aalaaf leera.* 2. *ᶜaar (i ᵓiᶜaara//nᶜaar).* He loaned me an interesting book. *ᶜaarni ktaab ᵊmfiid ᵊktiir.*

to **loathe** - *kəreh (a karah//nkarah).* I loathe snakes. *bəkrah ᵊl-ḥayaaya.*

local - 1. *maḥalli*.* The local papers say nothing about the accident. *ž-žaraayed ᵊl-maḥalliyye maa ᶜam təḥki šii ᶜan ᵊl-ḥaadse.* — He wasn't familiar with local conditions. *maa kaan ᶜando ᵓəṭṭilaaᶜ ᶜal-ᵓaḥwaal ᵊl-maḥalliyye.* 2. *daaxli*.* How much is a local call? *b-qaddeeš l-ᵊmxaabara d-daaxliyye?* 3. *mawḍiᶜi*.* A local anesthetic will do. *t-taxdiir ᵊl-mawḍiᶜi bikaffi.*

local (train) - *treen~* (pl. *-aat~*) *ᵊḍ-ḍawaaḥi.* Does the local stop there? *treen ᵊḍ-ḍawaaḥi biwaqqef ᵊhniik?*

to **locate** - *laqa (-ylaaqi ø).* I couldn't locate him. *maa qdərt laaqii.* -- I can't locate the trouble. *maa bəqder laaqi ween ᵊl-ɛəṭᵊl.*

located - *ḥaakem, ṣaayer.* Where is your new store located? *ween ḥaakem maḥallak ᵊž-ždiid?*

location - *mawqeɛ* pl. *mawaaqeɛ, markaz* pl. *maraakez.* The location of the hotel is ideal. *mawqeɛ ᵊl-ʔoteel məmtaaz mən kəll ᵊn-nawaaḥi.*

**Most of the film was shot on location in the Nile Valley. *ʔaktar ᵊl-fəlᵊm ᵊttaaxad b-maḥall-ma žaret ᵊl-qəṣṣa b-waadi n-niil.*

lock - **1.** *ġaal* pl. *-aat.* The lock of the front door needs oiling. *ġaal baab ᵊṣ-ṣqaaq bəddo tazyiit.* **2.** *qəfᵊl* pl. *qfuule* and *qfaal.* Have you noticed that the lock for the chain is gone? *šəfᵊt ʔənno qəfl ᵊž-žanziir raaḥ?* -- He keeps everything under lock and key. *byəḥfaẓ kəll šii taḥt ᵊl-qəfᵊl wᵊl-məftaaḥ.*

to lock - **1.** *ġalaq (e ġalq//nġalaq), qafal (e qafl//nqafal).* Don't forget to lock the door when you leave. *laa tənsa maa təġleq ᵊl-baab lamma bətruuḥ.* **2.** *qafal ɛala.* I locked it in my desk. *qafalt ɛalée b-dərž ṭaawəlti.* **3.** *tšarbak.* When the two cars hit each other their bumpers locked. *lamma s-sayyaarteen ṭṣaadamu maɛ baɛḍon ᵊṭ-ṭabboonaat tabáɛon ᵊtšarbaku.*

to lock out - *daqqar ᵊl-baab ɛala.* Don't lock me out in case I'm late. *laa ddaqqer ɛaliyyi l-baab ʔiza ṣadaf w-ᵊtʔaxxart.*

to lock up - *ḥabas (e ḥabs//nḥabas).* They locked him up overnight. *ḥabasúu l-leele.*

locomotive - *qaaṭra* pl. *-aat, maakiina* pl. *-aat.*

locust - (insect) *žraade* coll. *žraad* pl. *-aat.*

to **lodge** - **1.** *nəzel (e nzuul).* I'm lodging at the Jezira Hotel. *ʔana naazel b-ʔoteel ž-žaziire.* **2.** *ɛəleq (a ɛalqa).* A piece of wood is lodged in the machine. *fii šaqfet xašab ɛalqaane bᵊl-maakiina.* **3.** *rafaɛ (a rafᵊɛ), qaddam.* He lodged a complaint with the authorities. *rafaɛ šakwa ləṣ-ṣəlṭaat.*

log - *žəzᵊɛ* pl. *žzuuɛ.* The logs were floating down the river. *ž-žzuuɛa kaanet faayše ɛala wəšš ᵊn-nahr.*

**He sat there like a (bump on a) log. *kaan qaaɛed ᵊhniik mətl ᵊl-looḥ.*

**I slept like a log. *nəmᵊt mətl ᵊl-qatiil.*

logic - *manṭeq.*

logical - *manṭiqi*.*

logician - *manṭiqi** pl. *manaaṭiqa.*

London - *landan, londra.*

lonely - **1.** *muuḥeš, mənfə́red.* The lighthouse keeper lives a lonely life. *ḥaares ᵊl-manaara biɛiiš ɛiiše muuḥše.* **2.** *mənɛə́zel, məṭṭarref.* This place is quite lonely in winter. *hal-maḥall ᵊktiir mənɛə́zel bᵊš-šəte.*

lonesome - *məstawḥeš.* She feels very lonesome. *šaaɛra b-ḥaala ktiir məstawᵊḥše.*

to be lonesome for - *štaaq la-.* I'm very lonesome for you. *ʔana ktiir məštaq-lak.*

long - **1.** *ṭawiil* pl. *ṭwaal, bɛiid* pl. *bɛaad.* We had to make a long detour. *nžabarna naɛmel doora ṭawiile.* -- It's a long way to the top of the mountain. *ṭ-ṭariiq ṭawiil la-raas ᵊž-žabal.* **2.** *mədde ṭawiile.* Did you stay long at the party? *qaɛadt mədde ṭawiile bᵊl-ḥafle?* or ***ṭawwalᵊt bᵊl-ḥafle?* (cf. below, to stay, etc., a long time.)

**The room is twenty feet long. *l-ʔuuḍa ṭuula ɛašriin qadam.*

**So long! (said by the person leaving; to a man) *xaaṭrak,* (to a woman) *xaaṭrek,* (to a group of people) *xaaṭərkon;* (said by the person or persons staying behind) *maɛ ᵊs-salaame* (answered, in turn, by the person leaving with *ʔaḷḷa ysallmak, ʔaḷḷa ysallmek, ʔaḷḷa ysalləmkon,* respectively).

long after - *baɛᵊd (mən) ... b-zamaan.* He got there long after we did. *wəṣel baɛᵊd mənna b-zamaan.* -- The borders remained closed long after the war. *l-ᵊḥduud tammet ᵊmsakkara baɛd ᵊl-ḥarb ᵊb-zamaan.*

a long time - *mədde ṭawiile, waqᵊt ṭawiil.* The trip took a long time. *s-safra ʔaxdet mədde ṭawiile.*

to do, perform, work at, etc., **for a long time** - *ṭawwal b-.* Did you work long last night? *ṭawwalt bᵊš-šəġl ᵊmbaarḥa bᵊl-leel?*

to stay, remain, etc., **(a) long (time)** - *ṭawwal.* Did you stay long at the party? *ṭawwalt bᵊl-ḥafle?*

(a) long (time) ago - *mən zamaan.* That was a long time ago. *haada ṣaar mən zamaan.* — I knew that long ago. *ɛrəfᵊt haada mən zamaan.*

all ... long - *ṭuul~...* The child cried all night long. *l-walad bəqi yəbki ṭuul ᵊl-leel.* -- We had been in the garden all day long. *bqiina bᵊž-žneene ṭuul ᵊn-nhaar.*

as long as - **1.** *qadd-ma.* You can keep it as long as you wish. *btəqder txallii maɛak qadd-ma bəddak.* **2.** *ma-daam, ṭaala-ma.* It doesn't bother me as long as the work gets done. *maa bihəmmni ma-daam bişiir ᵊš-šəġᵊl.* -- As long as you're here, you might as well have dinner with us. *ṭaala-ma ʔənte hoon leeš maa btəqɛod tətɛašša maɛna?*

how long - *qaddeeš.* How long shall we wait? *qaddeeš bəddna nəstanna?*

in the long run - **1.** *ɛala ṭuul.* I won't be able to stand that in the long run. *maa bətḥammal haš-šii ɛala ṭuul.* **2.** *maɛ ᵊl-mədde.* Everything will work out in the long run. *kəll šii raḥa yəṭlaɛ mniiḥ maɛ ᵊl-mədde.*

to **long** - *štaaq.* I'm longing to see my parents again. *ʔana məštaaq šuuf ʔəmmi w-ʔabi mn ᵊždiid.* -- He's longing for home. *huwwe məštaaq ləl-waṭan.*

long-distance call - *mxaabara* (pl. *-aat*) *xaaržiyye.* Operator, I'd like to make a long-distance call. *ṣanṭraal, bəddi ʔaɛmel mxaabara xaaržiyye.*

longer - **1.** *ʔaṭwal.* This table is longer than that one. *haṭ-ṭaawle ʔaṭwal mən hadiik.* **2.** *mədde ʔaṭwal.* He wanted to stay longer, but I was sleepy. *kaan bəddo yəbqa mədde ʔaṭwal bass ʔana kənᵊt naɛsaan.*

not ... any longer - *maa ɛaad (u ø)* (in personal construction). I can't stand it any longer. *maa ɛaad fiyyi ʔətḥammə́la* or *maa ɛədt ʔətḥammə́la.* -- They don't speak to each other any longer. *maa ɛaadu yəḥku maɛ baɛḍon.* -- If you keep treating him like this he won't listen to you any longer. *ʔiza bəttamm ᵊtɛaamlo heek maa laḥa yɛuud yəsmaɛ mənnak.*

long-suffering - *ṣabuur.* I must say, she's a long-suffering wife! *bəddak ᵊl-ḥaqiiqa? hiyye žooze ṣabuura ktiir!*

long-winded - *məshab.* It was a long-winded speech. *kaan ᵊxṭaab məshab.*

look - **1.** *naẓra* pl. *-aat.* You can see with one look that the town is dirty. *btaɛref mən naẓra waaḥde ʔənno l-balad wəsxa.* -- I'd like to have a look at the house before I buy it. *bəddi ʔəlqi naẓra ɛal-beet qabᵊl-ma ʔəštrii.* **2.** *taṭliiɛa* pl. *-aat.* He gave her an angry look. *ṭṭallaɛ ɛaleeha taṭliiɛet ġaḍab.*

**Take a good look! *ṭṭallaɛ mniiḥ!*

looks - *heeʔa.* To judge by his looks, he's a prize fighter. *mən heeʔto btaɛref ʔənno mlaakem məḥtə́ref.* -- I don't like his looks. *maa bḥəbb heeʔto.* -- From the looks of things it may take much longer than we thought. *ᵊl-heeʔa ʔənno haš-šaġle bədda waqᵊt ʔaṭwal məm-ma ftakarna.*

to look - **1.** *ṭṭallaɛ (taṭliiɛa).* I took the book when he wasn't looking. *ʔaxadt l-ᵊktaab lamma maa kaan ɛam yəṭṭallaɛ.* -- Don't look down if it makes you dizzy. *laa təṭṭallaɛ la-taḥᵊt ʔiza bədduux.* -- Don't look now! *laa təṭṭallaɛ hallaq!* -- I enjoy looking at pictures. *bḥəbb ʔəṭṭallaɛ ɛaṣ-ṣuwar.* -- Don't look at me. I didn't do it! *laa təṭṭallaɛ ɛaliyyi. muu ʔana yalli saaweeta!* -- She didn't so much as look at me. *maa ṭṭallaɛet ɛaliyyi ḥatta w-laa taṭliiɛa.* -- May I look at your identification? *məmken ʔəṭṭallaɛ ɛala* (or ***šuuf*) *hawiitak?* **2.** *šaaf (u ø), ṭṭallaɛ.* Look, a falling star! *šuuf, nəžm ʔabu danab!* -- Look, I told you a hundred times: don't do it! *šuuf, qəlt-ə́llak miit marra laa taɛmə́la.* **3.** *naẓar (o naẓar).* We'll have to look into the matter. *laazem nənẓor b-hal-masʔale* or *hal-masʔale bədda naẓar.*

**You look well. *maašaaḷḷa heeʔtak mniiḥa.*

**These shoes are cheap, and they look it too. *haṣ-ṣabbaaṭ ᵊrxiiṣ w-ᵊmbayyen ɛalée heek.*

**It looks like rain. *mbayyen bədda tənzel maṭar* or *ẓ-ẓaaher bədda tšatti.*

to look after - *ɛaṭa (-yaɛṭi ø) baalo ɛala, ɛtana b-.* Do you have someone to look after the child? *fii ḥada yaɛṭi baalo ɛal-walad?*

to look down on - *ḥtaqar, zdara.* You mustn't look down on people just because they're poor. *ḥaraam təḥtə́qer ᵊn-naas laʔənnon fəqara.*

to look down one's nose at - *zdara, ḥtaqar.* She looks down her nose at everyone. *btəzdə́ri kəll ᵊn-naas.*

to look for - *fattaš ɛala, dawwar ɛala.* We're looking for rooms. *ɛam nfatteš ɛala ʔuwaḍ ləl-ʔəžra.*

**He's always looking for trouble. *bixaaneq ḥatta xyaalo.*

to look forward to - *tšawwaq la-.* We're looking

forward to our vacation. *Eam nətšawwaq la-fərṣətna.* -- I'm looking forward to meeting you. *ʔana mətšawweq əktiir ʔəštəmeE fiik.*

to look on - *tfarraž.* I was just looking on. *ʔana kənt mətfarrež bass.*

**They look on her as a stranger. *byəEtəbruuha ġariibe.*

look out! - *ʔoEa* (f. *ʔoEi* pl. *ʔoEu*), *ʔəṣḥa* (f. *ʔəṣḥi* pl. *ʔəṣḥu*), *diir baalak* (f. *diiri baalek* pl. *diiru baalkon*).

to look out on - *ṭall (ə ə) Eala, ʔašraf Eala.* The big window looks out on a garden. *š-šəbbaak l-əkbiir biṭəll Eala žneene.*

to look over - *faḥaṣ (a faḥəṣ//nfaḥaṣ).* Will you look over these papers? *Emeel maEruuf fḥaṣ-li hal-əwraaq.*

to look up - **1.** *rafaE (a rafəE) raaso.* He didn't even look up when I called him. *ḥatta maa rafaE raaso waqət ṣaraxt-əllo.* **2.** *zaar (u zyaara).* Look me up some time, won't you? *zuurni waqət bišəḥḥ-əllak ʔiza bətriid.* **3.** *raažaE, ṭṭallaE Eala.* I have to look up this word in a dictionary. *laazem raažeE hal-kəlme bəl-qaamuus.* **4.** *tḥassan.* Things are beginning to look up. *l-ʔawḍaaE badet tətḥassan.*

**Every boy needs someone to look up to. *kəll ṣabi laazmo šaxəṣ ykən-lo qədwe.*

lookout - *raqiib* pl. *rəqaba.* A lookout was placed on every hill. *ḥaṭṭu raqiib Eala kəll raas haḍabe.*

**It's your lookout now. *ʔənte ṣṭəfel la-ḥaalak hallaq.*

to be on the lookout for - *xalla Eeeno Eala, ṭṭallaE Eala.* I'll be on the lookout for you. *bxalli Eeeni Ealeek* or *raḥa bəṭṭallaE Ealeek.*

loom - *nool* pl. *nwaal.*

loophole - *maxraž* pl. *maxaarež, maxlaṣ* pl. *maxaaleṣ.* Many loopholes have been left in the law. *fii maxaarež ktiire b-hal-qaanuun.*

loose - **1.** *mərxi*.* The button is loose. *z-zərr mərxi.* -- The nail is loose. *l-bəsmaar mərxi.* -- You must have a screw loose! *fii bərġi mərxi b-Eaqlak!* **2.** *faltaan.* Is the dog allowed to run around loose? *btətərku l-kalb yruuḥ la-hoon w-hoon faltaan?* -- She has a loose tongue. *lsaana faltaan.* **3.** *farəṭ* (invar.). Do you sell the coffee loose or in packages? *bətbiiE əl-bənn farəṭ ʔaw bəl-baakeetaat?*

to cut loose - *ṣaar (i) harž w-marž.* The boys cut loose the minute the teacher steps out of the room. *b-daqiiqet-ma yətrok əl-ʔəstaaz əṣ-ṣaff l-əwlaad biṣiiru harž w-marž.*

to **loosen** - *ḥalḥal.* Can you loosen this screw? *btəqder əṭḥalḥel hal-bərġi?* -- I want to loosen my shoelaces. *bəddi ḥalḥel šawwaaṭaat ṣabbaaṭi.*

loot - *ġaniime* pl. *ġanaayem.* The thieves hid the loot in a tree. *l-ḥaraamiyye xabbu l-ġaniime b-šažara.*

to loot - *nahab (a nahəb//ntahab).* The enemy looted the town. *l-ʔaEdaaʔ nahabu l-balad.*

lopsided - *maEwuuž.* The picture's hanging lopsided. *ṣ-ṣuura mEallaqa maEwuuže.*

to **lose** - **1.** *ḍayyaE, ḍawwaE.* I lost my pencil again. *ḍayyaEət qalami marra taanye* or ****Eaad əl-qalam ḍaaE mənni kamaan.** -- After a few steps he lost his balance. *baEəd kam xaṭwe ḍayyaE tawaazno* (or ****ḍaaE tawaazno**). **2.** *xəser (a xsaara), fəqed (a fəqdaan//nfaqad).* He lost his entire fortune during the war. *xəser kəll sáruto ʔiyyaam əl-ḥarb.* -- They lost a son in the war. *fəqdu walad bəl-ḥarb.* **3.** *xəser.* I'm afraid he'll lose the game. *xaayə́f-lak yəxṣar əl-ləEbe.* **4.** *xaṣṣar.* This speech lost him the election. *hal-xəṭbe xaṣṣarə́to l-ʔəntixaab.* **5.** *qaṣṣar, ʔaxxar.* My watch loses three minutes a day. *saaEti Eam əṭqaṣṣer tlatt daqaayeq kəll yoom.*

**I'm losing my hair. *Eam əyhərr šaEri.*

**He lost his life in the fire. *maat bəl-ḥariiqa.*

**I've lost all my strength. *ḥaṭṭet kəll quwwti.*

**If you leave soda water standing it will lose its strength. *ʔiza bətxalli ṣ-ṣooda qaaEde bətruuḥ quwwə́ta.*

**I've lost sight of him lately. *maa Eədt šəfto b-hal-ʔiyyaam.*

**I lost track of them after the war. *nqaṭEet ʔaxbaarhon Eanni baEd əl-ḥarb.*

lost - **1.** *ḍaayeE, mafquud.* I hope you'll find the lost object again. *nšaaḷḷa tlaaqi l-ġaraḍ əḍ-ḍaayeE.* — We'll never make up for this lost opportunity. *b-ḥayaatna maa mnəqder nEawweḍ Ean hal-fərṣa ḍ-ḍaayEa.* **2.** *xaaser, xasraan.* It was a lost game from the very beginning. *kaanet qaḍiyye xaaṣra mn əl-ʔasaas.* **3.** *ġarqaan.* He was lost in thought. *kaan ġarqaan bət-tafkiir.*

**For heaven's sake, don't look like a lost sheep! *ḥaaže baqa tkuun mətəl yalli mḍawweE ḥmaaret xaalto!*

**Since his wife's death he's completely lost. *mən waqət maatet marto maa Eaad yəṭlaE əb-ʔiido šii.*

to be or **get lost** - **1.** *ḍaaE (i ḍyaaEa).* My shirt was lost in the laundry. *qamiiṣi ḍaaE bəl-maṣbaġa.* -- I hope nothing is lost in the moving. *nšaaḷḷa maa yḍiiE šii bən-naqle.* -- I'm completely lost in this maze of details. *ḍəEət tamaaman b-kətret hat-tafṣiilaat.* **2.** *raaḥ (u ə), ḍaaE.* My things got lost in the fire. *raaḥet əġraaḍi bəl-ḥariiqa.* **3.** *ḍaaE, taah (u tawahaan).* Don't get lost on your way home! *ʔəṣḥa ḍḍiiE əb-ṭariiqak Eal-beet!*

to lose one's temper - *ġəḍeb (a ġaḍab), ġtaaẓ, ḥəmeq (a ḥamqa).* He loses his temper easily. *byəġḍab b-sərEa.*

to lose one's way - *ḍaaE (i ḍyaaEa), taah (u tawahaan).* Don't lose your way! *ʔəṣḥa ḍḍiiE!*

loser - *xaṣraan* pl. *-iin.*

loss - **1.** *ḍyaaEa* pl. *-aat.* The loss of a cheap watch like that is not worth all this excitement. *ḍyaaEet saaEa rxiiṣa mətəl hayye maa bədda kəll haḍ-ḍažže.* **2.** *xṣaara* pl. *xaṣaayer.* They suffered heavy losses. *ṣaabə́ton xaṣaayer faadḥa.* — I sold the house at a loss. *bəEt əl-beet b-əxṣaara.*

to be at a loss - *ḥtaar.* He's never at a loss for an excuse. *huwwe maa byəḥtaar ʔabadan ʔiza laazmo šii Eəzər.* -- She's never at a loss for an answer. *maa btəḥtaar ʔabadan ʔiza laazə́ma šii žawaab.* -- I'm at a loss to explain his absence. *ʔana məḥtaar fasser ġeebto.*

lot - **1.** *šaqfet~* (pl. *šəqaf~*) *ʔarḍ.* How big is your lot? *qəddeeš masaaḥet šaqfet ʔarḍak?* **2.** *ḥaẓẓ, naṣiib.* I don't envy his lot. *maa bəḥəsdo Eala ḥaẓẓo.* **3.** *šaḥne* pl. *-aat.* I'll send the books in three separate lots. *bəbEə́t-lak əl-kətəb Eala tlətt šaḥnaat.*

**He's a bad lot. *ḅaḅa ḥasan huwwe.*

**They are a fine lot. *hənne ʔərṭet ḅaḅa ḥasan Eal-maṣḅuuṭ.*

lots of - *ktiir əktiir.* She has lots of money. *Eanda maṣaari ktiir əktiir.* -- We had lots of fun at the dance. *tsalleena ktiir əktiir bəl-ḥafle r-raaqṣa.*

a lot - **1.** *ktiir.* We like him a lot. *mənḥəbbo ktiir.* **2.** *b-əktiir.* She's a lot better than people think. *hiyye ʔaḥsan b-əktiir məm-ma byəftəkruuha n-naas.*

a lot of - *ktiir.* I still have a lot of work. *ləssa Ealiyyi šəġl əktiir.*

to draw lots - *ḍarab (o ḍarəb) qərEa, Eəmel qərEa.* Let's draw lots. *xalliina nəḍrob qərEa.*

loud - **1.** *Eaali.* She has a loud, unpleasant voice. *ʔəlha ṣooṭ Eaali bəšeE.* **2.** *b-ṣooṭ Eaali.* Don't talk so loud! *laa təḥki b-ṣooṭ Eaali heek!* **3.** *mbahraž, žaareḥ.* I don't like loud colors. *maa bḥəbb l-əlwaan l-əmbahraže.*

loudspeaker - *mkabber~* (pl. *-aat~*) *ṣooṭ, həbbarloor* pl. *-aat.*

to **lounge around** - *tkaslan.* I like to lounge around the house on Sundays. *bḥəbb ʔətkaslan bəl-beet yoom əl-ʔaḥad.*

louse - *qamle* coll. *qaməl* pl. *-aat.*

love - *ḥəbb.* Love is blind. *l-ḥəbb ʔaEma.*

**You can't get it for love or money. *maa btəqder təḥṣal Ealeeha laa b-ərxiiṣ w-laa b-ġaali.*

in love - *Eašqaan, ṭaabeṣ bəl-ġaraam.* He must be in love. *laazem ykuun Eašqaan.*

to fall in love with - *waqeE (-yəqaE* and *-yuuqaE wquuE) əb-ġaraam~...* He's fallen in love with her. *waaqeE əb-ġaraama.* — The two met and fell in love. *t-tneen šaafu baEḍon w-waqEu b-ġaraam baEḍon.*

to love - **1.** *ḥabb (ə ḥəbb//nḥabb),* (passionately) *Eəšeq (a Eəšəq//nEašaq).* He loves her very much. *biḥəbba ktiir əktiir* or *byəEšə́qa ktiir.* **2.** *ḥabb.* I love apples. *bḥəbb ət-təffaaḥ.* -- I love to dance. *ya ʔaḷḷa šuu bḥəbb ʔərqoṣ!*

**Would you like a cup of coffee? - I'd love one! *šaay Eala baalak taaxod fənžaan qahwe? - ʔaḥabb Eala qalbi!*

lovely - *ktiir ḥəlu.* They have a lovely home. *Eandon beet əktiir ḥəlu.* -- That was a lovely evening! *waḷḷa kaanet əs-sahra ktiir ḥəlwe.*

lover - *Eašiiq* pl. *Eəššaaq, maEšuuq* pl. *-iin.*

low - **1.** *waaṭi.* Do you want shoes with high or low heels? *bəddek kəndra b-kaEb Eaali walla waaṭi?* — He made a low bow. *nḥana ḥanye waaṭye.* -- She spoke in a low voice. *ḥaket əb-ṣooṭ waaṭi.* -- That was low of him. *hal-Eamal kaan waaṭi mənno.* -- He always gets low marks. *daayman byaaxod Ealaamaat*

waatye. -- I have a low opinion of him. *Eandi fəkra waatye Eanno.* 2. *waati, xafiif.* His pulse is low. *nabdo waati.* -- You have very low blood pressure. *fii Eandak dagt damm waati ktiir.*
**Our funds are running low. *ʔamwaalna Eala wašak təxloṣ.*
**That plane is flying too low. *haṭ-ṭayyaara mwaṭṭye ktiir ᵊktiir.*
**The sun is quite low already. *š-šamᵊs ṣaaret maayle ləl-ᵊġruub.*
**Put the car in low (gear). *xalli s-sayyaara Eal-brəmyeer.*
**I feel very low today. *ʔana haaṭeṭ ᵊl-yoom.*
lower - 1. *ʔawṭa.* This chair is lower than that one. *hal-kərsi ʔawṭa mən hadaak.* 2. *taḥtaani*.* Put it on the lower shelf. *ḥəṭṭa Ear-raff ᵊt-taḥtaani.*
to lower - 1. *nazzal.* Lower the lifeboats. *nazzlu ġawaareb ᵊn-nažaat.* -- Please lower the blinds. *balla nazzel ᵊš-šarraaraat.* 2. *waṭṭa.* He lowered his voice when he saw her come in. *waṭṭa ṣooṭo waqᵊt šaafha žaaye.* — He lowered himself in their eyes. *waṭṭa ḥaalo qəddaamon.* 3. *xaffaḍ, nazzal, waṭṭa.* They will lower the prices some day, I'm sure. *ʔakiid ləssa bixaffḍu l-ʔasEaar šii yoom.*
loyal - *məxleṣ.* I've always been a loyal friend, haven't I? *kənᵊt daayman ṣaaḥeb məxleṣ, mu heek?* — You couldn't have a more loyal friend. *muu məmken ykən-lak ṣaaḥeb ʔaxlaṣ mən heek.* -- He has always been loyal to the government. *huwwe daayman kaan məxleṣ ləl-ᵊḥkuume.*
loyalty - *ʔəxlaaṣ, wafaaʔ.* You can depend on his loyalty. *btəqder təEtəmed Eala ʔəxlaaṣo.* -- Nobody questioned his loyalty to the government. *maa ḥada šakk ᵊb-ʔəxlaaṣo ləl-ᵊḥkuume.*
to **lubricate** - *šaḥḥam*/*tšaḥḥam.* Please lubricate the car. *balla šaḥḥəm-li s-sayyaara.*
lubrication - *tašḥiim.*
lucid - 1. *waaḍeḥ.* He gave a lucid summary of the discussion. *Eaṭa muužaz waaḍeḥ ləl-ᵊmnaaqaše.* 2. *ṣaafi.* Even the insane have their lucid moments. *ḥatta l-mažaniin btəžiihon ʔawqaat ṣaafye.*
luck - *ḥaẓẓ, baxt.* My luck has changed. *nqalab ḥaẓẓi.* -- Now you try your luck! *žarreb ḥaẓẓak ʔənte baqa!* -- It's not merely a matter of luck. *l-masʔale muu masʔalt ḥaẓẓ bass.* -- It was his (good) luck to be chosen. *kaan mən (ḥəsᵊn) ḥaẓẓo ʔənnon xtaarúu.* -- That was bad luck! *kaan haada ḥaẓẓ Eaaṭel!*
**Did you have any luck! *twaffaqᵊt šii?*
**Good luck! *ʔaḷḷa maEak!* or *mwaffaq nšaaḷḷa!*
**I wish you all the luck in the world. *bətmannda-lak kəll xeer.*
in luck - *maḥẓuuẓ.* You're in luck! *ʔənte maḥẓuuẓ.*
out of luck - *muu maḥẓuuẓ.* I'm out of luck! *ʔana maa-li maḥẓuuẓ.*
luckily - *mən ḥəsn˜ ᵊl-ḥaẓẓ, la-ḥəsn˜ ᵊl-ḥaẓẓ.* Luckily she didn't see me. *mən ḥəsn ᵊl-ḥaẓẓ maa šaafətni.*
lucky - 1. *saEiid.* It was a lucky coincidence. *kaanet mṣaadafe saEiide.* 2. *maḥẓuuẓ.* You can consider yourself lucky. *ʔənte laazem təEtəber ḥaalak maḥẓuuẓ.* -- You're a lucky fellow. *ʔənte waaḥed maḥẓuuẓ.* -- You lucky dog! *maašaaḷḷa qaddeešak maḥẓuuẓ!*
to be lucky - *nḥaẓẓ.* You were lucky! *nḥaẓẓeet waḷḷa!*
lucrative - *mərbeḥ, mdərr.* He runs a lucrative business. *Eando tižaara mərᵊbḥa.*
ludicrous - *məḍḥek.* We found ourselves in a ludicrous situation. *nḥaṭṭeena b-ḥaale məḍᵊḥke.*
luggage - *Eafᵊš, šanaati* (pl.). We stowed our luggage on the back seat of the car. *ḥaṭṭeena Eafᵊšna bᵊl-maqEad ᵊl-warraani tabaE ᵊs-sayyaara.*
lukewarm - *faater.* Take a lukewarm bath. *xood ḥammaam faater.* -- He's very lukewarm about the whole thing. *huwwe faater naaḥ hal-masʔale kəlla.*
lull - *xmuud.* We went out during the lull in the storm. *ṭləEna la-barra b-ᵊxmuud ᵊl-Eaaṣfe.*
to lull - *xammad, sakkan.* Her singing lulled the boy to sleep. *ġnaaha xammad ᵊl-walad ḥatta naam.*
lullaby - *tahliil* pl. *-aat.*
lumber - *xašab.* How much lumber will be needed for the bookshelves? *qaddeeš laazəmna xašab la-rfuuf ᵊl-kətᵊb?*
lump - 1. *kətle* pl. *kətal, kabtuule* pl. *kabatiil.* What are you going to do with that lump of clay? *šuu bəddak tsaawi b-hal-kətlet ᵊṭ-ṭiin?* 2. *dəmmale* pl. *damaamel.* He has a big lump on his forehead. *fii dəmmale kbiire b-ᵊžbiino.*
lump of sugar - *qəṭEet˜* (pl. *qəṭaE˜*) *səkkar.* I take only one lump of sugar in my coffee. *baaxod qəṭEet səkkar waaḥde bass ᵊb-qahᵊwti.*
lump sugar - *səkkar šəqaf, səkkar mqaṭṭaE.* Do you have lump sugar? *fii Eandak səkkar šəqaf?*
lump sum - *mablaġ ʔəžmaali* pl. *mabaaleġ ʔəžmaaliyye, mablaġ šaqfe waaḥde.* You'll receive a lump sum of 1500 pounds. *btəqbaḍ-lak mablaġ ʔəžmaali ʔalf w-xams miit leera.*
lunar - *qamari*.*
lunatic - *mažnuun* pl. *mažaniin, madduub* pl. *mažadiib.* He's acting like a lunatic. *Eam yəštəġel šəġᵊl mažaniin.*
lunatic asylum - *məstašfa˜* (pl. *məstašfayaat˜*) *mažaniin.*
lunch - *ġada* pl. *ʔəġᵊdye.* It's time for lunch. *ṣaar waqt ᵊl-ġada.*
to lunch - *tġadda.* Will you lunch with me? *btətġadda maEi?*
lung - *riʔa* pl. *-aat.* His left lung was seriously affected. *riʔato š-šmaal kaanet mṣaabe ʔiṣaabe xaṭiira.* -- Your lungs are all right. *riʔateenak saalmiin maa fiihon šii.*
**The little fellow yelled at the top of his lungs. *ṭ-ṭəfl Eayyaṭ mən žuwwaat qalbo.*
to **lure** - *ʔaġra.* They lured him away from his work with a promise of money. *ʔaġrúu yaEṭúu maṣaari ḥatta yətrok šəġlo.*
to **lurk** - *trabbaṣ.* Who knows what dangers lurk in the darkness? *miin byaEref ġeer ʔaḷḷa šuu l-ʔaxṭaar ᵊl-mətrabbṣa bᵊl-Eətme?*
luxury - 1. *taraf, rafaaha.* They lived in unbelievable luxury. *Eaašu b-taraf maa byətsaddaq.* 2. *luks* (invar.). He rented one of the luxury apartments on the other end of town. *staʔžar šaqqa luks bᵊn-naaḥye t-taanye bᵊl-balad.*
lye - *qəli.*
lying - *kəzᵊb.* Lying won't get you anywhere. *l-kəzᵊb maa biwaṣṣlak la-šii.*

M

macaroni - *maEkaroone.*
mace - (spice) *žoozt˜ ᵊṭ-ṭiib.*
machine - *maakiina* pl. *-aat* and *makaayen, ʔaale* pl. *-aat.* The machine is working again. *l-maakiina ražEet təštəġel.* -- This store has a wide selection of machine parts. *hal-maxzan fii taškiile kbiire mən qəṭaE ᵊl-maakiinaat.*
machinery - 1. *maakiinaat* (pl.), *ʔaalaat* (pl.). The country imports a great deal of heavy machinery every year. *l-ᵊblaad btəstawred kammiyye kbiire mn ᵊl-maakiinaat ᵊs-saqiile kəll səne.* 2. *žihaaz* pl. *ʔažhize.* He knows the workings of the government machinery. *byaEref kiif byəštəġel žihaaz l-ᵊḥkuume.*
machine gun - *raššaaš(e)* pl. *-aat.*
mad - 1. *mažnuun* pl. *mažaniin.* He must be mad! *laazem ykuun mažnuun!* -- He drove like mad. *saaq mətl ᵊl-mažaniin.* 2. *kalbaan.* He was bitten by a mad dog. *Eaḍḍo kalᵊb kabbaan.*
**He was raving mad. *kaan Eam yfuur fawaraan mn ᵊl-ġeeẓ.*
to be mad about - 1. *žann (ə žnuun, žnaan) b-.* She's mad about him. *hiyye žaanne fii.* 2. *žann Eala, maat (u ø) Eala.* My boy is mad about ice cream. *ʔəbni bižənn Eal-buuẓa.*
to be mad at - *zəEel (a zaEal) mən.* She's mad at me again. *rəžEet zəElet mənni kamaan.*
to drive mad - *žannan.* This noise is driving me mad! *haḍ-ḍažže Eam ᵊdžannənni!*
**The heat is driving me mad. *š-šoob Eam yəhləkni* (or *Eam ymawwətni*).
madam - *madaam, xaanom.* Is somebody waiting on you, madam? *fii ḥada Eam yəxᵊdmek, yaa madaam?*
maddening: This noise is maddening. *haḍ-ḍoože bədžannen.* -- He has the maddening habit of never letting you finish your sentence. *fii Eaade bədžannen maa bixalliik ᵊtxalleṣ kalaamak.*

madhouse - *Eaṣfuuriyye* pl. *-aat.* It's always like a madhouse in here. *hal-maḥall daayman mət*ᵊ*l Eaṣfuuriyye.*

madman - *maǰnuun* pl. *maǰaniin.*

magazine - **1.** *maǰalle* pl. *-aat.* Where can I buy the magazine? *mneen bəštə́ri l-maǰalle?* **2.** *məšṭ* pl. *mšaaṭ.* How many bullets does the magazine hold? *kam ṛṣaaṣa byəsaE hal-məšṭ?*

magic - **1.** *saEbara* pl. *-aat.* Do you expect me to do it by magic? *məṇṭəẓərni ʔaEmə́la bᵊz-zaEbara?* **2.** *səḥᵊr.* The magic of his smile puts everyone at ease. *səḥᵊr ʔəbtisaamto bixalli l-waaḥed yəšEor b-ʔərtiyaaḥ.* -- The door opened as if by magic. *l-baab nfataḥ kaʔənno fii səḥᵊr.* **3.** *səḥri*.* There's no magic formula for losing weight. *maa fii waṣfe səḥriyye la-tanqiiṣ ᵊl-wazᵊn.* **4.** *saaḥer, səḥri*.* He has a magic smile. *ʔəlo ʔəbtisaame saaḥra.*

magician - *mšaEweʒ* pl. *-iin.*

magistrate - *qaaḍi* pl. *qəḍaat.*

magnet - *maǧnaṭiiṣ* pl. *-aat.*

magnetic - *maǧnaṭiiṣi*.*

magnificent - **1.** *Eaẓiim.* You have a magnificent view from the top of the mountain. *fii Eandak manẓar Eaẓiim mən Eala raas ᵊǰ-ǰabal.* **2.** *faxᵊm.* The architecture of this city is magnificent. *binaayaat hal-madiine faxme.*

to **magnify** - *kabbar.* This lens magnifies six times. *hal-Eadase bətkabber sətt ʔaḍEaaf.*

magnifying glass - *mkabbra* pl. *-aat.* You can only see it with a magnifying glass. *maa btəqder ᵊtšuufa ʔəlla b-ᵊmkabbra.*

maid - *ṣaanEa* pl. *-aat* and *ṣənnaaE, xaadme* pl. *-aat, xaddaame* pl. *-aat.* We let our maid go. *xalaṣna mən ṣaanEətna.*

mail - *bariid, boosṭa.* The mail is delivered at four o'clock. *l-bariid byətwazzaE ᵊs-saaEa ʔarbEa.* -- Is there any mail for me? *fii ʔəli šii bariid?* -- The package will be sent to you by mail. *ṭ-ṭarᵊd biráḥ-lak bᵊl-bariid.*

mails - *bariid.* The mails were held up by the storm. *l-bariid ᵊtʔaxxar ᵊb-sabab ᵊl-Eaaṣfe.*

by return mail - *b-Eood(e)t˜ ᵊl-bariid, b-ᵊrǰuuE˜ ᵊl-bariid.* He answered by return mail. *ǰaawab b-Eoodt ᵊl-bariid.*

to mail - *ḥaṭṭ (ə ḥaṭaṭ) ... bᵊl-boosṭa* (or *bᵊl-bariid*). Did you mail that package? *ḥaṭṭeet hat-ṭarᵊd bᵊl-boosṭa?* -- Please mail the letter for me. *ḥəṭṭ-ə́lli hal-maktuub bᵊl-boosṭa, mən faḍlak.*

mailbox - *sanduuq˜* (pl. *sanadiiq˜*) *boosṭa.*

mailman - *bosṭaǰi* pl. *-iyye.*

main - **1.** *raʔiisi*.* That's one of our main problems. *hayye waaḥde mən mašaakəlna r-raʔiisiyye.* -- Did you inquire at the main office? *staxbarᵊt mn ᵊl-maktab ᵊr-raʔiisi?* **2.** *qasṭal˜* (pl. *qasaaṭel˜*) *ʔəmmaaye, qasṭal raʔiisi.* The main has burst. *qasṭal ᵊl-ʔəmmaaye nfaxat.*

main thing - *ʔahamm˜ šii.* You've forgotten the main thing. *nsiit ʔahamm šii.*

in the main - **1.** *Eala wažh˜ ᵊl-Eumuum.* The discussion revolved in the main around two questions. *Eala wažh ᵊl-Eumuum l-ᵊmnaaqaše daaret ḥawaali masʔalteen.* **2.** *bᵊl-ʔəǰmaal.* I agree with him in the main. *ʔana mattə́feq maEo bᵊl-ʔəǰmaal.*

mainly - *Eal-ǧaaleb, bᵊl-ʔaktar.* He comes mainly on Tuesdays. *byəǰi Eal-ǧaaleb yoom ᵊt-talaata.* -- He's mainly handling administrative matters. *bᵊl-ʔaktar biEaaleǰ ʔumuur ʔidaariyye.*

to **maintain** - **1.** *ʔakkad.* He maintains that he was there. *Eam yʔakked ʔənno kaan ᵊhniik.* **2.** *ḥaafaẓ Eala.* They can't maintain their present living standard. *maa fiihon yḥaafẓu Eala məstáwa l-maEiiše yalli Eaayšiin Ealeeha hallaq.*

maintenance - *ṣyaane, mḥaafaẓa (Eala).* Maintenance of the car alone costs me fifty pounds a month. *ṣyaanet ᵊs-sayyaara* (or *l-ᵊmḥaafaẓa Eas-sayyaara*) *waḥda bətkallə́fni xamsiin leera bᵊš-šahr.*

major - **1.** *raaʔed* pl. *rəwwaad.* Has anyone seen the Major? *ḥada šaaf ᵊr-raaʔed?* **2.** *taxaṣṣoṣ, ʔəxtiṣaaṣ.* What's your major in college? *šuu taxaṣṣuṣak bᵊl-kəlliyye?* **3.** *raʔiisi*.* Our major aim at present is industrialization. *hadafna r-raʔiisi bᵊl-waqt ᵊl-ḥaaḍer huwwe t-taṣniiE.* **4.** *maǰoor.* The piece is in F major. *l-maqṭuuEa bi-faa maǰoor.*

major part - **1.** *məEẓam, ʔaktar.* The major part of my income goes for rent. *məEẓam daxli biruuḥ ʔəǰret beet.* **2.** *door raʔiisi* pl. *ʔadwaar raʔiisiyye.* He played a major part in this. *ləEeb door raʔiisi b-hal-qaḍiyye.*

majority - **1.** *ʔaksariyye, ʔaǧlabiyye.* The majority was against the proposal. *l-ʔaksariyye kaanet ḍədd ᵊl-ʔəqtiraaḥ.* **2.** *məEẓam, ʔaktar, ʔaksariyye.* The majority of the students were sick. *məEẓam ᵊṭ-ṭəllaab kaanu marḍa.*

make - **1.** *maarka* pl. *-aat.* What make is your radio? *šuu maarket ᵊr-raadyo tabaEak?* **2.** *modeel* pl. *-aat, maarka* pl. *-aat.* What make is your car? *šuu modeel* (or *maarkèt*) *sayyaartak?*

to make - **1.** *Eəmel (-yaEmel Eamal//nEamal), saawa//tsaawa.* Shall I make tea or coffee? *ʔaEmel qahwe wəlla šaay?* -- This chair is made of very expensive wood. *hal-kərsi maEmuul mən xašab ᵊktiir ǧaali.* -- Did you make the cake yourself? *saaweeti l-gaato waḥdek?* -- I'm having a suit made for myself. *Eam saawi* (or ***faṣṣel*) *ṭaqᵊm ʔəli.* -- You'll have to make a few changes. *laazem ᵊtsaawi šwayyet taEdiilaat.* -- They made him chairman. *Eəmlúu raʔiis.* — Money alone doesn't make you a great man. *l-maṣaari waḥda maa btaEᵊmlak rəǰǰaal Eaẓiim.* -- He made a friend of an enemy. *Eəmel mən Eaduww ṣaaḥeb.* -- They made starch from wheat. *Eəmlu naša mn ᵊl-qamᵊḥ.* -- She made a long story out of this incident. *Eəmlet mən hal-ḥaadse qəṣṣa kbiire.* -- I think you're making a mountain out of a molehill. *b-raʔyi Eam taEmel mən ḥabbe qəbbe.* — He's made a good reputation for himself. *saawa la-ḥaalo səmEa mniiḥa.* — The car makes at least 90 kilometers per hour. *s-sayyaara btaEmel təsEiin kiilomətr bᵊs-saaEa Eal-qaliili.* -- Five times four makes twenty. *xamse b-ʔarbEa bətsaawi Eəšriin.* **2.** *ṣanaE (a ṣənᵊE), fabrak, Eəmel, saawa.* What do they make in that factory? *šuu byəṣnaEu b-hal-maṣnaE?* **3.** *ṭaleE (a ø).* He would make a good father. *mbayyen Ealée byəṭlaE ʔabb ᵊmniiḥ.* **4.** *maraq (o mruuq) mən, faat (u foote) b-.* Do you think the piano will make the window? *btəftə́ker l-ᵊbyaano byəmroq mn ᵊš-šəbbaak?* **5.** *ləḥeq (a lḥuuq), laḥḥaq.* Do you think we'll make the train? *btəEtə́qed mnəlḥaq ᵊt-treen?* **6.** *ṭabb (ə ø) b-.* If we start out early, we can make Homs by evening. *ʔiza mšiina bakkiir mənṭabb ᵊb-ḥəmᵊṣ nawaaḥi l-masa.* **7.** *dabbar.* I'll never make it! *maa byəṭlaE ᵊb-ʔiidi dabbə́ra ʔabadan!* -- He made it! *dabbára waḷḷa!* **8.** *ṭaalaE, saḥab (a saḥᵊb), Eəmel, saawa.* How much do you make a week? *qaddeeš bəṭṭaaleE bᵊǰ-ǰəmEa?* **9.** *ǧaṣab (o ǧaṣᵊb), ǰabar (o/e ǰabᵊr).* Nobody can make me go there. *maa ḥada fii yəǧṣəbni ruuḥ la-hniik.* **10.** *xalla.* That conversation has made me change my mind. *hal-ᵊmḥaadase xallətni ǧayyer raʔyi.*

**He's got it made. *ʔaḷḷa waṣṣalo.*

**What do you make of that? *šuu btəfham mən haš-šii?* or *šuu bətfasser haš-šii?*

**I can make neither head nor tail of this story. *maa-li fahmaan hal-qəṣṣa ʔawwə́la mən ʔaaxə́ra.*

**You made a good choice. *ntaqeet ᵊš-šii l-maẓbuuṭ.*

**She made a clean breast of what she had done. *Etarfet ᵊb-kəll šii saawto.*

**He made a complete confession. *Etaraf ʔəEtiraaf kaamel.*

**Does it make any difference? *btəfreq šii?*

**It doesn't make any difference! *maa Elee šii!* or *maEleeš!*

**It makes no difference in my plans. *maa biʔasser Eala mašaariiEi šii.*

**If you do that you'll surely make a fool of yourself. *ʔiza btaEmel heek bətbahdel ḥaalak ʔakiid.*

**He won't make a fool of me a second time. *maa fii yəstaḥmərni marra taanye.*

**Don't make such a fuss! *ḥaaǰe tkabbə́ra!* or *ḥaaǰe ṭṭabbel w-ᵊdzammer fiiha!*

**I wish you wouldn't make such a fuss over him! *ya-reetak maa ṭṭabṭə́b-lo hal-qadd!*

**He'll never make a go of it. *b-ḥayaato maa byətwaffaq ᵊb-haš-šii.*

**How does he make his living? *šloon byərbaḥ maEiišto?*

**You made a terrible mistake! *ǧləṭṭ ǧalṭa faẓiiEa!*

**Do you think he'll make a speech after dinner? *šloon šaayef? byəlqi kəlme baEd ᵊl-Eaša?*

**She is only making believe that she doesn't know. *Eaamle ḥaala ʔənno maa btaEref.*

**Nobody can make me believe that. *maa ḥada byəqder yəqnəEni b-haš-šii.*

**Why don't we make friends? *leeš maa mnətṣaaḥab?*

**He doesn't make friends easily. *maa biṣaaḥeb ᵊn-naas b-ᵊshuule.*

**I made good the damage. *εawwaḍᵊt εan ᵊḍ-ḍarar.*
**He'll never make good! *b-ḥayaato maa byətwaffaq!*
**They don't seem to make any headway at all. *ẓ-ẓaaher maa εam yətqaddamu bᵊl-marra.*
**When will the results be made known? *ʔeemta raḥa yəεᵊlnu n-nataayež?*
**She made known her intention to leave her husband. *kašfet εan niyyə́ta ʔənno bədda tətrok žooza.*
**He makes no bones about his stand. *maa bixalli šii mxabba b-mawqə́fo.*
**They made peace again. *režεu tṣaalaḥu taani marra.*
**Why don't you make peace with him? *leeš maa bətṣaalḥo?*
**He made the rounds of the house before he locked it. *daar ᵊl-beet kəllo qabᵊl-ma yəqᵊflo.*
**Does this make sense to you? *haš-šii šaayfo maεquul šii?*
**We can make time if we take the side road. *mnəxtə́ṣer waqᵊt ʔiza ʔaxadna ṭ-ṭariiq ᵊž-žannaabi.*
to have something made – *waṣṣa εala šii.* I'd like to have a table made for this room. *bəddi waṣṣi εala ṭaawle la-hal-ʔuuḍa.*
**Where can I have a suit made around here? *ween fiini faṣṣel badle hoon?*
**I'd like to have my bed made no later than 10 o'clock. *bəddi taxti yṣiir qabl ᵊs-saaεa εašara.*
to make as if or **as though** – *εəmel ḥaalo (kaʔənno).* He made as if he didn't understand me. *εəmel ḥaalo kaʔənno maa fəhem εaliyyi.* -- I made as though I were asleep. *εmәlᵊt ḥaali (kaʔənni) naayem.*
to make off – *fələt (a falataan), harab (o harab), šammaε l-ᵊftiile.* They've made off with our car. *fəltu b-sayyaarətna.*
to make out – **1.** *fakfak.* Can you make out the date on the postmark? *btəqder ᵊtfakfek ᵊt-taariix yalli εala damġet ᵊl-boosṭa?* **2.** *mayyaz.* Can you make out who's coming there? *btəqder ᵊtmayyez miin žaaye mn ᵊhniik?* **3.** *malla, εabba.* Have you made out the application blank? *malleet ᵊṭ-ṭalab?* **4.** *ṭaleε (a ∅).* How did you make out yesterday? *šloon ṭlaεᵊt ᵊmbaarḥa?* or ***šuu kaanet ᵊn-natiiže maεak ᵊmbaarḥa?* **5.** *saawa, εəmel (-yaεmel εamal).* Please make out our bill. *mən faḍlak saawī-lna l-faatuura.* -- Make out the check payable to me. *εmeel ᵊš-šakk la-ʔamri.* **6.** *fəhem (a fəhm).* Can you make out what he means? *fahmaan šuu εam yəqṣoḍ?*
to make over – **1.** *qalab (e qalᵊb//nqalab).* Do you know of anyone who could make over this old coat for me? *btaεrə́f-li ḥada fii yaqlə́b-li hal-manṭo l-εatiiq?* **2.** *ṭawwab.* Her father made over the farm to her. *ʔabuuha ṭawwáb-ᵊlha l-mazraεa.*
to make up – **1.** *saawa, εəmel (-yaεmel εamal).* Make up a list of all the things you need. *saawi liista b-kəll l-ᵊġraaḍ yalli laazə́mtak.* -- Can you make up a bouquet of roses for me? *fiik ᵊtsaawī-li baaqet ward?* **2.** *εəmel, šakkal, rakkab.* Make up a sentence with the word 'no'. *εmeel žəmle fiiha kəlmet "laʔ".* **3.** *katab (o ktaabe), ʔallaf.* Did he make up the speech himself? *huwwe katab ᵊl-xiṭaab la-ḥaalo?* **4.** *fabrak, xtaraε, laffaq.* Did you make up the story? *ʔənte yalli fabrakt ᵊl-qəṣṣa?* **5.** *ʔallaf, šakkal.* A technician and three assistants make up the entire staff. *fanni waaḥed w-tlətt ᵊmsaaεdiin biʔallfu heeʔet l-ᵊmwaẓẓafiin kəlla.* **6.** *εawwaḍ εan.* I'll make up the hour I lost tomorrow. *bεawweḍ bəkra εan ᵊs-saaεa yalli ḍayyaεta.* **7.** *tṣaalaḥu.* They've made up again. *rəžεu tṣaalaḥu mn ᵊždiid.*
**I made up my mind not to accept the offer. *εtamadt maa ʔəqbal ᵊl-εarᵊḍ.*
**Come on, make up your mind! *yaḷḷa, εtəmed baqa: ya heek ya heek!* or *xallə́sna baqa: εtəmed!*
**We'll have to make up our minds soon. *laazem nəεtə́med ᵊb-εažale: ya heek ya heek.*
**I can't make up my mind. *ʔana məḥtaar maa-li εaaref šuu saawi.*
**I haven't made up my mind yet. *ləssaani mxooṭar.*
to make oneself up – **1.** *tḥammaret w-ᵊtboodaret, tġandaret.* She always makes herself up very carefully before she goes out. *daayman ᵊbtətḥammar w-ᵊbtətboodar εala ʔaaxer daqqa qabᵊl-ma təṭlaε mn ᵊl-beet.* **2.** *ḥaṭṭ maakiyaaž.* The clown is making himself up for the afternoon show. *l-ᵊmharrež εam yḥəṭṭ maakiyaaž mənšaan ḥaflet baεd ᵊḍ-ḍəhᵊr.*
to make up for – **1.** *ṣallaḥ.* You can't make up for past mistakes. *maa btəqder ᵊtṣalleḥ ᵊl-ġalṭaat ᵊl-maaḍye.* **2.** *εawwaḍ εan.* I have to make up for the lost time. *laazem εawweḍ εan ᵊl-waqt ᵊḍ-ḍaayeε.*

makeshift – *mwaqqat.* This is just a makeshift arrangement. *haada tartiib ᵊmwaqqat bass.*
make-up – **1.** *ḥəmra w-boodra, maakiyaaž.* She uses an awful lot of make-up. *btəḥəṭṭ ḥəmra w-boodra šii ktiir.* -- Shall I put on a little more make-up? *ḥəṭṭ maakiyaaž ʔaktar šwayye?* **2.** *ṭabiiεa* pl. *ṭabaayeε, ṭabᵊε* pl. *ʔaṭbaaε.* It's not in his make-up to lie. *muu mən ṭabiiεto yəkzeb.*
makings: The boy has the makings of an actor. *l-walad maxluuq ykuun mumassel.* -- The situation has the makings of a major crisis. *l-waḍᵊε fii kəll ᵊl-εawaamel yalli bətʔaddi la-ʔazme xaṭiira.*
malaria – *malaarya.*
male – *dakar* pl. *dkuura.* Is that dog a male or a female? *hal-kalb dakar walla ʔəntaaye?*
male nurse – *mmarreḍ* pl. *-iin.*
malicious – *xabiis* pl. *xəbasa.* That was a malicious remark. *hayy kaanet ᵊmlaaḥaẓa xabiise.* -- Malicious people might say that ... *n-naas ᵊl-xəbasa məmken yquulu ʔənno ...*
malignant – *xabiis.* He died from a malignant tumor. *maat mən waram xabiis.*
Malta – *maalṭa.*
Maltese – *maalṭi**.
mammoth – **1.** *žabbaar, ḍaxᵊm.* They are embarking on a mammoth project. *mbaašriin b-mašruuε žabbaar.* **2.** *maamuut* pl. *-aat.* There is the skeleton of a mammoth on display at the museum. *fii heekal maamuut maεruuḍ bᵊl-matḥaf.*
man – **1.** *rəžžaal* pl. *ržaal, zalame* pl. *zəlᵊm.* Who's that man? *miin har-rəžžaal?* -- He's a very capable man. *huwwe zalame ktiir šaaṭer.* -- Tell the men to unload the furniture. *quul lər-ržaal ynazzlu l-mobiilya.* **2.** *nafar* pl. *ʔanfaar, žəndi* pl. *žnuud.* One officer and four men volunteered. *ṭṭawwaεu ẓaabeṭ w-ʔarbaε ʔanfaar.* **3.** *l-ʔənsaan.* Man is a rational animal. *l-ʔənsaan ḥaywaan naaṭeq.*
**He's not the man for it. *huwwe muu qadd haš-šaġle.*
man in the street – *ražol~ ᵊš-šaareε.* What does the man in the street say about it? *šuu εam yquul ražol ᵊš-šaareε b-hal-masʔale?*
men's room – *tuwaleet lər-ržaal.*
to **manage** – **1.** *daar (i ʔidaara).* Who manages the plantation? *miin εam ydiir ᵊl-mazraεa?* -- He managed the store for six years. *daar ᵊl-maxzan məddet sətt ᵊsniin.* **2.** *dabbar.* How did you manage to get the tickets? *kiif dabbart ᵊdžiib ᵊt-tazaaker?* -- I can't manage the children. *muu ṭaaleε ᵊb-ʔiidi dabber l-ᵊwlaad.* -- Wasn't that cleverly managed? *šaayef qaddeeš mdabbara b-ḥənke!* **3.** *dabbar ḥaalo, maššа ḥaalo.* Can you manage on your salary? *btəqder ᵊddabber ḥaalak ᵊb-maεaašak?* -- We have to manage very carefully on our small salary. *laazem ndabber ḥaalna b-ʔəntibaah b-maεaašna l-qaliil.*
management – *ʔidaara* pl. *-aat.* I'm going to complain to the management. *raḥ ʔəštə́ki ləl-ʔidaara.*
manager – *mudiir* pl. *mədara.* I'd like to speak to the manager of this hotel. *bəddi ʔəḥki maε mudiir ᵊl-ʔoteel.*
**His wife is a good manager. *marto mdabbra mniiḥ.*
mandate – **1.** *tafwiiḍ* pl. *tafawiiḍ.* Has he a mandate from the people? *maεo tafwiiḍ mn ᵊš-šaεᵊb?* **2.** *ʔəntidaab* pl. *-aat.* In what year did the French mandate in Syria end? *b-ʔanu səne xalaṣ ᵊl-ʔəntidaab l-ᵊfrənsaawi b-suuriyya?*
**That country was a mandate for twenty years. *hal-ᵊblaad kaan məntádab εaleeha εəšriin səne.*
mandatory – *ʔəžbaari**. It is mandatory to submit a written application. *ʔəžbaari taqdiim ṭalab xaṭṭi.*
mandatory power – *dawle* (pl. *duwal*) *məntadabe.*
maneuver – *mnaawara* pl. *-aat.* They're holding military maneuvers along the border. *εam yaεᵊmlu mnaawaraat εaskariyye εala ṭuul l-ᵊḥduud.*
to **manhandle** – *ṭabbaš.* The gang manhandled him roughly. *l-ᵊεṣaabe ṭabbašə́to taṭbiiš.*
mania – *hawas.*
manifesto – *manifeesto* pl. *manifeestoyaat.*
mankind – *l-ʔənsaaniyye, l-bašariyye.*
man-made – *mən ṣanε~ ᵊl-ʔənsaan.*
manner – **1.** *ṭariiqa.* I liked the manner in which he went about the job. *εažbətni ṭ-ṭariiqa yalli məši fiiha b-haš-šəġᵊl.* **2.** *ṣuura.* He presented the case in an exaggerated manner. *εaraḍ ᵊl-qaḍiyye b-ṣuura fiiha ktiir ᵊmbaalaġa.*
in this manner, in that manner – **1.** *εala hal-mənwaal, εala haš-ṣuura.* Continue in this manner. *xalliik εala hal-mənwaal.* **2.** *b-haš-ṣuura, heek.* In this manner they managed to get the house

without paying a penny. *b-haṣ-ṣuura ʔaxadu l-beet bala-ma yədfaεu w-laa nḥaase.*

manners - *ʔadab.* She has no manners. *maa εandha ʔadab.* -- Don't you have any manners! *šuu hal-qəllet əl-ʔadab!* -- It's about time somebody taught the boy some manners. *ḥal-lo baqa ḥada yεallem hal-walad šwayyet ʔadab.*

manual - 1. *yadawi**. His manual skill is amazing. *mahaarto l-yadawiyye məḍəhše.* -- He's earning a living by manual labor. *biṭaaleε maεiišto b-εamal yadawi.* 2. *daftar˜* (pl. *dafaater˜*) *taεliimaat, daliil* pl. *dalaayel.* I'll have to consult the manual again. *laazem raažeε daftar ət-taεliimaat taani marra.* -- Look it up in the teacher's manual. *raažəεa b-daliil l-əmεallem.*

to **manufacture** - *ṣanaε (a ṣənəε, ṣanəε//nṣanaε).* What do they manufacture here? *šuu byəṣnaεu hoon?*

manufacturer - 1. *ṣaaḥeb˜ fabriika* pl. *ṣḥaab˜ fabaarek.* Many wealthy manufacturers live in this town. *fii ṣḥaab fabaarek ʔaġnya ktiir saakniin b-hal-balad.* 2. *məntež* pl. *-iin.* He is a well-known manufacturer of farm machinery. *huwwe məntež maεruuf ləl-ʔaalaat əz-ziraaεiyye.*

manure - *zəbəl.*

manuscript - 1. *maxṭuuṭ* pl. *-aat.* The library is said to have a large collection of manuscripts. *biquulu ʔənno l-maktabe fiiha mažmuuεet maxṭuuṭaat əkbiire.* 2. *nəsxa* (pl. *nəsax*) *ʔaṣliyye.* The manuscript should go to press no later than Wednesday. *n-nəsxa l-ʔaṣliyye laazem ətruuḥ εaṭ-ṭabəε qabəl yoom əl-ʔarbεa.*

many - *ktiir* (invar.), (with pl. of animate beings) *ktaar,* (with pl. of abstract nouns or inanimate things) *ktiire.* I have many reasons. *εandi ʔasbaab əktiir* (or *əktiire*). -- She has many relatives. *ʔəla qaraaybiin əktaar* (or *əktiir*).

many a - *ktiir mən* (with foll. pl.). Many a man owes his success to his wife. *ktiir mn ər-ržaal madyuuniin əb-nažaaḥon la-nəswaanhon.* -- Many a person has fallen for that already. *ktiir mn ən-naas sabaq w-ənxadaεu b-haš-šii.* -- I've passed here many a time. *maraqət mən hoon əktiir mn əl-marraat.*

a good many - *ktiir* (invar.). He knows a good many people there. *byaεref naas əktiir əhniik.* -- I've been there a good many times. *kənt əhniik marraat əktiir.*

a great many - *ktiir əktiir* (invar.). He has a great many books. *εando kətb əktiir əktiir.* -- He has done that a great many times. *εəmə́la haš-šaġle marraat əktiir əktiir.*

how many - *kam* (with foll. sg.). How many tickets do you want? *kam tazkara bəddak?* -- How many students do you have? *kam ṭaaleb εandak?*

map - *xaarṭa* pl. *-aat, xariiṭa* pl. *xaraayeṭ.* I want a map of Asia. *bəddi xaarṭa la-ʔaasya.* -- Don't you have a bigger map of the town? *maa εandak xaarṭa ʔakbar mən hayy ləl-balad?* -- Where can I get a road map of Lebanon? *ween blaaqi xaarṭa la-ṭəroq ləbnaan?*

to map out - *xaṭṭaṭ.* Have you mapped out your route yet? *xaṭṭaṭət ṭariiq safərtak wəlla ləssa?*

marble - 1. *rxaam, marmar.* The statue is made of marble. *t-təmsaal msaawa mn ər-rxaam.* -- Two rows of marble pillars support the ceiling. *ṣaffeen rakaayez marmar ḥaamliin əs-saqəf.* 2. *daḥale* coll. *daḥal* pl. *-aat.* I used to play marbles too. *w-ʔana kamaan kənt ʔəlεab bəd-daḥal.*

March - *ʔaadaar, maars.* I plan to stay here till March. *naawi ḍall hoon la-ʔaadaar.*

march - 1. *məšwaar* pl. *mašawiir.* We still have a long march ahead of us. *ləssa baaqʔi-lna məšwaar ṭawiil qəddaamna.* 2. *marš* pl. *-aat* and *mruuše.* The band began with a march. *ž-žooqa badet əb-marš.*

to steal a march on - *sabaq (e/o sabəq).* He stole a march on all of us. *sabaqna kəllna.*

to march - 1. *məši (i məši).* Did you see the soldiers marching? *šəft əž-žunuud maašyiin?* 2. *maššа.* He marched the platoon to the drill ground. *maššа l-faṣiile la-saaḥt ət-tadriib.*

mare - *faraṣa* pl. *fraaṣ.*

margin - 1. *haameš* pl. *hawaameš.* Leave a wider margin on the left side. *xalli haameš ʔaεraḍ εaš-šmaal.* 2. *rəbəḥ* pl. *ʔarbaaḥ, maksab* pl. *makaaseb.* We're operating on a very small margin. *εam nəštəġel əb-rəbəḥ başiiṭ əktiir.* 3. *mažaal.* You'd better allow a margin for incidental expenses. *ʔaḥsan-lak ətxalli mažaal lən-natriyyaat.* 4. *farəq.* We won by a narrow margin. *rbəḥna b-farq əẓġiir.*

marital - *zooži*, ziiži*.*

marjoram - *mardaqūuš.*

mark - 1. *εalaame* pl. *-aat, ʔišaara* pl. *-aat.* Make a mark after the names of those present. *ḥəṭṭ εalaame žamb ʔəsəm kəll waaḥed ḥaaḍer.* 2. *εalaame* pl. *-aat.* He always got good marks in mathematics. *daaymaan ḥaṣṣal εala εalaamaat εaalye bər-riyaaḍiyyaat.* 3. *laṭεa* pl. *ləṭaε.* Where did you get those black-and-blue marks? *mneen žəbət hal-ləṭaε əs-sooda wəz-zarqa?* 4. *mark* pl. *-aat.* How much is the exchange rate of the mark today? *qaddeeš səεr əl-mark əl-yoom?*

**He made his mark in the world. *twaffaq bəd-dənye.*
**I don't feel quite up to the mark today. *ʔana šaaεer b-ḥaali muu εala baεḍi l-yoom.*

mark of identification - *εalaame* (pl. *-aat*) *mmayyze.* Do you have any special marks of identification? *fii b-žəsmak šii εalaame mmayyze?*

to mark - 1. *ʔaššar εala, εallam εala.* I've marked the important parts of the article. *ʔaššarət εal-ʔaqsaam əl-muhəmme bəl-maqaale.* -- I marked that date red on the calendar. *εallamət εala hat-taariix bəl-ʔaḥmar bər-rəznaama.* 2. *εallam εala.* Mark my words. *εallem εala kalaami!* 3. *εallam.* They've marked the roads well around here. *εallamu ṭ-ṭəroq əmniiḥ əb-hal-qaraani.* 4. *ḥaṭṭ εalaame mmayyze εala.* Have you marked your laundry? *ḥaṭṭeet εalaame mmayyze εala ġasiilak?* 5. *ṣallaḥ.* When will you mark our examination papers? *ʔeemta bəddak ətṣalleḥ ʔawraaq əl-ʔəmtiḥaan tabaεna?*

**The day marks the fiftieth anniversary of the company. *l-yoom haada bikuun εibaara εan əl-εiid əl-xamsiini ləš-šərke.*

to mark down - 1. *qayyad//tqayyad.* I've marked down the things I want. *qayyadət kəll šii bəddi-yáa.* 2. *xaffaḍ səεr˜ ...* The coats have been marked down from forty to thirty dollars. *l-manṭoyaat mxaffaḍ səεron mən ʔarəbεiin dolaar la-tlaatiin.*

market - 1. *suuq* (f. and m.) pl. *swaaq.* Everything is cheaper at the market. *kəll šii ʔarxaṣ bəs-suuq.* -- They bought it on the black market. *štaruuha bəs-suuq əs-sooda.* -- This tooth paste has been put on the market only recently. *hal-maεžuun əs-snaan tnazzal εas-suuq mən məddе qariibe bass.* -- There's no market here for bicycles. *maa fii suuq ləl-bəsəkleetaat hoon.* -- That item has been off the market for a year. *has-sələεa ṣar-la səne mafquude mn əs-suuq.*

to be in the market for - *dawwar εala.* Are you in the market for a good car? *εam əddawwer εala sayyaara mniiḥa?* -- She's still in the market (for a husband). *ləssaaha εam əddawwer εala šii εariis.*

to market - *rawwaž.* It's difficult to market this product in the Middle East. *ṣaεb ətrawwež hal-mantuuž bəš-šarq əl-ʔawṣaṭ.*

to do one's marketing - *tbaḍḍaε.* She does her marketing usually in the morning. *εaadatan btətbaḍḍaε bəṣ-ṣabaaḥ.*

marmalade - *maεquud˜ bərdqaan, mrabba˜ bərdqaan.*

marriage - *žwaaz, zwaaž, ziiže.* She has a daughter from her first marriage. *ʔəlha bənət mən əžwaaza l-ʔawwal.* -- Before her marriage she worked in an office. *qabl əžwaaza kaanet təštəġel əb-maktab.*

to **marry** - 1. *džawwaz, dzawwaž.* Is she going to marry him? *raḥa tədžawwazo?* 2. (Christian) *zawwaž//dzawwaž, žawwaz//džawwaz,* (Muslim) *katab (o ø) əktaab˜ ...* Who married you? *miin zawwažkon?* or *miin katab əktaabkon?* — Were you married in church? *dzawwažtu bəl-əkniise?*

married - *mədzawwež, mədžawwez.* They've been married over a year. *ṣar-lon mədzawwžiin ʔaktar mən səne.*

to get married - *džawwaz, dzawwaž.* When are you getting married? *ʔeemta raḥa tədžawwazu?*

Mars - 1. (god) *maars.* 2. *l-marriix.*

marshal - (military) *maršaal* pl. *-aat* and *-iyye, mušiir* pl. *-iin.*

martyr - *šahiid* pl. *šəhada.*

marvelous - *εaẓiim* pl. *-iin* and *εəẓama.* He's a marvelous teacher. *huwwe mεallem εaẓiim.* -- We had a marvelous dish of taboulé at their house. *ʔakalna tabbuule εaẓiime b-beeton.*

masculine - *mzakkar.* "*ktaab*" is masculine in Arabic. "*ktaab*" *bəl-εarabi mzakkar.*

**She has a lot of masculine traits. *ʔəla ktiir ṣifaat zakar.*

to **mash** - *xabaṣ (o xabəṣ//nxabaṣ), maεas (a maεəs// mmaεas).* Have you mashed the potatoes yet? *xabaṣti l-baṭaaṭa wəlla ləssa?*

mashed potatoes - *baṭaaṭa buré.*

Mass - *qəddaas* pl. *qadadiis.* She went to Mass.

raahet Eal-qəddaas.

mass - *kammiyye* pl. *-aat.* He's collected a mass of material about it. *žamaE kammiyyaat mn ᵊl-mawaadd Ean hal-mawḍuuE.*

**Television can be used as a means of mass education. *t-televəzyoon məmken ʔəstəEmaalo ka-waasṭa la-taEliim Eaammet ᵊn-naas.*

the masses - *l-žamahiir* (pl.), *Eaammet˜ ᵊš-šaEb.* He has the masses behind him. *ž-žamahiir kəlla warḍa.*

to mass - *ḥašad (o ḥašᵊd//nḥašad* and *ḥtašad).* Turkey massed two divisions along the border. *tərkiyya ḥašdet farᵊqteen Eala ṭuul l-ᵊḥduud.*

massage - **1.** *masaaž* pl. *-aat.* I have a massage regularly every week. *baEmel masaaž ᵊb-ʔəntiẓaam kəll žəmEa.* **2.** *tamsiid.* A mild massage should relieve the headache. *tamsiid laṭiif bᵊl-ġaaleb bixaffef wažaE ᵊr-raas.*

to massage - *Eəmel masaaž la-, massad.* The doctor told me to massage my knee. *qal-li l-ḥakiim ʔaEmel masaaž la-rəkᵊbti.*

master - **1.** *ṣaaḥeb* pl. *ṣḥaab.* The dog was sitting at the feet of his master. *l-kalb kaan qaaEed taḥt ᵊqdaam ṣaaḥbo.* **2.** *mEallem* pl. *-iin.* In the shop he met the master and his two apprentices. *bᵊl-waršе laqa l-ᵊmEallem w-ṣanaEiito t-tneen.* **3.** *sayyed* pl. *ʔasyaad.* He is master of his own time. *huwwe sayyed waqto.* **4.** *mhaymen Eala.* He remained master of the situation. *bəqi mhaymen Eal-ḥaale.* **5.** *mbarrez b-.* This writer is a master of the short story. *hal-kaateb mbarrez b-fann ᵊl-qəṣṣa.*

master of ceremonies - *raʔiis˜* (pl. *rəʔasa˜*) *tašriifaat.*

master bedroom - *ʔuudet˜* (pl. *ʔuwaḍ˜*) *noom ᵊkbiire.*

master switch - *məftaaḥ raʔiisi* pl. *mafatiiḥ raʔiisiyye.*

to master - **1.** *ʔatqan.* Do not study lesson three until you have mastered lesson two. *laa tədros ᵊd-dars ᵊt-taalet qabᵊl-ma tkuun ʔatqant ᵊd-dars ᵊt-taani.* **2.** *baraE (a barᵊE) b-.* He's mastered the art of flattery. *huwwe baareE b-fann l-ᵊmmaalaqa* or ***xaatem kəll ᵊbwaab l-ᵊmmaalaqa.*

mastermind - *dmaaġ.* He is the mastermind of the whole project. *huwwe dmaaġ ᵊl-mašruuE kəllo.*

to mastermind - *dabbar.* He masterminded the whole plot. *dabbar l-ᵊmʔaamara mən ʔawwə́la la-ʔaaxə́ra.*

masterpiece - *təḥfe* pl. *təḥaf.*

mat - *ḥaṣiire* pl. *ḥəṣᵊr.*

match - **1.** *kəbriite* coll. *kəbriit* pl. *kabariit.* Give me a box of matches, please. *Eaṭiini Eəlbet kəbriit mən faḍlak.* **2.** *mubaarḍa(t)* pl. *mubaarayaat.* Who won the match? *miin rəbeḥ ᵊl-mubaarḍa?*

**These colors aren't a good match. *hal-ʔalwaan maa btətnaasab* (or *maa binaasbu baEḍon* or *maa biruuḥu maE baEḍon) mniiḥ.*

a match for - *qadd˜* ... He's a match for anybody in drinking. *huwwe qadd kəll waaḥed bᵊš-šərᵊb.* — I'm no match for him. *ʔana maa-li qaddo.* — I think you're a good match for your brother in chess. *bẓənnak qadd ʔaxuuk w-ᵊzyaade bᵊš-šaṭranž.*

to match - **1.** *raaḥu (u ø) maE baEḍon, tnaasabu maE baEḍon.* I think the two rugs match beautifully. *bəEtəqed has-səžžaadteen raayḥiin maE baEḍon ᵊktiir ᵊmniiḥ.* — I bought a number of ties and socks to match. *štareet Eəddet ᵊkraavaat w-ᵊžraabaat biruuḥu maE baEḍon.* **2.** *waffaq been.* Let him match his deeds with his words. *xallíi ywaffeq been ʔafEaalo w-ʔaq̃waalo.* **3.** *ṭəleE (a ø) qadd˜.* I'll match him any time. *bəṭlaE qaddo ʔeemta-ma kaan.*

**You'll never be able to match this shade. *maa btəqder ʔabadan džiib hal-loon mətᵊl hal-loon.*

material - **1.** *maadde* pl. *mawaadd.* We use only the best materials. *mnəstaEmel ʔaḥsan ᵊl-mawaadd bass.* — He's collecting material for a book. *Eam yžammeE mawaadd mənšaan ᵊktaab bəddo yəkᵊtbo.* **2.** *qmaaš* pl. *-aat* and *ʔaqmiše.* Can you wash this material? *hal-ᵊqmaaš byənġə́sel?* **3.** *maaddi*.* She's only interested in material things. *maa bihəmma ġeer ᵊl-ʔašyaaʔ ᵊl-maaddiyye.* **4.** *ʔasaasi*, žawhari*.* There's no material difference between the two. *maa fii farᵊq ʔasaasi been ᵊt-tneen.*

materials - *ġraaḍ* (pl.). Please buy all the writing materials we will need. *mən faḍlak štari kəll ᵊġraaḍ l-ᵊktaabe yalli laazəmᵊtna.*

materialism - *maaddiyye.*

maternity clothes - *ʔawaaEi˜ l-ḥabal.*

maternity hospital - *məstašfa˜* (pl. *məstašfayaat˜*) *tawliid.*

mathematical - *riyaaḍi*.*

mathematics - *riyaaḍiyyaat* (pl.).

matinee - *maatiinée* pl. *maatiinaat.*

matter - **1.** *masʔale* pl. *masaaʔel, ʔamᵊr* pl. *ʔmuur, qaḍiyye* pl. *qaḍaaya.* I'll look into the matter. *bənẓor b-hal-masʔale.* — There are some personal matters that I'd like to talk to him about. *fii kam masʔale šaxṣiyye bəddi ʔəḥki maEo fiihon.* **2.** *masʔale, qaḍiyye.* It's a matter of life and death. *l-masʔale masʔalt ḥayaat ʔaw moot.* — It's not a matter of price. *l-masʔale muu masʔalt ᵊs-səEr.* — This is no laughing matter! *hayy masʔale maa bəḍḍaḥḥek!*

**Something's the matter with his lungs. *fii šii b-riʔatée.*

**What's the matter? *šuu ṣaayer?* or *šuu l-ᵊḥkaaye?* or *šuu l-qəṣṣa?*

**What's the matter with you? *šəbak* (f. *šəbek* or *šə́baki* pl. *šəbkon* or *šə́bakon)?*

**What's the matter with Ahmed today? *šəbo ʔaḥmad ᵊl-yoom?*

**You're only making matters worse. *ʔənte bass Eam ᵊdziid ᵊṭ-ṭiin balle.*

**You take matters too seriously. *ʔənte bətkabbə́ra ktiir.*

**You're carrying matters just a little too far. *Eam ᵊdzawwə́da šwayye.*

printed matter - *maṭbuuEaat* (pl.).

as a matter of course - *bᵊs-saliiq̃a.* I did it as a matter of course. *Eməlta bᵊs-saliiq̃a.*

as a matter of fact - *bᵊl-ḥaqiiqa, bᵊl-waaqeE.* As a matter of fact I wasn't even there. *bᵊl-ḥaqiiqa ʔana ḥatta maa kənt ᵊhniik.*

for that matter - *mən han-naaḥye, b-hal-ᵊxṣuuṣ.* For that matter he can stay where he is. *mən han-naaḥye xallíi yəbqa bᵊl-maḥall yalli huwwe fii.*

no matter how - **1.** *kiif-ma.* No matter how I figure it, the expenses always exceed the income. *kiif-ma ḥsabta, l-maṣariif daayman ʔaktar ᵊmn ᵊd-daxᵊl.* **2.** *qadd-ma.* No matter how smart you are, you won't guess this one. *qadd-ma kənᵊt zaki muu laḥa təḥzer hayy.*

no matter how much - *qadd-ma.* No matter how much you rush me, it won't get done any sooner. *qadd-ma Eažžalᵊtni haš-šaġle maa btəxloṣ ʔabkar.* — No matter how much money he pays, I won't sell the book. *qadd-ma byədfáE-li maṣaari maa bbiiE l-ᵊktaab.*

no matter what - **1.** *šuu-ma, ʔeeš-ma, mahma.* We're going, no matter what you say. *šuu-ma qəlᵊt ḥa-nruuḥ.* — No matter what I do, it doesn't please him. *šuu-ma Eməlt maa byəEᵊžbo.*

no matter when - *ʔeemta-ma.* No matter when he arrives he'll always be welcome. *ʔeemta-ma ʔəža daayman ʔahla w-sahla fii.*

no matter where - *ween-ma.* No matter where we are we keep running into other Americans. *ween-ma rəḥna byəṭlaE ᵊb-wəššna ʔameerkaan taanyiin.*

no matter who - *miin-ma.* No matter who said it, I couldn't care less. *miin-ma qaala maa bətEalleq Eala rəžli.* — No matter whom you saw, it was certainly not he. *miin-ma šəfto ʔakiid muu huwwe.*

no matter why - *mahma kaan sabab˜* ... No matter why he was late, it's still impolite. *mahma kaan sabab taʔaxxro bəttamm qəllet ʔadab.*

to matter - *faraq (e farᵊq).* It didn't really matter (to me). *bᵊl-ḥaqiiqa maa farqet maEi.* — Oh, come on, what does it matter! *xalləṣni baqa, šuu btəfreq!* — It doesn't matter what you say, I'll do it. *maa byəfreq maEi šuu Eam ᵊtquul, ḥa-saawiiha.*

**It doesn't matter. *maa bihəmm* or *maa Ealée šii.*

matter-of-fact - *waaq̃Ei*.* He's a matter-of-fact businessman. *huwwe ražol ʔaEmaal waaq̃Ei.*

mattress - *faršе* pl. *-aat* and *fərᵊš.*

mature - *naaḍež.* The boy is very mature for his age. *ṣ-ṣabi ktiir naaḍež bᵊn-nəsbe la-sənno.*

maturity - *nuḍuuž.*

maximum - **1.** *l-ḥadd ᵊl-ʔaq̃ṣa, ʔaq̃ṣa˜ ḥadd.* I'm willing to pay twenty pounds, but that's the maximum. *məstEədd ʔədfáE-lak Eəšriin leera, bass haada l-ḥadd ᵊl-ʔaq̃ṣa.* **2.** *ʔaq̃ṣa˜.* The maximum temperature around here is 100 degrees. *ʔaq̃ṣa ḥaraara hoon miit daraže.* — The maximum penalty for this crime is ten years in prison. *ʔaq̃ṣa Euq̃uube la-haž-žərᵊm Eašr ᵊsniin ḥabᵊs.*

May - *ʔayyaar, maayes, maayo.*

may - (no equivalent verb in Arabic, usually paraphrased with *məmken* or *bižuuz).* I may have said it. *məmken kuun qəlta.* — That may be so. *məmken haš-šii ykuun heek.* — I might go if they invite me. *məmken ruuḥ ʔiza Eazamuuni.* — May I keep this pencil? *məmken ʔəḥtə́feẓ b-hal-qalam?* or *fiini ʔəḥtə́feẓ ...* or *bəqder ʔəḥtə́feẓ ...* or *btəsmaḥ-li ʔəḥtə́feẓ ...* — Who might have done that? *miin məmken ykuun εəmel haš-šii* or *yaa-tára miin εəmel haš-šii.* — Be that as it may! *kiif-ma kaan!*

maybe - *məmken, yəmken, bišuuš.* Maybe they're not at home. *məmken muu bᵊl-beet hənne.*

mayor - *raʔiis~ baladiyye* pl. *rəʔasa~ baladiyyaat,* (of a village) *məxtaar* pl. *maxatiir.*

meadow - *marž* pl. *mruuž.*

meager - *ḍaʔiil.* The results were meager. *n-nataayež kaanet ḍaʔiile.*

meal - *waqεa* pl. *-aat, wažbe* pl. *-aat, ʔakle* pl. *-aat.* Three meals a day aren't enough for him. *tlatt waqεaat bᵊl-yoom maa bətkaffī.* — I haven't eaten a decent meal in weeks. *maa ʔakalt wa-laa ʔakle mətl ᵊl-εaalam mən ʔasabiiε w-ʔasabiiε.*

mean - *waaṭi, laʔiim, dani*.* That was a mean thing for him to do. *haada kaan εamal waaṭi mənno.* — That's a mean trick. *ləεbe waaṭye hayy!* — He's a mean old man. *huwwe ʔəxtyaar dani.*

**How can you be so mean to the poor man! *šuu had-danaawe mənnak b-ḥaqq har-rəžžaal ᵊl-məskiin!*

mean - *mətwaṣṣeṭ.* What is the mean temperature here during the summer? *šuu l-ḥaraara l-mətwaṣṣṭa* (or ***mέaddal ᵊl-ḥaraara*) *bᵊṣ-ṣeef hoon?*

to mean - **1.** *qaṣad* (*o qaṣᵊd*). I know he means well. *ʔana baεref* (*ʔənno*) *qaṣdo mniiḥ.* — You don't really mean that? *ʔənte maa-lak εam təqṣod haš-šii walla laʔ?* — I didn't mean any harm. *maa qaṣadt ʔayy šarr ʔabadan.* — That remark was meant for you. *hal-ᵊmlaaḥaẓa kənt ʔənte l-maqṣuuḍ fiiha.* **2.** *εana* (*i ø*). What do those signs mean? *hal-εalaamaat šuu btəεni?* — That doesn't mean much. *haada maa byəεni šii ktiir.* **3.** *εana, qaṣad.* What do you mean by that? *šuu btəεni* (or *btəqṣoḍ*) *b-haš-šii?* **4.** *nawa* (*i niyye*). I meant to call, but I forgot. *kənᵊt naawi saawī-lak talifoon, bass ᵊnsiit.* — What do you mean to do? *šuu naawi taεmel?* **5.** *hamm.* His friendship means a lot to me. *ṣadaaqto bəthəmmni ktiir.* — It means a lot to me to see him tonight. *bihəmmni ktiir šuufo l-leele.*

**You don't mean to say you saw everything? *maa bəddak ᵊtqəl-li ʔənnak šəfᵊt kəll šii?*

**Is this book meant for me? *hal-ᵊktaab ʔəli?*

I mean - *yaεni.* I'll pick you up at your house. I mean, you won't have to come all the way across town. *baaxdak mən beetak. yaεni, maa fii lzuum təži mən ʔawwal ᵊl-balad la-ʔaaxə́ra.* — I'm sure he'll lend you money. I mean, something in the vicinity of a hundred pounds or so. *mətʔakked ʔana ʔənno bidayynak maṣaari. yaεni b-ḥawaali miit leera.*

meaning - *maεna* pl. *maεaani.* This word has several meanings. *hal-kəlme ʔəla εəddet maεaani.* — What's the meaning of this? *šuu maεnaat* (or *maεna*) *haš-šaġle?* — I want the exact meaning of the word. *bəddi maεnaat* (or *maεna*) *l-kəlme l-maẓbuuṭ.*

meaningless - *bala maεna.* The sentence as it stands is meaningless. *ž-žəmle mətᵊl-ma hiyye bala maεna.*

meanness - *waṭaawe, laʔaame, danaawe.*

means - **1.** *waasṭa* pl. *waṣaayeṭ, wasiile* pl. *wasaayel.* It was just a means to an end. *maa kaanet ʔəlla waasṭa la-ġaaye.* — We traveled by practically every means of transportation. *saafarna taqriiban ᵊb-kəll wasaayel ᵊn-naqᵊl.* **2.** *ʔəmkaaniyyaat* (pl.). He doesn't have the means to do it. *maa εando l-ʔəmkaaniyyaat ysaawiiha.* — He lives beyond his means. *biεiiš fooq ʔəmkaaniyyaato.*

**She married a man of means. *džawwazet rəžžaal ġani.*

by all means - **1.** *mən kəll bədd.* By all means take the job! *mən kəll bədd ᵊqbaal ᵊš-šaġle.* **2.** *maεluum.* May I take it? - By all means! *məmken ʔaaxdo? - maεluum!*

by means of - *b-waasṭet~ ...* You can regulate it by means of a screw. *bədẓabbə́ṭa b-waasṭet šii bərġi.*

by no means - *ʔabadan, mnoob.* He's by no means stupid. *huwwe mu ḥmaar ʔabadan!*

ways and means - *ṭariiqa.* We have to find ways and means of helping him. *laazem ndawwer εala šii ṭariiqa nεaawno fiiha.*

in the **meantime** - *w-ᵊb-hal-mədde, w-ᵊb-hal-ʔasnaaʔ.* You can rest in the meantime. *w-ᵊb-hal-mədde fiik təstrə́ḥ-lak ᵊšwayye.*

meanwhile - *w-ᵊb-hal-mədde, w-ᵊb-hal-ʔasnaaʔ.* Meanwhile it had gotten too late. *w-ᵊb-hal-ʔasnaaʔ kaan faat ᵊl-waqt.*

measles - *ḥmeera.*

measly - *zahiid.* I can't get along on this measly salary. *maa bəqder dabber ḥaali b-hal-maεaaš ᵊz-zahiid.*

measure - **1.** *məqyaas* pl. *maqayiis, qyaas* pl. *-aat.* The meter is the standard measure of length in Syria. *l-mətᵊr huwwe l-məqyaas ᵊr-rasmi ləṭ-ṭuul b-suuriyya.* — Weights and measures. *maqayiis w-ʔawzaan.* **2.** *tadbiir* pl. *-aat* and *tadabiir.* We'll have to take strong measures. *laazem nəttə́xez tadabiir ṣaarme.*

measure of capacity - *məkyaal* pl. *makayiil.*

for good measure - *faḍle, εal-beeεa.* The vendor threw in an extra apple for good measure. *l-bayyaaε laḥaš təffaaḥa faḍle.* — They locked him up for five days and for good measure they revoked his license. *ḥabasúu xamᵊst iyyaam w-εal-beeεa ʔaxadúu-lo rəxṣet ᵊs-swaaqa tabaεo.*

to measure - *qaas* (*i qyaas//nqaas*). I measured the height of the window carefully. *qəsᵊt εəlu š-šəbbaak ᵊb-dəqqa.*

**How much does he measure around the waist? *qaddeeš ᵊqyaaso εand xaṣro?*

measurement - *qyaas* pl. *-aat.* Are these measurements correct? *hal-ᵊqyaasaat maẓbuuṭa?* — Did the tailor take your measurements? *l-xayyaaṭ ʔaxad ᵊqyaasak?*

meat - *laḥᵊm* and *laḥme* pl. *-aat* and *lḥuum* and *lḥuumaat.*

meat broth - *marqet~ laḥme.*

meat grinder - *farraamet~* (pl. *-aat~*) *laḥme, makiinet~* (pl. *-aat~*) *laḥme.*

Mecca - *makke.*

Meccan - *makki** pl. *-iyye, makkaawi** pl. *-iyye.*

mechanic - *mikaniiki* pl. *-iyye.*

mechanical - *mikaniiki*.*

mechanics - *mikaniik.*

medal - *madaalya* pl. *-aat, niišaan* pl. *nayašiin.*

to **meddle** - *ddaaxal.* He likes to meddle in other people's business. *biḥəbb yaddaaxal b-ᵊšʔuun ġeero.*

to **mediate** - *twaṣṣaṭ been.* A neutral commission mediated the opposing claims. *fii ləžne mḥaayde twaṣṣaṭet been ᵊl-ʔəddiεaaʔeen ᵊl-məḍḍaarbiin.*

mediation - *waṣaaṭa, tawaṣṣoṭ.*

mediator - *waṣiiṭ* pl. *wəṣaṭa.*

medical - *ṭəbbi*.* Look it up in the medical dictionary. *ruuḥ raažə́εa bᵊl-qaamuus ᵊṭ-ṭəbbi.*

medical school - *kəlliyyet~* (pl. *-aat~*) *ṭəbb.*

medical student - *ṭaaleb~* (pl. *ṭəllaab~*) *ṭəbb.*

medical treatment - *tadaawi, mεaalaže ṭəbbiyye.* I'm under medical treatment. *ʔana taḥt ᵊt-tadaawi* or ***ʔana εam ʔəddaawa.*

medicinal - *ṭəbbi*.* They use this drug only for medicinal purposes. *byəstaεmlu had-dawa la-ʔaġraaḍ ṭəbbiyye bass.*

medicine - **1.** *dawa* pl. *ʔədᵊwye.* This medicine tastes bitter. *had-dawa ṭaεᵊmto mərra.* — Have you taken your medicine yet? *ʔaxadt dawaak walla ləssa?* **2.** *ṭəbb.* My daughter is studying medicine. *bənti εam tədros ṭəbb.*

mediocre - *waṣaṭ* (invar.), *mətwaṣṣeṭ.* Their work is only mediocre. *εamálon muu ʔaktar mən waṣaṭ.*

Mediterranean Sea - *l-baḥr ᵊl-ʔabyaḍ ᵊl-mutawaṣṣeṭ, l-baḥr ᵊl-ʔabyaḍ, l-baḥr ᵊl-mutawaṣṣeṭ.*

medium - **1.** *waṣaṭ* (invar.). He's of medium height. *ṭuulo waṣaṭ.* — I'd like my steak medium rare. *bəddi l-bifteek tabaεi məstwiyye waṣaṭ.* **2.** *waasṭa* pl. *-aat* and *waṣaayeṭ, wasiile* pl. *wasaayel.* Through the medium of television. *b-waasəṭṭ ᵊt-televəzyoon.*

happy medium - *ḥall waṣaṭ.* It's hard to find a happy medium. *ṣaεb l-waaḥed ylaaqi ḥall waṣaṭ.*

medium-sized - *qyaas waṣaṭ* (invar.). He wears medium-sized shirts. *byəlbes qəmṣaan qyaas waṣaṭ.* — The medium-sized shoes are over there. *ṣ-ṣababiiṭ l-ᵊqyaas ᵊl-waṣaṭ ᵊhniike.*

meek - *ẓaliil* pl. *-iin* and *ʔaẓəlla.*

meekness - *ẓəll.*

to **meet** - **1.** *ṣaadaf.* Did you meet him on the street? *ṣaadafto bᵊš-šaareε?* **2.** *qaabal, laaqa.* He met us with a smile. *qaabalna b-ʔəbtisaame.* **3.** *tεarraf εala.* I just met him. *hallaq tεarraft εalée.* — Haven't we met before? *maa tεarrafna εala baεḍna mən qabᵊl?* **4.** *qaam* (*u qyaam*) *b-.* I can barely meet my expenses. *yaa-doobi quum ᵊb-maṣariifi.* — They couldn't meet their obligations. *maa qədru yquumu b-ʔəltizaamaaton.* **5.** *tlaaqa, tqaabal.* Let's meet in front of the theater. *xalliina nətlaaqa qəddaam ᵊs-siinama.* **6.** *žtamaε.* We meet once a week. *mnəžtə́meε marra bᵊž-žəmεa.* **7.** *ltaqa* (*-yəltə́qa*). The two ends don't meet. *ṭ-ṭarafeen maa byəltə́qu.*

**Will you meet them at the station? *bətruuḥ ᵊbtaaxədon (or badžiibon) mən l-ᵊmḥatta?*
**I'm very glad to meet you. *tšarrafna b-maᶜrəftak.*
**Pleased to meet you! *tšarrafna! ʔahla w-sahla!*
**Let's meet halfway in this matter. *mənnak šwayye w-mənni šwayye w-xalliina nəxsəma.*
**We have a deadline to meet. *fii ᶜanna waqt ᵊmḥaddad mədṭarriin nəxloṣ fii.*
to meet with - 1. *laqa (-ylaaqi ø), ṣaadaf.* Does that meet with your approval? *haada bilaaqi mwaafaqtak?* 2. *žtamaᶜ b-.* The President met with his advisors this morning. *r-raʔiis ᵊžtamaᶜ bᵊl-məstašaariin tabaᶜo l-yoom ᶜala bəkra.*
meeting - 1. *ʔəžtimaaᶜ* pl. *-aat.* There were five hundred people at the meeting. *kaan fii xamᵊs miit zalame bᵊl-ʔəžtimaaᶜ.* — I arranged for a meeting of the two. *dabbart ʔəžtimaaᶜ been ᵊt-tneen.*
melancholy - 1. *ḥaziin.* Why are you so melancholy today? *šəbak ḥaziin ᵊl-yoom?* 2. *sooda, kaʔaabe.* He has his moments of melancholy. *ʔəlo saaᶜaat btəžži fiiha s-sooda.*
melody - *naǵme* pl. *-aat.*
melon - *qaaquune* coll. *qaaquun* pl. *-aat.*
to **melt** - 1. *daab (u dawabaan).* The snow is all melted. *t-talᵊž kəllo daab.* 2. *dawwab.* Melt the sugar in a skillet. *ḥəṭṭ ᵊs-səkkar ᵊb-məqlaaye w-dawwbo.*
member - *ᶜəḍu* f. *ᶜəḍwe* pl. *ʔaᶜḍaaʔ.* Are you a member of this club? *ʔənte ᶜəḍu b-han-naadi?*
membership - 1. *ʔəntisaab.* Our membership is down to less than one hundred. *l-ʔəntisaab ᶜanna nəzel la-ʔaqall mən miyye.* 2. *ᶜəḍwiyye.* He kept his membership in the party secret. *katam sərr ᶜəḍwiito bᵊl-ḥəzᵊb.*
memorable: What a memorable day that was! *ya ʔaḷḷa šuu kaan ᵊl-yoom maa byəntəsa.* — It's a memorable date in my life. *haada taariix maa byəntəsa b-ḥayaati.*
memorandum - *məzakkra* pl. *-aat.*
to **memorize** - 1. *baṣam (o baṣᵊm).* Have you studied your lesson or just memorized it? *darasᵊt darsak wəlla bass baṣamto baṣᵊm?* 2. *ḥafaẓ (a ḥəfᵊẓ) ... ᶜal-ǵeeb.* He memorized the entire Koran. *ḥafaẓ ᵊl-q̈ərʔaan mən ʔawwalo la-ʔaaxro ᶜal-ǵeeb.*
memory - 1. *zaakra.* My memory is not what it used to be. *zaakərti muu mətᵊl-ma kaanet mən qabᵊl.* 2. *zəkra* pl. *zəkriyaat.* I have pleasant memories of this town. *ᶜandi zəkriyaat ᵊktiir ṭayybe ᶜan hal-balad.*
in memory of - *ᶜala zəkra˜ ..., ᶜala təzkaar˜ ...*
menace - *xaṭar* pl. *ʔaxṭaar.* He's a menace to society. *huwwe xaṭar ᶜal-məžtəmaᶜ.*
to **mend** - *rata (i rati//rtata).* When will you mend my shirts? *ʔeemta btərtī-li qəmṣaani?*
to mend one's ways - *ṣallaḥ ṭariiqto, ᶜaddal ṭariiqto.* You'll have to mend your ways. *laazem tṣalleḥ ṭariiqtak.*
mental - 1. *ᶜaqli*.* Many mental diseases can be cured these days. *ktiir ᵊmn ᵊl-ʔamraaḍ ᵊl-ᶜaqliyye məmken šifaaʔa b-hal-ʔiyyaam.* 2. *zəhni*.* It requires a complicated mental process. *hal-masʔale btəṭṭallab ᶜamaliyye zəhniyye mᶜaqqade.*
mentality - *ᶜaqliyye* pl. *-aat.*
to **mention** - *zakar (o zəkᵊr//nzakar).* He didn't mention the price. *maa zakar ᵊs-səᶜr* or ***maa qaal šii ᶜan ᵊs-səᶜr.* — I heard his name mentioned. *smə ᶜton ᶜam yəzᵊkru ʔəsmo.* — I would also like to mention that ... *w-ᵊbḥəbb kamaan ʔəzkor ʔənno ...* — That's not worth mentioning. *maa btəstḥəqq tənzəker* or *maa btəstḥəqq ᵊz-zəkᵊr.*
**Thank you very much! - Don't mention it. *šəkran ᵊktiir! - ᶜafwan!*
not to mention - *faḍlan ᶜan.* Their visit cost us a lot of money, not to mention the inconvenience it caused us. *zyaarəton kallafətna maṣaari ktiir faḍlan ᶜan ᵊl-ʔəzᶜaaž halli sabbabət-ᵊlna-yda.*
menu - *liistet˜* (pl. *-aat˜*) *ʔakᵊl, qaaymet˜* (pl. *qawaayem˜*) *ṭaᶜaam.*
merchandise - *bḍaaᶜa* pl. *baḍaayeᶜ.*
merchant - *taažer* pl. *təžžaar.*
merchant marine - *baḥriyye tižaariyye.*
mercury - 1. (metal) *zeebaq.* 2. (planet) *ᶜuṭaared.*
mercy - 1. *raḥme, ǵəfraan.* He pleaded for mercy. *ṭalab ᵊr-raḥme.* 2. *šafaqa, raḥme.* He has no mercy. *maa fii b-qalbo šafaqa (w-laa raḥme).*
mere - *mžarrad˜.* The mere thought of it disturbs me. *mžarrad ᵊt-tafkiir fiiha byəzᶜəžni.*
merely - *bass, maa ... ʔəlla.* I was merely joking. *kənᵊt bass ᶜam ʔəmzaḥ* or *maa kənᵊt ʔəlla ᶜam ʔəmzaḥ.* — It's merely a question of money. *l-masʔale maa hiyye ʔəlla masʔalt maṣaari.*
to **merge** - 1. *ltaqa.* The two roads merge at that point. *ṭ-ṭariiqeen byəltəqu b-han-nəqṭa.* 2. *damaž (o damž//ndamaž), ḍamm (ə ḍamm//nḍamm).* They're thinking of merging the two companies. *ᶜam yfakkru yədᵊmžu š-šərᵊkteen.*
merit - *miize* pl. *-aat.* A tour abroad has its merits. *s-syaaḥa bᵊl-xaarež ʔəla miizaata.*
to merit - *staḥaqq.* I think he merits a raise. *bəᶜtəqed byəstḥəqq zyaadet raateb.*
merry - *farḥaan.* They are a merry bunch. *hənne žamaaᶜa farḥaaniin.*
**Merry Christmas! - Merry Christmas to you! *ᶜiid miilaad saᶜiid! - ᶜiid saᶜiid w-ᵊmbaarak!*
mess - 1. *žalᶜaṣa.* Did you see the mess the painters left? *šəft ᵊž-žalᶜaṣa halli tarakuuha d-dahhaane?* 2. *xarbaṭa, laxbaṭa.* I can't find anything in this mess. *maa bəqder laaqi šii b-hal-xarbaṭa.* 3. *warṭa.* That's a fine mess we're in! *nəḥna waaqᶜiin ᵊb-warṭa ᶜal-maẓbuuṭ!*
**You certainly got yourself into a nice mess! *ḥatman warraṭṭ ḥaalak tawriiṭa malᶜuune!*
**The house is in an awful mess. *l-beet kəllo qaayem qaaᶜed.*
to mess up - 1. *waṣṣax//twaṣṣax.* Don't mess up the floor with your wet feet. *laa twaṣṣex ᵊl-ʔarḍ b-rəžleek ᵊl-mabluuliin!* 2. *xarbaṭ//txarbaṭ, laxbaṭ//tlaxbaṭ.* Who messed up the papers on my desk? *miin yalli xarbəṭ-li wraaqi ᶜaṭ-ṭaawle?*
message - *kəlme, xabar, risaale* pl. *rasaayel.* Is there a message for me? *fii šii ʔəli kəlme?* — He's not in. Can I take a message? *huwwe muu hoon. bətriid ballǵo šii risaale?*
messenger - *saaᶜi* pl. *suᶜaat.*
Messiah - *l-masiiḥ, s-sayyed ᵊl-masiiḥ.*
messy - 1. *mxarbaṭ, mlaxbaṭ.* His desk is always messy. *ṭaawəlto daayman mxarbaṭa.* 2. *mšarbak.* I don't want to get involved in a messy business like that. *maa bəddi ḥəṭṭ ʔəṣbaᶜti b-šaǵle mšarbake mətᵊl hayy.*
metal - *maᶜdan* pl. *maᶜaaden.*
metallic - *maᶜdani*.*
metaphor - *ʔəstiᶜaara* pl. *-aat.*
metaphoric(al) - *mažaazi*.*
meter - 1. *mətᵊr* pl. *mtaar.* Change these measurements into meters. *ǵayyer hal-maq̈ayiis la-mtaar.* 2. *wazᵊn* pl. *ʔawzaan.* The meter of this poem is very regular. *wazᵊn haš-šəᶜr ᵊktiir mənsažem.* 3. *saaᶜa* pl. *-aat, ᶜaddaad* pl. *-aat.* Every three months a man comes around to read the meter. *kəll tlətt əšhor byəži waaḥed yəqra s-saaᶜa.*
method - 1. *ṭariiqa* pl. *ṭəroq, ʔəsluub* pl. *ʔasaliib.* He's discovered a new method. *ktašaf ṭariiqa ždiide.* 2. *ʔənṭiẓaam.* There's method in his madness. *fii ʔənṭiẓaam b-ᵊžnuuno.*
microphone - *məkrofoon* pl. *-aat.*
microscope - *məkroskoob* pl. *-aat, məžhar* pl. *mažaaher.*
midday - *ḍəhᵊr.* The midday sun is very hot. *šamset ᵊḍ-ḍəhr ᵊktiir ḥaarra.*
middle - 1. *nəṣṣ, ʔawaaṣeṭ* (pl). I'm leaving the middle of next week. *ʔana msaafer ᵊb-ʔawaaṣeṭ ᵊž-žəmᶜa ž-žaaye.* 2. *xaṣr* pl. *xṣuur.* He's put on weight around the middle. *səmen šwayye naaḥ xaṣro.* 3. *waṣṭaani*, nəṣṣaani*.* Open the middle window. *ftaaḥ ᵊš-šəbbaak ᵊl-waṣṭaani.* 4. *waṣaṭ* (invar.), *mətwaṣṣeṭ, məᶜtədel.* He's a man of middle height. *huwwe waaḥed ṭuulo waṣaṭ.*
**He's in his middle forties. *ᶜəmro ḥawaali l-xamsda w-ʔarᵊbᶜiin.*
Middle Ages - *l-q̈uruun ᵊl-wəsṭa.*
middle class - *ṭ-ṭabaqa l-mətwaṣṣṭa.*
Middle East - *š-šarq̈ ᵊl-ʔawsaṭ.*
in the middle of - 1. *b-nəṣṣ˜ ..., b-waṣaṭ˜ ...* The man collapsed in the middle of the street. *r-rəžžaal wəqeᶜ ᵊb-nəṣṣ ᵊṭ-ṭariiq.* — There's a table in the middle of the room. *fii ṭaawle b-waṣaṭ ᵊl-ʔuuḍa.* 2. *b-nəṣṣ˜ ...* They woke us up in the middle of the night. *fayyaquuna b-nəṣṣ ᵊl-leel.* — He got up in the middle of things and walked out. *b-nəṣṣ ᵊš-šaǵle ḥamal ḥaalo w-məši.*
**I'm in the middle of packing. *naazel la-qaraqiiṭ ʔadaani ᵊb-ḍabb ᵊš-šanaati.*
middle-aged - *mətwaṣṣeṭ bᵊl-ᶜəmᵊr.* She's a middle-aged woman. *hiyye mara mətwaṣṣṭa bᵊl-ᶜəmᵊr.*
midnight - *nəṣṣ˜ (ᵊl-)leel.* It was past midnight when we returned home. *kaan ṣaar baᶜᵊd nəṣṣ ᵊl-leel lamma ržəᶜna ᶜal-beet.*
midwife - *daaye* pl. *-aat.*
might - *quwwe.* According to the proverb, might makes right. *mətᵊl-ma biquul ᵊl-matal: ᵊl-ḥaqq maᶜ*

ᵊl-quwwe.
might - see **may.**
mighty - 1. *qawi** pl. *qawaaya.* He dealt him a mighty blow. *ḍarabo ḍarbe qawiyye.* **2.** *ktiir.* I was mighty glad to see him again. *nbaṣaṭṭ ᵊktiir lamma šəfto taani marra* or ***qaddeeš ᵊnbaṣaṭṭ lamma ...*
migraine - *ṣudaaε.*
mild - 1. *maεtədel.* This is a mild climate. *haada manaax maεtədel.* **2.** *xafiif* pl. *xfaaf.* I'd like a mild tobacco. *bəddi šii dəxxaan xafiif.* — Instead of being punished he got away with a mild reproof. *εawaaḍ-ma kaan yətεaaďab nafad b-kam kəlmet taᵓniib ᵊxfaaf.*
mile - *miil* pl. *myaal* and *ᵓamyaal.* The village is three miles from here. *ḍ-ḍeeεa εala masaafet tlətt ᵊmyaal mən hoon.*
military - *εaskari*.* No military matters were discussed by the two delegations. *maa ṣaar baḥs ᵊb-masaaᵓel εaskariyye been ᵊl-wafdeen.* — He graduated from the Military Academy in Homs. *txarraž mn ᵊl-kəlliyye l-εaskariyye b-ḥəmᵊṣ.*
military police - *šərṭa ḥarbiyye.*
military service - *xədme εaskariyye, εaskariyye, žəndiyye.*
milk - *ḥaliib.* The milk has turned sour. *l-ḥaliib ḥammaḍ.* — The boy's beginning to lose his milk teeth. *ṣ-ṣabi bada ybaddel snaan ᵊl-ḥaliib.*
**There's no use crying over spilt milk. *halli ṣaar ṣaar, maa fii faayde mn ᵊl-bəke εal-maaḍi.*
milk products - *məntažaat˜ ᵓalbaan.*
to milk - *ḥalab (e/o ḥalᵊb//nḥalab).* Do you know how to milk a cow? *btaεref təḥleb baqara?*
mill - 1. *ṭaaḥuun(e)* (f.) pl. *ṭawaḥiin.* When are you going to take the wheat down to the mill? *ᵓeemta bəddak taaxod ᵊl-qamᵊḥ εaṭ-ṭaaḥuun?* **2.** *maṣnaε* pl. *maṣaaneε, maεmal* pl. *maεaamel.* We ordered the paper straight from the mill. *waṣṣeena εal-waraq raᵓsan mn ᵊl-maṣnaε.*
**That's grist to his mill. *ᵓəžžto daεme la-ḥəžžto.*
miller - *ṭaḥḥaan* pl. *-e* and *-iin.*
million - *malyoon* pl. *malayiin.* The company's assets exceed five million pounds. *mawžuudaat ᵊš-šərke bədziid εan xamᵊs malayiin leera.*
**I've got a million things to do before dinner. *fii εandi ᵓalf šağle laazem saawiiha qabl ᵊl-εaša.*
minaret - *maadne* pl. *mawaaden.*
mind - 1. *εaqᵊl* pl. *εquul* (with derogatory connotations *εaqlaat*), *zəhᵊn* pl. *ᵓazhaan.* He has a very keen mind. *εaqlo ktiir ḥaadd.* **2.** *εaqᵊl.* You can't be in your right mind! *laazem ᵊtkuun ᵊṭləεᵊt εan εaqlak!* **3.** *baal, xaaṭer.* On my way home the thought flashed through my mind. *b-ṭariiqi εal-beet ᵊl-fəkra xaṭret εala baali.* **4.** *baal, fəkr.* Keep your mind on your work. *xalli baalak b-šəğlak.* — What's on your mind? *šuu fii b-baalak?* or ***šuu qəṣṣtak?* — This has been on my mind for quite a while. *haš-šii b-baali mən zamaan.* — I have a good mind to tell him so. *žaaye b-baali qəl-lo heek.* — I'll keep you in mind. *bxalliik ᵊb-fəkri.* — His name slipped my mind. *ᵓəsmo ğaab εan baali.*
**He doesn't know his own mind. *maa byaεref šuu bəddo.*
**My mind isn't clear on what happened. *maa εandi fəkra waaḍḥa šuu ṣaar.*
**I've half a mind to leave tomorrow. *ᵓana mətxooṭer saafer bəkra.*
**She has her mind set on going shopping today. *mεannde ᵓəlla-ma tətsawwaq ᵊl-yoom.*
**Out of sight, out of mind. *bεiid εan ᵊl-εeen, bεiid εan ᵊl-qalᵊb.*
to my mind - *b-raᵓyi.* To my mind, she's the right person for the job. *b-raᵓyi hiyye ḥafr w-tanziil la-haš-šağle.*
to be out of one's mind - *žann (ə žnuun, žnaan).* Are you out of your mind? *šuu žanneet?* or *šuu žaanen ᵓənte?* — You must be completely out of your mind! *laazem ᵊtkuun žaanen εal-mazbuuṭ!*
to call to mind - *zakkar.* That calls to mind a story I know. *haada bizakkərni b-qəṣṣa baεrəfa.*
to change one's mind - *ğayyar fəkro.* I've changed my mind. *ğayyarᵊt fəkri.*
to have in mind - *fakkar b-.* Have you anyone definite in mind? *ᵓənte εam ᵊtfakker ᵊb-šaxṣ ᵊmεayyan?* — I have something else in mind. *εam fakker b-ğeer šii.*
to make up one's mind - *εtamad, ďarrar.* I made up my mind to stay after all. *bᵊr-ragᵊm εan kəll šii εtamadt ᵓəbqa.* — Come on, make up your mind! *yaḷḷa baqa, εtəmed : yaa heek yaa heek!*
**I can't make up my mind. *ᵓana məḥtaar maa-li εaaref šuu saawi.*
**I haven't made up my mind yet. *ləssaani mxooṭar.*
to mind - 1. *htamm b-, εaṭa baalo εala.* Don't mind what he says. *laa təhtamm bi-kalaamo* or *laa taεṭi baalak εala kalaamo.* **2.** *εtana b-, daar (i ø) baalo εala.* Who's going to mind the baby? *miin bəddo yəεtəni bᵊl-beebẽe?* or *miin bəddo ydiir baalo εal-beebẽe?* **3.** *ṭaawaε.* He doesn't mind me any more. *maa εaad yṭaawəεni* or ***maa εaad yəsmaε kəlᵊmti.*
**I hope you don't mind my leaving now. *nšaaḷḷa maa fii maaneε εandak ᵓiza bruuḥ hallaq.*
**I don't mind going alone. *maa εandi maaneε ruuḥ waḥdi.*
**Mind your own business! *laa təddaaxal b-šii maa byəεniik!*
**Never mind, I'll do it myself. *maa bihəmm, baεmə́la la-ḥaali.*
**Shall I mail this letter now? - Never mind, it can wait till tomorrow. *ḥaṭṭ hal-maktuub b-sanduuq ᵊl-boosṭa hallaq? - maεleešii xallīi ystanna la-bəkra.*
**I'm sorry, I just broke the glass. - Oh, never mind, there are plenty more. *matᵓassef, hallaq kasart ᵊl-kaase. - ᵓe maεleešii, fii εanna šii ktiir.*
mine - 1. *manžam* pl. *manaažem.* There are a number of coal mines in that area. *fii εadad manaažem faḥm ᵊhniik.* **2.** *ləğᵊm* pl. *ᵓalğaam.* Their ship ran into a mine. *safiinə́ton ᵊṣṭadmet ᵊb-ləğᵊm.*
to mine - 1. *staxraž.* How much coal was mined during May? *qaddeeš ᵊstaxražu faḥᵊm bi-šahr ᵓayyaar?* **2.** *lağam (o lağᵊm//nlağam).* The enemy has mined all roads leading to the city. *l-εaduww lağamu kəll ᵊṭ-ṭəroq halli bətwaddi εal-balad.*
mine - *tabaεi, šiiti.* Is that cigarette mine? *has-sigaara tabaεi?* — In whose car are we going to go? - Mine, of course. *b-sayyaaret miin laḥa nruuḥ? - ṭabεan ᵊb-tabaεi.*
**He's an old friend of mine. *huwwe ṣaaḥeb qadiim ᵓəli.*
**Your room is to the right, mine is to the left. *ᵓuuḍtak εal-yamiin, ᵓuuḍti ᵓana εaš-šmaal.* — His brother is older than mine. *ᵓaxúu ᵓakbar mən ᵓaxi.*
miner - *mεadden* pl. *-iin.* The miners live near the mine. *l-ᵊmεaddniin saakniin qərb ᵊl-manžam.*
mineral - 1. *maεdan* pl. *maεaaden.* A number of valuable minerals are found in this area. *b-hal-manṭiqa fiiha εəddet maεaaden tamiine.* **2.** *maεdani*.* The soil is rich in mineral deposits. *t-tərbe ğaniyye b-rawaaseb maεdaniyye.*
minimum - 1. *l-ḥadd ᵊl-ᵓadna, ᵓadna˜ ḥadd.* Let's say, a hundred pounds is the minimum. *xalliina nquul miit leera huwwe l-ḥadd ᵊl-ᵓadna.* **2.** *ᵓadna˜, ᵓaqall˜.* The minimum wage is 20 pounds a week. *ᵓadna ᵓəžra εəšriin leera bᵊž-žəmεa.* — The minimum penalty is three days in prison. *ᵓadna εuďuube tlətt iyyaam ḥabᵊs.*
mining - *taεdiin.* The mining industry suffered most heavily. *ṣinaaεet ᵊt-taεdiin ᵊḍḍarraret ᵓaktar ᵊl-kəll.*
minister - 1. *qəssiis* and *qassiis* pl. *qasaawse,* loosely also *xuuri* pl. *xawaarne.* Our church has a new minister. *kniisətna ᵓəžaaha qəssiis ᵊždiid.* **2.** *waziir* pl. *wəzara.* Three ministers have resigned from his cabinet. *tlətt wəzara staεfu mən wazaarto.* **3.** *waziir ᵊmfawwaḍ* pl. *wəzara mfawwaḍiin.* He was appointed minister to Portugal. *εayyanúu waziir ᵊmfawwaḍ bᵊl-bərtuğaal.*
minor - 1. *qaaṣer* pl. *-iin.* No liquor will be served to minors. *muu masmuuḥ taqdiim l-ᵊxmuur ləl-qaaṣriin.* — As long as the boy is a minor, his uncle will be his guardian. *maa-daam ᵊṣ-ṣabi ləssə́a qaaṣer εammo bikuun ᵊl-waṣi εalẽe.* **2.** *minoor.* This piece is in A minor. *hal-maqṭuuεa bi-laa minoor.* **3.** *ṭafiif, zahiid.* I made only minor changes. *saaweet tağyiiraat ṭafiife bass.* — That's a minor matter. *hayy masᵓale ṭafiife.*
minority - *ᵓaqalliyye* pl. *-aat.* We were in the minority. *kənna ᵓaqalliyye.*
mint - *naεnaε.* The tea contains mint. *š-šaay fii naεnaε.*
mint - *daaᵓərt˜ daqq˜ ᵊl-εəmle.* The mint is on the other side of town. *daaᵓərt daqq ᵊl-εəmle bᵊṭ-ṭaraf ᵊt-taani mn ᵊl-balad.*
**They made a mint on that deal. *ṭələ́ε-lon kənz ᵊb-haṣ-ṣafďa.*
minute - 1. *daqiiqa* pl. *daqaayeq.* I'll be back in five minutes. *bəržaε baεᵊd xamᵊs daqaayeq.* — Just

a minute, please. *mən faḍlak, daqiiqa!* — I'll drop in for a minute. *bəši bšuufak šii daqiiqa.* — The minute hand of my watch has come off. *Ɛaqrab əd-daqaayeq tabaƐ saaƐti ṭaleƐ mən maṭraḥo.*

minutes - *maḥdar* pl. *maḥaader.* The secretary will read the minutes of the last meeting. *s-səkrəteer raḥa yəqrđa-lna maḥdar əž-žalse s-saabqa.*

the minute - *b-daqiiqet-ma.* I'll call you the minute I know. *bsaawři-lak talifoon əb-daqiiqet-ma ʔaƐref.*

minute - *daqiiq.* It was so minute you could hardly see it. *kaan hal-qadd daqiiq bəl-kaad ətšuufo.* — I have checked every minute detail. *faḥaṣət kəll ət-tafarruƐaat əd-daqiiqa.*

miracle - 1. *məƐəžze* pl. *-aat, ʔəƐžuube* pl. *ʔaƐažiib.* This machine is a miracle of human ingenuity. *hal-maakiina məƐəžze mən məƐəžzaat əl-ʔəbdaaƐ əl-ʔənsaani.* -- It's almost a miracle that he was saved. *kaʔənna məƐəžze kaanet nažaato.* 2. *məƐəžze* pl. *-aat.* The saint is credited with a number of miracles. *l-wali byənəsbúu-lo Ɛəddet məƐəžzaat.*

mirage - *saraab.*

mirror - *mraaye* pl. *-aat* and *maraaya.*

to **miscalculate** - *ʔaxṭaʔ b-, ġəleṭ (a ø) b-.* I miscalculated the time of arrival. *ʔaxṭaʔt əb-waqt əl-wuṣuul.*

miscarriage - 1. *ṭərəḥ* pl. *ṭruuḥa.* She had a miscarriage only a few weeks ago. *ʔəžaaha ṭərəḥ* (or ***ṭərḥet) mən tlətt ʔarbaƐ žəmaƐ.* 2. *suuʔ˜ ʔəstəƐmaal.* His acquittal was a flagrant miscarriage of justice. *tabrəʔto kaanet suuʔ ʔəstəƐmaal faadeḥ ləl-Ɛadaale.*

miscellaneous - *mətnawweƐ, mətfarreƐ.* The appendix lists a number of miscellaneous phrases. *z-zeel fii Ɛadad əmn əl-Ɛibaaraat əl-mətnawwƐa.*

miscellaneous expenses - *natriyyaat* (pl.). Let's set aside 50 dollars for miscellaneous expenses. *xalliina nḥəṭṭ Ɛala žanab xamsiin dolaar lən-natriyyaat.*

mischief - *šeeṭane, Ɛafrate, malƐane.* That boy is full of mischief. *hal-walad malaan šeeṭane.*

miser - *bxiil* pl. *bəxala, šaḥiiḥ* pl. *-iin.*

miserable - 1. *məžwi*, ḥaqiir.* They live in a miserable shack. *saakniin əb-kuux məžwi.* 2. *taƐiis.* She makes life miserable for him. *msaawiit-əllo ḥayaato taƐiise* or ***Ɛam ətnaġġəṣ-lo ḥayaato.* 3. *məzri*.* What miserable weather! *qaddeeš haṭ-ṭaqəṣ məzri!*

**I feel miserable today. *šaayef ḥaali mətl əz-zəft əl-yoom.*

misery - *taƐaase, bəʔs.* They lived in utter misery. *Ɛaašu b-taƐaase w-bəʔs.*

misfortune - *mṣiibe* pl. *maṣaayeb.* It won't be a great misfortune if you don't get it. *muu raḥa tkuun əmṣiibe kbiire ʔiza maa ḥṣəlt Ɛaleе.*

misgivings - *riibe.* From the very beginning I had certain misgivings about the man. *mən ʔawwal əl-ʔamər kaan Ɛandi šwayyet riibe b-haz-zalame.*

to **misinterpret** - *ġəleṭ (a ø) b-tafsiir˜ ...* He misinterpreted my remark to mean that I wasn't interested in the job. *ġəleṭ əb-tafsiir əmlaaḥaẓti kaʔənno maa-li raayed ʔəqbal əš-šaġle.*

to **misjudge** - *ġəleṭ (a ø) bəl-ḥəkəm Ɛala.* We mustn't misjudge the seriousness of the situation. *laazem maa nəġlaṭ əb-ḥəkəmna Ɛala xṭuuret əl-wadəƐ.*

to **mislay**: I've mislaid my glasses. *nsiit ween ḥaṭṭeet kəzəlki.* — Be sure not to mislay these papers. *ʔəṣḥa tḥəṭṭ hal-əwraaq ween-ma kaan.*

to **mislead** - *ḍallal//ḍḍallal, xadaƐ (a xidaaƐ//nxadaƐ).* You misled me into thinking that your offer was meant seriously. *ḍallaltni w-xalleetni ʔəftəker ʔənnak kənət žaaded əb-Ɛarḍak.*

misleading - *mḍallel.* The report contains a number of misleading statements. *t-taqriir byəḍḍamman Ɛəddet bayaanaat mḍalləle* (or ***bayaanaat fiiha taḍliil).*

misprint - *ġalaṭ maṭbaƐi* pl. *ʔaġlaaṭ maṭbaƐiyye.*

Miss - *ʔaanise* pl. *-aat* and *ʔawaanes, madəmwazeel* pl. *-aat.* How do you do, Miss Khouri. *tšarrafna yaa ʔaanise xuuri.*

to **miss** - 1. *ʔaxṭaʔ.* You've missed the target. *ʔaxṭaʔt əl-hadaf.* 2. *maa laḥḥaq.* I missed him at the station. *maa laḥḥaqto bəl-əmḥaṭṭa.* — Do you think I'll miss my train? *btəƐtəqed maa blaḥḥeq ət-treen?* 3. *ḍawwaƐ.* Our house is so easy to find, you can't miss it. *beetna hayyen tlaaqĩi, maa fiik əḍḍawwƐo.* 4. *fawwat, rawwaḥ Ɛaleе.* Don't miss the picture. *la tfawwet əl-fələm!* or *laa trawweḥ Ɛaleek əl-fələm!* 5. *štaaq la-.* I'll miss you terribly. *raḥa ʔəštdq-lak əktiir.*

**You haven't missed anything. *maa raaḥ Ɛaleek šii.*

**He missed hitting me by a hair. *maa ṣəfi beeno w-been ʔənno yṣiibni ʔəlla šaƐra.*

**You missed the point. *faatak maġza l-qəṣṣa.*

missing - 1. *ḍaayeƐ.* The child has been missing for three days. *l-walad ṣar-lo ḍaayeƐ tlətt iyyaam.* 2. *naaqeṣ.* One suitcase is missing. *fii šanta waaḥde naaqṣa.*

missile - (rocket) *ṣaaruux* pl. *ṣawariix.* Intercontinental ballistic missile. *ṣaaruux Ɛaaber* (pl. *ṣawariix Ɛaabərt) əl-qaarraat.*

mission - 1. *bəƐse* pl. *-aat.* A military mission is at present touring the country. *fii bəƐse Ɛaskariyye Ɛam yduur l-əblaad bəl-waqt əl-ḥaader.* 2. *tabšiiriyye* pl. *-aat, ʔərsaaliyye* pl. *-aat.* This Catholic mission was established fifty years ago. *hat-tabšiiriyye l-katuliikiyye tʔassaset mən xamsiin səne.* 3. *muhəmme* pl. *-aat.* They were sent on a special mission into the desert. *baƐatuuhon əb-muhəmme xaaṣṣa ləṣ-ṣaḥra.*

missionary - *mbaššer* pl. *-iin.*

mist - *ḍabaab, ġṭeeṭa.*

mistake - *ġalṭa* pl. *-aat, ġalaṭ* pl. *ʔaġlaaṭ.* How could I make such a mistake? *yaa ʔaḷḷa, kiif əƐməlt hal-ġalṭa?* -- There must be some mistake. *laazem ykuun fii ġalaṭ.*

**Make no mistake about it. This is a serious matter. *ʔəṣḥa təxdaƐ nafsak! hayy masʔale xaṭiira.*

**Sorry, my mistake. *Ɛafwan, ʔana ġalṭaan.*

by mistake - *bəl-ġalaṭ.* Sorry, I took it by mistake. *Ɛafwan, ʔaxadta bəl-ġalaṭ.*

to mistake - 1. *fəhem (a ø) ... ġalaṭ.* Please don't mistake me. *bətražžaak laa təfhamni ġalaṭ.* 2. *gəleṭ (a ġalaṭ).* Sorry, I mistook you for someone else. *mətʔassef əġləṭṭ beenak w-been waaḥed taani.*

**There's no mistaking his intention. *niyyaato waaḍḥa ləl-Ɛayaan.*

mistaken - *xaaṭeʔ, maġluuṭ.* That's a mistaken belief. *haada ʔəƐtiqaad xaaṭeʔ.*

**It was a case of mistaken identity. *kaanet əl-masʔale masʔalet ġalaṭ bəl-hawiyye.*

to be mistaken - *ġəleṭ (a ġalaṭ).* There you're mistaken. *hoon ʔənte ġalṭaan.*

to **mistreat** - *Ɛaamal ... b-qasaawe.* The children were mistreated. *Ɛaamalu l-əwlaad b-qasaawe.*

mistress - *ṣaaḥbe* pl. *-aat.* The dog didn't recognize his mistress. *l-kalb maa Ɛəref ṣaaḥəbto.* — Everybody knows he has a mistress. *kəll ən-naas əbtaƐref ʔənno Ɛando ṣaaḥbe.*

to **misunderstand** - *fəhem (a ø) ... ġalaṭ.* Don't misunderstand me! *laa təfhamni ġalaṭ.*

misunderstanding - 1. *suuʔ˜ fəhəm.* It must be a misunderstanding on my part. *laazem ykuun haada suuʔ fəhəm mənni.* 2. *suuʔ˜ tafaahom.* The conference failed due to a basic misunderstanding between the two parties. *fəšel əl-muʔtamar b-sabab suuʔ tafaahom ʔasaasi been əṭ-ṭarafeen.*

to **mix** - 1. *xalaṭ (o xaləṭ//nxalaṭ), mazaž (e mazəž//mmazaž).* I mixed yellow and red. *xalaṭṭ ʔaṣfar w-ʔaḥmar (maƐ baƐḍon).* — Shall I mix some glue? *ʔəxloṭ šii ġəre?* 2. *xtalaṭ, xaalaṭ, Ɛaašar.* We don't mix much with our neighbors. *maa mnəxtəleṭ əktiir maƐ žiiraanna* or *maa mənxaaleṭ* (or *mənƐaašer) žiiraanna ktiir.* 3. *raaḥu (u ø) maƐ baƐḍon.* Pickles and whipped cream don't mix. *l-əmxallal wəl-kreem maa biruuḥu maƐ baƐḍon.*

to mix in - *ddaaxal.* Don't mix in, this is none of your business. *laa təddaaxal, maa bəddak haš-šaġle maa bətxəṣṣak.* — She likes to mix in other people's business. *bətḥəbb təddaaxal b-əšʔuun ġeera.*

to mix someone up in - *daxxal b-, warraṭ b-.* Don't mix me up in your argument. *laa ddaxxəlni b-əxnaaqak.*

to mix up - *xarbaṭ//txarbaṭ.* Don't mix up the cards. *laa txarbeṭ əš-šadde.* — Don't mix me up! *laa txarbəṭni!*

to get mixed up - 1. *xarbaṭ.* You got me all mixed up now. *xarbaṭtni Ɛal-maḍbuuṭ hallaq.* 2. *txarbaṭ.* I got all mixed up after a while. *baƐda txarbaṭṭ Ɛal-maḍbuuṭ.*

to get someone mixed up in - *daxxal, warraṭ.* Don't get me mixed up in your sordid affairs. *laa ddaxxəlni b-šaġlaatak l-əmƐətte.*

mixture - 1. *xaliiṭ, maziiž.* He's a mixture of stupidity and arrogance. *huwwe xaliiṭ ḥamrane w-šoofet ḥaal.* 2. *maxluuṭa* pl. *-aat.* The mixtures are left standing over night. *l-maxluuṭaat btəntərek la-waḥda ṭuul əl-leel.*

mix-up - *xaṛbaṭa, ḷaxbaṭa.* There was an awful mix-up. *kaan fii xaṛbaṭa faẓiiεa.* — There's been a mix-up in the coats. *ṣaar fii xarbaṭa bᵊl-kababiid.*
to **moan** - *ʔann (ə ʔaniin), tʔawwah.* I could hear him moaning in the next room. *kənᵊt εam ʔəsmaεo yʔənn bᵊl-ʔuuḍa t-taanye.* — Quit moaning. *ḥaaštak ʔaniin!*
mob - *ruεaaε.* The mob almost lynched him. *r-ruεaaε kaanu raḥa yəšᵊnqúu.*
**There's a mob of people waiting for you. *fii εaalam ᵊktiir (or naas ᵊktiir) εam yəstannuuk.*
to mob - *faεaṣ (a faεᵊṣ//nfaεaṣ), šaqqaf.* He was nearly mobbed by the crowd. *ž-žamhuur kaanu raḥa yəfεaṣúu faεᵊṣ (or yšaqqfúu šəqaf).*
**The stores are always mobbed before Christmas. *l-maxaazen εala ṭuul mazḥuume bᵊz-zabaayen qabᵊl εiid ᵊl-miilaad.*
Mocha - *l-muxa.*
mockery - *maṣxara.* The past elections were a mockery of democracy. *l-ʔəntixaabaat ᵊl-ʔaxiire kaanet maṣxara mən maṣaaxer ᵊd-diimuqraaṭiyye.*
model - 1. *numuuzaž* pl. *namaazež.* He's working on the model of a bridge. *εam yaεmel numuuzaž la-žəsr.* 2. *modeel* pl. *-aat.* This is a 1940 model. *hayy modeel sənt ʔarᵊbεiin.* — She was a photographer's model before she became an actress. *kaanet modeel taṣwiir qabᵊl-ma tṣiir mumassile.* 3. *manukaan* pl. *-aat, εaarəḍt˜* (pl. *εaarḍaat*)˜ *ʔazyaaʔ.* She's a model in a fashionable dress shop. *btəštġel manukaan b-maḥall faxᵊm ləl-ʔalbise.* 4. *numuuzaži*.* The government is setting up a number of model villages. *l-ᵊḥkuume εam təbni εadad ᵊmn ᵊl-qura n-numuuzažiyye.* 5. *numuuzaži*, misaali*.* She's a model housewife. *hiyye rabbet beet numuuzažiyye.*
moderate - *məεtədel.* The store charges moderate rates. *l-maxzan bibiiε ᵊb-ʔasεaar məεtədle.* — He has moderate political views. *ʔaaraaʔo s-siyaasiyye məεtədle.*
**He's a man of moderate means. *huwwe rəžžaal ḥaalo εala qaddo.*
to moderate - *daar (i ø).* Who's going to moderate the discussion? *miin bəddo ydiir l-ᵊmnaaqaše?*
modern - 1. *ḥadiis, εala ʔaaxer mooḍa.* She has a modern kitchen. *εanda maṭbax ḥadiis (or maṭbax εala ʔaaxer mooḍa).* 2. *εaṣri*.* The strain of modern life is too much for them. *ḍaġṭ ᵊl-ḥayaat ᵊl-εaṣriyye maa-lon εam yəqᵊdru yətḥammalúu.*
3. *ḥadiis.* Modern art confuses me. *l-fann ᵊl-ḥadiis bixarbəṭni.* 4. *məḥdas* pl. *-iin.* He's an authority on the Moderns in Arabic literature. *huwwe siqa bᵊl-məḥdasiin bᵊl-ʔadab ᵊl-εarabi.*
to **modernize** - *saawa ... εala ʔaḥdas ṭiraaz.* We want to modernize our offices. *bəddna nsaawi makaatəbna εala ʔaḥdas ṭiraaz.*
modest - *mətwaaḍeε.* She's a very modest person. *hiyye mara ktiir mətwaaḍεa.* — We welcome all contributions, no matter how modest they may be. *mənraḥḥeb ᵊb-kəll ᵊt-tabarruεaat mahma kaanet mətwaaḍεa.*
modesty - *tawaaḍoε.*
modification - *taεdiil* pl. *-aat.*
to **modify** - *εaddal//tεaddal.* They modified the original plan several times. *εaddalu l-xəṭṭa l-ʔaṣliyye εəddet marraat.*
moist - *rəṭeb.* The ground is still moist. *l-ʔarḍ ləssaaha raṭbe.*
moisture - *rṭuube.*
molar - *dərᵊs* pl. *draas.*
mold - *εafne.* There was a layer of mold on the cheese. *ž-žəbne kaanet ᵊmġaṭṭaaye bᵊl-εafne.*
to mold - *εaffan.* Bread tends to mold in damp weather. *l-xəbᵊz bᵊṭ-ṭaqṣ ᵊr-rəṭeb biεaffen.*
mold - *qaaleb* pl. *qawaaleb.* You can use this mold for the cake. *fiiki təstaεᵊmli hal-qaaleb ləl-gaato.*
to mold - *kawwan//tkawwan.* Such environmental factors mold the minds of the youngsters. *heek εawaamel ᵊl-biiʔa bətkawwen εaqliyyaat ᵊl-ʔaḥdaas.*
moldy - *mεaffen.* The bread is moldy. *l-xəbz ᵊmεaffen.*
mole - *xəld* pl. *xluud(e).* We've a mole in our garden. *fii xəld b-ᵊžneenətna.*
mole - *xaal* pl. *xiilaan, šaame* pl. *-aat.* He has a large mole on his cheek. *fii xaal ᵊkbiir ᵊb-xaddo.*
mole - *bənṭ* pl. *bnuuṭa.* We swam out to the end of the mole. *sabaḥna la-ʔaaxer ᵊl-bənṭ.*
moment - *laḥẓa* pl. *-aat.* Wait a moment. *stanna laḥẓa.* — Just a moment! *laḥẓa bass!* — I'll give you your change in a moment. *baεṭiik l-ᵊkmaale baεᵊd laḥẓa.*
**Be ready to leave at a moment's notice. *xalliik ḥaaḍer ᵊtruuḥ b-ᵊmžarrad ʔayy ʔəšεaar.*
at the moment - *bᵊl-waqt ᵊl-ḥaaḍer.* At the moment I can't give you any further information. *bᵊl-waqt ᵊl-ḥaaḍer maa bəqder ʔaεṭiik maεluumaat ᵊzyaade.*
momentary - *xaaṭef.* I felt a momentary pain in the chest. *ʔəžaani wažaε xaaṭef ᵊb-ṣədri.*
momentous - *xaṭiir.* A momentous decision like this requires a lot of thinking. *qaraar xaṭiir mətᵊl haad byəṭṭallab tafkiir ᵊktiir.*
monastery - *deer* pl. *dyuura.*
Monday - *(yoom˜) ᵊt-taneen.*
money - 1. *εəmle, maṣaari* (pl.). Do you take American money? *btəqbal εəmle ʔameerkaaniyye?* 2. *maṣaari* (pl.). He has money to burn. *εando maṣaari maa btaakəla n-niiraan.* — He made a lot of money during the war. *εəmel maṣaari ktiir ʔiyyaam ᵊl-ḥarb.* — How much money did you make on it? *qaddeeš ᵊrbəḥt maṣaari fiiha?*
**You can't get that for love or money. *maa btəqder təḥṣal εala haš-šii w-laa b-maal qaaruun.*
**He's got a good wad of money in the bank. *εando qəršeen ᵊmnaaḥ bᵊl-bank.*
money-changer - *ṣarraaf* pl. *-e.*
money lender - *dayyaan (pl. -e) bᵊl-faayez.*
money order - *ḥawaale* pl. *-aat.*
monk - *raaheb* pl. *rəhbaan.*
monkey - *saεdaan* pl. *saεadiin, qərᵊd* pl. *qruud(e).*
monkey wrench - *məftaaḥ ʔəngliizi* pl. *mafatiiḥ ʔəngliiziyye.*
monologue - *manalooğ* pl. *-aat.*
to **monopolize** - *staʔsar b-.* He tends to monopolize the conversation. *biḥəbb yəstaʔser bᵊl-ḥadiis.*
monopoly - *ʔəḥtikaar* pl. *-aat.* The tobacco monopoly is in the hands of the government. *ʔəḥtikaar ᵊd-dəxxaan ᵊb-ʔiid l-ᵊḥkuume.*
to have a monopoly - *ḥtakar.* The company has a monopoly in the production of agricultural machinery. *š-šərke məḥtəkra ʔəntaaž ᵊl-ʔaalaat ᵊz-ziraaεiyye.*
monotonous - 1. *εala watiire waaḥde, εala namaṭ waaḥed.* The monotonous tune made me sleepy. *n-naġme εala watiire waaḥde naεεasətni.* — Day in, day out, the same monotonous work. *yoom baεᵊd yoom nafs ᵊš-šəġᵊl εala watiire waaḥde.* 2. *εala šəkᵊl waaḥed.* The area around here is very monotonous. *l-ʔaraaḍi hoon kəlla εala šəkᵊl waaḥed.*
month - *šahr* pl. *ʔəšhor* and *šhuur,* after numbers 3 - 10 *əšhor.* He came last month. *ʔəža š-šahr ᵊl-maaḍi.* — The repair will take three-and-a-half months. *t-taṣliiḥ byaaxod tlatt əšhor w-nəṣṣ.*
monthly - 1. *šahri*.* You can pay the amount in monthly installments. *btədfaε ᵊl-mablaġ εala ʔaqṣaaṭ šahriyye.* 2. *šahriyyan, kəll šahr, mšaahara.* The money will be collected monthly. *l-maṣaari btənžə́ba šahriyyan.* 3. *mažalle (pl. -aat) šahriyye.* He writes for a well-known monthly. *byəktob maqaalaat ᵊb-mažalle šahriyye maεruufe.*
monument - *naṣᵊb* pl. *ʔanṣaab.*
mood: He's in a good mood today. *žaaye keefo l-yoom.* — He was in a nasty mood when I last saw him. *ʔaaxer marra šəfto kaan εam yxaaneq ᵊxyaalo.* — I'm not in the mood for that. *muu žaay εala baali haš-šii.* — They are not in the mood for laughing. *muu žaay εala baalon yəḍḥaku.*
moody - *nəked.*
moon - *qamaṛ* pl. *qmaaṛ.* There's a ring around the moon tonight. *fii haale ḥawaali l-qamaṛ ᵊl-leele.*
**The moon's out tonight. *l-leele məqᵊmra.*
**I hear from her once in a blue moon. *bəsmaε ʔaxbaara yaa-dooba marra bᵊl-εəmᵊr.*
full moon - *badr* pl. *bduur(a).*
new moon - *hlaal* pl. *-aat.*
moonlight - *ḍaww˜ qamaṛ.* We sat in the moonlight in the garden. *qaεadna bᵊž-žneene taḥᵊt ḍaww ᵊl-qamaṛ.*
mop - *mamsaḥa* pl. *mamaaseḥ.* Take a wet mop. *xədi mamsaḥa mabluule.*
to mop - *masaḥ (a masᵊḥ).* He mopped his forehead. *masaḥ ᵊžbiino.*
to mop (up) - *masaḥ (a masᵊḥ//mmasaḥ).* Did you mop the floor? *masaḥti l-ʔarḍ?*
moral - 1. *ʔaxlaaqi*.* This is a moral question. *hayy masʔale ʔaxlaaqiyye.* 2. *maεnawi*.* I consider it a moral obligation. *bəεtəbə́ra waažeb maεnawi.* 3. *εəbra* pl. *εəbar.* And the moral of the story is ... *wᵊl-εəbra b-hal-qəṣṣa ʔənno ...*
morals - *ʔaxlaaq* (pl.). He has no morals at all. *maa εando ʔaxlaaq ʔabadan.*
morale - *maεnawiyyaat* (pl.). The morale of the troops was excellent. *maεnawiyyaat ᵊž-žnuud kaanet məmtaaze.*
more - 1. *zyaade, ʔaktar.* He's asking for more money. *εam yəṭlob maṣaari zyaade.* 2. *ʔazwad, ʔaktar.* He

asked for more money than his brother did. *ṭalab maṣaari ʔaẓwad mən ʔaxu.* — His salary is more than mine. *maεaašo ʔaẓwad mən maεaaši.* — She makes 50 pounds more than I do. *btaεmel xamsiin leera ʔaktar mənni* or *maεaaša ʔaẓwad mən maεaaši b-xamsiin leera.* **3.** *kamaan.* Give me two more bottles of wine, please. *εaṭiini qanniinteen nbiit kamaan ʔiza bətriid.* — Won't you have some more soup? *maa bəddak kamaan šwayyet šooraba?* **4.** (elative): She's more beautiful than her sister. *hiyye ʔaḥla mən ʔəxta.* — There's nothing more disturbing ... *maa fii šii ʔazεaž mən* ... (or *məzεež ʔaktar mən...*). — This store is usually more crowded in the afternoon than it is in the morning. *hal-maxzan εaadatan bikuun maεžuuq ʔaktar baεd ᵊḍ-ḍəhᵊr mən εala bəkra.* — That's more likely. *εal-ʔaržaḥ* (or *εal-ʔaġlab*) *heek.*

more and more - *ʔaktar w-ʔaktar.* He got more and more involved in the matter. *twarraṭ ʔaktar w-ʔaktar bᵊl-masʔale.* — This business is getting more and more complicated. *haš-šaġle εam tətεaqqad ʔaktar w-ʔaktar.* — Everything is getting more and more expensive. *kəll šii εam yəġla ʔaktar w-ʔaktar.*

more or less - *εala wažh ᵊl-εumuum, bᵊl-ʔəžmaal.* I believe that report is more or less true. *bəεtəqed hat-taqriir εala wažh ᵊl-εumuum ṣaḥiiḥ.*

not any more - **1.** *maa εaad* (inflected). I don't care any more. *maa εədt ʔəhtamm.* — We didn't see him any more. *maa εədna šəfnda.* **2.** *laa εaad* (inflected). Don't do that any more! *laa εədt taεmel haš-šii ʔabadan!* — Don't go and see him any more. *laa εədtu dzuurdu ʔabadan!*

once more - *taani marra, marra taanye, kamaan marra.* Try once more. *žarreb taani marra.*

the more ... the ... - *kəll-ma ... ʔaktar kəll-ma ... ʔaktar.* The more I give him the more he wants. *kəll-ma baεṭii ʔaktar kəll-ma byəṭlob ʔaktar.* — The more I see him the more I like him. *kəll-ma bšuufo ʔaktar kəll-ma bḥəbbo ʔaktar.*

**The more, the merrier. *z-zyaade ʔaḥsan mn ᵊn-nəqṣaan.*

what's more - *w-ʔaktar mən heek, w-ᵊzyaade εala heek.* What's more, I don't believe him. *w-ʔaktar mən heek maa bsaddqo.*

moreover - *w-ᵊzyaade εala heek, w-ʔaktar mən heek.*

morning - **1.** *ṣabaaḥ.* Good morning! *ṣabaaḥ ᵊl-xeer!* answer: *ṣabaaḥ ᵊl-xeeraat.* — It's a beautiful morning, isn't it? *haṣ-ṣabaaḥ ḥəlu, muu heek?* **2.** *ṣəbᵊḥ, ṣabaaḥ.* He works from morning till night. *byəštəġel mn ᵊṣ-ṣəbᵊḥ ləl-masa.* **3.** *qabl ᵊḍ-ḍəhᵊr.* He slept all morning. *naam kəll qabl ᵊḍ-ḍəhᵊr.* **4.** *εala bəkra.* I'll see you tomorrow morning. *bšuufak bəkra εala bəkra.*

in the morning - *bᵊṣ-ṣabaaḥ, ṣ-ṣəbᵊḥ, εala bəkra.* She's only here in the morning. *hiyye maa bətkuun hoon ʔəlla bᵊṣ-ṣabaaḥ.* — I'll see you in the morning. *bšuufak εala bəkra.*

**We danced till one in the morning. *raqaṣna ḥatta s-saaεa waaḥde baεᵊd nəṣṣ ᵊl-leel.*

this morning - *l-yoom εala bəkra, ṣabaaḥ ᵊl-yoom, l-yoom ᵊṣ-ṣəbᵊḥ.* There was a lot to do this morning. *kaan fii šəġl ᵊktiir ᵊl-yoom εala bəkra.*

Moroccan - *maraakši** pl. *-iyye, məġᵊrbi** pl. *maġaarbe.*

Morocco - *maraakeš, l-mamlake l-məġᵊrbiyye.*

mortal - **1.** *mumiit, qaatel, ḍaadi.* That was a mortal blow to the industry of the country. *kaanet ḍarbe mumiite la-ṣinaaεet l-ᵊblaad.* **2.** *laduud* pl. *-iin.* They are mortal enemies. *hənne εaduwwiin laduudiin la-baεḍon ᵊl-baεᵊḍ.* **3.** *bašar* (invar.). That isn't for ordinary mortals. *haada muu la-bašar mətli w-mətlak.*

**We are all mortal. *kəllna zaayliin.*

mortality - *nəsbet˜ wafayaat.* Mortality was unusually high that year. *nəsbet ᵊl-wafayaat kaanet εaalye εala ġeer εaade has-səne.*

mortar - **1.** *muune.* Mortar is made out of lime and sand. *l-muune bisaawuuha mn ᵊl-kəls wᵊr-ramᵊl.* **2.** *haawen* pl. *hawaawiin.* Pound the garlic in the mortar. *dəqqi t-tuum bᵊl-haawen.* **3.** *madfaε* (pl. *madaafeε*) *haawen.* The platoon is equipped with two mortars and one machine gun. *l-faṣiile mžahhaze b-madfaεeen haawen w-raššaaš waaḥed.*

mortgage - *rahniyye* pl. *-aat, rahᵊn* pl. *rhuun.* The interest on the mortgage is due. *l-faayde εar-rahniyye stḥaqqet.*

to mortgage - *rahan (o/e rahᵊn//nrahan).* He had to mortgage his house. *nžabar yərhon beeto.*

mosaic - *moozayiik.*

Moscow - *moosko.*

Moslem - *məslem* pl. *-iin,* f. *məsᵊlme* pl. *-aat.*

mosque - *masžed* pl. *masaažed,* (large) *žaameε* pl. *žawaameε.*

mosquito - *naamuuse* coll. *naamuus* pl. *-aat.*

most - **1.** *ʔaktar šii.* That's the most I can pay. *haada ʔaktar šii bəqder ʔədfaεo.* — What did you like most? *šuu ḥabbeet ʔaktar šii?* **2.** *ʔaktar˜.* Most people went home early. *ʔaktar ᵊn-naas raaḥu εala byuuton bakkiir.* — Who did the most work? *miin ᵊštaġal ʔaktar ᵊš-šəġᵊl?* — Most of those present were against the proposal. *ʔaktar ᵊl-ḥaaḍriin kaanu ḍədd ᵊl-ʔəqtiraaḥ.* — I did most of his work. *štaġalᵊt ʔaktar šəġlo.* — Most of them never showed up. *ʔaktdron maa ʔəžu ʔabadan.* — Most of the day I'm at the office. *ʔaktar ᵊn-nhaar ʔana bᵊl-maktab.* — He's on the road most of the time. *ʔaktar ᵊl-ʔawqaat huwwe msaafer.* **3.** (elative): This is the most beautiful church I've ever seen. *hayy ʔaḥla kniise šəfta.* — She's the most intelligent student I ever had. *hiyye ʔazka ṭaalbe darrasta.* **4.** *ktiir.* The talk was most interesting. *l-ḥadiis kaan ᵊktiir ṭariif.*

at (the) most - *εal-ʔaktar.* I can pay fifteen pounds at most. *bəqder ʔədfaε xamᵊsṭaεšar leera εal-ʔaktar.* — At the most it's worth ten pounds. *εal-ʔaktar btəswa εašᵊr leeraat.*

for the most part - *bᵊl-ʔaktar.* For the most part I agree with him. *bᵊl-ʔaktar ʔana mwaafeq maεo.*

to make the most of - *stafaad mən.* We'd better make the most of our time. *ʔaḥsdn-ᵊlna nəstfiid mən waqᵊtna.*

mostly - **1.** *ʔaktar ᵊl-marraat, ʔaktar ᵊl-ʔawqaat, ʔaktar ᵊl-ʔaḥyaan.* He's mostly right. *ʔaktar ᵊl-marraat maεo ḥaqq.* **2.** *bᵊl-ʔaktar.* The audience consisted mostly of women. *ž-žamaaεa kaanet ᵊmʔallafe bᵊl-ʔaktar mən nəswaan.*

Mosul - *l-muuṣel.*

moth - **1.** (clothes) *εətte* coll. *εətt* pl. *-aat.* **2.** (large, nocturnal) *farraaše* coll. *farraaš* pl. *-aat.*

moth ball - *ḥabbet˜* (coll. *ḥabb˜* pl. *-aat˜*) *naftaliin.*

mother - **1.** *ʔəmm* pl. *-aat* and *ʔəmmahaat, waalde* pl. *-aat.* She takes care of us like a mother. *btəεtəni fiina mətᵊl ʔəmm.* **2.** *ʔəmm.* Necessity is the mother of invention. *l-ḥaaže ʔəmm ᵊl-ʔəxtiraaε.*

to mother - *εtana b-* ... *mətᵊl ʔəmm.* She mothers him all the time. *εala ṭuul btəεtəni fii mətᵊl ʔəmm.*

motherhood - *ʔumuume.*

mother-in-law - *ḥamaaye* (with pron. suff. *ḥamaat-*) pl. *ḥamawaat.*

motion - **1.** *ḥarake* pl. *-aat.* You can barely feel the motion of the ship. *bᵊl-kaad ᵊtḥəss ᵊb-ḥaraket ᵊl-baaxra.* **2.** *ʔəqtiraaḥ* pl. *-aat.* I'd like to make a motion. *bəddi qaddem ʔəqtiraaḥ.*

to be in motion - *tḥarrak.* The train was still in motion. *t-treen kaan ləssda εam yətḥarrak.*

to set in motion - **1.** *ḥarrak, mašša.* The action of the pistons sets the flywheel in motion. *ḥaraket ᵊl-bəstoonaat bətḥarrek ᵊl-ḥaddaafe.* **2.** *mašša.* Lowering of tariffs set the economic recovery in motion. *taxfiiḍ ᵊr-rsuum ᵊž-žəmrukiyye maššet ᵊl-ʔənmaaʔ ᵊl-ʔəqtiṣaadi.*

to motion - *εəmel ʔišaara la-, ʔaššar la-.* He motioned the taxi to stop. *εəmel ʔišaara lət-taksi la-ywaqqef.*

motionless - *bala ḥarake.*

motion picture - *fəlᵊm* pl. *flaam* and *ʔaflaam* and *fluume.*

motive - *baaεes* pl. *bawaaεes.*

motor - *motoor* pl. *-aat, mḥarrek* pl. *-aat.* I let the motor run. *xalleet ᵊl-motoor εam yəštəġel.*

motor bike - *ṭəqṭeeqa* pl. *-aat* and *ṭaqaṭiiq.*

motorboat - *šaxtuura* (pl. *šaxatiir*) *εal-banziin.*

motorcycle - *mootosiikᵊl* pl. *-aat.*

motorman - *sawwaaq˜* (pl. *-iin˜*) *traam.*

motto - *šiεaar* pl. *-aat.*

to **mount** - **1.** *rəkeb (a rəkᵊb).* He mounted his horse and rode off. *rəkeb ᵊḥṣaano w-məši.* **2.** *ṭaleε (a ṭluuε) εala.* He mounted the platform to make a speech. *ṭaleε εal-mənaṣṣa la-yəlqi xiṭaab.* **3.** *rakkab//trakkab.* The machines will be mounted on concrete blocks. *l-maakiinaat raḥa yətrakkabu εala qawaaεed beetoon.* — I'd like to have this photograph mounted and framed. *bəddi-yaak trakkəb-li haṣ-ṣuura w-ᵊtbarwəza.* **4.** *εəli (a ø).* Costs are mounting fast. *t-takaliif εam təεla b-εažale.*

mounted police - *šərṭa xayyaale.*

mountain - *žabal* pl. *žbaal.* How high is that mountain? *qaddeeš εəluww haž-žabal?*

**Don't make a mountain out of a molehill. *laa tsaawi mən ᵊl-ḥabbe qəbbe.*

mountainous - *žabali**.
mourning - (Christian) *ḥdaad,* (Muslim) *ḥəz°n.* She went to parties before the period of mourning was over. *raaḥet ʕal-ʕazaayem qab°l-ma təmḍa məddet l-°ḥdaad.*
to be in mourning - *ḥadd (ə ḥdaad), ḥazen (a ḥəz°n).* He's in mourning. *huwwe ḥaaded.*
mouse - *faar* pl. *fiiraan.*
mousetrap - *maṣyade* pl. *maṣaayed.*
mouth - **1.** *təmm* pl. *tmaam.* I've got a bad taste in my mouth. *fii ṭaʕme ʕaaṭle b-təmmi.* — The story passed from mouth to mouth. *l-qəṣṣa məšyet mən təmm la-təmm.* — They live from hand to mouth. *ʕaayšiin mən ʕəbbon la-təmmon.* — The dog stopped at the mouth of the cave. *l-kalb waqqaf ʕand təmm l-°mġaara.* **2.** *maṣabb* pl. *-aat.* Souédieh is at the mouth of the Orontes. *s-sweediyye waaqʕa ʕala maṣabb nahr °l-ʕaaṣi.* **Don't look a gift horse in the mouth. *ʕəmrak laa tfalli hdiyye, xəda ʕala ʕəllaata.* **Why are you so down in the mouth? *leeš maqbuuḍ?* or *šəbak maa-lak ʕala baʕḍak?*
mouthpiece - **1.** *lsaan˜ ḥaal.* That newspaper acts as a government mouthpiece. *haž-žariide bətmassel lsaan ḥaal l-°ḥkuume.* **2.** *bazbuuze* pl. *bazabiiz.* The mouthpiece of my pipe needs cleaning. *bazbuuzet °l-ġalyuun tabaʕi laazə́ma tanḍiif.*
mouthwash - *mayyet˜ ġarġara.*
movable - *mətḥarrek.*
move - **1.** *ḥarake* pl. *-aat.* Every move I make hurts. *kəll ḥarake bsaawiiha btəžaʕ.* — He can't make a move without asking his wife. *maa byəqder yaʕmel ḥarake bala-ma yšaawer marto* or ***maa byəqder yətḥarrak* (or *yḥarrek qašše*) *bala-ma ...* — Don't make a move or I'll shoot! *maa taʕmel ḥarake bqawweṣ!* — He checkmated me after 24 moves. *mawwat šaahi baʕ°d ʔarbʕa w-ʕəšriin ḥarake.* **2.** *xaṭwe* pl. *-aat.* He made a very shrewd move. *xaṭa* (or *ʕəmel*) *xaṭwe kəlla dahaa?.* **It's your move, you're in check. *doorak* (or *ləʕbak*), *kəšš!* **They're forever on the move. *maa byəhdu, ʕala ṭuul byəḥ°rku.*
to move - **1.** *ḥarrak//tḥarrak.* She can't move her foot. *maa btəqder °tḥarrek rəžla.* **2.** *tḥarrak.* I can't move. *maa fiini ʔətḥarrak.* **3.** *ǧtaraḥ, ṭalab (o ṭalab).* I move we adjourn. *bəǧtə́reḥ narže? °ž-žalse.* **4.** *ʔassar b-* or *ʕala//tʔassar.* The story moved them deeply. *l-qəṣṣa ʔassaret fiihon °ktiir.* — I was moved to tears. *tʔassar°t la-daražet °l-bake.* **5.** *ʕaašar.* They move in the best circles. *biʕaašru ʔaʕla ṭ-ṭabaqaat* or ***biruuḥu w-°byəžu maʕ °z-zawaat.* **6.** *ntaqal, naqal (o naqle).* We're moving on October first. *bəddna nəntə́qel b-ʔawwal təšriin °l-[illegible]al.* — Do you know where they're moving to? *btaʕ[illegible]f la-ween raḥa yəntəqlu?* — The new tenants are moving in next week. *l-məstaʔ°žriin °ž-žədad raḥa yəntəqlu ləl-beet °ž-žəmʕa ž-žaaye.* — When are you moving out? *ʔeemta raḥa təntə́qel?* **7.** *qaam (i ø).* You'll have to move your car. *laazem tqiim sayyaartak mən hoon.* **I just moved. It's your turn. *lʕəb°t. doorak.* **We moved heaven and earth to get it. *qəmna d-dənye w-ḥaṭṭeenaaha la-nəḥṣal ʕalée.*
moving - *m°asser.* He told us a very moving story. *ḥakḍa-lna ḥkaaye ktiir °m°assra.*
to move along - *tqaddam, tḥarrak.* Things are finally moving along now. *w-ʔaxiiran l-°ʔmuur ʕam tətqaddam.*
to move away - **1.** *ntaqal, raḥal (a raḥiil).* They moved away a long time ago. *ntaqalu mən zamaan.* **2.** *qaam (i ø).* Move the table away, please. *qiim °ṭ-ṭaawle, mən faḍlak.*
to move back - *ʔaxxar la-wara.* Move your chair back a little. *ʔaxxer kərsiik la-wara šwayye.* — Move back, folks! *ʔaxxru la-wara yaa žamaaʕa!*
to move forward - *qaddam.* Can you move forward a little? *fiik °tqaddem šwayye?* — Now move your foot forward. *hallaq qaddem rəžlak la-qəddaam.*
to move on - *ntaqal.* We'll now move on to the next chapter. *hallaq mnəntə́qel ləl-faṣl °ž-žaaye.* **Move on! *yaḷḷa mən hoon!*
movement - **1.** *ḥarake* pl. *-aat.* His movements are closely watched. *ʕam yraaqbu kəll ḥarake mən ḥarakaato.* — He never belonged to any political movement. *b-ḥayaato maa ntama la-ʔayy ḥarake siyaasiyye.* **2.** *faṣl* pl. *fṣuul.* That theme is from the second movement of the Fifth Symphony. *ḥan-naġme b°l-faṣl °t-taani tabaʕ °s-sinfuuniyye l-xaamse.* **3.** *ʔawaayel* (pl.), *ʔaalaat* (pl.). My watch has a Swiss movement. *saaʕti ʔawaayə́la swiisriyye.*
movie - **1.** *fəl°m* pl. *flaam* and *ʔaflaam* and *fluume.* Is there a good movie playing tonight? *fii fəl°m mniiḥ °l-leele?*
movies - *siinama* pl. *-aat.* We rarely go to the movies. *qəllet-ma nruuḥ ʕas-siinama.*
to **mow** - **1.** *ḥaṣad (o ḥaṣ°d//nḥaṣad).* It'll take two men at least a week to mow this field of wheat. *zal°mteen bəddon ʕal-ʔaqalli žəmʕa la-yəḥ°ṣdu ḥaqlet hal-qam°ḥ.* **2.** *qaṣṣ (ə qaṣṣ//nqaṣṣ), qaṭaʕ (a qaṭ°ʕ//nqaṭaʕ).* Tell the gardener to mow the grass. *quul ləž-žneenaati yqəṣṣ °l-ḥašiiš.*
mowing machine - *ḥaṣṣaaḍe* pl. *-aat.*
Mr. - **1.** *s-sayyed ...* Could I speak to Mr. Haddad? *bəqder ʔəḥki maʕ °s-sayyed ḥaddaad?* **2.** *sayyed ...* Mr. Smith, I'd like you to meet my friend Ali. *sayyed smiis, bḥəbb ʕarrfak ʕala rafiiqi ʕali.* **3.** *siyaadet˜ ...* Mr. Consul General, may I present... *siyaadet °l-qənṣol °l-ʕaamm, btəsmaḥ-li qaddem...*
Mrs. - **1.** *madaam* (preceding family name), *xaanom* (following given name, a respectful but slightly less formal address than *madaam*); e.g., a lady by the name of *Suʕaad Kamaal* would be addressed or referred to either as *madaam Kamaal* or *Suʕaad xaanom.* **2.** *s-sayyde..., madaam...* May I speak with Mrs. Khuri, please? *məmken ʔəḥki maʕ °s-sayyde xuuri* (or *maʕ madaam xuuri*), *mən faḍlak?*
much - **1.** *ktiir.* I haven't much time. *maa ʕandi waqt °ktiir.* **2.** *b-°ktiir.* I feel much better today. *ḥaases ḥaali ʔaḥsan b-°ktiir °l-yoom.* — She is much prettier than I had expected. *hiyye ʔaḥla b-°ktiir məmma kən°t mənṭə́ẓer.* **Much ado about nothing. *dooše bala sabab.*
how much - *qaddeeš.* How much will it cost me? *qaddeeš ḥa-tkallə́fni?* — How much time will it take? *qaddeeš btaaxod waq°t?* — Think of how much money we've spent already! *tṣawwar qaddeeš ṣarafna maṣaari la-hallaq!*
that much, this much - *hal-qadd, qadd heek.* I didn't ask for that much. *maa ṭalab°t hal-qadd.* — That much we know. *hal-qadd °mnaʕref.* — What are you going to do with that much money? *šuu bəddak taʕmel °b-qadd heek maṣaari?*
very much - *ktiir.* We didn't like him very much. *maa ḥabbeenda ktiir.* — Thank you very much. *šəkran °ktiir.*
mucus - *mxaaṭ.*
mud - *ṭiin, waḥ°l.* The car got stuck in the mud. *s-sayyaara ġarzet b°ṭ-ṭiin.* — All the roads were covered with mud after the rain. *kəll °ṭ-ṭəroq kaanet malaane ṭiin baʕd °l-maṭar.*
to **muddle** - *xarbaṭ, laxbaṭ, šawwaš.* The wine had muddled her thinking. *l-xam°r xarbáṭ-la tafkiira.*
to muddle through - *dabbar ḥaalo.* We ran into no end of obstacles, but somehow we managed to muddle through. *ṣaadafna maṣaaʕeb maa-la ʔaaxer bass kiif-ma kaan dabbarna ḥaalna.*
muddy - **1.** *malaan˜ ṭiin.* Your shoes are muddy. *ṣabbaaṭak malaan ṭiin.* **2.** *mʕakkar, ʕəker.* This water is muddy. *hal-mayy mʕakkara.*
muezzin - *m°adden* pl. *-iin.*
mufti - **1.** *məfti* pl. *mafaati.* The mufti will announce his decision next week. *l-məfti ḥa-yəʕlen fatḍa ž-žəmʕa ž-žaaye.* **2.** *madani.* He wore mufti the last time I saw him. *ʔaaxer marra šəfto fiiha kaan laabes madani.*
muggy - *ʕəbeq.* It's awfully muggy today. *d-dənye ʕəbqa ktiir °l-yoom.*
mule - *baġ°l* pl. *bġaal,* f. *baġle* pl. *-aat.*
mule driver - *baġġaal* pl. *-e.*
to **mull** - *qallab...b°l-ʕaq°l.* He mulled over the suggestion before approving it. *qallab °l-ʔəǧtiraaḥ °b-ʕaqlo qab°l-ma waafaq ʕalée.*
multiple - **1.** *mətʕadded, ʕadiid.* This act will have multiple consequences. *hal-ʕamal ḥa-ykə́n-lo nataayež mətʕadd°de.* **2.** *ḍəʕ°f* pl. *ʔaḍʕaaf.* Find the numbers that are multiples of five. *laaqi l-ʔaʕdaad yalli hiyye ʔaḍʕaaf °l-xamse.*
multiplication - **1.** *takaator.* The rate of multiplication of rabbits is amazing. *nəsbet takaator °l-ʔaraaneb šii mədheš.* **2.** *ḍarb.* Children learn multiplication after addition and subtraction. *l-°wlaad byətʕallamu ḍ-ḍarb baʕd °ž-žam°ʕ w°ṭ-ṭar°ḥ.*
multiplication table - *žadwal˜* (pl. *žadaawel˜*) *ḍarb.*
to **multiply** - **1.** *ḍarab (o ḍarb//nḍarab).* Multiply three by four! *ḍroob tlaate b-ʔarbʕa.* **2.** *tkaatar.* The population multiplies at an alarming speed. *ʕadad °s-səkkaan ʕam yətkaatar °b-sərʕa mər°ʕbe.*
to **mumble** - *barbar.* He always mumbles in his beard.

Eala tuul bibarber la-haalo.
mummy - *muumye* pl. *-aat.*
mumps - *ʔabu˜ kaEᵊb.* The boy had the mumps two weeks ago. *l-walad tələE-lo* (or *kaan maEo*) *ʔabu kaEᵊb mən žəmᵊEteen.*
Munich - *muniix.*
municipal - *baladi**. There are municipal elections coming up. *fii ʔəntixaabaat baladiyye žaaye Ean qariib.*
munitions - *zaxiire* pl. *zaxaayer.* He works in a munitions factory. *byəštəġel ᵊb-maEmal zaxiire.*
murder - (*haadset˜*) *qatᵊl* pl. *hawaades qatᵊl.* The murder was not discovered until a few days later. *haadəst ᵊl-qatᵊl maa nkašfet ʔəlla baEᵊd kam yoom.*
to murder - *qatal* (*o qatᵊl//nqatal*). There is a rumor that he murdered his business partner. *fii ʔišaEa ʔənno qatal ᵊšriiko bᵊš-šəġᵊl.* — She murdered that song. *qatlet* (or **harqet diin*) *hal-ġanniyye.* — He murders the Arabic language. *byəqtol* (or ***byəhreq diin*) *ᵊl-luġa l-Earabiyye.*
murderer - *qaatel* pl. *qatale.*
murky - *məEtem.*
murmur - **1.** *barbara, hamhame.* The crowd received him with a murmur of approval. *ž-žamᵊE staqbalo b-barbara bəddəll Eal-ᵊmwaafaqa.* **2.** *xariir.* In the distance, we could hear the murmur of the stream. *mən Eala bəEᵊd smaEna xariir ᵊs-saaʔel.*
**There was a murmur of discontent. *kaan fii tazammor.*
to murmur - *barbar.* He murmured something I couldn't understand. *barbar šii maa hsənᵊt ʔəfhamo.*
muscle - *Eadale* pl. *-aat.*
muscular - *Eadali**. The child suffers from muscular dystrophy. *l-walad ᵊmsaab ᵊb-wahᵊn Eadali.*
**He has a muscular physique. *bənito kəlla Eadalaat.*
museum - *mathaf* pl. *mataahef.*
mushroom - *fətra* coll. *fətᵊr* pl. *-aat.* Are these mushrooms poisonous? *hal-fətr ᵊmsəmm?*
**Around here new houses are popping up like mushrooms. *b-han-nawaahi l-binaayaat ᵊž-ždiide Eam tənboz mətl ᵊl-fəžᵊl.*
music - **1.** *muusiiqa.* Where's the music coming from? *l-muusiiqa žaaye mneen?* — I like the music of Beethoven. *bhəbb muusiiqet bəthooven.* — Who's giving you music lessons? *miin Eam yaEtiik ᵊdruus muusiiqa?* **2.** *noot.* I didn't bring my music with me. *maa žəbt ᵊn-noot tabaEi.*
to set to music - *lahhan.* This poem is beautifully set to music. *haš-šəEr ᵊmlahhan talhiin həlu.*
musical - **1.** *muusiiqi**. Do you play any musical instrument? *btaEref təlEab Eala šii ʔaale muusiiqiyye?* **2.** *rwaaye* (pl. *-aat*) *muusiiqiyye.* I haven't been to a musical for years. *sar-li sniin maa rəhᵊt Eala rwaaye muusiiqiyye.*
**He's a very musical person. *Eando ʔədᵊn muusiiqiyye.*
musician - *muusiiqaar* and *muusiiqi* pl. *muusiiqiyyiin.*
Muslim - *məslem* pl. *-iin,* f. *məsᵊlme* pl. *-aat.*
muslin - *moosliin.*
must - *laazem* + imperf. without *b-*. He must be sick. *laazem ykuun ᵊdEiif.* — I mustn't be late. *laazem maa ʔətʔaxxar.* — You must never forget that. *laazem maa tənsa haš-šii ʔabadan.*
**There is no such thing as must. *maa fii šii bᵊd-dənye ʔəsmo "hatᵊm".*
**This dam is a must for the development of agriculture in this region. *has-sadd laa bədd mənno la-tanmiit ᵊz-ziraaEa b-hal-mantiqa.*
mustache - *šawaareb* (sg. and pl.).
mustard - *xardal.*
musty - *mənten.* These old rooms have a musty smell. *hal-ʔuwad ᵊl-qadiime riihəta mənᵊtne.*
mute - *ʔaxras* f. *xarsa* pl. *xərᵊs* and *xərsaan.* The poor fellow is a mute. *hal-məskiin ʔaxras.*
to **mutilate** - *šawwah//tšawwah.* He was badly mutilated in a traffic accident. *tšawwah ᵊktiir ᵊb-haades ʔəstidaam.*
mutiny - *tamarrod* pl. *-aat, Eəsyaan.* A mutiny broke out on the ship. *saar fii tamarrod Eal-baaxra.*
to mutiny - *tmarrad.* Several Army units mutinied. *Eəddet wəhdaat ᵊmn ᵊž-žeeš ᵊtmarradet.*
to **mutter** - *barbar.* He muttered something under his breath. *barbar šii b-soot waati.*
mutton - *lahᵊm˜ ġanam, lahᵊm˜ xaaruuf.*
mutual - *mətbaadel.* This treaty provides for mutual aid in case of war. *hal-ᵊmEaahade btəštəret ᵊmsaaEade mətbaadle b-haalet harb.* — It will be to our mutual advantage. *bətkuun la-maslahətna l-mətbaadle.*
**He's a mutual friend of ours. *huwwe saahebna nəhna t-tneen.*
muzzle - *kammaame* pl. *-aat.* Dogs are not allowed on the street without muzzles. *muu masmuuh ləl-ᵊklaab yəmšu bᵊt-tariiq bala kammaamaat.*
to muzzle - *kammam//tkammam.* That dog ought to be muzzled. *hal-kalb laazem yətkammam.*
my - **1.** *-i,* (after vowels) *-yi.* This is my picture. *hayy suurti.* — I have to wash my hands. *laazem ġassel ʔidayyi.* **2.** *tabaEi, šiiti.* My secretary will call you back. *l-kaatbe tabaEi bəttalfən-lak.* — My radio is broken again. *r-raadyo tabaEi xəreb taani marra.*
myrrh - *tiib.*
myself - **1.** *la-haali, b-nafsi.* I'll do it myself. *ʔana la-haali baEməla.* — I make my bed myself. *bsaawi taxti la-haali.* **2.** *haali, nafsi.* I cut myself shaving this morning. *žarahᵊt haali s-səbᵊh w-ʔana Eam ʔəhleq.* **3.** *-i* (*-yi*). The responsibility is on myself. *l-masʔuuliyye Ealiyyi ʔana.*
**I'm going to buy myself a pair of shoes. *laha ʔəštri-li sabbaat ᵊždiid.*
**I'm not myself today. *maa-li Eala baEdi l-yoom.*
by myself - **1.** *la-haali, la-wahdi, b-nafsi.* I assembled the radio all by myself. *rakkabt ᵊr-raadyo kəllo la-haali.* **2.** *la-haali, wahdi.* I don't like being at home all by myself. *maa bhəbb ʔəqEod bᵊl-beet la-haali.*
mysterious - **1.** *ġaamed.* We received a mysterious telephone call last night. *ʔəžaana talifoon ġaamed ᵊmbaarha bᵊl-leel.* **2.** *ġariib.* Who is that mysterious woman you always talk about? *miin hiyye hal-mara l-ġariibe yalli Eam təhki Eanha Eala tuul?* — Where's that mysterious noise coming from? *mneen žaaye haṣ-soot ᵊl-ġariib?*
mystery - **1.** *sərr ġaamed* pl. *ʔasraar ġaamda.* The police never solved the mystery. *š-šərta ʔabadan maa hallet ᵊs-sərr ᵊl-ġaamed.* **2.** *sərr məġlaq* pl. *ʔasraar məġlaqa.* How he managed it is a mystery to me. *kiif dabbəra sərr məġlaq Ealiyyi.*
mystery story - *qəssa* (pl. *qəsas*) *booliisiyye.*
mysticism - *tasawwof, suufiyye.*
myth - *xuraafe* pl. *-aat.* Many myths have a historical foundation. *ktiir ᵊmn ᵊl-xuraafaat ʔəlon ʔasᵊl taariixi.*

N

nag - *gdiiš* pl. *kədᵊš.* The old nag could hardly pull the wagon. *l-ᵊgdiiš ᵊl-qadiim bᵊl-kaad qəder yžərr ᵊl-Earabaaye.*
to **nag** - *naqq* (*ə naqq*) *Eala* (*qalb-...*). She kept nagging me. *dallet ᵊtnəqq Ealiyyi* (or *Eala qalbi*).
nail - **1.** *bəsmaar* pl. *basamiir, məsmaar* pl. *masamiir.* Don't hammer the nail in all the way. *laa ddəqq ᵊl-bəsmaar la-ʔaaxro.* **2.** *dəfᵊr* pl. *ʔadafiir.* I just broke my nail. *hallaq ᵊnkasar dəfri.*
**He always hits the nail on the head. *huwwe daayman bižiiba masbuut.*
to nail - *basmar, masmar.* Please nail the board to the wall. *balla basmer ᵊl-looh Eal-heet.*
to nail down - *ʔalzam.* It's difficult to nail him down to anything. *saEᵊb təlᵊzmo b-šii.*
naked - **1.** *Earyaan, mgallat.* He claims he saw a naked woman leave the room. *biquul ʔənno šaaf mara Earyaane taalEa mn ᵊl-ʔuuda.* **2.** *bᵊz-zalt.* The children ran around naked. *l-ᵊwlaad kaanu faltaaniin bᵊz-zalt.* **3.** *mžarrad.* On a clear day you can see the town from here with the naked eye. *b-yoom saahi btəqder ᵊtšuuf ᵊl-balad mən hoon bᵊl-Eeen l-ᵊmžarrade.*
name - **1.** *ʔəsᵊm* pl. *ʔasmaaʔ* and *ʔasaami.* His name sounds familiar to me. *kaʔənni samEaan ʔəsmo.* — What's your name, please? *šu ʔəsmak ᵊl-kariim?* — I know him only by name. *baEᵊrfo bᵊl-ʔəsᵊm bass.* — He's the head of the company in name only. *huwwe*

raʔiis ᵊš-šərke bᵊl-ʔəsᵊm bass. -- I haven't a cent to my name. maa ɛandi w-laa qərš (ᵊmqayyad) ᵊb-ʔəsmi or **maa bəmlek ᵊn-nḥaase. 2. ʔəsᵊm, səmɛa, ṣiiṭ. He has made quite a name for himself in literary circles. bana ʔəsᵊm laa baʔs fii bᵊl-ʔawsaaṭ ᵊl-ʔadabiyye.

family or **last name** - ʔəsm˜ ᵊl-ɛeele, kənye pl. -aat. What's your family name? šuu ʔəsᵊm ɛeeltak or šuu kənitak?

first or **given name** - ʔəsᵊm ʔawwalaani. What's his first name? šuu ʔəsmo l-ʔawwalaani?

to name - samma//tsamma. He named his son Mahmud. samma ʔəbno maḥmuud. -- They named the baby after his father. sammu l-walad ɛala ʔəsᵊm ʔabúu. -- Can you name all the planets? btəqder ᵊtsammᵊi-li kəll ᵊl-kawaakeb ᵊs-sayyaara? or **btəqder tqəl-li ʔasmaaʔ kəll ᵊl-kawaakeb ᵊs-sayyaara? -- Name your own price. sammᵊi-li s-səɛᵊr yalli biwaafqak.

namely - yaɛni. I have only one wish, namely to go home soon. maa ɛandi ʔəlla rəġbe waaḥde, yaɛni (or **w-hiyye) bəddi ruuḥ ɛal-beet ɛan qariib.

nap - ġafwe pl. -aat, sahwe pl. -aat. Grandfather used to take a nap after lunch. žəddi kaanet ɛaadto yaaxə́d-lo ġafwe baɛd ᵊl-ġada.

napkin - fuuṭa pl. fuwaṭ.

Naples - naapoli.

narrow - dayyeq. This is a narrow street haada ṭariiq dayyeq. -- He has very narrow views on education. ʔafkaaro ᵊktiir dayyqa ɛan ᵊš-šuʔuun ᵊt-tarbawiyye.

**He had a narrow escape. nafad ᵊb-ɛəžbe.

to narrow - 1. daaq (i ø). The road narrows just beyond the bridge. ṭ-ṭariiq bidiiq raʔsan baɛd ᵊž-žəsᵊr. 2. dayyaq. Narrow the sleeves a little. dayyə́q-li l-ᵊkmaam šwayye.

to narrow down to - nḥaṣar b-. The question has narrowed down to this: Is it worth while or not? l-masʔale nḥaṣret b-han-nəqṭa: məḥᵊrze š-šaġle wəlla laʔ?

nasty - 1. malɛuun. Do you always have such nasty weather? fii ɛandkon daayman ṭaqᵊs malɛuun heek? -- 2. waaṭi. He said a few very nasty things about her. ḥaka kam mlaaḥaẓa waaṭye ɛanha. -- He's a real nasty fellow. huwwe zalame waaṭi ɛan ḥaqa.

**Don't be so nasty! ḥaaštak waṭaawe!

**That was very nasty of you! kaanet ᵊktiir waṭaawe mənnak!

to get nasty - ṭwaaṭa. She can get very nasty when you contradict her. lamma tɛaakə́sa fiiha təṭwaaṭa ktiir.

nation - 1. šaɛb pl. šəɛuub. The whole nation mourned his death. š-šaɛᵊb kəllo kaan ḥaznaan ɛalée. 2. ʔəmme pl. ʔəmam. The United Nations. (heeʔet˜) ᵊl-ʔəmam ᵊl-məttáḥide.

national - 1. ǧawmi*. This is against our national interest. haada ḍədd maṣlaḥətna l-ǧawmiyye. -- The national emblem of Syria. š-šiɛaar ᵊl-ǧawmi tabaɛ suuriyya. 2. waṭani*. The band played the national anthem. ž-žooqa daqqet ᵊn-našiid ᵊl-waṭani. -- I have a checking account at the National Bank. ɛandi ḥsaab žaari bᵊl-baṇk ᵊl-waṭani. 3. raɛiyye pl. raɛaaya. There were only French and Egyptian nationals on the ship. kaan fii bass raɛaaya frənsaawiyyiin w-məṣriyyiin bᵊl-baaxra.

nationalism - ǧawmiyye.

nationalist - ǧawmi* pl. -iyyiin.

nationality - žənsiyye pl. -aat.

nationalization - taʔmiim pl. -aat.

to **nationalize** - ʔammam. Egypt nationalized the Suez Canal Company in 1956. maṣr ʔammamet šərket ǧanaat ᵊs-swees sənt səttáa w-xamsiin.

native - 1. ʔahli*, baladi*. That's a native custom. hayye ɛaade ʔahliyye. 2. maḥalli*. The native troops quelled the riot. ž-žnuud ᵊl-maḥalliyye qaḍet ɛaš-šaġab. 3. ʔaṣli*. He never returned to his native country. maa ražeɛ la-waṭano l-ʔaṣli ʔabadan. -- What's your native language? šuu lúġatak ᵊl-ʔaṣliyye?

**He's a native of Germany. huwwe ʔaḷmaaṇi l-mawled.

**You speak French almost like a native. btəḥki l-luġa l-frənsaawiyye taqriiban mətᵊl ʔahla.

natives - ʔahaali (pl.). The natives of the island were very friendly. ʔahaali ž-žaziire kaanu ləṭafa ktiir.

natural - ṭabiiɛi*. That's quite natural! haada ṭabiiɛi tamaaman! -- The fruit in this picture looks very natural. l-fawaaki b-haṣ-ṣuura mbayyne ṭabiiɛiyye ktiir. -- He has a natural talent for painting. ɛando mawhibe ṭabiiɛiyye bᵊr-rasme. -- Their department of natural science is especially famous. daaʔərt ᵊl-ɛuluum ᵊṭ-ṭabiiɛiyye tabdə́ɛon mašhuura b-šəkᵊl xaaṣṣ.

naturally - 1. ṭabɛan, bᵊṭ-ṭabᵊɛ. Naturally we want you to come. ṭabɛan mənriidak təži. 2. b-ṣuura ṭabiiɛiyye, biduun taṣannoɛ. She behaves very naturally. btəṭṣarraf ᵊb-ṣuura ṭabiiɛiyye.

**She has a naturally friendly disposition. hiyye ṭabiiɛə́ta maḥbuube.

nature - 1. ṭabiiɛa. He enjoys the beauties of nature. biḥəbb žamaal ᵊṭ-ṭabiiɛa. 2. ṭabiiɛa, ṭabᵊɛ. It's not his nature to lie. muu mən ṭabiiɛto yəkzeb or **muu mafṭuur ɛal-kəzᵊb. 3. ṭabiiɛa, maahiyye. I can't tell you anything about the nature of my job. maa fiini qəl-lak šii ɛan ṭabiiɛet šəġli.

by nature - bᵊl-fəṭra. He's lazy by nature. huwwe kaslaan bᵊl-fəṭra or **huwwe mafṭuur ɛal-kaslane.

naughty - məʔzi*. You're a very naughty child. ʔənte walad məʔzi ktiir.

**Oh, oh, I hear you were pretty naughty at the party last night. tsk, tsk, sməɛᵊt ʔənnak šaṭṭeet ᵊktiir leelt ᵊmbaareḥ bᵊl-ḥafle.

nausea - žoošet˜ nafᵊs, laɛyet˜ nafᵊs. I was seized by sudden nausea. ntaabətni žoošet nafs ᵊmfaažʔa or **žaašet nafsi ɛala ġafle.

naval - baḥri*. Three naval units were dispatched to the Atlantic. tlatt wəḥdaat baḥriyye nbaɛtet ləl-muḥiiṭ ᵊl-ʔaṭlasi.

naval academy - kəlliyyet˜ ᵊl-baḥriyye.

naval officer - ḍaabeṭ˜ (pl. ḍəbbaaṭ˜) baḥriyye.

navy - baḥriyye. His son joined the navy a year ago. ʔəbno nḍamm ləl-baḥriyye mən səne.

navy blue - kəḥli*. My new suit is navy blue. taqmi ž-ždiid loono kəḥli.

near - 1. qariib pl. qraab. The station is quite near. l-ᵊmḥaṭṭa qariibe ktiir. -- Is there a hotel near here? fii šii ʔoteel qariib mən hoon? -- The hotel is conveniently located and there's a good restaurant near by. l-ʔoteel markazo mnaaseb w-fii maṭɛam ᵊmniiḥ qariib mənno. -- That's a little nearer the truth. haada ʔaqrab šwayye ləl-ḥaqiiqa. -- Is this the nearest way home? haada ʔaqrab ṭariiq ləl-beet? -- That's the nearest I can get in my estimate. haada ʔaqrab taqdiir məmken qaddro. 2. qariib˜, qərᵊb˜. Don't park your car near the bus stop. laa tṣəff sayyaartak qariib mawqef ᵊl-baaṣaat. -- They're standing near each other. waaqfiin qariib baɛḍon ᵊl-baɛḍ. — It was near midnight when we got home. kaan qariib nəṣṣ ᵊl-leel lamma wṣəlna ɛal-beet.

to bring (take, move, etc.) **near** ... - qarrab ɛala. Move the table near the window. qarreb ᵊṭ-ṭaawle ɛaš-šəbbaak.

to go (come, draw, etc.) **near** ... - qarrab ɛala, qtarab mən. Don't go near the fire. laa tqarreb ɛan-naar.

nearby - mžaawer. We had lunch at a nearby restaurant. tġaddeena b-maṭɛam mžaawer.

Near East - š-šarǧ ᵊl-ʔadna.

nearly - 1. ɛala wašak, taqriiban. I'm nearly finished. ɛala wašak ʔəxloṣ or taqriiban laḥa ʔəxloṣ. 2. taqriiban. It was nearly a year before we heard from him again. maḍa taqriiban səne la-ḥatta ɛədna sməɛna mənno šii.

**I nearly made the train, but ... kənt laḥa laḥḥeq ᵊt-treen laaken ...

**It isn't nearly as good as it used to be. haš-šii muu mniiḥ mətᵊl-ma kaan mən qabᵊl, laa mən qariib w-laa mən baɛiid.

neat - 1. mrattab. His desk always looks neat. maa bətšuuf ṭaawəlto ʔəlla mrattabe. -- That was a neat presentation of the subject. haada kaan ɛarḍ ᵊmrattab ləl-mawḍuuɛ. 2. mhandam, mrattab. She always looks neat. maa bətšuufa ʔəlla mhandame. 3. ẓariif. That was a neat trick you played on him. hayy kaanet ḥiile ẓariife yalli ʔənte lɛəbta ɛalée. 4. nḍiif. You did a very neat job on that. ɛməlᵊt šaġle ktiir nḍiife. -- The dictionary distinguishes itself by its neat format. l-ǧaamuus byəmtaaz ᵊb-taṣmiimo n-nḍiif.

necessarily - bᵊḍ-ḍaruura. This does not necessarily mean that you'll have to go there. haada muu maɛnaato bᵊḍ-ḍaruura ʔənno laazem ᵊtruuḥ la-hniik. — Necessarily, the whole process entails a certain amount of inconvenience. bᵊḍ-ḍaruura, l-ɛamaliyye kəlla laḥa təžleb šwayyet ʔəzɛaaž.

necessary - 1. *ḍaruuri*, laazem.* Can you raise the necessary funds? *btəqder ᵊddabber ᵊl-ʔamwaal ᵊḍ-ḍaruuriyye?* 2. *ḍaruuri*.* That won't be necessary. *haada maa bikuun ḍaruuri.*
**I'll stay if it's absolutely necessary. *btamm ʔiza laa bədd.*

necessity - 1. *ḍaruura* pl. *-aat.* There's no necessity for it. *maa fii ʔəlo ḍaruura.* -- Necessity knows no law. *ḍ-ḍaruuraat tubiiḥ ᵊl-maḥẓuuraat.* 2. *ḥaaže.* Necessity is the mother of invention. *l-ḥaaže ʔəmm ᵊl-ʔəxtiraaɛ.*

neck - 1. *raqbe* pl. *-aat.* Put that scarf around your neck. *ləff hal-laḥše ɛala raqᵊbtak.* -- He fell down the stairs and broke his neck. *wəqeɛ mən ɛad-daraž w-ᵊnqaṣfet raqᵊbto.* -- The bottle has a very narrow neck. *l-qanniine raqbə́ta ktiir dayyqa.*
2. *deekoltée* (invar.). My dress has a low neck. *fəṣṭaani ʔəlo deekoltée waaṭi.*
**He's dead from the neck up. *maa ɛando šii bᵊṭ-ṭaabeq ᵊl-fooqaani.*
**Why stick your neck out when nobody cares? *leeš la-txarbeq ḥaalak ʔiza maa ḥada maṭšuuš?*

necklace - *ṭooq* pl. *ṭwaaq, ɛaqᵊd* pl. *ɛquude.*

necktie - *graafe* pl. *-aat, kraave* pl. *-aat.*

need - 1. *ḥaaže.* There's a great need for warm woolens. *fii ḥaaže qawiyye ləl-ʔalbise ṣ-ṣuufiyye t-tqiile.* -- We're in dire need of a good translator. *nəḥna b-ḥaaže maasse la-mtaržem ᵊmniiḥ.*
2. *ḥaaže* pl. *-aat.* He has few needs. *ḥaažaato qaliile.* 3. *diiq.* You're certainly a friend in need. *ʔənte waḷḷa sadiiq ɛand ᵊd-diiq.*
if need be - *ʔiza fii ḍaruura.* I'll go myself if need be. *ʔiza fii ḍaruura bruuḥ ᵊb-nafsi.*
to need - *ḥtaaž.* We have all we need. *ɛanna kəll šii mnəḥtaažo* or ***ɛanna kəll šii byəlzamna.* -- I need some rest. *bəḥtaaž šwayyet raaḥa* or ***laazəmni šwayyet raaḥa.* -- We'll need more time if we are to finish the job. *bəddna nəḥtaaž* (or ***bəddo yəlzamna*) *waqᵊt ʔaktar ʔiza bəddna nxalleṣ ᵊš-šaġle.* -- This suit needs to be cleaned. *hal-badle btəḥtaaž* (or ***laazə́ma* or *bədda*) *tanḍiif.* -- The car needed new tires. *s-sayyaara ḥtaažet* (or ***ləzə́ma* or *kaan bədda*) *kawašiik žədad.*
**That's all we needed! *haada yalli naaqəṣna!*

needle - 1. *ʔəbre* pl. *ʔəbar.* I can't thread the needle. *maa fiini ḍəmm ᵊl-ʔəbre.* 2. *ɛaqrab* pl. *ɛaqaareb.* The speedometer needle climbed to 50, 60, 70 ... *ɛaqrab ᵊl-kiilomətraaž ṭəlɛet la-xamsiin w-səttiin w-sabɛiin ...*
**For two days we were on pins and needles. *bqiina yoomeen ɛala ʔaḥarr mn ᵊž-žamᵊr.*
knitting needle - *sannaara* pl. *-aat.*

needless - *bala lzuum, bala muužeb, bala ḍaruura.* That's a needless waste of time. *haada ḍyaaɛet waqt bala lzuum.*
**Needless to say, you'll stay at our house when you come to Damascus. *maa fii daaɛi nəḥki ʔənno bəddak tənzel ɛanna lamma btəži ɛaš-šaam.*

negative - 1. *balloora* pl. *-aat.* The negative is much clearer than the print. *l-balloora ʔawḍaḥ b-ᵊktiir mn ᵊṣ-ṣuura.* 2. *salbi*.* The result of the test was negative. *natiižet ᵊl-faḥᵊṣ kaanet salbiyye.* -- I expected a negative answer. *twaqqaɛᵊt žawaab salbi.*
negative particle - *ʔadaat˜* (pl. *ʔadawaat˜*) *nafi.* "*laa*", for instance, is a negative particle. *masalan "laa" ʔadaat nafi.*

neglect - *ʔəhmaal.* The house shows signs of neglect. *l-beet ᵊmbayyen ɛalée l-ʔəhmaal.*
to neglect - 1. *ʔahmal* and *hamal* (*e ʔəhmaal// nhamal*). He's been neglecting his work lately. *ɛam yəhmel šəġlo b-hal-ʔiyyaam ᵊl-ʔaxiire.* 2. *nəsi* (*a nəsyaan*). Don't neglect to water the plants. *laa tənsa maa təsqi šaqaf ᵊz-zriiɛa.*

to **negotiate** - *tfaawaḍ ɛala.* They are negotiating a cease-fire. *ɛam yətfaawaḍu ɛala tawqiif ḍarb ᵊn-naar.*

negotiation - *mfaawaḍa* pl. *-aat.* Negotiations were broken off after a week. *l-ᵊmfaawaḍaat ᵊnqaṭɛet baɛᵊd žəmɛa.*

Negress - *zənžiyye* pl. *-aat, ɛabde* pl. *-aat.*

Negro - *zənži* pl. *znuuž, ɛabᵊd* pl. *ɛabiid.*

neighbor - *žaar* f. *žaara* pl. *žiiraan.* How do you like our new neighbors? *kiif laqeet žiiraanna ž-žədad?*

neighborhood - 1. *žiire, ḥaara, ḥayy.* Many artists live in our neighborhood. *ktiir ᵊmn ᵊl-fannaaniin saakniin ᵊb-žiirətna.* 2. *žiwaar, žiire.* The whole neighborhood was there. *kəll ᵊž-žiwaar kaanu hniik.*

neither - *w-laa ...* Neither of the two was there. *w-laa waaḥed mn ᵊt-tneen kaan ᵊhniik.* -- Neither of the (two) boys was there. *w-laa ṣabi mn ᵊṣ-ṣabiyyeen kaan ᵊhniik.* -- Neither of the (two) girls was there. *w-laa bənᵊt mn ᵊl-bənteen kaanet ᵊhniik.* -- Neither answer is correct. *w-laa žawaab mn ᵊž-žawaabeen maẓbuuṭ.* -- I haven't seen him. - Neither have I. *ʔana maa šəfto.* - *w-laa ʔana.*
neither ... nor - *laa ... w-laa.* Neither he nor I will be there. *laa ʔana w-laa huwwe laḥa nkuun ᵊhniik.* -- She's neither pretty nor does she come from a rich family. *laa hiyye ḥəlwe w-laa ɛeelə́ta ʔaġniya.*

nephew - (brother's son) *ʔəbᵊn˜* (pl. *wlaad˜*) *ʔaxx,* (sister's son) *ʔəbᵊn˜* (pl. *wlaad˜*) *ʔəxᵊt.*

Neptune - (planet) *naptuun.*

nerve - *ɛaṣab* pl. *ʔaɛṣaab.* That noise is getting on my nerves. *haḍ-ḍoože ɛam təlɛab ɛala ʔaɛṣaabi* or ***haḍ-ḍoože ɛam ᵊtnarvəzni.* -- He has nerves of iron. *ʔaɛṣaabo mən ḥadiid.*
**Some nerve! *ʔamma waqaaḥa!*

nervous - 1. *ɛaṣabi*.* Who was that nervous fellow who just left? *miin has-zalame l-ɛaṣabi halli raaḥ hallaq?* -- He had a nervous breakdown. *ṣaar maɛo ʔənhiyaar ɛaṣabi.* 2. *mnarvez.* What are you so nervous about? *šuu ṣaayə́r-lak hal-qadd ᵊmnarvez?*
to get nervous - *narvaz.* He gets terribly nervous every time he has to speak in public. *binarvez ᵊktiir kəll-ma byəḥki b-žamᵊɛ.*
to make nervous - *narvaz.* It makes me nervous when you look over my shoulder while I work. *bətnarvəzni waqt ᵊbtəṭṭallaɛ mən fooq raasi ɛaliyyi w-ʔana ɛam ʔəštə́ġel.*

nest - *ɛəšš* pl. *ɛšaaš.*

net - *šabake* pl. *-aat.* The nets were full of fish. *š-šabakaat kaanet malaane samak.*

net - *ṣaafi.* My weekly salary is fifty pounds net. *maɛaaši bᵊž-žəmɛa xamsiin leera ṣaafi.* -- What was your net profit last year? *šuu kaan rəbḥak ᵊṣ-ṣaafi* (or *ṣaafi˜ ʔarbaaḥak*) *ᵊs-səne l-maaḍye?*
to net - *darr* (*ə darr*), *rabbaḥ.* That store doesn't net much. *hal-maxzan maa bidərr ᵊktiir.* -- How much does the business net you a year? *qaddeeš ᵊš-šəġᵊl bidərr-ə́llak* (or *birabbḥak*) *bᵊs-səne?*

the **Netherlands** - *hoolanda.*

neutral - *mḥaayed, ḥiyaadi*.* Sweden was neutral during the First World War. *s-sweed kaanet ᵊmḥaayde* (or ***kaanet ɛal-ḥiyaad*) *waqt ᵊl-ḥarb ᵊl-ɛaalamiyye l-ʔuula.*
in neutral - *mboomar.* The car's in neutral now. *s-sayyaara mboomara hallaq.*
to shift into neutral - *boomar.* Don't shift into neutral going downhill. *laa tboomer bᵊn-nzuul.*

neutrality - *ḥiyaad.*

never - 1. *maa ... ʔabadan, maa ... b-ḥayaat-* + pron. suff. I'll never go there again. *maa laḥa ruuḥ baqa la-hniik ʔabadan* or *b-ḥayaati maa laḥa ruuḥ baqa la-hniik.* -- I've never claimed anything of the sort. *ʔana maa ddaɛeet ᵊb-šii mətᵊl haad ʔabadan* or *b-ḥayaati maa ddaɛeet ᵊb-šii mətᵊl haad.* -- You're never alone in this place. *ʔənte muu waḥdak ʔabadan ᵊb-hal-maḥall* or *b-ḥayaatak maa bətkuun waḥdak ᵊb-hal-maḥall.* -- Will you go to his party tomorrow? - Never again! *laḥa truuḥ la-ɛando ɛal-ḥafle bəkra?* - *ʔabadan maa bɛiida.* 2. *ʔabadan bᵊl-marra.* Are you going to speak to him again? - Never! *laḥa tḥaakii marra taanye?* - *ʔabadan!*
**Now or never! *yaa hallaq yaa bala!*

nevertheless - *maɛ zaalek, maɛ kəll haš-šii.* Nevertheless I still can't believe it. *maɛ zaalek ləssa maa ɛam bəqder saddə́qa.*

new - *ždiid* pl. *ždaad* and *žədad.* Are these new shoes? *haṣ-ṣabbaaṭ ᵊždiid?* -- I see you have a new maid. *šaayef fii ɛandkon ṣaanɛa ždiide.* -- What are your plans for the new year? *šuu bərnaamžak ləs-səne ž-ždiide?* -- I feel like a new man. *ḥaases kaʔənni xalqaan ᵊždiid.* -- What's new? *šuu fii ždiid?* or ***šuu l-ʔaxbaar?*
**Happy New Year! *kəll ɛaam w-ʔənte* (f. *ʔənti* pl. *ʔəntu*) *b-xeer!*
new moon - *hlaal.* There'll be a new moon next week. *l-ᵊhlaal laḥa yhəll ᵊž-žəmɛa ž-žaaye.*
New Year's - *raas˜ ᵊs-səne.* We spent New Year's Eve at the house of some friends. *maḍḍeena leelt raas ᵊs-səne ɛand ᵊṣḥaab.* -- New Year's Day comes on a Monday. *yoom raas ᵊs-səne byəḥkom yoom ᵊt-taneen.*

news - *xabar* pl. *ʔaxbaar.* The news came entirely unexpectedly. *l-xabar maa kaan ɛal-baal wᵊl-xaaṭer.* -- We'll have to break the news to him gently.

laazem ᵊnqəl-lo l-xabar ᵊb-taʔanni. -- Did you listen to the eight o'clock news? *sməɛᵊt šii ʔaxbaar ᵊs-saaɛa tmaane?*

**That isn't news to me. *haada muu šii ždiid ɛaliyyi.*

newscast - *našret˜* (pl. *-aat˜*) *ʔaxbaar.*

newspaper - *žariide* pl. *žaraayed.*

newsreel - *manaaẓer* (pl.).

newsstand - *baṣṭet˜* (pl. *-aat˜*) *žaraayed.*

next - **1.** *žaaye* (invar.). We're leaving next month. *(nəḥna) msaafriin ᵊš-šahr ᵊž-žaaye.* -- Next time do it right. *l-marra ž-žaaye saawiiha maẓbuuṭ.* -- I have to get off at the next stop. *bəddi ʔənzel bᵊl-mawqef ᵊž-žaaye.* -- **2.** *baɛdeen.* Next I have to go to the Post Office. *baɛdeen laazem ruuḥ ɛal-boosṭa.* -- What shall I do next? *šuu bəddi ʔaɛmel baɛdeen?*

**Who's next? *door˜ miin?* or *la-miin ᵊd-door?*

next door to - *žamb˜* ... The tailor lives next door to us. *l-xayyaaṭ saaken žambna.* -- We live next door to the school. *nəḥna saakniin žamb ᵊl-madrase.* -- Our next-door neighbor is a university professor. *žaarna (yalli) žambna ʔəstaaz žaamɛa.*

next to - *b-žamb˜* ... Sit down next to me! *ɛood ᵊb-žambi!* -- They live next to the church. *hənne saakniin ᵊb-žamb l-ᵊkniise.*

next to nothing - *ʔašwa mən bala.* He knows next to nothing about Arabic. *maɛrəfto bᵊl-ɛarabi ʔašwa mən bala.* -- He has next to nothing. *halli maɛo ʔašwa mən bala.*

the next day - *taani yoom, bᵊl-yoom ᵊt-taali.* The next day he got sick. *taani yoom ḍaɛef.*

to **nibble** - *naqwab.* He kept nibbling at the cake. *ḍall ynaqweb bᵊl-gaato.*

nice - **1.** *ḥəlu.* She wears nice clothes. *btəlbes ʔawaaɛi ḥəlwe.* **2.** *laṭiif* pl. *-iin* and *ləṭafa* and *lṭaaf, ḥabboob.* He's a very nice man. *huwwe zalame laṭiif ᵊktiir.* **3.** *laṭiif, ḥəlu.* That wasn't very nice of him. *maa kaanet laṭiife mənno ʔabadan.*

**Did you have a nice time? *šloon mbaṣaṭᵊt?* or *šloon ᵊtsalleet?*

**I asked him in a nice way to give it to me. *saʔalto b-kəll laṭaafe ʔənno yaɛṭiini-yda.*

nicely - *mniiḥ.* You did that quite nicely. *ɛməlta mniiḥ laa baʔs fiiha.* -- She came through the operation nicely. *ṭəlɛet ᵊmn ᵊl-ɛamaliyye mniiḥ.*

niece - (brother's daughter) *bənᵊt˜* (pl. *banaat˜*) *ʔaxx,* (sister's daughter) *bənᵊt˜* (pl. *banaat˜*) *ʔəxᵊt.*

night - **1.** *leel.* We stayed up till late in the night. *ḍalleena sahraaniin la-waqᵊt mətʔaxxer bᵊl-leel.* -- I haven't been able to sleep at night lately. *maa ɛam bəḥsen naam bᵊl-leel ᵊmʔaxxaran.* **2.** *leele* pl. *layaali.* It was a pleasant summer night. *kaanet leele ṣeefiyye ḥəlwe.* **3.** *leeli**. He works as a night watchman at a large department store. *byəštəġel ḥaares leeli b-maġzan ᵊkbiir.*

**Good night! *təṣbeḥ* (f. *təṣᵊbḥi* pl. *təṣᵊbḥu*) *ɛala xeer!* -- (reply:) *tlaaqi l-xeer!*

nights - *bᵊl-leel.* He works nights. *byəštəġel bᵊl-leel.*

last night - *leelt˜ ᵊmbaarḥa, l-leele l-maaḍye.* We had unexpected company last night. *leelt ᵊmbaarḥa ʔəžaana zuwwaar maa kaanu ɛala baalna.* -- Did you sleep well last night? *nəmt ᵊmniih ᵊl-leele l-maaḍye?*

tomorrow night - **1.** *bəkra ɛašiyye.* They're going to the movies tomorrow night. *raayḥiin bəkra ɛašiyye ɛas-siinama.* **2.** *leelet˜ bəkra.* Tomorrow night is the longest night of the year. *leelet bəkra ʔaṭwal leele bᵊs-səne.* -- Tomorrow night we're staying with friends in Amman. *leelet bəkra mənbaata ɛand ᵊṣḥaab ᵊb-ɛammaan.*

night club - *kabarée* pl. *kabareeyaat.*

nightgown - *qamiiṣ˜* (pl. *qəmṣaan˜*) *noom.*

nightingale - *bəlbol* pl. *balaabel.*

nightshirt - *qamiiṣ˜* (pl. *qəmṣaan˜*) *noom.*

nine - **1.** *təsɛa.* Nine and six makes fifteen. *təsɛa w-sətte bisaawu xamᵊṣṭaɛš.* -- There are nine of us in class. *nəḥna təsɛa bᵊṣ-ṣaff.* **2.** *təsᵊɛ.* He owes me nine pounds. *ʔəli maɛo təsᵊɛ leeraat.* **3.** *təsᵊɛt.* I lived there for nine months. *sakant ᵊhniik təsᵊɛt əšhor.* -- My visa expires in nine days. *viizti btəxloṣ məddə́ta baɛᵊd təsᵊɛt iyyaam.* -- She inherited nine thousand pounds from her aunt. *wərtet təsᵊɛt aalaaf leera mən ɛammə́ta.* **4.** *s-saaɛa təsɛa.* Is nine a convenient time for you? *s-saaɛa təsɛa binaasbak?* -- The train leaves at half past nine. *t-treen byəmši s-saaɛa təsɛa w-nəṣṣ.*

nineteen - **1.** *təsaṭaɛš.* So far there are nineteen of us for the chartered flight. *la-ḥadd hallaq ṣarna təsaṭaɛš yalli bəddna naaxod ṭayyaara skaarsa.* **2.** *təsaṭaɛšar.* Nineteen people got killed in the explosion. *təsaṭaɛšar zalame qətlu bᵊl-ʔənfižaar.*

nineteenth - **1.** *t-təsaṭaɛš.* It's his nineteenth birthday. *haada ɛiid miilaado t-təsaṭaɛš.* -- We arrived on June the nineteenth. *wṣəlna b-təsaṭaɛš ᵊḥzeeraan.* **2.** *t-taaseɛ ɛašar.* He died in the early nineteenth century. *maat ᵊb-ʔawaaʔel ᵊl-qarn ᵊt-taaseɛ ɛašar.*

ninetieth - *t-təsɛiin, t-təsɛiini**. He celebrated his ninetieth birthday in good health. *ḥtafal ᵊb-ɛiid miilaado t-təsɛiin(i) b-ṣaḥḥa məmtaaze.*

ninety - *təsɛiin.*

ninth - **1.** *taaseɛ.* It's the ninth house from the corner. *huwwe l-beet ᵊt-taaseɛ* (or *huwwe taaseɛ beet*) *mn ᵊs-suuke.* **2.** *təsɛa.* He was born on June ninth. *wəled ᵊb-təsɛa ḥzeeraan.*

one ninth - **1.** *təsᵊɛ* pl. *ʔatsaaɛ.* That's eight ninths of the total amount. *haada tmən ʔatsaaɛ ᵊl-mablaġ kəllo.*

nip - *šaffe* pl. *-aat, darra* pl. *-aat.* Give me a little nip of that whisky. *ḥəṭṭ-ə́lli šaffe zġiire mən hal-wəski.*

to nip in the bud - *qaḍa (i qaḍa//nqaḍa) ɛala ... b-mahdo.* The uprising was nipped in the bud. *nqaḍa ɛas-sawra b-mahda.*

no - **1.** *laʔ.* Answer yes or no. *quul yaa ʔee yaa laʔ.* -- Do you always have to say no? *šuu daayman laazem ᵊtquul laʔ?* **2.** (no equivalent, rendered with negative clause:). He has no money. *maa (fii) ɛando maṣaari.* -- He gave me no answer. *maa žaawabni.* -- There is no such place. *maa fii heek maḥall.* -- There is no such thing as absolute justice. *maa fii šii ʔəsmo ɛadaale maṭlaqa.*

**No smoking, ladies and gentlemen! *mamnuuɛ ᵊt-tadxiin sayyidaati saadati!*

no good - *muu mniiḥ, mətl ᵊz-zəfᵊt.* This bicycle is no good at all. *hal-bəsᵊkleet muu mniiḥa ʔabadan* or *hal-bəsᵊkleet mətl ᵊz-zəfᵊt* or ****hal-bəsᵊkleet maa btəswa mnoob.**

no more - **1.** *maa ɛaad ..., maa bəqi ...* I have no more money. *maa ɛaad maɛi maṣaari.* **2.** *ḥaaže ... (baqa).* (Let's have) no more nonsense! *ḥaaže ʔakᵊl hawa baqa!* -- No more coffee, thanks. *ḥaažti qahwe, šəkran.*

no one - *maa ḥada.* No one said a word. *maa ḥada qaal kəlme.*

**I saw no one at the party I knew. *maa šəft ḥada bᵊl-ḥafle baɛᵊrfo.*

**I'm responsible to no one. *maa-li masʔuul qəddaam ḥada.*

no sooner - *maḥall-ma, ʔawwal-ma, saaɛet-ma.* No sooner did we arrive than the telephone rang. *maḥall-ma wṣəlna qaam ᵊt-talifoon ydəqq.*

no ... whatsoever - *maa ... w-laa ..., maa ... ʔabadan.* I have no doubt whatsoever. *maa ɛandi w-laa šakk* or *maa ɛandi šakk ʔabadan.* -- She gave me no reason whatsoever. *maa qaalə́t-li w-laa sabab* or *maa qaalə́t-li sabab ʔabadan.*

noble - **1.** *nabiil* pl. *nəbala, kariim* pl. *kraam.* That was very noble of you. *hayy kaanet šaġle nabiile ktiir mən naaḥak.* **2.** *nabiil.* He's of noble descent. *huwwe mən ʔaṣᵊl nabiil* or ****huwwe ʔaṣiil ᵊl-ḥasab wᵊn-nasab.**

nobody - *maa ḥada.* Nobody may leave this room. *maa ḥada masmə́ḥ-lo yəṭlaɛ mən hal-ʔuuḍa.* -- Nobody saw him. *maa ḥada šaafo.*

**I talked to nobody. *maa ḥakeet maɛ ḥada.*

nod - *hazzet˜* (pl. *-aat˜*) *raas.* He greeted us with a nod. *sallam ɛaleena b-hazzet raas.*

to nod - **1.** *hazz (ə hazz) raaso.* She nodded her head. *hazzet raasa.* -- The policeman nodded to us as we passed. *š-šərṭi hazz-ə́lna raaso lamma maraqna.* **2.** *kaba (i kabu).* He began to nod over his book. *bada yəkbi fooq ᵊktaabo.*

noise - **1.** *ḍoože, qarwaše.* Children, don't make so much noise! *ḥaažətkon ḍoože yaa wlaad!* **2.** *ḥəss.* Please don't make any noise! *balla laa ṭṭaaleɛ ḥəss ᵊmnoob!* **3.** *ṣooṭ* pl. *ṣwaaṭ, ḥəss.* Did you hear that strange noise? *šuu sməɛᵊt has-ṣooṭ ᵊl-ġariib?*

noisy - *mqarwaš.* That's a noisy office. *haada maktab ᵊmqarwaš.* -- Get rid of those noisy brats! *txallaṣ mən hal-ɛafariit l-ᵊmqarwašiin!*

to **nominate** - *ɛayyan//tɛayyan.* When do the parties nominate their candidates? *ʔeemta l-ʔaḥzaab raḥa tɛayyen mraššaḥiina?*

nomination - *taɛyiin* pl. *-aat.*

noncommissioned officer - *ḍaabeṭ˜* (pl. *ḍəbbaaṭ˜*) *ṣaff.*

none - **1.** *w-laa waaḥed, w-laa ḥada.* None of my friends could help me. *w-laa waaḥed mən ᵊṣḥaabi qəder ysaaεədni.* — None of the women knew anything about it. *w-laa waaḥde mn ᵊn-nəswaan kaan εanda xabar ᵊb-haš-šii.* **2.** *w-laa waaḥed.* None of these arguments has any bearing on the matter. *w-laa waaḥde mən hal-ḥəžaž ʔəla ʔayy εalaaq̈a bᵊl-mawḍuuε.*
 **None of your clothes fit me. *w-laa qəṭεa mən ʔawaaεiik btəži εaliyyi.*
 **That's none of your business. *haada maa bixəṣṣak ʔabadan!*
 **Don't ask me for money because I have none. *laa təṭlob mənni maṣaari laʔənno maa maεi.*
 **Don't expect dessert after dinner. There's none today. *laa tšədd ᵊryaaltak εal-ḥəlu baεd ᵊl-εaša. maa fii l-yoom.*

nonsense - *maṣxara, ʔakᵊl˜ hawa.* Enough of that nonsense! *ḥaaže maṣxara!* -- Come on, that's nonsense! *ʔamma hayye maṣxara!* or *ʔamma ʔakᵊl hawa haada!*
 **Don't talk such nonsense. *ḥaaštak ḥaki bala ṭaεme.*

noodles - *šεeeriyye.*

nor - *w-laa.* I'm neither for nor against this suggestion. *ʔana maa-li maε ᵊl-ʔəq̈tiraaḥ w-laa ḍəḍḍo.* -- I didn't go to the concert last night. - Nor did I. *maa rəḥᵊt εala ḥaflet ᵊl-muusiiq̈a leelt ᵊmbaareḥ.* - *w-laa ʔana.*

normal - **1.** *ṭabiiεi**. He's a normal child. *huwwe walad ṭabiiεi.* -- Both countries re-established normal relations not too long ago. *l-baladeen ʔaεaadu l-εalaq̈aat ᵊṭ-ṭabiiεiyye beenaaton mən mədde qariibe.* **2.** *εaadi**. That's his normal behavior. *haada taṣarrfo l-εaadi.*

normally - *bᵊl-εaade, εaadatan.* Normally, we go to Bloudane at this time of the year. *bᵊl-εaade mənruuḥ εala bluudaan b-hal-waqᵊt mn ᵊs-səne.*

noon - *ḍəhᵊr.* The weather cleared up around noon. *ṭ-ṭaqᵊs ṣəḥi ḥawaali ḍ-ḍəhr.*
 at noon - *ḍ-ḍəhᵊr.* She's seldom home at noon. *qaliil-ma tkuun ᵊḍ-ḍəhr bᵊl-beet.*

north - **1.** *šmaal.* The wind is coming from the north. *l-hawa žaaye mn ᵊš-šmaal.* **2.** *εaš-šmaal.* The road swings north on the other side of the village. *ṭ-ṭariiq biləff εaš-šmaal baεd ᵊḍ-ḍeeεa.* **3.** *šmaali**. The rooms on the north side are very cold in winter. *l-ʔuwaḍ bᵊṭ-ṭaraf ᵊš-šmaali bətkuun ᵊktiir baarde bᵊš-šəte.* -- There is a strong north wind today. *fii hawa šmaali qawi l-yoom.*
 north of - *b-ᵊšmaal˜.* Nebek is north of Damascus. *n-nəbᵊk waaqεa b-ᵊšmaal ᵊš-šaam.*

northeast - *šmaal šarqi.* The wind is coming from the northeast. *l-hawa žaaye mn ᵊš-šmaal š-šarqi.*

northeast(ern) - *šmaali* šarqi**. There were several border clashes along the northeastern frontier. *ṣaar fii εəddet ᵊmṣaadamaat εal-ᵊḥduud ᵊš-šmaaliyye š-šarqiyye.*

northern - *šmaali**. The northern part of the country is mostly a rural area. *ṭ-ṭaraf ᵊš-šmaali tabaε l-ᵊblaad ʔaktaro manṭiqa riifiyye.*

northwest - *šmaal ġarbi.* They live in the north west. *saakniin bᵊš-šmaal ᵊl-ġarbi.*

northwest(ern) - *šmaali* ġarbi**. The northwestern part of the country is thinly populated. *l-manṭiqa š-šmaaliyye l-ġarbiyye qaliilet ᵊs-səkkaan.*

Norway - *n-narweež.*

Norwegian - **1.** *narweeži**. Is she a Norwegian? *šu hiyye narweežiyye?* **2.** *narweeži* (invar.). I have a friend who speaks Norwegian. *ʔəli rfiiq byəḥki narweeži.*

nose - **1.** *mənxaar* and *məxxaar* pl. *manaxiir.* She has such a pretty little nose! *ya ʔaḷḷa qaddeeš mənxaara zġiir ḥəlu.* — The kid's nose is always running. *manaxiir ᵊl-walad daayman saayliin.* **2.** *ʔənf* pl. *ʔnuuf.* He sticks his nose into everything. *byəḥšor ʔənfo b-kəll šəġle.*
 **Just follow your nose! *xalliik maaši ḍəġri!*
 **You needn't turn up your nose at him. *muu laazem tətraffaε* (or *tətkabbar* or *tšuuf ḥaalak*) *εalée.*

nosebleed - *naziif ʔənfi.* I had a nosebleed this morning. *ṣaar maεi naziif ʔənfi l-yoom ᵊṣ-ṣəbᵊḥ* or ****nəzə́l-li damm mən manaxiiri l-yoom εala bəkra.**

nosy - *kattaar˜ ġalabe, fuḍuuli**. I wish his wife weren't so nosy! *ya-reet marto maa tkuun hal-qadd kattaaret ġalabe!*

not - **1.** *maa.* He didn't come. *maa ʔəža.* — Haven't you seen him yet? *ləssa maa šəfto?* **2.** *laa.* Do not go. *laa truuḥ.* — Don't forget our appointment. *laa tənsa mamεədna.* **3.** *muu, maa-l-* + pron. suff. That's not bad. *haada muu baṭṭaal* or *haada maa-lo baṭṭaal.* -- She's not coming. *maa-la žaaye* or *muu žaaye.* -- After all, I'm not a fool. *laa tənsa, ʔana maa-li* (or *muu*) *mažduub.*

to **notarize** - *saadaq//tsaadaq.* This document has to be notarized. *has-sanad laazem yətsaadaq εalée (mən q̈ibal kaateb εadᵊl).*

notary public - *kaateb˜* (pl. *kəttaab˜*) *εadᵊl.*

note - **1.** *mlaaḥaẓa* pl. *-aat.* The notes at the bottom of the page explain the rare words. *l-ᵊmlaaḥaẓaat yalli b-səfᵊl ᵊṣ-ṣafḥa bətfasser ᵊl-kəlmaat ᵊn-naadra.* **2.** *kəlme* pl. *-aat.* I received a note from her yesterday. *wəṣəlni mənha kəlme mbaareḥ.* **3.** *məzakkra* pl. *-aat.* The ambassador delivered a sharp note of protest. *s-safiir qaddam məzakkərt ʔəḥtižaaž qawiyye.* **4.** *nooṭa* pl. *-aat.* The next note is an A. *n-nooṭa ž-žaaye bətkuun ṣooṭ "laa".* **5.** *ranne.* There was a note of doubt in her voice. *kaan fii rannet šakk ᵊb-ṣooṭa.*
 notes - *rʔuus˜ ʔaq̈laam* (pl.). I have to check my notes before I can answer that. *laazem raažeε rʔuus ʔaq̈laami qabᵊl-ma žaawbak.* -- Did you take notes? *ʔaxadt-əllak šii rʔuus ʔaq̈laam?*
 (promissory) note - *kəmbyaale* pl. *-aat.* He gave me a note for the balance. *katáb-li kəmbyaale b-raṣiid l-ᵊḥsaab.*
 to make a note of something - *qayyad εando šii.* Make a note of the time he left. *qayyed εandak ʔeemta raaḥ.*
 to take note of - *laqaṭ (o laqᵊṭ), ntabah εala.* Have you taken note of what I told you? *laqaṭᵊt εanni šuu qəlt-əllak* or *ntabaht εala šuu qəlt-əllak?*
 to note - *laaḥaẓ.* Note the difference between the two. *laaḥeẓ ᵊl-farᵊq been ᵊt-tneen.*

notebook - **1.** *daftar˜* (pl. *dafaater˜*) *žeeb.* I want a little notebook with a calendar. *bəddi daftar žeeb ᵊzġiir fii rəznaama.* **2.** *safiine* pl. *safaayen, daftar* pl. *dafaater.* Have the notebooks been collected? *s-safaayen ᵊltammu?*

nothing - **1.** *maa ... šii.* Nothing came of it. *maa ʔəža mənha šii.* -- Can nothing be done? *maa fii šii byənεə́mel?* — There is nothing more for me to do here. *maa εaad fii šii ʔaεᵊmlo hoon.* **2.** *laa ... šii.* Tell him nothing! *laa tqəl-lo šii!* **3.** *muu ... šii, maa-l-* + pron. suff. ... *šii.* I see nothing. *muu šaayef šii* or *maa-li šaayef šii.* -- She knows nothing about it. *maa-la εarfaane šii εanha.* **4.** *muu šii, maa šii, w-laa šii.* What are you doing? - Nothing. *šuu εam taεmel? - muu šii.* — What did you find? - Nothing. *šuu laqeet? - w-laa šii.*
 **He means nothing to me. *maa-lo εandi ʔayy ʔahammiyye.*
 **Nothing doing! *məstaḥiil!*
 for nothing - *b-balaaš.* I got it for almost nothing. *ʔaxadta taqriiban ᵊb-balaaš.*
 nothing but - *maa ... ġeer, maa ... ʔəlla.* They got nothing but bread and water. *maa faat la-təmmon ġeer ᵊl-xəbᵊz wᵊl-mayy.*
 to make nothing of - *maa tqaḷḷan.* Make nothing of what he says. *laa tətqaḷḷan ḥakyo.*

notice - **1.** *ʔəεlaan* pl. *-aat.* Did you read the notice on the bulletin board? *qareet ᵊl-ʔəεlaan l-ᵊmεallaq εala looḥet ᵊl-ʔəεlaanaat?* **2.** *məhle.* The landlord gave us notice to move. *ṣaaḥeb ᵊl-beet εaṭaana məhle la-nəntə́qel.* — Our maid gave us notice last week. *ṣaanεətna εaṭətna məhle ʔənno bədda tətrek.*
 **The play got good notices. *t-təmsiiliyye nmadḥet bᵊž-žaraayed.*
 at a moment's notice - **1.** *εan-nadha.* I can be ready at a moment's notice. *raḥa kuun ḥaader εan-nadha.* **2.** *mən laḥẓə́ta.* They left for the airport at a moment's notice. *raaḥu εal-maṭaar mən laḥẓə́ta.*
 until further notice - *la-ʔažal ġeer ᵊmsamma, la-ʔəšεaar ʔaaxar.* This store will be closed until further notice. *hal-maxzan laḥa yətsakkar la-ʔážal ġeer ᵊmsamma.*
 without notice - *biduun ʔənzaar.* He was fired without notice. *qallaεúu biduun ʔənzaar.*
 to escape someone's notice - *faat (u fawaat) ḥada, falet (a falataan) mən ḥada.* I don't know how it escaped my notice. *maa baεref kiif haš-šii faatni* (or *fəlet mənni*).
 to take notice of - *ntabah εala, daar (i ø) baalo εala.* Take no notice of what he says. *laa təntə́beh εala šuu εam yəḥki* or *laa ddiir baalak εala ḥakyo.*

to notice - *laaḥaẓ, šaaf (u šoofe).* I noticed the mistake right away. *laaḥaẓt ᵊl-ġalaṭ ḥaalan.* -- I didn't notice the sign before. *maa laaḥaẓt ᵊl-ʔišaara mən qabᵊl.* -- I was so busy I scarcely noticed him. *kənᵊt mašġuul la-daraže bᵊl-kaad laaḥaẓto.*

**Everybody noticed his tie. *graafto laftet naẓar ᵊl-kəll.*

to **notify** - *xabbar.* You should have notified me in time. *kaan laazem txabbərni qabᵊl fawaat ᵊl-waqᵊt.*

notion - *fəkra* pl. *ʔafkaar.* I haven't the faintest notion what he wants. *maa ʕandi w-laa baṣiiṣ fəkra b-halli biriido.*

notions - *xərdawaat* (pl.). Is there a store near here that carries notions? *fii maḥall qariib mən hoon bibiiʕ xərdawaat?*

noun - *ʔəsᵊm* pl. *ʔasmaaʔ.*

nourishing - *mġazzi.* What you need is some nourishing food. *halli byəlzamak ʔakl ᵊmġazzi.*

nourishment - *ṭaʕaam, ġiza.* He hasn't taken any nourishment in days. *ṣar-lo kam yoom maa faat la-təmmo ʔayy ṭaʕaam.*

novel - **1.** *riwaaye* pl. *-aat.* Do you know of a good novel? *btaʕrəf-lak šii rwaaye ḥəlwe?* **2.** *badiiʕ.* That's a novel idea. *hayye fəkra badiiʕa.*

November - *təšriin ᵊt-taani.*

now - **1.** *hallaq.* I have to leave now. *laazem ruuḥ hallaq.* -- Are you satisfied now? *ʔənte raḍyaan hallaq?* **2.** ... *baqa.* Now look here! *šuuf baqa!* -- Now listen to me! *smaʕ-li baqa!*

now and then - *been waqt u-waqt.* I hear from him now and then. *ʕam ʔəsmaʕ mənno been waqt u-waqt.*

now that ... - *baʕᵊd-ma hallaq* ... Now that you mention his name, I do remember him. *baʕᵊd-ma hallaq qəlt-əlli ʔəsmo dzakkarto tamaam.*

by now - *la-hallaq.* He really ought to be here by now. *bᵊl-ḥaqiiqa laazem ykuun wəṣel la-hallaq.* -- We should know by now. *ṣaar laazem naʕref la-hallaq.*

from now on - *mən hallaq w-raayeḥ, mən hallaq w-ṭaaleʕ.* From now on I'll be more careful. *mən hallaq w-raayeḥ laḥa kuun ḥariiṣ ʔaktar.*

just now - *hallaq* (usually with raised intonation), *hal-laḥẓa.* I talked to him just now. *hallaq ḥaakeeto.*

up to (or **till**) **now** - *la-ḥadd hallaq.* I haven't noticed it up to now. *maa laaḥaẓto la-ḥadd hallaq.*

nowadays - *b-hal-ʔiyyaam.* Nowadays, people don't make this distinction any more. *b-hal-ʔiyyaam maa ʕaadet ᵊn-naas ᵊtfarreq heek tafriiq.*

nowhere - **1.** *maa* ... *b-maḥall.* He's nowhere to be seen. *maa byənšaaf ᵊb-maḥall.* **2.** *maa b-maḥall, muu b-maḥall, w-laa b-maḥall.* Where have you been? - Nowhere. *ween kənᵊt?* - *maa b-maḥall.*

nuclear - *ẓarri*, nawawi*.* The submarine is driven by nuclear energy. *l-ġawwaaṣa btəmši bᵊl-quwwe ẓ-ẓarriyye.*

nude - *mẓallaṭ, bᵊẓ-ẓalṭ* (invar.), *ʕaari.* The body was nude. *ž-žəsse kaanet mẓallaṭa.*

in the nude - *bᵊẓ-ẓalṭ.* The children ran around in the nude. *l-ᵊwlaad kaanu falṭaaniin bᵊẓ-ẓalṭ.*

nuisance - *šii məzʕež.* The flies are a real nuisance this summer. *d-dəbbaan šii məzʕež ᵊktiir ᵊb-haṣ-ṣeef.*

numb - *mxaddar.* My fingers are numb with cold. *ʔaṣabiiʕi mxaddara mən kətret ᵊl-bard.*

number - **1.** *nəmra* pl. *nəmar.* Did you write down the license number? *katabt nəmret ᵊs-sayyaara?* -- You can't bluff me, I've got your number! *maa fiik təbləfni, šaayef mən nəmᵊrtak ᵊktiir!* **2.** *ʕadad* pl. *ʔaʕdaad.* Take a number from one to ten. *xood ʕadad mən waaḥed la-ʕašra.* -- I found the information in Volume Three, Number Five. *laqeet ᵊl-maʕluumaat bᵊl-mužallad ᵊt-taalet, l-ʕadad ᵊl-xaames.* -- Quite a number of people have come. *ʕadad ᵊmniiḥ mn ᵊn-naas ʔəžu.*

to number - *nammar.* You forgot to number the cards. *nsiit ᵊtnammer l-ᵊkruute.*

numbered - *mnammar, mraqqam.* The seats aren't numbered. *l-maḥallaat muu mnammara.*

**His days are numbered. *ʔiyyaamo maʕduude.*

numeral - *ʕadad* pl. *ʔaʕdaad.* Can you read both Arabic and Roman numerals? *btaʕref təqra ʔaʕdaad ʕarabiyye w-roomaaniyye?*

nun - *raahbe* pl. *-aat.*

nurse - **1.** *mmarrḍa* pl. *-aat.* The nurse will be around in a minute to take your temperature. *l-ᵊmmarrḍa raḥa təži baʕd ᵊšwayye la-taaxod ḥaraartak.* **2.** *mrabbye* pl. *-aat.* The children are out in the park with the nurse. *l-ᵊwlaad bᵊl-ḥadiiqa maʕ l-ᵊmrabbye.*

male nurse - *mmarreḍ* pl. *-iin.*

to nurse - **1.** *ʕtana b-.* She nursed him back to health. *ʕtanet fii ḥatta šəfi.* **2.** *raḍḍaʕ.* Does she nurse the baby herself? *ʕam ᵊtraḍḍeʕ ᵊṭ-ṭəfᵊl mən ḥaliiba?*

nut - **1.** *žooze* coll. *žooz* pl. *-aat.* He's not allowed to eat nuts. *muu masməḥ-lo yaakol žooz.* **2.** *ʕaẓaqa* pl. *-aat.* This nut doesn't fit the bolt. *hal-ʕaẓaqa maa btədxol ᵊb-raas ᵊl-bərġi.* **3.** *mažnuun* pl. *mažaniin.* Who's that nut anyway? *miin hal-mažnuun haad qəl-li baqa?*

nuts - *mažnuun* pl. *mažaniin.* You must be nuts. *laazem ᵊtkuun mažnuun.*

to go nuts - *žann (ə žnaan, žnuun).* If this noise keeps up, I'll go nuts. *ʔiza ḍallet haḍ-ḍoože laḥa žənn.*

nylon - *nayloon.*

O

oak - *ballluuṭa* coll. *balluuṭ* pl. *-aat, šažaret˜* (coll. *šažar˜* pl. *ʔašžaar˜*) *balluuṭ.*

oar - *məždaaf* pl. *mažadiif.* The oars are in the boat. *l-məždaafeen bᵊš-šaxtuura.*

**He's always putting his oar in. *b-kəll ʕərᵊs ʔəlo qərᵊṣ.*

oasis - *waaḥa* pl. *-aat.*

oats - *šuufaan.* They plant a lot of oats here. *byəzraʕu šuufaan ᵊktiir b-hal-manṭiqa.*

obedience - *ṭaaʕa.*

obedient - *mṭiiʕ, ṭaayeʕ.*

to **obey** - **1.** *ṭaaʕ (i ṭooʕ, ʔiṭaaʕa//nṭaaʕ), ṭaawaʕ.* He doesn't obey me. *maa biṭiiʕni* or ****maa byəsmaʕ kəlᵊmti.** **2.** *ṭaaʕ (i).* I can't obey that order. *maa fiini ṭiiʕ hal-ʔamᵊr.*

object - **1.** *šii* pl. *ʔašyaaʔ.* He was struck on the head with a heavy object. *nḍarab ʕala raaso b-šii tqiil.* **2.** *qaṣᵊd, maqṣuud, ġaraḍ.* What's the object of that? *šuu l-qaṣᵊd mən haš-šaġle?* -- What do you suppose is his object in doing that? *šuu yaa-təra ykuun qaṣdo mən hal-ʕamal?*

to object to - *ʕtaraḍ ʕala, ʕaaraḍ b-.* I don't know why he should object to it. *maa-li ʕarfaan leeš bəddo yəʕtəreḍ ʕala haš-šaġle.* -- I hope you don't object to my smoking. *nšaalla maa btəʕaareḍ ᵊb-tadxiini* or ***nšaalla maa fii ʕandak maaneʕ ʔən daxxanᵊt.*

objection - **1.** *ʔəʕtiraaḍ* pl. *-aat.* He raised no objection. *maa saawa ʔayy ʔəʕtiraaḍ.* -- Are there any objections? *fii ʔayy ʔəʕtiraaḍ?* -- Have you any objection to my smoking? *fii ʕandak ʔayy ʔəʕtiraaḍ ʕala tadxiini?*

objective - **1.** *mədžarred.* I'll try to be as objective as possible. *bəddi ḥaawel kuun mədžarred qadd-ma fiyyi.* **2.** *mawḍuuʕi*.* Try to give an objective account of the incident. *ḥaawel ykuun sardak mawḍuuʕi ʕan ᵊl-ḥaades.* **3.** *hadaf* pl. *ʔahdaaf.* Our first objective is to ... *hadafna l-ʔawwal ʔənno* ...

objectively - *b-tažarrod.* Now let's look at the problem objectively. *xalliina nətmaʕʕan ᵊl-məšᵊkle b-tažarrod.*

obligation - **1.** *ʔəltizaam* pl. *-aat.* He can't meet his obligations. *maa byəqder ywaffi b-ʔəltizaamaato.* **2.** *mənniyye, ʔəltizaam.* We're under no obligation to him. *maa-lo ʕaleena mənniyye.*

to **oblige** - *qaddam maʕruuf la-.* I'm always glad to oblige you. *daayman məstʕədd qaddəm-lak maʕruuf.*

obliged - *mamnuun.* We're very much obliged to you. *mamnuuniin ʔəlak ᵊktiir.*

obliging - *xaduum.* He's always obliging. *huwwe daayman xaduum.*

observation - **1.** *mlaaḥaẓa, mšaahade.* He was taken to the hospital for observation. *ḥaṭṭuu bᵊl-məstašfa taḥt l-ᵊmlaaḥaẓa.* **2.** *mlaaḥaẓa* pl. *-aat.* That was a very clever observation you just made! *hayy kaanet ᵊmlaahaẓa kəlla zaka mənnak!*

observation post - *nəqṭet˜* (pl. *nəqaṭ˜*) *ᵊmraaq̈abe.*

to **observe** - **1.** *laahaẓ, šaaf (u šoofe).* Did you observe how she reacted? *laahaẓᵊt* (or *šəfᵊt*) *šuu kaan radd fəᶜla?* **2.** *tq̈ayyad b-, məši (i məši// nməša) ᶜala.* There are only a few rules which you have to observe. *fii kam q̈aaᶜde bass laazem təṭq̈ayyad fiiha* (or *təmši ᶜaleeha*). **3.** *ḥtafal b-.* What holidays do you observe? *šuu l-ʔaᶜyaad yalli btəḥtəflu fiiha?*

obstinate - *ᶜaniid* pl. *ᶜənada, mᶜaaned.*

obvious - **1.** *badiihi**. That's quite obvious. *haada badiihi tamaam.* — The obvious thing for you to do is keep out of their way. *š-šii l-badiihi yalli laazem taᶜᵊmlo xalliik ᵊbᶜiid ᶜannon.* **2.** *waadeḥ, mbayyen.* His motives are only too obvious. *bawaaᶜso ʔaktar mən waadḥa.*

obviously - *maa fii šakk.* She was obviously wrong. *maa fii šakk kaanet məxᵊṭʔa.* — That's obviously a mistake. *maa fii šakk haada ġalaṭ.*

occasion - **1.** *mnaasabe* pl. *-aat.* A dress like this can be worn for any occasion. *fəstaan mətᵊl haad byəltəbes ᵊb-kəll l-ᵊmnaasabaat.* — What's the occasion? *šuu l-ᵊmnaasabe?* **2.** *fərṣa* pl. *fəraṣ.* We had no occasion to talk to each other alone. *maa kaan ᶜanna fərṣa nəḥki maᶜ baᶜᵊdna waḥᵊdna.*

on the occasion of - *b-ᵊmnaasabet˜* ... They're giving a party on the occasion of their 30th anniversary. *bəddon yaᶜᵊmlu ḥafle b-ᵊmnaasabet ᶜiidon ᵊt-tlaatiini.*

occasional: We had fine weather except for an occasional thunderstorm. *kaan ᶜanna ṭaqᵊs ḥalu ʔəlla mən waqᵊt la-waqᵊt ṣaar šwayyet ᶜawaaṣef.* — Over the years we received an occasional letter from her. *ᶜala marr ᵊs-sniin ʔəžaana mənha mən waqᵊt la-waqᵊt šii kam maktuub.*

occasionally - *ʔaḥyaanan, been waqt w-waqᵊt, mən waqᵊt la-waqᵊt.* I see him occasionally. *bšuufo ʔaḥyaanan.*

occupation - **1.** *məhne* pl. *məhan, šaġle* pl. *-aat.* What's your occupation? *šuu məhᵊntak?* **2.** *ʔəḥtilaal.* Where were you during the occupation? *ween kənᵊt waqt ᵊl-ʔəḥtilaal?* — The occupation forces will be gradually withdrawn over the next five years. *q̈uwwaat ᵊl-ʔəḥtilaal laḥa tənsəḥeb tadriižiyyan ʔasna l-xamse sniin ᵊž-žaaye.*

to **occupy** - **1.** *ḥtall.* First the Americans occupied the town. *ʔawwal šii l-ʔamriikaan ᵊḥtallu l-balad.* **2.** *sakan (o sakan//nsakan) b-.* Who occupies the building at the present time? *miin halli saaken bᵊl-binaaye bᵊl-waqt ᵊl-ḥaader?* **3.** *šaġal (e ə// nšaġal), ʔaxad (-yaaxod ʔaxᵊd//nʔaxad).* School occupies all of my time. *l-madrase šaaġle kəll waqti.* — The camp occupies an area of ten thousand square meters. *l-ᵊmxayyam byəšġel masaaḥt ᶜašᵊrt aalaaf mətr ᵊmrabbaᶜ.*

occupied - **1.** *mašġuul.* The boss is occupied at the moment. *r-raʔiis hallaq mašġuul.* **2.** *maʔxuud, məttaaxed, mašġuul.* Is this seat occupied? *hal-kərsi maʔxuud?* **3.** *maskuun.* The house hasn't been occupied for years. *l-beet ṣar-lo sniin muu maskuun.* **4.** *məḥtall.* You need a special pass to go through the occupied territory. *laazmak rəxṣet ᵊmruur xaaṣṣa la-təqṭaᶜ ᵊl-manṭiqa l-məḥtalle.*

to keep occupied - *šaġal (e ə//nšaġal).* That will keep him occupied for a while. *haš-šaġle laḥa yəšᵊġlo la-waqᵊt.* — Oh, I keep myself occupied. *walḷa, daayman bəšġel ḥaali b-šii šaġle.*

to **occur** - **1.** *ṣaar (i ṣayaraan), žara (i žarayaan), ḥaṣal (e ḥṣuul), ḥadas (o ḥduus).* When did the accident occur? *ʔeemta ṣaaret ᵊl-ḥaadse?* **2.** *nəzel (e nzuul), ʔəža (-yəži žayye).* The name occurs twice in this chapter. *l-ʔəsᵊm naazel marrteen b-hal-faṣᵊl.* **3.** *xaṭar (o xaṭaraan, xṭuur) ᶜala baal-* ... It just didn't occur to me. *l-fəkra bᵊl-marra maa xaṭret ᶜala baali.* — That would never have occured to me. *haš-ši muu məmken ykuun xaṭar ᶜala baali.*

ocean - *muḥiiṭ* pl. *-aat.*

o'clock - *s-saaᶜa.* The train leaves at seven o'clock. *t-treen byəmši s-saaᶜa sabᶜa.*

octagon - *mtamman* pl. *-aat.*

October - *təšriin ᵊl-ʔawwal.*

oculist - *ḥakiim˜* (pl. *ḥəkama˜*) *ᶜyuun.*

odd - **1.** *šaazz* pl. *šawaazz, ġariib* pl. *ġəraba.* He's a very odd person. *huwwe zalame šaazz ᵊktiir.* — His behavior struck me as being odd. *laqeet taṣarrfo šaazz.* **2.** *mən fooq* ... It cost me thirty odd pounds. *kallafətni mən fooq ᵊtlaatiin leera.* **3.** *fardet˜* ... Have you seen an odd glove anywhere? *šaayəf-li šii fardet kaff b-ši qərne?* — I found an odd shoe in that old crate. *laqeet fardet ṣabbaaṭ ᵊb-has-saḥḥaara l-ᶜatiiqa.* **4.** *məfred.* Pick an odd number. *naqq̈i-lak šii ᶜadad məfred.* — We have only some odd pairs left. *ṣafyaan ᶜanna bass ᵊšwayyet ᵊžwaaz məfᵊrde.*

odd jobs - *šaġlaat lagane* (pl.). He does all the odd jobs around the house. *byaᶜmel kəll ᵊš-šaġlaat ᵊl-lagane l-mətᶜallqa bᵊl-beet.*

odds: The odds are in his favor. *ẓ-ẓuruuf maašye maᶜo.* — The odds are against us. *ẓ-ẓuruuf muu maašye maᶜna* or *ẓ-ẓuruuf ᶜam ᵊtᶜaakəsna.* — What can you do against such odds? *šuu bəddak taᶜmel maᶜ heek ṣuᶜuubaat?*

odds and ends - **1.** *šaġlaat ᵊẓġiire* (pl.). I still have some odds and ends to take care of. *ləssda-li šwayyet šaġlaat ᵊẓġiire laazem ʔaᶜməla.* **2.** *ġraaḍ ᵊmbaᶜzaqa* (pl.). I found all kinds of odds and ends in the drawer. *laqeet kəll ʔanwaaᶜ ᵊġraaḍ ᵊmbaᶜzaqa bᵊd-dərᵊž.*

at odds - *mətl ᵊl-kənne wᵊl-ḥamaaye.* He's at odds with everybody. *huwwe mətl ᵊl-kənne wᵊl-ḥamaaye maᶜ kəll waaḥed.*

of - **1.** *tabaᶜ.* The radio station of the government. *mḥaṭṭet ᵊl-ʔizaaᶜa tabaᶜ l-ᵊḥkuume.* — The Prime Minister of Syria. *raʔiis ᵊl-wazaara tabaᶜ suuriyya.* **2.** (*ʔiḍaafe* construction): A glass of milk. *kaaset˜ ḥaliib.* — Two kilos of apples. *kiiloween˜ təffaaḥ.* — A loaf of bread. *rġiif˜ xəbᵊz.* — The poems of Abu Nuwas. *ʔašᶜaar˜ ʔabu nawwaas.* — A dictionary of technical terms. *q̈aamuus˜ ʔəṣṭilaaḥaat fanniyye.* — A distance of four kilometers. *masaafet˜ ʔarbaᶜ kiilomətraat.* — A matter of minutes. *ḥkaayet˜ daqaayeq.* — Most of the country. *ʔaktar˜ l-ᵊblaad.* — South of Damascus. *žnuub˜ ᵊš-šaam.* **3.** *mən.* He's one of us. *huwwe waaḥed mənna.* — The book consists of four sections. *l-ᵊktaab mətʔallef mən ʔarbaᶜ ʔažzaaʔ.* — This watch is made of gold. *has-saaᶜa maᶜmuule mən dahab.* — That was very nice of her. *haada kaan ᵊktiir laṭiif mənha.* **4.** *b-.* His father died of a heart attack. *ʔabuu maat b-sakte qalbiyye.*

**A man of courage. *ražol ᶜando šažaaᶜa.*

**He's an old friend of mine. *huwwe rfiiq qadiim ʔəli.*

**Call me at a quarter of eight. *ᶜməl-li talifoon ᵊs-saaᶜa tmaane ʔəlla rəbᵊᶜ.*

**It tastes of vinegar. *fiiha ṭaᶜmet xall.*

off - (as adj., adv. and preposition without equivalent in Arabic): June is still three months off. *ləssa ṣafyaan tlətt əšhor la-ḥzeeraan.* — I'll have a week off soon. *žaayiini ᶜəṭlet ʔəsbuuᶜ ᶜan qariib.* — I may take a day off next week. *bižuuz ʔaaxəd-li yoom ᶜəṭle ž-žəmᶜa ž-žaaye.* — Hands off! *qiim ʔiidak!* — There's a button off your dress. *fii zərr waaqeᶜ mən fəstaanek.* — This item has been off the market for a year. *ṣar-lo səne haṣ-ṣənᵊf mafquud ᵊmn ᵊs-suuq.* — The head nurse is off duty from eight to twelve. *raʔiist ᵊl-mumarrḍaat maa ᶜanda dawaam mn ᵊt-tmaane lət-ṭnaᶜš.* — My question caught him off guard. *suʔaali ʔəžda mfaažaʔa.* — The ship anchored three miles off shore. *l-baaxra raset ᶜala masaafet tlətt ᵊmyaal ᶜan ᵊš-šaṭṭ.* — This is an off year for wheat. *has-səne sənt maḥᵊl mənšaan ᵊl-qamᵊḥ.* — His figures are way off. *ʔarq̈aamo ktiir ᵊbᶜiide ᶜan ᵊl-ḥaqiiqa.* — He was off in a flash. *qaam ġaab mətᵊl lamḥ ᵊl-baṣar.* — Our maid is off today. *ṣ-ṣaanᶜa mᶜaṭṭle l-yoom.* — The power is off. *l-kahraba maqṭuuᶜa.* — They aren't so badly off. *ḥaaləton muu baṭṭaale hal-qadd.* — They're very well off. *ḥaaləton ᵊl-maaliyye ktiir ᵊmniiḥa.* — He's a little off. *ᶜaqlo muu raakez.*

off and on - *mən waqᵊt la-waqᵊt, been waqt w-waqᵊt.* We have a little argument off and on. *mən waqᵊt la-waqt ᵊmnədžaadal maᶜ baᶜḍna šwayye.*

to **offend** - *ʔasaaʔ la-.* I hope I haven't offended you. *nšaaḷḷa kuun maa ʔasaʔt-əḷḷak.*

offense - **1.** *mxaalafe* pl. *-aat.* Is this your first offense? *hayy ʔawwal ᵊmxaalafe ᶜməlta?* **2.** *šarr.* She didn't mean any offense. *maa qaṣdet ʔayy šarr.*

to take offense - *ʔaxad ᶜala xaaṭro.* She took offense at my remark. *ʔaxdet ᶜala xaaṭra b-sabab ᵊmlaaḥaẓti.*

offensive - **1.** *muᶜiib.* I wouldn't consider it offensive behavior. *maa bəᶜtəber hat-taṣarrof taṣarrof muᶜiib.* **2.** *kariih.* It has an offensive odor. *riiḥəta kariiha.* **3.** *hužuumi**. The country has been stockpiling offensive weapons over the past few months. *l-ᵊblaad ṣar-la kam šahᵊr təddaxer ʔasliḥa hušuumiyye.* **4.** *hušuum* pl. *-aat.* In 1941 Germany launched an all-out offensive against the Soviet Union. *sənt waaḥed w-ʔarᵊbεiin ʔalmaanya šannet hušuum saaheq̈ ḍədd ᵊl-ʔəttiḥaad ᵊs-sovyeeti.*

offer - *εarᵊḍ* pl. *εruuḍ(a).* He made me a good offer. *qaddám-li εarḍ ᵊmniiḥ.*

to offer - **1.** *qaddam.* May I offer you a cup of coffee? *btəsmáḥ-li qaddə́m-lak fənžaan qahwe?* **2.** *εaraḍ (o εarᵊḍ//nεaraḍ) εala.* He offered me a hundred dollars for the radio. *εaraḍ εaliyyi miit dolaar bᵊr-raadyo.* -- She offered to get it for me. *εarḍet εaliyyi džəb-li-yda.* **3.** *ʔabda.* Did they offer any resistance? *ʔabdu ʔayy muq̈aawame?*

**What do you offer me for it? *šuu btaεṭiini fii?*

offhand - *mən raas-* or *mən εaql-* + pron. suff. of subj. I can't tell you that offhand. *maa bəqder qəl-lak haš-šii mən raasi.* -- He gave me an offhand answer. *εaṭaani žawaab mən raaso.*

office - **1.** *maktab* pl. *makaateb.* Come and see me in my office. *taεa šuufni b-maktabi.* **2.** *daayre* pl. *dawaayer.* Government offices close at five o'clock. *dawaayer l-ᵊḥkuume bətsakker ᵊs-saaεa xamse.* **3.** *waẓiife* pl. *waẓaayef.* He's running for public office. *εam yraššeḥ ḥaalo la-waẓiife εaamme.* -- He held office for a long time. *bəqi bᵊl-waẓiife mədde ṭawiile.*

**The whole office was invited. *kəll l-ᵊmwaẓẓaf-iin kaanu maεzuumiin.*

office hours - *saaεaat˜ ᵊd-dawaam.* What are your office hours? *ʔeemta saaεaat dawaamak?*

in office - *bᵊl-waẓiife.* How long has the mayor been in office? *qaddeeš ṣar-lo raʔiis ᵊl-baladiyye bᵊl-waẓiife?*

officer - **1.** *ẓaabeṭ* (and *ḍaabeṭ*) pl. *ẓəbbaaṭ (ḍəbbaaṭ).* He was an Army officer during the last war. *kaan ẓaabeṭ bᵊž-žeeš bᵊl-ḥarb ᵊl-maaḍye.* **2.** *šərṭi* pl. *šərṭa.* I asked the officer to direct me to the station. *saʔalt ᵊš-šərṭi ydəllni εal-ᵊmḥaṭṭa.* **3.** *εəḍu˜* (pl. *ʔaεḍaaʔ˜*) *maktab.* He was elected an officer of our club. *ntaxabúu εəḍu maktab ᵊn-naadi tabaεna.*

**Officer, how do I get to the airport? *yaa ʔaxi, ween ṭariiq ᵊl-maṭaar?*

officers - *maktab.* We elected new officers last night. *ntaxabna maktab ᵊždiid l-leele l-maaḍye.*

official - **1.** *mwaẓẓaf* pl. *-iin.* He's a State Department official. *huwwe mwaẓẓaf ᵊb-wazaart ᵊl-xaar-žiyye.* **2.** *rasmi*.* He paid me an official visit. *ẓar-li zyaara rasmiyye.* -- I'm here on official business. *ʔana hoon b-ᵊmhəmme rasmiyye.*

officially - *b-ṣuura rasmiyye, rasmiyyan.* It was announced officially. *ʔaεlanuuha b-ṣuura rasmiyye.*

often - *ktiir, marraat ᵊktiire.* Do you see him often? *bətšuufo ktiir?* -- Does this happen often? *haš-šii biṣiir ᵊktiir?*

how often - *kam marra, qaddeeš.* How often do you go to the movies? *kam marra bətruuḥ εas-siinama?*

oh - **1.** *haa.* Oh, really? *haa ṣaḥiiḥ?* -- Oh, is that so? *haa, heek lakaan?* **2.** *ʔeʔ.* Oh, well, let's forget about the whole thing. *ʔeʔ, ṭayyeb, xalliina nənsa haš-šaġle.* **3.** *waḷḷaahi.* Oh, I don't know! *waḷḷaahi maa baεref!* **4.** *yaa.* Oh miss, you dropped your handkerchief. *yaa ʔaanise waqqaεti maḥramtek.* -- Oh Ahmed, hand me that hammer, please. *yaa ʔaḥmad, naawəlni haš-šaakuuš baḷḷa.* -- Oh, my goodness! *yaa salaam!*

oh no - **1.** *laʔ ʔabadan.* You'll have to treat me to a movie tonight. - Oh no, I won't! *laazem təεzəmni εas-siinama hal-leele. - laʔ ʔabadan!* **2.** *laa tquula!* Ahmad was killed in an accident. - Oh no! How did it happen? *ʔaḥmad maat ᵊb-ḥaades sayyaara. - laa tquula! kiif ṣaaret ᵊl-qəṣṣa?*

oh yes - *mbala.* You're not going now, are you? - Oh yes, I am! *muu raayeḥ ʔənte hallaq? - mbala raayeḥ!*

oil - *zeet* pl. *zyuut.* Where can I get some olive oil? *ween blaaqi šwayyet zeet zeetuun?* -- They're prospecting for oil in the Jezirah. *εam ynaqqbu εaz-zeet bᵊž-žaziire.* -- The Arabian American Oil Company. *šərket ᵊz-zeet ᵊl-εarabiyye l-ʔameer-kiyye.*

**She paints in oils. *btərsom rasm zeeti.*

to oil - *zayyat.* The machine needs oiling. *l-maakiina bədda tazyiit.*

oil can - *mazyate* pl. *mazaayet.*

oilcloth - *məšammaε* pl. *-aat.*

oil painting - *ṣuura (pl. ṣuwar) zeetiyye.*

ointment - *marham* pl. *maraahem.*

O.K. - **1.** *mwaafaqa* pl. *-aat.* I need his O.K. *məḥtaaž ʔana mwaafaqto.* **2.** *tamaam.* Everything is O.K. now. *kəll šii ṣaar tamaam hallaq.* **3.** *ṭayyeb.* O.K., I'll talk to him about it. *ṭayyeb, bəḥki maεo b-hal-masʔale.*

**I'll go along if it's O.K. with you. *bruuḥ maεak ʔiza kaan maa fii εandak maaneε* (or *ʔiza biwaafqak*).

to O.K. - *waafaq εala, saadaq εala.* He has to O.K. it first. *bᵊl-ʔawwal laazem ywaafeq εaleeha.*

old - **1.** *ʔəxtyaar* pl. *-iyye, msənn.* He must be very old now. *laazem ykuun ʔəxtyaar ᵊktiir hallaq.* **2.** *kbiir* pl. *kbaar.* My sister is older than I. *ʔəxti ʔakbar mənni.* -- I'm five years older than my brother. *ʔana ʔakbar mən ʔaxi b-xams ᵊsniin* or ***bəkbar ʔaxi b-xams ᵊsniin.* **3.** *εatiiq* pl. *εətaq.* Is this an old model? *šuu hayy modeel εatiiq?* -- I've given away all my old clothes. *baxšašᵊt kəll ʔawaaεiyyi l-εətaq.* **4.** *qadiim* pl. *qədama.* They are old friends. *hənne ṣḥaab qədama.*

**How old are you? *qaddeeš εəmrak?*

**He's as old as I am. *huwwe mən εəmri* or *εəmro qadd εəmri.*

**He's as old as the hills. *(huwwe) εaayeš mən εahd ʔahl ᵊl-kahf.*

**That boy has an old head on his shoulders. *hal-walad εaqlo ʔakbar mən εəmro.*

old man - *ʔəxtyaar* pl. *-iyye.* He's an old man now. *ṣaar ʔəxtyaar hallaq.*

**I'll have to ask my old man for more money. *laazem ʔəsʔal ʔabi yaεṭiini maṣaari kamaan.*

old woman - *ʔəxtyaara* pl. *-aat, εažuuz* pl. *εažaayez.* She's an old woman now. *ṣaaret ʔəxtyaara hallaq.*

to get old - *xatyar.* I must be getting old. *εam xatyer.*

old-fashioned: She has such old-fashioned ideas. *εaqliita daqqa qadiime εan ḥaqa.* -- My grandfather is a very old-fashioned gentleman. *žəddi daqqa qadiime tamaam.* -- He wore an old-fashioned double-breasted suit. *kaan laabes badle mooḍa qadiime b-ṣaffeen ᵊzraar.*

oleander - *dəfᵊl.*

oleomargarine - *samᵊn nabaati.*

to **omit** - *ḥazaf (e ḥazᵊf//nḥazaf).* Omit that word! *ḥzeef hal-kəlme!* -- We have omitted several items which were on the list before. *ḥazafna εəddet nafdaat kaanu bᵊl-liista qable.*

Ommiad - *ʔamwi*.*

on - **1.** *b-.* On what day? *b-ʔanu yoom?* -- I live on Salhiye Street. *ʔana saaken b-šaareε ᵊṣ-ṣaalḥiyye.* -- The river is on the east. *n-nahᵊr bᵊš-šarᵊq.* -- Who's on the team? *mənu bᵊl-fariiq?* -- Is there anything interesting on the radio? *fii šii ḥəlu bᵊr-raadyo?* -- Do you sell on credit? *bətbiiε bᵊd-deen?* -- What are your ideas on that subject? *šuu fəkrak ᵊb-hal-mawḍuuε?* -- We saw the Ommiad Mosque on a tour through the city. *šəfna ž-žaameε ᵊl-ʔamwi b-žawle bᵊl-madiine.* -- When do you start on your trip? *ʔeemta btəbda b-rəḥᵊltak?* **2.** *εala.* He sat on the speaker's left. *kaan qaaεed εala šmaal ᵊl-xaṭiib.* -- The book is (lying) on the table. *l-ᵊktaab (maḥṭuuṭ) εaṭ-ṭaawle.* -- Put it on the table. *ḥəṭṭo εaṭ-ṭaawle.* -- If we make our calculations on this basis we'll never come to terms. *ʔiza εməlna ḥsaabna εala hal-ʔasaas maa-lna raḥa nəttə́feq ʔabadan.* -- This drink is on me. *hal-mašruub εaliyyi* (or ***εala ḥsaabi*). -- The joke's on you this time. *l-mazḥa εaleek hal-marra.* -- You can depend on it. *btəqder təεtə́med εaleeha.* -- I insist on it. *ʔana bṣərr εalée.* -- I'd like to know what they live on. *bḥəbb ʔaεref εala ʔeeš εaayšiin.* **3.** *εan.* It's a book on animals. *huwwe ktaab εan ᵊl-ḥaywaanaat.* **4.** *b-muužeb˜.* We decided to act on these grounds. *εtamadna naεmel bi-muužeb hal-ʔasbaab.* **5.** *mən.* I got this information on good authority. *ʔaxadᵊt hal-maεluumaat mən maṣdar mawsuuq.*

**Are you open on Saturday? *ʔəntu faatḥiin ᵊs-sabᵊt?*

**What's on for tonight? *šuu fii hal-leele?*

**The race is already on. *s-sbaaq maaši hallaq.*

**How long has the main feature been on? *qaddeeš ṣar-lo l-fəlᵊm šaġġaal* (or *maaši*)?

**Is the gas on? *l-ġaaz maftuuḥ?*

**I left one lamp on in the living room. *tarakᵊt balloora waaḥde šaaεle b-ʔuuḍet ᵊl-qaεde.*

**The heat's on now! *mšarbakiin hallaq!*

**He's on vacation just now. *ʔaaxed maʔẓuuniyye hallaq.*

on and on: She talks on and on. *bəḍḍall ᵊbtəḥki w-btəḥki.* -- The party went on and on. *l-ḥafle ṭawwalet w-ṭawwalet.*

and so on - *ʔila ʔaaxĭrihi.* I need paper, ink, and so on. *bəddi waraq w-ḥəbᵊr ʔila ʔaaxĭrihi.*

later on - *baɛdeen.* Can't we do it later on? *maa mnəqder naɛməla baɛdeen?*

once - 1. *marra (waaḥde).* I've seen him only once. *šəfto marra (waaḥde) bass.* -- He feeds the dog once a day. *biṭaɛmi l-kalᵊb marra bᵊl-yoom.* -- I've been here once before. *kənᵊt hoon marra mən qabᵊl.* -- Once doesn't count. *marra waaḥde ma btənḥəseb.* 2. *mən qabᵊl.* This was once the business section. *hal-qərne kaanet mən qabᵊl* (or ***b-zamaana*) *markaz ᵊt-tižaara.*

once (and) for all - *la-ʔawwal w-ʔaaxer marra.* Once and for all, no! *la-ʔawwal w-ʔaaxer marra, laʔ!*

once in a while - *been waqt u-waqt, ʔaḥyaanan, b-baɛḍ ᵊl-ʔawqaat.* Once in a while I like a good glass of wine. *been waqt u-waqt bḥəbb ʔəšrab kaas ᵊnbiit məmtaaz.*

once more - *marra taanye.* Let's try it once more. *xalliina nḥaawel marra taanye.*

once upon a time - *marra mən marraat.* Once upon a time there was a king ... *marra mən marraat kaan fii malek ...*

at once - 1. *fooq baɛḍo.* Everything came at once. *kəll šii ʔəža fooq baɛḍo.* 2. *sawa, b-fard marra, dafɛa waaḥde.* All these letters arrived at once. *kəll hal-makatiib wəṣlu sawa.* 3. *ḥaalan, fawran, ɛal-ḥaarek.* Come at once! *taɛa ḥaalan!*

this once - *hal-marra.* Forgive me this once. *saaməḥni hal-marra.*

one - 1. *waaḥed.* One of us can buy the tickets. *waaḥed mənna byəqder yəštəri t-tazaaker.* -- I've only one question to ask. *ɛandi suʔaal waaḥed bass bəddi ʔəsʔalo.* -- I prefer the more expensive one. *bfaḍḍel ᵊl-waaḥde l-ʔaġla.* -- One never knows. *l-waaḥed šuu biɛarrfo.* 2. *s-saaɛa waaḥde.* It's almost one. *raḥa tṣiir ᵊs-saaɛa waaḥde.*

**That's a tough one! *hayy məšᵊkle ɛawiiṣa.*

one another - *baɛḍ-* + pron. suff., *baɛḍ-* + pron. suff. *ᵊl-baɛᵊḍ.* They saw one another frequently. *šaafu baɛḍon marraat ᵊktiire.* -- We don't talk to one another any more. *maa ɛədna ɛam nəthaaku maɛ baɛḍna (ᵊl-baɛḍ).*

one after another - *waaḥed waaḥed, waaḥed wara waaḥed.* They left, one after another. *raaḥu waaḥed waaḥed.*

one at a time - *waaḥed waaḥed.* One at a time, please. *waaḥed waaḥed balla.*

one by one - *waaḥed waaḥed.* They came one by one. *ʔəžu waaḥed waaḥed.*

one day - *b-yoom mn ᵊl-ʔiyyaam.* One day I'll be back. *b-yoom mn ᵊl-ʔiyyaam bəržaɛ.*

one o'clock - *s-saaɛa waaḥde.* It's five minutes past one o'clock. *s-saaɛa waaḥde w-xamse.*

one of these days - 1. *b-hal-ʔiyyaam.* I'll see him one of these days. *laḥa šuufo b-hal-ʔiyyaam hayy.* 2. *ləssa byəži yoom.* One of these days you'll be sorry for it. *ləssa byəži yoom ḥa-təndam ɛaleeha.*

that one - *hadaak(e)* f. *hadiik(e).* That one is better. *hadaak ʔaḥsan.* -- Take that one! *xood hadaake!*

the one - *yalli.* The one with the glasses in the second row is my teacher. *yalli ḥaaṭeṭ kəzlok bᵊṣ-ṣaff ᵊt-taani ʔəstaazi.*

this one - *haada* f. *hayye.* This one is better. *haada ʔaḥsan.*

one-eyed - *ʔaɛwar* f. *ɛoora* pl. *ɛuur.*

onion - *baṣale* coll. *baṣal* pl. *-aat.*

only - 1. *l-waḥiid.* He's our only child. *huwwe ʔəbᵊnna l-waḥiid.* -- Am I the only woman here? *šuu ʔana l-mara l-waḥiide hoon?* 2. *bass, laaken.* I was going to buy it, only he told me not to. *kaan bəddi ʔəštriiha, bass qal-li laʔ.* 3. *bass.* This is only for you. *haada bass mənšaanak.* -- I got here only a moment ago. *wṣəlᵊt la-hoon mən daqiiqa bass.* 4. *bass, maa (muu) ... ʔəlla* (or *ġeer*). We have only two left. *ṣafyaan ɛanna bass ᵊtneen* or *muu ṣafyaan ɛanna ġeer ᵊtneen.* -- He met my brother only. *tɛarraf ɛala ʔaxi bass* or *maa tɛarraf ʔəlla ɛala ʔaxi.*

**If you could only help me! *yaa-reet təqder ᵊtsaaɛədni!*

not only ... but also - *muu bass ... (laaken) ... kamaan.* She's not only pretty but she's also intelligent. *muu bass ḥelwe, (laaken) zakiyye kamaan.*

open - 1. *maftuuḥ.* He must have come in through the open window. *laazem ykuun faat ᵊmn ᵊš-šəbbaak ᵊl-maftuuḥ.* 2. *faateḥ.* We're open from nine to six. *naḥna faatḥiin* (or ***mnaftaḥ*) *mn ᵊt-təsɛa ləs-sətte.* -- The dining room isn't open yet. *ṣaalet ᵊl-ʔakᵊl ləssaata muu faatḥa* (or ***ləssa maa fatḥet*). 3. *maftuuq.* The seam is open. *l-ᵊxyaaṭa maftuuqa.* 4. *ṭaleq.* He's in the open air all day long. *huwwe ṭuul ᵊn-nhaar bᵊl-hawa ṭ-ṭaleq.* 5. *makšuuf.* It was declared an open city during the war. *nɛalnet madiine makšuufe waqt ᵊl-ḥarb.* 6. *šaaġer, faadi.* Is the job still open? *š-šaġle ləssaata šaaġra?* 7. *taḥt ᵊl-baḥs.* That's still an open question. *hal-masʔale ləssaata taḥt ᵊl-baḥs.*

**When is the open season for hunting? *ʔeemta bikuun muusem ᵊṣ-ṣeeḍ?*

**He's always open to reasonable suggestions. *biraḥḥeb daayman bᵊl-ʔəqtiraaḥaat ᵊl-maɛquule.*

in the open - *bᵊl-hawa ṭ-ṭaleq.* You should spend more time in the open. *laazem tmaḍḍi-lak waqᵊt ʔaktar bᵊl-hawa ṭ-ṭaleq.*

**Why don't you come out in the open and say it? *leeš maa btəži w-tquula ɛal-makšuuf* (or *b-ṣaraaḥa*).

to open - 1. *fataḥ (a fatᵊḥ//nfataḥ).* Open the door, please. *balla ftaaḥ ᵊl-baab.* -- Open all the windows wide! *ftaaḥ kəll ᵊš-šababiik ɛala ʔaaxəra!* -- Open your books to page five. *ftaḥu kətᵊbkon ɛala ṣafḥa xamse.* -- Now open your mouth wide! *hallaq ftaaḥ təmmak la-ʔaaxro!* -- They opened an account at the National Bank. *fataḥu ḥsaab bᵊl-baŋk ᵊl-waṭani.* -- Take the opened box first. *xood ᵊs-sanduuq ᵊl-maftuuḥ ʔawwal.* -- They'll open the new store next Friday. *laḥa yaftaḥu l-maxzan ᵊž-ždiid yoom ᵊž-žəmɛa ž-žaaye.* -- The new road will soon be opened to traffic. *ṭ-ṭariiq ᵊž-ždiid laḥa yənfəteḥ ɛan qariib ləs-seer.* 2. *ftataḥ.* The Mayor opened the exposition. *raʔiis ᵊl-baladiyye ftataḥ ᵊl-maɛraḍ.* 3. *nfataḥ.* The door opens easily now. *l-baab byənfəteḥ b-ᵊshuule hallaq.* 4. *bada (a bdaaye).* When does the season open? *ʔeemta l-muusem byəbda?*

**Our bedroom opens onto a sunny balcony. *ʔuuḍet noomna btəṭlaɛ mənha la-balkoon məšmes.*

**Their living room opens onto the garden. *ʔuuḍet ᵊl-qaɛde tabəɛon btəṭlaɛ mənha ɛaž-žneene.*

opening - 1. *fatḥa* pl. *-aat.* The opening isn't big enough. *l-fatḥa muu kbiire kfaaye.* 2. *bdaaye.* We missed the opening of his speech. *raaḥ ɛaleena bdaayet xaṭᵊbto.* 3. *ʔəftitaaḥ.* Were you at the opening of the exhibition? *ḥaḍarᵊt ʔəftitaaḥ ᵊl-maɛraḍ?* 4. *šaaġer* pl. *šawaaġer.* We'll call you as soon as we have an opening. *laḥa nəttəṣel fiik waqᵊt yṣiir ɛanna šaaġer.* 5. *ʔawwal˜.* I liked the opening number best. *ɛažbətni ʔawwal nəmre ʔaktar ᵊl-kəll.* 6. *ʔəftitaaḥi*.* The meeting adjourned after a brief opening statement. *ž-žalse tʔažžalet baɛᵊd kəlme ʔəftitaaḥiyye qaṣiire.* -- Opening night is sold out. *tazaaker ᵊl-ḥafle l-ʔəftitaaḥiyye nafdet.*

opera - *ʔoopera* pl. *ʔooperayaat.* What opera do you like best? *ʔani ʔoopera bətḥəbba ʔaktar ᵊl-kəll?*

opera (house) - *daar˜* (pl. *duur˜*) *ᵊl-ʔoopera.* The opera house is near the City Hall. *daar ᵊl-ʔoopera qariibe mn ᵊl-baladiyye.*

to **operate** - 1. *saawa ɛamaliyye.* The doctor says he'll have to operate. *l-ḥakiim biquul ʔənno laazem ysaawi ɛamaliyye.* -- The doctor operated on her twice. *l-ḥakiim saawaa-la ɛamaliiteen.* 2. *šaġġal.* How do you operate this machine? *kiif bətšaġġel hal-ʔaale?*

to be operated - *štaġal.* This machine is operated by electricity. *hal-ʔaale btəštəġel ɛal-kahraba.*

operation - *ɛamaliyye* pl. *-aat.* That's her third operation. *hayy ɛamaliita t-taalte.* -- One machine does the whole process in a single operation. *fard ʔaale bətsaawi š-šaġle kəlla b-ɛamaliyye waaḥde.*

to put into operation - *šaġġal//tšaġġal.* This line was only recently put into operation. *hal-xaṭṭ šaġġaluu mən mədde qariibe bass.*

operetta - *ʔoopereet* pl. *-aat, mḥaawara* (pl. *-aat*) *ġinaaʔiyye.*

opinion - *raʔi* pl. *ʔaaraaʔ.* What's your opinion? *šuu raʔyak ʔənte?* -- I gave him my frank opinion. *qəlt-əllo raʔyi ṣ-ṣariiḥ.* -- In my opinion it was a waste of time. *b-raʔyi ʔana kaan taḍyiiɛ waqᵊt.* -- I'm of another opinion. *ʔana ɛandi ġeer raʔi.* -- We'll have to get the opinion of an expert. *laazem* *naaxod ra?i waaḥed xabiir.*

**I have a very high opinion of him. *?ana ?aaxed ̣ćanno naẓra ćaalye ktiir.*

opponent - *xaṣ*ᵊ*m* pl. *xṣuum(e)* and *?axṣaam.* He's a dangerous opponent. *huwwe xaṣ*ᵊ*m byənxaaf mənno.*

opportunity - **1.** *fərṣa* pl. *fəraṣ, mnaasabe* pl. *-aat.* When will you have an opportunity to see him? *?eemta laḥa yṣər-lak fərṣa tšuufo?* **2.** *fərṣa* pl. *fəraṣ.* This is a big opportunity for you. *hayy fərṣa kbiire ?əlak.*

opposite - **1.** *ćak*ᵊ*s.* That is just the opposite of what I meant. *haada tamaam ćak*ᵊ*s yalli bəćnii.* **2.** *mqaabel, mćaakes.* He came from the opposite direction. *?əža mn* ᵊ*ž-žəha l-*ᵊ*mqaable.* **3.** *mwaažeh~, mqaabel~.* We live opposite the library. *saakniin* ᵊ*mwaažeh* ᵊ*l-maktabe.*

opposition - **1.** *mćaaraḍa.* He's joined the opposition. *nḍamm ləl-*ᵊ*mćaaraḍa.* **2.** *mćaaraḍa, mćaakase.* The proposal met with unexpected opposition. *l-?əqtiraaḥ laqa mćaaraḍa ġeer məntḍaṛa.*

oppressive - **1.** *məhlek.* The heat's oppressive today *š-šoob məhlek* ᵊ*l-yoom.* **2.** *ṭaaġi.* They passed a number of oppressive laws. *ṭaalaću ćəddet q̈awaniin ṭaaġye.*

optical - *baṣari*.*

optician - *ćweenaati* pl. *-iyye.*

optimism - *tafaa?ol.*

optimist - *mətfaa?el* pl. *-iin.*

optimistic - *mətfaa?el.*

optometrist - *ćweenaati* pl. *-iyye.*

or - **1.** *?aw.* It's called the Abbasid Period or the Golden Age. *bisammúu l-ćaṣr* ᵊ*l-ćabbaasi ?aw* ᵊ*l-ćaṣr* ᵊ*z-zahabi.* **2.** *yaa, ?aw.* He's coming today or tomorrow. *(huwwe) žaaye l-yoom yaa bəkra.* **3.** *wəlla.* Are you going or not? *raayeḥ wəlla la??* — Did you go to the station or have you forgotten? *šuu rəḥ*ᵊ*t ćal-*ᵊ*mḥaṭṭa wəlla nsiit?*

**He's away for three or four days. *huwwe muu hoon la-tlat arbaćt iyyaam.*

or (else) - *wəlla.* Hurry up or you'll be late. *stačžel wəlla btət?axxar.* — You do it, or else ...! *raḥa tsaawiiha wəlla ...!*

either ... or - *(yaa) ... yaa, (yaa) ... yaa ?əmma.* I'll leave either today or tomorrow. *?ana msaafer (yaa) l-yoom yaa (?əmma) bəkra.* — It's either on the table or in the drawer. *huwwe yaa ćaṭ-ṭaawle yaa b*ᵊ*d-dər*ᵊ*ž.*

oral - *šafahi*, šafawi*.* She passed the oral examination. *nažḥet b*ᵊ*l-faḥṣ* ᵊ*š-šafahi.*

Oran - *wahraan.*

orange - **1.** *bərdqaane* coll. *bərdqaan* pl. *-aat.* How much are the oranges? *b-qaddeeš* ᵊ*l-bərdqaan?* — May I have some orange juice, please? *ḅaḷḷa ćaṭiini šwayyet ćaṣiir bərdqaan mən faḍlak.* **2.** *bərdqaani*.* Her dress was orange and white. *rooba kaan bərdqaani w-?abyaḍ.*

orchard - *bəstaan* pl. *basatiin.*

orchestra - *?orkeestra* pl. *-aat, fərqa* (pl. *fəraq) muusiiq̈iyye.* Our orchestra is giving twelve concerts this winter. *l-?orkeestra tabaćna (or fərqə́tna l-muusiiq̈iyye) bədda təḥyi ṭnaćšar ḥafle b-haš-šətwiyye.* **2.** (native Arab) *žooqa* pl. *-aat* and *žuwaq, noobet~* (pl. *-aat~*) *?aalaat.* They have a pretty good orchestra in that night club. *fii ćandon žooqa laa ba?*ᵊ*s fiiha b-hal-kabarée.* **3.** *ṣaale.* Are there any seats left in the orchestra? *ṣafyaan šii maḥall faaḍi b*ᵊ*ṣ-ṣaale?*

order - **1.** *?am*ᵊ*r* pl. *?awaamer.* Is this a request or an order? *haada rağa wəlla ?am*ᵊ*r?* — We have no orders to do that. *maa ćanna ?awaamer* ᵊ*nsaawi haš-šii.* — I'm just following orders. *?ana šaġ*ᵊ*lti naffez* ᵊ*l-?awaamer bass.* **2.** *ṭalabiyye* pl. *-aat.* They gave me an order for twelve dozen eggs. *ṭalabu mənni ṭalabiyyet beeḍ ṭnaćšar dazziine.* **3.** *ṭalab* pl. *-aat.* Three orders of fish, please! *tlətt ṭalabaat samak ?iza bətriid.* — Waiter, will you take my order? *garsoon, məmken qəl-lak ṭalabi?* **4.** *rahbane* pl. *-aat.* To what order does that monk belong? *la-?ani rahbane byəntə́seb har-raaheb?* **5.** *niẓaam.* Order was quickly restored. *ražžaću n-niẓaam* ᵊ*b-sərća.* — Order! Order! *niẓaam! niẓaam!* **6.** *tartiib.* Please put these cards back in their proper order. *ḅaḷḷa ražžə́ć-li hal-*ᵊ*kruut* ᵊ*b-tartiibon* ᵊ*l-maẓbuuṭ.*

**Line up in order of height! *nṣaffu b-ḥasab* ᵊ*ṭ-ṭuul!*

**I now call the meeting to order. *?ana hallaq bəftə́teḥ* ᵊ*ž-žalse.*

by order of - *b-?amr~.* By order of the Chief of General Staff. *b-?amr ra?iis ?arkaan* ᵊ*l-ḥarb ...*

in order - **1.** *b-maḥall-* + pron. suff. Your remark is quite in order. *mlaaḥaẓtak b-maḥalla tamaam.* **2.** *maẓbuuṭ.* His papers are in order. *wraaqo maẓbuuṭiin.*

in order to - *la-, mənšaan, (la-)ḥatta.* I've come from Aleppo in order to see you. *?žiit mən ḥalab la-šuufak.*

in short order - *b-sərća, b-ćažale, qawaam.* I disposed of it in short order. *txallaṣ*ᵊ*t mənno b-sərća.*

on order - *taḥt* ᵊ*ṭ-ṭalab.* We haven't that item right now but it's on order. *muu mawžuud haṣ-ṣən*ᵊ*f ćanna hallaq, bass taḥt* ᵊ*ṭ-ṭalab.*

out of order - *ćaṭlaan.* The fan is out of order. *l-marwaḥa ćaṭlaane.*

**You're out of order. *maa-lak ḥaqq təḥki.*

to order - **1.** *tafṣiil.* He has his suits made to order. *bisaawi ṭquumto tafṣiil.* **2.** *tuuṣaaye.* The table was made to order. *ṭ-ṭaawle nšaġlet tuuṣaaye.*

to put in order - *handaz, rattab.* Put your room in order before the company arrives. *handez ?uuḍtak qab*ᵊ*l-ma yəžu ḍ-ḍyuuf.* — He's putting his affairs in order. *ćam yratteb ?ašġaalo.*

to order - **1.** *?amar (o ?am*ᵊ*r//n?amar).* Who ordered you to do this? *miin ?amárak tsaawi haš-šii?* — He ordered their arrest. *?amar* ᵊ*b-ḥabson.* **2.** *ṭalab (o ṭalab//nṭalab).* Order the taxi for six o'clock. *ṭləb-li t-taksi ləs-saaća sətte.* **3.** *waṣṣa ćala.* This is not the book I ordered. *muu haada l-*ᵊ*ktaab yalli waṣṣeet ćalée.*

to order around - *t?ammar ćala.* Stop ordering me around! *ḥaaštak tət?ammar ćaliyyi!*

ordinary - *ćaadi*.* He's just an ordinary mechanic. *huwwe ćibaara ćan mikaniiki ćaadi.*

out of the ordinary - *xaarež ćan* ᵊ*l-ma?luuf.* That's quite out of the ordinary. *haada šii xaarež ćan* ᵊ*l-ma?luuf tamaam.*

ore - *(maćdan) xaam* pl. *maćaaden xaam.* Iron ore is found in this area. *xaam* ᵊ*l-ḥadiid mawžuud b-hal-manṭiqa.*

organ - **1.** *?ərġon* pl. *?araaġen.* She plays the organ in our church. *bəddəqq ćal-?ərġon b-*ᵊ*kniisətna.* **2.** *ćəḍu* pl. *?aćḍaa?.* The eye is a very delicate organ. *l-ćeen ćəḍu ktiir ḥassaas.* **3.** *lsaan~ ḥaal.* The paper is the organ of the Socialist Party. *ž-žariide lsaan ḥaal* ᵊ*l-ḥəzb* ᵊ*l-?əštiraaki.*

organic - *ćəḍwi*.*

organization - (body) *mnaẓẓame* pl. *-aat.*

to **organize** - **1.** *naẓẓam//tnaẓẓam.* The whole thing was poorly organized. *š-šaġle kəlla kaanet* ᵊ*mnaẓẓame tanẓiim ćaaṭel.* **2.** *nṭaẓamu b-*ᵊ*nq̈aabe.* All the employees in our office have organized. *kəll l-*ᵊ*mwaẓẓafiin* ᵊ*b-daayrətna nṭaẓamu b-*ᵊ*nq̈aabe.*

**We'll call you up as soon as we get ourselves organized. *məntalfə́n-lak baćᵊd-ma nrasteq ḥaalna.*

Orient - *š-šar*ᵊ*q.*

oriental - *šarqi*.*

orientalist - *məstašreq* pl. *-iin.*

origin - **1.** *maṣdar* pl. *maṣaader.* What's the origin of this story? *šuu maṣdar hal-qəṣṣa?* **2.** *?aṣ*ᵊ*l* pl. *?ṣuul.* Have you read "The Origin of Species"? *qareet* ᵊ*ktaab "?aṣl* ᵊ*l-?anwaać?"*

original - **1.** *?aṣ*ᵊ*l* pl. *?ṣuul.* The original of this picture doesn't exist any more. *?aṣ*ᵊ*l haṣ-ṣuura maa ćaad mawžuud.* **2.** *nəsxa* (pl. *nəsax) ?aṣliyye.* I'd like to see the original of the contract. *bəddi šuuf* ᵊ*n-nəsxa l-?aṣliyye tabać* ᵊ*l-kəntraat.* **3.** *?aṣli*.* The original plan was altogether different. *l-xəṭṭa l-?aṣliyye kaanet kəlla ġeer heek.* — Is that the original text? *haada n-naṣṣ* ᵊ*l-?aṣli?* **3.** *məbtə́kar.* He has very original ideas. *ćando ?afkaar məbtə́kara ktiir.*

originally - *b*ᵊ*l-?asaas, b*ᵊ*l-?aṣ*ᵊ*l, ?aṣlan.* He wanted to be a doctor originally. *b*ᵊ*l-?asaas kaan bəddo yṣiir doktoor.*

orphan - *yatiim* f. *yatiime* pl. *yətama* and *?aytaam.*

orphan asylum - *daar~* (pl. *duur~*) *?aytaam.*

orphanage - *daar~* (pl. *duur~*) *?aytaam.*

other - **1.** *taani.* How do I get to the other side of the river? *kiif bəqder ćaddi la-ṭaraf* ᵊ*n-nahṛ* ᵊ*t-taani?* — I can't tell one from the other. *maa bəqder ?aćref waaḥed mn* ᵊ*t-taani.* **2.** *taani, ġeer~* Have you any other books? *fii ćandak ?ani kət*ᵊ*b taanye?* or *fii ćandak ġeer hal-kət*ᵊ*b?* or *fii ćandak šii kət*ᵊ*b ġeera?* — He has no consideration for other people. *maa ćando mraaćaa lən-naas* ᵊ*t-taanyiin* or *ma ćando mraaćaa la-ġeero* (or *ləl-ġeer* or *la-naas ġeero*). **3.** *ġeer~.* On the shelf are no other books than mine. *ćar-raff maa* *fii kət^ə b ġeer kətbi.* -- No students other than those who fulfilled their requirements will be admitted. *maa fii təllaab laha yənqablu ġeer yalli stawfu š-šuruuṭ ^əl-maṭluube.*

among other things - *w-b^əž-žəmle.* Among other things he mentioned that ... *w-b^əž-žəmle zakar ʔənno ...* or ***w-^əb-žəmlet ma zakar zakar ʔənno ...*

each other - *baƐḍ-* + pron. suff. *^əl-baƐḍ* (or *baƐḍ-* + pron. suff. alone). Do you see each other every day? *bətšuufu baƐḍkon (^əl-baƐḍ) kəll yoom?* -- We see each other every day. *mənšuuf baƐḍna (l-baƐḍ) kəll yoom.* -- You have to help each other. *laazem tsaaƐdu baƐḍkon ^əl-baƐḍ.* — They have no consideration for each other. *maa fii Ɛandon ^əmraaƐda la-baƐḍon (^əl-baƐḍ).* -- They have nothing to do with each other. *maa fii been baƐḍon ʔayy Ɛalaaqa* or ***maa fii ʔayy Ɛalaaqa beenaaton.*

every other - *kəll* + noun in dual. The meetings are held every other day. *ž-žalsaat btənƐə́qed kəll yoomeen* (or ***yoom ʔee yoom laʔ*).

on the one hand ... on the other hand - *mən žəha ... w-mən žəha taanye.* On the one hand he wants it finished, on the other hand he doesn't give us the material. *mən žəha bəddo-yaana nxallə́sa, w-mən žəha taanye maa Ɛam yaƐṭiina l-mawaadd.*

somehow or other - *n-kaan heek ʔaw heek.* He must have forgotten it somehow or other. *n-kaan heek ʔaw heek, laazem ykuun ^ənsiiha.* -- Somehow or other we'll finish the job next month. *n-kaan heek ʔaw heek, bəddna nxalleṣ ^əš-šəġl ^əš-šahr ^əž-žaaye.*

the other day - *mən kam yoom, hadaak ^əl-yoom.* I saw your friend the other day. *šəf^ət ṣaaḥbak mən kam yoom.*

otherwise - **1.** *ġeer heek.* What would you do otherwise? *šuu bəddak taƐmel ġeer heek?* **2.** *b^əl-baqiyye.* Otherwise I'm satisfied with him. *b^əl-baqiyye ʔana raḍyaan mənno.*

ought - *l-mafruuḍ ...* You ought to tell him about it. *l-mafruuḍ ^ətqəl-lo Ɛanha.* -- At least, he ought to give them a call. *l-mafruuḍ Ɛal-ʔaqall ytalfə́n-lon.*

**You ought to be ashamed of yourself. *stəḥi Ɛala ḥaalak!* or *Ɛeeb Ɛaleek!*

our - **1.** *-na.* Our dog is full of fleas. *kalbna malaan baraġiit.* **2.** *tabaƐna, šiitna.* The accident happened on our corner. *l-ḥaades ṣaar Ɛand ^əs-suuke tabaƐna.*

ours - *tabaƐna, šiitna.* This is ours. *hayy tabaƐna.*

**He's an old friend of ours. *huwwe rfiiq qadiim ʔəlna.*

**Their house is larger than ours. *beeton ʔawsaƐ mən beetna.*

ourselves - **1.** *b-naf^əsna, la-ḥaalna.* Let's do it ourselves. *xalliina nsaawiiha b-naf^əsna.* -- We make our beds ourselves. *mənsaawi txuutətna la-ḥaalna.* **2.** *ḥaalna.* We saw ourselves on the television screen. *šəfna ḥaalna Ɛala šaašet ^ət-telefəzyoon.* -- We're just hurting ourselves. *nəḥna bass Ɛam nəʔzi ḥaalna.* **3.** *-na (nəḥna).* This is strictly between ourselves. *hayye šəġle xaaṣṣa beenaatna (nəḥna).* -- The responsibility is on ourselves. *l-masʔuuliyye Ɛaleena (nəḥna).*

out - **1.** *barra.* They're out in the garden. *hənne barra b^əž-žneene.* — Usually, we're out in the country this time of the year. *Ɛaadatan mənkuun barra b^ər-riif b-hal-faṣ^əl mn ^əs-səne.* **2.** *məṭfi*.* The lights are out. *l-ʔəḍ^əwye məṭfiyye.* — The stove is out. *ṣ-ṣoobya məṭfiyye.* **3.** *muu mawžuud.* They were out when we called them. *kaanu muu mawžuudiin lamma daqqeenda-lon talifoon.* **4.** *məstaḥiil.* The raise is definitely out. *zyaadet ^əl-maƐaaš ḥatman məstaḥiile.*

**Let's eat out tonight! *xalliina naakol b^əl-maṭƐam ^əl-leele.*

**We send our laundry out. *mnəbƐat ġasiilna Ɛal-masbaġa.*

**You should see a doctor before the week is out. *laazem ^ətšuuf doktoor qab^əl-ma tənda ž-žəmƐa.*

**The new edition isn't out yet. *ṭ-ṭabƐa ž-ždiide ləssa maa ṣadret.*

**I added it twice and I'm still out three dollars. *žamaƐto marrteen w^əl-^əḥsaab ləssaato naaqeṣ tlətt dolaaraat.*

**Out with it! *ṭaalə́Ɛa baqa!*

**One of these days I'll have it out with him. *byəži yoom bṣaffi ḥsaabi maƐo.*

out of - **1.** *barraat~.* He took me out of turn. *ʔaxadni barraat ^əd-door.* — Prices are much lower out of season. *l-ʔasƐaar ʔawṭa ktiir barraat ^əl-muusem.* -- The situation is beginning to get completely out of hand. *l-ḥaale Ɛam tabda taṭlaƐ barraat ʔiidna mnoob.* -- I hope this isn't out of your way. *nšaaḷḷa maa tkuun barraat ṭariiqak.* -- He's been out of jail for two weeks. *ṣar-lo barraat ^əl-ḥab^əs žəm^əƐteen.* — I'm coming from out of town. *ʔana žaaye mən barraat ^əl-balad.* **2.** *xaarež Ɛan, barraat~.* That's out of my bailiwick. *haada xaarež Ɛan ʔəxtiṣaaṣi.* -- This solution is definitely out of the question. *hal-ḥall ḥatman xaarež Ɛan ^ən-niṭaaq.*

**He came out of the house. *ṭəleƐ mn ^əl-beet.*

**She's been out of bed only two days. *ṣar-la yoomeen bass qaayme mn ^ət-tax^ət.*

**We are out of this brand. *xaaleṣ has-sən^əf mən Ɛanna.*

**I'm afraid we're out of gas. *xaayə́f-lak ykuun ^əl-banziin xalaṣ maƐna.*

**Sorry, the book is out of print. *mətʔassef, hal-^əktaab nafdet ṭab^əƐto.*

**You're out of step. *ʔənte mxarbeṭ ^əb-mášitak.*

**She's out of work. *hiyye Ɛaaṭle Ɛan ^əl-Ɛamal.*

**I've been out of touch with him for over a year now. *ṣar-li hallaq mənqə́ṭeƐ Ɛanno ʔaktar mən səne.*

**The ball was out of reach. *ṭ-ṭaabe kaanet maa btənṭaal.*

**A car is completely out of reach for us now. *muu b-ʔəmkaaniyyaatna b^əl-marra nətḥammal sayyaara hallaq.*

**Straw hats are out of fashion. *ṭawaaqi l-qašš maa Ɛaadet Ɛal-mooḍa.*

**The piano is out of tune. *l-byaano raaḥ duuzaano.*

**The elevator is temporarily out of order. *l-ʔaṣanṣoor mƐaṭṭal ^əmwaqqatan.*

**I did it out of pity. *Ɛməlta šafaqa.*

**He did it out of spite. *saawaaha žakaara.*

out of doors - *taḥt ^əs-sama.* It's too cold to sit out of doors. *ktiir bar^əd təqƐod taḥt ^əs-sama.*

to be out for - *rakaḍ (o rak^əḍ) wara.* She's only out for a good time. *raakḍe wara t-təslaaye bass.* -- He's out for a record. *huwwe raakeḍ wara raq^əm qiyaasi.*

out-and-out - *Ɛaṭ-ṭaalƐa w^ən-naazle.* You're an out-and-out liar. *ʔənte kazzaab Ɛaṭ-ṭaalƐa w^ən-naazle.*

outbreak - **1.** *nšuub.* At the outbreak of the war ... *waqt ^ənšuub ^əl-ḥarb ...* **2.** *ẓhuur.* The papers report an outbreak of cholera in that area. *ž-žaraayed Ɛam təktob Ɛan ^əẓhuur ^əl-koleera b-hal-manṭiqa.*

outdoors - *taḥt ^əs-sama.* It's too cold to sit outdoors. *ktiir bar^əd təqƐod taḥt ^əs-sama.*

outfit - **1.** *ṭaq^əm* pl. *ṭquume.* If you want to go skiing, I'll let you borrow my outfit. *ʔiza bəddak truuḥ Ɛas-skii la-Ɛiirak ṭaqmi.* **2.** *kəswe* pl. *-aat.* My wife bought the children new spring outfits. *marti štaret ləl-^əwlaad kəswe ždiide lər-rabiiƐ.* **3.** *wəḥda* pl. *-aat.* Corporal *SaƐiid* was transferred to another outfit. *l-Ɛariif saƐiid ^əntaqal la-wəḥde ždiide.* **4.** *žamaaƐa* pl. *-aat.* I wouldn't work for an outfit like that. *b-ḥayaati maa bəštə́ġel maƐ žamaaƐa mən han-nəmre.*

to outfit - *kasa (i kəswe//nkasa).* The children have to be outfitted from head to foot. *l-^əwlaad laazem yənkəsu mən raason la-qaddə́mon.*

to outgrow - The children have outgrown their clothes. *l-ʔawaaƐi ṣəġret Ɛal-^əwlaad.* — The girl has outgrown dolls. *l-bən^ət maa Ɛaadet ^əzġiire təlƐab b^əl-ləƐab.*

outlet - **1.** *maṣraf* pl. *maṣaaref.* The lake has two outlets. *l-buḥayra ʔəla maṣrafeen.* -- Children have to have an outlet for their energies. *l-^əwlaad bəddon maṣraf la-ṭaaqə́ton.* **2.** *briiz* pl. *-aat.* We need another outlet in this room. *laazəmna briiz taani b-hal-ʔuuḍa.*

outline - **1.** *malaameḥ* (pl.), *xyaal* (pl. *-aat.*) We could see the outlines of the mountains in spite of the mist. *kənna šaayfiin malaameḥ ^əž-žbaal maƐ ^əḍ-ḍabaab.* **2.** *mxaṭṭaṭ* pl. *-aat.* Have you made an outline yet of what you're going to say? *Ɛməlt ^əmxaṭṭaṭ la-halli bəddak ^ətquulo?* **3.** *məxtáṣar* pl. *-aat, muužaz* pl. *-aat.* What I want is a brief outline of Arab history. *š-šii yalli bəddi-yda huwwe məxtáṣar Ɛan taariix ^əl-Ɛarab* (or *muužaz taariix ^əl-Ɛarab*).

outlook - **1.** *tabašiir* (pl.). The outlook for the future isn't very bright. *tabašiir ^əl-məstaqbal muu ktiir mniiḥa.* **2.** *wəžhet~* (pl. *-aat~*) *naẓar.* That experience has changed her outlook on child rearing. *hat-təžribe ġayyarə́t-la wəžhet naẓra b-tarbiyet* *ᵊl-ʔaṭfaal.* **3.** *tafkiir.* He has a very narrow outlook. *tafkiiro ktiir maḥduud.*

out-of-the-way – *naaʔi.* He lives in an out-of-the-way part of the city. *byəskon b-qərne naaʔye mn ᵊl-balad.*

outrage – **1.** *ṛaziile* pl. *ṛazaayel.* During the last years of his reign he committed innumerable outrages against his people. *bᵊs-sniin ᵊl-ʔaxiire mən ɛahᵊd ḥəkmo rtakab ṛazaayel laa tuḥṣa b-ḥaqq šaɛbo.* **2.** *kəfᵊr, ẓəlᵊm, ṛazaale.* It's an outrage that he should charge such prices! *kəfᵊr ʔənno yḥaṭṭeṭ ᵊn-naas heek ʔasɛaar!*

outraged – *ḥaaneq.* The bystanders were outraged by his behavior. *l-mətfarržiin kaanu ḥaanqiin ɛala taṣarrfo.*

outrageous – **1.** *šaaʔen.* Everyone was shocked by his outrageous behavior. *kəll waaḥed ᵊstahžan suluuko š-šaaʔen.* **2.** *žnuuni*.* They charge outrageous prices in that store. *byəṭᵊlbu ʔasɛaar ᵊžnuuniyye b-hadaak ᵊl-maxzan.*

outright – *ṣərᵊf* (invar.). That's an outright lie. *hayye kəzbe ṣərᵊf.*

outside – **1.** *barraaniyye, barraani.* The outside of the building is drab and gray. *barraaniit ᵊl-binaaye ʔašhab baahet.* **2.** *barraani*.* Do you have an outside cabin? *ɛandak kabiin barraani?* **3.** *barra.* It's cold outside. *d-dənye barᵊd barra.* **4.** *barraat˜.* He lives outside the city. *byəskon barraat ᵊl-balad.*

outside of – *maa ɛada˜.* I don't trust anyone here outside of you. *maa buusaq b-ḥada hoon ma ɛadaak ʔənte.*

at the outside – *ɛala ʔaktar taɛdiil, ɛal-ʔaktar.* At the outside, I give him five days to live. *ɛala ʔaktar taɛdiil maa laha yɛəš-lo ʔaktar mən xamᵊst iyyaam.*

from the outside – *mən barra.* The house looks very pretty from the outside. *l-beet manẓaro ḥəlu mən barra.*

outstanding – *baarez.* He's an outstanding scholar. *huwwe ɛaalem baarez.*

**We have three hundred forty-two dollars in outstanding debts with this company. *ʔəlna tlaat miyye w-ᵊtneen w-ʔarᵊbɛiin dolaar b-zəmmet haš-šərke.*

**I have a lot of money outstanding. *ʔəli maṣaari ktiir ᵊb-zəmmet ᵊn-naas.*

oven – *fərᵊn* pl. *fruune* and *fraan.*

over – **1.** *ɛala.* Your jacket is hanging over the chair. *žaakeetak mɛallaq ɛal-kərsi.* **2.** *fooq.* Don't pull the cover over your head. *laa təsḥab ᵊl-ġaṭa fooq raasak.* — My room is over the kitchen. *ʔuudti fooq ᵊl-maṭbax.* **3.** *mən fooq.* The plane passed over the tree tops. *ṭ-ṭayyaara marqet mən fooq ruus ᵊs-sažar.* — Why don't you jump over the ditch? *leeš maa bətnəṭṭ mən fooq ᵊl-xandaq?* **4.** *mən, ɛabr.* We traveled over the new road to Palmyra. *saafarna mn ᵊṭ-ṭariiq ᵊž-ždiid la-tədmor.* **5.** *ɛabr.* The news came over the air. *l-xabar ntašar ɛabr (mawžaat) ᵊl-hawa.* **6.** *fooq ᵊmmən˜.* There is no one over me at the office. *maa fii ḥada fooq ᵊmmənni bᵊl-maktab.* **7.** *ʔaktar mən.* Is it over three miles? *šu, ʔaktar mən tlətt ʔamyaal?*

**The lecture was way over my head. *l-ᵊmḥaadara kaanet ʔaɛla b-ᵊktiir mən məstawaayi* or *l-ᵊmḥaadara faatet ɛaliyyi bᵊṭ-ṭərreeši.*

over again – *kamaan marra, taani marra, marra taanye.* Do it over again. *saawiiha kamaan marra.*

over and above – *fooq, ɛalaawe ɛala.* You'll receive certain allowances over and above your regular salary. *laha təqbaḍ taɛwiiḍaat ᵊmɛayyane fooq maɛaašak ᵊl-ɛaadi.*

over and over again – *marraat w-marraat, ʔamraaran, miraaran w-takraaran.* He asked the same question over and over again. *saʔalni nafs ᵊs-suʔaal marraat w-marraat.*

over here – **1.** *hoon(e).* She's over here. *hiyye hoone.* **2.** *la-hoon(e).* Come over here. *taɛa la-hoon.*

over there – **1.** *hniik(e).* What's that over there? *šuu haada yalli hniik?* **2.** *la-hniik.* Go over there and see for yourself. *ruuḥ la-hniik w-šuuf ᵊb-nafsak.*

all over – **1.** *b-kəll qərne, b-kəll maṭraḥ.* I've looked all over. *dawwarᵊt bi-kəll qərne.* **2.** *kəll.* He traveled all over the country. *daar l-ᵊblaad kəlla.* — She trembled all over. *kaanet ɛam tərtažž kəlla.*

**It's all over. *kəll šii xalaṣ* or *xalṣet ᵊš-šaġle.*

to be over – *xalaṣ (o xluuṣ).* When is the show over? *ʔeemta l-ḥafle btəxloṣ?*

to get something over with – **1.** *xallaṣ šii.* Let's get this business over with. *xalliina nxalleṣ haš-šaġle baqa.* **2.** *xalaṣ (o xalaaṣ) mən šii.* Let's ask him and get it over with. *xalliina nəsʔalo w-nəxloṣ mənha baqa.*

overcoat – *manṭo* pl. *manṭohaat* and *manṭoyaat* and *manaaṭi, kabbuud* pl. *kababiid.*

to **overcome** – *tġallab ɛala.* She had many difficulties to overcome. *kaan laazem tətġallab ɛala ṣuɛuubaat ᵊktiire.*

to be overcome – **1.** *ġaṭṭ ɛala qalbo.* I was almost overcome by gas. *kaan laḥa yġəṭṭ ɛala qalbi mn ᵊl-ġaaz.* **2.** *tʔassar.* She was so overcome, she couldn't talk. *kaanet mətʔassra la-daražet ʔənno maa qədret təḥki.*

to **overdo** – **1.** *zaad (i zyaade), ṭabaš (o ṭabᵊš), kattar.* I'm allowed to play tennis as long as I don't overdo it. *masmuḥ-li ʔəlɛab tanəs ma-daam maa ziid fiiha.* — He always overdoes it. *huwwe daayman biziida.*

to **overlook** – **1.** *səhi (a sahu) ɛan.* He must have overlooked it. *laazem ykuun səhi ɛanha.* **2.** *tġaaḍa ɛan.* Shall I overlook his mistake? *bəddak-yaani ʔətġaaḍa ɛan ġalᵊṭṭo?*

overnight – *b-leele w-ḍəḥaaha.* He got rich overnight. *ṣaar zangiil b-leele w-ḍəḥaaha* (or ***b-leele maa fiiha ḍaww qamar*).

to stay overnight – *baat (a byaate) leele.* I intend to stay there overnight. *b-niiti baat ᵊhniik leele.*

to **overrule** – *radd (ə radd//nradd* and *rtadd).* The judge overruled the objection. *l-ḥaakem radd ᵊl-ʔəɛtiraaḍ.*

oversight – *sahwe* pl. *-aat, zalle* pl. *-aat.* That must have been an oversight. *laazem kaanet hayy sahwe.*

to **oversleep** – *tʔaxxar bᵊn-noom(e).* I overslept this morning. *l-yoom ɛala bəkra tʔaxxarᵊt bᵊn-noome.*

to **overthrow** – *qalab (e qalᵊb//nqalab).* That's the second time this year the government was overthrown. *hayy taani marra has-səne nqalbet fiiha l-ᵊḥkuume.*

overtime – *saaɛaat ʔiḍaafiyye* (pl.). I had to work overtime. *ḍṭarreet ʔəštəġel saaɛaat ʔiḍaafiyye.* — He worked five hours overtime. *štaġal xamᵊs saaɛaat ʔiḍaafiyye.*

to **owe**: How much do I owe you? *qaddeeš ʔəlak maɛi?* — We owed her about 200 pounds. *kan-la maɛna ḥawaali miiteen leera.* — She owes everything to him. *hiyye madyənt-əllo b-kəll šii.* — He owes me a lot in this life. *madyən-li ktiir b-hal-ḥayaat.*

owl – *buume* coll. *buum* pl. *-aat* and *buwam.*

own: Are these your own things? *hayy ᵊġraaḍak ʔənte?* — That was his own doing, not mine. *haada kaan ɛamalo huwwe, muu ɛamali (ʔana).* — It's his own fault. *hayy xaṭiiʔto huwwe.* — Can I have a room of my own? *məmken taɛṭuuni ʔuuḍa ʔəli waḥdi?* — My brother had a car of his own at that time. *ʔaxi kan-lo sayyaara ʔəlo waḥdo b-hadiik ᵊl-ʔiyyaam.* — He's been on his own ever since he was sixteen. *ṣar-lo məstqəll ᵊb-ḥaalo mən waqᵊt kaan ɛəmro səṭṭaɛš.*

on one's own (hook) – *ɛala masʔuuliit-* + pron. suff. Then I'll do it on my own hook. *ʔizan baɛməla ɛala masʔuuliiti.*

to own – *malak (e/o məlk).* He owns a house. *byəmlek beet* or ***ɛando beet.* — Who owns this lot? *miin halli byəmlek haš-šaqfet ᵊl-ʔarḍ?* or ***miin ṣaaḥeb haš-šaqfet ᵊl-ʔarḍ?*

owner – *ṣaaḥeb* pl. *ṣḥaab, maalek* pl. *-iin.*

ox – *toor* pl. *twaar* and *tiiraan.*

oxygen – *ʔoksižeen.*

oyster – *maḥaara* coll. *maḥaar* pl. *-aat.*

P

pace - 1. *xaṭwe* pl. *-aat*. The garden is about twenty paces wide and thirty-five long. *ž-žneene taqriiban ʕəšriin xaṭwe ʕarḍ ᵊb-xamsda w-ᵊtlaatiin ṭuul.* 2. *sərʕa*. He sets the pace. *huwwe yalli biʕayyen ᵊs-sərʕa.*
  to keep pace with - *žaara*. I can't keep pace with him. *maa fiini žaarii.*
  to pace - *tmašša*. He paced up and down the room. *tmašša bᵊl-ʔuuḍa raayeḥ žaaye.*
  to pace off - *qaas (i qyaas) ᵊb-xaṭwaato*. Pace off a hundred feet. *qiis ᵊb-xaṭwaatak masaafet miit qadam.*

Pacific (Ocean) - *l-muḥiiṭ ᵊl-haadi, l-muḥiiṭ ᵊl-baasifiiki.*

pack - 1. *sərbe* pl. *sərab*. They went at the food like a pack of hungry wolves. *laḥašu ḥaalon ʕal-ʔakᵊl kaʔənnon sərbet dyaab.* 2. *ḥəzme* pl. *ḥəzam*. The donkeys were loaded down with heavy packs. *l-ḥamiir kaanu mḥammaliin ḥəzam tqiile ktiir.*
  **Where is that new pack of cards? *ween haš-šadde ž-ždiide?*
  **That's a pack of lies! *haada kəzb ᵊb-kəzᵊb.*
  to pack - 1. *ḍabb (ə ḍabb//nḍabb)*. Have you packed your trunk yet? *ḍabbeet sanduuqak wəlla ləssa?* -- My things are all packed. *kəll ᵊġraaḍi maḍbuubiin.* 2. *zarak (o zark//nzarak), taras (o tarᵊs//ntaras)*. They shouldn't pack us into the train this way. *ʕeeb ʕaleehon yəzᵊrkuuna heek zark bᵊt-treen.*
  packed - 1. *matruus, maʕžuuq, mazḥuum*. The bus was packed this morning. *l-baaṣ ᵊl-yoom ʕala bəkra kaan matruus tars.* 2. *maḥṭuuṭ*. The sardines are packed in olive oil. *s-sardiin maḥṭuuṭ ᵊb-zeet zeetuun.*
  to pack in - *zarak (o zarak//nzarak)*. We were packed in like sardines. *kənna mazruukiin mətl ᵊs-sardiin.*
  to pack up - *ḍabb (ə ḍabb), ṣarr (ə ṣarr), ḥazam (o ḥazᵊm)*. He packed up his things and left. *ḍabb ᵊġraaḍo w-məši.*

package - 1. *ṭard* pl. *ṭruude*. The mailman brought a package for you. *l-boosṭaži žab-lak ṭard.* 2. *baakeet* pl. *-aat*. Do you sell the coffee loose or in packages? *bətbiiʕ ᵊl-bənn farṭ wəlla bᵊl-baakeetaat?*

pact - *mʕaahade* pl. *-aat, miisaaq̈* pl. *mawasiiq̈*.

pad - 1. *ṭərraaḥa* pl. *ṭarariiḥ*. Do you have a pad for your typewriter? *ʕandak ṭərraaḥa ləl-ʔaale l-kaatbe tabaʕak?* 2. *daftar* pl. *dafaater*. I wrote his telephone number down on the pad. *qayyadᵊt nəmret talifoono ʕad-daftar.* 3. *ṣṭamba* pl. *-aat*. I've got the stamp but I can't find the pad. *l-xatᵊm maʕi bass maa laqeet ᵊṣ-ṣṭamba.*
  to pad - *ḥaša (i ḥaši//nḥaša)*. I want the shoulders padded. *bəddi l-ᵊktaaf məḥšiyye.*

padding - *ḥašwe* pl. *-aat*.

padlock - *qəfᵊl* pl. *qfaal*.

page - *ṣafḥa* pl. *-aat*. The book is two hundred pages long. *l-ᵊktaab miiteen ṣafḥa.*

pail - *ṣaṭᵊl* pl. *ṣṭuul(e)*. Get a pail of water! *žiib ṣaṭᵊl mayy.*

pain - *wažaʕ* pl. *ʔawžaaʕ, ʔalam* pl. *ʔaalaam*. I feel a sharp pain in my back. *ḥaases wažaʕ šadiid b-ḍahri.*
  to take pains - *ʔažhad ḥaalo*. She takes great pains with her work. *btəžhed ḥaala ktiir ᵊb-šəġla.*

painful - 1. *muužeʕ, məʔlem*. Was the operation very painful? *l-ʕamaliyye kaanet ᵊktiir muužʕa?* 2. *məḥrež*. It's painful to watch him. *šii məḥrež ʔənnak ᵊtšaahdo.*

paint - *dhaan* pl. *-aat*. The paint is still wet. *d-dhaan ləssda maa nəšef.*
  to paint - 1. *dahan (a dhaan//ndahan), dahhan*. Why don't you paint the house white? *leeš maa btədhan ᵊl-beet ʔabyaḍ?* 2. *ṣawwar*. She paints in oils. *bətṣawwer taṣwiir zeeti.*

paintbrush - *foršaaye* pl. *-aat* and *faraaši*.

painter - 1. *rassaam* pl. *-iin*. He's a famous painter. *huwwe rassaam mašhuur.* 2. *dahhaan* pl. *-iin*. The painters will be through with the kitchen by tomorrow. *d-dahhaaniin bixallṣu l-maṭbax bəkra.*

painting - 1. *looḥa* pl. *-aat*. That's a beautiful painting. *hayy looḥa ḥəlwe.* 2. *taṣwiir*. I'm especially interested in Italian painting. *bəhtəmm ᵊb-ṣuura xaaṣṣa bᵊt-taṣwiir ᵊṭ-ṭəlyaani.* 3. *dhaan, tadhiin*. Painting the house was hard. *dhaan ᵊl-beet kaan ṣaʕᵊb.*

pair - *žooz* pl. *žwaaz, zoož* pl. *zwaaž*. I bought myself a pair of gloves. *štareet žooz ᵊkfuuf.*

pajamas - *biižaama* pl. *-aat*.

pal - *rfiiq* pl. *rəfaqa*. You're a real pal. *ʔənte rfiiq ʕan ṣaḥiiḥ.*
  to pal around - *tṣaaḥab*. They've palled around for years. *hənne mətṣaaḥbiin mən zamaan.*

palace - *qaṣᵊr* pl. *qṣuur(a)*.

palate - *saqf˜ (pl. squufet˜) ᵊl-ḥalq*.

pale - 1. *ʔaṣfar* f. *ṣafra* pl. *ṣəfᵊr, baahet, šaaḥeb*. You look so pale today. *waḷḷa loonak ʔaṣfar ᵊl-yoom.* 2. *baahet*. It's a pale blue. *l-loon ʔazraq baahet.*
  to turn pale - *ṣfarr*. When he heard that, he turned pale. *lamma səmeʕ haš-šaġle ṣfarr.*

Palestine - *falasṭiin*.

Palestinian - *falasṭiini**.

pallor - *ʔəṣfiraar, šuḥuub*.

palm - 1. *naxle* coll. *naxᵊl* pl. *-aat*. These palms grow as high as thirty feet. *han-naxᵊl məmken yəṭwal la-ḥadd ᵊtlaatiin qadam ᵊʕluww.* 2. *kaff* pl. *kfuuf*. My palm is all calloused. *kaffi kəllo damaamel.*
  to grease the palm - *barṭal, raša (i rašwe)*. They had to grease a lot of palms in order to achieve their purpose. *nžabaru ybarᵊṭlu naas ᵊktiir ḥatta yəṣalu la-ġaraḍon.*
  to palm off - *lazzaq*. He palmed off his old books on me. *lazzaqni kətbo l-ʕatiiqa talziiq.*

Palm Sunday - *ʔaḥad ᵊš-šaʕaniin*.

Palmyra - *tədmor*.

paltry - *zahiid, ḍaʔiil*.

pan - (frying pan) *məqlaaye* pl. *-aat*, (saucepan) *ṭanžara* pl. *ṭanaažer*. Did you wash the pots and pans too? *ġasalti kamaan ᵊṭ-ṭanaažer wᵊl-məqlaayaat?*
  to pan out - *ṭəleʕ (a ṭluuʕ)*. How did your scheme pan out? *kiif ṭəleʕ mašruuʕak?*
  to pan out badly - *fəšel (a fašal)*.
  to pan out well - *nažaḥ (a nažaaḥ)*.

Panama - *panama*.

Panama Canal - *q̈anaat panama*.

pane - *looḥ˜ (pl. lwaaḥ˜) balloor*. The storm blew in several panes. *l-ʕaaṣfe kassaret ʕəddet ᵊlwaaḥ balloor.*

panic - *žazaʕ, fazaʕ*. The crowd was seized by a sudden panic. *l-ḥašᵊd stawla ʕalée žazaʕ ᵊmfaaže?.*
  to panic - *žəzeʕ (a žazaʕ), fəzeʕ (a fazaʕ)*. Don't panic, everything's going to straighten out all right. *laa təžzaʕ, kəll šii raḥa tkuun nihaayto xeer.*

panel - 1. *ḥašwe* pl. *-aat*. One of these days we'll have to replace the lower door panel. *bəddna šii yoom ᵊngayyer ᵊl-ḥašwe t-taḥtaaniyye tabaʕ ᵊl-baab.* 2. *ḥalaq̈a* pl. *-aat*. She is a regular member of the panel on a Thursday-night television program. *hiyye ʕəḍwe daayme b-ḥalaq̈et bərnaamež televəzyoon kəll xamiis ᵊl-masa.*
  to panel - *xaššab*. She wants to panel the library in oak. *bədda txaššeb ᵊl-maktabe b-xašab balluuṭ.*

paneling - *taxšiib*.

panorama - *baanoraama* pl. *-aat, manẓar ʕaamm* pl. *manaaẓer ʕaamme*.

to pant - *lahat (a lahataan)*. He came panting up the stairs. *ṭəleʕ ʕad-daraž w-huwwe ʕam yəlhat.*

panther - *fahᵊd* pl. *fhuud(e)*.

pantry - *beet (pl. byuut) muune*.

pants - *banṭaloon* and *banṭaroon* pl. *-aat*. I have to have my pants pressed. *banṭalooni laazmo l-kawi.*-- I bought a suit with two pairs of pants. *štareet badle maʕ banṭalooneen.*

papacy - *l-baabawiyye*.

papal - *baabawi**.

paper - 1. *waraq*. Do you have some paper? *ʕandak šii waraq?* -- May I have a paper bag for these books? *btəsmaḥ-li b-kiis waraq la-hal kətᵊb?* 2. *waraqa* coll. *waraq* pl. *-aat* and *wraaq*. Some important papers are missing. *fii wraaq ᵊmhəmme ḍaayʕa.* 3. *hawiyye* pl. *-aat*. May I see your papers please? *btəsmaḥ-li b-hawiitak ʔiza bətriid.* 4. *žariide* pl. *žaraayed*. Where is today's paper?

ween šariitt ᵊl-yoom?

sheet of paper - *waraqa* pl. *-aat* and *wraaq.*

to paper - *warraq//twarraq.* This room hasn't been papered in five years. *ṣaar la-hal-ʔuuḍa xams ᵊsniin maa twarraqet.*

paper mill - *maɛmal˜* (pl. *maɛaamel˜*) *waraq.*

paper money - *ɛəmle waraqiyye.*

paperweight - *taqqaalet˜* (pl. *-aat˜*) *waraq.*

paprika - *fəlfel ʔarnaʔuuṭi.*

parachute - *barašuut* pl. *-aat, mẓalle* pl. *-aat.*

parade - *ʔəstəɛraaḍ* pl. *-aat.* They plan a big parade. *b-niyyə́ton ysaawu ʔəstəɛraaḍ ᵊkbiir.*

paradise - *žanne* pl. *-aat.*

paragraph - **1.** *faqra* pl. *-aat.* This is the beginning of a new paragraph. *hoone bidaayet faqra ždiide.* **2.** *maadde* pl. *mawaadd.* Paragraph eight of the contract stipulates that ... *l-maadde t-taamne tabaɛ ᵊl-kəntraato bətnəṣṣ ʔənno ...*

parallel - **1.** *xaṭṭ ᵊmwaazi* pl. *xṭuuṭ ᵊmwaazye.* Draw a parallel to this line. *rsoom xaṭṭ ᵊmwaazi la-hal-xaṭṭ.* **2.** *masal q̄iyaasi* pl. *ʔamsaal q̄iyaasiyye.* Let me give you a parallel from Roman history. *xalliini žəb-lak masal q̄iyaasi mən taariix ᵊr-ruumaan.* **3.** *mwaazi, mḥaazi.* I parked the car in a parallel street. *ṣaffeet ᵊs-sayyaara b-šaareɛ ᵊmwaazi.*

to run parallel to - *məši (i ə) b-ᵊmḥaazaat˜..., məši b-ᵊmwaazaat˜* ... The road runs parallel to the river. *ṭ-ṭariiq maaši b-ᵊmḥaazaat ᵊn-nahr.*

paralysis - *šalal.*

to **paralyze** - *šall (ə šall, šalal//nšall).* The air raid paralyzed the entire city. *l-ġaara ž-žawwiyye šallet ᵊl-madiine kəlla šall.* -- Traffic was completely paralyzed. *ḥaraket ᵊs-seer ᵊnšallet tamaaman.* -- I was paralyzed with fear. *nšalleet mn ᵊl-xoof.*

paralyzed - *mašluul.* She's been paralyzed ever since she had that stroke. *ṣar-la mašluule mən waqᵊt-ma ṣaar maɛa ʔənfižaar bᵊd-dmaaġ.*

paramount - *ʔaɛẓam* f. *ɛəẓma* pl. *ɛəẓaama.* That's of paramount importance. *haš-šaġle ʔəla ʔahammiyye ɛəẓma.*

parasol - *šamsiyye* pl. *šamaasi.*

paratrooper - *(žəndi) mẓalli* pl. *(žnuud) ᵊmẓalliyyiin.*

parcel - *baakeet* pl. *-aat.* You forgot your parcels. *nsiit ᵊl-baakeetaat tabaɛak.*

by **parcel post** - *b-ṭard bariidi.* I'm sending it to you by parcel post. *bəbɛat-lak-yda b-ṭard bariidi.*

parcel-post window - *šəbbaak ᵊṭ-ṭruud ᵊl-bariidiyye.*

pardon - *ɛafu.* He was refused a pardon. *rafaḍu l-ɛafu ɛanno.*

**I beg your pardon! *ɛafwan!* or *laa twaaxəzni!*

**Beg pardon. *ɛafwan!*

**(I beg your) pardon? *naɛam?*

to pardon - *ɛafa (i ɛafu//nɛafa) ɛan.* The President pardoned him at the last moment. *r-raʔiis ɛafa ɛanno b-ʔaaxer daqiiqa.*

**Pardon me! What time is it, please? *ɛafwan! qaddeeš ᵊs-saaɛa mən faḍlak?*

to **pare** - *qaššar.* Shall I pare an apple for you? *qaššə́r-lak šii təffaaḥa?*

parenthesis - *hlaal* pl. *-aat.* Put the word in parentheses. *ḥəṭṭ ᵊl-kəlme been ᵊhlaaleen.*

parents - *ʔəmm w-ʔabb.* Both my parents are still living. *ʔəmmi w-ʔabi tneenaaton ləssaahon ṭayybiin.*

Paris - *baariiz.*

Parisian - *baariizi*.*

parish - *ṭaayfe* pl. *ṭawaayef.* Our parish has a new pastor. *ṭaayfətna ʔəžaaha xuuri ždiid.*

park - *baark* pl. *-aat, ḥadiiqa* pl. *ḥadaayeq.* There is a beautiful park in the center of the city. *fii baark ḥəlu b-nəṣṣ ᵊl-madiine.*

to park - *ṣaff (ə ṣaff), barrak.* You can park your car here. *fiik ᵊtṣəff sayyaartak hoon.*

parking lot - *fasḥa* (pl. *-aat*) *la-ṣaff˜ ᵊs-sayyaaraat.* There is a parking lot across the street. *fii fasḥa la-ṣaff ᵊs-sayyaaraat qaaṭeɛ ᵊš-šaareɛ.*

parking place - *maḥall* (pl. *-aat*) *la-ṣaff ᵊs-sayyaara.* It took me almost half an hour to find a parking place. *bqiit taqriiban nəṣṣ saaɛa la-laqeet maḥall la-ṣaff sayyaarti.*

parliament - *ḅarlamaan* pl. *-aat.*

parliamentary - *ḅarlamaani*.*

parlor - *ṣaaloon* pl. *-aat.*

parrot - *babġaaʔ* pl. *babġawaat.*

parsley - *baqduunes.*

parson - *xuuri* pl. *xawaarne.*

part - **1.** *qəsᵊm* pl. *ʔaqsaam, žəzᵊʔ* pl. *ʔažzaaʔ.* That part of the work isn't finished yet. *hal-qəsᵊm mn ᵊš-šəġᵊl ləssa maa xalaṣ.* **2.** *žəzᵊʔ* pl. *ʔažzaaʔ.* This little screw is a very important part of the machine. *hal-bərġi ẓ-ẓġiir huwwe žəzʔ ᵊktiir ᵊmhəmm la-hal-maakiina.* **3.** *qəsᵊm.* The fence is part wood and part stone. *l-xəṣṣ qəsᵊm xašab w-qəsᵊm ḥažar.* **4.** *qəṭɛa* pl. *qəṭaɛ.* We'll have to order these parts from the factory. *laazem ᵊnwaṣṣi ɛala hal-qəṭaɛ mn ᵊl-maṣnaɛ.* **5.** *door* pl. *ʔadwaar.* He's playing an important part in the country's political life. *ɛam yəlɛab door ᵊmhəmm b-ḥayaat l-ᵊblaad ᵊs-siyaasiyye.*

**What part of the country do you come from? *mən ʔayy manṭiqa mən l-ᵊblaad ʔənte?*

parts - *manṭiqa.* I haven't traveled much in these parts. *maa dərt ᵊktiir b-hal-manṭiqa.*

for my part, for your part, etc. *bᵊn-nəsbe ʔəli, bᵊn-nəsbe ʔəlak,* etc., *mən žəhti, mən žəhtak,* etc. I for my part have no objection. *bᵊn-nəsbe ʔəli ʔana maa ɛandi maaneɛ.* -- For my part, you can go. *bᵊn-nəsbe ʔəli btəqder truuḥ.*

for the most part - **1.** *b-ʔaksariit-* + pron. suff., *ɛal-ġaaleb.* His company is made up for the most part of volunteers. *sariito mʔallafe b-ʔaksariita mən məṭṭawwɛiin.* **2.** *ɛal-ġaaleb, ʔaktar ᵊl-ʔawqaat.* For the most part the weather has been nice this summer. *ɛal-ġaaleb kaan ᵊṭ-ṭaqᵊṣ ḥəlu haṣ-ṣeefiyye.*

in part - *žəzʔiyyan.* I agree with you in part. *ʔana mwaafeq maɛak žəzʔiyyan.*

on the part of - *mən ṭaraf˜..., mən qəbal˜..., mən naḥiit˜...* That was a grave mistake on the part of the government. *hayy kaanet ġalṭa faẓiiɛa mən ṭaraf l-ᵊḥkuume.*

spare part - *ʔaksəswaar* (invar.), *qəṭɛet˜* (pl. *qəṭaɛ˜*) *taġyiir.* Can you get spare parts for my bicycle? *btəqder džəb-li ʔaksəswaar ləl-bəsᵊkleet tabaɛi?*

to take part - *štarak.* Are you going to take part in the discussion? *laḥa təštə́rek bᵊl-ᵊmnaaq̄aše?*

to take someone's part - *tḥayyaz la-, ṣaff (ə ə) maɛ, ʔaxad žaaneb˜* ... He always takes his brother's part. *daayman byətḥayyaz la-ʔaxúu.*

to part - **1.** *tfaaraq.* They parted as friends. *tfaaraqu ṣḥaab.* -- We parted at the corner. *tfaaraqna ɛand ᵊs-suuke.* **2.** *faraq (o farᵊq).* He parts his hair on the left side. *byəfroq šaɛro ɛal-yasaar.*

to part with - *səxi (a saxa, saxaawe) b-.* I wouldn't part with that book for any price. *maa bəsxa b-hal-ᵊktaab w-laa b-ʔayy taman.*

partial - **1.** *žəzʔi*.* It was only a partial success. *maa kaan ʔəlla nažaaḥ žəzʔi.* **2.** *mətḥayyez.* He tries not to be partial. *biḥaawel ʔənno maa ykuun mətḥayyez.*

to be partial to - *faḍḍal.* He's always been partial to his youngest daughter. *ṭuul ɛəmro bifaḍḍel bənto ẓ-ẓġiire.* -- He's partial to blondes. *bifaḍḍel ᵊš-šəqᵊr.*

partiality - *taḥayyoz.*

partially - **1.** *nawɛan maa, la-daraže.* You're partially right. *maɛak ḥaqq nawɛan maa.* **2.** *žəzʔiyyan.* It's only partially finished. *bass žəzʔiyyan xalaṣ.*

to **participate** - *štarak (b-).* Who's going to participate in the competition? *miin laḥa yəštə́rek bᵊl-ᵊmsaabaqa?*

participle: Active participle. *ʔəsᵊm faaɛel.* -- Passive participle. *ʔəsᵊm mafɛuul.*

particle - **1.** *zarra* pl. *-aat.* There is not a particle of truth in that story. *maa fii w-laa zarra mn ᵊṣ-ṣəḥḥa b-hal-qəṣṣa.* **2.** *ʔadaat* pl. *ʔadawaat.* "muu" is a negative particle. *"muu" ʔadaat nafi.*

particular - **1.** *tafṣiil* pl. *-aat* and *tafaṣiil.* For further particulars you should write to the publishers. *mənšaan ᵊt-tafaṣiil ᵊl-ʔiḍaafiyye ktoob lən-naašer.* -- My wife will give you all the particulars. *marti laḥa taɛṭiik kəll ᵊt-tafaṣiil.* **2.** *xaaṣṣ.* Is he a particular friend of yours? *huwwe rfiiq xaaṣṣ ʔəlak?* **3.** *b-ɛeen-* + pron. suff., *(b-)zaat-* + pron. suff. This particular dress costs more. *hal-fəṣṭaan ᵊb-ɛeeno bikallef ʔaktar.* **4.** *mʔannaf, mnaqnaq.* My husband is very particular about his food. *žoozi ktiir ᵊmʔannaf ᵊb-ʔaklo.* **5.** *mwanwan.* He's very particular about his ties. *huwwe mwanwan ᵊktiir b-ᵊkraafaato.*

in particular - *xaaṣṣatan, ɛal-ᵊxṣuuṣ.* I remember one man in particular. *bədzakkar xaaṣṣatan waaḥed rəžžaal.*

**Are you looking for anything in particular? *ɛam ᵊddawwer ɛala šii mɛayyan?*

particularly - *xaaṣṣatan, ɛal-ᵊxṣuuṣ.* He's particularly interested in science. *humme byəhtamm xaaşşatan b*ᵊ*l-Eɛuluum* ᵊ*t-ţabiiEiyye.*

partly: The house is only partly rented. *hal-beet baEdo mᵊaǧǧar w-baEdo muu mᵊaǧǧar.* -- The story is only partly true. *hal-qəşşa baEda şahiih w-baEda kəzᵊb.*

partner - *šriik* pl. *šəraka.* My partner is coming back tomorrow. *šriiki raaǧeE bəkra.* -- My partner and I have been winning every game. *ʔana w-ᵊšriiki Eam nərbah kəll doora la-hadd hallaq.*

partnership - *šaraake, šərke.*

partridge - *hağale* coll. *hağal* pl. *-aat.*

party - **1.** *həzᵊb* pl. *ʔahzaab.* What party do you belong to? *b-ʔanu həzᵊb ʔənte daaxel?* **2.** *ţaraf* pl. *ʔaţraaf.* Neither of the two parties appeared at the trial. *w-laa waahed mn ᵊţ-ţarafeen ʔəǧa Eal-ᵊmhaakame.* **3.** *hafle* pl. *-aat, Eaziime* pl. *Eazaayem.* She likes to give big parties. *bəthəbb taEmel haflaat ᵊkbiire.* -- Good night. It was a lovely party. *walla kaanet hafle ǧamiile. təsᵊbhu Eala xeer.*

to be a party to - *kan-lo ʔiid b-.* I won't be a party to that. *maa bikən-li ʔiid b-haš-šağle.*

party line - *talifoon məštárak.* We have a party line. *Eanna talifoon məštárak.*

Pashto - *pəšti, pəštu.*

pass - **1.** *maEbar* pl. *maEaaber, mamarr* pl. *-aat.* The pass is snowed under in winter. *l-maEbar btətraakam Ealée t-tluuǧ bᵊš-šəte.* **2.** *warqet*˜ (pl. *wraaq*˜) *muruur.* You'll need a pass to get by the gate. *bəddak warqet muruur la-tfuut mn ᵊl-bawwaabe.* **3.** *maʔzuuniyye* pl. *-aat.* He has a weekend pass. *Eando maʔzuuniyye mənšaan ʔaaxer ᵊǧ-ǧəmEa hayy.*

to pass - **1.** *waafaq Eala.* The House passed the bill unanimously. *l-mağles waafaq Eala mašruuE ᵊl-qaanuun bᵊl-ʔəǧmaaE.* **2.** *naǧah (a naǧaah) b-, maraq (o ∅) b-.* Did you pass your examination? *naǧahᵊt bᵊl-fahᵊş?* **3.** *marraq.* The play was finally passed by the censor. *l-ᵊmraaqeb marraq bᵊl-ʔaaxiir ᵊr-riwaaye.* -- The professor passed everybody in the class. *l-ʔəstaaz marraq kəll ᵊţ-ţəllaab bᵊş-şaff.* **4.** *tmarraq.* The buckets passed from man to man. *ş-şţuule tmarraqet mən rəǧǧaal la-rəǧǧaal.* **5.** *naawal.* Will you please pass the bread? *mən fadlak naawəlni l-xəbᵊz.* -- Can I pass you anything? *bəddak naawlak šii?* **6.** *qaţaE (a ∅) Eala, maraq Eala.* You passed the red light. *qaţaEt Ead-daww ᵊl-ʔahmar.* **7.** *maraq mən, marr (ə ∅) mən.* The train passes here at three o'clock. *t-treen byəmroq mən hoon ᵊs-saaEa tlaate.* **8.** *marr qəddaam.* I pass this bank building every day. *kəll yoom ᵊbmərr qəddaam hal-bank.* **9.** *ntaqlet məlkiit*˜... The farm passes from father to son. *l-mazraEa məlkiita btəntéqel mn ᵊl-ʔabb ləl-ʔəbᵊn.* **10.** *madda, qada (i ∅).* He passes most of the time reading. *bimaddi ʔaktar ʔawqaato bᵊl-ʔqraaye.* **11.** *mada (a ∅).* The days pass quickly when you're busy. *l-ʔiyyaam btəmda b-sərEa waqt ᵊl-waahed bikuun mašğuul.* **12.** *ţəleE (a ţalEa).* Keep to the right, pass on the left! *xalliik Eal-yamiin w-ᵊţlaE Eal-yasaar.* **13.** *ţəleE qəddaam.* I wouldn't pass this car if I were you. *law kənt ᵊb-mahallak maa bəţlaE qəddaam has-sayyaara.* **14.** *ʔaşdar.* The court will pass sentence today. *l-mahkame btəşder həkma l-yoom.* **15.** *thawwal.* Their attitude passed from annoyance to anger. *mawqéfon thawwal mən zaEal la-ğadab.*

**It's your turn. I passed. *ləEbak. daqqeet* (or *paas*).

to pass around - *marraq.* They passed the bottle around. *marraqu l-qanniine (Eal-haadriin).*

to pass away - *maat (u moot(ə)).* Her mother passed away last week. *ʔəmma maatet ᵊǧ-ǧəmEa l-maadye.*

to pass by - *maraq (o ∅) mən qəddaam, marr (ə ∅) mən qəddaam.* He passed right by me without seeing me. *maraq mən qəddaami biiduun-ma yšuufni.*

to pass judgment on - *hakam (o həkᵊm) Eala.* Don't pass judgment too quickly on him. *laa təhkom Ealée b-tahawwor.*

to pass off - *marraq.* He tried to pass off an imitation as the original. *haawal ymarreq šii taqliid ka-ʔaşli.*

to pass on - **1.** *waşşal (ᵊl-kalaam).* Don't pass this on. *laa twaşşel hal-qəşşa* or *laa twaşşel šuu hakeet.* **2.** *maat (u moot(ə)).* I didn't know his mother passed on. *maa Erəfᵊt ʔənno ʔəmmo maatet.*

to pass out - *ğəmi (a ∅) Eala qalbo.* Several people passed out from the heat. *fii Eəddet ʔašxaaş ğəmi Eala qalbon mn ᵊš-šoob.*

to pass through - **1.** *maraq (o ∅) mən, nafad (o ∅) mən.* You can't pass through there. *maa fiik təmroq mən hoon.* **2.** *maraq mən, marr (ə ∅) mən.* Does the bus pass through here? *l-baaş byəmroq mən hoon?* -- We can pass through here. *mnəqder ᵊnmərr mən hoon.* **3.** *marraq mən.* Pass the rope through here. *marreq ᵊl-habᵊl mən hoon.*

to pass up - *fawwat.* You ought not to pass up an opportunity like that. *haraam Ealeek ᵊtfawwet fərşa mətᵊl hayye.*

to let pass - **1.** *marraq.* The censor let the letter pass. *l-ᵊmraaqeb marraq ᵊl-maktuub.* **2.** *fawwat, marraq.* The guard didn't let me pass. *l-haares maa fawwatni.* **3.** *maššа.* Don't be offended; let it pass. *laa taaxod Eala xaaţrak; maššiiha.*

passable - *saalek, maaši.* Is the road ahead passable? *ţ-ţariiq qəddaam saalek?*

**The work is passable. *š-šəğᵊl yaEni maaši haalo.*

passage - **1.** *mamarr* pl. *-aat, mamraq* pl. *mamaareq.* We had to go through a dark passage. *nǧabarna nəmši mən mamarr Eətme.* **2.** *maqţaE* pl. *maqaaţeE.* He read us an interesting passage from his book. *qara Ealeena maqţaE ţariif mn ᵊktaabo.*

**I've made the passage eight times between New York and Le Havre. *qaţaEt ᵊl-muhiiţ tmən marraat been niyoork wᵊl-haavᵊr.*

passenger - **1.** *raakeb* pl. *rəkkaab.* The bus holds only thirty passengers. *l-baaş byəsaE bass tlaatiin raakeb.* **2.** *msaafer* pl. *-iin.* All passengers are required to go through customs inspection. *kəll l-ᵊmsaafriin Ealeehon yəmᵊrqu bᵊl-gamaarek.*

passenger car - *sayyaara* pl. *-aat.*

passenger list - *qaaʔəmt*˜ (pl. *qawaaʔem*˜) *ᵊmsaafriin.*

passenger train - *treen*˜ (pl. *-aat*˜) *rəkkaab.*

passer-by - *maareq* pl. *-iin.* A passer-by must have picked it up. *šii waahed maareq laazem ykuun ʔaxəda.*

passing - **1.** *wafaat, moot.* The whole nation mourned his passing. *l-ᵊblaad kəlla həznet Eala wafaato.* **2.** *waqti*, mwaqqat.* That's just a passing fancy with her. *haš-šağle ʔəla Eibaara Ean fazlake waqtiyye.* **3.** *naaǧeh.* I got passing grades in all my subjects. *haşalt Eala Ealaamaat naaǧha b-kəll mawaaddi.*

in passing - *Eal-maaši.* In passing I'd like to say that ... *bəddi quul Eal-maaši ʔənno ...*

passion - **1.** *šahwe* pl. *-aat.* He's a man of strong passions. *humme şaaheb šahwaat qawiyye.* **2.** *walaE.* He had a passion for music. *kan-lo walaE bᵊl-muusiiqa.*

passive - **1.** *salbi*.* All they can put up is passive resistance. *kəll šii byəţlaE b-ʔiidon ᵊmqaawame salbiyye.* **2.** *şiiğet*˜ *ᵊl-mağhuul.* What's the passive of this verb? *šuu şiiğet ᵊl-mağhuul la-hal-fəEᵊl?*

**He's just a passive onlooker. *huwwe mətfarreǧ bass.*

Passover - *Eiid ᵊl-fəşᵊh, fţiir.*

passport - *basboor* pl. *-aat, ǧawaaz*˜ (pl. *-aat*˜) *safar.*

past - **1.** *l-maadi.* That's a thing of the past. *haada šii bᵊl-maadi.* **2.** *maadi.* Where were you this past week? *ween kənt ᵊǧ-ǧəmEa l-maadye?* **3.** *mən qəddaam.* He walked right past me without seeing me. *marr mən qəddaami biduun-ma yšuufni.*

**It's five minutes past twelve. *s-saaEa ţnaEš w-xamse.*

**The worst part of the trip is past. *ʔaşEab marhale bᵊs-safra madet.*

**I'm past that stage now. *dǧaawazᵊt haţ-ţoor hallaq.*

**I wouldn't put it past him. *maa bəstabEəda Eanno.*

**It's way past bedtime. *faat waqt ᵊn-noom mən zamaan.*

past tense - *siiğet*˜ *ᵊl-maadi.*

in the past - *bᵊl-maadi, mən qabᵊl.* That has often happened in the past. *haš-šii hadas miraaran bᵊl-maadi.*

paste - *ləzzeeq.* I'll have to buy some wallpaper and paste. *laazem ʔəštəri šwayyet waraq ləl-hiiţaan w-ləzzeeq.*

to paste - *lazzaq.* Paste these labels on the jars. *lazzeq hal-ʔetiketaat Eal-qaţramiizaat.*

pasteurized - *mbastar, mEaqqam.*

pastime - *təslaaye* pl. *-aat.*

pastor - *xuuri* pl. *xawaarne.*

pastry - *həlwiyyaat* (pl.)

pastry shop - *dəkkaanet*˜ (pl. *dakakiin*˜) *həlwiyyaat.*

pasture - *marЄa* pl. *maraaЄi*. Are the cows still in the pasture? *lǝssaahon ᵊl-baqaraat bᵊl-marЄa?*
to **pat** - *ṭabṭab*. He patted him encouragingly on the shoulder. *ṭabṭáb-lo Єala kǝtfo la-yšaǧǧЄo*. -- He patted the dog. *ṭabṭab Єal-kalb*.
patch - **1.** *rǝqЄa* pl. *rǝqaЄ*. I'll have to put a new patch on. *laazem ḥaṭṭ rǝqЄa ǧdiide*. **2.** *lazqa* pl. *-aat*. He wore a patch over his eye for days. *kaan ḥaaṭeṭ lazqa Єala Єeeno mǝddet ᵓiyyaam*.
to patch - (put patches on) *raqqaЄ*, (mend) *qaṭab (o qaṭᵊb)*. Mother patched my trousers. *ᵓǝmmi raqqaЄǝt-li banṭarooni*.
to patch up - *faḍḍ (ǝ faḍḍ//nfaḍḍ)*. Have they patched up their quarrel yet? *faḍḍu l-xilaaf beenaaton wǝlla lǝssa?*
patchwork - *šǝǧᵊl ǧalЄaṣa*.
patent - *baraaᵓa* pl. *-aat*. I've applied for a patent on my invention. *ṭalabᵊt baraaᵓa mǝnšaan ᵓǝxtiraaЄi*.
to patent - *saǧǧal*. You ought to have your method patented. *laazem tsaǧǧel ṭariiqtak hayye*.
patent leather - *ǧǝlᵊd lammaaЄ*.
path - *darb* pl. *druub(e)*, *ṭaaruuq* pl. *ṭawariiq*. A narrow path leads to the river. *fii darb dayyeq biwaddi Єan-nahr*.
patience - **1.** *ṣabᵊr*, *ṭuulet˜ baal*. This kind of work needs patience. *heek šǝǧᵊl bǝddo ṣabᵊr*. **2.** *ṣabᵊr*. Finally, I lost patience. *bᵊl-ᵓaaxiir nafad ṣabri*.
to have patience - *ṣabar (o ṣabᵊr)*, *ṭawwal baalo*. Have a little patience with him. *ṣbǝr-lak Єalée šwayye*.
patient - **1.** *mariiḍ* pl. *mǝraḍa*. There are two more patients waiting outside, doctor. *fii kamaan mariiḍeen Єam yǝnṭǝṛu barra, ya doktoor*. **2.** *ṣabuur*, *ṭawiil˜ baal*. He's very patient. *huwwe ktiir ṣabuur*.
patio - *dyaar* pl. *-aat*.
patriot - *waṭani* pl. *-iyyiin*.
patriotic - *waṭani**.
patriotism - *waṭaniyye*.
patrol - *dooriyye* pl. *-aat*. We sent a patrol out to reconnoiter. *baЄatna dooriyye lǝl-ᵓǝstǝkšaaf*.
to patrol - *ṭaaf (u ṭawaaf) b-*. A policeman patrols these streets all night long. *waaḥed šǝrṭi biṭuuf b-haš-šawaareЄ ṭuul ᵊl-leel*.
pattern - **1.** *rasme* pl. *-aat*, *taqliime* pl. *-aat*. This rug has a pretty pattern. *rasmet has-sǝǧǧaade ktiir ḥǝlwe*. **2.** *baṭroon* pl. *-aat*. Where did you get the pattern for your new dress? *mneen ǧǝbti l-baṭroon tabaЄ fǝsṭaanek ᵊǧ-ǧdiid?* **3.** *namaṭ*, *mǝnwaal*. His reactions follow a fairly predictable pattern. *radd fǝЄlo byǝtbaЄ namaṭ mǝmken Єaadatan tanabbᵓo*. **4.** *namaṭ* pl. *ᵓanmaaṭ*. Anthropology is concerned, among other things, with the study of cultural patterns. *l-ᵓantroboloožya btǝhtamm, bᵊl-ᵓiḍaafe la-ᵓašya taanye, b-diraaset ᵊl-ᵓanmaaṭ ᵊl-ḥaḍaariyye*. **5.** *wazᵊn* pl. *ᵓawzaan*. The word "*ḥawaass*" is built on the pattern "*fawaaЄel*". *kǝlmet "ḥawaass" Єala wazᵊn "fawaaЄel"*.
pause - *waqfe* pl. *-aat*. After a short pause the speaker continued. *baЄᵊd waqfe qaṣiire l-xaṭiib ᵊstarsal ᵊb-xiṭaabo*.
to pause - *waqqaf*. He paused briefly before he answered. *waqqaf ᵊšwayye qabᵊl-ma yǝǧaaweb*.
to **pave** - *Єabbad//tЄabbad*. Our street has finally been paved. *bᵊl-ᵓaaxiir tЄabbad šaarǝЄna*.
to pave the way - *mahhad ᵊṭ-ṭariiq*. If you have somebody to pave the way for you, it's easy enough to get ahead. *ᵓiza fii waaḥed bimahhǝd-lak ᵊṭ-ṭariiq bišiir ᵓashǝl-lak tǝtqaddam*.
pavement - **1.** *wǝšš˜ ᵊṭ-ṭariiq*. The pavement is very bumpy. *wǝšš ᵊṭ-ṭariiq ᵊmЄaqwar ᵊktiir*. **2.** *blaaṭ*. The pavement in our courtyard needs repair. *blaaṭ ᵊdyaarna laazmo tarmiim*.
paw - *rǝǧᵊl* pl. *rǝǧleen*. The dog has hurt his paw. *l-kalb ǧaraḥ rǝǧlo*.
pawn - *beedaq* pl. *bayaadeq*. You've already lost four pawns. *ṣǝrt xaṣraan la-hallaq ᵓarbaЄ bayaadeq*.
to pawn - *rahan (e/o rahᵊn//rtahan)*. He had to pawn his radio. *nǝǧbar yǝrhen ᵊr-raadyo tabaЄo*.
pawnshop - *maḥall˜ (pl. -aat˜) ruhuunaat*.
pawn ticket - *waṣᵊl˜ (pl. wṣuulaat˜) rahᵊn*.
pay - *maЄaaš*, *raateb*. How is the pay on your new job? *kiif ᵊl-maЄaaš ᵊb-šǝǧlak ᵊǧ-ǧdiid?*
to pay - **1.** *dafaЄ (a dafᵊЄ//ndafaЄ)*. How much did you pay for your car? *qaddeeš dafaЄᵊt ḥaqq ᵊs-sayyaara?* -- We had to pay for it dearly. *nǝǧbarna nǝdfaЄ tamǝna ǧaali*. -- I'll pay the balance in weekly installments. *bǝdfaЄ ᵊr-raṣiid Єala ᵓaqṣaaṭ ᵓǝsbuuЄiyye*. **3.** *nafaЄ (a ø)*, *faad (i ø)*. That doesn't pay. *haš-šii maa byǝnfaЄ*.
**You couldn't pay me to do that. *maa bsaawiiha w-laa b-ᵓayy taman*.
to pay attention - see **attention**.
to pay a visit - see **visit**.
to pay one's respects - see **respect**.
to pay back - *raǧǧaЄ*. I'll pay you back the twenty pounds on Monday. *braǧǧǝЄ-lak ᵊl-Єǝšriin leera yoom ᵊt-taneen*.
to pay down - *dafaЄ (a dafᵊЄ) salaf*. All you have to do is pay down a hundred pounds. *kǝll halli laazmak ᵓǝnno tǝdfaЄ miit leera salaf*.
to pay for itself - *ṭaalaЄ ḥaqqo*. This machine will pay for itself in five months. *hal-maakiina bǝṭṭaaleЄ ḥaqqa b-ṣarf xamᵊst ǝšhor*.
to pay off - *saddad*. He paid off all his debts. *saddad kǝll ᵊdyuuno*.
to pay out - **1.** *dafaЄ (a dafᵊЄ//ndafaЄ)*. They pay out huge sums at the end of every month. *Єam byǝdfaЄu mabaaleǧ ṭaaᵓile b-ᵓaaxer kǝll šahᵊr*. **2.** *raxa (i raxi)*, *ḥall (ǝ ḥall)*. Pay out the rope slowly. *ᵓǝrxi l-ḥabᵊl šwayye šwayye*.
to pay up - *saddad*. In a month I'll have it all paid up. *baЄᵊd šahᵊr bkuun saddadt kǝll šii*.
pay day - *yoom˜ (pl. ᵓiyyaam˜) ᵊl-qabḍ*.
payment - **1.** *dafᵊЄ*. We request prompt payment. *narǧu d-dafᵊЄ ḥaalan*. **2.** *dafЄa* pl. *-aat*, *qǝsṭ* pl. *ᵓaqṣaaṭ*. I still have three more payments to make on my car. *lǝssa baqyaan Єaliyyi tlǝtt dafЄaat mǝn ḥaqq sayyaarti*. **3.** *dafЄa* pl. *-aat*. We have received your payment. *wǝṣlǝtna dafᵊЄtak*.
payroll - *boodro* pl. *boodroyaat*.
pea - *bazaalyaaye* coll. *bazaalya*.
peace - **1.** *salaam*, *ṣǝlḥ*. Our goal is lasting peace. *hadafna s-salaam ᵊd-daaᵓem*. **2.** *huduuᵓ*. If I could only work in peace! *ya-reet ᵓǝqder ᵓǝštǝǧel b-huduuᵓ!* **3.** *ᵓamᵊn*. The army is maintaining peace and order. *ǧ-ǧeeš Єam yḥaafeẓ Єal-ᵓamᵊn wᵊn-niẓaam*. **4.** *r-raaḥa l-Єaamme*. He was arrested for disturbing the peace. *waqqafúu la-ᵓǝǧlaaǧo r-raaḥa l-Єaamme*.
**I'm doing it just to keep (the) peace. *bsaawiiha bass la-ᵓǝtfaada l-xiṣaam*.
**He doesn't give me any peace. *maa birayyeḥ baali ᵓabadan*.
**Oh, leave me in peace! *Єiif Єanni baqa!* or *ḥǝll Єan diini baqa!* or *frǝqni baqa!*
peace conference - *mǝᵓtamar˜ (pl. -aat˜) ṣǝlḥ*.
Peace Corps - *wǝḥdaat˜ ᵊs-salaam (pl.)*, *fǝrqet˜ ᵊs-salaam*.
to make peace - **1.** *ṣaalaḥ*, *tṣaalaḥ maЄ*. Why don't you make (your) peace with him? *leeš maa bǝtṣaalḥo?* **2.** *tṣaalaḥ*. The two countries made peace at last. *d-dawᵊlteen bᵊl-ᵓaaxiir ᵊtṣaalaḥu*.
peaceful - **1.** *raayeq*, *haadi*. Everything is so peaceful around here. *faẓaaЄa qaddeeš kǝll šii raayeq hoon*. **2.** *sǝlmi**. We want to achieve our purpose by peaceful means. *raaydiin nḥaqqeq ǧaayǝtna bᵊl-wasaaᵓel ᵊs-sǝlmiyye*. **3.** *msaalem*. Look, I'm a peaceful man, but ... *ftaḥ Єeenak, ᵓana waaḥed ᵊmsaalem, bass ...*
peach - *dǝrraaqne* coll. *dǝrraaqen* pl. *-aat*. These peaches are very juicy. *had-dǝrraaqnaat maawiyyaat ᵊktiir*.
peacock - *ṭaawuus* pl. *ṭawawiis*.
peak - **1.** *ǧǝmme* pl. *ǧǝmam*, *zarwe* pl. *-aat*, *raas* pl. *ruus*. We climbed to the peak of the mountain. *tsallaqna ǧ-ǧabal lǝl-ǧǝmme*. **2.** *zarwe*, *ᵓooǧ*. He was then at the peak of his power. *kaan waqta b-zarwet ṣǝlṭaano*.
peanut - *fǝstqaayet˜ Єabiid* coll. *fǝstoq˜ Єabiid* pl. *fǝstqaayaat Єabiid*.
pear - *nǧaaṣa* coll. *nǧaaṣ* pl. *-aat*. How much is a kilo of pears? *qaddeeš kiilo n-nǧaaṣ?*
pearl - *luuliyye* coll. *luulu* pl. *luuliyyaat*.
peasant - *fallaaḥ* pl. *-iin*.
pebble - *ḥaṣwe* coll. *ḥaṣu*, *ḥaṣa* pl. *ḥaṣwaat*. The path is covered with pebbles. *d-darᵊb mafruuš ḥaṣu*.
peculiar - **1.** *ǧariib*, *šaaḍḍ*. He's a peculiar fellow. *huwwe zalame ǧariib*. **2.** *xaaṣṣ b-*. His dialect is peculiar to that region. *lahᵊǧto xaaṣṣa b-haadiik ᵊl-manṭiqa*.
peculiarity - *xaaṣṣiyye* pl. *-aat*. This is a peculiarity of his style. *hayy xaaṣṣiyye mǝn xaaṣṣiyyaat ᵓǝsluubo*.
peddler - *bayyaaЄ mǝdǧawwel* pl. *bayyaaЄiin mǝdǧawwliin*.
pedestrian - *maaši* pl. *mušaat*.
pediatrician - *ḥakiim˜ (pl. ḥǝkama˜) l-ᵓaṭfaal*.
pediatrics - *ṭǝbb˜ ᵊl-ᵓaṭfaal*.

peel - *qəšre* coll. *qəšᵊr* pl. *qšuur(a)*. These oranges have a thick peel. *hal-bərdqaanaat qəšrə́ton smiike.*
to peel - **1.** *qaššar.* I have to peel the potatoes. *laazem qaššer ᵊl-baṭaaṭaat.* **2.** *qašar (o qašaraan).* My skin is peeling. *žəldi ɛam yəqšor.* -- The paint is peeling off the ceiling. *d-dhaan ɛam yəqšor mən ɛas-saqᵊf.*
peep - **1.** *ṣooṭ* pl. *ṣwaaṭ.* I don't want to hear another peep out of you. *maa bəddi ᵊəsmaɛ mənnak w-laa ṣooṭ.* **2.** *taṭliiɛa* pl. *-aat.* Take a peep into the room. *ṭṭalləɛ-lak taṭliiɛa ɛal-ᵊuuḍa.*
to peep - *tnaawaq, tlaṣlaṣ.* He peeped through the hole in the fence. *tnaawaq mn ᵊl-bəxᵊš halli bᵊl-xəṣṣ.*
peeved - *zaɛlaan.* She was peeved about the remark you made. *kaanet zaɛlaane mn ᵊmlaaḥaṣtak.*
peg - **1.** *watad* pl. *wtaad.* Drive a peg in the ground so you can tie up the goat. *dəqq watad bᵊl-ᵊarḍ ḥatta tərboṭ ᵊl-ɛanze.* -- This small tent needs only three pegs. *hal-xeeme ẓ-ẓẓiire laazə́ma bass ᵊtlətt əwtaad.* **2.** *xaazuuq* pl. *xawaziiq.* Hang your jacket on the peg in the wall. *ɛalleq žaakeettak ɛal-xaazuuq bᵊl-ḥeeṭ.* -- We use a peg to plug the drain of the basin. *mnəstaɛmel xaazuuq la-nsədd balluuɛet ᵊl-baḥra.* **3.** *məftaaḥ* pl. *mafatiiḥ.* One peg of my violin keeps working loose. *məftaaḥ mən mafatiiḥ ᵊl-kamanža tabaɛi biḥall ᵊbyərxi.* **4.** *bəsmaar* (pl. *basamiir*) *xašab.* The boards are held together by pegs. *l-lwaaḥ mšabbake b-baɛḍa b-basamiir xašab.*
**He's a square peg in a round hole. *maa byənfaɛ laa ləl-xall w-laa ləl-xardal.*
**That should take him down a peg! *haš-šii biṭaqṭə́q-lo raqᵊbto šwayy* or *haš-šii bikassə́r-lo raqᵊbto šwayy* or *haš-šii bikassə́r-lo manaafso.*
pelican - *ᵊabu˜ žraab.*
pelvis - *ḥawḍ* pl. *ḥwaaḍ.*
pen - **1.** *riiše* pl. *riyaš.* This pen is for drawing only. *har-riiše bass lər-rasm.* **2.** *stiilo* pl. *stiiloyaat, qalam˜* (pl. *qlaam˜*) *ḥəbᵊr.* I forgot my pen at home. *nsiit ᵊstiilooyi bᵊl-beet.* **3.** *zriibe* pl. *zaraayeb.* We'll have to build a larger pen for the pigs. *laazem nəbni zriibe ᵊakbar ləl-xanaziir.*
penal code - *ǧaanuun˜ ᵊl-ɛuǧuubaat, ǧaanuun˜ ᵊž-žazaaᵊ.*
penalty - *ɛuǧuube* pl. *-aat.* The penalty is ten years' imprisonment. *l-ɛuǧuube ɛašr ᵊsniin bᵊs-səžᵊn.*
under penalty of law - *taḥᵊt ṭaaᵊəlt ᵊl-ɛuǧuubaat.* Crossing the tracks is forbidden under penalty of law. *l-maši ɛas-səkke mamnuuɛ taḥᵊt ṭaaᵊəlt ᵊl-ɛuǧuubaat.*
pencil - *qalam* pl. *qlaam, qalam˜ ᵊrṣaaṣ.* Give me that pencil, please. *ɛaṭiini hal-qalam mən faḍlak.*
pending - **1.** *mɛallaq.* The matter is still pending. *l-qaḍiyye ləssaata mɛallaqa.* **2.** *rahn˜ ...* Pending further investigation ... *rahn ᵊt-taḥqiiqaat ᵊl-ᵊiḍaafiyye ...*
to **penetrate** - **1.** *xaraq (o xarᵊq).* The bullet penetrated his right thigh. *r-rṣaaṣa xarqet faxdo l-yamiin.* **2.** *tɛammaq b-, tġalġal b-, tbaḥḥar b-.* He easily penetrates the complexities of the subject. *b-ᵊshuule byətɛammaq b-taɛqiidaat ᵊl-mawḍuuɛ.*
pension - *taǧaaɛod* (invar.) He gets a pension from the government. *byaaxod taǧaaɛod mən l-ᵊḥkuume.*
to pension - *ᵊaḥaal ɛat-taǧaaɛod.* He was pensioned last year. *ᵊuḥiil ɛat-taǧaaɛod ᵊs-səne l-maaḍye.*
Pentecost - *(ɛiid˜) ᵊl-ɛanṣara.*
people - **1.** *šaɛᵊb* pl. *šɛuub.* He has the support of the people. *huwwe ḥaaṣel ɛala taᵊyiid ᵊš-šaɛᵊb.* -- Can you name the most important peoples of Asia? *btəqder tsammii-li ᵊahamm ᵊšɛuub ᵊaasya?* **2.** *naas.* What will people say? *ya-tə́ra n-naas šuu raḥa tquul?* -- You have to take people as they are. *laazem təqbal ᵊn-naas mətᵊl-ma hənne.* **3.** *naas, ɛaalam.* Were there many people at the meeting? *kaan fii naas ᵊktiir bᵊl-ᵊəžtimaaɛ?* **4.** *ɛaammet˜ ᵊn-naas.* He's a man of the people. *huwwe rəžžaal mən ɛaammet ᵊn-naas.* **5.** *ᵊahᵊl.* I want you to meet my people. *bəddi ɛarrfak ɛala ᵊahli.* **6.** *ᵊahᵊl, ᵊahaali* (pl.) The people of this city suffered terribly during the war. *ᵊahᵊl hal-madiine tɛazzabu ktiir ᵊiyyaam ᵊl-ḥarb.*
**I knew only a handful of people at the party. *ɛrəfᵊt bass kam šaxᵊṣ bᵊl-ḥafle.*
**His people are Armenian. *ᵊaṣlo ᵊarmani.*
pep - *našaaṭ.* Where do you get your pep? *mneen žaayᵊi-lak han-našaaṭ?* -- He's full of pep today. *huwwe l-yoom malaan našaaṭ.*
to pep up - *naššaṭ.* I need something to pep me up. *laazəmni šii ynaššəṭni.*

pepper - *fəlfol.* Pass me the pepper, please. *baḷḷa naawəlni l-fəlfol.*
per - **1.** *b-.* How much are these eggs per dozen? *qaddeeš hal-beeḍaat bᵊd-dazziine?* -- He makes seven thousand dollars per annum. *biṭaaleɛ sabᵊɛt aalaaf doolaar bᵊs-səne.* **2.** *ɛala.* We paid fifty piasters per person. *dafaɛna xamsiin qərᵊš ɛaš-šaxᵊṣ.*
per cent - *bᵊl-miyye.* The cost of living has risen ten per cent. *takaliif ᵊl-maɛiiše rtafɛet ɛašara bᵊl-miyye.* -- A ten-per-cent service charge is included. *bᵊl-miyye ɛašara rasᵊm xədme daaxle.* -- Our bank pays two per cent interest. *l-bank tabaɛna byədfaɛ bᵊl-miyye tneen faayde.*
percentage - *nəsbe miᵊawiyye.*
perfect - **1.** *kaamel.* Nothing is perfect. *maa fii šii kaamel.* **2.** *ɛat-tamaam* (invar.). That's perfect nonsense. *hayy maṣxara ɛat-tamaam.* -- He speaks perfect French. *byəḥki frənsaawi ɛat-tamaam.*
**He's a perfect stranger to me. *huwwe ġariib ɛanni tamaam.*
to perfect - *taqan (e ᵊətqaan//ntaqan), tammam// ttammam, ᵊakmal.* The method hasn't been perfected yet. *ṭ-ṭariiqa ləssaaha maa ntaqnet.*
perfection - *kamaal.*
perfectly - *ɛat-tamaam, tamaaman, ɛal-maẓbuuṭ.* He was perfectly satisfied. *kaan raḍyaan ɛat-tamaam.* -- He's perfectly willing to do it. *huwwe məstɛədd tamaaman ysaawiiha.* -- He did it perfectly the first time. *saawaaha ɛal-maẓbuuṭ la-ᵊawwal marra.*
**I know him perfectly well. *ᵊana baɛᵊrfo mniiḥ.*
perfidious - *xaayen* pl. *xawane.*
perfidy - *xyaane.*
to **perform** - **1.** *ɛəmel (-yaɛmel ø//nɛamal), saawa// tsaawa.* Who performed the operation? *miin ɛəmel ᵊl-ɛamaliyye?* **2.** *qaam (u qyaam) b-.* The acrobats performed the most difficult feats. *l-bahlawaanaat qaamu b-ᵊaṣɛab nəmar bahlawaaniyye.*
performance - *ɛarᵊḍ.* Did you enjoy the performance? *tsalleet bᵊl-ɛarᵊḍ?*
perfume - *ɛəṭᵊr* pl. *ɛṭuur(a).* She always buys the most expensive perfumes. *daayman btəštə́ri ᵊaġla ɛṭuur.*
to perfume - *ɛaṭṭar//tɛaṭṭar.* He used to perfume his beard. *kaanet ɛaadto yɛaṭṭer ləḥᵊyto.*
perhaps - *bižuuz, məmken, žaayez, yəmken.* Perhaps I'll come along. *bižuuz ᵊəži maɛkon.*
period - **1.** *mədde* pl. *mədad.* He worked here for a short period. *štaġal hoon mədde qaṣiire.* **2.** *fatra* pl. *-aat.* It's the most interesting period in American history. *hiyye ᵊaṭraf fatra b-taariix ᵊameerka.* **3.** *nəqṭa* pl. *nəqaṭ.* You forgot to put a period here. *nsiit ᵊtḥəṭṭ nəqṭa hoon.* **4.** *ḥəṣṣa* pl. *ḥəṣaṣ, dars* pl. *druus.* I have the third period free. *maa ɛandi šii b-taalet ḥəṣṣa.*
period of grace - *məhle* pl. *məhal.* The period of grace expires on the tenth. *l-məhle btəntə́hi b-ɛaašer yoom.*
periodic(al) - *dawri*.* We must learn to face periodic setbacks. *laazem nətɛallam ᵊnwaažeh nakṣaat dawriyye.*
periodical - *mažalle* pl. *-aat, našra* (pl. *-aat*) *dawriyye.* They publish a number of periodicals. *byənᵊšru ɛəddet mažallaat.*
periodically - *dawriyyan.* The fever returns periodically. *ṣ-ṣxuune btəržaɛ dawriyyan.*
perjury - *šahaade kaazbe.* She committed perjury. *šəhdet šahaade kaazbe.*
permanent - **1.** *bərmanaan.* I need a permanent. *laazəmni bərmanaan.* **2.** *daaᵊem.* I have no permanent address. *maa ɛandi ɛənwaan daaᵊem.* -- This is a permanent job. *hayy waẓiife daaᵊime.*
permission - *ᵊəzᵊn.* Did you get his permission? *ᵊaxadt ᵊəzᵊn mənno?*
to ask permission - *staᵊzan mən, ṭalab (o ø) ᵊəzᵊn mən.* Ask your father's permission first. *staᵊzen mən ᵊabuuk bᵊl-ᵊawwal.*
permit - *rəxṣa* pl. *rəxaṣ, maᵊzuuniyye* pl. *-aat, ᵊižaaze* pl. *-aat.* You need a permit to play tennis here. *bəddak rəxṣa la-təlɛab tanəs hoon.*
to permit - *samaḥ (a samaaḥ) b-.* I can't permit that. *maa bəqder ᵊəsmaḥ b-haš-šii.* -- No one is permitted to enter this building. *maa ḥada masmə́ḥ-lo yədxol hal-binaaye.* -- Is smoking permitted? *t-tadxiin masmuuḥ?*
perpendicular - *ɛaamuudi*, raᵊsi*.*
to **perpetuate** - *xallad.* He perpetuated his name through his good works. *xallad ᵊəsmo b-ḥasanaato.*
to **persecute** - *ḍṭahad.* The religious minority was cruelly persecuted. *ḍṭahadu l-ᵊaǧalliyye d-diiniyye b-waḥšiyye.*

persecution – *ʔədṭihaad* pl. *-aat.*
perseverance – *mwaaẓabe.*
to **persevere** – *waaẓab, daawam.* If we persevere through all difficulties the job will get done. *ʔiza waaẓabna raġᵊm kəll ᵊṣ-ṣuƐuubaat ᵊl-Ɛamal biṣiir.*
Persia – *blaad˜ ᵊl-fərs, blaad ᵊl-Ɛažam, ʔiiraan.*
Persian – **1.** *faarsi* pl. *-iyyiin* and *fərs, Ɛažami* coll. *Ɛažam* pl. *-iyye, ʔiiraani* pl. *-iyyiin.* **2.** (language) *faarsi.*
person – *šaxᵊṣ* pl. *ʔašxaaṣ, zalame* pl. *zəlᵊm.* They paid fifty piasters per person. *dafaƐu xamsiin qərᵊš Ɛaš-šaxᵊṣ.* -- He's a very kind person. *huwwe zalame laṭiif ᵊktiir.*
**What a nice person she is! *qaddeeš laṭiife hiyye!*
**What sort of a person is he? *šuu ṣifaato huwwe?* or *šuu btaƐrə́f-li Ɛanno?*
in person – *šaxṣiyyan, bᵊz-zaat.* Please deliver this to him in person. *Ɛmeel maƐruuf sallem haš-šii ʔəlo šaxṣiyyan.*
juristic (or **artificial**) **person** – *šaxᵊṣ maƐnawi* pl. *ʔašxaaṣ maƐnawiyye, šaxᵊṣ ḍaanuuni* pl. *ʔašxaaṣ ḍanuuniyye.*
natural person – *šaxᵊṣ ḥaḍiiḍi* pl. *ʔašxaaṣ ḥaḍiiḍiyye.*
personal – **1.** *šaxṣi**, *xṣuuṣi**. He asks too many personal questions. *byəsʔal ᵊktiir ʔasʔile šaxṣiyye.* -- He would like to discuss a personal matter with you. *biriid ᵊyḥaakiik b-šaġle xṣuuṣiyye.* **2.** *xaaṣṣ.* They're my personal belongings. *hayy ᵊġraaḍi l-xaaṣṣa.*
personality – *šaxṣiyye* pl. *-aat.* A number of famous personalities attended the celebration. *fii Ɛadad mn ᵊš-šaxṣiyyaat ᵊš-šahiira ḥədru l-ʔəḥtifaal.* -- She has a pleasant personality. *Ɛanda šaxṣiyye faatne.*
personally – **1.** *šaxṣiyyan.* I don't know him personally. *maa baƐᵊrfo šaxṣiyyan.* **2.** *bᵊz-zaat, šaxṣiyyan.* I'd like to speak to him personally. *bəddi ʔəḥki maƐo bᵊz-zaat.*
personal pronoun – *ḍamiir* pl. *ḍamaayer.*
personnel – *mwaẓẓafiin* (pl.) We don't have enough personnel. *maa fii Ɛanna mwaẓẓafiin ᵊkfaaye.*
personnel office – *maktab˜* (pl. *makaateb˜*) *ʔəstəxdaam.*
to **persuade** – *qanaƐ (e ʔəqnaaƐ//nqanaƐ).* He persuaded me to go. *qanaƐni ruuḥ.*
persuasion – **1.** *ʔəqnaaƐ.* Gentle persuasion will do the trick. *l-ʔəqnaaƐ ᵊl-laṭiif bimašši l-ḥaal.* **2.** *mabaadeʔ* (pl.) Nobody knows exactly his political persuasion. *maa ḥada Ɛarfaan Ɛal-maẓbuuṭ mabaadʔo s-siyaasiyye.*
pessimism – *tašaaʔom.*
pessimist – *mətšaaʔem* pl. *-iin.*
pessimistic – *mətšaaʔem.*
pest – **1.** *ḥašara* pl. *-aat.* Insect pests destroyed the whole crop this year. *l-ḥašaraat xarrabu l-maḥṣuul kəllo has-səne.* **2.** *ʔaafe* pl. *-aat.* You're such a pest! *yaa laṭiif šuu ʔənnak ʔaafe!*
to **pester** – *naqar (o naqᵊr) raas˜* ... Stop pestering me! *ḥaaštak tənqə́r-li raasi!*
**He's pestering me to death with his questions! *Ɛam yəhləkni b-ʔasʔəlto.*
pet – **1.** *ḥaywaan* pl. *-aat.* We're not allowed to keep pets in our apartment. *muu masmə́ḥ-ᵊlna nəḥwa ḥaywaanaat bᵊl-ʔabartmaan tabaƐna.* **2.** *bəbbu˜ Ɛeen.* She's her mother's pet. *hiyye bəbbu Ɛeen ʔəmma.*
to pet – *dallal.* She's always been petted by everyone. *ṭuul Ɛəmra kəll ᵊn-naas bidallᵊluuha.*
petition – *Ɛariiḍa* pl. *Ɛaraayeḍ.* Why don't you get up a petition? *leeš maa btərfaƐu Ɛariiḍa?*
to petition – *qaddam Ɛariiḍa.* We petitioned the Minister of Education for a new school. *qaddamna Ɛariiḍa la-waziir ᵊl-maƐaaref ṭaalbiin fiiha madrase ždiide.*
Petra – *l-baṭra.*
petroleum – *batrool.*
petty – **1.** *ṭafiif, zahiid.* These are petty sums. *hayy mabaaleġ ṭafiife.* **2.** *taafeh.* He had a lot of petty objections. *Ɛtaraḍ ᵊktiir ʔəƐtiraaḍaat taafha.*
petty expenses – *natriyyaat* (pl.)
Pharaoh – *farƐoon* pl. *faraƐiin.*
pharaonic – *farƐooni**.
pharmaceutic(al) – *ṣaydali**.
pharmaceutics – *ṣaydale.*
pharmacist – *ṣaydali* pl. *ṣayaadle.*
pharmacology – *Ɛəlm ᵊṣ-ṣaydale.*
pharmacy – *ṣaydaliyye* pl. *-aat.*

phase – *marḥale* pl. *maraaḥel, ṭawr* pl. *ʔaṭwaar.* We're about to enter the second phase of the project. *nəḥna Ɛala wašak nədxol bᵊl-marḥale t-taanye ləl-mašruuƐ.*
the lunar phases – *ʔaškaal˜ ᵊl-qamar.*
phenomenon – *ẓaahira* pl. *ẓawaaher.* It's one of the most fascinating cultural phenomena. *hiyye ẓaahira mən ʔaƐžab ᵊẓ-ẓawaaher ᵊl-ḥaḍaariyye.*
philological – *luġawi**.
philologist – *luġawi* pl. *-iyyiin.*
philology – *Ɛəlm ᵊl-luġa.*
philosopher – *faylasuuf* pl. *falaasfe.*
philosophic(al) – *falsafi**.
philosophy – *falsafe* pl. *-aat.*
phone – *talifoon* pl. *-aat.* You're wanted on the phone. *ʔənte maṭluub Ɛat-talifoon.*
to phone – *talfan, saawa* or *Ɛəmel* or *ḍarab (o ḍarᵊb) talifoon.* Did anybody phone? *talfan ḥada šii?*
phonograph – *fənuuġraaf* pl. *-aat.*
phony – **1.** *mlaffaq.* That story sounds pretty phony to me. *hal-qəṣṣa mbayyənt-əlli mlaffaqa šwayye.* **2.** *xallaaṭ* pl. *-iin.* That guy's a phony! *haz-zalame xallaaṭ.*
phosphor – *fəṣfoor.*
phosphorous – *fəṣfoori**.
photograph – *ṣuura (šamsiyye)* pl. *ṣuwar (šamsiyye).* The wall was just covered with photographs and paintings. *l-ḥeeṭ kaan ᵊmġaṭṭa kəllo b-ṣuwar šamsiyye w-looḥaat.*
to photograph – *ṣawwar//tṣawwar.* Have you photographed the statue? *ṣawwart ᵊt-təmsaal?*
photographer – *mṣawwer* pl. *-iin.*
photography – *taṣwiir šamsi.*
phrase – **1.** *ḍool* pl. *ʔaḍwaal.* It's a common phrase in Arabic. *haada ḍool šaari bᵊl-Ɛarabi.* **2.** *mrakkab* pl. *-aat.* In Arabic it's a prepositional phrase. *haada mrakkab maƐ ḥarf ᵊž-žarr bᵊl-Ɛarabi.*
to phrase – *Ɛabbar Ɛan.* He phrases his thoughts well. *biƐabber Ɛan ʔafkaaro mniiḥ.*
physical – **1.** *badani**, *žasadi**, *žəsmaani**. Avoid every form of physical exertion. *tḥaaša kəll ʔəžhaad badani.* **2.** *ṭabiiƐi**, *fiiziyaaʔi**. This contradicts all physical laws. *haada binaaqeḍ kəll ᵊl-ḍawaniin ᵊṭ-ṭabiiƐiyye.*
physical exercises – *tamariin sweediyye* (pl.).
physician – *ḥakiim* pl. *ḥəkama, ṭabiib* pl. *ʔaṭəbba.*
physicist – *Ɛaalem˜* (pl. *Ɛəlama˜*) *fiiziya, fiiziyaaʔi* pl. *-iyyiin.*
physics – *fiiziya.* Nuclear physics has become very important since the war. *l-fiiziya n-nawawiyye ṣar-la ʔahammiyye kbiire mn ᵊl-ḥarb w-žaaye.*
physique – *bənye.* He has a powerful physique. *bənᵊyto qawiyye ktiir.*
pianist – *Ɛaazef˜* (pl. *-iin˜*) *byaano.*
piano – *byaano* pl. *byaanoyaat.* The piano is out of tune. *l-ᵊbyaano duuzaano manzuuƐ.*
pick – *maƐwal* pl. *maƐaawel.* The men were carrying picks and shovels. *r-ržaal kaanu ḥaamliin maƐaawel w-ᵊkreekaat.*
pick – *nəxbe, zəbde, xiire.* These men are the pick of the crop. *har-ržaal ḥənne nəxbet ᵊž-žamaaƐa.*
**I have three apples. Take your pick! *maƐi tlətt təffaaḥaat. naqqi-lak waaḥde.*
to pick – **1.** *qaṭaf (o qaṭᵊf//nqaṭaf).* Is the fruit ripe enough to pick? *l-fawaaki stawet ᵊkfaaye la-tənqəṭef?* **2.** *nakaš (o nkaaš), nakkaš.* Don't pick your teeth! *laa tənkoš ᵊsnaanak!* **3.** *naqqa, xtaar.* You certainly picked a nice time for an argument. *walḷa naqqeet waqt ᵊmnaaseb ᵊktiir ləl-ᵊxnaaq.* **4.** *našal (o/e našᵊl).* He's picked many a pocket. *našal naas ᵊktiir walḷa.*
**I have a bone to pick with you. *ʔəli ḥsaab ṣaffi maƐak.*
**Someone has picked this lock. *fii ḥada tḥaayal Ɛala hal-ġaal w-fataḥo.*
**They picked him to pieces. *maa xallu Ɛalée sətr ᵊmġaṭṭa.*
**Are you trying to pick a quarrel with me? *šuu Ɛam ᵊtḥaawel tətḥarraš bᵊš-šarr maƐi?*
to pick on – *ḥaṭṭ daabo w-daab˜* ... He's been picking on me all day. *ṣar-lo ṭuul ᵊn-nhaar ḥaaṭeṭ daabo w-daabi.*
to pick out – *naqqa, xtaar.* He picked out a very nice gift for his wife. *naqqa hdiyye ktiir ḥəlwe la-madaamto.*
to pick up – **1.** *qaam (i s).* Please pick up the paper from the floor. *mən faḍlak qiim ᵊl-waraqa mən Ɛal-ʔarḍ.* **2.** *šabak (o šabᵊk).* They picked up three girls on the road. *šabaku tlətt banaat*

Ɛaṭ-ṭariiq. 3. *kamaš (e kamᵊš//nkamaš), laqaṭ (o ə//ltaqaṭ).* The police picked up several suspects. *š-šərṭa kamšet Ɛəddet mašbuuhiin.* 4. *ṭaalaƐ, rakkab.* The bus stops here to pick up passengers. *l-baaṣ biwaqqef hoon la-yṭaaleƐ rəkkaab.* 5. *laqaṭ (o laqᵊṭ).* I picked up quite a bit of Italian on my trip. *laqaṭṭ ṭəlyaani mniiḥ ᵊb-safᵊrti.*
**The train gradually picked up speed. *t-treen bada yəsraƐ bᵊt-tadriiž.*

pickax - *maƐwal* pl. *maƐaawel.*

pickle - *mxallal (xyaar)* pl. *mxallal (xyaaraat).* Do you have pickles? *Ɛandak ᵊmxallal?*
in a pickle - *b-warṭa, b-maᵓzaq̇.* He's in a pretty pickle now. *huwwe waḷḷaahi waaqeƐ b-warṭa malƐuune.*
to put up pickles - *kabas (e kabᵊs) ᵊmxallal (ᵊxyaar).* Did you put up any pickles this year? *kabasti mxallal (ᵊxyaar) has-səne?*
to pickle - *kabas (e kabᵊs) ᵊmxallal (ᵊxyaar).* Did you do any pickling this year? *kabasti šii mxallal (ᵊxyaar) has-səne?*
pickled - *mxallal.* Buy a jar of pickled tomatoes. *štəri qaṭramiiz ᵊmxallal banadoora.*

pickpocket - *naššaal* pl. *-iin.*

picnic - *seeraan* pl. *sayariin, pəknek.*

picture - 1. *ṣuura* pl. *ṣuwar.* They have some beautiful pictures for sale. *fii Ɛandon šwayyet ṣuwar ḥəlwe ləl-beeƐ.* 2. *fəkra.* I have to get a clear picture of it first. *laazem yṣiir Ɛandi fəkra waadḥa bᵊl-ᵓawwal.* 3. *fəlᵊm* pl. *ᵓaflaam.* Was the picture good? *l-fəlᵊm kaan ḥəlu?*
**It was he who brought him into the picture in the first place. *huwwe halli kaan žaabo bᵊl-ᵓasaas.*
**She's been in pictures since she was a child. *ṣar-la mmassle siinamaaᵓiyye mən waqᵊt kaanet walad.*
picture book - *ktaab ᵊmṣawwar* pl. *kətb ᵊmṣawwara.*
picture gallery - *maƐraḍ˜* (pl. *maƐaareḍ˜*) *ṣuwar.*
picture post card - *kart˜ boosṭaal ᵊmṣawwar* pl. *kruut˜ boosṭaal ᵊmṣawwara.*
to give a picture of - *ṣawwar, Ɛaṭa ṣuura Ɛan.* He gave you a false picture of the situation. *ṣawwár-lak ᵊl-waḍᵊƐ ġalaṭ* or *Ɛaṭaak ṣuura xaaṭᵓa Ɛan ᵊl-waḍᵊƐ.*
to take a picture - *ṣawwar//tṣawwar, ᵓaxad ṣuura.* I haven't had my picture taken in years. *ṣar-li sniin maa tṣawwarᵊt.*
to picture - 1. *ṣawwar, waṣaf (-yuuṣef waṣᵊf//nwaṣaf).* He pictured it differently. *ṣawwára ġeer šəkᵊl.* -- This novel pictures life a thousand years ago. *har-riwaaye bətṣawwer ᵊl-ḥayaat mən qabᵊl ᵓalf səne.* 2. *tṣawwar.* I can't quite picture you as a politician. *maa-li Ɛam ᵓəqder ᵓətṣawwarak ka-siyaasi.*

piece - 1. *šaqfe* pl. *šəqaf, qəṭƐa* pl. *qəṭaƐ.* May I have a piece of cake? *btəsmáḥ-li b-šaqfet gaato?* -- Sew these two pieces together. *qṭoob haš-šaqᵊfteen maƐ baƐḍon.* 2. *maqṭuuƐa* pl. *-aat.* What is the name of the piece the orchestra is playing? *šuu ᵓəsm ᵊl-maqṭuuƐa halli l-ᵓorkeestra Ɛam ᵊddəqqa?*
**I gave him a good piece of my mind. *wabbaxto Ɛal-maṣbuuṭ.*
to fall to pieces - *faraṭ (o farᵊṭ).* The book is falling to pieces. *l-ᵊktaab Ɛam yəfroṭ farᵊṭ.*
to go to pieces - *nhaar.* She went completely to pieces. *nhaaret tamaaman.* -- Sooner or later their business is bound to go to pieces. *laa bədd Ɛaašilan ᵓaw ᵓaašilan ma yənhaar šəġlon.*
to take to pieces - *fakkak šaqfe šaqfe.* He took the whole radio to pieces. *fakkak ᵊr-raadyo kəllo šaqfe šaqfe.*
to tear to pieces - *šaraṭ (o šarṭ//nšaraṭ), šarraṭ šaqfe šaqfe.* Tear the letter to pieces and throw it away. *šrooṭ ᵊl-maktuub w-kəbbo.*

to do **piecework** - *štaġal bᵊl-qəṭƐa.* Do you also do piecework? *w-ᵊbtəštəġel ᵓənte šii kamaan bᵊl-qəṭƐa?*

pier - 1. *rṣiif* pl. *ᵓərᵊṣfe.* We were standing on the pier, waiting for the boat. *kənna waaqfiin Ɛar-rṣiif Ɛam nəstanna l-baaxra.* 2. *rakiize* pl. *rakaayez.* The bridge rests on four piers. *ž-žəsᵊr qaaƐed Ɛala ᵓarbaƐ rakaayez.*

pig - *xanziir* pl. *xanaziir.*

pigeon - *ḥamaame* coll. *ḥamaam* pl. *-aat.*

pigheaded - *Ɛaniid.* I wish he weren't so pigheaded! *ya-reet huwwe muu hal-qadd Ɛaniid* or ***ya-reet raaso muu hal-qadd məṭᵊl raas ᵊl-xanziir!*

pile - 1. *koome* pl. *-aat* and *kwaam, kədse* pl. *-aat.* The children shouldn't play on that pile of rocks. *l-ᵊwlaad ᵓaḥsán-lon maa yəlƐabu Ɛala koomet l-ᵊḥžaar hayy.* -- Here's a pile of letters to answer. *hayy kədset makatiib bədda žawaabaat.* -- That's a pile of money! *hayy koomet maṣaari!* 2. *rakiize* pl. *rakaayez.* The wharf rests on huge oak piles. *r-rṣiif qaaƐed Ɛala rakaayez ḍaxme mən xašab baḷḷuuṭ.*
**He made his pile during the war. *žammaƐ sarᵊwto waqt ᵊl-ḥarb.*
to pile - 1. *kawwam.* Pile the paper on the floor. *kawwem ᵊl-waraq Ɛal-ᵓarᵊḍ.* -- They'd piled the table with food. *kaanu mkawwmiin ᵊl-ᵓakᵊl Ɛaṭ-ṭaawle kwaam ᵊkwaam.* 2. *ndaḥaš.* The five girls piled into the small car and drove off. *l-banaat ᵊl-xamse ndaḥašu bᵊs-sayyaara ẓ-ẓġiire w-məšyu.*
to pile up - *tkawwam, tkaddas.* My debts are piling up. *dyuuni Ɛam tətkawwam.* -- The work keeps piling up on my desk. *š-šəġᵊl Ɛam yətkawwam Ɛala ṭaawəlti takwiim.*

pilgrim - *ḥažž* pl. *ḥəžžaaž, ḥažži* pl. *-iyye.*

pilgrimage - *ḥažž.* Are you going on the pilgrimage this year? *raayeḥ ᵓənte Ɛal-ḥažž has-səne?*

pill - *ḥabbe* coll. *ḥabb* pl. *-aat* and *ḥbuub.*

pillar - *Ɛadaaḍa* pl. *-aat.* A large pillar blocked my view of the stage. *fii Ɛaḍaaḍa kbiire manƐətni šuuf ᵊl-masraḥ.*

pillow - *mxadde* pl. *-aat.*

pillowcase - *beet˜ ᵊmxadde* pl. *byuut˜ ᵊmxaddaat.*

pilot - 1. *ṭayyaar* pl. *-iin.* He's a jet pilot. *huwwe ṭayyaar naffaase.* 2. *məršed* pl. *-iin.* That ship is waiting for the pilot. *hal-baaxra Ɛam təntẓer ᵊl-məršed.*

pimp - *Ɛarṣa* pl. *-aat.*

pimple - *ḥabbe* coll. *ḥabb* pl. *-aat* and *ḥbuub.*

pin - 1. *dabbuus* pl. *dababiis.* She stuck herself with a pin. *ġazzet ḥaala b-dabbuus.* 2. *šakle* pl. *-aat, brooš* pl. *-aat.* She wore a silver pin. *kaanet laabse šakle fəḍḍa.*
**I was on pins and needles. *kənᵊt qaaƐed Ɛala naar.*
to pin - *ḥašar (o ḥašᵊr//nḥašar).* The two men were pinned under the overturned auto. *r-ržaal ᵊt-tneen kaanu maḥšuuriin taḥt ᵊs-sayyaara l-maqluube.*
to pin down - *məsek (e masᵊk//nmasak).* We couldn't pin him down to anything definite. *maa qdərna nəmᵊsko w-laa b-šaġle mƐayyane.*
to pin on - 1. *šakal (o šakᵊl//nšakal).* I'll pin it on for you. *bəškə́l-lak-ydaha.* -- She pinned a flower on her dress. *šaklet warde Ɛala rooba.* 2. *labbas.* He tried to pin the crime on his companion. *ḥaawal ylabbes ᵊrfiiqo ž-žariime.*
to pin up - *šakkal (ᵊb-dababiis).* Let me pin up the hem first. *xalliini šakkə́l-lek ᵊd-daayer bᵊl-ᵓawwal.*

pinch - *nətfe* (pl. *nətaf*), *rašše* pl. *-aat.* Add a pinch of salt to the soup. *ḥəṭṭi nətfet məlᵊḥ bᵊš-šooraba.*
in a pinch - 1. *Ɛand ᵊḍ-ḍaruura, Ɛand ᵊl-ḥaaže.* In a pinch it'll do. *Ɛand ᵊḍ-ḍaruura bikaffi.* 2. *Ɛand ᵊd-diiq.* You can always count on him in a pinch. *fiik daayman təƐtə́med Ɛalée Ɛand ᵊd-diiq.*
to pinch - 1. *qaraṣ (o qarᵊṣ).* Don't pinch me! *laa təqrəṣni!* 2. *daayaq.* Where does the shoe pinch? *ween ᵊṣ-ṣabbaaṭ bidaayqak?* 3. *qaraṭ (o qarṭ//nqaraṭ).* I got my finger pinched in the door. *ᵓəṣbaƐti nqarṭet bᵊl-baab.*

pineapple - *ᵓananaas.*

pine (tree) - *ṣnoobara* coll. *ṣnoobar* pl. *-aat.* These pine trees are almost fifty years old. *haṣ-ṣnoobar Ɛəmron šii xamsiin səne.*

pink - *zahᵊr* (invar).

pious - *taqi* pl. *ᵓatqiya, ṣaaleḥ, naas malaaḥ* (invar.). His grandfather was a very pious man. *žəddo kaan rəžžaal ᵊktiir taqi.*
**That's no more than a pious wish. *hayy muu ᵓaktar mən ᵓəmniyye bariiᵓa w-xayaaliyye.*

pipe - 1. (small) *ᵓənbuub* pl. *ᵓanabiib,* (medium-sized) *buuri* pl. *bawaari,* (large) *qasṭal* pl. *qaṣaaṭel.* The pipe has burst. *l-ᵓənbuub ṭaqq.* 2. *ġalyuun* pl. *ġalayiin.* Do you smoke a pipe? *bəddaxxen ġalyuun?*
to pipe - *saḥab (a saḥᵊb//nsaḥab) bᵊl-ᵓanabiib.* We pipe our water from a spring. *mnəsḥab mayyətna mn ᵊl-Ɛeen bᵊl-ᵓanabiib.*

piracy - *q̇arṣane.*

pirate - *q̇ərṣaan* pl. *q̇araaṣne* and *q̇araṣiin.*

pistachio - *fəstqa* coll. *fəstoq* pl. *-aat.*

pistol - *fard* pl. *fruude, msaddas* pl. *-aat.*

piston - *pəstoon* pl. *-aat.*

pit - 1. *žuura* pl. *žuwar.* The ground is full of large pits. *l-ᵓarḍ malaane žuwar ᵊkbiire.*

2. *manðam* pl. *manaaðem*. Nobody was in the pit when the explosion occurred. *maa kaan fii hada bᵊl-manðam lamma ṣaar ᵊl-ʔənfiǧaar.*

pit - *bəzre* coll. *bəzᵊr* pl. *-aat* and *bzuur*. Don't swallow the pit. *laa təblaɛ ᵊl-bəzre.*

pitch - *zəfᵊt*. What's the difference between pitch and tar? *šuu l-farᵊq been ᵊz-zəfᵊt wᵊl-qaṭraan?*

pitch - *ramye* pl. *-aat*, *ḍarbe* pl. *-aat*. That was a good pitch. *hayy kaanet ramye mniiḥa.*

to pitch - *naṣab (o naṣᵊb//ntaṣab)*, *ḍarab (o ḍarᵊb//nḍarab)*. Where shall we pitch the tent? *ween nənṣob ᵊl-xeeme?*

to pitch in - *šammar ɛan ʔidée w-saaɛad*. We pitched right in. *šammarna ɛan ʔideena w-saaɛadna.*

pitcher - *ʔəbriiq* and *briiq* pl. *ʔabariiq*. Please get me a pitcher of water. *mən faḍlak šəb-li ʔəbriiq mayy.*

pitiable - *mḥazzen*. He played a pitiable role. *ləɛeb door ᵊmḥazzen* (or ***biḥazzen*).

pitiful - *məḥzen*. That was a pitiful sight. *kaan manẓar məḥzen.*

pity - *šafaqa*. I don't want your pity. *maa-li ɛaawez šafᵊqtak.*

**What a pity! *yaa xaṣaara!* or *yaa ḥaraam!*

to take pity - *šəfeq (a šafaqa)*. She took pity on him. *šəfqet ɛalée.*

it's a pity - *šii məʔsef*, *ʔasaf*, *(yaa) xaṣaara*. It's a pity you can't come. *šii məʔsef ʔənnak muu žaaye.*

to pity - *šəfeq (a šafaqa) ɛala*. She doesn't want to be pitied. *maa bədda ḥada yəšfaq ɛaleeha.* -- I pity them. *ʔana šafqaan ɛaleehon.*

place - 1. *maḥall* pl. *-aat*, *maṭraḥ* pl. *maṭaareḥ*. Please put it back in the same place. *balla raǧǧɛo la-maḥallo.* -- Do you know the place where we stopped reading? *btaɛref ᵊl-maṭraḥ yalli waqqafna ɛalée lamma kənna ɛam nəqra?* -- I wouldn't have done it in his place. *law kənt ᵊb-maḥallo maa kənᵊt ʔaɛməla.* -- Put yourself in my place! *ḥəṭṭ ḥaalak ᵊb-maḥalli w-šuuf!* 2. *maḥall*, *maṭraḥ*, *balad* pl. *blaad*. What's the name of this place? *šuu ʔəsᵊm hal-maḥall?* 3. *maḥall*, *maṭraḥ*, *maṭɛam* pl. *maṭaaɛem*. Can you recommend a good place to eat? *fiik ᵊtšiir ɛaleena b-maḥall ᵊmniiḥ naakol fii?* 4. *ṣaḥᵊn* pl. *ṣḥuun(e)*, (in a restaurant) *sarviis* pl. *-aat*. How many places did you set? *kam ṣaḥᵊn ḥaṭṭeeti ɛaṭ-ṭaawle?*

**His heart is in the right place. *huwwe zalame dəġri.*

in place of - *ɛawaaḍ~*, *badaal~*, *b-maḥall~*, *b-maṭraḥ~*. May I have another book in place of this one? *məmken ʔaaxod ᵊktaab ɛawaaḍ haada?*

in the first place - 1. *ʔawwal šii*. In the first place we can't leave until tomorrow. *ʔawwal šii maa mnəqder ᵊnsaafer la-bəkra.* 2. *bᵊl-ʔaṣᵊl*, *bᵊl-ʔawwal*. Who started all that trouble in the first place? *miin halli ballaš kəll hal-waǧaɛ ᵊr-raas bᵊl-ʔaṣᵊl?*

out of place - *muu b-maḥallo*. Your remark was out of place. *mlaaḥaẓtak kaanet muu b-maḥalla.* -- He was very much out of place. *wužuudo kaan muu b-maḥallo ʔabadan.*

to put someone in his place - *waqqaf ḥada ɛand ḥaddo*. Somebody ought to put him in his place. *laazem ḥada ywaqqfo ɛand ḥaddo.*

to take place - 1. *ṣaar (i ø)*. When will the wedding take place? *ʔeemta laḥa yṣiir ᵊl-ɛərᵊs?* 2. *žara (i ø)*, *ḥadas (o ø)*. Most of the story's action takes place in Baghdad. *ʔaktar ḥawaades ᵊl-qəṣṣa btəžri b-baġdaad.*

to place - 1. *ḥaṭṭ (ə ḥaṭaṭ//nḥaṭṭ)*. The table can be placed over there. *ṭ-ṭaawle məmken tənḥaṭṭ ᵊhniik.* 2. *waẓẓad (-yuuẓed ø) waẓiife la-*. We have placed all of our graduates. *waẓẓadna waẓaayef la-kəll ᵊl-mətxarržiin tabaɛna.*

**I've met him before but I can't place him. *šaayfo mən qabᵊl bass maa baɛref ween.*

plague - *ṭaaɛuun*.

plain - 1. *baṣiiṭ* pl. *-iin* and *bəṣaṭa*. They're plain people. *hənne žamaaɛa baṣiiṭiin.* -- We have a plain home. *ɛanna beet baṣiiṭ.* 2. *waaḍeḥ*, *ẓaaher*. It's quite plain that he's after her money. *šii waaḍeḥ ʔənno bəddo maṣariiha.* 3. *mbayyen*, *waaḍeḥ*, *ẓaaher*. It's as plain as the nose on your face. *haš-šii mbayyen mətᵊl ɛeen ᵊš-šams.*

**The airfield is in plain view. *l-maṭaar ẓaaher.*

**I told him the plain truth. *qəlt-éllo l-ḥaqiiqa b-ṣaraaḥa.*

**To put it in plain language ... *bᵊl-ɛarabi l-faṣiiḥ ...*

plains - *saḥᵊl* pl. *shuul(e)*. Many people prefer the mountains to the plains. *fii ktiir naas bifaḍḍlu ž-žbaal ɛas-shuul.*

plaintiff - *məddáɛi* pl. *-iin*.

plan - 1. *xariiṭa* pl. *xaraayeṭ*, *xaarṭa* pl. *-aat*. The plans for the house are ready. *xaraayeṭ ᵊl-beet ṣaaru ḥaaḍriin.* 2. *xəṭṭa* pl. *xəṭaṭ*, *mašruuɛ* pl. *mašariiɛ*. She has very ambitious plans. *ɛanda xəṭaṭ kəlla ṭumuuḥ.* -- Have you made any plans yet for the future? *ɛməlt šii xəṭaṭ ləl-məstaqbal wəlla ləssa?* -- What are your plans for tomorrow? *šuu mašariiɛak la-bəkra?*

floor plan - *mxaṭṭaṭ* pl. *-aat*.

to plan - 1. *ɛəmel xəṭṭa la-*. We planned the trip very carefully. *ɛməlna xəṭṭa ktiir madruuse la-safrətna.* 2. *nawa (i ø)*, *qaṣad (o ø)*. Where do you plan to spend the summer? *ween naawi tmaḍḍi ṣ-ṣeefiyye?* 3. *qassam*. He doesn't know how to plan his time. *maa byaɛref kiif yqassem waqto.*

to plan on - 1. *ɛtamad ɛala*. You'd better not plan on it. *ʔafḍál-lak maa təɛtəmed ɛaleeha.* 2. *dabbar ḥaalo*. On the salary I get, I have to plan very carefully. *ɛal-maɛaaš halli ɛam ʔaaxdo laazem dabber ḥaali b-tarawwi.*

plane - *ṭayyaara* pl. *-aat*. Did you come by plane? *ʔžiit bᵊṭ-ṭayyaara?*

plane - *məstáwa* pl. *məstawayaat*. The discussion was not on a very high plane. *l-ᵊmnaaqaše maa kaanet ɛala məstáwa ɛaali ktiir.*

plane - *faara* pl. *-aat*. I borrowed a plane from the carpenter. *stɛart faara mən ɛand ᵊn-naǧǧaar.*

to plane - *qašaṭ (o qašᵊṭ//nqašaṭ)*. These boards have to be planed. *hal-lwaaḥ laazem yənqᵊšṭu.*

planet - *kawkab sayyaar* pl. *kawaakeb sayyaara.*

plant - 1. *nabaat* pl. *-aat*. What kind of plants are they? *šuu nooɛ han-nabataat?* 2. *zriiɛa*. I water the plants every day. *bəsqi z-zriiɛa kəll yoom.* 3. *maṣnaɛ* pl. *maṣaaneɛ*, *maɛmal* pl. *maɛaamel*, *fabriika* pl. *fabaarek*. The manager showed me around the plant. *l-mudiir dawwarni bᵊl-maṣnaɛ.*

to plant - 1. *zaraɛ (a zarᵊɛ//nzaraɛ)*. We planted flowers in our garden. *zaraɛna zhuur b-ᵊžneenətna.* 2. *ḥaṭṭ (ə ø)*. He's planted some strange ideas in her head. *ḥaṭṭ-álla ʔafkaar ġariibe b-raasa.*

plantation - *mazraɛa* pl. *mazaareɛ*.

plaster - *kəlse*. The plaster on the wall is all cracked. *l-kəlse ɛal-ḥeeṭ kəlla šquuq.*

plaster (of Paris) - *žabṣiin*. This figure is made of plaster. *hat-təmsaal maɛmuul mən žabṣiin.*

(plaster) cast - *žabṣiin*. Her arm is still in a cast. *ʔiida ləssaata bᵊž-žabṣiin* or ***ʔiida ləssaata mžabṣane.*

to plaster - *kallas*. Have they finished plastering the walls yet? *xalaṣu takliis ᵊl-ḥiiṭaan wəlla ləssa?*

plastic - *blastiik* pl. *-aat*.

plastic surgery - *žiraaḥa tažmiiliyye*.

plate - 1. *ṣaḥᵊn* pl. *ṣḥuun(e)*. There's a crack in the plate. *fii šaɛᵊr bᵊṣ-ṣaḥᵊn.* 2. *balloora* pl. *-aat*. It's very difficult to get plates for this camera. *ṣaɛb ᵊktiir ᵊl-waaḥed ylaaqi ballooraat la-hal-kamera.* 3. *looḥa* pl. *-aat*. The illustration is on Plate Three. *ṣ-ṣuura ɛal-looḥa t-taalte.* 4. *ṭaqm~* (pl. *ṭquumet~*) *ᵊsnaan*. I didn't know she wore a plate. *maa-li ɛarfaan ʔənno hiyye ḥaaṭṭa ṭaqm ᵊsnaan.* 5. *raas* pl. *ruus*. How many plates are there on your stove? *kam raas fii bᵊṭ-ṭabbaax tabaɛek?*

platform - 1. *rṣiif* pl. *ʔərᵊṣfe*. Let's meet on the platform. *xalliina nšuuf baɛᵊḍna ɛar-rṣiif.* 2. *bərnaameǧ siyaasi* pl. *baraameǧ siyaasiyye*. The two parties agreed on a common platform. *l-ḥəzbeen ᵊttafaqu ɛala bərnaameǧ siyaasi mwaḥḥad.* -- The speakers were seated on the platform. *l-xəṭaba kaanu qaaɛdiin ɛal-ᵊmnaṣṣa.*

platinum - *blaatiin*.

platitude - *qawl məbtádal* pl. *ʔaqwaal məbtádale*. He spoke nothing but platitudes. *kəll yalli ḥakáa ʔaqwaal məbtádale.*

Plato - *ʔaflaaṭuun*.

platoon - *faṣiile* pl. *faṣaayel*.

platter - *ṣaniyye* pl. *ṣawaani*. The platter isn't big enough for the roast. *ṣ-ṣaniyye maa btəsaɛ ᵊr-roosto.*

plausible - *maɛquul*. This sounds like a plausible explanation. *haš-šarᵊḥ ẓaaher ɛalée šarᵊḥ maɛquul.*

play - 1. *ləɛᵊb* pl. *ʔalɛaab*. The children are completely absorbed in their play. *l-ᵊwlaad ġarqaaniin*

ᵊb-ləεbon. 2. *masraḥiyye* pl. *-aat, tamsiiliyye* pl. *-aat*. Are there any good plays in town? *fii šii masraḥiyyaat ḥəlwe εam təlεab bᵊl-balad?* 3. *ləεᵊb, laaš*. The steering wheel has too much play. *d-dərkəsyoon fii ləεb ᵊktiir.*
fair play - *ʔənṣaaf*. The union demands fair play in the company's employment policy. *n-naqaabe εam ᵊṭṭaaleb bᵊl-ʔənṣaaf b-siyaaset ᵊl-ʔəstəxdaam tabaε ᵊš-šərke.*
foul play - *talaaεob*. It looks to me as if there's some foul play going on in this place. *byəẓhár-li ʔənno fii šwayyet talaaεob εam yṣiir b-hal-maḥall.*
to play - 1. *ləεeb (a ləεᵊb)*. The children are playing in the garden. *l-ᵊwlaad εam yəlεabu bᵊž-žneene.* -- We played for money. *lεəbna εala maṣaari.* -- What's playing tonight? *šuu εam yəlεabu l-leele?* **2.** *daqq (ə daqq) εala*. He plays the violin very well. *bidəqq εal-kamanža ktiir ᵊmniiḥ.* 3. *massal door~...* He played Othello last night. *massal door ʔoteello leelt ᵊmbaareḥ.* -- Who's playing the lead? *miin εam ᵊymassel door ᵊl-baṭal?*
to play a joke (or **trick**) **on** - *ləεeb (a ə) daqq* (or *ḥiile*) *εala*. He played a joke on me. *ləεeb εaliyyi daqq.*
to play a role (or **part**) - *ləεeb (a ə) door, qaam (u ə) ᵊb-door*. He played an important role in the negotiations. *ləεeb door ᵊmhəmm bᵊl-ᵊmfaawaḍaat.*
to play around - 1. *qaṭṭaε waqᵊt*. You've been playing around long enough. *ṣar-lak εam ᵊtqaṭṭeε waqt ᵊkfaaye.* 2. *ləεeb (a ləεᵊb)*. Stop playing around with that radio! *ḥaaže təlεab b-har-raadyo!*
to play fair with - *ʔanṣaf maε*. He really didn't play fair with me. *waḷḷaahi maa ʔanṣaf maεi.*
to be played out - *faraṭ (o ə)*. After a hard day's work he's all played out. *baεᵊd šəġl ᵊnhaaṛ mədni byəfroṭ εal-ʔaaxiir.*
to play up - *barraz*. He played up her good qualities. *barraz mazaayaaha l-ᵊmniiḥa.*

player - *laεεiib* pl. *-e*. One of the players got hurt during the game. *fii waaḥed mn ᵊl-laεεiibe nžaraḥ ʔasna l-ᵊmbaarda.*

playing card - *waraqet~* (pl. *wraaq~*) *šadde*. I don't have any playing cards. *maa εandi wraaq šadde.*

plea - *ražaaʔ* pl. *ražawaat*. He ignored my plea. *tġaaḍa εan ražaaʔi.*

to **plead** - *twassal la-, traǧǧa*. She pleaded with him not to go. *twassalét-lo* (or *traǧǧto*) *ʔənno maa yruuḥ.*
**Do you plead guilty? *ʔənte məzneb?*
**I plead not guilty. *ʔana waḷḷaahi bari.*

pleasant - *laṭiif* pl. *ləṭafa*. She's a pleasant person. *hiyye waaḥde laṭiife.* -- We spent a very pleasant evening there. *maḍḍeena sahra laṭiife ktiir ᵊhniik.* -- That was a pleasant surprise. *hayy kaanet ᵊmfaažaʔa laṭiife.*
**It isn't pleasant for me to have to do this. *ʔana maa-li masruur ᵊb-εamali haš-šii.*
**Good-by! Have a pleasant trip! *ʔaḷḷa maεak! nšaaḷḷa tənbəṣeṭ ᵊb-has-safra!*

to **please - 1.** *εažab (e ə)*. How does this hat please you? *kiif hal-bərneeṭa btəεᵊžbak?* **2.** *raḍa (i ə)*. He's hard to please. *ṣaεᵊb tərḍii.* -- You can't please everybody. *maa fiik tərḍi kəll ᵊn-naas.*
**Do as you please. *saawi mətᵊl-ma bəddak* or *εala keefak.*
please - *baḷḷa* (invar.), *mən faḍlak, bətražžaak, εmeel maεruuf, ʔiza bətriid, ʔiza bətḥəbb*. Please shut the door. *baḷḷa sakkér-li l-baab.*
pleasing - *laṭiif*. She has a very pleasing voice. *ṣooṭa ktiir laṭiif.*
to be pleased - *rəḍi (a ə)*. He was pleased with the answer. *rəḍi bᵊž-žawaab.* **2.** *nbəṣaṭ*. He was very pleased when he saw me. *nbəṣaṭ ᵊktiir lamma šaafni.*

pleasure - 1. *baṣᵊṭ*. He never combines business with pleasure. *maa byəxloṭ ʔabadan ᵊš-šəġᵊl wᵊl-baṣᵊṭ.* **2.** *suruur*. The pleasure is all mine. *s-suruur ʔəli ʔana.* **3.** *suruur, mamnuuniyye*. I'll do it with pleasure. *baεméla b-kəll suruur.* **4.** *mətεa, lazze*. It was a real pleasure to watch him swim. *kaan mətεa εan ḥaqa tətfarraž εalée εam yəsbaḥ.*
**I got a lot of pleasure out of the work. *tmattaεt ᵊktiir b-haš-šəġᵊl.*
**It will be a pleasure to have you visit us. *mnənbəṣeṭ ᵊktiir ʔiza ʔᵊžiit zərtna.*

pleat - *ṭaεže* pl. *-aat*. Do you want the dress with or without pleats? *bəddək ᵊl-fəṣṭaan ᵊb-ṭaεžaat wəlla bala?*

to **pledge - 1.** *ʔaxad εahᵊd mən*. He pledged me to secrecy. *ʔaxad εahᵊd mənni ʔəktom ᵊs-sərr.* **2.** *tεahhad*. I pledged five dollars to the Red Cross. *tεahhadt ᵊb-xamᵊs doolaaraat ləṣ-ṣaliib ᵊl-ʔaḥmar.*

plentiful - *wafiir, ġaziir*.

plenty - *ktiir*. You have plenty of time. *εandak waqt ᵊktiir.* -- We had plenty to eat. *kaan εanna ʔakl ᵊktiir.* -- You have to get plenty of sleep. *laazmak noom ᵊktiir.*

pliers - *kammaaše* pl. *-aat*. I need a hammer and (a pair of) pliers. *laazəmni šaakuuš w-kammaaše.*

plot - 1. *ḥabke*. The story has an interesting plot. *l-qəṣṣa ʔəla ḥabke žazzaabe.* **2.** *mʔaamara* pl. *-aat*. The plot was discovered in time. *l-ᵊmʔaamara ktašafuuha qabl ᵊb-waqᵊt.* **3.** *šaqfe* pl. *šəqaf*. We bought a small plot of land in the suburbs. *štareena šaqfet ʔarḍ ᵊẓġiire bᵊḍ-ḍawaaḥi.*
to plot - *tʔaamar*. They plotted against the government. *tʔaamaru ḍəḍḍ l-ᵊḥkuume.*

plow - *məḥraat* pl. *maḥariit*. You need a heavier plow. *laazmak məḥraat ʔakbar mən haad.*
to plow - *ḥarat (o ḥarᵊt//nḥarat)*. I'll need all day to plow this field. *byaaxədni ṇ-ṇhaaṛ kəllo ḥatta ʔəḥrot hal-ḥaqle.*

to **pluck** - *nataf (o natᵊf)*. Did you pluck the chicken yet? *natafti ž-žaaže wəlla ləssa?*

plug - 1. *saddaade* pl. *-aat*. Pull the plug out of the drain. *qiim ᵊs-saddaade mn ᵊl-balluuεa.* **2.** *fiiš* pl. *-aat*. This lamp cord needs a new plug. *šriiṭ hal-lamḅa laazmo fiiš ᵊždiid.*
to plug in - *ḥaṭṭ (ə ḥaṭaṭ) ᵊl-fiiš*. Plug in the electric iron for me. *ḥəṭṭ-élli fiiš ᵊl-məkwaaye.*
to plug up - *sadd (ə sadd//nsadd)*. They had to plug up the hole with a piece of cloth. *nžabaru ysəddu l-bəxᵊš b-xərqa.*

plum - *xooxa* coll. *xoox* pl. *-aat*.

plumber - *ḥaddaad* pl. *-iin*.

plump - *mṭablaž, mεabba*. She's a little on the plump side. *hiyye šwayye mṭablaže.*

to **plunge - 1.** *ġaṭaṣ (o ġaṭᵊṣ)*. He plunged into the water. *ġaṭaṣ bᵊl-ṃayy.* **2.** *rama (i ə) ḥaalo*. He plunged into the burning house to save the baby. *rama ḥaalo εal-beet yalli εam yəḥtəreq la-yxalleṣ ᵊṭ-ṭəfᵊl.*

plural - *žamᵊε* pl. *žmuuε*.
broken plural - *žamᵊε~ taksiir, žamε ᵊmkassar*.
sound plural - *žamᵊε saalem*.

plus - *w-*. Five plus seven is twelve. *xamse w-sabεa ṭnaεš.*

plywood - *blakée*.

pneumonia - *zaat ᵊr-riʔa*.

pocket - *žeebe* pl. *-aat* and *žyuub*. Put this in your pocket. *ḥəṭṭ haada b-žeebtak.*
to pocket - *qašš (ə qašš)*. His partner pocketed all the profits. *šriiko qašš kəll ᵊl-ʔarbaaḥ.*

pocketbook - 1. *šanta* pl. *-aat, šantaaye* pl. *-aat* and *šanaaṭi*. The compact fell out of her pocketbook. *εəlbet ᵊl-boodra saltet mən šantéta.* **2.** *ktaab~* (pl. *kətᵊb~*) *žeeb*. This bookstore has an especially large selection of pocketbooks. *hal-maktabe fiiha taškiile kbiire εal-xuṣuuṣ mən kətb ᵊž-žeeb.*

pocketknife - *muus~* (pl. *mwaas~*) *žeeb*.

poem - *qəṭεa* (pl. *qəṭaε*) *šəεriyye*, (usually rather long) *qaṣiide* pl. *qaṣaayed*. This book contains all his poems. *hal-ᵊktaab fii kəll qəṭaεo š-šəεriyye* (or **kəll šəεro).

poet - *šaaεer* pl. *šəεara*.

poetry - *šəεᵊr*. She writes beautiful poetry. *btənẓom šəεᵊr ḥəlu.*

point - 1. *nəqṭa* pl. *nəqaṭ*. A straight line is the shortest distance between two points. *l-xaṭṭ ᵊl-məstaqiim huwwe ʔaqṣar masaafe been nəqᵊṭṭeen.* -- We've gone over the contract point by point. *raažaεna l-kəntraato nəqṭa nəqṭa.* -- Women are his weak point. *n-nəswaan hənne nəqṭet ᵊḍ-ḍəεᵊf fii.* -- Our team scored 23 points. *fariiqna sažžal tlaatḍa εəšriin nəqṭa.* **2.** *raas* pl. *ruus*. I broke the point of my knife. *kasarᵊt raas muusi.* **3.** *mawḍuuε*. Let's stick to the point. *xalliina žuwwaat ᵊl-mawḍuuε.* -- You missed the point. *faatak ᵊl-mawḍuuε.* -- That's beside the point. *haš-šii barraat ᵊl-mawḍuuε.* **4.** *daraže*. I can understand it up to a certain point. *fiini ʔəfhə́ma la-daraže.* -- The freezing point of alcohol is below that of water. *daražet ᵊt-tažallod tabaε ᵊl-kuḥuul ʔawṭa mən tabaε ᵊl-ṃayy.* -- The boiling point of water is 100 degrees centigrade. *daražet ᵊl-ġalayaan tabaε ᵊl-ṃayy miyye* santiġraad. 5. maziyye pl. mazaaya. He has his good points, too. mən naaḥye taanye, ʔəlo mazayᵊa l-ḥasane. 6. ṭaʕme. There is no point in that. haš-šii maa-lo ṭaʕme. 7. qaṣᵊḍ, ġaaye. I don't get the point. ʔana maa-li fahmaan ᵊl-qaṣᵊḍ.

**Mathematics is not his strong point. r-riyaaḍiyyaat maa xəlqet ʔəlo.

**Make it a point to be on time. xallii b-baalak təži ʕal-waqᵊt.

**In your case we can stretch a point. mənšaanak ʔənte maa ʕanna maaneʕ nətsaahal.

point of view - wəžhet˜ (pl. -aat˜) naẓar. Our points of view differ. wəžhaat naẓarna btəxtə́lef.-- From his point of view he's right. mən wəžhet naẓaro maʕo ḥaqq.

to the point - mṣiib, b-maḥallo. His comments are always to the point. mlaaḥaẓaato daayman ᵊmṣiibe (or b-maḥalla).

to come to the point - daxal ᵊb-žawhar ᵊl-mawḍuuʕ. Let's come to the point. xalliina nədxol ᵊb-žawhar ᵊl-mawḍuuʕ.

to be on the point of - kaan ʕala wašak ... We were on the point of leaving when company arrived. kənna ʕala wašak nəmši lamma ʔəžu ḍyuuf.

to point - 1. šaar (i š), dall (ə d). The arrow points north. s-sahᵊm bišiir ʕaš-šmaal. 2. ʔaššar ʕala, warža. Point to the man you mean. ʔaššə́r-li ʕar-rəžžaal (or waržiini r-rəžžaal) yalli b-fəkrak. 3. dall (ə d) ʕala. All signs point to a colder winter. kəll ᵊd-dalaaʔel bəddəll ʕala šətwiyye baarde.

to point out - ʔaššar ʕala, warža. Point out the place you told me about. ʔaššə́r-li ʕal-maḥall (or waržiini l-maḥall) yalli qəlt-ə́lli ʕanno.

pointed - 1. mrawwas, mbawwaz. Be careful with that pointed stick. ʔoʕa w-ʔənte ḥaamel hal-ʕaṣaaye l-ᵊmrawwase. 2. malġuum. She's always making pointed remarks. daayman btəṭlaʕ b-ᵊmlaaḥaẓaat malġuume.

poise - 1. ʔəttizaan. She never loses her poise. b-ḥayaata maa bəḍḍawweʕ ʔəttizaana. 2. razaane. She has a lot of poise for her age. ʕanda razaane ktiir bᵊn-nəsbe la-sənna.

poison - samm pl. smuum. Watch out! That jar contains poison. ʔəṣḥa! hal-qaṭramiiz fii samm.

poison gas - ġaaz saamm pl. ġaazaat saamme.

to poison - sammam/tsammam, samm (ə samm). Our dog has been poisoned. kalᵊbna tsammam.

poisonous - saamm, msəmm.

poker - 1. məḥraak pl. maḥariik. The poker is behind the stove. l-məḥraak wara ṣ-ṣoobya. 2. pooker. Do you play poker? btəlʕab pooker?

Poland - booloonya, boolanda.

polar - ḍ̌əṭbi*. The polar region. l-manṭiqa l-ḍ̌əṭbiyye. -- Polar bear. dəbb ḍ̌əṭbi.

polar star - nažmet ᵊl-ḍ̌əṭᵊb.

Pole - boolooni pl. -iyyiin and -iyye.

pole - 1. xašabe pl. -aat. Will the pole be long enough? l-xašabe ṭawiile kfaaye? 2. ʕaamuud pl. ʕawamiid. The car hit a telephone pole and burst into flame. s-sayyaara ḍarbet b-ʕaamuud talifoon w-ᵊltahbet. 3. zaane pl. -aat. The pole broke just as he went over the bar. z-zaane nkasret maʕo w-huwwe ʕam ynəṭṭ mən fooq ᵊt-taxšiibe.

pole - ḍ̌əṭᵊb pl. ʔaḍ̌ṭaab. How cold does it get at the poles? qaddeeš bişiir bard bᵊl-ḍ̌əṭbeen?

police - šərṭa, booliis. Call the police! ṣraax ləš-šərṭa!

police blotter - səžəll˜ (pl. -aat˜) waḍaaʔeʕ˜ ᵊš-šərṭa.

police station - karakoon pl. -aat, maxfar˜ (pl. maxaafer˜) šərṭa. Where is the nearest police station? ween ʔaqrab karakoon?

policeman - šərṭi pl. šərṭa, booliis (invar.).

policy - mabdaʔ pl. mabaadeʔ. I make it a policy to be on time. ʕaamə́la mabdaʔi ʔəži ʕal-waqᵊt. -- It's my policy to talk to every applicant myself. mabdaʔi ḥaaki kəll waaḥed mn ᵊl-məstadʕiin šaxṣiyyan.

policies - siyaase. We can't support his policies. maa mnəqder ᵊnʔayyed siyaasto.

policy - booliiṣa pl. bawaaleṣ. Don't let your policy lapse. laa txalli l-booliiṣa tabaʕak yfuut waqta.

Polish - 1. boolooni (invar.). He speaks an excellent Polish. byəḥki boolooni məmtaaz. 2. boolooni*. The Polish government has lodged a strong protest. l-ᵊḥkuume l-boolooniyye qaddamet ʔəḥtižaaž šadiid.-- She's Polish. hiyye boolooniyye.

polish - 1. booya. I need some brown polish for my new shoes. laazəmni šwayyet booya bənni la-ṣabbaaṭi š-ždiid. 2. tahziib. He still lacks polish. ləssa naaqṣo tahziib.

**I gave the knobs a good polish. lammaʕt ᵊṭ-ṭoobaat ᵊmniiḥ.

to polish - 1. booya (booyaaye). I didn't have time to polish my shoes. maa ṣaar ʕandi waqᵊt booyi ṣabbaaṭi. 2. lammaʕ. The silver needs polishing. l-fəḍḍiyye bədda talmiiʕ. 3. bardax. I haven't polished the furniture yet. ləssa maa bardaxt ᵊl-moobiilya.

polite - mʔaddab, mhazzab. He's not very polite. huwwe muu ktiir ᵊmʔaddab.

political - siyaasi*. Do you belong to any political party? btəntə́mi la-šii ḥəzᵊb siyaasi?

politician - siyaasi pl. -iyyiin.

politics - siyaase. I'm not interested in politics. maa bəhtamm bᵊs-siyaase.

polls - markaz˜ (pl. maraakez˜) ʔəntixaab. The polls close at 8 p.m. maraakez ᵊl-ʔəntixaab bətsakker ᵊs-saaʕa tmaane l-masa.

**80 percent of the population went to the polls. tmaaniin bᵊl-miyye mn ᵊs-səkkaan raaḥu w-ᵊntaxabu (or w-ṣawwatu).

polluted - mlawwat. Be careful, the water may be polluted. ʔəṣḥa l-mayy məmken ᵊtkuun ᵊmlawwate.

polygamy - taʕaddod˜ ᵊz-zawžaat.

pomegranate - rəmmaane coll. rəmmaan pl. -aat.

pond - bərke pl. bərak.

pool - bərke pl. bərak. The police found him lying in a pool of blood. š-šərṭa ləqᵊto waaqeʕ ᵊb-bərket damm.

(swimming) pool - masbaḥ pl. masaabeḥ, bərket˜ (pl. bərak˜) ᵊsbaaḥa. They have a big pool. ʕandon masbaḥ ᵊkbiir.

to pool - žammaʕ. If we pool our money we may have enough to buy a car. ʔiza mənžammeʕ maṣariina məmken yṣiir ʕanna kfaaye nəštə́ri sayyaara.

poor - 1. faqiir pl. fəqara. Many poor people live in this neighborhood. fii ktiir naas fəqara saakniin b-haž-žiire. -- This is poor soil for wheat. hat-tərbe faqiire ləl-qamᵊḥ. 2. məskiin pl. masakiin. The poor fellow is blind. haz-zalame l-məskiin ʔaʕma. 3. ḍʕiif pl. ḍəʕafa. He's very poor in arithmetic. huwwe ḍʕiif ᵊktiir bᵊl-ᵊḥsaab.

**According to the proverb the poor get poorer and the rich richer. mətᵊl-ma biquul ᵊl-matal: ᵊl-maal bižərr ᵊl-maal wᵊl-qamᵊl bižərr ᵊṣ-ṣiibaan.

Pope (or pope) - baaba pl. baabawaat.

poplar - ḥoora coll. ḥoor pl. -aat.

poppy - xašxaaš.

popular - 1. šaʕbi*. The program consists mostly of popular music. l-bərnaameš ʔaktaro mʔallaf mən muusiiqa šaʕbiyye. -- The store has popular prices. l-maxzan ʔasʕaaro šaʕbiyye. 2. maqṣuud, maʔmuum. It's a very popular restaurant. huwwe maṭʕam maqṣuuḍ ᵊktiir. 3. maḥbuub. He's very popular among his classmates. huwwe ktiir maḥbuub been rəfaqaat ṣaffo. 4. šaaʔeʕ. That's a popular notion, but it's wrong. hayy fəkra šaaʔiʕa bass ġalaṭ.

populated - maʕmuur, ʕaamer bᵊs-səkkaan, ʔaahel bᵊs-səkkaan. The industrial area is thickly populated. l-manṭiqa ṣ-ṣinaaʕiyye maʕmuura b-kasaafe (or ʕaamra b-səkkaan ᵊktaar).

population - səkkaan (pl.), ʔahaali (pl.). The population has almost doubled in the last twenty years. s-səkkaan taqriiban ḍḍaaʕafu bᵊl-ʕəšriin səne l-maaḍye.

porcelain - borsəleen, borsəlaan.

porch - varanda pl. -aat.

porcupine - niiṣ pl. nyaaṣ.

pore - (masaame) coll. pl. masaam, masaamaat.

pork - laḥᵊm˜ xanziir.

pork chop - kastaleetet˜ (pl. -aat˜) xanziir.

porosity - masaamiyye.

porous - masaami*.

port - miina pl. mawaani, marfaʔ pl. maraafeʔ. The ship will enter port at 6 p.m. l-baaxra bətfuut ʕal-miina s-saaʕa sətte l-masa.

port - portóo. I prefer port to sherry. bfaḍḍel ᵊl-portóo ʕaš-šeerii.

portable - portatiif (invar.). I bought myself a portable typewriter. štareet-ə́lli makanet ᵊktaabe portatiif.

porter - ḥammaal pl. -e and -iin. Shall I call a porter? ʔəṣrdx-lak la-ḥammaal?

portion - 1. kammiyye pl. -aat, (piece) šaqfe pl. šəqaf. Do they always serve such small portions?

daayman biqaddmu kammiyyaat hal-qadd ᵊẓġiire? 2. *qəsᵊm* pl. *ʔaqsaam, žəzᵊʔ* pl. *ʔažzaaʔ.* A large portion of the city was destroyed by the fire. *qəsm ᵊkbiir mn ᵊl-madiine txarrab b-natiižt ᵊl-ḥariiqa.*

Portugal - *l-bərtuġaal.*

Portuguese - 1. *bərtuġaali* (invar.). They're making a translation into Portuguese now. *ʕam yaʕᵊmlu taržame ləl-bərtuġaali hallaq.* 2. *bərtuġaali**. I like Portuguese sardines best. *bḥəbb ᵊs-sardiin ᵊl-bərtuġaali ʔaktar šii.* -- There were three Portuguese with me on the plane. *kaan fii tlətt bərtuġaaliyyiin maʕna bᵊṭ-ṭayyaara.*

position - 1. *waḍʕiyye.* He was sitting in a very uncomfortable position. *kaan qaaʕed ᵊb-waḍʕiyye ktiir muu mərᵊyḥa.* 2. *waḍʕiyye, waḍᵊʕ.* Leave every object in this room in its present position. *xalli kəll ġarad b-hal-ʔuuḍa b-waḍʕiito.* -- That leaves your rook in a very difficult position. *haada bixalli rəxxak ᵊb-waḍᵊʕ ṣaʕb ᵊktiir.* 3. *waḍᵊʕ.* I'm not in a position to pay right away. *ʔana maa-li b-waḍᵊʕ ʔədfaʕ ḥaalan.* 4. *markaz* pl. *maraakez, manṣeb* pl. *manaaṣeb, waẓiife* pl. *waẓaayef.* He has a good position with a wholesale house. *ʔəlo markaz ᵊmniiḥ ᵊb-maḥall beeʕ bᵊž-žəmle.* 5. *maqaam.* A man in your position has to be careful of his appearance. *rəžžaal ᵊb-maqaamak laazem ydiir baalo ʕala maẓharo.* 6. *markaz* pl. *maraakez.* What position does he play on the team? *šuu markazo bᵊl-fariiq?* 7. *markaz* pl. *maraakez, mawḍeʕ* pl. *mawaaḍeʕ.* The brigade had to abandon the forward positions. *l-liwaaʔ nžabar yətxalla ʕan ᵊl-maraakez ᵊl-ʔamaamiyye.* 8. *mawqef* pl. *mawaaqef.* What's your position on this subject? *šuu mawᵊqfak ʔənte mən hal-mawḍuuʕ?*

positive - 1. *ʔiižaabi**. I expect a positive answer. *ʔana mətʔammel b-žawaab ʔiižaabi.* 2. *mətʔakked, ʔakiid.* I'm positive that he was there. *ʔana mətʔakked ʔənno huwwe kaan ᵊhniik.*

positively - 1. *ʔakiid, mᵊʔakkad.* Do you know it positively? *btaʕᵊrfo ʔakiid?* 2. *ḥatman.* That's positively awful! *ḥatman haš-šii faẓiiʕ!*

to **possess** - *malak (o məlk).* That's all I possess. *haada kəll ma bəmlok.*

**What possessed you to do that? *šuu ṣar-lak ḥatta ʕməlt haš-šii?*

possession - *məlkiyye, məlk.* How long has that been in your possession? *qaddeeš ṣar-lo haš-šii b-məlkiitak* (or *məlkak*)?

**They lost all their possessions. *xəsru kəll yalli ʕandon.*

to take possession of - *ḥaṭṭ (ə ḥaṭaṭ) ʔiido ʕala, tmallak.* The new owner hasn't taken possession of the house yet. *l-maalek ᵊž-ždiid ləssa maa ḥaṭṭ ʔiido ʕal-beet.*

possibility - *ʔəmkaaniyye* pl. *-aat.* I see no other possibility. *maa-li šaayef fii ʔəmkaaniyye ġeer hayy.*

possible - 1. *məmken, žaayez.* That's quite possible. *haš-šii məmken.* 2. *məmken.* Let's consider every possible step. *xalliina nəftə́ker b-kəll xaṭwe məmᵊkne* (or *b-kəll xaṭwe məmken naʕmə́la*). -- If possible, give me a ring. *ʔiza məmken saawii-li talifoon* or ***ʔiza b-ʔəmkaanak saawii-li talifoon.*

possibly - *məmken, bᵊl-ʔəmkaan, b-ʔəmkaan-* + pron. suff. Could you possibly call me? *məmken tsaawii-li talifoon?* or *bᵊl-ʔəmkaan* (or *b-ʔəmkaanak*) *tsaawii-li talifoon?*

**He works as fast as he possibly can. *byəštə́ġel ᵊb-ʕažale qadd-ma byəṭlaʕ ᵊb-ʔiido.*

post - 1. *qaaʔime* pl. *qawaaʔem.* We need new posts for our fence. *laazəmna qawaaʔem ᵊždiide mənšaan ᵊl-xəṣṣ tabaʕna.* 2. *mawqeʕ* pl. *mawaaqeʕ.* A good soldier never deserts his post. *ž-žəndi l-ᵊmniiḥ maa byətrok mawᵊqʕo ʔabadan.*

to post - 1. *ḥaṭṭ (ə ḥaṭaṭ//nḥaṭṭ).* There were soldiers posted at the bridge. *kaan fii ʕaskar maḥṭuuṭiin ʕand ᵊž-žəsᵊr.* 2. *ʕallaq.* The order has been posted since yesterday. *l-qaraar ṣar-lo mʕallaq mn ᵊmbaareḥ.* -- Post the bill on the wall. *ʕalleq ᵊl-ʔəʕlaan ʕal-ḥeeṭ.*

postage - *ʔəžret~* (pl. *ʔžuuret~*) *bariid, rasᵊm~* (pl. *rsuumet~*) *bariid.* How much is the postage on a registered letter? *qaddeeš ʔəžret ᵊl-bariid ʕal-maktuub l-ᵊmsookar?*

**The letter didn't have enough postage. *l-maktuub maa kaan ʕalée ṭawaabeʕ ᵊkfaaye.*

**There is postage due on this letter. *hal-maktuub naaqeṣ ṭawaabeʕ.*

postage free - *xaaleṣ ᵊl-ʔəžra.* Official mail is postage free. *l-bariid ᵊr-rasmi xaaleṣ ᵊl-ʔəžra.*

postage stamp - *ṭaabeʕ~* (pl. *ṭawaabeʕ~*) *bariid, buule* coll. *buul* pl. *-aat.*

post(al) card - *kart~* (pl. *kruut~*) *bosṭaal.* Did you get my post card? *waṣlak kart ᵊl-bosṭaal tabaʕi?*

picture post card - *kart~ bosṭaal ᵊmṣawaar* pl. *kruut~ bosṭaal ᵊmṣawwara.* Let's send him a picture post card. *xalliina nəbʕə́t-lo kart bosṭaal ᵊmṣawwar.*

postal rates - *taʕriifet~ bariid, rsuumet~ bariid* (pl.).

posted - 1. *məṭṭə́leʕ.* He's pretty well posted. *huwwe məṭṭə́leʕ ᵊmniiḥ.* 2. *ʕala ʔəṭṭilaaʕ.* Keep me posted! *xalliini ʕala ʔəṭṭilaaʕ!*

poster - *ʔəʕlaan* pl. *-aat.* He draws very nice posters. *byərsom ʔəʕlaanaat ḥəlwe ktiir.*

postman - *boosṭaži* pl. *-iyye, mwazzeʕ~* (pl. *-iin~*) *bariid.*

postmark - *damġet~* (pl. *-aat~*) *bariid.* This postmark is illegible. *had-damġet ᵊl-bariid maa btənqəra.*

to postmark - *damaġ (o/e damᵊġ//ndamaġ).* The letter was postmarked May fifteenth. *l-maktuub kaan madmuuġ b-taariix xamaṣṭaaʕš ʔayyaar.*

post office - 1. *markaz~* (pl. *maraakez~*) *boosṭa, markaz~ bariid.* We have five post offices. *fii ʕanna xamᵊs maraakez boosṭa.* 2. *boosṭa.* The post office is open from nine to six. *l-boosṭa btəftaḥ mn ᵊt-təsʕa ləs-sətte.*

post-office box - *sanduuq~* (pl. *sanadiiq~*) *bariid, sanduuq~ boosṭa.*

to **postpone** - *ʔažžal//tʔažžal, ʔaxxar//tʔaxxar.* I can't postpone the appointment. *maa bəqder ʔažžel ᵊl-mawʕed.*

posture - *waqfe.* She has poor posture. *waqfə́ta muu mniiḥa.*

pot - 1. *ṭanžara* pl. *ṭanaažer.* There is a pot of soup on the stove. *fii ṭanžaret šooraba ʕaṭ-ṭabbaax.* 2. *ʔəbriiq* and *briiq* pl. *ʔabariiq.* Our coffee pot holds eight cups. *ʔəbriiq ᵊl-qahwe tabaʕna byesaʕ tmən fanažiin.*

potato - *baṭaṭaaye* coll. *baṭaaṭa* pl. *baṭaṭaat* and *baṭaṭaayaat.*

potential - 1. *məḥtə́mal.* You'd do well to consider him a potential enemy. *ʔaḥsə́n-lak təʕtəbro ʕaduww məḥtamal.* 2. *qədret~ ʔəntaaž.* The industrial potential of the country is enormous. *qədret ᵊl-ʔəntaaž ᵊṣ-ṣinaaʕi tabaʕ l-ᵊblaad haaʔile.*

potentially - *b-ᵊžbəllet-* + pron. suff. He's potentially a good worker, but he keeps frittering away his energy. *huwwe b-ᵊžbəllto šaġġiil ᵊmniiḥ, laaken bidaḷḷ ybadded našaaṭo hoon w-ᵊhniik.*

potter - *faaxuuri* pl. *-iyye, faaxərži* pl. *-iyye.*

pottery - *fəxxaar.*

poultry - *fraax* (pl.), *ṭyuur daažne* (pl.).

pound - 1. (metric) *nəṣṣ~ kiilo,* (otherwise) *liibra* pl. *-aat.* Our pound weighs a bit more than the American pound. *nəṣṣ ᵊl-kiilo tabaʕna ʔatqal b-ᵊšwayye mn ᵊl-liibra l-ʔameerkaaniyye.* -- I'd like three pounds of those apples over there. *bəddi kiilo w-nəṣṣ təffaaḥ mən haadaak.* 2. *leera* pl. *-aat, waraqa* pl. *-aat* and *wraaq.* This rug cost me 250 Syrian pounds. *has-səžžaade kallafətni miiteen w-xamsiin leera (suuriyye).*

**An ounce of prevention is worth a pound of cure. *dərham wiqaaye ʔaḥsan mən qanṭaar ʕilaaž.*

pound (sterling) - *leera* (pl. *-aat*) *ʔəngliiziyye.* How much is an English pound in Syrian money? *qaddeeš btəswa l-leera l-ʔəngliiziyye b-ʕəmle suuriyye?*

to **pound** - 1. *ṭaraq (o ṭarᵊq).* We pounded on the door for five minutes before they heard us. *ṭaraqna ʕal-baab məddet xamᵊs daqaayeq qabᵊl-ma səmʕuuna.* 2. *daqq (ə daqq).* I wish our upstairs neighbors wouldn't pound kubbah at seven in the morning. *ya-reet žiiraanna l-fawaaqne maa ydəqqu kəbbe s-saaʕa sabʕa ʕala bəkra.* 3. *xafaq (o xafaqaan), daqq.* His heart was pounding with excitement. *qalbo kaan ʕam yəxfoq mən kətᵊr hayažaano.*

to **pour** - 1. *ṣabb (ə ṣabb//nṣabb).* Please pour me a cup of coffee. *mən faḍlak ṣəbb-ə́lli fənžaan qahwe.* 2. *zaxx (ə zaxx).* It's pouring out. *ʕam ᵊdəxx barra.* 3. *ddaffaq.* The crowd was just then pouring out of the theater. *n-naas kaanu waqta ʕam yəddaffaqu mn ᵊt-tiyaatro.*

to pour out - *kabb (ə kabb//nkabb).* Pour it out! *kəbba baqa!*

**She poured her troubles out to me. *faššə́t-li qalba.*

poverty - *fəqər, qəlle.* He's living in great poverty. *huwwe Eaayeš əb-fəqər mədqeE.*

poverty-stricken - *faqiir* pl. *fəqara, məEser.*

powder - **1.** *boodra.* You've got too much powder on your nose. *fii boodra ktiir Eala mənxaarek.* **2.** *sfuuf.* Take one powder with a glass of water! *xood baakeet əsfuuf maE kaaset mayy.* **3.** *baaruud.* There is enough powder here to blow up the whole town. *fii baaruud hoon kaafi yənsof əl-balad kəlla.*

to powder - *boodar.* She powdered her nose. *boodaret mənxaara.*

powdered sugar - *səkkar boodra.*

power - **1.** *qədra, ṭaaqa.* That's beyond my power. *haada fooq qədərti.* **2.** *ʔəstiṭaaEa.* I'll do everything in my power. *baEmel kəll ma b-ʔəstiṭaaEti* or ***baEmel kəll žahdi.* **3.** *ṣəlṭa, ṣəlṭaan, nufuuz.* He wields a lot of power. *ʔəlo ṣəlṭa kbiire.* **4.** *quwwe.* The machine is operated by electric power. *l-makana btəštǵel Eal-quwwe l-kahrabaʔiyye.* -- The purchasing power of the local currency is very low. *l-quwwe š-širaaʔiyye tabaE əl-Eəmle l-maḥalliyye ktiir waaṭye.* **5.** *ḥəkəm.* How long were the Socialists in power? *qaddeeš bəqyu l-ʔəštiraakiyyiin bəl-ḥəkəm?* -- When did the Republicans come into power? *ʔeemta stalamu ž-žamhuuriyyiin əl-ḥəkəm?* **6.** *doole* pl. *duwal.* The foreign ministers of the three big powers met in Geneva. *wəzaraaʔ əl-xaaržiyye tabaE əd-duwal əl-kəbra t-tlaate žtamaEu b-žaneef.* **7.** *kahraba.* The power is turned off. *l-kahraba maqṭuuEa.*

powerful - *qawi** pl. *qawaaya* and *ʔaqwiya.* He has a powerful voice. *ʔəlo ṣooṭ qawi.* -- We're dealing with powerful enemies. *naḥna mwaažhiin ʔaEdaaʔ ʔaqwiya.*

powerless - *Eaažez.* I'm sorry, I'm powerless in this matter. *mətʔassef, Eaažez ʔana b-haš-šaǵle.*

practical - *Eamali*.* That plan isn't very practical. *hal-xəṭṭa muu Eamaliyye ktiir.* -- She's a practical woman. *hiyye mara Eamaliyye.*

practically - **1.** *b-ṣuura Eamaliyye, Eamaliyyan.* You have to look at things practically. *laazem təEtəber əl-ʔašya b-ṣuura Eamaliyye.* **2.** *Eamaliyyan.* I'm practically done. *Eamaliyyan ʔana xalaṣət.* -- We're practically there now. *Eamaliyyan wṣəlna hallaq.* -- It's practically the same. *Eamaliyyan nafs əš-šii.*

practice - **1.** *tamriin.* I'm a little out of practice. *naaqəṣni tamriin šwayye.* -- Practice makes perfect. *t-tamriin biwaṣṣel ləl-ʔətqaan.* **2.** *Eaade.* I've made it a practice to get to work on time. *Eməlta Eaadti ʔəži Eaš-šəǵəl Eal-waqət.*

**Dr. Hussein has a wide practice. *d-doktoor əḥseen Eando məraḍa ktaar.*

**He's in practice now. *Eam ymaares hallaq.*

**It's easy in theory but not in practice. *hayyne naẓariyyan bass ṣaEbe Eamaliyyan.*

to practice - **1.** *tmarran.* He's practicing on the piano. *Eam yətmarran Eal-byaano.* **2.** *ṭabbaq, Eəmel b-.* If he would only practice what he preaches. *ya-reeto bass yṭabbeq halli biquulo* (or *yaEmel b-halli biquulo*). **3.** *maaras, zaawal.* How long do you have to study before you can practice law? *qaddeeš laazmak diraase qabəl-ma yəsmaḥúu-lak tmaares l-əmḥaamda?* -- Since when has he been practicing medicine? *qaddeeš ṣar-lo Eam ymaares əṭ-ṭəbb?*

Prague - *braaǵ.*

praise - *madəḥ.* The praise went to his head. *l-madəḥ kabbar raaso.*

to praise - *madaḥ (a madəḥ/nmadaḥ), ʔasna Eala.* Everybody praises his work. *kəll ən-naas btəmdaḥ šəǵlo.* -- I don't want to praise myself, but... *maa bəddi ʔəsni Eala ḥaali laaken ...*

**He praised her to the skies. *nazzəla mn əs-sama.*

prank - *ḥiile* pl. *ḥiyal, ləEbe* pl. *ləEab, daqqa* pl. *-aat.* That's a silly prank. *hayy ḥiile baayxa.*

to **pray** - **1.** *ṣalla (ṣalaa(t)).* He was praying the midday prayer when I came to his house. *kaan Eam yṣalli ṣalaat əḍ-ḍəhər lamma ʔžiit la-beeto.* **2.** (Muslim) *daEa (i duEaaʔ),* (Christian) *ṣalla.* I'll pray for you. *bədEii-lak* or *bṣallii-lak* respectively.

prayer - *ṣalda(t)* pl. *ṣalawaat;* (of supplication) *duEaaʔ* pl. *-aat.*

to **preach** - **1.** (Protestant) *waEaẓ (-yuuEeẓ waEəẓ);* (Orth. Cath.) *karaz (e karz);* (Muslim) *xaṭab (o xəṭbe).* I've never heard our new pastor preach. *ləssa maa sməEət qassiisna ž-ždiid Eam yuuEeẓ.* **2.** *waEaẓ, karaz.* Who's going to preach the sermon next Sunday? *miin bəddo yuuEeẓ yoom əl-ʔaḥad əž-žaaye?* -- Stop preaching good manners if you don't have them yourself. *haaštak tuuEeẓ b-ḥəsn əs-suluuk ʔiza ʔənte nafsak maa-lak məṭḥalli fii.*

preacher - (Christian) *waaEeẓ* pl. *wəEEaaẓ;* (Muslim) *xaṭiib* pl. *xəṭaba.*

precaution - *ʔəḥtiyaaṭ* pl. *-aat.* You should take better precautions against fire. *laazem taaxod ʔəḥtiyaaṭaat ʔaḥsan mən hayy ḍədd əl-ḥariiq.*

to **precede** - *sabaq (o sabəq).* A strange silence preceded the storm. *hduww ǵariib sabaq əl-Eaaṣfe.*

precedent - *saabiqa* pl. *-aat.* That could constitute a dangerous precedent. *haada məmken yšakkel saabiqa xəṭra.*

precious - **1.** *tamiin.* Time is precious. *l-waqət tamiin.* **2.** *tamiin, nafiis.* She gave me a very precious gift. *Eaṭətni hdiyye tamiine ktiir.*

precious stone - *ḥažar kariim* (or *tamiin* or *nafiis*) pl. *ʔaḥžar kariime (tamiine, nafiise).* Emeralds are precious stones. *z-zmərrod ḥažar kariim.*

precise - **1.** *daqiiq.* It's impossible to give a precise definition of this word. *məstaḥiil taEṭi taEriif daqiiq la-hal-kəlme.* **2.** *məḥkam, daqiiq.* That's what I call precise work! *haada bəEtəbro Ean ḥaqa šəǵəl məḥkam.*

**Those were his precise words. *haadool kaanu kəlmaato bəl-ḥarf.*

precisely - *b-ṣuura daqiiqa.* Translate this paragraph as precisely as possible. *taržə́m-li hal-faqra b-ʔadaqq ṣuura məmə̄kne.*

**That's precisely what I had in mind. *haada š-šii b-Eeeno yalli kaan əb-fəkri.*

precision - **1.** *dəqqa.* The measurements must be taken with great precision. *l-əqyaasaat laazem təttaaxad b-dəqqa ktiir.* **2.** *daqiiq.* The company specializes in the manufacture of precision instruments. *š-šərke məxtaṣṣa b-ṣənE əl-ʔaalaat əd-daqiiqa.*

predecessor - *salaf* pl. *ʔaslaaf.* His predecessor was a retired army general. *salafo kaan ženeraal mətqaaEed.*

predicate - (nominal sentence) *xabar,* (verbal sentence) *fəEəl.*

to **predict** - *tnabbaʔ b-.* He predicted the revolt almost to the day. *tnabbaʔ bəs-sawra ḥatta taqriiban ləl-yoom yalli ṣaaret fii.*

preface - *mqaddame* pl. *-aat.*

to **prefer** - *faḍḍal.* I prefer my own brand. *bfaḍḍel əl-maarka tabaEi.* -- I prefer to wait until the weather is cooler. *bfaḍḍel ʔəntə́ẓer la-yboored əṭ-ṭaqṣ.* -- Would you prefer to go to the movies? *bətfaḍḍel əṭruuḥ Eas-siinama?* -- My brother prefers cats to dogs. *ʔaxi bifaḍḍel əl-qaṭaaṭ Eal-əklaab.*

preference - *ʔafḍaliyye.* I don't give preference to anyone. *maa ḥada ʔəlo Eandi ʔafḍaliyye.*

**I have no preference. *maa btəfreq maEi.*

pregnancy - *ḥabal, ḥaməl.*

pregnant - *ḥablaane, ḥaamel* and *ḥaamle* pl. *ḥawaamel.*

to become pregnant - *ḥəblet (a ḥabal), ḥamlet (e ḥaməl).*

prejudice - *taḥaamol, taḥayyoz, taḥazzob.* I have no prejudice against him. *maa fii Eandi taḥaamol Ealée.*

to be prejudiced against - *tḥaamal Eala, tḥayyaz ḍədd, tḥazzab ḍədd.* He's prejudiced against him. *huwwe mətḥaamel Ealée.*

to be prejudiced in favor of - *tḥayyaz la-, tḥazzab la-.* I think you're prejudiced in his favor. *bẓənnak ʔənte mətḥayyə́z-lo.*

preliminary - *tamhiidi*.* After a few preliminary remarks from the chairman, the discussion began. *baEəd kam kəlme tamhiidiyye mən qəbal ər-raʔiis badet l-əmnaaqaše.*

premature - *qabəl ʔawaan-* + pron. suff. I'm afraid that step was premature. *šaayə́f-lak hal-xaṭwe kaanet qabəl ʔawaana.*

premium - *qəsṭ* pl. *qsaaṭ* and *qsuuṭa.* I have to pay the premium on my insurance. *laazem ʔədfaE əl-qəsṭ tabaE booliiṣet əs-sookarta tabaEi.*

preparation - **1.** *taḥḍiir* pl. *-aat, tartiib* pl. *-aat.* I've made all the necessary preparations for the trip. *Emələt kəll ət-taḥḍiiraat əl-laazme mənšaan əs-safra.* **2.** *taḥḍiir, tahyiiʔ.* Plans are in preparation. *l-mašariiE taḥt əṭ-taḥḍiir.*

to **prepare** - **1.** *hayyaʔ.* You'd better prepare him for the bad news. *ʔaḥsə́n-lak əthayyʔo la-hal-xabar əl-Eaaṭel.* **2.** *ḥaḍḍar.* Who's going to prepare the meal? *miin laḥa yḥaḍḍer əl-ʔakle?* **3.** *ḥaḍḍar ḥaalo.* Did you prepare for tomorrow's exam? *ḥaḍḍarət ḥaalak ləl-faḥəṣ bəkra?* -- Prepare for the worst. *ḥaḍḍer ḥaalak la-ʔaswaʔ šii*

prepared - 1. *məstEədd.* Are you prepared to go with him? *ʔənte məstEədd truuḥ maEo?* 2. *məthaḍḍer, mhaḍḍar, ḥaaḍer.* I'm prepared for the worst. *ʔana məthaḍḍer la-ʔaswaʔ šii.*
preposition - *ḥarf˜* (pl. *ḥruuf˜*) *žarr.*
to **prescribe** - *waṣaf (-yuuṣef waṣəf//nwaṣaf).* The doctor prescribed these pills for me. *l-ḥakiim waṣáf-li hal-ḥabb.*
prescription - *raašeeta* pl. *-aat, waṣfe* pl. *-aat.* Where can I get this prescription filled? *ʔani ṣaydaliyye bətsaawi-li har-raašeeta?*
presence - *ḥḍuur.* The document has to be signed in our presence. *l-wasiiq̈a laazem təmmáḍa b-əḥḍuurna.*
presence of mind - *sərEet˜ əl-xaaṭer.* I admire your presence of mind. *ʔana məEžab b-sərEet xaaṭrak.*
present - *hdiyye* pl. *hadaaya.* Did you give him a present for his birthday? *Eaṭeeto hdiyye b-Eiid miilaado?*
present - 1. *l-ḥaaḍer.* We live in the present, not in the past. *nəḥna Eaayšiin bəl-ḥaaḍer, muu bəl-maaḍi.* 2. *ḥaaḍer.* All his friends were present. *kəll rəfaqaato kaanu ḥaaḍriin.* 3. *ḥaali*, ḥaaḍer, ʔaani*.* In my present position I can't do anything else. *b-waḍEiiti l-ḥaaliyye maa fiini ʔaEmel ġeer šii.*
at present - *bəl-waqt əl-ḥaaḍer, hallaq.* He's too busy to see you at present. *huwwe mašġuul əktiir, maa byəqder yšuufak bəl-waqt əl-ḥaaḍer.*
at the present time - *(b-)hal-ʔiyyaam, bəl-waqt əl-ḥaaḍer, hallaq.* That's hard to get at the present time. *ṣaEb əktiir l-əḥṣuul Eala haš-šii (b-)hal-ʔiyyaam.*
for the present - *mənšaan hallaq, mwaqqatan.* That will be enough for the present. *ḥaaže haada mənšaan hallaq.*
to **present** - 1. *ṭaalaE.* Each separate case presents new difficulties. *kəll ḥaale mənfərde bəṭṭaaleE maṣaaEeb əždiide.* 2. *qaddam, Earaḍ (e/o Earḍ//nEaraḍ)* Why don't you present the facts as they really are? *leeš maa bətqaddem əl-waq̈aaʔeE mətəl-ma hiyye?*
to present with - *hada (i ø//nhada).* My father presented him with a gold watch. *ʔabi hadda saaEa dahab.*
to **preserve** - *ḥaafaẓ Eala, ḥafaẓ (a ḥəfəẓ).* The library has preserved these manuscripts for centuries. *l-maktabe ṣar-la q̈uruun əmḥaafẓa Eala hal-maxṭuuṭaat.* -- He struggled hard to preserve his dignity. *Eəmel kəll žahdo ḥatta yəḥfaẓ karaamto.*
preserves - *mrabbayaat* (pl.), *mEaqqadaat* (pl.).
to **preside** - *traʔʔas.* Who's going to preside over next week's meeting? *miin bəddo yətraʔʔas ʔəžtimaaE əl-ʔəsbuuE əž-žaaye?*
presidency - *raʔaase.*
president - *raʔiis* pl. *rəʔasa.* He was president of the Arab Bank. *kaan raʔiis əl-bank əl-Earabi.* -- Washington was the first President of the United States. *waašənṭon kaan ʔawwal raʔiis ləl-wilaayaat əl-məttəḥde.*
press - 1. *ṣaḥaafe, ṣəḥufiyyiin* (pl.). Will the press be admitted to the conference? *masmuuḥ ləṣ-ṣaḥaafe təḥḍar l-məʔtámar?* 2. *makbas* pl. *makaabes.* Can you operate a press? *btaEref tšaġġel makbas?* 3. *maEṣara* pl. *maEaaṣer.* They have a large olive press in that village. *fii Eandon maEṣart zeetuun əkbiire b-haḍ-ḍeeEa.* 4. *maṭbaEa* pl. *maṭaabeE.* The manuscript is ready to go to press. *l-maxṭuuṭ žaahez yruuḥ Eal-maṭbaEa.*
**The film had a good press. *l-fələm madaḥúu bəž-žaraayed.*
in press - *taḥt əṭ-ṭabəE.* The book is in press now. *l-əktaab hallaq taḥt əṭ-ṭabəE.*
to press - 1. *kawa (i kawi//nkawa).* Ask Mommy to press your pants. *quul la-ʔəmmak təkwii-lak banṭaloonak.* 2. *laaḥaq, Eaššaz, daayaq.* His creditors are pressing him. *d-dayyaaniin tabaEo Eam ylaaḥqúu.* 3. *kabas (e kabs//nkabas).* Press the button. *kbees əz-zərr* or *kbees Eaz-zərr.*
**I wouldn't press the matter any further, if I were you. *law kənt əb-maḥallak maa bəmši b-hal-qaḍiyye ʔabEad mən heek.*
pressing - *məstaEžal.* I have a pressing argument. *Eandi mawEed məstaEžal.*
pressure - *ḍaġəṭ.* We work under constant pressure. *mnəštġel taḥət ḍaġəṭ maa byəftor.*
to put pressure on - *ḍaġaṭ (a ḍaġəṭ//nḍaġaṭ) Eala.* We'll have to put pressure on him. *laazem nəḍġaṭ Ealée.*

prestige - *heebe, maq̈aam, makaane.* He enjoys great prestige among these people. *ʔəlo heebe məḥtdrame been han-naas.*
to **presume** - *ẓann (ə ẓann).* I presume he is at home. *bẓənno bəl-beet.*
to **pretend** - 1. *Eəmel (-yaEmel ø) ḥaalo.* He pretended that he was a doctor. *Eəmel ḥaalo doktoor.*-- She pretended not to know a thing about it. *Eəmlet ḥaala muu Earfaane šii Eanha ʔabadan.* 2. *dẓaahar.* He's just pretending. *Eam yədẓaahar taẓaahor bass.*
pretense - 1. *ʔəddiEaaʔ.* It's an index with no pretense at completeness. *haada fahras maa fii ʔəddiEaaʔ əb-kamaalo.* 2. *ḥiile* pl. *ḥiyal.* His illness is only a pretense. *maraḍo maa huwwe ʔəlla ḥiile.*
pretext - *Eazər* pl. *ʔaEzaar.* He's just looking for a pretext. *Eam ydawwer bass Eala Eazər.*
pretty - 1. *ḥəlu.* She's a very pretty girl. *hiyye bənət ḥəlwe ktiir.* 2. *məḥtdram.* That's a pretty mess! *hayy xarbaṭa məḥtdrame waḷḷa!* 3. = rather (no equivalent; cf. very, enough, too, somewhat, and the like): That's a pretty cheap rug. *hayy səžžaade rxiiṣa.* -- The party was pretty dull. *l-ḥafle kaanet (yaEni) baayxa.*
**He's sitting pretty. *mrasteq ḥaalo.*
pretty good - *maa bo šii, laa baʔs fii.* He's a pretty good worker. *huwwe šaġġiil maa bo šii* (or *laa baʔs fii*). -- It tastes pretty good. *ṭaEméta maa baha šii* (or *laa baʔs fiiha*).
pretty much - *taqriiban.* He eats pretty much everything. *byaakol taqriiban kəll šii.* -- It's pretty much the same. *taqriiban nafs əš-šii.*
to **prevail** - 1. *nažaḥ (a ø).* We did everything we could but nothing prevailed. *Eməlna kəll halli byəṭlaE əb-ʔiidna, bass maa fii šii nažaḥ.* 2. *saad (u ø).* This opinion prevails at the moment. *har-raʔi saaʔed bəl-waqt əl-ḥaaḍer.* 3. *məši (i ø), žara (i ø), šaaE (i ø).* The custom still prevails in some areas. *l-Eaade ləssaata maašye b-baEḍ əl-manaaṭeq.*
to prevail (up)on - *qanaE (e ø), qannaE.* Can't we prevail on you to come along? *maa mnəqder nəqənEak təži maEna?*
to **prevent** - 1. *manaE (a manəE) wuq̈uuE˜...* I couldn't prevent it. *maa ṭəleE b-ʔiidi ʔəmnaE wuq̈uuEa.* -- You could have prevented that. *kaan b-ʔəmkaanak təmnaE wuq̈uuEo.* 2. *manaE.* Nobody is going to prevent you from doing it. *maa ḥada bəddo yəmnaEak taEmel haš-šii.*
previous - *saabeq.* I met him on a previous visit. *tEarrafət Ealée b-əzyaara saabqa.* -- He had no previous experience in that field. *maa kaan Eando xəbra saabqa b-hal-ḥaqəl.*
previously - *mən qabəl.* We'll proceed then as we previously agreed. *mənkammel baqa mətəl-ma ttafaqna mən qabəl.*
price - *səEər* pl. *ʔasEaar, taman* pl. *ʔatmaan.* The prices are very high here. *l-ʔasEaar hoon əktiir ġaalye.* -- I wouldn't do that for any price. *maa baEmə́la b-ʔayy səEər* (or **...*mahma kallaf əl-ʔamər*). -- That's all I have in this price range. *haada kəll halli Eandi b-niṭaaq̈ əl-ʔasEaar haada.*
cost price - *səEər˜* (pl. *ʔasEaar˜*) *kəlfe.* I'll sell it to you at cost price. *bbiiEak-yáa b-səEr əl-kəlfe.*
to price - *saEEar.* I priced this radio in several stores. *saEEart har-raadyo b-Eəddet maḥallaat.* -- This store prices its merchandise too high. *hal-maḥall bisaEEer əbḍaaEto ktiir ġaalye.*
price range - *niṭaaq̈˜* (pl. *-aat˜*) *ʔasEaar.* That's all I have in this price range. *haada kəll halli Eandi b-niṭaaq̈ əl-ʔasEaar haada.*
to **prick** - *šakk (ə šakk).* Stop pricking your little sister with that pin. *ḥaaže baqa tšəkk ʔəxtak əẓ-ẓġiire b-had-dabbuus.*
pride - 1. *Eəzzet˜ nafs.* Don't you have any pride? *šuu maa Eandak Eəzzet nafs?* 2. *kəbriyaaʔ* (f.), *šoofet˜ ḥaal.* His pride will be his undoing some day. *kəbriyaaʔo* (or *šoofet ḥaalo*) *ləssa btəxərbo.* 3. *faxər.* He's the pride of his parents. *huwwe faxr ʔəmmo w-ʔabúu.*
to take pride in - *Etazz b-, ftaxar b-.* He takes great pride in his work. *byəEtəzz əktiir əb-šəġlo.*
to pride oneself - *Etazz b-, ftaxar b-.* She prides herself on her good cooking. *btəEtəzz əb-ṭabxa ṭ-ṭayyeb.*
priest - *xuuri* pl. *xawaarne, qassiis* pl. *qasaawse.*
priesthood - *xawrane, kahnuut.* Her son entered priesthood at the age of 25. *ʔəbənha daxal bəl-xawrane lamma kaan Eəmro xamsda Eəšriin.*

primarily – *ʔawwal šii.* He's primarily interested in tennis. *ʔawwal šii huwwe haawi tanes.*
primary school – *madrase* (pl. *madaares*) *ʔəbtidaaʔiyye.*
prime – 1. *nooɛ ʔawwal* (invar.), *məmtaaz, faaxer.* That butcher only sells prime meat. *hal-laḥḥaam bibiiɛ laḥ°m nooɛ ʔawwal bass.* 2. *zahra.* He died in the prime of life. *maat °b-zahret ɛəmro.*
prime minister – *raʔiis˜ wazaara* pl. *rəʔasa˜ wazaaraat, raʔiis˜ wəzara.*
primitive – 1. *bidaaʔi**. This custom still prevails in some primitive societies. *hal-ɛaade ləssaaha maašye ɛand baɛḍ °l-məʒtamaɛaat °l-bidaaʔiyye.* 2. *baṣiiṭ.* He built himself a primitive boat. *saawa la-ḥaalo šaxtuura baṣiiṭa.*
primus stove – *baaboor˜ (bawabiir˜) kaaz, briimus* pl. *-aat.*
prince – *ʔamiir* pl. *ʔəmara, brəns* pl. *-aat.*
princess – *ʔamiira* pl. *-aat, brənsəs* pl. *-aat.*
principal – 1. *raʔiisi**. Is that the principal reason? *s-sabab °r-raʔiisi haada?* 2. *mudiir* pl. *mədara.* The principal called the teachers into his office. *l-mudiir ʒamaɛ l-°mɛallmiin °b-maktabo.* 3. *mablaġ ʔaṣli* pl. *mabaaleġ ʔaṣliyye.* Have you paid anything on the principal? *dafaɛt ʔayy šii ɛal-mablaġ °l-ʔaṣli?*
principality – *ʔamaara* pl. *-aat.*
principle – *mabdaʔ* pl. *mabaadeʔ.* I make it a principle to save some money every month. *ɛaaməla mabdaʔi ṣammed kəll šah°r šwayyet maṣaari.* — He is a man of principles. *huwwe raʒol ṣaaḥeb mabdaʔ.*
as a matter of principle – *mabdaʔiyyan.* I don't do such things as a matter of principle. *mabdaʔiyyan ʔana maa baɛmel heek ʔašya.*
print – 1. *ḥruuf* (pl.), *ṭbaaɛa.* The print in this book is very small. *ḥruuf hal-°ktaab ktiir °zġiire.* 2. *rasme* (pl. *rsuum*) *maṭbuuɛa.* The museum has a fine collection of prints. *l-matḥaf fii maʒmuuɛa ʒamiile rsuum maṭbuuɛa.* 3. *ṣuura* pl. *ṣuwar, nəsxa* pl. *nəsax.* How many prints shall I make of each negative? *kaam ṣuura bəddak mən kəll balloora?* 4. *fəṣṭaan °mnaqqaš* pl. *faṣaṭiin °mnaqqaše.* You always look good in a print. *daayman byəlbdq-lek fəṣṭaan °mnaqqaš.*
**Is the book still in print? *hal-°ktaab nafdet ṭab°ɛto wəlla ləssa?*
**That book is out of print. *hal-°ktaab nafdet ṭab°ɛto.*
**The title page is set in beautiful print. *ṣ-ṣafḥa l-ʔuula ṭbaaɛaata mnassaḍa həlu.*
to print – 1. *ṭabaɛ (a ṭab°ɛ//nṭabaɛ).* The programs still have to be printed. *l-baraameʒ ləssa laazəmon ṭab°ɛ.* 2. *katab (o z) b-°ḥruuf maṭbaɛiyye.* Please print your name. *mən faḍlak ktoob ʔəsmak b-°ḥruuf maṭbaɛiyye.* 3. *naqqaš, naqaš (o naq°š).* Can you show me a printed material? *fiik twarʒiini qmaaš °mnaqqaš?*
**The letter was printed in yesterday's paper. *l-maktuub ṭaleɛ °b-ʒariidt °mbaareḥ.*
printed matter – *maṭbuuɛaat* (pl.). What are the postage rates for printed matter? *šuu rsuum °l-bariid ɛal-maṭbuuɛaat?*
printer – *maṭbaɛʒi* pl. *-iyye, ṭabbaaɛ* pl. *-iin.*
print shop – *maṭbaɛa* pl. *maṭaabeɛ.*
priority – *ʔasbaqiyye.*
prism – *manšuur* pl. *manaašiir.*
prison – *səʒ°n* pl. *sʒuun, ḥab°s* pl. *ḥbuus.* The prison is heavily guarded. *s-səʒ°n fii ɛaləe ḥraase qawiyye.* — The court sentenced him to five years in prison. *l-maḥkame ḥakmet ɛaləe b-xams °sniin səʒ°n.*
prisoner – *maḥbuus* pl. *maḥabiis, saʒiin* pl. *səʒana.* A prisoner has just escaped. *fii waaḥed maḥbuus harab mən šwayye.*
prisoner of war – *ʔasiir* pl. *ʔəsara.*
to take prisoner – *ʔasar (e/o ʔas°r//nʔasar).* He was taken prisoner in France. *nʔasar b-°fransa.*
private – 1. *ɛaskari* pl. *ɛasaaker.* He was a private in the First World War. *kaan ɛaskari b°l-ḥarb °l-ɛaalamiyye l-ʔuula.* 2. *xaaṣṣ.* This is my private property. *haada məlki l-xaaṣṣ.* 3. *xṣuuṣi**, *xaaṣṣ.* Do you have a private entrance where you live? *fii ʔəlak madxal °xṣuuṣi b°l-maḥall yalli saaken fii?* — His private secretary got married last week. *səkrəteerto l-xaaṣṣa dzawwaʒet °ʒ-ʒəmɛa l-maaḍye.*
in private – *waḥd-* + pron. suff., *ɛala ʔənfiraad.* I'd like to talk to you in private. *bəddi ʔəḥki maɛak waḥ°dna.*
privation – *ḥərmaan.*
privilege – *ʔəmtiyaaz* pl. *-aat.* He was denied all privileges. *ḥaramuu mən kəll ʔəmtiyaazaato.*
**If you want to leave, it's your privilege. *ʔiza bəddak tətrok, haada mən ḥaqqak.*
**It would be a privilege to do it for you. *bisərrni saawii-lak-ydaha.*
prize – *ʒaayze* pl. *ʒawaayez.* Who won the first prize? *miin rəbeḥ °ʒ-ʒaayze l-ʔuula?*
probability – *ʔəḥtimaal* pl. *-aat.*
probable – *məḥtdmal, mraʒʒaḥ.* It might be possible, but it isn't very probable. *biʒuuz ykuun məmken, bass muu ktiir məḥtdmal.*
probably – *fii ʔəḥtimaal, məḥtdmal.* You'll probably meet him on the train. *fii ʔəḥtimaal °tšuufo b°t-treen.*
problem – 1. *məš°kle* pl. *mašaakel.* We all have our problems. *kəll waaḥed mənna ɛando mašaaklo.* — That's your problem. *hayy məškəltak ʔənte.* 2. *masʔale* pl. *masaaʔel.* I couldn't solve the second problem. *maa qdər°t ḥəll °l-masʔale t-taanye.* 3. *ṣaɛ°b.* She's a problem child. *hiyye bən°t ṣaɛbe.*
to proceed – *kammal.* Will the attorney for the defense please proceed? *byətfaḍḍal muḥaami d-difaaɛ w-bikammel?*
proceeds – *ʔiiraad* pl. *-aat.* The proceeds will go to charity. *l-ʔiiraad biruuḥ ləl-ʔaġraaḍ °l-xeeriyye.*
process – 1. *ṭariiqa* pl. *ṭəroq.* That process was worked out in our laboratory. *haṭ-ṭariiqa btakarnaaha b-maxbarna.* 2. *ɛamaliyye* pl. *-aat.* That will be a long drawn-out process. *hayy bətkuun ɛamaliyye bəṭṭuul.*
to process – 1. *waḍḍab//twaḍḍab, ḥaḍḍar//tḥaḍḍar.* The crude oil is then processed in various installations. *z-zeet °l-xaam mən baɛda ɛam yətwaḍḍab b-maṣaaneɛ məxtəlfe.* 2. *dawwar °mɛaamalet˜* ... The consulate is going to process your visa application. *l-qənṣliyye laḥa ddawwer °mɛaamalt °l-viiza tabaɛak.*
procession – *mawkeb* pl. *mawaakeb.*
to proclaim – *ʔaɛlan.* The fourth of July was proclaimed a holiday. *ʔaɛlanu yoom ʔarbaɛ tammuuz ɛəṭle.*
proclamation – *ʔəɛlaan* pl. *-aat;* (public notice) *balaaġ* pl. *-aat.*
to produce – 1. *ʔantaʒ.* We don't produce enough grain. *maa ɛam nənteʒ °ḥbuub °kfaaye.* — How many cars do they produce a month? *kam sayyaara byəntʒu b°ʒ-ʒah°r?* 2. *ʔabraz, ṭaalaɛ.* Can you produce any written proof? *fiik təbrez daliil xaṭṭi?* 3. *ʔaḥdas, sabbab.* The incident produced a political chain reaction. *l-ḥaades ʔaḥdas səlsəlt radd fəɛl syaasi.*
product – 1. *mantuuʒ* pl. *-aat.* They're selling agricultural products. *ɛam ybiiɛu mantuuʒaat ziraaɛiyye.* 2. *ḥaaṣel.* The product of five times four is twenty. *ḥaaṣel ḍar°b xamse b-ʔarbɛa ɛəšriin.*
production – *ʔəntaaʒ.*
productive – *xəṣeb, xaṣiib, məxṣeb.* He's a very productive writer. *huwwe kaateb xəṣeb °ktiir.*
profession – *məhne* pl. *məhan.* What's his profession? *šuu məh°nto?*
professional – *məḥtəref, məmtəhen.* He's a professional gambler. *huwwe mqaamer məḥtəref.*
**All of our friends are professional people. *kəll rəfaʔaatna ʔaṣḥaab məhan ḥərra.*
professor – *ʔəstaaz* pl. *ʔasaadze.*
assistant professor – *ʔəstaaz °msaaɛed.*
associate professor – *ʔəstaaz bala kərsi.*
full professor – *ʔəstaaz °b-kərsi.*
profit – *marbaḥ* pl. *maraabeḥ, rəb°ḥ* pl. *ʔarbaaḥ, maksab* pl. *makaaseb.* I sold it at a profit. *bəɛto b-marbaḥ.* — Does the business show any profit? *haš-šəġ°l ɛam yṭaaleɛ šii marbaḥ?*
**I don't expect to get any profit out of that. *maa-li mətwaqqeɛ ʔəstfiid mən haš-šaġle ʔabadan.*
to profit – *stafaad.* I didn't profit much by the lecture. *maa stafadt °b-šii ktiir mən l-°mḥaaḍara.*
**You profit from your mistakes. *btətɛallam mən ġalṭaatak.*
profitable – *mərbeḥ.* Is it a profitable business? *t-tiʒaara mər°bḥa?*
profound – *ɛamiiq, ġamiiq.* He inspired a profound confidence in all who worked with him. *kaan ɛam yuuḥi b-siqa ɛamiiqa b-kəll halli štaġalu maɛo.* — That was a very profound remark! *hayy kaanet °mlaaḥaẓa ɛamiiqa waḷḷa!*
program – *bərnaameʒ* pl. *baraameʒ, broogṛaam* pl. *-aat.*

The program sells for ten piasters. *l-bərnaamež byənbaaɛ b-ɛašr ᵊqruuš.* -- How did you like the program? *šloon ḥabbeet ᵊl-broograam?* -- What's on our program tonight? *šuu bərnaaməžna l-yoom?*
progress - *taqaddom.* The students are showing good progress. *ṭ-ṭəllaab ɛam ywaržu taqaddom ᵊmniiḥ.*
to make progress - *tqaddam.* Are you making any progress with your book? *ɛam tətqaddam b-ᵊktaabak šii?*
to progress - *tqaddam.* You've progressed a lot in the six weeks I've been away. *tqaddamt ᵊktiir bᵊs-sətt žəmaɛ yalli kənt ġaayeb fiiha.*
progressive - **1.** *taqaddumi*.* Their methods are progressive. *ʔasaliibon taqaddumiyye.* **2.** *məddarrež.* The evening came on in progressive stages. *l-leele ʔəžet ᵊb-maraaḥel məddarže.*
to **prohibit** - *manaɛ (a manᵊɛ//mmanaɛ).* The law prohibits the sale of liquor on Sunday. *l-qaanuun byəmnaɛ beeɛ ᵊl-xumuur yoom ᵊl-ʔaḥad.*
project - *mašruuɛ* pl. *mašariiɛ.* We're working on a project together. *ɛam nəštəgel ɛala mašruuɛ sawa.* -- The City is planning new housing projects. *l-baladiyye naawye tquum b-mašariiɛ sakan ᵊždiide.*
to project - **1.** *ɛaraḍ (o ɛarᵊḍ//nɛaraḍ).* The film was projected on the wall. *l-fəlm ᵊnɛaraḍ ɛal-ḥeeṭ.* **2.** *baraz (o bruuz).* The beams project from the wall. *ž-žsuura baarze mn ᵊl-ḥeeṭ.*
projecting - *baarez.*
projector - *broožektoor* pl. *-aat.*
to **prolong** - *ṭawwal.* You're only prolonging the agony. *ʔənte bass ɛam ᵊṭṭawwel ᵊl-ɛazaab.*
prominent - **1.** *məɛtəbar, baarez.* He's a prominent artist. *huwwe fannaan məɛtəbar.* **2.** *baarez.* He has a prominent chin. *daqno baarze.*
promise - **1.** *waɛᵊd* pl. *wɛuud.* You didn't keep your promise. *maa wafeet ᵊb-waɛdak.* **2.** *tabašiir* (pl.). These recent events hold out some promise of change. *hal-ḥawaades ᵊl-ʔaxiire fiiha tabašiir taġyiir.*
to promise - *waɛad (-yuuɛed waɛᵊd//nwaɛad) b-.* We promised him a present. *waɛadnəa b-ᵊhdiyye.* -- Promise me that you won't do it again. *wɛədni ʔənnak maa taɛməla taani marra.*
promising - *mbaššer bᵊl-xeer.* The project flopped after a very promising start. *l-mašruuɛ fəšel baɛᵊd bidaaye ktiir ᵊmbaššra bᵊl-xeer.*
promissory note - *kəmbyaale* and *kəmbyaaliyye* pl. *-aat.*
to **promote** - **1.** *raffaɛ//traffaɛ, raqqa//traqqa.* He was promoted to captain. *traffaɛ la-rətbet raʔiis.* **2.** *šaššaɛ, naššaṭ.* Most countries promote their foreign trade. *ʔaktar ᵊd-duwal bətšaššeɛ tižaarəton ᵊl-xaaržiyye.*
promotion - **1.** *tarfiiɛ* pl. *-aat, taraqqi* pl. *-iyaat.* The list of promotions was in yesterday's paper. *liistet ᵊt-tarfiiɛaat ṭəlɛet ᵊb-žariidt ᵊmbaareḥ.* **2.** *taššiiɛ, tanšiiṭ.* The new agreement stresses the promotion of cultural exchanges between the two countries. *l-ʔəttifaaq ᵊž-ždiid ɛam yrakkez ɛala taššiiɛ ᵊt-tabaadol ᵊs-saqaafi been ᵊl-baladeen.*
prompt - *ɛaažel, sariiɛ.* I expect a prompt reply. *mətwaqqeɛ žawaab ɛaažel.*
**He's prompt in paying his debts. *byədfaɛ dyuuno ɛal-waqᵊt.*
to prompt - *daɛa (i ø).* What prompted you to say that? *šuu yalli daɛaak ᵊtquul heek?*
promptly - **1.** *ɛad-daqiiqa, ɛat-tamaam.* We start promptly at five. *mənballeš ᵊs-saaɛa xamse ɛad-daqiiqa.* **2.** *ɛal-waqᵊt.* Make sure that this letter is mailed promptly. *xalli baalak hal-maktuub yənbəɛet ɛal-waqᵊt.* **3.** *ḥaalan, ɛal-foor, ɛal-ḥaarek.* He made the move and promptly lost the game. *ɛəmel ᵊn-naqle w-xəṣer ḥaalan.*
pronoun - see under **personal, relative,** etc.
to **pronounce** - **1.** *lafaẓ (o lafᵊẓ//ltafaẓ), naṭaq (o nəṭᵊq).* Am I pronouncing the word correctly? *ɛam ʔəlfoẓ ᵊl-kəlme maẓbuuṭ?* **2.** *ɛaṭa (-yaɛṭi ø).* The judge will pronounce sentence tomorrow. *l-qaaḍi byaɛṭi ḥəkmo bəkra.*
pronunciation - *lafᵊẓ, nəṭᵊq.* That's not the correct pronunciation. *haada muu l-lafẓ ᵊl-maẓbuuṭ.*
proof - **1.** *bərhaan* pl. *barahiin, daliil* pl. *ʔadəlle.* What proof do you have of that? *šuu bərhaanak ɛala haš-šaġle?* -- You have no proof. *maa fii ɛandak daliil.* --Can you furnish any written proof? *fiik ᵊdžiib šii bərhaan xaṭṭi?* **2.** *məswadde* pl. *-aat.* I've just finished reading proof on my new article. *hallaq xallaṣᵊt taṣḥiiḥ məswaddet maqaalti.*
prop - *sannaade* pl. *-aat.* One of the props is giving way. *fii sannade laḥa təqaɛ.*
to prop - *sanad (o sand//nsanad).* You'd better prop the tree before it falls. *ʔaḥsən-lak təsnod ᵊš-šažara qabᵊl-ma təqaɛ.*
propaganda - *diɛaaye, brobaġanda.*
propeller - *barawaane* pl. *-aat.*
proper - **1.** *mnaaseb, laayeq, mlaayem.* That isn't the proper way to handle people. *hayye muu ṭ-ṭariiqa l-ᵊmnaasbe yalli bətɛaamel fiiha n-naas.* -- That's not proper. *haada muu laayeq.* **2.** *mnaaseb.* This isn't the proper time to ask questions. *haada muu l-waqᵊt l-ᵊmnaaseb la-təsʔal fii suʔaalaat.* -- Everything at the proper time. *kəll šii b-waqto l-ᵊmnaaseb.* **3.** *nafs-* + pron. suff., *zaat-* + pron. suff. In 1937 the Japanese invaded China proper. *sənt sabɛda w-tlaatiin l-yaabaan haažamet ᵊṣ-ṣiin nafsa.*
properly - **1.** *ɛal-maẓbuuṭ.* I'll show you how to do it properly. *bwaržiik kiif bətsaawiiha ɛal-maẓbuuṭ.* **2.** *mətᵊl-ma laazem.* Can't you behave properly? *šuu maa fiik tətṣarraf mətᵊl-ma laazem?* or ***maa fiik tətṣarraf mətl ᵊl-ɛaalam wᵊn-naas?*
proper name - *ʔəsᵊm~* (pl. *ʔasmaaʔ~*) *ɛalam.*
property - **1.** *məlk, šyaat* (pl.). All the furniture is my property. *kəll ᵊl-moobiilya məlki* or ***kəll ᵊl-moobiilya tabaɛi.* **2.** *ɛaqaar* pl. *-aat.* He has a mortgage on his property. *fii rahniyye ɛala ɛaqaaṛo.*
prophet - *nabi* pl. *ʔanbiya.*
proportion - **1.** *tanaasob.* The proportions in that picture are all wrong. *t-tanaasob b-haṣ-ṣuura kəllo ġalaṭ.* **2.** *nəsbe.* Everybody is paid in proportion to what he does. *kəll waaḥed byəndəfəɛ-lo b-nəsbet šəġlo* (or ***ɛala ḥawa šəġlo*). -- His expenses are entirely out of proportion to his income. *maṣariifo muu b-nəsbet daxlo ʔabadan* or ***maṣariifo maa btətnaasab maɛ daxlo ʔabadan.*
proportional - **1.** *nəsbi*.* The graph shows the proportional distribution of rainfall. *l-ᵊmxaṭṭaṭ ᵊl-bayaani ɛam ywarži t-tawziiɛ ᵊn-nəsbi la-tasaaqoṭ ᵊl-ʔamṭaar.* **2.** *mətnaaseb.* His skill is proportional to his experience. *mahaarto mətnaaseb maɛ xəbᵊrto.*
proportioned - *mətnaaseb.* Her figure is well proportioned. *žəsma mətnaaseb tamaam.*
proposal - *ʔəqtiraaḥ* pl. *-aat, ɛarᵊḍ* pl. *ɛruuḍ(a).* He made me an interesting proposal. *qaddəm-li ʔəqtiraaḥ məġri.*
to **propose** - *qtaraḥ.* I propose that we go to the movies. *bəqtəreḥ ᵊnruuḥ ɛas-siinama.*
to propose to - *tqaddam la-.* He proposed to her at last. *tqaddəm-la l-ḥamdəlla.*
proposition - **1.** *ʔəqtiraaḥ* pl. *-aat, ɛarᵊḍ* pl. *ɛruuḍ(a).* He made him an excellent proposition. *ɛəməl-lo ʔəqtiraaḥ məmtaaz.* **2.** *šaġle.* Is it a paying proposition? *hayy šaġle məḥᵊrze?* -- That's going to be an expensive proposition. *haš-šaġle bədda tkuun məkᵊlfe ɛan ḥaqa.* **3.** *faraḍ* pl. *fruuḍ(a).* The proposition could not be verified. *hal-faraḍ maa ʔamkan ᵊt-taḥaqqoq mənno.*
proprietor - *maalek* pl. *məllaak, ṣaaḥeb* pl. *ṣḥaab.*
pros and cons - *maḥaasen w-masaaweʔ.* I first want to consider all the pros and cons of the proposal. *ʔawwal šii bəddi waazen been kəll maḥaasen w-masaaweʔ ᵊl-ʔəqtiraaḥ.*
prose - *nasᵊr.*
rhymed prose - *sažᵊɛ.*
prospect - **1.** *ʔamal* pl. *ʔaamaal.* What are his prospects of getting the job? *qaddeeš ʔamalo yəḥṣal ɛala hal-waẓiife?* **2.** *məstaqbal.* What are your prospects on that job? *šuu məstaqbalak b-hal-waẓiife?* **3.** *fəkra.* I don't like the prospect of having to work with that man at all. *maa-li ḥaabeb ʔabadan fəkret šəġli maɛ haz-zalame.*
to **protect** - **1.** *ḥama (i ḥmaaye//nḥama).* I wear these glasses to protect my eyes. *ḥaaṭeṭ ʔana hal-kəzlok la-ʔəḥmi ɛyuuni.* **2.** *ḥaafaẓ ɛala.* He'll protect your interests. *biḥaafeẓ ɛala maṣaalḥak.*
protection - *ḥmaaye.* There is no protection against that. *maa fii ḥmaaye ḍəḍḍa.*
protectorate - *maḥmiyye* pl. *-aat.*
protest - *ʔəḥtižaaž* pl. *-aat.* The country has lodged a formal protest with the Security Council. *d-doole qaddamet ʔəḥtižaaž rasmi la-mažles ᵊl-ʔamᵊn.*
to protest - **1.** *ḥtažž.* I protest against this kind of treatment. *ʔana bəḥtažž ɛala hal-ᵊmɛaamale.* **2.** *ʔakkad.* He protested his innocence throughout the trial. *ʔakkad baraaʔto ṭuul məddet l-ᵊmḥaakame.*
Protestant - *brootəsṭanṭi** coll. pl. *brootəsṭanṭ.*
Protestantism - *brootəsṭanṭiyye.*
protocol - *brootokool, tašriifaat* (pl.), *marasiim*

(pl.). Protocol requires that ... *l-brootokool byəṭṭallab ʔənno ...*
proud - **1.** *məftəxer, məƐtazz.* I am proud of you. *ʔana məftəxer fiik.* **2.** *mətkabber, šaayef ḥaalo.* He's considered a proud and pompous person. *b-raʔi n-naas huwwe waaḥed mətkabber w-mətbaššeh.*
**She's too proud to ask for other people's help. *nafsa Ɛaziize la-təṭlob mn ən-naas maƐuune.*
to **prove** - **1.** *barhan Ɛala, ʔasbat.* I can prove I didn't do it. *fiini barhen ʔənno maa saaweeta ʔana.* -- Can he prove his claim? *fii ybarhen Ɛala ʔəddiƐaaʔo?* or *fii yəsbet ʔəddiƐaaʔo?* **2.** *dall (ə ø) Ɛala, barhan Ɛala, ʔasbat.* That doesn't prove much. *haada maa bidəll Ɛala šii ktiir.*
to prove to be - *ṭəleƐ (a ø).* The rumor proved to be false. *l-ʔišaaƐa ṭəlƐet kaazbe.*
proverb - *matal* pl. *ʔamtaal.*
to **provide** - **1.** *mawwan.* They provided us with supplies to last two weeks. *mawwanuuna b-muune kaafye la-žəmƏƐteen.* **2.** *zawwad.* The company will provide you with the necessary equipment. *š-šərke bədzawwdak bət-tažhiizaat əl-laazme.*
to provide for - **1.** *Ɛaal (i ø), qaddam la-, qaam (u qyaam) b-.* He has to provide for the whole family. *Ɛalée yƐiil kəll əl-Ɛeele.* **2.** *ḥasab (o ø) əḥsaab la-.* The law provides for such special cases. *l-qaanuun byəḥsob əḥsaab la-ḥaalaat xaaṣṣa mən haš-šəkəl.* **3.** *ḥtaaṭ la-.* We should provide for a very cold winter. *laazem nəḥtaaṭ la-šətwiyye baarde ktiir.*
to provide against - *ḥtaaṭ ḍədd.* The measure is to provide against the spread of diseases. *hat-tadbiir ġaayto əl-ʔəḥtiyaaṭ ḍədd tafašši l-ʔamraaḍ.*
provided - *b-šarṭ, Ɛala šarṭ, šarṭ ʔənno.* I'll go, provided you come with me. *bruuḥ b-šarṭ ətruuḥ maƐi.*
providing - *b-šarṭ, Ɛala šarṭ, šarṭ ʔənno.* We'll leave tomorrow, providing we won't have heavy rain. *mənsaafer bəkra b-šarṭ maa tənzel maṭar ətqiile.*
province - **1.** *mḥaafaẓa* pl. *-aat.* Syria is divided into several provinces. *suuriyya mqassame la-Ɛəddet əmḥaafaẓaat.* **2.** *mqaaṭaƐa* pl. *-aat.* He was transferred to one of the western provinces. *naqalúu la-mqaaṭaƐa mən l-əmqaaṭaƐaat əl-ġarbiyye.*
provision - **1.** *naṣṣ* pl. *nṣuuṣ.* There is no provision in this contract for health insurance. *maa fii naṣṣ əb-hal-əmqaawale mənšaan əḍ-ḍamaan əṣ-ṣəḥḥi.* **2.** *band* pl. *bnuud, maadde* pl. *mawaadd.* According to this provision, you're required to register within three days. *ḥasab hal-band Ɛaleek ətsažžel ḥaalak ḍəmn ətlətt iyyaam.*
provisions - *muune.* Our provisions are running low. *muunətna Ɛam ətqəll.*
to **provoke** - **1.** *ʔasaar.* His remark provoked a roar of laughter. *mlaaḥaẓto ʔasaaret Ɛaaṣfe mn əḍ-ḍəḥək.* **2.** *tḥadda.* Don't provoke him any more. *ḥaaže təṭḥaddda baqa.*
prune - *xooxa mžaffafe* coll. *xoox əmžaffaf* pl. *xooxaat əmžaffafe.* I don't care much for prunes. *maa bḥəbb əktiir əl-xoox l-əmžaffaf.*
to **prune** - *šaffa//tšaffa.* The rosebushes need to be pruned. *l-ward bəddo təšfaaye.*
Prussia - *bruusya.*
Prussian - *bruusi*.*
psychiatrist - *ṭabiib nafsaani* pl. *ʔaṭəbba nafsaaniyye.*
psychiatry - *ṭəbb nafsaani.*
psychoanalysis - *taḥliil nafsaani.*
psychoanalyst - *mḥallel nafsaani* pl. *mḥalləliin nafsaaniyyiin.*
psychological - *psikolooži*, nafsaani*.*
psychologist - *psikolooži* pl. *-iyyiin.*
psychology - *psikoloožya, Ɛəlm~ ən-nafs.*
public - **1.** *naas, Ɛaalam.* Is this park open to the public? *hal-ḥadiiqa maftuuḥa lən-naas?* **2.** *ǧərraaʔ* (pl.). Such books will always find a public. *heek kətəb daayman bətlaaqi ǧərraaʔ.* **3.** *Ɛaamm.* Public opinion is against him. *r-raʔi l-Ɛaamm ḍəddo.* -- The new government has taken all measures to ensure public safety. *l-əḥkuume ž-ždiide Ɛəmlet kəll ət-tadabiir la-təkfal əl-ʔamn əl-Ɛaamm.* **4.** *Ɛmuumi*.* Is there a public telephone near here? *fii talifoon əƐmuumi b-han-nawaaḥi?* **5.** *Ɛalani*.* There is a public auction tomorrow. *fii bəkra mazaad Ɛalani.* **6.** *ḥkuumi*.* He sends his boy to a public school. *haaṭeṭ ʔəbno b-madrase ḥkuumiyye.*
**They say he embezzled public funds. *biquulu xtalas ʔamwaal əd-doole.*
public prosecutor - *məddaƐi Ɛaamm* pl. *məddaƐiin Ɛaammiin, naaʔeb Ɛaamm* pl. *nəwwaab Ɛaammiin.*
in public - *qəddaam əl-Ɛaalam.* That's no way to behave in public. *muu ḥeek əl-waaḥed byətṣarraf qəddaam əl-Ɛaalam.*
publication - **1.** *našər.* The publication of his thesis cost him a lot of money. *našər ʔəṭruuḥto kallafo maṣaari ktiir.* **2.** *našra* pl. *-aat, (manšuur)* pl. *manšuuraat.* The number of their publications is increasing month after month. *Ɛadad našraaton Ɛam yəzdaad šahər Ɛan šahər.*
publicity - *diƐaaye.* That's what I call clever publicity. *hayy Ɛan ṣaḥiiḥ diƐaaye ḥaazqa.* -- He gave me a lot of publicity. *Ɛəmə́l-li diƐaaye ktiir.*
to **publish** - *našar (o našər//ntašar), ṭaalaƐ.* He hopes to publish his new book very soon. *mətʔammel yənšor əktaabo ž-ždiid Ɛan qariib əktiir.* -- Who is going to publish your book? *miin laḥa yənšə́r-lak əktaabak?*
publisher - *naašer* pl. *-iin.*
publishing house - *daar~ (pl. duur~) našər.*
puddle - *waḥle* pl. *waḥəl.* Careful, don't step into that puddle! *ʔəṣḥa laa təmši b-hal-waḥle.*
puff - *saḥbe* pl. *-aat, nafxa* pl. *-aat.* I got sick after only one puff. *laƐet nafsi baƐəd saḥbe waaḥde (mn əs-siigaara).*
pull - **1.** *saḥbe* pl. *-aat, šadde* pl. *-aat.* One more pull, and we'll have it open. *kamaan saḥbe w-byənfə́teḥ.* **2.** *dafəš.* You need a lot of pull to get a job here. *bəddak dafš əktiir la-təḥṣal Ɛala šii šaġle hoon.*
to pull - **1.** *saḥab (a saḥəb), žarr (ə žarr).* Don't pull so hard. *laa təsḥab b-quwwe.* -- She pulled him away from the edge of the gorge. *saḥəbto mən ṭaraf əl-huwwe.* **2.** *qalaƐ (a qaləƐ//nqalaƐ).* The tooth must be pulled. *s-sənn laazem yənqə́leƐ.*
**Don't pull any funny stuff! *laa tətfaṣḥan!*
**Don't try to pull the wool over my eyes! *laa tḥaawel təstažədəbni!*
**He pulled a fast one on me. *ṣardƐa Ɛaliyyi.*
**I pulled a (big) boner. *saaweet-ə́llak ḍarəb ḥeewane ləl-Ɛama.*
**Pull over to the side! *ṣəff Ɛala žanab!*
to pull apart - **1.** *fakk (ə fakk//nfakku) Ɛan baƐḍon.* The two pieces are fitted in such a way that you can pull them apart easily. *l-qəṭəƐteen faaytiin b-baƐḍon b-šəkəl ʔənnak fiik ətfəkkon Ɛan baƐḍon b-əshuule.* **2.** *saḥab (a saḥəb//nsaḥabu) Ɛan baƐḍon.* We had to pull the two dogs apart by the scruff of their necks. *ḍṭarreena nəsḥab l-əklaab Ɛan baƐḍon mn ərqaabon.* **3.** *fakfak šaqfe šaqfe.* He had to pull the whole car apart before he found what was wrong. *nžabar yfakfek əl-Ɛarabiyye šaqfe šaqfe qabəl-ma laqa əl-Ɛəṭəl.*
to pull back - **1.** *saḥab la-wara, ražžaƐ la-wara.* He pulled me back from the curb. *saḥabni la-wara mn əl-kərb.* **2.** *qaam (i ø//nqaam), saḥab (a saḥəb// nsaḥab).* Pull back the curtains. *qiim əl-baraadi.*
to pull down - **1.** *nazzal.* Shall I pull down the shades? *nazzel əl-baraadi ž-žarraar?* **2.** *hadam (o hadəm//nhadam).* They're going to pull down all the old houses. *laḥa yəhədmu kəll l-əbyuut əl-Ɛatiiqa.*
to pull in - *wəṣel (-yəṣal wṣuul).* When did your train pull in? *ʔeemta t-treen tabaƐak wəṣel?*
to pull oneself together - *šadd ḥaalo.* Pull yourself together! *šədd ḥaalak baqa!*
to pull out - **1.** *qalaƐ (a qaləƐ//nqalaƐ), qaam (i ø//nqaam).* The children pulled out all the grass. *l-əwlaad qalaƐu kəll əl-ḥašiiš.* **2.** *məši (i məši), ṭəleƐ (a ṭluuƐ), tḥarrak.* The train will pull out any minute. *t-treen qarrab yəmši.*
to pull through - *nafad (o ø).* We were afraid she might not pull through. *xəfna ktiir maa tənfod.*
to pull up - **1.** *ʔəža w-waqqaf.* The car pulled up in front of the house. *s-sayyaara ʔəžet w-waqqafet qəddaam əl-beet.* **2.** *saḥab (a ø), žarr (ə ø).* Pull up a chair. *sḥab-lak kərsi.*
pulley - *bakara* pl. *-aat.*
pullover - *kanze* pl. *-aat.*
pulse - *nabəḍ, nabəṭ.* The nurse just took my pulse. *l-əmmarrḍa hallaq ʔaxdet nabḍi.*
pump - **1.** *ṭrəmbe* pl. *-aat, mḍaxxa* pl. *-aat.* We have a pump in the barnyard. *fii Ɛanna ṭrəmbe bəl-ḥooš.* **2.** *mənfaax* pl. *manafiix.* Somebody stole the pump from my bicycle. *fii ḥada saraq əl-mənfaax tabaƐ bəsəkleetti.*
to pump - **1.** *daqq (ə daqq).* Shall I pump some water from the well? *dəqq-ə́llak šwayyet mayy mn əl-biir?* **2.** *saḥab (a saḥəb//nsaḥab).* They pump

the oil into the waiting tankers. *byəshabu z-zeet la-ḥaamlaat ᵊl-batrool ᵊl-manṭᵊzra.* 2. *stanzal.* Don't let him pump you. *laa txallīi yəstanᵊzlak.*

to pump up – 1. *saḥab (a saḥᵊb//nsaḥab).* Our water is pumped up from the spring. *mayyətna mnəsḥába mn ᵊn-nabᵊƐ.* 2. *nafax (o nafᵊx//ntafax).* Will you please pump up the front tires? *ballа nfəx-li d-duulaabeen ᵊl-qəddaamaaniyye.*

pumpkin – *yaqṭiine* coll. *yaqṭiin* pl. *-aat.*

punch – 1. *ḍarbe* pl. *-aat, lakme* pl. *-aat.* The punch knocked him down. *ḍ-ḍarbe ṭarᵊḥto.* 2. *daafeƐ.* His speech lacked punch. *xiṭaabo kaan naaqṣo d-daafeƐ.*

to punch – 1. *baxaš (o/e baxᵊš//nbaxaš).* The conductor punched our tickets. *l-kəmᵊsyaari baxaš biileetaatna.* 2. *ḍarab (o ḍarb//nḍarab).* Shut up or I'll punch you in the nose! *xraas wəlla bəḍᵊrbak Ɛala wəššak!* or ***sədd niiƐak wəlla bəlweq ḥanakak!*

punch – *panš.* Would you like some more punch? *btaaxə́d-lak šwayyet panš kamaan?*

puncture – *banšara* pl. *-aat.* Is there a puncture in the tire? *fii banšara bᵊd-duulaab?*

to puncture – *baxaš (o/e baxᵊš//nbaxaš), baxwaš// tbaxwaš.* He has a punctured eardrum. *ṭablet ʔədno mabxuuše.*

to **punish** – *žaaza//džaaza, qaaṣaṣ//tqaaṣaṣ, Ɛaaq̈ab// tƐaaq̈ab.* You shouldn't punish the child for a little thing like that. *maa byəswa džaazi l-walad Ɛala šii taafeh mətᵊl haad.* -- I think he's been punished enough. *bẓənno džaaza kfaaye.*

punishment – *žaza, qṣaaṣ, Ɛiq̈aab, Ɛuq̈uube.* The punishment was too severe. *ž-žaza kaan ᵊktiir qaasi.*

**Our car took a lot of punishment on that trip. *sayyaarətna ḥtaraq diina b-has-safra.*

pupil – *təlmiiz* pl. *talamiiz,* also *talaamze.* She has twenty pupils in her class. *fii Ɛandha Ɛəšriin təlmiiz ᵊb-ṣaffa.*

pupil – *bəbbu* pl. *bəbbuyaat.* The pupil of the left eye is injured. *bəbbu l-Ɛeen ᵊš-šmaal mažruuḥ.*

puppet – *maryuneet* pl. *-aat.*

puppy – *kuut* pl. *kwaat, žaru* pl. *ʔəžᵊrwe.*

purchase – *šarwe* pl. *-aat.* We haven't made any major purchases lately. *maa saaweena šarwaat ᵊkbiire mᵊʔaxxaran.*

to purchase – *štara.* They purchased a house on the road to Beirut. *štaru beet Ɛala ṭariiq beeruut.*

pure – 1. *xaaleṣ* (invar.), *ṣərf* (invar.). The necktie is pure silk. *l-ᵊkraafe ḥariir xaaleṣ.* -- Do you have pure alcohol? *fii Ɛandkon kuḥuul ṣərf?* 2. *Ɛal-mazbuuṭ.* That's pure nonsense! *haada ʔakᵊl hawa Ɛal-mazbuuṭ!* or ***kəllo ʔakᵊl hawa haada!*

purple – *Ɛənnaabi*.*

purpose – 1. *maqṣuuḍ, qaṣᵊḍ, ġaaye, ġaraḍ.* What's the purpose of all these plans? *šuu l-maqṣuuḍ mən kəll hal-mašariiƐ?* 2. *qaṣᵊḍ, ġaaye.* What purpose did he have in doing that? *šuu kaan qaṣḍo mən Ɛamal haš-šii?* 3. *ġaaye* pl. *-aat, maqṣaḍ* pl. *maqaaṣeḍ, ġaraḍ* pl. *ʔaġraaḍ.* The tool can be used for many purposes. *l-ʔaale məmken ʔəstaƐmaala la-Ɛəddet ġaayaat.*

on purpose – 1. *Ɛan qaṣᵊḍ.* I left my coat home on purpose. *tarakᵊt manṭooyi bᵊl-beet Ɛan qaṣᵊḍ.* 2. *Ɛan Ɛamᵊd, Ɛan qaṣᵊḍ.* Did you do that on purpose? *Ɛməlt haš-šii Ɛan Ɛamᵊd?*

to accomplish (or **serve** or **fill**) **the purpose** – *qaam (u ø) bᵊl-ġaraḍ ᵊl-manšuud.* His intervention accomplished its purpose. *tadaxxlo qaam bᵊl-ġaraḍ ᵊl-manšuud.*

purse – 1. *šantet˜* (pl. *-aat˜*) *ʔiid.* This purse doesn't go well with my new dress. *haš-šantet ᵊl-ʔiid muu raayḥa maƐ fəsṭaani ž-ždiid.* 2. *žaayze* (pl. *žawaayez*) *maaliyye.* The purse was divided among the winners. *ž-žaayze twazzaƐet Ɛar-raabḥiin.*

(change) purse – *žəzdaan* pl. *žazadiin.* I have either mislaid or lost my change purse. *yaa maa baƐref ween ḥaṭṭeet žəzdaani yaa ḍawwaƐto.*

to **pursue** – *laaḥaq, taabaƐ.* I don't want to pursue the subject any further. *maa bəddi laaḥeq ᵊl-mawḍuuƐ ʔaktar.*

pus – *Ɛamal, q̈eeḥ.*

push – *dafše* pl. *-aat.* He gave me such a push that I nearly fell over. *dafašni dafše kənt laḥa ʔəqaƐ fiiha.*

to push – *dafaš (o dafᵊš//ndafaš).* Push the table over by the window. *dfooš ᵊṭ-ṭaawle naaḥ ᵊš-šəbbaak.* -- Don't push! *ḥaaše tədfoš yaa!* -- He was pushed way back. *ndafaš la-ʔaaxer ᵊl-kəll.* 2. *kabas (e kabᵊs//nkabas).* Did you push the button? *kabast ᵊz-zərr?* 3. *daḥaš (a daḥᵊš) ḥaalo, ndaḥaš, zdaḥam.* The crowd pushed into the elevator. *ž-žamaaƐa daḥašu ḥaalon bᵊl-ʔaṣanṣoor daḥᵊš.*

**He tried to push the blame on me. *ḥaawal yḥəṭṭ ᵊl-ḥaqq Ɛaliyyi.*

**I tried in vain to push my way through the crowd. *ḥaawalᵊt biduun faayde šəqq ṭariiqi bᵊl-ḥašᵊd.*

pustule – *basra* pl. *-aat* and *bsuur.*

to **put** – 1. *ḥaṭṭ (ə ḥaṭaṭ//nḥaṭṭ).* Put the table over there. *ḥəṭṭ ᵊṭ-ṭaawle hniik.* -- Did you put stamps on all the letters? *ḥaṭṭeet ṭawaabeƐ Ɛal-makatiib kəlla?* -- Where shall I put the trunks? *ween ḥəṭṭ ᵊs-sanadiiq?* -- Put an ad in the paper. *ḥəṭṭ ʔəƐlaan bᵊž-žariide.* -- Put it in writing. *ḥəṭṭa xaṭṭiyyan.* 2. *waḍaƐ (-yuuḍaƐ waḍᵊƐ//nwaḍaƐ), ḥaṭṭ.* That puts me in an embarrassing position. *haada byuuḍaƐni* (or ***bixalliini*) *b-waḍᵊƐ məḥrež.* -- I'll have to put an end to that nonsense. *laazem ʔuuḍaƐ ḥadd la-hal-masxara.* -- Can't you put a stop to that talk? *maa btəqder tuuḍaƐ ḥadd la-hal-Ɛalk?* -- Let's put the question to a vote. *xalliina nḥəṭṭ ᵊl-masʔale Ɛat-taṣwiit.*

**I wouldn't put any faith in that story. *law ᵊb-maḥallak maa bsaddeq hal-qəṣṣa ʔabadan.*

**Why don't you put it straight to him? *leeš maa bətqəl-lo-yḍaha b-kəll ṣaraaḥa?*

**Let me put it this way: I don't care. *w-ᵊb-kəlme ʔəxra: maa bihəmmni.*

**Put it this way: He doesn't like me and I don't like him. *b-kəlme ʔəxra: maa bḥəbbo w-laa biḥəbbni.*

**You stay put until I get back. *xalliik hoon la-ʔəržaƐ.*

**It's a feeling that is hard to put into words. *haada šuƐuur ṣaƐb ᵊt-taƐbiir Ɛanno b-kalaam.*

to put across – 1. *fahham.* I don't know how to put it across to him that ... *maa-li Ɛarfaan kiif bəddi fahhmo ʔənno ...* 2. *naha (i ø), xallaṣ.* Did you put the deal across? *naheet ᵊṣ-ṣafq̈a?*

to put aside (or **away**) – 1. *ṣammad, ḥaṭṭ Ɛala žanab.* She's been putting aside a little money each month. *ṣar-la madde Ɛam ᵊtṣammə́d-la šwayyet maṣaari kəll šahᵊr.* 2. *ḥaṭṭ (ə ḥaṭaṭ//nḥaṭṭ) Ɛala žanab.* Put your books away now and answer the following questions. *ḥəṭṭu kətᵊbkon Ɛala žanab hallaq w-žaawbu l-ʔasʔile l-ʔaatiye.*

to put away – 1. *qaam (i ø//nqaam).* Have you put your summer clothes away yet? *qəmti ʔawaaƐiiki ṣ-ṣeefiyye wəlla ləssa?* 2. *xabba//txabba, ḥafaẓ (a ḥəfᵊẓ//nḥafaẓ).* Put your jewelry away in a safe place. *xabbi maṣaaġek ᵊb-maḥall ʔamiin.*

to put back – *ražžaƐ.* Put the book back where you got it. *ražžeƐ l-ᵊktaab la-maṭraḥ-ma žəbto.*

to put by – *ṣammad, ḥaṭṭ Ɛala žanab.* I manage to put by a few pounds every month. *Ɛam yəṭlaƐ ᵊb-ʔiidi ṣammed kam leera kəll šahᵊr.*

to put down – 1. *ḥaṭṭ (ə ḥaṭaṭ//nḥaṭṭ).* Do you want me to put the box down here? *bəddak-yḍani ḥəṭṭ ᵊs-sanduuq hoon.* 2. *katab (o ø), ḥaṭṭ.* Put down your name and address. *ktoob ʔəsmak w-Ɛənwaanak.*

to put in – 1. *ṣaraf (o ṣarᵊf//nṣaraf), ḥaṭṭ (ə ḥaṭaṭ//nḥaṭṭ).* They put in a lot of time on that job. *ṣarafu waqt ᵊktiir Ɛala haš-šaġle.* 2. *rakkab, ḥaṭṭ.* Did they put in a new windowpane? *rakkabu looḥ balloor ᵊždiid?*

**Will you put in a word for me? *btəšfḍƐ-li?*

to put off – 1. *maaṭal b-.* I can't put off the matter any longer. *maa Ɛədt ᵊqder maaṭel b-haš-šaġle.* 2. *maaṭal.* Can't you put him off for a while? *maa fiik ᵊtmaaṭlo šwayye?* 3. *ʔaxxar, ʔažžal.* Let's put off the decision until tomorrow. *xalliina nᵊʔaxxer ᵊl-q̈araar la-bəkra.* -- I can't put off the appointment. *maa bəqder ʔažžel ᵊl-mawƐed.*

to put on – 1. *ḥaṭṭ (ə ḥaṭaṭ//nḥaṭṭ).* Put on a clean tablecloth! *ḥəṭṭi šlaalet ṭaawle ndiife!*-- Have you put on some water? *ḥaṭṭeet šwayyet mayy?* 2. *ləbes (e ləbᵊs//nlabas).* Put your hat on! *lbees bərneeṭṭak!* -- Which dress shall I put on? *ʔanu fəsṭaan ʔəlbes?* 3. *šaƐal (o/e šaƐᵊl//nšaƐal), fataḥ (a fatᵊḥ//nfataḥ).* Put on the light, please. *balla šƐool ᵊḍ-ḍaww.* 4. *zaad (i zyaade).* I've put on three kilos. *zədt ᵊtlatt kiiloyaat.* 5. *tṣannaƐ.* Don't you think her accent is put on? *maa btəftə́ker ʔənno lahžə́ta mətṣannaƐa?*

to put oneself out – *ġallab ḥaalo, zaƐaž (e ø) ḥaalo.* Don't put yourself out on my account. *laa tġalleb ḥaalak mənšaani.*

to put out – 1. *ṭafa (i ṭafi//nṭafa).* The fire

was put out quickly. ṭafu n-naar ᵊb-sərεa.
2. ṭafa, sakkar. Put out the light before you leave. ʔəṭfi ḍ-ḍaww qabᵊl-ma truuḥ. 3. ṭaalaε la-barra. Put him out if he makes too much noise. ṭaalεo la-barra ʔiza saawa qarwaše. 4. ṭaalaε, našar (o našᵊr//ntašar). Who's putting out your book? miin εam yṭaaləε-lak ᵊktaabak?

to put out(side) — ṭaalaε la-barra, ḥaṭṭ (ə ḥaṭaṭ//nḥaṭṭ) barra. Did you put the garbage out? ṭaalaεt ᵊz-zbaale la-barra?

to put over on — ləεeb (a ləεᵊb//ltaεab) εala. You can't put anything over on him. maa fiik taləεab εalée b-šii.

to put through — mašša. He put his own plan through. mašša xəṭṭᵊto huwwe.

to put together — 1. ḥaṭṭ (ə ḥaṭaṭ//nḥaṭṭu) maε baεḍon, rakkab maε baεḍon. Let's try to put these various pieces together. xalliina nžarreb ᵊnḥəṭṭ hal-qəṭaε ᵊl-məxtəlfe maε baεḍon. 2. ḍamm (ə ḍamm//nḍammu). He put his hands together as if he were about to pray. ḍamm ʔidée la-baεḍon kaʔənno raḥa yṣalli. 3. ḥaṭṭ sawa. Put them together in one room and you have the nicest row inside of five minutes. ḥəṭṭon sawa b-ʔuuḍa waaḥde w-maa byəmḍa xamᵊs daqaayeq ʔəlla btəsmaε la-xnaaqa məḥtḍrame.

**It wasn't so hard to find out; I just put two and two together. maa kaanet ᵊl-masʔale məεᵊžže, maa hiyye ʔəlla tneen w-tneen ʔarbεa.

to put up — 1. ḥaṭṭ (ə ḥaṭaṭ//nḥaṭṭ). New telephone poles are being put up. εam yḥəṭṭu εawamiid talifoon ᵊždiide. — We put up a fence around the house. ḥaṭṭeena xəṣṣ ḥawaali l-beet. — Who'll put up bail for him? miin laḥa yḥəṭṭ-əllo kafaale? — Each of them put up a thousand dollars. kəll waaḥed mənhon ḥaṭṭ ʔalf doolaar. 2. bana (i bina//nbana). This building was put up in six months. hal-binaaye nbanet ᵊb-sətt əšhor. 3. nazzal//tnazzal, ḥaṭṭ//nḥaṭṭ, waḍaε (-yuuḍaε waḍᵊε//nwaḍaε). The farm will be put up for sale this week. l-mazraεa laha tətnazzal εal-beeε haš-žəmεa. 4. rafaε (a rafᵊε//rtafaε). They've put up the price of butter again. rafaεu səεr ᵊz-zəbde taani marra. 5. ʔaawa. Can you put us up for the night? btəqder tʔaawiina εandak ᵊl-leele?

**They didn't put up a fight. maa daafaεu.

to put up to — ḥarraḍ εala. His friends put him up to it. rəfaqaato ḥarraḍu εala haš-šaġle.

to put up with — 1. hadam (o hadᵊm), tḥammal. I don't know why you put up with his insolence. maa baεref leeš εam təhḍom waqaaḥto. 2. ṣabar (o ṣabᵊr//nṣabar) εala, tḥammal. You have to put up with a few hardships. laazem təṣbor εala šwayyet mataaεeb.

put out — zaεlaan. He felt quite put out about it. kaan zaεlaan ᵊktiir mən haš-šaġle.

putty — maεžuune.

puzzle — ḥəzzeera pl. -aat, ləġᵊz pl. ʔalġaaz. Can you solve that puzzle? fiik ᵊtḥəll hal-ḥəzzeera? 2. ləġᵊz. That is a puzzle to me. haada ləġᵊz εaliyyi.

to puzzle — ḥayyar. His letter had us puzzled. maktuubo ḥayyarna.

to puzzle out — ḥall (ə ḥall//nḥall). I can't puzzle it out. maa-li qaader ḥəlla.

pyjama(s) — biižaama pl. -aat.

pyramid — haram pl. ʔahraam and ʔahraamaat.

Q

quack — dažžaal pl. -iin.

quadrangle — mrabbaε pl. -aat.

qualification — 1. ʔahliyye pl. mʔahhlaat. Do you think she has the necessary qualifications for the job? btəftəkəra εanda l-ᵊmʔahhlaat l-laazme ləš-šaġle? 2. taḥaffoẓ. I approve of it without qualification. ʔana mwaafeq εalée biduun taḥaffoẓ.

to **qualify** — 1. ḥaddad maεna˜ ... I'd like to qualify my previous statement to the effect that ... bəddi ḥadded maεna kalaami s-saabeq ʔənno ...
2. ʔahhal. That will hardly qualify him for this kind of work. haada muu məḥtdmal yʔahhlo la-han-nooε mn ᵊš-šəġᵊl.

**But she doesn't qualify for this position! laakənna hiyye muu ʔahᵊl la-hal-markaz!

qualified — ʔahᵊl (invar.). He is not qualified for this job. huwwe muu ʔahᵊl la-hal-waẓiife.

qualitative — nooεi*.

quality — 1. žəns pl. ʔažnaas, nooε pl. ʔanwaaε. Don't you have any better quality? maa fii εandak žəns ʔaḥsan? 2. miize pl. -aat, xəṣle pl. xəṣal, ṣifa pl. -aat. She has many good qualities. εanda εəddet miizaat ᵊmniiḥa. 3. ṭayaabe, žuude. We guarantee the quality of our product. mnəḍman ṭayaabet mantuužna. 4. keefiyye. It's a matter of quality, not of quantity. l-masʔale masʔalt keefiyye, muu masʔalt kammiyye.

quantitative — kammi*.

quantity — kammiyye pl. -aat. It's not the quantity but the quality that counts. l-ᵊmhəmm muu l-kammiyye, bass ᵊl-keefiyye. — Radios are now produced in large quantities. r-raadyoyaat εam tənṣəneε hallaq b-kammiyyaat ḍaxme.

in quantity — b-kətre, b-kammiyyaat. We buy in quantity. mnəštəri b-kətre.

quarantine — karantiina pl. -aat, maḥžar ṣəḥḥi pl. maḥaažer ṣəḥḥiyye. He has to remain in quarantine for two weeks. mažbuur yəqεod bᵊl-karantiina məddet žəmᵊεteen.

to quarantine — kartan//tkartan, ḥažar (o ḥažᵊr//nḥažar) εala. The health authorities had to quarantine the passengers of the ship. ṣ-ṣəlṭaat ᵊṣ-ṣəḥḥiyye ḍṭarret tkarten rəkkaab ᵊl-baaxra.

quarrel — xnaaq(a) pl. -aat and xanaayeq. Who started the quarrel? miin ballaš l-ᵊxnaaqa?

to quarrel — txaanaq. Let's not quarrel. maa bəddna nətxaanaq. — Why do you always have to quarrel with him? leeš daayman btətxaanaq maεo?

quarry — maḥžar pl. maḥaažer, maqlaε pl. maqaaleε.

quarter — 1. rəbᵊε pl. rbaaε. Each partner received a quarter of the profits. kəll ᵊšriik ʔaxad rəbε ᵊl-ʔarbaaḥ. — The company is prospecting for oil in the Empty Quarter. š-šərke εam ᵊtnaqqeb εaz-zeet bᵊr-rəbε ᵊl-xaali. — The train leaves at a quarter to three. t-treen byəmši s-saaεa tlaate ʔəlla rəbᵊε. — It's a quarter after ten already. ṣaaret ᵊs-saaεa εašara w-rebᵊε. 2. rəbᵊε (˜leera) pl. rbaaε (˜leera). This comb costs a quarter. hal-məšṭ ḥaqqo rəbᵊε leera.

quarters — maskan pl. masaaken, beet pl. byuut. Did you find decent quarters? laqeet-əllak maskan ᵊmniiḥ?

to quarter — sakkan. The soldiers were quartered in an old house. sakkanu l-εaskar b-beet εatiiq.

quarterly — kəll ᵊtlətt əšhor. I pay my insurance quarterly. bədfaε s-sookarta tabaεi kəll ᵊtlətt əšhor.

**The academy publishes a well-known quarterly. l-mažmaε εam yṭaaleε mažalle maεruufe btəṣdor kəll ᵊtlətt əšhor.

queen — 1. malake pl. -aat. Her Majesty, the Queen. žalaalet ᵊl-malake. 2. bənᵊt pl. banaat. I had a jack, a king, and three queens in my hand. kaan maεi šabb w-ʔəxtyaar w-ᵊtlətt banaat. 3. fərᵊz pl. fruuze, waziir pl. wəzara. I took the pawn with the queen. ʔakalt ᵊl-beedaq bᵊl-fərᵊz.

queer — šaazz. He's a queer bird. huwwe waaḥed šaazz. — What a queer idea! məlla fəkra šaazze!

to **quench** — rawa (i ə). I simply can't quench my thirst. šuu-ma baεmel maa-li εam ʔərwi εaṭaši.

question — 1. suʔaal pl. -aat and ʔasʔile. Have you any further questions? fii ʔəlak šii suʔaalaat taanye? — They asked a lot of questions. saʔalu suʔaalaat ᵊktiir. 2. šakk, riibe. There is no question about it. haš-šii maa fii šakk. — His honesty is beyond question. ʔamaanto maa fiiha riibe. 3. masʔale pl. masaaʔel. It was a question of saving a human life. l-masʔale kaanet masʔalet taxliiṣ ḥayaat bašariyye. — It's a question whether it's worth the trouble. l-masʔale hiyye ʔiza btəḥrez wəlla laʔ.

**Mr. Chairman, I call for the question! yaa ḥaḍret ᵊr-raʔiis ʔaržuuk ṭarḥ ᵊl-qaḍiyye εat-taṣwiiṭ.

**That's completely out of the question. haš-šii məstaḥiil.

**It's still an open question whether he'll do it or not. l-masʔale ləssaaha taḥt ᵊl-ʔaxd wᵊr-radd

ʔiza byaεməla wəlla laʔ.
question mark – *εalaamet˜* (pl. *-aat˜*) *ʔəstəfhaam.*
in question – *maεni*, maqṣuud.* The gentleman in question was not there. *s-sayyed əl-maεni maa kaan əhniik.*
to question – 1. *stažwab.* The police questioned him all night long. *š-šərṭa stažwabəto ṭuul əl-leel.* 2. *šakk (ø šakk) b-, rtaab b-, tsaaʔal εan.* I question his sincerity. *bšəkk əb-ʔəxlaaṣo.*
questionnaire – *liistet˜* (pl. *-aat˜*) *ʔasʔile.*
queue – *ṣaff* pl. *ṣfuuf, xaṭṭ* pl. *xṭuuṭ.* There was a long queue of people in front of the box office. *kaan fii ṣaff ṭawiil mn əl-εaalam qəddaam əl-giišée.*
to queue up – *ṣaffu (ø ø) ḥaalon.* Why are all those people queuing up there? *leeš kəll han-naas εam yṣəffu ḥaalon əhniik?*
quick – 1. *sariiε.* That was a quick decision. *haada kaan q̈araar sariiε.* 2. *šaaṭer.* He's very quick with numbers. *huwwe ktiir šaaṭer bəl-ʔaεdaad.*
**Be quick about it! *yaḷḷa staεžel (fiiha)!*
to quicken – *sarraε, staεžal b-.* He quickened his steps. *sarraε xaṭwaato.*
quickly – *b-sərεa, b-εažale.*
quickness – *sərεa, εažale.*
quicksilver – *zeebaq.*
quick-tempered – *nəzeq.* She is very quick-tempered. *hiyye nəzqa ktiir.*
quiet – 1. *hduuʔ, hduww.* I demand absolute quiet. *bəddi hduuʔ taamm.* — Quiet, please! *hduuʔ mən faḍəlkon!* 2. *haadi.* I live in a quiet neighborhood. *ʔana saaken əb-ḥayy haadi.*
to keep quiet – *tamm (a ø) saaket, sakat (o skuut).* Why didn't you keep quiet? *leeš maa tammeet saaket?*
to quiet (down) – 1. *hadda.* See if you can quiet her. *šuuf ʔiza fiik əthaddiiha.* 2. *hədi (a ø).* Let's wait till the excitement quiets down a bit. *xalliina nəstanna la-ḥatta yəhda l-əhyaaž šwayye.*
quilt – *lḥaaf* pl. *ləḥəf* and *ʔələḥfe.* The quilt isn't very warm. *l-lḥaaf maa bidaffi mniiḥ.*
quinine – *kiina.*
to quit – 1. *tarak (o/e tark), daššar, baṭṭal mən.* He quit his job yesterday. *tarak šaġəlto mbaareḥ.* 2. *tarak, daššar.* He quit right in the middle of the race. *tarak əb-nəṣṣ əs-sabaq.* 3. *waqqaf.* It's time to quit. *ṣaar waqt ənwaqqef.*
**Quit it! *ḥaaže baqa!* or *xalaṣna baqa!*
quite – 1. *tamaam.* Are you quite sure that you can't go? *ʔənte mətʔakked tamaam ʔənno maa fiik ətruuḥ?* — Have you finished reading the book? – Not quite. *xalaṣt əqraayet l-əktaab? – muu tamaam.* 2. *εan ḥaqa, εal-maḍbuuṭ.* That was quite an experience! *kaanet tažərbe εan ḥaqa!* 3. *ktiir.* That's quite possible. *ktiir žaayez* or *ktiir maεquul.* 4. (frequently not expressed at all:) It turned quite cold during the night. *ṣaaret əd-dənye bard ʔasnaaʔ əl-leel.*
quits – *xlaaṣ.* We're quits now. *ṣərna xlaaṣ hallaq.*
quorum – *niṣaab.*
quotation – 1. *ʔəstəšhaad* pl. *-aat.* His speech was full of quotations. *xiṭaabo kaan malaan ʔəstəšhaadaat.* 2. *səεər* pl. *ʔasεaar.* I follow the quotations of the stock market regularly. *btaabeε ʔasεaar əl-buurṣa b-ʔəntiẓaam.*
quotation mark – *εalaamet˜* (pl. *-aat˜*) *tanṣiiṣ.*
to quote – 1. *stašhad b-.* That passage's quoted on page ten. *hal-maqṭaε məstašhad fii bəṣ-ṣafḥa l-εaašra.* 2. *naqal (o naqəl//ntaqal) εan əlsaan˜ ..., stašhad b-.* Don't quote me. *laa tənqol εan əlsaani.* 3. *εaṭa (-yaεṭi ø).* What price did he quote you? *ʔayy səεər εaṭaak?*
quotient – *xaarež (˜ əl-q̈əsme).*

R

rabbi – *xaaxaam* pl. *-iyye, ḥaaxaam* pl. *-iyye.*
rabbit – *ʔarnab* pl. *ʔaraaneb.*
rabble – *ġawġaaʔ, ruεaaε.*
rabies – *kalab.*
race – 1. *sabaq* pl. *-aat, sbaaq* pl. *-aat.* When does the race start? *ʔeemta byəbda s-sabaq?* — Are you going to the bicycle races? *raayeḥ εala sabaq(aat) əl-bəsəkleetaat?* — He won the 400-meter race. *rəbeḥ əsbaaq l-ʔarbaε miyye.* 2. *sbaaq˜* (pl. *-aat˜*) *xeel.* I'm going to the races. *ʔana raayeḥ εala sbaaq əl-xeel.*
to race – 1. *rakad (o rakəd).* We raced to the nearest telephone. *rakadna la-ʔawwal talifoon.* 2. *tsaabaq.* Let's race. *xalliina nətsaabaq.* 3. *saabaq.* I'll race you to that tree over there. *bsaabqak la-hadiik əš-šažara hniik.* 4. *zawwar εala, zaayar.* Don't race the engine. *laa dzawwer εal-motoor.*
**The car raced through the streets. *s-sayyaara kaanet εam əṭṭiir ṭayaraan bəš-šawaareε.*
race – *εənṣor* pl. *εanaaṣer.* There is no such thing as a pure race. *maa fii šii ʔəsmo εənṣor xaaleṣ.*
racial – *εənṣuri*.*
racialism – *εənṣuriyye.*
rack – 1. *ṭarabeeza* pl. *-aat.* Put the books back on the rack. *ražžeε əl-kətəb εaṭ-ṭarabeeza.* 2. *raff* pl. *rfuuf.* Put your baggage up on the rack. *ḥəṭṭ šanaatiik εar-raff.* 3. *taεliiqa* pl. *-aat.* I hung my coat on the rack. *εallaqət manṭooyi εat-taεliiqa.*
to rack one's brains – *halak (e/o ø) ədmaaġo.* Don't rack your brains over it. *laa təhlek ədmaaġak fiiha.*
racket – 1. *qarwaše, ḍooše, šoošara.* The children are making an awful racket. *l-əwlaad εam yaεəmlu qarwaše faẓiiεa.* 2. *εawanṭa.* This whole business is nothing but a racket. *haš-šaġle maa hiyye ʔəlla εawanṭa b-εawanṭa.*
(tennis) racket – *mədrab* pl. *madaareb.* Her racket is much too heavy for you. *l-mədrab tabəεa ktiir ətqiil εaleeki.*
racketeer – *εawanṭaži* pl. *-iyye.*
radar – *raadaar.*
radiation – *ʔəšεaaε.*
radiator – *raadyatoor* pl. *-aat.* Our room has two radiators. *b-ʔuuḍətna fii raadyatooreen.* — Something is wrong with the radiator of my car. *fii šii manzuuε bər-raadyatoor tabaε sayyaarti.*
radical – 1. *radikaali** pl. *-iyyiin, məṭṭarref* pl. *-iin.* I consider him a radical. *bəεtəbro waaḥed radikaali huwwe.* 2. *ḥarf ʔaṣli* pl. *ḥruuf ʔaṣliyye.* What are the three radicals of this verb? *šuu l-əḥruuf əl-ʔaṣliyye t-tlaate tabaε hal-fəεəl?* 3. *məṭṭarref, radikaali*.* He has very radical views. *ʔəlo ʔaaraaʔ məṭṭarrfe ktiir.* 4. *žawhari*, ʔasaasi*.* He wants to make some radical changes. *bəddo yaεmel εəddet taġyiiraat žawhariyye.*
radicalism – *radikaaliyye.*
radio – 1. *raadyo, ʔizaaεa.* I heard the entire concert over the radio. *sməεt əl-koonseer kəllo bər-raadyo.* 2. *raadyo* pl. *raadyoyaat.* We bought ourselves a new radio. *štareena raadyo ždiid.* — Turn off the radio. *sakker ər-raadyo.*
radio station – *mḥaṭṭet˜* (pl. *-aat˜*) *ʔizaaεa, mḥaṭṭet˜ raadyo.* Have you seen the new radio station they're building outside of town? *šəft əmḥaṭṭet əl-ʔizaaεa ž-ždiide yalli εam yεammruuha barraat əl-balad?*
radish – *fəžle* coll. *fəžəl* pl. *-aat.* Shall I slice up the radish? *qaṭṭəε-lak əl-fəžle?*
(red) radish – *fəžle* coll. *fəžəl* pl. *-aat.* I'd like a bunch of radishes. *εaṭiini žərzet fəžəl.*
radius – 1. *nəṣṣ˜ q̈əṭər* pl. *nṣaaṣ˜ ʔaq̈ṭaar.* The circle's radius is approximately 50 cm. *nəṣṣ q̈əṭr əd-daayre taqriiban xamsiin ṣanti.* 2. *mada.* The plane has a radius of no more than 500 miles. *ṭ-ṭayyaara madaaha muu ʔabεad mən xaməs miit miil.*
raft – *ṭawwaafe* pl. *-aat.*
rafter – *žəsər* pl. *žsuur(a).*
rag – *xərqa* pl. *xruuq, šarṭuuṭa* pl. *šaraṭiiṭ.* Do you have a rag to dust the table? *fii εandak xərqa la-ʔəmsaḥ əṭ-ṭaawle?*
rags – *ʔawaaεi šaraṭiiṭ* (pl.), *ʔawaaεi mšarṭaṭa* (pl.). They were all (clad) in rags. *kaanu laabsiin kəllon ʔawaaεi šaraṭiiṭ.*
rage – *ġeeẓ, ʔəġtiyaaẓ, ġaḍab.* What's the cause of his rage? *šuu sabab ġeeẓo?*
**My father flew into a rage when I told him. *ʔabi ṭəleε diino lamma qəlt-əllo.*
**Brocade is all the rage nowadays. *r-rkiid ṣaayer εal-əbrookaar hal-ʔiyyaam.*
to rage – 1. *ġtaaẓ.* He raged like a stuck bull. *ġtaaẓ mətəl toor haayež.* 2. *εaṣaf (o εaṣəf), haaž (u hayažaan, hyaaž).* The storm raged all night

long. *l-ƹaaṣfe kaanet ƹam təƹṣof ṭuul ᵊl-leel.*
ragged - *mšarṭaṭ, mxazwaq.*
raid - 1. *ġaara* pl. *-aat.* We didn't have any air raids during the war. *maa ṣaar ƹanna ġaaraat žawwiyye waqt ᵊl-ḥarb.* 2. *mdaahame* pl. *-aat.* The police raid on the night club took place shortly before midnight. *mdaahamt ᵊš-šərṭa ləl-kabaréé žaret qabᵊl nəṣṣ ᵊl-leel b-ᵊšwayye.*
to raid - *daaham.* The police raided the place last night. *š-šərṭa daahamet ᵊl-maḥall leelt ᵊmbaareḥ.*
rail - *qaḍiib* pl. *qəḍbaan.* A loose rail seems to have caused the accident. *ẓ-ẓaaher ʔənno šii qaḍiib maḥluul kaan sabab ᵊl-ḥaades.*
railing - *darabziin* pl. *-aat.* Hold on to the railing. *mseek ᵊd-darabziin.*
railroad - 1. *səkket˜* (pl. *səkak˜*) *ḥadiid, səkke ḥadiidiyye.* They're building a new railroad now. *ƹam yƹammru səkket ḥadiid ᵊždiide hallaq.* 2. *treen, səkket˜ ḥadiid.* I prefer to go by railroad. *bfaḍḍel saafer bᵊt-treen.*
railroad crossing - *maƹbar˜* (pl. *maƹaaber˜*) *səkket˜ ḥadiid.*
railroad station - *mḥaṭṭet˜* (pl. *-aat˜*) *səkket˜ ḥadiid, mḥaṭṭet˜ treen.* I'm going to the railroad station. *raayeḥ ƹala mḥaṭṭet səkket ᵊl-ḥadiid* (or ***ƹal-ᵊmḥaṭṭa*).
railroad track - *xaṭṭ ḥadiidi* pl. *xṭuuṭ ḥadiidiyye.*
railway see **railroad.**
rain - *maṭar* (f.) pl. *ʔamṭaar, šəte.* We stayed home because of the rain. *bqiina bᵊl-beet b-sabab ᵊl-maṭar.*
to rain - *maṭṭaret, nəzlet (e nzuul) maṭar, šattet.* It rained hard all morning. *maṭṭaret ᵊb-šədde ṭuul ᵊṣ-ṣabaaḥ.*
**It's raining cats and dogs. *ƹam ᵊdəxx zaxx.*
rainbow - *qooṣ˜* (pl. *qwaaṣ˜*) *qazaḥ.*
raincoat - *mšammaƹ* pl. *-aat, tranškoot* pl. *-aat.*
rainfall - *huṭuul˜ ʔamṭaar.*
rainy - *məmṭer, maaṭer.* We've been having rainy weather for the past weeks. *ṭ-ṭaqᵊṣ kaan məmṭer ᵊž-žəmaƹ ᵊl-maaḍye.*
**The rainy season usually starts in the middle of December. *muusem ᵊl-maṭar ƹaadatan byəbda b-nəṣṣ kaanuun ᵊl-ʔawwal.*
**You should put away a little money for a rainy day. *xabbi qəršak ᵊl-ʔabyaḍ la-yoomak ᵊl-ʔaswad.*
raise - *zyaadet˜* (pl. *-aat˜*) *maƹaaš.* He got a raise. *ʔəžda zyaadet maƹaaš.*
to raise - 1. *rafaƹ (a rafᵊƹ//rtafaƹ* and *nrafaƹ).* They're raising the bridge. *ƹam yərfaƹu ž-žəsᵊr.* — All in favor, raise hands! *l-ᵊmwaafqiin yərfaƹu ʔideehon!* — They raised the building in six months. *rafaƹu l-binaaye b-sətt əšhor.* -- You don't have to raise your voice; I can hear you all right. *muu laazem tərfaƹ ṣooṭak, ƹam ʔəsmaƹak ᵊmniiḥ.* — The rent will be raised on October 1st. *l-ʔažaar laḥa yərtéfeƹ b-ᵊawwal təšriin ᵊl-ʔawwal.* — Finally, the court raised the injunction. *w-bᵊn-nihaaye l-maḥkame rafƹet ᵊl-ḥaẓᵊr.* 2. *dabbar, žamaƹ (a žamᵊƹ//nžamaƹ), lamm (ə lamm//ltamm).* I couldn't raise the money. *maa qdərt dabbər ᵊl-maṣaari.* 3. *zaraƹ (a zarᵊƹ//nzaraƹ).* They raise a lot of wheat here. *byəzraƹu qamḥ ᵊktiir hoon.* 4. *rabba.* She has raised nine children. *rabbet təsƹ ᵊwlaad.* — Most farmers here raise cattle. *ʔaktar l-ᵊmzaarƹiin hoon birabbu baqar.* 5. *ʔasaar.* Who raised the question? *miin ʔasaar ᵊl-masʔale?* 6. *qaddam.* I didn't hear you raise any objection then. *maa smaƹtak ƹam ᵊtqaddem ʔayy ʔəƹtiraaḍ ᵊb-waqta.* 7. *zaad (i ø) ƹala.* All right, I'll raise you five pounds. *ṭayyeb, bziid ƹaleek xamᵊs leeraat.*
to raise the roof - 1. *qaam (u ø) ᵊd-dənye w-ḥaṭṭa.* My father raised the roof because I took the car. *ʔabi qaam ᵊd-dənye w-ḥaṭṭa laʔənni ʔaxadt ᵊs-sayyaara.* 2. *qarwaš, ḍawwaš.* The kids are raising the roof again. *l-ᵊwlaad rəžƹu yqarᵊwšu taani marra.*
raisin - *zbiibe* and *zbiibaaye* coll. *zbiib* pl. *-aat.*
rake - *məšṭ.* We need a new rake for the garden. *laazəmna məšṭ ᵊždiid ləž-žneene.*
ram - 1. (male sheep) *kabᵊš* pl. *kbuuše.* 2. (battering-ram) *manžaniiq* pl. *mažaaneq.* 3. (of a pile driver) *mdaqq* pl. *-aat.*
Ramadan - *ramaḍaan* pl. *-aat.*
ramification - *tafarroƹ* pl. *-aat.*
at **random** - *ƹaṭ-ṭəffeeš, ƹala xiirt aḷḷa, kiif-ma kaan.* We chose these ten names at random. *naqqeena hal-ƹašᵊr ʔasaami ƹaṭ-ṭəffeeš.*
range - 1. *taškiile* pl. *-aat.* These shirts come in a large range of colors. *hal-qəmṣaan mawžuudiin ᵊb-taškiile waasƹa mn ᵊl-ʔalwaan.* 2. *ṭabbaax* pl. *-aat.* We just bought a new range. *maa-lna zamaan ᵊštareena ṭabbaax ᵊždiid.* 3. *mada.* The range of that interceptor is very limited. *mada hal-ᵊmṭaaride ktiir maḥduud.* 4. *marma.* The tanks were out of range of our guns. *d-dabbaabaat kaanu baraat marma madaafəƹna.* 5. *masmaƹ.* Quiet! Let's wait until he's out of range. *həṣṣ! xalliina nəstanna ḥatta yṣiir barraat masmaƹna.* 6. *səlᵊsle* pl. *salaasel.* The village is behind that range of mountains over there. *ḍ-ḍeeƹa wara səlsəlt haž-žbaal hayy.*
to range - *traawaḥ.* Prices range from one to five dollars. *l-ʔasƹaar btətraawaḥ been doolaar w-xamse.*
rank - 1. *mᵊʔanten.* Where is that rank smell coming from? *mneen žaaye har-riiḥa l-ᵊmʔantne?* 2. *faaheš.* That's rank ingratitude! *haada nəkraan žamiil faaheš!*
rank - 1. *rətbe* pl. *rətab.* What's that officer's rank? *šuu rətbet haẓ-ẓaabeṭ?*
**He's worked his way up from the ranks. *bana ḥaalo mən taḥt w-ṭaaleƹ.*
rape - *ʔəftiraas.* He's on trial for attempted rape. *ƹam yətḥaakam b-təhmet ᵊmḥaawalt ʔəftiraas.*
to rape - *ftaras.* She claims he raped her. *ƹam təddəƹi ʔənno ftarása.*
rapid - *sariiƹ.*
rare - 1. *naader.* That's a rare flower. *haz-zahr naader.* 2. *mdamma.* I'd like my steak rare. *bəddi l-bəfteek tabaƹi mdammaaye.*
rarely - *bᵊn-naader, qəllet-ma.* That rarely happens. *bᵊn-naader bətṣiir heek masʔale.*
rascal - *qərᵊd* pl. *qruud(e), ƹəfriit* pl. *ƹafariit.*
rash - 1. *ḥaraara, ṭafᵊḥ.* He has a rash on his face. *ṭaaləƹ-lo ḥaraara b-wəššo.* 2. *ṭaayeš, bala tarawwi.* I wouldn't make any rash promises. *law ᵊb-maḥallak maa baƹṭi wƹuud ṭaayše.*
raspberry - *tuutet˜* (coll. *tuut˜*) *syaaž, frambwaaz.*
rat - *žardoon* pl. *žaradiin.*
rate - 1. *taƹriife, ʔəžra* pl. *ʔžuur.* What are the rates for single rooms? *šuu t-taƹriife mənšaan ᵊl-ʔuwaḍ b-taxᵊt waaḥed?* -- What are the new rates for airmail? *šuu l-ᵊʔžuur ᵊž-ždiide tabaƹ ᵊl-bariid ᵊž-žawwi?* 2. *səƹᵊr* pl. *ʔasƹaar.* What's the rate of exchange today? *qaddeeš səƹr ᵊl-ƹəmle l-yoom?* 3. *mƹaddal.* The rate of interest is four per cent. *mƹaddal ᵊl-faaʔide ʔarbƹa bᵊl-miyye.* -- The birth rate is on the increase. *mƹaddal l-ᵊwlaade ƹam yəzdaad.* -- At this rate we'll never get done. *ƹala hal-ᵊmƹaddal b-ḥayaatna maa mnəxloṣ.*
first-rate, second-rate, etc. - *daraže ʔuula, daraže taanye,* etc. It's definitely a first-rate hotel. *mᵊʔakkad hal-ʔoteel daraže ʔuula.*
at any rate - *ƹala kəll ḥaal, ƹala kullin.* At any rate, I'd like to see you. *ƹala kəll ḥaal bḥəbb šuufak.*
to rate - *ƹadd (ə ø//nƹadd).* Many critics rate him as the most important author of this generation. *fii nəqqaad ᵊktiir biƹəddúu ʔahamm kaateb b-haž-žiil.*
rather - *šwayye, nawƹan maa.* (in most instances, not expressed at all; cf. pretty, very, somewhat, and the like). The play was rather long. *t-tamsiiliyye ṭaalet šwayye.*
**I would rather wait. *bfaḍḍel ʔəntéẓer.*
**I'd rather die than give in. *bfaḍḍel muut ƹan ʔənni sallem* or *bfaḍḍel ᵊl-moot ƹan ᵊt-tasliim.*
ration - 1. *ḥəṣṣa* pl. *ḥəṣaṣ.* Our rations consisted of bread and soup. *ḥəṣaṣna kaanet xəbᵊz w-šooraba.* 2. *taƹyiine* pl. *-aat.* The platoon will receive rations for three days. *l-faṣiile laḥa taaxod taƹyiinaat la-tlətt iyyaam.*
ration card - *biṭaaqet˜* (pl. *-aat˜*) *ʔiƹaaše.*
to ration - *qannan.* Sugar was rationed during the war. *s-səkkar kaan ᵊmqannan ʔiyyaam ᵊl-ḥarb.*
rational - 1. *ƹaaqel.* Man is sometimes called the rational animal. *l-ʔənsaan b-baƹḍ ᵊl-ʔaḥyaan bisammúu ḥayawaan ƹaaqel.* 2. *maƹquul.* That's a rational way of looking at it. *hayy ṭariiqa maƹquule lən-naẓar fiiha.* -- That phenomenon has a rational explanation. *haẓ-ẓaahira ʔəla tafsiir maƹquul.* -- He's not capable of rational argumentation. *maa byəṭlaƹ b-ʔiido yžaadel ᵊmžaadale maƹquule.*
rationalism - *l-mazhab ᵊl-ƹaqli.*
to **rationalize** - *sawwaġ, barrar.* You can rationalize

any action if you put your mind to it. *fiik ᵊtsawweġ ʔayy εamal ʔiza ḥaṭṭeet fəkrak.*
to **rattle** - 1. *qarqaε b-.* Do you have to rattle the dishes that way? *šuu ḍaruuri tqarqeε bᵊṣ-ṣḥuun heek?* 2. *xaḍwaḍ.* Stop rattling the doorknob! *ḥaaže txaḍweḍ ṭaabet ᵊl-baab!*
to rattle on - *εallak (εlaak), latlat.* She can rattle on like that for hours. *fiiha tεallek heek saaεaat w-saaεaat.*
to get rattled - *xarbaṭ, laxbaṭ.* Don't get me rattled. *laa txarbəṭni.*
to **rave** - *haaž (u hayažaan, hyaaž).* He raved like a madman. *haaž mətl ᵊl-mažnuun.*
to rave about - *žann (ə žnuun, žnaan) b-, ṭaar (i ø) εaqlo b-.* Everyone raves about his new book. *kəll ᵊn-naas εam yžənnu b-ᵊktaabo ž-ždiid.*
raw - 1. *nayy.* The meat is almost raw. *l-laḥme ləssaaha taqriiban nayye.* 2. *xaam* (invar.). We import the raw materials from Turkey. *mnəstawred ᵊl-mawaadd ᵊl-xaam mən tərkiyya.* 3. *məltəheb.* My throat is raw. *žoozet ḥalqi məltəhbe.*
**He got a raw deal. *εaamalúu mεaamale kəlla ḥeef w-ẓəlᵊm.*
ray - 1. *šεaaε* pl. *ʔašəεεa.* Ordinary glass keeps out ultraviolet rays. *l-balloor ᵊl-εaadi byəmnaε nafaad ᵊl-ʔašəεεa fooq ᵊl-banafsažiyye.* 2. *bṣiiṣ.* There's still a ray of hope. *ləssa fii bṣiiṣ ʔamal.*
rayon - *ḥariir ʔəṣṭinaaεi.*
razor - *muus˜* (pl. *mwaas˜*) *ᵊḥlaaqa.* I have to strop my razor. *laazem sənn muus ᵊḥlaaqti.*
razor blade - *šafra* pl. *-aat.* Please buy me a dozen razor blades. *baḷḷa štrii-li dazziinet šafraat.*
safety razor - *maakiint˜* (pl. *-aat˜*) *ᵊḥlaaqa.* I can't find my safety razor. *maa-li εam laaqi maakiint ᵊḥlaaqti.*
reach - 1. *marma.* The ship was careful to stay out of reach of the shore batteries. *s-safiine kaanet ḥariiṣa ʔənna təbqa barraat marma baṭṭaariyyaat ᵊs-saaḥel.* 2. *manaal.* A car like that is out of reach for a man with an average income. *sayyaara mətᵊl hayy ʔabεad mən manaal waaḥed ʔəlo daxᵊl mətwaṣṣeṭ.*
to reach - 1. *madd (ə ø) ʔiido la-.* The little fellow reaches for everything he sees. *ẓ-ẓġiir bimədd ʔiido la-kəll šii bišuufo.* -- She reached for her gun. *maddet ʔiida la-farda.* -- I reached into my pocket. *maddeet ʔiidi la-žeebti.* 2. *wəṣel (-yəṣal* and *-yuuṣal wṣuul) la-.* We reached the city at daybreak. *wṣəlna ləl-balad εand ᵊṭluuε ᵊḍ-ḍaww.* -- The rumor even reached us. *l-ʔišaaεa wəṣlətna ḥatta ʔəlna.* -- Millions of people are reached by the radio. *malayiin mn ᵊn-naas εam yəṣalúu-lon b-waasəṭṭ ᵊr-raadyo.* 3. *ṭaal (u ø).* Can you reach that shelf? *fiik ᵊṭṭuul har-raff?* 4. *ttaṣal b-.* There was no way of reaching him. *maa kaan məmken ᵊl-ʔəttiṣaal fii.* 5. *naawal.* Please reach me the salt. *mən faḍlak naawəlni l-məlᵊḥ.* 6. *mtadd la-.* The garden reaches all the way to the river. *ž-žneene btəmtadd la-ḥadd ᵊn-nahr.*
reaction - *radd fəεᵊl.* What was his reaction? *šuu kaan radd ᵊl-fəεᵊl εando?*
reactionary - *rağεi*.*
to **read** - 1. *qara (a qraaye//nqara).* You should read this book. *bənṣaḥak təqra hal-ᵊktaab.* -- Please read the article to me. *baḷḷa qraa-li hal-maq̈aale.* -- Read it aloud. *qraaha b-ṣooṭ εaali.* -- This reads like a fairy tale. *haš-šii kaʔənno l-waaḥed byəqra xuraafe.* 2. *naṣṣ (ə ø) εala.* The text reads differently. *n-naṣṣ binəṣṣ εala šii ġeero.* 3. *warža, farža.* The thermometer reads thirty-five degrees. *miizaan ᵊl-ḥaraara εam ywarži xamsda w-ᵊtlaatiin daraže.*
**Was my name read? *ṭaleε ʔəsmi?*
reader - 1. *q̈aareʔ* pl. *q̈ərraaʔ.* Our newspaper has more than a million readers. *žariidətna ʔəlha ʔaktar mən malyoon q̈aareʔ.* 2. *ktaab˜* (pl. *kətᵊb˜*) *q̈iraaʔa.* Do you have my Spanish reader? *εandak ktaab ᵊl-q̈iraaʔa l-ʔəṣbaani tabaεi?*
readily - *biduun taraddod, εal-ḥaarek, qawaam.* He readily admitted it. *εtaraf fiiha biduun taraddod.* -- She consented readily. *rəḍyet qawaam.*
reading - *q̈iraaʔa.* He got an A in reading. *ʔaxad "žayyed žəddan" bᵊl-q̈iraaʔa.*
ready - 1. *ḥaaḍer.* When will dinner be ready? *ʔeemta l-εaša bikuun ḥaaḍer?* -- I don't have much ready cash. *maa fii εandi maṣaari ḥaaḍra ktiir.* 2. *məstεədd, mətḥaḍḍer, ḥaaḍer.* I'm ready for anything. *ʔana məstεədd la-ḥayaḷḷa šii.*
**Keep your tickets ready! *xallu biileetaatkon ᵊb-ʔideekon!*
**She's always ready with an answer. *daayman žawaaba εala raas ᵊlsaana.*
ready-made - *ḥaaḍer, žaahez.* Do you buy your suits ready-made? *btəštəri badlaatak ḥaaḍra?* -- I bought this dress ready-made. *štareet har-roob žaahez.*
real - 1. *ḥaqiiqi*.* What was the real reason? *šuu kaan ᵊs-sabab ᵊl-ḥaqiiqi?* -- That's not his real name. *haada muu ʔəsmo l-ḥaqiiqi.* 2. *ʔaṣli*.* Is this real silk? *haada ḥariir ʔaṣli?* 3. *εal-maẓbuuṭ.* That's what I call a real friend. *haada ḥalli bsammi̇i sadiiq εal-maẓbuuṭ.*
**That never happens in real life. *haš-šii ʔabadan maa biṣiir bᵊl-ḥayaat.*
**It was a real pleasure to listen to him. *bᵊl-ḥaqiiqa kaan laziiz ᵊktiir ᵊl-ʔəstimaaε ʔəlo.*
real estate - *məlk* pl. *ʔamlaak, εaq̈aar* pl. *-aat.*
reality - 1. *waaq̈eε.* It sounds all right in theory, but reality is a little different. *bᵊn-naẓariyye btəẓhar mniiḥa, bass ᵊl-waaq̈eε šwayye ġeer šəkᵊl.* 2. *ḥaqiiqa, waaq̈eε.* In reality, he's a very nice man. *bᵊl-ḥaqiiqa huwwe zalame ktiir laṭiif.*
to **realize** - 1. *ḥaqqaq.* He never realized his ambition to become a doctor. *b-ḥayaato maa ḥaqqaq maṭmaḥo ʔənno yṣiir doktoor.* 2. *ḥaqqaq, ḥaṣal (a ḥṣuul) εala.* He realized quite a profit on that deal. *ḥaqqaq rəbᵊḥ məḥtərám b-haṣ-ṣafq̈a.* 3. *ḥass (ə ø).* I didn't realize it was so late. *maa ḥasseet εal-waqt qaddeeš maḍa b-sərεa.* -- I never realized the danger. *maa kənᵊt ḥaases bᵊl-xaṭar ʔabadan.* 4. *dəri (a ø), εəref (-yaεref ø).* Does he realize how sick he is ? *daryaan huwwe qaddeešo ḍεiif?* -- He doesn't realize how much work is involved. *muu εarfaan huwwe qaddeeš ᵊl-masʔale bədda šəġᵊl.*
**I simply can't realize he's dead. *maa εam yfuut ᵊb-εaqli ʔənno maat.*
really - 1. *εan ḥaqa, εan ṣaḥiiḥ, ḥaqiiqatan.* Do you really mean it? *εan ḥaqa ʔənte btəεniiha?* 2. *bᵊl-ḥaqiiqa.* He is really younger than he looks. *huwwe bᵊl-ḥaqiiqa ʔaẓġar məmma byəẓhar.* -- I really wanted to stay at home. *bᵊl-ḥaqiiqa kənᵊt bəddi ʔəbqa bᵊl-beet.* 3. *saddeq* (to a woman *saddqi,* to a group *saddqu*). It really isn't very far. *saddeq muu bεiid.* -- That's really too much! *saddeq haš-šii fooq ᵊṭ-ṭaaqa.*
rear - 1. *qafa.* The rear of the house is being painted. *εam yədhanu qafa l-beet.* 2. *warraani*, xalfi*.* The rear windows haven't been cleaned yet. *š-šababiik ᵊl-warraaniyye ləssa maa tnaḍḍafu.*
in the rear - *bᵊl-qafa, wara.* The emergency exit is in the rear. *maxraž ᵊn-nažaat bᵊl-qafa.*
to **rearrange** - *εaad (i ʔiεaadet˜) tartiib˜ ...* You ought to rearrange the furniture. *laazem ᵊtεiid tartiib ᵊl-mobiilya.*
reason - 1. *sabab* pl. *ʔasbaab.* She really has no reason for acting like that. *waḷḷaahi maa εanda sabab tətṣarraf heek taṣarrof.* -- He was dismissed without any reason. *ṣarafúu mn ᵊl-xədme biduun ʔayy sabab.* -- Is that the reason you didn't go? *la-has-sabab maa rəḥᵊt?* -- That's the reason I didn't ask. *haada s-sabab yalli maa xallaani ʔəsʔal.* 2. *daaεi* pl. *dawaaεi, sabab* pl. *ʔasbaab.* He gave me no reason for complaint. *maa εaṭaani ʔayy daaεi ləš-šakwa.* 3. *ṣawaab, εaqᵊl.* We brought him to reason. *ražžaεnáa ləṣ-ṣawaab* (or *la-εaqlo*). -- Please, listen to reason! *mənšaan ʔaḷḷa baqa, ržaaε la-εaqlak!* -- If this keeps up, I'll lose my reason. *ʔiza haš-šii bəddo ytamm biṭiir εaqli.*
**It stands to reason that he would want to check those figures first. *šii maεquul ʔənno bəddo yətḥaqqaq mən hal-ʔarq̈aam bᵊl-ʔawwal.*
to reason - 1. *ḥaažaž.* You can't reason with him. *maa fiik ᵊtḥaažžo.* 2. *εallal.* He reasoned that the burglar must have escaped through the window. *εallal ʔənno laazem ykuun l-ḥaraami harab mn ᵊš-šəbbaak.*
reasonable - 1. *εaaqel.* She's a very reasonable person. *hiyye sətt εaaqle ktiir.* 2. *maεquul.* That's a reasonable fee. *hayy taεriife maεquule.*
reasonably - 1. *b-ʔasεaar mətḥaawde.* You can get books very reasonably here. *fiik təštəri kətᵊb hoon ᵊb-ʔasεaar mətḥaawde.* 2. *nooεan maa.* He speaks reasonably good French. *byəḥki frənsaawi nooεan maa mniiḥ* -- The hotel is reasonably

comfortable. *l-ʔoteel nooƐan maa məryeḥ.*
rebellion - *Ɛəṣyaan, sawra* pl. *-aat, tamarrod.*
to **recall** - **1.** *stadƐa.* The ambassador has been recalled. *stadƐu s-safiir.* **2.** *dzakkar.* Do you recall whether he was there? *Ɛam tədzakkar ʔiza kaan ᵊhniik?*
receipt - **1.** *ʔəstilaam.* Have you acknowledged the receipt of his letter? *xabbarto b-ʔəstilaam maktuubo?* **2.** *waṣᵊl* pl. *wṣuulaat.* Please give me a receipt. *bətražžaak Ɛaṭiini waṣᵊl.* **3.** *waared* pl. *-aat, ʔiiraad* pl. *-aat.* The receipts were low today. *l-waardaat ᵊl-yoom kaanet qaliile.*
to receipt - *maḍa (i ʔəmḍa* and *maḍi//mmaḍa).* Please receipt this bill. *mən faḍlak mḍii-li hal-faatuura* (and *Ɛala hal-faatuura).*
to **receive** - **1.** *stalam.* Did you receive my telegram? *stalamᵊt barqiiti?* **2.** *qabaḍ (a qabᵊḍ//nqabaḍ).* Have you received your salary yet? *qabaḍṭ maƐaašak wəlla ləssa?* **3.** *staqbal.* We were cordially received. *staqbaluuna b-kəll ḥaraara w-ləṭᵊf.*
receiver - **1.** *sammaaƐa* pl. *-aat.* You left the receiver off the hook. *maa ražžaƐt ᵊs-sammaaƐa Ɛat-talifoon.* **2.** *məstə́lem* pl. *-iin.* Write the receiver's name legibly. *ktoob ʔəsm ᵊl-məstə́lem b-wuḍuuḥ.*
recent - **1.** *ḥadiis.* Television is a comparatively recent invention. *t-televəzyoon nəsbiyyan ʔəxtiraaƐ ḥadiis.* **2.** *ždiid* pl. *ždaad.* Don't you have any recent issues? *maa fii Ɛandak ʔaƐdaad ᵊždaad?*
recently - *mʔaxxaran, mn ᵊždiid, mən mədde qariibe.* I saw him only recently. *mʔaxxaran šəfto* or ***maa-li zamaan šəfto.*
reception - **1.** *tarḥiib.* He gave us a warm reception. *raḥḥab fiina tarḥiib ḥaarr.* **2.** *ʔəstəqbaal.* Reception is very poor today. *l-ʔəstəqbaal ᵊḍƐiif ᵊktiir ᵊl-yoom.* **3.** *ḥaflet˜* (pl. *-aat˜*) *ʔəstəqbaal.* Have you been invited to the reception? *nƐazamᵊt Ɛala ḥaflet ᵊl-ʔəstəqbaal?*
recess - **1.** *ʔəstiraaḥa* pl. *-aat, fərṣa* pl. *fəraṣ.* We have a short recess at ten in the morning. *fii Ɛanna ʔəstiraaḥa qaṣiire s-saaƐa Ɛašara Ɛala bəkra.* **2.** *Ɛəṭle* pl. *Ɛəṭal, fərṣa* pl. *fəraṣ.* Mid-term recess is only five days this year. *hal-Ɛaam Ɛəṭlet nəṣṣ ᵊs-səne bass xamᵊst iyyaam.*
recipe - *waṣfe* pl. *-aat.* Do you have a simple recipe for a cake? *fii Ɛandek waṣfe sahle la-šii gaato?*
to **recite** - **1.** *qara (a qraaye//nqara), sammaƐ.* She recited some of her own poems. *qaret šwayye mən šəƐra.* **2.** *sammaƐ Ɛal-ġeeb, qara Ɛal-ġeeb.* He can recite whole sections of the Koran. *fii ysammeƐ ʔažzaaʔ kaamle mn ᵊl-q̈ərʔaan Ɛal-ġeeb.*
reckless - *ṭaayeš.* He's a reckless driver. *huwwe sawwaaq ṭaayeš.*
recognition - **1.** *taqdiir.* He didn't get the recognition he deserved. *maa ḥaṣal Ɛat-taqdiir yalli stḥaqqo.* **2.** *ʔəƐtiraaf.* Recognition of the new government by our country is expected any day now. *l-ʔəƐtiraaf bᵊl-ᵊḥkuume ž-ždiide mən q̈ibal ḥukuumətna mənṭə́ẓar been ᵊl-yoom wᵊt-taani.*
**The United States has not yet extended its recognition of the new regime. *l-wilaayaat ᵊl-məttəḥde ləssa maa Ɛtarfet bᵊl-ᵊḥkuume ž-ždiide.*
in recognition of - *ʔəƐtiraafan b-.* In recognition of his great services ... *ʔəƐtiraafan b-xədmaato l-baahira ...*
to **recognize** - *Ɛəref (-yaƐref ø//nƐaraf).* I recognize him by his voice. *baƐᵊrfo mən ṣooto.* -- You have grown so much I almost wouldn't have recognized you. *kbərᵊt la-daraže ʔənni kənᵊt maa laḥa ʔəƐᵊrfak.* **2.** *qaddar.* Everybody recognizes his great merits. *kəll ᵊn-naas biqaddru ʔafḍaalo l-ᵊkbiire.* **3.** *Ɛtaraf b-.* I refuse to recognize this claim. *bərfoḍ ʔəƐtə́ref b-hal-ʔəddiƐaaʔ.*
to **recommend** - **1.** *waṣṣa b-.* I recommended her highly to him. *waṣṣeeto fiiha ktiir.* **2.** *naṣaḥ (a ø) b-, šaar (i ø) b-.* Can you recommend a good dentist around here? *fiik tənṣaḥni (or tšiir Ɛaliyyi) b-ṭabiib ᵊsnaan ᵊmniiḥ b-han-nawaaḥi?* **3.** *naṣaḥ.* I recommend that you stay in bed for two days. *bənṣaḥak təbqa bᵊl-farše šii yoomeen.*
recommendation - *tuuṣaaye, tawṣiye.* I did it on your recommendation. *saaweeta b-muužeb tuuṣaaytak.*
reconnaissance - *ʔəstəkšaaf, ʔəstəṭlaaƐ.*
reconnaissance plane - *ṭayyaaret˜* (pl. *-aat˜*) *ʔəstəkšaaf.*
record - **1.** *raq̈am q̈iyaasi** pl. *ʔarq̈aam q̈iyaasiyye.* He broke all records in free-style swimming. *ḍarab kəll ᵊl-ʔarq̈aam ᵊl-q̈iyaasiyye bᵊs-sbaaḥa l-ḥərra.* **2.** *qeed* pl. *qyuud.* I can't find any record of that bill. *maa-li Ɛam laaqi ʔayy qeed la-hal-faatuura.* **3.** *kwaane* pl. *-aat, ʔəsṭwaane* pl. *-aat.* They have a good selection of classical records. *fii Ɛandon taškiile mniiḥa mən l-ᵊkwaanaat l-ᵊklaasiikiyye.* **4.** *q̈iyaasi*.* We had a record crop this year. *kaan fii Ɛanna maḥṣuul q̈iyaasi has-səne.*
**He has a criminal record. *ʔəlo sawaabeq bᵊl-ʔəžraam.*
**That was the worst earthquake on record. *kaanet ʔalƐan zalzale ḥadset.*
**The ambassador insisted that his comments be considered strictly off the record. *s-safiir ʔaṣarr ʔənno taƐliiqaato təttaaxad ḥatman b-ṣuura ġeer rasmiyye.*
**What I told you was meant to be off the record (= confidential). *yalli qəlt-əllak-yāa qaṣaḍt fii maa yəṭlaƐ mənnak* (or ***qaṣaḍṭ fii yəbqa beenaatna).*
**I want to go on the record as saying that ... *bəddi hal-ḥaki yətsažžal Ɛaliyyi ʔənno ...*
records - *səžəllaat* (pl.), *qyuud* (pl.). All the records were destroyed. *s-səžəllaat kəlla təlfet.*
to keep a record of - *qayyad, ḥafaẓ (a ḥəfᵊẓ) liista b-.* Keep a careful record of all expenses. *qayyed ᵊb-dəqqa kəll šii btəṣᵊrfo* or *ḥfaaẓ liista daqiiqa b-kəll šii btəṣᵊrfo.*
to make a record of - *sažžal, qayyad.* The secretary made a record of everything. *s-səkərteera sažžalet kəll šii.*
to record - *sažžal.* Have you recorded everything he said? *sažžalᵊt kəll šii qaalo?*
to **recover** - **1.** *ṭaab (i ø), šafi (a šifa), tƐaafa.* He recovered quickly from his illness. *ṭaab ᵊb-sərƐa mən maraḍo.* **2.** *staržaƐ, staradd.* Did you finally recover your watch? *bᵊl-ʔaaxiir staržaƐᵊt saaƐtak?* -- He recovered his balance immediately. *Ɛal-ḥaarek staržaƐ tawaazno.*
recovery - **1.** *šifa.* He's on the road to recovery. *huwwe Ɛala ṭariiq ᵊš-šifa.* **2.** *ʔəstiƐaade, ʔəstəržaaƐ.* Recovery of the space capsule proved extremely difficult in the heavy sea. *ʔəstiƐaadet safiinet ᵊl-faḍaaʔ bᵊl-baḥr ᵊl-haayež kaanet ṣaƐbe ktiir.*
recreation - *tarfiih.* What kind of recreation do you advise, doctor? *šuu btənṣaḥ lət-tarfiih, doktoor?* -- The company is expanding its recreation center. *š-šərke Ɛam ᵊtwasseƐ markaz ᵊt-tarfiih tabƐ̣a.*
recruit - *(žəndi) məstažədd* pl. *(žnuud) məstažəddiin.* We had about 50 recruits in our company. *kaan fii šii xamsiin məstažədd b-sariyyətna.*
to recruit - *žannad.* The Navy is recruiting single men between the ages of 18 and 25. *l-baḥriyye Ɛam ᵊdžanned ᵊl-Ɛazzaabiyye halli been tmanṭaƐš w-xamsda w-Ɛəšriin.*
red - **1.** *ʔaḥmar* f. *ḥamra* pl. *ḥəmᵊr.* I want to buy a red hat. *bəddi ʔəštrži-li bərneeṭa ḥamra.* **2.** *(loon) ʔaḥmar* pl. *ʔalwaan ḥəmᵊr.* Red is not becoming to her. *l-ʔaḥmar maa byəlbə́q-la.*
**He makes me see red. *bifawwer dammi* or *biṭaaleƐ diini.*
**I saw red when I heard that. *ṭəleƐ ᵊd-damm la-raasi waqt ᵊsməƐᵊt haš-šii.*
Red Army - *ž-žeeš ᵊl-ʔaḥmar.*
Red Crescent - *l-hilaal ᵊl-ʔaḥmar.*
Red Cross - *ṣ-ṣaliib ᵊl-ʔaḥmar.*
Red Sea - *l-baḥr ᵊl-ʔaḥmar.*
to become or **turn red** - *ḥmarr.*
to **reduce** - **1.** *nazzal, xaffaḍ.* We've reduced the prices ten per cent. *nazzalna l-ʔasƐaar Ɛašara bᵊl-miyye.* **2.** *qallal, nazzal, xaffaḍ.* We have to reduce our expenses. *laazem ᵊnqallel maṣariifna.* **3.** *nəzel (e ø), naqeṣ (a ø).* I've reduced a lot. *nzəlt ᵊktiir.*
reel - *karraar* pl. *-aat.*
to **refer to** - **1.** *ḥaal* or *ʔaḥaal (i ʔiḥaale//nḥaal) la-.* I was referred to the manager. *ʔaḥaaluuni ləl-mudiir.* **2.** *šaar* or *ʔašaar (i ʔišaara//nšaar) la-.* She referred to it in her book. *ʔašaaret ʔəla b-ᵊktaaba.*
referee - *ḥakam* pl. *ḥəkkaam.*
reference - **1.** *maržeƐ* pl. *maraažeƐ.* You may give me as a reference. *fiik təzkərni ka-maržeƐ.* **2.** *šahaade* pl. *-aat.* He has very good references. *Ɛando šahaadaat ᵊmniiḥa.* -- May I see your references? *məmken šuuf šahaadaatak?*
reference book - *maržeƐ* pl. *maraažeƐ.*
referendum - *ʔəstəftaaʔ* pl. *-aat.*
to **refine** - *ṣaffa//tṣaffa, karrar//tkarrar.* The oil is

refined before being shipped overseas. *z-zeet ɛam yətsaffa qabᵊl-ma yənšəhen bᵊl-baḥᵊr.*
refinery - *məṣfaaya* pl. *-aat, maṣfa* pl. *maṣaafi, maɛmal˜* (pl. *maɛaamel˜*) *takriir.*
to **reflect** - *ɛakas (o/e ɛakᵊs//nɛakas).* The white sand reflected the heat of the midday sun. *r-raml ᵊl-ʔabyaḍ ɛakas ḥaraaret šams ᵊḍ-ḍəhᵊr.*
reflection - *xyaal* pl. *-aat, ṣuura* pl. *ṣuwar.* You can see your reflection in the water. *fiik ᵊtšuuf ᵊxyaalak bᵊl-mayy.*
**That's no reflection on you. *ʔənte muu l-maqṣuuḍ b-haš-šii.*
reform - *ʔəṣlaaḥ* pl. *-aat.* He introduced many reforms. *ɛəmel ʔəṣlaaḥaat ᵊktiire.*
to reform - 1. *ʔaṣlaḥ//nṣalaḥ.* He's always trying to reform the world. *daayman ɛam yḥaawel yəṣleḥ ᵊl-ɛaalam.* 2. *nṣalaḥ.* I'm sure he'll reform. *ʔana mətʔakked ʔənno laḥa yənṣəleḥ.*
reformer - *məṣleḥ* pl. *-iin.*
refreshment - *mraṭṭeb* pl. *-aat.* Refreshments were served during the intermission. *qaddamu mraṭṭbaat ʔasnaaʔ ᵊl-ʔəstiraaḥa.*
refreshment room - *buufée* pl. *buufeeyaat.*
refrigerator - *barraade* pl. *-aat.*
refugee - *laažeʔ* pl. *-iin.*
to **refund** - *raǧǧaɛ, radd (ə radd//nradd).* I'll refund your expenses. *brəǧǧəɛ-lak maṣariifak.*
refusal - *rafᵊḍ.* I didn't expect a refusal from him. *maa ntaẓarᵊt mənno rafᵊḍ.*
to **refuse** - *rafaḍ (o rafᵊḍ//nrafaḍ* and *rtafaḍ).* He doesn't refuse me anything. *maa byərfəḍ-li šii.* -- He refuses to accept my resignation. *ɛam yərfoḍ yəqbal ʔəstiq̈aalti.* -- What'll happen if I refuse to let you take it? *šuu biṣiir yaɛni ʔiza rafaḍṭ xalliik taaxəda?*
regard - 1. *xṣuuṣ.* In that regard, I agree with you. *b-hal-ᵊxṣuuṣ mwaafeq ʔana maɛak.* 2. *ʔəɛtibaar.* He has no regard at all for others. *maa ɛando ʔəɛtibaar ʔabadan ləl-ġeer.*
regards - *taḥiyyaat* (pl.). Give my regards to your wife. *balleġ taḥiyyaati ləs-sətt* or ***sallə́m-li ɛal-madaam.*
with (or **in**) **regard to** - *b-ᵊxṣuuṣ˜ ..., bᵊn-nəsbe la-.* With regard to wages, our policy has remained essentially the same. *b-ᵊxṣuuṣ ᵊl-ʔužuur xəṭṭətna ɛal-ᵊɛmuum ḍallet mətᵊl-ma hiyye.*
to regard - 1. *ɛtabar, ḥasab (o ø//nḥasab).* I regard him as an authority in this field. *bəɛtəbro ḥəǧǧe b-hal-ḥaqᵊl.* 2. *ɛtabar.* I regard him highly. *bəɛtəbro ktiir.*
regardless of - *b-ṣarf ᵊn-naẓar ɛan.* Each member pays the same fees regardless of the size of his income. *kəll ɛəḍu byədfaɛ nafs ᵊr-rasᵊm b-ṣarf ᵊn-naẓar ɛan daxlo.* -- We'll go ahead with our plans regardless of what he says. *laḥa nəmši b-xəṭaṭna b-ṣarf ᵊn-naẓar ɛan halli ɛam yquulo.*
regiment - *katiibe* pl. *kataayeb.*
region - *manṭiqa* pl. *manaaṭeq, ʔəq̈liim* pl. *ʔaq̈aliim.*
regional - *ʔəq̈liimi*.*
register - *səǧǧəll* pl. *-aat, daftar* pl. *dafaater.* Did you sign the register? *maḍeet ᵊs-səǧəll?*
(cash) register - *sanduuq* pl. *sanadiiq.* Did you take any money out of the register? *ʔaxadt maṣaari šii mn ᵊs-sanduuq?*
to register - 1. *saǧǧal//tsaǧǧal, qayyad// tqayyad.* He's not registered at this hotel. *huwwe muu msaǧǧal ᵊb-hal-ʔoteel.* 2. *saǧǧal ḥaalo, tsaǧǧal.* Where do you register here ? *ween ᵊl-waaḥed bisaǧǧel ḥaalo hoon?* -- I couldn't vote because I forgot to register. *maa qdərᵊt ṣawweṭ laʔənno səhi ɛan baali ʔətsaǧǧal.* -- Have you registered with the police? *saǧǧalᵊt ḥaalak b-daaʔərt ᵊš-šərṭa?* 3. *saǧǧal.* How many degrees does the thermometer register? *kam daraže msaǧǧel miizaan ᵊl-ḥaraara?* 4. *sookar, saǧǧal.* Where do you register letters ? *ween bisookru l-makatiib?*
registered - 1. *msaǧǧal, maḍmuun, msookar.* I got a registered letter today. *stalamt ᵊl-yoom maktuub ᵊmsaǧǧal.* 2. *msaǧǧal.* That's a registered trade-mark. *hayy maarka msaǧǧale* (or *ɛalaame msaǧǧale*).
regret - 1. *ʔasaf.* I decline with regret. *bərfoḍ maɛ ᵊl-ʔasaf.* 2. *nadam.* His regret came too late. *nadamo kaan baɛᵊd fawaat ᵊl-ʔawaan.*
**Mrs. Khouri sends her regrets. *madaam xuuri btəɛtəzer laʔənna maa btəqder təži.*
to have regrets - *nədem (a nadam), tnaddam.* I'd rather wait than have regrets later. *bfaḍḍel ʔəntə́ẓer ɛan ʔənni ʔəndam baɛdeen.*
to regret - 1. *nədem (a nadam), tnaddam.* I've always regretted not having traveled much. *ʔana daaymaan nadmaan laʔənni maa saafart ᵊktiir.* -- I don't regret having said it. *ʔana maa-li nadmaan la-qooli haš-šii.* 2. *tʔassaf.* I regret to tell you that your thesis is rather weak. *mətʔassef qəl-lak ʔənno ʔəṭruuḥtak šwayye ḍɛiife.*
regrettable - *məḥzen.* This is a regrettable mistake. *hayy ġalṭa məḥᵊzne.*
regular - 1. *ɛaadi*.* The regular price is five pounds. *s-səɛr ᵊl-ɛaadi xamᵊs leeraat.* 2. *ṭabiiɛi*, ɛaadi*.* His pulse is regular. *nabḍo ṭabiiɛi.* 3. *məntə́ẓem, mnaẓẓam.* He leads a very regular life. *ɛaayeš ɛiiše ktiir məntaẓme.* -- The committee meets at regular intervals. *l-ləžne btəžtə́meɛ b-faṭraat məntaẓme.* 4. *niẓaami*.* They are units of the regular army. *haadool waḥdaat bᵊž-žeeš ᵊn-niẓaami.* 5. *mdaawem.* Is he a regular customer? *huwwe zbuun ᵊmdaawem šii?* 6. *q̈iyaasi*.* Is this plural form regular? *ṣiiġet ᵊž-žamᵊɛ hayy q̈iyaasiyye?* 7. *ḍəġri* (invar.). She has beautiful regular teeth. *snaana ḥəlwe ḍəġri.* -- He's a regular fellow. *huwwe zalame ḍəġri.*
regularly - *b-ʔəntiẓaam.* He pays regularly. *byədfaɛ b-ʔəntiẓaam.*
to **regulate** - *ɛaddal, ẓabbaṭ.* I can't regulate the temperature. *maa fiini ɛaddel ᵊl-ḥaraara.*
regulation - *niẓaam* pl. *ʔanẓime.* That's against police regulations. *haada ḍəḍḍ ʔanẓəmt ᵊš-šərṭa.* -- I'm sticking to regulations. *ɛam ʔətbaɛ l-ʔanẓime.*
rehearsal - *broova* pl. *-aat.* Why weren't you at (the) rehearsal? *leeš maa kənᵊt bᵊl-broova?*
to **reject** - *rafaḍ (o rafᵊḍ//nrafaḍ* and *rtafaḍ).* They rejected my application for a scholarship. *rafaḍu ṭalab ᵊl-mənḥa šiiti.*
relapse - *nakse* pl. *-aat.* She was getting better, but all of a sudden she had a relapse. *kaanet ɛam tətḥassan ḥaalə́ta laaken fažʔatan ṣar-la nakse.*
related - *mətɛalleq b-* + pron. suff. He's competent in organic chemistry and related fields. *huwwe fahmaan bᵊl-kiimya l-ɛəḍwiyye w-bᵊl-ʔabḥaas ᵊl-mətɛallqa fiiha.* -- That question is not even related to the topic under discussion. *has-suʔaal maa-lo ḥatta mətɛalleq bᵊl-mawḍuuɛ halli ɛam nəbḥaso.*
to be related - *qəreb (a qaraabe).* We're related on my mother's side. *mnəqrab baɛᵊḍna mən naaḥiit ʔəmmi* or ***nəḥna qaraaybiin mən naaḥiit ʔəmmi.* -- Are you related to him? *btəqrabo šii?*
relation - 1. *ɛalaaqa* pl. *-aat.* I don't see any relation between the two incidents. *maa-li šaayef ʔani ɛalaaqa been ᵊl-ḥaadᵊsteen.* -- The relations between the two countries are strained. *l-ɛalaaqaat been ᵊd-doolteen mətwattra.* 2. *qaraayeb* pl. *-iin.* I have a lot of relations there. *fii ʔəli ktiir qaraaybiin ᵊhniik.*
relationship - 1. *qaraabe.* What's his relationship to the Khouris? *šuu qaraabto b-beet ᵊl-xuuri?* 2. *ɛalaaqa.* There is a close relationship between cost and price. *fii ɛalaaqa qariibe been ᵊl-kəlfe wᵊs-səɛᵊr.* -- I'd prefer to keep our relationship a platonic one. *bfaḍḍel xalli ɛalaaqətna ɛəzriyye.*
relative - 1. *qaraayeb* pl. *-iin.* They are close relatives of ours. *hənne qaraaybiin ᵊqraab ʔəlna* or *hənne qaraaybiinna mniiḥ.* 2. *nəsbi*.* Everything in life is relative. *kəll šii bᵊd-dənye nəsbi.*
relative clause - 1. (syndetic) *ṣilet˜* (pl. *-aat˜*) *ᵊl-mawṣuul.* 2. (asyndetic) *ṣifa* pl. *-aat.*
relative pronoun - *ʔəsᵊm mawṣuul* pl. *ʔasmaaʔ mawṣuule.*
relatively - *nəsbiyyan, bᵊn-nəsbe.* He's relatively young. *nəsbiyyan huwwe ẓġiir.*
relativity - *nəsbiyye.*
to **relax** - 1. *raxa (i raxi//rtaxa).* Relax your muscles. *ʔərxi ɛaḍalaatak.* 2. *rtaaḥ, straaḥ.* I can't relax until it's finished. *maa bərtaaḥ la-təxloṣ.* 3. *raaq (u ø), hədi (a ø).* Relax! Nobody's going to hurt you. *ruuq, maa ḥada birə́d-lak suuʔ.*
relaxation - *raaḥa.* He plays golf for relaxation. *byəlɛab golf lər-raaḥa.*
release - 1. *ʔəxlaaʔ˜ sabiil, ʔəfraaž ɛan.* The lawyer has applied for her release. *l-muḥaami ṭalab ʔəxlaaʔ sabiila* (or *ᵊl-ʔəfraaž ɛanha*). 2. *našra* pl. *-aat.* Have you seen the latest press release of the President's office? *qareet ʔaaxer našra ləṣ-ṣaḥaafe mən maktab ᵊr-raʔiis?*

to release - **1.** *ʔaxla sabiil˜ ..., ʔafraž ɛan.* The police released him right away. *š-šərṭa ʔaxlet sabiilo ɛal-ḥaarek.* **2.** *ḥall (ə ḥall//nḥall), fakk (ə fakk//nfakk), raxa (i raxi//rtaxa).* Release the safety catch. *ḥəll (dəqr) ᵊt-taʔmiin.* -- He forgot to release the brake. *nəsi yḥəll l-ᵊfraam.* **3.** *samaḥ (a samaaḥ) ᵊb-našᵊr˜ ...* The press department hasn't released the text of the speech yet. *daaʔərt ᵊṣ-ṣaḥaafe ləssa maa samḥet ᵊb-našᵊr naṣṣ ᵊl-xiṭaab.*

relevant - *mətɛalleq bᵊl-mawḍuuɛ.* Give me all the relevant details of the case. *ɛaṭiini kəll ᵊt-tafaṣiil ᵊl-mətɛallqa b-mawḍuuɛ ᵊl-qaḍiyye.* -- I don't think that's a relevant question. *maa bẓənn has-suʔaal mətɛalleq bᵊl-mawḍuuɛ.* -- That point is not relevant to the question. *han-nəqṭa maa-la mətɛallqa b-mawḍuuɛ ᵊl-masʔale* (or ***maa-la ɛalaaqa bᵊl-masʔale*).

reliable - **1.** *yuɛtamad ɛalée.* She's a very reliable person. *hiyye waaḥde yuɛtamad ɛaleeha mniiḥ.* -- That's a reliable firm. *hayy šərke yuɛtamad ɛaleeha.* **2.** *mawsuuq̈ fii.* I got it from a reliable source. *ḥṣəlt ɛalée mən maṣdar mawsuuq̈ fii.*

relief - **1.** *faraž.* I bet it's a relief to have it off your mind. *laa šakk ʔənna faraž yalli qəmt ᵊš-šaġle mən baalak.* **2.** *fakke, faraž.* No relief from the heat is in sight. *maa fii fakke qariibe mən haš-šoobe.* **3.** *ʔəsɛaaf.* Within hours, relief teams moved into the flood area. *baɛᵊd saaɛaat qaliile raaḥet fəraq̈ ʔəsɛaaf la-manṭəqt ᵊl-fayaḍaan.* -- They want to organize a relief committee. *bəddon yʔallfu ləžnet ʔəsɛaaf. yʔallfu ləžnet ʔəsɛaaf.*

to be on relief - *ɛaaš (i ɛiiše) ɛal-ʔiɛaanaat.* He's been on relief ever since he was laid off. *ɛaayeš ɛal-ʔiɛaanaat mən yoom-ma ṭaalaɛúu mn ᵊl-xədme.*

to give relief - *rayyaḥ, kannan.* Did the medicine give you any relief? *rayyaḥak šii d-dawa?*

to relieve - **1.** *kannan, xaffaf.* This will relieve your headache. *haada bikannən-lak wažaɛ raasak.* -- Isn't there anything to relieve his pains? *maa fii šii yxaffə́f-lo wažaɛo?* **2.** *xallaṣ//txallaṣ.* I'm glad I've been relieved of that worry. *ʔana farḥaan yalli txallaṣᵊt mən hal-hamm.* **3.** *baddal//tbaddal.* The guard is relieved at twelve o'clock. *l-ḥaras byətbaddal ᵊs-saaɛa ṭnaɛᵊš.*

to relieve one another - *tnaawabu.* We relieve one another. *mnətnaawab (maɛ baɛᵊḍna).*

religion - *diin* pl. *ʔadyaan, dayaane* pl. *-aat.* What is your religion? *šuu diinak?*

religious - **1.** *məddayyen.* He's very religious. *huwwe məddayyen ᵊktiir.* **2.** *diini*.* He belongs to a religious order. *huwwe mən rahbane diiniyye.* -- That's a religious question. *hayy masʔale diiniyye.* **3.** *šarɛi*.* All religious courts have been abolished in Egypt. *kəll ᵊl-maḥaakem ᵊš-šarɛiyye ltaġet ᵊb-maṣᵊr.*

religiously - **1.** *b-kəll ʔamaane.* I take the pills religiously twice a day. *baaxod ᵊl-ḥabbaat ᵊb-kəll ʔamaane marrteen bᵊl-yoom.* **2.** *ɛal-ḥarf.* You don't have to follow these rules religiously. *muu laazem ᵊṭṭabbeq hal-q̈awaaɛed ɛal-ḥarf.*

to **rely on** - *ɛtamad ɛala, ttakal ɛala.* You can't rely on him. *maa fiik təɛtə́med ɛalée.*

**Rely on it! He'll be late as usual. *xood mənni* (or *ɛallem ɛala kalaami*)! *bəddo yətʔaxxar mətᵊl ɛaadto.*

to **remain** - **1.** *bəqi (a ø), ṣəfi (a ø).* Only five remain. *bass xamse baqyaaniin.* -- There remains nothing else for us to do but to wait. *maa ṣəfi ɛaleena šii naɛmel ʔəlla nəntə́ẓer.* **2.** *bəqi, ḍall (a ø), tamm (a ø).* That's not going to remain that way. *haš-šii maa laḥa yəbqa heek.* -- On Friday, the store remains open till 10 p.m. *yoom ᵊž-žəmɛa l-maḥall biḍall faateḥ ləs-saaɛa ɛašara bᵊl-leel.*

**Remain seated please. *xalliik qaaɛed mən faḍlak.*

**That remains to be seen. *ləssa mənšuuf.*

remaining - *baaqi, baqyaan.* What did you do with the remaining cards? *šuu ɛmə́lt bᵊl-ᵊkruut ᵊl-baaqye* (or ***b-baqiit l-ᵊkruut*)?

remark - *mlaaḥaẓa* pl. *-aat.* That remark wasn't called for. *hal-ᵊmlaaḥaẓa maa kaanet laazme.*

remarkable - *mədheš.* What's so remarkable about it? *šuu fii šii mədheš ᵊb-haš-šaġle yaɛni?*

remedy - *dawa* pl. *ʔədʔwye.* That's a good remedy for colds. *haada dawa mniiḥ lər-rašᵊḥ.* -- There's no remedy for that. *maa fii dawa la-haš-šii.*

household remedy - *waṣfe* pl. *-aat.* That's an old household remedy. *hayy waṣfe qadiime.*

to remedy - *daawa//ddaawa, ṣallaḥ//tṣallaḥ.* I don't know how that can be remedied. *maa baɛref kiif haš-šii byəddaawa.*

to **remember** - **1.** *dzakkar.* It was in May, as far as I remember. *ṣaaret ᵊb-maayes ɛala-ma bədzakkar.* -- I simply can't remember his name. *šuu-ma baɛmel maa-li ɛam ʔədzakkar ʔəsmo.* -- He always remembers us at Christmas. *daayman byədzakkarna b-ɛiid ᵊl-miilaad.* -- Remember to turn out the light. *dzakkar təṭfi ḍ-ḍaww* or ***laa tənsa maa təṭfi ḍ-ḍaww.* **2.** *sallam.* Remember me to your mother. *sallə́m-li ɛala ʔəmmak.*

to **remind** - *zakkar.* He reminded me of my promise. *zakkarni b-waɛdi.* -- Remind me about it later. *zakkərni fiiha baɛdeen.* -- She reminds me of my sister. *bədzakkərni b-ʔəxti.*

**That reminds me, I have to do some shopping. *b-hal-ᵊmnaasabe, laazem ʔəštríi-li kam šaġle.*

reminder - *muzakkara* pl. *-aat.* I'll send him a reminder if he doesn't pay by tomorrow. *laḥa ʔəbɛə́t-lo muzakkara ʔiza maa dafaɛ mən hoon la-bəkra.*

remnant - *faḍle* pl. *-aat.* How much do you want for those three remnants? *qaddeeš bəddak b-hat-tlətt faḍlaat?*

remote - *bɛiid.* There's a remote possibility that ... *fii ʔəmkaaniyye bɛiide ʔənno ...*

**I haven't the remotest idea what you mean. *maa ɛandi ʔayy fəkra šuu btəɛni.*

to **remove** - **1.** *qaam (i qayamaan//nqaam).* Please remove your hat. *mən faḍlak qiim bərneeṭṭak.* -- Remove everything from the desk. *qiim kəll šii mən ɛaṭ-ṭaawle.* -- He was removed from office. *nqaam mən waẓiifto.* **2.** *qaam, zaal (i ø).* That cleaner will remove all stains. *hal-ᵊmnaḍḍef biqiim kəll ʔanwaaɛ ᵊl-bəqaɛ.* -- This should remove all doubt. *maɛquul haada yziil kəll šakk.*

to **renew** - *žaddad.* I have to renew my lease. *laazem žadded ʔižaari.* -- Have you renewed your passport yet? *žaddadt žawaaz safarak wəlla ləssa?*

renewal - *taždiid.* The renewal of my subscription is coming up. *tažiid ʔəštiraaki qarbaan.*

to **renovate** - *handaz.* Only two years ago they renovated the whole building. *mən sənteen bass handazu l-binaaye kəlla.*

rent - *ʔažaar* pl. *-aat, ʔižaar* pl. *-aat.* How much rent do you pay for your apartment? *qaddeeš btədfaɛ ʔažaar l-ʔabaarṭmaan tabaɛak?* -- Do you have rooms for rent? *fii ɛandkon ʔuwaḍ ləl-ʔažaar?*

to rent - **1.** *staʔžar.* I rented a room for three months. *staʔžarᵊt ʔuuḍa la-tlətt əšhor.* **2.** *ʔažžar.* Do you rent rooms? *bətʔažžer ʔuwaḍ?* -- All rooms are rented. *kəll ᵊl-ʔuwaḍ mʔažžara.*

repair - **1.** *taṣliiḥ* pl. *-aat.* The car needs only minor repairs. *s-sayyaara laazə́ma bass taṣliiḥaat baṣiiṭa.* **2.** *tarmiim* pl. *-aat.* The road needs repair urgently. *ṭ-ṭariiq laazmo tarmiim b-ɛažale.*

**The watch is beyond repair. *s-saaɛa maa ɛaadet tətṣallaḥ.*

to repair - **1.** *ṣallaḥ//tṣallaḥ.* I want to have these shoes repaired. *bəddi ṣalleḥ haṣ-ṣabbaaṭ.* **2.** *rammam//trammam.* We repaired the house last year. *rammamna l-beet ɛaamnawwal.*

to **repeat** - *ɛaad (i ø//nɛaad).* Repeat what I just said! *ɛiid yalli hallaq ʔana qəlto.* -- Repeat these words after me. *ɛiid hal-kəlmaat baɛdi.* -- Children repeat everything they hear. *l-ᵊwlaad biɛiidu kəll šii byəsmaɛúu.*

to **repent** - *nədem (a nadam).*

to **replace** - **1.** *ʔaxad maḥall˜ ..., qaam (u ø) maqaam˜ ...* We haven't been able to get anyone to replace her. *maa-lna qaadriin nlaaqi waaḥde taaxod maḥalla.* **2.** *baddal//tbaddal.* We're thinking of replacing these radiators with oil stoves. *ɛam nəftə́ker ᵊnbaddel har-raadyatooraat b-ṣoobaat maazoot.* -- They had to replace him with a man from out of town. *nžabaru ybaddlúu b-waaḥed mən barraat ᵊl-balad.* -- This pipe has to be replaced by a new one. *hal-buuri laazem yətbaddal b-waaḥed ᵊždiid.* **3.** *ɛawwaḍ//tɛawwaḍ.* These glasses can't be replaced. *hal-kaasaat maa byətɛawwaḍu.*

replacement - *tabdiil.* The pump will need replacement pretty soon. *ṭ-ṭrəmbe bədda tabdiil ɛan qariib.*

**We're looking for a replacement for our secretary. *ɛam ᵊndawwer ɛala waaḥde badaal* (or *ɛawaaḍ*) *səkərteerətna.*

reply - *žawaab* pl. *-aat* and *ʔažwibe.* I never received a reply to my letter. *maa stalamt ʔabadan žawaab ɛala maktuubi.*

to reply - *žaawab.* He replied that they would be glad to come. *žaawab ʔənno b-kəll suruur byəžu.*
report - *taqriir* pl. *taqariir.* I've already read the report. *sabaq w-qareet ᵊt-taqriir.* -- When will you make your report? *ʔeemta laḥa taʕmel taqriirak?*
to report - **1.** *ʕaṭa (-yaʕṭi ə //nʕaṭa) xabar ʕan.* Have you reported the incident? *ʕaṭeet xabar ʕan ᵊl-ḥaades?* **2.** *xabbar ʕan, ʕaṭa xabar ʕan.* Somebody must have reported him to the police. *fii ḥada laazem ykuun xabbar ᵊš-šərṭa ʕanno.* **3.** *qaabal.* To whom do I report? *miin laazem qaabel?* **4.** *tqaddam la-, ḥəḍer (a ḥḍuur) qəddaam.* Tell the soldier to report to his company commander. *quul ləl-ʕaskari yətqaddam la-qaaʔed sariito.*
report card - *daftar˜ (pl. dafaater˜) ʕalaamaat.*
reporter - *məxber* pl. *-iin.*
to **represent** - **1.** *twakkal ʕan, massal.* Who is representing the defendant? *miin mətwakkel ʕan ᵊl-məddaʕa ʕaléʼe?* **2.** *massal.* He represents a well-known German company. *bimassel šərke ʔalmaaniyye maʕruufe.* -- What does this symbol represent? *har-ramᵊz šuu bimassel?*
representative - **1.** *mmassel* pl. *-iin, wakiil* pl. *wəkala.* He is the European representative of a big concern. *huwwe l-ᵊmmassel ᵊl-ʔawrəbbi tabaʕ šərke ḍəxme.* **2.** *naaʔeb* pl. *nəwwaab.* Who's the representative from your district? *miin naaʔeb manṭəqtak?* **3.** *tamsiili*.* Does the country have a representative form of government? *l-ᵊblaad ʔəla niẓaam ḥəkᵊm tamsiili?* **4.** *mmassel.* Their opinion is not necessarily representative of the general feeling among the population. *raʔyon muu ḍaruuri ykuun ᵊmmassel ləš-šuʕuur ᵊl-ʕaamm been ᵊs-səkkaan.*
reproach - *mʕaatabe, ʕtaab* pl. *-aat.* I didn't mean that as a reproach. *maa ʕaneet haš-šii mʕaatabtak.*
to reproach for - *laam (u loom//nlaam) ʕala.* My mother is always reproaching me for my extravagance. *ʔəmmi daayman bətluumni ʕala baʕzaqti.*
reptile - *zaḥḥaafe* pl. *-aat* and *zawaaḥef.*
republic - *žamhuuriyye* pl. *-aat.*
republican - *žamhuuri*.*
reputation - *səmʕa, ṣiit.* He has a good reputation. *səmᵊʕto mniiḥa.*
**He has a reputation for being a good worker. *masmuuʕ ʕanno ʔənno šaġġiil ᵊmniiḥ.*
request - *raža* and *ražaaʔ* pl. *ražaʔaat* and *ražawaat, ṭalab* pl. *-aat.* Has he granted your request? *qəbə́l-lak ražaaʔak?* -- I am coming to you at the request of a friend. *ʔana žaayiik binaaʔan ʕala raža sadiiq.*
to request - *ṭalab (o ṭalab//nṭalab).* I must request you to leave this place. *ʔana məḍṭarr ʔəṭlob mənnak tətrok hal-maḥall.* -- I'm going to request three more copies. *bəddi ʔəṭlob tlatt nəsax taanyaat.*
to **require** - **1.** *ṭṭallab, qtaḍa.* A thing like that requires careful study. *šii mən haš-šəkᵊl byəṭṭallab diraase daqiiqa.* **2.** *ḥtaaž, ṭṭallab, bədd- + pron. suff., laazem- + pron. suff.* How much money does that require? *haš-šii qaddeeš byəḥtaaž maṣaari?* -- How much time will that require? *qaddeeš haš-šaġle btəṭṭallab waqᵊt?* -- That requires no proof. *haš-šii maa bəddo bərhaan.* **3.** *štaraṭ, ṭṭallab.* Do you require a deposit? *btəštə́reṭ šii raʕbuun?*
requirement - **1.** *šarṭ* pl. *šruuṭ.* That's the first requirement for this job. *haada ʔawwal šarṭ la-hal-waẓiife.* **2.** pl. *məṭṭallabaat.* A thorough knowledge of English is the most important requirement. *maʕᵊrfe taamme bᵊl-ʔəngliizi hiyye ʔahamm ᵊl-məṭṭallabaat.* -- Does he meet our requirements? *huwwe ḥaayez ʕala məṭṭallabaatna?*
rescue - **1.** *ʔənqaaz.* The rescue teams worked day and night. *fəraq ᵊl-ʔənqaaz štaġlet leelt ᵊnhaar.* **2.** *taxliiṣ, ʔənqaaz.* Nobody came to his rescue. *maa ḥada ʔəža la-taxliiṣo.* **3.** *xalaaṣ, nažaat.* His rescue was almost a miracle. *xalaaṣo kaan ʕibaaratan ʕan məʕᵊžze.*
to rescue - *xallaṣ, nažža, ʔanqaz.* They rescued only a handful of passengers. *xallaṣu bass kam waaḥed mn ᵊr-rəkkaab.*
research - *baḥᵊs* pl. *ʔabḥaas.* Are you teaching or doing research? *ʕam ᵊtʕallem wəlla ʕam taʕmel ʔabḥaas?*
resemblance - *mšaabaha, tašaaboh.* There's a strange resemblance between the two. *fii mšaabaha ġariibe been ᵊt-tneen.*
to **resemble** - *šəbeh (a šəbᵊh).* Don't you think he resembles his mother? *maa bədḍənn ʔənno byəšbah ʔəmmo?*
reservation - **1.** *ḥažᵊz.* Reservations are now being accepted. *hallaq ʕam yəqbalu ḥažᵊz.* -- I couldn't get a reservation on that train. *maa qdərᵊt ʔaʕmel ḥažᵊz b-hat-treen.* -- We wired the hotel for reservations. *ʕmalna taliġraaf ləl-ʔoteel yaʕmə́l-lna ḥažᵊz.* -- Make five reservations for us. *ʕmə́l-lna ḥažᵊz la-xamᵊs ʔašxaaṣ.* **2.** *taḥaffoẓ* pl. *-aat.* I'll accept the proposal with due reservations. *bəqbal ᵊl-ʔəqtiraaḥ maʕ kəll ᵊt-taḥaffoẓ(aat).*
reserve - **1.** *ʔəḥtiyaaṭi.* I'm afraid we'll have to dig into our reserves. *xaayə́f-lak laazem naaxod mn ᵊl-ʔəḥtiyaaṭi tabaʕna.* -- The country's oil reserves are estimated at almost one billion barrels. *ʔəḥtiyaaṭi z-zeet tabaʕ l-ᵊblaad mqaddar qariib mən balyoon barmiil.* **2.** *ʔəḥtiyaaṭ.* He's a reserve officer. *huwwe ẓaabeṭ ʔəḥtiyaaṭ.* **3.** *taḥaffoẓ.* Nothing can disturb his reserve and equanimity. *maa fii šii byəzʕež taḥaffẓo w-rabaaṭet žaʔšo.*
reserves - *quwwaat ʔəḥtiyaaṭiyye* (pl.). The defense ministry is calling up part of the reserves. *wazaart ᵊd-difaaʕ ʕam tədʕi qəsᵊm mn ᵊl-quwwaat ᵊl-ʔəḥtiyaaṭiyye.*
to reserve - *ḥažaz (e ḥažᵊz//nḥažaz).* Don't forget to reserve seats for us. *laa tənsa maa təḥžə́z-ᵊlna maḥallaat.* -- Is this table reserved? *haṭ-ṭaawle maḥžuuze?*
reserved - *mətḥaffeẓ.* I found him very reserved. *šəfto ktiir mətḥaffeẓ.*
reservoir - *xazzaan* pl. *-aat, ḥaawuuẓ* pl. *ḥawawiiẓ.*
residence - **1.** *maḥall˜ (pl. -aat˜) ʔiqaame.* State your residence and telephone number. *zkoor maḥall ʔiqaamtak w-nəmret talifoonak.* **2.** *beet, maskan.* Operator, try his residence if his office doesn't answer. *ṣanṭraal, baḷḷa žarrə́b-li beeto ʔiza maktabo maa bižaaweb.*
resident - *muqiim* pl. *-iin.* How long have you been an alien resident in this country? *qaddeeš ṣar-lak muqiim ʔažnabi b-hal-ᵊblaad?*
residential area - *manṭqet˜ (pl. manaaṭeq˜) sakan.*
to **resign** - *staʕfa, staqaal.* He resigned as chairman. *staʕfa mn ᵊr-raʔaase.* -- I've resigned from the club. *staʕfeet mn ᵊn-naadi.*
resignation - **1.** *ʔəstiqaale* pl. *-aat.* We demand his resignation. *mnəṭlob ʔəstiqaalto.* -- He handed in his resignation today. *qaddam ʔəstiqaalto l-yoom.* **2.** *ʔəstəslaam.* The villagers accept their hard lot with resignation. *ʔahl ᵊḍ-ḍeeʕa byəqbalu qəsmə́ton mən ʔaḷḷa b-ʔəstəslaam.*
resin - *ṣamᵊġ.*
to **resist** - **1.** *qaawam, maanaʕ b-.* He was shot while resisting arrest. *qawwaṣúu w-huwwe ʕam yqaawem tawqiifo.* **2.** *qaawam.* I couldn't resist the temptation. *maa ṭəleʕ b-ʔiidi qaawem ᵊl-ʔəġraaʔ.*
resistance - *mqaawame.* He didn't put up any resistance. *maa warža ʔayy ᵊmqaawame.*
to **resole** - *ḥaṭṭ (ə ḥaṭaṭ//nḥaṭṭ) naʕl ᵊždiid.* I'm having my shoes resoled. *ʕam ḥəṭṭ naʕl ᵊždiid la-ṣabbaaṭi.*
resolute - *ḥaazem.* My grandmother was a very resolute lady. *səṭṭi kaanet sətt ḥaazme ktiir.*
resoluteness - *ḥazᵊm, ʕazᵊm.*
resolution - *qaraar* pl. *-aat.* The resolution was adopted unanimously. *l-qaraar waafaqu ʕaléʼe bᵊl-ʔəžmaaʕ.*
resort - *malža.* As a last resort I can always turn to him. *biḍall daayman ʔaaxer malža bəltəží-lo.*
summer resort - *maṣyaf* pl. *maṣaayef.* Do you know a nice summer resort? *btaʕrə́f-li šii maṣyaf ḥəlu?*
winter resort - *mašta* pl. *mašaati.* Are you going to your favorite winter resort this year? *raayeḥ has-səne la-maštaak l-ᵊmfaḍḍal?*
to resort - *ltaža, laža(ʔ) (a lžuuʔ).* I don't want to resort to force. *maa bəddi ʔəltə́ži ləl-ʕənf.* -- We had to resort to drastic measures. *ḍṭarreena nəlžaʔ la-tadabiir ṣaarme.*
resource - *mawred* pl. *mawaared.* I have exhausted all my financial resources. *stanfazᵊt kəll mawaardi l-maaliyye.* -- The area is rich in natural resources. *l-manṭiqa bətfiiḍ bᵊl-mawaared ᵊṭ-ṭabiiʕiyye.*
respect - *ʔəḥtiraam* pl. *-aat, ʔəʕtibaar* pl. *-aat.* He has won the respect of everyone. *ḥəṣel ʕala ʔəḥtiraam ᵊl-kəll.*
in every respect - *mən kəll naaḥye.* We were satisfied in every respect. *kənna raḍyaaniin mən kəll naaḥye.*
in many respects - *mən ᵊktiir nawaaḥi, b-nawaaḥi ktiire.* In many respects I agree with you. *mən ᵊktiir nawaaḥi ʔana məttə́feq maʕak.*

to pay one's respects to - *qaddam ʔəḥtiraamaato la-*. Don't forget to pay your respects to the ambassador. *laa tənsa maa tqaddem ʔəḥtiraamaatak la-ḥaḍret ᵊs-safiir.*

to respect - *ḥtaram*. I respect your opinion. *bəḥtérem raʔyak.* -- You must respect your elders. *laazem təḥtérem kbaarak.*

respected - *məЄtábar, məḥtáram*. He is a respected businessman. *huwwe ražol ʔaЄmaal məЄtábar.*

respectable - *məḥtáram*. These are respectable people. *hənne naas məḥtaramiin.*

respective: The two scholars are considered the leading authorities in their respective fields. *l-Єaalmeen byəЄtəbruuhon kəll waaḥed mənhon maržeЄ b-ḥaqlo.*

respectively - *b-hat-tartiib*. He and his younger brother won first and second prizes respectively. *huwwe w-ʔaxúu ẓ-ẓgiir rəbḥu ž-žaayze l-ʔuula wᵊt-taanye b-hat-tartiib.*

respiration - *tanaffos*.

respiratory organs - *ʔaЄḍaaʔ˜ tanaffos* (pl.).

responsibility - *masʔuuliyye*. I'll take the responsibility. *baaxod ᵊl-masʔuuliyye.* -- He has no sense of responsibility. *maa Єando ʔayy šuЄuur bᵊl-masʔuuliyye.*

responsible - **1.** *masʔuul*. You are responsible for it. *ʔənte masʔuul Єanha.* -- I'm not responsible for anything. *ʔana maa-li masʔuul Єan šii.* -- You can't hold him responsible for the accident. *maa fiik tḥəṭṭo masʔuul Єan ᵊl-ḥaades.* **2.** *masʔuul Єan taṣarrfaato*. He's not quite responsible any more. *maa Єaad masʔuul tamaam Єan taṣarrfaato.* **3.** *fii masʔuuliyye*. It's a more responsible job. *hiyye šağle fiiha masʔuuliyye ʔaktar.*

rest - *baaqi, baqiyye*. Eat some now and save the rest. *kəl-lak šwayye hallaq w-xabbi l-baaqi.* -- You raise the money and I'll do the rest. *ʔənte žmaaЄ ᵊl-maṣaari w-ʔana baЄmel ᵊl-baaqi.* -- Where are the rest of the boys? *ween baqiit l-ᵊwlaad?*

rest - *raaḥa*. It's amazing what an hour's rest can do for you. *ğariib šuu btaЄmél-lak saaЄet raaḥa.* -- I went to the mountains for a rest. *rəḥᵊt Єaž-žbaal lər-raaḥa.*

to be at rest - *waqqaf*. Wait till the pointer is at rest. *ntéẓer la-ḥatta ywaqqef ᵊl-Єaqrab.*

to put one's mind at rest - *rayyaḥ baal˜* ... This will put your mind at rest. *haada laḥa yrayyéḥ-lak baalak.*

to take a rest - *staraaḥ*. Let's take a short rest. *xalliina nəstriiḥ ᵊšwayye.*

to rest - **1.** *rtaaḥ, staraaḥ*. Rest awhile. *rtaḥ-lak šwayye.* **2.** *rayyaḥ*. Try to rest your eyes. *ḥaawel rayyeḥ ᵊЄyuunak.* **3.** *ḥaṭṭ (ə ḥaṭaṭ// nḥaṭṭ)*. Rest your foot on this chair. *ḥəṭṭ ʔəžrak Єala hal-kərsi.*

**The ladder was resting against the wall. *s-səllom kaan masnuud Єal-ḥeeṭ.*

**The whole responsibility rests on him. *kəll ᵊl-masʔuuliyye Єalée.*

**The decision rests with you. *l-q̈araar Єaleek.*

**Rest assured that I'll take care of it. *tʔakkad ʔənni laḥa diir baali Єaleeha.*

**Let the matter rest! *xalli l-qəṣṣa təhda.*

restaurant - *maṭЄam* pl. *maṭaaЄem*. Is there a good restaurant around here? *fii šii maṭЄam ᵊmniiḥ ᵊb-han-nawaaḥi?*

restless - *ḍažraan, mətmalmel*.

to **restore** - **1.** *raǎžaЄ la-niṣaab-* + pron. suff. The police had to restore order. *ḍṭarret ᵊš-šərṭa traǎžeЄ ᵊn-niẓaam la-niṣaabo.* **2.** *raǎžaЄ//traǎžaЄ*. All the stolen goods were restored. *kəll l-ᵊğraaḍ ᵊl-masruuqa traǎžaЄet.*

to **restrain** - *ḍağaṭ (a ḍağᵊṭ) Єala, ẓabaṭ (o ẓabᵊṭ)*. She couldn't restrain her curiosity. *maa qədret təḍğaṭ Єala kətret ğalbəta.*

to **restrict** - *qayyad, ḥaddad*. The government is going to restrict the import of foreign cars to one hundred per year. *l-ᵊḥkuume laḥa tqayyed ʔəstiiraad ᵊs-sayyaaraat ᵊl-ʔažnabiyye la-miyye bᵊs-səne.*

restriction - *taqyiid* pl. *-aat, qeed* pl. *qyuud*. There are still many restrictions on foreign trade. *ləssa fii taqyiidaat ᵊktiire Єat-tižaara l-xaaržiyye.*

rest room - *beet˜* (pl. *byuut˜*) *mayy, beet˜ ʔadab, beet˜ xala, marḥaaḍ* pl. *maraḥiiḍ, l-xaareǰ.*

result - *natiiže* pl. *nataayež*. The results were very satisfactory. *n-nataayež kaanet ᵊktiir mərḍiyye.* -- The result was that ... *n-natiiže kaanet ʔənno ...*

to result from - *nataž (o ø) Єan*. The explosion resulted from a leak in the fuel tank. *l-ʔənfižaar nataž Єan nazazaan ᵊb-dabbo l-banziin.*

to result in - *ʔadda la-, ʔantaž*. The elections resulted in an overwhelming victory of the People's Party. *l-ʔəntixaabaat ʔaddet la-nažaaḥ baaher la-ḥəzb ᵊš-šaЄb.*

to **resume** - *staʔnaf*. The two parties will resume negotiations before long. *ṭ-ṭarafeen laḥa yəstaʔᵊnfu mfaawaḍaaton Єan qariib.*

resumption - *ʔəstəʔnaaf*.

retail - *bᵊl-ᵊmfarraq*. He sells wholesale and retail. *bibiiЄ bᵊž-žəmle w-bᵊl-ᵊmfarraq.* -- He has a retail business somewhere on the other side of town. *Єando tižaara bᵊl-ᵊmfarraq b-qərne bᵊṭ-ṭaraf ᵊt-taani mn ᵊl-balad.*

retail price - *səЄᵊr˜* (pl. *ʔasЄaar˜*) *ᵊmfarraq*. What's the retail price? *šuu səЄr l-ᵊmfarraq?*

to retail - *nbaaЄ bᵊl-ᵊmfarraq*. This coat retails at about thirty dollars. *hal-manṭo byənbaaЄ b-ḥawǎali tlaatiin doolaar bᵊl-ᵊmfarraq.*

retailer - *taažer˜* (pl. *təžžaar˜*) *ᵊmfarraq*.

to **retire** - **1.** *nsaḥab*. He has retired from public life. *nsaḥab mn ᵊl-ḥayaat ᵊl-Єaamme.* **2.** *tq̈aaЄad*. He'll be able to retire next year. *b-ʔəmkaano yətq̈aaЄad ᵊs-səne ž-žaaye.*

retirement - *taq̈aaЄod*.

retouch - *rootaše* pl. *-aat, reetuuš* pl. *-aat*. The picture needs a few retouches here and there. *ṣ-ṣuura laazəma šwayyet rootaše hoon w-ᵊhniik.*

to retouch - *rootaš*. Don't retouch the picture too much. *laa trooteš ᵊṣ-ṣuura ʔaktar mn ᵊl-lzuum.*

retreat - *taraažoЄ*. The retreat was orderly. *t-taraažoЄ kaan ᵊb-ʔəntiẓaam.*

to retreat - *traažaЄ*. The battalion retreated in the face of the enemy tanks. *l-foož traažaЄ qəddaam dabbaabaat ᵊl-Єaduww.*

return - **1.** *ʔiiraad* pl. *-aat, ḥaaṣel* pl. *ḥawaaṣel, maḥṣuul* pl. *maḥaṣiil*. How much of a return did you get on your investment? *qaddeeš ʔəžaak ʔiiraad mən tawẓiif ʔamwaalak?* **2.** *ražЄa* pl. *-aat*. I found many things changed on my return. *laqeet ʔašya ktiir ᵊtğayyaret baЄᵊd ražᵊЄti.*

returns - **1.** *nataayež* (pl.). Have the election returns come in yet? *ẓahret nataayež ᵊl-ʔənti-xaabaat wəlla ləssa?* **2.** *ʔiiraad, reeЄ*. The returns on the ticket sales alone run up to 1,500 pounds. *l-ʔiiraad mən beeЄ ᵊt-tazaaker waḥdo byəṭlaЄ ʔalf w-xamᵊs miit leera.*

**I wish you many happy returns of the day. *bətmannda-lak ʔiyyaam saЄiide.*

**Many happy returns of the day! *qbaal ʔiyyaam saЄiide!*

return ticket - *tazkaret˜* (pl. *tazaaker˜*) *raǎЄa, tazkaret˜ ʔiyaab*. I didn't use my return ticket. *maa staЄmalt tazkart ᵊr-raǎЄa tabaЄi.*

in return for - *mqaabel˜*. We ought to buy them a present in return for their hospitality. *ḥəlu ʔənno nəštríi-lon ᵊhdiyye mqaabel ḍyaafəton.*

by return mail - *b-ᵊržuuЄ ᵊl-booṣṭa*. If possible, answer by return mail. *ʔiza məmken žaaweb b-ᵊržuuЄ ᵊl-booṣṭa.*

income tax return - *taṣriiḥ˜* (pl. *taṣariiḥ˜*) *ḍariibet˜ ᵊd-daxᵊl*. You have to file your income tax return this week. *laazem tqaddem taṣriiḥ ḍariibet daxlak haž-žəmЄa.*

to return - **1.** *ražeЄ (a ržuuЄ, raǎЄa)*. When did you return? *ʔeemta ržəЄᵊt?* -- I've returned to my original idea. *ržəЄᵊt la-fəkᵊrti l-ʔaṣliyye.* **2.** *raǎžaЄ*. Don't forget to return the book. *laa tənsa maa traǎžeЄ l-ᵊktaab.* **3.** *radd (ə radd)*. She didn't return my visit. *maa raddət-li zyaarti.*

revenge - *ʔəntiq̈aam*. Her revenge was cruel. *ʔəntiq̈aama kaan qaasi la-daraže.*

to take revenge - *ntaq̈am, ʔaxad (b-)taar*. It's too late for you to take revenge on him. *faat ᵊl-ʔawaan təntéq̈em mənno.*

to revenge - *ʔaxad (b-)taar*. Their team wants to revenge their defeat of last year. *fariiqon bəddo yaaxod taar xṣaarəton tabaЄ ᵊs-səne l-maaḍye.*

reverse side - *qafa, ḍahᵊr*. Don't forget to fill in the reverse side of the card. *laa tənsa maa tЄabbi qafa l-kart.*

review - *taq̈riiẓ* pl. *taq̈ariiẓ*. The book had good reviews in all the newspapers. *l-ᵊktaab ṣar-lo taq̈ariiẓ ᵊmniiḥa b-kəll ᵊž-žaraayed.*

review lesson - *dars˜* (pl. *druus˜*) *ᵊmraažaЄa*.

to review - **1.** *naqad (o naqᵊd//nnaqad), ntaqad*. Who's going to review the book? *miin laḥa yənqod l-ᵊktaab?* **2.** *staЄraḍ*. The general will review the troops of the southern sector. *ž-ženeraal laḥa yəstaЄreḍ quwwaat ᵊl-manṭiqa ž-žanuubiyye.*

3. *raažaε.* I want you to review lessons five and six for tomorrow. *bəddi-yðakon ᵊtraažεu d-darseen ᵊl-xaames wᵊs-saades la-bəkra.*

to **revise** - 1. *naq̈q̈aḥ, hazzab.* Who's going to revise the dictionary? *miin laḥa ynaq̈q̈eḥ ᵊl-q̈aamuus?* 2. *ʔaεaad ᵊṇ-ṇaẓar b-.* Do you think the new administration will revise the immigration laws? *btəεtəqed ʔənno l-ᵊḥkuume ž-ždiide laḥa tεiid ᵊṇ-ṇaẓar ᵊb-q̈awaniin ᵊl-həžra?*

revolt - *tamarrod* pl. *-aat.* There are rumors of an army revolt in the north. *ṭaalεa ʔišaaεaat εan tamarrod bᵊž-žeeš bᵊš-šmaal.*

to revolt - *tmarrad, saar (u sawra).* They had good reason to revolt. *kaan maεon kəll ᵊl-ḥaqq ʔənno yətmarradu.*

revolting - *kariih, məqref.*

revolution - 1. *sawra* pl. *-aat.* The country has gone through two revolutions in five years. *l-ᵊblaad εaanet sawᵊrteen b-ᵊxlaal xams ᵊsniin.* 2. *doora* pl. *-aat, laffe* pl. *-aat.* How many revolutions does this motor make per minute? *kam doora byaεmel hal-motoor bᵊd-daqiiqa?* 3. *dawaraan.* Of course, they have to take the revolution of the planets into account. *ṭabiiεi laazem yəḥᵊsbu ḥsaab la-dawaraan ᵊl-kawaakeb ᵊs-sayyaara.*

to **revolve** - *daar (u dawaraan).* It all revolves around the question whether ... *š-šağle kəlla bədduur ḥawl ᵊl-masʔale ʔiza kaan ...*

revolver - *fard* pl. *fruude, msaddas* pl. *-aat.* The police found the revolver not far from the scene of the crime. *š-šərṭa laqet ᵊl-fard b-qərne muu bεiide εan makaan ᵊž-žariime.*

revolving door - *baab dawwaar* pl. *bwaab dawwaara.*

reward - *mkaafaa(t)* pl. *mkaafayaat.* He was promised a substantial reward. *waεadúu b-ᵊmkaafaat məḥᵊrze.*

to reward - *kaafa//tkaafa.* The company rewarded him for his faithful services. *š-šərke kaafto la-ʔəxlaaṣo bᵊl-εamal.*

rhetoric - *εəlm ᵊl-balaağa, εəlm ᵊl-bayaan.*

rheumatism - *ruumatəzm(a).*

rhinoceros - *karkadann* pl. *-aat.*

rhombus - *mεayyan* pl. *-aat.*

rhubarb - *raawand.*

rhyme - *q̈aafye* pl. *q̈awaafi.* The kasida contains several imperfect rhymes. *l-qaṣiide fiiha εəddet q̈awaafi muu maẓbuuṭa.* -- Rhyme is one of the characteristics of Arabic poetry. *l-q̈aafye mən miizaat ᵊš-šəεr ᵊl-εarabi.*

**His suggestion has neither rhyme nor reason. *ʔəq̈tiraaḥo maa-lo ṭaεme w-laa maεna.*

to rhyme with - *kaan εala q̈aafiit˜* ... The fourth line doesn't rhyme with the third. *raabeε beet muu εala q̈aafiit ᵊt-taalet.*

rib - 1. *ḍəlᵊε* pl. *ʔaḍlaaε.* He's so thin you can see his ribs. *huwwe nḥiif la-daraže bətšuuf ʔaḍlaaεo.* 2. *siix* pl. *siyax.* The wind broke one of the ribs of my umbrella. *l-hawa kasar siix mən siyax šamsiiti.*

ribbon - 1. *šriiṭa* pl. *šaraayeṭ.* She was wearing a blue ribbon in her hair. *kaanet ḥaaṭṭa šriiṭa zarqa εala šaεra.* 2. *šriiṭ* pl. *šaraayeṭ.* I need a new ribbon for my typewriter. *laazəmni šriiṭ ᵊždiid la-maakiint l-ᵊktaabe tabaεi.*

rice - *rəzz.* I'd like a pound of rice. *εaṭiini nəṣṣ kiilo rəzz.*

rich - 1. *ğani** pl. *ʔağniya, zangiil* pl. *zanagiil.* He comes from a very rich family. *huwwe mən εeele ğaniyye ktiir.* 2. *ṭayyeb, ğani*, xəṣeb.* It's rich soil. *l-ʔarḍ ṭayybe.* 3. *dəsem.* The food is too rich for me. *l-ʔakl dəsem εaliyyi ktiir.*

to get rich - *ğəni (a ø).* You won't get rich overnight. *maa laḥa təğna b-leele w-ḍəḥaaha.*

rickets - *ksaaḥ ᵊl-ʔaṭfaal.*

rickety - *mxalwaε.*

to get **rid of** - *txallaṣ mən.* We want to get rid of this old sofa. *bəddna nətxallaṣ mən hal-kanabe l-εatiiqa.*

riddle - *ləğᵊz* pl. *ʔalğaaz, ḥazzeera* pl. *-aat* and *ḥazaziir.*

ride - *rəkbe* pl. *-aat.* It's only a short ride by bus. *bass rəkbe qaṣiire bᵊl-baaṣ.*

**He gave me a ride all the way. *rakkabni ṭuul ᵊṭ-ṭariiq.*

**Can I give you a ride? *waṣṣəlak?*

**I'll take you for a ride tomorrow afternoon. *baaxdak bəkra baεd ᵊḍ-ḍəhr məšwaar bᵊs-sayyaara.*

**Boy, did she take him for a ride! *yaa laṭiif, qaddeeš ləεbet εalée!*

to ride - 1. *rəkeb (a rkuub, rəkᵊb, rəkbe// nrakab).* Do you know how to ride a motorcycle? *btaεref tərkab motosəkᵊl?* -- We rode in a beautiful car. *rkəbna b-sayyaara ḥəlwe.* -- Stop riding me! *ḥaaže tərkabni baqa!* 2. *məši (i məši).* This car rides smoothly. *has-sayyaara btəmši b-ᵊnεuume.*

to ride away - *məši (i məši).* He mounted his horse and rode away. *rəkeb ᵊḥṣaano w-məši.*

ridiculous - *məḍḥek.* That's a ridiculous attitude! *haada mawqef məḍḥek* (or ***mawqef biḍaḥḥek*)!

**Don't be ridiculous! *ḥaaštak maṣxara baqa!*

rifle - *baaruude* pl. *bawariid.*

right - 1. *ḥaqq* pl. *ḥquuq.* I insist on my rights. *bṣərr εala ḥquuqi.* -- I have as much a right to it as you do. *ʔəli ḥaqq fii qadd-ma ʔəlak.* 2. *ḥaqq.* You have no right to say that. *maa-lak ḥaqq təḥki heek.* -- He's right. *maεo ḥaqq* or *εando ḥaqq.* -- Do you think she's right? *btəftəker εandha ḥaqq?* 3. *yamiin* (invar.). I've lost my right glove. *ḍayyaεᵊt fardet kfuufi l-yamiin.* -- Politically, he's leaning to the right. *bᵊs-siyaase bimiil naaḥ ᵊl-yamiin.* 4. *q̈aaʔem.* A right angle has ninety degrees. *zaawye q̈aaʔime təsεiin daraže.* 5. *mnaaseb, mwaafeq.* He came just at the right time. *ʔəža tamaam bᵊl-waqt l-ᵊmnaaseb.* -- We'll leave tomorrow if the weather is right. *məndaššer bəkra ʔiza ṭ-ṭaqṣ ᵊmwaafeq.* 6. *maẓbuuṭ.* Are we going the right way? *maašyiin nəḥna bᵊṭ-ṭariiq ᵊl-maẓbuuṭ?* -- That's the right answer. *haada ž-žawaab ᵊl-maẓbuuṭ.* -- You didn't do the right thing. *maa εməlt ᵊš-šii l-maẓbuuṭ.* -- That's right. *maẓbuuṭ.* -- Only part of what you say is right. *bass šii mən kalaamak maẓbuuṭ.* 7. *ḍəğri, raʔsan, mbaašaratan.* I'm coming right home from the office. *žaaye mn ᵊl-maktab ḍəğri εal-beet.* 8. *raʔsan, mbaašaratan.* The house is right next to the church. *l-beet raʔsan žamb l-ᵊkniise* or ***l-beet b-ləzᵊq l-ᵊkniise.* 9. *ḥaalan, raʔsan, mbaašaratan.* We're going right after dinner. *raḥa nruuḥ ḥaalan baεd ᵊl-εaša.*

**You can't be in your right mind! *ʔənte muu məmken tkuun ᵊb-εaqlak!*

**It serves him right! *xaržo!*

**I'll be right there. *hallaq bəži.*

**Stay right there! *xalliik ᵊhniik!*

**He's right here next to me. *huwwe hoon žambi.*

**The porch runs right around the house. *l-varanda mḥaawṭa l-beet kəllo.*

**Go right straight ahead. *xalliik maaši ḍəğri.*

**They fought right to the bitter end. *ḥaarabu la-ʔaaxer ramaq.*

right of way - *ḥaqq ᵊl-muruur.*

right away - 1. *hallaq, ḥaalan, εal-ḥaarek.* Let's go right away or we'll be late. *xalliina nruuḥ hallaq walla mnətʔaxxar.* 2. *bᵊl-ḥaal, ḥaalan, b-saaεəta.* That's what I thought right away. *haada yalli ftakarto bᵊl-ḥaal.*

right now - *hallaq.* I'm busy right now. *ʔana mašğuul hallaq.*

right off - 1. *εal-ḥaarek.* I can't answer that right off. *maa fiini žaaweb haš-šii εal-ḥaarek.* 2. *bᵊl-ḥaal, ḥaalan, b-saaεəta.* That's what I thought right off. *haada yalli ftakarto bᵊl-ḥaal.*

all right - 1. *ṭayyeb.* All right, I'll do it if you want me to. *ṭayyeb, baεməla ʔiza bəddak.* -- We got there all right, but how! *ṭayyeb, wṣəlna la-hniik, bass kiif!* -- That's true all right, but nevertheless ... *ṭayyeb, haada maẓbuuṭ, bass maε heek ...* 2. *tamaam.* Is everything all right? *šuu kəll šii tamaam?* -- Everything will turn out all right. *kəll šii laḥa ykuun tamaam.* -- Is that all right with you? *haada tamaam maεak?*

**That's all right! (In reply to an apology) *baṣiiṭa!* or *maεleeši!*

**I think it's quite all right. *bẓənn maεleeši.*

**He knows why all right. *saddeq huwwe byaεref leeš.*

**I'll get even with you, all right! *saddeq ləssa bṣaffi ḥsaabi maεak!*

**I'd like to go, all right, but it's impossible. *žaaye εala baali ruuḥ, bass məstaḥiil.*

**He'll be all right again in a few days. *biṭiib b-hal-kam yoom.*

on the right - *εal-yamiin.* Take the road on the right. *xood ᵊṭ-ṭariiq εal-yamiin* (or *εala yamiinak*).

rightful - *šarεi*.* He is the rightful owner of the house. *huwwe ṣaaḥeb ᵊl-beet ᵊš-šarεi.*

right-hand - *yamiin* (invar.). The school is on the right-hand side of the street. *l-madrase bᵊṭ-ṭaraf ᵊl-yamiin mn ᵊš-šaareε.*

**He's the boss's right-hand man. *huwwe ʔiid ᵊr-raʔiis ᵊl-yamiin.*

rightist - *yamiini*.* The rightist parties support the

bill. *l-ʔaḥzaab ᵊl-yamiiniyye bətʔayyed mašruuε ᵊl-qaanuun.*

rim - 1. *šambar* pl. *šanaaber.* The rim of my glasses is broken. *šambar kəzᵊlki maksuur.* 2. *žanṭ* pl. *žnuuṭa.* The rim of the wheel is all bent out of shape. *žanṭ ᵊd-duulaab kəllo mṭaεwaž.*

ring - 1. *xaatem* pl. *xawaatem.* She wears a ring on her right middle finger. *laabse xaatem b-ʔaṣbaεta l-wəṣṭa l-yamiin.* 2. *ḥalaqa* pl. *-aat.* I can't find my key ring. *maa-li εam laaqi ḥalqet mafatiiḥi.* 3. *ḥalbe* pl. *-aat.* It's only a two-ring circus. *s-sərk ʔəlo bass ḥalᵊbteen.* -- We had seats near the ring. *maḥallaatna kaanet qəddaam ᵊl-ḥalbe.*

ring - *raane, ṭanne, daqqa.* That bell has a peculiar ring. *haž-žaraṣ ʔəlo ranne ġariibe.*

to give a ring - *saawa talifoon, ḍarab (o ḍ) talifoon, talfan.* Give me a ring tomorrow. *saawii-li talifoon bəkra.*

to ring - 1. *ṭanṭan, rann (ə raniin).* The noise is still ringing in my ears. *l-qarwaše ləssaaha εam ᵊṭṭanṭen b-ʔədni.* 2. *rann, ṭann (ə ṭniin), daqq (ə daqq).* The phone just rang. *hallaq rann ᵊt-talifoon.* -- Have you rung the bell? *daqqeet ᵊž-žaraṣ?*

**Somehow it doesn't ring true. *maa baεref leeš, laaken mbayyen εaleeha muu ṣaḥiiḥa.*

to ring up - *talfan, saawa talifoon.* Ring him up next week. *talfə́n-lo ž-žəmεa ž-žaaye.*

ring finger - *banṣar* pl. *banaaṣer.*

ringleader - *raʔiis˜ εiṣaabe* pl. *rəʔasa˜ εiṣaabaat.*

rinse - *faḍḍa* pl. *-aat.* Two rinses will be enough. *faḍḍᵊteen bikaffu.*

to rinse - 1. *faḍḍ (ə faḍḍ//nfaḍḍ).* I rinse my wash twice. *bfəḍḍ ġasiili marrteen.* 2. *ġasal (e ġasᵊl//nġasal), xasal (e xasᵊl//nxasal).* Be sure to rinse your denture after each meal. *laa tənsa maa təġsel ṭaqm ᵊsnaanak baεᵊd kəll waqεa.*

to rinse out one's mouth - *tmaḍmaḍ.* Rinse out your mouth with a little salt and water. *tmaḍmaḍ b-šwayyet mayy w-məlᵊḥ.*

riot - 1. *šaġab.* Two people were killed in the riot. *tneen qətlu bᵊš-šaġab.* 2. *tarkiibe.* He's a riot. *huwwe tarkiibe.*

riots - *ʔəḍṭiraabaat* (pl.). I'm afraid there'll be riots. *xaayə́f-lak yṣiir fii ʔəḍṭiraabaat.*

rip - *šaqq* pl. *šquuqa.* You have a rip in your skirt. *fii šaqq ᵊb-tannuurtek.*

to rip - 1. *šaqq (ə šaqq//nšaqq), šaraṭ (o šarᵊṭ// nšaraṭ).* I ripped my pants climbing the fence. *šaqqeet banṭalooni w-ʔana εam ʔətεarbaš εal-xəṣṣ.* 2. *fataq (o/e fatᵊq//nfataq).* I have to rip the seams. *laazem ʔəfteq ᵊl-lafqaat.*

to rip open - *šaqq (ə šaqq//nšaqq), šaraṭ (o šarᵊṭ//nšaraṭ).* I nearly ripped my hand open. *kənt laḥa šəqq ʔiidi.*

ripe - *məstə́wi, naaḍež.* The apples aren't ripe yet. *t-təffaaḥ muu məstə́wi ləssa.*

**She lived to a ripe old age. *εammaret la-šaafet wəld wəlda.*

to **ripen** - *stawa, naḍaž (o nḍuuž).* The apricots are already beginning to ripen. *l-məšmoš εam yəbda yəstə́wi.*

to **rise** - 1. *ṭaleε (a ṭluuε, ṭalεa).* The sun rises early. *š-šams εam təṭlaε bakkiir.* -- Over there the road rises again. *hniik ᵊṭ-ṭariiq byəṭlaε kamaan.* 2. *rtafaε.* The river is rising fast. *n-nahᵊr εam yərtə́feε ᵊb-sərεa.* 3. *rtafaε, ṭaleε.* Prices are still rising. *l-ʔasεaar ləssaaha εam tərtə́feε.* 4. *qabb (ə qabb).* The cake is rising. *l-gaato εam yqəbb.* 5. *qaam (u qyaam).* All rose from their seats. *kəllon qaamu mən karaasiihon.* 6. *traffaε, ddarraž.* He rose from the ranks. *ḍall yətraffaε mən ʔasfal martabe.*

to rise up - *rtafaε.* A huge column of smoke rose up over the town. *εaamuud haaʔel mn ᵊd-dəxxaan ᵊrtafaε fooq ᵊl-balad.*

risk - *mžaazafe* pl. *-aat, mxaaṭara* pl. *-aat.* I can't take such a risk. *maa fiini žaazef heek ᵊmžaazafe* (or ... *xaaṭer heek ᵊmxaaṭara*).

at the risk of one's life - *mxaaṭer ᵊb-ḥayaato, mžaazef ᵊb-ḥayaato.* We escaped at the risk of our lives. *harabna mxaaṭriin ᵊb-ḥayaatna.*

to run the risk of - 1. *žaazaf b-, xaaṭar b-.* He ran the risk of losing all his money. *žaazaf b-ᵊxṣaaret kəll maṣarii.* 2. *εarraḍ ḥaalo.* If you go out in this weather you run the risk of catching cold. *ʔiza btəṭlaε b-heek ṭaqᵊṣ bətεarreḍ ḥaalak taaxod barᵊd.*

to risk - 1. *žaazaf b-, xaaṭar b-.* He risked his life to save her. *žaazaf ᵊb-ḥayaato la-yxallə́ṣa.* -- He's risked his entire fortune. *xaaṭar ᵊb-kəll sarᵊwto.* 2. *tεarraḍ.* If we stay any longer, we'll risk being late for the party. *ʔiza qaεadna ʔaktar mən heek mnətεarraḍ nətʔaxxar εal-ḥafle.*

risky - *məxṭer, xəṭer.* That's a risky business. *hayy šaġle məxᵊṭra.*

rival - *mnaafes* pl. *-iin, mzaaḥem* pl. *-iin.* They have always been rivals. *daayman kaanu mnaafsiin (baεḍon ᵊl-baεḍ).*

rivalry - *mnaafase* pl. *-aat, tanaafos* pl. *-aat, mzaaḥame* pl. *-aat, tazaaḥom* pl. *-aat.*

river - *nahᵊr* pl. *nhuura* and *ʔənhor.* What's the name of this river? *šuu ʔəsᵊm han-nahᵊr?*

river bed - *mažra˜ nahᵊr* pl. *mažaari˜ nhuura.*

rivet - *tabšiime* pl. *-aat.* One of the rivets has worked loose. *tabšiime mn ᵊt-tabšiimaat ᵊrtaxet.*

to rivet - *baššam.* The worker is riveting the struts together. *š-šaġġiil εam ybaššem ᵊr-rakaayez maε baεḍon.*

roach - *ṣarṣuur* pl. *ṣaraṣiir.* Our kitchen is teeming with roaches. *maṭbaxna εam yəġli bᵊṣ-ṣaraṣiir.*

road - *ṭariiq* pl. *ṭəroq,* also *ʔəṭᵊrqa.* Where does this road go to? *haṭ-ṭariiq la-ween biwaddi?* -- He's on the road to recovery. *huwwe εala ṭariiq ᵊš-šifa.* -- Have one more drink for the road. *šrab-lak qadaḥ taani mənšaan ᵊṭ-ṭariiq.*

to go on the road - *džawwal.* Our salesman is going on the road next week. *l-bayyaaε tabaεna laḥa yədžawwal ᵊž-žəmεa ž-žaaye.* -- Is the whole cast going on the road? *l-fərqa kəlla laḥa tədžawwal?*

roar - 1. *hadiir.* You can hear the roar of the waterfall from here. *fiik təsmaε hadiir ᵊš-šallaal mən hoon.* 2. *zaʔiir.* It sounded more like the roar of a lion. *ṣ-ṣooṭ kaan ʔaqrab la-zaʔiir ᵊl-ʔasad.* 3. *žaεiir.* You could hear his roar for half a mile. *kaan fiik təsmaε žaεiiro mən εala nəṣṣ kiilomətᵊr.*

to roar - 1. *karr (ə karr).* The audience roared with laughter. *l-məstəmεiin karru mn ᵊḍ-ḍəḥᵊk.* 2. *žaεar (o žaεiir).* ''Shut up!'' he roared at me. *"xraas!" žaεar fiyyi.* 3. *zaʔar (o zaʔiir).* A lion roared in the distance. *fii ʔasad zaʔar mən εala bəεᵊd.* 4. *hadar (o hadiir).* We heard the torrent roaring deep down in the gorge. *sməεna hadiir ᵊs-seel mən səfl ᵊl-haawye.*

roast - 1. *roosto.* The roast is tough today. *r-roosto qaasi l-yoom.* 2. *mḥammar.* Do you like roast duck? *bətḥəbb ᵊl-baṭṭ l-ᵊmḥammar?* -- We had roast chicken for dinner. *ʔakalna farariiž ᵊmḥammara εal-εaša.*

to roast - *ḥammar.* You didn't roast the meat long enough. *maa ḥammarti l-laḥme kfaaye.*

roast beef - *roosto.*

to **rob** - *nahab (a nahᵊb//ntahab).* The two men are reported to have robbed a bank. *biquulu ʔənno t-tneen nahabu bank.* -- I've been robbed. *nahabuuni.* -- They'll rob you of your last cent. *byənhabu mənnak ʔaaxer qərš.*

robbery - *nahᵊb, salb.* He was convicted of robbery. *žarramúu bᵊn-nahᵊb.* -- That's highway robbery. *haada nahᵊb.*

robe - *roob-də-šaambᵊr* pl. *rwaab-də-šaambᵊr.* Please get me my robe and slippers. *balla žiibii-li r-roob-də-šaambᵊr wᵊš-šaḥḥaaṭa tabaεi.*

rock - 1. *ṣaxᵊr* pl. *ṣxuur(a).* They had to blast the rock. *nžabaru yənᵊsfu ṣ-ṣaxᵊr.* 2. *ḥažar* pl. *ḥžaar(a).* He was throwing rocks. *kaan εam yərmi ḥžaara.*

rock crystal - *krəstaal.*

rock salt - *məlᵊḥ ṣaxri* pl. *ʔamlaaḥ ṣaxriyye.*

on the rocks - 1. *xarbaan.* Their marriage is on the rocks. *ziižə́ton xarbaane.* 2. *seek* (invar.). I'd like a whiskey on the rocks. *εaṭiini wəski seek.*

to **rock** - 1. *hazhaz.* The floor rocked under our feet. *l-ʔarḍ hazhazet taḥᵊt ʔəžreena.* 2. *tražraž, hazhaz.* The boat's rocking. *š-šaxtuura εam tətražraž.* 3. *hazz (ə hazz//nhazz).* She rocked the cradle until the baby fell asleep. *hazzet ᵊs-sriir ḥatta naam ᵊl-beebé.*

**The situation is bad enough already; don't rock the boat. *l-ḥaale εaaṭle kfaaye hallaq, laa tsaawi šii yʔazzə́ma ʔaktar.*

to make rock - *hazz (ə hazz).* The explosion made

the whole house rock. *l-ʔənfižaar hazz ᵊl-beet mən ʔasaaso.*
rocket - *ṣaaruux* pl. *ṣawariix.*
rocking chair - *kərsi hazzaaz* pl. *karaasi hazzaaze.*
rocky - *ṣaxri*.*
rod - 1. *qaḍiib* pl. *qəḍbaan.* The parts are connected by an iron rod. *l-qəṭaᶜ mawṣuule maᶜ baᶜḍa b-qaḍiib ḥadiid.* 2. *qaṣabe* pl. *-aat,* also *qṣaab.* Get your rod and let's go fishing. *xood qaṣᵊbtak w-yalla nruuḥ nəṭṣayyaḍ.*
lightning rod - *qaḍiib˜* (pl. *qəḍbaan˜*) *ṣaaᶜqa.* Most churches have lightning rods. *ʔaktar ᵊl-kanaayes ᶜaleehon qəḍbaan ṣaaᶜqa.*
rodent - *ǧaareḍ* pl. *ǧawaareḍ.*
role - *door* pl. *ʔadwaar.* His role in the whole affair is pretty mysterious. *dooro b-haš-šaǧle kəlla ǧaameḍ šwayye.* -- What role did she play in the scandal? *šuu d-door yalli ləᶜᵊbto b-hal-ᵊfḍiiḥa?*
roll - 1. *laffe* pl. *-aat.* He used up a whole roll of wrapping paper. *stahlak laffe kaamle mən waraq ᵊṣ-ṣarr.* 2. *karraar* pl. *-aat.* I'll have to get another roll of film. *laazəmni karraar fəlᵊm taani.* 3. *ṣanḍwiiše* (pl. *-aat*) *mdawwara,* coll. *ṣanḍwiiš ᵊmdawwar.* Shall I get bread or rolls? *žiib xəbᵊz wəlla ṣanḍwiiš ᵊmdawwar?*
to call the roll - *qara (a qraayet˜//nqaret) ᵊl-ʔasaami.* Have they called the roll yet? *qaru l-ʔasaami wəlla ləssa?*
to roll - 1. *daḥraž.* Don't roll the barrel. *laa ddaḥrež ᵊl-barmiil.* 2. *ddaḥraž.* The ball rolled under the table. *ṭ-ṭaabe ddaḥražet taḥt ᵊṭ-ṭaawle.* 3. *laff (ə laff).* I roll my own cigarettes. *bləff sigaaraati.* 4. *hazhaz yamiin w-ᵊšmaal.* The ship was rolling heavily. *l-baaxra kaanet ᶜam ᵊthazhez ᵊb-šədde yamiin w-ᵊšmaal.* 5. *daḥal (o daḥᵊl// ndaḥal).* The lawn needs rolling. *l-gazoon laazmo daḥᵊl.* 6. *raqqaṣ.* Stop rolling your eyes like an idiot. *ḥaaže traqqeṣ ᵊᶜyuunak mətl ᵊl-mažnuun.*
**He's rolling in money. *huwwe ᶜando maṣaari maa btaakəla n-niiraan.*
to roll out - *raqqaq.* Roll the dough out thin. *raqqᵊqi l-ᶜažiine rqiiq.*
to roll up - *laff (ə laff//ltaff* and *nlaff).* We rolled up the rug. *laffeena s-səžžaade.*
to roll up one's sleeves - *šammar ᶜan sawaaᶜdo.* Roll up your sleeves and get down to work. *šammer ᶜan sawaaᶜdak w-quum ᵊštəğel.*
roller - 1. *ʔəṣṭwaane* pl. *-aat.* The typewriter needs a new roller. *maakiinet l-ᵊktaabe laazəma ʔəṣṭwaane ždiide.* 2. *madḥale* pl. *madaaḥel.* Don't leave the roller on the lawn. *laa txalli l-madḥale ᶜal-gazoon.* 3. *duulaab* pl. *dawaliib.* The heavy machine had to be moved on rollers. *nžabaru yənᵊqlu l-ʔaale t-tqiile ᶜala dawaliib.* 4. *karraar* pl. *-aat.* Can you fix the roller on that shade? *fiik ᵊtṣalləḥ-li l-karraar tabaᶜ hal-bərdaaye?*
roller skate - *fardet˜ batinaaž* pl. *batinaaž.*
rolling pin - *šoobak* pl. *šawaabek.*
Roman - *ruumaani** pl. *ruumaan.*
Roman Catholic - *laatiini** pl. *laatiin.*
Romania - *ruumaanya.*
Romanian - *ruumaani*.*
romantic - *roomanṭiiki*.*
Rome - *rooma.*
roof - *ʔəsṭuuḥ* pl. *ʔasaṭiiḥ.* I think the roof is leaking. *bẓənn ᵊl-ʔəsṭuuḥ ᶜam ynaffed mayy.*
**He's so poor he doesn't have a roof over his head. *faqiir la-daraže l-məskiin maa-lo maʔwa.*
**It was already past midnight and we still had no roof over our heads. *kaanet ṣaaret baᶜᵊd nəṣṣ ᵊl-leel w-ləssa maa kənna laqeena maʔwa nrəḥ-lo.*
roof garden - *ḥadiiqet˜* (pl. *ḥadaayeq˜*) *saṭᵊḥ.*
roof of the mouth - *saqf˜* (pl. *squuf(et)˜*) *ᵊl-ḥalᵊq.* I burned the roof of my mouth. *ladaᶜᵊt saqᵊf ḥalqi.*
rook - *rəxx* pl. *rxaax.* Too bad I can't move my rook! *yaa xaṣaara maa fiini ḥarrek rəxxi!*
room - 1. *ʔuuḍa* pl. *ʔuwaḍ, ġərfe* pl. *ġəraf.* Where can I get a furnished room? *ween bəqder laaqi ʔuuḍa mafruuše?* 2. *maḥall.* Is there any room left for my baggage? *safyaan šii maḥall la-šanatiyyi?* -- How can I make corrections if you don't leave room on your paper? *kiif bsaawi taṣḥiiḥaat ʔiza maa bətxalli maḥall b-warᵊqtak?* 3. *mažaal, maḥall.* There's no room for argument here. *maa fii mažaal ləž-žadal hoon.*
room and board - *ʔakl u-noom.* What do they charge for room and board? *qaddeeš biḥaasbu ʔakl u-noom?*
to do a room - *saawa ʔuuḍa.* My room hasn't been done yet. *ʔuuḍti ləssa maa tsaawet.*
to make room - 1. *faḍḍa maḥall.* Move the table to the right to make room for the arm-chair. *dfooš ᵊṭ-ṭaawle ᶜal-yamiin ḥatta tfaḍḍi maḥall ləl-qəlṭoq.* 2. *fasaḥ (a fasᵊḥ) mažaal.* He resigned from the faculty to make room for a younger man. *staǧaal mən səlk ᵊl-ʔasaadze la-yəfsaḥ mažaal la-waaḥed ʔaẓġar mənno.*
to room - *sakan (o ø).* They room together. *saakniin sawa.*
roomy - *waaseᶜ.* We have a roomy apartment. *ᶜanna ʔabarṭmaan waaseᶜ.*
rooster - *diik* pl. *dyaak* and *dyuuke.*
root - 1. *šərᵊš* pl. *šruuš(e).* The roots of this tree are very deep. *šruuš haš-šažara ġamiiqa ktiir.* -- The root of the tooth is decayed. *šərš ᵊs-sənn msawwes.* 2. *žəzᵊr* pl. *žzuur(a).* What's the square root of twelve? *šuu ž-žəzr ᵊt-tarbiiᶜi la-ṭnaᶜš?* 3. *ʔaṣᵊl* pl. *ʔṣuul.* What's the root of the word "ʔənsaan"? *šuu ʔaṣᵊl kəlmet "ʔənsaan"?* 4. *ʔaṣᵊl, manšaʔ, manbaᶜ.* Money is the root of all evil. *l-maṣaari ʔaṣᵊl kəll ᵊš-šruur.*
to take root - 1. *šarraš, ḍarab (o ḍarb) šruuš.* How can you tell whether the rosebush has taken root? *kiif btaᶜref ʔiza l-warde šarrašet?* 2. *tʔaṣṣal.* The custom never really took root. *l-ᶜaade bᵊl-ḥaqiiqa maa tʔaṣṣalet ʔabadan.*
to root out (or **up**) - *staʔṣal, qaḍa (i qaḍa// nqaḍa) ᶜala.* We must root out intolerance. *laazem nəstaʔṣel ᶜadam ᵊt-tasaamoḥ.*
rooted to the spot - *mbasmar ᵊb-maḥallo.* He stood there as if rooted to the spot. *waqqaf ᵊhniik kaʔənno mbasmar ᵊb-maḥallo.*
rope - 1. *ḥabᵊl* pl. *ḥbaal.* He let himself down the rope. *nəzel ᶜal-ḥabᵊl.* -- Give him enough rope and he'll hang himself. *rxii-lo l-ḥabᵊl šwayye w-šuufo kiif byəxreb ḥaalo.* 2. *ḥable* pl. *-aat* and *ḥbaal.* He was leading the calf by a rope. *kaan ᶜam yžərr ᵊl-ᶜəžᵊl b-ḥable.*
**He knows all the ropes. *byaᶜref kəll ᵊl-ḥiyal* or *byaᶜref ᵊl-madaaxel wᵊl-maxaarež.*
**I'm at the end of my rope. *nafdet kəll ḥiyali.*
to rope in - *ḥašar (ə/o ḥašᵊr//nḥašar).* Don't let him rope you in! *laa txallīi yəḥᵊšrak!*
to rope off - *ḥawwaq b-ᵊḥbaal.* The police had roped off the street for the parade. *š-šərṭa kaanet ḥawwaqet ᵊš-šaareᶜ b-ᵊḥbaal mənšaan ᵊl-ʔəstəᶜraaḍ.*
rosary - *masbaḥa* pl. *masaabeḥ.*
rose - *warde* coll. *ward* pl. *-aat* and *wruud.*
rosebud - *zərr˜* (pl. *zraar˜*) *warᵊd.*
rosebush - *warde* pl. *-aat* and *wruud, šažaret˜* (pl. *-aat˜*) *ward.*
rosemary - *ḥaṣa lbaan.*
rose water - *maawarᵊd.*
roster - *žadwal˜* (pl. *žadaawel˜*) *ʔasaami.*
rosy - 1. *wardi*.* You can already see a rosy glow in the east. *ṣaar fiik ᵊtšuuf waḥᵊž wardi bᵊl-mašreq.* -- What rosy cheeks those children have! *məlla xduud wardiyye fii ᶜand hal-ᵊwlaad!* 2. *zaahi, zaaher.* These are not exactly rosy prospects. *hal-ʔaamaal maa fiik ᵊtsammīi-hon ʔaamaal zaahye.*
**He always has a rosy outlook on life. *daayman byəṭṭallaᶜ taṭliiᶜet ᵊl-mətfaaʔel ᶜal-ḥayaat.*
to **rot** - *ᶜaffan.* The fruit is rotting on the trees. *l-fawaaki ᶜam ᵊtᶜaffen ᶜaš-šažar.*
to **rotate** - 1. *daar (u dawaraan), laff (ə laff).* Does the moon rotate on its axis? *biduur ᵊl-qamar šii ḥawl nafso?* -- This gear rotates counter-clockwise. *hal-ᵊmsannan biduur ᵊb-ᶜaks ᶜaqaareb ᵊs-saaᶜa.* 2. *ġayyar//tġayyar, baddal//tbaddal.* The troops stationed along the eastern boarders are rotated every six months. *l-ǧuwwaat l-ᵊmraabṭa ᶜala ṭuul l-ᵊḥduud ᵊš-šarqiyye btətġayyar kəll sətt əšhor.* 3. *tnaawab.* They work in rotating shifts. *byəštəġlu b-dooraat mətnaawbe.*
rotation - 1. *dawaraan.* The flywheel's rotation opens and closes the valves. *dawaraan ᵊṭ-ṭaara l-ḥaddaafe byəftaḥ w-bisakker ᵊṣ-ṣabbaabaat.* 2. *doora.* Farmers in this area have adopted crop rotation only recently. *l-ᵊmzaarᶜiin b-hal-manṭiqa bədyu yətbaᶜu niẓaam ᵊd-doora z-ziraaᶜiyye mn ᵊždiid.* 3. *tanaawob.* The paratroop unit was relieved within the regular schedule of rotation. *wəḥdet ᵊl-maẓalliyyiin tġayyaret ḥasab bərnaamež ᵊt-tanaawob ᵊl-ᶜaadi.*
rotten - 1. *mᶜaffen.* The peaches are rotten.

d-dərraaqnaat mεaffniin. 2. *mtaxtex.* The beam was rotten through and through. *l-εaḍaaḍa kaanet *mtax*txa ləl-εaḍ*m.* 3. *faased.* The whole government is rotten. *l-*ḥkuume kəlla faasde.*
4. *baayex *ktiir.* We saw a rotten film last night. *šəfna fəl*m baayex *ktiir *mbaareḥ εašiyye.*
5. *waaṭi.* They played a rotten trick on us. *ləεbu εaleena ləεbe waaṭye.*
rouge - *ḥəmra.*
rough - 1. *xəšen.* Why are your hands so rough? *leeš ʔideek hal-qadd xəšniin?* 2. *xəšen, žəreš.* He has a rough voice. *ṣooṭo xəšen.* 3. *wəεer.* The road gets very rough after five kilometers. *ṭ-ṭariiq baε*d xam*s kiilomətraat biṣiir *ktiir wəεer.*
4. *ġaliiẓ.* She isn't used to such rough work. *hiyye muu mətεawwde εala šəġ*l ġaliiẓ mən han-nooε.*
5. *xaam* (invar.), *ġašiim* (invar.). The bench is made of rough planks. *l-maqεad msaawa mn *lwaaḥ xašab xaam.* 6. *haayež.* The sea's pretty rough today. *l-baḥ*r haayež *l-yoom.* 7. *taqriibi**. This will give you a rough idea. *haada byaεṭiik fəkra taqriibiyye.* -- That's only a rough estimate. *haada muu ʔaktar mən taxmiin taqriibi.*
**You've got to treat him rough. *laazem *tεaamlo b-*xšuune.*
rough draft (or **copy**) - *məswadde* pl. *-aat.*
to rough it - *txašwan, txawšan.* I feel like going out in the desert and really roughing it. *žaaye εala baali ruuḥ εaṣ-ṣaḥra w-ʔətxašwan εan ḥaqa.*
roughly - *taqriiban.* Can you tell me roughly how much it will be? *fiik *tqəl-li taqriiban qaddeeš bikallef?*
roughneck - *žəl*f* pl. *žlaaf.*
Roumania see **Romania.**
round - 1. *žoole* pl. *-aat.* He was knocked out in the first round. *nṭaraḥ mən ʔawwal žoole.*
2. *doora* pl. *-aat.* How about another round of drinks? *šuu raʔykon b-dooret mašruub taanye?*
3. *fašake* coll. *fašak* pl. *-aat.* The man was carrying a gun and twenty rounds of ammunition. *r-rəžžaal kaan ḥaamel fard w-εəšriin fašake.*
4. *ṭalqa* pl. *-aat.* The battery fired some fifteen rounds at the retreating ship. *l-baṭṭaariyye ʔaṭlaqet šii xam*ṣṭaεšar ṭalqa εal-baaxra l-harbaane.* 5. *mdawwar.* They have a round table in the dining room. *fii εandon ṭaawle mdawwara b-ʔuuḍṭ *l-ʔakl.* 6. *ṣaḥiiḥ, taamm.* Forget about the fractions, give me only round numbers. *treek l-*ksuur εala žanab, εaṭiini bass ʔaεdaad ṣaḥiiḥa.*
7. *taamm.* Let's make it a round figure. *xalliina nsaawiiha εadad taamm.* 8. *məḥrez, məḥtḍram.* He's made a round sum in the deal. *ṭaalḍε-lo mablaġ məḥrez b-haṣ-ṣafqa.* 9. *daayer˜, ḥawaali˜.* The dog had a piece of rope round its neck. *l-kalb kaan εando ḥable daayer raq*bto.*
**He's just coming round the corner. *leeko žaaye εand *s-suuke.*
all the year round - *εala madaar *s-səne, ṭuul *s-səne, mn *l-ḥool ləl-ḥool.* I live here all the year round. *bəskon hoon εala madaar *s-səne.*
in round numbers - *taqriiban, εat-taqriib.* In round numbers there were two hundred people present. *taqriiban kaan fii miiteen zalame.*
to go round - *daar (u dawaraan).* Is there enough coffee to go round? *fii qahwe kfaaye dduur εaleena kəllna?* -- The wheel goes round and round and round. *d-duulaab εam yduur w-yduur w-yduur.*
to make the rounds - 1. *daar (u dawaraan).* The book is making the rounds among the students. *l-*ktaab εam yduur been *ṭ-ṭəllaab.* 2. *daar εala ʔalson *n-naas.* The story is making the rounds in town. *l-qəṣṣa εam *dduur εala ʔalson *n-naas b*l-balad.*
to round off - 1. *ḥaff (ə ḥaff//nḥaff).* Round off the edges a little. *ḥəff-ə̀lli l-ʔaṭraaf šwayye.* 2. *kammal, ṭabbaq.* Let's round off the number to 400. *xalliina nkammel *l-εadad la-ʔarbaε miyye* or *xalliina nṭabbeq *l-εadad εala ʔarbaε miyye.*
to round out - *kammal, tammam.* I need this to round out my collection. *laazəmni haš-šii la-kammel mažmuuεti.*
to round up - 1. *žammaε, žamaε (a žam*ε//nžamaε), lamm (ə lamm//nlamm).* See if you can round up the rest of the group. *šuuf ʔiza btəqder *džammeε baqiit *ž-žamaaεa.* 2. *žamaε, žammaε.* Do you think he can round up enough votes for this bill? *btəεtə́qed fii yəžmaε ʔaṣwaaṭ *kfaaye la-mašruuε hal-qaanuun?*
roundabout way - *doora* pl. *-aat, laffe* pl. *-aat.* They took a roundabout way to get there. *εəmlu doora la-yəṣalu la-hniik.*
in a roundabout way - *qiil εan qaal.* I heard it in a roundabout way. *sməεta qiil εan qaal.*
round-table conference - *məʔtamar˜* (pl. *-aat˜*) *ṭaawle məstadiire.*
round trip - *safra* (pl.*-aat*) *rooḥa ražεa, safra zihaab w-ʔiyaab.* How much is the round trip? *qaddeeš *s-safra rooḥa ražεa?*
round-trip ticket - *tazkaret˜* (pl. *tazaaker˜*) *zihaab w-ʔiyaab, tazkaret˜ rooḥa ražεa.* I saved a lot on my round-trip ticket. *waffart *ktiir *b-tazkə̀ret z-zihaab w*l-ʔiyaab tabaεi.*
route - *ṭariiq* pl. *ṭəroq* and *ṭərqaat,* also *ʔəṭ*rqa.* Which route did you take? *ʔanu ṭariiq ʔaxadto?* -- In winter, the planes fly the southern route. *b*š-šəte, ṭ-ṭayyaaraat btaaxod *ṭ-ṭariiq *ž-žanuubi.*
routine - *ruutiin.* Most of what I do is routine. *ʔaktar šəġli ruutiin (b-ruutiin).* -- That's a routine check-up. *haada faḥ*ṣ ruutiin.* -- After some time you acquire a certain amount of routine. *baε*d waq*t biṣiir εandak daraže mniiḥa mn *r-ruutiin.*
row - 1. *xnaaqa* pl. *-aat* and *xanaayeq.* My neighbors had a terrible row last night. *žiiraani ṣaar fii εandon xnaaqa faẓiiεa *mbaarḥa εašiyye.* -- I had a row with him. *ṣaar fii xnaaqa beeni w-beeno.*
to kick up a row - *qaam (i ∅) *d-dənye w-ḥaṭṭa.* You don't have to kick up a row because of such a minor mistake. *muu laazem *tqiim *d-dənye w-*tḥəṭṭa mənšaan ġalṭa ẓġiire mət*l hayy.*
row - *ṣaff* pl. *ṣfuuf.* We had seats in the first row. *kənna qaaεdiin b*ṣ-ṣaff *l-ʔawwalaani.*
in a row - *b*t-tawaali, b*t-tataaboε.* He won three times in a row. *rəbeḥ tlətt marraat b*t-tawaali* or ***rəbeḥ tlətt marraat wara baεḍon *l-baε*ḍ.*
to **row** - *žazzaf.* We rowed about a mile on the lake. *žazzafna ḥawaali miil b*l-buḥayra.*
rowboat - *šaxtuura* pl. *šaxatiir.*
royal - *malaki**.
royalty - *ʔəsar maalke* (pl.). Practically all of Europe's royalty attended the wedding. *taqriiban kəll *l-ʔəsar *l-maalke tabaε ʔawrəbba ḥəḍru l-εər*s.*
royalties - *εaaʔidaat* (pl.). The royalties from his latest book should increase his income considerably. *l-mənṭə́ḍar ʔənno l-εaaʔidaat mən *ktaabo l-ʔaxiir *dziid daxlo zyaade mniiḥa.*
rub - *εəqde.* Here's the rub! *hoon *l-εəqde!*
to rub - 1. *ḥakk (ə ḥakk).* My shoes rub at the heel. *ṣabbaaṭi biḥəkk naaḥ *l-kaε*b.* 2. *farak (o far*k//nfarak).* Keep rubbing it until it shines. *xalliik εam təfrə́ka ḥatta təlmaε.* 3. *farak, farrak.* He rubbed his hands to keep them warm. *farak ʔidée ḥatta yxalliihon dafyaaniin.* 4. *dalak (o dal*k//ndalak), farak.* Rub his back with alcohol. *dlək-lo ḍahro b*s-sbeetro.*
**Be careful not to rub him the wrong way. *ʔəṣḥa tədεas εala karaεiibo.*
to rub against - 1. *tḥaswas εala.* The cat rubbed against my leg. *l-qaṭṭa tḥaswaset εala rəžli.*
2. *ḥaswas εala.* He rubbed his back against the cabinet. *ḥaswas ḍahro εal-*xzaane.*
to rub down - *ḥass (ə ḥass//nḥass).* Tell him to rub down the horse. *qəl-lo yḥəss l-*ḥṣaan.*
to rub in - *farak (o far*k//nfarak), dalak (o dal*k//ndalak).* Rub the salve in well. *frook *l-marham *mniiḥ.*
**I know I'm wrong but you don't have to rub it in. *ʔana εarfaan ḥaali ġalṭaan, bass maa fii lzuum *tεiid w-təfteq fiiha.*
to rub off - *masaḥ (a mas*ḥ//mmasaḥ).* Rub off that lipstick on your cheek. *msaaḥ hal-ḥəmret *š-šəfaf mən εala xaddak.*
**He's been around lawyers so long that some of it has rubbed off on him. *εaašar *l-muḥaamiin mədde ṭawiile ḥatta ʔənno nṣabaġ šwayye b-ṣəbġə́ton.*
to rub out - *masaḥ (a mas*ḥ//mmasaḥ), maḥa (i maḥi//mmaḥa).* You forgot to rub out the price. *nsiit təmsaḥ *s-səε*r.*
rubber - 1. *kawšuuk.* These tires are made of synthetic rubber. *hal-kawašiik maεmuule mən kawšuuk ʔəṣṭinaaεi.* 2. *gaalooš* pl. *gawaliiš.* I lost one of my rubbers yesterday. *ḍayyaε*t fardet gaalooši mbaareḥ.*
rubber band - *maṭṭaaṭa* pl. *-aat, məġġeeṭa* pl. *-aat.*
rubbish - *zbaale.* Rubbish keeps piling up in our

backyard. *z-zbaale εam tətkawwam b-qafa beetna.* — Don't talk such rubbish! *laa təḥki heek ᵊzbaale!* or ***laa təḥki ṭaaleε naazel!*

rubble - *ʔanq̈aaḍ* (pl.).

ruble - *ruubᵊl* pl. *-aat.*

ruby - *yaaquute* coll. *yaaquut* pl. *-aat.*

rudder - *daffe* pl. *-aat.*

ruddy - *ḥəmraawi*, ʔaḥmar* f. *ḥamra* pl. *ḥəmᵊr.*

rude - 1. *žəfeṣ, šəres, qaliil˜* (pl. *qlaal˜*) *ʔadab.* Don't be so rude! *laa tkuun hal-qadd žəfeṣ!* 2. *bala ʔadab.* That was a very rude remark. *hal-ᵊmlaaḥaẓa kaanet ᵊktiir bala ʔadab.*

rudeness - *qəllet˜ ʔadab.* His rudeness is inexcusable. *qəllet ʔadabo maa-lha εazᵊr.*

rudimentary - *ʔawwali*, ʔəbtidaaʔi*.*

rudiments - *ʔawwaliyyaat* (pl.).

rug - *səžžaade* coll. *səžžaad* pl. *-aat* and *sažažiid.*

rugged - 1. *wəεer.* The country up there is pretty rugged. *l-ʔarḍ ᵊhniik ᵊktiir wəεra.* 2. *qawi*.* That boy's got a rugged constitution. *hal-walad tarkiibo qawi.*

ruin - *xaraab.* You'll be the ruin of me. *bəddak ᵊtkuun ʔaṣᵊl xaraabi.*

ruins - *xaraayeb* (pl.), *ʔaasaar* (pl.). They discovered the ruins of an old temple. *ktašafu xaraayeb heekal qadiim.*

in ruins - *xarbaan.* The city is in ruins. *l-madiine xarbaane kəlla.*

to ruin - *xarab* (*e xarᵊb//nxarab* and *xəreb a xaraab*), *nazaε* (*a nazᵊε//ntazaε*). The frost will ruin the crop. *s-saqεa laḥa təxreb ᵊl-maḥṣuul.* — He's ruining his health. *εam yəxreb ṣaḥḥto.* — They were ruined by the war. *xərbu b-sabab ᵊl-ḥarb.* — His new suit is completely ruined. *badᵊlto ž-ždiide ntazεet tamaam.*

rule - 1. *ḥəkᵊm.* In the 16th century Spain, too, was under the rule of the Hapsburgs. *bᵊl-q̈arn ᵊs-saades εašar sbaanya kamaan kaanet taḥᵊt ḥəkᵊm ʔəsret hapsburk.* 2. *q̈aaεde* pl. *q̈awaaεed.* The exception proves the rule. *š-šaazz bisabbet ᵊl-q̈aaεde.* — I'm sticking to the rules. *ʔana mətmassek bᵊl-q̈awaaεed.* — That's against the rules of the game. *haada ḍədd q̈awaaεed ᵊl-ləεbe.*

as a rule - *εaadatan.* As a rule, I don't drink whisky. *εaadatan maa bəšrab wəski.*

to rule - 1. *ṣayṭar εala, ḥakam* (*o ḥəkᵊm// nḥakam*). They wanted to rule the entire world. *kaan bəddon yṣayṭru εal-εaalam kəllo.* — What do you mean by the ''ruling class?'' *šuu btəεni bᵊt-ṭabaqa l-ḥaakme?* 2. *ḥakam.* He ruled for nineteen years. *ḥakam məddet təsaṭaεšar səne.*

**He rules the roost. *ʔəlo ṣoole w-doole.*

to rule out - *nafa* (*i nafi//ntafa*). This doesn't rule out the other possibility. *haada maa byənfi l-ʔəmkaaniyye t-taanye.*

ruler - 1. *ḥaakem* pl. *ḥəkkaam.* He's an absolute ruler. *huwwe ḥaakem məṭlaq̈.* 2. *maṣṭara* pl. *maṣaaṭer.* The ruler is too short. *l-maṣṭara ktiir qaṣiire.*

rum - *room, ram.*

Rumania see **Romania.**

Rumanian see **Romanian.**

to **rumble** - 1. *qarqaε.* We heard the cannon rumbling in the distance. *sməεna l-madaafeε εam ᵊtqarqeε mən bεiid.* 2. *karkar.* My stomach is rumbling. *məεᵊdti εam ᵊtkarker.*

to **rummage** - *nakwaš, baḥwaš.* He's rummaging around in the trunks. *εam ynakweš bᵊs-sanadiiq.*

rumor - *ʔišaaεa* pl *-aat.* The rumor spread like wildfire. *hal-ʔišaaεa ntašret mətl ᵊl-kəzᵊb.*

it's rumored - *fii ʔišaaεa.* It's rumored that she was kicked out. *fii ʔišaaεa ʔənno tqallaεet.*— It's been rumored for quite some time. *fii ʔišaaεa b-hal-ᵊxṣuuṣ mən məde.*

rumpus - *ġooše, šoošara, qarwaše, ḍoože.*

run - 1. *məšwaar* pl. *mašawiir.* The run takes five hours. *l-məšwaar byaaxod xamᵊs saaεaat.* 2. *rakᵊd.* I'm still exhausted from the run. *ləssaani halkaan mn ᵊr-rakᵊd.* 3. *rakde* pl. *-aat.* There was a run on the bank. *ṣaar fii rakde εal-bank.* 4. *tansiile* pl. *-aat* and *tanasiil.* You've got a run in your stocking. *fii tansiile b-ᵊžraabtek.*

**He must have had a run of luck. *laazem ykuun ḥakamo ḥazz ᵊmniiḥ.*

**The play has had an unusually long run. *ləεbu t-tamsiiliyye la-mədde ṭawiile εala ġeer εaade.*

**When he heard steps behind him he broke into a run. *lamma səmeε xaṭwaat ᵊb-qafda bada yərkod.*

average run - *waṣaṭ.* He's above the average run. *huwwe fooq ᵊl-waṣaṭ.*

in the long run - *maε ᵊl-waqᵊt.* In the long run you'll get tired of that. *maε ᵊl-waqᵊt bətməll haš-šii.*

to run - 1. *rakad* (*o rakᵊd*). Don't run so fast. *laa tərkod b-hal-εažale.* — I ran after him, but I couldn't catch up to him. *rakadt warda bass maa lḥəqto.* 2. *məši* (*i maši*). How often does this bus run? *kəll qaddeeš hal-baaṣ byəmši?* — There is a train running between Homs and Aleppo. *fii treen byəmši been ḥəmᵊṣ w-ḥalab.* — The road runs right by my house. *ṭ-ṭariiq maaši raʔsan b-žamb beeti.*— Why do you keep the motor running? *leeš bətxalli l-motoor maaši?* 3. *žara* (*i žarayaan*). Every room has running water. *kəll ʔuuḍa fiiha mayy žaarye.* 4. *mtadd.* The railroad track runs due north from here. *xaṭṭ ᵊt-treen byəmtadd dəġri naaḥ ᵊš-šmaal mən hoon.* 5. *štaġal, ləεeb* (*a ləεᵊb*). How many weeks has this play been running? *kam žəmεa ṣar-la hat-tamsiiliyye εam təštəġel?* 6. *ḥall* (*ə ø*). The color runs. *l-loon biḥəll.* 7. *šarr* (*ə ø*), *saal* (*i sayalaan*). I've such a cold that my nose has been running for two weeks now. *maεi rašᵊḥ malεuun la-daraže ʔənno manaxiiri ṣar-la žəmᵊεteen εam ᵊtšərr.* 8. *šaġġal, maššа.* Can you run a washing machine? *fiik ᵊtšaġġel šii ġassaale?* 9. *maššа, daar* (*i ʔidaara*). He's been running the business for three years. *ṣar-lo tlətt ᵊsniin εam ymašši š-šəġᵊl.* 10. *maššа, fataḥ* (*a fatᵊḥ*). They're going to run a road through our property. *bəddon ymaššu ṭariiq b-ʔarᵊḍna.* 11. *marraq.* Run the rope through this loop. *marreq ᵊl-ḥabᵊl b-hal-εəqde.* 12. *haššal, qallaε.* They ran him out of town. *haššalu mn ᵊl-balad.*

**Does that run in the family? *haš-šii mawžuud bᵊl-εeele?*

**He's running a high fever. *fii maεo ṣxuune qawiyye.*

**My horse ran last. *ḥṣaani ṭaleε ᵊl-ʔaaxraani.*

**These apples don't run any larger. *hat-təffaaḥ maa byəži ʔakbar mən heek.*

to run across - *ṣaadaf.* Maybe I'll run across him someday. *məmken ṣaadfo šii yoom.*

to run aground - *žanaḥ* (*a žnuuḥ*). My boat ran aground. *šaxtuurti žanḥet.*

to run along - 1. *tmaaša maε.* The boundary runs along the ridge. *l-ᵊḥduud btətmaaša maε ḍahr ᵊž-žabal.* 2. *waaza, ḥaaza.* The road runs along the shore of the lake. *ṭ-ṭariiq biwaazi šaṭṭ ᵊl-buḥayra.* 3. *tmaššа.* Run along now, children. *yaḷḷa yaa wlaad, tmaššu!*

to run around - *εaṭwaṭ.* Where have you been running around again? *ween kənᵊt εam ᵊtεaṭweṭ kamaan?* — He's running around with a bad crowd. *εam yεaṭweṭ maε žamaaεa ḅaaḅa ḥasan.*

to run away - *harab* (*o harabaan, hriibe*). My dog ran away. *kalbi harab.* — When he saw us, he ran away. *waqᵊt šaafna harab.* — His wife has run away. *marto harbet.*

**His imagination ran away with him. *mxayyilaato žarᵊfto maεa.*

to run down - 1. *našar* (*o našᵊr*), *ḥaka* (*i ḥaki*) *εala.* She's always running her friends down behind their backs. *daayman εam tənšor rəfaqaata b-ḍahron.* 2. *daεas* (*a daεᵊs//ndaεas*). He was run down by a truck. *ndaεas ᵊb-kamyoon.*

to run dry - *našef* (*a našafaan*). The well ran dry last summer. *l-biir nəšef ᵊṣ-ṣeef ᵊl-maaḍi.*

to run for - *raššaḥ ḥaalo, traššaḥ.* Who's running for mayor? *miin mraššeḥ ḥaalo raʔiis baladiyye?*

to run into - 1. *ṣadam* (*o ṣadᵊm*). He ran the car into a tree. *ṣadam ᵊs-sayyaara b-šažara.* 2. *ṣaadaf.* You'll never guess who I ran into at the post office. *ʔabadan maa laḥ yəži b-baalak miin ṣaadaft bᵊl-boosṭa.* 3. *ġaṭaṣ* (*o ġaṭᵊṣ*). He's running into debt. *εam yəġṭoṣ bᵊd-dyuun.* 4. *balaġ* (*o ø*). The casualties ran into the thousands. *l-xaṣaayer balġet ʔaalaaf w-ʔaalaaf.*

to run low - *kaan εala wašak yəxloṣ, qall* (*ə ø*), *xaff* (*ə ø*). My money is running low. *maṣariyyi εala wašak təxloṣ.*

to run off - *šammaε ᵊl-xeeṭ, farḍka.* He ran off with the club's funds. *šammaε ᵊl-xeeṭ maε ʔamwaal ᵊn-naadi.*

to run on - 1. *ṭaal* (*u ø*). His speech ran on and on. *xiṭaabo ṭaal w-ṭaal.* 2. *tamm* (*a ø*) *maaši.* The engine ran on even after I turned the switch off. *l-motoor tamm maaši ḥatta baεᵊd-ma sakkart ᵊl-məftaaḥ.*

to run out - *xalaṣ (o ø), nafad (o nafaad).* Our supply of sugar has run out. *muunet ᵊs-səkkar tabaƐna xalṣet.* — We ran out of ammunition. *xalṣet zaxiirətna.*

to run over - 1. *ṭaff (ə ṭaff), ṭaaf (u ø).* Watch out that the bathtub doesn't run over. *ʔəṣḥa yṭəff ᵊl-baanyo.* 2. *raažaƐ.* Run over your part before the rehearsal. *raažeƐ doorak qabl ᵊl-broova.* 3. *daƐas (a daƐᵊs//ndaƐas).* He was run over by a truck. *ndaƐas ᵊb-kamyoon.*

to run short of: I'm running short of cash. *xaafef maƐi n-naqdi.* — I'm afraid he's running short of new ideas. *šaayə́f-lak xaaffe maƐo l-ʔafkaar ᵊž-ždiide.*

to run through - 1. *txallal.* The theme runs through the whole novel. *l-mawḍuuƐ byətxallal ᵊr-riwaaye kəlla.* 2. *qaṭaƐ (a qaṭᵊƐ).* The boundary runs through a palm grove. *l-ᵊḥduud btəqṭaƐ ḥaqlet naxiil.* 3. *raažaƐ.* I'll run through these reports over the weekend. *braažeƐ hat-taqariir b-ʔaaxer ᵊž-žəmƐa.*

to run up - *rakad (o rakᵊd) la-fooq.* Run up to your room and get me the scissors. *rkood (or **nəṭṭ) la-fooq la-ʔuuḍtak w-žəb-li l-ᵊmqaṣṣ.* **We've run up a terrific bill at the hotel. *ṭaleƐ Ɛaleena ḥsaab faẓiiƐ bᵊl-ʔoteel.*

to run wild - 1. *fannak.* They just let the children run wild. *Ɛam yfalltu l-ᵊwlaad yfannku.* 2. *twaḥḥaš.* The dog has run wild since his master died. *l-kalb ᵊtwaḥḥaš mən waqᵊt maat ṣaaḥbo.*

run-down - 1. *mharmaš, faareṭ.* The house is run-down. *l-beet ᵊmharmaš.* 2. *manhuuk.* She looks terribly run-down. *faẓaaƐa hee ʔə́ta šuu manhuuke.*

rung - *daraže* pl. *-aat.* The top rung of the ladder is broken. *ʔaƐla daraže bᵊs-səllom maksuura.*

runner - 1. *Ɛaddaaʔ* pl. *-iin, rakkiid* pl. *-e.* He's a famous runner. *huwwe Ɛaddaaʔ mašhuur.* 2. *saaƐi* pl. *-yiin.* They sent the message by runner. *baƐatu r-risaale maƐ saaƐi.* 3. *lyaan* pl. *-aat.* She tripped on the runner in the hall. *tfarkašet bᵊl-lyaan bᵊl-kooridoor.* 4. *ḥadd* pl. *ḥduud(e).* One of the runners on my sled is broken. *ḥadd mən ᵊḥduudet məzlaaǧi maksuur.*

rupee - *rəbbiyye* pl. *-aat.*

rupture - *ftaaq* pl. *-aat.* He has a rupture. *maƐo ftaaq.*

rural - *riifi*, ǧarawi*.*

ruse - *ḥiile* pl. *ḥiyal, xədƐa* pl. *xədaƐ.* We had to resort to a ruse. *ḍṭarreena nəlža la-šii ḥiile.*

rush - 1. *Ɛažale.* What's your rush? *leeš hal-Ɛažale?* -- There's no rush about it. *maa fii lzuum ləl-Ɛažale* or *maa fii Ɛažale fiiha.* 2. *Ɛažqa, ṭaḥᵊš.* Let's wait till the rush is over. *xalliina nəstanna la-təxloṣ ᵊl-Ɛažqa.*

rush hour - 1. *saaƐet˜* (pl. *-aat˜*) *Ɛažqa.* During the rush hours everything is overcrowded. *ʔasna saaƐaat ᵊl-Ɛažqa kəll šii bikuun mazḥuum.* 2. *Ɛažqa, zaḥme.* You'd better not go during the rush hour. *ʔaḥsə́n-lak maa truuḥ waqt ᵊl-Ɛažqa.*

rush job - *šaġle* (pl. *-aat) məstaƐžale.* Can you do a rush job for me? *fiik taƐmə́l-li šaġle məstaƐžale?*

in a rush - 1. *məstaƐžel.* I'm in a terrible rush. *ʔana məstaƐžel ᵊktiir.* 2. *b-Ɛažale, b-sərƐa.* You can see it was done in a rush. *šii baayen ʔənno nƐamlet ᵊb-Ɛažale.*

to rush - 1. *Ɛažžal, staƐžal.* Don't rush me, I'll do it. *laa tƐažžəlni, baƐmə́la.* 2. *rakad (o ø) b-.* They rushed him to the hospital. *rakadu fii Ɛal-məstašfa.* 3. *baƐat (a ø//nbaƐat) b-sərƐa.* They rushed the message to the President's office. *baƐatu r-risaale b-sərƐa la-maktab ᵊr-raʔiis.* 4. *staƐžal.* I packed early because I didn't want to rush. *ḍabbeet šanatiyyi bakkiir laʔənni maa rədt ʔəstaƐžel.* — Don't rush, we have lots of time. *laa təstaƐžel, fii Ɛanna waqt ᵊktiir.* 5. *rakad (o rakᵊd).* They rushed to the bank. *rakadu Ɛal-bank.* 6. *ṭaleƐ (a ṭluuƐ).* The blood rushed to his head. *ṭaleƐ ᵊd-damm la-raaso.*

to rush at - *ʔasraƐ naaḥ.* He rushed at me. *ʔasraƐ naaḥi.*

to rush oneself - *tsarraƐ.* Don't rush yourself. *laa tətsarraƐ.*

to rush through - *salaq (o salᵊq//nslaq).* They rushed the bill through. *salaqu mašruuƐ ᵊl-ǧaanuun salᵊq.*

Russia - *ruusya.*

Russian - 1. *ruusi** pl. *ruus.* His father is a Russian. *ʔabúu ruusi.* — Is this the Russian Embassy? *hayye s-safaara r-ruusiyye?* 2. *ruusi.* He speaks a good Russian. *byəḥki ruusi mniiḥ.* — Translate that into Russian. *taržem haada lər-ruusi.*

rust - *ṣəḍe.* Before you paint the roof gutters scrape off the rust. *qabᵊl-ma ddahhen ᵊl-mazariib qḥaaṭ ᵊṣ-ṣəḍe Ɛanhon.*

to rust - *ṣaḍḍa.* Oil the machine or it will rust. *zayyet ᵊl-ʔaale w-ʔəllà bətṣaḍḍi.*

to **rustle** - *xašxaš, xarxaš.* I thought I heard something rustling. *kaʔənni smaƐᵊt šii Ɛam yxašxeš.*

rusty - 1. *mṣaḍḍi.* He scratched his hand on a rusty nail. *xadaš ʔiido b-bəsmaar ᵊmṣaḍḍi.* — The lock is all rusty. *l-qəfᵊl kəllo mṣaḍḍi* (or ***kəllo ṣəḍe*). 2. *taqlaan.* I'm afraid my French is a little rusty. *šaayə́f-lak ʔənno fransaawiiti šwayye taqlaane.*

rut - 1. *taləm* pl. *tlaam.* The road is full of ruts. *ṭ-ṭariiq malaan ᵊtlaam* (or ***kəllo mtallam*). 2. *ruutiin.* I simply have to get out of this rut. *kəll maa hunaalek laazem ʔəxloṣ mən har-ruutiin.*

ruthless - *bala šafaqa.* He's an utterly ruthless man. *huwwe šaxᵊṣ bala šafaqa ʔabadan.*

rye - *žaawadaar.*

S

sabbatical year - *sənt˜* (pl. *sniin˜*) *ʔiifaad.*

sabotage - *sabotaaž, taxriib.* There were a few scattered acts of sabotage. *ṣaar fii Ɛəddet ḥawaades sabotaaž hoon w-hoon.*

to sabotage - *xarrab.* He thinks someone is trying to sabotage his plans. *byəƐtə́qed fii ḥada Ɛam yḥaawel yxarrə́b-lo xəṭaṭo.*

saccharine - *səkkariin.*

sack - *kiis* pl. *kyaas.* I want a sack of potatoes. *bəddi kiis baṭaaṭa.*

to sack - *nahab (a nahᵊb//ntahab).* The enemy sacked the town. *l-Ɛaduww nahab ᵊl-balad.*

sacrament - *sərr* pl. *ʔasraar.*

sacred - 1. *mḥarram.* Nothing is sacred to him. *maa Ɛando šii mḥarram.* 2. *mǧaddas.* It is our sacred duty to defend our country. *waažəbna l-ᵊmǧaddas ᵊndaafeƐ Ɛan ᵊblaadna.*

sacrifice - *taḍḥiye* pl. *-aat.* They made many sacrifices for their children. *Ɛəmlu taḍḥiyaat ᵊktiire mənšaan ᵊwlaadon.*

at a sacrifice - *b-ᵊxṣaara.* I sold my car at a sacrifice. *bəƐᵊt sayyaarti b-ᵊxṣaara.*

to sacrifice - *ḍaḥḥa b-.* She sacrificed her life for him. *ḍaḥḥet ᵊb-ḥayaata la-ʔažlo.*

sacrilege - *ʔəntihaak˜ ḥərme.*

sad - 1. *ḥaznaan.* Why does he look so sad? *leeš hal-qadd huwwe ḥaznaan?* 2. *məḥzen, ḥaziin.* That's a real sad story. *hal-qəṣṣa məḥᵊzne Ɛan ḥaqa.* 3. *məḥzen, taƐiis.* The business is in a pretty sad state. *t-tižaara b-ḥaale məḥᵊzne waḷḷa.*

to feel sad - *ḥəzen (a ḥəzᵊn).* We all felt very sad when we heard of his illness. *kəlliyyaatna ḥzənna ktiir lamma sməƐna xabar maraḍo.*

to make feel sad - *ḥazzan.* Such a thing makes me feel real sad. *heek šii biḥazzənni ktiir.*

saddle - 1. (horse, camel) *sarᵊž* pl. *sruuž(e).* Can you ride without a saddle? *fiik tərkab bala sarᵊž?* 2. (donkey, mule, usually made of wood) *žlaal* pl. *-aat.* Tell him to adjust the mule's saddle. *qəl-lo yrakkez ᵊžlaal ᵊl-baġᵊl.*

saddle bags - *xərᵊž* pl. *xruuže.*

to saddle - *saraž (o sarᵊž//nsaraž).* Do you know how to saddle a horse? *btaƐref kiif təsrož ᵊl-xeel?*

to saddle with - *ḥammal, labbas.* He saddled me with all his troubles. *ḥammalni kəll mašaaklo.*

safe - 1. *sanduuq˜* (pl. *sanadiiq˜*) *ḥadiid.* The burglars tried to open the safe but failed. *l-ḥaramiyye ḥaawalu yəftaḥu sanduuq ᵊl-ḥadiid bass maa qədru.* 2. *ʔamiin.* You're perfectly safe around here. *ʔənte ʔamiin tamaam ᵊb-han-nawaaḥi.*

— This neighborhood isn't quite safe. *hal-maḥalle maa-la ʔamiine ktiir.* — Is the bridge safe? *ž-žəsər ʔamiin?*
**That's a safe guess. *mražžaḥ haada.*
**To be on the safe side, let's ask him again. *mən ḍabiil əl-ʔəḥtiyaaṭ xalliina nəsʔalo taani marra.*
safe and sound - *ṣaaġ saliim* (invar.). He's back safe and sound. *rəžeᶜ ṣaaġ saliim.*
safe-deposit box - *sanduuq˜* (pl. *sanadiiq˜*) *ḥadiid.*
safely - 1. *b-ʔamaan, b-salaame.* They arrived safely. *wəṣlu b-ʔamaan.* 2. *bət-taʔkiid.* I can safely predict that nothing's going to come of it. *ʔana bətnabbaʔ bət-taʔkiid maa fii šii laḥa yəṭlaᶜ mənha.*
safety - 1. *salaame.* This is for your own safety. *haada mənšaan salaamtak ʔənte.* 2. *ʔamən.* We can't guarantee public safety in that area. *maa mnəqder nəḍman əl-ʔamn əl-ᶜaamm əb-hadiik əl-manṭiqa.*
safety belt - *ḥzaam˜* (pl. *ʔaḥzimet˜*) *nažaat.*
safety pin - *šakkaale* pl. *-aat.*
safety razor - *ʔaalet˜* (pl. *-aat˜*) *əḥlaaqa, maakiinet˜* (pl. *-aat˜*) *əḥlaaqa.*
to bring to safety - *nažža//tnažža.* First they brought the children to safety. *ʔawwal šii nažžu l-əwlaad.*
saffron - *zaᶜfaraan.*
to **sag** - *habaṭ (o hbuuṭ).* The bookshelf sags in the middle. *raff əl-kətəb haabeṭ əmn ən-nəṣṣ.*
sail - *širaaᶜ* pl. *-aat.* The wind tore the sail. *l-hawa šarraṭ əš-širaaᶜ.*
to set sail - *ʔabḥar.* We set sail at daybreak. *ʔabḥarna maᶜ əl-fažər.*
to sail - *məši (i məši), saafar.* The boat sails at five. *l-baaxra btəmši s-saaᶜa xamse.*
**We go sailing every Sunday. *mənruuḥ məšwaar bəl-baḥər kəll ʔaḥad.*
**Do you know how to sail a boat? *btaᶜref ətmašši markab širaaᶜi?*
sailboat - *markab širaaᶜi* pl. *maraakeb širaaᶜiyye.*
sailor - *baḥḥaar* pl. *-a, baḥri* pl. *-iyye.*
saint - (Christian) *qəddiis* pl. *-iin,* (Muslim) *wali* pl. *ʔawliya.*
sake - see under **for**
salad - *ṣalaṭa* pl. *-aat.*
salad dressing - *soos˜* (pl. *-aat˜*) *ṣalaṭa.*
salary - *maᶜaaš* pl. *-aat, raateb* pl. *rawaateb.* How can you manage on that salary? *kiif fiik ətmašši haalak əb-hal-maᶜaaš?*
sale - 1. *beeᶜ.* The sale of alcohol to children is prohibited. *mamnuuᶜ beeᶜ əl-mašruubaat əl-kuḥuuliyye ləl-əwlaad.* — Our neighbor's house is for sale. *beet žiiraanna ləl-beeᶜ.* 2. *beeᶜa* pl. *-aat.* We made only three sales this morning. *ʔəžaana bass tlatt beeᶜaat has-ṣabaaḥ.* 3. *mabiiᶜ* pl. *mabiiᶜaat.* Sales of cotton have doubled this year. *mabiiᶜaat əl-qəṭən doobalet has-səne.* 4. *rəxṣa* pl. *rəxaṣ, ʔokazyoon* pl. *-aat.* I bought this coat at a sale. *štareet hal-manṭo b-rəxṣa.*
salesclerk - *bayyaaᶜ* pl. *-iin,* f. *bayyaaᶜa* pl. *-aat.*
saleslady - *bayyaaᶜa* pl. *-aat.*
salesman - *bayyaaᶜ* pl. *-iin.* We had to hire extra salesmen. *ḍṭarreena nwaẓẓef bayyaaᶜiin əzyaade.* — One of our salesmen will call on you tomorrow. *waaḥed mən bayyaaᶜiinna (l-mədžawwliin) byəmroq ᶜaleek bəkra.*
saleswoman - *bayyaaᶜa* pl. *-aat.*
saliva - *ryaale, bzaaq.*
salmon - *samaket˜* (coll. *samak˜* pl. *ʔasmaak˜* and *samakaat˜*) *sleemaan.*
salon - *ṣaaloon* pl. *-aat.*
saloon - *baar* pl. *-aat.*
salt - 1. *mələḥ* pl. *ʔamlaaḥ.* May I have the salt, please? *məmken ətnaawəlni l-mələḥ mən faḍlak?* 2. *maaleḥ.* The plant is found only in salt water. *n-nabaat maa byənwəžed ʔəlla b-mayy maalḥa.* 3. *mmallaḥ.* Do you have salt fish? *fii ᶜandak samak əmmallaḥ?*
**Take what the article says with a grain of salt. *fhaam məḥtawayaat əl-maḍaale b-šwayyet taḥaffoẓ.*
salt cellar - *mamlaḥa* pl. *mamaaleḥ.*
salt shaker - *mamlaḥa* pl. *mamaaleḥ.*
to salt - *mallaḥ//tmallaḥ.* Oh dear, I forgot to salt the soup. *yaa salaam nsiit malleḥ əš-šooraba.*
to salt away - *xabba, ddaxar, ḥaṭṭ ... ᶜala žanab.* He salted away a tidy sum. *xabba kam qərš əmnaaḥ.*
salty - *maaleḥ.* The fish is awfully salty. *s-samak maaleḥ əktiir.*
same - 1. *nafs˜, zaat˜.* I can be back on the same day. *fiini ʔəržaᶜ əb-nafs əl-yoom.* — They arrived at the same time. *wəṣlu b-zaat əl-waqət.* — We're the same age. *nəḥna b-nafs əl-ᶜamər.* — The same man called three times. *nafs ər-rəžžaal talfan tlatt marraat.* — He said exactly the same (thing). *qaal tamaam nafs əš-šii.* 2. *mətəl baᶜḍ-* + pron. suff. Except for the color these two patterns are exactly the same. *law-laa l-loon han-naqəšteen mətəl baᶜḍon tamaam.* — The two pictures are not the same. *ṣ-ṣuurteen muu mətəl baᶜḍon.* — That's all the same to me. *kəlla mətəl baᶜḍa bən-nəsbe ʔəli.*
**Thanks, the same to you! *wəl-qaayel, šəkran!*
**After the air raid, the town has never been the same again. *baᶜd əl-ġaara ž-žawwiyye l-balad maa ᶜaadet mətəl-ma kaanet ʔabadan.*
**After that experience he'll never be the same. *baᶜəd hat-tažrube muu raḥa yᶜuud mətəl-ma kaan mən qabəl ʔabadan.*
all the same - *maᶜ kəll zaalek, maᶜ haada.* All the same, it's a good idea. *maᶜ kəll zaalek hiyye fəkra mniiḥa.*
sample - 1. *maṣṭara* pl. *maṣaaṭer, ᶜaayne* pl. *-aat.* Do you have a sample of the material with you? *maᶜak maṣṭara mən l-əqmaaš hoon?*
sanatorium - *maṣaḥḥ* pl. *-aat.*
sanction - 1. *ʔəstəḥsaan, rəḍa.* A custom which enjoys the sanction of society. *ᶜaade bətlaaqi ʔəstəḥsaan əl-məžtamaᶜ.* 2. *ᶜuḍuube* pl. *-aat.* The cabinet voted unanimously for economic sanctions against the country. *mažles əl-wəzara ḍarrar bəl-ʔəžmaaᶜ farḍ ᶜuḍuubaat ʔəḍtiṣaadiyye ᶜal-əblaad.*
to sanction - *staḥsan, rəḍi (a rəḍa) ᶜala.* The Church has never sanctioned that practice. *l-əkniise b-ḥayaata maa staḥsanet (or rəḍyet ᶜala) hal-ᶜaade.*
sand - 1. *raməl* pl. *rmaal.* Let's lie in the sand. *xalliina nəssaṭṭaḥ ᶜar-raməl.* 2. *raməl* pl. *-aat.* Why don't you take this sand away? *leeš maa bətqiim har-ramlaat mən hoon?*
to sand - *farak (e/o farək//nfarak) ... b-waraq əqzaaz.* You'll have to sand the table before you finish it. *laazem təfrek əṭ-ṭaawle b-waraq əqzaaz qabəl-ma tbardəxa.*
sandal - *ṣanḍal* pl. *ṣanaaḍel.*
sandpaper - *waraq˜ əqzaaz.*
sandstorm - *ᶜaaṣfe* (pl. *ᶜawaaṣef*) *ramliyye.*
sandwich - *ṣaanḍwiiše* pl. *-aat.* Take a few sandwiches along. *xəd-lak kam ṣaanḍwiiše maᶜak.*
to sandwich in - *zarak (o zarək//nzarak), xabaṣ (o xabəṣ//nxabaṣ).* He was sandwiched in between two stout women. *kaan mazruuk been tənteen nəswaan əsmaan.*
sandy - *mərmel, ramli*.*
sane - 1. *ᶜaaqel.* Sometimes I think he's not quite sane. *ʔiyyaam əbḥasseb ʔənno huwwe muu ᶜaaqel.* 2. *maᶜquul.* If you ask me that's not a very sane decision. *ʔiza bəddak raʔyi haada muu ḍaraar maᶜquul əktiir.*
sanitary - *ṣəḥḥi*.* They prepare the food under the strictest sanitary conditions. *biḥaḍḍru l-ʔakəl b-ʔadaqq əš-šruuṭ əṣ-ṣəḥḥiyye.* — Drinking from the same cup isn't sanitary. *š-šərəb mən nafs əl-kaase muu ṣəḥḥi.*
sanitary napkin: no generic name, rather referred to by brand name, e.g., *kooteks, tampaks,* etc.
sanitation - *ᶜnaaye ṣəḥḥiyye.* They don't know the first thing about sanitation. *maa byaᶜərfu šii ᶜan l-əᶜnaaye ṣ-ṣəḥḥiyye.*
sanity - *salaamet˜ ᶜaqəl.* I doubt his sanity. *bšəkk əb-salaamet ᶜaqlo.*
sapphire - *yaaquute zarqa* coll. *yaaquut ʔazraq* pl. *yaquutaat zərəq.*
sarcasm - *tahakkom.*
sarcastic - 1. *məthakkem.* Don't be so sarcastic. *laa tkuun hal-qadd məthakkem.* 2. *tahakkumi*.* He silenced him with a few sarcastic remarks. *xarraso b-kam mlaaḥaẓa tahakkumiyye.*
sardine - *sardiin* (invar.).
Satan - *š-šeeṭaan.*
satellite - 1. *qamar ʔəṣṭinaaᶜi* pl. *ʔaqmaar ʔəṣṭinaaᶜiyye.* The United States has put another satellite into orbit. *l-wilaayaat əl-məttəḥde ʔaṭlaqet qamar ʔəṣṭinaaᶜi taani ḥawl əl-ʔarḍ.* 2. *taabᶜa* pl. *tawaabeᶜ.* Russia and its satellites voted against the resolution. *ruusya w-tawaabəᶜa ṣawwatu ḍədd əl-ḍaraar.*
satin - *sataan, ʔaṭlaṣ.*
satire - *hižaaʔ, hažu.*
satirical - *hižaaʔi*.*
satisfaction - 1. *lazze.* I don't get any satisfaction

out of that kind of work. *maa baš∈or ᵊb-ʔayy lazze b-heek šəğᵊl.* 2. *suruur.* It gives me great satisfaction to hear that. *byəḥṣal-li s-suruur ʔənni ʔəsma∈ haš-šii.* 3. *rəḍa.* Was everything settled to your satisfaction? *kəll šii ṣaar ḥasab rəḍaak?*
**We like to give our customers complete satisfaction. *bəddna nərḍi zabaayənna ∈al-maẓbuuṭ.*
satisfactory – *mərḍi*.* His condition is satisfactory. *ḥaalto mərḍiyye.*
**This room is quite satisfactory. *hal-ʔuuḍa laa baʔᵊs fiiha.*
to **satisfy** – 1. *kafa (i ø).* Your answer doesn't satisfy me. *žawaabak maa byəkfiini.* 2. *raḍa (i ʔərḍaaʔ//nraḍa).* You can't satisfy everybody. *maa fiik tərḍi kəll ᵊn-naas* or *maa byərḍi n-naas ʔəlla ʔaḷḷa.* 3. *qaam (u qyaam) b-.* Are you prepared to satisfy all the conditions of the contract? *ʔənte məst∈ədd ᵊtquum ᵊb-kəll ᵊšruuṭ ᵊl-kəntraato?*
to be satisfied – 1. *rəḍi (a raḍa).* I am not satisfied with my new apartment. *maa-li raḍyaan ∈al-ʔabarṭmaan taba∈i ž-ždiid.* — Are you satisfied now? *rḍiit hallaq?* 2. *ktafa.* We'll have to be satisfied with less. *laazem nəktəfi b-ʔaqall.*
Saturday – *(yoom˜) ᵊs-sabᵊt.*
Saturn – *zuḥal* (f.).
sauce – *soos* pl. *-aat, ṣalṣa* pl. *-aat.*
saucepan – *ṭanžara* pl. *ṭanaažer.*
saucer – *ṣaḥᵊn˜ fənžaan* pl. *ṣḥuun˜ fanažiin.*
flying saucer – *ṭabaq ṭaayer* pl. *ʔaṭbaaq ṭaayra.*
saucy – *wəqeḥ, qaliil* (pl. *qlaal*) *ḥaya.*
sausage: no generic term in Arabic. *maqaaneq* (pl.), actually, small sausages made of mutton, or the French *soosisoon* are used as the closest equivalents.
savage – 1. *waḥši*.* Savage rituals. *ṭuquus waḥšiyye.* 2. *mətwaḥheš* pl. *-iin.* The savages of the rain forest. *mətwaḥḥšiin ᵊl-ġaabaat ᵊl-ʔəstiwaaʔiyye.*
to **save** – 1. *ʔanqaz.* He saved her life. *ʔanqəz-la ḥayaata.* 2. *xabba, ḥafaẓ (a ḥəfᵊẓ).* Could you save this for me until tomorrow? *fiik ᵊtxabbi-li hayy ∈andak la-bəkra?* 3. *ḥafaẓ (a ḥəfᵊẓ).* Would you save a seat for me, please? *btəḥfəẓ-li šii maḥall ʔiza bta∈mel ma∈ruuf?* — Why do you save these old papers? *leeš ∈am təḥfaẓ haž-žaraayed ᵊl-qadiime?* — She'll do anything to save face. *bta∈mel kəll šii la-təḥfaẓ karaaməta.* 4. *waffar.* You could have saved (yourself) the trouble. *kaan fiik ᵊtwaffer ∈ala ḥaalak hat-ta∈ab.* — You saved me a trip to the office. *waffart ∈aliyyi məšwaar ∈al-maktab.* — You'll save time if you do it my way. *bətwaffer waqᵊt ʔiza bətsaawiiha bᵊṭ-ṭariiqa taba∈i.* — I saved almost a hundred dollars by going by boat. *waffarᵊt taqriiban miit dolaar b-safᵊrti bᵊl-baaxra.* 5. *ṣammad, waffar.* On a salary like this it's impossible to save any money. *b-ma∈aaš mətᵊl haad məstaḥiil ᵊl-waaḥed yṣammed maṣaari.*
**Save your breath. *bala ḥaki.*
savings – *taṣmiidaat* (pl.), *tawfiiraat* (pl.). He has used up all (of) his savings. *stahlak kəll ᵊt-taṣmiidaat taba∈o.*
savings account – *ḥsaab˜* (pl. *-aat˜*) *taṣmiid.*
saw – *mənšaar* pl. *manaašiir.* Could I borrow a saw? *fiini ʔəsta∈iir mənšaar?*
to saw – *našar (o našᵊr//ntašar).* He's been sawing wood all morning. *ṣar-lo ∈am byənšor xašab kəll ∈ala bəkra.*
sawdust – *nšaara.*
sawmill – *manšara* pl. *manaašer.*
say – *kəlme.* I wish I had a say in this matter. *ya-reet ʔəli kəlme b-hal-qaḍiyye.* — Who really has the say around here? *bᵊl-ḥaqiiqa l-kəlme la-miin hoon?*
to say – *qaal (u qool//nqaal).* What did you say? *šuu qəlᵊt?* — What do you say to that! *šuu bətquul ᵊb-haš-šii!* — She left the room without saying a word. *tarket ᵊl-ʔuuḍa b-ġeer-ma tquul kəlme.* — I would like to say something in that connection. *bḥəbb quul šii b-hal-ᵊxṣuuṣ.* — The papers didn't say a thing about it. *ž-žaraayed maa qaalu šii ∈anna.* — What does that sign say? *hal-ʔišaara šuu bətquul?* — I'll meet you, (let's) say, in an hour. *bšuufak xalliina nquul ba∈ᵊd saa∈a.* — They say he speaks several languages. *bquulu byəḥki ∈əddet luġaat.* — The word isn't said in polite company. *l-kəlme maa btənqaal qəddaam ᵊn-naas ᵊl-ʔawaadem.* — He's said to be rich. *biquulu ʔənno ġani.*
**There's much to be said for his suggestion. *fii maḥaasen ᵊktiir la-ʔəqtiraaḥo.*
**He has nothing to say around here. *maa-lo kəlme hoon.*
**I said good-by to him yesterday. *wadda∈to mbaareḥ.*
**We said a silent prayer at his grave. *ṣalleena b-qalᵊbna ∈and qabro.*
**It takes a lot of time, to say nothing of the expense. *btaaxod waqt ᵊktiir hayy faḍlan ∈an ᵊl-maṣruuf.*
**Needless to say, I can't afford to buy this car. *maa bədda ḥaki, maa fiini ʔəštəri has-sayyaara.*
**You can say that again! *waḷḷaahi ma∈ak ḥaqq!*
**That goes without saying. *haada mafhuum.*
saying – *qool* pl. *ʔaqwaal.* That's a very common saying. *haada qool šaaye∈ ᵊktiir.*
scaffold – *sqaale* pl. *-aat* and *saqaayel.* He fell from the scaffold. *wəqe∈ mən ∈as-sqaale.*
scale – 1. *daražaat* (pl.). The scale on the thermometer shows both Fahrenheit and centigrade. *daražaat miizaan ᵊl-ḥaraara fiiha faarənhayt w-santigraad.* 2. *məqyaas* pl. *maqayiis.* One centimeter on the map's scale corresponds to five kilometers. *ṣ-ṣantimətr ᵊl-waaḥed ∈ala məqyaas l-xariiṭa bisaawi xamᵊs kiilomətraat.* 3. *žadwal* pl. *žadaawel.* The United States has a higher scale of wages than any other country in the world. *l-wilaayaat ᵊl-məttəḥde fiiha žadwal ʔužuur ʔa∈la mən ʔayy doole bᵊl-∈aalam.* 4. *səllom* pl. *salaalem.* My neighbor has been practicing scales on the piano all morning. *žaari ṣar-lo ∈am yətmarran salaalem ∈al-byaano kəll ∈ala bəkra.*
to scale – 1. *darraž//ddarraž.* Wages are scaled according to seniority. *l-ʔužuur ᵊmdarraže ḥasab ᵊl-ʔaqdamiyye.* 2. *t∈arbaš ∈ala.* He tried to scale the prison wall. *ḥaawal yət∈arbaš ∈ala suur ᵊs-səžᵊn.*
scale – *ḥaršafe* pl. *ḥaraašef.* It is a popular belief that the scales of a fish mean good luck. *∈aammet ᵊš-ša∈b ᵊbtə∈təqed ʔənno ḥaraašef ᵊs-samak btəžlob ḥaẓẓ sa∈iid.*
to scale – *qaam (i qayamaan) ḥaraašef˜...* Clean and scale the fish properly. *naḍḍfi w-qiimi ḥaraašef ᵊs-samak ∈al-maẓbuuṭ.*
scales – *miizaan* pl. *mayaziin.* Put the meat on the scales. *ḥəṭṭ ᵊl-laḥme bᵊl-miizaan.*
scalp – *žəldet˜ raas.*
scandal – *fḍiiḥa* pl. *faḍaayeḥ.*
scapegoat – *kabš˜ ᵊl-fidaaʔ.*
scar – *šaṭᵊb* and *šəṭᵊb* pl. *šṭuube, nədbe* pl. *-aat.* He has a scar on his right cheek. *fii šaṭᵊb ∈ala xaddo l-yamiin.*
scarce – *qaliil.* Eggs are scarce at this time of (the) year. *l-beeḍ qaliil ᵊb-hal-ʔiyyaam ᵊmn ᵊs-səne.*
to become scarce – *qall (ə ø).* Food has become scarce. *l-ʔakᵊl qall.*
scarcely – *bᵊl-kaad.* I scarcely know him. *bᵊl-kaad ba∈ᵊrfo.*
scarcity – *qəlle.* There's a scarcity of good professors in that field. *fii qəllet ʔasaadze mnaaḥ ᵊb-hal-ḥaqᵊl.*
scare – *rə∈be* pl. *-aat.* You gave me an awful scare. *xalleetni ʔərtə∈eb rə∈be faẓii∈a.*
to scare – 1. *xawwaf, ra∈ab (e ø).* The dog scared me. *l-kalᵊb xawwafni.* 2. *xaaf (a xoof), rta∈ab.* I scare easily. *bxaaf ᵊb-sər∈a.*
**The explosion scared me stiff. *l-ʔənfižaar mawwatni mn ᵊl-xoof.*
to scare up – *dabbar.* Where did he scare up the money? *mneen qəder ydabber hal-maṣaari?*
scarf – *ʔišaarb* pl. *-aat.*
scarlet fever – *ḥəmma qərməziyye.*
to **scatter** – 1. *tfarṭa∈, tšattat.* The crowd scattered when the police arrived. *ž-žam∈ ᵊtfarṭa∈ waqt əlli wəṣlet ᵊš-šərṭa.* 2. *farṭa∈, laḥwaš.* I wish you wouldn't scatter the books all over the floor. *ya-reetak maa tfarṭe∈ ᵊl-kətᵊb ∈al-ʔarᵊḍ hoon w-ᵊhniik.*
scattered – 1. *mbaḥtar.* There are only a few scattered villages in the area. *fii bass kam ḍee∈a mbaḥtariin bᵊl-manṭiqa.* 2. *mfarṭa∈, mlaḥwaš.* The papers were scattered all over the desk. *l-ᵊwraaq kaanu mfarṭa∈iin ∈aṭ-ṭaawle kəlla.* 3. *mətnaaser.* The radio predicted scattered showers. *r-raadyo qaal ʔənno bəddo yṣiir zaxxaat maṭar mətnaasra.*
scene – 1. *mašhad* pl. *mašaahed.* That's in the third scene of the second act. *haada bᵊl-mašhad ᵊt-taalet bᵊl-faṣl ᵊt-taani.* 2. *makaan, mawqe∈.* The police arrived five minutes later at the scene of the crime. *l-boliis wəṣel ba∈ᵊd xamᵊs daqaayeq la-makaan ᵊž-žariime.* 3. *fərže* pl. *fəraž.* Don't make a scene in front of all these people. *laa ta∈məl-lna fərže qəddaam kəll ᵊn-naas.*

behind the scenes - *wara l-kawaliis.* Nobody knows what's going on behind the scenes. *maa ḥada byaƐref šuu ṣaayer wara l-kawaliis.*

scenery - 1. *deekoor.* Who designed the scenery? *miin ṣammam ᵊd-deekoor?* 2. *manaaẓer* (pl.). You can find some beautiful scenery a few miles out of town. *fiik ᵊtlaaqi manaaẓer žamiile Ɛala baƐᵊd kam miil ᵊmn ᵊl-balad.*

scent - *ḥaasset˜ šamm.* Our dog has a keen scent. *kalbna Ɛando ḥaasset šamm ḥaadde.*

to scent - *šamm (ə šamm//nšamm).* The dogs have scented the fox. *l-ᵊklaab šaammiin ᵊt-taƐlab.*

schedule - 1. *bərnaamež* pl. *baraamež.* We'll have to work out a schedule if we want to finish on time. *laazem naƐmel bərnaamež ʔiza bəddna nxalleṣ Ɛal-waqᵊt.* 2. *žadwal˜* (pl. *žadaawel˜*) *mawaƐiid.* Check the schedule to see when the bus leaves. *raažeƐ žadwal ᵊl-mawaƐiid ḥatta tšuuf ʔeemta byəmši l-baaṣ.*

on schedule - *Ɛal-waqᵊt.* The train arrived on schedule. *t-treen waṣel Ɛal-waqᵊt.*

to schedule - *ḥaddad, Ɛayyan.* The meeting is scheduled for tomorrow. *l-ʔəžtimaaƐ mḥaddad bəkra.* — We have tentatively scheduled the appointment for Thursday. *mabdaʔiyyan ḥaddadna l-ᵊmqaabale l-xamiis.*

scheme - 1. *mašruuƐ* pl. *mašariiƐ.* Has he thought up a new scheme? *dabbar šii mašruuƐ ᵊždiid?* 2. *tansiiq, tartiib.* We've changed the color scheme. *ġayyarna tansiiq ᵊl-ʔalwaan.*

to scheme - *dabbar dasaayes, ḥayyak ᵊmʔaamaraat.* They're always scheming. *daaʔiman Ɛam ydabbru dasaayes.*

scholar - *Ɛaliim* pl. *Ɛəlama,* f. *Ɛaliime* pl. *-aat.*

scholarship - 1. *kafaaʔa Ɛəlmiyye.* The university is known for the high degree of scholarship it maintains. *ž-žaamƐa mašhuura b-kafaaʔəta l-Ɛəlmiyye l-Ɛaalye.* 2. *mənḥa* (pl. *mənaḥ*) *diraasiyye.* He was in Egypt on a Fulbright Scholarship. *kaan ᵊb-məṣr ᵊb-mənḥa diraasiyye tabaƐ fulbrayt.*

school - *sərᵊb* pl. *ʔasraab.* We sighted a school of dolphins a little while ago. *šəfna sərᵊb darfiil mən šwayye.*

school - 1. *madrase* pl. *madaares.* Boarding school. *madrase daaxliyye.* - Elementary school. *madrase ʔəbtidaaʔiyye.* - Private school. *madrase xaaṣṣa.* - Public school. *madrase ḥkuumiyye.* - Secondary school. *madrase saanawiyye.* 2. *mazhab* pl. *mazaaheb, madrase* pl. *madaares.* He's a leading exponent of the realistic school of painting. *huwwe mən ʔaƐlaam mazhab ᵊl-waaqƐiyye lət-taṣwiir.*

law school - *kəlliyyet˜* (pl. *-aat˜*) *ḥuquuq, madraset˜* (pl. *madaares˜*) *ḥuquuq.*

medical school - *kəlliyyet˜* (pl. *-aat˜*) *ṭəbb.*

schoolmate - *rfiiq˜* (pl. *rəfaqaat˜* and *rfaaq˜*) *madrase.*

sciatica - *Ɛərq˜ ᵊl-ʔansar.*

science - *Ɛəlᵊm* pl. *Ɛluum.*

scientific - *Ɛəlmi*.*

scientist - *Ɛaalem* pl. *Ɛəlama,* f. *Ɛaalme* pl. *-aat.*

(pair of) **scissors** - *mqaṣṣ* pl. *-aat.*

to **scold** - *xaanaq.* My mother scolded me. *ʔəmmi xaanaqətni.*

scolding - *xnaaqa* pl. *xanaayeq.*

scoop - 1. *maġrafe* pl. *maġaaref.* I can't find the ice-cream scoop. *maa-li Ɛam laaqi maġraft ᵊl-buuẓa.* 2. *ġarfe* pl. *-aat.* Give me one scoop of vanilla ice cream and one scoop of pistachio. *Ɛaṭiini ġarfet vaneella w-ġarfet fəstoq.*

scooter - 1. (motor) *skuuter* pl. *-aat, vespa* pl. *vespayaat.* 2. (children's) *zəḥḥeeṭa* pl. *-aat.*

scope - *niṭaaq* pl. *-aat.* This goes far beyond the scope of such a dictionary. *haada xaareǰ ᵊktiir Ɛan niṭaaq heek qaamuus.*

to **scorch** - *ladaƐ (a ladᵊƐ//ltadaƐ).* I nearly scorched my dress. *kənt laḥa ʔəldaƐ roobi.* -- The sun is scorching (hot). *š-šamᵊs laadƐa.*

score - *natiiže* pl. *nataayež, skoor.* What's the score up to now? *qaddeeš ᵊn-natiiže la-hallaq?* — She had the highest score in the English test. *naalet ʔaḥsan natiiže bᵊl-faḥṣ ᵊl-ʔəngliizi.*

**I want you to know the score before you sign the paper. *bəddi-ydak taƐref ḥaqaayeq ᵊl-ḥaale qabᵊl-ma təmḍi l-waraqa.*

scores - *Ɛašaraat* (pl.). Scores of people died in that epidemic. *Ɛašaraat ᵊn-naas maatu b-hal-wabaaʔ.*

on that score - 1. *b-han-naaḥye, b-hal-ᵊxṣuuṣ.* You don't need to worry on that score. *maa laazem ᵊtšaġġel baalak b-han-naaḥye.* 2. *la-has-sabab, məšaan heek.* We can't excuse him on that score. *maa mnəqder nəƐᵊzro la-has-sabab.*

to keep score - *qayyad.* Who's keeping score in this game? *miin Ɛam yqayyed ᵊb-hal-ləƐbe?*

to settle a score with - *ṣaffa ḥsaab maƐ.* I have a score to settle with that fellow. *ʔəli ḥsaab laazem ṣaffīi maƐ haz-zalame.*

to score - 1. *saǰǰal.* He scored five points. *saǰǰal xamᵊs nəqaṭ.* 2. *fawwat, saǰǰal.* Who scored that goal? *miin fawwat hal-gool?*

scorpion - *Ɛaqrab* pl. *Ɛaqaareb.*

Scot - *skotlandi** pl. *-iyye* and *-iyyiin.*

Scotch - *skotlandi*.*

Scotchman - *skotlandi* pl. *-iyye* and *-iyyiin.*

Scotland - *skotlanda.*

Scotsman - *skotlandi* pl. *-iyye* and *-iyyiin.*

Scottish - *skotlandi*.*

scoundrel - *saafel* pl. *-iin.*

to **scour** - *farak (o farᵊk//nfarak).* You'll have to scour the pans thoroughly. *laazem təfᵊrki l-maqaali mniiḥ.*

scout - *kaššaaf* pl. *-e.* A local scout accompanied the patrol. *fii kaššaaf maḥalli raafaq ᵊd-dooriyye.*

boy scout - *kaššaaf* pl. *-e.*

girl scout - *kaššaafe* pl. *-aat.*

to scout - *stakšaf.* Let's scout the territory. *xalliina nəstakšef ᵊl-manṭiqa.*

scrambled eggs - *beeḍ maxfuuq.*

scrap - 1. *faḍle* pl. *-aat.* Give the scraps to the dog. *Ɛaṭi l-faḍlaat ləl-kalᵊb.* 2. *qṣaaṣe* pl. *-aat* and *qaṣaayeṣ.* That's only a scrap of paper. *haada bass ᵊqṣaaṣet waraq.* 3. *xnaaqa* pl. *-aat.* They had an awful scrap last night. *ṣaar beenaaton ᵊxnaaqa faẓiiƐa mbaareḥ Ɛašiyye.*

scrap metal - *maƐdan* (pl. *maƐaaden*) *xərḍa.* He deals in scrap metal. *bitaažer ᵊb-maƐaaden xərḍa.*

to scrap - *kabb (ə kabb//nkabb).* After two years they scrapped the whole project. *baƐᵊd sənteen kabbu l-mašruuƐ kəllo.*

scrape - *warṭa* pl. *-aat.* Those boys are always getting into some kind of scrape. *hal-ᵊwlaad daayman biwaqqƐu ḥaalon b-šii warṭa.*

to scrape - *qašaṭ (o qašᵊṭ//nqašaṭ), šaṭab (o/e šaṭᵊb//nšaṭab).* He scraped his knees on the rock. *qašaṭ rəkabo bᵊṣ-ṣaxra.*

to scrape along - *qandaq Ɛala ḥaalo.* We had to scrape along on very little money this month. *nǰabarna nqandeq Ɛala ḥaalna b-maṣaari ktiir qaliile bᵊš-šahr ᵊl-maaḍi.*

to scrape off - *qašaṭ (o qašᵊṭ//nqašaṭ).* Scrape the paint off first. *ʔawwal šii qšooṭ ᵊd-dhaan.*

to scrape together - *žammaƐ.* I couldn't scrape the money together. *maa ḥsənt žammeƐ ᵊl-maṣaari.*

scratch - *xadᵊš* pl. *xduuš(e), xamᵊš* pl. *xmuuš(e).* Where did you get that scratch on your cheek? *mən ʔeeš hal-xadᵊš Ɛala xaddak?* — We escaped without a scratch. *nažeena bala w-laa xadᵊš.*

from scratch - *mən laa-šeeʔ.* After the fire he had to start from scratch. *baƐd ᵊl-ḥariiqa ḍṭarr yəbda mən laa-šeeʔ.*

to scratch - 1. *žaraḥ (a ø//nžaraḥ).* This pen scratches. *har-riiše btəžraḥ.* 2. *xadaš (o xadᵊš//nxadaš).* Be careful not to scratch the furniture. *diir baalak maa təxdoš ᵊl-moobiilya.* 3. *xarmaš, xamaš (o xamᵊš//nxamaš).* Is the cat going to scratch if I pet her? *hal-qaṭṭa bətxarmeš ʔiza bəlƐab maƐa?* 4. *ḥakk (ə ḥakk//nḥakk).* Stop scratching yourself in public. *ḥaaže tḥəkk ḥaalak qəddaam ᵊn-naas.*

to scratch out - *šaṭab (o/e šaṭᵊb//nšaṭab).* Scratch out the last sentence. *šṭoob ᵊž-žəmle l-ʔaaxraaniyye.*

scream - *ṣarxa* pl. *-aat.* I thought I heard a scream *kaʔənni smaƐᵊt ṣarxa.*

**He's a scream! *huwwe tarkiibe!*

to scream - *ṣarax (a ṣraax* and *ṣriix), zaƐaq (a zaƐᵊq).* The child screamed with fright. *ṭ-ṭəfᵊl ṣarax mən xoofo.*

screen - 1. *baravaan* pl. *-aat.* Undress behind the screen. *šlaaḥ wara l-baravaan.* 2. *šaaše* pl. *-aat.* He looks older on the screen. *mbayyen ʔakbar Ɛaš-šaaše.* 3. *šəbbaak* (pl. *šababiik*) *mənxol.* We need new screens in the living room. *laazəmna šababiik mənxol ᵊždiide la-ʔuudet l-ᵊqƐuud.*

screen door - *baab* (pl. *bwaab*) *mənxol.*

to screen - 1. *xtabar.* The applicants are carefully screened. *ṭ-ṭaalbiin byəxtəbruuhon ᵊb-kəll dəqqa.* 2. *ḥaṭṭ mənxol b-.* We're thinking of screening the veranda. *Ɛam ᵊnfakker ᵊnḥəṭṭ mənxol bᵊl-veeranda tabaƐna.*

to screen off - *ḥaṭṭ baravaan b-.* She wants to screen off this end of the room. *bədda tḥəṭṭ* haravaan ᵊb-hal-qərne mn ᵊl-ʔuuḍa.

screw - bərġi pl. baraaġi. These screws need tightening. hal-baraaġi laazmon šadd. — He's got a screw loose. fii bərġi b-raaso maḥluul.

to screw - 1. baram (o barᵊm//mbaram). Don't forget to screw the cap onto the pen. laa tənsa ma təbrom ġaṭa s-stiilo. 2. sabbat ... b-baraaġi. Screw the board to the wall. sabbet ᵊl-looḥ ɛal-ḥeeṭ ᵊb-baraaġi.

**If I can screw up enough courage, I'll ask for a raise. ʔiza byəṭlaɛ ᵊb-ʔiidi šədd ḥeeli kfaaye bəṭlob zyaadet maɛaaš.

screw driver - mfakk pl. -aat.

to **scribble** - 1. xarbaš, šaxbar. It's terrible the way he scribbles. faẓaaɛa šuu bixarbeš. 2. katab (o ktiibe//nkatab). I saw him scribble notes throughout the lecture. šəfto ɛam yəktob ruʔuus ʔaqlaam ṭuul l-ᵊmḥaaḍara.

to scribble up - xarbaš, šaxbar. The kids have scribbled up the whole wall. l-ᵊwlaad xarbašu l-ḥeeṭ kəllo.

to **scrub** - farak (o/e farᵊk//nfarak). We had to scrub every floor in the house. nžabarna nəfrok ʔarḍ ᵊl-beet kəlla. — I want you to scrub your hands before dinner. bəddi-yđak təfrok ʔideek qabl ᵊl-ɛaša.

scruples - ḍamiir. He has no scruples when it comes to furthering his own ends. maa ɛando ḍamiir waqt ᵊl-qəṣṣa fiiha manfaɛa ʔəlo.

sculptor - naḥḥaat pl. -iin, naqqaaš pl. -iin, massaal pl. -iin.

sculpture - 1. naḥᵊt. He is studying sculpture and painting. ɛam yədros ᵊn-naḥᵊt wᵊr-rasᵊm. 2. təmsaal pl. tamasiil. There's a modernistic sculpture in front of the new post office. fii təmsaal ᵊmn ᵊl-fann ᵊl-ḥadiis qəddaam binaayet ᵊl-bariid ᵊž-ždiide.

scythe - mḥašš pl. -aat.

sea - baḥᵊr pl. bḥuura and bḥaar. A storm broke out at sea. ṭəlɛet ɛaaṣfe ɛal-baḥᵊr. — He's never been to sea. b-ḥayaato maa rəkeb ᵊl-baḥᵊr. — Bloudane is some 1600 m above sea level. bluudaan ḥawaali ʔalf w-sətt miit mətᵊr ɛan saṭḥ ᵊl-baḥᵊr.

**He went to sea before he was twenty. daxal ᵊl-baḥriyye qabᵊl-ma yṣiir ɛəmro ɛəšriin.

sea mile - miil baḥri pl. ʔamyaal baḥriyye.

seagull - lawras˜ (pl. lawaares˜) baḥᵊr. A flock of seagulls followed the ship. sərb mən lawras ᵊl-baḥᵊr ləḥeq ᵊl-baaxra.

seal - faqme pl. -aat. We watched them feed the seals. tfarražna ɛaleehon ɛam yṭaɛmu l-faqmaat.

seal - 1. xətᵊm pl. xtuume. The papers bore the official seal. l-ᵊwraaq kaan ɛaleehon ᵊl-xətm ᵊr-rasmi. 2. xətm˜ (pl. xtuumet˜) ᵊrṣaaṣ. Somebody must have broken the seal on the door. fii ḥada laazem ykuun kasar ᵊl-xətm ᵊr-rṣaaṣ ɛal-baab.

to seal - 1. xatam (o xatᵊm//nxatam). Have you sealed the letter? xatamt ᵊl-maktuub? 2. ḥakkam taskiir˜ ... You have to seal the jars while the fruit is still hot. laazem ᵊtḥakkmi taskiir ᵊl-qaṭramiizaat waqt ᵊl-fawaaki ləssaata ṣəxne.

sealing wax - šamᵊɛ ʔaḥmar.

seam - 1. lafqa pl. -aat, xyaaṭa pl. -aat. Rip open the seam. ftəqi l-lafqa. 2. sabale pl. -aat. The seam of your right stocking isn't straight. sablet ᵊžraabtek ᵊl-yamiiniyye muu ḍəġri.

seamless - bala sabale. I want a pair of seamless stockings. bəddi žooz ᵊžraabaat bala sabale.

seamstress - xayyaaṭa pl. -aat.

seaplane - ṭayyaara (pl. -aat) maaʔiyye.

seaport - marfaʔ baḥri pl. maraafeʔ baḥriyye.

search - taftiiš pl. -aat. The police made a thorough search. š-šərṭa qaamet ᵊb-taftiiš daqiiq.

to search - 1. fattaš, dawwar. We searched for him everywhere. fattašna ɛanno b-kəll qərne. — I've searched everywhere for a good apartment. dawwart ᵊb-kəll qərne ɛala šaqqa mniiḥa. 2. fattaš, nabbaš. We'll have to search you. laazem mənfattšak. — I've searched the whole house. nabbašt ᵊl-beet kəllo.

searchlight - prožektoor pl. -aat. Searchlights lit up the harbor. l-marfaq ḍawwəlu prožektooraat.

seashore - šaṭṭ˜ ᵊl-baḥᵊr. We spent part of the summer at the seashore. maḍḍeena qəsᵊm mn ᵊṣ-ṣeefiyye ɛala šaṭṭ ᵊl-baḥᵊr.

to be **seasick** - daax (u dawaxaan, dooxa) bᵊl-baḥᵊr. I was terribly seasick on my last trip. dəxᵊt dooxa faẓiiɛa bᵊl-baḥᵊr b-raḥᵊlti l-ʔaaxraaniyye.

seasickness - dawaxaan˜ baḥᵊr, dooxet˜ baḥᵊr.

season - 1. faṣᵊl pl. fṣuul(e), faṣl˜ ᵊs-səne. Which season do you like best? ʔanu faṣᵊl bətḥəbb ʔaktar šii? 2. faṣᵊl pl. fṣuul(e), waqᵊt pl. ʔawqaat. This is the best season for skiing. haada ʔaḥsan faṣᵊl ləs-skii. 3. muusem pl. mawaasem. The hotel had an excellent season this year. l-ʔoteel kaan ɛando muusem ɛaẓiim has-səne. — Apricots are not yet in season. ləssa maa ʔəža muusem ᵊl-məšmoš.

to season - tabbal. What did you season the meat with? b-ʔeeš tabbalt ᵊl-laḥme?

seasoned - 1. mtabbal. This kind of food must be properly seasoned. han-nooɛ ᵊmn ᵊl-ʔakᵊl laazem ykuun ᵊmtabbal ᵊmniiḥ. 2. mḥannak. They were seasoned troops. kaanu žnuud ᵊmḥannakiin.

seat - 1. maqɛad pl. maqaaɛed. This seat needs fixing. hal-maqɛad bəddo taṣliiḥ. 2. maḥall pl. -aat, maqɛad pl. maqaaɛed. There's still a free seat. ləssa fii maḥall faaḍi. — This seat is taken. hal-maqɛad maʔxuud. — Don't forget to reserve seats for us. laa tənsa ma təḥžəz-ᵊlna maḥallaat. 3. xərᵊž pl. xruuže. The pants are too tight in the seat. xərž ᵊl-banṭaloon dayyeq ᵊktiir. 4. maqarr pl. -aat. The seat of government is in Beirut. maqarr l-ᵊḥkuume b-beeruut.

to have (or **take**) **a seat** - qaɛad (o qɛuud). Please have a seat. tfaḍḍal ɛood.

to seat - 1. qaɛɛad. Seat the children in the front row. qaɛɛed l-ᵊwlaad bᵊṣ-ṣaff ᵊl-ʔawwalaani. — How many people can you seat in your living room? kam zalame fiik ᵊtqaɛɛed b-ʔuuḍṭ l-ᵊqɛuud tabaɛak? 2. wəseɛ (-yəsaɛ siɛa), ttasaɛ la-. The theater seats five hundred people. l-masraḥ byəsaɛ (or byəttəseɛ la-) xamᵊs miit zalame.

to be seated - qaɛad (o qɛuud). Won't you be seated? maa bətḥəbb təqɛod? or tfaḍḍal ɛood.

second - 1. saaniyye pl. sawaani. He ran a hundred yards in ten seconds. rakad miit yaard ᵊb-ɛašᵊr sawaani. 2. takke pl. -aat. Wait a second. ntəẓer takke! 3. taani. Will you please give me the second book from the left? məmken mən faḍlak taɛṭiini l-ᵊktaab ᵊt-taani mn ᵊš-šmaal? — This is my second time in Damascus. hayy ᵊl-marra t-taanye bəži ɛaš-šaam. — This product is second to none. hal-mantuuž maa-lo taani.

in the second place - taani šii, taaniyan. In the first place I have no time, and in the second place I don't want to go anyway. ʔawwal kəll šii maa maɛi waqᵊt w-taani šii maa bəddi ruuḥ.

to second - ʔayyad//tʔayyad. I second the motion. bʔayyed ᵊl-ʔəqtiraaḥ.

secondary - saanawi*. Let's forget for the time being all secondary considerations. bᵊl-waqt ᵊl-ḥaaḍer xalliina nənsa kəll ᵊl-ʔəɛtibaaraat ᵊs-saanawiyye. — His son's in secondary school now. ʔəbno hallaq bᵊl-madrase s-saanawiyye.

**These things are of secondary importance. hal-ᵊʔmuur ʔahammiyyə̀ta bᵊd-daraže t-taanye.

second-class - daraže taanye. Give me one second-class ticket to Aleppo, please. ɛaṭiini tazkara daraže taanye la-ḥalab mən faḍlak.

secondhand - 1. məstaɛmal. I bought the book secondhand. štareet l-ᵊktaab məstaɛmal. — We bought a secondhand washing machine. štareena ġassaale məstaɛmale. 2. qiil ɛan qaal. I got the story secondhand. sməɛᵊt hal-qəṣṣe qiil ɛan qaal.

secondly - taaniyan, taani šii. In the first place I don't like potatoes, secondly, I'm not hungry at all. ʔawwal šii maa bḥəbb ᵊl-baṭaaṭa, taaniyan, ʔana maa-li žuuɛaan ʔabadan.

second-rate - daraže taanye (invar.). It's definitely a second-rate hotel. ḥatman ʔənno ʔoteel daraže taanye.

secret - 1. sərr pl. ʔasraar. Let me in on the secret. šaarəkni bᵊs-sərr. — Can you keep a secret? fiik təḥfaẓ sərr? — This is one of their trade secrets. haada waaḥed mən ʔasraar məhnə̀ton. — His good manners certainly are the secret of his success. ḥəsᵊn ʔadabo ḥatman huwwe sərr nažaaḥo. 2. sərri*. They have a secret plan. ɛandon xəṭṭa sərriyye. — He was elected by a secret ballot. ntaxabùu b-ʔəqtiraaɛ sərri.

**She keeps no secrets from me. maa bətxabbi ɛanni šii.

in secret - bᵊs-sərr. They signed the Peace Treaty in secret. maḍu mɛaahadt ᵊs-salaam bᵊs-sərr.

to keep secret - ḥafaẓ (a ḥəfᵊẓ) sərr˜ ... They kept the marriage secret for six months. ḥafaẓu sərr ᵊz-zawaaž məddet sətt əšhor.

to make a secret of - xabba. He makes no secret of it. maa bixabbiiha.

secretary - səkᵊrteer pl. -iyye, f. səkᵊrteera pl. -aat.

secretary general - səkᵊrteer ɛaamm, ʔamiin ɛaamm.

secretly - bᵊs-sərr. They met secretly. žtamaɛu

bəs-sərr.
sect - *ṭaayfe* pl. *ṭawaayef.*
section - 1. *ğəsəm* pl. *ʔağsaam.* You'll find it in Chapter One, Section Three. *bətlaaqiiha bəl-faṣl əl-ʔawwal əl-ğəsm ət-taalet.* 2. *žəzəʔ* pl. *ʔažzaaʔ, ğəsəm* pl. *ʔağsaam.* I was brought up in this section of the country. *rbiit b-haž-žəzəʔ mən l-əblaad.* 3. *ḥayy* pl. *ʔaḥyaaʔ.* He lives in one of the nicest sections of the town. *saaken əb-ḥayy mən ʔaḥla ʔaḥyaaʔ əl-balad.* 4. *fağara* pl. *-aat.* You have violated Section 242 of the Penal Code. *xaalaft əl-fağara miiteen tneen w-ʔarəbʕiin mən ğaanuun əl-ʕuğuubaat.* 5. *ğiṭaaʕ* pl. *-aat.* This is a horizontal section of the rocket. *haada mağṭaʕ ʔəfği ləṣ-ṣaaruux.* 6. *ḥəzz* pl. *ḥzuuz.* Would you like a section of my orange? *bətḥəbb šii ḥəzz mən bərdqaanti?*
sector - *ğiṭaaʕ* pl. *-aat.* The city of Berlin is divided into four sectors. *madiinet barliin maqsuume la-ʔarbaʕ ğiṭaaʕaat.*
secure - *mʔamman.* Nobody feels secure these days. *maa ḥada šaaʕer əb-ḥaalo mʔamman* (or **...*šaaʕer ʔənno b-ʔamaan) hal-ʔiyyaam.* — His position with the company is secure. *waẓiifto bəš-šərke mʔammane.*
 to secure - 1. *ʔamman//tʔamman.* His future is secured. *məstaqbalo mʔamman.* 2. *ḥəṣel (a ḥṣuul) ʕala.* We've finally secured a loan. *ʔaxiiran ḥaṣalna ʕala ğarḍ.*
 **Is the boat secured? *š-šaxtuura marbuuṭa mniiḥ?*
security - 1. *ʔamaan.* It gives us a sense of security. *btaʕṭiina šʕuur bəl-ʔamaan.* — The latest step constitutes a serious threat to our country's security. *l-xaṭwe l-ʔaxiira ʕibaara ʕan tahdiid xaṭiir la-ʔamaan əblaadna.* 2. *kafaale* pl. *-aat, ḍamaane* pl. *-aat.* What security can you give me? *šuu l-kafaale halli fiik taʕṭiini-ydaha?* 3. *rahən* pl. *rhuune, ḍamaane* pl. *-aat.* I had to leave my watch as security. *nžabarət xalli saaʕti ka-rahən.*
 social security - *ḍamaan ʔəžtimaaʕi.*
 securities - *ʔawraaq maaliyye* (pl.). He's invested most of his money in securities. *stasmar ʔaktariit ʔamwaalo b-ʔawraaq maaliyye.*
sedative - *msakken* pl. *-aat.*
to **see** - 1. *šaaf (u šoofe//nšaaf).* I can't see a thing. *maa-li šaayef šii.* — I'd like to see more of you. *bḥəbb šuufak ʔaktar.* — I can't see over his head. *maa fiini šuuf mən fooq raaso.* — Try to see it my way. *ḥaawel ətšuufa mən wəžhet naẓari.* — I don't see it that way. *maa-li šaayef əl-masʔale heek.* — That remains to be seen. *mənšuuf baqa.* — You see? I told you. *šəfət? qəlt-əllak.* — Why don't you see a lawyer about it? *leeš maa bətšə́f-lak muḥaami b-əxṣuuṣa?* — You'd better see a doctor. *l-ʔafḍal tšəf-lak doktoor.* — Do you see now what I mean? *šəfət hallaq šuu bəqṣoḍ?* — Do you see the point? *šaayef əl-mağza?* — See what can be done about it. *šuuf šuu məmken yənʕə́mel fiiha.* — All we can do is wait and see. *kəll šii fiina nsaawi huwwe mnənṭə́ẓer w-ənšuuf šuu biṣiir.* — Wait and see. *stanna w-šuuf.* 2. *šaaf, ṭṭallaʕ ʕala.* May I see your passport? *məmken šuuf basbboorak?* 3. *šaaf, tfarraž ʕala.* I would like to see the town. *bḥəbb šuuf əl-balad.* — We've just seen a good movie. *muu mən zamaan tfarražna ʕala fələm ḥəlu.* 4. *šaaf, qaabal.* I can't see him until tomorrow. *maa fiini šuufo qabəl bəkra.* 5. *laaḥaẓ.* Anybody should be able to see that. *ḥayaḷḷa waaḥed laazem ylaaḥeẓ haš-šii.* 6. *tʔakkad.* I'm here to see that everything goes according to schedule. *ʔžiit la-hoon la-ʔətʔakkad ʔənno kəll šii maaši ḥasab əl-xəṭṭa.*
 **Oh, I see! *ʔaa, fhəmt ʕaleek!*
 **You see, I love that girl. *ʕaṭeet baalak šloon? ʔana bḥəbb hal-bənət.*
 **So I walked up to that guy, see, and hit him. *fa-mšiit la-naaḥ haz-zalame, fhəmt ʕaliyyi šloon? w-haffeeto.*
 **See me tomorrow. *taʕa la-ʕandi bəkra.*
 **See you again. *naraakum.*
 **He makes me see red. *biṭaaleʕ əd-damm la-raasi.*
 **He has seen better days. *mbayyen ʕalé ʔənno kan-lo zamaan.*
 **These clothes have seen a lot of wear. *hal-ʔawaaʕi ʔaklet daʕk əktiir.*
 **The country has seen a lot of progress lately. *l-əblaad tqaddamet əktiir əb-hal-ʔiyyaam.*
 **I'm glad to see you! *ʔahla w-sahla!*
 **May I see you home? *məmken raafqek* (or *waṣṣlek*) *ʕal-beet?*
 **I'll see you to the door. *braafqak* (or *bwaṣṣlak*) *ləl-baab.*
 to see off - *waddaʕ.* We saw them off on the boat. *waddaʕnaahon ʕal-baaxra.*
 to see through - 1. *fəhem (a fəhəm) ḥaqiiqet˜ ...* Anybody can see through that guy. *ḥayaḷḷa waḥed fii yəfham ḥaqiiqet haš-šaxəṣ.* 2. *saaʕad.* I'll see you through. *laḥa saaʕdak (la-txalleṣ).*
 **Do you have enough money to see you through? *fii ʕandak maṣaari kaafye la-ddabber ḥaalak?*
 **The glass is hard to see through. *ṣaʕb əl-waaḥed yšuuf mən hal-əqzaaz.*
 to see to it - *tʔakkad.* Please see to it that this letter is mailed today. *mən faḍlak ətʔakkad ʔənno hal-maktuub laḥa yənbə́ʕet əl-yoom.* — See to it that you are on time. *tʔakkad ətkuun ʕal-waqət.* — I'll see to it that she gets the letter. *laḥa ʔətʔakkad ʔənna təstə́lem əl-maktuub.*
seed - *bəzre* coll. *bəzər* pl. *-aat* and *bzuur.* Did you buy any seeds? *štareet bəzər šii?* — Some types of oranges have no seeds. *baʕḍ ʔanwaaʕ əl-bərdqaan maa-lon bəzər.*
 to seed - *zaraʕ (a zarəʕ//nzaraʕ), baddar.* When did you seed the garden? *ʔeemta zaraʕt əž-žneene?*
seeder - *mabdara* pl. *mabaader, baddaara* pl. *-aat.*
seedless - *bala bəzər.* Are those seedless oranges? *hal-bərdqaanaat bala bəzər?*
seedy - *məhri*, məhtə́ri*.* His clothes look seedy. *ʔawaaʕi məhriyye.* — He looked pretty seedy this morning. *kaan əmbayyen ʕalé məhri l-yoom əṣ-ṣəbəḥ.*
to **seem** - 1. *baan (a ø) ʕalé, bayyan ʕalé, ẓahar (a ø) ʕalé.* She seemed to be seriously ill. *baan ʕaleeha ʔənno kaanet ḍaʕfaane tamaam.* — You don't seem to understand. *mbayyen ʕaleek maa-lak ʕam təfham.* 2. *ẓahar.* It seems I have interrupted your conversation. *ʕala-ma yəẓhar qaaṭaʕt-ə́lkon ḥadiiskon.* — He's coming, it seems, tomorrow. *ʕala-ma yəẓhar ḥa-yəži bəkra.* — It would seem so! *ʕala-ma yəẓhar heek!* — It seemed best to compromise. *ẓahar ʔənno ʔafḍal šii l-ʔəttifaaq ʕala ḥall waṣaṭ.* -- That seems peculiar to me. *haš-šii byəẓhə́r-li ğariib.*
to **seep** - *nazz (ə nazz).* Water keeps seeping into the cellar. *l-mayy bəḍḍall bətnəzz ləl-qabu.*
seesaw - *ʔabiilo žaʕiiṣo* (invar.).
segregation - *tafriqa.* We don't have racial segregation in this country. *maa fii ʕanna tafriqa ʕənṣuriyye b-hal-əblaad.*
to **seize** - 1. *masak (e masək//mmasak).* He seized the rope with both his hands. *masak əl-ḥable b-ʔideeno.* 2. *ḥažaz (o ḥažəz//nḥažaz) ʕala.* They seized his papers. *ḥažazu ʕala wraaqo.* 3. *ṣaadar, ḥažaz ʕala.* The government has seized all his property. *l-əḥkuume ṣaadaret kəll ʔamlaako.* 4. *ntahaz.* If I don't seize this opportunity it may be too late. *ʔiza maa ntahazt hal-fərṣa bižuuz ykuun faat əl-waqət.* 5. *ʔaxad (-yaaxod ʔaxəd//ttaaxad).* He was seized by fear. *ttaaxad bəl-xoof.*
seizure - *mṣaadara.*
seldom - *naader* (invar.), *naadiran, qəllet-ma.* I seldom use his telephone. *naader bəstaʕmel talifoono.*
to **select** - 1. *xtaar.* Have you selected anything yet? *xtərt-əllak šii wəlla ləssa?* 2. *naqqa//tnaqqa.* I selected only the best fruits. *naqqeet bass ʔaḥsan əl-fawaaki.*
selection - 1. *taškiile* pl. *-aat.* We have a big selection of shirts. *ʕanna taškiilet qəmṣaan əkbiire.* 2. *məntaxabaat* (pl.). The book contains a selection of contemporary poetry. *l-əktaab byəḥtə́wi ʕala məntaxabaat əmn əš-šəʕr əl-ḥadiis.* 3. *ʔəntixaab.* It is the principle of natural selection that guarantees the survival of the species. *mabdaʔ əl-ʔəntixaab əṭ-ṭabiiʕi huwwe yalli byəkfal bağaaʔ əž-žənəs.*
self-confidence - *səğa bən-nafs.* She has no self-confidence whatsoever. *maa ʕanda ʔayy səğa bən-nafs.*
self-confident - *waaseğ mən nafs-* + pron. suff. I wish he were a little more self-confident. *ʕala waah law kaan waaseğ mən nafso šwayye ʔaktar.*
self-conscious - *xažuul.* He's very self-conscious when he's around us. *huwwe ktiir xažuul waqət bikuun beenaatna.*
self-contradictory - *mətnaağeḍ.* The two statements are self-contradictory. *t-taṣriiḥeen mətnaağḍiin.*

self-control - *ḍabᵊṭ˜ ʔaεṣaab.* It takes a lot of self-control to stand this questioning. *bədda ḍabᵊṭ ʔaεṣaab maaken la-yəthammal ᵊl-waaḥed heek ʔəstənṭaaq.*
self-defense - *difaaε εan ᵊn-nafs.*
self-explanatory - *mafhuum.* The questions are self-explanatory. *l-ʔasʔile mafhuume* (or ***maa bədda tafsiir*).
self-government - *ḥəkᵊm zaati.*
selfish - *ʔanaani*.*
selfishness - *ʔanaaniyye.*
self-made man - *εiṣaami* pl. *-iyyiin.*
self-respect - *ʔəḥtiraam˜ ᵊn-nafᵊs.* Don't you have any self-respect? *maa εandak ʔayy ʔəḥtiraam la-nafsak?*
self-winding - *ʔotomaatiik* (invar.).
to **sell** - **1.** *baaε (i beeε//mbaaε).* Did you sell your old piano? *bəεᵊt šii l-byaano l-εatiiq tabaεak?* — You wouldn't sell me your car, would you? *maa-lak ḥa-tbiiεni sayyaartak, muu heek?* — Sorry, we're all sold out. *εadam muʔaaxaze bəεna kəll yalli εanna.* — He sold us out to the enemy. *baaεna ləl-εaduww.* **2.** *mbaaε.* These shoes sell well. *haṣ-ṣababiiṭ εam təmbaaε ᵊmniiḥ.* — This suit usually sells for thirty-five dollars. *hal-badle εaadatan btəmbaaε b-xamsda w-tlaatiin dolaar.*
**He's been trying to sell us the idea for quite a while now. *ṣar-lo mədde εam yḥaawel yəqnaεna bᵊl-fəkra.*
semester - *faṣᵊl* pl. *fṣuul(e).* I studied in Beirut for three semesters. *darasᵊt b-beeruut tlətt ᵊfṣuule.*
semiannual - *nəṣᵊf sanawi*.*
semicircle - *nəṣṣ˜* (pl. *nṣaaṣ˜*) *duwweera, nəṣᵊf˜* (pl. *ʔanṣaaf˜*) *daaʔira.*
semicolon - *faaṣle* (pl. *fawaaṣel*) *manquuṭa.*
seminar - *seminaar* pl. *-aat, ḥalaqa* pl. *-aat.*
semiofficial - *šəbᵊh˜ rasmi*.* It's a semiofficial news agency. *hiyye wakaalet ʔanbaaʔ šəbᵊh rasmiyye.*
Semite - *saami** pl. *-iyyiin.*
Semitic - *saami*.*
Semitics - *saamiyyaat* (pl.), *diraasaat saamiyye* (pl.).
senate - *mažles˜* (pl. *mažaales˜*) *šyuux.*
senator - *šeex* pl. *šyuux, sanatoor* (invar.).
to **send** - *baεat (a baεᵊt//mbaεat).* Send it by mail. *bεáta bᵊl-bariid.* — I want to send him a telegram. *bəddi ʔabεát-lo barqiyye.* — Have you sent for the doctor? *baεatᵊt wara d-doktoor?* — To which college did you send your son? *la-ʔayy žaamεa baεatᵊt ʔəbnak?*
**Send him in. *xallīi yfuut.*
to send back - *ražžaε.* We'll send the book back in a few days. *mənražžəε-lak l-ᵊktaab baεᵊd kam yoom.* — Send him back to where he came from. *ražžεo mən maḥall-ma ʔəža.*
to send in - *baεat (a baεᵊt//mbaεat).* Don't forget to send in your application before the fifteenth of the month. *laa tənsa maa təbεat ṭalabak qabᵊl xamᵊṣṭaεš ᵊš-šahᵊr.*
to send off - *baεat (a baεᵊt//mbaεat).* When did you send the package off? *ʔeemta baεatt ᵊṭ-ṭarᵊd?*
to send one's regards to - *sallam εala.* He sends you his regards. *bisallem εaleek.*
to send out - *baεat (a baεᵊt//mbaεat).* Shall I send him out for some ice cream? *ʔəbεato yžiib šwayyet buuẓa?*
to send up - *baεat (a baεᵊt//mbaεat), ʔaṭlaq.* When did they send up the rocket? *ʔeemta baεatu ṣ-ṣaaruux?*
sender - *mərsel* pl. *-iin.*
senior - *ʔakbar bᵊs-sənn.* He's my senior in age. *huwwe ʔakbar mənni bᵊs-sənn.*
**He's a senior member of the faculty. *huwwe mən ʔaqdam ʔaεdaaʔ ᵊl-heeʔa t-tadriisiyye.*
seniority - *ʔaqdamiyye.*
sensation - *šεuur.* Believe me, hunger is not a pleasant sensation. *saddeq ᵊž-žuuε muu šεuur ḥəlu.*
**His speech created a sensation. *xiṭaabo qaam ᵊd-dənye w-ḥaṭṭa.*
**Some papers are after sensation only. *baεḍ ᵊž-žaraayed ġaayə́ton bass ʔisaaret ᵊl-εawaaṭef.*
sense - **1.** *ḥaasse* pl. *ḥawaass.* Man has five senses. *l-ʔənsaan ʔəlo xamᵊs ḥawaass.* **2.** *šεuur, ʔəḥsaas.* It gives us a sense of security. *btaεṭiina šεuur bᵊl-ʔamaan.* **3.** *šεuur.* That guy has no sense of responsibility whatsoever. *haz-zalame maa εando ʔayy ᵊšεuur bᵊl-masʔuuliyye.* **4.** *maεna* pl. *maεaani.* I never use the word in that sense. *b-ḥayaati maa bəstaεmel ᵊl-kəlme b-hal-maεna.* — The paragraph doesn't make sense. *l-faqara maa-la maεna.*
**Do I make sense? *εam təfham εaliyyi?*
**There's no sense in waiting any longer, let's go. *maa fii faayde mnənṭə́zer ʔaktar; yaḷḷa, xalliina nruuḥ.*
**I must have been out of my senses when I agreed to it. *laazem kənt mažnuun lamma waafaqᵊt εala haš-šaġle.*
**I hope he has sense enough to take a taxi. *nšaaḷḷa ykuun fəṭer w-yaaxod taksi.*
sense of humor - *rooḥ˜ ᵊn-nəkte.* He has no sense of humor. *maa εando rooḥ ᵊn-nəkte.*
in a sense - *mən naaḥye, b-naaḥye mn ᵊn-nawaaḥi.* In a sense, I'm responsible. *mən naaḥye ʔana masʔuul.*
to sense - *šaεar (o šεuur).* I sensed right away that something was wrong. *šaεarᵊt εal-ḥaarek ʔənno fii šii muu mažbuuṭ.*
senseless - **1.** *bala maεna.* We lost hours with senseless discussions. *ḍawwaεna saaεaat w-saaεaat b-ᵊmnaaqašaat bala maεna.* **2.** *bala waεi.* The blow knocked him senseless. *ḍ-ḍarbe xallə́to bala waεi.*
sensible - *εaaqel, raakez.* She's a sensible person, she'll understand your problem. *hiyye waaḥde εaaqle, ʔakiid ḥa-tətfahham məškəltak.*
sensitive - *ḥassaas.* I'm very sensitive to cold. *ʔana ḥassaas ᵊktiir ləl-barᵊd* or ***bətʔassar qawaam bᵊl-barᵊd* or ***ʔana barriid ᵊktiir.* — We use highly sensitive instruments in our work. *mnəstaεmel ʔaalaat ᵊktiir ḥassaase b-šəġᵊlna.*
sentence - **1.** *žəmle* pl. *žəmal.* I didn't understand the last sentence. *maa fhəmt ᵊž-žəmle l-ʔaaxraaniyye.* **2.** *ḥəkᵊm* pl. *ʔaḥkaam.* The judge has already pronounced sentence. *l-qaaḍi ṣaar εaaṭi l-ḥəkᵊm.*
to sentence - *ḥakam (o ḥəkᵊm//nḥakam).* They sentenced him to five years in prison. *ḥakamúu xams ᵊsniin ḥabᵊs.*
sentiment - **1.** *εaaṭfe* pl. *εawaaṭef.* His poetry is characterized by too much sentiment. *šəεro byəttə́ṣef ᵊb-kətret ᵊl-εawaaṭef.* **2.** *šεuur.* Your remark has offended his religious sentiments. *mlaaḥaẓtak žarḥet ᵊšεuuro d-diini.*
sentimental - *εaaṭifi*.* He came here for sentimental reasons. *ʔəža la-hoon la-ʔasbaab εaaṭifiyye.* — I like sentimental music. *bḥəbb ᵊl-muusiiqa l-εaaṭifiyye.*
sentimentalist - *εawaaṭfi* pl. *-iyye.*
sentry - *ḥaares* pl. *ḥərraas.* The sentry didn't let me pass. *l-ḥaares maa xallaani ʔəmroq.*
separate - *mənfə́red.* Could we have separate rooms? *məmken taεṭiina ʔuwaḍ mənfərde?* — We made a separate agreement with them. *εməlna ʔəttifaaq mənfə́red maεon.*
**Put these letters in a separate file. *ḥəṭṭ hal-makatiib b-ᵊmṣannaf la-ḥaalo.*
to separate - **1.** *farraq//tfarraq.* The kids are fighting, you'd better separate them. *l-ᵊwlaad εam yətqaatalu, l-ʔafḍal ᵊtfarrə́qon.* **2.** *faraq (o farᵊq//nfaraq), faraz (o farᵊz//nfaraz).* Separate the red beads from the blue ones. *frooq ᵊl-xarazaat ᵊl-ḥəmᵊr εan ᵊz-zərᵊq.* **3.** *faṣal (e faṣᵊl//nfaṣal).* Separate the boys and the girls for the next game. *fṣeel ᵊṣ-ṣəbyaan εan ᵊl-banaat ləl-ləεbe ž-žaaye.* **4.** *nfaṣal.* They separated after seven years of marriage. *nfaṣalu (εan baεḍon) baεᵊd-ma ṣar-lon mədžawwziin sabε ᵊsniin.* — My parents are separated. *ʔabi w-ʔəmmi mənfəṣliin εan baεḍon.*
separately - *la-waḥd-* + pron. suff. Can you buy each volume separately? *fiik təštə́ri kəll ᵊmžallad la-waḥdo?*
September - *ʔeeluul.*
Serbia - *blaad˜ ᵊṣ-ṣərᵊb.*
Serbian - *ṣərbi** coll. pl. *ṣərᵊb.*
sergeant - *raqiib* pl. *rəqaba.*
serial - **1.** *mətsalsel.* What's the serial number on the engine? *šuu r-raqam ᵊl-mətsalsel εal-motoor?* **2.** *qəṣṣa* (pl. *qəṣaṣ*) *mətsalᵊsle.* The magazine's starting a new serial in its next issue. *l-ᵊmžalle raḥa təbda qəṣṣa mətsalᵊsle ždiide b-εaddda l-qaadem.*
series - *səlsle.* He's going to give a series of lectures. *laḥa yaεṭi səlslet ᵊmḥaaḍaraat.*
serious - **1.** *žaddi.* He is a serious business man. *huwwe ražol ʔaεmaal žaddi.* **2.** *xəṭer, məxṭer.* I understand his illness is serious. *εala-ma fhəmᵊt maraḍo xəṭer.* **3.** *mhəmm.* That's a serious mistake. *hayy ġalṭa mhəmme.* — A serious project like this requires careful planning. *mašruuε ᵊmhəmm mətᵊl haada byəṭṭallab taxṭiiṭ daqiiq.*
**He never made a serious attempt to keep his promise. *εəmro maa ḥaawal εan žadd yuufi b-waεdo.*

**Why are you so serious today? *leeš kəll hal-qadd qaabəḍa l-yoom?*
**Are you serious? *mən kəll ɛaqlak?*
**You can't be serious. *muu maɛquul ᵊtkuun qaaṣəḍa.*

seriously - 1. *b-žadd.* I'm seriously considering getting married. *ɛam fakker b-žadd ʔənni ʔədzawwaž.* -- Don't take it so seriously. *laa taaxəda kəll hal-qadd ᵊb-žadd.* 2. *ktiir.* She is seriously ill. *hiyye ḍɛiife ktiir.*

sermon - 1. *waɛẓa* pl. *-aat.* Our minister gave a good sermon on Sunday. *qəssiisna ɛamel waɛẓa mniiḥa yoom ᵊl-ʔaḥad.* 2. *ɛiẓa* pl. *-aat, mawɛiẓa* pl. *-aat.* She's always ready with a sermon. *daayman fii ɛala raas ᵊlsaana ɛiẓa.*

serum - *maṣᵊl* pl. *mṣuule.*

servant - 1. *xaadem* f. *xaadme* pl. *xəddaam.* She has to get along without servants now. *laazem ᵊddabber ḥaala biduun xəddaam hallaq.* 2. *ʔžiir* pl. *ʔəžara.* I'm not your servant. *ʔana maa-li ʔžiirak.*
civil servant - *mwaẓẓaf ᵊḥkuumi* pl. *mwaẓẓafiin ᵊḥkuumiyyiin.*

serve - *sarviis.* Whose serve is it? *sarviis miin?*
to serve - 1. *xadam (ə xədme//nxadam).* He served me loyally for many years. *xadamni b-ʔəxlaaṣ la-ɛəddet ᵊsniin.* -- He served in the Navy. *xadam bᵊl-baḥriyye.* -- You'll be served in a moment. *hallaq byəži ḥada la-xədᵊmtak.* 2. *ɛabad (o ɛbaade//nɛabad).* He dedicated his life to serving God. *karras ḥayaato la-ɛbaadet ṛabbo.* 3. *qaddam.* Shall I serve the drinks now? *qaddem ᵊl-mašruub hallaq?* 4. *qaḍa (i qaḍa).* He's serving a four-year term in prison. *ɛam byəqḍi ḥəkᵊm ʔarbaɛ ᵊsniin bᵊl-ḥabᵊs.* -- Did it serve your purpose? *qaḍət-lak ġaraḍak?*
**That serves you right! *xaržak!*
**That sofa will have to serve as a bed. *haṣ-ṣoofa laazem tustaɛmal ɛawaaḍ taxᵊt.*
**The accident will serve to remind you to be more careful from now on. *l-ḥaadse raḥa dzakkrak ᵊtkuun ḥazer ʔaktar mən hallaq w-raayeḥ.*
**Dinner is served! *l-ɛaša ḥaaḍer!*

service - 1. *xədme* pl. *-aat.* The service is bad in this restaurant. *l-xədme ɛaaṭle b-hal-maṭɛam.* -- The company guarantees free service for the first six months. *š-šərke btəkfal l-xədme b-balaaš la-ʔawwal sətt əšhor.* -- He received many rewards for his faithful services to the company. *ḥəṣel ɛala žawaaʔez ᵊktiire məšaan xədmaato l-məxᵊlṣa ləš-šərke.* -- How long have you been in the service? *qaddeeš ṣar-lak bᵊl-xədme (l-ɛaskariyye)?* 2. *tazwiid.* The water service of the city is excellent. *tazwiid ᵊl-balad bᵊl-mayye məmtaaz.* 3. *qəddaas* pl. *qadadiis.* Let's meet in front of the church after the service. *xalliina nəžtə́meɛ qəddaam l-ᵊkniise baɛd ᵊl-qəddaas.* 4. *ɛbaade.* He spent his life in the service of God. *maḍḍa ḥayaato b-ᵊɛbaadet ṛabbo.* 5. *ṭaqᵊm* pl. *ṭquum(e).* Two pieces of my dinner service are broken. *qəṭᵊɛteen mən ṭaqm ᵊs-səfra tabaɛi maksuuriin.*
**Can I be of any service to you? *btəʔmor šii?*
**It's given me good service. *xadmətni mniiḥ.*
**This bus is out of service. *hal-baaṣ maa ɛam yəštəġel.*
burial service - (Muslim) *žnaaze,* (Christian) *žənnaaz.*
civil service - *xədme madaniyye.*
service station - *mḥaṭṭet˜* (pl. *-aat˜*) *banziin.*

session - 1. *žalse* pl. *-aat.* The session lasted two hours. *ž-žalse staḥmalet saaɛteen.* 2. *darᵊs* pl. *druus, ḥəṣṣa* pl. *ḥəṣaṣ.* I have two sessions a week with that professor. *ɛandi darseen bᵊž-žəmɛa maɛ hal-ʔəstaaz.*

set - 1. *ṭaqᵊm* pl. *ṭquum(e), seerᵊi* pl. *seeriyyaat.* We have a whole set of these ash trays. *fii ɛanna ṭaqᵊm kaamel mən haš-ṣḥuun ᵊs-sigaara.* 2. *seerᵊi* pl. *seeriyyaat.* There's only one stamp missing in that set. *fii bass ṭaabeɛ waaḥed naaqeṣ ᵊb-has-seerᵊi.* 3. *door* pl. *dwaar, set* (invar.). He won in three sets. *rəbeḥ b-ᵊtlatt ᵊdwaar* (or *b-ᵊtlaate set*). 4. *žihaaz* pl. *ʔəžhize.* He sold his old radio and bought a new set. *baaɛ ᵊr-raadyo l-ɛatiiq tabaɛo w-štara žihaaz ᵊždiid.* 5. *šəlle* pl. *šəlal.* She's a familiar figure among the diplomatic set. *hiyye šaxṣiyye maʔluufe b-šəllet ᵊd-diblumaasiyyiin.* 6. *qəṭɛet˜* (pl. *qəṭaɛ˜*) *deekoor* coll. *deekoor.* The sets for the film were designed by one of our best artists. *deekoor ᵊl-fələᵊm ṣammamo fannaan mən ʔaḥsan fannaaniinna.*
(all) set - *ḥaaḍer (ɛat-tamaam).* Everything is all set. *kəll šii ḥaaḍer ɛat-tamaam.*
dead set on - *mayyet ɛala, ṭaaqeq ɛala.* He's dead set on it. *mayyet huwwe ɛaleeha.*
to set - 1. *ḥaṭṭ (ə ḥaṭaṭ//nḥaṭṭ).* Set the box on the desk! *ḥəṭṭ ᵊl-ɛəlbe ɛaṭ-ṭaawle.* -- Tell the maid to set the table! *quul ləš-ṣaanɛa tḥəṭṭ ᵊṭ-ṭaawle.* -- He's set his heart on it. *ḥaṭṭ qalbo fiiha.* -- The wheels are set close together. *d-dawaliib maḥṭuuṭiin ᵊqraab la-baɛḍon.* 2. *naṣab (o naṣᵊb//ntaṣab).* He got caught in the trap he'd set himself. *ltaqaṭ bᵊl-faxx halli huwwe naṣabo.* 3. *ẓabbaṭ, rabaṭ (o rabᵊṭ).* I set my watch by the station clock this morning. *ẓabbaṭṭ saaɛti l-yoom ɛala bəkra ɛala saaɛet l-ᵊmḥaṭṭa.* -- I set my watch five minutes ahead. *rabaṭṭ saaɛti xamᵊs daqaayeq la-qəddaam.* -- Set the alarm for seven. *rbooṭ l-ᵊmnabbeh ɛas-saaɛa sabɛa.* 4. *ẓabbaṭ.* Set the oven on 400 degrees. *ẓabbeṭ ᵊl-fərᵊn ɛala ʔarbaɛ miit daraže.* 5. *ɛayyan//tɛayyan, ḥaddad//tḥaddad.* Why don't you set the time for the party? *leeš maa ʔənte bətɛayyen mawɛed ᵊl-ḥafle?* -- The judge set bail at 5,000 pounds. *l-qaaḍi ɛayyan ᵊl-kafaale b-xamᵊst aalaaf leera.* -- He set the price at fifty dollars. *ɛayyan ᵊs-səɛᵊr ɛala xamsiin dolaar.* -- The meeting has been set for nine o'clock. *l-ʔəžtimaaɛ tɛayyan ɛas-saaɛa təsɛa.* 6. *žabbar.* The doctor will have to set your arm. *d-doktoor laazem yžabbə́r-lak ʔiidak.* 7. *nazzal//tnazzal.* I'd like to have these diamonds set in platinum. *bəddi hal-ʔalmaasaat yətnazzalu ɛala blaatiin.* 8. *ṣaff (ə ṣaff//nṣaffet) ḥruuf˜...* I'm afraid this page will have to be set again. *xaayə́f-lak haṣ-ṣafḥa ḥruufa laazem tənṣaff mən ʔawwal w-ᵊždiid.* -- The title page is set in beautiful print. *ṣ-ṣafḥa l-ʔuula ḥruufa maṣfuufe ḥəlu.* 9. *ḥarraḍ//tḥarraḍ, wazz (ə wazz//nwazz).* They wouldn't hesitate to set brother against brother. *maa bəstabɛed ɛanhon ʔənno yḥarrḍu l-ʔaxx ɛala ʔaxu.* 10. *wažžah.* Set the sails to the wind! *wažžeh ᵊš-širaaɛ ᵊb-ʔəttižaah ᵊr-riiḥ!* 11. *hayyaž.* He set the dogs on me. *hayyaž l-ᵊklaab ɛaliyyi.* 12. *qaɛad (o qɛuud) ɛal-beeḍ(aat).* Is the hen setting? *r-rəqqa qaaɛde ɛal-beeḍaat?* 13. *ġarab (o/e ġruub).* The sun has already set. *š-šamᵊs ṣaaret ġaarbe.* 14. *qəsi (a ø).* The concrete hasn't set yet. *l-baṭoon ləssa maa qəsi.* 15. *žamed (a žmuud).* The gelatine takes two hours to set. *ž-žalatiin bəddo saaɛteen la-yəžmad.* 16. *nəšef (a našafaan).* Don't touch the picture; the paint has to set first. *laa tədqor ᵊl-looḥa; z-zeet laazem bᵊl-ʔawwal yənšaf.*
**Go ahead and set a good example! *ruuḥ w-xalliik qədwe mniiḥa!*
**The second scene is set in a garden. *l-mašhad ᵊt-taani byəḥdos b-ᵊžneene.*
**She has her mind set on going shopping today. *mɛannde ʔəlla-ma tətsawwaq ᵊl-yoom.*
to set aside - 1. *ḥaṭṭ (ə ḥaṭaṭ//nḥaṭṭ) ɛala žanab.* Set this aside for me. *ḥəṭṭ-ə́lli hayye ɛala žanab.* -- I'll try to set a day aside for you. *bḥaawel ḥəṭṭ-ə́llak šii yoom ɛala žanab.* -- Let's set aside all political differences. *xalliina nḥəṭṭ kəll ᵊl-ʔəxtilaafaat ᵊs-siyaasiyye ɛala žanab.* 2. *xaṣṣaṣ.* I think we have enough money set aside for the trip. *bəɛtəqed xaṣṣaṣna maṣaari kaafye lər-raḥle.* -- Let's set Tuesdays aside for our weekly meetings. *xalliina nxaṣṣeṣ kəll talaata la-ʔəžtimaaɛaatna l-ʔəsbuuɛiyye.*
to set back - 1. *ɛaṭṭal//tɛaṭṭal, ʔaxxar//tʔaxxar.* The loss of one of our best engineers has set us back considerably. *fəqdaan waaḥed mən ʔaḥsan ᵊmhandsiinna ɛaṭṭalna ktiir.* 2. *ʔaxxar//tʔaxxar,ražžaɛ//tražžaɛ.* Don't forget to set your watch back an hour. *laa tənsa maa tʔaxxer saaɛtak saaɛa.*
to set down - 1. *ḥaṭṭ (ə ḥaṭaṭ//nḥaṭṭ).* Set the box down gently. *ḥəṭṭ ᵊṣ-ṣanduuq ɛala mahlak.* 2. *katab (o ø//nkatab).* Set down your conditions and then we'll see. *ktoob ᵊšruuṭak w-baɛdeen mənšuuf.* 3. *nasab (o nasᵊb//ntasab).* You have to set it down to his lack of experience. *laazem tənsə́ba la-qəllet xəbᵊrto.*
to set in - *ḥall (ə ḥluul), bada (a bdaaye).* The rainy season set in early this year. *muusem ᵊl-ʔamṭaar has-səne ḥall ɛala bakkiir.*
to set off - 1. *fažžar//tfažžar.* They didn't have time to set off the charge. *maa ṣaar maɛon waqᵊt la-yfažžru d-dakke.* 2. *sabbab.* His innocent remark set off a whole chain of events. *mlaaḥaẓto l-barii ʔa sabbabet sənsəlt ḥawaades ṭawiile ɛariiḍa.* 3. *ʔabraz, ʔaẓhar.* The black dress sets off her beautiful skin to advantage. *r-roob ᵊl-ʔaswad*

byəbrez šamaal bəšrə́ta tamaam.

to set out - 1. *tarak (o/e tarᵊk).* We set out at five in the morning. *tarakna s-saaɛa xaamse ṣ-ṣəbᵊḥ.* -- He set out for home on Monday. *tarak ɛal-beet yoom ᵊt-taneen.* 2. *zaraɛ (a zarᵊɛ//nzaraɛ).* Did you set out the tomato plants? *zaraɛᵊt šatlaat ᵊl-banadoora?*

to set up - 1. *rakkab//trakkab.* The new machines have just been set up. *l-makanaat ᵊž-ždiide maa ṣar-lon zamaan ᵊmrakkabiin.* 2. *naṣab (o naṣᵊb// ntaṣab).* The workers are setting up a fence around the construction site. *š-šaġġiile ɛam yənᵊṣbu ḥaažez ḥawaali manṭəqt ᵊl-ʔənšaaʔaat.* 3. *ʔallaf//tʔallaf.* Parliament will set up a special committee to look into this sordid mess. *l-barlamaan laḥa yʔallef ləžne xaaṣṣa la-tənẓor b-hal-ᵊfḍiiḥa l-wəṣxa.* 4. *ʔassas.* His father set him up in business. *ʔabúu ʔassaso bᵊš-šəġᵊl.*

**They are going to set up housekeeping as soon as they return from their honeymoon. *laḥa yquumu bᵊl-beet ʔawwal-ma byəržaɛu mən šahr ᵊl-ɛasal.*

to set upon - *ṭabaq (o ṭabqa) b-.* The gang set upon him in a dark alley. *l-ᵊɛṣaabe ṭabqet fii b-ḥaara məɛᵊtme.*

setback - *dafše* (pl. *-aat*) *la-wara.* Their project suffered several setbacks in a row. *mašruuɛon ɛaana ɛəddet dafšaat la-wara b-qafa baɛḍon.*

setting - 1. *saruiis* (invar.). Do we have enough settings for everybody? *fii ɛanna saruiis ᵊkfaaye ləl-kəll?* 2. *tanziil.* The setting of this ruby is lovely. *tanziil hal-yaaquute l-ḥamra təḥfe.* 3. *masraḥ* pl. *masaareḥ.* The setting of the story is a fictitious country of the Far East. *masraḥ ᵊl-qəṣṣa balad xayaaliyye bᵊš-šarq ᵊl-ʔaqṣa.*

to **settle** - 1. *ṣaffa//tṣaffa, sawwa//tsawwa.* We must settle our accounts today. *laazem ᵊnṣaffi ḥsaabaatna l-yoom.* -- The matter has to be settled as soon as possible. *l-qaḍiyye laazem tətṣaffa b-ʔasraɛ-ma yəmken.* -- They managed to settle all claims before the year was out. *qədru ysawwu kəll l-ᵊmṭaalabaat qabᵊl nihaayt ᵊs-səne.* 2. *sawwa// tsawwa, qarrar//tqarrar.* We settled that question a long time ago. *sawweena hal-mawḍuuɛ mən zamaan.* 3. *naha (i nahi//ntaha).* That settles the matter. *haada byənhi l-qaḍiyye.* 4. *ḥasam (e/o ḥasᵊm// nḥasam).* You must settle that between yourselves. *laazem təḥᵊsmuuha beenaatkon.* -- Can you settle their argument? *fiik təḥsom ᵊmžaadaləton?* 5. *tṣaafa.* He settled with his creditors. *tṣaafa maɛ dayyaanto.* -- We settled for two hundred dollars. *tṣaafeena ɛala miiteen dolaar.* 6. *stawṭan.* Many Arabs settled in Latin America. *ktiir ᵊmn ᵊl-ɛarab stawṭanu b-ʔameerka l-laatiiniyye.* 7. *habaṭ (o hbuuṭ* and *habaṭaan).* The wall has settled a little. *l-ḥeeṭ habaṭ šwayye.* 8. *rassab, xadar (o xadᵊr).* Wait until the tea has settled. *ntəẓer ḥatta š-šaay yrasseb.*

to settle down - 1. *rakaz (o rakᵊz), rakan (o rakᵊn).* It's about time for him to give up this kind of life and settle down. *ḥan-lo ybaṭṭel hal-ɛiiše halli ɛaayə́ša w-yərkoz.* -- Now settle down to work! *hallaq ᵊrkoon baqa w-štəġel!*

to settle oneself - *kankan.* On Sunday I like to settle myself in my chair and smoke my pipe. *yoom ᵊl-ʔaḥad ᵊbḥəbb kanken ᵊb-kanabaayti w-daxxen ġalyuuni.*

settlement - 1. *ʔəttifaaq* pl. *-aat.* They couldn't reach a settlement. *maa ḥəsnu yuuṣalu la-ʔəttifaaq.* 2. *məstaɛmara* pl. *-aat.* That village is an old settlement. *hal-qarye məstaɛmara qadiime.*

settler - *məstaɛmer* pl. *-iin.* The first European settlers came to the country some 300 years ago. *l-məstaɛᵊmriin l-ʔawrəbbiyyiin ᵊl-ʔawwaliin ʔəžu ləl-ᵊblaad mən ḥawaali tlaat miit səne.*

setup - *tanẓiim* pl. *-aat.* There is a lot wrong with the setup of our company. *fii ktiir ʔaxṭaaʔ ᵊb-tanẓiim šərkətna.*

seven - 1. *sabɛa.* Five and seven make twelve. *xamse w-sabɛa bisaawu ṭnaɛš.* -- There are seven of us in class. *nəḥna sabɛa bᵊṣ-ṣaff.* 2. *sabᵊɛ.* You owe me seven pounds. *ʔəli maɛak sabᵊɛ leeraat.* 3. *sabᵊɛt.* We have only seven days to go. *baaqᵊi-lna sabᵊɛt iyyaam bass.* -- The car cost me seven thousand pounds. *s-sayyaara kallafətni sabᵊɛt aalaaf leera.* 4. *s-saaɛa sabɛa.* Is seven a convenient time for you? *s-saaɛa sabɛa binaasbak?* -- The plane leaves at seven sharp. *ṭ-ṭayyaara btəmši s-saaɛa sabɛa ɛat-takke.*

seventeen - 1. *sabaṭaɛš.* So far there are seventeen of us for the chartered flight. *la-ḥadd hallaq ṣərna sabaṭaɛš yalli bəddna naaxod ṭayyaara skaarsa.* 2. *sabaṭaɛšar.* He spent seventeen years in Africa. *maḍḍa sabaṭaɛšar səne b-ʔafriiqya.*

seventeenth - 1. *s-sabaṭaɛš.* It's her seventeenth birthday. *haada ɛiid miilaada s-sabaṭaɛš.* -- We arrived on July the seventeenth. *wṣəlna b-sabaṭaɛš tammuuz.* 2. *s-saabeɛ ɛašar.* He died at the end of the seventeenth century. *maat ᵊb-ʔawaaxer ᵊl-qarn ᵊs-saabeɛ ɛašar.*

seventh - 1. *saabeɛ.* It's the seventh house from the corner. *huwwe l-beet ᵊs-saabeɛ* (or *saabeɛ beet*) *mn ᵊs-suuke.* 2. *sabɛa.* I was born on February seventh. *wlədt ᵊb-sabɛa šbaaṭ.*

one seventh - *səbᵊɛ* pl. *ʔasbaaɛ.* That's six sevenths of the total amount. *haada sətt ʔasbaaɛ ᵊl-mablaġ kəllo.*

seventieth - *s-sabɛiin, s-sabɛiini*.* She celebrated her seventieth birthday in good health. *ḥtaflet ᵊb-ɛiid miilaada ᵊs-sabɛiin(i) b-ṣaḥḥa məmtaaze.*

seventy - *sabɛiin.*

several - *ɛəddet˜* ... I'd like to stay here for several days. *ḥaabeb ʔəbqa hoon ɛəddet ʔiyyaam.* -- I've been there several times. *rəḥᵊt la-hniik ɛəddet marraat.* -- She's several years older than he. *hiyye ʔakbar mənno b-ɛəddet ᵊsniin.*

severe - 1. *qaasi.* It was a very severe winter. *kaanet šətwiyye qaasye ktiir.* -- The punishment was very severe. *l-qaṣaaṣ kaan qaasi ktiir.* -- It was a severe test for man and machine. *kaan ʔəmtiḥaan qaasi ləl-ʔənsaan wᵊl-ʔaale.* 2. *qawi*, šadiid.* He has a severe case of pneumonia. *maɛo ʔiṣaabe qawiyye b-zaat ᵊr-riʔa.* -- She complains of severe pains. *ɛam təški mən ʔaalaam qawiyye.*

to **sew** - *xayyaṭ//txayyaṭ.* She sews her own dresses. *bətxayyeṭ faṣaṭiina la-ḥaala.* -- Now sew the two ends together. *hallaq xayyṭi ṭ-ṭarafeen sawa.*

to sew on - *rakkab, xayyaṭ.* Would you sew on that button for me? *məmken ᵊtrakkbᵊi-li haz-zərr?*

sewer - *siyaaʔ* pl. *-aat.*

sewing machine - *maakiinet˜* (pl. *-aat˜*) *xyaaṭa.*

sex - *žənᵊs.* In your application state age and sex. *b-ṭalabak zkoor ᵊl-ɛəmᵊr wᵊž-žənᵊs.* -- It's one of those cheap magazines full of crime and sex. *waaḥde mən hal-mažallaat ᵊr-rxiiṣa halli malaane ʔəžraam w-žənᵊs.*

sex appeal - *žaazbiyye žənsiyye.*

sexy: She's a very sexy girl. *hiyye bənᵊt bətsiir ᵊš-šahwe ktiir* or *hiyye bənᵊt ɛanda ktiir žaazbiyye žənsiyye.* -- That dress sure is sexy! *faṣaaɛa šuu bihayyež har-roob.*

shabby - 1. *mhargal.* His suit looks shabby. *badᵊlto mhargale.* -- He hangs out in all kinds of shabby places. *mdaawem ɛala kəll ʔanwaaɛ ᵊl-maḥallaat l-ᵊmhargale.* 2. *mlaɛwan.* Don't try those shabby tricks on me. *laa tmašši hal-ḥiyal l-ᵊmlaɛwane ɛaliyyi.* 3. *mšaršaḥ.* Does he expect us to thank him for his shabby contribution? *šuu bəddo-ydana nəšᵊkro ɛala tabarrɛo l-ᵊmšaršaḥ?*

**That was very shabby of him. *bᵊl-ḥaqiiqa kaanet šaršaḥa mənno.*

shack - *kuux* pl. *kwaax.*

shade - 1. *fayy* pl. *-aat.* Let's stay in the shade. *xalliina nəbqa bᵊl-fayy.* 2. *bərdaaye* pl. *baraadi.* Pull down the shades! *nazzel ᵊl-baraadi.* 3. *wažᵊh* pl. *ʔawžoh* and *wžuuh.* The party includes every shade of leftism. *l-ḥəzᵊb byəšmol ɛala kəll ʔawžoh ᵊl-yasaar.* 4. *nətfe, šwayye.* This red is a shade too dark. *hal-ʔaḥmar ġaameq nətfe.*

**There's a shade of difference in the meaning of the two expressions. *fii farᵊq laa yuzkar been maɛna t-taɛbiireen.*

**Those carnations come in all shades of red. *hal-qərənfol byəži b-kəll šii fii ʔalwaan ḥamra.*

to shade - 1. *ẓallal//dẓallal, xayyam//txayyam.* This oak shades the house in the afternoon. *hal-balluuṭa bədẓallel ᵊl-beet baɛd ᵊḍ-ḍəhᵊr.* 2. *ẓallal//dẓallal.* It would look nicer if you shaded the drawing. *bətbayyen ʔaḥla ʔiza ẓallalt ᵊr-rasme.* 3. *tmaazaž.* The colors shade into each other. *l-ʔalwaan btətmaazaž maɛ baɛḍa.*

shadow - 1. *ẓəll* pl. *ẓlaal* and *ʔaẓlaal.* The trees cast long shadows. *š-šažaraat ɛaamliin ẓlaal ṭawiile.* 2. *xyaal.* He follows me like a shadow. *byəlḥaqni mətl ᵊxyaali.* -- He's afraid of his own shadow. *bixaaf mən ᵊxyaalo.*

**There is not a shadow of doubt about it. *maa fii ʔadna šakk fiiha.*

shadow play - *karakooz* pl. *-aat.*

to shadow - *raaqab.* They hired a detective to shadow him. *staxdamu taḥarri la-yraaqbo.*

shady - *mašbuuh*. What kind of shady business is he engaged in now? *šuu š-šaġle l-mašbuuha halli Ɛam yəštəġəla hallaq?*
**Let's try to find a shady place. *xalliina nḥaawel ᵊnlaaqi maḥall fayy*.
**It's shady over here. *hoon fayy*.

to **shake** - 1. *hazz (ə hazz//nhazz)*. He shook his head. *hazz raaso*. — The earthquake shook everything within a radius of two miles. *z-zalzale hazzet kəll šii Ɛala masaafet miileen*. — You have to shake the apples from the tree. *laazem ᵊthazz ᵊt-təffaaḥaat mən Ɛaš-šažara*. 2. *xaḍḍ (ə xaḍḍ//nxaḍḍ)*. Shake the bottle well before opening it. *xaḍḍ ᵊl-qanniine mniiḥ qabᵊl-ma təftaḥa*. 3. *ražaf (e ražafaan)*. I was still shaking half an hour after the accident. *kənt ləssaani Ɛam bəržef baƐd ᵊl-ḥaadse b-nəṣṣ saaƐa*. 4. *htazz, rtažž*. The whole ground shook. *kəll ᵊl-ʔarḍ ᵊhtazzet*.
**Come on, shake a leg! *yaḷḷa xəffa!*
to shake hands - *tṣaafaḥ*. Let's shake hands. *xalliina nətṣaafaḥ*.
to shake hands with - *ṣaafaḥ, tṣaafaḥ maƐ*. He shook hands with the prime minister. *ṣaafaḥ raʔiis ᵊl-wəzara*.
to shake someone's hand - *ṣaafaḥ ḥada*. He shook my hand cordially. *ṣaafaḥni b-ḥaraara*.

shaky - *mḍaƐḍaƐ*. I'm still shaky. *ləssaani mḍaƐḍaƐ*. — The table looks pretty shaky, don't you think? *maa bədzənn ʔənno ṭ-ṭaawle mḍaƐḍaƐa šwayye?*

shall - 1. imperfect without b-: Shall I wait? *ʔəstanna?* — Shall we leave the door open? *nxalli l-baab maftuuḥ?* — Shall he wait? *yəstanna šii?* 2. imperfect with b- or *laha (raha)*: We shall see who's right. *mənšuuf miin maẓbuuṭ*. — I shall never go there. *b-ḥayaati maa-li raha ruuḥ la-hniik*.
should - see alphabetically.

shallow - 1. *faayeš*. The lake is very shallow at this point. *l-buḥayra ktiir faayše b-hal qərne*. — Put it in a shallow bowl. *ḥəṭṭa b-zəbdiyye faayše*. 2. *saṭḥi**. She's a shallow person. *hiyye mara saṭḥiyye*. — What is a cocktail-party but two hours of shallow conversation! *daxlak šuu ḥaflet kokteel ʔəlla saaƐteen ḥaki saṭḥi!*

shame - 1. *ḥaya, xažal*. Haven't you any shame? *maa Ɛandak ʔayy ḥaya?* 2. *Ɛeeb*. It's a shame the way he treats us. *Ɛeeb ᵊṭ-ṭariiqa halli biƐaaməlna fiiha*. — Shame on you! *Ɛeeb Ɛaleek!*
**What a shame you can't come! *yaa ləl-ʔasaf maa fiik təži!*

shameless - 1. *bala ḥaya, bala xažal, qaliil˜ (pl. qlaal˜) ḥaya; qaliil˜ xažal*. She's a shameless hussy, if you ask me. *ʔiza bəddak raʔyi hiyye waaḥde waaṭye bala ḥaya* (or *qaliilet ḥaya*). 2. *žaaʔer*. Take the shameless exploitation by the landlords of the critical housing situation! *xood masalan ᵊl-ʔəstəġlaal ᵊž-žaaʔer la-ʔazmet ᵊs-sakan mən ṭaraf ʔaṣḥaab l-ᵊbyuut*.

shampoo - *šampu* (invar.).

shape - 1. *šakᵊl* pl. *ʔaškaal, heeʔa* pl. *-aat*. Could you describe its shape as precisely as possible? *fiik tuuṣef ᵊb-kəll daqqa šakla?* 2. *ḥaale* pl. *-aat*. The building is in very good shape. *l-binaaye b-ḥaale ktiir ᵊmniiḥa*. — I'm in bad shape. *ḥaalti malƐuune*. — What shape is the car in? *šuu ḥaalt ᵊs-sayyaara?*
**Is everything in shape? *kəll šii maẓbuuṭ?*
out of shape - *mṭaƐwaž, mlaƐbaž*. The hat's all out of shape. *l-bərneeṭa kəlla mṭaƐwaže*.
to take shape - *tkawwan, tšakkal*. His plan is taking shape. *xəṭṭᵊto Ɛam tətkawwan* or ****xəṭṭᵊto b-ḥeez ᵊt-takwiin**.
to shape - 1. *kawwan, šakkal*. It's fun to watch a potter shape a lovely vase out of a lump of clay. *maa fii ʔaḥla mn ᵊl-waaḥed yətfarraž Ɛal-faaxuuri w-huwwe Ɛam ykawwen mašrabiyye ḥəlwe mən kabtuulet fəxxaar*. 2. *ṣaaġ (i ṣyaaġa//nṣaaġ)*. The board of directors shapes the company's policy. *mažles ᵊl-ʔidaara huwwe halli biṣiiġ syaaset ᵊš-šərke*.
to shape up - *tkawwan, tšakkal*. The project is gradually shaping up. *l-mašruuƐ šwayye šwayye Ɛam tətkawwan*.

shapeless - *bala šakᵊl*.

share - 1. *ḥəṣṣa* pl. *ḥəṣaṣ*. Everybody has to pay his share. *kəll waaḥed laazem yədfaƐ ḥəṣṣto*. 2. *naṣiib*. He's had his share of luck in business. *ʔəžda naṣiibo mn ᵊl-ḥaẓẓ bᵊt-tižaara*. 3. *sahᵊm* pl. *ʔashom*. How many shares did you buy? *kam sahm ᵊštareet?*
to share - 1. *tšaarak b-*. Let's share the cake. *xalliina nətšaarak bᵊl-gaatoo*. 2. *šaarak*. Let me share this beer with you. *xalliini šaarkak ᵊb-hal-biira*.
**We shared many happy hours together. *qaḍeena ktiir saaƐaat saƐiide sawa*.

shareholder - *msaahem* pl. *-iin*.

shark - *ġərᵊš* pl. *ʔaġraaš*.

sharp - 1. *ḥadd*. Do you have a sharp knife? *maƐak səkkiine ḥadde?* 2. *maaken*. It takes a sharp mind to play chess real well. *bədda dmaaġ maaken la-ḥatta yəḥsen ᵊl-waaḥed yəlƐab šaṭranž Ɛat-tamaam*. — The accident happened in a sharp curve. *l-ḥaades ḥadas Ɛala kuuƐ maaken*. 3. *waxxaaz*. Suddenly he felt a sharp pain. *fažʔatan šaƐar ᵊb-ʔalam waxxaaz*. 4. *laazeƐ*. A sharp wind was blowing in our faces. *kaan fii riiḥ laazƐa Ɛam tənsof ᵊb-wəššna*. — She has a sharp tongue. *ʔəla lsaan laazeƐ*. 5. *ḥədeq*. He's a sharp guy. *huwwe šaxᵊṣ ḥədeq* or ****huwwe ʔaxu ʔəxto**. 6. *šadiid*. The ambassador delivered a sharp note of protest. *s-safiir ᵊtqaddam ᵊb-muzakkaret ʔəḥtižaaž šadiide*. 7. *Ɛat-takke, Ɛat-tamaam*. We have to be there at five o'clock sharp. *laazem ᵊnkuun ᵊhniik ᵊs-saaƐa xamse Ɛat-takke*.
**Keep a sharp eye on him. *xalli Ɛeenak maftuuḥa Ɛalée*.
**He's a sharp dresser. *huwwe labbiis*.

to **sharpen** - 1. *sann (ə sann//nsann), šallax//džallax*. This knife needs sharpening. *has-səkkiine bədda sann*. 2. *bara (i bari//mbara)*. Sharpen the pencil for me, please. *brii-li l-qalam mən faḍlak*.

sharpener - *barraaye* pl. *-aat*. I've ruined all my pencils using this sharpener. *nazaƐᵊt kəll ʔaqlaami b-hal-barraaye*.

shave - *ḥlaaqa* pl. *-aat, ḥlaaqet˜ daqᵊn*. I guess I need a shave. *bəƐtəqed laazəmni ḥlaaqa*.
**That was a close shave! *waḷḷa ʔaḷḷa satar!*
to give a shave - *ḥalaq (e ḥlaaqa//nḥalaq)*. The barber gave me a good shave. *l-ḥallaaq ḥalaq-li ḥlaaqa mniiḥa*.
to shave - *ḥalaq (e ḥlaaqa//nḥalaq) la-*. When my arm was broken my wife had to shave me every morning. *waqt-əlli kaanet ʔiidi maksuura marti ḍṭarret təḥləq-li kəll yoom Ɛala bəkra*. — Do you shave every morning? *btəḥleq kəll yoom Ɛala bəkra?*

shaving cream - *ṣaabuun˜ ᵊḥlaaqa*.

shaving lotion - *koloonya ləl-ᵊḥlaaqa*.

shawl - *šaal* pl. *-aat*.

she - *hiyye*.

to **shear** - *žazz (ə žazz//nžazz)*. They shear the sheep early in spring. *bižəzzu l-ġanam ᵊb-ʔawwal ᵊr-rabiiƐ*.

(pair of) **shears** - 1. (sheep) *mžazz* pl. *-aat*. 2. (hedges) *mqaṣṣ* pl. *-aat*.

shed - *taxšiibe* pl. *-aat*. Put the tools back in the shed. *ražžeƐ ᵊl-Ɛədde Ɛat-taxšiibe*.

to **shed** - 1. *sakab (o sakᵊb//nsakab)*. She shed bitter tears. *sakbet ᵊdmuuƐ mərra*. 2. *ʔalqa*. That sheds some light on the matter. *haš-šii byəlqi šwayyet nuur Ɛal-qaḍiyye*. 3. *safak (o safᵊk//nsafak)*. Not a drop of blood was shed in the revolution. *maa nsafak w-laa nəqṭet damm bᵊs-sawra*. 4. *šalaḥ (a šalᵊḥ//nšalaḥ)*. As soon as I got into my room I shed all my clothes. *ʔawwal-ma fətt Ɛala ʔuuḍṭi šalaḥᵊt kəll ʔawaƐiyyi*.

sheep - 1. *raas ġanam* coll. *ġanam* pl. *ruus ġanam*. Three sheep are missing from the flock. *naaqeṣ tlatt ruus ġanam ᵊmn ᵊṭ-ṭarᵊš*. 2. *xaaruuf* pl. *xawariif*. They slaughtered several sheep for the banquet. *dabaḥu Ɛəddet xawariif ləl-Ɛaziime*.
sheep pen - *zriibet˜* (pl. *-aat˜* and *zaraayeb˜*) *ġanam*.

sheepish - *baliid*. He stood there with a sheepish expression on his face. *kaan waaqef ᵊhniik w-Ɛala wəššo taƐbiira baliide*.

sheer - 1. *Ɛal-maẓbuuṭ*. That's sheer nonsense. *haada ʔakᵊl hawa Ɛal-maẓbuuṭ*. — That would be sheer madness. *haada bikuun ᵊžnaan Ɛal-maẓbuuṭ*. 2. *qaasi*. It's a sheer drop to the rocks below. *nazle qaasye ləṣ-ṣaxraat taḥᵊt*. 3. *šaffaaf, mžalli, mlaali*. I'd like something sheerer. *bəddi šii bikuun šaffaaf ʔaktar*.

sheet - 1. *šaršaf* pl. *šaraašef*. Shall I change the sheets, too? *ġayyer ᵊš-šaraašef kamaan?* 2. *ṭabaqa* pl. *-aat*. The road is covered with a sheet of ice. *ṭ-ṭariiq ᵊmġaṭṭa b-ṭabaqet žaliid*.
**She turned as white as a sheet. *ṣaar wəšša ʔabyaḍ mətl ᵊl-ḥeeṭ*.
sheet of paper - *waraqa* pl. *-aat* and *wraaq*.
cookie sheet - *ṣeeniyyet˜* (pl. *ṣawaani˜*) *baskoot*.

shelf - *raff* pl. *rfuuf*. The shelves are empty. *r-rfuuf faaḍye*.

shell - 1. *qəšre* coll. *qəšər* pl. *qšuur*. Hazelnuts have a hard shell. *qəšr əl-bəndoq qaasi.* — Throw the egg shells in the garbage. *lḥooš qšuur əl-beeḍ əb-tanket əz-zbaale.* **2.** *ǧəmble* pl. *ǧanaabel, ǧaziife* pl. *ǧazaayef.* The shell exploded in front of our house. *l-ǧəmble nfažret qəddaam beetna.* **3.** *ṣadafe* coll. *ṣadaf* pl. *-aat.* The beach is covered with shells. *š-šaṭṭ malyaan ṣadaf.*

**He came out of his shell only at the end of our conversation. *maa ṭəleɛ mən ɛəzəlto ʔəlla b-ʔaaxer əmḥaadasətna.*

to shell - 1. *faṣṣaṣ//tfaṣṣaṣ, faṣfaṣ//tfaṣfaṣ.* The peas have to be shelled. *l-bazaalya laazem tətfaṣṣaṣ.* **2.** *faqqaš//tfaqqaš.* You shell the nuts while I take care of the batter. *ʔənti faqqši ž-žooz been-ma ʔana saawi l-ɛažiinaat.* **3.** *ḍarab (o ḍarəb//nḍarab) .., bəl-madfaɛiyye.* The enemy shelled the capital. *l-ɛaduww ḍarab əl-ɛaaṣme bəl-madfaɛiyye.*

shellac - *kamaleeka.*

shelter - 1. *maʔwa.* We found shelter in a hut during the storm. *laqeena maʔwa b-kuux ʔasnaaʔ əl-ɛaaṣfe.* **2.** *malžaʔ* pl. *malaažeʔ.* Where is the nearest shelter in case of attack? *ween ʔaqrab malžaʔ b-ḥaalet ġaara žawwiyye?*

to shelter - *ʔawwa//tʔawwa.* They sheltered and fed us. *ʔawwuuna w-ṭaɛmuuna.*

shepherd - *raaɛi* pl. *ruɛaat.*

sherbet - *šaraab žaamed.*

sherry - *šeeri* (invar.).

shield - *dərəɛ* pl. *druuɛa.* They banged their swords on the shields as a sign of approval. *daqqu b-əsyuufon ɛala druuɛə́ton ɛalaamet əmwaafaqa.*

to shield - *ḥama (i ḥmaaye//nḥama).* You ought to shield your eyes against the sun. *laazem təḥmi ɛyuunak mn əš-šaməs.* -- He must be shielding somebody. *laazem ykuun ɛam byəḥmi ḥada.*

shift - 1. *noobe* pl. *-aat.* Our workers work in three shifts. *ɛəmmaalna byəštəġlu ɛala tlatt noobaat.* **2.** *taġyiir* pl. *-aat, tabdiil* pl. *-aat.* This will mean a shift in my plans. *haš-šii maɛnaato taġyiir əb-xəṭaṭi.* **3.** *taḥwiil* pl. *-aat.* His death meant quite a shift of responsibility in the company. *mooto sabbab taḥwiil əkbiir bəl-masʔuuliyye bəš-šərke.*

to shift - 1. *ġayyar//tġayyar.* You'd better shift into second. *l-ʔafḍal ətġayyer ləd-doozyeem.* **2.** *naqal (o naqəl//ntaqal).* We have to shift the meeting to Tuesday. *laazem nənqol əl-ʔəžtimaaɛ la-yoom ət-talaata.* **3.** *tḥawwal.* The wind has shifted. *r-riiḥ əṭḥawwalet.*

to shift for oneself - *dabbar ḥaalo.* I've always had to shift for myself. *mən ṭuul ɛəmri nžabarət dabber ḥaali la-ḥaali.*

shin - *qaṣbet˜ rəžəl* pl. *qaṣbaat˜ rəžleen.* I bumped my shin against the table. *ṭaraqət qaṣbet rəžli bəṭ-ṭaawle.*

shine - *talmiiɛa.* See if you can take the shine out of these pants. *šuuf ʔiza fiik ətrawweḥ ət-talmiiɛa mən hal-banṭaloon.*

**We'll come, rain or shine. *šattet wəlla maa šattet laḥ nəži.*

**Where can I get a shoe shine around here? *ween bəqder laaqi booyaži b-han-nawaaḥi?*

**He's taken a shine to her. *ṣaaret təɛəžbo ktiir.*

to shine - 1. *lamaɛ (a lamaɛaan).* Her eyes were shining with joy. *kaanet ɛyuuna ɛam təlmaɛ əmn əl-faraḥ.* **2.** *baddaɛ, barraz.* He's good in all his subjects, but mathematics is where he shines. *huwwe mniiḥ əb-kəll mawaaddo laaken bər-ryaaḍiyyaat mbaddeɛ.* **3.** *booya//tbooya.* I have to shine my shoes. *laazem booyi ṣabbaaṭi.* **4.** *lammaɛ//tlammaɛ.* Tell the maid to shine all the pots and pans in the kitchen. *quul ləṣ-ṣaanɛa tlammeɛ kəll əṭ-ṭanaažer wəl-maqaali yalli bəl-maṭbax.*

**When I woke up in the morning the sun was shining, and now we have rain. *lamma fəqt əṣ-ṣəbəḥ š-šaməs kaanet ṭaalɛa w-hallaq naazle maṭar.*

**He's a pretty good student, but he's no shining light. *huwwe təlmiiz maa bo šii bass maa-lo faṭḥal.*

shiny - *lammaaɛ, lammiiɛ.*

ship - *baaxra* pl. *bawaaxer, safiine* pl. *səfon.* When does the ship leave? *ʔeemta btəmši l-baaxra?*

to ship - *šaḥan (a šaḥən//nšaḥan).* Hasn't the case been shipped yet? *ləssa maa nšaḥan əṣ-ṣanduuq?* — Why don't you ship these goods by rail? *leeš maa btəšḥan hal-əbḍaaɛa bət-treen?*

shipment - *šaḥne* pl. *-aat.* We've just received a new shipment of shoes. *šii-ʔənno ʔəžətna šaḥnet ṣababiiṭ əždiide.*

shipping - *šaḥən.* Shipping these things by plane will cost you a fortune. *šaḥən hal-əġraaḍ bəṭ-ṭayyaara bikallfak sarwe.*

shipping agency - *šərket˜* (pl. *-aat˜*) *šaḥən, wakaalet˜* (pl. *-aat˜*) *šaḥən.*

to **shirk** - *tharrab mən, tmallaṣ mən.* He's been shirking his duty as long as I can remember. *ṣar-lo ɛam yətharrab mən waažbaato mən ʔawwal maɛrəfti fii.*

shirt - *qamiiṣ* pl. *qəmṣaan.* Are my shirts back from the laundry? *rəžɛu qəmṣaani mən ɛand əl-kawwa?* -- He would give you the shirt off his back. *walla byəšləḥ-lak qamiiṣo.*

**Keep your shirt on, I'll be right there. *ṭawwel baalak, hallaq bəži.*

to **shiver** - *ražaf (e ražafaan).* The child shivered with cold. *ṭ-ṭəfəl ražaf mən əl-barəd.*

shock - *ṣadme* pl. *-aat, hazze* pl. *-aat.* His death was a great shock to us all. *mootto kaanet ṣadme kbiire la-ʔəlna kəllna.*

**I got a shock when I plugged in the lamp. *tkahrabət lamma dahašt əbriiz əḍ-ḍaww.*

shock absorber - *ʔamatəsoor* pl. *-aat.*

to shock - *hazz (ə hazz//nhazz), ṣadam (o ṣadəm//nṣadam).* We were shocked by the news. *l-xabar hazzna hazz.*

shocking - 1. *məxžel, məxzi.* Everybody commented on her shocking behavior. *kəll ən-naas ɛallaqu ɛala taṣarrə́fa l-məxžel.* **2.** *faẓiiɛ, məfžeɛ.* Official reports played down the shocking details of the massacre. *t-taqariir ər-rasmiyye xaffafet ət-tafaṣiil əl-faẓiiɛa tabaɛ əl-madbaḥa.*

shock - *koome* pl. *-aat.* They stacked up the wheat in shocks. *kawwamu l-qaməḥ koomaat.*

shoe - 1. (men's) *ṣabbaaṭ* pl. *ṣababiiṭ,* a single shoe *fardet˜ ṣabbaaṭ,* (ladies') *kəndra* pl. *kanaader, skarbiine* pl. *-aat.* We have just the shoe for you, sir. *ɛanna ṣabbaaṭ ġaraḍak tamaam, yaa beek.* -- You didn't have to throw your shoe at the cat. *maa kaan fii ləzuum təlḥoš (fardet˜) ṣabbaaṭak ɛal-qaṭṭa.* **2.** *ḥadwe* pl. *-aat.* The horse lost one shoe. *ḍaaɛet ḥadwe mən l-əḥṣaan.*

**I wouldn't want to be in his shoes. *maa bəddi kuun əb-maḥallo.*

to shoe - *rakkab ḥadwaat la-.* The blacksmith is going to shoe our horses today. *l-ḥaddaad raḥa yrakkeb ḥadwaat la-ʔəḥṣənətna l-yoom.*

shoehorn - *šakazak* pl. *-aat, sakažak* pl. *-aat, karata* pl. *-aat.*

shoelace - *šawwaaṭa* pl. *-aat, šriiṭ˜* (pl. *šaraayeṭ˜*) *ṣabbaaṭ.*

shoemaker - *kəndarži* pl. *-iyye.*

shoe polish - *booya.*

shoot - 1. *ɛərəq* pl. *ɛruuq.* Our rosebush has two new shoots. *wardətna ṭaalə́ɛ-la ɛərqeen əždaad.* **2.** *ġarse* pl. *-aat.* I'll give you a shoot of this azalea. *baɛṭiik ġarse mən hal-ʔaḍaalya.*

to shoot - 1. *qawwaṣ//tqawwaṣ.* Don't shoot! *laa tqawweṣ!* -- He was shot yesterday night. *tqawwaṣ əmbaareḥ ɛašiyye.* **2.** *ṣawwar.* They're shooting in Studio Five. *ɛam yṣawwru bəs-stuudyo nəmra xamse.*

**Come on, shoot, let's hear the good news! *yalla nṭooq xalliina nəsmaɛ əl-ʔaxbaar əs-saarra.*

**The car shot past us. *s-sayyaara qaṭɛet ɛanna mətl ər-riiḥ.*

to shoot dead - 1. *qatal (o qatəl//nqatal) b-ərṣaaṣ.* They shot him dead. *qatalúu b-ərṣaaṣ.*

to shoot down - 1. *qawwaṣ//tqawwaṣ.* He shot him down in cold blood. *qawwaṣo mən ġeer-ma traff-ə́llo ɛeen.* **2.** *ṣaqqaṭ//tṣaqqaṭ.* They shot down four of our airplanes. *ṣaqqaṭu ʔarbaɛ mən ṭayyaaraatna.*

to shoot up - *šabb (ə šabbe).* How the boy has shot up in the last year! *ya laṭiif qaddeeš šabb haṣ-ṣabi* (or ***qaddeeš haṣ-ṣabi šamaṭ ṭuul*) *mən ɛaamnawwal.*

shop - *dəkkaan* (f.) pl. *dakakiin, maxzan* pl. *maxaazen.* There are many shops on this street. *fii ktiir dakakiin ɛala haš-šaareɛ.* — He was found dead in his shop. *laqúu mayyet əb-dəkkaanto.*

**I wish they wouldn't always talk shop. *ɛala waaḥ ybaṭṭlu yəḥku ɛan šəġlon ɛaṭ-ṭaalɛa wən-naazle.*

shop window - *vətriin(a)* pl. *-aat, waažha* pl. *-aat.*

to shop - *tsawwaq, tbaḍḍaɛ.* We usually shop on Friday morning. *ɛaadatan mnətsawwaq əž-žəmɛa ṣ-ṣəbəḥ.*

**She spent all afternoon shopping for clothes. *maḍḍet kəll baɛd əḍ-ḍəhər ɛam əddawwer ɛala ʔawaaɛi.*

**I want to shop around a little before I buy a car. *bəddi dawwə́r-li šwayye qabəl-ma ʔəštə́ri sayyaara.*

to go shopping - *tsawwaq, tbaḍḍaƐ.* I'll go shopping with you if you pay for everything. *bətsawwaq maƐak ʔiza btədfaƐ ḥaqq kəll šii.*
shopping - *taswiiq, tabḍiiƐ, šəre.* Shopping isn't easy in a strange city. *t-taswiiq muu hayyen ᵊb-madiine maa btaƐrə́fa.*
to do one's shopping - *tsawwaq, tbaḍḍaƐ.* I'll do my shopping after work. *raḥa ʔətsawwaq baƐd ᵊš-šəġᵊl.*
shore - *šaṭṭ* pl. *šṭuuṭ, šaaṭeʔ* pl. *šawaaṭeʔ.* How far is it to the shore? *qaddeeš mən hoon ləš-šaṭṭ?*
short - **1.** *kontaak.* There must be a short in the radio. *laazem ykuun fii kontaak bᵊr-raadyo.* **2.** *qaṣiir* pl. *qṣaar.* It's only a short way from here. *kəlla masaafe qaṣiire mən hoon.* — We stayed there for just a very short time. *qaƐadna hniik mədde ktiir qaṣiire bass.* -- She wears her dresses too short. *fasaṭiina qaṣiire ktiir.* -- You can get short wave too on this radio. *btəqder ᵊdžiib ᵊl-moože l-qaṣiire Ɛala har-raadyo kamaan.* -- She writes pretty good short stories. *btəktob qəṣaṣ qaṣiire laa baʔᵊs fiiha.* -- He's rather short. *huwwe qaṣiir ᵊšwayye.*
**I am three pounds short. *naaqəṣni tlətt leeraat.*
**Right now, I am short of money. *bᵊl-waqt ᵊl-ḥaader naaqəṣni maṣaari.*
**The government will take all necessary steps short of declaring war. *l-ᵊḥkuume laḥa taaxod kəll ᵊt-tadabiir ᵊl-laazme maa Ɛada ʔəƐlaan ᵊl-ḥarᵊb.*
**She seems to have a short memory. *mbayyen Ɛaleeha zaakərta ḍƐiife.*
**Come on, make it short! *yaḷḷa, xtəṣə́ra!*
shorts - *šoort* pl. *-aat, banṭaloon qaṣiir* pl. *banṭaloonaat ᵊqṣaar.* We bought six pairs of shorts. *štareena sətt šoortaat.*
short cut - **1.** *ṭariiq~* (pl. *ṭəroq~*) *ᵊmqaaṭaƐa.* He knows a short cut to the beach. *byaƐref ṭariiq ᵊmqaaṭaƐa ləš-šaṭṭ.* **2.** *ṭariiqa* (pl. *ṭəroq*) *məxtṣ́ara.* There's no short cut in language learning. *maa fii ṭariiqa məxtṣ́ara b-taƐallom ᵊl-luġaat.*
in short - *məxtṣ́ar mufiid, wᵊl-xulaaṣa.* In short, I can't leave before Saturday. *məxtṣ́ar mufiid, maa fiini ʔətrek qabl ᵊs-sabᵊt.*
to make a long story short - *bala ṭuul~ siire.* To make a long story short, it's settled. *bala ṭuul siire, ntahet ᵊl-qəṣṣa.*
to cut short - **1.** *xtaṣar, qaṣṣar.* They had to cut their trip short. *ḍṭarru yəxtəṣru raḥlə́ton.* **2.** *xarras, sakkat.* I opened my mouth to apologize, but he cut me short. *fataḥt təmmi la-ʔəƐtə́zer bass xarrasni.*
to fall short of - *qaṣṣar Ɛan.* The project fell short of what the government had promised before. *l-mašruuƐ qaṣṣar Ɛan halli waƐᵊdto l-ᵊḥkuume.*
to run short - see **run**.
shortage - *naqᵊṣ, Ɛažᵊz.* We're facing an acute shortage of teachers. *Ɛam ᵊnwaažeh naqᵊṣ ḥaadd bᵊl-ᵊmƐallmiin.*
shortcoming - *naaqṣa* pl. *nawaaqeṣ.* The house has many shortcomings. *l-beet fii nawaaqeṣ ᵊktiir.*
to **shorten** - *qaṣṣar.* Shorten the pants for me, please. *qaṣṣə́r-li l-banṭaloon mən faḍlak.*
shorthand - *ʔəxtizaal.*
shortly - **1.** *baƐd ᵊšwayye, Ɛan qariib.* He'll be here shortly. *laḥa ykuun hoon baƐd ᵊšwayye.* **2.** *b-ᵊšwayye.* He arrived shortly before I did. *wəṣel qabᵊl-ma ʔuuṣal b-ᵊšwayye.*
shortsighted - *qaṣiir~ naẓar.* That was a very shortsighted decision. *kaan qaraar ᵊktiir qaṣiir naẓar.*
short-tempered - *nəzeq.*
short-term - *qaṣiir~* (pl. *qṣaar~*) *ʔažal.* The banks decided to raise the interest on short-term loans. *l-ᵊbnuuke qarraret tərfaƐ ᵊl-faaʔide Ɛal-ᵊqruuḍ ᵊl-qaṣiiret ᵊl-ʔažal.*
shot - **1.** *ṭalqa* pl. *-aat, qwaaṣa* pl. *-aat.* Did you hear a shot? *sməƐᵊt ṭalqa?* -- He fired three shots. *qawwaṣ tlətt ṭalqaat.* **2.** *ḍarbe* pl. *-aat.* That was a good shot! *waḷḷa ḍarbe mḥakkame!* **3.** *ʔəbre* pl. *ʔəbar.* Are you getting shots? *Ɛam taaxod ʔəbar?* **4.** *ṣuura* pl. *ṣuwar.* We got beautiful shots of the lake. *ʔaxadna ṣuwar həlwe ləl-buḥayra.* **5.** *ṣayyiib* pl. *-e.* He's a good shot. *huwwe ṣayyiib ᵊmniiḥ.*
**I wouldn't mind a shot of whiskey now. *maa Ɛandi maaneƐ ᵊb-qadaḥ wəski hallaq.*
**He thinks he's a big shot. *mḥasseb ḥaalo ʔakaaber.*
to take a shot at - *qawwaṣ Ɛala.* Somebody took a shot at him. *fii ḥada qawwaṣ Ɛalée.*
shotgun - *žəfᵊt* pl. *žfuute.*
should - *laazem* + imperfect without *b-*. I should know because I saw it with my own eyes. *laazem ʔaƐref laʔənni šəfta b-Ɛeeni.* -- You shouldn't have believed it. *maa kaan laazem tsaddə́qa.* — He shouldn't worry, he's got all the money in the world. *maa laazem yəhtamm, maƐo maṣaari ʔaḷḷa.* -- I think you should see the film. *bəƐtə́qed laazem ᵊtšuuf ᵊl-fəlᵊm.* -- You shouldn't do that. *laazem maa taƐmel haš-šii.* — You shouldn't have said that. *kaan laazem maa tquul haš-šii.*
I should like to, we should like to - *žaaye Ɛala baali ..., žaaye Ɛala baalna ..., ḥaabeb ..., ḥaabbiin ...* I should like to start out early. *žaaye Ɛala baali ʔəmši Ɛala bakkiir.* -- We should like to meet your family. *ḥaabbiin nətƐarraf Ɛala ʔahlak.*
**How should I know? *šuu Ɛarrafni?*
**I should say so! *maa bədda kalaam!* or *biduun šakk!*
shoulder - **1.** *kətᵊf* pl. *ktaaf.* He has very broad shoulders. *Ɛalée ktaaf ᵊktiir Ɛariiḍa.* -- This coat is too tight in the shoulders. *hal-kabbuud dayyeq ᵊktiir Ɛand l-ᵊktaaf.* -- I'd like a shoulder cut. *bəddi šaqfet kətᵊf.* **2.** *Ɛaateq* pl. *Ɛawaateq.* As usual, all the responsibility rests on my shoulders. *mətl ᵊl-Ɛaade l-masʔuuliyye kəlla məlqaat Ɛala Ɛaatqi.*
**I gave it to him straight from the shoulder. *dažžeet-əllo-yáaha dažž ᵊb-wəššo.*
**Why did you give him the cold shoulder? *leeš naššafᵊt wəššak fii?*
**We'll have to put our shoulders to the wheel. *laazem nḥəṭṭ kəll žahᵊdna Ɛaš-šəġᵊl.*
to shoulder - *tḥammal.* Why should I shoulder the blame for it? *leeš laazem ʔana ʔətḥammal ᵊl-loom Ɛaleeha?*
shout - *ṣarxa* pl. *-aat.* Where did that shout come from? *mneen ṭəlƐet haṣ-ṣarxa?*
to shout - *Ɛayyaṭ, ṣarax* (*a ṣarᵊx* and *ṣriix*). You don't have to shout! *maa fii lzuum ᵊtƐayyeṭ!*
to shout down - *xarras//txarras, sakkat//tsakkat.* The speaker was shouted down by the crowd. *l-xaṭiib xarraso ž-žamᵊƐ.*
shouting - *Ɛyaaṭ, ṣraax.* Your shouting is getting on my nerves. *Ɛyaaṭak Ɛam yəḍrob Ɛala Ɛaṣabi.*
shove - *dafše* pl. *-aat.* He gave me such a shove that I nearly fell over. *dafašni dafše kaan laḥa waqqaƐni.*
to shove - *daffaš//ddaffaš, dafaš* (*o dafᵊš// ndafaš*). Stop shoving me! *ḥaaštak ᵊddaffəšni.*
to shove around - *tnahtar b-, tnaftar b-.* No one's going to shove me around from now on. *maa raḥ xalli ḥada yətnahtar fiyyi mən hallaq w-raayeḥ.*
shovel - *kreek* pl. *-aat.* You'll need a pickax and a shovel. *byəlzamak maƐwal w-kreek.* -- Throw another two shovels of coal on the fire. *ḥəṭṭ-ə́llak kreekeen faḥᵊm kamaan Ɛan-naar.*
to shovel - *žaraf* (*o žarᵊf//nžaraf*). We had to shovel a path through the snow. *nžabarna nəžrof mamarr bᵊt-talᵊž.*
show - **1.** *Ɛarᵊḍ* pl. *Ɛruuḍ.* We spent all afternoon at the automobile show. *maḍḍeena kəll baƐd ᵊḍ-ḍəhr ᵊb-Ɛarḍ ᵊs-sayyaaraat.* -- How did you like yesterday's fashion show? *kiif šəfᵊt Ɛarḍ ᵊl-ʔazyaaʔ tabaƐ ᵊmbaareḥ?* **2.** *nimerо́o* pl. *nimeroyaat.* The night club has an unusually good show. *l-kabarée fii nimerо́o qaliil mənno.* **3.** *fəlᵊm* pl. *ʔaflaam* and *flaam.* Between trains I took in a show. *been ᵊt-treen wᵊt-taani rəḥt ᵊḥḍərt-ə́lli fəlᵊm.* **4.** *ḥafle* pl. *-aat.* When does the afternoon show start? *ʔeemta btəbda ḥaflet baƐd ᵊḍ-ḍəhᵊr?* **5.** *siinama.* They go to the show at least once a week. *biruuḥu Ɛal-maqalli marra bᵊl-ʔəsbuuƐ Ɛas-siinama.* **6.** *bərnaamež* pl. *baraamež.* The best television shows are usually in the winter. *ʔaḥsan baraamež televəzyoon Ɛaadatan ʔasnaaʔ ᵊš-šəte.* **7.** *tamsiil.* Her crying was just for show. *bəkaaha kaan kəllo tamsiil.* **8.** *maẓaaher* (pl.). He bought that expensive car just for show. *štara has-sayyaara l-ġaalye bass ləl-maẓaaher.*
**The United States dispatched several naval units as a show of strength. *l-wilaayaat ᵊl-məttáḥide baƐtet Ɛəddet qəṭaƐ baḥriyye la-twarži quwwə́ta.*
to show - **1.** *warža//twarža, ʔarža//tʔarža, farža// tfarža.* Show me how to do it. *waržiini kiif saawiiha.* -- I'll show them! *waḷḷa la-waržiihon!* -- She showed herself extremely kind when I met her. *ʔaržet ḥaala ktiir laṭiife waqt-əlli tƐarraft Ɛaleeha.* -- This shows the truth of what I said. *haš-šii biwarži ṣəḥḥet kalaami.* **2.** *dall* (*ə dalle//ndall*) *Ɛala.* Could you show me the way? *btəqder ᵊddəllni*

ɛaṭ-ṭariiq? -- The plan shows intelligence. *l-xəṭṭa bəddəll ɛala zaka.* **3.** *ɛaraḍ (o ɛarᵊḍ//nɛaraḍ).* What are they showing at the movies this evening? *šuu ɛam yəɛᵊrḍu bᵊs-siinamayaat ᵊl-leele?* **4.** *raafaq.* I'll show you to the door. *braafqak ləl-baab.* **5.** *baan (a ø), bayyan.* Only his head showed above the water. *bass raaso kaan baayen fooq ᵊl-mayy.* -- Does the spot show? *l-fəššaaye mbayyne šii?*

**Show some sense, man! *xalliik maɛquul yaa zalame!*

**He doesn't dare show himself again around here. *maa baqa yəstarži ybayyen hoon.*

to show around - *dawwar.* She's showing her guests around town. *ɛam ᵊddawwer zuwwaara ᵊl-balad* or *******ɛam ᵊtwarži zuwwaara ɛal-balad.*

to show off - 1. *tmanfax.* He's just showing off. *huwwe bass ɛam yətmanfax.* **2.** *tbaaha b-.* He likes to show his children off. *biḥəbb yətbaaha b-ᵊwlaado.*

to show up - 1. *ʔəža (-yəži žayye).* Nobody showed up. *maa ḥada ʔəža.* **2.** *ẓahar (a ẓhuur).* Yellow shows up well against black. *l-ʔaṣfar byəẓhar ᵊmniiḥ ɛal-ʔaswad.* **3.** *kašaf (e kašᵊf// nkašaf).* The incident showed him up as the coward that he essentially is. *l-ḥaadse kašᵊfto ɛala ḥaqiiqto w-huwwe ʔənno žabaan.*

showcase - *vitriin(a)* pl. *-aat.*

shower - 1. *maṭara* pl. *-aat, zaxxet˜* (pl. *-aat˜*) *maṭar.* We were caught in a heavy shower. *ɛləqna b-maṭara qawiyye.* **2.** *duuš* pl. *dwaaš.* Does your new apartment have a shower? *fii duuš bᵊl-ʔabaarṭmaan tabaɛak ᵊž-ždiid?* -- I just have to take a shower and get dressed. *bass ɛaliyyi ʔaaxod duuš w-ʔəlbes.*

to shower - 1. *ṭamar (o ṭamᵊr//nṭamar).* Their friends showered them with presents. *ṣḥaabon ṭamaruuhon bᵊl-hadaaya.* **2.** *ʔaxad duuš.* I shower every day before going to bed. *baaxod duuš kəll yoom qabᵊl-ma naam.*

show-off - *bahwarži* pl. *-iyye.* He's a big show-off. *huwwe bahwarži kbiir.*

showroom - *ṣaalet˜* (pl. *-aat˜*) *ɛarᵊḍ.*

shrewd - 1. *ḥədeq.* He's a shrewd businessman. *huwwe ražol ʔaɛmaal ḥədeq* or *******huwwe ražol ʔaɛmaal ʔaxu ʔəxto.* **2.** *hənek, mḥannak.* That was a very shrewd move. *kaanet xaṭwe ḥənke tamaam.*

shrill - *ḥadd.* She has a shrill voice. *ṣooṭa ḥadd.* -- The sound of that door bell is awfully shrill. *faẓaaɛa šuu ṣooṭ žaraṣ hal-baab ḥadd.*

shrimp - *qreedse* coll. *qreedes* pl. *-aat.* We're having shrimp for dinner. *ɛaamliin qreedes ɛal-ɛaša.*

**He's a little shrimp. *huwwe ṣarṣuur.*

shrine - *ḥaram* pl. *ʔaḥraam.*

to **shrink** - *kašš (ə kašš).* Does this material shrink? *hal-ᵊqmaaš bikəšš šii?*

**You have to shrink the material before you work on it. *laazem ᵊtxalli l-ᵊqmaaš ykəšš qabᵊl-ma təštəġel ɛalée.*

to shrink from - *tharrab mən.* He shrinks from any responsibility. *byətharrab mən ʔaxᵊd ʔayy masʔuuliyye.*

shrub - *šužayra* pl. *-aat,* (hedge) *syaaž* pl. *-aat.*

shrug - *hazzet˜* (pl. *-aat˜*) *kətᵊf.* He answered me with a shrug. *žaawabni b-hazzet kətᵊf.*

to shrug - 1. *hazz (ə hazz).* She shrugged her shoulders. *hazzet ᵊktaafa.* **2.** *hazz kətfo* (or *ᵊktaafo*). He shrugged and walked away. *hazz kətfo w-məši.*

to **shudder** - *ražaf (o ražafaan).* I shudder when I think of the consequences. *bəržof kəll-ma bəṣfon bᵊl-ɛawaaqeb.*

shuffle - 1. *xalṭa* pl. *-aat, xarbaṭa* pl. *-aat.* I still say he won by a crooked shuffle. *ləssaani bquul rəbeḥ mən xalṭa maxšuuše.* **2.** *taɛdiil* pl. *-aat* and *taɛadiil.* I heard the news of the cabinet shuffle last night over the radio. *sməɛᵊt xabar taɛdiil ᵊl-wazaara mbaareḥ ɛašiyye ɛar-raadyo.*

**My suggestion must have got lost in the shuffle. *ʔəqtiraaḥi laazem ykuun ḍaaɛ bᵊl-ɛažqa.*

to shuffle - 1. *daqq (ə daqq//ndaqq), xarbaṭ// txarbaṭ, xalaṭ (o xalᵊṭ//nxalaṭ).* Let me shuffle the cards first. *ʔawwal xalliini dəqq ᵊš-šadde.* **2.** *šaḥḥaṭ.* Quit shuffling, you're ruining your shoes. *ḥaaže tšaḥḥeṭ, ɛam tənzaɛ ṣabbaaṭak.*

to **shut - 1.** *sakkar//tsakkar, taras (o tarᵊs//ntaras).* Please shut the door. *mən faḍlak sakker ᵊl-baab.* **2.** *sakkar.* Shut your books now. *sakkru kətᵊbkon hallaq.* -- Shut your mouth! *sakker təmmak!* **3.** *zarab (e/o zriibe//nzarab), ḥabas (o/e ḥabᵊs// nḥabas).* Who shut the dog in the garage? *miin zarab ᵊl-kalb bᵊl-garaaž?*

to shut down - *sakkar//tsakkar.* At last, they had to shut down the entire factory. *ʔaxiiran ᵊnžabaru ysakkru kəll ᵊl-maɛmal.*

to shut in - *zarab (e/o zriibe//nzarab), ḥabas (e/o ḥabᵊs//nḥabas).* Someone must have shut the cat in while we were gone. *laazem ḥada zarab ᵊl-qaṭṭa b-ᵊgyaabna.* -- He's been shut in for three months because of his illness. *ṣar-lo tlatt əšhor maḥbuus ᵊb-sabab maraḍo.*

to shut off - 1. *sakkar//tsakkar.* Shut off the water. *sakker l-mayy.* **2.** *qaṭaɛ (a qaṭᵊɛ//nqaṭaɛ).* The Electric Company shut off our lights. *šərket ᵊl-kahraba qaṭɛet ᵊl-kahraba ɛaleena.*

to shut up - 1. *sakkar//tsakkar.* They've shut up their house for the winter. *sakkaru beeton ɛaš-šəte.* **2.** *zarab (e/o zriibe//nzarab), ḥabas (o/e ḥabᵊs// nḥabas).* Shut the cat up for the night. *zreeb ᵊl-qaṭṭa ləṣ-ṣəbᵊḥ.* **3.** *xəres (a xaras).* Aw, shut up! *ʔaa xraas!*

shutter - 1. *ʔabažoor* pl. *-aat.* Open the shutters, please. *ftaaḥ ᵊl-ʔabažooraat mən faḍlak.* **2.** *dyafraam* pl. *-aat.* The shutter in my camera is stuck. *d-dyafraam ᵊb-ʔaalet ᵊt-taṣwiir tabaɛi ɛalqaan.*

shy - *xažuul.* Don't be so shy! *laa tkuun hal-qadd xažuul.*

**I'm a bit shy on cash this month. *mqaṣṣra maɛi l-maṣaari šwayye haš-šahᵊr.*

to shy - *žəfel (a žafalaan).* The horse shied at the car. *l-ᵊḥṣaan žəfel ᵊmn ᵊs-sayyaara.*

to shy away from - *džannab, tḥaaša.* All his life he's shied away from hard work. *ṭuul ɛəmro džannab ᵊš-šəġl ᵊṣ-ṣaɛᵊb.*

Sicilian - *ṣəqəlli*.*

Sicily - *ṣəqəlya.*

sick - *mariiḍ* pl. *mərada, ḍɛiif* pl. *ḍəɛafa.* She sat up all night with her sick baby. *sahret kəll ᵊl-leel maɛ ṭəfla l-mariiḍ.* -- The sick are given the best of care. *ḍ-ḍəɛafa məɛtána fiihon ʔaḥsan ʔəɛtəna.*

**We laughed ourselves sick. *mətna mn ᵊḍ-ḍəḥᵊk.*

**I'm sick and tired of that guy. *ṭaaleɛ diini mən haz-zalame.*

**I'm getting just a little sick and tired of his stale jokes. *badet təlɛi maɛi mən nəkato l-baayxa.*

to be (or **get**) **sick - 1.** *stafraġ, raažaɛ.* I felt I was going to be sick when I saw that blood. *ḥasseet bəddi ʔəstafreġ lamma šəfᵊt kəll had-damm.* **2.** *ḍəɛef (a ḍaɛaf), məreḍ (a maraḍ).* He got sick a month ago and hasn't been back to work since. *ḍəɛef mən šahᵊr w-maa rəžeɛ ɛaš-šəġᵊl mən waqto.* -- How long has she been sick? *qaddeeš ṣar-la ḍaɛfaane?*

to feel sick - 1. *ḥass (ə ø) ḥaalo marḍaan* (or *ḍaɛfaan*). I don't know what's wrong with me, I feel sick all over. *maa baɛref šə-bni ḥaases ḥaali kəlli marḍaan.* **2.** *ləɛyet (i ø) nafso.* All of a sudden I felt sick (to my stomach). *ɛala ġafle ləɛyet nafsi.* -- I get sick when I look at him. *kəll-ma bšuufo btəlɛi nafsi.*

to make sick - 1. *laɛa (i laɛayaan) nafs˜ ...* Liquor on an empty stomach invariably makes me sick. *l-mašruub ɛala məɛde faaḍye daayman byəlɛi nafsi.* **2.** *laɛɛa nafs˜ ...* Doesn't that magazine make you sick? *balla hal-mažalle maa bətlaɛɛi-lak nafsak?*

sickle - *manžal* pl. *manaažel.*

sickness - *maraḍ* pl. *ʔamraaḍ, ḍaɛaf.*

side - 1. *ṭaraf* pl. *ʔaṭraaf, žəha* pl. *-aat.* Put this side up. *qleeb haṭ-ṭaraf la-fooq.* -- On this side of the street there are only a few houses. *ɛala haž-žəha mn ᵊš-šaareɛ fii kam beet bass.* -- They live on the other side of town. *saakniin ɛaž-žəha t-taanye mn ᵊl-balad.* **2.** *žanᵊb* pl. *žnaab, žanab* pl. *-aat, ṭaraf* pl. *ʔaṭraaf.* He sat on my left side. *qaɛad ɛala žanbi š-šmaal.* **3.** *žaaneb* pl. *žawaaneb.* The event had a bright side, too. *l-ḥaadse kan-la kamaan žaaneb məfreḥ.* **4.** *saaq* pl. *siiqaan.* The three roads form a triangle with two equal sides. *ṭ-ṭəroq ᵊt-tlaate bišakklu msallas mətsaawi s-saaqeen.* **5.** *xaaṣra* pl. *xawaaṣer.* I nearly split my sides laughing. *kaanu xawaaṣri laḥa yṭəqqu mn ᵊḍ-ḍəḥᵊk.* **6.** *žannaabi*, žaanibi*.* We entered through a side door. *fətna mən baab žannaabi* -- About a mile from here you come to a little side road. *ḥawaali miil mən hoon btəṣal la-ṭariiq žaanibi zġiir.* **7.** *saanawi.* The negotiations bogged down on side issues. *l-ᵊmfaawaḍaat waqqafet ᵊb-sabab mawaḍiiɛ saanawiyye.*

**My grandfather on my mother's side left me this house. *žəddi ʔabu ʔəmmi tarák-li hal-beet.*
**She is a thorn in his side. *hiyye šooke b-Ƹeeno.*
**He is on our side. *huwwe maƸna.*
**To be on the safe side, I asked him again. *mən ǧabiil ʔl-ʔəḥtiyaaṭ saʔalto marra taanye.*
side by side - *b-žanb baƸḍ* + pron. suff. For a while we walked side by side without saying a word. *mšiina ḥəṣṣa b-žanb baƸʔḍna biduun-ma nəḥki kəlme.* -- The two houses stand side by side on top of a hill. *l-beeteen ʔb-žanb baƸḍon Ƹala raas haḍbe.* -- Muslim troops fought side by side with Christian units. *ž-žnuud ʔl-məsʔlmiin ḥaarabu b-žanb baƸḍon maƸ ʔl-wəḥdaat ʔl-masiiḥiyye.*
on the side - *Ƹala žanab.* He does something else on the side. *byəštəġel šaġle taanye Ƹala žanab.*
to take sides - *tḥayyaz.* It's difficult to take sides on this question. *ṣaƸb ʔl-waaḥed yətḥayyaz (la-ṭaraf) ʔb-hal-masʔale.*
to side with - *ʔəža maƸ, tḥayyaz la-.* Why do you always side with him? *leeš daayman btəži maƸo (or btətḥayyáz-lo)?*
sideburn - *saalef* pl. *sawaalef.*
sidecar - *sitkaar* pl. *-aat.*
sidewalk - *rṣiif* pl. *ʔarʔṣfe.*
sideward - *Ƹala žanab.* The oncoming car swerved sideward to avoid the child. *s-sayyaara ž-žaaye kasret Ƹala žanab la-tətfaada l-walad.*
sideways - **1.** *mn ʔṭ-ṭaraf.* Seen sideways, the house looks bigger than it is. *lamma btəṭṭallaƸ Ƹal-beet ʔmn ʔṭ-ṭaraf bibayyen ʔakbar məmma huwwe.* **2.** *žannaabi* (invar.), *bʔl-warʔb.* You'll never get the table through the door sideways. *b-ḥayaat maa btəqder ʔtfawwet ʔṭ-ṭaawle žannaabi mn ʔl-baab.*
siege - *mḥaaṣara* pl. *-aat, ḥiṣaar* pl. *-aat.*
sieve - (coarse) *ġərbaal* pl. *ġarabiil,* (fine) *mənxol* pl. *manaaxel.*
to **sift** - **1.** (finely) *naxal (o naxʔl//ntaxal),* (coarsely) *ġarbal//tġarbal.* The flour has to be sifted first. *ṭ-ṭḥiin bəddo yəntáxel bʔl-ʔawwal.* **2.** *maḥḥaṣ.* The prosecution is still sifting the evidence. *l-məddaƸi l-Ƹaamm ləssaato Ƹam ymaḥḥeṣ ʔl-ʔadəlle.*
sigh - *tanhiide* pl. *-aat.* She gave a sigh of relief. *tnahhadet tanhiidet xalaaṣ.*
to sigh - *tnahhad.* What are you sighing about? *Ƹala ʔeeš Ƹam tətnahhad?*
sight - **1.** *naẓar, baṣar.* He nearly lost his sight in the accident. *taqriiban faqad naẓaro bʔl-ḥaades.* — The car was already out of sight when I got to the corner. *s-sayyaara kaanet ġaabet Ƹan-naẓar lamma wṣəlt Ƹas-suuke.* **2.** *manẓar* pl. *manaaẓer, šoofe* pl. *-aat.* The dead bodies were a terrible sight. *ž-žəsas kaan manẓ́ra bišayyeb ʔr-raas.* — You're quite a sight in that dirty dress! *ṭalƸa šoofe b-hal-fəsṭaan ʔl-wəsex!* **3.** *manẓar* pl. *manaaẓer.* Have you seen the sights of the town? *tfarražʔt Ƹala manaaẓer ʔl-balad?* **4.** *niišaan* pl. *nayašiin.* The sight of this gun needs adjusting. *niišaan hal-baaruude laazə́ma taẓbiiṭ.*
**I recognized you at first sight. *Ƹrəftak ʔawwal-ma šəftak.*
**They have orders to shoot him on sight. *maƸon ʔawaamer yqawwṣúu ʔawwal-ma bišuufúu.*
**Get out of my sight! *nqəleƸ mən wəšši!*
**Out of sight, out of mind. *bƸiid Ƹan ʔl-Ƹeen, bƸiid Ƹan ʔl-qalʔb.*
at sight - *Ƹaṭ-ṭalab.* The draft is payable at sight. *l-kəmbyaale təndə́feƸ Ƹaṭ-ṭalab.*
by sight - *bʔl-wəšš, bʔš-šoofe.* I know him only by sight. *baƸʔrfo bʔl-wəšš bass.*
in sight - *mbayyen.* The end is not yet in sight. *l-ʔaaxra ləssaaha muu mbayyne.*
to catch sight of - *lamaḥ (a lamʔḥ//nlamaḥ).* As soon as he caught sight of you, he vanished. *ʔawwal-ma lamaḥak ʔxtafa.*
to lose sight of - *səhi (a sahu) Ƹan.* We shouldn't lose sight of one important factor, namely ... *laazem maa nəsha Ƹan Ƹaamel waaḥed ʔmhəmm, w-huwwe ...*
sight-seeing: Did you do a lot of sight-seeing when you were in Damascus? *tfarražʔt Ƹal-balad ʔktiir waqt əlli kənʔt bʔš-šaam?* — I'll be glad to take you sight-seeing on my day off. *b-kəll mamnuuniyye hžawwlak bʔl-balad yoom Ƹəṭʔlti.*
sight-seeing tour - *žawle* (pl. *-aat*) *siyaaḥiyye.* They've all kinds of sight-seeing tours in and around the city. *Ƹandon mən kəll ʔanwaaƸ ʔž-žawlaat ʔs-siyaaḥiyye žuwwaat ʔl-balad w-ḥawaleeha.*
sight-seeing trip - *raḥle* pl. *-aat.* We went on a sight-seeing trip to Jerusalem. *rəḥna raḥle Ƹal-qədʔs.*
sign - **1.** *lawḥa* pl. *-aat.* What does the sign over the door say? *šuu maktuub Ƹal-lawḥa halli fooq ʔl-baab?* **2.** *ʔišaara* pl. *-aat, Ƹalaame* pl. *-aat* and *Ƹalaayem.* Cross out the plus sign above. *šxaaṭ ʔišaart ʔž-žamʔƸ fooq.* — There's a traffic sign ahead. *fii Ƹalaamet seer qəddaam.* — What does this sign in front of the word stand for? *šuu maƸnaat hal-ʔišaara halli qəddaam ʔl-kəlme?* **3.** *ẓaahra* pl. *ẓawaaher, baadra* pl. *bawaader, Ƹalaame* pl. *Ƹalaayem.* Is that a good sign? *daxlak hayy ẓaahra mniiḥa?* — All signs point to an early winter. *kəll ʔl-bawaader Ƹam ʔddəll Ƹala šətwiyye mbakkra.* — There was no sign of life in the village. *maa kaan fii ʔayy Ƹalaayem ḥayaat bʔl-ǧarye.* **4.** *ʔišaara* pl. *-aat.* He gave us a sign to follow him. *Ƹaṭaana ʔišaara nəlḥaqo.*
sign of the zodiac - *bərʔž* pl. *ʔabraaž* and *bruuže.* What sign of the zodiac were you born under? *b-ʔayy bərž ʔwlədt?*
to sign - *maḍa (i ʔəmḍa//nmaḍa), waǧǧaƸ// twaǧǧaƸ.* He forgot to sign the letter. *nəsi yəmḍi l-maktuub.* -- Please sign your name on the last line. *mən faḍlak waǧǧeƸ ʔəsmak Ƹas-saṭr ʔl-ʔaaxraani.* -- Don't forget to sign in. *laa tənsa maa təmḍi waqt əlli btəži.* -- I forgot to sign out last night. *nsiit ʔəmḍi qabʔl-ma ruuḥ ʔmbaareḥ Ƹašiyye.*
to sign off - *waqqaf.* When does the radio station sign off? *ʔeemta bətwaqqef mḥaṭṭet ʔl-ʔizaaƸa?*
to sign over - *ṭawwab//ṭṭawwab.* He signed over the business to his son. *ṭawwab ʔš-šəġʔl la-ʔəbno.*
to sign up for - *sažžal.* I signed up for three courses. *sažžalt b-ʔtlətt mawaḍiiƸ.*
signal - **1.** *ʔišaara* pl. *-aat.* We agreed on a signal. *ttafaqna Ƹala ʔišaara.* — I'll give you the signal. *ʔana baƸṭiik ʔl-ʔišaara.* — He went through the signal. *maa waqqaf Ƹal-ʔišaara.* **2.** *Ƹalaame* pl. *-aat, ʔišaara* pl. *-aat.* This was the signal for the attack. *hayy kaanet Ƹalaamet ʔl-hužuum.*
Signal Corps - *silaaḥ˜ ʔl-ʔišaara.*
to signal - *ʔaššar.* He signaled me to come over. *ʔaššə́r-li ʔəži.*
signature - *ʔəmḍa* pl. *ʔəmḍayaat, tawǧiiƸ* pl. *tawaǧiiƸ.* The letter has no signature. *l-maktuub maa Ƹalée ʔəmḍa.*
significance - **1.** *ʔahammiyye.* Most people don't realize the full significance of the party split. *ʔaktar ʔn-naas maa biqaddru tamaam ʔahammiyyet ʔl-ʔənšiǧaaǧ bʔl-ḥəzʔb.* **2.** *maġza* pl. *maġaazi, maƸna* pl. *maƸaani.* After reading that letter, his words have taken on a new significance. *baƸd ʔqraayet ʔl-maktuub kalaamo ṣar-lo maġza ždiid.*
significant - *mhəmm.* He has written a number of significant books in this field. *katab Ƹəddet kətb ʔmhəmme b-hal-ḥaǧʔl.*
silence - *sukuut, ṣamʔt, sukuun.* A long silence followed his words. *kalaamo təbƸo sukuut ṭawiil.* — They listened in silence. *stamaƸu b-sukuun.* — There was complete silence in the room. *kaan fii ṣamʔt taamm bʔl-ʔuuḍa.*
to silence - *sakkat//tsakkat.* I couldn't silence him. *maa ḥsənʔt sakkto.*
silent - **1.** *ṣaameṭ.* We said a silent prayer at his grave. *ṣalleena ṣalḍa ṣaamṭa Ƹala qabro.* — She used to play in silent pictures. *kaanet ʔtmassel bʔs-siinama ṣ-ṣaamṭa.* **2.** *saaken, haadi.* We walked through the silent streets. *mšiina bʔš-šawaareƸ ʔs-saakne.* **3.** *sakuuti*, haadi.* He's a silent man. *huwwe zalame sakuuti.*
silent partner - *šriik muuṣi* pl. *šəraka muuṣiyyiin.*
to be silent - **1.** *sakat (o sukuut).* Why are you so silent? *leeš kəll hal-qadd saaket?* **2.** *sakat, ṣamaṭ (o ṣamʔṭ).* The newspapers were silent about the accident. *ž-žaraayed saktet Ƹan ʔl-ḥaades.*
silk - **1.** *ḥariir* pl. *ḥaraayer.* How much is this silk? *b-qaddeeš hal-ḥariir?* **2.** *ḥariir* (invar.). You simply can't get silk stockings. *mustaḥiil təḥṣali Ƹala žraabaat ḥariir.*
silkworm - *duudet˜* (coll. *duud˜* pl. *-aat˜*) *qazz, duudet˜ ḥariir.*
silky - *ḥaraayri*, ḥariiri*.*
silly - **1.** *maayeƸ.* Don't mind her, she's a silly girl. *laa təhtamm-ə́lla, hiyye bənʔt maayƸa.* **2.** *saxiif.* I've had enough of your silly jokes. *šbəƸʔt mən nəkatak ʔs-saxiife.*

**Don't be so silly! *bala myuuεa!*
silver - 1. *fəḍḍa.* The price of silver has gone up. *səεr ᵊl-fəḍḍa rtafaε.* — She's wearing a silver ring. *laabse xaatem fəḍḍa.* 2. *fəḍḍiyye.* You forgot to put the silver on the table. *nsiiti tḥəṭṭi l-fəḍḍiyye εaṭ-ṭaawle.*
**Would you change this pound note into silver? *məmken təṣrə́f-li hal-leera?*
similar - 1. *mšaabeh, mmaasel.* I know of a similar case. *baεref qaḍiyye mšaabha.* 2. *mətšaabeh.* The two dresses are similar. *l-fəsṭaaneen mətšaabhiin.*
similarity - *šabah, mšaabaha.* The similarity between the original and the imitation is striking. *š-šabah been ᵊl-ʔaṣli wᵊt-taqliid šii mədheš.*
to **simmer** - 1. *thadda.* Let the soup simmer for five minutes. *xalli š-šooraba təthadda šii xamᵊs daqaayeq.* 2. *baqbaq.* When the water simmers take it off the fire. *lamma l-mayy bətbaqbeq nazzə́la mən εan-naar.*
simple - *baṣiiṭ* pl. *bəṣaṭa.* Let me ask you a simple question. *xalliini ʔəsʔalak suʔaal baṣiiṭ.* — She wears very simple clothes. *btəlbes ʔawaaεi baṣiiṭa ktiir.* — Her reasoning is a little simple once in a while. *taεliila baṣiiṭ šwayye baεḍ ᵊl-ʔawqaat.* — We are simple people. *nəḥna žamaaεa bəṣaṭa.*
**That's the simple truth. *hayy ᵊl-ḥaqiiqa b-εeena.*
simplicity - *baṣaaṭa.* The house is simplicity itself. *l-beet huwwe l-baṣaaṭa b-εeena.*
**For the sake of simplicity let's say that ... *la-tabṣiiṭ ᵊl-masʔale xalliina nquul ʔənno ...*
to **simplify** - *baṣṣaṭ//tbaṣṣaṭ.* It would simplify things if you could come in your own car. *kənt bətbaṣṣeṭ ᵊl-məšᵊkle law kənt ᵊbtəži b-sayyaartak ʔənte.*
simply - 1. *b-baṣaaṭa.* They live very simply. *biεiišu b-kəll baṣaaṭa.* 2. *ḥatman.* That's simply impossible! *mustaḥiil ḥatman!* 3. *bᵊl-marra, εal-maẓbuuṭ.* We're simply exhausted. *nəḥna halkaaniin bᵊl-marra.*
**I simply couldn't come. *waḷḷaahi maa qdərᵊt ʔəži.*
simultaneous - *ʔaani*.* He's excellent in simultaneous translation. *huwwe məmtaaz bᵊt-taržame l-ʔaaniyye.*
**They say he can play up to thirty simultaneous games. *biquulu ʔənno fii yəlεab la-ḥadd tlaatiin ləεbe b-ʔaan waaḥed.*
simultaneously - *b-ʔaan waaḥed, b-nafs ᵊl-waqᵊt.*
sin - *zanᵊb* pl. *znuub, xaṭiiʔa* pl. *xaṭaaya.*
since - 1. *mən.* He has not been here since Monday. *maa ʔəža la-hoon mən yoom ᵊt-taneen.* — We've visited Syria several times since the war. *zərna suuriyya εəddet marraat mən (ʔiyyaam) ᵊl-ḥarᵊb.*
2. *mən waqᵊt-ma.* I haven't seen anybody since I got back. *maa šəfᵊt ḥada mən waqᵊt-ma ržəεᵊt.* — I haven't eaten a thing since I had lunch. *maa ḥaṭṭeet ᵊb-təmmi šii mən waqᵊt-ma tġaddeet.* 3. *mən waqta.* We haven't heard from him (ever) since. *mən waqta maa ʔəžaana ʔayy xabar mənno.* 4. *b-ḥees, bi-ma ʔənno, la-ʔənno.* Since I didn't have the money I couldn't go. *b-ḥees maa kaan εandi l-maṣaari maa qdərᵊt ruuḥ.*
sincere - *məxleṣ.* He has always been a sincere friend. *ṭuul ḥayaato kaan ṣadiiq məxleṣ.* — I think he's sincere about his offer. *bəεtə́qed ʔənno məxleṣ ᵊb-εarḍo.*
**Is that your sincere opinion? *haada raʔyak b-ʔəxlaaṣ?*
**It's my sincere wish that he'll succeed. *bətmanna b-kəll ʔəxlaaṣ ʔənno yənžaḥ.*
**Give her my sincere regards. *sallə́m-li εaleeha ktiir ᵊs-salaam.*
sincerely - 1. *mən kəll qalb-* + pron. suff. I sincerely hope you'll be able to come. *bətʔammal mən kəll qalbi ʔənnak təḥsen təži.* — We're sincerely sorry that you can't come. *nəḥna mən kəll qalbna mətʔassfiin ʔənnak maa fiik təži.* 2. *εan ḥaqa, mən kəll εaql-* + pron. suff. You sincerely believe it? *εan ḥaqa (or mən kəll εaqlak) bətṣaddə́qa?*
to **sing** - 1. *ġanna.* Sing me that song again. *ġanniī-li hal-ġənniyye marra taanye.* 2. *ġarrad, zaqzaq.* The birds sing all day in front of my window. *l-εaṣafiir ṭuul ᵊn-nhaar biġarrdu qəddaam šəbbaaki.*
**He sang your praises all evening long. *ṭuul ᵊs-sahra kaan εam yənfoš fiik.*
to **singe** - *šalwaṭ.* I nearly singed my hair. *kənt laḥa šalweṭ šaεri.*

singer - *mġanni* pl. *-iyyiin,* f. *mġannye* pl. *-aat.*
single - 1. *ʔaεzab* f. *εazba* pl. *εəzbaan.* Are you married or single? *ʔənte mžawwaz wəlla ʔaεzab?* 2. *fardet˜...* I found a single glove on the floor. *laqeet fardet kaff εal-ʔarḍ.* 3. *farᵊd˜..., waaḥed.* He made a single mistake. *εəmel farᵊd ġalṭa (or ġalṭa waaḥde).* 4. *w-laa.* He didn't make a single mistake. *maa εəmel w-laa ġalṭa.*
**I looked through every single drawer, but couldn't find it. *ṭṭallaεt ᵊb-kəll dərᵊž waaḥed waaḥed laaken maa laqeeta.*
to single out - *naqqa//tnaqqa.* Why did they single you out? *leeš naqquuk ʔənte?*
singular - 1. *məfrad.* "*mara*" is the singular of "*nəswaan*". "*mara*" *məfrad* "*nəswaan*". 2. *fariid.* His singular discoveries have established his fame in this field. *ʔəktišaafaato l-fariide ʔawžadet ṣiito b-hal-ḥaqᵊl.*
sink - 1. *mažla* pl. *mažaali.* The dishes are still in the sink. *l-ᵊṣḥuun ləssaaton bᵊl-mažla.* 2. *balluuεa* pl. *-aat.* Don't throw it into the sink. You'll stop it up. *laa təlḥə́ša bᵊl-balluuεa, btəṣṭə́ma.*
to sink - 1. *ġəreq (a ġaraq).* The ship sank in ten minutes. *l-baaxra ġərqet ᵊb-εašᵊr daqaayeq.* 2. *habaṭ (o hbuuṭ), xafas (o xafasaan).* The house has sunk twenty centimeters. *l-beet habaṭ εəšriin ṣanṭi.* 3. *ġaṭas (o ġaṭᵊs).* My feet sank in the snow. *rəžliyyi ġaṭasu bᵊt-talᵊž.* 4. *ġaab (i ġyuub* and *ġayabaan).* The sun sank rapidly behind the mountains. *š-šamᵊs ġaabet ᵊb-sərεa wara ž-žbaal.* — This voice sank to a whisper. *ṣooto ġaab la-ṣaffa mətᵊl wašwaše.* 5. *ġarraq//tġarraq.* They sank three enemy ships. *ġarraqu tlett bawaaxer ləl-εaduww.* 6. *waẓẓaf, ḥaṭṭ (ə ḥaṭaṭ* and *ḥaṭaṭaan).* They sank all their money in the restaurant. *waẓẓafu kəll maṣariihon bᵊl-maṭεam.*
**The doctor said he's sinking rapidly. *d-doktoor qaal ʔənno ḥaalto εam təddahwar ᵊb-sərεa.*
sinner - *məzneb* pl. *-iin.*
sinus - *žeeb* pl. *žyuub.* I've had sinus trouble ever since I was a child. *mən ṣaġari bišə́r-li mašaakel bᵊž-žyuub.*
sinusitis - *ʔəltihaab˜ ᵊž-žyuub.*
sip - *maṣṣa* pl. *-aat, šafṭa* pl. *-aat.* Let me have a sip of your drink. *xalliini ʔaaxə́d-li maṣṣa mən kaasak.*
to sip - *mazmaz//tmazmaz.* We sat in the shade and sipped cold lemonade. *qaεadna bᵊl-fayy w-mazmazna leemunaaḍa baarde.*
siphon - *siifoon* pl. *-aat.*
sir - 1. *ya beek, ya siidna.* Excuse me, sir. *εafwan ya beek.* -- What can I do for you, sir? *šuu btəʔmor ya siidna.* 2. *sayyidi.* Have the platoon fall in in five minutes. - Yes, sir! *ṣaff ᵊl-faṣiile baεᵊd xamᵊs daqaayeq. - ʔamrak sayyidi.* 3. *ya beek.* Yes sir(ee), my mother was quite a woman! *w-ᵊḥyaatak ya beek ʔəmmi kaanet sətt qaliil mənna.*
siren - *zammuur˜* (pl. *zamamiir˜*) *xaṭar.*
sirup - 1. *mayye.* Those pears are preserved in their own sirup. *han-nžaaṣaat maḥfuuẓiin ᵊb-mayyə́ton.* 2. *qaṭᵊr.* Pancakes with sirup, please. *qaṭaayef maε qaṭᵊr mən faḍlak.*
sister - 1. *ʔəxt* pl. *ʔəxwaat banaat.* Do you have any sisters? *εandak šii ʔəxwaat banaat?* -- All my brothers and sisters came home for the weekend. *kəll ʔəxwaati ṣ-ṣəbyaan wᵊl-banaat ʔəžu εal-beet la-ymaḍḍu l-εəṭle l-ʔəsbuuεiyye.* 2. *raahbe* pl. *-aat.* The sisters at the convent will be able to help you in this matter. *r-raahbaat bᵊd-deer byəṭlaε ᵊb-ʔiidon ysaaεduuk ᵊb-hal-qəṣṣa.*
sister-in-law - 1. (brother's wife) *mart˜ ʔaxx* pl. *nəswaan˜ ʔəxwaat, kənne mart˜ ʔaxx* pl. *kanaayen nəswaan˜ ʔəxwaat.* 2. (husband's or wife's sister) *bənt˜ ʔəḥma* pl. *banaat˜ ʔəḥma.* 3. (husband's brother's wife) *səlfe* pl. *salaayef.*
to **sit** - 1. *qaεad (o qεuud* and *qaεde,* imperative *εood* f. *εədi* pl. *εədu).* We sat in the front row. *qaεadna bᵊṣ-ṣaff ᵊl-qəddaamaani.* 2. *nεaqad.* Does the court sit today? *l-maḥkame btənεə́qed ᵊl-yoom šii?* 3. *ʔaxad pooz.* I sit for the painter twice a week. *baaxod pooz ləṛ-rassaam marrteen bᵊž-žəmεa.*
**He sat in Parliament for four years. *bəqi bᵊl-barlamaan ʔarbaε ᵊsniin.*
to sit around - *qaεad (o qεuud* and *qaεde) εala žanab.* The third day I got bored stiff from sitting around and doing nothing. *bᵊl-yoom ᵊt-taalet ṭələε diini mn ᵊl-qaεde εala žanab bala šaġle w-laa εamle.*
to sit down - *qaεad (o qaεde,* imperative *εood* f. *εədi* pl. *εədu).* Sit down please. *εood mən faḍlak.*

-- He walked in just as we sat down to eat. *ʔəža ʔawwal-ma qaʕadna la-naakol.*
to sit in on - *ḥađer (a ḥđuur).* I sat in on all conferences. *ḥđərᵊt kəll ᵊl-məʔtamaraat.*
to sit up - **1.** *žalas (o žluus).* He tried to sit up in bed. *ḥaawal yəžlos bᵊt-taxᵊt.* -- Sit up straight! *žloos!* **2.** *səher (a sahar).* We sat up all night waiting for him. *sharna ṭuul ᵊl-leel mnənṭəṛo.* -- I sat up with him all night. *shərt maʕo ṭuul ᵊl-leel.*
sitting - *žalse* pl. *-aat.* How many sittings did it take to finish the portrait? *kam žalse ʔaxdet ᵊr-rasme la-xalṣet?* -- When is the next sitting of the court? *ʔeemta ž-žalse ž-žaaye tabaʕ ᵊl-maḥkame?*
sitting room - *ʔuuḍet˜* (pl. *ʔuwaḍ˜*) *ᵊqʕuud.*
situation - **1.** *mawqef* pl. *mawaaqef.* It was a very embarrassing situation. *kaan mawqef ᵊktiir məḥrež.* -- She saved the situation. *hiyye ʔanqazet ᵊl-mawqef.* **2.** *waḍᵊʕ* pl. *ʔawḍaaʕ, ḥaale* pl. *-aat* and *ʔaḥwaal.* The economic situation of the country is quite serious. *l-waḍʕ ᵊl-ʔəqtiṣaadi tabaʕ l-ᵊblaad xəṭer ᵊktiir.* -- The situation has gotten out of hand. *l-ḥaale xaržet ʕan ṭawra.*
six - **1.** *sətte.* Five and six make eleven. *xamse w-sətte bisaawu ʔidaʕš.* -- There are six of us in class. *nəḥna sətte bᵊṣ-ṣaff.* **2.** *sətt.* I paid six pounds for the tickets. *dafaʕᵊt sətt leeraat ləl-biṭaaqaat.* -- We have only six days to go. *baaqii-lna sətt iyyaam bass.* -- He lost almost six thousand pounds in the deal. *xəser taqriiban sətt aalaaf leera bᵊṣ-ṣafqa.* **3.** *s-saaʕa sətte.* Is six a convenient time for you? *s-saaʕa sətte binaasbak?* -- I'll pick you up at six at your house. *baaxdak ᵊs-saaʕa sətte mən beetak.*
**It's six of one and half a dozen of another. *kiif-ma baramta məṭᵊl baʕḍa.*
sixteen - **1.** *səṭṭaʕš.* The number of dead has climbed to sixteen. *ʕadad ᵊl-mawta ṭəleʕ ʕala səṭṭaʕš.* **2.** *səṭṭaʕšar.* He spent sixteen years in Africa. *maḍḍa səṭṭaʕšar səne b-ʔafriiqya.*
sixteenth - **1.** *s-səṭṭaʕš.* It's his sixteenth birthday. *haada ʕiid miilaado ᵊs-səṭṭaʕš.* -- He arrived on July the sixteenth. *wəṣel b-səṭṭaʕš tammuuz.* **2.** *s-saades ʕašar.* He was born at the end of the sixteenth century. *wəled ᵊb-ʔawaaxer ᵊl-qarn ᵊs-saades ʕašar.*
sixth - **1.** *saades.* It's the sixth house from the corner. *huwwe l-beet ᵊs-saades* (or *saades beet*) *mn ᵊs-suuke.* **2.** *sətte.* I was born on May the sixth. *wlədt b-sətte ʔayyaar.*
one sixth - *sədᵊs* pl. *ʔasdaas.* That's one sixth of my salary. *haada sədᵊs maʕaaši.*
sixtieth - *s-səttiin, s-səttiini*.* His sixtieth birthday is coming up. *ʕiid miilaado s-səttiin(i) žaaye.*
sixty - *səttiin.*
size - **1.** *qyaas* pl. *-aat.* What size do you wear? *šuu l-ᵊqyaas halli btəlᵊbso?* -- Do you have these shirts in another size? *fii ʕandak mən hal-qəmṣaan ᵊb-ġeer ᵊqyaas?* -- Everything is arranged according to size. *kəll šii mnaẓẓam ḥasab l-ᵊqyaas.* **2.** *ḥažᵊm* pl. *ʔaḥžaam.* What size book will it be? *qaddeeš raḥa ykuun ḥažᵊm l-ᵊktaab?*
to size up - **1.** *qaddar//tqaddar.* How do you size up the situation? *kiif bətqadder ᵊl-waḍᵊʕ?* **2.** *ʔaxađ fəkra ʕan.* They invited their new neighbors for coffee so they could size them up. *ʕazamu žiiraanon ᵊž-ždadad ʕala fənžaan qahwe la-yaaxdu fəkra ʕanhon.*
skeleton - *haykal ʕaḍmi* pl. *hayaakel ʕaḍmiyye.*
skeptic - *mətšakkek* pl. *-iin.*
skeptical - *šakuuk.* Don't be so skeptical! *laa tkuun kəll hal-qadd šakuuk!*
skepticism - *taškiik, laa-ʔadriyye.*
sketch - **1.** *krooki* pl. *krookiyaat.* Make me a sketch of the house. *rsəm-li krooki ləl-beet.* **2.** *skatš* pl. *-aat.* The students performed several humorous sketches. *ṭ-ṭəllaab ləʕbu kam ᵊskatš məḍḥek.*
ski - *skii* pl. *skiyyaat.* These skis come from Norway. *has-skiyyaat mən narweež.*
to ski - *ʕəmel skii.* I never learned how to ski. *ʕəmri maa tʕallamᵊt kiif ʔaʕmel skii.*
to skid - *dzaḥlaq.* The car started to skid. *s-sayyaara badet tədzaḥleq.*
skill - *mahaara, baraaʕa.* That requires a lot of skill. *haš-šii byəṭṭallab mahaara ktiire.*
skilled - **1.** *maaher, šaaṭer.* He is a skilled mechanic. *huwwe miikaniiki maaher.* **2.** *mdarrab.* A skilled laborer makes about a pound and a half an hour. *l-ʕaamel l-ᵊmdarrab biṭaaleʕ ḥawaali leera w-nəṣṣ bᵊs-saaʕa.*
skillet - *məqlaaye* pl. *maqaali.*
skillful - *maaher, šaaṭer.* She is also a skillful dressmaker. *hiyye kamaan xayyaaṭa maahra.*
skillfully - *b-mahaara.* You got yourself out of that situation very skillfully. *xallaṣᵊt ḥaalak mən hal-waḍʕ ᵊb-mahaara ktiire.*
to skim - **1.** *qašš (ə qašš) zafret˜ ...* Did you skim the soup? *qaššeet zafret ᵊš-šooraba?* **2.** *qašš qəšṭet˜ ...* I skimmed the milk. *qaššeet qəšṭet ᵊl-ḥaliib.*
to skim through - *ṭṣaffaḥ.* I just skimmed through the book. *ṭṣaffaḥᵊt l-ᵊktaab bass.*
skin - **1.** *žəlᵊd* pl. *žluud.* She has a very sensitive skin. *ʕanda žəlᵊd ḥassaas ktiir.* -- How many skins will you need for the coat? *kam žəlᵊd byəlzamak ləl-manṭo?* **2.** *qəšre.* These apples have a very thick skin. *hat-təffaaḥaat qəšrə́ton ᵊsmiike ktiir.*
**He has a thick skin. *huwwe mtamseḥ.*
**I passed the exam by the skin of my teeth. *nažaḥᵊt bᵊl-faḥᵊṣ ya kabbe ya daʕse.*
**He thought of nothing but saving his own skin. *maa fakkar ʔəlla b-salaamto.*
**Well, it's no skin off my nose. *muu ʔana halli bənḍarr.*
to skin - *salax (a salᵊx//nsalax).* Let me show you how to skin the rabbit. *xalliini waržiik kiif ᵊbtəslax ᵊl-ʔarnab.* -- If you do that again, I'll skin you alive. *ʔiza btaʕmə́la taani marra bəslax žəldak ʕaḍmak.*
to skip - **1.** *qaffa//tqaffa, šaṭaḥ (a šaṭᵊḥ//nšaṭaḥ).* Let's skip a few pages. *xalliina nqaffii-lna kam ṣafḥa.* -- I skipped second grade. *šaṭaḥt ᵊṣ-ṣaff ᵊt-taani.* **2.** *naṭṭ (ə naṭṭ).* Can you skip rope? *btaʕref ᵊtnəṭṭ bᵊl-ḥable?*
**We skipped breakfast this morning. *maa trawwaqna l-yoom ʕala bəkra.*
skirt - *xarraaṭa* pl. *-aat, tannuura* pl. *tananiir.*
skull - *žəmᵊžme* pl. *žamaažem.*
sky - *sama* (f.) pl. *samawaat.* How does the sky look today? *kiif ᵊs-sama l-yoom?* -- He praised her to the skies. *nafdža ləs-sama.*
**The news came out of a clear sky. *l-xabar ṭəleʕ mən qalb ᵊḍ-dənye.*
skyscraper - *naaṭḥet˜* (pl. *-aat˜*) *saḥaab.*
slack - **1.** *mərxi*.* The rope's too slack. *l-ḥabᵊl mərxi ktiir.* **2.** *kaased.* Business is slack right now. *š-šəġᵊl kaased bᵊl-waqt ᵊl-ḥaaḍer.*
slacks - *bantaloon* pl. *-aat.*
to become slack - **1.** *rtaxa.* The rope's become slack overnight. *l-ḥabl ᵊrtaxa ʔasnaaʔ ᵊl-leel.* **2.** *traaxa.* He's become slack in his work lately. *ʕam yətraaxa b-šəġlo b-hal-ʔiyyaam.*
to slacken - **1.** *raxa (i raxi//nraxa).* Slacken the rope a little! *ʔərxi l-ḥable šwayye!* **2.** *traaxa.* Don't slacken your pace now, we're almost finished. *laa tətraaxa hallaq, taqriiban ṣəṛna xaalṣiin.* **3.** *rtaxa.* The sails slackened visibly. *l-ʔašriʕa rtaxet ᵊb-šəkᵊl ẓaaher.* **4.** *xaff (ə xafafaan).* Sales slacken over the summer months. *l-mabiiʕaat bətxəff ʔasnaaʔ ʔašhor ᵊṣ-ṣeef.*
to slam - *xabaṭ (o xabᵊṭ//nxabaṭ).* He slammed the box on the floor. *xabaṭ ᵊṣ-ṣanduuq ʕal-ʔarᵊḍ.* -- She slammed the door right in my face. *xabṭet ᵊl-baab ᵊb-nəṣṣ diin wəšši.*
slander - *ʔəftə́ra, tašhiir.* That's absolute slander. *haada ʔəftə́ra ʕal-maẓbuuṭ.*
to slander - *ftara ʕala, šahhar b-.* She's not above slandering other people. *muu bʕiid ʕanna təftə́ri ʕan-naas* (or *tšahher bᵊn-naas*).
slap - **1.** *kaff* pl. *kfuuf, laṭše* pl. *-aat.* She answered him with a slap in the face. *žaawabə́to b-kaff ʕala wəššo.* **2.** *xabṭa* pl. *-aat.* That remark was like a slap in the face. *hal-ᵊmlaaḥaẓa kaanet mətl ᵊl-xabṭa ʕar-raas.*
to slap - *laṭaš (o laṭᵊš//nlaṭaš) ʕala, ṣafaq (o ṣafᵊq//nṣafaq) ʕala.* I'll slap your hand if you touch it. *bəlᵊṭšak ʕala ʔiidak ʔiza tədqə́ra.* -- She slapped his face. *laṭašto ʕala wəššo.*
slash - *šarᵊṭ* pl. *šruuṭa.* Have you noticed that long slash in our mattress? *šəft ᵊš-šarṭ ᵊṭ-ṭawiil ᵊb-faršətna?*
to slash - *šaraṭ (o šarᵊṭ//nšaraṭ).* Somebody slashed the tires with a knife. *fii ḥada šaraṭ ᵊd-dawaliib ᵊb-səkkiin.*
slate - **1.** *ʔarduwaaz.* Few houses are covered with slate. *qaliil mən l-ᵊbyuut masqufe b-ʔarduwaaz.* **2.** *looḥ˜* (pl. *lwaaḥ˜*) *ḥažar.* The children are still writing on slates. *l-ᵊwlaad ləssaahon ʕam yəkᵊtbu ʕala lwaaḥ ḥažar.*
**He has a clean slate. *maaḍii nḍiif.*

slaughter – **1.** *dabᵊḥ.* The slaughter of an animal has to be performed according to strict ritual requirements. *dabḥ ᵊl-ḥaywaanaat laazem ysiir ḥasab Ɛaadaat ᵊmḥaddade.* **2.** *madbaḥa* pl. *madaabeḥ.* The battle turned into a slaughter. *l-maƐrake ṣaaret madbaḥa.*

to slaughter – *dabaḥ (a dabᵊḥ//ndabaḥ).* We always slaughter a lamb for the Big Bayram. *daayman mnədbaḥ xaaruuf Ɛal-Ɛiid l-ᵊkbiir.*

slaughterhouse – *maslax* pl. *masaalex.*

Slav – *slaavi** coll. pl. *slaav.*

slave – *Ɛabᵊd* pl. *Ɛabiid.* He treats them like slaves. *biƐaamə́lon mətl ᵊl-Ɛabiid.* -- He's become a slave of hasheesh. *ṣaar Ɛabᵊd ləl-ḥašiiš.*

to slave – *halak (e ø) ḥaalo, šəqi (a šaqi).* I've slaved enough today. *halakt ḥaali* (or *šqiit*) *kfaaye l-yoom.*

slavery – *Ɛubuudiyye.*

Slavic – *slaavi**.

sleep – *noom.* He walks in his sleep. *byəmši b-noomo.*

**I didn't get enough sleep last night. *maa nəmt ᵊkfaaye leelt ᵊmbaareḥ.*

to sleep – *naam (a noom).* Did you sleep well? *nəmt ᵊmniiḥ?* -- I didn't sleep a wink. *maa nəmᵊt w-laa ġəmḍə́t-li Ɛeen.* -- Sleep on it before you decide. *naam Ɛaleeha qabᵊl-ma tqarrer.*

sleeper – *vagon-li* (invar.). Does the train have a sleeper? *fii vagon-li bᵊt-treen?*

**He's a light sleeper. *noomo xafiif.*

sleeping car – *vagon-li* (invar.).

sleeping sickness – *maraḍ˜ ᵊn-noom.*

sleepy – *naƐsaan.* I'm still sleepy. *ləssaani naƐsaan.*

to get sleepy – *nəƐes (a naƐas).* After lunch I usually get awfully sleepy. *baƐd ᵊl-ġada Ɛaadatan bənƐas ᵊktiir.*

to make sleepy – *naƐƐas.* The heat is making me sleepy. *š-šoob Ɛam ynaƐƐəsni.*

sleeve – *kəmm* pl. *kmaam.* The sleeves are too short. *l-ᵊkmaam ᵊqṣaar ᵊktiir.*

**He laughed up his sleeve. *ḍəḥek ᵊb-Ɛəbbo.*

**What's he got up his sleeve? *šuu b-baalo?*

slender – *rafiiƐ, naḥiif.* She's very slender. *hiyye rafiiƐa ktiir.*

to get slender – *rəfeƐ (a rafaƐaan), nəḥef (a naḥafaan).* He's gotten very slender. *rəfeƐ ᵊktiir.*

to make slender – *naḥḥaf, raffaƐ.* If that diet doesn't make you slender I don't know what will. *ʔiza har-režiim maa-lo raḥa ynaḥḥfak maa baƐref šuu binaḥḥfak.*

slice – *qəṭƐa* pl. *qəṭaƐ.* How many slices of bread shall I cut? *kam qəṭƐet xəbᵊz ʔəqṭaƐ?*

to slice – *qaṭṭaƐ.* Do you want to slice the roast? *bəddak ᵊtqaṭṭeƐ ᵊr-roosto?*

slide – **1.** *slayd* pl. *-aat.* Someday I have to show you the slides I brought back from Damascus. *šii yoom bəddi waržiik ᵊs-slaydaat halli žəbton maƐi mn ᵊš-šaam.* **2.** *zəḥleeqa* pl. *-aat.* The children are in the garden playing on the slide. *l-ᵊwlaad bᵊž-žneene Ɛam yədzaḥlaqu Ɛaz-zəḥleeqa.*

to slide – *salat (o salataan).* The package slid from her arm. *l-ḥəzme saltet mən ʔiida.*

**Let's let things slide awhile. *xalliina nətrok ᵊl-ʔumuur taaxod mašraaha la-mədde.*

to slide down – **1.** *dzaḥlaq Ɛala.* He slid down the banister. *dzaḥlaq Ɛad-daraabziin.* **2.** *daḥkal.* Slide the package down to me. *daḥkə́l-li l-ḥəzme.*

to slide in – *daḥaš (a daḥᵊš//ndaḥaš).* Maybe you can slide it in sideways. *barki fiik tədḥə́ša bᵊl-warᵊb.*

slight – **1.** *baṣiiṭ.* There's a slight difference. *fii farᵊq baṣiiṭ.* **2.** *xafiif.* He has a slight cold. *Ɛando rašᵊḥ xafiif.* **3.** *naḥiif, rafiiƐ.* She's very slight. *hiyye naḥiife ktiir.*

**I haven't the slightest doubt. *maa Ɛandi ʔadna šakk.*

to slight – *stahaan b-.* She felt they had slighted her. *ḥasset ʔənno stahaanu fiiha.*

slim – **1.** *naḥiif, rafiiƐ.* She's very slim. *hiyye naḥiife ktiir.* **2.** *ḍƐiif.* His chances are very slim. *ʔamalo ktiir ᵊḍƐiif.*

slip – **1.** *ġalṭa* pl. *-aat.* Did I make a slip? *Ɛməlt šii ġalṭa?* **2.** *zalle* pl. *-aat.* It was just a slip of the tongue. *kaanet zallet ᵊlsaan bass.* **3.** *wəšš* pl. *wšuuš.* Our pillows need new slips. *mxaddaatna laazə́mon wšuuš ᵊždiide.* **4.** *šalḥa* pl. *-aat.* Your slip is showing. *šalᵊḥtek ᵊmbayyne.* **5.** *šatle* coll. *šatᵊl* pl. *-aat.* The slips have grown fast during the last few days. *š-šatlaat kəbru b-sərƐa xilaal ᵊl-ʔiyyaam ᵊl-ʔaxiire.* **6.** *šaqfe* pl. *šəqaf.* I wrote the address on a slip of paper. *katabt ᵊl-Ɛənwaan Ɛala šaqfet waraq.*

to give someone the slip – *zamaṭ (o zmiiṭ) mən ʔiid˜ ..., fəlet (a falataan) mən.* He's given us the slip again. *zamaṭ mən ʔiidna marra taanye.*

to slip – **1.** *zaḥaṭ (a zḥiiṭ), zaḥlaq.* I slipped on a banana peel. *zaḥaṭṭ Ɛala qəšret mooze.* **2.** *zəleq (a zalaqaan), zall (ə zalal).* Even good speakers can slip. *ḥatta l-xəṭaba l-ᵊmnaaḥ byəzlaqu.* **3.** *salat (o salataan), fəlet (a falataan).* It slipped out of my hand. *saltet mən ʔiidi.* **4.** *salḥab.* When he heard her voice he slipped out the back door. *lamma səmeƐ ṣooṭa salḥab mən ᵊl-baab ᵊl-warraani.* **5.** *raaḥ (u ø) Ɛan.* It slipped my mind completely. *raaḥet Ɛan baali bᵊl-marra.* **6.** *raaḥ mən ʔiid˜ ...* Don't let the chance slip. *laa txalli l-fərṣa truuḥ mən ʔiidak.* **7.** *nəzel (e nzuul).* Prices have slipped a little. *l-ʔasƐaar nəzlet šwayye.* **8.** *marraq.* He slipped him some money. *marrdq-lo šwayyet maṣaari.* **9.** *labbas.* He slipped the ring on her finger. *labbas ᵊl-xaatem Ɛala ʔəṣbaƐta.*

**Wait until I slip into a coat. *stannaani la-ʔəlḥoš Ɛaliyyi kabbuud.*

to slip away – *salḥab.* Let's slip away. *xalliina nsalḥeb.*

to slip by – *maraq (o mruuq).* Her birthday slipped by without my realizing it. *Ɛiid miilaada maraq biduun-ma ʔəntə́beh.*

to slip on – *ḥaṭṭ Ɛalə́e ..., laḥaš (o laḥᵊš) Ɛalə́e ...* Let me slip on a dress. *xalliini ḥəṭṭ Ɛaliyyi fəsṭaan.*

to slip out – *fəlet ᵊmn ᵊlsaan˜ ...* I really didn't want to tell him, but it just slipped out. *waḷḷaahi maa kənt bəddi qəl-lo laaken fəltet mən ᵊlsaani.*

to slip up – **1.** *xabbaṣ.* I slipped up badly on the second question. *xabbaṣᵊt Ɛal-mazbuuṭ bᵊs-suʔaal ᵊt-taani.* **2.** *səhi (a sahu* and *sahayaan).* I don't know why I slipped up on her name and didn't invite her. *maa baƐref kiif ᵊshiit Ɛan ʔəsma w-maa Ɛazamta.*

slipper – *baabuuže,* (pair) *baabuuž* pl. *bawabiiž, fardet˜ šaḥḥaaṭa,* (pair) *šaḥḥaaṭa* pl. *-aat.* I can't find my slippers in the bedroom. *maa Ɛam bəqder laaqi baabuuži b-ʔuuḍt ᵊn-noom.*

slippery – *mzeebeq.* The roads are very slippery. *t-təroq ᵊktiir ᵊmzeebqa.* -- The fish was so slippery I couldn't hold it. *s-samake kaanet ᵊmzeebqa la-daraže maa ḥsənᵊt ʔəmsə́ka.*

slit – *fatḥa* pl. *-aat.* Make the slit a bit longer. *Ɛmeel ᵊl-fatḥa šwayy ʔaṭwal.*

to slit – *šaraṭ (o šarᵊṭ//nšaraṭ).* You'd better slit the box along the edge. *l-ʔafḍal təšroṭ ᵊl-Ɛəlbe Ɛala ṭuul ᵊl-kanaar.*

slob – *šaršuuḥ* pl. *šarašiiḥ.*

slope – *mənḥə́dar* pl. *-aat.* Is the slope very steep? *l-mənḥə́dar qawi ktiir?*

to slope – *nḥadar.* The terrain slopes down to a broad valley. *l-ʔaraaḍi btənḥə́der la-waadi waaseƐ.*

sloppy – **1.** *mšaršaḥ, ʔašram* f. *šarma* pl. *šərᵊm.* I wish you wouldn't be so sloppy. *ya-reetak maa kənᵊt hal-qadd mšaršaḥ.* **2.** *mšaršaḥ.* Her clothes always look sloppy. *ʔawaƐiiha daayman ᵊmšaršaḥa.* **3.** *qaayem qaayed.* Why does his desk have to be so sloppy? *leeš daayman ṭaawəlto qaayme qaaƐde?* **4.** *mfaškal, mƐafšak.* Sloppy work won't get you anywhere. *š-šəġᵊl l-ᵊmfaškal maa bifiidak ᵊb-šii.*

Slovak – *slovaaki** pl. *-iyyiin.*

Slovakia – *slovaakya.*

Slovene – *sloveeni** pl. *-iyyiin.*

Slovenia – *sloveenya.*

Slovenian – *sloveeni**.

slow – **1.** *baṭiiʔ.* He's a slow worker. *huwwe šaġġiil baṭiiʔ.* -- We're making slow progress only. *Ɛam nətqaddam taqaddom baṭiiʔ bass.* **2.** *xafiif, haadi.* Cook the soup over a slow fire. *ṭboox ᵊš-šooraba Ɛala naar xafiife.*

**Drive slow! *suuq Ɛala mahlak!*

**How do you explain the slow market we're having right now? *kiif bətfasser kasaad ᵊs-suuq yalli nəḥna fii hallaq?*

**She's slow in catching on. *btaaxə́da mədde la-təstawƐeb ᵊš-šii.*

to be slow – **1.** *rakad (o rəkdaan), kəsed (a kasaad), fatar (o ftuur).* The market is slow this time of the year. *s-suuq byərkod ᵊb-heek ʔiyyaam ᵊmn ᵊs-səne.* **2.** *qaṣṣar, ʔaxxar.* Your watch is slow. *saaƐtak ᵊmqaṣṣra.*

to slow down - 1. *xaffaf ᵊs-sərƐa.* Slow down when you come to a crossing. *xaffef ᵊs-sərƐa lamma btuuṣal la-mṣallabiyye.* -- He slowed down the car to look back. *xaffaf sərƐet ᵊs-sayyaara la-yəṭṭallaƐ la-wara.* 2. *qaṣṣar.* He's slowing down in his work. *Ɛam biqaṣṣer ᵊb-šəġlo.* 3. *ʔaxxar.* That has slowed us down considerably. *haš-šii ʔaxxarna ktiir.*

slowly - 1. *Ɛala mahl-* + pron. suff. I can understand him when he speaks slowly. *bəfham Ɛalée waqt ᵊbyəḥki Ɛala mahlo.* -- Drive slowly. *suuq Ɛala mahlak!* 2. *šwayye šwayye.* He slowly regained consciousness. *ṣəḥi šwayye šwayye.* -- Slowly it dawned on me that she had no intention of keeping her promise. *šwayye šwayye tbayydn-li ʔənno muu b-fəkra ʔabadan tuufi b-waƐda.*

slowness - *baṭaaʔa, bəṭᵊʔ.*

sly - *ḥarbuuq.*

small - 1. *ẓġiir* pl. *ẓġaar.* The room is rather small. *l-ʔuuḍa šwayye ẓġiire.* -- They have three small children. *Ɛandon tlatt ᵊwlaad ᵊẓġaar.* -- His generosity made me feel small. *karamo xallaani ʔəšƐor ᵊb-ḥaali ẓġiir.* 2. *baṣiiṭ.* The difference is very small. *l-farᵊq baṣiiṭ ᵊktiir.* -- That's no small matter. *hayye maa-la qəṣṣa baṣiiṭa.*

**That's small comfort. *šuu haad? taksiir Ɛaliyyi?*

small change - *fraaṭa.* I haven't any small change. *maa maƐi fraaṭa.*

small talk - *ṭaqq˜ ḥanak, Ɛlaak.* All she's good at is small talk. *maa btənfaƐ ʔəlla la-ṭaqq ᵊl-ḥanak.*

smallpox - *žədri.*

smart - 1. *šiik* (invar.). That's a smart dress. *haada fəsṭaan šiik waḷḷa.* 2. *zaki** pl. *ʔazkiya.* I think he's a very smart boy. *bəƐtə́qed ʔənno walad zaki ktiir.* 3. *ḥazeq.* Surprisingly, he came up with a very smart answer. *la-dahᵊšti ṭaleƐ ᵊb-žawaab ḥazeq.*

**That was very smart of you. *waḷḷa kaanet šaṭaara mənnak.*

to smart - *ḥaraq (e ḥarᵊq).* My eyes are smarting from the smoke. *Ɛyuuni Ɛam byəḥᵊrquuni mn ᵊd-dəxxaan.* -- Her hand still smarts from the slap she gave him. *ʔiida ləssaata Ɛam təḥrə́qa mn ᵊl-kaff yalli ḍarᵊbto-yə́a.*

to **smash** - *ṭaḥbaš//ṭṭaḥbaš.* The boys smashed the window. *ṣ-ṣəbyaan ṭaḥbašu š-šəbbaak.* -- I found the lamp on the floor smashed to bits. *laqeet ᵊl-lambadeer Ɛal-ʔarḍ ᵊmṭaḥbaš ṭaḥbaše.* -- His car was smashed in the accident. *sayyaarto ṭṭaḥbašet bᵊl-ʔəṣṭidaam.*

smell - *riiḥa* pl. *rawaayeḥ.* What's that smell? *šuu har-riiḥa?*

to smell - *šamm (ə šamm//nšamm).* Do you smell gas? *šaamem ġaaz?* -- He smelled the plot and got away in time. *šamm riiḥet l-ᵊmʔaamara w-nafad qabᵊl fawaat ᵊl-waqᵊt.*

**The roses smell beautifully. *l-wardaat riiḥə́ton ḥəlwe.*

**The whole thing smells to high heaven. *haš-šaġle riiḥə́ta waaṣle ləs-sama.*

smile - *ʔəbtisaame* pl. *-aat.* She has a charming smile. *Ɛanda ʔəbtisaame ḥəlwe.*

**She was all smiles. *kaan wəšša kəllo Ɛam ᵊtbassam.*

to smile - *btasam, tbassam.* Why are you smiling? *leeš Ɛam təbtə́sem?* -- She smiled at you. *tbassamə́t-lak.* -- He smiled at my words. *btasam Ɛala kalaami* (or *lamma sameƐ kalaami*).

smoke - 1. *dəxxaan.* Where's that smoke coming from? *mneen žaaye had-dəxxaan?* 2. *sigaara* pl. *sagaayer.* Could I have a smoke please? *btəsmáḥ-li b-sigaara mən faḍlak?*

**His plans went up in smoke. *tbaxxaret mašariiƐo.*

to smoke - *daxxan//ddaxxan.* Do you smoke? *bəddaxxen?* -- I don't smoke a pipe. *maa bdaxxen ġalyuun.* -- The stove is smoking again. *ṣ-ṣooba ražƐet Ɛam ᵊddaxxen.* -- We either dry or smoke the fish. *ya mənyabbes ya məndaxxen ᵊs-samak.* -- This smoked glass is very beautiful. *hal-ᵊqzaaz l-ᵊmdaxxan ktiir ḥəlu.*

to **smolder** - *Ɛass (ə Ɛass).* Hours after the fire the beams were still smoldering. *baƐd ᵊl-ḥariiqa b-saaƐaat l-Ɛawaareḍ kaanu ləssaahon Ɛam yƐəssu.*

smooth - 1. *naaƐem, maales.* I'll take the box with the smooth surface. *baaxod ᵊl-Ɛəlbe halli wəšša naaƐem.* -- She has smooth hair. *Ɛanda šaƐᵊr naaƐem.* 2. *naaƐem.* I can't get a smooth shave with this blade. *maa bəqder ʔəḥleq ḥlaaqa naaƐme b-haš-šafra.* 3. *haadi, raayeq.* The sea was very smooth. *l-baḥᵊr kaan haadi ktiir.*

**He's a smooth talker. *huwwe ḥəles məles.*

to smooth down - *mallas//tmallas.* Smooth down your hair! *malles šaƐraatak!*

to smooth out - 1. *mallas//tmallas.* Smooth out the tablecloth. *malles šaršaf ᵊṭ-ṭaawle.* 2. *Ɛaddal//tƐaddal.* We have to smooth out a few points before we sign the contract. *laazem ᵊnƐaddel kam nəqṭa bᵊl-Ɛaqᵊd qabᵊl-ma nəmḍii.*

smoothly - *b-ᵊshuule.* Everything went smoothly. *kəll šii məši b-ᵊshuule.*

to **smother** - 1. *xtanaq.* We nearly smothered. *kənna laḥa nəxtə́neq.* 2. *xanaq (o xanᵊq//nxanaq).* They were about to smother the kitten in the blanket. *kaanu raḥa yəxᵊnqu l-qaṭṭa ᵊẓ-ẓġiire bᵊl-ᵊḥraam.*

to **smuggle** - *harrab//tharrab.* He got caught when he tried to smuggle liquor across the border. *nkamaš w-huwwe Ɛam yḥaawel yharreb məšruub Ɛal-ᵊḥduud.*

smuggler - *mharreb* pl. *-iin.*

smuggling - *tahriib.*

snack - *ləqme* pl. *ləqam.* Let's have a snack before we leave. *xalliina naakə́l-lna ləqme qabᵊl-ma nəmši.*

snacks - *maaza.* The hostess served little snacks with the drinks. *sətt ᵊl-beet qaddamet maaza maƐ ᵊl-məšruub.*

snail - (slug) *bazzaaqa* coll. *bazzaaq* pl. *-aat,* (with house) *ḥalazoone* coll. *ḥalazoon* pl. *-aat.*

snake - *ḥayye* pl. *-aat* and *ḥayaaya, ḥanaš* pl. *ḥnaaš.*

snap - 1. *faqše* pl. *-aat.* He called the boy with a snap of his fingers. *naada ləl-walad b-faqšet ʔaṣabiiƐo.* 2. *ṭaqše* pl. *-aat.* The lock closed with a snap. *l-qəfᵊl tsakkar ᵊb-ṭaqše.* 3. *kabsoone, kabšoone* coll. *kabsoon, kabšoon* pl. *-aat.* I have to sew snaps on my dress. *laazem xayyeṭ kabsoonaat ᵊb-fəsṭaani.* 4. *ṣuura* pl. *ṣuwar.* I'd like to take a snap of you. *ḥaabeb ʔaaxə́d-lak ṣuura.* 5. *ləƐbe.* That's a snap for me. *hayy ləƐbe bᵊn-nəsbe ʔəli.*

**We had a cold snap two days ago. *mən yoomeen ʔəžaana fatra baarde.*

**The exam was a snap. *l-faḥᵊṣ kaan hayyen ᵊktiir.*

**There's no snap to that song. *hal-ġənniyye maa-la ṭaƐme.*

**Don't make snap judgments. *laa tətsarraƐ ᵊb-ḥəkmak.*

to snap - 1. *nqaṭaƐ.* That rubber band is sure to snap. *hal-maṭṭaaṭa ʔakiid bədda tənqə́ṭeƐ.* 2. *qaṣaf (e qaṣᵊf//nqaṣaf), qaṣṣaf.* The storm snapped the trees like match sticks. *l-Ɛaaṣfe qaṣfet ᵊš-šažar mətᵊl Ɛuud ᵊl-kəbriit.* 3. *naqaf (o naqᵊf) b-.* Stop snapping that rubber band. *ḥaaštak tənqof b-hal-maṭṭaaṭa.* 4. *faqaš (o faqᵊš) b-.* He snapped his fingers to call the waiter. *faqaš b-ʔaṣabiiƐo la-ynaadi ləl-garṣoon.*

**The lock snapped shut. *l-qəfᵊl tsakkar ᵊb-ṭaqše.*

**Snap out of it! *qtəṣə́ra!* or *ləffa!*

to snap at - 1. *nahaš (a nahᵊš).* The dog snapped at me. *l-kalb nahašni.* 2. *ntatar b-.* I don't know why he snapped at me like that. *maa-li Ɛarfaan leeš ᵊntatar fiyyi heek.*

snappy - *ḥayawi**. He's a snappy fellow. *huwwe zalame ḥayawi.*

**Make it snappy! *xəffa!*

snapshot - *ṣuura* pl. *ṣuwar.*

to **snatch** - *xaṭaf (o xaṭᵊf//nxaṭaf).* Why did you snatch the envelope away from him? *leeš xaṭaft ᵊẓ-ẓarᵊf mənno?*

to **sneak** - *salḥab.* I sneaked out of the house. *salḥabt ᵊmn ᵊl-beet.* -- He must have sneaked in while I wasn't looking. *laazem ykuun salḥab la-žuwwa bᵊl-waqt yalli kənt maa Ɛam ʔəṭṭallaƐ fii.*

**Don't trust him, he's a sneak. *laa tʔammno, huwwe mən taḥᵊt la-taḥᵊt.*

to **sneer** - *stahzaʔ.* You have no reason to sneer at the poor fellow. *maa-fii lzuum təstahzeʔ ᵊb-hal-məskiin.*

to **sneeze** - *Ɛaṭṭaṣ.* He's been sneezing all morning. *ṣar-lo Ɛam yƐaṭṭeṣ kəll Ɛala bəkra.*

**That's nothing to sneeze at! *waḷḷa muu maḍḥake!*

to **sniff** - *šamšam.* I wish you'd stop sniffing the food like that. *ḥaaštak ᵊtšamšem ᵊl-ʔakᵊl heek.*

to **snore** - *šaxar (o šxiir).* You mean you never snore? *Ɛam ᵊtqəl-li ʔənno maa btəšxor ʔabadan?*

snow - *talᵊž* pl. *tluuž.* How deep is the snow? *qaddeeš səmk ᵊt-talᵊž?*

to snow - *talžet (e talᵊž).* It snowed all night. *talžet ṭuul ᵊl-leel.*

**They were snowed in for a whole week. *nḥabasu bᵊt-talᵊž žəmƐa.*

**Our garage is completely snowed under. *karaažna maṭmuur Ɛal-ʔaaxiir bᵊt-talᵊž.*

**We're snowed under with work. *nəḥna ġaaṭsiin la-qaraqiiṭ ʔadaanna bəš-šəġəl.*
snowball – *kərret˜* (pl. *-aat˜*) *talᵊž.*
snowflake – *nədfet˜* (pl. *-aat˜*) *talᵊž.*
snowstorm – *Eaaṣfe* (pl. *Eawaaṣef*) *talžiyye.*
to **snub** – *zabal (o zabᵊl//nzabal).* Everybody snubbed him at the party. *l-kəll zabalúu bᵊl-ḥafle.*
so – **1.** *heek.* So they say. *heek biquulu.* -- Isn't it so? *muu heek?* -- I suppose so. *bẓənn heek.* -- I told you so. *qəlt-əllak heek* or ***maa qəlt-əllak?* -- Is that so? *lakaan heek?* (sarcastically) *heek baqa!* **2.** *baqa.* So you think it's a good idea. *btəftəker baqa fəkra mniiḥa.* **3.** *kamaan, t-taani.* I'm leaving now. - So am I. *ʔana raayeḥ hallaq.* - *w-ʔana kamaan* or *w-ʔana t-taani* (f. *t-taanye,* etc.). -- If I can do it, so can you. *ʔiza ʔana byəṭlaE b-ʔiidi ʔaEməla w-ʔənte kamaan.* **4.** *qaddeeš.* You look so pale! *qaddeešak šaaheb!* -- You're so kind! *qaddeešak laṭiif!* -- They're so rich! *qaddeešon ʔaġniya!* -- The town is so beautiful! *qaddeeš ᵊl-balad ḥəlwe!*

**So I see. *šaayef.*

**So what? *yaEni šuu biṣiir?*

**So long. (said by the person leaving) *xaaṭrak!* (to a woman: *xaaṭrek!* to a group: *xaaṭərkon!*), (said by the person staying behind) *maE ᵊs-salaame!*

**So much the better. *ʔažet Eala rəžleeha.*

**How are things? - So far, so good. *kiif ᵊl-ʔaḥwaal?* - *la-hallaq* (or *la-hoon*) *l-ḥamdəlla kəll šii maaši mniiḥ.*

so so – *nəṣṣ Eala nəṣṣ, heek w-heek, nəṣṣ˜ waaḥde.* How are you? - Thanks, so so. *kiifak?* - *l-ḥamdəlla nəṣṣ Eala nəṣṣ.* -- It's a so-so translation. *hiyye taržame nəṣṣ Eala nəṣṣ.*

so as to – *ḥatta, la-ḥatta, la-, mənšaan.* I did some of the work so as to make things easier for you. *Eməlt baEḍ ᵊš-šəġᵊl ḥatta hawwə́na Ealeek.*

so much – **1.** *hal-qadd.* Not so much pepper, please. *muu hal-qadd fəlfol ʔiza bətriid.* **2.** *qaddeeš.* I missed you so much! *qaddeeš məštaq-lak!* **3.** *la-daraže ..., hal-qadd.* We have so much work that we have to hire extra help. *fii Eanna šəġᵊl la-daraže* (or *fii Eanna hal-qadd šəġᵊl*) *ʔənno laazem ᵊnžiib msaaEdiin ʔiḍaafiyyiin.* -- I ate so much I couldn't sleep. *taqqalᵊt bᵊl-ʔakᵊl la-daraže maa qdərᵊt naam.*

**So much has already been written about that subject. *nkatab šii ktiir b-hal-mawḍuuE!*

**So much about your work. Now to your salary. *ḥaažətna mən šəġlak baqa. xalliina nəḥki b-maEaašak.*

**Thanks ever so much. *šəkran žaziilan.*

so that – *ḥatta, la-ḥatta, la-, mənšaan.* I'm telling you so that you'll know. *Eam qəl-lak ḥatta taEref.*

and so on (or **forth**) – *ʔila ʔaaxírihi, w-ma žarr.* All his uncles, aunts, cousins and so forth were there. *kəll ᵊEmuumo w-Eammaato w-wlaad ᵊEmuumo ʔila ʔaaxírihi kaanu hniik.*

not so ... as ... – **1.** *muu ... qadd ...* Our living room is not so big as yours. *ʔuuḍet ᵊqEuudna muu kbiire qadd ʔuuḍətkon.* **2.** *muu ... qadd-ma ...* He's not so old as you would think. *Eəmro muu kbiir qadd-maa-lak faaker.*

or so – *ḥawaali.* I need five dollars or so. *laazəmni ḥawaali xamᵊs dolaaraat.*
to **soak** – *naqaE (a naqᵊE//ntaqaE).* We soak the laundry overnight. *mnənqaE ᵊl-ġasiil ṭuul ᵊl-leel.*

to soak up – *maṣṣ (ə maṣṣ//mmaṣṣ).* The sponge will soak it up. *s-sfənže batməṣṣa.*

soaked – *mbalbal, mabluul.* We came home soaked. *ržəEna Eal-beet ᵊmbalbaliin* or ***ržəEna Eal-beet wᵊl-mayy Eam təzrob mən rəžleena.*

to get soaked – *tsaqsaq.* I got soaked to the skin. *tsaqsaqᵊt Eat-tamaam.*
soap – *ṣaabuun* (f.) pl. *ṣawabiin.* I want a cake of soap. *bəddi qaaleb ṣaabuun* or ***bəddi ṣaabuune.*

to soap – *ṣooban.* Soap your hands well to get the grease off. *ṣooben ʔideek ᵊmniiḥ ḥatta trawweḥ ᵊš-šaḥᵊm.*
soap factory – *maṣbane* pl. *maṣaaben.*
sob – *ʔannet˜* (pl. *-aat˜*) *bəke.*

to sob – *tnahnah.*
sobbing – *nahnaha, ʔaniin bəke.*
sober – **1.** *ṣaḥyaan.* He is never quite sober. *b-ḥayaatak maa bətšuufo ʔəlla nəṣṣ ṣaḥyaan.* **2.** *raziin.* He gave us a sober appraisal of our situation. *qaddə́m-əlna taqdiir raziin la-ḥaalətna.*

to sober up – **1.** *ṣəḥi (a ṣ).* He sobered up quickly. *ṣəḥi b-sərEa.* **2.** *ṣaḥḥa.* That coffee will sober him up. *hal-qahwe bətṣaḥḥii.*
so-called – **1.** *mazEuum.* These so-called patriots are working against the best interests of their country. *haadool ᵊl-mazEuumiin waṭaniyyiin Eam yəštəġlu ḍədd maṣlaḥt ᵊblaadon.* **2.** *maa yudEaa.* What exactly is the area comprised by the so-called "Fertile Crescent"? *šuu l-manṭiqa bᵊẓ-ẓabṭ yalli bəddammə́na maa yudEaa "l-hilaal ᵊl-xaṣiib"?*
soccer – *futbool, kəret˜ ᵊl-qadam.* Soccer is a very popular sport in Syria. *l-futbool sboor ᵊktiir məntə́šer b-suuriyya.*
sociable – *maEᵊšraani*.*
social – *ʔəžtimaaEi*.* Social conditions have changed tremendously. *l-ʔaḥwaal ᵊl-ʔəžtimaaEiyye tġayyaret b-ṣuura haaʔile.*
socialism – *ʔəštiraakiyye.*
socialist – *ʔəštiraaki*.*
society – **1.** *žamEiyye* pl. *-aat.* He's a member of many learned societies. *huwwe Eəḍu b-Eəddet žamEiyyaat Eəlmiyye.* **2.** *məžtəmaE.* You owe it to society. *haada waažbak naaḥ ᵊl-məžtəmaE.* -- Her name appears frequently on the society page. *ʔəsᵊmha byəẓhar marraat ᵊktiire b-ṣafḥet ᵊl-məžtəmaE.* -- He doesn't feel at ease in high society. *maa byərtaaḥ b-məžtəmaE ᵊṭ-ṭabaqaat ᵊr-raaqye.*
sociological – *soosyolooži*.*
sociology – *Eəlm˜ ᵊl-ʔəžtimaaE, soosyoloožya.*
sock – *žraabe* pl. *-aat.* I want three pairs of socks. *bəddi tlətt ᵊžwaaz ᵊžraabaat.*
Socrates – *səqraaṭ.*
soda – *ṣooda.* I put some soda in my wash. *ḥaṭṭeet šwayyet ṣooda b-ġasiili.* — Bring me a bottle of soda. *žəb-li qanniinet ṣooda.*

baking soda – *karbonaat˜ ᵊṣ-ṣooda.* Use one teaspoon of baking soda. *staEmel maElaqet šaay karbonaat ᵊṣ-ṣooda.*
sofa – *kə́nabe* pl. *-aat, kanabaaye* pl. *-aat.*
soft – **1.** *ṭari*, raxu.* Is the ground soft? *l-ʔarḍ ṭariyye?* **2.** *waaṭi.* She sang in a soft voice. *ġannet ᵊb-ṣooṭ waaṭi.* **3.** *xafiif.* A soft light would be better. *ḍaww xafiif bikuun ʔaḥsan.* **4.** *nayy.* He's terribly soft. *faẓiiE qaddeešo nayy.* **5.** *ḥassaas.* That's a soft spot with him. *hayy nəqṭa ḥassaase fii.* **6.** *hayyen.* He's got a soft job. *Eando šağle hayyne.*

**Pretty soft (for him)! *kəll šii žaayíi mətl ᵊs-samne wᵊl-Easal!*

to get soft – **1.** *ṭəri (a ṭaraawe).* The butter got too soft. *z-zəbde ṭəryet ᵊktiir.* **2.** *trahhal.* Take up some physical exercise, you're getting soft. *saawíi-lak šii tamariin ryaaḍiyye, Eam tətrahhal.* **3.** *raqqaq qalbo.* Now, don't you get soft with him. *ʔəṣḥa traqqeq qalbak Ealée.*
soft-boiled – *brəšt* (invar.). I'd like two soft-boiled eggs. *bəddi beeḍteen ᵊbrəšt.*
soft drink – *kaẓooẓa* pl. *-aat* coll. pl. *kaẓooẓ.*
soil – *tərbe* pl. *tərab, ʔarḍ* (f.) pl. *ʔaraaḍi.* The soil here is very fertile. *t-tərbe hoon ᵊktiir xəṣbe.*

to soil – *waṣṣax.* You soiled your suit. *waṣṣaxᵊt badᵊltak.*
soirée – *swarée* pl. *swareyaat, sahra* pl. *-aat.*
solar – *šamsi*.*
solder – *lḥaam* pl. *-aat.* What do you use for solder? *šuu btəstaEmel lḥaam?*

to solder – *laḥam (e/o lḥaam//nlaḥam).* You'd better solder the pipes together. *ʔaḥsə́n-lak təlḥem ᵊl-buuriyeen maE baEḍon.*
soldering iron – *laḥḥaame* pl. *-aat.*
soldier – *Easkari* coll. *Easkar* pl. *Easaaker, žəndi* pl. *žnuud.*
sole – **1.** *baṭn˜ ᵊl-qadam* pl. *bṭuunet˜ l-ᵊqdaam.* I have a blister on my sole. *fii faqfuule b-baṭᵊn qadami.* **2.** *naEᵊl* pl. *nEaal.* The soles of the brown shoes are worn through. *naEl ᵊṣ-ṣabbaaṭ ᵊl-bənni nfaxat.*

to sole – *ḥaṭṭ (ə ḥaṭaṭ˜) nəṣṣ naEᵊl la-.* I have to have my shoes soled. *laazem ḥəṭṭ nəṣṣ naEᵊl la-ṣabbaaṭi.*
sole – *waḥiid.* He's the sole heir. *huwwe l-waares ᵊl-waḥiid.* -- He was the sole survivor. *kaan ᵊl-waḥiid halli bəqi ṭayyeb.*

**He came here for the sole purpose of meeting you. *ʔəža la-hoon bass mənšaan yətEarraf Ealeek.*
solely – *(b-)məfrad-* + pron. suff., *waḥd-* + pron. suff. He's solely responsible for it. *huwwe b-məfrado* (or *waḥdo*) *masʔuul Ean haš-šii.*
solemn – **1.** *rasmi*.* He gave me his solemn promise that... *waEadni waEᵊd rasmi ʔənno...* **2.** *rahiib,*

muhiib. It was a solemn moment when he rose to speak. *kaanet lahza rahiibe lamma waqqaf yaxtob.* — The coronation was a solemn ceremony. *t-tatwiiž kaan ʔəhtifaal muhiib.* 3. *raziin.* What's the matter with you? You look so solemn. *šəbak? heeʔtak raziin ᵊl-yoom.*

solid - 1. *qawi*.* Is the ice solid? *ž-žaliid qawi?* — This chair doesn't seem very solid to me. *hal-kərsi mbayyə́n-li muu qawi ktiir.* 2. *kaamel.* We waited a solid hour for him. *stanneenda saaᶜa kaamle.* — He talked to me for three solid hours. *hakaani tlatt saaᶜaat kaamle.* 3. *xaaleṣ.* The statue is made of solid gold. *t-təmsaal maᶜmuul mn ᵊd-dahab ᵊl-xaaleṣ.* 4. *žamaad* pl. *-aat.* We distinguish between solids, liquids and gases. *mənfarreq been ᵊž-žamaadaat wᵊs-sawaaʔel wᵊl-ġaaziyyaat.*

**The lake is frozen solid. *l-buhayra mžallde mətl ᵊṣ-ṣaxr.*

solidarity - *tadaamon.*

solitary confinement - *habᵊs ʔənfiraadi.*

solution - 1. *hall* pl. *hluul.* That's the solution of the problem. *haada hall ᵊl-məšᵊkle.* 2. *mahluul* pl. *-aat.* You need a stronger solution. *bəddak mahluul ʔaqwa mən heek.*

to **solve** - *hall (ə hall//nhall).* I can't solve the riddle. *maa fiini həll ᵊl-həzzeera.*

solvency - *qədra ᶜad-dafᵊᶜ.*

solvent - *qaader ᶜad-dafᵊᶜ.*

some - 1. *šii.* There must be some way of finding out. *laazem ykuun fii šii tariiqa la-naᶜref.* — I've seen you some place before. *šəftak b-šii mahall mən qabᵊl.* 2. *kam.* Give me some matches. *ᶜatiini kam kəbriite.* 3. *šwayyet˜.* He lent me some money. *dayyanni šwayyet maṣaari.* 4. *baᶜd˜.* Some people can't stand noise. *fii baᶜᵊd naas maa byəthammalu d-dooše.* — Some of us are going by train and some by boat. *baᶜᵊdna raayhiin bᵊt-treen w-baᶜᵊdna bᵊl-markab.* 5. *hawaali.* We stayed some two or three hours. *bqiina hawaali saaᶜteen ᵊtlaate.*

**I need some stockings. *laazəmni žraabaat.*

**Boy, that's some jalopy! *daxiil ʔalla, məlla təmbor!*

some day - 1. *ləssa byəži yoom.* You'll regret that some day. *ləssa byəži yoom btəndam ᶜala haš-šii.* 2. *šii yoom.* I hope to meet him some day. *bətʔammal ʔətᶜarraf ᶜalée šii yoom.*

some ... or other - *šii.* It's in some book or other on that shelf. *mamžuud ᵊb-šii ktaab ᶜar-raff.*

somebody - 1. *hada, waahed.* Somebody asked for you. *fii hada saʔal ᶜannak.* — If somebody calls, tell him I'll be back in an hour. *ʔiza hada talfə́n-li qəl-lo bəržaᶜ baᶜᵊd saaᶜa.* — Somebody must have opened the envelope. *laazem ykuun fii hada fatah ᵊz-zarᵊf.* 2. *hada, šii hada, šii waahed.* You have to trust somebody. *laazem təsaq ᵊb-hada.*

somehow - 1. *b-šii tariiqa.* We'll fix it somehow. *mənsalləha b-šii tariiqa.* 2. *b-tariiqa mn ᵊt-təroq.* The letter got lost somehow. *l-maktuub ᵊb-tariiqa mn ᵊt-təroq daaᶜ* or ***l-maktuub daaᶜ maa baᶜref šloon.*

somehow or other - *b-tariiqa mn ᵊt-təroq.* Somehow or other he always gets what he wants. *b-tariiqa mn ᵊt-təroq daayman byəhsal ᶜala yalli bəddo-yda.*

someone - 1. *hada, waahed.* Is there someone here who can play the piano? *fii hada hoon byaᶜref ydəqq ᶜal-byaano?* — There's someone at the door who wants to talk to you. *fii hada ᶜal-baab biriid yəhki maᶜak.* 2. *hada, šii hada, šii waahed, šii farᵊd.* Someone has to take the responsibility. *šii hada laazem yaaxod ᵊl-masʔuuliyye ᶜala ᶜaatqo.*

something - 1. *šii.* Something's going on in that building. *fii šii ṣaayer b-hal-binaaye.* — That's something to think about. *haada šii məhrez naftə́ker fii.* — Is something the matter? *fii šii?* -- Something's up. *fii šii ṣaayer.*

**He knows something about medicine. *byəfham bᵊt-təbb.*

something of - *nooᶜan maa.* He's something of an expert in that field. *huwwe nooᶜan maa xabiir b-hal-haql.*

something or other - *šii.* Something or other reminded me of home. *fii šii zakkarni b-baladi.*

sometime - 1. *šii yoom.* Why don't you come around sometime? *leeš maa btəži dəuurna šii yoom.* 2. *b-šii waqᵊt.* She'll be here sometime today. *laha təṣal b-šii waqt ᵊl-yoom.*

sometime or other - *b-šii waqᵊt mn ᵊl-ʔawqaat.* I'd like to read it sometime or other. *bhəbb ʔəqraaha b-šii waqᵊt mn ᵊl-ʔawqaat.*

sometimes - *(b-)baᶜd˜ ᵊl-ʔawqaat, ʔahyaanan.* Sometimes it gets very hot here. *b-baᶜd ᵊl-ʔawqaat hoon bišiir šoob ᵊktiir.* -- Sometimes I wake up in the middle of the night. *ʔahyaanan bfiiq ᵊb-sawaad ᵊl-leel.*

somewhat - *šwayye.* I feel somewhat tired. *ʔana taᶜbaan ᵊšwayye.*

somewhere - 1. *b-šii mahall, b-šii qərne.* I saw it somewhere but I don't remember where. *šəfto b-šii mahall bass maa-li ᶜam ʔədzakkar ween.* 2. *la-šii mahall, la-šii qərne.* Let's go somewhere tonight. *xalliina nrəh-ᵊlna la-šii mahall ᵊl-leele.*

somewhere else - 1. *b-ġeer˜ mahall, b-ġeer˜ qərne.* Let's meet somewhere else. *xalliina nəštə́meᶜ b-ġeer mahall.* 2. *la-ġeer˜ mahall, la-ġeer˜ qərne.* Let's go somewhere else where we're alone. *xalliina nruuh la-ġeer mahall hatta nkuun la-haalna.*

son - *ʔəbᵊn* pl. *wlaad, walad* pl. *wlaad,* (politely of another person's son) *mahruus* pl. *mahariis.*

song - *ġənniyye* pl. *-aat* and *ġanaani.* Do you know the song? *btaᶜref šii l-ġənniyye?*

**He always gives me the same song and dance. *daayman byətlə́ᶜ-li b-nafs ᵊl-fanti.*

for a song - *b-balaaš, ləqta.* We bought the chair for a song. *štareena l-kərsi b-balaaš.*

son-in-law - *ṣəhᵊr* pl. *ʔəṣᵊhra.* He's his son-in-law, not his brother-in-law. *huwwe ṣəhro - žooz bənto - muu ṣəhro žooz ʔəxto.*

soon - 1. *ᶜan qariib.* Come again soon. *ᶜiida ᶜan qariib.* 2. *bakkiir.* It's too soon to tell what's the matter with him. *bakkiir ləssa naᶜref šuu haakmo.*

**I'd just as soon not go. *ləssaani mxootar been ruuh w-maa ruuh.*

as soon as - *ʔawwal-ma, b-ᵊmžarrad-ma, b-haal-ma.* Let me know as soon as you get here. *ᶜatiini xabar ʔawwal-ma təṣal la-hoon.*

sooner - 1. *ʔabkar.* Can you leave a little sooner? *btəqder tətrok ʔabkar šwayye?* 2. *b-waqᵊt ʔaqrab.* Do you think we can get together sooner than that? *btaᶜtə́qed fiina nəštə́meᶜ b-waqᵊt ʔaqrab mən heek?*

**The sooner you come, the better. *qadd-ma bakkart bᵊž-žayye bikuun ʔahsan.*

**He'd sooner die than give in. *bifaddel ᵊl-moot ᶜan ᵊl-ʔəstəslaam.*

no sooner ... than - *b-ᵊmžarrad-ma, b-haal-ma.* He no sooner mentioned her name than she appeared. *b-ᵊmžarrad-ma zakar ʔəsma hadret.*

**No sooner said than done. *l-kəlme maa btənqaal ʔəlla bətlaaqᵊiha tnaffazet.*

sooner or later - *ᶜaažilan ʔaw ʔaažilan, ʔawwalta ʔaw ʔaaxerta, n-maa kaan hallaq bikuun baᶜdeen.* Sooner or later we'll have to make up our minds. *ᶜaažilan ʔaw ʔaažilan laazem ᵊnhətt haalna ᶜala qaraar.*

soot - *šəhhaar.*

to **soothe** - *hammad, kannan.* This salve will soothe the pain. *hal-marham bihammed ᵊl-wažaᶜ.*

sooty - *mšahher, mšahwar.*

sore - 1. *žarᵊh* pl. *žruuh(a).* The sore is pretty well healed up. *ž-žarᵊh taab ᵊmniih.* 2. *məltə́heb.* I have a sore thumb. *baahmi məltə́heb.* — He has a sore throat. *halqo məltə́heb.* 3. *hassaas.* That's a sore spot with him. *hayye nəqta hassaase fii.* — You've touched a sore spot. *ʔənte daqarᵊt nəqta hassaase.* 4. *zaᶜlaan.* Are you sore at me? *ʔənte zaᶜlaan mənni?*

**Don't touch my arm, it's still sore. *laa tədqor ʔiidi, ləssaaha btəžaᶜni.*

**My muscles are still sore. *ᶜadalaati ləssaaton šaaddiin.*

to get sore - 1. *zəᶜel (a zaᶜal).* You needn't get sore right away. *maa fii lzuum təzᶜal ᶜal-haarek.* 2. *wažeᶜ (-yəžaᶜ* and *-yuužaᶜ wažaᶜ).* My feet got sore from all that walking. *rəžlayyi wažᶜətni mən kətr ᵊl-maši.*

sorrow - *həzᵊn* pl. *ʔahzaan, ġamm* pl. *ġmuum.* She can't get over her sorrow. *maa ᶜam təġder təsla həzna.*

sorry - 1. *məhzen, maʔsef.* They're in a sorry state. *hənne b-haale məhᵊzne.* 2. *mətʔassef.* I'm really sorry. *ʔana mətʔassef mən kəll qalbi.* — I'm sorry to say that can't be done. *ʔana mətʔassef (or **maᶜ ᵊl-ʔasaf) haš-šii muu məmken yṣiir.* 3. *zaᶜlaan, mətʔallem.* I'm sorry for her. *ʔana zaᶜlaan ᶜaleeha.* 4. *ᶜafwan.* Sorry! Did I hurt you? *ᶜafwan! ʔallamtak šii?*

sort - *nooᶜ* pl. *ʔanwaaᶜ, šəkᵊl* pl. *ʔaškaal.* I can't get along with that sort of person. *maa-li ᶜam ʔəqder ʔəslok maᶜ šaxᵊṣ mən han-nooᶜ.* — I said nothing of the sort. *maa qəlt šii mən han-nooᶜ*

ʔabadan. — What sort of car do you want to buy? *šuu nooƐ ᵊs-sayyaara yalli bəddak təštriiha?*
**He's a decent sort. *huwwe zalame ḍəġri.*
**She's not a bad sort. *hiyye muu baṭṭaale.*
**You'll do nothing of the sort! *laa təḥlam taƐmel heek šii!*
sort of - *nooƐan maa.* She's sort of attractive. *hiyye nooƐan maa žazzaabe.* — I'm sort of glad I didn't go. *ʔana nooƐan maa mabṣuuṭ yalli maa rəḥᵊt.* — I had sort of a hunch that something was going to happen. *kənᵊt nooƐan maa šaaƐer b-šii bəddo yṣiir.* — I sort of knew that it was going to happen. *nooƐan maa kənᵊt Ɛarfaan ʔənno haš-šii bəddo yṣiir.*
all sorts of things - *kəll šii byəxṭor Ɛal-baal.* He promised me all sorts of things. *waƐadni b-kəll šii byəxṭor Ɛal-baal.*
to sort - *ṣannaf//tṣannaf.* Have the stockings been sorted? *tṣannafu ž-žraabaat?*
soul - **1.** *rooḥ* pl. *(ʔa)rwaaḥ.* God have mercy on his soul. *ʔaḷḷa yarḥam rooḥo.* **2.** *nafᵊs* pl. *nfuus,* also *ʔənfos,* (after numerals 3-10) *ənfos, nasame* pl. *-aat.* The population of the village doesn't exceed a hundred souls. *səkkaan ᵊḍ-ḍeeƐa maa byədžaawazu l-miit nafs.*
**There wasn't a soul to be seen in the streets. *maa kaan fii d-doomari bᵊš-šawaareƐ.*
**He's thrown himself into it heart and soul. *lahaš ḥaalo fiiha ǧalban w-ǧaaliban.*
sound - **1.** *saliim.* He has a sound constitution. *bənᵊyto saliime.* **2.** *matiin, maaken.* The house is old but sound. *l-beet Ɛatiiq bass matiin.* **3.** *saalem.* Arabic distinguishes a sound from a broken plural. *l-luġa l-Ɛarabiyye btətmayyaz b-žamᵊƐ saalem w-žamƐ ᵊmkassar.* **4.** *maƐquul, ṣaḥiiḥ, mniiḥ.* That's a sound bit of advice. *hayye naṣiiḥa maƐquule.* — That's a sound argument. *hayye ḥəžže maƐquule.*
**He's sound asleep. *huwwe ġaaṭeṭ bᵊn-noom.*
safe and sound - **1.** *bᵊs-salaame.* He returned safe and sound. *rəžeƐ bᵊs-salaame.* **2.** *saalem mƐaafa.* Everybody is safe and sound. *l-kəll saalmiin ᵊmƐaafayiin.*
sound - **1.** *ṣoot* pl. *(ʔa)ṣwaat.* Light travels faster than sound. *ḍ-ḍaww byənṭəqel ʔasraƐ mn ᵊṣ-ṣoot.* — Some sounds of Arabic are very hard for an English-speaking person to pronounce. *baƐᵊḍ ʔaṣwaat ᵊl-luġa l-Ɛarabiyye lafẓon ṣaƐb ᵊktiir Ɛala halli byəḥku ʔəngliizi.* **2.** *ḥəss, ṣoot* pl. *(ʔa)ṣwaat.* What was that sound? *šuu kaan hal-ḥəss?* **3.** *daqqa, ṣoot.* At the sound of a trumpet everybody got up from his seat. *Ɛala daqqet boorazaan kəll waaḥed mn ᵊl-qaaƐdiin waqqaf.* **4.** *ṣooti*.* The jets crashed the sound barrier several times. *n-naffaasaat ᵊxtarqet ᵊl-ḥaažez ᵊṣ-ṣooti Ɛəddet marraat.*
**I recognized her by the sound of her voice. *Ɛrəfta mən ṣoota.*
**She didn't utter a sound. *maa fatḥet təmma w-laa b-kəlme.*
**She didn't know we were within sound of her voice. *maa kaanet Ɛarfaane ʔənna kənna Ɛala masmaƐ mən ṣoota.*
to sound - **1.** *daqq (ə daqq, daqqe).* A bell sounded and everybody left the room. *daqq žaraṣ fa-kəll waaḥed tarak ᵊl-ʔuuḍa.* **2.** *ẓahar (a ẓhuur), baan (a ø), bayyan.* That sounds very strange. *haš-šii ẓaaher ktiir ġariib.* — The report sounds good. *t-taǧriir ᵊmbayyen ᵊmniiḥ.*
**That sounds funny to me. *haš-šii ġariib bᵊn-nəsbe ʔəli.*
**The whole story sounds fishy to me. *l-qəṣṣa kəlla bᵊn-nəsbe ʔəli fiiha ləƐbe.*
to **sound out** - *šass (ə šass) nabᵊḍ˜ ..., stamzaž.* I'll have to sound him out first. *bᵊl-ʔawwal laazem šəss nabḍo* (or *laazem ʔəstamᵊzžo*).
soundproof - *Ɛaazel ḍədd ᵊṣ-ṣooṭ.* Are the studios soundproof? *s-stuudyoyaat Ɛaazliin ḍədd ᵊṣ-ṣooṭ?*
to soundproof - *Ɛazal (e Ɛazᵊl//nƐazal) Ɛan ᵊṣ-ṣooṭ.* We're going to soundproof these walls. *laḥa nəƐzel hal-ḥiiṭaan Ɛan ᵊṣ-ṣooṭ.*
soup - *šooraba* pl. *-aat.*
sour - **1.** *ḥaamoḍ.* This wine is very sour. *han-nbiid ᵊktiir ḥaamoḍ.* **2.** *naašef.* Why do you make such a sour face? *leeš wəššak naašef hal-qadd?*
sour grapes - (literally and figuratively) *ḥəṣrom.* You say he didn't want the job? - I suspect it's a question of sour grapes. *Ɛam ᵊtquul ʔənno maa raad ᵊl-waẓiife? - b-raʔyi ʔana hiyye ḥəṣrom ʔəlo.*
to turn sour - *ḥammaḍ, faraṭ (o farᵊṭ).* The milk turned sour. *l-ḥaliib ḥammaḍ.*
source - **1.** *maṣdar* pl. *maṣaaḍer, manbaƐ* pl. *manaabeƐ.* I have it from a good source. *ʔažaani l-xabar mən maṣḍar mawsuuǧ.* **2.** *maṣḍar* pl. *maṣaaḍer.* Don't rely too much on secondary sources in your thesis. *laa təƐtəmed ᵊb-zyaade Ɛala maṣaaḍer saanawiyye b-ʔəṭruuḥtak.* **3.** *maṣdar, manbaƐ, ʔaṣᵊl* pl. *ʔṣuul.* Have you found the source of the trouble? *laqeet maṣdar ᵊl-məškel?*
**The Rhine has its source in the Swiss Alps. *nahr ᵊr-reen byənboƐ mn ᵊžbaal ᵊl-ʔalb ᵊs-swiisriyye.*
south - **1.** *žanuub, žnuub.* The wind is coming from the south. *l-hawa žaaye mn ᵊž-žanuub.* **2.** *naaḥ ᵊž-žanuub.* The arrow points south. *s-sahᵊm bidəll naaḥ ᵊž-žanuub.* **3.** *Ɛaž-žanuub.* I want to go south for the winter. *bəddi ruuḥ Ɛaž-žanuub məddet ᵊš-šəte.*
south of - *b-žanuub˜ ...* He lives south of here. *saaken ᵊb-žanuub hoon.*
South Africa - *žanuub˜ ʔafriiǧya.*
South America - *žanuub˜ ʔamriika, ʔamriika ž-žanuubiyye.*
southeast - *žanuub˜ šarᵊq, žanuub šarqi*.* The village is some 20 km southeast of Damascus. *ḍ-ḍeeƐa waaqƐa ḥawaali Ɛəšriin kiilomətᵊr žanuub šarq ᵊš-šaam.* — The southeast is mostly desert. *ž-žanuub ᵊš-šarqi ʔaktaro ṣaḥra.*
Southeast Asia - *žanuub˜ šarq˜ ʔaasya.*
southern - *žanuubi*, žnuubi*.* This plant is found only in southern regions. *han-nabaat byənwəžed bass bᵊl-manaaṭeq ᵊž-žanuubiyye.*
southwest - *žanuub˜ ġarb, žanuub ġarbi*.* Qatana is located southwest of Damascus. *qaṭana waaqƐa žanuub ġarb ᵊš-šaam.* — The southwest is mostly mountains. *ž-žanuub ᵊl-ġarbi ʔaktaro žbaal.*
souvenir - *suuvəniir* (invar.). I want to buy some souvenirs here. *bəddi ʔəštri-li šwayyet suuvəniir mən hoon.*
sovereign - *zaat˜* (pl. *zawaat˜*) *syaade.* The Sudan has been a sovereign state since 1955. *s-suudaan doole zaat syaade mən sənt ʔalf w-təsaƐ miyye w-xamsṭa w-xamsiin.*
Soviet - *səvyeeti*, səfyeeti*, səfyaati*.* The Soviet government has delivered a stiff protest. *l-ᵊḥkuume s-səvyeetiyye baƐtet ʔəḥtižaaž šadiid.*
Soviet Russia - *ruusya s-səvyeetiyye.*
Soviet Union - *l-ʔəttiḥaad ᵊs-səvyeeti.*
sow - *xanziire* pl. *xanaziir.* Our sow had twelve baby pigs yesterday. *xanziirətna ʔəžaaha ṭnaašar xanziir ᵊẓġaar ᵊmbaareḥ.*
to **sow** - *zaraƐ (a zarᵊƐ//nzaraƐ).* As ye sow, so shall ye reap. *halli btəzraƐo btəḥᵊṣdo.* — That fellow's been sowing discord all along. *haz-zalame ṣar-lo zamaan Ɛam yəzraƐ ᵊbzuur ᵊl-fətne been ᵊn-naas.*
soya - *ṣooya.*
space - **1.** *maḥall, makaan.* The desk takes up too much space. *ṭ-ṭaawle btaaxod maḥall b-ᵊzyaade.* — Is there still space for my bag? *ləssa fii maḥall la-šantaayti?* **2.** *masaaḥa* pl. *-aat.* The floor space of the building is more than 300 square meters. *masaaḥet ʔarḍ hal-binaaye ʔaktar mən tlaat miit mətr ᵊmrabbaƐ.* **3.** *faḍaaʔ.* Science is learning more and more about the secrets of outer space. *l-Ɛəlᵊm Ɛam yəktəšef ʔaktar w-ʔaktar ʔasraar ᵊl-faḍaaʔ ᵊl-xaarži.* **4.** *faḍa.* He just sat there staring out into space. *qaƐad ᵊhniik Ɛam ybaḥleq bᵊl-faḍa.* **5.** *faraaġ* pl. *-aat.* Leave a double space after each sentence. *trook faraaġeen baƐᵊd kəll žəmle.*
in the space of - *b-məddet˜...* He did the work in the space of two weeks. *xallaṣ ᵊš-šaġle b-məddet ʔəsbuuƐeen.*
to space: The posts are spaced a foot apart. *l-Ɛawamiid bəƐd ᵊl-waaḥed Ɛan ᵊt-taani qadam.* — Space the last two words in line two. *baƐƐed been ᵊḥruuf ᵊl-kəlᵊmteen ᵊl-ʔaaxraaniyyaat bᵊṣ-ṣaṭr ᵊt-taani.*
spacious - *fasiiḥ, waaseƐ.*
spade - **1.** *rafᵊš* pl. *rfuuše.* Grab a spade and dig. *xəd-lak rafᵊš w-ᵊḥfoor.* **2.** *basṭooni* pl. *basṭooniyyaat.* I bid two spades. *bsammi tneen basṭooni.*
**Why don't you call a spade a spade? *leeš maa bətsammi l-ʔašyaaʔ b-ʔasmaaʔa?*
spaghetti - *sbageetti.*
Spain - *sḅaanya.*
Spaniard - *sḅanyooli* pl. *-iyye, sḅaani* pl. *-iyye.*
Spanish - *sbanyooli*, sbaani*.*
to **spank** - *ḍarab (o ḍarᵊb//nḍarab), ṭaƐma qaṭle// ʔakal qaṭle.* I have a good mind to spank him for it. *žaaye Ɛala baali ʔəḍᵊrbo* (or *ṭaƐmi qaṭle*) *b-sabḅa.*
to **spare** - **1.** *waffar.* You can spare yourself the trouble. *fiik ᵊtwaffer Ɛala ḥaalak ᵊl-ġalabe.* — Nobody was spared. *maa waffaru ḥada.* **2.** *baqqa*

Ɛala. He was the only one whose life was spared. *kaan ᵊl-waḥiid halli baqqu Ɛala ḥayaato.* 3. *staġna Ɛan.* Can you spare this pencil? *fiik təstaġni Ɛan hal-qalam?* 4. *Ɛaaf (i ø) mən, xallaṣ mən.* Spare me the details. *Ɛiifni mn ᵊt-tafaṣiil.*
**He spared no expense. *bazal ᵊr-rxiiṣ wᵊl-ġaali.*
**Can you spare a minute? *faaḍi šii daqiiqa?*
**I'm sorry, but I don't have a minute to spare. *mətˀassef bass maa-li faaḍi w-laa daqiiqa.*

spare part - *qəṭƐet˜* (pl. *qəṭaƐ˜*) *ġyaar, ˀaksəswaar* (invar.). Can you get spare parts for your radio? *fiik ᵊdžiib qəṭaƐ ġyaar lər-raadyo tabaƐak?*

spare time - *waqᵊt˜ faraaġ.* What do you do in your spare time? *šuu btaƐmel ᵊb-waqᵊt faraaġak?*

spare tire - *stəbne* pl. *-aat.* We never travel without a spare tire. *maa mənsaafer ˀabadan bala stəbne.*

sparingly - *b-ˀəqtiṣaad, b-tawfiir.* Use it sparingly. *staƐᵊmlo b-ˀəqtiṣaad* or ***waffer ᵊb-ˀəstəƐmaalo* or ***qtəṣed ᵊb-ˀəstəƐmaalo.*

spark - *šaraara* coll. *šaraar* pl. *-aat.* The sparks flew in every direction. *š-šaraar tnaasar ᵊb-kəll žəha.* — The fire was started by a spark. *l-ḥariiq sabbabə́to šaraara.*

to **sparkle** - *baraq (o barᵊq).*

sparkler - *ḍaww˜ ᵊl-leel* (invar.).

spark plug - *buuži* pl. *buužiyaat.* I need a new spark plug for my car. *laazəmni buuži ždiid la-sayyaarti.*

sparrow - *Ɛaṣfuur duuri* pl. *Ɛaṣafiir duuriyye.*

spasm - *tašannož* pl. *-aat.*

to **speak** - *ḥaka (i ḥaki//nḥaka).* Do I speak clearly enough? *Ɛam ˀəḥki b-ᵊwḍuuḥ ᵊkfaaye?* -- Do you speak German? *btəḥki ˀalmaani?* -- We're not on speaking terms. *maa-lna Ɛam nəḥki maƐ baƐᵊḍna.*
**It's nothing to speak of. *maa fii šii byəstḥəqq ᵊz-zəkᵊr.*
spoken - *məḥki**. You have to distinguish between the spoken and the written language. *laazem ᵊtfarreq been ᵊl-luġa l-məḥkiyye* (or ***luġet ᵊl-ḥaki*) *wᵊl-luġa l-maktuube* (or ***luġet l-ᵊktaabe*).
frankly speaking - *b-kəll ṣaraaḥa.* Frankly speaking, I never liked that guy. *b-kəll ṣaraaḥa b-ḥayaati maa ḥabbeet haz-zalame.*
generally speaking - *Ɛal-ᵊƐmuum, bᵊl-ˀəžmaal.* Generally speaking, people were friendly. *Ɛal-ᵊƐmuum ᵊn-naas kaanu ˀaniisiin.*
strictly speaking - *Ɛala wažh˜ ᵊt-taḥdiid.* Strictly speaking, it is not the same. *Ɛala wažh ᵊt-taḥdiid muu nafs ᵊš-šii.*
to speak to - *ḥaka (i ḥaki) maƐ, ḥaaka.* May I speak to you? *məmken ˀəḥki maƐak* (or *ḥaakiik*)? — I'll speak to him about your application. *bḥaakii-lak-yəa b-ᵊxṣuuṣ ṭalabak.*
to speak up - 1. *Ɛalla ṣooṭo, rafaƐ (a rafᵊƐ) ṣooṭo.* Speak up! We can't hear you. *Ɛalli ṣooṭak! maa-lna Ɛam nəsmaƐak.* 2. *fataḥ (a ø) təmmo.* Why didn't you speak up? *leeš maa fataḥᵊt təmmak?*
to speak up for - *ḥaka (i ḥaki) la-ṣaaleḥ˜...* Nobody spoke up for him. *maa ḥada ḥaka la-ṣaalḥo.*

speaker - 1. *xaṭiib* pl. *xəṭaba.* He's an excellent speaker. *huwwe xaṭiib məmtaaz.* 2. *xaṭiibe* pl. *-aat.* She's an excellent speaker. *hiyye xaṭiibe məmtaaze.* 3. *mkabber˜* (pl. *-aat˜*) *ṣooṭ, həbbarloor* pl. *-aat.* The radio is equipped with two speakers. *r-raadyo mžahhaz b-ᵊmkabbreen ṣooṭ.*

spear - *rəmᵊḥ* pl. *rmaaḥ* and *rmuuḥ.*

special - 1. *xaaṣṣ, maxṣuuṣ.* I'm saving it for a special occasion. *ˀana mxalliiha la-mnaasabe xaaṣṣa.* 2. *xaaṣṣ.* That's a special case. *hal-qaḍiyye ˀəla waḍᵊƐ xaaṣṣ.* — Have you seen the special edition of the magazine? *šəft ᵊl-Ɛadad ᵊl-xaaṣṣ tabaƐ ᵊl-mažalle?* — I have to follow a special diet. *laazem ˀəttə́beƐ ḥəmye xaaṣṣa.* -- He's a special friend of ours. *huwwe sadiiq xaaṣṣ ˀəlna.*

special delivery - *məstaƐžal.* Mail this letter special delivery. *bƐaat hal-maktuub məstaƐžal.* — I received a special-delivery letter this morning. *stalamᵊt maktuub məstaƐžal ᵊl-yoom Ɛala bəkra.*

specialist - *ˀəxtiṣaaṣi** pl. *-iyyiin.*

specialization - 1. *taxaṣṣoṣ.* We live in an age of specialization. *nəḥna Ɛaayšiin ᵊb-Ɛaṣr ᵊt-taxaṣṣoṣ.* 2. *ˀəxtiṣaaṣ.* What's your field of specialization? *šuu ḥaqᵊl ᵊl-ˀəxtiṣaaṣ tabaƐak?*

to **specialize** - *txaṣṣaṣ.* What did you specialize in? *b-ˀeeš txaṣṣaṣᵊt?*
specialized - *ˀəxtiṣaaṣi**. He's an excellent physicist, but only in a narrow specialized field. *huwwe fiizyaaˀi məmtaaz, laaken bass ᵊb-ḥaqᵊl ˀəxtiṣaaṣi dayyeq.*

specialty - *ˀəxtiṣaaṣ* pl. *-aat.* Taboulé is their specialty. *t-tabbuule ˀəxtiṣaaṣon.* -- Children's diseases are his specialty. *ˀəxtiṣaaṣo ˀamraaḍ ᵊl-ˀaṭfaal.*

species - *žənᵊs* pl. *ˀažnaas, nooƐ* pl. *ˀanwaaƐ.*

specific - 1. *nooƐi*, žənsi**. Let us consider the specific differences between the dog and the wolf. *xalliina nəbḥas ᵊl-fawaareq ᵊn-nooƐiyye been ᵊl-kalb wᵊd-diib.* 2. *nooƐi**. The specific gravity of gold is 19.3. *s-səql ᵊn-nooƐi tabaƐ ᵊd-dahab təsaṭaƐš faaṣle tlaate.* 3. *mƐayyan.* Give me a specific example of what you have in mind. *Ɛaṭiini masal ᵊmƐayyan Ɛala halli b-fəkrak.*

specification - *taƐyiin* pl. *-aat.* Customs regulations require a specification of the contents. *ˀanəmt ᵊl-gəmrok btəṭṭallab taƐyiin ᵊl-məḥtawayaat.*
specifications - 1. *ˀawṣaaf* (pl.). The builder didn't follow the engineer's specifications. *l-banna maa ttabaƐ ᵊl-ˀawṣaaf tabaƐ l-ᵊmhandes.* 2. *šruuṭ* (pl.). Bids that do not comply with the ministry's specifications will be rejected. *btərtə́feḍ l-ᵊƐruuḍ yalli maa btəttə́feq ḥarfiyyan maƐ ᵊšruuṭ ᵊl wazaara.*

to **specify** - *xaṣṣaṣ, ḥaddad.* Specify your expenses below. *xaṣṣeṣ maṣariifak taḥᵊt.*

specimen - *Ɛaayne* pl. *-aat.* Bring a specimen of your urine along. *žəb-li Ɛaaynet boolak.*

spectacle - 1. *fərže* pl. *fəraž, mašhad* pl. *mašaahed.* I saw a most curious spectacle this morning. *šəfᵊt Ɛala bəkra fərže ktiir ġariibe.* 2. *manẓar, fərže.* He made a spectacle of himself at the party last night. *Ɛəmel ḥaalo manẓar qəddaam ᵊn-naas bᵊs-sahra leelt ᵊmbaareḥ.*

spectator - *mətfarrež* pl. *-iin, mšaahed* pl. *-iin.*

speculation - 1. *ˀəftiraaḍ* pl. *-aat.* All this speculation about a possible rapprochement is completely baseless. *kəll hal-ˀəftiraaḍ Ɛan taqaarob məḥtə́mal maa-lo ˀasaas ˀabadan.* 2. *mḍaarabe* pl. *-aat.* He made a fortune through speculation on the stock market. *Ɛəmel sarwe bl-ᵊmḍaarabaat bᵊs-suuq ᵊl-maaliyye.*

speculator - *mḍaareb* pl. *-iin.*

speech - 1. *nəṭᵊq.* He lost his speech after the accident. *faqad ᵊn-nəṭᵊq b-natiižt ᵊl-ḥaadse.* 2. *xiṭaab* pl. *-aat, xəṭbe* pl. *xəṭab, kəlme* pl. *-aat.* That was a very good speech. *haada kaan xiṭaab ᵊktiir ᵊmniiḥ.* 3. *kalaam.* Don't pay any attention to his pretty speeches. *laa taƐṭi baalak la-kalaamo ẓ-ẓariif.*

to be **speechless** - *xəres (a xaras), tbalkam.* He was speechless with fear. *xəres mən šəddet xoofo.*
to leave speechless - *xarras, balkam.* Such insolence leaves me speechless. *heek waqaaḥa bətxarrəsni.*
**He stared at me in speechless astonishment. *baḥlaq fiyyi w-mən dahᵊšto maa Ɛaad fii yəḥki.*

speed - *sərƐa.* The train was going at full speed. *t-treen kaan maaši b-ˀaqṣa sərᵊƐto.* — We are moving at a good speed now. *nəḥna maašyiin hallaq b-sərƐa mniiḥa.*
speed limit - *ˀaqṣa sərƐa, s-sərƐa l-qəṣwa.* The speed limit is thirty-five miles an hour. *ˀaqṣa sərƐa xamsə́a w-ᵊtlaatiin miil bᵊs-saaƐa.*
to put on speed - *šahhal, ˀasraƐ.* Let's put on a little speed. *xalliina nšahhəl-lna šwayye.*
to speed - *ˀasraƐ.* You're speeding now. *Ɛam təsreƐ hallaq.*
to speed up - *šahhal.* Can you speed things up a little? *fiik tšahhə́l-li l-qaḍiyye šwayye?*

speedometer - *kiilomətraaž* pl. *-aat.*

speedy - *Ɛaažel.* I wish you a speedy recovery. *bətmannə́a-lak šifa Ɛaažel.*
**Let's make a speedy trip downtown. *xalliina nənxə́ṭef Ɛal-balad.*

spell - *səḥᵊr.* She's completely under his spell. *hiyye ġarqaane b-səḥro Ɛat-tamaam.*

spell - 1. *noobe* pl. *-aat.* Does she often get spells like that? *btəžiiha noobaat ᵊktiir heek?* 2. *bərha* pl. *bərahaat, mədde* pl. *mədad.* He worked for a short spell. *štaġal bərha qaṣiire.*
cold spell - *moožet˜* (pl. *-aat˜* and *mwaaž˜*) *bard.* We had another cold spell early in spring. *ˀəžaana moožet bard kamaan ᵊb-ˀawwal ᵊr-rabiiƐ.*
hot spell - *šoobe* pl. *-aat, moožet˜* (pl. *-aat˜* and *mwaaž˜*) *ḥarr.* How long do you think this hot spell will last? *qaddeeš ᵊbtəƐtə́qed haš-šoobe bədda təbqa?*

to **spell** - *hažža.* Please spell your name. *Ɛmeel maƐruuf hažži ˀəsmak.* -- How do you spell that word? *kiif bəthažži hal-kəlme?*

to **spend** - **1.** *ṣaraf (o/e ṣarᵊf//nṣaraf).* We spent a lot of money. *ṣarafna koomet maṣaari.* **2.** *ṣaraf, ḥaṭṭ.* I can't spend any more time on this. *maa bəqder ʔəṣrof waqᵊt ʔaktar mən heek Ɛala haš-šağle.* **3.** *ṃaḍḍa, qaḍa (i s), qaḍḍa.* I'd like to spend my vacation here. *ḥaabeb ṃaḍḍi fərᵊṣti hoon.*

spent - *manhuuk.* When I come home in the evening I feel completely spent. *waqᵊt bəršaƐ Ɛal-beet ᵊl-masa bkuun manhuuk ləl-ʔaaxiir.*

sphere - **1.** *kəra* pl. *-aat.* The earth is not a perfect sphere. *l-ʔarḍ muu kəra Ɛat-tamaam.* **2.** *manṭiqa* pl. *manaaṭeq.* The coastal area used to be within the British sphere of influence. *l-manṭiqa s-saaḥliyye kaanet ḍəmᵊn manṭiqet ᵊn-nufuuz l-ᵊbriiṭaani.* **3.** *niṭaaq.* That's outside his sphere of activity. *haada xaareš niṭaaq našaato.*

spherical - *kərawi**. Spherical geometry. *handase kərawiyye.*

Sphinx - *ʔabu˜ l-hool.*

spice - *bhaar* pl. *-aat,* pl. *tawaabel.* Do you use spices much in your cooking? *bətḥəṭṭi bhaaraat ᵊktiir ᵊb-ṭabxek?*

to spice - *bahhar, tabbal.* The meat is highly spiced. *l-laḥme mbahhara ktiir.*

spicy - **1.** *mbahhar zyaade.* Spicy food doesn't agree with me. *l-ʔakl l-ᵊmbahhar zyaade maa biwaatiini.* **2.** *mfalfal ᵊmƐaṣfar.* He's always ready with a little spicy story. *daayman Ɛala raas ᵊlsaano ḥkaaye mfalfale mƐaṣfara* (or ***ḥkaaye kəlla fəlfol w-ᵊbhaar*).

spider - *Ɛankabuute* coll. *Ɛankabuut* pl. *-aat.*

to **spill** - **1.** *dalaq (o dalᵊq//ndalaq).* Who spilled the milk? *miin dalaq ᵊl-ḥaliib?* **2.** *kabb (ə kabb//nkabb), dalaq.* The waiter spilled soup on my dress. *l-garṣoon kabb šooraba Ɛala roobi.*

**There's no use crying over spilt milk. *ṃayye w-ᵊnsafḥet* or *yalli faat maat.*

to **spin** - **1.** *ġazal (o ġazᵊl//nġazal).* The thread is spun unevenly. *l-xeeṭ maġzuul muu bᵊt-tasaawi.* **2.** *daar (u dawaraan).* My head is spinning. *raasi Ɛam yduur.* **3.** *dawwar.* Spin the wheel once. *dawwer ᵊd-duulaab marra.*

to spin around - *dawwar.* He picked me up and spun me around. *rafaƐni w-dawwarni.*

**She spun around when she heard my voice. *ltaftet ᵊb-Ɛašale lamma səmƐet ṣooti.*

to spin out - *maṭmaṭ.* He can't tell a story without spinning it out indefinitely. *maa fii yəḥki qəṣṣa ʔəlla-ma ymaṭməṭa bala ʔaaxra.*

spinach - *sabaanex.*

spinal column - *Ɛaamuud faqari* pl. *Ɛawamiid faqariyye.*

spinal cord - *nəxaaƐ šawki.*

spindle - *maġzal* pl. *maġaazel.*

spine - (backbone) *səlsəlet˜* (pl. *salaasel˜*) *ḍahᵊr.*

spinning mill - *maġzal* pl. *maġaazel, maƐmal˜* (pl. *maƐaamel˜*) *ġazᵊl.*

spinning wheel - *duulaab˜* (pl. *dawaliib˜*) *ġazᵊl.*

spinster - *Ɛaanes* pl. *Ɛawaanes.*

spiny - *šawki**.

spiral - *ḥalazooni**. A spiral staircase leads to the top of the minaret. *fii daraš ḥalazooni biwaṣṣel la-raas ᵊl-maadne.*

spirit - **1.** *ruuḥ, rooḥ* pl. *(ʔa)rwaaḥ.* The spirit is willing, but the flesh is weak. *ʔammaa r-ruuḥ fa-mustaƐidd wa-ʔammaa l-šasad fa-ḍaƐiif.* -- The natives believe in evil spirits. *s-səkkaan ᵊl-maḥalliyiin biʔaamnu bᵊl-ʔarwaaḥ ᵊš-šarriire.* **2.** *qalb.* I was with you in spirit. *kənt maƐak bᵊl-qalb* (or *b-qalbi*). **3.** *nafsiyye.* That's the proper spirit! *hayy ᵊn-nafsiyye l-maṭbuuṭa!*

in good spirits - *mfarfeš.* I hope you're in good spirits. *nsaaḷḷa ʔənte mfarfeš?*

in high spirits - *mšaqreq.* She's in high spirits. *hiyye mšaqᵊrqa.*

in low spirits - *mfastek.* He seemed to be in low spirits. *baan Ɛaléé mfastek.*

spirit level - *zeebaq* pl. *-aat.*

spiritual - *ruuḥi**. There's a spiritual bond between them. *fii raabṭa ruuḥiyye beenaaton.*

spiritualism - *ʔəstəḥḍaar˜ ᵊl-ʔarwaaḥ.*

spit - *siix* pl. *syaax.* We need a few more spits for the meat. *laazəmna kamaan kam siix ləl-laḥme.*

spit - *bzaaq.* Let me wipe the spit off the baby's face. *xalliini ʔəmsaḥ l-ᵊbzaaq mən Ɛala wəšš ᵊl-beebée.*

to spit - *bazaq (o bazᵊq).* She spat in his face. *bazqet ᵊb-wəššo.*

spite - *nakaaye, šakar.* He did it just for spite. *saawaaha bass lən-nakaaye.*

in spite of - *bᵊr-raġᵊm mən* (or *Ɛan*). I went in spite of the rain. *rəḥᵊt bᵊr-raġᵊm mn ᵊl-maṭar.*

to spite - *šaakar.* Are you doing that just to spite me? *Ɛam taƐmel haš-šii bass la-ḥatta dšaakərni?*

spittle - *bzaaq.*

to **splash** - **1.** *ṭaraš (o ṭarᵊš), ṭarṭaš.* The water splashed in all directions. *l-ṃayy ṭaršet ᵊb-kəll ᵊš-šəhaat.* **2.** *ṭarṭaš.* The boy was splashing happily in the water. *l-walad kaan Ɛam yṭarṭeš bᵊl-ṃayy farḥaan.* **3.** *ṭarraš, ṭarwaš.* A car splashed me with mud. *fii sayyaara ṭarrašətni bᵊṭ-ṭiin.*

splendid - *faaxer, Ɛaẓiim.* That was a splendid idea! *hayy kaanet fəkra faaxra.*

splinter - **1.** *qašše* pl. *-aat.* I've got a splinter under my nail. *faatet qašše taḥᵊt ḍəfri.* **2.** *šaẓiyye* pl. *šaẓaaya.* You can still see the marks of bomb splinters on the walls. *ləssaak fiik ᵊtšuuf ʔaasaar šaẓaaya l-qanaabel Ɛal-ḥiiṭaan.*

to splinter - *ṭaḥmaš.* The board splintered when I hit it with the hammer. *l-looḥ ṭaḥmaš waqᵊt daqqeeto bᵊš-šaakuuš.*

split - **1.** *ʔənšiqaaq* pl. *-aat.* There was a split in the party. *ṣaar fii ʔənšiqaaq bᵊl-ḥəzᵊb.* **2.** *fətᵊq* pl. *ftuuqa.* You've got a split in your pants. *fii fətᵊq b-banṭaloonak.*

to split - **1.** *šaqq (ə šaqq//nšaqq).* The lightning split the tree from top to bottom. *s-saaƐqa šaqqet ᵊš-šašara mən fooq la-taḥᵊt.* **2.** *nšaqq, šaqq.* The table top has split in the middle. *ḍahr ᵊṭ-ṭaawle nšaqq bᵊn-nəṣṣ.* **3.** *nšaqq.* The party has split into three groups. *l-ḥəzb ᵊnšaqq la-tlatt fəraq.* **4.** *tqaasam.* They split the profit. *tqaasamu l-marbaḥ.* **5.** *qassam, qasam (e qəsᵊm// nqasam).* We split the profit three ways. *qassamna l-marbaḥ la-tlatt ḥəṣaṣ.* **6.** *nfataq.* Your pants have split at the seam. *banṭaloonak ᵊnfataq Ɛand l-ᵊxyaaṭa.*

**Now you're just splitting hairs. *hallaq badeet ᵊddaqqeq tadqiiqaat bala ṭaƐme.*

**I nearly split my sides laughing. *kənt laḥa ṭəqq mn ᵊḍ-ḍəḥᵊk.*

**I have a splitting headache. *Ɛandi wašaƐ raas bišannen.*

to split open - *nšaqq.* The ground split open and a jinni appeared. *l-ʔarḍ ᵊnšaqqet w-ṭaleƐ mənha šənni.*

to split up - **1.** *šaqqaf, qaṭṭaƐ.* Split up some wood. *šaqqéf-lak šwayyet ḥaṭab.* **2.** *nšaqq.* The party split up a year ago over internal differences. *l-ḥəzb ᵊnšaqq mən səne b-sabab xilaafaat daaxliyye.*

to **spoil** - **1.** *nazaƐ (a nazᵊƐ//ntazaƐ).* She's spoiled my whole fun. *nazƐét-li kəll maraaqi.* **2.** *ntazaƐ.* The apples are beginning to spoil. *t-təffaaḥaat Ɛam yəbdu yəntəzƐu.* **3.** *dallal, šaṭṭaṭ.* You're spoiling him. *Ɛam ᵊddallᵊlo.*

spoke - (metal) *siix* pl. *syaax,* (wood) *ʔəṣᵊbƐa* pl. *ʔaṣabiiƐ.* I put two new spokes in the front wheel. *ḥaṭṭeet siixeen ᵊšdaad bᵊd-duulaab ᵊl-qəddaamaani.*

spokesman - *naaṭeq* (pl. *-iin*) *b-ᵊlsaan˜..., mətḥaddes* (pl. *-iin*) *b-ᵊlsaan˜...* A spokesman of the Foreign Ministry declared that... *naaṭeq b-ᵊlsaan wazaart ᵊl-xaaršiyye ṣarraḥ ʔənno...*

sponge - *sfənše* coll. *sfənš* pl. *-aat.* Where did you buy that sponge? *mneen ᵊštareet has-sfənše?*

sponge diving - *ṣeed˜ ᵊsfənš.*

to sponge on - *ṭṭaffal Ɛala, ttaaqal Ɛala.* You've been sponging on him long enough. *ḥaaštak təṭṭaffal Ɛaléé.*

sponger - *ṭufayli* pl. *-iyye.*

sponsor - **1.** *kafiil* pl. *kəfala.* To join this club you must have a sponsor. *laazem ykən-lak kafiil la-təltəḥeq ᵊb-han-naadi.* **2.** *mumawwel* pl. *-iin.* They are looking for a sponsor for their TV show. *Ɛam ydawwru Ɛala mumawwel la-bərnaaməšon ᵊt-televəzyooni.* **3.** *šbiin* pl. *šabaayen.* One of my friends is going to be the baby's sponsor. *waaḥed mən rəfaqaati laḥ ykuun ᵊšbiin ᵊl-walad.*

to sponsor - *mawwal.* This program is sponsored by the Syrian Commercial Industrial Corporation. *hal-bərnaameš mawwaləto š-šərke l-xumaasiyye.*

spoon - *maƐlaqa* pl. *maƐaaleq.*

sport(s) - *spoor.* Do you go in for sports? *btəlƐab ᵊs-spoor?*

**Be a sport. *xalliik ᵊmsaayer.*

poor sport - *mḥayyeṣ* pl. *-iin.* Don't be a poor sport. *laa tkuun ᵊmḥayyeṣ.*

sportsman - *riyaaḍi* pl. *-iyyiin.*

spot - **1.** *laṭxa* pl. *-aat, bəqƐa* pl. *bəqaƐ.* You have a spot on your tie. *fii laṭxa b-ᵊkraaftak.* **2.** *maḥall* pl. *-aat, qərne* pl. *qaraani.* I stood on the same spot for a solid hour. *waqqaft saaƐa* *kaamle b-nafs ᵊl-maḥall.* -- He stood there as if rooted to the spot. *kaan waaqef ᵊhniik kaʔanno mbasmar ᵊb-ʔarᵊnto.* 3. *nəqṭa* pl. *nəqaṭ.* That's a sore spot with him. *hayy nəqṭa ḥassaase fii.* -- You've touched a sore spot. *daqarᵊt nəqṭa ḥassaase.* 4. *nətfe, nəqṭa, damɛa.* How about a spot of tea? *šuu raʔyak ᵊb-nətfet šaay?*

**A cup of coffee would just hit the spot. *fənžaan qahwe hallaq bikuun ᵊb-maḥallo ḥafr w-tanziil.*

on the spot - 1. *b-daqiiqə́ta.* They fired him on the spot. *qallaɛúu b-daqiiqə́ta.* 2. *ḥaaḍer.* I was right on the spot when it happened. *kənᵊt ḥaaḍer lamma ḥadset.* 3. *mətḥayyer.* Now I'm on the spot. *hallaq ʔana mətḥayyer.*

to put on the spot - *ɛallaq.* I'll ask him a question that's going to put him on the spot. *raḥa ʔəsʔalo suʔaal ɛallqo fii.* -- That kind of puts us on the spot as far as paying the installments is concerned. *haš-šii ɛallaqna b-ᵊxṣuuṣ dafᵊɛ l-ᵊqṣuuṭa.*

to spot - 1. *laqaṭ (o laqᵊṭ//ltaqaṭ).* I spotted him in the crowd. *laqaṭto mən been ᵊn-naas.* -- I could spot him anywhere. *bəḥsen ʔəlᵊqṭo ween-ma kaan.* 2. *faraq (e ø), kamaš (e kamᵊš//nkamaš), laqaṭ.* I spotted the mistake immediately. *faraqt ᵊl-ġalṭa ɛal-ḥaarek.*

spotted - *mnaqqaṭ, mlaṭṭaɛ.*

spout - *buuz* pl. *bwaaz, təmm* pl. *tmaam.* The spout of this teapot clogs up easily. *buuz hal-ʔəbriiq ᵊš-šaay byənsə́ṭem b-ᵊshuule.*

to spout - 1. *ddaffaq.* The water was spouting from the roof gutter. *l-mayye kaanet ɛam təddaffaq mn ᵊl-məzraab.* 2. *ṭaaleɛ.* The chimney spouted thick clouds of smoke. *l-madxane ṭaalɛet ᵊġyuum kasiife mn ᵊd-dəxxaan.*

to **sprain** - *fakaš (e fakᵊš//nfakaš).* She sprained her ankle. *fakšet kaaḥə́la* or *nfakaš kaaḥə́la.*

spray - 1. *baxxaaxa* pl. *-aat.* The paint is applied with a spray. *d-dhaan ɛam yḥaṭṭúu b-waaṣəṭṭ baxxaaxa.* 2. *sprée.* Can you recommend a good hair spray? *fiiki tənṣaḥiini b-ᵊspree mniiḥ?*

to spray - 1. *rašš (ə rašš//nrašš), baxx (ə baxx//nbaxx).* We have to spray the peach trees. *laazem ᵊnrašš šažaraat ᵊd-dərraaqen.* 2. *baxx.* Spray the paint as evenly as possible. *baxx ᵊd-dhaan bᵊt-tasaawi qadd-muu məmken.*

spread - *ʔəntišaar, sarayaan.* They tried to check the spread of the disease. *ḥaawalu ywaqqfu ʔəntišaar ᵊl-maraḍ.*

to spread - 1. *ḥaṭṭ (ə ḥaṭaṭ//nḥaṭṭ), faraš (o ø).* Spread some honey on the bread. *ḥəṭṭ-əllak (or frəš-lak) šwayyet ɛasal ɛal-xəbze.* -- Spread a piece of canvas over the crates. *frəš-lak šaqfet xaam ɛas-saḥaḥiir.* 2. *wazzaɛ//twazzaɛ.* The payments were spread over several years. *d-dafɛaat ᵊtwazzaɛet ɛala ɛəddet ᵊsniin.* 3. *našar (o našᵊr//ntašar), ballaġ//tballaġ.* My brother has run over to our neighbors to spread the good news. *ʔaxi rakad la-ɛand žiiraanna la-yənšor ᵊl-xabar l-ᵊmsərr.* 4. *baššar b-.* He wants to become a priest and spread the word of God. *biḥəbb yṣiir xuuri w-ybaššer b-kəlmet ʔaḷḷa.* 5. *ntašar.* The fire is spreading rapidly. *l-ḥariiqa ɛam təntə́šer b-sərɛa.* -- The news spread quickly. *l-xabar ᵊntašar b-sərɛa.*

to spread out - 1. *faraš (o farᵊš//nfaraš), fataḥ (a fatᵊḥ//nfataḥ).* Spread the map out. *frooš ᵊl-xariiṭa.* 2. *mtadd.* We saw the whole valley spread out below us. *šəfna l-waadi kəllo məmtadd taḥᵊtna.*

spring - 1. *rabiiɛ.* We arrived in spring. *wṣəlna bᵊr-rabiiɛ.* 2. *nabᵊɛ* pl. *nbuuɛa.* There's a spring behind our house. *fii nabᵊɛ b-qafa beetna.* 3. *zəmbə́rak* pl. *-aat, raṣṣoor* pl. *-aat.* The spring in my watch is broken. *zəmbə́rak saaɛti maksuur.* 4. *mqaṣṣ* pl. *-aat.* I'm afraid the car needs new springs. *xaayə́f-lak ᵊs-sayyaara laazə́ma mqaṣṣaat žədad.* 5. *raffaas* pl. *-aat.* Don't sit in that chair, its springs are coming out. *laa taqɛod ɛala hal-kəltoq; raffaasaato ɛam yəṭlaɛu.*

spring cleaning - *taɛziilet˜* (pl. *-aat˜*) *ṣeef.*

to spring - 1. *naṭṭ (ə naṭṭ), qafaz (e qafᵊz).* He sprang from his seat. *naṭṭ mən kərsíi.* 2. *nabaɛ (o nabᵊɛ).* All the rumors spring from one and the same source. *kəll ᵊl-ʔišaaɛaat btənboɛ mən nafs ᵊl-manbaɛ.* 3. *faažaʔ b-.* He sprang the news on us at dinner. *faažaʔna bᵊl-xabar ɛal-ɛaša.*

**New houses spring up like mushrooms. *byuut ᵊždiide ɛam təṭlaɛ mətl ᵊl-fəžᵊl.*

sprinkle - *nafnafe.* It didn't really rain, it was just a sprinkle. *maa nəzlet ᵊl-maṭar ᵊktiir, bass kaanet nafnafe.*

to sprinkle - *rašš (ə rašš//rtašš* and *nrašš).* Have the streets been sprinkled yet? *š-šawaareɛ ᵊrtaššu wəlla ləssa?* -- The lawn still has to be sprinkled. *l-ḥašiiš kamaan bəddo rašš.* -- Sprinkle the cake with sugar. *rəšš šwayyet səkkar ɛal-gaato* or *rəšš ᵊl-gaato b-šwayyet səkkar.*

sprinkler - *raššaaše* pl. *-aat.* Be sure to turn the sprinkler off when you go out in the garden. *laa tənsa maa tsakker ᵊr-raššaaše waqt ᵊbtəṭlaɛ ɛaž-žneene.*

spur - *məhmaaz* pl. *mahamiiz.* Don't use the spurs on that horse. *laa tədqor hal-ᵊḥṣaan ᵊb-məhmaazak.*

**He won his spurs as a research chemist by helping to develop a new plastic. *ḥəṣel ɛala markazo ka-baaḥes kiimaawi b-ᵊmsaahamto b-taṭwiir blaastiik ᵊždiid.*

on the spur of the moment - *ʔərtižaaliyyan, biduun tarawwi.* I made the decision on the spur of the moment. *ɛməlt ᵊl-qaraar ʔərtižaaliyyan.*

to spur on - *ḥass (e ø//nḥass), dafaɛ (a dafᵊɛ//ndafaɛ).* Maybe a reward would spur him on. *bižuuz šii mkaafáa tḥəsso.*

spy - *žaasuus* pl. *žawasiis, daasuus* pl. *dawasiis.* He was convicted as a foreign spy. *žarramúu b-koono žaasuus ʔažnabi.*

to spy on - *džassas ɛala.* I wish our neighbor would stop spying on us. *ya-reet žaarna ybaṭṭel yədžassas ɛaleena baqa.*

squabble - *mnaaqara* pl. *-aat.* What was that squabble all about? *ɛan šuu kaanet l-ᵊmnaaqara?*

to squabble - *tnaaqar.* I wish they would stop their silly squabbling. *ya-reeton ybaṭṭlu yətnaaqaru ɛaṭ-ṭaalɛa wᵊn-naazle.*

squad - 1. (military) *ḥaḍiira* pl. *ḥaḍaayer.* 2. (police) *fərqa* pl. *fəraq.*

squad car - *sayyaaret˜* (pl. *-aat˜*) *dooriyye.*

squadron - 1. (aviation) *sərᵊb* pl. *ʔasraab.* 2. (navy) *ʔəsṭool* pl. *ʔasaṭiil.*

square - 1. *saaḥa* pl.*-aat.* Our front windows look out on a large square. *šababiikna l-qəddaamaaniyye biṭəllu ɛala saaḥa kbiire.* 2. *mrabbaɛ* pl. *-aat.* That's not a square, that's a rectangle. *haada muu mrabbaɛ, məsṭaṭiil.* 3. *mrabbaɛ.* I'd like a square box. *bəddi sanduuq ᵊmrabbaɛ.* -- The rug is four meters square. *s-səžžaade ʔarbaɛ ᵊmtaar ᵊmrabbaɛa.* 4. *tarbiiɛi*.* The square root of nine is three. *ž-žazr ᵊt-tarbiiɛi tabaɛ təsɛa tlaate.* 5. *məḥtə́ram.* I haven't eaten a square meal in days. *maa ʔakalᵊt waqɛa məḥtə́rame mən ʔiyyaam.*

**He's a square fellow. *huwwe zalame ɛala salaamto.*

to square - 1. *sawwa//tsawwa.* This squares our accounts. *haada bisawwi ḥsaabaatna.* 2. *rabbaɛ.* Square the speed and divide the result by four. *rabbeɛ ᵊs-sərɛa w-qassem ᵊl-ḥaaṣel ɛala ʔarbɛa.*

squash - 1. (zucchini) *kuusaaye* coll. *kuusa* pl. *kuusaayaat.* 2. (large, gourd-like) *yaqṭiine* coll. *yaqṭiin* pl. *-aat.*

to **squash** - 1. *maɛas (a maɛᵊs//mmaɛas).* I squashed the cake. *maɛast ᵊl-gaato.* 2. *haras (o harᵊs//nharas).* I squashed my finger in the door. *harast ʔəṣbaɛti bᵊl-baab.*

to **squeal** - *zaqzaq.* The child squealed with joy. *ṭ-ṭəfᵊl zaqzaq mən faraḥo.*

squeamish - *msoodan.*

to **squeeze** - 1. *šadd (ə šadd//nšadd) ɛala, ɛaṣar (o ɛaṣᵊr//nɛaṣar).* Don't squeeze my hand so hard. *laa tšədd ɛala ʔiidi kəll hal-qadd.* 2. *ɛaṣar.* I'll squeeze the oranges. *ʔana bəɛṣor ᵊl-bərdqaanaat.* 3. *daḥaš (a daḥᵊš//ndaḥaš).* I can't squeeze another thing into my trunk. *maa fiyyi ʔədḥaš ʔayy šii taani b-sanduuqi.*

to squeeze out - *ɛaṣar (o ɛaṣᵊr//nɛaṣar).* Squeeze out the sponge. *ɛṣoor ᵊs-sfənže.*

squint - (strabismus) *ḥawal.*

squint-eyed - *ʔaḥwal* f. *ḥoola* pl. *ḥuul.*

squirrel - *sənžaabe* coll. *sənžaab* pl. *-aat.*

to **stab** - *ṭaɛan (a ṭaɛᵊn//nṭaɛan).* He was stabbed in the brawl. *nṭaɛan bᵊl-ᵊxnaaqa.* -- He's just waiting for a chance to stab me in the back. *bass ɛam yənṭə́zer fərṣa ḥatta yəṭɛanni mn ᵊl-xalf.* -- He was found stabbed to death. *laqúu maṭɛuun ṭaɛne qaatle.*

stability - *sabaat, ʔəstəqraar.* What the country needs is a period of economic stability. *halli laazem ləl-ᵊblaad bᵊl-ḥaqiiqa huwwe sabaat ʔəqtiṣaadi la-šii mədde.*

stable - *yaaxor* pl. *yawaxiir, ʔəsṭabᵊl* pl. *-aat.*

Where are the stables? *ween ᵊl-yawaxiir?*
stable - *məstaqərr, saabet.* They haven't had a stable government for years. *ṣar-lon ᵊsniin bala ḥkuume məstaqərra.* — A stable currency is absolutely necessary. *ʕəmle saabte ḥaaže laa bədd mənha.*
stack - *sətfe* pl. *sətaf.* I had to go through a whole stack of newspapers to find the article. *nžabarᵊt raažeʕ sətfe kaamle mn ᵊž-žaraayed ḥatta laqeet ᵊl-maqaale.*
to stack - *sattaf.* Stack these books somewhere on the floor. *sattə́f-li hal-kətᵊb b-šii qərne ʕal-ʔarḍ.*
stadium - *malʕab* pl. *malaaʕeb, staad* pl. *-aat.*
staff - 1. *mwaẓẓafiin* (pl.). He dismissed part of his staff. *qallaʕ baʕḍ ᵊmwaẓẓafiino.* 2. *heeʔet˜ ᵊmwaẓẓafiin.* She's not a member of the staff. *hiyye muu b-heeʔet l-ᵊmwaẓẓafiin.* 3. *ʔarkaan˜ ḥarb* (pl.). The general brought along his entire staff. *ž-ženeraal žaab kəll ʔarkaan ḥarbo.*
staff officer - *ẓaabeṭ˜* (pl. *ẓəbbaaṭ˜*)*ʔarkaan˜ ḥarb.*
stage - 1. *masraḥ* pl. *masaareḥ, marsaḥ* pl. *maraaseḥ.* Our theater has a modern stage. *t-tyaatro tabaʕna ʔəlo masraḥ ḥadiis.* 2. *marḥale* pl. *maraaḥel, ṭoor* pl. *ʔaṭwaar.* That depends on what stage the work is in. *haada byətwaqqaf ʕal-marḥale halli l-ʕamal fiiha.*
to stage - 1. *ʕaraḍ (o/e ʕarḍ//nʕaraḍ).* The play was good, but it was poorly staged. *t-tamsiiliyye kaanet ᵊmniiḥa, bass ʕarḍa kaan baṭṭaal.* 2. *saawa, ʔaḥya.* They staged a birthday party for him. *saawə́a-lo ḥafle la-ʕiid miilaado.*
to stagger - 1. *ṭṭarmax, trannaḥ.* I saw him stagger out of the bar. *šəfto ṭaaleʕ mn ᵊl-baar ʕam yəṭṭarmax.* 2. *ṭarmax.* The blow staggered him. *ḍ-ḍarbe ṭarmaxə́to.*
**The prices are staggering. *l-ʔasʕaar bəddawwex.*
stagnant - *raaked.*
stain - *bəqʕa* pl. *bəqaʕ, laṭxa* pl. *-aat* and *ləṭax,* (of food) *fəššaaye* pl. *fašaaši,* (of ink) *dabġa* pl. *-aat.* I can't get the stain out of my dress. *maa fiini qiim ᵊl-bəqʕa mən roobi.*
to stain - 1. *bardax.* I'm going to stain the bookcases. *bəddi bardex xazaayen ᵊl-kətᵊb.* 2. *baqqaʕ, laṭṭax, fašša, dabbaġ* (cf. **stain** n.). You've stained your vest. *baqqaʕᵊt ṣədriitak.* — The tablecloth is all stained. *ġaṭa ṭ-ṭaawle mfašša.*
staircase - *daraž* pl. *draaž.*
stairs - *daraž* pl. *draaž.* Take the stairs to your right. *ṭlaaʕ ʕad-daraž ʕala yamiinak.*
stairway - *daraž* pl. *draaž.*
stake - 1. *xaazuuq* pl. *xawaziiq.* You drive the stakes into the ground. *yaḷḷa ʔənte bəddəqq ᵊl-xawaziiq bᵊl-ʔarḍ.* 2. *rahᵊn* pl. *rhuune.* They doubled the stakes. *doobalu r-rhuune.*
**There's too much at stake. *fiiha ktiir ᵊmʔaayase.*
**His life is at stake. *ḥayaato b-mahabb ᵊr-ryaaḥ.*
**It's my money that is at stake, not yours. *maṣariyyi ʔana halli ʕam yətġaamar fiiha, muu maṣariik ʔənte.*
to stake - *žaazaf b-, xaaṭar b-.* It would be foolish to stake your reputation on such a project. *bətkuun žadbane mənnak ʔiza badžaazef b-səmᵊʕtak mənšaan heek mašruuʕ.*
stale - 1. *baayet.* Give that stale bread to the beggar. *ʕaṭi hal-xəbz ᵊl-baayet ləš-šaḥḥaad.* 2. *baayex.* I'm getting sick and tired of his stale jokes. *ʔana maalel mən nəkato l-baayxa.*
stalemate - 1. *maaneʕ.* If you move to that field, it'll be a stalemate. *ʔiza btətḥarrak la-hal-beet bišiir maaneʕ.* 2. *taʕaadol.* The two powers have reached a nuclear stalemate. *d-doolteen wəṣlu la-taʕaadol nawawi.*
stalk - *saaq* pl. *siiqaan.* The corn stalks grow as tall as seven feet. *siiqaan ᵊd-dəra byəṣal ṭuulon la-ḥadd sabʕ ᵊqdaam.*
to **stall** - 1. *nṭafa, ṭafa (i ṭafi).* The motor's stalled again. *l-motoor ᵊnṭafa marra taanye.* 2. *ṭafa (i ṭafi//nṭafa).* She stalls the engine at every intersection. *btəṭfi l-motoor b-kəll mafraq ṭəroq.* 3. *tharrab.* Come on, quit stalling, I want an answer. *yaḷḷa ḥaaštak tətharrab, bəddi žawaab.*
stallion - *faḥᵊl* pl. *fḥuul, ḥṣaan* pl. *ʔəḥᵊṣne.*
to **stammer** - 1. *taʔtaʔ, tlaʕsam.* He stammers when he's excited. *bitaʔteʔ lamma bikuun məthayyež.* 2. *tlažlaž.* She stammered an apology. *tlažlažet ᵊb-kəlmet ʔəʕtizaar.*

stamp - 1. *ṭaabeʕ* pl. *ṭawaabeʕ, buule* coll. *buul* pl. *-aat.* Five air-mail stamps, please. *xamᵊs ṭawaabeʕ bariid žawwi btaʕmel maʕruuf.* 2. *xətᵊm* pl. *xtuume, damġa* pl. *-aat.* Have you seen the ''received'' stamp somewhere around here? *šəft xətm ᵊl-waarde b-han-nawaaḥi?* 3. *kuboon* pl. *-aat.* Do they give stamps at that gas station? *byaʕṭu kuboonaat ᵊb-hal-ᵊmḥaṭṭet ᵊl-banziin?* 4. *ṭaabeʕ.* His latest book bears the stamp of his inimitable style. *ktaabo l-ʔaxiir byəḥmel ṭaabeʕ ʔəsluubo halli maa byətqallad.*
to stamp - 1. *xatam (o xatᵊm//nxatam), damaġ (a damᵊġ//ndamaġ).* Did you stamp the box ''fragile?'' *xatamt ᵊs-sanduuq "qaabil lil-kasr"?* -- I stamped all the documents. *xatamᵊt kəll ᵊl-wasaayeq.* 2. *dabak (o dabᵊk) b-.* She stamped her foot. *dabket ᵊb-rəžla.*
to stamp out - 1. *ṭafa (i ṭafi) b-rəžlée.* He stamped out the fire. *ṭafa n-naar ᵊb-rəžlée.* 2. *staʔṣal.* All opposition was ruthlessly stamped out. *staʔṣalu kəll ᵊmʕaaraḍa biduun raḥme w-laa šafaqa.*
stand - 1. *baṣṭa* pl. *-aat.* They have a stand on the market. *fii ʔəlon baṣṭa bᵊs-suuq.* 2. *kərsi˜* (pl. *karaasi˜*) *šhuud.* Will the witness take the stand, please. *byətfaḍḍal ᵊš-šaahed la-kərsi š-šhuud?* 3. *siibe* pl. *-aat* and *siyab.* I'm going to buy a stand for my camera. *laḥa ʔəštəri siibe mənšaan ᵊl-kdameera tabaʕi.* 4. *manṣab* pl. *manaaṣeb.* The vase would look nicer if it were on a stand. *l-vaaz byəṭlaʕ ʔaḥla law byənḥaṭṭ ʕala manṣab.* 5. *mawqef* pl. *mawaaqef.* There's a taxi stand at the corner. *fii mawqef taksi ʕas-suuke.* — He's changed his stand on this matter several times. *ġayyar mawᵊqfo mən hal-masʔale ʕəddet marraat.*
stands - *mdarraž* pl. *-aat.* We watched the race from the stands. *kənna ʕam ᵊnšaahed ᵊs-sbaaq mən l-ᵊmdarraž.*
to stand - 1. *waqqaf.* Don't let him stand outside. *laa txallīi ywaqqef barra.* -- Stand (right) where you are. *xalliik waqqef b-maḥallak.* -- Stand aside for a moment please. *waqqef ʕala žanab laḥẓa ʔiza bətriid.* — We can't stand aside when our country needs us. *maa mnəqder nwaqqef ʕala žanab lamma blaadna btəḥtdž-ᵊlna.* -- Stand it in the corner. *waqqə́fa bᵊz-zaawye.* 2. *ḥtamal, tḥammal, ḍaayan ʕala.* I can't stand it any longer there. *maa ʕaad fiyyi ʔəḥtə́mel hal-maḥall.* -- She can't stand the cold. *maa fiiha təḥtə́mel ᵊl-bard.* 3. *kaan qaayem, kaan naafez.* What I said the other day still stands. *halli qəlto hadaak ᵊl-yoom ləssa qaayem.*
**I want to know where I stand. *bəddi ʔaʕref ḥaali ween.*
**You can have it as it stands for 50 dollars. *fiik taaxə́da matᵊl-ma hiyye b-xamsiin dolaar.*
**As things stand, you haven't got a chance of winning. *ḥasab ᵊl-ʔawḍaaʕ ᵊl-ḥaaliyye maa fii ʕandak ʔayy ʔamal tərbaḥ.*
**He stands in good with the boss. *ʕalaaqto ṭayybe b-raʔiiso.*
to stand by - 1. *waqqaf ʕala žanab.* He stood by doing nothing. *waqqaf ʕala žanab maa ʕəmel šii.* 2. *waqqaf maʕ.* You know that I'll stand by you in case of trouble. *ʔənte btaʕref ʔənni bwaqqef maʕak ʔiza fii ʕandak mašaakel.* 3. *tmassak b-.* I stand by my decision. *ʔana mətmassek ᵊb-qaraari.* 4. *bəqi (a ø) ʕala.* You can count on him to stand by his word. *fii təʕtə́med ʕalée yəbqa ʕala kəlᵊmto.*
**The operator told me to stand by for a long-distance call. *ṣ-ṣanṭraal qal-li ʔənṭə́ẓer laʔənno fii mxaabara xaaržiyye žaaye.*
**Army units are standing by to deal with all emergencies. *wəḥdaat ᵊž-žeeš ʕala ʔəstəʕdaad la-mwaažahet kəll ᵊṭ-ṭawaareʔ.*
to stand for - 1. *naaṣar, ʕaaḍad, daafaʕ ʕan.* He stands for equality. *binaaṣer mabda l-ᵊmsaawaat.* 2. *qaam (u ø) ʕawaaḍ˜.* P.O.B. stands for ''post office box''. *ṣaad bee bətqum ʕawaaḍ "sanduuq bariid".* 3. *haḍam (o ø).* I won't stand for that! *maa bəhḍom haš-šii!*
to stand on - *ṣarr (ə ʔəṣraar) ʕala.* I stand on my rights. *ʔana bṣərr ʕala ḥquuqi.*
to stand on end - 1. *waqqaf.* My hair stood on end. *waqqaf šaʕᵊr raasi.* 2. *waqqaf ... ʕala ʕarḍo.* Stand the crate on end in the corner. *waqqef ᵊs-saḥḥaara ʕala ʕarḍa bᵊl-qərne.*
to stand out - 1. *žalab (e/o ø) ᵊn-naẓar, lafat (e/o) ᵊn-naẓar.* She stands out in a crowd. *btəžleb*

ᵊn-naẓar w-law kaanet been miit ẓulume. 2. barraz, baddaᶜ. He stands out in physics. ᶜam ybarrez bᵊl-fiizya. 3. ẓahar (a ẓhuur), bayyan. Underline all proper names so they stand out from the rest of the text. ḥaṭṭ xaṭṭ taḥᵊt kəll ʔasmaaʔ ᵊl-ᶜalam ḥatta yəẓharu mən baqiit ᵊn-naṣṣ.

to stand up - 1. waqqaf. Don't bother standing up. laa tġalleb ḥaalak ᵊtwaqqef. 2. ḍaayan ᶜala. Do you think these shoes will stand up under hard wear? bədzənn ʔənno haṣ-ṣabbaaṭ biḍaayen ᶜal-ʔəstəᶜmaal ᵊt-tqiil? 3. baᶜaṣ (a baᶜᵊṣ//nbaᶜaṣ). She stood me up at the last minute. baᶜṣətni b-ʔaaxer daqiiqa.

to stand up for - daafaᶜ ᶜan, ᶜaaḍad, ḥaama ᶜan. If we don't stand up for him, nobody will. ʔiza nəḥna maa daafaᶜna ᶜanno maa ḥada bidaafeᶜ ᶜanno.

to stand up to - rafaᶜ (a ø) ṣooṭo qəddaam˜. Why don't you stand up to your boss once in a while? leeš maa btərfaᶜ ṣooṭak qəddaam raʔiisak mən marra la-marra?

standard - 1. maᶜyaar pl. maᶜayiir, maqyaas pl. maqayiis. You can't judge him by ordinary standards. maa btəqder təḥkom ᶜalée b-məᶜyaar ᶜaadi. -- Their standards are very high. maᶜayiiron ktiir ᶜaalye. 2. ᶜaadi*. We carry all standard sizes. ᶜanna kəll l-ᵊqyaasaat ᵊl-ᶜaadiyye.

standard of living - məstawa˜ (pl. məstawayaat˜) l-maᶜiiše. Their standard of living is lower than ours. məstawa maᶜiišə́ton ʔawṭa mən tabaᶜna.

standing - 1. maq̈aam pl. -aat. He has a high standing in the community. ʔəlo maq̈aam marmuuq̈ b-maḥallto. 2. raaked. It's standing water. hayy ṃayye raakde. 3. saari. It'll remain a standing offer for ten days. byəbqa ᶜarḍ saari ᶜašᵊrt iyyaam. 4. daaʔem. The country can't afford a standing army. l-ᵊblaad maa btətḥammal žeeš daaʔem.

**They have only standing room left. maa fii ᶜandon ġeer maḥallaat ᶜal-waaqef.

of long standing - mən qadiim, mən zamaan, mən ᶜahd ᵊbᶜiid. They are friends of long standing. ṣar-lon ᵊṣḥaab mən qadiim.

standpoint - wəžhet˜ (pl. -aat˜) ṇaẓar.

to come to a **standstill** - twaqqaf, waqqaf, tᶜaṭṭal. All operations came to a standstill. kəll ᵊl-ᶜamaliyyaat ᵊtwaqqafet.

star - 1. nažme pl. nžuum. The sky is full of stars. s-sama malaane nžuum. 2. nažᵊm f. nažme pl. nžuum. She's a famous movie star. hiyye nažme siinamaaʔiyye mašhuura.

**He's my star pupil. huwwe ʔalmaᶜ talamiizi.

**You can thank your lucky stars that it wasn't worse. škoor ṛabbak halli maa kaanet ʔalᶜan mən heek.

starch - naša. Mix some starch for the shirts. xlaṭ-li šwayyet naša ləl-qəmṣaan.

to starch - našša. Did you starch the shirts? naššeeti l-qəmṣaan?

starchy - našawi*. Starchy food doesn't agree with me. l-ʔakl ᵊn-našawi maa biwaatiini or **n-naša-wiyyaat maa biwaatuuni.

to **stare** - baḥlaq. He just stared into space. maa saawa šii ʔəlla baḥlaq bᵊs-sama. -- She stared at me. baḥlaqet fiyyi.

starling - zarzuur pl. zaraziir.

start - 1. bdaaye pl. -aat, badye pl. -aat. We got off to a bad start. badeena bdaaye ᶜaaṭle. 2. ʔawwal, bdaaye. I read the book from start to finish in one day. qareet l-ᵊktaab mən ʔawwalo la-ʔaaxro (or mən ᵊbdaayto la-nihaayto) b-fard yoom.

to give someone a start - naqqaz ḥada. You gave me quite a start. waḷḷaahi naqqazᵊtni.

**It was his father who gave him a start in the company. kaan ʔabúu yalli fatáḥ-lo ṭ-ṭariiq bᵊš-šərke.

to start - 1. bada and bədi (a bdaaye, badye), ballaš. The concert has just started. l-konseer hallaq bada. — How did the fire start? kiif ᵊl-ḥariiqa badet? — At the corner the car started to skid. ᶜand ᵊs-suuke s-sayyaara badet təẓḥaṭ. 2. tḥarrak. The train started slowly. t-treen ᵊtḥarrak ᶜala mahlo. 3. mašša, šaġġal. Start the motor. mašši l-motoor. 4. šaᶜᶜal. Let's start a fire. xalliina nšaᶜᶜel ṇaaṛ. 5. ṭaalaᶜ, ṭaleᶜ (a ø) b-. Who started this rumor? miin ṭaalaᶜ hal-ʔišaaᶜa?

**Leave it to me, I'll start the ball rolling. trək-li-yáaha, ʔana bmaššiiha.

starting - mən ... w-ṭaaleᶜ, mən ... w-raayeḥ, ʔəbtidaaʔan mən. Starting today the bus will stop here. mn ᵊl-yoom w-ṭaaleᶜ ᵊl-baaṣ biwaqqef hoon.

to start out - 1. bada and bədi (a bdaaye, badye), ballaš. He started out at a good pace. bada b-sərᶜa laa baʔᵊs fiiha. 2. tarak (o/e tarᵊk), məši (i məši). They started out bright and early in the morning. taraku ṣ-ṣəbᵊḥ bakkiir.

to start (up) - mašša, šaġġal. Start up this machine! maššíi-li hal-maakiina!

starter - marš pl. -aat. Something's wrong with the starter of my car. fii šii manzuuᶜ ᵊb-marš sayyaarti.

to **startle** - naqqaz. The noise startled me. l-ḥəss naqqazni.

to be startled - naqaz (o naqᵊz). I was startled by the shot. naqazt mən ṭalqet ᵊṛ-ṛṣaaṣ.

starvation - žuuᶜ.

to **starve** - žaaᶜ (u žuuᶜ). Thousands of people starved during the war. ʔaalaaf mn ᵊn-naas žaaᶜu waqt ᵊl-ḥarᵊb. -- We didn't starve. maa žəᶜna.

starved - mayyet mn ᵊž-žuuᶜ, halkaan mn ᵊž-žuuᶜ. When are we going to eat? I'm starved. ʔeemta laḥa naakol? ʔana mayyet mn ᵊž-žuuᶜ.

to starve out - žawwaᶜ, mawwat žuuᶜ. They wanted to starve us out. raadu yžawwᶜuuna (or ymawwtuuna žuuᶜ).

to starve to death - 1. həlek (a halaak) mn ᵊž-žuuᶜ, maat (u moot) mn ᵊž-žuuᶜ. They almost starved to death. kaanu laḥa yəhláku mn ᵊž-žuuᶜ. 2. žawwaᶜ ləl-moot. The enemy conquered the fortress after having starved the defenders to death. l-ᶜaduww fataḥ ᵊl-qalᶜa baᶜᵊd-ma žawwaᶜ l-ᵊmdaafᶜiin ᶜanna ləl-moot.

state - 1. wilaaye pl. -aat. Alaska is the largest state in the U.S.A. ʔalaaska ʔakbar wilaaye bᵊl-wilaayaat ᵊl-məttáḥide. 2. doole pl. duwal. The railroads are owned by the state. s-səkak ᵊl-ḥadiidiyye məlk ᵊd-doole. 3. ḥaale pl. -aat, waḍᵊᶜ pl. ʔawḍaaᶜ. I'm in a very bad state. ʔana b-ḥaale malᶜuune ᶜan ḥaqa. 4. ḥkuumi*. It's a state institution. hayy ᵊmʔassase ḥkuumiyye.

state of affairs (or **things**) - ʔawḍaaᶜ (pl.). Anything is better than the present state of affairs. ḥayaḷḷa šii bikuun ʔaḥsan mn ᵊl-ʔawḍaaᶜ ᵊl-ḥaaḍra.

to state - 1. zakar (o zəkᵊr//nzakar). You just stated that you were not there. ləssa hallaq zakart ʔənnak maa kənt ᵊhniik. 2. šaraḥ (a šarᵊḥ//nšaraḥ), fannad//tfannad. I thought he stated it plainly. ẓanneet ʔənno šaráḥa b-ᵊwḍuuḥ.

statement - 1. taṣriiḥ pl. -aat, bayaan pl. -aat. His statements are not to be trusted. taṣriiḥaato maa byənwə́seq fiiha. 2. kašf˜ ᵊḥsaab pl. kšuuf˜ ᵊḥsaabaat. My bank sends me a statement every month. l-ḅaṇk tabaᶜi byəbᶜə́t-li kašf ᵊḥsaab kəll šahᵊr.

statesman - ražol˜ (pl. rižaal˜) doole.

static - paraziit. There's so much static I can't get a single station. fii paraziit la-daraže ʔənno maa bəqder žiib w-laa mḥaṭṭa.

station - mḥaṭṭa pl. -aat. Get off at the next station. nzeel bᵊl-ᵊmḥaṭṭa ž-žaaye. -- What stations can you get on your radio? šuu l-ᵊmḥaṭṭaat halli bədžiiba bᵊr-raadyo tabaᶜak? -- I'll wait for you in front of the main station. bəstannaak qəddaam l-ᵊmḥaṭṭa ᵊr-raʔiisiyye.

to station - waqqaf, ḥaṭṭ (ə ḥaṭaṭ). The police stationed a man at the door. š-šərṭa waqqafet šərṭi qəddaam ᵊl-baab.

stationed - mraabeṭ. The troops stationed along the northern border are being reinforced. ž-žnuud l-ᵊmraabṭiin ᶜala ṭuul l-ᵊḥduud ᵊš-šmaaliyye ᶜam tətᶜazzaz.

stationery - 1. qərṭaaṣiyye. You can get these pencils at the stationery store. fiik ᵊtlaaqi hal-ᵊqlaam ᵊb-maxzan ᵊl-qərṭaaṣiyye. 2. waraq, waraq˜ ᵊktaabe. Could I borrow some air-mail stationery? məmken ʔəstᶜiir šwayyet waraq bariid žawwi?

statue - təmsaal pl. tamasiil.

status - 1. maq̈aam. It's all a matter of social status. kəll ᵊl-qəṣṣa qəṣṣet maq̈aam ʔəžtimaaᶜi. 2. waḍᵊᶜ. What's your marital status? šuu waḍᶜak ᵊz-zawži?

stay - ʔiq̈aame pl. -aat, qaᶜde pl. -aat. Our stay in the mountains was very pleasant. ʔiq̈aamətna bᵊž-žbaal kaanet ᵊktiir ᵊmsərra.

to stay - baqi (a ø), qaᶜad (o qaᶜde), tamm (a ø) ḍall (a ø). How long will you stay? qaddeeš laḥa təbqa? -- I stayed there several months. bqiit ᵊhniik kam šahᵊr. -- Our boy had to stay after school. ʔəbᵊnna nžabar yəbqa bᵊl-madrase baᶜd ᵊd-druus. -- He has to stay in bed. laazem

yəbqa bᵊl-farše.
to stay at - *nəzel (e nzuul, nazle) b-.* Are you staying at the hotel? *ʔənte naazel bᵊl-ʔoteel?*
to stay away - **1.** *ġaab (i ġyaab, ġeebe).* You've stayed away a long time. *ġəbᵊt mədde ṭawiile yaa!* **2.** *baʕʕad.* Stay away from that man. *baʕʕed ʕan har-rəžžaal.*

to stay up - *bəqi (a ø) sahraan.* Our children stay up until nine o'clock. *wlaadna byəbqu sahraaniin ləs-saaʕa təsʕa.*
to stay with - *nəzel (e nzuul, nazle) ʕand.* Are you staying with friends? *ʔənte naazel ʕand šii ṣḥaab?*
steady - **1.** *saabet.* This needs a steady hand. *haš-šii bəddo ʔiid saabte.* — The ladder isn't steady. *s-səllom muu saabet.* **2.** *saabet, daayem.* I'm looking for steady work. *ʕam dawwer ʕala šaġle saabte.* **3.** *daayem.* He's one of our steady customers. *huwwe waaḥed mən zabayiinna d-daaymiin.* **4.** *mətwaaṣel.* We kept up a good steady pace. *ḥaafazna ʕala sərʕa mətwaaṣle laa baʔᵊs fiiha.* — He's made steady progress. *tqaddam taqaddom mətwaaṣel.*
steak - *bəfteek.*
to **steal** - *saraq (o sərqa//nsaraq).* They stole all my money. *saraqúu-li kəll maṣaariyyi.*
to steal away - *ẓamaṭ (o ẓamᵊṭ).* We stole away in the middle of the party. *ẓamaṭna b-nəṣṣ ᵊl-ḥafle.*
steam - **1.** *buxaar.* The laundry is always full of steam. *l-maṣbuġa daayman ʕaayme bᵊl-buxaar.* — We have steam heat at home. *t-tədfaaye ʕanna bᵊl-beet ʕal-buxaar.* **2.** *buxaari*.* Steam engine. *ʔaale buxaariyye.*
**You'll have to get up some steam if you want to get done. *laazem ᵊtḥəṭṭ šwayyet žahᵊd ʔiza bəddak təxloṣ.*
to let off steam - *fašš (ə fašš//nfašš) xəlqo.* Don't mind him, he's just letting off steam. *laa ykən-lak fəkre, ʕam yfəšš xəlqo bass.*
to steam - **1.** *tbaxxar.* The kettle is steaming. *l-ʔəbriiq ʕam yətbaxxar.* **2.** *habbal.* I prefer to steam my vegetables. *bfaḍḍel habbel ᵊl-xəḍar tabaʕaati.*
steamer - *baaxra* pl. *bawaaxer.* The steamer sails at ten o'clock. *l-baaxra btəmši s-saaʕa ʕašara.*
steamroller - *madḥale* pl. *madaaḥel.*
steel - *buulaad.* The bridge is built entirely of steel. *ž-žəsᵊr məbni kəllo mən buulaad.* — The steel mill shut down because of the strike. *maṣnaʕ ᵊl-buulaad sakkar ᵊb-sabab ᵊl-ʔəḍraab.*
steelyard - *qabbaan ruumaani* pl. *qabbaanaat ruumaaniyye.*
steep - **1.** *waaqef.* Be careful, the stairs are steep. *ntəbeh, ᵊd-daraž waaqef.* **2.** *ʕaali.* The price is too steep for me. *s-səʕᵊr ʕaali ktiir ʕaliyyi.*
to **steep** - *ḥall (ə ḥall//nḥall).* Let the tea steep a little longer. *xalli š-šaay yḥəll kamaan šwayye.*
steeple - *bərž* pl. *ʔabraaž* and *bruuž(e).* The steeples of the church are visible from afar. *ʔabraaž l-ᵊkniise bibayynu mən ʕala bəʕᵊd.*
steer - *toor məxṣi* pl. *twaar məxṣiyye.* There are about a hundred steers in the herd. *fii ḥawaali miit toor məxṣi bᵊl-qaṭiiʕ.*
to **steer** - **1.** *waǧǧah.* Steer the boat to shore. *waǧǧeh ᵊl-markab ləš-šaṭṭ.* **2.** *ẓabbaṭ b-.* I can steer a car, but I don't know how to shift gears. *baʕref ẓabbeṭ bᵊs-sayyaara, bass maa baʕref ġayyer.*
to steer clear of - *tḥaaša.* You'd better steer clear of that fellow! *ʔaḥsdn-lak tətḥaaša haz-zalame.*
steering wheel - *dərkəsyoon* pl. *-aat.*
stem - **1.** *ʕərᵊq* pl. *ʕruuq(a).* Don't cut the stems too short. *laa tqəṣṣ l-ᵊʕruuqa qṣaar.* **2.** *ʕənᵊq* pl. *ʕnaaq.* Watch out, don't break the stem of the glass. *ʔəṣḥak takser ʕənq ᵊl-kaase.*
stenographer - *məxtəzel* pl. *-iin.*
stenography - *ʔəxtizaal.*
step - **1.** *daraže* pl. *-aat.* The steps are carpeted. *d-daražaat mġaṭṭaayiin bᵊs-səǧǧaad.* **2.** *xaṭwe* pl. *-aat.* He took one step forward. *ʔaxad xaṭwe la-qəddaam.* **3.** *tadbiir* pl. *-aat* and *tadabiir.* We'll take the necessary steps in this matter. *laḥa naaxod ᵊt-tadbiiraat ᵊl-laazme b-hal-qaḍiyye.*
**You're out of step again. *šaʕak ᵊmxarbeṭ marra taanye.*
**He's out of step with the times. *maa bisaayer ᵊl-waqᵊt.*
**Watch your step! *ʔoʕak!*
step by step - *daraže daraže, xaṭwe xaṭwe.* We built up our business step by step. *baneena šəġᵊlna daraže daraže.*
to step - **1.** *waqqaf.* Perhaps if you step on a chair you might be able to reach it. *barki ʔiza waqqafᵊt ʕal-kərsi fiik təṭdla.* **2.** *daʕas (a daʕᵊs).* I stepped into a puddle. *daʕasᵊt bᵊl-waḥᵊl.* **3.** *faat (u foote).* I saw him step into the store. *šəfto faayet ʕal-maxzan.*
**Step lively! *yaḷḷa ḥrook!*
to step aside - *raaḥ (u ø) ʕala žanab.* Step aside! *ruuḥ ʕala žanab!*
to step back - *rəžeʕ (a ø) la-wara.* Step back a bit. *ržaaʕ la-wara šwayye.*
to step forward - *qaddam.* Will all volunteers step forward please. *kəll yalli bəddon yəṭṭawwaʕu yətfaḍḍalu yqaddmu.*
to step in - **1.** *faat (u foote) la-žuwwa.* They just stepped in for a moment. *faatu la-žuwwa bass lahẓa.* **2.** *ddaaxal.* The President himself may have to step in. *bižuuz ᵊr-raʔiis nafso yəḍṭarr yəddaaxal.*
to step off - *nəzel (e nzuul, nazle) mən.* He just stepped off the train. *hallaq nəzel mn ᵊt-treen.*
to step over - **1.** *ntaqal.* Step over to the other side please. *ntəqel ʕaž-žanab ᵊt-taani mən faḍlak.* **2.** *džaawaz, tʕadda.* Don't step over this line. *laa tədžaawaz hal-xaṭṭ.*
to step out - *xaṭa (i xaṭwe) la-barra.* No one is allowed to step out. *maa ḥada masmᵊḥ-lo yəxṭi la-barra.*
to step up - **1.** *zaad (i zyaade//nzaad).* We'll have to step up the pace a bit. *laazem ᵊnziid ᵊs-sərʕa šwayye.* **2.** *tqaddam.* A strange man stepped up to me on the street. *šaxᵊṣ ġariib tqaddam mənni bᵊš-šaareʕ.*
stepbrother - *ʔaxx* (pl. *ʔəxwaat*) *mn ᵊl-ʔabb* or *mn ᵊl-ʔəmm* respectively. My stepbrother lives in Aleppo. *ʔaxi mən ʔabi saaken ᵊb-ḥalab.*
stepdaughter - *bənt˜* (pl. *banaat˜*) *ᵊz-zoož* or *ᵊz-zoože* respectively. Her stepdaughter is married to an American. *bənt zooža mədžawwze ʔameerkaani.*
stepfather - *žooz˜* (pl. *žwaaz˜*) *ᵊl-ʔəmm,* sometimes only *ʕamm* pl. *ʕmuum(e)* and *ʕmaam.* His stepfather died a year ago. *žooz ʔəmmo maat mən səne.*
stepmother - *maret˜* (pl. *nəswaan˜*) *ᵊl-ʔabb,* sometimes only *xaale* pl. *-aat.* Our stepmother is much younger than our father. *mart ʔabuuna ʔaẓġar b-ᵊktiir mən ʔabuuna.*
stepsister - *ʔəxt* (pl. *ʔəxwaat*) *mn ᵊl-ʔabb* or *mn ᵊl-ʔəmm* respectively. Does your stepsister go to the same school you go to? *ʔəxtak mən ʔabuuk bətruuḥ ʕala nafs ᵊl-madrase yalli bətrᵊḥ-la ʔənte?*
stepson - *ʔəbn˜* (pl. *wlaad˜*) *ᵊz-zoož* or *ᵊz-zoože* respectively. Her stepson studies medicine at A.U.B. *ʔəbᵊn zooža ʕam yədros ṭəbb bᵊž-žaamʕa l-ʔameerkiyye b-beeruut.*
sterile - **1.** *qaaḥel, maaḥel, məždeb.* Most of the land is sterile. *ʔaktar ᵊl-ʔarḍ qaaḥle.* **2.** *ʕaaqer.* The doctor's examination showed that he's sterile. *faḥṣ ᵊṭ-ṭabiib ʔaẓhar ʔənno huwwe ʕaaqer.* **3.** *ʕaqiim.* The article is a hodgepodge of sterile ideas. *l-maqaale xalṭ balṭ kəlla ʔafkaar ʕaqiime.*
sterility - *qaḥᵊl, maḥᵊl, ʕəqᵊr, ʕəqᵊm* (cf. **sterile**).
to **sterilize** - *ʕaqqam.* Have you sterilized the instruments yet? *ʕaqqamt ᵊl-ʔadawaat walla ləssa?*
sterilizer - *mʕaqqem* pl. *-aat.*
sterling - **1.** *starliini*.* How much is the pound sterling? *qaddeeša l-leera s-starliiniyye?* **2.** *ṣaafi, xaaleṣ.* That's sterling silver. *haada fəḍḍa ṣaafye.*
stern - **1.** *qaasi.* We have a very stern teacher. *fii ʕanna mʕallem qaasi ktiir.* — His boss gave him a stern look. *raʔiiso ṭṭallaʕ ʕalée taṭliiʕa qaasye.* **2.** *ṣaarem.* He takes a stern view of the whole affair. *byaaxod mawqef ṣaarem mən haš-šaġle.*
stern - *mᵊʔaxxara* pl. *-aat.* The stern of the ship was slightly damaged. *mᵊʔaxxart ᵊs-safiine ṣaaba ḍarar baṣiiṭ.*
stethoscope - *sammaaʕa* pl. *-aat.*
stew - *mnazzale* pl. *-aat.* Who wants a second helping of stew? *miin bəddo ṣaḥn ᵊmnazzale taani?*
**He's in a stew again. *huwwe maḍṭéreb mn ᵊždiid.*
to stew - *ṭabax (o ṭabᵊx//nṭabax).* Shall I stew the chicken or roast it? *ʔəṭbox ᵊž-žaaže wəlla ḥammára?*

steward - **1.** (ship) *garṣoon* pl. *-aat* and *garaṣiin.* **2.** (airline) *mḍiif* pl. *-iin.*
stewardess - *mḍiife* pl. *-aat.*
stick - **1.** *ʕaṣaaye* pl. *-aat* and *ʕəṣi,* (smaller)

qaḍiib pl. *qəḍbaan*. He hit me with a stick. *ḍarabni b-ƐaṣAaye*. 2. *Ɛuude* pl. *Ɛiidaan*. Put a few more sticks on the fire. *ḥəṭṭ-əllak kam Ɛuude kamaan bᵊn-naar*.

**You can tell right away that he's from the sticks. *fiik təqᵊfro ḥaalan ʔənno žaaye mn ᵊš-šool*.

to stick - 1. *šakk (ə šakk)*, *šakwak*. Something is sticking me. *fii šii Ɛam yšəkkni*. 2. *šakk*. I stuck my finger. *šakkeet ʔəṣbaƐṭi*. 3. *lazaq (o lazᵊq//nlazaq)*. Don't forget to stick a stamp on the envelope. *laa tənsa maa təlzoq buule Ɛaẓ-ẓarf*. 4. *ḥaṭṭ (ə ḥaṭaṭ//nḥaṭṭ)*. Just stick it in your pocket. *bass ḥəṭṭa b-žeebtak*. 5. *ləzeq (a ø)*. This stamp doesn't stick. *haṭ-ṭaabeƐ maa-lo Ɛam yəlzaq*. 6. *Ɛəleq (a ø)*. The door always sticks in damp weather. *l-baab daayman byəƐlaq bᵊr-rṭuube*. -- Nothing sticks in his mind. *maa fii šii byəƐlaq ᵊb-zəhno*.

**Stick around while I finish my work. *xalliik ᵊb-han-nawaaḥi been-ma xalleṣ šəğli*.

stuck - *Ɛalqaan*. Now I'm stuck. *hallaq ʔana Ɛalqaan*.

to get stuck - 1. *Ɛəleq (a ø)*. My car got stuck in the mud. *sayyaarti Ɛəlqet bᵊṭ-ṭiin*. -- Everything was going smoothly, but then we got stuck. *kəll šii kaan maaši mətl ᵊs-samne wᵊl-Ɛasal, bass baƐdeen ᵊƐləqna*. 2. *rookab*, *Ɛəleq*. One of the typewriter keys got stuck again. *fii məftaaḥ mən mafatiiḥ ᵊl-maakiina rookab taani marra*. 3. *txoozaq*. He got stuck with that car. *txoozaq ᵊb-has-sayyaara*.

to stick by - 1. *tmassak b-*. He'll always stick by his principles. *daayman byətmassak ᵊb-mabaadʔo*. 2. *saanad*, *ṣaff (ə ø) maƐ*. He's a man who'll always stick by his friends. *huwwe rəžžaal daayman bisaaned ᵊṣḥaabo*.

to stick it out - 1. *tḥammāl(h)a*. Try and stick it out a little longer. *žarreb tətḥammə́la kamaan šwayye*. 2. *saabar*. He encouraged me to stick it out. *šažžaƐni saaber*.

to stick one's nose into - *ddaaxal b-*, *daxxal ḥaalo b-*. He sticks his nose into everything. *byəddaaxal ᵊb-kəll šii*. -- Don't stick your nose into other people's business. *laa ddaxxel ḥaalak b-ᵊšʔuun ğeerak*.

to stick out - 1. *baraz (o bruuz)*. Watch out! There's a nail sticking out over there. *ʔoƐak! fii bəsmaar baarez ᵊhniik*. 2. *ṭaalaƐ*. If you stick out your tongue once more I'll spank you. *ʔiza bəṭṭaaleƐ lsaanak taani marra bṭaƐmiik qatle*.

to stick out one's neck - *xarbaq ḥaalo*. Why should I stick my neck out and take the rap? *leeš ḥatta xarbeq ḥaali w-ʔaakə́la?*

to stick to - 1. *tmassak b-*, *tšabbas b-*. I stick to my opinion. *ʔana bətmassak ᵊb-raʔyi*. 2. *rakaz (e/o rkuuz) b-*, *sabat (o/e sabaat) Ɛala* and *b-*. He can't stick to anything. *maa fii yərkez ᵊb-šii*. 3. *laazam*, *ltazam*. Stick to the original. *laazem ᵊl-ʔaṣᵊl*. 4. *ḥaṭṭ ḥaalo Ɛala* or *b-*. Let's stick to business. *xalliina nḥəṭṭ ḥaalna Ɛaš-šağle*.

to stick together - 1. *šaddu maƐ baƐḍon*. You can't do a thing against them because they'll always stick together. *maa fiik taƐmə́l-lon šii laʔənno daayman bišəddu maƐ baƐḍon* (or **laʔənno daayman hənne ʔiid waaḥde*). 2. *ləzqu maƐ baƐḍon*. The two bills must have stuck together when I took them out of the wallet. *l-warᵊqteen laazem ykuunu ləzqu maƐ baƐḍon waqᵊt ṭalaƐton mn ᵊl-maḥfaẓa*.

to stick up - *baraz (o bruuz)*, *ṭəleƐ (a ṭluuƐ)*. Watch out! There's a nail sticking up over there! *ʔoƐak! fii bəsmaar baarez ᵊhniik*.

stuck up - *šaayef ḥaalo*, *mƐanṭaẓ*. She's so stuck up she won't even talk to us. *šaayfe ḥaala la-daraže maa btətnaazal ᵊtḥaakiina*.

sticker - *ʔetikeet* pl. *-aat*.

sticky - 1. *mdabbeq*, *dəbeq*. My fingers are all sticky from the honey. *ʔaṣabiiƐi mdabbqiin Ɛal-maẓbuuṭ mn ᵊl-Ɛasal*. 2. *Ɛəbeq*, *mƐabbeq*. It's awfully sticky today. *faẓaaƐa qaddeeš ᵊž-žaww Ɛəbeq ᵊl-yoom*.

stiff - 1. *žaamed*. When it dries out it turns into a stiff mass. *waqt ᵊbtənšaf bətṣiir maadde žaamde*. 2. *yaabes*. He always wears stiff collars. *daayman byəlbes qabbaat yaabse*. 3. *mṣannaž*. I have a stiff neck. *raqᵊbti mṣannaže*. -- My legs are stiff from all this sitting. *ražlayyi mṣannažiin mən kətr ᵊl-qaƐde*. 4. *mətrassem*, *rasmi**. Don't be so stiff. *laa tkuun hal-qadd mətrassem*. 5. *ṣaƐb*, *qaasi*. Was it a stiff examination? *šuu kaan ṣaƐb ᵊl-faḥᵊṣ?* 6. *Ɛaali*. They charge you stiff prices in that store. *byəṭᵊlbu mənnak ʔasƐaar Ɛaalye b-hal-maxzan*. 7. *ṣaarem*. The ambassador delivered a stiff note from his government. *s-safiir qaddam mzakkara ṣaarme mn ᵊḥkuumto*.

still - *raaken*. At night, the streets are still and quiet. *bᵊl-leel ᵊš-šawaareƐ bətkuun raakne haadye*.

to hold still - *rakan (e rakne)*. Hold still a minute! *rkə́n-lak šwayye baqa!*

to keep still - *sakat (o skuut)*, *tamm (a ø) saaket*. Why didn't you keep still? *leeš maa sakatᵊt?* or **leeš maa xalleet təmmak saaket?*

still - 1. *ləssa*, *ləssaa(t)˜* + pron. suff. I'm still of the same opinion. *ləssaani mən nafs ᵊr-raʔi*. -- They're still in Rome. *ləssaaton b-rooma*. -- Do you still think so? *ləssaak btəftə́ker heek?* 2. *maƐ zaalek*, *bᵊr-rağᵊm Ɛan heek*. Still, I think you did the right thing. *maƐ zaalek bəƐtə́qed ʔana ʔənnak ᵊƐməlt ᵊš-šii l-maẓbuuṭ*.

to stimulate - 1. *ḥarrak*, *nabbah*. The drug stimulates blood circulation. *d-dawa biḥarrek ᵊd-doora d-damawiyye*. 2. *ʔasaar*. The lecture was quite stimulating. *l-ᵊmḥaaḍara kaanet musiira nooƐan maa*.

to sting - *qaraṣ (o qarᵊṣ//nqaraṣ)*. I was stung by a bee. *qarṣətni naḥle*.

stingy - *bxiil* pl. *bəxala*, *mqatter*, *šaḥiiḥ*. Don't be so stingy! *laa tkuun hal-qadd ᵊbxiil!*

stipend - *mənḥa* pl. *mənaḥ*.

to stipulate - *štaraṭ*. Article 4 stipulates that the contracting parties will aid each other in a case of outside aggression. *l-maadde r-raabƐa btəštə́reṭ ʔənno ṭ-ṭarafeen ᵊl-mətƐaaqdeen yƐaawnu baƐḍon b-ḥaalet ʔəƐtidaaʔ xaarži*.

stir - *ḥarake*. There was a stir in the crowd when he got up to speak. *ṣaar fii ḥarake lamma qaam yəxṭob*.

to stir - 1. *ḥarrak*. If you had stirred the soup it wouldn't have burned. *law ḥarrakt ᵊš-šooraba maa kaanet ᵊḥtarqet*. 2. *tḥarrak*. He's stirring now. *Ɛam yətḥarrak hallaq*. 3. *tḥarrak*, *ḥarak (o ḥarake)*. Don't stir! *laa tətḥarrak!*

stirring - *mᵊʔasser*. It was a stirring speech. *kaan xiṭaab ᵊmʔasser*.

to stir up - *ʔasaar*. As was to be expected, his remarks stirred up a lot of trouble. *mətᵊl-ma kaan məntə́ẓar ᵊmlaaḥaẓaato ʔasaaret mašaakel ᵊktiire*.

stirrup - *rkaab* pl. *-aat*.

stitch - *qəṭbe* pl. *qəṭab*. Don't make such big stitches. *laa tsaawi qəṭab ᵊkbiire hal-qadd*. -- I lost a stitch. *ḍawwaƐᵊt qəṭbe*. -- When is the doctor going to take out the stitches? *ʔeemta d-doktoor laḥa yqiim ᵊl-qəṭab?*

**I haven't done a stitch of work today. *maa saaweet ᵊl-yoom w-laa nətfet šəğᵊl*.

to stitch - *qaṭab (o qaṭᵊb//nqaṭab)*. Did you stitch the hem yet? *qaṭabti d-daayer wəlla ləssa?*

to stitch on - *qaṭab (o qaṭᵊb//nqaṭab)*. Stitch on the pockets. *qṭəbi ž-žiyab*.

stock - 1. *muune* pl. *-aat* and *muwan*. I want to lay in a stock of soap. *bəddi mawwen muunet ṣaabuun*. 2. *mawžuudaat* (pl.). I'll look through my stock and see if I have it. *bəṭṭallaƐ bᵊl-mawžuudaat Ɛandi w-ᵊbšuuf ʔiza Ɛandi-yə́aha*. 3. *sahᵊm* pl. *ʔashom* and *shuume*. I advise you not to buy these stocks. *bənṣaḥak maa təštə́ri hal-ʔashom*.

in stock - *mawžuud*. What sizes do you have in stock? *šuu l-ᵊqyaasaat ᵊl-mawžuude Ɛandak?*

out of stock - *xaaleṣ*, *naafed*. It's out of stock, but we have reordered it. *xaalṣa, bass waṣṣeena Ɛaleeha mn ᵊždiid*. -- Sorry, we're all out of stock. *mətʔassfiin, xaalṣa kəll ᵊbḍaaƐətna*.

to take stock - *žarad (o žarᵊd//nžarad)*. Next week we're going to take stock. *ž-žəmƐa ž-žaaye bəddna nəžrod*.

to take (or **put**) **stock in** - *ḥaṭṭ qiime la-*, *ʔaxad ʔahammiyye la-*. I don't put much stock in what he says. *maa bḥəṭṭ la-kalaamo qiime ktiir*.

to stock - *xalla stook mən*. We don't stock that brand. *Ɛaadatan maa mənxalli stook mən hal-maarka*.

to stock up on - *mawwan*, *tmawwan b-*. Did you stock up on coal? *mawwanᵊt faḥᵊm?* -- We're pretty well stocked. *mmawwaniin mniiḥ nəḥna*.

stockbroker - *səmsaar˜* (pl. *samaasret˜*) *ʔashom*.

stock exchange - *boorṣa* pl. *-aat*.

stockholder - *ḥaamel˜* (pl. *-iin˜*) *ʔashom*. I'm a stockholder in that company. *ʔana ḥaamel ʔashom b-haš-šərke*.

stocking - (men's and women's) *žraabe* pl. *-aat*, (women's only) *fardet˜ kalsaat* pl. *kalsaat*. I'd like three pairs of stockings. *bəddi tlətt ᵊžwaaz ᵊžraabaat*.

stocktaking - *žarᵊd*.

stomach - *məƐde* pl. *məƐad*. He has an upset stomach.

məᶜᵊdto mxarbaṭa.
**I'm sick to my stomach. *nafsi ᶜam təlᶜi.*
to stomach - *ḥadam (o ḥadᵊm//nhadam).* I can't stomach that fellow. *ʔana maa bəhḍom haz-zalame.*
stomach-ache - *wažaᶜ- məᶜde.* I have a stomach-ache. *maᶜi wažaᶜ məᶜde.*
stone - **1.** *ḥažar(a)* pl. *ḥžaar(a).* Who threw that stone? *miin rama hal-ḥažar?* -- Let me see this beautiful stone on your ring. *xalliini šuuf hal-ḥažar ᵊl-ḥəlu b-xaatmak.* -- He killed two birds with one stone. *ḍarab ᶜaṣfuureen ᵊb-ḥažar waaḥed.* **2.** *ḥažar.* The kitchen has a stone floor. *l-maṭbax ʔarḍo ḥažar.* **3.** *šaahde* pl. *šawaahed.* We had a beautiful stone put on his grave. *ḥaṭṭeena šaahde ktiir ḥəlwe ᶜala qabro.* **4.** *bəzre* coll. *bəzᵊr* pl. *-aat* and *bzuur.* These plums have big stones. *hal-xoox bəzro kbiir.*
**He left no stone unturned. *maa xalla ḥiile maa saawaaha.*
Stone Age - *l-ᶜaṣr ᵊl-ḥažari.*
to stone - *ražam (o ražᵊm) b-ᵊḥžaara.* The people in that village almost stoned us. *ʔahl ᵊḍ-ḍeeᶜa kaanu laḥa yərᵊžmuuna bᵊl-ᵊḥžaara.*
stonecutter - *ṣaayeġ* pl. *ṣiyyaaġ.*
stonemason - *naḥḥaat* pl. *-e* and *-iin.*
stony - **1.** *məḥžer.* We crossed a stretch of stony terrain. *qaṭaᶜna qəṭᶜet ʔaraaḍi məḥᵊžra.* **2.** *ḥažari*, ṣaxri*.* He listened with a stony face. *kaan ᶜam yəstəmeᶜ ᵊb-wəšš ḥažari.*
stoop - *ḥanye.* Do you see the man with the stoop over there? *šaayəf-lak har-rəžžaal ʔabu l-ḥanye hniik?* -- He walks with a slight stoop. *byəmši b-ḥanye baṣiiṭa.*
to stoop - **1.** *nḥana.* He stooped to pick up the newspaper. *nḥana la-yərfaᶜ ᵊž-žariide.* **2.** *danna ḥaalo, waṭṭa ḥaalo.* I don't think she'd stoop to anything like that. *maa bẓənnha bəddanni ḥaala la-šii mətᵊl haad.*
stop - **1.** *mawqef* pl. *mawaaqef, mḥaṭṭa* pl. *-aat.* You have to get off at the next stop. *laazem tənzel bᵊl-mawqef ᵊž-žaaye.* **2.** *waqfe* pl. *-aat.* We have a ten-minute stop in Hama. *fii ᶜanna waqfe ᶜašᵊr daqaayeq b-ḥama.*
to bring to a stop - *waqqaf.* He brought the car to a full stop. *waqqaf ᵊs-sayyaara tamaam.*
to put a stop to - *ḥaṭṭ ḥadd la-.* We'll have to put a stop to that practice. *laazem nḥaṭṭ ḥadd la-hat-taṣarrof.*
to stop - *waqqaf.* Stop the car at the next crossing! *waqqef ᵊs-sayyaara bᵊl-mafraq ᵊž-žaaye.* -- We were stopped by the police. *waqqafətna š-šərṭa.* -- Please stop that noise. *baḷḷa waqqef haḍ-ḍoože.* -- I instructed the bank to stop the check. *ʔamart ᵊl-bank ywaqqef ᵊš-šakk.* -- The bus stops on the other side of the street. *l-baaṣ biwaqqef ᶜaṭ-ṭaraf ᵊt-taani mn ᵊš-šaareᶜ.* -- We stopped at a small inn overnight. *waqqafna leele b-lookanda zġiire.* -- Where are we going to stop? *ween laḥa nwaqqef?* -- My watch has stopped. *saaᶜti waqqafet.*
**He stops at nothing. *maa ᶜando raadeᶜ.*
**Stop it! *ḥaaže baqa!*
**Stop jumping around. *ḥaaže (or ḥaaštak) naṭwaṭa (or tnaṭweṭ).*
to stop over at - *maraq (o marqa) ᶜala.* Why don't you stop over at my place on the way? *leeš maa btəmroq ᶜaleena b-ṭariiqak?*
to stop short - **1.** *waqqaf ᶜala ġafle.* The car ahead of me had stopped short. *s-sayyaara yalli qəddaami kaanet waqqafet ᶜala ġafle.* **2.** *qaaṭaᶜ.* I stopped him short before he could say more. *qaaṭaᶜto qabᵊl-ma yəqder yəḥki ʔaktar.*
to stop someone from - *manaᶜ (a manᵊᶜ//mmanaᶜ) ḥada (ᶜan).* I couldn't stop him from mailing the letter. *maa qdərt ʔəmnaᶜo yəbᶜat ᵊl-maktuub.*
to stop up - *ṣaṭam (o ṣaṭᵊm//nṣaṭam).* You're going to stop up the sink. *laḥa təṣṭom ᵊl-balluuᶜa.*
stopper - *saddaade* pl. *-aat.*
stop watch - *kroonomətr* pl. *-aat.*
storage - *maxzaniyye.* How much did they charge you for storage? *qaddeeš kallafuuk maxzaniyye?*
storage battery - *baṭṭaariyye* pl. *-aat.*
store - **1.** *maxzan* pl. *maxaazen, dəkkaan* (f.) pl. *dakakiin, maḥall* pl. *-aat.* I know a store where you can buy that. *baᶜrəf-lak maxzan fiik təštəri mənno haš-šii.* -- The stores are open until seven o'clock. *l-maxaazen faatḥa (or **s-suuq faateḥ) ləs-saaᶜa sabᶜa.* -- I'm sure I saw it in his store. *ʔana mətʔakked šəfta b-dəkkaanto.* **2.** *muune* pl. *-aat* and *muwan, daxiire* pl. *-aat.* We have quite a store of food in the pantry. *fii ᶜanna munnet ʔakl ᵊmniiḥa b-beet ᵊl-muune.*
in store for - *mxabba la-.* Who knows what is in store for us? *miin byaᶜref šuu mxabbda-lna?*
to have (or **hold**) **in store for** - *xabba la-.* No one knows what the future holds in store for the present generation. *maa ḥada byaᶜref šuu l-məstaqbal mxabbi ləž-žiil ᵊl-ḥaaḍer.* -- He had a pleasant surprise in store for them. *kaan mxabbʼi-lon ᵊmfaažaʔa ẓariife.*
to store - *xazan (e xazᵊn//nxazan), ḥafaẓ (a ḥəfᵊẓ//nḥafaẓ).* Where shall I store the potatoes? *ween bəddi ʔəxzen ᵊl-baṭaaṭa?*
to store up - *ddaxar.* I stored up a lot of energy during my vacation. *ddaxarᵊt quwwe mniiḥa waqᵊt ᶜəṭᵊlti.*
storehouse - *maxzan* pl. *maxaazen, ᶜambar* pl. *ᶜanaaber.*
storekeeper - *dəkkanži* pl. *-iyye.*
stork - *(ḥažž) laglag* pl. *lagaaleg.*
storm - *ᶜaaṣfe* pl. *ᶜawaaṣef, zoobaᶜa* pl. *zawaabeᶜ.* There was a big storm last night. *ṣaar fii ᶜaaṣfe kbiire mbaareḥ bᵊl-leel.*
to storm - **1.** *ᶜaṣaf (e ᶜaṣᵊf).* It is storming outside. *ᶜam təᶜṣef ᵊd-dənye barra.* **2.** *hažam (o hžuum).* She stormed into my room, a letter in her hand. *hažmet ᶜala ʔuuḍti w-ᵊb-ʔiida maktuub.* **3.** *ǧtaḥam, nǧaḍḍ ᶜala.* Infantry stormed the fortress. *l-mušaat ǧtaḥmet ᵊl-ḥəṣᵊn.*
**My father was storming for an hour when I told him about it. *ʔabi tamm ṭaaleᶜ xəlqo saaᶜa lamma ḥakeet-əllo ᶜan haš-šaġle.*
stormy - *ᶜaaṣef.*
story - *qəṣṣa* pl. *qəṣaṣ, ḥkaaye* pl. *-aat* and *ḥakaaya.* The whole story sounds improbable. *mbayyen ᶜal-qəṣṣa kəlla ʔənna məstaġrabe.* -- I wish I could tell you the whole story. *ya-reet fiini qəl-lak ᵊl-qəṣṣa mən ʔawwəla la-ʔaaxəra.* -- It's always the same old story. *daayman nafs ᵊl-qəṣṣa (or **nafs ᵊn-naġme).*
**That's another story. *hayy masʔale taanye.*
story - *ṭaabeq* pl. *ṭawaabeq.* The house has five stories. *l-beet ʔəlo ʔarbaᶜ ṭawaabeq.* -- It's a two-story building. *hiyye binaaye b-ṭaabqeen.*
storyteller - *ḥakawaati* pl. *-iyye.*
stove - **1.** *ṭabbaax* pl. *-aat.* Put the beans on the stove. *ḥəṭṭi l-faaṣuuliyye ᶜaṭ-ṭabbaax.* **2.** *ṣooba* pl. *-aat, ṣoobya* pl. *-aat.* This one mazoot stove will never heat the room properly. *haṣ-ṣoobet ᵊl-maazoot ᵊl-waaḥde maa bəddaffi l-ʔuuḍa ʔabadan ᶜal-maẓbuuṭ.*
straight - **1.** *məstaǧiim, ḍəgri* (invar.). Draw a straight line. *rsoom xaṭṭ məstaǧiim.* -- He's always been straight with me. *daayman kaan ḍəgri maᶜi.* -- He promises to go straight. *byuuᶜed yṣiir məstaǧiim.* **2.** *ḍəgri.* Is my hat on straight? *bərneeṭṭi ḍəgri?* **3.** *ḍəgri, žaales.* Stand up straight, boys. *waqqfu ḍəgri (or žaalsiin) ya wlaad.* -- Can't you sit straight? *šuu maa fiik təqᶜod žaales?* **4.** *ḍəgri, raʔsan.* Our house is straight across from the church. *beetna ḍəgri mwaažeh l-ᵊkniise.* -- Go straight home. *ruuḥ ḍəgri ᶜal-beet.* **5.** *maẓbuuṭ.* He can't think straight, much less talk straight. *maa fii yfakker maẓbuuṭ b-ṣarf ᵊn-naẓar ᶜan ḥakyo.* -- You didn't get me straight. *maa fhəmᵊtni maẓbuuṭ.* -- Now get me straight. *fhaam ᶜaliyyi maẓbuuṭ baqa.* **6.** *ᶜal-maẓbuuṭ.* See if you can get the story straight. *šuuf ʔiza fiik ᵊdžiib ᵊl-qəṣṣa ᶜal-maẓbuuṭ.* **7.** *seek* (invar.). I take my whiskey straight. *bəšrab ᵊl-wəski tabaᶜi seek.*
**Now let's get this straight once and for all. *xalliina nwaḍḍeḥ haš-šaġle beenaatna la-ʔawwal w-ʔaaxer marra.*
**He worked for fifteen hours straight. *štaġal xamᵊṣṭaᶜšar saaᶜa bala waqfe.*
straight ahead - *ḍəgri.* Keep straight ahead! *xalliik maaši ḍəgri.*
to set straight - *nawwar.* Can you set me straight on this? *fiik ᵊtnawwərni b-haš-šaġle?*
to straighten - **1.** *massad, rakkaz.* Straighten the tablecloth. *massed ġaṭa ṭ-ṭaawlę.* **2.** *qawwam, žallas.* You can straighten these nails and use them over again. *fiik ᵊtqawwem hal-basamiir w-təstaᶜməlon taani marra.*
to straighten out - **1.** *dabbar, rakkaz, ẓabbaṭ.* Did you straighten out everything? *šuu dabbarᵊt kəll šii?* **2.** *nṣalaḥ.* He'll straighten out if you give him a chance. *byənṣəleḥ ʔiza ᶜaṭeeto mažaal.*
to straighten up - **1.** *rattab.* Will you please straighten up the room? *mən faḍlak ratteb ᵊl-ʔuuḍa*

ʾiza batriid. 2. šallas ḥaalo. Why do you stand like that? Straighten up! leeš heek waaqef? šalles ḥaalak!

strain - 1. ʾažhaad. He couldn't stand the strain. maa qader yatḥammal ᵊl-ʾažhaad. -- She's been under considerable strain lately. mʾasser Ɛaleeha l-ʾažhaad ᵊktiir ᵊb-hal-madde l-ʾaxiire. 2. šadd, taqᵊl. I don't think the rope will stand the strain. maa baƐtqed ᵊl-ḥabᵊl biḍaayen bᵊš-šadd.

**It's a strain to read this small print. šii mažhed ᵊqraayet hal-ᵊḥruuf ᵊẓ-ẓġiire matl ᵊn-namᵊl.

to strain - 1. ʾažhad. I strained my eyes. ʾažhadt ᵊƐyuuni. 2. falaš (e/o falš//nfalaš). I strained a ligament in my foot. falašᵊt watar (or nfalaš watar) ᵊb-rəžli. 3. madd (ə ø) naẓaro. He strained to see what was going on at his neighbor's house. madd naẓaro la-yšuuf šuu kaan ṣaayer Ɛand žiiraano. 4. šadd (ə šadd). The dog was straining at the leash. l-kalb kaan Ɛam yšadd ᵊr-rasan. 5. ṣaffa. Did you strain the soup? ṣaffeeti š-šooraba?

strained - matwatter. At the moment our relations are somewhat strained. bᵊl-waqt ᵊl-ḥaaḍer Ɛalaaqaatna matwattra nooƐan maa.

to strain oneself - 1. ʾažhad nafso. He never strains himself. b-ḥayaato maa byažhed nafso. 2. mbaraq. He must have strained himself. laazem ykuun ᵊmbaraq.

strainer - maṣfaaye pl. -aat and maṣaafi.

straits - maḍiiq̈ pl. maḍaayeq̈. The Straits of Bab el Mandeb link the Red Sea and the Indian Ocean. maḍiiq̈ baab ᵊl-mandab byaṣel ᵊl-baḥr ᵊl-ʾaḥmar bᵊl-muḥiiṭ ᵊl-həndi.

**I've been in financial straits all month. ṣar-li kall haš-šahᵊr ʾiidi muu waaṣle.

strand - xaṣle pl. xaṣal. A strand of hair keeps falling in her face. fii xaṣlet šaƐᵊr battamm naazle Ɛala wašša.

to **strand** - žanaḥ (a žnuuḥ). The ship stranded on the Lebanese coast. l-baaxra žanḥet Ɛaš-šaṭṭ ᵊl-ləbnaani.

strange - ġariib pl. ġarabe. All this is strange to me. kall haada ġariib Ɛaliyyi. -- What a strange question! qaddeeš suʾaal ġariib! -- There is something strange about this house. fii šii ġariib b-hal-beet. -- That's strange! šii ġariib!

strangeness - ġaraabe.

stranger - ġariib pl. ġaraba. Who was the stranger? miin kaan hal-ġariib? -- I'm a stranger here. ʾana ġariib hoon.

to **strangle** - xanaq (e/o xanᵊq//nxanaq). He strangled her with a piece of rope. xanáqa b-ḥable.

strap - 1. qšaaṭ pl. qašᵊṭ. Put the strap around the suitcase. ḥaṭṭ l-ᵊqšaaṭ daayer ᵊš-šanta. 2. kammaaše pl. -aat. Some buses don't even provide straps to hold on to. fii baaṣaat maa fiiha ḥatta kammaašaat l-waaḥed yasnod ḥaalo Ɛaleeha. 3. ḥammaale pl. -aat. The strap of your slip is showing. ḥammaalet šalᵊḥtek baayne.

strategic - stratiiži*.

strategy - stratiižiyye pl. -aat.

stratosphere - ṭ-ṭabaq̈a ṭ-ṭəhruuriyye.

straw - 1. qašš. The mat is made of straw. l-ḥaṣiire maƐmuule mən qašš. 2. qašše pl. -aat. She brushed a straw from his sleeve. nafḍet qašše mən Ɛala kəmmo. -- A desperate man will grasp at any straw. l-ʾənsaan ᵊl-yaaʾes byatƐallaq ᵊb-qašše. 3. maṣṣaaṣa pl. -aat, šalamoonaaye pl. -aat. Can I please have a straw? məmken tnaawəlni maṣṣaaṣa mən faḍlak?

**That's the last straw! haada ṭafaḥ ᵊl-keel.

strawberry - freezaaye coll. freez pl. freezaayaat.

stray - 1. ṭaayeš. He was hit by a stray bullet. nṣaab b-ᵊrṣaaṣa ṭaayše. 2. šaared. She keeps bringing stray cats home. bəddall ᵊdžiib qaṭaaṭ šaarde Ɛal-beet.

stream - 1. nahr pl. nhuura and ʾanhaar. There's a small stream winding through the valley. fii nahr ᵊẓġiir ᵊmƐawwaž maareq bᵊl-waadi. 2. seel pl. syuul, maškaak pl. mašakiik. Did you see the stream of cars? šəfᵊt seel ᵊs-sayyaaraat?

to stream - 1. zarab (o zarᵊb), šarr (ə šarr). The sweat was just streaming down his brow. l-Ɛaraq kaan Ɛam yəzrob mn ᵊžbiino. 2. ddaffaq. People came streaming out of the stadium. ddaffaqu l-Ɛaalam mən l-ᵊmdarraž.

**We had to walk in the streaming rain. nžabarna nəmši taḥᵊt seel ᵊl-maṭar.

streamlined - ʾansiyaabi*.

street - šaareƐ pl. šawaareƐ. I met him on the street. ṣaadafto bᵊš-šaareƐ. -- I used to live on this street. kənᵊt saaken b-haš-šaareƐ. -- He was put out on the street. qallaƐúu Ɛaš-šaareƐ. -- The street lights go on at dark. ʾaḍᵊwyet ᵊš-šawaareƐ btəšƐel Ɛand l-ᵊġruub.

dead-end street - ṭariiq̈ (pl. ṭəroq̈) sadd.

one-way street - ṭariiq̈ (pl. ṭaroq̈) ʾattižaah waaḥed.

streetcar - tramwaay pl. -aat. Are we taking the streetcar? raḥa naaxod ᵊt-tramwaay?

strength - 1. ḥeel, quwwe. I haven't the strength to do it. maa-li ḥeel ʾaƐməla. 2. quwwe. He doesn't know his own strength. maa byaƐref qaddeeš quwwto. -- I've lost all my strength. ḍayyaƐᵊt quwwti kəlla. -- We had underestimated the strength of the enemy. staxaffeena b-quwwet ᵊl-Ɛaduww.

on the strength of - binaaʾan Ɛala. He was hired on the strength of your recommendation. staxdamúu binaaʾan Ɛala tuuṣaaytak.

to **strengthen** - qawwa//tqawwa, daƐam (e daƐᵊm//ndaƐam). The cultural agreement will strengthen the ties between the two countries. l-ʾattifaaq̈ ᵊs-saq̈aafi raḥa yqawwi r-rawaabeṭ been ᵊl-baladeen.

strenuous - məžhed, matƐeb. That's a strenuous job. hayy šaġle məžᵊhde.

stress - 1. ḍaġᵊṭ. I doubt if the rope can stand that much stress. bšəkk ʾənno l-ḥable fiiha taḥammal heek ḍaġᵊṭ. 2. šədde, ḍaġᵊṭ. The stress of the work is getting too much for him. šəddet ᵊš-šəġᵊl ṣaaret fooq ṭaaqto. 3. nabra. The stress is on the last syllable. n-nabra Ɛala ʾaaxer maq̈ṭaƐ.

to stress - 1. ḥaṭṭ ʾahammiyye Ɛala. She stressed two things in particular. ḥaṭṭet ʾahammiyye Ɛala šaġᵊlteen ᵊxṣuuṣan. 2. ḥaṭṭ ᵊn-nabra Ɛala. The second syllable is stressed. l-maqṭaƐ ᵊt-taani (maḥṭuuṭ) Ɛalée n-nabra.

stretch - 1. marḥale pl. maraaḥel. We had to run the last stretch. nžabarna narkod ʾaaxer marḥale. 2. fasḥa pl. -aat. There's a stretch of wasteland behind our house. fii fasḥet ʾarḍ buur b-qafa beetna.

at a stretch - fard saḥbe, bala waqfe. He works about ten hours at a stretch. byaštaġál-lo šii Ɛašᵊr saaƐaat fard saḥbe.

to stretch - 1. wassaƐ. Can you stretch my shoes a little bit? fiik ᵊtwassáƐ-li ṣabbaaṭi natfe? 2. madd (ə madd//mmadd). Stretch a rope between the two posts. madd ḥable been ᵊl-q̈aaʾəmteen. 3. šadd (ə šadd//nšadd). Don't stretch the rope so tight. laa tšədd ᵊl-ḥable kəll hal-qadd. 4. raxa (i ø). The gloves will stretch. l-ᵊkfuuf lassa byarxu. 5. mtadd. The park stretches from here all the way down to the seashore. l-baark byamtadd mən hoon w-naazel ləš-šaṭṭ. 6. tmaṭmaṭ. He yawned and stretched when he got up from the couch. ttaawab w-ᵊtmaṭmaṭ waqᵊt qaam mən Ɛal-kanabe.

to stretch out - 1. mtadd. The wheat fields stretch out for miles. ḥquul ᵊl-qamᵊḥ btamtadd Ɛala masaafet ʾamyaal w-ʾamyaal. 2. tmaṭraq, tṣaṭṭaḥ. I'd like to stretch out a bit. ḥaabeb ʾatmaṭráq-li šwayye. 3. madd (ə madd). Stretch out your arm. madd ʾiidak.

stretcher - naqqaale pl. -aat. They carried him out on a stretcher. ḥamalúu la-barra Ɛala naqqaale.

strict - ṣaarem, šadiid. His father is very strict. ʾabúu ktiir ṣaarem. -- They have strict regulations. fii Ɛandon ʾanẓime šadiide.

strictly - 1. bataatan, maṭlaq̈an. Smoking is strictly forbidden. t-tadxiin mamnuuƐ bataatan. 2. Ɛat-tamaam, b-kəll daqqa. We'll adhere strictly to the stipulations of the contract. bəddna nəttəbeƐ šruuṭ ᵊl-ʾəttifaaqiyye Ɛat-tamaam.

strictly speaking - Ɛala wažh ᵊt-taḥdiid. Strictly speaking, it's not the same. Ɛala wažh ᵊt-taḥdiid muu nafs ᵊš-šii.

strike - ʾəḍraab pl. -aat. How long did the strike last? qaddeeš daawam ᵊl-ʾəḍraab? -- The strike has been going on for four weeks. l-ʾəḍraab ṣar-lo məstmərr ʾarbaƐ žəmaƐ.

to go on strike - ʾaḍrab (-yəḍreb and -yʾaḍreb). We're going on strike tomorrow. laha nʾaḍreb bəkra.

to strike - 1. ʾaḍrab (-yəḍreb and -yʾaḍreb). Why are the workers striking? leeš ᵊl-Ɛəmmaal məḍᵊrbiin? 2. daqq (ə daqq). The clock just struck ten. s-saaƐa hallaq daqqet Ɛašara. 3. ḍarab (o ḍarb//nḍarab). Who struck you? miin ḍarabak? -- He struck him a blow with his cane. ḍarabo ḍarbe b-Ɛaṣaayto. 4. šaḥaṭ (a šaḥᵊṭ//nšaḥaṭ). Strike a match. šḥaaṭ kəbriite. 5. ṣṭaḍam b-, ḍarab b-.

The ship struck a rock. l-baaxra ṣaḍmet b-ṣaxra.
6. ṣaab (i ʔiṣaabe), nəzel (e nzuul) ɛala. Did the lightning strike anywhere? s-saaɛqa ṣaabet šii maḥall?
**Does that strike a familiar note? maa byəẓhár-lak haada šii maʔluuf?
**He must have struck oil, the way he's throwing money away. laazem ykuun ṭaaleɛ ɛala wəššo kənz la-ḥatta ɛam ykəbb ᵊl-maṣaari kabb.
**It strikes me he's acting very strangely. ɛam yətṣarraf ᵊb-šəkᵊl ġariib ᵊktiir.

striking - 1. mbahraž. She likes to wear striking colors. bətḥəbb təlbes ʔalwaan ᵊmbahraže.
2. mədheš, ɛažiib. There's a striking resemblance between the two. fii šabah mədheš been ᵊt-tneen.

to strike dead - qatal (o qatᵊl//nqatal and qətel a qatᵊl). He was struck dead by lightning. qətel ᵊb-saaɛqa or qatᵊlto saaɛqa.

to strike off - šaṭab (o šaṭᵊb//nšaṭab), Strike his name off the list. šṭoob ʔəsmo mn ᵊl-liista.

to strike out - šaṭab (o šaṭᵊb//nšaṭab), qaam (i qayamaan//nqaam). Strike out the first paragraph. šṭoob ᵊl-faq̈ra l-ʔawwalaaniyye.

to strike up a conversation - fataḥ (a fatᵊḥ) ḥadiis. I tried to strike up a conversation with the girl. ḥaawalt ʔəftaḥ ḥadiis maɛ ᵊl-bənᵊt.

to strike up a friendship - ḍarab (o ø) ṣəḥbe. The two of them struck up a friendship very quickly. tneenaaton ḍarabu ṣəḥbe maɛ baɛḍon b-sərɛa ktiir.

to strike one's eye - lafat (e ø) naẓar˜ ḥada, žalab (e/o žalb) naẓar˜ ḥada. That was the first thing that struck my eye. haada kaan ʔawwal šii lafat naẓari.

string - 1. šriiṭ pl. šaraayeṭ. This string is too short. haš-šriiṭ qaṣiir maa bikaffi. 2. watar pl. wtaar. I have to buy a new string for my violin. laazem ʔəštṛi watar ᵊždiid ləl-kamanža tabaɛi.
3. ḥabᵊl pl. ḥbaal. How much would you guess this string of pearls costs? qaddeeš bətqadder hal-ḥabl ᵊl-luulu bikallef?
**He's still attached to her apron strings. ləssáa mɛallaq b-ᵊdyaala.
**She has three men on the string. mɛallqa tlətt ᵊržaal.
**You can't get that job without pulling some strings. maa fiik təḥṣal ɛala haš-šaġle bala waasṭa.

to string - 1. laḍam (o laḍᵊm//nlaḍam). Where can I have my pearls strung? ween bəqder ʔəlḍom ᵊl-luuliyyaat tabaɛi? 2. faṣṣaṣ. Please help me string the beans. b-ᵊḥyaatek saaɛdiini faṣṣeṣ ᵊl-faaṣuuliyye. 3. madd (ə madd//mmadd). How are you going to string the wire? kiif bəddak ᵊtmədd əš-šriiṭ? 4. rakkab ᵊwtaar b-, ḥaṭṭ wtaar la-. Would you string this violin for me? məmken baḷḷa trakkəb-li wtaar b-hal-kamanža?

string bean - ḥabbet˜ faaṣuuliyye coll. faaṣuuliyye pl. ḥabbaat˜ faaṣuuliyye.

strip - šəqfe ṭawiile pl. šəqaf ᵊṭwaal. Cut the paper into strips. qaṭṭeɛ ᵊl-waraq šəqaf ᵊṭwaal. -- A narrow strip of land. šəqfet ʔarḍ dayyqa w-ṭawiile.

stripe - qalam pl. qlaam. The tie has red and white stripes. l-ᵊkraafe fiiha qlaam ḥəmr w-biiḍ.

striped - mqallam. She's wearing a striped dress. laabse roob ᵊmqallam.

stroke - 1. šaxṭa pl. -aat. Erase the strokes on the margin. ʔəmḥi š-šaxṭaat mən ɛal-haameš. 2. šaxṭa pl. -aat, žarra pl. -aat. With one stroke of the pen he suspended the constitution. b-šaxṭet qalam ɛallaq ᵊd-dastuur. 3. naqṭa (pl. nəqaṭ) ɛad-dmaaġ. Her father had another stroke yesterday. ʔabuuha ʔəžžato naqṭa ɛad-dmaaġ taani marra mbaareḥ.
**I haven't done a stroke of work on my book for three weeks. maa ɛməlt w-laa nətfe mn ᵊš-šəġᵊl b-ᵊktaabi mən tlətt žəmaɛ.
**At one stroke everything was changed. mən qalb ᵊd-dənye kəll šii tġayyar.
**It was a real stroke of luck to get this apartment. kaan ɛan ḥaqa šaanṣ ᵊmniiḥ ʔənno ḥṣəlna ɛala hal-beet.

at the stroke of - ɛad-daqqa. He arrived at the stroke of four. ʔəža s-saaɛa ʔarbɛa ɛad-daqqa.

to stroke - laḥmas//tlaḥmas. Our cat loves to be stroked. qaṭṭətna bətḥəbb yətlaḥmás-la (or bətḥəbb ᵊl-laḥmase).

stroll - mašye pl. -aat, təmšaaye pl. -aat, gazdara pl. -aat. First I'd like to take a stroll through the town. bᵊl-ʔawwal ḥaabeb ʔaɛməl-li mašye bᵊl-balad.

to stroll - tmašša, tmašwar, gazdar. Let's stroll through the town. xalliina nətmašša bᵊl-balad.

strong - 1. qawi* pl. qawaaya. He has strong hands. ʔidée qawaaya. -- She needs stronger glasses. laazə́ma kəzlok ʔaqwa mən heek. -- Of course, that's a very strong argument in his favor. ṭabiiɛi, hayy ḥəžže ktiir qawiyye b-ṣaalḥo. 2. maaken, qawi*. Is this ladder strong enough? has-səllom maaken ᵊkfaaye? -- Those are good strong chairs. hal-karaasi maakniin ᵊmnaaḥ. 3. tqiil. I don't want my coffee so strong. maa bəddi qahᵊwti tqiile hal-qadd.

strop - msann (˜ muus) pl. -aat (˜ ᵊmwaas). Where did I put my razor strop? ween ḥaṭṭeet ᵊmsann ᵊl-muus tabaɛi?

to strop - sann (ə sann//nsann). You'd better strop the razor before you shave. ʔaḥsán-lak ᵊtsənn ᵊl-muus qabᵊl-ma təḥleq.

structure - tarkiib pl. -aat, kyaan pl. -aat.

struggle - niḍaal pl. -aat. It was a hard struggle. waḷḷaahi kaan niḍaal qaasi. -- It's been a hard struggle for me lately. ṣar-li mədde ɛam naaḍel qaasi.

to struggle - ṣaaraɛ, ɛaarak. We had to struggle against the tide. nžabarna nṣaareɛ ᵊt-tayyaar. -- I've been struggling with this problem for some time. ṣar-li mədde ɛam ɛaarek b-hal-məšᵊkle.

stub - 1. ɛəqᵊb pl. ʔaɛqaab. Throw that old pencil stub away. kəbb hal-ɛəqb ᵊl-qalam ᵊl-ɛatiiq.
2. ʔaruume pl. -aat. You must still have the stub of this check, or don't you? laazem ykuun ləssa ɛandak ʔaruumet ᵊš-šakk, walla laʔ?

stubborn - ɛaniid. He's terribly stubborn. faẓaaɛa šuu ɛaniid huwwe.

student - 1. ṭaaleb pl. ṭəllaab and ṭalabe. How many students are there at the medical school? kam ṭaaleb fii b-kəlliit ᵊṭ-ṭəbb? 2. təlmiiz pl. talamiiz and talaamze. He's one of the best students in high school. huwwe mən ʔaḥsan talamiiz ᵊl-madrase s-saanawiyye.

studio - stuudyo pl. stuudyoyaat.

study - 1. diraase pl. -aat. Has he finished his studies? xallaṣ diraasto? 2. baḥᵊs pl. ʔabḥaas and bḥuus, diraase pl. -aat. He has published several studies in that field. našar ɛəddet ʔabḥaas ᵊb-hal-ḥaq̈ᵊl. 3. maktabe pl. -aat and makaateb. My husband is in the study. žoozi bᵊl-maktabe.

to study - 1. daqqaq b-. We studied the map before we started. daqqaqna bᵊl-xariiṭa qabᵊl-ma mšiina. 2. daras (o diraase), tɛallam. He's studying Chinese. ɛam yədros ṣiini. 3. daras (o darᵊs, diraase//ndaras), baḥas (a baḥᵊs//nbaḥas). We'll study the question further. laḥa nədros ᵊl-masʔale ʔaktar.

studied - maqṣuuḍ. He looked at the car with studied indifference. ṭṭallaɛ ɛas-sayyaara b-ɛadam mbaaláa maqṣuuḍ.

stuff - ġraaḍ (pl.). Throw that old stuff away. kəbb hal-ᵊġraaḍ ᵊl-ɛatiiqa.
**He has the stuff of a singer in him. ɛando mawhəbt ᵊl-ġəne.
**Now we'll see what stuff he's made of. hallaq mənšuuf mən šuu ṭiine mažbuul.

to stuff - 1. ḥaša (i ḥaši//nḥaša). He stuffs animals for the museum. byəḥši ḥaywaanaat mənšaan ᵊl-matḥaf. -- We had stuffed eggplant for lunch. kaan ġadaana beetənžaan məḥši. 2. ḥaṭṭ (ə ḥaṭaṭ//nḥaṭṭ). Stuff cotton in your ears. ḥəṭṭ-ə́llak šii qəṭne b-ʔadaneek.

to stuff oneself - ḥaša (i ḥaši) ḥaalo, taxam (o taxᵊm) ḥaalo. Don't stuff yourself. laa təḥši ḥaalak.

to stuff up - sadd (ə sadd//nsadd). My nose is all stuffed up. manaxiiri ɛan ḥaqa masduude.

stuffing - ḥašwe pl. -aat. Would you give me the recipe for the stuffing? məmken taɛṭiini l-waṣfe tabaɛ ᵊl-ḥašwe? -- The stuffing of the hassock is coming out. ḥašwet ᵊṭ-ṭərraaḥa ɛam təṭlaɛ.

to **stumble** - tfarkaš. I stumbled over the garden hose. tfarkašᵊt b-barbiiš ᵊž-žneene.

stumbling block - ɛasra pl. -aat.

to **stun** - zahal (e zhuul//nzahal). We were stunned by the news. waḷḷa l-xabar zahalna.

stupid - 1. ʔaḥmaq f. ḥamqa pl. ḥəmᵊq, ġabi* pl. ʔaġbiya. He isn't at all stupid. huwwe muu ʔaḥmaq ʔabadan. 2. saxiif. That's a stupid question. haada suʔaal saxiif ɛan ḥaqa.

stupidity - ḥamaaqa, ġabaawe, saxaafe. (cf. stupid).

sturdy - 1. maaken, matiin. That's a sturdy table. hayy ṭaawle maakne. 2. ḍayaan (invar.). I need a pair of sturdy shoes for the winter. laazəmni *ṣabbaaṭ ḍayaan ləš-šəte.*

sty - *šaḥḥaad.* I'm getting a sty on my left eye. *ṭaaləč-li šaḥḥaad əb-čeeni š-šmaal.*

style - 1. *ʔəsluub* pl. *ʔasaliib.* He has a very poor style. *ʔəsluubo ktiir əḍčiif.* 2. *mooḍa* pl. *-aat.* It's the latest style. *hayy ʔaaxer mooḍa.* — Combs are in style again. *l-əmšaaṭ ṭaalča mooḍəton taani marra.* — Straw hats are out of style. *baraniiṭ əl-qašš raaḥet mooḍəton.*
**Let's go out tonight and dine in style. *xalliina nəṭlač əl-yoom čašiyye nətčaššda-lna čaša mrattab.*

stylish - *čal-mooḍa.* She always wears stylish clothes. *btəlbes ʔawaači čal-mooḍa čala ṭuul.*

subcommittee - *ləžne* (pl. *ləžaan*) *farčiyye.*

subconscious - *laa-šučuuri*.* It was a subconscious reaction. *kaan radd fəčəl laa-šučuuri.*

subconsciously - *bala šučuur.* Subconsciously, I raised my hands to shield my eyes. *bala šučuur rafačət ʔidayyi la-ʔəḥmi čyuuni.*

subject - 1. *mawḍuuč* pl. *-aat* and *mawaḍiič.* I'm not familiar with that subject. *ʔana maa-li məṭṭəleč čala hal-mawḍuuč.* 2. *maadde* pl. *mawaadd, mawḍuuč* pl. *mawaḍiič.* What subjects did you like best in high school? *šuu l-mawaadd halli ḥabbeeta ʔaktar šii bəl-madrase s-saanawiyye?* 3. *(račiyye)* pl. *račaaya.* He is a British subject. *huwwe mn ər-račaaya l-briiṭaaniyye.* 4. (of a nominal sentence) *məbtəda* pl. *məbtadayaat,* (of a verbal sentence) *faačel* pl. *-iin.* "ktaab" is the subject of this sentence. *"ktaab" huwwe məbtada b-haž-žəmle.*
subject to - 1. *mčarraḍ la-.* He's subject to melancholic depressions. *huwwe mčarraḍ la-noobaat soodaawiyye.* 2. *xaaḍeč la-, mčarraḍ la-.* This schedule is subject to change. *hat-tawqiit xaaḍeč lət-taġyiir.* -- These prices are subject to change without notice. *hal-ʔasčaar xaaḍča lət-taġyiir biduun ʔənzaar.*
to subject to - *čarraḍ//tčarraḍ la-.* They were subjected to every kind of humiliation. *tčarraḍu la-ʔihaanaat b-kəll əl-ʔalwaan.*

subjective - *šaxṣi*.* That is, of course, a very subjective appraisal of the situation. *bəṭ-ṭabəč haada taqdiir əktiir šaxṣi lel-ḥaale.*

submachine gun - *rəššeeš* pl. *-aat, tomigaan* pl. *-aat.*

submarine - *ġawwaaṣa* pl. *-aat.*

to **submit** - *qaddam, rafač (a rafəč//rtafač).* I'll submit my report on Monday. *bqaddem taqriiri ət-taneen.*
**His mother had to submit to an operation. *ʔəmmo nžabret tačmel čamaliyye.*

subpoena - *mzakkaret˜* (pl. *-aat˜*) *ʔəḥḍaar.*

to **subscribe** - 1. *štarak b-.* I subscribe to both papers. *bəštərek bəž-žariidteen.* 2. *ktatab b-.* The government has invited the public to subscribe to war bonds. *l-əḥkuume dačet əš-šačəb yəktəteb b-sanadaat əl-ḥarəb.* 3. *waafaq čala, məši (i ø) mač.* I can't subscribe to this viewpoint. *maa fiini waafeq čala hal-wəžhet ən-naẓar.*

subscription - *ʔəštiraak* pl. *-aat; ʔəktitaab* pl. *-aat.* (cf. **subscribe**).

substance - 1. *žoohar.* The two ideas are the same in substance. *l-fəkərteen waaḥed mən ḥays əž-žoohar.* 2. *xulaaṣa, zəbde.* The substance of his words was that he wants more money. *xulaaṣet kalaamo kaanet ʔənno bəddo maṣaari ʔaktar.* 3. *maadde* pl. *mawaadd.* The detergent contains a poisonous substance. *l-əmnaḍḍef fii maadde saamme.*

substantial - 1. *məḥtəram, mniiḥ.* He lost a substantial sum of money. *xəser mablaġ məḥtəram.* 2. *žoohari*.* I don't see any substantial difference between the two. *maa-li šaayef ʔənu farəq žoohari been ət-tneen.*

substantially - *žoohariyyan, bəž-žoohar.* The two are substantially alike. *t-tneen žoohariyyan mətəl bačḍon.*

substitute - *naaʔeb* pl. *nuwwaab.* If you can't be here tomorrow, send a substitute. *ʔiza maa fiik təḥḍar bəkra bčaat naaʔeb čannak.*
as a substitute for - *čawaaḍ˜..., badaal˜...* Margarine is frequently used as a substitute for butter. *s-samne n-nabaatiyye məstačmale ktiir čawaaḍ əz-zəbde.*
to substitute - 1. *baddal, stabdal.* I'll substitute green for red. *laḥa baddel əl-ʔaḥmar bəl-ʔaxḍar.* 2. *naab (u nyaabe) čan, qaam (u qyaam˜) maqaam˜...* Can you substitute for me today? *fiik ətnuub čanni l-yoom?* or *fiik ətquum maqaami l-yoom?*

subtle - *daqiiq.* Notice the subtle distinction the author is making. *šuuf ət-tamyiiz əd-daqiiq halli čaamlo l-əmʔallef.* -- It's sometimes impossible to bring out the subtle shades of meaning of a given word. *b-bačḍ əl-ʔawqaat məstaḥiil əl-waaḥed ywarži l-əfruuq əd-daqiiqa la-mačna kəlme mčayyane.*

to **subtract** - *ṭaraḥ (a ṭarəḥ//nṭaraḥ).* You should have subtracted 30 from the sum, not added it. *kaan laazem təṭraḥ tlaatiin mn əl-mažmuuč, muu təžmačo.*

subtraction - *ṭarəḥ.*

suburb - *ḍaaḥye* pl. *ḍawaaḥi.*

subway - *meetro* pl. *meetroyaat.*

to **succeed** - 1. *xalaf (e/o ø//nxalaf).* Who succeeded him in office? *miin xalafo b-markazo?* 2. *nažaḥ (a nažaaḥ).* He succeeds in everything he undertakes. *byənžaḥ əb-kəll šii bisaawīi.* -- You'll never succeed in convincing him. *b-ḥayaatak maa btənžaḥ əb-ʔəqnaačo.*

success - *nažaaḥ, fooz.* Congratulations on your success! *bhanniik čala nažaaḥak.*
to be a success - *nažaḥ (a nažaaḥ).* The play wasn't much of a success. *t-tamsiiliyye maa nažḥet hal-qadd.*

successful - *naažeḥ, mwaffaq.*

successive - *mətwaali, məttaabeč.*

successor - *xaliife* pl. *xəlafa.* Our ambassador in France was appointed his successor. *safiirna b-fransa tčayyan xaliifto.*

such - 1. *heek, ... mətəl heek, mətəl˜...* Such statements are hard to prove. *heek ʔaqwaal* (or *ʔaqwaal mətəl heek* or *mətəl hal-ʔaqwaal*) *ṣačəb ʔəsbaata.* — She would never say such a thing. *məstaḥiil ətkuun qaalet heek šii.* — I heard some such thing. *smečət mətəl haš-šii.* — Such a word doesn't even exist. *ḥatta maa fii mətəl hal-kəlme.* — I've never heard such nonsense before. *b-ḥayaati maa smečət heek ʔakəl hawa.* 2. *hal-qadd.* They pay him such a small salary that he has to get a second job. *byədfačuu-lo hal-qadd mačaaš əzġiir ḥatta ʔənno mažbuur ylaaqi šaġle taanye.* -- Don't be in such a hurry. *laa tkuun hal-qadd məstačžel.*
**It's been such a long time that I can't remember any more. *maḍa čaleeha zamaan əktiir maa čaad fiini ədzakkdra.*
**It's been such a long time since I saw you last. *qaddeeš maḍa zamaan čala ʔaaxer marra šəftak fiiha.*
**He's such a bore! *qaddeešo bimallel!*
such as - 1. *mətəl˜...* Adjectives such as "taaza", "čaal", etc. remain unchanged. *ṣifaat mətəl "taaza", "čaal" ʔila ʔaaxirihi byəbqu čala ṣiiġa waaḥde.* 2. *mətəl-ma.* Leave it such as it is. *trəka mətəl-ma hiyye.* 3. *masalan, mətəl ʔeeš.* I could give you several reasons for it. - Such as? *bəḥsen ʔačṭiik čəddet ʔasbaab la-haš-šaġle. - masalan?*
as such - *b-ḥadd zaato* (or *zaata, zaaton* respectively). The work as such isn't difficult. *š-šaġle b-ḥadd zaata muu ṣačbe.*
such and such - *flaani*, kaza w-kaza* (invar.). He went to such and such a place that the man had pointed out to him. *raaḥ ləl-maḥall l-əflaani halli z-zalame dallo čalée.*

to **suck** - 1. *maṣṣ (ə maṣṣ//mmaṣṣ).* Stop sucking your thumb. *ḥaaštak ətməṣṣ baahmak.* 2. *rəḍeč (a rḍaača).* Look at the cute little lamb sucking from its mother's breast. *šuuf hal-xaaruuf əz-zġiir čam yərḍač mən bəzz ʔəmmo.*

sucker - *mġaffal* pl. *-iin.* He's waiting for some sucker to buy his old jalopy. *čam yəstanna šii waaḥed əmġaffal yəštəri mənno əṭ-ṭəmbor tabačo.*

Sudan - *s-suudaan.*

Sudanese - *suudaani*.*

sudden - *fəžaaʔi*.* There's been a sudden change in the weather. *ṣaar fii taġyiir fəžaaʔi bəṭ-ṭaqəs.*
all of a sudden - *mən qalb əd-dənye, čala ġafle.* All of a sudden I remembered that I had to mail a letter. *mən qalb əd-dənye dzakkart ʔənno kaan laazem ḥəṭṭ maktuub bəl-boosṭa.*

suddenly - *fažʔatan, čala ġafle, mən qalb əd-dənye.* Suddenly everything disappeared. *fažʔatan kəll šii xtafa.*

suds - *ġsaalet˜ ṣaabuun,* (froth) *raġwet˜ ṣaabuun.*

to **sue** - 1. *qaam (i qayamaan˜//nqaamet) dačwa čala.* We sued him for damages. *qəmna čalée dačwa b-ṭalab ət-tačwiiḍaat.* 2. *ṭaalab.* They'll sue for peace. *bəddon yṭaalbu bəs-salaam.*

suet - *šaḥəm.*

to **suffer** - 1. *tčazzab, tʔallam.* Did she suffer very much? *tčazzabet əktiir?* 2. *tkabbad.* They suffered heavy losses. *tkabbadu xaṣaayer faadḥa.*

sufficient - *kaafi, kfaaye* (invar.). Do we have

sufficient provisions for the trip? *fii Ɛanna muune kaafye mənšaan ᵊs-safra?*
to be sufficient - *kaffa, kafa (i kfaaye).* Will the food be sufficient for so many guests? *l-ʔakᵊl bikaffi la-hal-Ɛadad mn ᵊḏ-ḏyuuf?*
sufficiently - *kfaaye.*
to **suffocate** - 1. *xtanaq.* I nearly suffocated. *kənᵊt laḥa ʔəxtə́neq.* 2. *xanaq (e xanᵊq//xtanaq).* Open the windows, the heat in this room is suffocating. *ftaaḥ ᵊš-šababiik, š-šoob b-hal-ʔuuḍa Ɛam yəxneq xanᵊq.*
Sufi - *ṣuufi* pl. *-iyye.*
Sufism - *ṣ-ṣuufiyye.*
sugar - *səkkar.* Please pass me the sugar. *marrə́q-li s-səkkar mən faḍlak.*
sugar bowl - *səkkariyye* pl. *-aat.*
sugar cane - *qaṣab˜ maṣṣ,* (a stalk) *qaṣabet˜ maṣṣ* pl. *-aat˜ maṣṣ.*
sugar loaf - *raas˜* (pl. *ruus˜*) *səkkar.*
sugar refinery - *maƐmal˜* (pl. *maƐaamel˜*) *səkkar.*
sugar tongs - *malqaṭ˜* (pl. *malaaqeṭ˜*) *səkkar.*
to **suggest** - 1. *q̈taraḥ.* I suggest that we go to the movies. *bəq̈tə́reḥ ᵊnruuḥ Ɛas-siinama.* — I'll suggest it at the next meeting. *laḥa ʔəq̈tərə́ḥa bᵊš-žalse l-qaadme.* — It was he who suggested it to me. *kaan huwwe halli q̈tarə́ḥa Ɛaliyyi.* 2. *laṭṭaš.* Are you suggesting that I'm wrong? *šuu Ɛam ᵊtlaṭṭeš ʔənni ġalṭaan?* 3. *waḥa (-yuuḥi ø) b-.* Does this suggest anything to you? *haada byuuḥí-lak ᵊb-šii?*
suggestion - 1. *ʔəq̈tiraaḥ* pl. *-aat.* May I make a suggestion? *məmken qaddem ʔəq̈tiraaḥ?* 2. *ʔišaara, naṣiiḥa.* At his suggestion, we stayed in Beirut overnight. *binaaʔan Ɛala ʔišaarto bətna l-leele b-beeruut.*
suicide - *ʔəntiḥaar* pl. *-aat.* The number of suicides has been increasing over the past few years. *Ɛadad ᵊl-ʔəntiḥaaraat Ɛala ʔəzdiyaad bᵊs-sniin ᵊl-ʔaaxraaniyye.*
to commit suicide - *ntaḥar, qatal (o qatᵊl) ḥaalo.* She's said to have committed suicide. *biquulu ʔənna ntaḥret* (or *qatlet ḥaala*).
suit - 1. *badle* pl. *-aat, ṭaqᵊm* pl. *ṭquum(e).* He needs a new suit. *laazmo badle ždiide.* 2. *tayyoor* pl. *-aat.* How do you like her gray suit? *kiif bətḥəbb tayyoora r-rṣaaṣi?* 3. *daƐwa* pl. *daƐaawi.* If we do not hear from you by Monday, we shall bring suit. *ʔiza maa btəžží-lna kəlme mənnak qabl ᵊt-taneen mənqiim Ɛaleek daƐwa.* — Did the company win the suit? *š-šərke rəbḥet ᵊd-daƐwa šii?* 4. *loon* pl. *lwaan.* Diamonds is his strongest suit. *d-diinaari ʔaqwa loon Ɛando.*
to follow suit - *ləḥeq (a lḥuuq) ᵊl-loon.* For instance, when I play clubs you have to follow suit. *masalan, ʔiza bəlḥoš sbaati laazem təlḥaq ᵊl-loon.* 2. *ləḥeq (a lḥuuq).* If he takes one, I'll follow suit. *ʔiza huwwe ʔaxad waaḥde ʔana bəlḥaqo.*
to suit - 1. *raḍa (i ʔərḍaaʔ).* It's hard to suit everybody. *ṣaƐᵊb tərḍi kəll ᵊn-naas* or *maa ḥada byərḍi n-naas ʔəlla ʔaḷḷa.* 2. *waafaq.* Which day would suit you best? *ʔanu yoom biwaafqak ʔaḥsan?* 3. *waata, ʔəža Ɛala.* Does this suit your taste? *haš-šii biwaati zooqak* (or *byəži Ɛala zooqak*)? 4. *ʔəža Ɛala, raaḥ la-.* Red doesn't suit you. *l-ʔaḥmar maa byəži Ɛaleek* (or *maa birə́ḥ-lak*).
**Suit yourself. *Ɛala keefak!*
to suit something to - *Ɛamel šii ynaaseb* (or *ywaafeq*). The book is suited to the age of the children. *l-ᵊktaab maƐmuul ynaaseb sənn l-ᵊwlaad.*
to be suited for - *ṣalaḥ (e ṣalaaḥ) la-.* Is she suited for this kind of work? *ṣaalḥa hiyye la-heek nooƐ mn ᵊš-šəġᵊl?*
suitable - *mwaafeq, mnaaseb, laayeq.* We can find a suitable apartment. *mnəġder ᵊnlaaqi ʔaḅarṭmaan ᵊmwaafeq.*
suitcase - *šanta* pl. *šanaati, šantaaye* pl. *-aat.*
sulfate - *səlfaat* pl. *-aat.*
sulfur - *kəbriit.*
sulfuric acid - *ḥaamoḍ˜ kəbriit.*
to **sulk** - *bawwaz, ḥaran (o ḥarᵊn).* It won't get you anywhere if you just sit in the corner and sulk. *maa fii ʔifaade ʔabadan ʔiza bəttamm qaaƐed ᵊmbawwez.*
sullen - *Ɛaabes.*
sultan - *ṣəlṭaan* pl. *ṣalaṭiin.*
sultanate - *ṣalṭane* pl. *-aat.*
sultry - *Ɛəbeq.* It's awfully sultry today. *faẓaaƐa šuu ṭ-ṭaqᵊṣ Ɛəbeq ᵊl-yoom* or ***faẓaaƐa šuu Ɛbuuq ᵊl-yoom.*

sum - 1. *mablaġ* pl. *mabaaleġ.* I still owe him a small sum. *ləssa Ɛaliyyi mablaġ ᵊẓġiir ʔəlo.* 2. *mažmuuƐ* pl. *-aat.* Multiply the sum of the principal and the interest by twelve. *ḍroob mažmuuƐ ᵊl-mablaġ ᵊl-ʔaṣli wᵊl-faayde b-ᵊṭnaƐš.*
to sum up - *laxxaṣ.* Let me sum up briefly. *xalliini laxxeṣ b-ʔəxtiṣaar.*
**To sum up, he's no good at all. *xulaaṣt ᵊl-ḥadiis, huwwe maa byəswa ʔabadan.*
summary - *xulaaṣa* pl. *-aat, mlaxxaṣ* pl. *-aat, məxtə́ṣar* pl. *-aat.*
summer - 1. *ṣeef.* Does it get hot here in summer? *bətšawweb hoon bᵊṣ-ṣeef?* 2. *ṣeefiyye* pl. *-aat, ṣeef.* Do you have any plans for this summer? *Ɛandak šii mašariiƐ la-haṣ-ṣeefiyye?*
summer resort - *maṣyaf* pl. *maṣaayef.* Do you know a nice summer resort in that section? *btaƐrə́f-lak šii maṣyaf ḥalu b-hal-manṭiqa?*
to spend the summer - *ṣayyaf.* We spent the summer in Bloudane. *ṣayyafna b-bluudaan.*
sun - *šamᵊs* (f.) pl. *šmuus.* The sun has just gone down. *š-šams hallaq ġaabet.* — The midday sun is very hot. *šamset ᵊḍ-ḍəhr ᵊktiir ḥaarra.*
sun lamp - *šamᵊs ʔəṣṭinaaƐi* pl. *šmuus ʔəṣṭinaaƐiyye.*
to sun oneself - *šammas ḥaalo.* I'm sunning myself. *Ɛam šammes ḥaali.*
sunbeam - *šƐaaƐ˜* (pl. *ʔašəƐƐet˜*) *šamᵊs.*
sunburn - *ḥarqet˜ šamᵊs.* I came back with a severe sunburn. *ržəƐᵊt maƐi ḥarqet šamᵊs.*
Sunday - *yoom˜* (pl. *ʔiyyaam˜*) *ᵊl-ʔaḥad, l-ʔaḥad* pl. *-aat.* Wait till Sunday. *nṭəẓer la-yoom ᵊl-ʔaḥad.* — We always go to church on Sunday. *daayman mənruuḥ Ɛal-ᵊkniise yoom ᵊl-ʔaḥad.*
sundial - *saaƐa* (pl. *-aat*) *šamsiyye.*
sundown - *ġruub˜ ᵊš-šamᵊs, ġyaab˜ ᵊš-šamᵊs.* We came back at sundown. *ržəƐna maƐ ᵊġruub ᵊš-šamᵊs.*
sunflower - *dawwaar˜ ᵊl-qamar.*
sunlight - *ḍaww˜ ᵊš-šamᵊs.*
Sunnite - *sənni** pl. *sənne.*
sunny - *məšmes.* The front rooms are sunny. *l-ʔuwaḍ ᵊl-qəddaamaaniyye məšᵊmse.*
sunrise - *ṭluuƐ˜ ᵊš-šamᵊs.* We started out at sunrise. *mšiina maƐ ᵊṭluuƐ ᵊš-šamᵊs.*
sunset - *ġruub˜ ᵊš-šamᵊs, ġyaab˜ ᵊš-šamᵊs.*
sunshine - *ḍaww˜ ᵊš-šamᵊs.*
sunstroke - *ḍarbet˜ šamᵊs.* I almost had a sunstroke. *kaan laḥa yṣər-li ḍarbet šamᵊs.*
superficial - *saṭḥi**.
superfluous - *fooq ᵊl-lzuum.* These are superfluous expenses in my opinion. *b-raʔyi hayy maṣariif fooq ᵊl-lzuum.*
superior - 1. *raʔiis* pl. *rəʔasa.* Is he your superior? *huwwe raʔiisak?* 2. *məmtaaz, xaareq, faaxer.* This material is of superior quality. *hal-ᵊqmaaš žəns məmtaaz.* 3. *mətfawweq.* We fought against an enemy superior in number and equipment. *ḥaarabna ḍəḍḍ Ɛaduww mətfawweq bᵊl-Ɛədde wᵊl-Ɛadad.*
superiority - *tafawwoq.*
superstition - 1. *xuraafaat* (pl.), *ʔəƐtiqaad bᵊl-xuraafaat.* Superstition is still widespread in the country. *l-xuraafaat ləssaaha šaayƐa ktiir bᵊl-ᵊblaad.* 2. *xuraafe* pl. *-aat.* That's an old superstition. *hayy xuraafe Ɛatiiqa.*
superstitious - *xuraafi**. She clings to all kinds of superstitious beliefs. *btətmassak b-ʔəƐtiqaadaat xuraafiyye mən kəll ᵊl-ʔalwaan.*
**Don't be so superstitious. *laa təƐtə́qed hal-qadd bᵊl-xuraafaat.*
**The superstitious peasants in the area claim that the ruins are haunted. *l-fallaaḥiin ᵊb-hal-manṭiqa halli byəƐtəqdu bᵊl-xuraafaat biquulu ʔənno l-xaraabaat maskuune.*
supervision - *ʔəšraaf.* They are under constant supervision. *hənne taḥᵊt ʔəšraaf mətwaaṣel.*
supervisor - *məšref* pl. *-iin.*
supper - *Ɛaša* pl. *ʔəƐᵊšye.* I've been invited for supper. *nƐazamt Ɛal-Ɛaša.*
to have (or **eat**) **supper** - *tƐašša.* What time do you usually have supper? *b-ʔayy saaƐa Ɛaadatan btətƐaššu?*
supplement - *məlḥaq̈* pl. *-aat* and *malaaḥeq̈.* A supplement to the dictionary will come out soon. *laḥa yəṭlaƐ məlḥaq̈ ləl-q̈aamuus Ɛan qariib.*
supply - 1. *mawžuudaat* (pl.). We still have a big supply of bicycles. *ləssa fii Ɛanna mawžuudaat ᵊktiir mn ᵊl-bəsᵊkleetaat.* 2. *tamwiin.* Our supply lines were under constant threat from submarines and aircraft. *xṭuuṭ tamwiinna kaanet taḥᵊt tahdiid*

daa⁽em mən ⁹l-ġawwaaṣaat w⁹t-ṭayyaaraat.
supplies - *mέaddaat* (pl.), *zaxaayer.* On the fifth day of battle, the troops were running out of supplies. *b⁹l-yoom ⁹l-xaames ləl-maέrake ž-žunuud nafdet mέaddaaton.*
supply and demand - *έarḍ w-ṭalab.* It's simply a question of supply and demand. *b-kəlme waaḥde l-mas⁹ale mas⁹alt έarḍ w-ṭalab.*
to supply - 1. *zawwad.* Our bakery supplies all the big hotels. *l-maxbaze tabaέna bədzawwed kəll ⁹l-⁹oteelaat l-⁹kbaar.* -- He always supplies us with cigarettes. *daayman bizawwədna b⁹s-sigaaraat.*
2. *qaam b-.* We have enough shoes to supply any demand. *fii έanna ṣababiiṭ ⁹kfaaye la-nquum b-⁹ayy ṭalab.*
support - 1. *ta⁹yiid, mέaaḍada.* You can count on my support. *fiik təέtə́med έala ta⁹yiidi ⁹əlak.* 2. *⁹iέaale.* He's responsible for the support of his former wife. *huwwe mas⁹uul έan ⁹iέaalet marto l-⁹mṭallaqa.* 3. *rakiize* pl. *rakaayez.* The supports of the platform are rather weak. *rakaayez ⁹l-minaṣṣa muu qawiyye.*
**Can you offer any evidence in support of your statement? *byəṭlaέ b-⁹iidak tqaddem ⁹ayy bərhaan y⁹ayyed ⁹ifaadtak?*
to support - 1. *⁹ayyad.* He's being supported by all parties. *kəll ⁹l-⁹aḥzaab ⁹m⁹ayyədto.* -- I'll support your plan. *⁹ana b⁹ayyed xəṭṭ⁹tak.* 2. *έaal (i ⁹iέaale).* He has to support his parents. *laazem yέiil ⁹abúu w-⁹əmmo.* 3. *sanad (o san⁹d//nsanad), ḥamal (e ḥam⁹l//nḥamal).* One huge pillar supports the entire ceiling. *fii έaḍaada ḍaxme waaḥde saande s-saq⁹f kəllo.*
to support oneself - *tkaffal b-ḥaalo, έaal (i ⁹iέaalet˜) ḥaalo.* I have had to support myself ever since I was fifteen. *nžabart ⁹ətkaffal b-ḥaali mən waq⁹t kaan έəmri xam⁹ṣṭaέ⁹š.*
to **suppose** - 1. *faraḍ (o ø), ftaraḍ.* Let's suppose that I'm right. *xalliina nəfroḍ ⁹ənno maέi ḥaqq.* — Suppose I give him the money. Then what? *frooḍ έaṭeeto l-maṣaari. w-baέdeen šuu?* 2. *ftakar, έtaqad, ẓann (ə ẓann).* I suppose he's already gone. *bəftə́ker ⁹ənno raaḥ w-xalaṣ.* -- I suppose so. *bẓənn heek.*
**Suppose you wait till tomorrow. *šuu ra⁹yak ⁹iza stanneet la-bəkra?*
to be supposed to - *l-mafruuḍ b- ... (⁹ənno).* He's supposed to be rich. *l-mafruuḍ fii ⁹ənno ġani.* -- Her sister is supposed to be very intelligent. *l-mafruuḍ ⁹b-⁹əxta ⁹ənna zakiyye ktiir.* — I'm supposed to go out tonight, but I'm too tired. *l-mafruuḍ fiyyi ⁹əṭlaέ ⁹əshar ⁹l-leele, bass ⁹ana taέbaan ⁹ktiir.*
to **suppress** - *xanaq (e/o xan⁹q//nxanaq).* For many years the government has suppressed freedom of speech. *mən sniin ⁹ktiire ṣar-la l-⁹ḥkuume xaanqa ḥərriit ⁹l-kalaam.*
supremacy - *haymane.*
supreme commander - *q̈aa⁹ed ⁹aέla.*
sure - 1. *m⁹akkad, ⁹akiid, saabet.* That's a sure thing. *haada šii m⁹akkad.* 2. *maέluum, ⁹akiid.* Sure, I'll do it. *maέluum bsaawiiha.* 3. *⁹akiid.* I'd sure like to see him. *⁹akiid ḥaabeb šuufo.* 4. *b-kəll ta⁹kiid, biduun šakk, maέluum.* Have you locked the garage door? - Sure! *daqqar⁹t baab ⁹l-garaaž? - b-kəll ta⁹kiid.* 5. *⁹akiid, mət⁹akked, mən kəll bədd.* He's sure to be back at nine o'clock. *⁹akiid byəržaέ ⁹s-saaέa təsέa.*
sure enough - 1. *b⁹l-fəέ⁹l.* You thought it would rain, and sure enough it did. *ftakart ⁹ənno bədda tənzel maṭar, w-b⁹l-fəέ⁹l nəzlet.* 2. *maέluum.* Did you catch the train? - Sure enough! *laḥḥaqt ⁹t-treen? - maέluum!*
for sure - *m⁹akkad, ⁹akiid.* Be there by five o'clock for sure. *m⁹akkad kuun ⁹hniik ⁹s-saaέa xamse.* — I know it for sure. *baέ⁹rfa ⁹akiid.*
to be sure - *ṭayyeb.* It's done, to be sure, but how? *ṭayyeb, tsaawet, bass kiif?*
to be sure of - 1. *kaan mət⁹akked mən.* Are you sure of that? *⁹ənte mət⁹akked mən haš-šii?* 2. *kaan waaseq̈ mən* (or *b-*). He's not very sure of himself. *huwwe muu waaseq̈ ⁹ktiir mən ḥaalo.*
be sure not to - *⁹əṣḥa..., diir baalak maa...* Be sure not to forget your umbrella. *⁹əṣḥa tənsa šamsiitak* or *diir baalak maa tənsa šamsiitak.*
be sure to - *⁹əṣḥa maa..., diir baalak ...* Be sure to come tomorrow! *⁹əṣḥa maa təži bəkra!* or *diir baalak təži bəkra!*
to make sure - 1. *tḥaqqaq (mən), t⁹akkad (mən).* Make sure that you have everything. *tḥaqqaq ⁹ənno ṣaar έandak kəll šii.* -- I just wanted to make sure that everything was all right. *⁹ana kaan kəll halli bəddi-yáa ⁹ənno ⁹atḥaqqaq kəll šii maaši maẓbuuṭ.* 2. *xalla baalo, daar baalo.* Make sure that he gets one too. *xalli baalak ⁹ənno huwwe kamaan yaaxod waaḥde.* -- Make sure that it doesn't happen again. *xalli baalak haš-šii maa yṣiir taani marra.*
surely - 1. *b-kəll ta⁹kiid, biduun šakk, maέluum, lakaan.* Will you be there? - Surely. *raḥa tkuun ⁹hniik? - b-kəll ta⁹kiid.* 2. *b-kəll ta⁹kiid, biduun šakk, maέluum.* He can surely do that. *b-kəll ta⁹kiid byəṭlaέ b-⁹iido yaέmel haš-šii.* 3. *mən kəll bədd.* I surely thought it would be done. *ftakar⁹t ⁹ənno mən kəll bədd laḥa təxloṣ.* 4. *⁹akiid.* I surely ought to know that! *⁹akiid laazem ⁹aέrə́fa!*
surface - *ṣaṭ⁹ḥ* pl. *ṣṭuuḥ.* The surface of the road is pretty bad at some places. *ṣaṭḥ ⁹ṭ-ṭariiq έaaṭel b-baέḍ ⁹l-qaraani.*
on the surface - *ṣaṭḥiyyan.* On the surface, the question looks easy. *ṣaṭḥiyyan ⁹l-mas⁹ale mbayyne hayyne.*
surgeon - *žarraaḥ* pl. *-iin.*
surgery - 1. *žiraaḥa, ṭəbb žiraaḥi.* He specializes in surgery. *huwwe mətxaṣṣeṣ b⁹ž-žiraaḥa.* 2. *έamaliyye žiraaḥiyye.* The doctor says she'll need surgery. *d-doktoor qaal ⁹ənno laazə́ma έamaliyye (žiraaḥiyye).*
surgical - *žiraaḥi*.*
to **surpass** - *faaq (u ø) έan.* The figures surpass the wildest imagination. *l-⁹arq̈aam bətfuuq έan ḥadd ⁹t-taṣawwor.*
surplus - *faa⁹eḍ.* They have a surplus of manpower. *fii έandon faa⁹eḍ mn ⁹l-yad ⁹l-έaamle.* — The country has bought several thousand tons of American surplus wheat. *l-⁹blaad štaret ⁹aalaaf ⁹l-⁹aṭnaan mən faa⁹eḍ ⁹l-qam⁹ḥ ⁹l-⁹ameerki.*
surprise - 1. *mfaaža⁹a* pl. *-aat.* I've got a surprise for you. *fii έandi mfaaža⁹a ⁹əlak.* 2. *dahše.* Think of my surprise when I opened the door and there was my brother. *tṣawwar qaddeeš kaanet dah⁹šti lamma fataḥt ⁹l-baab w-šəft qəddaami ⁹axi.* -- Later I learned, to my surprise, that he was right. *baέdeen la-dah⁹šti έrəf⁹t ⁹ənno kaan ⁹mḥəqq.*
**You'll get the surprise of your life. *raḥa tšuuf šoofe bəṭṭayyə́r-lak έaqlak.*
to catch by surprise - *daaham, baaġat.* The rain caught me by surprise. *l-maṭar daahamətni.*
to take by surprise - *⁹axad έala ġafle.* You took me completely by surprise. *⁹axadtni έala ġafle tamaam.*
to surprise - 1. *faaža⁹, baaġat.* I wanted to surprise you. *kaan bəddi faaž⁹ak.* 2. *dahaš (o/e dahše//ndahaš).* Nothing surprises me any more. *maa έaad fii šii yədhəšni.*
surprising - 1. *mfaaže⁹, fižaa⁹i*.* He made another one of his surprising decisions. *έəmel q̈araar taani mən q̈araaraato l-⁹mfaaž⁹a.* 2. *mədheš.* A surprising number of the women are still illiterate. *ləssa fii έadad mədheš mn ⁹n-naswaan ⁹əmmiyyiin.*
to be surprised - 1. *ndahaš (b-), tέažžab (mən), staġrab.* I was very much surprised that he came. *ndahašt ⁹ktiir ⁹ənno ⁹əža.* -- I'm not surprised at anything you do. *maa bəndə́heš b-⁹ayy šii btaέ⁹mlo ⁹ənte.* 2. *tέažžab (mən), ndahaš (b-).* I'm surprised at you. *⁹ana mətέažžeb mənnak.* -- You'll be surprised to see how he's changed. *btəndə́heš kiif ⁹tġayyar.*
to **surrender** - *staslam, sallam.* The enemy surrendered. *l-έaduww staslam.*
to **surround** - *ḥaawaṭ, ḥaaṭ (i ⁹iḥaaṭa) b-.* A high fence surrounds the tennis court. *fii ḥaažez έaali biḥaaweṭ saaḥet ⁹t-tanəs.* -- They surrounded us on all sides. *ḥaawaṭuuna mən kəll žiha.*
survey - 1. *mas⁹ḥ.* The land survey is almost finished. *masḥ ⁹l-⁹araaḍi έala wašak yəxloṣ.* 2. *kaš⁹f* pl. *kšuuf(e).* The government is making a survey of the damage caused by the flood. *l-⁹ḥkuume έam taέmel kašf ⁹l-⁹aḍraar halli sabbə́ba l-fayaḍaan.*
to survey - 1. *masaḥ (a mas⁹ḥ//mmasaḥ).* They have to survey the land before they can put a road through. *laazem yəmsaḥu l-⁹araaḍi qab⁹l-ma ymarrqu ṭariiq fiiha.* 2. *staέraḍ.* The author surveys the entire field of Hanafi law. *l-⁹m⁹allef byəstaέreḍ kəll baab ⁹l-mazhab ⁹l-ḥanafi.*
surveyor - *massaaḥ* pl. *-iin.*
survival - *baq̈aa⁹.* He maintains that the survival of mankind depends on nuclear disarmament. *bi⁹akked*

ʔənno baqaaʔ ᵊl-bašariyye mətwaqqef ʕala nazᵊʕ ᵊs-silaaḥ ᵊz-zarri.

to **survive** - *bəqi (a baqayaan) ṭayyeb (baʕᵊd).* Only a handful of people survived the catastrophe. *bass byənʕaddu ʕal-ʔaṣaabeʕ halli bəqyu ṭayybiin baʕd ᵊl-kaarse.*

suspect - *mašbuuh* pl. *-iin.* The police picked him up as a likely suspect in the holdup. *l-booliis kamašo ka-mašbuuh ᵊmraššaḥ bᵊt-tašliiḥa.*

to suspect - *štabah b-.* Do you suspect anything? *btəštəbeh ᵊb-šii?* — I suspect him. *bəštəbeh fii huwwe.*

to **suspend** - **1.** *waqqaf.* The bank has suspended all payments. *l-bank waqqaf kəll ᵊd-dafʕaat.* **2.** *kaff (ə kaff//nkaffet) ʔiid˜...* He was suspended (from work) for a week. *nkaffet ʔiido la-məddet ʔəsbuuʕ.* **3.** *ṭarad (o ṭarᵊd//nṭarad).* They suspended him from classes for the rest of the year. *ṭaradúu mn ᵊl-madrase la-nhaayet ᵊs-səne.*

suspender - *šayyaale* pl. *-aat.*

suspense - *balbale.* I can't stand the suspense any longer. *maa ʕədt ʔəthammal hal-balbale.*

**The story is full of suspense. *l-qəṣṣa mwattre ləl-ʔaʕṣaab.*

suspension - *tawqiif.* Next time it may mean the suspension of your driving license. *l-marra ž-žaaye yəmken ᵊtʔaddi la-tawqiif šahaadet ᵊs-swaaqa tabaʕak.*

suspension bridge - *žəsr ᵊmʕallaq* pl. *žsuur(a) mʕallaqa.*

suspicion - *šəbha* pl. *-aat.* What aroused your suspicion? *šuu halli ʔasaar šəbᵊhtak?*

**I have my suspicions. *ʔana maštəbeh.*

suspicious - **1.** *ẓanuun.* He's a suspicious fellow. *huwwe zalame ẓanuun.* **2.** *mašbuuh fii, məštəbah fii.* That looks suspicious to me. *haš-šii mbayyən-li mašbuuh fii.*

to get suspicious - *štabah.* I immediately got suspicious. *raʔsan ᵊštabahᵊt.*

Swahili - *sawaahili*.*

swallow - *snuunu* (invar.). The swallows have returned early this year. *s-snuunu rəžeʕ bakkiir has-səne.*

swallow - *balʕa* pl. *-aat,* (of drink) *karʕa* pl. *-aat.* One swallow of that poison and you're dead. *balʕa waaḥde mən has-samm btəqᵊtlak.*

to swallow - **1.** *balaʕ (a balᵊʕ//mbalaʕ).* My throat is so sore I can't swallow. *ḥalqi ʕam yəžaʕni maa-li ʕam ʔəqder ʔəblaʕ.* **2.** *karaʕ (a karᵊʕ//nkaraʕ)* He downed the whiskey in one swallow. *karaʕ ᵊl-wəski karʕa waaḥde.* **3.** *hadam (o hadᵊm).* He had to swallow a lot. *walla nšabar yəhdom šii ktiir.*

**He swallows everything he hears. *bisaddeq kəll šii byəsmaʕo.*

swamp - *məstanqaʕ* pl. *-aat.* How far does the swamp go? *qaddeeš byəmtadd hal-məstanqaʕ?*

to be swamped with - *ġaṭaṣ (e/o ġaṭᵊṣ) b-, ġəreq (a ġaraq) b-.* I was swamped with work last week. *kənᵊt ġaaṭeṣ bᵊš-šəġᵊl ᵊž-žəmʕa l-maaḍye.*

swan - *bažʕa* coll. *bažaʕ* pl. *bažʕaat.*

swarm - **1.** *kooše* pl. *-aat* and *kuwaš.* They went after him like a swarm of bees. *rakadu warda mətᵊl koošet dababiir.* **2.** *sərᵊb* pl. *sraab.* We saw a huge swarm of locusts down south. *šəfna sərᵊb haaʔel mn ᵊž-žraad bᵊž-žanuub.* **3.** *raff* pl. *-aat.* Look at that swarm of pigeons over there. *šəf-lak har-raff ᵊl-ḥamaam ᵊhniik.*

to swarm - *ʕažž (ə ʕažž, ʕžiiž).* The swamp swarms with mosquitoes. *l-məstanqaʕ ʕam yʕəžž bᵊn-naamuus.* — People were swarming all over the place. *n-naas kaanu ʕam yʕəžžu bᵊl-maḥall ʕažž.*

swastika - *ṣaliib maʕkuuf* pl. *ṣəlbaan maʕkuufe.*

swatter - *qattaalet˜* (pl. *-aat˜*) *dəbbaan.*

to **sway** - **1.** *tmaayal.* The trees swayed in the wind. *š-šažar tmaayal bᵊl-hawa.* **2.** *zaḥzaḥ.* Nothing can sway him after his mind is made up. *maa fii šii bizaḥᵊzḥo baʕᵊd-ma yəʕtəmed ʕala šii.* **3.** *ʔassar b-* or *ʕala//tʔassar.* She's very easily swayed. *hiyye btətʔassar b-ᵊshuule.*

to **swear** - **1.** *ḥalaf (e ḥəlfaan).* She swears she's telling the truth. *ʕam təḥlef ʔənna ʕam təḥki ṣ-ṣaḥiiḥ.* — I swear by God I didn't do it. *bəḥləf-lak b-ʔaḷḷa ʔənni maa saaweeta.* — Can you swear to that? *btəḥlef ʕala haš-šii?* **2.** *sabb (ə sabb).* He swears like a trooper. *bisabb ʕaṭ-ṭaalʕa wᵊn-naazle.*

to swear in - *ḥallaf//tḥallaf.* Has the witness been sworn in yet? *š-šaahed tḥallaf walla ləssa?*

sweat - *ʕaraq.* He wiped the sweat from his brow. *masaḥ ᵊl-ʕaraq mən ʕala žbiino.*

to sweat - *ʕəreq (a ʕaraq).* I'm sweating all over. *ʕam ʔəʕraq kəlli.* — I sweated over that article for almost a week. *ʕrəqᵊt ʕala hal-maqaale taqriiban žəmʕa.*

sweater - *kanze* pl. *-aat.*

Swede - *sweedi** pl. *-iyyiin, ʔəswəži** pl. *-iyyiin.*

Sweden - *(blaad˜) s-sweed, ʔəswež.*

Swedish - *sweedi*, ʔəswəži*.*

to **sweep** - **1.** *qašš (ə qašš//nqašš), kannas.* Did you sweep the bedroom? *qaššeeti ʔuuḍṭ ᵊn-noom?* **2.** *žaržar ʕala, šaḥaṭ (a šaḥᵊṭ) ʕala.* Your dressing gown sweeps the ground. *r-roobdəšaambᵊr tabaʕak ʕam yžaržer ʕal-ʔarḍ.*

**He swept her off her feet. *ʔaxad-la ʕaqla.*

to sweep up - *kannas, qašš (e qašš//nqašš).* Sweep up that dirt in the corner. *kanneš hal-waṣax mn ᵊl-qərne.*

sweet - **1.** *ḥəlu.* These apples are very sweet. *hat-təffaaḥaat ḥəlwe ktiir.* **2.** *laṭiif* pl. *ləṭafa.* She's a very sweet girl. *hiyye bənt laṭiife ktiir.*

**She has a sweet tooth. *bətḥəbb ᵊl-ḥəlu.*

sweets - *ḥəlu, ḥalwiyyaat* (pl.). I don't care much for sweets. *maa bḥəbb ᵊl-ḥəlu ktiir.*

to **swell** - *wərem (-yəram* and *-yuuram waram).* My ankle is all swollen. *kaaḥli kəllo warmaan.*

**Does he have a swollen head! *waḷḷa raaṣo manfuux ᵊktiir!*

swelling - *waram* pl. *ʔawraam.* Has the swelling gone down? *l-waram xaff?*

to **swerve** - *zaaġ (i zawaġaan).* The car swerved to the right and hit a tree. *s-sayyaara zaaġet naaḥ ᵊl-yamiin w-ḍarbet ᵊb-šažara.*

swim - *sbaaḥa.* It's a great afternoon for a swim. *waḷḷa nhaar təḥfe ləs-sbaaḥa.*

to take a swim - *sabaḥ (a sbaaḥa).* He takes a swim every morning. *byəsbaḥ kəll yoom ʕala bəkra.*

to swim - **1.** *sabaḥ (a sbaaḥa).* Do you know how to swim? *btaʕref təsbaḥ?* — The meat is swimming in gravy. *l-laḥme ʕam təsbaḥ bᵊl-maraqa sbaaḥa.* **2.** *qaṭaʕ (a qaṭᵊʕ)...sbaaḥa.* Can you swim the lake? *fiik təqṭaʕ ᵊl-buḥayra sbaaḥa?*

**My head is swimming. *raasi daayex.*

**Things were swimming before my eyes. *d-dənye ġabbašet b-ᵊʕyuuni.*

swimming - *sbaaḥa.* Don't forget to bring your swimming trunks. *laa tənsa maa džiib ᵊlbaas ᵊs-sbaaḥa tabaʕak.*

swimming pool - *masbaḥ* pl. *masaabeḥ.*

swindle - *xədʕa* pl. *xədaʕ.* A lot of people fell for the swindle. *fii naas ᵊktiir məšyet ʕaleehon ᵊl-xədʕa.*

to swindle - *ġašš (ə ġašš//nġašš), xadaʕ (a xidaaʕ//nxadaʕ).* They swindled him out of all his savings. *ġaššúu w-šallaḥúu kəll šii waffaro.*

swindler - *naṣṣaab* pl. *-iin, ġaššaaš* pl. *-iin.*

swine - *xanziir* pl. *xanaziir.*

swing - *maržuuḥa* pl. *maražiiḥ.* We have a swing in our garden. *fii ʕanna maržuuḥa bᵊž-žneene.*

in full swing - *b-ʕəzz-* + pron. suff. The party is in full swing. *l-ḥafle b-ʕəzza.*

to swing - **1.** *tmaržaḥ.* You'll fall off if you swing so high. *btəqaʕ ʔiza tmaržaḥt b-ᵊʕluww hal-qadd.* **2.** *maržaḥ.* She swings her arms when she walks. *bətmaržeḥ ʔideeha w-hiyye maašye.* **3.** *naas (u nawasaan).* The pendulum swings thirty times a minute. *n-nawwaas binuus tlaatiin noose bᵊd-daqiiqa.*

to swing around - **1.** *duur (i dawaraan//ndaar).* Swing the car around. *diir ᵊs-sayyaara.* **2.** *daar (u doora) ᵊb-sərʕa, ltafat ᵊb-sərʕa.* He swung around when he heard her voice. *daar ᵊb-sərʕa lamma səmeʕ ṣooṭa.*

Swiss - *swiisri*, swiisraani*.*

switch - **1.** *məftaaḥ* pl. *mafatiiḥ.* The switch is next to the door. *l-məftaaḥ žamb ᵊl-baab.* **2.** *mqaṣṣ* pl. *-aat.* The last car jumped the track at the switch. *ʔaaxer fargoon ṭaleʕ ʕan ᵊl-xaṭṭ ʕand l-ᵊmqaṣṣ.* **3.** *taḥwiil, tabaddol.* Have you noticed the surprising switch in their policy? *laaḥaẓt ᵊt-taḥwiil l-ᵊmfaažeʔ b-ᵊsyaasəton?*

to switch - **1.** *ḥawwal//tḥawwal.* The train was switched to another track. *t-treen ᵊtḥawwal la-xaṭṭ taani.* **2.** *tbaadal (maʕ).* Let's switch places. *xalliina nətbaadal maḥallaatna.*

3. *xarbaṭ b-.* I don't know how we switched coats. *maa baʕref kiif xarbaṭna b-kababiidna.*

to switch off - *ṭafa (i ṭafi//nṭafa).* Switch off the light. *ʔəṭfi ḍ-ḍaww.*

to switch on - **1.** *šaʕal (e šaʕᵊl//nšaʕal), fataḥ*

(a fat^{ə}h//nfatah). Switch on the light. š*ε*eel ^{ə}d-daww. 2. fatah. Switch on the ignition. ftaah ^{ə}l-kəntaak.
Switzerland - *swiisra.*
sword - *seef* pl. *syuuf.*
sycamore - *žəmmeeze* coll. *žəmmeez* pl. *-aat.*
syllable - *maq̈taε* pl. *maq̈aateε.* The accent is on the first syllable. *n-nabra εal-maq̈taε ^{ə}l-ʔawwal.*
symbol - *ram^{ə}z* pl. *rmuuz.*
symbolic - *ramzi*.*
symmetrical - *mətnaaseq̈.*
symmetry - *tanaasoq̈.*
to **sympathize with** - *šaεar (o šεuur) maε.* I can sympathize with you. *ʔana bəšεor maεak.*
sympathy - **1.** *šafaqa.* I have no sympathy for her. *maa-li šafaqa mnoob naaha.* **2.** *taεziye* pl. *taεaazi.* (You have) my sincere sympathy. *taεaziyyi l-haarra (ʔəlak).*
symphony - *sənfooniyye* pl. *-aat.*
symphonic - *sənfooni*.*
symptom - **1.** *εaared* pl. *εawaared.* Headaches can be a symptom of eye strain. *wažaε ^{ə}r-raas məmken ykuun εaared la-ʔəžhaad ^{ə}l-εeen.* **2.** *zaahra* pl. *zawaaher.* Juvenile crime is a symptom of social instability. *žaraayem ^{ə}l-ʔahdaas hiyye zaahra mən zawaaher εadam ^{ə}l-ʔəstəq̈raar ^{ə}l-ʔəžtimaaεi.*
synagogue - *kniis* pl. *kanaayes.*
synonym - *mraadef* pl. *-aat.*
synonymous - *mətraadef.*
synopsis - *mlaxxas* pl. *-aat.*
synthetic - *ʔəstinaaεi*.*
syphilis - *sefles, zəhri, marad ʔafranži.*
Syria - *suuriyya.*
Syriac - *səryaani*.*
Syrian - *suuri*.*
system - **1.** *tariiqa* pl. *təroq, ʔəsluub* pl. *ʔasaliib.* I have a better system. *εandi tariiqa ʔahsan.* **2.** *nizaam* pl. *-aat,* also *ʔanzime.* Their whole economic system is outmoded. *nizaamon ^{ə}l-ʔəq̈tisaadi b-mažmuuεo raah εahdo.* **3.** *žihaaz* pl. *ʔəž^{ə}hze.* Those fumes have a harmful effect on the respiratory system. *had-daxaxiin ʔəla taʔsiir ^{ə}mdərr εala žihaaz ^{ə}t-tanaffos.*
**My system can't take it. *haš-šii maa biwaatiini.*
systematic - *manhaži*.* The article gives a systematic presentation of the subject. *l-maq̈aal byəεred ^{ə}l-mawduuε εard manhaži.*
systematically - *b-ʔəntizaam, b-suura məntdzame.* We must attack the problem systematically. *laazem nεaaləž ^{ə}l-məš^{ə}kle b-ʔəntizaam.*

T

table - **1.** *taawle* pl. *-aat.* Put the table in the middle of the room. *hətt ^{ə}t-taawle b-nəss ^{ə}l-ʔuuda.* **2.** *səfra* pl. *səfar.* They were at table when I phoned. *kaanu εas-səfra lamma εmə lt talifoon.* **3.** *žadwal* pl. *žadaawel.* The figures are given in the Table on page 20. *l-ʔarq̈aam mawžuude b^{ə}ž-žadwal εala safhet εəšriin.*
**Now the tables are turned. *hallaq ^{ə}tgayyaret ^{ə}l-ʔahwaal.*
table of contents - *fahras* pl. *fahaares.* Look it up in the table of contents. *raažəεa b^{ə}l-fahras.*
table tennis - *ping-pong, kuret˜ ^{ə}t-taawle.*
tablecloth - *saršaf˜* (pl. *šaraašef˜*) *taawle, gata˜* (pl. *ʔəg^{ə}tyet˜*) *taawle.*
tablespoon - *maεlaqet˜* (pl. *maεaaleq˜*) *šooraba, maεlaqa kbiire.*
tablet - **1.** *daftar˜* (pl. *dafaater˜*) *məswadde.* Write it down on your tablet. *ktəba b-daftar ^{ə}l-məswadde tabaεak.* **2.** *habbe* pl. *-aat* and *hbuub.* Did you take your tablets on time? *ʔaxadt ^{ə}hbuubak εal-waq^{ə}t?*
tack - **1.** (thumb tack) *pineez* pl. *-aat.* Tacks won't hold on this wall. *l-pineezaat maa byəεlaqu b-hal-heet.* **2.** *bəsmaar ^{ə}zgiir* pl. *basamiir ^{ə}zgaar.* Hand me a handful of those (carpet) tacks. *naawəlni kamše mən hal-basamiir ^{ə}z-zgaar.*
to tack - **1.** *sarraž.* Tack the hem before you sow it! *sarrži d-daayer qab^{ə}l-ma txayyti.* **2.** *masmar//tmasmar, basmar//tbasmar.* He tacked the carpet down to the floor. *masmar ^{ə}s-səžžaade b^{ə}l-ʔar^{ə}d.* **3.** *sabbat ... b^{ə}l-pineez.* Tack the map on the wall. *sabbet ^{ə}l-xaarta εal-heet b^{ə}l-pineez.*
to **tackle** - *εaalaž.* You've tackled the problem the wrong way. *εaalažt ^{ə}l-məš^{ə}kle b-tariiqa galat.*
tact - *labaaqa.* This task requires a considerable amount of tact. *hal-^{ə}mhəmme btəttallab labaaqa ktiire.*
tactful - *ləbeq.* A tactful person would have said nothing. *waahed ləbeq maa kaan qaal šii.*
**I don't think that was a very tactful answer. *maa bəεtəqed haž-žawaab kaan bidəll εala labaaqa.*
tactical - *taktiiki*.*
tactics - *taktiik.*
taffeta - *tafta.*
tag - **1.** *bitaaq̈a* pl. *-aat.* Please remove the price tag before wrapping it. *balla qiim ^{ə}l-bitaaq̈a halli εaleeha s-səε^{ə}r qab^{ə}l-ma tləffa.* **2.** *plaak* pl. *-aat.* Our dog lost his tag. *kalbna daawaε ^{ə}l-plaak tabaεo.*
to play tag - *ləεeb (a ləε^{ə}b) daqra* (or *daqqa*). The children played tag all afternoon. *l-^{ə}wlaad ləεbu daqra kəll baεd ^{ə}d-dəh^{ə}r.*
tail - *danab* pl. *dnaab.* My dog has a short tail. *kalbi danabo qasiir.*
**I can't make head or tail of the story. *maa-li fahmaan ^{ə}l-qəssa ʔawwalta mən ʔaaxərta.*
**Head(s) or tail(s)? *tərra walla naq^{ə}š?*
tails - *fraak* pl. *-aat.* The gentlemen wore tails. *r-ržaal kaanu laabsiin fraak.*
tail light - *daww˜* (pl. *ʔəd^{ə}wyet˜*) *stoop.*
at the tail end of - *b-ʔaaxer˜ ...* We arrived at the tail end of the first act. *wsəlna b-ʔaaxer ^{ə}l-fasl ^{ə}l-ʔawwal.*
tailor - *xayyaat* pl. *-iin.*
take - *reeε.* The take ran to fifty thousand dollars. *r-reeε wəsel la-xamsiin ʔalf dolaar.*
to take - **1.** *ʔaxad (-yaaxod ʔax^{ə}d//ttaaxad).* Who took my ties? *miin ʔaxad kraafaati?* -- Why don't you take the bus? *leeš maa btaaxod ^{ə}l-baas?* -- He wants to take me to dinner. *bəddo yaaxədni εal-εaša.* -- Who's taking her to the station? *miin laha yaaxəda εal-^{ə}mhatta?* -- We took many pictures. *ʔaxadna suwar ^{ə}ktiire.* -- Did the doctor take your temperature this morning? *ʔaxad ^{ə}d-doktoor haraartak ^{ə}l-yoom εala bəkra?* -- He took a deep breath. *ʔaxad nafas gamiiq.* -- Let's take a quick dip. *xalliina naaxəd-^{ə}lna šii gatsa sariiεa.* -- Let's take a walk. *xalliina naaxəd-^{ə}lna məšwaar.* -- We've taken all the necessary precautions. *ʔaxadna kəll ^{ə}l-ʔəhtiyaataat ^{ə}l-laazme.* -- Take my advice. *xood nasiihti.* -- Don't take it so seriously! *laa taaxəda žaddiyye hal-qadd.* -- All seats are taken. *kəll ^{ə}l-mahallaat maʔxuude* (or *məttaaxde*). -- You'll have to take my word for it. *laa bədd taaxod kalaami siq̈a.* -- He took me at my word. *ʔaxadni εala kalaami.* -- These figures are taken from his latest book. *hal-ʔarq̈aam maʔxuudiin mən ʔaaxer ^{ə}ktaab ʔəlo.* -- My last smallpox vaccination didn't take. *maa ʔaxad ʔaaxer tatεiim ʔəli ləž-žədri.* **2.** *ʔaxad, thammal.* How long will it take? *qaddeeš raha taaxod?* -- That takes too much time. *btəthammal waqt ^{ə}ktiir* or ***haš-šii bəttawwel ^{ə}ktiir.* -- I'll take the responsibility. *ʔana bəthammal ^{ə}l-masʔuuliyye.* **3.** *htaaž, bədd- +* pron. suff. That doesn't take much brains. *haš-šii maa btəhtaaž* (or *maa bəddo*) *zaka ktiir.* -- The whole thing will take a little patience. *l-qəssa bədda* (or *btəhtaaž*) *šwayyet sab^{ə}r.* **4.** *masak (e mas^{ə}k//mmasak).* She took the child by the hand. *masket ^{ə}l-walad ^{ə}b-ʔiido.*
**Take a seat, please. *tfaddal εood!*
**I take it you don't like it. *εala-ma yəzhar muu εaažəbtak.*
**I take it you're in trouble again. *εala-ma yəzhar ʔənnak ^{ə}b-šii warta kamaan.*
**I don't take to him. *maa byəxrot məšti.*
**How did he take to your suggestion? *kiif kaan mawq̈fo mən ʔəq̈tiraahak?*
to take after - *taleε (a talεa) la-.* He takes after his father. *taaleε la-ʔabúu.*
to take along - *ʔaxad (-yaaxod ø) ... maεo.* What else do you want to take along? *šuu kamaan bəddak taaxod maεak?* -- Why don't you take me along? *leeš maa btaaxədni maεak?*

to take away - 1. *ˀaxad (-yaaxod ˀaxᵊd//ttaaxad).* The policeman took him away. *l-booliis ˀaxado.* -- Two men came this morning and took the sofa away. *ˀəža rəžžaaleen ᵊl-yoom Ɛala bəkra w-ˀaxadu ṣ-ṣoofa.* 2. *qaam (i qayamaan//nqaam).* Please, take this box away. *mən faḍlak qiim has-sanduuq (mən hoon).*

to take back - 1. *staržaƐ.* You can take it back, I won't need it any more. *fiik təstaržə́Ɛa maa Ɛaadet təlzamni.* 2. *raǧǧaƐ//traǧǧaƐ.* Take it back to where you found it. *raǧǧə́Ɛa maṭraḥ-ma laqeeta.* -- We already hired someone else so we can't take him back now. *ṣərna mwaẓẓfiin zalame taani maa Ɛaad fiina hallaq nraǧǧə́Ɛo.* -- The store refused to take back the shoes I bought. *l-maḥall maa qəbel yraǧǧə́Ɛ-li ṣ-ṣabbaaṭ yalli štareeto.* -- Can you take me back to town with you? *fiik traǧǧəƐni maƐak Ɛal-balad?* 3. *saḥab (a saḥᵊb).* I take back what I said. *bəsḥab yalli qəlto.*

**The sight of these students takes me back to my days in Paris. *manẓar hat-talamiiz bizakkərni b-ˀiyyaami b-baariiz.*

to take down - 1. *nazzal//tnazzal.* Take the picture down from the wall. *nazzel ᵊṣ-ṣuura mən Ɛal-ḥeeṭ.* 2. *ˀaxad (o ˀaxᵊd//ttaaxad).* Why don't you take down my address? *leeš maa btaaxod Ɛənwaani.* -- Who's taking down the minutes? *miin Ɛam yaaxod maḥḍar ᵊž-žalse?* 3. *kabas (e kabᵊs//nkabas).* I took him down a peg or two. *kabasto kabse maatne.*

to take in - 1. *ṭaalaƐ.* He doesn't take in much more than a few pounds per day. *maa biṭaaleƐ ˀaktar mən kam leera bᵊl-yoom.* 2. *dayyaq//ddayyaq.* Will you take this dress in at the waist? *bəddayyqí-li hal-fəsṭaan Ɛand xaṣro?* 3. *ˀaxad (-yaaxod ˀaxᵊd//ttaaxad).* I have taken in my neighbor's boy while she is away. *ˀaxadt ˀəbᵊn žaarətna b-ᵊġyaaba.* 3. *ġašš (ə ġašš//nġašš).* Have you been taken in again? *marra taanye nġaššeet?*

to take for - *ḥassab.* Sorry, I took you for someone else. *Ɛafwan ḥassabtak zalame taani.* -- What do you take me for? *šuu mḥassəbni?*

to take off - 1. *qaam (i qayamaan//nqaam).* Would you please take off your hat, madam? *məmken ᵊtqiimi bərneeṭtek ya madaam?* 2. *šalaḥ (a šalᵊḥ//nšalaḥ).* Do you mind if I take off my coat? *fii maaneƐ ˀəšlaḥ žaakeeti?* 3. *ṭaar (i ṭayaraan).* When does the plane take off? *ˀeemta raḥa ṭṭiir ᵊṭ-ṭayyaara?* 4. *məši (i maši), tḥarrak.* When do you intend to take off for Bloudane? *ˀeemta naawi təmši la-bluudaan?*

to take on - 1. *staxdam, waẓẓaf.* I hear the factory is taking on some new men. *sməƐt ˀənno l-maƐmal raḥa yəstaxdem Ɛəmmaal ᵊždaad.* 2. *ˀaxad (-yaaxod ˀaxᵊd//ttaaxad).* I took on a new job yesterday. *ˀaxadt šaġle ždiide mbaareḥ.*

**He can take on anyone of you. *huwwe qadd ḥayaḷḷa waaḥed beenaatkon.*

**A dining car will be taken on in Aleppo. *Ɛarabet maṭƐam ḥa-təndaaf lət-treen ᵊb-ḥalab.*

to take out - 1. *ˀaxad (-yaaxod ˀaxᵊd//ttaaxad).* Did you take out the money that was in the box? *ˀaxadt šii l-maṣaari halli kaanet bᵊl-Ɛəlbe?* 2. *qaam (i qayamaan//nqaam).* Take out the comma in the first line. *qiim ᵊl-faaṣle bᵊṣ-ṣaṭr ᵊl-ˀawwalaani.* 3. *Ɛazam (e Ɛaziime//nƐazam).* He wants to take us out to dinner some night. *bəddo yəƐzəmna Ɛal-Ɛaša šii leele.*

**You don't have to take it out on me. *maa fii lzuum ᵊtfəšš xəlqak fiyyi.*

to take over - 1. *ˀaxad (-yaaxod ˀaxᵊd//ttaaxad).* He took over my job. *ˀaxad waẓiifti.* 5. *stalam.* Who has taken over the management of the factory? *miin ᵊstalam ˀidaaret ᵊl-maƐmal?* -- You take over from here. *stəlem mən hoon.*

to take up - 1. *ˀaxad (-yaaxod ˀaxᵊd//ttaaxad), ˀakal (-yaakol ˀakᵊl//ttaakal).* The dresser takes up too much space. *l-biiró byaaxod maḥall ᵊktiir.* 2. *ˀaxad.* I'll take you up on that. *ləssa baaxdak Ɛala kalaamak.* -- You'll have to take up that matter with someone else. *laazem taaxod hal-q̈aḍiyye la-Ɛand šaxᵊṣ taani.* 3. *bada (a bdaaye) Ɛala.* I think I'll take up a foreign language this year. *raˀyi ˀəbdá-li Ɛala šii luġa ˀažnabiyye has-səne.* 4. *tƐaamal.* I wouldn't take up with these people if I were you. *law kənt maṭraḥak maa bətƐaamal maƐ haž-žamaaƐa.*

tale - *ḥkaaye* pl. *-aat* and *ḥakaaya, rwaaye* pl. *-aat, qəṣṣa* pl. *qəṣaṣ.* I like the tales of Sindbad the Sailor best. *bḥəbb ˀaktar šii ḥkaayaat səndibaad ᵊl-baḥri.*

talent - *mawhibe* pl. *mawaaheb.* He's a man of many talents. *huwwe šaxᵊṣ ṣaaḥeb mawaaheb ᵊktiire.*

talk - 1. *xiṭaab* pl. *-aat.* His talk was much too long. *xiṭaabo kaan ṭawiil Ɛan ᵊl-lzuum.* 2. *ḥadiis* pl. *ˀaḥadiis.* A talk with him might help. *ḥadiis maƐo yəmken yfiid.* -- Her marriage is the talk of the town. *zawaaža ḥadiis ᵊl-balad.* -- I had a heart-to-heart talk with him. *ḥakeet maƐo ḥadiis ᵊmn ᵊl-qalb ləl-qalb.* 3. *mḥaadase* pl. *-aat.* Both sides decided to break off their talks. *ṭ-ṭarafeen q̈arraru qaṭᵊƐ l-ᵊmḥaadasaat.* 4. *ḥaki.* What kind of talk is that from an intelligent fellow like you?! *šuu diin hal-ḥaki mən zalame zaki mətlak?!* -- Oh that's just talk! *xaḷḷəsni haada kəllo ḥaki.*

small talk - *taqq˜ ḥanak, Ɛlaak.* There wasn't anything interesting, just small talk. *maa kaan fii šii mhəmm, kəllo taqq ḥanak.*

to talk - *ḥaka (i ḥaki).* Don't you think he talks too much? *maa btəftə́ker ˀənno byəḥki ktiir?* -- We talked French all the time. *ḥakeena frənsaawi ṭuul ᵊl-waqᵊt.* -- What were they talking about? *Ɛala ˀeeš kaanu Ɛam yəḥku?* -- Look who's talking. *šuuf miin Ɛam yəḥki!* -- Now, you're talking. *hallaq Ɛam təḥki!* -- Now you're talking sense. *hallaq Ɛam təḥki šii maƐquul.* -- People in the neighborhood are beginning to talk. *n-naas bᵊl-ḥaara badet təḥki.* -- Stop talking shop! *ḥaaže təḥku Ɛaš-šəġᵊl!*

**Talking of books, have you seen his latest novel? *Ɛala zəkr ᵊl-kətᵊb, šəft šii rwaayto l-ˀaxiire?*

to talk back - *radd (ə radd) žawaab.* Spank him if he talks back. *ḍrəbo ˀiza radd žawaab.*

to talk into - *qannaƐ.* Do you suppose we can talk them into coming with us? *btəƐtə́qed fiina nqannə́Ɛon yəžu maƐna?* -- He has talked himself into believing that he's sick. *qannaƐ haalo ˀənno ḍƐiif.*

to talk over - *baḥas (a baḥᵊs//nbaḥas).* Talk the matter over with him. *bḥaas ᵊl-qaḍiyye maƐo.*

to talk up - *raġġab.* We're going to talk the project up to him this evening. *laḥa nraġġbo l-mašruuƐ ᵊl-yoom Ɛašiyye.*

tall - *ṭawiil* pl. *ṭwaal.* What's that tall building over there? *šuu hal-binaaye ṭ-ṭawiile hniik?* -- She's tall and thin. *hiyye ṭawiile w-rafiiƐa.*

**How tall are you? *qaddeeš ṭuulak?*

tall story - *qəṣṣa (pl. qəṣaṣ) xuraafiyye, xuraafe* pl. *-aat.* You don't expect me to believe that tall story, do you? *maa-lak mənṭəzərni saddeq hal-qəṣṣa l-xuraafiyye ˀaa?*

Talmud - *talmuud.*

tamarind - *tamᵊr həndi.*

tambourine - *daff* pl. *dfuuf.*

tame - 1. *ˀaliif, mᵊˀaalef.* The pigeons are so tame they eat out of your hand. *l-ḥamaamaat ˀaliifiin la-daraže byəžu byaaklu mən ˀiidak.* 2. *haadi.* They played a pretty tame match. *ləƐbu mbaaráa haadye tamaam.*

to tame - *rawwaḍ//trawwaḍ, wallaf//twallaf.* Lions are much easier to tame than tigers. *tarwiiḍ l-ᵊˀsuude ˀashal b-ᵊktiir mən tarwiiḍ ᵊn-nmuura.*

to tame down - *rakaz (o rakᵊz).* He's tamed down a lot since he left school. *ktiir rakaz mən baƐᵊd-ma tarak ᵊl-madrase.*

tan - 1. *samaar.* Where did you get that nice tan? *mnən-lak has-samaar ᵊl-ḥəlu?* 2. *beež* (invar.). I lost my tan gloves. *ḍawwaƐt ᵊkfuufi l-beež.*

to tan - 1. *dabaġ (a dabᵊġ//ndabaġ).* What do you use in tanning hides? *šuu btəstaƐmel la-dabġ ᵊž-žluud?* 2. *smarr.* She tans easily. *btəsmarr b-ᵊshuule.*

**I tanned his hide. *ṭaƐmeeto qatle maakne.*

tangerine - *yuusfaaye ˀafandiyye* coll. *yuusef ˀafandi* pl. *yuusfaayaat ˀafandiyye.*

tango - *tango.*

tank - 1. *dabbo* pl. *dabboyaat.* There's only a gallon of gasoline left in the tank. *ṣafyaan bass galoon banziin bᵊd-dabbo.* 2. *rəzᵊrwaar* pl. *-aat.* We used up all the hot water in the tank. *staƐmalna kəll ᵊl-mayy ᵊṣ-ṣəxne halli bᵊr-rəzᵊrwaar.* 3. *dabbaabe* pl. *-aat.* A column of tanks led the attack. *ratiil ᵊmn ᵊd-dabbaabaat qaad l-ᵊhžuum.*

tank truck - *siiteern* pl. *-aat.*

tanker - *ḥaamlet˜ (pl. -aat˜) zeet, naaq̈let˜ (pl. -aat˜) zeet.*

tanner - *dabbaaġ* pl. *-a.*

tap - *ḥanafiyye* pl. *-aat.* The tap is dripping. *l-ḥanafiyye Ɛam təzrob.*

on tap - *farṭ* (invar.). Do they really have beer on tap? *ṣaḥiiḥ fii Ɛandon biira farṭ (ᵊmn ᵊl-barmiil)?*

to tap - **1.** *daqar (o daqᵊr//ndaqar).* Why, they haven't begun to tap the country's enormous resources! *walla ləssa maa badu yadᵊqru mawaared l-ᵊblaad ᵊl-mahuule!* **2.** *raaq̈ab.* They tapped his telephone line. *raaq̈abu talifoono.*

tap - *ḥadwe* pl. *-aat.* Don't forget to put taps on my shoes. *laa tənsa maa tḥəṭṭ-ə́lli ḥadwaat εala ṣabbaaṭi.*

to tap - **1.** *naqqar//tnaqqar.* He tapped on the window. *naqqar εaš-šəbbaak.* **2.** *daqq (ə daqq//ndaqq).* She tapped me on the shoulder. *daqqə́t-li εala kətfi.*

tape - **1.** *ləzzeeqa* pl. *-aat.* Should I put some tape over the cut? *ḥəṭṭ šii šaqfet ləzzeeqa εaž-žərᵊḥ?* **2.** *šriiṭ* pl. *šaraayeṭ.* I'd like five meters of the white tape. *laazəmni xams ᵊmtaar ᵊmn ᵊš-šriiṭ ᵊl-ʔabyaḍ.* -- Where are the tapes with the dance music? *ween ᵊš-šaraayeṭ halli εaleehon ᵊl-muusiiq̈a r-raaqṣa?*

**I've got his speech on tape at home. *εandi xiṭaabo msažžal bᵊl-beet.*

scotch tape - *šriiṭ ləzzeeq.*

tape measure - *mazuura* pl. *-aat.*

tape recorder - *ʔaalet~* (pl. *-aat~*) *tasžiil, msažžel* pl. *-aat.*

to tape - **1.** *sažžal//tsažžal.* They taped the entire conversation. *sažžalu l-ᵊmḥaadase kəlla.* **2.** *ləzzaq.* Tape the package well before you mail it. *ləzzeq ᵊṭ-ṭard ᵊmniiḥ qabᵊl-ma təbεato bᵊl-bariid.*

tapeworm - *duude waḥiide.*

tar - *zəfᵊt.*

target - *hadaf* pl. *ʔahdaaf.*

tariff - **1.** *taεriife* (pl. *-aat*) *žəmrukiyye.* How much is the tariff on cotton? *qaddeeš ᵊt-taεriife ž-žəmrukiyye εal-qəṭᵊn?* **2.** *ʔəžret~* (pl. *ʔžuur~*) *safar.* The railway tariffs went up again. *raddet ᵊrtafεet ᵊʔžuur ᵊs-safar bᵊt-treen.*

tart - *tart* pl. *-aat.* She makes delicious tarts. *btaεmel tartaat laziize.*

tart - *mazz.* The apples have a tart taste. *t-təffaahaat ṭaεmə́ton mazze.*

tartar - **1.** *ṭarṭiir.* **2.** (on teeth) *qaaluuḥ.*

Tartar - *tatari** coll. pl. *tatar.*

task - *šaġle* pl. *-aat, mhəmme* pl. *-aat.* He is equal to his task. *huwwe ṭaaleε qadd šaġᵊlto.*

to take to task - *ḥaasab.* I'll take him to task for his lies. *bəddi ḥaasbo εala kəzbaato.*

taste - **1.** *ṭaεme* pl. *-aat.* This meat has a peculiar taste. *hal-laḥme ṭaεmə́ta ġariibe.* -- Just a taste of success has made him overbearing. *šii-ʔənno daaq ṭaεmet ᵊn-nažaaḥ w-ṣaar šaayef ḥaalo qadd ᵊd-dənye.* **2.** *zooq* pl. *ʔazwaaq.* She has good taste. *εanda zooq ḥəlu.* -- I would have given you credit for better taste. *kənt ᵊmfakker εandak zooq ʔaḥla mən heek.*

**That has given us a taste of what could happen to all of us. *haš-šii εaṭaana fəkra εan šuu məmken yṣər-ᵊlna kəllna.*

**Suit your own taste. *εala keefak!*

**I just want a taste of it. *bəddi duuqa bass.*

in bad taste - *bala zooq.* That remark was really in bad taste. *hal-ᵊmlaaḥaẓa kaanet ḥaqiiqatan bala zooq.*

in good taste - *b-zooq.* She is always dressed in good taste. *daayman btəlbes b-zooq* or ***daayman məzᵊwqa b-ləbsa.*

to taste - *daaq (u dawaqaan//ndaaq).* Just taste this coffee! *bass duuq hal-qahwe!*

**The soup tastes good. *š-šooraba ṭaεmə́ta ṭayybe.*

**It tastes of vinegar. *ṭaεmə́ta xall.*

tasteful - *məzweq.* She's known as a tasteful hostess. *maεruufe ʔənna sətt beet məzᵊwqa.* -- Look at the tasteful display in the window. *šuuf hal-εarḍ ᵊl-məzweq bᵊl-waažha.*

tasteless - **1.** *bala ṭaεme.* The food is tasteless. *l-ʔakᵊl bala ṭaεme.* **2.** *bala zooq.* He's loudmouthed and tasteless. *huwwe mboožaq w-bala zooq.* -- What a tasteless remark! *ʔamma ḥaki bala zooq!*

tattered - *naazel kətte, mšarṭaṭ, mhalhel, mšaqwaq.* We saw lots of children in tattered clothes. *šəfna wlaad ᵊktiir ʔawaaεiihon naazle kətte.*

Taurus Mountains - *žbaal~ ṭooroos.*

tavern - *xəmmaara* pl. *-aat.*

tax - *ḍariibe* pl. *ḍaraayeb.* Have you paid your taxes yet? *dafaεt ᵊḍ-ḍaraayeb yalli εaleek walla ləssa?*

tax collector - *žaabi~* (pl. *žubaat~*) *ḍaraayeb.*

to tax - *ḥaṭṭ (ə ḥaṭaṭ//nḥaṭṭet) ḍariibe εala.* The government is taxing the farmers very heavily. *l-ᵊḥkuume εam ᵊtḥəṭṭ ḍariibe εaalye ktiir εal-fallaaḥiin.*

**This merchandise is taxed heavily. *hal-ᵊbḍaaεa εaleeha ḍariibe εaalye.*

tax-exempt - *məεfi mn ᵊḍ-ḍaraayeb.* Donations to charity are tax-exempt. *ṣ-ṣadaq̈aat məεfiyye mn ᵊḍ-ḍaraayeb.*

taxi - *taxi* pl. *taxiyaat.*

taxpayer - *daafeε~* (pl. *-iin~*) *ḍaraayeb.*

tea - *šaay.* Can I have another cup of tea? *məmken ʔaaxod fənžaan šaay taani?* -- I invited him to tea. *εazamto εaš-šaay.*

to teach - **1.** *εallam//tεallam.* Who taught you that? *miin εallamak haš-šii?* -- Will you teach me Arabic? *bətεalləmni εarabi?* -- That's what I was taught. *haada yalli tεallamto* or *heek εallamuuni.* -- I'll teach him not to disturb me again. *walla la-εallmo ḥatta maa yəzεažni marra taanye.* **2.** *εallam, darras.* He teaches in a boys' school. *biεallem ᵊb-madraset ṣəbyaan.*

**That will teach him a lesson! *haada raḥ ykən-lo darᵊs.*

teacher - *mεallem* pl. *-iin,* f. *mεallme* pl. *-aat.*

teaching - **1.** *taεliim, tadriis.* How do you like teaching? *kiif ᵊmlaaqi t-taεliim?* **2.** *εaq̈iide* pl. *εaq̈aaʔed.* Later on, he became fascinated by the teaching of Gandhi. *baεdeen ᵊttaaxad ᵊb-εaq̈aaʔed ġaandi.*

teacup - *fənžaan~* (pl. *fanažiin~*) *šaay.*

teakettle - *ʔəbriiq~* (pl. *ʔabariiq~*) *šaay.*

teakwood - *xašab~ saaž.*

team - *fariiq* pl. *fəraq.* Our team has won every game this year. *fariiqna rəbeḥ kəll l-ᵊmbaarayaat has-səne.* -- We're a team of five working on the dictionary. *nəḥna fariiq ᵊmʔallaf mən xamᵊs ʔašxaaṣ εam nəštə́ġel εal-q̈aamuus.*

to team up - *džammaε.* We teamed up in groups of four players. *džammaεna kəll ʔarbaε laεεiibe maε baεḍon.*

teamwork - **1.** *tafaahom.* We can still win the game with a little more teamwork. *ləssa fiina nərbaḥ l-ᵊmbaarḍa b-šwayyet tafaahom zyaade.* **2.** *taεaawon.* Only perfect teamwork will enable us to finish the job on time. *bass ᵊt-taεaawon ᵊl-maẓbuuṭ bimakkənna mən ʔətmaam ᵊš-šaġle εal-waqᵊt.*

teapot - *ʔəbriiq~* (pl. *ʔabariiq~*) *šaay.*

tear - *xazᵊq* pl. *xzuuqa, šaqq* pl. *šquuqa.* Can this tear be mended? *hal-xazᵊq məmken ratyo?*

to tear - **1.** *xaṭaf (o xaṭᵊf//nxaṭaf).* She tore the letter out of his hand. *xaṭfet ᵊl-maktuub mən ʔiido.* **2.** *šaraṭ (o šarᵊṭ//nšaraṭ), šaqq (ə šaqq// nšaqq).* Don't tear your clothes on that nail. *laa təšroṭ ʔawaaεiik b-hal-məsmaar!* **3.** *nxazaq, nšaqq.* The dress is tearing at the sleeve. *l-fəsṭaan εam yənxə́zeq εand ᵊl-kəmm.* -- Be careful, these stamps tear easily. *ntəbeh haṭ-ṭawaabeε btənšaqq b-ᵊshuule.*

to tear along - *šaffaṭ.* The car tore along at a tremendous speed. *s-sayyaara šaffaṭet ᵊb-sərεa faẓiiεa.*

to tear apart - *nakat (o nakᵊt).* The critics tore his book apart. *n-naq̈q̈aad nakatúu-lo ktaabo.*

to tear down - *habbaṭ//thabbaṭ.* They tore the house down last year. *habbaṭu l-beet ᵊs-səne l-maaḍye.*

to tear off - **1.** *qaṭaε (a qaṭᵊε//nqaṭaε).* Tear off the coupon. *qṭaaε ᵊl-kuupoon.* **2.** *qalaε (a qalᵊε//nqalaε), qabaε (a qabᵊε//nqabaε).* Who tore off the poster? *miin qalaε ᵊl-ʔəεlaan?* **3.** *nqaṭaε.* The button tore off. *z-zarr nqaṭaε.*

to tear open - *šaraṭ (o šarᵊṭ//nšaraṭ) šaqq (ə šaqq//nšaqq).* Who tore the package open? *miin šaraṭ l-baakeet?*

to tear out - *šaraṭ (o šarᵊṭ//nšaraṭ), šaqq (ə šaqq//nšaqq).* Who tore out this page? *miin šaraṭ has-ṣafḥa?*

to tear up - *šaqšaq.* I hope you tore that letter up. *bətʔammal ᵊtkuun šaqšaqᵊt hal-maktuub.*

tear - *damεa* pl. *-aat* coll. pl. *dmuuε.* Tears won't help you. *d-dmuuε maa raḥa tfiidak.*

to tear - *dammaε.* My eyes are tearing. *εyuuni εam ᵊddammeε.*

to tease - *ḥarqaṣ, žaakar.* Everyone teases him when he's late for work. *l-kəll biḥarᵊqṣo waqᵊt byəži mətʔaxxer εaš-šəġᵊl.* -- The children always tease her about her stutter. *l-ᵊwlaad daayman bižaakruuha εala taʔtaʔə́ta.* -- Don't tease the dog. *laa tḥarqeṣ ᵊl-kalb.*

teaspoon - *maεlaqet~* (pl. *maεaaleq~*) *šaay, maεlaqa ẓġiire.*

technical - *fanni*.* The broadcast was called off for

technical reasons. *l-ʔizaaƐa ltaǧet la-ʔasbaab fanniyye.* -- I didn't understand all the technical terms. *maa fhəmᵊt kəll ᵊl-məṣṭalaḥaat ᵊl-fanniyye.*

technician - *fanni* pl. *-iyyiin.*

technique - *ʔəsluub* pl. *ʔasaliib.*

technology - *taknolooǯya.*

tedious - *mməll.* What a tedious lecture! *ʔamma mḥaaḍara mməlle!*

teenager - *mraaheq* pl. *-iin,* f. *mraahqa* pl. *-aat.*

teens - *Ɛəmr˜ ᵊmraahaqa.* She must be in her teens by now. *laazem tkuun ṣaaret ᵊb-Ɛəmr l-ᵊmraahaqa hallaq.*

telegram - *barqiyye* pl. *-aat, taliǧraaf* pl. *-aat.*

to **telegraph** - *baƐat (a baƐᵊt) barqiyye, baraq (e barᵊq).* Did he telegraph you? *baƐát-lak barqiyye?* or *bardq-lak?*

telegraph office - *maktab˜ (pl. makaateb˜) taliǧraaf, maktab˜ barᵊq.*

telegraph pole - *Ɛaamuud˜ (pl. Ɛawamiid˜) taliǧraaf.*

telephone - *talifoon* pl. *-aat.* May I use your telephone, please? *məmken ʔəstaƐmel talifoonak btaƐmel maƐruuf?* -- He does all his business by telephone. *byaƐmel kəll šəǧlo bət-talifoon.*

telephone booth - *ǧərfet˜ (pl. ǧəraf˜) talifoon ləl-Ɛumuum.*

telephone call - *mxaabara* pl. *-aat.* You had an important telephone call while you were out. *ʔəǯətak mxaabara mhəmme b-ᵊǧyaabak.*

telephone directory - *daliil˜ (pl. dalaayel˜) talifoon, daliil˜ haatef.*

telephone line - *xaṭṭ˜ (pl. xṭuuṭ˜) talifoon.*

telephone number - *nəmret˜ (pl. nəmar˜) talifoon.*

telephone operator - *Ɛaamlet˜ (pl. -aat˜) ṣanṭraal.*

to telephone - *talfan, Ɛəmel talifoon.* Did anyone telephone me? *ḥada talfán-li?* or *ḥada Ɛəmə́l-li talifoon?*

telescope - *talaskoob* pl. *-aat, naaḍuur* pl. *nawaḍiir.*

television - **1.** *televəzyoon.* I saw it on television. *šəfta Ɛat-televəzyoon.* **2.** *televəzyooni*.* What's your favorite television program? *šuu l-bərnaameǯ ᵊt-televəzyooni l-ᵊmfaḍḍal Ɛandak?*

television set - *televəzyoon* pl. *-aat.*

to **tell** - *qaal (u qool//nqaal).* Tell him your name. *qəl-lo šuu ʔəsmak.* -- Tell me, what are you doing tonight? *qəl-li, šuu Ɛaamel ᵊl-leele?* -- He told me to give you this letter. *qal-li (la-)ʔaƐṭiik hal-maktuub.* -- Did they tell you anything about their plans? *qaalúu-lak šii Ɛan mašariiƐon?* -- I wish I could tell you the whole story. *ya-reet ʔəqder qəl-lak kəll ᵊl-qəṣṣa.* -- I could have told you that in advance. *kənt ᵊbqəl-lak-yáaha salaf.*

**You can tell by his voice that he has a cold. *mbayyen mən ṣooṭo ʔənno mraššeḥ.*

**To tell the truth, I don't know. *(bəddak) l-ḥaqiiqa maa baƐref.*

**Can your little boy tell time yet? *ʔəbnak ᵊz-zġiir byaƐref bᵊs-saaƐa wəlla ləssa?*

**Who can tell? *miin byaƐref?*

**You can never tell what goes on in a criminal's mind. *maa fiik taƐref ʔabadan šuu biduur ᵊb-baal ᵊl-məǯrem.*

**I can't tell the one from the other. *maa bəqder farreq ᵊl-waaḥed Ɛan ᵊt-taani.*

**How can you tell the difference? *kiif btəqder taƐref ᵊl-farᵊq?*

**A person's clothes tell much of his personality. *ʔawaaƐi š-šaxᵊṣ bəddəll ᵊktiir Ɛala šaxṣiito.*

**I told him off all right. *naqarto bahdale Ɛal-keef.*

to tell apart - *farraq, mayyaz.* How can you tell those two apart? *kiif btəqder ᵊtfarreq hat-tneen Ɛan baƐḍ?*

to tell on someone - *fasad (e fasᵊd//nfasad) Ɛala.* I'm going to your mother and tell on you. *laḥa ruuḥ ʔəfsed Ɛaleek la-ʔəmmak.*

temper - *xəlᵊq.* He has a vicious temper. *xəlqo dayyeq.* -- He loses his temper easily. *byəṭlaƐ xəlqo qawaam.*

temperament - *ṭabᵊƐ* pl. *ʔaṭbaaƐ.* She got her temperament from her mother. *ʔaaxde ʔaṭbaaƐa mən ʔəmma.*

temperature - **1.** *daraǯet˜ ḥaraara.* What's the temperature outside? *qaddeeš darǯet ᵊl-ḥaraara barra?* **2.** *ḥaraara.* The nurse took his temperature. *l-ᵊmmarrḍa ʔaxdə́t-lo ḥaraarto.* -- She has been running a high temperature for three days now. *ṣar-la tlətt iyyaam maƐa ḥaraara Ɛaalye.*

temple - *haykal* pl. *hayaakel, maƐbad* pl. *maƐaabed.* Did you visit the temples of Baalbek? *zərt šii hayaakel bƐalbak?*

temple - *ṣədᵊǧ* pl. *ʔaṣdaaǧ.* He's getting gray at the temples already. *Ɛam yšiib Ɛand ʔaṣdaaǧo.*

temporarily - *mwaqqatan.* The line is temporarily disconnected. *l-xaṭṭ mwaqqatan maqṭuuƐ.*

temporary - *waqti*, mwaqqat.* This is only a temporary solution. *haada ḥall waqti bass.*

to **tempt** - *ʔaǧra.* Your offer doesn't tempt me a bit. *Ɛarḍak maa byəǧriini ʔabadan.* -- The food looks tempting. *l-ʔakᵊl məǧri.*

**I was tempted to tell him the truth. *ʔəǯa Ɛala baali qəl-lo l-ḥaqiiqa.*

temptation - *ʔəǧraa ʔ.*

ten - **1.** *Ɛašara.* Two times five make ten. *tneen ᵊb-xamse bisaawu Ɛašara.* -- There are ten of us in class. *nəḥna Ɛašara bᵊṣ-ṣaff.* **2.** *Ɛašᵊr.* Would you lend me ten pounds? *bəddayyənni Ɛašᵊr leeraat?* **3.** *Ɛašᵊrt.* We have only ten days to go. *baaqii-lna Ɛašᵊrt iyyaam bass.* -- Some ten thousand people were there. *ḥawaali Ɛašᵊrt aalaaf zalame kaanu hniik.* **4.** *s-saaƐa Ɛašara.* Is ten a convenient time for you? *s-saaƐa Ɛašara binaasbak?* -- The train leaves at ten. *t-treen byəmši s-saaƐa Ɛašara.*

tenant - *məstaʔǯer* pl. *-iin.* He has been our tenant for ten years. *ṣar-lo məstaʔǯer Ɛanna Ɛašr ᵊsniin.*

to **tend** - **1.** *maal (i mayalaan).* He tends to be partial. *bimiil lət-taḥayyoz.* **2.** *Ɛaṭa baalo Ɛala, ntabah la-.* Who's going to tend the furnace? *miin raḥa yaƐṭi baalo Ɛal-ᵊwǯaaq?* **3.** *raƐa (i raƐi* and *rƐiyye//nraƐa).* In his youth he tended his father's sheep. *b-šabaabo raƐa ǧanam ʔabúu.*

**Tend to your own business! *laa təddaaxal ᵊb-šii maa byəƐniik!*

tendency - **1.** *meel* pl. *myuul.* He has a tendency to exaggerate. *Ɛando meel ləl-ᵊmbaalaǧa.* **2.** *ʔəttiǯaah* pl. *-aat.* The present tendency among smaller nations is away from military alliances. *l-ʔəttiǯaah ᵊl-ḥaaḍer ləd-duwal ᵊz-zġiire ʔənna təthaaša l-ʔaḥlaaf ᵊl-Ɛaskariyye.*

tender - **1.** *ṭari.* The meat is so tender you can cut it with a fork. *l-laḥme ṭariyye la-daraǯe fiik təqṭáƐa bᵊš-šooke.* **2.** *ḥanuun.* She spoke to the child in a tender voice. *ḥaaket ᵊl-walad b-ṣooṭ ḥanuun.* **3.** *mdammel.* My arm's still tender where I bruised it. *ʔiidi ləssaata mdammle maḥall-ma ṭaraqta.*

tendon - *watar* pl. *wtaar.*

tennis - *tanəs.* Where's my tennis racket? *ween raakeet ᵊt-tanəs tabaƐi?* -- I love to play tennis. *waḷḷa bḥəbb ʔəlƐab tanəs.*

tense - **1.** *mətwatter.* The situation was tense. *l-ḥaale kaanet mətwattra.* **2.** *mnarvez.* Everybody was tense at the meeting. *l-kəll kaanu mnarᵊvziin bᵊl-ʔəǯtimaaƐ.*

tension - *tawattor.* There's always tension between them. *daayman fii tawattor beenaaton.*

high tension - *voltaaž Ɛaali.* Don't touch it, it looks like a high tension wire. *laa tədᵊqro, mbayyen Ɛalée šriiṭ voltaažo Ɛaali.*

tent - *xeeme* pl. *xiyam,* (very large) *ṣiiwaan* pl. *ṣawawiin.*

tentative - *mabdaʔi*, ʔawwali*.* That's a tentative plan only, mind you. *laa tənsa hayye xəṭṭa mabdaʔiyye bass.*

tentatively - *mabdaʔiyyan.* The meeting is tentatively scheduled for 4:00. *mabdaʔiyyan ᵊǯ-ǯalse tḥaddadet ᵊs-saaƐa ʔarbƐa.*

tenth - **1.** *Ɛaašer.* It's the tenth house from the corner. *huwwe l-beet ᵊl-Ɛaašer* (or *Ɛaašer beet*) *mn ᵊs-suuke.* **2.** *Ɛašara.* We'll leave on July tenth. *msaafriin ᵊb-Ɛašara tammuuz.*

one tenth - *Ɛəšᵊr* pl. *Ɛšaar.* One tenth of my salary goes for taxes. *Ɛəšᵊr maƐaaši biruuḥ ḍaraayeb.*

term - **1.** *šarᵊṭ* pl. *šruuṭ.* The terms of the contract don't provide for such a thing. *šruuṭ ᵊl-kəntraat maa bətnəṣṣ Ɛala heek šii.* **2.** *faṣl* pl. *fṣuul.* When does the new term at the university begin? *ʔeemta l-faṣl ᵊǯ-ǯdiid biballeš bᵊǯ-ǯaamƐa?* **3.** *doora* pl. *-aat, mədde* pl. *mədad.* His term will end in October. *doorto btəxloṣ ᵊb-təšriin ᵊl-ʔawwal.* **4.** *məṣṭalaḥ* pl. *-aat, ʔəṣṭilaaḥ* pl. *-aat.* Do you know the technical term for it? *btaƐref šii l-məṣṭalaḥ ᵊl-fanni ʔəla?* **5.** *Ɛibaara* pl. *-aat.* It's a common term of endearment. *hiyye Ɛibaaret tadliil šaayƐa.*

**He gave us very good terms when we bought the house. *raaƐaana ktiir lamma štareena l-beet.*

**I told him in no uncertain terms what I think of him. *qəlt-ə́llo bᵊl-ᵊmšabrah šuu raʔyi fii.*

**We're not on speaking terms. *maa Ɛam naḥki maƐ baƐdna.*

**We've been on bad terms ever since. *ṣar-ᵊlna madzaaƐliin mən waqta.*

**I'm on good terms with him. *Ɛalaaqti fii mniiḥa.*

to come to terms - *ttafaq.* We've been trying to come to terms about this question for months now. *ṣar-ᵊlna ʔəšhor Ɛam ᵊnḥaawel nəttəfeq Ɛala hal-masʔale.*

to **terminate** - *laġa* and *ʔalġa (i ʔəlġaa//ltaġa* and *nlaġa).* If worse comes to worse, we'll have to terminate their contracts. *b-ʔalƐan ᵊl-ḥaalaat laazem nəlġi Ɛŭuudon.*

terminology - *məṣṭalaḥaat* (pl.), *ʔəṣṭilaaḥaat* (pl.).

termite - *namle beeḍa* coll. *namᵊl ʔabyaḍ* pl. *namlaat biiḍ.*

terrace - *ṣṭeeḥa* pl. *-aat, teeraas* pl. *-aat.*

terrain - *ʔaraaḍi* (pl.).

terrible - **1.** *faẓiiƐ.* Wasn't that a terrible storm last night? *maa kaanet Ɛaaṣfe faẓiiƐa ᵊl-leele l-maaḍye?* **2.** *malƐuun.* The weather is terrible. *ṭ-ṭaqᵊṣ malƐuun.*

to **terrify** - *raƐƐab.* He terrified me. *raƐƐabni.*

territorial - *ʔəqliimi*.*

territory - *manṭiqa* pl. *manaaṭeq.*

terror - *rəƐᵊb.* We were speechless with terror. *rṭabaṭ ᵊlsaanna mən kətr ᵊr-rəƐᵊb.*

terrorism - *ʔərhaab.*

terrorist - *ʔərhaabi** pl. *-iin.*

to **terrorize** - *našar (o našr) ᵊr-rəƐᵊb b-.* They terrorized the population for years. *našaru r-rəƐᵊb bᵊl-ʔahaali la-sniin w-ᵊsniin.*

test - **1.** *faḥᵊṣ* pl. *fḥuuṣ(a).* You have to take a test before you get a driver's license. *laazem taƐmel faḥᵊṣ qabᵊl-ma taaxod rəxṣet ᵊswaaqa.* -- The blood test showed he had a rare disease. *faḥṣ ᵊd-damm warža ʔənno Ɛando maraḍ naader.* **2.** *ʔəmtiḥaan* pl. *-aat, faḥᵊṣ* pl. *fḥuuṣ(a).* Did you pass all your tests? *nažaḥᵊt b-kəll ʔəmtiḥaanaatak?* -- I have an English test today. *Ɛandi faḥᵊṣ ʔəngliizi l-yoom.* -- I had to take a shorthand test before they hired me. *nžabart ʔaaxod ʔəmtiḥaan bᵊl-ʔəxtizaal qabᵊl-ma ywaẓẓfuuni.* **3.** *tažrube* pl. *tažaarob.* The material withstood the severest tests. *l-maadde tḥammalet ʔaqṣa ʔanwaaƐ ᵊt-tažaarob.*

**The car has stood the test well. *s-sayyaara ʔasbatet ḥaala mniiḥa.*

to test - **1.** *mtaḥan.* The teacher, as a rule, tests the students at the end of each week. *l-ᵊmƐallem Ɛaadto yəmtəḥen ᵊt-talamiiz ᵊb-ʔaaxer kəll žəmƐa.* **2.** *faḥaṣ (a faḥᵊṣ//nfaḥaṣ).* You'd better test your brakes. *ʔaḥsán-lak təfḥaṣ fraamaatak.*

testament - *wṣiyye* pl. *-aat.* She wasn't mentioned in his testament. *maa nzakret b-ᵊwṣiito.*

the New Testament - *l-Ɛahd ᵊž-ždiid.*

the Old Testament - *l-Ɛahd ᵊl-qadiim, t-tooraat.*

to **testify** - *šəhed (a šahaade).* Have you anything further to testify? *fii Ɛandak šii zyaade bəddak təšhad Ɛalée?* -- The woman testified to his good character. *l-mara šəhdet b-ʔaxlaaqo l-ᵊmniiḥa.*

testimony - *šahaade* pl. *-aat.* Her testimony changed the whole course of the trial. *šahaadə́ta ġayyaret mažra l-ᵊmḥaakame kəlla.*

tetanus - *tatanos, kuzaaz.*

text - **1.** *naṣṣ* pl. *nṣuuṣ.* The Latin text is followed by a Greek translation. *n-naṣṣ ᵊl-laatiini baƐdo taržame yuunaaniyye.* **2.** *matᵊn.* Take it out of the text and use it for a footnote. *qiima mn ᵊl-matᵊn w-ᵊƐməla ḥaašye.*

textbook - *ktaab diraasi* pl. *kətᵊb diraasiyye.*

textile - *mansuuž* pl. *-aat.* Did they show textiles at the fair? *kaanu Ɛaarḍiin šii mansuužaat bᵊl-maƐraḍ?* -- There's mostly textile industry in this area. *ʔaktar ᵊṣ-ṣinaaƐa b-hal-manṭiqa ṣinaaƐet mansuužaat.*

than - *mən.* He's older than his brother. *huwwe ʔakbar mən ʔaxúu.* -- I appreciate him now more than ever. *bqaddro hallaq ʔaktar mən ʔayy waqten kaan.*

**I'd rather stay home than go to that dull game. *bfaḍḍel ʔəqƐod bᵊl-beet Ɛan ʔənno ruuḥ Ɛala hal-ᵊmbaaráa l-mumalle.*

**None other than the president himself answered the phone. *maa ḥada žaawab ᵊt-talifoon ʔəlla r-raʔiis nafso.*

to **thank** - *šakar (o šəkᵊr//nšakar), tšakkar.* Thank him for me. *škər-li-yáa.* -- I haven't thanked her for the present yet. *ləssa maa tšakkarta Ɛal-ᵊhdiyye.* -- I'd thank you to keep your mouth shut. *bkuun šaaker ʔiza bəddall saaket.*

**You have only yourself to thank for this mess. *l-faḍᵊl ʔəlak b-hal-xarbaṭa.*

**And who do we have to thank for breaking the window? *w-la-miin ᵊl-faḍl ᵊb-kasr ᵊš-šəbbaak?* -- Thank God! *nəškor ʔaḷḷa!* or ***l-ḥamdu ləllaah!*

**Thank goodness! *l-ḥamdəlla!*

**Thank heaven(s)! *l-ḥamdəlla!*

**Thank you. *šukran* or *mamnuun.*

**Thank you very much. *šukran žaziilan* or *mamnuun ᵊktiir.*

thankful - *mamnuun.* We are very thankful to you. *nəḥna mamnuuniinak ᵊktiir.* -- He's thankful even for little favors. *bikuun mamnuun ḥatta Ɛala maƐruuf baṣiiṭ.*

thankless: That's a thankless job if you want my opinion. *ʔiza bəddak raʔyi hayye šaġle maa-lak raḥa tətqaddar Ɛaleeha.* -- He wastes his time with all kinds of thankless chores. *biḍawweƐ waqto b-šaġlaat maa ḥada biqaddər-lo-yáaha.*

thanks - *šəkᵊr, tašakkor* pl. *-aat.* I don't expect any thanks. *maa Ɛam ʔəntə́ẓer ʔayy šəkᵊr.* -- Many thanks. *ʔalf šəkᵊr* or *tašakkuraat* or *mətšakker ᵊktiir.*

**Thanks a lot. *mətšakker ᵊktiir* or *šukran žaziilan.*

thanks to - *l-faḍᵊl la-.* Thanks to him I was able to go. *l-faḍᵊl ʔəlo qdərᵊt ruuḥ.* -- Thanks to your intervention he wasn't fired. *l-faḍᵊl la-tadaxxlak halli maa tsarraḥ.* -- It's no thanks to him that I'm here. *l-faḍᵊl muu ʔəlo b-wužuudi hoon.*

that - **1.** *haad(a)* f. *hayy(e), haadi.* What's that? *šuu haada?* -- That's what caused the mistake. *haada yalli sabbab ᵊl-ġalṭa.* -- I'll come tomorrow, that is, if it doesn't rain. *bəži bəkra, haada ʔiza maa šattet.* -- That reply of his was really uncalled for. *žawaabo haada ḥaqiiqatan maa kan-lo muužeb.* -- Who was that at the door? *miin haada halli kaan Ɛal-baab?* -- That's my little sister. *hayy ʔəxti ẓ-ẓġiire.* -- That question you should never have asked! *has-suʔaal haada maa kənt laazem təsʔalo ʔabadan.* -- I'll never make <u>that</u> mistake again! *b-ḥayaati maa raḥa Ɛiid hal-ġalṭa hayy!* **2.** *hadaak* f. *hadiik.* Why do you want this one? Take that. *leeš bəddak haada? xood hadaak.* -- That day I lost my nerves. *b-hadaak ᵊl-yoom faqadt ʔaƐṣaabi.* -- Who's that girl over there? *miin hal-bənt hadiik?* **3.** *ha-* + def. article. Just look at that magnificent view! *ṭṭallaƐ Ɛala hal-manẓar ᵊl-Ɛaẓiim!* -- Where did you buy that dress? *mneen ᵊštareeti har-roob?* -- What was that word again? *šuu kaanet hal-kəlme yalli qəlta?* **4.** *haš-šaġle, haš-šii.* I can't worry about that. *maa bəqder ʔəšġel baali b-haš-šaġle.* -- What will you get by that? *šuu raḥa təstfiid mən haš-šaġle?* -- I'm responsible for that. *ʔana masʔuul Ɛan haš-šii.* -- There's some truth in that. *fii šii mn ᵊl-ḥaqiiqa b-haš-šii.* -- That's been bothering me for quite a while. *haš-šii ṣar-lo Ɛam ydaayəqni mədde.* **5.** *heek.* At that price you could have gotten a better car. *b-heek səƐᵊr kənt ᵊštareet sayyaara ʔaḥsan.* -- You don't expect me to believe that nonsense, do you? *maa-lak mənṭəẓərni saddeq heek xuzaƐbalaat muu heek?* -- That's life. *heek (ḥaal) ᵊd-dənye.* -- When I saw that I had to speak up. *waqᵊt šəft heek maa ḥsənᵊt ʔəlla-ma ʔəḥki.* -- That's what they say. *heek biquulu.* -- Why did you have to do that? *leeš saaweet heek?* **6.** *hal-qadd.* I didn't know she was that beautiful. *maa kənt Ɛarfaan hiyye hal-qadd ḥəlwe.* -- Anyone that stupid shouldn't be admitted to a university. *šaxᵊṣ hal-qadd ᵊḥmaar maa laazem yənqəbel ᵊb-žaamƐa.* -- He's not that bright, you know. *huwwe muu (kəll) hal-qadd zaki, btaƐref.* **7.** *halli, yalli.* Who's the man that just came in? *miin ᵊr-rəžžaal halli faat hallaq?* -- Is this the bus that leaves at two? *haada huwwe l-baaṣ halli byəmši s-saaƐa tənteen?* **8.** *ʔənn-* + pron. suff., *ʔənno* (invar.). I'm sorry that this happened. *ʔana mətʔassef ʔənno haš-šii ḥadas.* -- She didn't tell that she'd be late. *maa qaalə́t-li ʔənna* (or *ʔənno*) *raḥa tətʔaxxar.*

**That's that! *ntahet!*

**They talked about this and that. *ḥaku ʔaškaal w-ʔalwaan.*

**How about that? Now he doesn't want the job! *šuu raʔyak?! hallaq ṣaar maa bəddo l-waẓiife!*

**We leave an hour earlier. How about that? *mnəmši ʔabkar ᵊb-saaƐa. šuu raʔyak?*

that's why - *mən heek, mənšaan heek.* That's why I never go to the movies. *mən heek maa bruuḥ ʔabadan* *ƹas-siinama.*

after that - *baƹdeen.* After that we went to a café. *baƹdeen rəḥna ƹala qahwe.*

at that - **1.** *ƹand hoon.* Let's leave it at that. *xalliina nətrə́ka ƹand hoon.* -- We'll let it go at that for the time being. *mənxalliiha ƹand hoon bᵊl-waqt ᵊl-ḥaader.* **2.** *fooq haada.* And it will mean a lot of work at that. *w-fiiha kamaan šəġl ᵊktiir fooq haada.* **3.** *maƹ haada, maƹ zaalek.* Even at that I'd say he's a good worker. *maƹ haada kəllo ləssaani bquul ʔənno šaġġiil ᵊmniiḥ.* **4.** *kamaan.* It's not a bad idea at that! *kamaan, maa-la fəkra baṭṭaale.*

thaw - *dawabaan˜ talᵊž.* This year the thaw set in rather early. *dawabaan ᵊt-talᵊž has-səne ṣaar ƹala bakkiir.*

to thaw - **1.** *daab (u dawabaan).* The ice is already beginning to thaw. *ž-žaliid ƹam yəbda yduub.* **2.** *dawwab.* Don't forget to thaw the meat before cooking it. *laa tənsi maa ddawweb ᵊl-laḥme qabᵊl-ma təṭᵊbxiiha.* **3.** *tlaḥlaḥ.* He was very reserved at first, but after a while he began to thaw. *kaan ᵊktiir mətḥaffeẓ bᵊl-ʔawwal, baƹdeen ᵊtlaḥlaḥ.*

the - *l-* (assimilating to the sun letters). You'd better stay in the house. *ʔaḥsán-lak təbqa bᵊl-beet.* -- Where is the blue dress? *ween ᵊr-roob ᵊl-ʔazraq?*

the ... the - *kəll-ma ... kəll-ma.* The more you give him the more he wants. *kəll-ma ƹaṭeeto ʔaktar kəll-ma byəṭlob ʔaktar.* -- The sooner they pay us the better. *kəll-ma ƹažžalúu-lna bᵊd-dafᵊƹ kəll-ma kaan ʔaḥsan.*

theater - **1.** *masraḥ* pl. *masaareḥ.* They're presenting a good play in the new theater. *fii tamsiiliyye mniiḥa bᵊl-masraḥ ᵊž-ždiid.* **2.** *siinama* pl. *siinamaayaat.* There's an old film at the theater down the street. *fii fəlᵊm qadiim bᵊs-siinama halli ƹaš-šaareƹ taḥt ᵊšwayye.* **3.** *tamsiil.* She appreciates good theater. *bətqadder ᵊt-tamsiil l-ᵊmniiḥ.*

theft - *sərqa* pl. *-aat.*

their - **1.** *-(h)on.* Do you know their address? *btaƹref ƹanwaanon šii?* -- Tell the kids to wash their hands. *quul ləz-zġaar yġasslu ʔiidee(h)on.* **2.** *tabáƹon, šiiton.* Who's their new secretary? *miin ᵊs-səkᵊrteera ž-ždiide tabáƹon?* -- We bought their dining set. *štareena ṭaqm ᵊṣ-ṣəfra tabáƹon.*

theirs - *tabáƹon, šiiton.* Those books are all theirs. *hal-kətᵊb kəllon tabáƹon.*

**Are you a friend of theirs? *ʔənte sadiiq ʔəlon šii?*

**Our house isn't as big as theirs. *beetna muu kbiir qadd beeton.*

**We'll go in our car, and they'll take theirs. *nəḥna mənruuḥ b-sayyaarətna w-hənne biruuḥu b-sayyaarə́ton.*

theme - *mawḍuuƹ* pl. *mawaḍiiƹ.* Why did you pick that theme? *leeš naqqeet hal-mawḍuuƹ?*

themselves - **1.** *la-ḥaalon, b-nafson.* They have to make the beds themselves. *laazem ysaawu t-txuut la-ḥaalon.* **2.** *ḥaalon, nafson.* They are working themselves to death. *qaatliin ḥaalon bᵊš-šəġᵊl.* **3.** *-(h)on.* They discussed the matter among themselves. *baḥasu l-masʔale beenaaton.*

by themselves - **1.** *la-ḥaalon, la-waḥdon, b-nafson.* Did they really do all that work by themselves? *ƹan ḥaqa ƹəmlu kəll haš-šəġᵊl la-ḥaalon?* **2.** *la-ḥaalon, waḥdon.* I don't dare leave the children by themselves in the house. *maa bəstarži xalli l-ᵊwlaad la-ḥaalon bᵊl-beet.*

then - **1.** *baƹdeen.* What did he do then? *šuu ƹəmel baƹdeen?* -- Then what happened? *baƹdeen šuu ṣaar?* **2.** *waqta.* Did he talk to you about it then or later? *ḥakda -lak ƹaleeha waqta wəlla baƹdeen?* -- She was busy then, but she might be free now. *kaanet mašġuule waqta, barki faaḍye hallaq.* -- I'll wait until then to decide. *bənṭəẓer la-waqta la-qarrer.* **3.** *lakaan, baqa.* Then everything is settled. *lakaan kəll šii tsawwa.* -- Was he there, too? Then he must know the whole story. *huwwe kaan ᵊhniik kamaan? lakaan laazem ykuun byaƹref kəll ᵊl-qəṣṣa.* -- Well, then, let's go. *ʔee baqa xalliina nəmši.*

then and there - *b-saaƹə́ta.* Why didn't you mention it then and there? *leeš maa zakarta b-saaƹə́ta?*

by then - *saaƹə́ta, waqta.* Call Tuesday. We'll know by then. *talfen ᵊt-talaata. saaƹə́ta mnaƹref.*

(every) now and then - *mən waqᵊt la-waqᵊt, baƹḍ ᵊl-ʔaḥyaan.* We go to the movies now and then. *mənruuḥ ƹas-siinama mən waqᵊt la-waqᵊt.*

theologian - *ƹaalem˜* (pl. *ƹəlama˜*) *laahuut,* (specif., Muslim) *faqiih* pl. *fəqaha.*

theological - *laahuuti**, (specif., Muslim) *fəqhi**.

theology - *laahuut,* (specif., Muslim) *fəqᵊh.*

theoretical - *naẓari**.

theory - *naẓariyye* pl. *-aat.*

there - **1.** *hniik(e).* Have you ever been there? *kənt ᵊhniik šii?* -- You can still find an old copy here and there. *ləssa fiik ᵊtlaaqi nəsxa qadiime hoon w-hniik.* -- Fill it up to there. *ƹabbiiha la-hniik.* **2.** *la-hniik(e).* They go there because it's cheaper. *biruuḥu la-hniik la-ʔənno ʔarxaṣ.*

**There, that's enough now! *lək, ḥaaže baqa.*

**I have to admit, you've got me there. *laazem ʔəƹtə́ref ʔənnak laqaṭni.*

**There you're wrong! *b-hayy ʔənte ġalṭaan!*

**I'm afraid he's not quite all there. *xaayə́f-lak ykuun ƹando bərġi faltaan.*

**There, there! Everything will be all right. *ṭawwel baalak! kəll šii raḥa yəmši mniiḥ.*

**There you are! I was looking all over for you. *leekak* (or *šaƹak*)*! nakatt ᵊd-dənye ƹaleek.*

**There you are! It's all done. *leeka! xalṣet.*

**Have you seen my fountain pen? - There you are. *šəft ᵊstiilooyi šii? - leeko* (or *šaƹo*).

**There you are! Now you're sneezing! *šəfᵊt! hayy ƹam ᵊtƹaṭṭeṣ.*

there is, there are - *fii.* There is no such thing. *maa fii heek šii.* -- Is there anything I can do? *fii šii bəqder ʔaƹᵊmlo?* -- There are a few good hotels in town. *fii kam ʔoteel ᵊmniiḥ bᵊl-balad.*

then and there - *b-saaƹə́ta.* I decided then and there to take it. *qarrart ᵊb-saaƹə́ta ʔənni ʔaaxə́da.*

therefore - *mən heek, mənšaan heek, li-zaalek.* Therefore you think he's lying. *mən heek ʔənte mfakkro ƹam yəkzeb.*

thermometer - *miizaan˜* (pl. *mawaziin˜*) *ḥaraara, tarmumətᵊr* pl. *-aat.*

thermos bottle - *tərmos* pl. *taraames.*

these - **1.** *hadool(e), hadoon.* I like these better. *bḥəbb hadoole ʔaktar.* -- Give me some of these and some of those. *ƹaṭiini kam waaḥed mən hadool w-kam waaḥed mən hadənk.* -- Are these the right books? *hadool ᵊl-kətb ᵊl-maẓbuuṭiin?* **2.** *ha-* + def. article. These girls are here to study English. *hal-banaat žaayiin la-hoon la-yədᵊrsu ʔəngliizi.* -- How much are these peaches? *b-qaddeeš had-daraaqen?* **3.** *hayy(e).* These are hard times. *hayy ʔiyyaam ṣaƹbe.* -- These are questions which don't concern me. *hayye masaaʔel maa bətxəṣṣni.* **4.** *heek.* These things are hard to understand. *heek ʔašya ṣaƹᵊb fahma.* -- These people would kill a man without batting an eye. *heek naas byəqᵊtlu zalame biduun-ma trəff-ə́llon ƹeen.*

thesis - **1.** *ʔəṭruuḥa* pl. *-aat.* He's still working on his doctoral thesis. *ləssáa ƹam yəštə́ġel ƹala ʔəṭruuḥt ᵊd-doktorá̄a tabaƹo.* **2.** *faraḍiyye* pl. *-aat.* The entire work is based on the thesis that ... *l-ᵊmʔallaf kəllo məbni ƹala faraḍiyyet ʔənno ...*

they - *hənne.*

thick - **1.** *smiik* pl. *smaak.* They gave us some thick soup for lunch. *ġadduuna šooraba smiike.* -- This board isn't thick enough. *hal-looḥ ᵊl-xašab maa-lo smiik ᵊhfaaye.* — I need some thick material for a winter suit. *laazəmni qmaaše smiike la-badle šətwiyye.* -- The work consists of five thick volumes. *l-ᵊktaab ᵊmʔallaf mən xams ᵊmžalladaat ᵊsmiike.* **2.** *txiin* pl. *txaan.* We were unable to roll the thick log away. *maa ḥsənna ndarkel ᵊž-žəzᵊƹ ᵊt-txiin.* -- What's that thick roll you're carrying? *šuu hal-laffe t-txiine halli ḥaamə́la?* -- He's so thick he wouldn't understand the hint. *ƹaqlo txiin la-daraže maa byəfham ᵊt-talmiiḥa.* **3.** *ƹabi** pl. *ƹabaaya, kasiif.* Look what thick hair the baby has! *šuuf qaddeeš ᵊl-beebée šaƹraato ƹabaaya.* -- The house is surrounded by a thick hedge. *l-beet ḥawaléé syaaž ƹabi.* **4.** *kasiif.* The forest was so thick we nearly lost our way. *l-ġaabe kaanet kasiife la-daraže kənna raḥa nḍawweƹ ṭariiqna.* -- The thick smoke burned our eyes. *d-dəxxaan ᵊl-kasiif ḥarǎq-ᵊlna ƹyuunna.* **5.** *tqiil.* He has a thick foreign accent. *ƹalée lakne ʔažnabiyye tqiile.*

**The asphalt is several centimeters thick. *z-zəfᵊt səmko ƹəddet ṣanṭimətraat.*

**They're as thick as thieves. *hənne mətᵊl ṭiiẓeen b-ᵊlbaas.*

**I'll go through thick and thin for him. *bətḥammal ᵊs-samm wᵊd-damm la-ʔažlo.*

**Wherever there's a fight, he's in the thick of

it. kəll ᵊxnaaqa batlaaqii b-nəṣṣ diin ᵊl-maᶜmaᶜa.

to **thicken** - **1.** səmek (a samakaan). The cream will thicken as it cools. l-ᵊkreem byəsmak ᶜal-ᵊbruud. **2.** sammak//tsammak. Thicken the sauce with a little cornstarch. sammki ṣ-ṣalṣa b-ᵊšwayyet naša.

thief - **1.** ḥaraami* pl. -iyye. He was an accomplished thief at the age of twelve. kaan ḥaraami mhannak waqᵊt kaan ᶜəmro tnaᶜš. **2.** saareq pl. -iin. The police caught the car thief a few hours later. š-šərṭa kamšet saareq ᵊs-sayyaara baᶜᵊd šii kam saaᶜa.

**They're as thick as thieves. hənne matᵊl ṭiizeen b-ᵊlbaas.

thigh - faxᵊd pl. fxaad.

thimble - kəšᵊtbaan pl. kašatbiin.

thin - **1.** rqiiq pl. rqaaq. I'm looking for some thin paper. ᶜam dawwer ᶜala waraq ᵊrqiiq. **2.** rafiiᶜ pl. rfaaᶜ. nahiif pl. nəḥafa. She is very thin now. rafiiᶜa ktiir hallaq. **3.** rafiiᶜ. He has a high thin voice. ṣooto ᶜaali rafiiᶜ. **4.** xafiif. He has thin hair. šaᶜro xafiif. -- It's hard to breathe in this thin air. ṣaᶜb ᵊt-tanaffos ᵊb-hal-hawa l-xafiif. **5.** mriiq pl. mraaq. Don't add more water, the soup's too thin already. laa dziid mayy kamaan, š-šooraba mən ġeer šii mriiqa. -- That's a pretty thin excuse. haada ᶜəzr ᵊdᶜiif tamaam.

**I'll go through thick and thin for him. bət-ḥammal ᵊs-samm wᵊd-damm la-ᵊaẑlo.

to thin - **1.** xaff (ə xəffaan). His hair is thinning. šaᶜro ᶜam bixəff. **2.** marraq//tmarraq. I'm going to thin the sauce a little. raḥa marreq ᵊṣ-ṣalṣa šwayye.

to thin out - xaff (ə xəffaan). Let's wait until the crowd thins out. xalliina nənṭəẑer la-ḥatta txəff ᵊl-ᶜaẑqa.

thing - **1.** šii pl. ᵊašyaaᵊ and ᵊašya. There is no such thing. maa fii heek šii. -- That's the very thing I want. haada š-šii halli bəddi-yáa b-zaato. -- You shouldn't have said a thing like that. maa kaan laazem ᵊtquul heek šii. -- We didn't know a thing about their marriage. maa ᶜrəfna šii ᶜan žwaazəton. -- I don't know the first thing about chemistry. maa baᶜref w-laa šii ᶜan ᵊl-kiimya. -- We haven't done a thing all week. ᵊəlna žəmᶜa maa saaweena šii. -- You're seeing things. ᵊənte ᶜam tətxayyal ᵊašyaaᵊ. **2.** šii pl. ᵊašyaaᵊ, šaġle pl. -aat. We'll do that first thing in the morning. mnaᶜməla ᵊawwal šii ᶜala bəkra. -- We've heard a lot of nice things about you. sməᶜna ktiir šaġlaat ẓariife ᶜannak. -- That's an entirely different thing. hayy bᵊl-marra ġeer šaġle. -- Some funny things are going on there. fii šaġlaat ġariibe ᶜam ᵊtṣiir ᵊhniik. **3.** šaġle pl. -aat, qaḍiyye pl. qaḍaaya, qəṣṣa pl. qəṣaṣ, šii pl. ᵊašyaaᵊ. What's that thing I hear about you? šuu haš-šaġle halli sməᶜnaaha ᶜannak? -- I don't want to get involved in that kind of thing. maa bəddi ᵊətxarbaq ᵊb-heek šaġle. -- It's the same old thing over again. nafs ᵊl-qəṣṣa mən ᵊawwal w-ᵊždiid or **rəžᶜet ḥaliime la-ᶜaadəta l-qadiime. **4.** ġaraḍ pl. ġraaḍ. Have you packed all your things yet? ḍabbeet kəll ᵊġraaḍak wəlla ləssa? -- You can leave your things in the trunk of the car. fiik tətrok ᵊġraaḍak ᵊb-sanduuq ᵊs-sayyaara.

**It all adds up to the same thing. kəlla btəṭlaᶜ matᵊl baᶜḍa.

**How are things? šloon ᵊl-ᵊaḥwaal?

**You poor thing! yaa məskiin!

**This time it's the real thing. hal-marra ᶜan ḥaqa w-ḥaqiiq.

**He certainly knows a thing or two about business. laa šakk ᵊənno fahmaan bᵊt-tižaara.

**I'm going to tell him a thing or two! laḥa rəṣṣo raṣṣa maẓbuuṭa!

**Among other things he told me ... w-bᵊẑ-ẑəmle qal-li ...

**Well of all things, what are you doing here? mən kəll fii maḥallaat bᵊd-dənye, šuu žaabak la-hoon?

**Of all things! Who does he think he is? daxiil ᶜərḍak! miin ᵊmḥasseb ḥaalo.

to **think** - **1.** fakkar. He's never really learned how to think. bᵊl-ᵊaṣᵊl maa tᶜallam kiif yfakker. -- Now he thinks differently. hallaq ṣaar yfakker ġeer šakᵊl. -- Think twice before you quit your job. fakker maẓbuuṭ qabᵊl-ma tətrok šaġᵊltak. **2.** fakkar, ftakar, ṣafan (o ṣafᵊn). What are you thinking about? b-ᵊeeš ᶜam ᵊtfakker? -- I've been thinking about it all afternoon. ṣar-li ᶜam fakker fiiha kəll baᶜd ᵊḍ-ḍahr. -- She thinks of him all day long. bətfakker fii ṭuul ᵊn-nhaar. -- I'm only thinking of your interests. ᵊana bass ᶜam fakker ᵊb-maṣaalḥak. -- I'd think better of it, if I were you. law kənt ᵊb-maṭraḥak bəṣfon fiiha ᵊaktar. -- I thought better of it and stayed at home. ṣafanᵊt fiiha w-ᵊbqiit bᵊl-beet. **3.** ḥassab, ẓann (ə ẓann), fakkar, ftakar. We thought he was gone. ḥassabna ᵊənno raaḥ or ḥassabnáa raaḥ. -- That's what you think! heek ᵊənte badẓənn! -- He thinks he's very clever. mḥasseb ḥaalo zaki ktiir. -- I thought you were someone else. ḥassabtak ẓalame taani. **4.** ᶜtaqad, ẓann, ftakar. Don't you think it's too warm? maa btəᶜtəqed ᵊənno šoob ᵊktiir? -- I think the price is too high. bẓənn ᵊənno s-səᶜᵊr ġaali ktiir. **5.** ᶜtabar. He thought it a bad joke. ᶜtabára nakte bala ṭaᶜme.

**What do you think of that fellow? šuu raᵊyak ᵊb-haẓ-ẓalame?

**We think better of him since we know the whole story. tḥassan raᵊina fii baᶜᵊd-ma ᶜrəfna kəll ᵊl-qəṣṣa.

**I can't think of his address right now. maa ᶜam bədzakkar ᶜənwaano hallaq.

**Think nothing of it! basiiṭa!

**He thinks nothing of driving all night. maa btəfreq maᶜo ᵊiza bisuuq kəll ᵊl-leel.

**I wouldn't think of doing it. maa byəxṭor ᶜala baali saawiiha.

**He thinks only in terms of money. byəḥseb kəll šii bᵊl-maṣaari.

**That's wishful thinking. hayy tamanniyaat w-ᵊaḥlaam.

to think over - ṣafan (o ṣafᵊn) b-, tfakkar b-, ẓaan (i ø) ... b-baalo. He's still thinking it over. ləssaato ᶜam yəṣfon fiiha or ləssaato ᶜam yẓiina b-baalo. -- Think it over and let me know your decision. ṣfoon fiiha (or ẓiina b-baalak) w-qəl-li qaraarak.

to think up - ṭəleᶜ (a ṭalᶜa) b-. I'm sure you can think up some excuse. ᵊana ᵊakiid ᵊənno fiik tətláᶜ-lak b-šii ᶜəẑᵊr. -- Whoever thought up that story must be crazy. miin-ma ṭəleᶜ b-hal-qəṣṣa laazem ykuun bala ᶜaqᵊl.

third - **1.** taalet. It's the third street from here. huwwe š-šaareᶜ ᵊt-taalet (or taalet šaareᶜ) mən hoon. **2.** tlaate. We'll leave on the third of August, mənsaafer b-ᵊtlaate ᵊaab. **3.** taalitan, taalet šii. First it's expensive, second it's impractical, and third it's difficult to get. ᵊawwalan ġaali, taaniyan muu ᶜamali w-taalitan ṣaᶜᵊb l-ᵊḥṣuul ᶜaleeha.

one third - təlᵊt pl. tlaat. Only two thirds of the water is actually put to use. bass təlteen ᵊl-mayy ᶜam təstaġall.

third-class - daraže taalte, teerse. Give me one third-class ticket to Aleppo. ᶜaṭiini tazkara daraže taalte la-ḥalab.

thirdly - taalitan, taalet šii.

thirst - **1.** ᶜaṭaš. I can't quench my thirst. maa fiini ᵊəṭfi ᶜaṭaši. **2.** taᶜaṭṭoš. This thirst for knowledge is unusual in someone his age. hat-taᶜaṭṭoš ləl-ᶜəlᵊm muu šii ᶜaadi la-waaḥed ᵊb-ᶜəmro.

thirsty - ᶜaṭšaan. I'm very thirsty. ᵊana ᶜaṭšaan ᵊktiir.

thirteen - **1.** tləṭṭaᶜš. All together, there are thirteen of us in our family. l-kəll bᵊl-kəll, nəḥna tləṭṭaᶜš bᵊl-ᶜeele. **2.** tləṭṭaᶜšar. He worked thirteen years for the company. štaġal tləṭṭaᶜšar səne ləš-šərke.

thirteenth - **1.** t-tləṭṭaᶜš. Tomorrow is his thirteenth birthday. bəkra ᶜiid miilaado t-tləṭṭaᶜš. -- We arrived on March the thirteenth. wṣəlna b-ᵊtləṭṭaᶜš ᵊaadaar. **2.** t-taalet ᶜašar. He's the most famous poet of the thirteenth century. huwwe ᵊašhar šaaᶜer bᵊl-qarn ᵊt-taalet ᶜašar.

thirtieth - t-tlaatiin, t-tlaatiini*. The company is celebrating its thirtieth anniversary. š-šərke ᶜam təḥtəfel ᵊb-ᶜiida t-tlaatiin(i).

thirty - tlaatiin.

this - **1.** haad(a) f. hayy(e), haadi. What's this? šuu haad? -- This is just what I wanted to avoid. haada bᵊz-zaat halli kənt raayed ᵊtfaada. -- Is this the same picture I saw on your desk? hayye nafs ᵊṣ-ṣuura halli šəfta ᶜala maktabak? -- No one could anticipate this problem. maa ḥada qəder yətwaqqaᶜ hal-məšᵊkle hayy. -- This aunt of mine I'm telling you about got married when she was eighteen. ᶜammti hayye halli ᶜam bəḥkii-lak *ɛanha džawwazet lamma kaan ɛəmra tmənṭaɛšar səne.* **2.** *ha-* + def. article. Do you know this man? *btaɛref har-rəžžaal?* -- Cross out this word. *šxaaṭ hal-kəlme.* -- This time I'll let it go. *hal-marra bmašSiiha.* -- Come here this minute. *taaɛa la-hoon had-daqiiqa.* **3.** *haš-šii, haš-šağle.* What do you think of this? *šuu raʔyak ᵊb-haš-šii?* -- What do you conclude from this? *šuu btəstantež mən haš-šii?* -- This takes a lot of time. *haš-šii byaaxod waqt ᵊktiir.* **4.** *heek.* This is what I heard: He's getting married next month. *heek ᵊsmaɛᵊt: raha yədžawwaz ᵊš-šahr ᵊž-žaaye.* -- This is his usual behavior. *heek taṣarrfo l-ɛaadi.* -- The poem goes like this: ... *heek ᵊl-qaṣiide: ...* **5.** *hal-qadd.* I didn't think she'd be this stupid. *maa kənt ᵊmhassəba hal-qadd žadbe.*

**They talked about this and that. *ḥaku ʔaškaal w-ʔalwaan.*

**To this day I don't know what he wanted. *la-ḥadd ᵊl-yoom maa baɛref šuu kaan bəddo.*

**My only condition is this:... *šarṭi l-waḥiid huwwe...*

this afternoon - *l-yoom baɛd ᵊḍ-ḍəhᵊṛ.* I'm going to see him this afternoon. *raḥa ruuḥ šuufo l-yoom baɛd ᵊḍ-ḍəhᵊṛ.*

this evening - *l-yoom ɛašiyye.* We have no time this evening. *maa ɛanna waqt ᵊl-yoom ɛašiyye.*

this morning - *l-yoom ᵊṣ-ṣəbᵊḥ, l-yoom ɛala bəkra.* I met her on the street this morning. *ltaqeet fiiha bᵊṭ-ṭariiq ᵊl-yoom ᵊṣ-ṣəbᵊḥ.*

this noon - *l-yoom ᵊḍ-ḍəhᵊṛ.* They're coming to our house this noon. *žaayiin la-ɛanna l-yoom ᵊḍ-ḍəhᵊṛ.*

thorn - *šooke* coll. *šook* pl. *-aat.* The dog seems to have a thorn in his paw. *ɛala-ma yəẓhar ᵊl-kalb fii šooke b-rəžlo.* -- That fellow's been a thorn in my side for a long time. *haz-zalame ṣar-lo mədde mətl ᵊš-šooke b-xaaṣərti.*

thorny - **1.** *malaan šook.* The garden is surrounded by a thorny hedge. *ž-žneene ḥawaleeha syaaž malaan šook.* **2.** *šaaʔek.* Let's set that thorny question aside for a moment. *xalliina nḥəṭṭ has-suʔaal ᵊš-šaaʔek ɛala žanab šwayye.* -- The road to success can be thorny sometimes. *ṭariiq ᵊn-nažaaḥ šaaʔek ʔiyyaam.*

thorough - **1.** *mtaqqan.* He's very thorough in everything he does. *huwwe mtaqqan ᵊktiir ᵊb-kəll šii byaɛᵊmlo.* **2.** *daqiiq.* Each machine has to pass a thorough test. *kəll maakiina laazem təžtaaz faḥᵊṣ daqiiq.*

thoroughly - **1.** *b-ʔətqaan, b-dəqqa.* We checked the engine thoroughly and couldn't find a thing. *faḥaṣna l-motoor ᵊb-ʔətqaan w-maa kənna nlaaqi šii.* **2.** *ɛat-tamaam, ɛal-ʔaaxiir.* I was thoroughly exhausted after the long walk. *kənᵊt faareṭ ɛat-tamaam baɛd ᵊl-mašye ṭ-ṭawiile.*

those - **1.** *hadənk(e).* Why don't you leave these and take those? *leeš maa btətrok hadool w-ᵊbtaaxod hadənke?* -- Those apples look fresher than these. *hadənk ᵊt-təffaaḥaat ᵊmbayyen ɛaleehon taaza ʔaktar mən hadool.* **2.** *hadənk(e), hadool(e), hadoon.* I never buy anything but those. *b-ɛəmri maa bəštə́ri ʔayy šii ʔəlla hadənk.* -- Who were those people you were talking to? *miin hadool ᵊn-naas halli kənt ɛam təḥki maɛon?* -- Those were the best students I ever had. *hadool kaanu ʔaḥsan talamiiz maraqu ɛaliyyi.* -- Are those the books you ordered? *hadool ᵊl-kətᵊb halli ṭalabton?* **3.** *hadiik, hadənk.* We didn't have any money in those days. *maa kaan maɛna w-laa qərᵊš hadiik ᵊl-ʔiyyaam.* -- Who lives in those houses over there? *miin saaken ᵊb-hadənk l-ᵊbyuut?* **4.** *hadaak.* Who bought those shoes? *miin ᵊštara hadaak ᵊṣ-ṣabbaaṭ?* — Who's are those glasses there? *la-miin hadaak ᵊl-kəzlok?* **5.** *heek.* Those people have no conscience at all. *heek naas maa ɛandon ḍamiir ʔabadan.* — Those things can't be explained. *heek ʔašyaaʔ muu məmken šarḥa.*

though - **1.** *maɛ ʔənno* (invar.), *maɛ ʔənn-* + pron. suff. Though he knew it he didn't tell me anything about it. *maɛ ʔənno kaan ɛarfaana maa qal-li šii ɛanna.* — He'll probably win the election though the opposition is powerful. *l-məḥtə́mal ʔənno yənžaḥ bᵊl-ʔəntixaabaat maɛ ʔənno (or maɛ ʔənna) l-ᵊmɛaaraḍa qawiyye.* **2.** *laaken.* I'll do it! Not now, though. *bsaawiiha! laaken muu hallaq.* -- You've ordered it, though, haven't you? *laaken waṣṣeet ɛaleeha, muu heek?*

as though - *ka-ʔənno* (invar.), *ka-ʔənn-* + pron. suff. It looks as though it may rain. *mbayyen ka-ʔənno raḥa təmṭer.*

even though - *maɛ ʔənno* (invar.), *maɛ ʔənn-* + pron. suff. He went there even though I warned him against it. *raaḥ la-hniik maɛ ʔənni nabbahto maa yruuḥ.*

thought - **1.** *tafkiir* pl. *-aat.* The very thought of it makes me sick. *məžarrad ᵊt-tafkiir fiiha bilaɛɛi-li nafsı.* **2.** *fəkra* pl. *ʔafkaar.* What a noble thought! *məlla fəkra nabiile!* -- You must have read my thoughts. *laazem ᵊtkuun qareet ʔafkaari.* -- He was lost in thought. *kaan šaared ᵊb-ʔafkaaro.* -- Sorry, I don't follow your line of thought. *ɛafwan, maa ɛam bəḥsen ʔətbaɛ səlsəlt ʔafkaarak.*

to give thought to - **1.** *ṣafan (o ṣafᵊn) b-, tfakkar b-, zaan (i ø) ... b-baalo.* I'll have to give this matter some thought. *laazem ʔəṣfon šwayye b-hal-mawḍuuɛ* or *laazem ziin hal-mawḍuuɛ ᵊb-baali šwayye.* **2.** *fakkar b-.* Don't give it another thought! *laa baqa tfakker fiiha.*

**Don't give it a thought! *hmə́la!*

to show thought for - *raaɛa.* Can't you show a little thought for others? *maa fiik ᵊtraaɛi ġeerak šwayye?*

thoughtful - *ġarqaan bᵊt-tafkiir.* Why do you look so thoughtful? *šə-bak ġarqaan bᵊt-tafkiir?*

**Not all children are so thoughtful toward their elders. *muu kəll l-ᵊwlaad hal-qadd ᵊbyəɛtəbru halli ʔakbar mənhon.*

**It's very thoughtful of you to bring me flowers. *ktiir ləṭᵊf mənnak ʔənnak təftə́ker w-ᵊdžəb-li haz-zhuur.*

thoughtless - *ṭaayeš, msahhem.* He's just a thoughtless young fellow. *maa huwwe ʔəlla šabb ṭaayeš.*

**A thoughtless remark brought on the whole trouble. *mlaaḥaẓa biduun tafkiir sabbabet ᵊl-məšᵊkle kəlla.*

thousand - *ʔalf* pl. *ʔluuf* and *ʔaalaaf,* after numerals 3 to 10 *aalaaf.* There were a thousand or more people there. *kaan fii ḥawaali ʔalf zalame ʔaw ʔaktar ᵊhniik.* — We saw thousands of people waiting for the King to pass by. *šəfna ʔaalaaf ᵊn-naas ɛam byənṭəẓru l-malek yəmroq.* -- Thousands and thousands of people attended the convention. *ʔluuf ᵊmʔallafe mn ᵊn-naas ḥəḍru l-mahražaan.* -- The car cost me more than seven thousand pounds. *s-sayyaara kallafətni ʔaktar mən sabᵊɛt aalaaf leera.*

thousandth - **1.** *l-ʔalf.* The thousandth ship has passed through the new canal. *l-baaxra l-ʔalf marqet bᵊl-qanaat ᵊž-ždiide.* **2.** *ʔalfi**. The city has just celebrated its thousandth anniversary. *l-madiine maa-la zamaan məḥtəfle b-ɛiida l-ʔalfi.*

one thousandth - *waaḥed ɛala ʔalf.* The instrument is accurate to five thousandths of a millimeter. *dəqqet l-ʔaale xamse ɛala ʔalf ᵊmn ᵊl-məllimətᵊr.*

thrashing - *qatle* pl. *-aat.* Did he ever get a thrashing! *yaa ʔaḷḷa ʔakal qatle məḥtə́rame!*

thread - **1.** *xeeṭ* pl. *xiiṭaan.* Have you a needle and thread? *ɛandak ʔəbre w-xeeṭ?* -- His life hung by a thread. *ḥayaato kaanet ᵊmɛallaqa b-xeeṭ.* **2.** *snaan* (pl.). The thread on this screw is worn out. *baayẓa snaan hal-bərġi.* **3.** *mažra.* I've lost the thread of your argument. *ḍaaɛ mənni mažra mḥaažažtak.*

to thread - *laḍam (o laḍᵊm//nlaḍam).* I'll thread the needle for you. *bəldə́m-lak ᵊl-ʔəbre.*

threat - *tahdiid* pl. *-aat.* Your threats won't get you anywhere with me. *tahdiidaatak maa bətwaṣṣlak la-natiiže maɛi.*

to **threaten** - *haddad//thaddad.* He threatened to leave if he didn't get a raise. *haddad ʔənno yətrok ʔiza maa ɛaṭúu ɛalaawe.* — The entire city was threatened by the epidemic. *l-madiine kəlla kaanet ᵊmhaddade bᵊl-wabaaʔ.*

**It's threatening to rain. *raḥa yənzel maṭaṛ.*

three - **1.** *tlaate.* Three times nine is twenty-seven. *tlaate b-təsɛa bisaawu sabɛda ɛəšriin.* -- Three of us will stay here. *tlaate mənna byəbqu hoon* or *tlaatətna mnəbqa hoon.* **2.** *tlətt.* I called you three times. *talfant-ə́llak tlətt marraat.* --We'll leave in three days. *mənsaafer baɛd ᵊtlətt iyaam.* -- The population is a little over three thousand people. *ɛadad ᵊs-səkkaan ʔaktar b-ᵊšwayye mən tlətt aalaaf zalame.* **3.** *s-saaɛa tlaate.* Is three a convenient time for you? *s-saaɛa tlaate binaasbak?* -- We have to be at the airport at three. *laazem ᵊnkuun bᵊl-maṭaar ᵊs-saaɛa tlaate.*

to **thresh** - *daras (o darᵊs* and *draase//ndaras).* We'll start threshing the wheat tomorrow. *mnəbda nədros ᵊl-qamḥaat bəkra.*

threshing machine - *darraase* pl. *-aat.*

threshold - *barṭuuše* pl. *baraṭiiš,* (also fig.) *ɛatabe* pl. *-aat.*

thrifty - *məqtəṣed, ʔidaari*.* She's a thrifty housewife. *hiyye sətt beet məqtəṣde.*

thrill - *našwe* pl. *-aat.* I still remember the thrill of my first plane flight. *ləssaani mədzakker našwet ʔawwal rəkbe bᵊṭ-ṭayyaara.*

to **thrive** - 1. *zdahar.* Business is thriving this time of the year. *t-tižaara btəzdəher b-hal-waqt ᵊmn ᵊs-səne.* 2. *tnaššaṭ.* He seems to thrive on hardships. *εala-ma yəẓhar byətnaššaṭ εal-mataaεeb.*

**The children are thriving. *l-ᵊwlaad εam yəkbaru mətl ᵊl-kəzᵊb.*

thriving - *naažeḥ.* They built up a thriving export business. *banu tižaaret taṣdiir naažḥa.*

throat - *ḥalᵊq* pl. *ḥluuq.* The doctor examined my throat. *d-doktoor faḥaṣ-li ḥalqi.* -- She wanted to say something, but the words stuck in her throat. *kaanet bədda tquul šii laaken ᵊl-kəlme εəlqet ᵊb-ḥalqa.* -- My throat is dry. *ḥalqi našfaan.* -- I have a sore throat. *ḥalqi εam yuužaεni.*

**He almost jumped down my throat. *maa bəqi ʔəlla ydəqq b-xawaniiqi.*

**He'd cut your throat for a pound. *byədbaḥak εala leera.*

to clear one's throat - *tnaḥnaḥ.* He cleared his throat and continued in a loud voice. *tnaḥnaḥ w-kammal b-ṣooṭ εaali.*

throne - *εarᵊš* pl. *εruuš(e).*

through - 1. *b-.* We went through the woods. *maraqna bᵊl-ġaabe.* -- We strolled through the quiet streets. *tmašwarna bᵊš-šawaareε ᵊl-haadye.* 2. *mən.* The thief fled through the window. *l-ḥaraami harab mn ᵊš-šəbbaak.* -- We entered through a narrow opening in the fence. *fətna mən ṭaaqa zġiire bᵊl-xəṣṣ.* 3. *mən εala ṭariiq^.* Let's go out through the garden. *xalliina nəṭlaε mən εala ṭariiq ᵊž-žneene.* 4. *mən wara.* We heard their voices through the (closed) door. *sməεna ʔaṣwaaṭon mən wara l-baab.* 5. *ṭuul^.* We laughed through the whole film. *ḍḍaḥḥakna ṭuul ᵊl-fəlᵊm.* 6. *b-sabab^.* The work was held up two weeks through his illness. *š-šəġl ᵊtεaṭṭal žəmᵊεteen b-sabab ḍaεafo.* 7. *b-waasəṭt^, εan ṭariiq^.* I got this book through a friend in Damascus. *ʔəžaani hal-ᵊktaab ᵊb-waaṣəṭṭ ṣadiiq ʔəli bᵊš-šaam.* 8. *fard saḥbe* (invar.). I booked a through ticket to Athens. *ḥažažᵊt tazkara fard saḥbe la-ʔatiina.* -- Isn't there a through flight to London? *maa fii ṭayyaara fard saḥbe la-landan?*

through street - *ṭariiq* (pl. *ṭəroq*) *naafde.*

through and through - *εal-ʔaaxiir.* We were soaked through and through. *saqsaqna bᵊl-mayy εal-ʔaaxiir.* -- He's evil through and through. *huwwe šarriir εal-ʔaaxiir* or ***huwwe kəllo šarr.*

to be through - *xallaṣ.* I'll be through work at five o'clock. *bxalleṣ ᵊš-šəġᵊl s-saaεa xamse.* -- I'm nearly through with the book. *taqriiban xallaṣᵊt l-ᵊktaab.*

**I am through with him. *ntaha kəll šii beeni w-beeno.*

**If you ever do that again, we're through. *ʔiza btaεmel haš-šii marra taanye kəll šii beenaatna byəntəhi.*

**He's been through a lot. *maraq εala raaso šii ktiir.*

throughout - *ṭuul^.* You can get these vegetables throughout the whole year. *fiik ᵊtlaaqi hal-xədra ṭuul ᵊs-səne.*

**This hotel is famous throughout the world. *hal-ʔoteel mašhuur bᵊl-εaalam kəllo.*

**I discovered mistakes throughout the article. *laqeet ʔaġlaaṭ ᵊb-kəll ᵊl-maqaale.*

throw - *laḥše* pl. *-aat, ramye* pl. *-aat.* That was some throw. *məlla laḥše!* -- His house is only a stone's throw from the station. *beeto bass laḥšet ḥažar εan l-ᵊmḥaṭṭa.*

to throw - 1. *rama (i rami//nrama* and *rtama), laḥaš (o laḥᵊš//nlaḥaš).* Let's see how far you can throw the ball. *xalliina nšuuf la-ween fiik tərmi ᵊṭ-ṭaabe.* -- The horse threw him. *l-ᵊḥṣaan ramda.* -- He threw a pair of fours. *laḥaš w-žaab dərži.* -- She practically threw herself at him. *taqriiban laḥšet ḥaala εalée.* -- Let me just throw a coat on. *bass xalliini ʔəlḥoš kabbuud εala ktaafi.* 2. *sakkar//tsakkar.* Throw the main switch before you leave. *sakker məftaaḥ ᵊl-kahraba r-raʔiisi qabᵊl-ma truuḥ.* 3. *wažžah//twažžah.* Throw that light this way, please. *wažžeh han-nuur la-hoon, mən faḍlak.* 4. *εəmel (-yaεmel εamal//nεamal).* Let's throw a party next week. *xalliina naεmel ḥafle ž-žəmεa ž-žaaye.* 5. *ḥayyar//tḥayyar.* His quick answer threw me for a minute. *žawaabo s-sariiε ḥayyarni laḥẓa.*

**When she hears the news she'll throw a fit. *lamma bədda təsmaε ᵊl-xabar laḥa tqiim ᵊqyaame.*

**I thought my suggestion was wonderful but he threw cold water on it. *ftakarᵊt ʔəqtiraaḥi kaan εaẓiim laaken huwwe fannado tafniid.*

to throw around - *laḥwaš//tlaḥwaš.* I wish you wouldn't throw your clothes around like that. *ya-reetak maa bətlaḥweš ʔawaεiik heek.*

to throw away - *kabb (ə kabb//nkabb).* Throw the papers away. *kəbb l-ᵊwraaq!*

to throw down - *rama (i rami//nrama* and *rtama).* Throw down a pillow to me. *rmii-li mxadde.*

to throw in - 1. *ḥaṭṭ εal-beeεa.* Throw in a couple of tires and I take the car. *ḥəṭṭ kawšuukeen εal-beeεa la-ʔaaxod ᵊs-sayyaara.* 2. *laḥaš (o laḥᵊš //nlaḥaš).* Don't forget to throw in a clove of garlic when the soup boils. *laa tənsi maa təlᵊḥši sənn tuum bᵊš-šooraba lamma təġli.*

to throw out - 1. *kabb (ə kabb//nkabb).* I threw the old shoes out. *kabbeet ᵊṣ-ṣabbaṭ ᵊl-εatiiq.* 2. *qallaε//tqallaε.* She almost threw me out. *maa bəqi ʔəlla tqalləεni.*

to throw out of court - *radd (ə radd//rtadd).* The case was thrown out of court for lack of evidence. *rtaddet ᵊd-daεwa la-εadam wužuud ʔadəlle.*

to throw over - 1. *laḥaš (o laḥᵊš//nlaḥaš), rama (i rami//nrama* and *rtama).* Can you throw it over to me? *fiik təlḥəš-li-yaha?* 2. *baaε (i beeε//mbaaε).* She threw him over for a sailor. *baaεto mənšaan baḥḥaar.*

to throw up - 1. *laḥaš (o laḥᵊš) ... bᵊl-hawa.* She threw up her arms in dismay. *laḥšet ʔideeha bᵊl-hawa mn ᵊl-yaʔᵊs.* 2. *rafaε (a rafᵊε//nrafaε* and *rtafaε).* They threw up a temporary bridge after the flood. *rafaεu žəsr ᵊmwaqqat baεd ᵊṭ-ṭawafaan.* 2. *raažaε, stafraġ, tqaaya.* I throw up every time I ride on the train. *kəll-ma bərkab bᵊt-treen ᵊbraažeε.*

**That's the second time you've thrown that up to me. *hayy taani marra btəftəḥ-li has-siire.*

thumb - *baahem* pl. *bawaahem.* I burned my thumb. *ḥaraqᵊt baahmi.*

**I don't know what's happening, I'm all thumbs. *maa baεref šuu ṣaayer-li l-yoom, ʔana mfaškal tamaam.*

**He's too much under his wife's thumb. *huwwe ktiir taḥᵊt baaṭ marto.*

to thumb through - *tṣaffaḥ.* I only thumbed through the book. *bass ᵊtṣaffaḥᵊt l-ᵊktaab.*

thunder - *raεᵊd.* Did you hear the thunder last night? *sməεᵊt ᵊr-raεᵊd leelt ᵊmbaareḥ?*

**A thunder of applause greeted the speaker. *εaaṣəft tasfiiq ḥayyet ᵊl-xaṭiib.*

to thunder - 1. *raεad (o raεᵊd).* It's beginning to thunder. *badet tərεod.* 2. *ṣaεwaṭ.* You shouldn't have let him thunder at you like that. *maa kaan laazem txalli yṣaεweṭ εaleek heek.*

thunderbolt - *ṣaaεiqa* pl. *ṣawaaεeq.*

thunderstorm - *εaaṣfe* (pl. *εawaaṣef*) *raεdiyye.*

Thursday - *(yoom^) xamiis.*

thus - *haakaza, heek.* Thus we can say that ... *haakaza mnəqder ᵊnquul ʔənno ...*

thyme - *zaεtar.*

tick - *qraade* coll. *qraad* pl. *qərdaan.* The woods are full of ticks and mosquitoes. *l-ġaabe malaane qraad w-naamuus.*

to **tick** - *taktak.* My watch has stopped ticking. *saaεti waqqafet ᵊttaktek.*

ticket - 1. *tazkara* pl. *tazaaker, biṭaaqa* pl. *-aat.* Can you get us three tickets for that show? *fiik džəb-ᵊlna tlətt tazaaker la-hal-ḥafle?* -- You can buy a ticket on the train. *fiik təštəri tazkara εat-treen.* -- I want a round-trip ticket to Aleppo. *bəddi tazkara rooḥaražεa la-ḥalab.* 2. *qaaʔime* pl. *qawaaʔem.* I'm voting the Republican ticket. *εam ṣawwet la-qaaʔəmt ᵊž-žamhuuriyyiin.* 3. *ẓabᵊṭ* pl. *ẓbuuṭa.* I just got a ticket for speeding. *hallaq ʔakalt ẓabᵊṭ la-ʔənni məsreε.*

to **tickle** - *karkar.* He wouldn't laugh even if you tickled him. *maa byəḍḍaḥḥak w-law karkarto.*

ticklish - *ḥassaas.* That's a ticklish question. *hayye masʔale ḥassaase.*

to be ticklish - *tkarkar, ġaar (a ø).* Are you ticklish? *btətkarkar šii?*

tide - *madd w-žazᵊr.* There's a strong tide in the bay. *fii madd w-žazᵊr qawi bᵊl-xaliiž.*

high tide - *madd.* It was high tide when our ship left the harbor. *kaan fii madd lamma baaxrətna tarket ᵊl-boor.*

low tide - *žazᵊr.* You can walk out to the island at low tide. *btəqder təmši ləž-žaziire waqᵊt ᵊž-žazᵊr.*

to tide over - *madd (ə madd) maε.* Twenty pounds will tide me over until Monday. *εəšriin leera bimaddu maεi la-yoom ᵊt-taneen.*

tidy - **1.** *mrattab.* Your desk is always so tidy. *maktabak daayman ᵊmrattab.* -- He's a tidy worker. *huwwe šaġġiil ᵊmrattab.* -- His clothes aren't expensive but he always looks tidy. *ʔawaεʼi muu ġaalye bass daayman ᵊmrattab.* **2.** *məḥtdram.* He saved a tidy sum over the years. *ṣammad mablaġ məḥtdram maε marr l-ᵊsniin.*

to tidy up - *rattab//trattab.* I've got to tidy up my room a little. *laazem ratteb ʔuudti šwayye.*

tie - **1.** *graave* and *graafe* and *graavaat* pl. *graavataat.* He wears loud ties. *byəlbes graavataat ʔalwaana faaqεa.* **2.** *raabṭa* pl. *rawaabeṭ.* He broke all family ties when he left the country. *qaṭaε kəll rawaabṭo l-εaaʔiliyye b-tarko l-ᵊblaad.* **3.** *taεaadol.* The game ended in a tie. *l-ᵊmbaarda ntahet bᵊt-taεaadol.*

to tie - **1.** *rabaṭ (o rabᵊṭ//nrabaṭ).* Just a minute, I have to tie my shoelaces. *laḥẓa bəddi ʔərboṭ šawwaaṭaat ṣabbaaṭi.* -- They tied the goat to a stake. *rabaṭu l-εanze b-watad.* -- Tie the two ends together. *rbooṭ ᵊṭ-ṭarafeen sawa.* -- Tie the rope around the tree. *rbooṭ ᵊl-ḥable daayer maduur ᵊš-šažara.* **2.** *rabaṭ, εaqad (o εaqᵊd// nεaqad).* Let me tie a knot in the middle. *xalliini ʔərboṭ εəqde bᵊn-nəṣṣ.* **3.** *rabaṭ, rabbaṭ.* My hands are tied in this matter. *ʔidayyi marbuuṭiin ᵊb-haš-šaġle.*

**We plan to tie the knot soon. *naawyiin nədzawwaž εan qariib.*

to tie down - *rabaṭ (o rabᵊṭ//nrabaṭ).* I don't want to tie myself down by buying a house. *maa bəddi ʔərboṭ ḥaali b-šarwet beet.* -- I'm terribly tied down all day long. *faẓaaεa šuu marbuuṭ ʔana ṭuul ᵊn-nhaar.* -- Make sure to tie the cover down well. *diir baalak tərboṭ ᵊl-ġaṭa mniiḥ.*

to tie in - *ṭṭaabaq.* Her visit ties in very well with my plans. *zyaarə́ta məṭṭaabqa tamaam maε bərnaamži.*

to tie on - *waṣal (-yuuṣel waṣᵊl//nwaṣal).* Tie on another piece of string! *wṣə́l-lak šaqfet ḥable taanye.*

to tie up - **1.** *rabaṭ (o rabᵊṭ//nrabaṭ).* Please tie the package up for me. *mən faḍlak ᵊrbəṭ-li r-rəzme.* -- Did you tie up the boat? *rabaṭṭ ᵊš-šaxtuura?* **2.** *rabaṭ, ḥažaz (e/o ḥažᵊz//nḥažaz).* He ties up the telephone for hours. *byərboṭ ᵊt-talifoon saaεaat w-saaεaat.*

to be or get tied up - **1.** *rtabaṭ.* Are you tied up this evening? *ʔənte martə́beṭ ᵊb-šii l-leele?* **2.** *εəleq (a εalqa).* I got tied up in heavy traffic. *εləqt ᵊb-εažqet ᵊs-seer.*

**Most of his money is tied up in oil. *ḥaaṭeṭ ʔaktar maṣarʼi b-mašariiε zeet.*

tiger - *nəmᵊr* pl. *nmuura.*

tight - **1.** *dayyeq.* This jacket is too tight for me. *haž-žaakeet dayyeq ᵊktiir εaliyyi.* **2.** *mašduud.* The rope is too tight. *l-ḥabᵊl mašduud ᵊktiir.* **3.** *εal-maẓbuuṭ.* Shut your eyes tight. *sakker ᵊεyuunak εal-maẓbuuṭ!* -- Is the jar sealed tight? *l-qaṭramiiz maxtuum εal-maẓbuuṭ?* **4.** *ḥarež.* I've been in tight spots before. *maraqt ᵊb-mawaaqef ḥarže mən qabᵊl.* **5.** *sakraan.* Boy, was he tight last night! *yaa laṭiif šuu kaan sakraan leelt ᵊmbaareḥ!*

**Sleep tight! *naam malaat ᵊžfuunak!*

**He's very tight with his money. *ʔiido šadiide ktiir εala maṣarʼi.*

**You have to tie your shoelaces tighter. *laazem ᵊtšədd šawwaaṭaat ṣabbaaṭak ʔaktar.*

**He swore that the boat was tight. *ḥalaf ʔənno š-šaxtuura maa btəzrob.*

**Just sit tight until I come back. *xalliik qaaεed εala maḥallak la-ḥatta ʔəržaε.*

**The best thing for us to do is sit tight until we hear from him. *ʔafḍal šii ʔəlna ʔənna nəbqa matᵊl-ma nəḥna la-ḥatta nəsmaε mənno.*

**Hold me tight! *εbəṭni!*

to tighten - *šadd (ə šadd//nšadd).* Tighten the rope. *šədd ᵊl-ḥabᵊl!* -- Can you tighten the screw a little? *fiik ᵊtšədd ᵊl-bərġi šwayye?*

**We'll have to tighten our belts this year. *laazem ᵊnqatter ᵊktiir has-səne.*

tile - **1.** (floor) *blaaṭa* coll. *blaaṭ* pl. *-aat.* **2.** (wall) *porsaleene* coll. *porsaleen* pl. *-aat.* **3.** (roof) *qarmiide* coll. *qarmiid* pl. *qaramiid.*

to tile - *ballaṭ.* They've finished tiling the first floor. *ṣaaru mxallṣiin tabliiṭ ᵊṭ-ṭaabeq ᵊl-ʔawwal.*

tilelaying - *tabliiṭ.*

tiler - *ballaaṭ* pl. *-iin.*

till - **1.** *la-, la-ḥatta.* Wait till I come back. *nṭẓer la-ʔəržaε.* **2.** *la-.* I won't be able to see you till next week. *maa raḥa ʔəḥsen šuufak ləž-žəmεa ž-žaaye.*

to **tilt** - *mayyal//tmayyal.* If you tilt the bottle, you may be able to get it out. *ʔiza mayyalt ᵊl-qanniine yəmken fiik ᵊṭṭaalə́εa.* -- Tilt your head back. *mayyel raasak la-wara.* -- Don't tilt your chair so far back. *laa tmayyel kərsiik kəll hal-qadd la-wara.*

timber - **1.** *xašab* pl. *ʔaxšaab.* They floated the timber down the river. *xallu l-xašab yfuuš εala wəšš ᵊn-nahᵊr.* **2.** *ḥərᵊš* pl. *ʔaḥraaš.* The mountains are covered with timber. *ž-žbaal ᵊmġaṭṭaaye bᵊl-ʔaḥraaš.*

time - **1.** *waqᵊt* pl. *ʔawqaat.* It's time to leave. *ṣaar waqᵊt nəmši.* -- It is lunch time. *ṣaar waqt ᵊl-ġada.* -- These are hard times. *hayy ʔawqaat ṣaεbe.* -- The time is up tomorrow. *bəkra byəxloṣ ᵊl-waqᵊt.* -- We have no time to lose. *maa εanna waqt ᵊndawwεo.* -- We had good weather all the time. *ṣaadafna ṭaqᵊṣ ḥalu ṭuul ᵊl-waqᵊt.* -- Half the time he doesn't do a thing. *nəṣṣ ᵊl-waqᵊt maa byəštə́ġel šaġle.* -- Where have you been keeping yourself all this time? *ween hal-ġeebe kəll hal-waqᵊt?* -- At that time I thought differently about it. *b-hadaak ᵊl-waqᵊt fakkarᵊt fiiha ġeer šəkᵊl.* -- We got there at the same time. *wṣəlna la-hniik b-nafs ᵊl-waqᵊt.* -- He comes to see us from time to time. *mən waqᵊt la-waqᵊt byəži yzuurna.* -- The winner's time was 11 seconds. *waqt ᵊl-ʔawwal kaan ḥdaεšar saanye.* -- He ran the mile in record time. *ḍarab raqam qiyaasi bᵊl-waqᵊt yalli rakad fii l-miil.* -- I finished the job in record time. *ḍarabᵊt raqam qiyaasi bᵊl-waqᵊt yalli xallaṣᵊt fii š-šaġle.* -- Now's your time to take revenge. *hallaq ᵊl-waqᵊt la-taaxod ᵊb-taarak.* -- This is a good time to buy a car. *hallaq waqt ᵊmnaaseb ləl-waaḥed yəštə́ri sayyaara.* -- Does your watch keep good time? *saaεtak btəẓboṭ ᵊl-waqᵊt?* -- Give me time to think it over. *εaṭiini waqᵊt la-fakker fiiha.* -- Take your time, there's no rush. *xood waqtak, maa fii εažale.* -- Such a job takes time. *šaġle matᵊl heek btaaxod* (or *btaakol*) *waqᵊt.* -- You'll know it in good time. *bᵊl-waqt l-ᵊmnaaseb btədra fiiha.* -- Let's leave it for the time being. *xalliina nətrə́ka bᵊl-waqt ᵊl-ḥaaḍer.* **2.** *tawqiit.* Do you have daylight-saving time in your country? *fii εandkon tawqiit ṣeefi b-ᵊblaadkon?* -- That corresponds to eight o'clock Baghdad time. *haada biwaafeq ᵊs-saaεa tmaane ḥasab tawqiit bəġdaad.* **3.** *mədde* pl. *mədad.* How much time did you spend in jail? *qaddeeš kaanet ᵊl-mədde yalli maḍḍeeta bᵊl-ḥabᵊs?* -- I spent a short time in the library today. *maḍḍeet mədde qaṣiire bᵊl-maktabe l-yoom.* -- We've been corresponding for some time now. *ṣar-ᵊlna mədde εam nətkaatab.* -- I lived with them for a long time. *εəšt maεon mədde ṭawiile.* -- We could have finished the job in half the time. *kaan ᵊb-ʔəmkaanna nxalleṣ ᵊš-šaġle b-nəṣṣ ᵊl-mədde.* **4.** *zamaan* pl. *-aat.* It happened a long time ago. *ḥadset mən zamaan ᵊktiir.* -- There was a time when I didn't like vegetables. *b-zamanaati maa kənᵊt ḥəbb ᵊl-xəḍar.* -- I haven't seen him for a long time. *mən zamaan ᵊktiir maa šəfto.* -- I haven't been to their house in a long time. *ṣar-li zamaan maa rəḥt la-εandon εal-beet.* **5.** *εaṣr* pl. *εuṣuur, waqᵊt* pl. *ʔawqaat, ʔiyyaam* (pl.). He was the most famous musician of his time. *kaan ʔašhar musiiqaar b-εaṣro.* -- The mosque dates from the time of the Fatimids. *ž-žaameε byəržaε la-εaṣr ᵊl-faaṭimiyyiin.* **6.** *ʔiyyaam* (pl.). That writer is before my time. *hal-kaateb qabᵊl ʔiyyaami.* -- In time of war a lot of irregularities happen. *b-ʔiyyaam ᵊl-ḥarb ʔašya ktiire ġeer ʔəεtiyaadiyye btəḥdos.* -- You can depend on him in time of need. *fiik təεtə́med εalée (b-)ʔiyyaam ᵊl-ḥaaže.* -- Time will tell. *l-ʔiyyaam ᵊbtəsbet.* **7.** *saaεa* pl. *-aat.* What time is it? *qaddeeš ᵊs-saaεa?* -- What time do we eat? *ʔayy saaεa* (or ***ʔeemta*) *raḥa naakol?* --

Can you tell me the correct time? *fiik ᵊtqəl-li qaddeeš ᵊs-saaε a bᵊḍ-ḍabᵊṭ?* -- Can your little boy tell time yet? *ʔəbnak ᵊz-zġiir ṣaar yaεref bᵊs-saaεa?* -- She has to make up time at the office. *εaleeha saaεaat laazem ᵊtεawwáḍa bᵊl-maktab.*. 8. *marra* pl. *-aat.* This is my first time here. *hayye ʔawwal marra ʔəli hoon.* -- Each time I see him I get a strange feeling. *kəll marra bšuufo* (or ***kəll-ma šəfto*) *bəšεor b-ᵊšεuur ġariib.* -- Next time come a little earlier. *l-marra ž-žaaye taεa ʔabkar šwayye.* -- If he did it one time he'll do it again. *ʔiza saawaaha marra bisaawiiha marra taanye.* -- I asked him any number of times not to do it. *kam marra ṭalabᵊt mənno maa yaεmə́la!* -- I've asked him time after time not to do it. *ṭalabt mənno marra baεᵊd marra ʔənno maa ysaawiiha.* -- I've tried it time and again, but without success. *žarrabta marra baεᵊd marra biduun ʔayy nažaaḥ.* -- I've been many times at his house. *rəḥt la-εando εal-beet marraat ᵊktiire.*

**I had the time of my life. *yaa laṭiif šuu nbaṣaṭṭ.*

**They gave him a hard time about losing the book. *ḥaraqu diino la-ʔənno ḍawwaε l-ᵊktaab.*

**Try to keep time to the music. *ḥaawel təmši εad-daqqa.*

**She's behind the times in her thinking. *hiyye ktiir mətʔaxxra b-tafkiira.*

**Hand them to me two at a time. *naawəlni-ydahon tneen ᵊtneen.*

**Have them come in four at a time. *fawwə́ton ʔarbεa ʔarbεa.*

**Two times two equals four. *tneen b-ᵊtneen ʔarbεa.*

at times - *b-baεḍ ᵊl-ʔawqaat, ʔaḥyaanan.* At times I work fourteen hours at a stretch. *b-baεḍ ᵊl-ʔawqaat bəštə́ġel ʔarbaεṭaεšar saaεa fard saḥbe.* — I see him at times. *bšuufo ʔaḥyaanan.*

in due time - *waqt biḥiin ᵊl-waqᵊt.* I'm sure we'll come to an agreement in due time. *ʔana mətʔakked ʔənno mnəṣal la-ʔəttifaaq waqt biḥiin ᵊl-waqᵊt.*

in no time - *raʔsan.* He finished in no time. *xallaṣ raʔsan.* -- I'll be back in no time. *bəržaε raʔsan.* -- He'll be famous in no time. *raʔsan raḥa yənšə́her.*

in time - *εal-waqᵊt.* We arrived at their house in time to see them off. *wṣəlna εal-waqᵊt la-beeton la-nwaddə́εon.*

on time - 1. *εal-waqᵊt.* Please be on time. *mən faḍlak kuun εal-waqᵊt.* 2. *bᵊt-taqṣiiṭ.* He bought the car on time. *štara s-sayyaara bᵊt-taqṣiiṭ.*

to have a good time - *nbasaṭ.* Did you have a good time? *nbasaṭṭ šii?* -- Have a good time, boys! *nšaaḷḷa tənbəṣṭu yaa šabaab!*

to time - *waqqat//twaqqat.* Let's time the meeting so it doesn't conflict with next week's conference. *xalliina nwaqqet ᵊl-ʔəžtimaaε ᵊb-šakᵊl ʔənno maa yətεaaraḍ maε məʔtə́mar ᵊž-žəmεa ž-žaaye.* -- The conference was well timed. *l-məʔtə́mar kaan tawqiito mnaaseb.* -- Time my speech for me so I don't go over ten minutes. *waqqə́t-li kəlᵊmti la-ḥatta maa dziid εan εašᵊr daqaayeq.* -- He timed his visit to catch everybody at home. *waqqat zyaarto b-šakᵊl la-yəžtə́meε ᵊb-kəll ʔahl ᵊl-beet.*

timely - *b-waqto, b-maḥallo.* That's a timely topic. *haada mawḍuuε b-waqto.* -- Everyone thinks it was a most timely visit. *l-kəll byəεtəqdu ʔənno kaanet zyaara ktiir ᵊb-maḥalla.*

timetable - *žadwal˜* (pl. *žadaawel˜*) *mawaεiid.*

timid - *xažuul.*

timidity - *xažal.*

tin - 1. *qaṣdiir.* The price of tin went up last week. *səεr ᵊl-qaṣdiir rtafaε ž-žəmεa l-maaḍye.* 2. *tanak.* Most cans are made of tin. *ʔaktariit ᵊl-εəlab msaawaaye mən tanak.* 3. *εəlbe* pl. *εəlab.* Give me a tin of tobacco. *εaṭiini εəlbet təmbaak.*

tinsmith - *sankari* pl. *-iyye.*

tiny - 1. *zġiir* (pl. *zġaar*) *ᵊktiir.* I live in a tiny room. *saaken b-ʔuuḍa zġiire ktiir.* 2. *ṭaqmuuš* pl. *ṭaqamiiš.* You'd never expect to find so much courage in a tiny fellow like that. *εəmro l-waaḥed maa byənṭə́zer kəll haš-šažaaεa mən zalame ṭaqmuuš mətᵊl heek.*

tip - 1. *raas* pl. *ruus.* They landed on the northern tip of the island. *nəzlu εala raas ᵊž-žaziire š-šmaali.* -- The word is on the tip of my tongue. *l-kəlme εala raas ᵊlsaani.* -- The tips of her fingers were cold as ice. *ruus ʔaṣabiiεa kaanet baarde mətl ᵊt-talᵊž.* -- The tip of your nose is all red. *raas mənxaarak kəllo ʔaḥmar.* 2. *buuz* pl. *bwaaz.* My shoes are worn at the tips. *ṣabbaaṭi məhri mən buuzo.*

tip - 1. *taεliime* pl. *-aat.* Where did you get the tip on that horse? *mneen ʔaxadt hat-taεliime εala hal-ᵊḥṣaan?* 2. *baxšiiš* pl. *baxašiiš.* How much of a tip shall I give the waiter? *qaddeeš ʔaεṭi baxšiiš ləl-garṣoon?*

to tip - *baxšaš//tbaxšaš.* Did you tip the porter? *baxšašt ᵊl-ḥammaal šii?*

to tip off - *εaṭa ... taεliime.* Somebody must have tipped them off about the raid. *fii ḥada laazem ykuun εaṭaahon taεliime εala ḥamlet l-ᵊmdaahame.* -- Who tipped you off about the house? *miin εaṭaak taεliime εala hal-beet?*

to **tip** - *mayyal.* Tip your head a little to the left. *mayyel raasak šwayye εaš-šmaal.*

to tip over - *qalab (o qalᵊb), nqalab.* The boat tipped over. *š-šaxtuura qalbet.*

on **tiptoe** - *εala ruus ᵊl-ʔaṣabiiε.* The children came in on tiptoe. *l-ᵊwlaad faatu εala ruus ʔaṣabiiεon.*

to tiptoe - *məši (i məši) εala ruus ʔaṣabiiεo.* You don't need to tiptoe. *maa fii lzuum təmši εala ruus ʔaṣabiiεak.*

tire - *kawšuuk* pl. *kawašiik, duulaab* pl. *dawaliib.* My rear tires are a little low. *kawašiiki l-warraaniyye ḥaaṭṭiin šwayye.* -- On the way back we had a flat tire. *nəḥna w-raažεiin banšar maεna kawšuuk.*

to tire - 1. *təεeb (a taεabaan).* I tire very easily in this hot weather. *bətεab b-ᵊshuule b-haṭ-ṭaqs ᵊl-məšweb.* 2. *taεab (e ʔətεaab//ntaεab).* These long sessions tire me. *haž-žalsaat ᵊt-ṭawiile btətεəbni.*

tired - *taεbaan.* He looks tired. *heeʔto taεbaan.*

to get tired of - *mall (ə malal) mən, zəheq (a zahaqaan) mən.* I'm tired of doing the same thing over and over again. *ʔana maalel mn ᵊmsaawaat nafs ᵊš-šii marra baεᵊd marra.* -- I'm so tired of this place! *faẓaaεa šuu ʔana zahqaan mən hal-maḥall!*

tired out - *halkaan.* I'm all tired out from the trip. *ʔana halkaan mn ᵊs-safra.*

tiresome - *mətεeb.* What a tiresome business! *məlla šaġle mətᵊεbe!*

title - 1. *εənwaan* pl. *εanawiin.* Do you know the title of the book? *btaεref εənwaan l-ᵊktaab?* 2. *laqab* pl. *ʔalqaab.* Just what is his exact title? *šuu laqabo εal-maẓbuuṭ?* 3. *məlkiyye* pl. *-aat.* You have to bring the title to the car for registration. *laazem ᵊdžiib məlkiit ᵊs-sayyaara mənšaan ᵊt-tasžiil.*

to - 1. *la-.* How far is it to his house? *qaddeeš ᵊl-masaafe la-beeto?* -- We are going to Cyprus this summer. *raayḥiin la-qəbroṣ* (or ***εala qəbroṣ*) *haṣ-ṣeefiyye.* -- They drive to town twice a week. *bisuuqu ləl-balad* (or ***εal-balad*) *marrteen bᵊž-žəmεa.* -- I'm in my office from 9 to 12. *ʔana b-maktabi mn ᵊt-təsεa lət-ṭnaεš.* -- To this day I couldn't find out what he really wanted. *la-hal-yoom haada* (or ***la-ḥadd ᵊl-yoom*) *maa ḥsənᵊt ʔaεref šuu ḥaqiiqatan kaan bəddo.* -- To date I haven't heard a thing. *la-hallaq maa sməεᵊt šii.* -- He went through his fortune to the last cent. *ṣaraf sarᵊwto la-ʔaaxer baara.* -- They're trusting to the point of carelessness. *byuusaqu bᵊn-naas la-daražet ᵊl-ʔəhmaal.* -- They beat him slowly to death. *ḍarabúu šwayye šwayye la-maat.* -- The paper burnt to ashes. *l-waraqa ḥtarqet la-ṣaffet ṣafwe.* -- Explain that to me! *fassə́r-li haš-šii!* -- Send it to me. *bεat-li-yaaha.* -- I'll give it to my boss. *baεṭiiha la-raʔiisi.* -- I'm writing to my father. *εam ʔəktob la-ʔabi.* -- What did he do to you? *šuu saawda-lak?* -- What I want is a room to myself. *halli bəddi-yáa ʔuuḍa la-ḥaali.* -- There's one car to every five families. *fii sayyaara waaḥde la-kəll xamᵊs εaaʔilaat.* -- Do you have a key to this desk? *maεak məftaaḥ la-hal-maktab* (or ***tabaε hal-maktab*)? -- To an artist the island is a paradise. *la-waaḥed fannaan ᵊž-žaziire mətl ᵊl-fardoos.* -- To the (trained) ear of a musician this kind of music has its attractions. *la-ʔəzᵊn waaḥed muusiiqi han-nooε ᵊmn ᵊl-muusiiqa ʔəla žaazbiita.* -- To our surprise he passed the exam. *la-dahšətna nažaḥ bᵊl-faḥᵊṣ.* -- The score at half time was four to nothing. *natiižet ᵊš-šooṭ ᵊl-ʔawwal kaanet ʔarbεa la-laa-šeeʔ.* -- Two to one you're wrong. *braahnak tneen la-waaḥed ʔənte ġalṭaan.* -- No one came to our aid. *maa ʔəža ḥada la-msaaεadətna.* — The whole idea seems rather strange to us. *l-fəkra kəlla ẓaahrə́t-ᵊlna ġariibe šwayye.* -- He's blind to what's going on around him. *huwwe ʔaεma la-halli εam yəžri* *ḥawalée.* 2. *la-ɛand.* Why do you come to me? Go to him! *leeš əbtəži la-ɛandi? ruuḥ la-ɛando.* -- Go to the neighbors and ask them. *ruuḥ la-ɛand əž-žiiraan w-əsʔálon.* -- Why don't you go to a doctor? *leeš maa bətruuḥ la-ɛand ṭabiib?* 3. *ɛala.* I must go to bed. *laazem ruuḥ ɛat-taxət.* -- Let's go to the exhibition. *xalliina nruuḥ ɛal-maɛraḍ.* -- Apply this ointment to the inflamed area. *ḥəṭṭ hal-marham ɛala maḥall əl-ʔəltihaab.* -- Take the first turn to your left. *xood ʔawwal lafte ɛala šmaalak.* -- We danced to the music of the band. *raqaṣna ɛala muusiiqet əl-ʔorkeestra.* 4. *maɛ.* To me he's always polite. *huwwe daayman əmʔaddab maɛi.* -- They were very kind to me. *kaanu ktiir laṭiifiin maɛi.* 5. *b-.* What do you say to this? *šuu raʔyak əb-haš-šii?* -- I told him to his face that he was a liar. *qəlt-əllo b-wəššo ʔənno kazzaab.* -- That's all there is to it. *haada kəll maa fii bəl-ʔamər.* -- There's nothing to it. *maa fiiha šii.* 6. *bən-nəsbe la-.* To me, it's a grave mistake. *bən-nəsbe ʔəli ġalṭa faẓiiɛa.* -- To her, it's a matter of little importance. *bən-nəsbe ʔəla qaḍiyye ʔəla ʔahammiyye ḍaʔiile.*

**It's ten minutes to four. *s-saaɛa ʔarbɛa ʔəlla ɛašara.*

**Let's drink to our country. *xalliina nəšrab naxb əblaadna.*

**The dog tore the rug to pieces. *l-kalb habbaš əs-səžžaade šəqaf.*

**The car is falling to pieces. *s-sayyaara ɛam ətharher šaqfe šaqfe.*

toad - *ḍəfḍaɛa* pl. *ḍafaaḍeɛ.*

toadstool - *xəbz˜ əl-qaaq.*

toast - 1. *xəbz əmqammar, xəbz əmḥammaṣ.* I'd like my toast buttered. *bəddi l-xəbz l-əmqammar tabaɛi ykuun madhuun bəz-zəbde.* 2. *naxəb* pl. *nxaab.* Let's drink a toast to the newlyweds. *xalliina nəšrab naxb əl-ɛariis wəl-ɛaruus.*

to toast - 1. *qammar//tqammar, ḥammaṣ//tḥammaṣ.* Shall I toast the bread? *qammer əl-xəbəz?* 2. *šəreb (a šərəb) naxəb˜ ...* Let's toast the hostess. *xalliina nəšrab naxəb ṣaaḥəbt əl-beet.*

tobacco - (general term and plant) *dəxxaan* pl. *-aat, təbəġ* pl. *tbuuġ,* (fine, for cigarettes) *təton,* (coarse, specif. for narghile) *təmbaak.*

today - 1. *l-yoom.* What's on the menu today? *šuu fii ɛala liistet əl-ʔakl əl-yoom?* -- I haven't read today's paper yet. *ləssa maa qareet žariidet əl-yoom.* 2. *(b-)hal-ʔiyyaam.* Life today is very complicated. *l-ḥayaat hal-ʔiyyaam əmɛaqqade ktiir.*

toe - 1. *ʔəṣbaɛ˜ (pl. ʔaṣabiiɛ˜) rəžəl.* My toes are frozen. *ʔaṣabiiɛ rəžlayyi mžalldiin.* 2. *buuz* pl. *bwaaz.* I want a shoe with a rounder toe. *bəddi ṣabbaaṭ buuzo mdawwar ʔaktar.*

**I didn't mean to step on anybody's toes. *maa qaṣadt ʔədɛas ɛala karaɛiib ḥada.*

**I have to be on my toes all the time. *ɛala ṭuul laazem kuun ɛala ʔəhbet əl-ʔəstəɛdaad.*

toffee - *karameel,* (a piece) *karameele* pl. *-aat.*

together - *sawa, maɛ baɛḍ-* + pron. suff. You see them together most of the time. *bətšuufon sawa* (or *maɛ baɛḍon*) *ʔaktar əl-waqət.* -- We work very well together. *mnəštəġel əktiir əmniiḥ maɛ baɛḍna.* -- I saw you enter the house together. *šəftkon faaytiin ɛal-beet sawa* (or *maɛ baɛḍkon*).

together with - *maɛ.* The heat, together with the humidity, makes everyone so tired. *š-šoob maɛ ər-rṭuube bixalli n-naas tətɛab kəll hal-qadd.*

toilet - *twaleet* pl. *-aat.* The toilets are to your left. *t-twaleetaat ɛala šmaalak.*

toilet paper - *waraq˜ twaleet.*

token - 1. *ɛarbuun* pl. *ɛarabiin.* He gave it to me as a token of his friendship. *ɛaṭaani-yaaha ka-ɛarbuun sadaaqto.* 2. *ʔəsmi*.* They offered only token resistance. *maa waržu ʔəlla mqaawame ʔəsmiyye.*

tolerable - *maḥmuul, məḥtámal.* The heat here is tolerable. *š-šoob hoon maḥmuul.*

tolerance - *tasaamoḥ.*

tolerant - *mətsaameḥ.*

to tolerate - *ḥtamal, tḥammal.* How long are you going to tolerate this behavior of his? *la-ʔeemta raḥa təḥtəmel taṣarrfo haada?*

toll - *rasəm* pl. *rsuum(e).* You have to pay a toll on this bridge. *laazem tədfaɛ rasəm ɛala haž-žəsər.*

tomato - *banadooraaye* coll. *banadoora* pl. *-aat* and *banadoorayaat.*

tomato juice - *ɛaṣiir˜ banadoora.*

tomato paste - *rəbb˜ banadoora.*

tomato sauce - *ṣalṣet˜ banadoora.*

tomb - *qabər* pl. *qbuur.* He placed a wreath on the Tomb of the Unknown Soldier. *ḥaṭṭ ʔəkliil ɛala qabr əž-žəndi l-mažhuul.*

tombstone - *šaahde* pl. *šawaahed.*

tomcat - *haaruun* pl. *hawariin.*

tomorrow - *bəkra, bukra.* I'll be back tomorrow. *bəržaɛ bəkra.* -- It'll be in tomorrow's paper. *raḥa tkuun əb-žariidet bəkra.* -- I won't see him till tomorrow morning. *maa-li raḥa šuufo la-bukra ɛala bukra.* -- It will be ready the day after tomorrow. *bikuun ḥaaḍer baɛəd bukra.*

ton - *ṭoon* pl. *ṭnaan.*

tone - 1. *ṣooṭ.* This violin has a beautiful tone. *hal-kamanža ṣooṭa ḥəlu ktiir.* 2. *naġəm* pl. *ʔanġaam.* Gypsy music is based on the five-tone scale. *l-muusiiqa l-ġažariyye məbniyye ɛala səllom ʔəlo xaməs ʔanġaam.* 3. *lahže.* You mustn't speak to her in such a tone. *ḥaraam ɛaleek təḥki maɛa b-hal-lahže.*

tongs - *malqaṭ* pl. *malaaqeṭ.*

tongue - *lsaan* pl. *-aat.* She has a sharp tongue. *ʔəla lsaan laazeɛ.* -- Just a minute! I have his name on the tip of my tongue. *ṭawwel baalak! ʔəsmo ɛala raas əlsaani.* -- The tongue of my left shoe has come off. *salat əlsaan fardet ṣabbaaṭi š-šmaal.*

**Hold your tongue! *skət-lak šwayye!*

tonic - 1. *mqawwi* pl. *-yaat.* If you take that tonic you're sure to feel better. *ʔiza ʔaxadt hal-əmqawwi ʔakiid əbtəšɛor əb-ḥaalak ʔaḥsan.* 2. *toniik* (invar.). Can you recommend a good hair tonic? *fiik tənṣaḥni toniik šaɛr əmniiḥ?* -- Gin and tonic, please. *mən faḍlak žənn w-toniik.*

tonight - 1. *l-yoom ɛašiyye, l-yoom əl-masa.* What shall we do tonight? *šuu raḥa nsaawi l-yoom ɛašiyye?* 2. *l-leele.* I'm sleeping at my aunt's house tonight. *naayem b-beet xaalti l-leele.*

tonnage - *ḥmuule.* What's the tonnage of this ship? *qaddeeš əḥmuulet hal-baaxra?*

tonsil - *bənt˜ ʔədən* pl. *banaat˜ ʔadaan.* My tonsils are swollen. *naaẓliin banaat ʔadaani.*

too - 1. *kamaan, l-ləxər* f. *l-ləxra* pl. *l-ləxriin, r-rəxər* f. *r-rəxra* pl. *r-rəxriin.* May I come, too? *məmken ʔəži ʔana kamaan?* -- I thought so, too. *ʔana ẓanneet heek kamaan* or *ʔana l-ləxər ẓanneet heek.* 2. *ktiir.* It's too hot for this time of the year. *šoob əktiir la-hal-waqət mən əs-səne.* -- Don't stay away too long. *laa tġiib əktiir.* -- Our stay here was all too short. *b-kəll ʔasaf qaɛdətna hoon kaanet məxtəṣara ktiir.* -- The play was none too good. *t-tamsiiliyye maa kaanet əktiir əmniiḥa.* -- The dress is too long for you. *l-fəsṭaan əktiir ṭawiil ɛaleeki.* -- He's much too old to work. *ʔəxtyaar əktiir, muu xarž əš-šəġəl.*

**The table is a little too long for this room. *ṭ-ṭaawle ṭawiile šwayye ɛala hal-ʔuuḍa.*

**The dress is a little too expensive. *l-fəsṭaan ġaali šwayye.*

**But you never told me! - I did, too! *ʔabadan maa qəlt-əlli! - qəlt-əllak w-nəṣṣ!*

**You didn't wash your hands. - I did, too! *maa ġassalt ʔideek. - ġassalton w-nəṣṣ!*

tool - *ʔadaat* pl. *ʔadawaat.* A hammer is a useful tool around the house. *š-šaakuuš ʔadaat əmfiide bəl-beet.* -- This man is only a tool of his party. *har-rəžžaal maa huwwe ʔəlla ʔadaat (ṣammaaʔ) la-ḥəzbo.*

tools - *ɛədde.* He packed up his tools and left. *ḍabb ɛəddto w-məši.*

tooth - *sənn* pl. *snaan.* This tooth hurts. *has-sənn ɛam yuužaɛni.* -- The saw has a broken tooth. *l-mənšaar fii sənn maksuur.*

**She has a sweet tooth. *bətḥəbb əl-ḥəlu.*

**We fought against it tooth and nail. *ɛaaraḍnaaha b-ʔiideenna w-rəžleenna.*

back tooth - *dərəs* pl. *draas.* I had one of my back teeth pulled. *qalaɛət dərəs mən ədraasi.*

canine tooth - *naab* pl. *nyaab.*

wisdom tooth - *dərs˜ əl-ɛaqəl.*

toothache - *wažaɛ˜ əsnaan.*

toothbrush - *fəršaayet˜ (pl. faraaši˜) snaan.*

toothpaste - *dawa˜ snaan, maɛžuun˜ əsnaan.*

toothpick - *nakkaašet˜ (pl. -aat˜) əsnaan.*

top - 1. *raas* pl. *ruus.* The storm broke off the top of our big tree. *l-ɛaaṣfe qaṣfet raas šažrətna l-əkbiire.* -- How far is it to the top of this mountain? *qaddeeš l-masaafe la-raas haž-žabal?* -- She was standing at the top of the stairs. *kaanet waaqfe ɛala raas əd-daraž.* -- You'll find that passage at the top of page 32. *bətlaaqi hal-maqṭaɛ b-raas əṣ-ṣafḥa tneen w-tlaatiin.* -- His name is at the top of the list. *ʔəsmo ɛala raas əl-qaaʔime.*

2. *kabbuud* pl. *kababiid*. I want to put down the top of the car. *bəddi nazzel kabbuud s-sayyaara*. 3. *bəlbol* pl. *balaabel*. Do you know how to spin a top? *btaƐref tədrob bəlbol?* 4. *fooqaani**. There's still one room vacant on the top floor. *ləssa fii ʔuuḍa waaḥde faaḍye bəṭ-ṭaabeq əl-fooqaani*. — It's in the top drawer. *mawžuude bəd-dərž əl-fooqaani*.
**I don't know why he blew his top. *maa baƐref leeš ṭəleƐ xəlqo*.
**I slept like a top last night. *nəmət mətl qatiil leelt əmbaareḥ*.
**When we have a problem we always go to the top. *kəll-ma bikuun Ɛanna məšəkle mənruuḥ la-ʔaƐla waaḥed*.
**She looked pretty from top to toe. *kaanet ṭaaləƐt-əlla mən farqa la-raas qaddma*.
**You're tops with me. *bən-nəsbe ʔəli maa fii baƐdak ḥada*.
**He's tops in his field. *maa fii ʔaḥsan mənno b-ḥaqlo*.
**She shouted at the top of her voice. *ṣarxet əb-ʔaƐla ṣooṭa*.
**The little boy yelled at the top of his lungs. *l-walad əẓ-ẓġiir Ɛayyaṭ mən əṣmiim Ɛaqlo*.
**This is top quality. *haada mən ʔaṣnaaf ər-rəfəƐ*.
**That's top secret. *haada sərri ždan*.
**We drove at top speed all the way down here. *kəll əṭ-ṭariiq la-hoon səqna Ɛala ʔaaxer sərƐa*.
from top to bottom – *mən fooq la-taḥət*. We searched the house from top to bottom. *fattašna l-beet mən fooq la-taḥət*.
on top – *Ɛal-wəšš*. Take the towel on top. *xood əl-baškiir halli Ɛal-wəšš*. — The lightweight things should be on top. *l-əġraaḍ əl-xafiife laazem ətkuun Ɛal-wəšš*.
on top of – 1. *Ɛala raas˜..., Ɛala wəšš˜...* Hand me the book which is on top of the stack. *naawəlni l-əktaab halli Ɛala raas əl-koome*. 2. *Ɛala ḍahər˜...* I left the bottle on top of the refrigerator. *xalleet əl-qanniine Ɛala ḍahr əl-barraade*. 3. *fooq˜, Ɛalaawe Ɛala, zyaade Ɛala, bəl-ʔiḍaafe Ɛala*. On top of it all he's stupid! *fooq kəll šii huwwe ḥmaar*. — On top of being lazy, he's never on time. *Ɛalaawe Ɛala kaslanto huwwe daayman mətʔaxxer*.
**Boy, am I sitting on top of the world! *daxiil Ɛərdak šuu ʔənni mƐoorem!*
to top – *faaš (u fawašaan) Ɛala*. That tops everything! *haada bifuuš Ɛala kəll šii!* 2. *faaq (u ø) Ɛala*. That tops any idea they ever had. *hayye bətfuuq ʔayy fəkra taanye ṭəlƐu fiiha*. 3. *tfawwaq b-*. He tops his class. *huwwe mətfawweq əb-ṣaffo* or ***huwwe l-ʔawwal* (or *brənži*) *b-ṣaffo*.
**Let's top the cake with some whipped cream. *xalliina nḥəṭṭ Ɛala wəšš əl-gaatóo šwayyet kreema*.
to top off – *xatam (o xatəm//nxatam)*. Let's top off the evening with a glass of wine. *xalliina nəxtom əs-sahra b-qadaḥ ənbiit*.
**To top it off he stole my wallet. *fooq kəll haš-šii saraq žəzdaani*.

topcoat – *bardosiil* pl. *-aat, maanṭo* pl. *maanṭoyaat*.
topic – *mawḍuuƐ* pl. *mawaḍiiƐ*.
topnotch – *mən ʔawwal baab, brənži* (invar.). He's a topnotch chemist. *huwwe kiimyaaʔi mən ʔawwal baab*.
**He comes from one of the topnotch families here. *huwwe mən ʔaḥsan əl-Ɛiyal hoon*.
topography – *topoġraafya*.
topsy-turvy – *fooqaani taḥtaani*. Everything was topsy-turvy. *kəll šii kaan fooqaani taḥtaani*. — They turned everything topsy-turvy. *qalabu kəll šii fooqaani taḥtaani*.
torch – *mašƐal* pl. *mašaaƐel*.
torment – *Ɛazaab*.
torpedo – *ṭərbiid* and *ṭorbiid* pl. *-aat*.
torture – *taƐziib*. Some of the prisoners were subjected to torture. *baƐḍ əl-ʔəsara tƐarraḍu lət-taƐziib*.
**It was torture just to watch them. *l-fərže Ɛaleehon bass kaanet təḥreq əl-qalb*.
to torture – *Ɛazzab//tƐazzab*. You must never torture animals. *ʔabadan maa laazem ətƐazzeb əl-ḥaywaanaat*.
to toss – 1. *laḥaš (o laḥəš//nlaḥaš), rama (i rami//nrama* and *rtama)*. He tossed his hat on the couch. *laḥaš bərneeṭṭo Ɛal-kanabaaye*. 2. *tabbal//ttabbal*. Toss the salad thoroughly before you serve it. *tabbli s-salaṭa mniiḥ qabəl-ma tqaddmiiha*. 3. *fann (ə fann//nfann)*. Let's toss a coin. *xalliina nfənn əfrang*. 4. *ḥarak (o ḥarake)*. The child tossed in his sleep all night long. *l-walad ḥarak əb-noomo ṭuul əl-leel*.

total – 1. *mažmuuƐ*. Subtract ten from the total. *ṭraaḥ Ɛašra mn əl-mažmuuƐ*. — My total earnings for the month were two hundred pounds. *mažmuuƐ daxli b-haš-šahər kaan miiteen leera*. 2. *kəlli*, kaamel, taamm*. Unfortunately, the car was a total loss. *la-suuʔ əl-ḥaẓẓ əs-sayyaara kaanet xṣaara kəlliyye*. 3. *šaamel*. And they are prepared to wage total war, if necessary. *hənne məstƐəddiin yšənnu ḥarb šaamle ʔiza ləzem əl-ʔamər*.
to total – *žamaƐ (a žaməƐ//nžamaƐ)*. Let's total our expenses for the month. *xalliina nəžmaƐ maṣariifna ləš-šahər*.
**His income totals two thousand pounds a year. *mažmuuƐ daxlo ʔalfeen leera bəs-səne*.
touch – 1. *daqra* pl. *-aat*. The alarm system goes off at the slightest touch. *l-əmnabbeh byəštəġel mən ʔaqalla daqra*. 2. *ʔəttiṣaal*. Keep in touch with me. *xalliik Ɛala ʔəttiṣaal fiyyi*. — We've been in close touch since the war. *ṣar-əlna Ɛala ʔəttiṣaal mətwaaṣel mən waqt əl-ḥarəb*. 3. *rašše, nətfe*. The soup still needs a touch of salt. *š-šooraba ləssa laazəma raššet məlәḥ*. 4. *nətfe, ʔaasaar* (pl.). The children have a touch of the flu. *l-əwlaad maƐon nətfet rašəḥ*.
**My dentist has a very light touch. *ṭabiib l-əsnaan tabaƐi ʔiido xafiif əktiir*.
**The flowers add the final touch to the room. *z-zhuur bikammlu žamaal əl-ʔuuḍa*.
to get in touch with – *ttaṣal b-*. I have to get in touch with him right away. *laazem ʔəttəṣel fii Ɛal-ḥaarek*.
to touch – 1. *daqar (o daqər//ndaqar)*. Please don't touch that! *mən faḍlak laa tədqor haš-šii*. — I never touch liquor. *b-ḥayaati maa bədqor əl-mašruub*. 2. *ʔassar//tʔassar*. I was deeply touched by his kindness. *tʔassart əktiir mən laṭaafto*. 3. *mass (ə mass//mmass)*. The scandal will touch a lot of people. *l-faḍiiḥa raḥa tməss naas əktiir*.
**I touched him for five pounds. *saʔalto ydayyənni xaməs leeraat*.
**Don't mind him! He's a little touched. *laa təntəkəš-lo, Ɛaqlaato bixəḍḍu šwayye*.
touching – *mʔasser*. You should have heard the touching story he told me! *ya-reetak əsməƐt əl-qəṣṣa l-əmʔassra yalli qal-li-ydaha!*
to touch off – *ʔasaar*. His remarks touched off a violent argument. *mlaaḥaẓaato ʔasaaret mžaadale ḥaamye*.
to touch on – *ṭaraq (o ṭarəq//nṭaraq)*. She only touched briefly on the matter. *ṭarqet əl-mawḍuuƐ bass əšwayye*.
to touch up – *rootaš//trootaš*. The picture hasn't been touched up yet. *ṣ-ṣuura ləssa maa trootašet*.
touchy – 1. *naquuz, naquuzi**. I don't know why he's so touchy. *maa baƐref leeš hal-qadd huwwe naquuz*. 2. *ḥareš, ḥassaas*. That's a touchy subject with them. *haada mawḍuuƐ ḥareš maƐon*.
**He's touchy about his academic standing. *byətʔassar lamma btəḥki Ɛan maqaamo ž-žaamƐi*.
tough – 1. *qaasi*. The meat is awfully tough. *l-laḥme ktiir qaasye*. 2. *ṣaƐəb*. That's a tough job. *hayy šaġle ṣaƐbe*. — It was a tough contest but we won. *kaanet əmbaarda ṣaƐbe w-maƐ zaalek ərbəḥna*. — That's a tough nut to crack. *hayy məšəkle ṣaƐb ḥalla*. 3. *šaluud*. They're concentrating the toughest troops along the border. *Ɛam yəḥəšdu ʔašlad əž-žunuud Ɛala madd l-əḥduud*.
**Don't be too tough on him, he's only a child. *laa tšaddəda Ɛalée, huwwe ləssda walad*.
**We had a tough time convincing him. *b-kəll əṣƐuube qannaƐnda*.
tough guy – *zgərt* pl. *-iyye, Ɛammak xaalak* (invar.). He's known as a tough guy. *huwwe maƐruuf ʔənno zgərt*.
**Stop acting the tough guy with me. *ḥaaštak tətmanfax Ɛaliyyi*.
tough luck – *ḥaẓẓ Ɛaaṭel*. He had tough luck. *ḥakamo ḥaẓẓ Ɛaaṭel*.
tour – 1. *žawle* pl. *-aat, raḥle* pl. *-aat*. He made a tour through Europe and Asia. *Ɛəmel žawle b-ʔawrəbba w-ʔaasya*. — The ballet is now on tour through the Middle East. *l-balée Ɛaamle hallaq žawle bəš-šarq əl-ʔawsaṭ*. 2. *doora* pl. *-aat, barme* pl. *-aat, laffe* pl. *-aat*. They took us on a tour through the factory. *ʔaxaduuna b-doora bəl-maƐmal*.
to tour – *daar (u doora) b-, žaal (u žawalaan) b-, laff (ə laff) b-*. The orchestra toured the whole Middle East. *l-ʔorkeestra daaret əb-kəll əš-šarq əl-ʔawsaṭ*.

tourism - *syaaḥa.*
tourist - 1. *saayeḥ* pl. *suwwaaḥ.* Many tourists come here during the summer. *fii suwwaaḥ əktiir byəžu la-hoon ʔasnaaʔ əṣ-ṣeef.* — He works as a tourist guide in summer. *byəštəġel daliil suwwaaḥ bəṣ-ṣeef.* 2. *syaaḥi*.* The trip is about 300 pounds in tourist class. *s-safra bətkallef ḥawaali tlaat miit leera daraže syaaḥiyye.*
tournament - *mbaarḍa* pl. *mbaarayaat.*
toward(s) - 1. *naaḥ.* His back was toward me. *ḍahro kaan naaḥi.* — He ran toward me. *rakaḍ naaḥi.* 2. *nawaaḥi.* I'll be there towards evening. *bkuun əhniik nawaaḥi l-masa.* 3. *tižaah.* He was very nice toward me. *kaan əktiir laṭiif tižaahi.* 4. *mənšaan.* I'm putting away money toward a new car. *εam ḥəṭṭ maṣaari εala žanab mənšaan sayyaara ždiide.* 5. *b-sabiil˜...* His efforts towards mediation failed miserably. *mažhuudaato b-sabiil ət-tawaṣṣoṭ fəšlet fašal zariiε.*
towel - 1. (small, for the hands) *baškiir* pl. *bašakiir.* 2. (large, for bath or beach) *manšafe* pl. *manaašef.*
dish towel - *baškiir˜* (pl. *bašakiir˜*) *maṭbax.*
tower - *bərž* pl. *braaž* and *bruuž(e).*
town - 1. *balad* (f.) pl. *blaad.* What's the name of this town? *šuu ʔəsəm hal-balad?* — When will you be in town? *ʔeemta bətkuun bəl-balad?* — He skipped town. *farḍka mn əl-balad.* — My husband is out of town. *žoozi barraat əl-balad.* — The whole town marched in the parade. *l-balad kəlla məšyet bəl-ʔəstəεraaḍ.* 2. *baladiyye.* The town plans to build a new jail. *l-baladiyye naawye tεammer səžn əždiid.*
**Let's spend this last night on the town. *xalliina nəḥyiiha ʔəsmo hal-leele ʔaaxer leele ʔəlna hoon.*
toy - 1. *ləεbe* pl. *ləεab.* I'll bring him a toy. *raḥa žəb-lo ləεbe.* 2. *ləεbe* (invar.). The children were simply delighted at the toy train I brought them. *l-əwlaad mbaṣaṭu ktiir bət-treen əl-ləεbe halli žəbt-əllon-yəda.*
to toy - *žoožal, laaš (u ø), laak (u ø).* I've been toying with the idea of taking a long vacation. *ʔana εandi fəkra b-raasi εam žoožəla ʔənno ʔaaxod εəṭle ṭawiile.*
trace - *ʔasar* pl. *ʔaasaar.* Traces of poison were found in the wine. *laqu ʔaasaar samm bən-nbiit.* — He disappeared without a trace. *xtafa biduun-ma yətrok ʔasar.*
to trace - 1. *kazz (ə kazz//nkazz).* I want you to trace the map carefully. *bəddi-yaak ətkəzz əl-xariiṭa b-taʔanni.* 2. *ġtafa ʔasar˜...* The police hasn't been able to trace the murder weapon. *š-šərṭa maa qədret təġtəfi ʔasar silaaḥ əž-žariime.* 3. *tεaqqab.* We traced the story to him. *tεaqqabna l-qəṣṣa la-wṣəlna ʔəlo.*
track - 1. *ʔasar* pl. *ʔaasaar.* The tracks lead to a shed. *l-ʔaasaar waṣṣalet la-taaxšiibe.* — I've completely lost track of him. *ḍawwaεət kəll ʔasaro.* 2. *rṣiif* pl. *ʔarəṣfe.* The train will arrive on Track Two. *t-treen byuuṣal εar-rṣiif nəmro tneen.* 3. *səkke* pl. *səkak.* The railroad track is being repaired. *səkket əl-ḥadiid εam tətṣallaḥ.* 4. *xaṭṭ* pl. *xṭuuṭ.* Only two cars went off the track. *bass εarəbteen ṭəlεu εan əl-xaṭṭ.* 5. *žanziir* pl. *žanaziir.* The shell hit the track of the tank. *l-qaziife ṣaabet žanziir əd-dabbaabe.*
**You're on the right track. *ʔənte εaṭ-ṭariiq əl-maẓbuuṭ.*
**I'm afraid you're entirely off the track. *šaayəf-lak ʔənte taayeh εal-ʔaaxiir.*
**Keep close track of all your expenses. *xalli b-fəkrak maẓbuuṭ kəll maṣariifak.*
**Let's not lose track of our principal aim. *xalliina maa nənsa hadafna r-raʔiisi.*
to track - 1. *laaḥaq.* They've been tracking a criminal for weeks now. *ṣar-lon ʔasabiiε εam ylaaḥqu məžrem.* 2. *rašam (o rašəm//nrašam).* The children tracked mud all over the rug. *l-əwlaad rašamu ṭiin malaat əs-səžžaade.*
to track down - 1. *ṭabb (ə ṭabb) b-, ṭabaq (o ṭabəq) b-.* The police tracked him down in Aleppo. *l-boliis ṭabbu fii b-ḥalab.* 2. *laqa (-ylaaqi ø).* I don't know now where I saw it, but I think I can track it down for you. *maa baεref hallaq ween šəfto bass baεtəqed fiini laaqii-lak-yəda.*
tractor - *traktoor* pl. *-aat, žarraar* pl. *-aat.*
trade - 1. *tižaara.* Our trade with the Far East has fallen off. *tižaarətna nəzlet maε əš-šarq əl-ʔaqṣa.* 2. *šaġle* pl. *-aat, ṣanεa* pl. *-aat.* I'm a butcher by trade. *šaġəlti laḥḥaam.* — The boy has to learn a trade. *l-walad laazem yətεallam ṣanεa.* 3. *mdaakaše, mbaadale.* I got this car in a trade. *ḥṣəlt εala has-sayyaara mdaakaše.*
**No man is born a master of his trade. *maa ḥada byəži mən baṭən ʔəmmo mətεallem.*
**My competitor across the street is taking away my trade. *mzaaḥmi halli qaaṭeε əš-šaareε εam yžərr-əlli kəll zabaayni.*
to trade - 1. *daakaš, baadal.* I've traded my typewriter for a bicycle. *daakašt əl-ʔaale l-kaatbe tabaεi b-bəskleet.* 2. *taažar.* They're trading mostly in hides and furs. *εam ytaažru ʔaktar šii bəž-žluud wəl-faru.*
to trade in - *daakaš, baadal.* I want to trade this car in for a new one. *bəddi daakeš has-sayyaara b-sayyaara ždiide.*
trade-mark - *marka* (pl. *-aat*) *tižaariyye.*
tradition - 1. *εaade* pl. *-aat.* It's said to be an old local tradition. *biquulu hayye εaade maḥalliyye qadiime* (or ***hayy mn ət-taqaliid əl-maḥalliyye l-qadiime*). 2. *taqaliid* (pl.). His thinking is deeply rooted in tradition. *tafkiiro mətʔaṣṣel bət-taqaliid.* — Many of the old traditions are being forgotten by the young generation. *ktiir mn ət-taqaliid əl-qadiime εam byənsaaha ž-žiil əž-ždiid.*
Prophetic tradition - *ḥadiis nabawi.* He has devoted a lifetime to the study of Prophetic traditions. *maḍḍa kəll εəmro yədros əl-ḥadiis ən-nabawi.*
traditional - *taqliidi*.* This is a traditional holiday in this country. *haadi εəṭle taqliidiyye b-hal-əblaad.*
traffic - 1. *seer.* Traffic on Sundays is heavy. *s-seer maεžuuq ʔiyyaam əl-ʔaḥad.* 2. *tižaara.* Traffic in dope has increased a great deal in the last few years. *tižaaret l-əmxaddiraat zaadet əktiir b-hal-kam səne l-ʔaxiira.*
**At present, the road is closed to traffic. *bəl-waqt əl-ḥaader əṭ-ṭariiq əmsakkar.*
traffic division - *maṣlaḥt˜ əs-seer.*
traffic jam - *εažqet˜ seer.*
traffic light - *ḍaww˜* (pl. *ʔəḍwiit˜*) *seer.*
traffic sign - *εalaamet˜* (pl. *-aat˜*) *seer.*
traffic signal - *ʔišaaret˜* (pl. *-aat˜*) *seer.*
tragedy - 1. *maʔsaat* pl. *maʔaasi, faažεa* pl. *fawaažeε.* His untimely death is a great tragedy for the country. *mootto qabəl ʔawaano maʔsaat əkbiire ləl-waṭan.* 2. *maʔsaat* pl. *maʔaasi.* I'm taking a course on Shakespeare's tragedies. *εam ʔaaxod darəs b-maʔaasi šekspiir.*
tragic - 1. *məfžeε.* She died in a tragic accident. *maatet əb-ḥaades məfžeε.* 2. *məḥzen.* He's best in tragic roles. *huwwe ʔaḥsan šii bəl-ʔadwaar əl-məḥəzne.*
trail - *ṭaaruuq* pl. *ṭawariiq.* There's a trail leading to the village. *fii ṭaaruuq biwaddi εaḍ-ḍeeεa.*
**The police are on his trail. *š-šərṭa εam ətlaaḥqu εaḍ-daεse.*
to trail - 1. *tεaqqab, laaḥaq.* Somebody trailed me all the way home. *fii ḥada tεaqqabni kəll ṭariiqi εal-beet.* 2. *šaḥaṭ (a šaḥəṭ).* Her long skirt trailed on the ground. *tannuurəta ṭ-ṭawiile kaanet εam təšḥaṭ εal-ʔarḍ.*
train - 1. *treen* pl. *-aat.* When does the train leave? *ʔeemta raḥa yəmši t-treen?* — I prefer to go by train. *bfaḍḍel ruuḥ bət-treen.* 2. *deel* pl. *dyaal.* Two little girls carried the train of her gown. *bənteen əẓġaar ḥamalúu-la deel rooba.*
to train - 1. *darrab//ddarrab.* He trains circus animals. *bidarreb ḥaywaanaat ləs-sərk.* 2. *marran// tmarran, darrab//ddarrab.* The hospital is training nurses during the summer. *l-məstašfa εam ymarren mumarriḍaat ʔasnaaʔ əṣ-ṣeef.* 3. *ddarrab, tmarran.* He's been training for the fight for weeks. *ṣar-lo ʔasabiiε εam yəddarrab mənšaan l-əmbaarḍa.*
training - 1. *tadriib.* It requires thorough training to handle such a machine. *bədda tadriib daqiiq ḥatta yəqder əl-waaḥed yšaġġel heek maakiina.* 2. *tamriin.* Where did he receive his medical training? *ween saawa tamriino ṭ-ṭəbbi?*
traitor - *xaayen* pl. *xawane.*
tramp - *sarsari** pl. *-iyye, nawari** coll. pl. *nawar.*
to **trample** - *daεεas//ddaεεas.* They nearly trampled him to death. *daεεasúu kaan laḥa ymuut.*
tranquilizer - *dawa mhaddi l-ʔaεṣaab* pl. *ʔədəwye mhaddye l-ʔaεṣaab.*

transaction - *εamaliyye* pl. *-aat.*
transatlantic - *εəbr ᵊl-ʔaṭlanṭi.* They have a transatlantic flight every day. *fii εandon ṭayyaara εəbr ᵊl-ʔaṭlanṭi kəll yoom.*
transfer - 1. *naql.* I have asked for a transfer to the main office. *ṭalabᵊt naqli ləl-maktab ᵊr-raʔiisi.* 2. *taḥwiil.* The transfer of the money will take some time. *taḥwiil ᵊl-maṣaari bəddo yaaxod waqᵊt.*
to transfer - 1. *ġayyar.* Where do we transfer to go downtown? *ween mənġayyer la-ḥatta nruuḥ εal-balad?* 2. *naqal (o/e naqᵊl//ntaqal).* They transferred him to another outfit. *naqalúu la-wəḥde taanye.* — He had the money transferred to her name. *naqal ᵊl-maṣaari la-ʔəsma.* 3. *ḥawwal//tḥawwal.* Can I transfer money to Egypt? *fiini ḥawwel maṣaari la-maṣᵊr?*
to **transform** - *ḥawwal//tḥawwal.* Marriage has transformed her into a real woman. *z-zwaaž ḥawwəla la-mara εan ṣaḥiiḥ.*
transformation - *taḥwiil* pl. *-aat.*
transformer - *transformatoor* pl. *-aat, mḥawwel* pl. *-aat.*
transformer station - *mḥaṭṭet˜* (pl. *-aat˜*) *taḥwiil.*
transfusion - *naqᵊl.* A quick blood transfusion would have saved her life. *naqᵊl damm ᵊb-sərεa kaan xalləṣ-la ḥayaata.*
transistor - *transistoor* pl. *-aat.*
transit - *ṭranziit.* The merchandise is in transit. *l-ᵊbḍaaεa bᵊṭ-ṭranziit.*
transit visa - *taʔšiiret˜* (pl. *-aat˜*) *ṭranziit, taʔšiiret˜ muruur.*
transition - *ʔəntiqaal* pl. *-aat.*
transitional - *ʔəntiqaali*.*
transitive - *mətεaddi.* The verb "*qalab*" is both transitive and intransitive. *fəεᵊl "qalab" mətεaddi w-laazem.*
to **translate** - *taržam//ttaržam.* How would you translate this word? *kiif bəttaržem hal-kəlme?*
translation - *taržame* pl. *-aat.* I think it's a very good translation of his book. *bəεtəqed hayy ᵊktiir taržame mniiḥa la-ktaabo.* — In some sessions they have simultaneous, in others consecutive translation. *b-baεḍ ᵊž-žalsaat bikuun fii taržame ʔaaniyye w-ᵊb-baεḍa bikuun fii taržame məttaabεa.*
translator - *mtaržem* pl. *-iin.*
transmission - *transməsyoon* pl. *-aat.* Something seems to be wrong with the transmission of my car. *εala-ma yəẓhar fii šii εəṭᵊl bᵊt-transməsyoon tabaε sayyaarti.*
transmitter - *raadyo muziiε* pl. *raadyoyaat muziiεa.*
transparent - 1. *šaffaaf.* I don't particularly care for these transparent curtains. *maa-li ḥaabeb ᵊktiir hal-baraadi š-šaffaafe.* 2. *mafḍuuḥ, makšuuf.* His reason for going to the meeting was very transparent. *sabab rooḥto ləl-ʔəžtimaaε kaan ᵊktiir mafḍuuḥ.*
transport - 1. *naqᵊl.* Our primary concern was the transport of troops. *hammna r-raʔiisi kaan naql ᵊž-žunuud.* 2. *naqle* pl. *-aat.* Another transport of fifteen thousand men is expected tomorrow. *naqle taanye mᵊʔallafe mən xamᵊṣṭaεšar ʔalf nafar mənṭəẓara bəkra.* 3. *naaqle* pl. *-aat.* Two troop transports were sunk by submarines. *naaqᵊlteen žunuud ġarraqəton ᵊl-ġawwaaṣaat.*
to transport - *naqal (o/e naqᵊl//ntaqal).* How were the troops transported? *kiif ᵊž-žunuud naqaluuhon?*
transportation - *rəkᵊb.* We'll provide transportation to and from the school. *mənqaddem rəkᵊb ləl-madrase w-mənna.* — Transportation is no problem. I have my own car. *r-rəkᵊb muu məšᵊkle ʔəli, εandi sayyaara xṣuuṣiyye.*
trap - *faxx* pl. *fxuuxa* and *fxaax.* The police set a trap for him. *š-šərṭa naṣabúu-lo faxx.* — He walked into the trap. *waqeε bᵊl-faxx.* — Every morning we check the traps. *kəll yoom εala bəkra mnəfḥaṣ l-ᵊfxaax.*
to trap - 1. *laqaṭ (o laqᵊṭ//nlaqaṭ* and *ltaqaṭ).* Yesterday we trapped a mouse in the basement. *mbaareḥ laqaṭna faara bᵊl-qabu.* 2. *waqqaε.* I tried to trap him in a lie. *žarrabᵊt waqqεo b-kəzbe.*
to get trapped - *nḥaṣar, nḥabas.* He got trapped under a fallen girder. *nḥaṣar taḥᵊt žəsᵊr ḥadiid waqaε εalée.*
trash - *zbaale.* Burn the trash! *ḥreeq ᵊz-zbaale!* — I wouldn't waste my money on such trash. *b-maḥallak maa bḍawweε maṣariyyi εala zbaale mən han-nooε.*
trash can - *tanaket˜* (pl. *-aat˜*) *ᵊzbaale.*
travel - 1. *safar.* Travel in winter is difficult. *s-safar bᵊš-šəte ṣaεᵊb.* 2. *safra* pl. *-aat* and *ʔasfaar, raḥle* pl. *-aat.* Let him tell you about his travels. *xallii yxabbrak εan safraato.* — Have you ever read Ibn Batuta's travels? *qareet šii raḥlaat ʔəbᵊn baṭṭuuṭa?*
travel agency - *wakaalet˜* (pl. *-aat˜*) *safriyyaat, maktab˜* (pl. *makaateb˜*) *safar.*
to travel - 1. *saafar, daar (u ø), žaal (u žawalaan).* I have traveled a lot in my time. *b-zamaani saafart ᵊktiir.* — He has traveled all over Europe. *daar ʔawrəbba kəlla* or *saafar* (or *žaal*) *ᵊb-ʔawrəbba kəlla.* 2. *məši (i məši).* He must have been traveling sixty miles an hour. *laazem kaan ykuun maaši səttiin miil bᵊs-saaεa.*
tray - *ṣaniyye* pl. *ṣawaani.* Put the glasses on the tray. *ḥəṭṭ ᵊl-kaasaat εaṣ-ṣaniyye.*
ash tray - *ṣaḥᵊn˜* (pl. *ṣḥuun˜*) *sigaara.* Where's my ash tray? *ween ṣaḥᵊn sigaarti?*
treacherous - 1. *xaayen.* Believe me, he's a treacherous man. *saddəqni huwwe zalame xaayen ᵊktiir.* 2. *məxṭer.* Watch out, the stairs are treacherous. *ʔoεa, d-daražaat məxᵊṭriin.*
tread - *zyaaq* (pl.). The tread of the right front tire is all worn out. *zyaaq ᵊd-duulaab ᵊl-qəddaamaani l-yamiini daabu.*
treason - *xyaane.*
treasure - *kənz* pl. *knuuz(e).*
treasurer - *xaazen* pl. *-iin, ʔamiin˜* (pl. *ʔəmana˜*) *sanduuq.*
treasury - *xazaane, xaziine.*
treat - *lazze* pl. *-aat.* It's a treat to read his books. *lazze l-waaḥed yəqra kətbo.*
**Now the treat's on me. *hallaq doori bᵊd-dafᵊε.*
**Let's make it Dutch treat. *xeeṭ məṭṭo halli εalée šii biḥəṭṭo.*
to treat - 1. *εaamal//tεaamal.* He treats me like a child. *biεaaməlni kaʔənni walad.* 2. *daawa, εaalaž, ṭabbab, ḥakkam.* Dr. Hakeem is treating me. *d-doktoor ḥakiim εam ydaawiini.* 3. *εaalaž.* I don't quite agree with the way he treats the subject. *maa bwaafeq tamaaman εaṭ-ṭariiqa halli εam yεaalež fiiha l-mawḍuuε.* 4. *dafaε (a dafᵊε) εan.* He treated everybody. *dafaε εan kəll waaḥed.* 5. *εazam (o εaziime//nεazam).* Come on, I'll treat you to a bottle of champagne. *yaḷḷa, taεa bəεᵊzmak εala qanniinet šampanya.*
**She treats everything like a big joke. *btaaxod kəll šii kaʔənno mazᵊḥ.*
to treat lightly - *staxaff b-.* You shouldn't treat that so lightly. *ʔaḥsən-lak maa təstaxaff bi-haš-šağle hal-qadd.*
treatment - 1. *mεaamale.* I can't complain about bad treatment. *maa fiini ʔətšakka mn ᵊmεaamale εaṭle.* 2. *mεaalaže.* I don't go along with his treatment of the subject. *maa bwaafeq εala mεaalažto ləl-mawḍuuε.*
medical treatment - *mdaawda, tadaawi, ḥəkme, mεaalaže ṭəbbiyye.* What he needs is proper medical treatment. *halli laazmo mdaawda maẓbuuṭa.*
treaty - *mεaahade* pl. *-aat.* The commercial treaty was renewed for another five years. *l-ᵊmεaahade t-tižaariyye džaddadet la-xams ᵊsniin taanyaat.*
tree - *šažara* coll. *šažar* pl. *-aat* and *ʔəššaar, sažara* coll. *sažar* pl. *-aat* and *ʔasžaar.* They cut down three trees for firewood. *qaṭaεu tlatt šažaraat ləl-ḥaṭab.* — He can trace back his family tree to the 16th century. *fii yəržaε ᵊb-šažaret ᵊl-εaaʔile tabaεo ləl-qarn ᵊs-saades εašar.*
**He doesn't see the forest for the trees. *ʔəhtimaamo bᵊt-tafaṣiil εam ynassli ləbb ᵊl-mawḍuuε.*
tree nursery - *maštal* pl. *mašaatel.*
trellis - *sqaale* pl. *-aat.*
to **tremble** - *ražaf (o ražafaan).* He trembled with fear. *ražaf mn ᵊl-xoof.*
tremendous - *haaʔel, mahuul, εaẓiim.* That's a tremendous difference. *haada farᵊq haaʔel.* — I saw a tremendous film last night. *šəft-əllak fəlᵊm εaẓiim leelt ᵊmbaareḥ.*
tremor - 1. *ražafaan,* (as noun of instance) *ražfe* pl. *-aat.* Did you notice the tremor in his hand? *laaḥaẓt ražafaan ʔiido?* 2. *hazze* pl. *-aat.* They counted four major tremors during the earthquake. *εaddu ʔarbaε hazzaat ᵊkbiire ʔasnaaʔ ᵊz-zəlzaal.*
trench - *xandaq* pl. *xanaadeq.* Civilians were forced to dig trenches. *l-madaniyyiin nžabaru yəḥᵊfru xanaadeq.*
trench coat - *tranškoot* pl. *-aat.*
trend - *ʔəttižaah* pl. *-aat.*
to **trespass** - *txaṭṭa.* You were trespassing on my property. *kənt εam tətxaṭṭa ʔarḍi.*
tress - *žđiile* pl. *žadaayel.*

trial - **1.** *mḥaakame* pl. *-aat.* The trial will start tomorrow. *l-ᵊmḥaakame raḥa təbda bukra.* — When is your case coming up for trial? *ʔeemta qaḍiitak laḥa təbda mḥaakamta?* — The case was never brought to trial. *l-qaḍiyye ɛəmro maa žara fiiha mḥaakame.* **2.** *tažriib.* They sent me the merchandise for a week's free trial. *baɛatú-li l-ᵊbḍaaɛa tažriib la-məddet žəmɛa b-balaaš.* — I took the records on trial. *ʔaxadt ᵊl-ʔəsṭwaanaat lət-tažriib.* **3.** *bala mən ɛand ʔaḷḷa.* I find his company a real trial. *šaayef ṣəḥᵊbto bala mən ɛand ʔaḷḷa.*

**He's on trial for murder. *ɛam yəthaakam ᵊb-žariimet qatᵊl.*

to give a trial - *žarrab//džarrab.* Why don't you give the car a trial? *leeš maa bədžarreb ᵊs-sayyaara?* — We usually give them a week's trial before we hire them. *ɛaadatan mənžarrə́bon žəmɛa qabᵊl-ma nwaẓẓə́fon.*

triangle - *msallas* pl. *-aat.*

triangular - *mtallat.*

tribal - *ɛašaayri*, q̈abali*.*

tribe - *ɛašiire* pl. *ɛašaayer, q̈abiile* pl. *q̈abaayel.*

tribunal - *maḥkame* pl. *maḥaakem.*

tributary - *raafed* pl. *rawaafed.* The tributary empties into the river a few miles from here. *r-raafed biṣəbb bᵊn-nahᵊr ɛala baɛᵊd kam miil mən hoon.*

tribute - *ʔataawe.* The Ottoman Empire demanded tribute from all the countries under its domain. *l-ʔəmbaraṭooriyye ᵊl-ɛəsmaaniyye farḍet ʔataawe ɛala kəll ᵊd-duwal halli waaqɛa taḥᵊt ṣəlṭə́ta.*

to pay tribute to - *karram//tkarram.* We are gathered tonight to pay tribute to a great scholar. *məžtəmɛiin nəḥna l-leele la-nkarrem ɛallaame kbiir.*

trick - **1.** *ḥiile* pl. *ḥiyal.* Don't try your tricks on me! *laa džarreb ḥiyalak ɛaliyyi!* — I'm on to his tricks. *baɛref kəll ḥiyalo.* **2.** *ləɛbe* pl. *ləɛab, ḥiile* pl. *ḥiyal.* Do you know any card tricks? *btaɛref šii ləɛab bᵊš-šadde?* — It's a trick I learned a long time ago. *hiyye ləɛbe tɛallamta mən zamaan.* **3.** *ləġᵊz* pl. *lġuuze.* There's a trick to making a good cake. *fii ləġᵊz la-msaawaat gaato mniiḥ.* **4.** *fatte* pl. *-aat.* Who took that last trick? *miin rəbeḥ ʔaaxer fatte?*

**He knows all the tricks of the trade. *byaɛref kəll madaaxel w-maxaarež ᵊṣ-ṣanɛa.*

**A safety pin will do the same trick. *šakkaale bətfiid nafs ᵊn-natiiže.*

**That'll do the trick. *haada d-dawa š-šaafi.*

**That's a mean trick! *haada ḍarᵊb waaṭi!*

to trick - *ləɛeb (a ləɛᵊb) ɛala, ḥtaal ɛala.* He tricked me again. *ləɛeb ɛaliyyi marra taanye.* — He tricked me into signing. *ləɛeb ɛaliyyi la-ḥatta ʔəmḍi.* — He tricked her out of the money. *ləɛeb ɛaleeha w-xalláṣa maṣariiha.*

tricktrack - *ṭaawəlt˜ zahᵊr.*

tricky - **1.** *dəqᵊr, ḥareš.* That's a tricky question. *haadi masʔale dəqra.* **2.** *mlaɛwan.* Be careful, he's a tricky fellow! *ʔəntə́beh, huwwe zalame mlaɛwan* (or ***huwwe ḥiyalži)!*

tricot - *triiko.*

tricycle - *bəsᵊkleet(e)* (pl. *-aat*) *b-tlətt dawaliib.*

trifle - *šii taafeh* pl. *ʔašya taafha.* I wouldn't bother with such trifles. *ɛawaaḍak ʔana maa bəhtamm b-heek ʔašya taafha.*

a trifle - *šwayye ẓġiire.* The trousers are a trifle too long. *l-banṭaloon ṭawiil šwayye ẓġiire.*

to trifle with - *staxaff b-.* He won't be trifled with. *maa fiik təstaxəff fii.*

trifling - *zahiid.* He paid a trifling sum for the car. *dafaɛ mablaġ zahiid ḥaqq ᵊs-sayyaara.*

trigger - *znaad* pl. *-aat, diik* pl. *dyaak.* Go ahead, pull the trigger! *yaḷḷa, šədd ᵊz-znaad!*

trigonometry - *ɛəlm˜ ᵊmsallasaat.*

triliteral - *sulaasi*.*

trim - *mrattab.* She always looks very trim. *hiyye daaʔiman heeʔə́ta mrattabe.*

to trim - **1.** *šakkal//tšakkal, zawwaq//dzawwaq.* The hat is trimmed with feathers. *l-bərneeṭa mšakkale b-riiš.* **2.** *qaṣṣ (ə qaṣṣ//nqaṣṣ).* The gardener trimmed the lawn and the rosebushes. *ž-žneenaati qaṣṣ ᵊl-ḥašiišaat wᵊl-ᵊwruud.* **3.** *qaṣqaṣ.* Shall I trim your eyebrows? *qaṣqə́ṣ-lak ḥawaažbak?*

trip - *məšwaar* pl. *mašawiir, safra* pl. *-aat, raḥle* pl. *-aat.* How was your trip? *kiif kaan məšwaarak?* — On the trip back I visited some friends. *ʔana w-raažeɛ b-məšwaari zərt baɛᵊḍ l-ᵊṣḥaab.* — Have a pleasant trip! *nšaḷḷa btənbəṣeṭ b-məšwaarak!* — The trip there was quicker than the trip back. *bᵊs-safra kaanet ᵊr-rooḥa ʔasraɛ mn ᵊr-ražɛa.* — How much is the round trip? *qaddeeš bətkallef ᵊs-safra rooḥa ražɛa?*

to trip - **1.** *tfarkaš.* Don't trip on the stairs. *laa tətfarkaš ɛad-daraž.* **2.** *farkaš.* He tripped me. *huwwe farkašni.*

to trip up - **1.** *ġəleṭ (a ġalaṭ).* I must have tripped up somewhere. *laazem kuun ġləṭṭ ᵊb-šii maḥall.* **2.** *waqqaɛ.* He's easy to trip up with a clever question or two. *hayyen ɛaleek ᵊtwaqqɛo b-šii suʔaal suʔaaleen ḥəzqiin.*

tripartite - *sulaasi*.*

triumph - *naṣᵊr, fooz.*

trivial - **1.** *taafeh.* The author has a tendency to get lost in all kinds of trivial matters. *l-ᵊmʔallef ɛando ʔəstəɛdaad yḍiiɛ ᵊb-masaaʔel taafha.* **2.** *zahiid.* It's only a trivial sum that you have to contribute. *kəll maa hunaalek mablaġ zahiid halli laazem tətbarraɛ fii.*

triviality - **1.** *tafaaha.* The triviality of the problem doesn't warrant all this excitement. *tafaahet ᵊl-məšᵊkle maa bətbarrer kəll hal-hoože.* **2.** *taafha* pl. *tawaafeh.* Let's not waste our time with such trivialities. *xalliina maa nḍawweɛ waqᵊtna ɛala heek tawaafeh.*

troop - **1.** *ʔərṭa* pl. *ʔəraṭ.* I passed a troop of children on my way back. *maraqt ᵊb-ʔərṭet ᵊwlaad ᵊb-ražᵊɛti.* **2.** *ḥaẓiira* pl. *-aat* and *ḥaẓaayer.* Two troops of boy scouts went to a summer camp. *ḥaẓiirteen ᵊmn ᵊl-kaššaafe raaḥu ɛala maxyam ṣeefi.* **3.** *žnuud* (pl.), *ɛaskar* (coll.). The radio reported troop movements along the border. *r-raadyo qaal ʔənno fii taḥarrukaat ᵊžnuud ɛala ṭuul l-ᵊḥduud.*

troops - *žnuud* (pl.), *ɛaskar* (coll.). The government moved troops into the city to quell the student riots. *l-ᵊḥkuume nazzalet ᵊžnuud ɛal-balad la-ḥatta təqmaɛ ʔəḍṭiraabaat ᵊṭ-ṭəllaab.*

tropic - *madaar* pl. *-aat.* The Tropic of Cancer. *madaar˜ ᵊṣ-ṣaraṭaan.* The Tropic of Capricorn. *madaar˜ ᵊž-žadi.*

tropics - *manaaṭeq ʔəstiwaaʔiyye* (pl.), *manaaṭeq ḥaarra* (pl.).

tropical - *ʔəstiwaaʔi*.* He's a specialist in tropical diseases. *huwwe ʔəxtiṣaaṣi bᵊl-ʔamraaḍ ᵊl-ʔəstiwaaʔiyye.*

trouble - **1.** *səqle, ġalabe.* Why all this trouble? You didn't have to bring me flowers. *leeš kəll has-səqle? maa kaan fii lzuum džəb-li zhuur.* — It was no trouble at all. *maa kaan fii ġalabe ʔabadan.* — Thank you for all you've done for me. - No trouble at all. *katter xeerak ɛala kəll šii ɛmə́lt-əlli-yḍa. - maa fii ġalabe* (or ***taɛabak raaḥa*). **2.** *ġalabe, mašaakel* (pl.). If he tries to make trouble, throw him out. *ʔiza bada ysaawi ġalabe qallɛo.* **3.** *mašaakel* (pl.). I've never known anyone with so many troubles. *b-ḥayaati maa ɛrəft waaḥed ɛando mašaakel qaddo.* — He's been in trouble as long as I've known him. *mən waqᵊt-ma baɛᵊrfo waaqeɛ ᵊb-mašaakel.* **4.** *warṭa.* Boy, I'm in real trouble! *daxiil ɛərḍak, ʔana waaqeɛ b-warṭa malɛuune!* **5.** *məšᵊkle, ɛəlle, mṣiibe.* The trouble with him is, he's a liar. *məškəlto ʔənno kazzaab.* **6.** *hamm* pl. *hmuum.* She always tells her troubles to me. *daayman btəškī-li hmuuma.* **7.** *maraḍ.* He suffers from heart trouble. *ɛando maraḍ qalb.* **8.** *ḥawaades* (pl.). There's usually trouble in that section of town. *ɛaadatan biṣiir ḥawaades ᵊb-hal-manṭiqa mn ᵊl-balad.* — The police are always ready for trouble around here. *l-bawaliis daayman ɛala ḥaḍar ləl-ḥawaades ᵊb-han-nawaaḥi.*

**What's the trouble? *šuu l-qəṣṣa?*

**They didn't even take the trouble to write us. *ḥatta maa ʔazɛažu ḥaalon yəkᵊtbū-lna.*

to give trouble - *ġallab.* Sorry to have given you so much trouble. *mətʔassef ʔənni ġallabtak kəll hal-ġalabe.* — The patient gives me lots of trouble. *l-mariiḍ ɛam yġallə́bni ktiir.*

to go (or put oneself) to trouble - *ġallab ḥaalo, ɛazzab ḥaalo.* Don't go to any trouble for me, please. *bətražžaak laa tġalleb ḥaalak məšaani.* — Don't put yourself to any trouble. *laa tġalleb ḥaalak.* — Why should I go to all that trouble? *leeš la-ɛazzeb ḥaali kəll hal-ɛazaab?*

to have trouble - *tġallab.* I had a lot of trouble about it. *tġallabt ᵊktiir ᵊb-sabáha.* — We've had trouble with this man before. *tġallabna maɛ har-rəžžaal mən qabᵊl.*

**I'm always having trouble with my teeth. *snaani daayman biġallbuuni.*

to trouble - **1.** *ġallab//tġallab.* I'm sorry, but

I'll have to trouble you again. *ɛadam m'aaxaze, laḥa ġallbak marra taanye.* — May I trouble you for a match? *mənken ġallbak b-kəbriite?* — My arm has been troubling me ever since my accident. *'iidi ṣar-la ɛam 'tġalləbni mən waqt 'l-ḥaades tabaɛi.* 2. *daayaq, zaɛaž (e zaɛ'ž).* What's troubling you? *šuu mdaayqak?* or *šuu zaaɛžak?*

troubled - 1. *mašġuul˜ 'l-baal.* I've been very troubled about his health lately. *ktiir mašġuul baali ɛala ṣaḥḥto b-hal-'iyyaam.* 2. *məḍṭəreb.* We're living in troubled times. *ɛaayšiin 'b-'iyyaam məḍṭərbe.* 3. *mšawwaš.* That man has a troubled mind. *haz-zalame fəkro mšawwaš.* 4. *mɛazzab.* He has a troubled conscience. *wəždaano mɛazzab.*

troublemaker - *mašaakəlži* pl. *-iyye.*

troublesome - *məzɛež.*

trousers - 1. (Western style) *banṭaloon* and *banṭaroon* pl. *-aat.* 2. (native) *šərwaal* pl. *šarawiil.*

trousseau - *žhaaz˜ 'l-ɛaruus.*

trowel - *maɛlaqa* pl. *maɛaaleq.*

truce - *hədne.*

truck - *kamyoon* pl. *-aat.*

truck farmer - *bəstaani* pl. *basaatne.*

truck garden - *bəstaan* pl. *basatiin.*

true - 1. *mazbuuṭ, ṣaḥiiḥ.* Is that story true? *hal-qəṣṣa mazbuuṭa šii?* 2. *'akiid.* Dark clouds are always a true sign of rain. *l-'ġyuum 'l-ġaatme daa'iman daliil 'akiid ɛal-maṭar.* 3. *saadeq.* You'll find him a true friend. *bətlaaqīi sadiiq saadeq.* 4. *məxleṣ.* He stayed true to his principles. *bəqi məxleṣ la-mabaad'o.* 5. *ɛal-mazbuuṭ, ɛan ṣaḥiiḥ, ɛan ḥaqa.* He is a true poet. *huwwe šaaɛer ɛal-mazbuuṭ.*

**True to his word, he didn't tell anyone. *wafaa'an b-waɛdo maa ḥaka la-ḥada.*

to hold true - *ṣaḥḥ (ə ø).* That doesn't hold true in our case. *haš-šii maa biṣəḥḥ 'b-waḍ'ɛna.*

truffle - *kəmaaye* coll. *kəme* pl. *kəmaayaat.*

truly - *ḥaqiiqatan, b'l-ḥaqiiqa.* I am truly sorry. *'ana ḥaqiiqatan mət'assef.*

trumpet - *booraẓaan* pl. *-aat.*

trunk - 1. *žəz'ɛ* pl. *žzuuɛa, saaq* pl. *siiqaan.* The trunk of the tree is completely hollow. *žəzɛ 'š-šažara faaḍi ɛal-'aaxiir.* 2. *žəz'ɛ* pl. *žzuuɛa.* The human body consists of head, trunk, and limbs. *žəsm 'l-'ənsaan m'allaf mən raas w-žəz'ɛ w-'aṭraaf.* 3. *xarṭuum* pl. *xaraṭiim.* Suddenly, the elephant raised his trunk and squirted water at us. *faž'atan 'l-fiil rafaɛ xarṭuumo w-raššna b-mayy.* 4. *sanduuq* pl. *sanadiiq.* Are the trunks packed? *s-sanadiiq maḍbuube šii?* — Get the spare tire from the trunk. *žiib 'r-rəseerv mn 's-sanduuq.*

trunks - *mayyǒo* pl. *mayyohaat.* These trunks are too tight. *hal-mayyǒo dayyeq 'ktiir.*

trust - 1. *siqa.* I'm putting my trust in you. *ḥaaṭeṭ siqati fiik.* 2. *'amaane.* He put the money in trust for her. *wadaɛ 'l-maṣaari 'amaane 'əla.*

to trust - 1. *'amman, wəseq (-yuusaq siqa//nwasaq) b-.* I don't trust him. *maa b'ammno* or *maa buusaq fii.* -- Can you trust me until payday? *bət'ammənni la-yoom 'd-daf'ɛ?* -- You can trust all your money to him. *fiik 't'ammno ɛala kəll maṣariik* or *fiik tuusaq fii b-kəll maṣariik.* — Can I trust him to send me all the merchandise? *bəḥsen 'ammno* (or *'uusaq fii*) *yəbɛdt-li kəll l-'bḍaaɛa?* 2. *ɛtamad.* You shouldn't trust too much to your memory. *maa laazem təɛtəmed 'ktiir ɛala zaakərtak.*

**I trust you slept well. *nšaaḷḷa tkuun nəmt 'mniiḥ.*

trustworthy - *mawsuuq fii.* The maid is absolutely trustworthy. *ṣ-ṣaanɛa mawsuuq fiiha tamaam.* — I have it from a trustworthy source. *'ažətni mən maṣdar mawsuuq fii.*

truth - 1. *ḥaqiiqa* pl. *ḥaqaayeq.* That's the truth. *hayy 'l-ḥaqiiqa.* — I told him the plain truth. *qəlt-əllo l-ḥaqiiqa ɛala ḥabbəta.* — We don't have to argue about such simple truths. *maa fii lzuum 'nhaažež ɛala heek ḥaqaayeq waaḍḥa.* 2. *ṣaḥḥa.* Do you think there's any truth in that story? *bədḍənn 'ənno fii 'asar mn 'ṣ-ṣaḥḥa b-hal-qəṣṣa?*

**To tell the truth, I don't know. *b-kəll ṣaraaḥa, maa baɛref.*

try - *mḥaawale* pl. *-aat, tažrube* pl. *tažaarob.* He made it on the first try. *nažaḥ mən 'awwal 'mḥaawale.* — It was a good try anyway. *ɛala kəllen kaanet 'mḥaawale mniiḥa.*

**Let's have another try. *xalliina nḥaawel marra taanye.*

to try - 1. *žarrab//džarrab, ḥaawal.* I'd like to try it. *žaaye ɛala baali žarrəba.* — Did you ever try hunting? *žarrabt šii b-ṣayaatak təṣṭaad?* — Try to do better next time. *žarreb taɛmel 'aḥsan l-marra ž-žaaye.* — He tries to get out of all hard work. *biḥaawel yətmaḷḷaṣ mən kəll 'š-šəġl 'ṣ-ṣaɛ'b.* -- That thing was never tried before. *haš-šii ɛəmro maa džarrab mən qab'l.* 2. *naẓar (o naẓar) b-.* Which judge is trying the case? *'anu qaaḍi ɛam byənẓor b'd-daɛwa?*

**The fellow really tries my patience. *haz-zalame ɛam yṭaaleɛ diini.*

**My patience was sorely tried. *waṣlet maɛi la-təsɛda w-təsɛiin.*

trying - *ḥərež.* We've had some trying days lately. *ḥakmətna 'iyyaam ḥərže m'axxaran.*

to try on - *qaas (i qayasaan* and *qyaas).* I'd like to try that suit on again. *bḥəbb qiis hal-badle marra taanye.*

to try out - *žarrab//džarrab.* I'd like to try out the car first. *bḥəbb 'awwal žarreb 's-sayyaara.*

Tuareg - *ṭawaarqi** coll. pl. *ṭawaareq.*

tub - 1. *baanyo* pl. *baanyoyaat.* Did you wash the (bath) tub? *ġasalt 'l-baanyo?* 2. *lagan* pl. *-aat.* The wash is still in the tub. *l-ġasiil ləssa b'l-lagan.*

tube - 1. *kabsuule* pl. *-aat, 'əṣbaɛ* pl. *'aṣaabeɛ* and *'aṣabiiɛ.* I want a large tube of tooth paste. *bəddi kabsuulet maɛžuun 'snaan 'kbiir.* 2. *lamba* pl. *-aat, balloora* pl. *-aat.* My radio needs new tubes. *r-raadyo tabaɛi laazmo lambaat ždad.* 3. *kawšuuk žuwwaani* pl. *kawašiik žuwwaaniyye.* I need a new tube for my bicycle. *laazəmni kawšuuk žuwwaani ždiid la-bəs'kleetti.* 4. *'ənbuub* pl. *'anabiib, barbiiš* pl. *barabiiš.* He had to be fed through a tube. *nžabaru yġazzúu b-waaṣəṭṭ 'ənbuub.* 5. *barbiiš* pl. *barabiiš.* He siphoned the gasoline out of the tank with a rubber tube. *saḥab 'l-banziin mn 'd-dabbo b-waaṣəṭṭ barbiiš kawšuuk.* 6. *'ənbuub* pl. *'anabiib.* One of the glass tubes is broken. *'ənbuub mən 'anabiib l-'qzaaz maksuur.*

tuberculosis - *səll, səll tadarruni.* He has tuberculosis. *maɛo səll.*

tuck - *ġabne* pl. *-aat.* The dress needs some tucks at the waist. *l-fəṣṭaan laazmo kam ġabne b-xaṣro.*

to tuck - 1. *daḥaš (a daḥ'š//ndaḥaš).* Let me tuck the blanket around you. *xalliini 'ədḥaš l-'ḥraam ḥawaleek.* 2. *kamkar.* She tucked the children in bed. *kamkaret l-'wlaad b't-tax't.*

to tuck in - *fawwat.* Tuck in your shirt. *fawwet qamiiṣak.*

Tuesday - *(yoom˜) 't-talaata.* I'll be back on Tuesday. *bəržaɛ 't-talaata.*

tug - 1. *natše* pl. *-aat.* He freed himself with one tug at the rope. *xallaṣ ḥaalo b-natše waaḥde b'l-ḥab'l.* 2. *žarraara* pl. *-aat.* Two tugs are towing the liner. *fii žarraarteen ɛam yžərru l-baaxra.*

to tug at - *natwaš, žaržar, šadšad, šadwad.* Stop tugging at me! *ḥaaže tnatwəšni.*

tuition - *qəṣ'ṭ* (pl. *qṣaaṭ).* Is tuition very high at your college? *l-qəṣ'ṭ ġaali ktiir b'l-kəlliyye tabaɛak?*

**He has to dance to her tune. *mažbuur yəmši ɛala keefa.*

**He pays installments on the house to the tune of 2,000 pounds a month. *byədfaɛ qṣuuṭa ɛal-beet mablaġ 'alfeen leera b'š-šah'r.*

tulip - *zahret˜ tuuliib* coll. *tuuliib* pl. *zahraat˜ tuuliib.*

tulle - *tuul.*

to **tumble** - *tkarfat.* He tumbled down the stairs. *tkarfat mən ɛad-daraž.*

tumor - *waram* pl. *'awraam.*

tuna - *ṭoon.*

tune - *naġme* pl. *-aat, daqqa* pl. *-aat.* Do you know that tune? *btaɛref han-naġme?* — He can't carry a tune. *maa fii yəmši ɛan-naġme.*

out of tune - 1. *barraat 'n-naġme.* She always sings out of tune. *bətġanni daayman barraat 'n-naġme.* 2. *muu mdoozan.* The piano is out of tune. *l-byaano muu mdoozan.*

to tune - *doozan//ddoozan.* The piano needs tuning. *l-byaano laazmo doozane.*

to tune in - *ẓabbaṭ.* You haven't tuned the station in properly. *maa ẓabbaṭṭ l-'mḥaṭṭa mniiḥ.*

to tune up - 1. *doozan.* The orchestra is tuning up. *l-'orkeestra ɛam 'ddoozen.* 2. *ɛayyar//tɛayyar.* I'm looking for a good mechanic to tune up my engine. *ɛam dawwer ɛala məkanəsyaan 'mniiḥ yɛayyər-li motoori.*

Tunis - *tuunes.*

Tunisia - *tuunes.*

Tunisian - *tuunsi* pl. *-iyyiin* and *-iyye.*
tunnel - *tuneel* pl. *-aat, nafaq̈* pl. *ʔanfaaq̈.*
turban - *laffe* pl. *-aat.*
turbine - *tərbiin* pl. *-aat* and *tarabiin.*
Turk - *tərki** coll. pl. *tərᵊk* pl. *traak.*
Turkey - *tərkiyya.*
turkey - *diik˜* (pl. *dyuuk˜*) *ḥabaš.*
Turkish - 1. *tərki.* Do you know Turkish? *btaεref tərki?* 2. *tərki**. It's a Turkish costume. *haada zayy tərki.*
Turkoman - *tərkmaani** coll. pl. *tərkmaan.*
turmeric - *kərkom.*
turn - 1. *barme* pl. *-aat, doora* pl. *-aat, laffe* pl. *-aat.* Try two turns to the right. *šarreb barᵊmteen εal-yamiin.* 2. *laffe* pl. *-aat, kuuε* pl. *kwaaε, kərᵊb* pl. *kruube, barme* pl. *-aat.* Here the road makes a turn. *hoone fii laffe bᵊṭ-ṭariiq.* 3. *lafte* pl. *-aat.* Make a left turn at the next corner. *εmeel lafte εala šmaalak εas-suuke ž-žaaye* or ****lfeet εala yasaarak εas-suuke ž-žaaye.* 4. *door* pl. *dwaar.* It's my turn now. *hallaq doori ʔana.* — The teacher, in his turn, claimed that... *l-ᵊmεallem b-dooro ddaεa ʔənno...* — You're talking out of turn. *εam təhki muu b-doorak.* 5. *maṭlaε.* The author was widely read at the turn of the century. *l-ᵊmʔallef kaanet kətbo tənqára ktiir b-maṭlaε hal-q̈arᵊn.*
**One good turn deserves another. *l-ḥasane bᵊl-ḥasane.*
**She never forgets a good turn. *εəmra maa btənsa mniiḥa.*
**We took a turn around the park while waiting for you. *baramna ḥawaali l-ḥadiiqa w-naḥna εam nənṭəẓrak.*
at every turn - *b-kəll xaṭwe.* We encountered difficulties at every turn. *waažahna ṣεuubaat ᵊb-kəll xaṭwe.*
by turns - *bᵊt-tanaawob.* I felt hot and cold by turns. *ʔəžaani bardiyye wᵊ-ṣxuune bᵊt-tanaawob.* — The two secretaries answer the phone by turns. *s-səkrəteerteen bižaawbu εat-talifoon bᵊt-tanaawob.*
in turn - *bᵊd-door.* You will be called up in turn. *byəṣraxúu-lkon bᵊd-door.*
to a turn - *εala ḥabbe, εala ḥabbet-* + pron. suff. The meat is cooked to a turn. *l-laḥme stawet εala ḥabbe* (or *εala ḥabbə́ta*).
to take turns - *tnaawab.* We'll take turns at the wheel. *mnətnaawab bᵊs-swaaqa.*
to turn - 1. *dawwar, baram* (*o barᵊm//nbaram*). I can't turn the key. *maa fiini dawwer ᵊl-məftaaḥ.* 2. *dawwar, daar* (*i ø//ndaar*), *baram.* A donkey walks round and round and turns the mill stone. *fii ḥmaar biduur w-biduur w-bidawwer ḥažar ᵊṭ-ṭaaḥuun.* 3. *daar* (*i ø//ndaar*). She turned her back on me. *daarə́t-li ḍahra.* — Turn your head a little to the right. *diir raasak šwayye εal-yamiin.* — He turned tail and ran. *daar danabo w-harab.* 4. *qalab* (*e qalᵊb//nqalab*), *qallab.* Turn the meat every five minutes or so. *qləbi l-laḥme kəll xamᵊs daqaayeq yaεni.* 5. *qalab.* Now turn the page. *hallaq qleeb ᵊṣ-ṣafḥa.* — Please turn to page ten. *qleeb balla ləṣ-ṣafḥa εašara.* — I turned the whole house upside down. *qalabt ᵊl-beet kəllo fooqaani taḥtaani.* 6. *ḥawwal, qalab.* You can always turn your stocks into money. *daayman fiik tḥawwel ʔasᵊhmak la-maṣaari.* 7. *lawa* (*i lawi// ltawa*). It's the second time today that I turned my ankle. *hayye l-marra t-taanye l-yoom yalli bəlwi fiiha kaaḥli.* 8. *fallat.* Next time I'm going to turn the dogs on him. *l-marra ž-žaaye laḥa fallet l-ᵊklaab εalée.* 9. *daar* (*u dawaraan*). The wheel turns on a vertical axle. *d-duulaab biduur εala məḥwar εaamuudi.* — The whole argument turns on that question. *kəll l-ᵊmnaaq̈aše bədduur ḥawl hal-masʔale.* 10. *ndaar, ltafat.* The woman turned to my friend and asked him a question. *l-mara ndaaret naaḥ rfiiqi w-saʔᵊlto suʔaal.* 11. *ltaža la-, raažaε.* I don't know to whom to turn. *maa baεref la-miin bəddi ʔəltəži* (or ... *miin bəddi raažeε*). 12. *lafat* (*e lafte*). Turn left at the intersection. *lfeet εaš-šmaal εal-ᵊmṣallabiyye.* — Turn down this road. *lfeet ᵊb-haṭ-ṭariiq.* 13. *ḥawwal, tḥawwal.* He turned to medicine after he flunked out of law school. *ḥawwal ləṭ-ṭəbb baεᵊd-ma ṣaqaṭ bᵊl-ᵊḥquuq.* 14. *tḥawwal, qalab.* The discussion turned into a brawl. *l-ᵊmnaaq̈aše tḥawwalet la-xnaaqa.* 15. *ṣaar* (*i ø*). It was so cold, the water turned to ice. *kaan bard la-daraže l-mayy ṣaaret buuẓ.* 16. *ḥammaḍ.* The weather is so hot that the cream has turned. *ṭ-ṭaqᵊṣ məšweb la-daraže l-qəšṭa ḥammaḍet.*
**I didn't expect you to turn on me too. *maa ntaẓaṛt mənnak tətlaε ḍəḍḍi ʔənte l-ləxᵊr.*
**He's just turned twenty. *ləssa ṭaabeq ᵊl-εəšriin.*
**The leaves are already turning red. *l-waraq ṣaar yəḥmarr.*
**The milk turned sour. *l-ḥaliib ḥammaḍ.*
**He turned pale when they told him the news. *ṣafran lamma xabbarúu.*
**My stomach turns at the thought of it. *nafsi btəlεi b-ᵊmžarrad-ma ʔəftə́ker fiiha.*
**His behavior turns my stomach. *taṣarrfo bilaεεi nafsi.*
**Now the tables are turned. *hallaq tġayyaret ᵊl-ʔiyyaam.*
**Don't let flattery turn your head. *laa txalli t-tamliiq yəlεab b-raasak.*
to turn around - 1. *daar* (*i ø//ndaar*), *baram* (*o barᵊm//nbaram*). Let's turn the table around. *xalliina ndiir ᵊṭ-ṭaawle.* 2. *daar* (*u dawaraan*), *ndaar.* Turn around! *duur!* 3. *ltafat.* He turned around when he heard his name. *ltafat lamma səmeε ʔəsmo.*
to turn back - 1. *rəžeε* (*a ražεa*). Let's turn back. *xalliina nəržaε.* — Turn back to page 35 and look at the diagram. *ržaaε la-ṣafḥa xamsə́a w-ᵊtlaatiin w-šuuf ᵊr-rasm ᵊl-bayaani.* 2. *traažaε.* We gave our word and we can't turn back now. *εaṭeena kəlmətna w-maa fiina nətraažaε hallaq.* 3. *qalab* (*e qalᵊb//nqalab*). Don't forget to turn back the covers on your bed. *laa tənsa maa təqleb ᵊl-ʔəġᵊṭye εan taxtak.* 4. *raǧǧaε ... la-wara.* You can't turn back the clock. *maa fiik ᵊtražžeε ᵊs-saaεa la-wara.*
to turn down - 1. *rafaḍ* (*o rafᵊḍ//nrafaḍ* and *rtafaḍ*). My application was turned down. *ṭalabi rtafaḍ.* — She turned him down. *rafᵊḍto.* 2. *waṭṭa, xaffaf.* Will you turn down the radio, please? *waṭṭi r-raadyo ʔiza bətriid.*
to turn in - 1. *radd* (*ə radd//nradd*), *ražžaε// tražžaε.* Of course, you'll have to turn in the wallet you found. *ṭabiiεi laazem ᵊtrədd ᵊž-žəzdaan yalli laqeeto.* 2. *qaddam//tqaddam, sallam// tsallam.* The application must be turned in by the 15th. *ṭ-ṭalab laazem yətqaddam qabᵊl xamᵊṣṭaεš ᵊš-šahᵊr.* — He turned in his resignation. *qaddam ʔəstiq̈aalto.* 3. *raaḥ εal-farše.* We ought to turn in early tonight. *ʔaḥsan ᵊnruuḥ εal-farše bakkiir ᵊl-leele.*
to turn off - *ṭafa* (*i ṭafi//nṭafa*). Why did you turn off the heat? *leeš ṭafeet ᵊš-šoofaaž?* — Did you turn off the gas? *ṭafeet ᵊl-gaaz?* — Turn off the light in the hall. *ʔəṭfi ḍ-ḍaww bᵊṣ-ṣoofa.*
to turn on - *fataḥ* (*a fatᵊḥ//nfataḥ*), *šaεal* (*e šaεᵊl//nšaεal*). Why don't you turn on the light? *leeš maa btəftaḥ ᵊḍ-ḍaww?* — I forgot to turn on the radio. *nsiit ʔəftaḥ ᵊr-raadyo.*
**He can really turn on the charm when he wants to. *lamma biriid byəqder yətlaaṭaf la-ʔaaxer daraže.*
to turn out - 1. *ṭəleε* (*a ø*). Things turned out worse than I had expected. *l-ʔawḍaaε ṭəlεet ʔalεan məmma kənᵊt məntə́ẓer.* — It turned out that I was right. *ṭəleε ʔənno kaan maεi ḥaqq.* — The cake didn't turn out well. *l-gaatə́o maa ṭəleε mniiḥ.* — He turned out to be very nice. *ṭəleε ᵊktiir laṭiif.* 2. *ntaha.* How did the elections turn out? *kiif ᵊntahet ᵊl-ʔəntixaabaat?* — It all turned out for the best. *kəll šii ntaha εala ʔaḥsan maa yuraam.* 3. *tbayyan.* It turned out to be a mistake. *tbayyan ʔənna kaanet ġalṭa.* 4. *ʔəža, ḥəḍer* (*a ḥḍuur*). The family turned out in full force. *l-εeele ʔəžet mn ᵊkbiira la-ẓġiira.* — A large crowd turned out for the meeting. *žamε ᵊkbiir ḥəḍer ᵊl-ʔəžtimaaε* (or *ʔəža ləl-ʔəžtimaaε*). 5. *ṭaalaε.* They've turned me out of my room. *ṭaalaεuuni mən ʔuuḍti.* — The factory turns out 500 pairs of shoes a day. *l-maεmal biṭaaleε xamᵊs miit žooz ṣabbaaṭ bᵊl-yoom.* 6. *ṭafa* (*i ṭafi// nṭafa*). Turn out the light when you leave the room. *ʔəṭfi ḍ-ḍaww lamma tətrok ᵊl-ʔuuḍa.*
**My plan didn't turn out well. *xəṭṭᵊti maa naǧḥet.*
to turn over - 1. *sallam//tsallam.* All weapons have to be turned over to the police. *kəll ᵊl-ʔasliḥa laazem tətsallam ləš-šərṭa.* — He turned over his business to his son. *sallam šəġlo la-ʔəbno.* 2. *qalab* (*e qalᵊb//nqalab*). I nearly turned over the table. *kənt laḥa ʔəqleb ᵊṭ-ṭaawle.* — He promised to turn over a new leaf and never

tell another lie. *waɛad ʔənno yəqleb ṣafḥa ždiide w-ᵊb-ḥayaato maa yəkzeb marra taanye.* 3. *nqalab, qalab.* Our boat almost turned over. *šaxtuurətna kaanet laḥa tənqəleb.* 4. *qallab.* Turn it over in your mind before you give me your answer. *qalləba* (or ***luuka* or ***žoožəla*) *b-ɛaqlak qabᵊl-ma taɛṭiini žawaab.*

to turn up - 1. *bayyan.* He's always turning up where you don't want him. *daayman bibayyen maṭraḥ-ma maa-bəddak-yda ykuun.* 2. *žadd (ə ø).* Maybe something will turn up by next week. *barki bižədd šii ž-žəmɛa ž-žaaye.* 3. *ɛalla.* Would you turn up the volume a little? *məmken ᵊtɛalli r-raadyo šwayye.*

**He turned up his nose at it. *šaaf ḥaalo ɛaleeha.*

turner - *xarraaṭ* pl. *-iin.*
turnery - 1. (work) *xraaṭa.* 2. (shop) *maxraṭa* pl. *maxaareṭ.*
turning point - *nəqṭet˜ taḥawwol.*
turnip - *raas˜ ləfᵊt* coll. *ləfᵊt* pl. *ruus˜ ləfᵊt.*
turpentine - *tərbanṭiin.*
turquoise - *feeruuzi*.*
turret - *bərᵊž* pl. *bruuž(e).*
turtle - *zəlᵊḥfe* pl. *zalaaḥef.*
tusk - *naab* pl. *nyaab.*
tutor - *mɛallam ᵊxṣuuṣi* pl. *mɛallmiin ᵊxṣuuṣiyye.* When I was sixteen I had a tutor in mathematics. *waqᵊt kaan ɛəmri səṭṭaɛš tɛallamt ᵊr-riyaaḍiyyaat ɛala mɛallem ᵊxṣuuṣi.*
tuxedo - *smooken* (invar.).
tweezers - *malqaṭ* pl. *malaaqeṭ.*
twelfth - 1. *ṭ-ṭnaɛš.* It was his twelfth accident. *haada kaan ᵊl-ʔaksiḍaan ᵊṭ-ṭnaɛᵊš tabaɛo.* -- He left on the twelfth of June. *saafar b-ᵊṭnaɛš ᵊḥzeeran.* 2. *t-taani ɛašar.* He died at the end of the twelfth century. *maat ᵊb-ʔawaaxer ᵊl-q̈arn ᵊt-taani ɛašar.*

one twelfth - *waaḥed mən ṭnaɛš.* He owns one twelfth of the building. *byəmlok waaḥed mən ṭnaɛš mn ᵊl-binaaye.* -- Two twelfths equal one sixth. *tneen mən ṭnaɛš bisaawu sədᵊs.*

twelve - 1. *ṭnaɛš.* Twelve and six are eighteen. *ṭnaɛš w-sətte tmənṭaɛš.* -- There are twelve of us in class. *nəḥna ṭnaɛš bᵊṣ-ṣaff.* 2. *ṭnaɛšar.* I lived there for twelve years. *ɛəšt ᵊhniik ṭnaɛšar səne.* 3. *s-saaɛa ṭnaɛš.* Is twelve a convenient time for you? *biwaafqak ᵊs-saaɛa ṭnaɛš?* -- The train leaves at twelve. *t-treen byəmši s-saaɛa ṭnaɛš.*
twentieth - 1. *l-ɛəšriin.* After all, we're living in the twentieth century. *laa tənsa, nəḥna ɛaayšiin bᵊl-q̈arn ᵊl-ɛəšriin.* 2. *l-ɛəšriini*, l-ɛəšriin.* They're celebrating their twentieth anniversary. *ɛam yəḥtəflu b-ɛiidon ᵊl-ɛəšriini.*

one twentieth - *waaḥed mən ɛəšriin.*

twenty - *ɛəšriin.* There are no more than twenty houses in our street. *maa fii ʔaktar mən ɛəšriin beet b-šaarəɛna.*
twice - 1. *marrteen.* I was invited there twice. *nɛazamt la-hniik marrteen.* 2. *b-marrteen.* He's twice as old as she is. *huwwe ʔakbar mənha b-marrteen.* -- I paid twice as much. *dafaɛᵊt ʔaktar b-marrteen.* -- That way it will take twice as long. *b-haṭ-ṭariiqa btətḥammal ʔaṭwal ᵊb-marrteen.*
twig - *ġəṣᵊn* pl. *ʔaġṣaan.*
twin - *šaqq˜* (or *fardet˜*) *toom* dual *toom* pl. *twaam.* I can't tell those twins apart. *maa bəq̈der farreq been hat-toom.* -- His twin brother died last year. *ʔaxdu šaqq ᵊt-toom maat ɛaamnawwal.* -- Have you met his twin sister? *tɛarraft ɛala ʔəxto šaqq ᵊt-toom?* -- He has a twin brother. *ʔəlo ʔaxx, huwwe wiyyda toom.* -- She's his twin sister. *hiyye wiyyda toom.* -- She bore him twins twice. *žaabət-lo toomeen.*

**It's a small plane with a twin engine. *hiyye ṭayyaara ẓġiire b-ᵊmḥarrikeen.*
twine - *xeeṭ* (pl. *xiiṭaan*) *maṣṣiiṣ.* I need some more twine to tie this package. *laazəmni kamaan šwayyet xiiṭaan maṣṣiiṣ la-ʔərboṭ hal-baakeet.*
to **twist** - 1. *dawwar, baram (o barᵊm//nbaram).* She twisted her ring on her finger. *dawwaret ᵊl-xaatem b-ʔəṣbəɛa.* 2. *lawa (i lawi//ltawa).* Stop twisting my arm. *ḥaaže təlwii-li ʔiidi.* -- I nearly twisted my arm. *kənt laḥa ʔəlwi ʔiidi.* 3. *ɛarwaž.* The road twists through the mountains. *ṭ-ṭariiq biɛarwež bᵊž-žbaal.*

**She can twist him around her little finger. *bətlaɛɛbo ɛala ruus ʔaṣabiiɛa.*

**All right, you've twisted my arm; I'll have a drink now. *ṭayyeb, ġalabtni; baaxəd-li qadaḥ hallaq.*

two - 1. *tneen* f. *tənteen.* Two of my books got lost. *tneen mən kətbi ḍaaɛu.* 2. *tneen* pl. *-aat.* Add up the four twos in the right column. *žmaaɛ ᵊt-tneenaat ᵊl-ʔarbɛa halli bᵊl-xaane ɛal-yamiin.* -- Only the two of us went on that trip. *bass tneenaatna ɛməlna har-raḥle.* 3. *s-saaɛa tənteen.* Two is a very convenient time for me. *s-saaɛa tənteen ᵊktiir ᵊmnaasbe ʔəli.* -- He said he'd be here at two. *qaal ʔənno bikuun hoon ᵊs-saaɛa tənteen.* 4. dual: Can you lend me two pounds? *fiik təqrədni leerteen?* -- The first two items have been canceled. *n-nafᵊdteen ᵊl-ʔawwalaaniyye nšaṭabu.*

**She didn't actually tell me, but I can put two and two together. *hiyye bᵊl-waaq̈eɛ maa qaalət-li laaken fiini ʔəḥzer.*

in (or **by**) **twos** - *tneen tneen* f. *tənteen tənteen.* The children lined up in twos. *l-ᵊwlaad nṣaffu tneen tneen.*

in two - *šaqᵊfteen.* Cut it in two. *qṭaɛa šaqᵊfteen.*

type - 1. *nooɛ* pl. *ʔanwaaɛ.* What type of shoe do you wear? *šuu nooɛ ᵊṣ-ṣababiiṭ halli btəlbəsa?* -- He's not the type to run after girls. *maa-lo mn ᵊn-nooɛ yalli byərkod wara l-banaat.* 2. *tiip.* He's not my type. *maa-lo mn ᵊt-tiip tabaɛi.* 3. *ṭbaaɛa, ḥruuf* (pl.). The type is too small. *ṭ-ṭbaaɛa ktiir ᵊẓġiire.*

to type - 1. *ṭabaɛ (a ṭabᵊɛ, ṭbaaɛa).* Can you type? *btaɛref təṭbaɛ?* -- Will you type these letters for me, please? *məmken baḷḷa təṭbəɛ-li hal-makatiib?*

typesetter - *ṣaffaaf˜* (pl. *-iin˜*) *ᵊḥruuf, mnaḍḍeḍ* pl. *-iin.*
typewriter - *ʔaale* (pl. *-aat*) *kaatbe.*
typhoid - *tifoʔiid.*
typhus - *tiifos.*
typical - *ḥayy.* This is a typical example of red tape. *haada misaal ḥayy ɛan ᵊl-biiruq̈raaṭiyye.*

**That's typical of him. *haada misaal ḥayy ɛanno.*

**You might say, he's the typical college student. *fiik ᵊtquul ʔənno huwwe misaal ṭəbq ᵊl-ʔaṣᵊl ɛan ṭəllaab ᵊž-žaamɛa.*

**He dresses like a typical professor. *byəlbes mətᵊl ʔəstaaz ɛal-maẓbuuṭ.*

typist: He's a good typist. *huwwe byəṭbaɛ ᵊmniiḥ ɛal-ʔaale l-kaatbe.* -- She's a typist at the bank. *btəṭbaɛ ɛal-ʔaale l-kaatbe bᵊl-baṇk.* -- We need two more typists. *laazəmna kamaan tneen yəṭbaɛu ɛal-ʔaale l-kaatbe.*
typographical - *maṭbaɛi*.* There are five or six typographical errors on every page. *fii xamᵊs sətt ġalṭaat maṭbaɛiyye ɛala kəll ṣafḥa.*
typography - *ṭbaaɛa.*
tyrannical - *ṭaaġiye* pl. *ṭəġaat.*
tyranny - *ṭəġyaan.*
tyrant - *ṭaaġiye* pl. *ṭəġaat.*
Tyre - *ṣuur.*

U

udder - *dərra* pl. *dərar.*
ugly - *qabiiḥ, bəšeɛ, šaniiɛ.* That's an ugly picture. *haṣ-ṣuura qabiiḥa.* -- They're spreading ugly rumors about him. *ɛam yənᵊšru ʔišaaɛaat bəšɛa ɛanno.*
ulcer - *qarḥa* pl. *-aat.*
ultraviolet rays - *ʔašəɛɛa fawq̈ ᵊl-banafsaži.*
umbrella - *šamsiyye* pl. *šamaasi.*
umpire - *ḥakam* pl. *ḥəkkaam.*
to be **unable** - *maa ṭəleɛ (a ø) b-ʔiid-* + pron. suff., *maa tmakkan, maa qəder (e ø), maa ḥəsen (e ø).* His father was unable to pay his debts. *ʔabuu maa ṭəleɛ ᵊb-ʔiido yədfaɛ dyuuno.* -- I'm sorry I'm unable to

give you that information. *mət?assef muu taaleƐ b-?iidi ?aƐtiik hal-maƐluumaat.*

unanimous – 1. *məžmeƐ.* The assembly was unanimous in approval. *ž-žamƐiyye kaanet məž?mƐa Ɛal-?mwaafaqa.* 2. *məžmaƐ Ɛalée.* It is the unanimous opinion of all concerned that ... *r-ra?i halli məžmaƐ Ɛalée mən taraf kəll ?l-məxtassiin ?ənno ...*

unanimously – *b?l-?əžmaaƐ.* He was elected unanimously. *ntaxabúu b?l-?əžmaaƐ.*

unbearable: It's an unbearable situation. *hayy haale maa btənhámel.* -- The heat is getting unbearable. *š-šoob maa Ɛaad Ɛam yənhámel.*

unbiased – *muu məthazzeb, muu məthayyez.* On this subject he's quite unbiased. *huwwe b-hal-mawduuƐ muu məthazzeb ?abadan.*

uncertain – 1. *muu m?akkad, muu mhaqqaq.* His trip is still uncertain. *saf?rto ləssaaha muu m?akkade.* 2. *mxootar.* I'm still uncertain whether I'll go. *ləssaani mxootar ?iza raha ruuh wəlla la?.*

in no uncertain terms – *b?l-?mšabrah.* I told him in no uncertain terms what I thought of him. *qəltállo b?l-?mšabrah šuu ra?yi fii.*

uncle – 1. (father's brother) *Ɛamm* pl. *Ɛmuum(e)* and *Ɛmaam.* 2. (mother's brother) *xaal* pl. *xwaal.*

uncomfortable – 1. *muu məryeh.* That's an uncomfortable chair. *hal-kərsi muu məryeh.* 2. *məhrež.* We found ourselves in a real uncomfortable situation. *wažadna haalna b-haale məh?rže Ɛan haqa.*

uncommon – 1. *ġeer ma?luuf.* He's employing uncommon methods to get results. *Ɛam yəstaƐmel ?asaliib ġeer ma?luufe la-yəhsal Ɛan-nataayež ?l-matluube.* 2. *naader.* The museum has a number of uncommon archeological items. *l-mathaf fii Ɛəddet qətaƐ ?asariyye naadra.*

**It's not uncommon to find him in a bar early in the morning. *muu šii Ɛažiib ?ənnak tlaaqíi b?l-baaraat mən Ɛand Ɛala bəkra.*

unconscious – *muu waƐyaan, ġaayeb, faaqed˜ ?l-waƐi.* He's still unconscious. *ləssáa muu waƐyaan.*

to be unconscious of – *maa šaƐar (o šƐuur) b-, maa hass (ə həss) b-.* He was unconscious of the real danger. *maa kaan šaaƐer b?l-xatar ?l-haqiiqi.* -- She's unconscious of what's going on around her. *maa-la haasse b-halli saayer hawaleeha.*

unconsciously: Unconsciously, he reached for a cigarette. *biduun-ma yəšƐor madd ?iido la-yaaxod sigaara.* -- She did it unconsciously. *Ɛəmlə́ta biduun-ma təšƐor.*

undecided – 1. *mxootar, mətradded.* I'm still undecided. *ləssaani mxootar.* 2. *muu mqarrar.* It's still undecided. *š-šaġle ləssaata muu mqarrara.*

under – 1. *tah?t.* Slip the letter under the door. *dhaaš ?l-maktuub taht ?l-baab.* -- The slippers are under the bed. *š-šahhaataat taht ?t-tax?t.* -- Are you under medical treatment? *?ənte taht l-?mƐaalaže t-təbbiyye?* -- He's under constant surveillance. *huwwe taht ?mraaqabe mətwaasle.* -- The troops fought exceptionally well under his command. *ž-žnuud haarabu ktiir ?mniih tah?t qiyaadto.* -- The project is under consideration. *l-mašruuƐ taht ?l-bah?s.* -- The road is under construction. *t-tariiq taht ?t-taƐbiid.* -- The new decree comes under emergency measures. *l-marsuum ?ž-ždiid byəži taht ?t-tadabiir ?t-taar?a.* -- Any income under 600 dollars is tax free. *?ayy dax?l tah?t sətt miit dolaar maa fii Ɛalée dariibe.* -- Children under the age of six are admitted free. *l-?wlaad halli mən taht ?s-sətte bifuutu b-balaaš.* -- The recruiting officer rejected him because he was still under age at that time. *daabet ?t-tažniid rafado la?ənno kaan taht ?s-sənn ?b-waqta.* 2. *taht ?iid˜ ...* He has five employees working under him. *fii Ɛando xams ?mwazzafiin byəštəġlu taht ?iido.* 3. *b-.* Put the item under "Miscellaneous". *hatt ?n-nafde b?n-natriyyaat.* -- You'll find the book under "General Economics". *bətlaaqi l-?ktaab ?b-qəs?m "?l-?əqtisaad ?l-Ɛaamm".* -- Under the circumstances I will accept your apology. *b?z-zuruuf ?l-haadra bəqbal ?əƐtizaarak.* -- She's traveling under an assumed name. *Ɛam ?tsaafer ?b-?əs?m məstaƐaar.* 4. *b-hasab˜ ..., b-muužeb˜ ...* Under the new law, taxes will be higher. *b-hasab ?l-qaanuun ?ž-ždiid ?d-daraayeb laha tkuun ?aƐla.* -- Under the contract, he cannot be fired without due notice. *b-hasab ?l-kontraat muu məmken sarfo mn ?l-xədme biduun ?əšƐaar waažeb.*

**Don't forget that you are under oath. *laa tənsa ?ənnak haalef yamiin.*

**Is everything under control? *kəll šii maaši mazbuut?*

**I was under the impression that he wanted to go. *kənt ?mhasseb ?ənno bəddo yruuh.*

underclothes – *?awaaƐi tahtaaniyye* (pl.), *?awaaƐi žuwwaaniyye* (pl.).

to **underestimate** – *st(a)xaff b-.* Don't underestimate his influence. *laa təstaxəff b-tuul baaƐo.*

underground – *taht˜ ?l-?ard.* The underground shelter will cost some two million pounds. *l-malža taht ?l-?ard bikallef hawaali malyooneen leera.*

to **underline** – 1. *hatt (ə hatat) xatt taht˜ ...* Underline the first two words. *hətt xatt taht ?l-kəl?mteen ?l-?awwalaaniyyaat.* 2. *šaddad Ɛala.* The prime minister underlined the importance of that project. *ra?iis ?l-wazaara šaddad Ɛala ?ahammiyyet hal-mašruuƐ.*

underneath – 1. *tah?t˜.* I found the ball underneath the bed. *laqeet ?t-taabe taht ?t-tax?t.* 2. *tah?t.* She wore a flimsy blouse and nothing underneath. *kaanet laabse bluuz šaffaaf w-maa fii šii tah?t.* -- Try to get at it from underneath. *haawel təlqə́ta mən tah?t.*

undershirt – *qamiis tahtaani* pl. *qəmsaan tahtaaniyye.*

underside – *səf?l.* The underside of the table is not painted. *səfl ?t-taawle muu mdahhan.*

to **understand** – *fəhem (a fəh?m//nfaham).* He doesn't understand Russian. *maa byəfham ruusi.* -- I can't understand how it happened. *maa fiini ?əfham kiif saaret.* -- Will you say that again? I didn't understand you. *fiik tƐiid yalli qəlto? maa fhəmt Ɛaleek.* -- My wife doesn't understand me. *marti maa btəfham Ɛaliyyi.* -- I understand from his letter that he likes his work. *fhəm?t mən maktuubo ?ənno haabeb šəġlo.* -- I understand that you are leaving tomorrow. *fhəm?t ?ənnak msaafer bəkra.* -- It's understood that you will stay with us. *mafhuum ?ənnak laha təbqa maƐna.*

understanding – *mətfaahem.* I explained the problem and he proved very understanding. *šarahtə́llo l-məš?kle w-təleƐ mətfaahem ?ktiir.*

understanding – 1. *?əttifaaq* pl. *-aat.* It was our understanding that you would let me know before you act. *kaan ?əttifaaqna ?ənnak txabbərni qab?l-ma taƐmel šii.* 2. *tafaahom.* Their organization tries to further better understanding among the nations of the world. *mnazzamə́ton Ɛam ?thaawel dziid mən hasn ?t-tafaahom been ?šƐuub ?l-Ɛaalam.*

to **undertake** – 1. *qaam (u qyaam) b-.* I hope you're not planning to undertake that trip alone. *mət?ammal ?ənnak maa-lak ?mfakker ?tquum b-har-rahle la-haalak.* 2. *tƐahhad b-, tkaffal b-.* The school undertakes to provide textbooks free of charge. *l-madrase btətƐahhad ?b-tazwiid kətb ?t-təllaab b-balaaš.*

undertaker – *daffaan* pl. *-iin.*

underwear – *?awaaƐi tahtaaniyye* (pl.), *?awaaƐi žuwwaaniyye* (pl.).

to **undo** – 1. *fakk (ə fakk//nfakk).* Help me undo this knot. *saaƐədni fəkk hal-Ɛəqde.* 2. *zaal (i zayalaan//nzaal).* You can't undo the wrong you've done. *maa fiik ?dziil ?š-šarr halli saaweeto ka?ənno maa saar.*

undoubtedly – *biduun šakk, laa šákk, biduun reeb.*

to **undress** – 1. *šallah.* I'll undress the children. *laha šalleh l-?wlaad.* 2. *šalah (a šal?h).* The bell rang just as I was undressing. *ž-žaras daqq b-daqiiqet-ma kənt Ɛam ?əšlah.*

uneasy – 1. *muu mərtaah, məddaayeq.* I feel uneasy in his company. *bəšƐor ?b-haali muu mərtaah b-rəf?qto.* 2. *məkreb.* I have an uneasy feeling that the project will be a flop. *Ɛandi šuƐuur məkreb ?ənno l-mašruuƐ raha yəfšal.*

unemployed – *Ɛaatel Ɛan ?l-Ɛamal, mbattel.* She's unemployed now. *hiyye Ɛaatle Ɛan ?l-Ɛamal hallaq.*

unemployment – *bataale.* Unemployment is rising in this country. *(nəsbet) ?l-bataale Ɛam ?dziid b-hal-?blaad.* -- How much do you have to pay for unemployment insurance? *qaddeeš laazem tədfaƐ ta?miin ḍədd ?l-bataale?*

uneven – 1. *taaleƐ naazel, muu məstə́wi*.* The floor in that room is rather uneven. *?ard hal-?uuda taalƐa naazle.* 2. *mətfaawet.* His works are of uneven quality. *?əntaažo mətfaawet b?ž-žuude.* 3. *muu mətsaawi.* The legs of the table seem to be uneven. *ražleen hat-taawle Ɛala-ma yəzhar muu mətsaawyiin.*

unexpected – 1. *muu məntə́zar.* Last night we had unexpected guests. *leelt ?mbaareh ?əžaana zəwwaar muu məntazariin.* 2. *muu b?l-həsbaan, muu məntə́zar.* Those were unexpected expenses. *hayy kaanet masariif muu b?l-həsbaan.*

unfortunate - 1. *muu mwaffaq.* That was an unfortunate idea. *hayy kaanet fəkra muu mwaffaqa.* 2. *yu?sáf-lo.* That's an unfortunate mistake! *hayy ġalṭa yu?sáf-la.*

unfortunately - *la-suu? ᵊl-ḥaẓẓ, maᶜ ᵊl-?asaf.* Unfortunately, I arrived late. *la-suu? ᵊl-ḥaẓẓ ?žiit mət?axxer.*

unfounded - *maa-lo ?asaas.* Your fears are unfounded. *maxaawfak maa-la ?asaas.*

ungrateful - *naaker˜ ᵊž-žamiil, muu mqadder ᵊl-maᶜruuf* I've never seen such an ungrateful person. *b-ḥayaati maa šəfᵊt zalame naaker ᵊž-žamiil matᵊl haad.*
**That was very ungrateful of you. *haada kaan nəkraan žamiil mənnak.*

unhappy - 1. *zaᶜlaan.* She's very unhappy about it. *hiyye zaᶜlaane ktiir mən haš-šii.* 2. *muu mwaffaq.* You made a somewhat unhappy choice. *tənqaaytak kaanet šwayye muu mwaffaqa.* 3. *muu mabṣuuṭ.* I'm unhappy in this environment. *?ana maa-li mabṣuuṭ b-hal-bii?a.* 4. *baa?es, mᶜattar.* He's leading an unhappy life. *ᶜaayeš ḥaayaat baa?se.*

unharmed - *saalem.* He escaped unharmed. *nafad saalem.*

unhealthy - *muu ṣəḥḥi*.* The climate here is unhealthy. *l-manaax hoon muu ṣəḥḥi.*

uniform - 1. *badle* (pl. *-aat*) *rasmiyye.* We got new uniforms. *?əžaana badlaat rasmiyye ždiide.* 2. *mətᶜaadel, ᶜala watiire waaḥde.* His scholastic achievements are of a uniform quality. *žuudet nataayžo d-diraasiyye mətᶜaadle.*

unimportant - 1. *muu mhəmm, maa-lo ?ahammiyye.* That's an unimportant question. *hayy mas?ale muu mhəmme* (or *maa-la ?ahammiyye*). 2. *taafeh.* He had an unimportant part in the play. *kan-lo door taafeh bᵊt-tamsiiliyye.*

union - 1. *?əttiḥaad* pl. *-aat.* In union there is strength. *l-q̈uwwe bᵊl-?əttiḥaad.* -- It belongs to the Union of Soviet Socialist Republics. *hiyye taabᶜa la-?əttiḥaad ᵊž-žamhuuriyyaat ᵊl-?əštiraakiyye s-sovyeetiyye.* 2. *naq̈aabe* pl. *-aat.* Do you belong to a union? *?ənte mənt̆əseb la-šii naq̈aabe?*

unique - *waḥiid mən nooᶜo, fariid, maa-lo masiil.* The statue is a unique piece of art. *t-təmsaal qəṭᶜa fanniyye waḥiide mən nooᶜa.* -- He's unique as a scholar. *huwwe ᶜaalem waḥiid mən nooᶜo.*

unit - *waḥde* pl. *-aat.* The book is divided into twelve units. *l-ᵊktaab mqassam la-ṭnaᶜšar waḥde.* -- He's been assigned to another unit. *ntaqal la-waḥde taanye.* -- The ohm is the unit of electrical resistance. *l-?oom huwwe waḥdet l-ᵊmqaawame l-kahrabaa?iyye.* -- The doctor gave him an injection of 20,000 units of penicillin. *d-doktoor ᶜaṭáa ?əbret banisiiliin ᶜəšriin ?alf waḥde.*
units - *?aaḥaad* (pl.). Numbers are divided into units, tens, hundreds, etc. *l-?aᶜdaad btənq̆əsem la-?aaḥaad, ᶜašaraat, mii?aat ?ila ?aaxírihi.*

to **unite** - 1. *žamaᶜ (a žamᵊᶜ//nžamaᶜ).* This marriage will unite the two families. *haz-zwaaž byəžmaᶜ ᵊl-ᶜeelteen.* 2. *ttaḥad.* We'll never get anywhere unless we unite. *maa byəṭlaᶜ ᵊb-?iidna šii ?abadan ?əlla ?iza ttaḥadna.*
united - *məttə́ḥed.* The entire country stands united behind the President. *l-ᵊblaad kəlla məttəḥde wara r-ra?iis* (or ** ... *ṣaff waaḥed wara r-ra?iis*). -- The United States of America. *l-wilaayaat ᵊl-məttəḥde l-?ameerkiyye.* -- The United Nations. *l-?əmam ᵊl-məttəḥde* (or *ᵊl-məttə́ḥide*).

unity - *waḥde, ?əttiḥaad.*

universal - 1. *ᶜaamm.* The project met with universal acceptance. *l-mašruuᶜ ṣaadaf ᵊq̈buul ᶜaamm.* 2. *ᶜaalami*.* Think how many people have tried to create a universal language. *ftəker b-ᶜadad ᵊn-naas halli ḥaawalu yaxᵊlqu luġa ᶜaalamiyye.*

university - 1. *žaamᶜa* pl. *-aat.* He studied at American University of Beirut. *daras b-žaaməᶜt beeruut ᵊl-?ameerkiyye.* 2. *žaamᶜi*.* A lot of university students live in my neighborhood. *fii təllaab žaamᶜiyyiin ᵊktiir saakniin ᵊb-ḥayyna.*

unjust - *ẓaalem.* That was an unjust decision. *haada kaan q̈araar ẓaalem.*

unless - *?əlla ?iza.* We're coming unless it rains. *laḥa nəži ?əlla ?iza nəzlet ᵊl-maṭar.*

unlike - *b-ᶜaks˜* ... Unlike my elder brother, I went to college. *b-ᶜaks ?axi l-ᵊkbiir ?ana daxalt ᵊž-žaamᶜa.*
**It's unlike anything I've seen before. *maa byəšbah ?ayy šii šəfto b-ḥayaati.*
**That's quite unlike him. *haada ġariib ᶜanno* or *haada muu mən ᶜaadto* (or *mən ṭabᶜo*).
**The two sisters are as unlike as they can be. *l-?əxteen byəxtəlfu ᶜan baᶜḍon kəll ᵊl-?əxtilaaf.*

unlikely - *muu məḥtə́mal, bᶜiid ᶜan ᵊl-ᶜaqᵊl.* That's very unlikely. *haada muu məḥtə́mal ?abadan.*

to **unload** - 1. *farraġ//tfarraġ, faḍḍa//tfaḍḍa.* They haven't unloaded the truck yet. *ləssa maa farraġu l-kamyoon.* -- Don't forget to unload the rifle. *laa tənsa ma tfarreġ ᵊl-baaruude.* 2. *nazzal// tnazzal, farraġ//tfarraġ, faḍḍa//tfaḍḍa.* Has the cargo been unloaded? *tnazzalet ᵊš-šaḥne?*

to **unlock** - *fataḥ (a fatᵊḥ˜//nfataḥ) qəfᵊl˜* ... Unlock the door! *ftaaḥ qəfl ᵊl-baab.*

unlucky - *manḥuus.* It was an unlucky coincidence. *kaanet ṣədfe manḥuuse.* -- I don't know why I'm so unlucky. *maa baᶜref leeš ḥaẓẓi manḥuus hal-qadd.*

unnecessary - *muu ḍaruuri*, muu laazem, maa-lo lzuum.* That's entirely unnecessary. *haš-šii muu ḍaruuri mnoob.*

to **unpack** - *faḍḍa//tfaḍḍa, farraġ//tfarraġ.* After you've unpacked the boxes throw them away. *baᶜᵊd-ma tfaḍḍi ᵊl-ᶜəlab kəbbon.*
**I am just unpacking my things. *?ana ᶜam ṭaaleᶜ ᵊġraaḍi mn ᵊš-šanta* (or *mn ᵊṣ-ṣanduuq* or *mn ᵊs-saḥḥaara*, etc.).

to **untie** - *fakk (ə fakk//nfakk).* Can you untie this knot for me? *fiik ᵊtfəkk-ə́lli hal-ᶜəqde?* -- Wait till I untie the package. *stanna ḥatta fəkk ᵊl-baakeet.* -- My shoe is untied. *fardet ṣabbaaṭi mafkuuke.*

until - 1. *la-.* Wait until tomorrow. *stanna la-bəkra.* -- He will not give us his answer until next week. *maa byaᶜṭiina žawaabo ləž-žəmᶜa ž-žaaye.* -- This store will be closed until further notice. *hal-maxzan ᵊmsakkar la-?əšᶜaar ?aaxar.* 2. *la-, la-ḥatta.* We waited in the car until she came back. *stanneena bᵊs-sayyaara la-rəžᶜet.*

unusual - 1. *muu ma?luuf, ġeer ?əᶜtiyaadi*.* This is an unusual name. *haada ?əsᵊm muu ma?luuf.* 2. *naader.* There are a number of unusual paintings on display at the gallery. *fii ᶜəddet loohaat naadra maᶜruuḍa bᵊl-maᶜraḍ.* 3. *šaaẓẓ, ġariib.* His unusual behavior at the party has become the talk of the town. *taṣarrfo š-šaaẓẓ bᵊl-ḥafle ṣaar ḥadiis ᵊl-balad kəlla.*

to **unveil** - *kašaf (o kašᵊf˜//nkašaf) ᵊs-sitaar ᶜan, ?azaaḥ ᵊs-sitaar ᶜan.* The President himself unveiled the monument. *r-ra?iis b-zaato kašaf ᵊs-sitaar ᶜan ᵊn-naṣᵊb.*

unwise - *muu ḥakiim.* I think it was an unwise decision. *bẓənn ?ənno kaan q̈araar muu ḥakiim.*
**That was very unwise on your part. *taṣarrfak maa kaan fii ḥəkme ?abadan.*

up - 1. *fooq.* I'm up here. *?ana hoon fooq.* -- What's he doing up there? *šuu ᶜam yaᶜmel ᵊhniik fooq?* 2. *ṭaaleᶜ.* You can get a nice room for fifty pounds and up. *fiik ᵊtlaaqi ?uuḍa mniiḥa mən xamsiin leera w-ṭaaleᶜ.* -- The town is located twenty miles up the river. *l-balad waaqᶜa ᶜəšriin miil ṭaaleᶜ mn ᵊn-nahᵊr.*
**Is he up yet? *faaq wəlla ləssa?*
**He's up and around again. *qaam ᶜala rəžlée l-ḥamdəlla w-rəžeᶜ yəṭfattal.*
**What's up? *šuu fii maa fii?*
**Your time is up. *xalaṣ waqtak.*
**Prices are up. *l-?asᶜaar ᵊrtafᶜet.*
**His name is up for election. *?əsmo beenaat l-ᵊmraššaḥiin ləl-?əntixaabaat.*
**She's up against severe criticism. *ᶜam ᵊtwaažeh naq̈ᵊd laazeᶜ.*
**Hands up! *rfaaᶜ ?ideek!*
**Chin up! *šədd ḥeelak!*
**Shut up! *xraas!*
**They're hard up. *məndaaqiin hənne.*
**We all have our ups and downs. (in one's luck) *yoom ?əlak yoom ᶜaleek;* (in one's work, mood, etc.) *kəllna ?əlna ?iyyaam raayqa w-?iyyaam ᶜəkre.*
up to - 1. *la-, la-ḥadd˜* ... Up to now he hasn't answered. *la-hallaq maa žaawab.* -- They're paying salaries up to 8,000 pounds per year. *ᶜam yədfaᶜu maᶜaašaat la-ḥadd tmənt aalaaf leera bᵊs-səne.* -- Because of the snowstorm trains were up to two hours late. *b-sabab ᵊl-ᶜaaṣfe t-talžiyye t?axxaret ᵊt-treenaat la-ḥadd saaᶜteen.* -- During the flood the water rose up to here. *waqt ᵊl-fayaḍaan ᵊl-mayy wəṣlet la-ḥadd hoon.* 2. *la-.* The decision is up to you. *l-q̈araar ?əlak (?ənte).* -- If it were up to him ... *law kaanet ᵊl-mas?ale ᶜaa?ide ?əlo* ... -- It's up to her. *l-qool ?əla.*
**What's he up to this time? *šuu ṭaaleᶜ ᵊb-raaso hal-marra?*
**I'm not quite up to par today. *?ana muu ᶜala baᶜḍi l-yoom.*

up and down - **1.** *sərri mərri.* He was walking up and down the room. *kaan maaši sərri mərri bᵊl-ʔuuḍa.* **2.** *ṭaaleε naazel.* Stop running up and down those stairs! *ḥaažtak ṭaaleε naazel εala had-daraž!* -- When the plane hit the storm it began to pitch up and down. *lamma ṭ-ṭayyaara waažahet ᵊl-εaaṣfe ṣaaret təlεab ṭaalεa naazle.* -- The man kept moving the lantern up and down. *z-zalame tamm ylawweḥ bᵊl-faanuus ṭaaleε naazel.* **3.** *mən fooq la-taḥᵊt.* He looked her up and down. *ṭṭallaε εaleeha mən fooq la-taḥᵊt.*

uphill - **1.** *bᵊṭ-ṭalεa, bᵊṭ-ṭluuε.* Going uphill, the engine knocks sometimes. *bᵊṭ-ṭalεa, s-sayyaara bətqaṭṭeš.* **2.** *ṭluuε* (invar.). The road is uphill from here to the next village. *ṭ-ṭariiq ṭluuε mən hoon ləḍ-ḍeeεa ž-žaaye.*

**At this stage of the project the going is all uphill. *b-hal-marḥale mn ᵊl-mašruuε ᵊš-šəġᵊl kəllo ṣaεᵊb.*

upkeep - *ṣiyaane.* The upkeep on my car is too expensive. *ṣiyaanet sayyaarti ġaalye ktiir.*

upon - see **on.**

upper - **1.** *fooqaani*.* The fire started on one of the upper floors. *l-ḥariiqa badet ᵊb-ṭaabeq ᵊmn ᵊṭ-ṭawaabeq ᵊl-fooqaaniyye.* -- Write the page number in the upper right-hand corner. *ḥəṭṭ nəmret ᵊṣ-ṣafḥa bᵊl-qərne l-fooqaaniyye εal-yamiin.* **2.** *ʔaεla* f. *εəlya.* They own quite a lot of land in the upper Jezirah. *byəmᵊlku ʔaraaḍi ktiir bᵊž-žaziire l-εəlya.* -- I've never been to the upper Jordan valley. *b-ḥayaati maa zərt ᵊl-manṭiqa l-εəlya mən waadi l-ʔərdon.*

**Both their families belong to the upper class of the city. *εeelteenon tneenaaton mən ṭabqet ᵊl-ʔakaaber bᵊl-madiine.*

Upper Egypt - *ṣ-ṣaεiid, l-wažh ᵊl-qəbli.*

to **uproot** - **1.** *qalaε (a qalᵊε//nqalaε).* The storm uprooted several trees. *l-εaaṣfe qalεet εəddet ʔašžaar.* **2.** *staʔṣal.* The new regime has vowed to uproot corruption and favoritism. *l-ᵊḥkuume ž-ždiide tεahhadet ᵊb-ʔəstəʔṣaal ᵊr-rašwe wᵊl-maḥsuubiyye.*

upset - *məḍṭə́reb.* He was all upset. *kaan məḍṭə́reb ᵊktiir.*

**I have an upset stomach. *fii maεi suuʔ haḍᵊm.*

to upset - **1.** *qalab (e qalᵊb//nqalab).* Be careful or you'll upset the pitcher. *ʔəṣḥa, baεdeen ᵊbtəqleb l-ʔəbriiq.* -- You're upsetting the boat. *laḥa təqleb ᵊš-šaxtuura.* -- The arms shipments are apt to upset the balance of power. *šaḥnaat ᵊl-ʔasliḥa muu bεiid ʔənno təqleb tawaazon ᵊl-ʔəwa.* **2.** *farkas, farkaš.* The rain upset our plans. *l-maṭar farkaset xəṭaṭna.* **3.** *zaεaž (e zaεaž//nzaεaž).* Nothing ever upsets him. *maa fii šii bᵊd-dənye byəzᵊεžo.*

upside down - *εal-maqluub, fooqaani taḥtaani.* That picture is upside down. *haṣ-ṣuura maḥṭuuṭa εal-maqluub.*

to turn upside down - *qalab (e qalᵊb//nqalab) fooqaani taḥtaani.* They turned the whole house upside down. *qalabu l-beet kəllo fooqaani taḥtaani.*

upstairs - **1.** *fooq.* She's upstairs with her mother. *hiyye fooq maε ʔəmma.* **2.** *la-fooq.* Go upstairs and get it. *ṭlaaε la-fooq žiiba.* **3.** *fooqaani*.* The upstairs apartment is vacant. *l-ʔabarṭmaan ᵊl-fooqaani faaḍi.*

up-to-date - *εala ʔaaxer mooḍa.* She has an up-to-date kitchen. *εanda maṭbax εala ʔaaxer mooḍa.*

**I'm not up-to-date on that matter. *ʔana maa-li məṭṭə́leε εala ʔaaxer taṭawwuraat hal-qaḍiyye.*

uranium - *ʔoranyoom.*

urge - *rəġbe.* I felt the urge to tell him what I thought of him. *šaεart ᵊb-rəġbe* (or ***ktiir ʔəža εala baali*) *qəl-lo šuu raʔyi fii.*

to urge - *εaṣṣaḍ εala.* She urged us to stay a little longer. *εaṣṣaḍet εaleena nəbqa kamaan šwayye.* -- If you urge her a bit, she'll do it. *ʔiza εaṣṣaḍt εaleeha šwayye btaεmə́la.*

urgency - *εažale.* Let me remind you of the urgency of this matter. *xalliini zakkrak ᵊb-εažalet hal-qaḍiyye.*

urgent - *məstaεžal.* I have an urgent request. *εandi ṭalab məstaεžal.* -- Is it very urgent? *haš-šii ktiir məstaεžal?*

urinary bladder - *masaane* pl. *-aat.*

to **urinate** - *bawwal.*

urine - *bool.*

urologist - *ṭabiib˜* (pl. *ʔaṭəbba˜*) *ʔamraaḍ booliyye.*

urology - *εəlm˜ ᵊl-ʔamraaḍ ᵊl-booliyye.*

use - **1.** *ʔəstəεmaal.* The use of strong detergents may hurt the fabric. *ʔəstəεmaal l-ᵊmnaḍḍfaat ᵊl-qawiyye məmken ᵊḍḍərr l-ᵊqmaaš.* **2.** *faayde.* It's no use hurrying. *l-εažale maa fiiha faayde.* -- What's the use of arguing? *šuu l-faayde mn ᵊl-ʔaxd wᵊr-radd?* -- It's no use, we've got to do it. *maa fii faayde* (or ***maa fii samara*), *mažbuuriin naεmə́la.*

**I have no use for two. *tneen maa byəlzamuuni.*

**He lost the use of his arm in the accident. *maa qəder yəstaεmel ʔiido baεd ᵊl-ʔaksiḍaan.*

**Have you any use for an old typewriter? *btənfaεak šii ʔaale kaatbe εatiiqa?*

**She has the use of the car while they're gone. *btəqder təstaεmel ᵊs-sayyaara b-ᵊġyaabə́ton.*

**I have no use for him. *maa byəεžəbni.*

in use - *məstaεmal.* That's no longer in use. *haada maa εaad məstaεmal.*

to be of use to - *faad (i ʔifaade, faayde), nafaε (a nafᵊε).* Will that information be of any use to you? *hal-maεluumaat bətfiidak šii?*

to make use of - **1.** *staεmal.* Don't they make any use of the enormous water resources? *maa byəstaεᵊmlu maṣaader ᵊl-miyaah ᵊl-haaʔile ʔabadan?* -- Feel free to make use of our excellent library. *xood ḥərriitak w-ᵊstaεmel maktabətna l-məmtaaze.* **2.** *staġall, stafaad mən.* Make good use of your summer vacation. *staġəll ʔižaaztak ᵊṣ-ṣeefiyye mniiḥ.* **3.** *ntahaz, staġall, stafaad mən.* He made good use of the opportunity. *ntahaz ᵊl-fərṣa mniiḥ.*

**Please don't make any use of this information. *bətražžaak laa təfši* (or *tbuuḥ ᵊb-*) *hal-maεluumaat.*

to put to good use - *stasmar ᵊmniiḥ.* One day, we'll put the money to good use. *ləssa byəži yoom mnəstasmer fii l-maṣaari mniiḥ.*

to use - *staεmal.* We'll use this room as a bedroom. *mnəstaεmel hal-ʔuuḍa ʔuuḍet noom.* -- What tooth paste do you use? *šuu maεžuun ᵊs-snaan yalli btəstaεᵊmlo?*

to use up - *stahlak, stanfad.* We have used up all the soap we had in the house. *stahlakna kəll ᵊṣ-ṣaabuun halli bᵊl-beet.* -- I've used up all my energy. *stahlakᵊt kəll našaaṭi.*

**I have used up all my money. *ṣaraft kəll maṣariyyi.*

**We've used up all our cigarettes. *daxxanna kəll sigaraatna.*

I used to, we used to, etc. - *kənt, kənna,* etc. + imperf. without *b-*. I used to live here. *kənt ʔəskon hoon.* -- We used to go to the movies very often. *kənna nruuḥ εas-siinama ktiir.* -- He used to eat in a restaurant before he was married. *kaan yaakol bᵊl-maṭεam qabᵊl-ma yədžawwaz.*

used to - *mətεawwed εala, məεtaad εala.* I'm not used to hard work. *ʔana maa-li mətεawwed εaš-šəġl ᵊl-məžhed.* -- She's used to getting up at seven o'clock. *hiyye mətεawwde tfiiq ᵊs-saaεa sabεa.*

to get used to - **1.** *tεawwad εala, εtaad εala.* I can't get used to daylight-saving time. *maa-li εam ʔəqder ʔətεawwad εat-tawqiit ᵊṣ-ṣeefi.* **2.** *εawwad εala.* I've got my children used to putting their things away. *εawwadt ᵊwlaadi yḍəbbu ġraaḍon.*

useful - *mufiid, naafeε.* I've found this book very useful. *šəft hal-ᵊktaab ᵊktiir mufiid.*

**She makes herself useful around the house. *bəthəbb ᵊtsaaεed ᵊb-šəġl ᵊl-beet.*

usefulness - *nafᵊε, manfaεa.*

useless - **1.** *maa fii faayde, maa fii samara.* It's useless to try to convince him. *maa fii faayde džarreb təqᵊnεo.* **2.** *maa-lo faayde.* It's a useless book. *ktaab maa-lo faayde.* -- This map is useless to me. *hal-xariiṭa maa-la faayde ʔəli* or ***hal-xariiṭa maa btənfaεni ʔabadan.* -- I feel completely useless around here. *ḥaases kaʔənno maa-li faayde hoon.*

usher - *daliil* f. *daliile* pl. *ʔadəllaaʔ.* The usher will show you to your seats. *d-daliil raḥa yaaxədkon la-karasiikon.*

to usher - *dall (ə dall//ndall).* We were ushered to our seats. *ndalleena la-maḥallaatna.*

usual - *εaadi*, ʔəεtiyaadi*.* Our usual hours are from 8 to 3. *saaεaatna l-εaadiyye mn ᵊt-tmaane lət-tlaate.* -- We'll meet at the usual place. *mnəžtə́meε bᵊl-maḥall ᵊl-ʔəεtiyaadi.*

as usual - *mətl ᵊl-εaade, ka-l-εaade.* It's raining, as usual. *naazle maṭar, mətl ᵊl-εaade.*

usually - *εaadatan.* I usually visit them twice a week. *εaadatan bzuuron marrteen bᵊž-žəmεa.*

usurer - *fawaayzi* pl. *-iyye.*

usury - *faayez.*

uterus - *raḥᵊm* pl. *ʔarḥaam.*

utilities: The rent is 150 pounds, including utilities. *l-ᵓəžra miyye w-xamsiin leera daaxel fiiha l-kahraba wᵊl-mayy wᵊl-ġaaz.*
public utilities - *maraafeq̈ ɛaamme.*
utmost - *ġaayet˜* ... The matter is of the utmost importance. *l-masᵓale hiyye b-ġaayet ᵊl-ᵓahammiyye.*
to do one's utmost - *ɛəmel ġaayet˜ žahdo.* We did our utmost. *ɛməlna ġaayet žahᵊdna.*

utter - *ɛat-tamaam, ɛal-maẓbuuṭ, bᵊl-marra.* Things are in a state of utter confusion in our office. *l-ᵓawḍaaɛ ᵊb-maktabna b-ḥaalet xarbaṭa ɛat-tamaam.*
to utter - *lafaẓ (o lafᵊẓ//ltafaẓ), tlaffaẓ.* I couldn't utter a single word. *maa qdərᵊt ᵓəlfoẓ w-laa kəlme.*
utterly - *bᵊl-marra, ɛat-tamaam, ɛal-maẓbuuṭ.* I was utterly disappointed in him. *xayydb-li ᵓamali bᵊl-marra.*

V

vacancy - **1.** *šaaġer* pl. *šawaaġer, maḥall faaḍi* pl. *maḥallaat faaḍye.* We'll let you know when we have a vacancy. *mnaɛṭiik xabar waqᵊt biṣiir ɛanna šaaġer.* **2.** *maḥall faaḍi, ᵓuuḍa* (pl. *ᵓuwaḍ*) *faaḍye.* The hotel across the street doesn't have any more vacancies. *l-ᵓoteel halli qaaṭeɛ ᵊš-šaareɛ maa ɛaad fii maḥall faaḍi.*
vacant - **1.** *faaḍi.* The apartment has been vacant for a week. *l-ᵓabarṭmaan ṣar-lo faaḍi žəmɛa.* -- Next to our house there is still a vacant lot. *ləssa fii šaqfet ᵓarḍ faaḍye žamb beetna.* **2.** *šaaġer, faaḍi.* We have no position vacant at the moment. *maa fii ɛanna waẓiife šaaġra bᵊl-waqt ᵊl-ḥaaḍer.*
to **vacate** - *faḍḍa, ᵓaxla.* When are you going to vacate the apartment? *ᵓeemta laḥa tfaḍḍi l-ᵓabarṭmaan?*
vacation - **1.** *ɛəṭle* pl. *ɛəṭal, fərṣa* pl. *fəraṣ.* The children are looking forward to their summer vacation. *l-ᵊwlaad mətšawwqiin ᵊktiir ləl-ɛəṭle ṣ-ṣeefiyye.* **2.** *ᵓižaaze* pl. *-aat, ɛəṭle* pl. *ɛəṭal, maᵓzuuniyye* pl. *-aat.* She's on vacation. *hiyye bᵊl-ᵓižaaze* or *hiyye ᵓaaxde ɛəṭle* (or *maᵓzuuniyye*) or ***hiyye mužaaze* (or *maᵓzuune*).
to **vaccinate** - *ṭaɛɛam//ṭṭaɛɛam, laq̈q̈aḥ//tlaq̈q̈aḥ.* The school requires that all children be vaccinated. *l-madrase btəṭṭallab ᵓənno kəll l-ᵊwlaad yəṭṭaɛɛamu.*
vaccination - *taṭɛiim* pl. *-aat, talq̈iiḥ* pl. *-aat.*
vaccine - *ṭəɛᵊm* pl. *ṭɛuume, liq̈aaḥ* pl. *-aat.*
vacuum - *faraaġ.*
vacuum cleaner - *məkᵊnse* (pl. *makaanes*) *ɛal-kahraba.*
vagabond - *mətšarred* pl. *-iin.*
vagrancy - *tašarrod.*
vagrant - *mətšarred.*
vague - *mubham, məbham.* He gave me a vague answer. *ɛaṭaani žawaab mubham.*
vaguely - *b-ᵓəbhaam.* He talked to me vaguely about some plans of his. *ḥakaa-li b-ᵓəbhaam ɛan baɛᵊḍ xaṭaṭo.*
**I remember him vaguely. *bᵊl-kaad bədzakkaro.*
vain - **1.** *qaabeḍ ḥaalo, šaayef ḥaalo, maġruur.* She's terribly vain. *faẓaaɛa šuu qaabḍa ḥaala.* **2.** *faašel.* He made a vain attempt to hide his ignorance. *ḥaawal ᵊmḥaawale faašle la-yxabbi žahlo.*
in vain - *ɛabas.* The doctor tried in vain to save the boy's life. *d-doktoor ḥaawal ɛabas yxalleṣ ḥayaat ᵊṣ-ṣabi.*
to be in vain - *raaḥ suda, raaḥ ɛabas, raaḥ ɛal-faaḍi.* All our efforts were in vain. *kəll žuhuudna raaḥet suda.*
valid - **1.** *ṣaaleḥ.* Your argument isn't valid. *ḥəžžətak muu ṣaalḥa.* **2.** *maɛmuul fii, ṣaaleḥ.* Your visa isn't valid any more. *l-viiza tabaɛak maa ɛaad maɛmuul fiiha* (or *maa ɛaadet ṣaalḥa*).
validity - **1.** *ṣaḥḥa.* I doubt the validity of his claim. *bšəkk ᵊb-ṣaḥḥet zaɛmo.* **2.** *ɛamal b-.* The validity of the passport expires after six months. *l-ɛamal bᵊl-basboor byəntəhi baɛᵊd sətt əšhor.*
valley - *waadi* pl. *wədyaan.*
valuable - **1.** *tamiin, mətmen.* That's a valuable ring. *haada xaatem tamiin.* **2.** *q̈ayyem.* We thank you for your valuable suggestions. *mnəšᵊkrak ɛala ᵓəq̈tiraaḥaatak ᵊl-q̈ayyme.*
valuables - *ġraad tamiine* (pl.), (jewelry) *mžawharaat* (pl.). You'd better lock your valuables in the safe. *ᵓafḍál-lak təḥfaẓ ᵊġraadak ᵊt-tamiine b-sanduuq ᵊl-ḥadiid.*
value - *qiime* pl. *qiyam.* This merchandise has no value. *hal-ᵊbḍaaɛa maa-la qiime.* -- The information is of no value to me. *hal-maɛluumaat maa-la qiime bᵊn-nəsbe ᵓəli.* -- I don't attach any value to his opinions. *maa bɛalleq ᵓayy qiime la-ᵓaaraaᵓo.*
to value - **1.** *qaddar.* I value his friendship very highly. *bqadder sadaaqto kəll ᵊt-taqdiir.* **2.** *qaddar, xamman.* What do you value your house at? *qaddeeš bətqadder beetak?*
valve - *ṣubaab* pl. *-aat, ṣabbaab* pl. *-aat.*
vanilla - *vaneella.*
to **vanish** - **1.** *xtafa.* My pencil has vanished. *qalami xtafa.* **2.** *zaal (u zawaal), xtafa.* After three days, the symptoms vanished. *baɛᵊd tlətt iyyaam zaalet ᵊl-ᵓaɛraaḍ.*
vanity - *šoofet˜ ḥaal, ġruur.* His vanity is almost proverbial. *šoofet ḥaalo bətkaad ᵊtkuun maḍrab ᵊl-masal.*
vapor - *buxaar* pl. *-aat.*
variable - **1.** *mətfaawet.* We can't hold the prices steady because our costs are variable. *maa fiina nḥaafeẓ ɛala sabaat ᵊl-ᵓasɛaar la-ᵓənno takaliifna mətfaawte.* -- Projects of this sort usually meet with variable success. *l-mašariiɛ mən haš-šəkᵊl ɛaadatan bətlaaqi nažaaḥ mətfaawet.* **2.** *mətqalleb.* That part of the country has quite variable weather. *han-naaḥye mən l-ᵊblaad žawwa šwayye mətqalleb.*
variety - **1.** *taškiile* pl. *-aat.* We have a wide variety of shirts. *ɛanna taškiilet qəmṣaan ᵊkbiire.* **2.** *nooɛ* pl. *ᵓanwaaɛ, šəkᵊl* pl. *ᵓaškaal.* How many varieties of apples grow in your orchard? *kam nooɛ mn ᵊt-təffaaḥ fii b-bəstaanak?*
**Their discussion covered a wide variety of subjects. *baḥson tnaawal mawaḍiiɛ ᵊktiire ɛala ᵓəxtilaaf ᵓanwaaɛa.*
for the sake of variety - *taġyiir˜ šəkᵊl.* For the sake of variety let's stay at home. *xalliina nəbqa bᵊl-beet taġyiir šəkᵊl.*
various - **1.** *mətnawweɛ.* I have various reasons. *ɛandi ᵓasbaab mətnawwɛa.* **2.** *məxtəlef.* The table was decorated with various kinds of flowers. *ṭ-ṭaawle kaanet ᵊmzawwaqa b-ᵓanwaaɛ məxtəlfe mn ᵊz-zhuur.*
varnish - *varniiš.* How long does it take the varnish to dry? *qaddeeš byəthammal ᵊl-varniiš la-yənšaf?*
to varnish - *dahan (a dahᵊn//ndahan)* ... *bᵊl-varniiš.* We have just varnished the floor. *hallaq ləssa dahanna l-ᵓarḍ bᵊl-varniiš.*
to **vary** - *xtalaf.* The prices vary from place to place. *l-ᵓasɛaar btəxtəlef been ᵊl-maḥall wᵊt-taani.* -- The color varies slightly from that of the car we had before. *l-loon byəxtəlef šwayye ɛan loon ᵊs-sayyaara halli kaanet ɛanna mən qabᵊl.*
varied - *mətnawweɛ.*
vase - *vaaz* pl. *-aat, mazhariyye* pl. *-aat.*
vaseline - *vaazliin, wazaliin.*
veal - *laḥᵊm˜ ɛəžᵊl.*
vegetable - **1.** *xəḍra* pl. *xəḍrawaat* and *xəḍar.* We need fresh vegetables. *laazəmna xəḍar taaza.* -- We usually serve a vegetable dish with the meat. *ɛaadatan mənqaddem ṣaḥᵊn xəḍra maɛ ᵊl-laḥme.* **2.** *nabaati*.* My mother cooks mostly with vegetable shortening. *ᵓaktar ᵊl-ᵓawqaat maama btəṭbox ᵊb-samne nabaatiyye.*
veil - **1.** (covering the whole head) *ġaṭa* pl. *ᵓəġᵊṭye, mandiil* pl. *manadiil.* **2.** (leaving eyes exposed) *ltaam* pl. *-aat.* **3.** (diaphanous, worn by city women) *boonée* pl. *booneeyaat.*
to veil oneself - *tḥažžab, tġaṭṭa, tlattam* (cf. **veil**).
vein - **1.** *wariid* pl. *ᵓawride.* The serum has to be injected into the vein. *l-maṣᵊl laazem yənɛaṭa bᵊl-wariid.* **2.** *ɛərᵊq* pl. *ɛruuq.* You can clearly see the veins of the leaf. *fiik ᵊtšuuf b-ᵊwḍuuḥ ɛruuq ᵊl-waraqa.*
velvet - *məxmal.*
venereal disease - *maraḍ tanaasuli* pl. *ᵓamraaḍ tanaasuliyye.*

Venetian - *bəndoqi**. The painter belongs to the Venetian school. *r-rassaam mn ᵊl-mazhab ᵊl-bəndoqi.*
vengeance - *ʔəntiqaam.*
Venice - *l-bəndoqiyye, vəniisya.*
vent - *mahwa* pl. *mahaawi, ṭaaqet˜* (pl. *-aat˜*) *hawa.* Open the vent! *ftaaḥ ᵊl-mahwa!*
**She gave vent to her anger. *faššet xəlqa.*
ventilation - *təhwaaye.*
ventilator - *marwaḥa* pl. *maraaweḥ.*
venture - *mžaazafe* pl. *-aat, mxaaṭara* pl. *-aat.* It was a dangerous venture. *kaanet ᵊmžaazafe xəṭra.*
to venture - *starža, džaasar, džarraʔ.* I wouldn't venture to go out in this weather. *ʔana maa bəstarži ʔəṭlaε b-heek ṭaqᵊṣ.* -- I was the only one who ventured out on the ice. *kənt ʔana waḥdi bass halli džaasar yəṭlaε εaž-žaliid.*
**Nothing ventured, nothing gained. *bala mžaazafe maa fii rəbᵊḥ.*
Venus - **1.** (goddess) *vinuus.* **2.** (planet) *z-zahra.*
veranda - *varanda* and *baranda* pl. *-aat, balkoon* pl. *-aat* and *balakiin.*
verb - *fəεᵊl* pl. *ʔafεaal.*
verbal - **1.** *šafahi**. We made a verbal agreement. *saaweena ʔəttifaaq šafahi.* **2.** *fəεli**. Arabic distinguishes verbal sentences and nominal sentences. *l-luġa l-εarabiyye bətmayyez been ᵊž-žəmle l-fəεliyye wᵊl-ʔəsmiyye.*
verdict - *qaraar* pl. *-aat.* Everybody expects the jury to bring in a verdict of ''not guilty''. *l-kəll εam yətwaqqaε ʔənno l-ᵊmḥallafiin laha yṭaalεu qaraar "barii".*
verdigris - *žənzaar.*
on the **verge of** - *εala wašak˜* ... She's on the verge of a breakdown. *hiyye εala wašak ʔənhiyaar εaṣabi.* -- I was on the verge of telling him. *kənt εala wašak qəl-lo* or **maa ṣafi šii ʔəlla qəl-lo.*
to verge on - *qəreb (a ə) la-.* His behavior verges on madness. *taṣarrfo byəqrab ləž-žnaan.*
to **verify** - **1.** *tḥaqqaq mən, tsabbat mən.* Have someone verify these figures. *xalli ḥada yətḥaqqaq mən hal-ʔarqaam.* **2.** *sabbat, ḥaqqaq.* That only verifies our previous theory. *haada bass bisabbet naẓariitna s-saabqa.*
vermicelli - *šεeeriyye.*
vermouth - *varmuut.*
verse - **1.** *byaat˜ šəεᵊr* (pl.). The play is written in verse. *t-tamsiiliyye manẓuume b-byaat šəεᵊr.* **2.** *beet* pl. *byaat.* Let's sing only the first verse. *xalliina nġanni l-beet ᵊl-ʔawwal bass.*
version - **1.** *riwaaye* pl. *-aat.* I heard another version. *sməεt riwaaye ġeera.* **2.** *naṣṣ* pl. *nṣuuṣ.* This edition differs considerably from the original version. *haṭ-ṭabεa btəxtəlef la-daraže mniiha εan ᵊn-naṣṣ ᵊl-ʔaṣli.*
versus - *ḍədd.*
vertebra - *faqra* pl. *-aat.*
vertebral column - *εaamuud faqari* pl. *εawamiid faqariyye.*
vertical - *εaamuudi**.
very - **1.** *ktiir.* The bank is not very far from here. *l-baŋk muu bεiid ᵊktiir mən hoon.* -- We're very much satisfied. *nəḥna ktiir raḍyaaniin.* **2.** *mžarrad˜* ... The very thought of that is unpleasant to me. *mžarrad ᵊt-tafkiir b-haš-šii byəzεəžni.* **3.** *b-εeen-* + pron. suff., *b-zaat-* + pron. suff. He is the very man you want. *huwwe r-rəžžaal yalli bəddak-yda b-εeeno.* **4.** (doubled demonstrative:) I have to see him this very evening. *laazem šuufo hal-leele hayy.* -- I haven't been able to learn the truth to this very day. *maa ṭəleε b-ʔiidi ʔaεref ᵊl-ḥaqiiqa la-han-nhaar haada.*
**She left the very next day. *saafaret baεᵊd b-ᵊnhaar waaḥed.*
**He came the very next morning. *ʔəža baεd ᵊb-yoom εala bəkra.*
**This cloth is of the very best quality. *haš-šuux ʔaḥsan mən ṣənfo maa fii.*
vessel - *markab* pl. *maraakeb, safiine* pl. *səfon.* Several large vessels were docked in the harbor. *kaan fii εəddet maraakeb ᵊkbiire raabṭa bᵊl-marfaʔ.*
blood vessel - *εərᵊq˜* (pl. *εruuq˜*) *damm.*
vest - *ṣədriyye* pl. *ṣadaari.*
veterinarian - (*ṭabiib*) *bayṭari* pl. (*ʔaṭəbba*) *bayaaṭra.*
veterinary science - (*εəlm˜ ᵊl-*) *bayṭara.*
veto - **1.** *ḥaqq˜ ᵊl-viito.* The chairman has the veto. *r-raʔiis ʔəlo ḥaqq ᵊl-viito.* **2.** *viito* pl. *viitoyaat.* That's the second veto he brought in against the proposal. *haada l-viito t-taani halli ṭəleε fii ḍədd ᵊl-ʔəqtiraaḥ.*
to veto - *staεmal ḥaqq ᵊl-viito ḍədd* ... Russia was the only country to veto the proposed measure. *ruusya kaanet ᵊd-doole l-waḥiide yalli staεmalet ḥaqq ᵊl-viito ḍədd ᵊt-tadbiir ᵊl-məqtáraḥ.*
vibration - *ʔəhtizaaz, ʔərtižaaž.*
vice - *raziile* pl. *razaaʔel.* Prostitution is a common vice in those port cities. *d-daεaara raziile šaayεa b-hal-mawaani.*
vice- - *naaʔeb˜* pl. *nuwwaab˜*, e.g., vice-consul *naaʔeb˜ qənṣol* pl. *nuwwaab˜ qanaaṣel,* vice-president *naaʔeb˜ raʔiis* pl. *nuwwaab˜ raʔiis* (or *rəʔasa* respectively).
vicinity - *žiwaar, qərᵊb.* There are good restaurants in the vicinity of the railroad station. *fii maṭaaεem mniiḥa b-žiwaar ᵊmḥaṭṭet səkket ᵊl-ḥadiid.*
vicious - *šəres.* That dog is vicious. *hal-kalb šəres.* -- He has a vicious temper. *ṭabεo šəres.*
**It's a vicious circle. *hayy ḥalaqa məfraġa.*
victim - *ḍaḥiyye* pl. *ḍaḥaaya.* He was the victim of a plot. *kaan ḍaḥiyyet ᵊmʔaamara.*
victor - *ġaaleb* pl. *-iin, manṣuur* pl. *-iin, məntəṣer* pl. *-iin.*
victorious - *ẓaafer, mẓaffar.* Our victorious armies have entered the enemy's capital. *žyuušna ẓ-ẓaafra daxlet εaaṣəmt ᵊl-εaduww.*
victory - *naṣᵊr, ẓafar, ʔəntiṣaar* pl. *-aat.*
Vienna - *vyanna.*
view - **1.** *manẓar* pl. *manaaẓer, naẓaara.* You have a nice view from here. *εandak manẓar ᵊktiir ḥəlu mən hoon.* **2.** *raʔi* pl. *ʔaraaʔ.* Our views differ. *ʔaraaʔna btəxtəlef.* -- Do you know anything about his political views? *btaεref ʔayy šii εan ʔaraaʔo s-siyaasiyye?*
point of view - *wəžhet˜* (pl. *-aat˜*) *naẓar.* From my point of view, he was wrong. *b-wəžhet naẓari kaan ᵊl-ḥaqq εalée.*
in view of - *bᵊn-naẓar la-.* In view of the tense situation, they were advised not to enter the country. *bᵊn-naẓar la-tawattor ᵊl-ḥaale naṣaḥuuhon maa yfuutu εal-ᵊblaad.*
in plain view - *baayen mətᵊl εeen ᵊš-šamᵊs, ẓaaher mətl ᵊl-kaff.* The enemy positions were in plain view of our observation posts. *maraakez ᵊl-εaduww kaanet baayne mətᵊl εeen ᵊš-šamᵊs qəddaam nəqaṭ l-ᵊmraaqabe tabaεna.*
on view - *maεruuḍ ləl-fərže.* Pictures are on view in the lobby of the theater. *fii ṣuwar maεruuḍa ləl-fərže b-madxal ᵊs-siinama.*
to come into view - *baan (a ə), ẓahar (a ə).* The ship finally came into view. *w-ʔaxiiran ᵊl-baaxra baanet.*
to view - *naẓar (o naẓar) b-.* We view the situation with great concern. *εam nənẓor bᵊl-waḍε ᵊb-ʔəhtimaam baaleġ.*
vile - *šaniiε, məqref.* Where's that vile smell coming from? *mneen žaaye har-riiḥa š-šaniiεa?*
villa - *vəlla* pl. *vəllayaat.*
village - *ḍeeεa* pl. *ḍiyaε, qarye* pl. *qəra.*
vinegar - *xall.*
vineyard - *karᵊm* pl. *kruum(e).*
to **violate** - *xaalaf.* That's not the first time he's violated the law. *hayy muu ʔawwal marra bixaalef fiiha l-qaanuun.*
violation - *mxaalafe* pl. *-aat.*
violent - **1.** *εaniif, šadiid.* We had a violent argument. *txaanaqna xnaaqa εaniife.* **2.** *εaniif.* He's a very violent person. *huwwe zalame ktiir εaniif.* **3.** *ġeer ṭabiiεi**. He died a violent death. *maat moote ġeer ṭabiiεiyye.*
violin - *kamanža* pl. *-aat.*
violinist - *kamanžaati* pl. *-iyye, εaazef˜* (pl. *-iin˜*) *kamanža.*
virgin - *bənt bəkᵊr* pl. *banaat bəkkar.*
the Virgin Mary - *maryam ᵊl-εadra* (and *ᵊl-εazra*).
virgin soil - *ʔarḍ* (pl. *ʔaraaḍi*) *bəkᵊr.*
virtue - *faḍiile* pl. *faḍaaʔel.* Can you name the cardinal virtues? *fiik ᵊtεədd-əlli l-faḍaaʔel ᵊl-ʔawwaliyye?*
virus - *vairoos* pl. *-aat.*
visa - *viiza* (f.) pl. *viizayaat, taʔšiira* pl. *-aat, sima* pl. *-aat.*
vise - *malzame* pl. *malaazem.*
visibility - *rəʔya.* Visibility was very bad that day. *kaanet ᵊr-rəʔya ktiir εaaṭle b-hadaak ᵊn-nhaar.*
visible - *malḥuuẓ, ẓaaher ləl-εayaan.* His health shows visible improvement. *ṣaḥḥto fiiha taḥasson malḥuuẓ.*
**On a clear day, the mountains are clearly visible from here. *b-yoom ṣaaḥi ž-žbaal btənšaaf mən hoon ᵊb-kəll ᵊwḍuuḥ.*

vision - 1. *naẓar*. His vision is getting poor. *naẓaro ɛam yxəff*. 2. *baɛ°d˜ naẓar, baɛ°d˜ baṣar*. He's a man of great vision. *ɛando baɛ°d naẓar °ktiir*.
visit - *zyaara* pl. *-aat*. That was an unexpected visit! *hayy kaanet zyaara muu b°l-ḥəsbaan*.
to pay a visit - *zaar (u zyaara//nzaar), ɛamel zyaara*. He paid me a visit last week. *zaarni* (or *ɛəmə́l-li zyaara*) *ž-žəmɛa l-maadye*.
to visit - 1. *zaar (u zyaara//nzaar)*. He wanted to visit you. *kaan bəddo yzuurak*. -- Have you visited our museum yet? *zərt °l-matḥaf tabaɛna wəlla ləssa?* 2. *nazel (e nzuul, nazle) ɛand˜ ..., zaar ɛand˜ ...* He's visiting us. *huwwe naazel ɛanna*.
visitor - 1. *zaayer* pl. *zuwwaar, ḍeef* pl. *ḍyuuf*. We're having visitors tonight. *žaayiinna zuwwaar °l-yoom ɛašiyye*. 2. *zaayer* pl. *zuwwaar*. She's not yet allowed to receive visitors. *ləssa muu məsmə́ḥ-la təstaqbel zuwwaar*.
vital - *ḥayawi**. The bombings have wiped out most of the vital centers of the enemy. *l-ġaaraat °ž-žawwiyye maḥet °aktar °l-maraakez °l-ḥayawiyye ɛand °l-ɛaduww*. -- It does not affect our vital interests. *maa-la ta°siir ɛala maṣaaləḥna l-ḥayawiyye*.
**It's of vital importance. *°əlo °ahammiyye baalġa*.
Bureau of Vital Statistics - *daa°ərt˜ °n-nufuus*.
vitality - *ḥayawiyye*.
vivid - *ḥayy*. He has a vivid imagination. *°əlo mxayyale ḥayye*.
vocabulary - 1. *žadwal˜* (pl. *žadaawel˜*) *kəlmaat*. You'll find a vocabulary at the end of each lesson. *bətlaaqi žadwal kəlmaat b-°aaxer kəll dars*. 2. *məfradaat* (pl.). The vocabulary of Russian has changed radically since the Revolution of 1917. *məfradaat °l-luġa r-ruusiyye ṣaar fiiha taġyiir °asaasi mən waq°t sawret °alf w-təsaɛ miyye w-ṣabaṭaɛš*.
**His vocabulary in French is rather limited. *ɛadad °l-kəlmaat halli byaɛrə́fa b°l-fransaawi maḥduud nooɛan maa*.
vocal - 1. *ṣooti**. Something's wrong with his vocal cords. *fii ɛəlle b-°awtaaro ṣ-ṣootiyye*. 2. *ġinaa°i** I'm very fond of vocal music. *bḥəbb °l-muusiiqa l-ġinaa°iyye ktiir*.
vodka - *voodka*.
voice - 1. *ṣoot* pl. *°aṣwaat*. His voice was barely audible. *ṣooto b°l-kaad °nsamaɛ*. -- Sometimes I listen to the broadcasts of the Voice of America. *°aḥyaanan bəsmaɛ °izaaɛaat ṣoot °ameerka*. 2. *kəlme, qool*. I wish I had a voice in this matter! *ya-reet kan-li kəlme b-haš-šaġle*.
to voice - *ɛabbar ɛan*. Everyone voiced his opinion. *kəll waaḥed ɛabbar ɛan ra°yo*.
void - *baaṭel*. The passport is void now. *l-basboor ṣaar baaṭel hallaq*.
null and void - *baaṭel˜ °l-mafɛuul*. The contract is null and void. *l-kontraat baaṭel °l-mafɛuul*.
to void - *laġa (i °əlġa//ltaġa* and *nlaġa)*. I'll void the check. *laḥa °əlġi š-šakk*.
volcanic - *bərkaani**.
volcano - *bərkaan* pl. *barakiin*.
volt - *voolṭ* pl. *-aat*.
voltage - *voolṭaaž*.
volume - 1. *mžallad* pl. *-aat*. The book was published in two volumes. *l-°ktaab ntašar b-°mžalladeen*. -- Volume Fifteen of this magazine is missing. *l-°mžallad l-xaames ɛašar mən hal-mažalle mafquud*. 2. *ḥaž°m* pl. *°aḥžaam*. The volume of the cylinder is 500 cm³. *ḥažm °l-°əsṭwaane xam°s miit ṣanṭimətr °mkaɛɛab*. 3. *kammiyye*. Our office handles a great volume of correspondence every month. *maktabna biquum b-kammiyye kbiire mən l-°mraasalaat kəll šah°r*. 4. *ṣooṭ*. The volume control doesn't work. *ɛyaar °ṣ-ṣooṭ maa ɛam yəštə́ġel*.
**Please turn up the volume (on the radio) a little. *ballа ɛalli r-raadyo šwayye*.
voluntary - *°əxtiyaari**. All our funds come from voluntary contributions. *kəll °amwaalna btəži mən tabarruɛaat °əxtiyaariyye*.
volunteer - *məṭṭawweɛ* pl. *-iin*. Can you get some volunteers to do it? *fiik °džiib kam məṭṭawweɛ yaɛ°mluuha?*
to volunteer - *ṭṭawwaɛ*. Who'll volunteer for this job? *miin laḥa yəṭṭawwaɛ la-haš-šaġle?*
**He has volunteered his services. *qaddam xəd°mto biduun raža*.
to **vomit** - *raažaɛ, naṭaq (o nṭaaq), stafraġ*.
vote - 1. *ṣoot* pl. *°aṣwaaṭ*. He was elected by a majority of 2000 votes. *ntaxabúu b-°aġlabiit °alfeen ṣooṭ*. 2. *taṣwiiṭ*. The motion was put to a vote. *l-°əqtiraaḥ nwaḍaɛ ɛat-taṣwiiṭ*. 3. *ḥaqq˜ °t-taṣwiiṭ*. Minors have no vote. *l-qaaṣriin maa-lon ḥaqq °t-taṣwiiṭ*.
to vote - 1. *ṣawwat, ntaxab*. I couldn't vote the last time. *maa qdər°t ṣawweṭ °aaxer marra*. -- For whom did you vote? *la-miin ṣawwatt?* or *miin °ntaxab°t?* 2. *ṣawwat*. Shall we vote on it? *nṣawweṭ ɛaleeha?* 3. *xaṣṣaṣ, qarrar*. The board voted five hundred dollars for relief. *l-mažles xaṣṣaṣ xam°s miit dolaar ləl-°əsɛaaf*.
**The proposal was voted down. *l-°əqtiraaḥ maa ḥaaz °l-°aṣwaaṭ °l-laazme*.
voter - *naaxeb* pl. *-iin*.
to **vouch for** - *ḍəmen (a ḍamaan), kəfel (a kafaale)*. I vouch for him. *bəḍmano*. -- Of course, I can't vouch for that bit of information. *ṭabiiɛi maa bəqder °əkfal (ṣaḥḥet) hal-xabar*.
to **vow** - *tɛahhad*. He vowed not to do it again. *tɛahhad maa yɛiida taani marra*.
voyage - *safra* (pl. *-aat*) *baḥriyye, raḥle* (pl. *-aat*) *baḥriyye*.
vulgar - 1. *šaršuuḥ*. I won't have anything to do with that vulgar fellow. *maa bəddi °ayy ɛalaaqa maɛ haz-zalame š-šaršuuḥ*. 2. *bazii°*. I wish he wouldn't use such vulgar language. *ya-reeto maa yəstaɛmel heek luġa bazii°a*.
vulture - *nəs°r* pl. *nsuura*.

W

to **wade** - *xaaḍ (u xooḍ), xawwaḍ*. I wouldn't wade into the stream if I were you. *law kənt °b-maḥallak maa bxuuḍ b-han-nah°r*.
wadi - *waadi* pl. *wədyaan*.
wage(s) - *°əžra* pl. *°əžrawaat* and *°žuur*. Are you satisfied with your wages? *raḍyaan °b-°əž°rtak?* -- They're negotiating for new wage rates in the textile industry. *ɛam yətfaawaḍu mənšaan fi°aat °°žuur °ždiide b-ṣinaaɛet °n-nasiiž*.
to wage - *šann (ə šann)*. They can't wage a long war. *maa fiihon yšənnu ḥarb ṭawiile*.
wagon - *ɛarabaaye* pl. *-aat*. Hitch the horses to the new wagon. *rbooṭ °l-°əḥ°ṣne b°l-ɛarabaaye ž-ždiide*.
Wahhabi - *wahhaabi* pl. *-iyye*.
Wahhabism - *l-wahhaabiyye*.
waist - *xaṣ°r* pl. *xṣuura*. I took the pants in at the waist. *dayyaqt °l-banṭaloon ɛand °l-xaṣ°r*. -- Strip to the waist! *šlaaḥ la-xaṣrak!*
wait - *°ənṭiẓaar*. It was a long wait. *kaan °ənṭiẓaar ṭawiil*.
**We have an hour's wait before the train gets in. *laazem nənṭə́ẓer saaɛa la-yəṣal °t-treen*.
to lie in wait - *trabbaṣ, traṣṣad*. They were lying in wait for us. *kaanu ɛam yətrabbaṣúu-lna*.
to wait - *stanna, nṭaẓar*. Wait a moment. *stannа́-lak daqiiqa*. -- Have you been waiting long? *ṣar-lak ɛam tənṭə́ẓer zamaan?* -- Wait and see. *stanna w-šuuf*. -- I'm sorry to keep you waiting. *laa t°aaxəzni xalleetak tənṭə́ẓer*. -- I'll wait for you until five o'clock. *bəstannaak la-ḥadd °s-saaɛa xamse*. -- We'll wait (with the) dinner for him. *mnəstannа́ ɛal-ɛaša*. -- Wait for his answer. *stanna ḥatta yəži žawaabo*. -- Go to bed. Don't wait up for me. *ruuḥ naam. laa təstannaani*.
**That can wait till tomorrow. *haš-šaġle fiiha təbqa la-bəkra*.
**I can hardly wait to see him! *°ana mətl °n-naar ɛala-ma šuufo*.
**I can hardly wait for the day. *maa-li msaddeq °eemta yəži hadaak °n-nhaar*.
to wait on - *xadam (o xədme//nxadam)*. Will you please wait on me now? *fiik balla təxdəmni hallaq?*

waiter - *garṣoon* pl. *garaṣiin* and *garṣooniyye*. Call the waiter. *ṣraax ləl-garṣoon.*
 head waiter - *ra?iis˜* (pl. *rə?asa˜*) *garṣooniyye, mət°r* pl. *mtuura.*
waiting room - **1.** *ṣaḷoon˜* (pl. *-aat˜*) *?ənṭiẓaar.* Is there a waiting room at the station? *fii ṣaḷoon ?ənṭiẓaar b°l-°mḥaṭṭa?* **2.** *ġərfet˜* (pl. *ġəraf˜*) *?ənṭiẓaar.* How many patients are there still in the waiting room? *kam mariiḍ ləssa fii b-ġərfet °l-?ənṭiẓaar?*
waitress - *garṣoone* pl. *-aat.*
to **wake** - *fayyaq, ṣaḥḥa, waƐƐa.* Please wake me at seven o'clock. *baḷḷa fayyəqni s-saaƐa sabƐa.*
 to wake up - **1.** *fayyaq, ṣaḥḥa, waƐƐa.* The noise woke me up. *ḍ-ḍoože fayyaqətni.* **2.** *faaq (i fayaqaan), ṣəḥi (a ə), wəƐi (-yuuƐa waƐayaan).* I didn't wake up until eight this morning. *maa fəqt °l-yoom Ɛala bəkra ləs-saaƐa tmaane.* **3.** *wəƐi, ṣəḥi.* It's high time you woke up to the fact that ... *?aan °l-?awaan tuuƐa Ɛala ḥaqiiqet ?ənno ...*
walk - **1.** *məšwaar* pl. *mašawiir.* Did you have a nice walk? *Ɛməlt məšwaar ḥəlu?* -- Let's go for a walk. *xalliina naƐməl-lna məšwaar* or ***xalliina nətmašwár-°lna šwayye.* -- Would you like to take a walk? *bətriid taƐmə́l-lak məšwaar?* **2.** *mašye* pl. *-aat, məšwaar* pl. *mašawiir.* It's a long walk to the station. *waḷḷa mašye ṭawiile ləl-°mḥaṭṭa.* **3.** *mašye.* You can recognize him by his walk. *fiik taƐ°rfo mən mašito.*
 to walk - **1.** *məši (i maši).* Shall we walk or take the bus? *nəmši wəlla naaxod °l-baaṣ?* -- Can the baby walk yet? *bada ṭ-ṭəf°l yəmši wəlla ləssa?* **2.** *mašwar, mašša.* Did you walk the dog? *mašwart °l-kal°b šii?*
 to walk down - *nəzel (e nzuul, nazle).* We were walking down the stairs. *kənna Ɛam nənzel mən Ɛad-daraž.*
 **I saw him walk down the street a while ago. *šəfto maaši b°ṭ-ṭariiq mən šwayye.*
 to walk in - *faat (u foote).* I didn't wait, I just walked in. *maa stanneet, fətt w°s-salaam.*
 to walk out - *ṭəleƐ (a ṭluuƐ, ṭalƐa).* He turned on his heels and walked out. *daar ḍahro w-ṭəleƐ.*
 to walk out on - *daššar.* Our maid walked out on us. *ṣaanƐətna daššarətna.*
 to walk up - *ṭəleƐ (a ṭluuƐ, ṭalƐa).* He can't walk up the stairs. *maa byəḥsen yəṭlaƐ Ɛad-daraž.*
 **Let's walk up the street. *xalliina nəmši mən haž-žiha b°š-šaareƐ.*
wall - **1.** *ḥeeṭ* pl. *ḥiiṭaan.* Hang the picture on this wall. *Ɛalleq °ṣ-ṣuura Ɛala hal-ḥeeṭ haad.* -- Only the walls are still standing. *bass °l-ḥiiṭaan ṣəfyet waaqfe.* **2.** *suur* pl. *?aswaar.* You can still see parts of the ancient city wall. *ləssa la-hal-?iyyaam bətšuuf ?ažzaa? mən suur °l-madiine l-Ɛatiiq.* **3.** *židaar* pl. *žədraan.* Excessive gastric acid affects the stomach walls. *zyaadet l-°ḥmuuḍa l-məƐdiyye bət?asser Ɛala žədraan °l-məƐde.*
wallet - *maḥfaẓa* pl. *maḥaafeẓ, žəzdaan* pl. *žazadiin.* I lost my wallet. *ḍaaƐet maḥfaẓti.*
wallpaper - *waraq˜ ḥiiṭaan.*
walnut - *žooze* coll. *žooz* pl. *-aat.*
 walnut tree - *žooze* coll. *žooz* pl. *-aat.*
waltz - *vaals* pl. *-aat.*
want - **1.** *rəġbe* pl. *-aat, ḥaaže* pl. *-aat.* My wants are very modest. *rəġbaati ktiir mətwaaḍƐa.* **2.** *Ɛawz.* Many people in the world have never known freedom from want. *fii bašar °ktiir b°l-Ɛaalam b-ḥayaaton maa Ɛərfu l-ḥərriyye mn °l-Ɛawz.*
 for want of - *la-Ɛadam˜ wžuud˜ ...* I'll take it for want of something better. *baaxə́da la-Ɛadam wžuud šii ?aḥsan.*
 to want - *raad (i ?iraade), (kaan) bədd-* + pron. suff. He knows what he wants. *byaƐref šuu biriid* (or ... *šuu bəddo*). -- How much do you want for these three remnants? *qaddeeš bəddak b-hat-tlətt faḍlaat?* -- I want to go swimming. *bəddi ruuḥ ?əsbaḥ.* -- She doesn't want to. *maa bədda.*
 wanted - **1.** *maṭluub.* He is wanted by the police. *maṭluub huwwe mn °š-šərṭa.* **2.** *marġuub fii.* I don't feel wanted around here. *šaaƐer °b-ḥaali maa-li marġuub fiyyi hoon.*
war - *ḥar°b* (m. and f.) pl. *ḥruub.* Where were you during the last war? *ween kən°t ?iyyaam °l-ḥarb °l-maaḍye?*
 War Ministry - *wazaaret˜* (pl. *-aat˜*) *°l-ḥarbiyye.*
 war profiteer - *ġani˜* (pl. *?aġniyaa?˜*) *ḥar°b.*
ward - *qaawuuš* pl. *qawawiiš.* He had to be put in the ward because all the rooms were taken. *nžabaru yḥəṭṭúu b°l-qaawuuš la?ənno kəll °l-?uwaḍ °ttaaxadet.*
 **She'll be my ward until she comes of age. *bəḍḍall taḥt °wṣaayti la-təbloġ °s-sənn.*
wardrobe - *xzaanet˜* (pl. *xazaayen˜*) *?awaaƐi.* What are your shoes doing in my wardrobe? *šuu ḥaṭṭ ṣabbaaṭak b-°xzaanet ?awaƐiyyi?*
 **She bought herself a complete new wardrobe. *ṭaqmet ḥaala mən farqa la-raas qaddáma ṭaq°m kaamel °ždiid.*
warehouse - *Ɛanbar* pl. *Ɛanaaber, dabbo* pl. *dabboyaat, məstawdaƐ* pl. *-aat.*
warm - **1.** *šoob.* It's very warm today. *šoob °ktiir °l-yoom.* **2.** *dafyaan.* Are you warm enough? *dafyaan °kfaaye ?ənte?* **3.** *daafi.* Sitting in this warm room makes me sleepy. *l-qaƐde b-hal-?uuḍa d-daafye bətnaƐƐəsni.* **4.** *ṣəx°n.* Is there enough warm water left? *bəqi mayy ṣəxne kaafye wəlla la??* **5.** *ḥaarr.* He greeted me with a warm handshake. *sallam Ɛaliyyi b-°mṣaafaḥa ḥaarra.*
 to warm - **1.** *daffa.* Warm your feet before the fire. *daffi rəžleek Ɛan-naar.* **2.** *ṣaxxan.* Warm the plates before you put the fried eggs on them. *ṣaxxni ṣ-ṣḥuun qab°l-ma təs°kbi l-beeḍ °l-məqli fiihon.*
 to warm oneself - *ddaffa, daffa ḥaalo.* Come in and warm yourself by the fire. *fuut °ddaffa žamb °n-naar.*
 to warm up - *ṣaxxan.* Please, warm up the soup for me. *baḷḷa ṣaxxnīi-li š-šooraba.*
 **I can't warm up to him. *maa Ɛam yfuut la-qalbi.*
warmth - *ḥaraara.*
to **warn** - **1.** *ḥazzar, nabbah.* They warned me against him. *ḥazzaruuni mənno.* **2.** *?anzar (e and -y?anzer), ḥazzar, nabbah.* I warn you, don't do that again. *b?anzrak laa taƐməla taani marra.*
warning - *?ənzaar* pl. *-aat, taḥziir* pl. *-aat.* Let that be a warning to you! *xalli haš-šii ykuun ?ənzaar ?əlak!*
to **warp** - *qawwaṣ, lawa (i lawi).* This wood will warp. *hal-xašab biqawweṣ.*
Warsaw - *varsoovya.*
warship - *safiine* (pl. *səfon*) *ḥarbiyye.*
wart - *taaluule* pl. *tawaliil.*
wash - *ġasiil, xasiil.* The wash hasn't come back from the laundry. *l-ġasiil ləssa maa rəžeƐ mn °l-maṣbaġa.*
 to wash - **1.** *ġasal (e ġas°l//nġasal), xasal (e xas°l//nxasal).* I have to wash my shirts. *laazem ?əġsel qəmṣaani.* **2.** *ġassal, xassal, ġasal, xasal.* May I wash my hands? *məmken ġassel ?idayyi?* **3.** *žala (i žali//nžala).* Who's going to wash the dishes? *miin bəddo yəžli ṣ-ṣḥuun?* **4.** *masaḥ (a mas°ḥ//mmasaḥ).* Why haven't you washed the floor yet? *leeš maa masaḥti l-?arḍ ləssa?* **5.** *nġasal, nxasal.* Does this material wash? *hal-°qmaaš byənġə́sel?* **6.** *ġassal, xassal.* I didn't have time to wash this morning. *maa ṣar-li waq°t ġassel Ɛala bəkra.*
 to wash away - **1.** *žaraf (o žar°f//nžaraf).* Last spring the flood washed away the dam. *b°r-rabiiƐ °l-maaḍi s-seel žaraf °s-sadd.* **2.** *nžaraf.* The shack washed away in the flood. *l-kuux nžaraf b°l-fayaḍaan.*
 to wash down - **1.** *ṣarraf//tṣarraf.* You can wash it down the sink. *fiik °tṣarrə́fa b°l-balluuƐa.* **2.** *dafaš (o daf°š//ndafaš).* I wish I had a glass of beer to wash down this spicy food! *Ɛala waaḥ kaaset biira tədfoš hal-?akle l-malaane bhaaraat.*
 to wash off - **1.** *qaam (i qayamaan//nqaam) b°l-mayy, ṭaalaƐ b°l-mayy.* Do you think you can wash it off? *bədzənn fiik tqiima b°l-mayy?* **2.** *qaam (i qayamaan//nqaam), ṭaalaƐ.* The rain has washed off most of the paint. *l-maṭar qaamet ?akṭar °d-dhaan.*
 to wash out - **1.** *qaam (i qayamaan//nqaam), ṭaalaƐ, rawwaḥ.* Try to wash out the stain with hot water. *žarreb qiim °l-baqƐa b-mayy səxne.* **2.** *ḥaffar.* The heavy rains have washed out the roads in the mountains. *l-?amṭaar °š-šadiide ḥaffaret °ṭ-ṭəroq b°ž-žbaal.*
 **He looks all washed out. *mbayyen Ɛaafiito Ɛadmaane.*
 **I feel all washed out today. *šaayef ḥaali ḥaaṭet °ktiir °l-yoom.*
 to wash up - **1.** *ġassal, xassal.* I'd like to wash up before supper. *bəddi ġassel qabl °l-Ɛaša.* **2.** *qadaf (o qad°f//nqadaf) (b-).* The sea washed up a lot of dead fish on the beach. *l-baḥ°r qadaf (b-)samak mayyet °ktiir Ɛaš-šaṭṭ.*
 **He's all washed up as a politician. *nṭafa b-miidaan °s-siyaase.*
 **Our vacation plans are all washed up. *xəṭaṭna*

tabaε ᵊl-εaṭle kəlla fartet.
washbasin – *maġsale* pl. *maġaasel, maxsale* pl. *maxaasel.*
washbowl – *ṭəšᵊt* pl. *ṭšuuṭa.*
washcloth – *liife* pl. *liyaf.*
washer – **1.** *žəlde* pl. *-aat.* The faucet needs a new washer. *l-ḥanafiyye laazə́ma žəlde ždiide.* **2.** *ġassaale* pl. *-aat.* Put the clothes in the washer. *ḥəṭṭ ᵊl-ʾawaaεi bᵊl-ġassaale.*
washing – **1.** *ġasle* pl. *-aat, xasle* pl. *-aat.* The curtains need a good washing. *l-baraadi laazə́mon ġasle maakne.* **2.** *ġasiil, xasiil.* Tell her to hang out the washing. *qəl-la tənšor ᵊl-ġasiil.*
washing machine – *ġassaale* pl. *-aat.*
washtub – *lagan* pl. *-aat.*
wasp – *zəlᵊqṭa* pl. *zalaaqeṭ.*
waste – **1.** *tabziir, baεzaqa.* That's sheer waste. *haada tabziir ṣərf.* **2.** *ḍyaaεa.* It's a waste of time and energy. *ḍyaaεet waqt w-žahᵊd.* **3.** *εaadem.* The river is contaminated with a lot of waste materials from the chemical plant. *n-nahr ᵊmwaṣṣax b-mawaadd εaadme mn ᵊl-maṣnaε ᵊl-kiimaawi.*
**Haste makes waste. *l-εažale mn ᵊš-šeeṭaan.*
to go to waste – *raaḥ (u ø) kabb.* A good cook doesn't let anything go to waste. *ṭ-ṭabbaax l-ᵊmniiḥ maa bixalli šii yruuḥ kabb.*
to lay waste – *xarrab, dammar.* The storm has laid waste the entire area. *l-εaaṣfe xarrabet ᵊl-manṭiqa kəlla.*
to waste – **1.** *ḍayyaε, ḍawwaε.* He wastes a lot of time talking. *biḍayyeε waqt ᵊktiir bᵊl-ḥaki.* **2.** *baεzaq, bazzar, baddad.* He'll be a poor man if he keeps wasting his money like that. *ləssa byəšḥad ʾiza bitamm ybaεzeq maṣaari heek.*
**Don't waste your breath. *laa tġalleb ḥaalak!*
wastebasket – *sallet˜ (pl. -aat˜ and səlal˜) məhmalaat.*
watch – *saaεa* pl. *-aat.* By my watch it's five. *εala saaεti (s-saaεa) xamse.*
**The police are keeping close watch over his activities. *š-šərṭa εam ᵊtraaqeb ḥarakaato mraaqabe daqiiqa.*
to watch – **1.** *raaqab.* I've been watching him for some time. *ṣar-li madde εam raaqbo.* -- That fellow needs close watching. *haz-zalame laazmo mraaqabe daqiiqa.* **2.** *tfarraž εala, raaqab.* Watch how I do it. *tfarraž εaliyyi kiif baεmə́la.* -- I like to watch children at play. *bḥəbb ʾətfarraž εal-ᵊwlaad w-hənne εam yəlεabu.* **3.** *šaaf (u ø), šaahad, tfarraž εala.* I watched the game on television. *šəft ᵊl-ləεbe bᵊt-televəzyoon.* **4.** *xalla εeeno εala, raaqab.* Who's going to watch the children? *miin bəddo yxalli εeeno εal-ᵊwlaad (or yraaqeb l-ᵊwlaad)?*
**Watch your step on your way out. *ʾoεa təqaε w-ʾənte ṭaaleε.*
**Watch your step, or you may find yourself in real trouble. *ʾoεa walla btəqáε-lak waqεa sooda.*
to watch out – *waεi (-yuuεa ø), ṣəḥi (a ø), daar (i ø) baalo, ntabah.* Watch out when you cross the street. *ʾoεa w-ʾənte εam təqṭaε ᵊš-šaareε.*
to watch (out) for – **1.** *ttallaε εala, xalla εeeno εala.* I'll be watching out for you at the station. *bəttallaε εaleek (or bxalli εeeni εaleek) bᵊl-ᵊmḥaṭṭa.* **2.** *ṣəḥi (a ø), waεi (-yuuεa ø), daar (i ø) baalo mən.* Watch out for that fellow! *ʾəṣḥa mən haz-zalame!*
watchdog – *kalb˜ (pl. klaab˜) ᵊḥraase.*
watchmaker – *saaεaati* pl. *-iyye.*
watchman – *ḥaares* pl. *ḥərraas, ġafiir* pl. *ġəfara, xafiir* pl. *xəfara.*
watchtower – *bərž˜ (pl. braaž˜ and bruuž˜) ᵊmraaqabe.*
water – **1.** *mayy(e)* pl. *-aat.* Please give me a glass of water. *balla εaṭiini kaaset mayy.* **2.** *miyaah* (pl.). The main problem in the Middle East is that of water. *l-məšᵊkle l-ʾasaasiyye bᵊš-šarq ᵊl-ʾawṣaṭ hiyye məškəlt ᵊl-miyaah.*
**He can barely keep his head above water. *bᵊz-zoor mmašši ḥaalo.*
**This time we're really in hot water. *hal-marra wqəεna b-warṭa εal-mazbuuṭ.*
water carrier – *ṣaqqa* pl. *ṣaqqaaye.*
water pipe – *ʾargiile* pl. *ʾaragiil.* I've never smoked a water pipe in all my life. *b-ḥayaati maa šrəbᵊt ʾargiile.*
water wheel – *naaεuura* pl. *nawaεiir.* Have you seen the famous water wheels of Hama? *šəft nawaεiir ḥama l-mašhuura?*
to water – **1.** *ṣaqa (i ṣaqi//nṣaqa).* I water the garden every day. *bəṣqi ž-žneene kəll yoom.* **2.** *rawa (i rawi//nrawa), šarrab, ṣaqa.* Have you watered the horses yet? *raweet ᵊl-ʾəḥᵊṣne walla ləssa?* **3.** *dammaε, damaε (a damᵊε).* My eyes are watering. *εyuuni εam ᵊddammeε.*
**The cake makes my mouth water. *l-gaatóo εam yṭaffef riiqi.*
to water down – *xaffaf mən ḥaddet˜ ...* He watered down his speech before delivering it. *xaffaf mən ḥəddet xiṭaabo qabᵊl-ma ʾalqáa.*
waterfall – *šallaal* pl. *-aat.*
watermelon – *baṭṭiixa (ḥamra)* coll. *baṭṭiix (ʾaḥmar)* pl. *-aat (ḥəmᵊr).*
waterproof – *ḍədd ᵊl-mayy.* Is this coat waterproof? *hat-trənškoot ḍədd ᵊl-mayy?*
waterskin – *qərbe* pl. *qərab.*
watt – *waaṭ* pl. *-aat.*
wave – **1.** *moože* coll. *moož* pl. *-aat* and *mwaaž.* The waves are very high today. *l-moož ᵊktiir εaali l-yoom.* -- Does your radio have short wave? *r-raadyo tabaεak fii moože qaṣiire?* -- A wave of enthusiasm swept the country. *moože mn ᵊl-ḥamaase εammet l-ᵊblaad.* **2.** *taεže* pl. *-aat.* He has a natural wave in his hair. *fii taεže ṭabiiεiyye b-šaεro.*
to wave – **1.** *rafraf.* The flags were waving in the breeze. *l-ʾaεlaam kaanet εam ᵊtrafref bᵊl-hawa.* **2.** *lawwaḥ b-, loolaḥ b-.* Somebody was waving a handkerchief. *fii ḥada kaan εam ylawweḥ ᵊb-maḥrame.* -- I waved to him. *loolaḥt-ə́llo.*
wavy – *mmawwaž, mtaεεaž.* He has wavy dark hair. *šaεro mmawwaž ʾaswad.*
wax – *šamᵊε.* Some wax got spilled on the tablecloth. *fii šwayyet šamᵊε nəzel εala žlaalet ᵊṭ-ṭaawle.*
to wax – *lammaε.* Has the maid waxed the floor? *l-xaadme lammaεet ᵊl-ʾarḍ?*
wax paper – *waraq ᵊmšammaε.*
way – **1.** *ṭariiq* pl. *ṭəroq* and *ʾəṭᵊrqa.* Is this the right way to town? *haada ṭ-ṭariiq ᵊl-mazbuuṭ ləl-balad?* -- Are you going my way? *ṭariiqak εala ṭariiqi?* **2.** *ṭariiqa* pl. *ṭəroq.* That's no way to treat people. *muu heek ᵊṭ-ṭariiqa yalli bətεaamel fiiha n-naas.* -- There are different ways of doing things. *fii ṭəroq məxtəlfe la-εamal ᵊš-šii ᵊl-waaḥed* or *kəll waaḥed ʾəlo ṭariiqto la-εamal ᵊl-ʾašya.* -- Is this the right way to do it? *heek ᵊṭ-ṭariiqa l-mazbuuṭa ḥatta bətṣiir fiiha?* -- There are ways and means of finding out. *fii ṭəroq w-ʾasaliib la-maεrᵊft ᵊl-ḥaqiiqa.* **3.** *ṭabᵊε* pl. *ṭbaaε.* Don't mind him, that's just his way. *laa təntəbə́h-lo heek ṭabεo wᵊs-salaam.* **4.** *namaṭ, mənwaal.* Everything is going along (in) the same old way. *kəll šii maaši εala nafs ᵊn-namaṭ.*
**I'm afraid he's in a bad way. *šaayə́f-lak ʾənno ḥaalto εaaṭle.*
**Everything turned out the way they wanted it. *kəll šii ṣaar matᵊl-ma kaan bəddon.*
**Have it your own way! *ṣṭəfel, εmeel ḥalli bəddak-yáa.*
**Let him have his (own) way. *trəko εala keefo.*
**He has a way with women. *huwwe ḥarbuuq maε ᵊn-nəswaan* or *suuqo maaši maε ᵊn-nəswaan.*
**Do you know your way around here? *εarfaan ᵊl-madaaxel wᵊl-maxaarež hoon?*
**He paid my way. *dafaε εanni.*
**I paid my own way. *dafaεt εan ḥaali.*
**I don't see my way clear to buy it now. *maa-li εarfaan kiif bəqder ʾəštriiha hallaq.*
**That's the way he wants it. *heek bəddo.*
**This way in, please! *mən hoon ᵊl-foote, mən faḍᵊlkon.*
**What have you got in the way of radios? *šuu fii εandak mən ʾanwaaε ᵊr-raadyo?*
**Christmas is still a long way off. *εiid ᵊl-miilaad ləssáa mṭawwel ᵊktiir.*
**New York is still a long way off. *nyuu-yoork ləssaaha bεiide.*
**He's come a long way since I knew him in school. *tqaddam ᵊktiir mən waqt ᵊεrəfto bᵊl-madrase.*
**The plane was way off its course. *ṭ-ṭayyaara kaanet ṭaalεa ktiir εan ṭariiqa.*
**We're way behind in our work. *mətʾaxxriin ᵊktiir b-šəġᵊlna.*
**The place is way out in the country. *l-maḥall ᵊbεiid ᵊktiir bᵊl-barriyye.*
way out – **1.** *maxraž* pl. *maxaarež.* Which is the way out? *ween ᵊl-maxraž?* **2.** *maxraž, mafarr, manfad.* I don't see any other way out. *maa-li šaayef ʾayy maxraž ġeer haad.*
right of way – **1.** *ṭ-ṭariiq.* The car on your right has the right of way. *s-sayyaara εala yamiinak ʾəla ṭ-ṭariiq.* **2.** *ḥaqq ᵊl-muruur.* The oil company is negotiating for the right of way for their pipeline. *šərket ᵊz-zeet εam ᵊtfaaweḍ mənšaan ḥaqq ᵊl-muruur la-ʾanabiiba.*

across the way - *bᵊl-wəšš.* His house is just across the way. *beeto tamaam bᵊl-wəšš.*

a long way from - *bɛiid ɛan.* The school is a long way from our house. *l-madrase bɛiide ɛan beetna.* -- His latest speech is a long way from his former promises. *xiṭaabo l-ʔaaxraani bɛiid ᵊktiir ɛan ᵊwɛuudo s-saabqa.*

by the way - *b-hal-ᵊmnaasabe.* By the way, are you coming with us tonight? *b-hal-ᵊmnaasabe, ʔənte maɛna l-leele?*

by way of - **1.** *ɛan ṭariiq˜* ... We went by way of Athens. *rəḥna ɛan ṭariiq ʔatiina.* **2.** *ɛala sabiil˜* ... He said it by way of a joke. *qaala ɛala sabiil ᵊn-nəkte.*

in a way - *mən žiha.* In a way he's right. *mən žiha maɛo ḥaqq.* -- In a way I am responsible. *mən žiha ʔana masʔuul.*

in no way - *maa ... bᵊl-marra, maa ... ʔabadan, maa ... mnoob.* This is in no way better than the other one. *haada muu ʔaḥsan bᵊl-marra mn ᵊt-taani.*

in the way - *bᵊṭ-ṭariiq.* Why don't you remove this old typewriter? It's only in the way. *leeš maa bətqiim hal-makana l-ɛatiiqa? hiyye bass qaaɛde bᵊṭ-ṭariiq.* -- What's he doing here? He's in everybody's way. *šuu ʔəlo ɛamal huwwe hoon? waaqef ᵊb-ṭariiq kəll waaḥed.*

in what way - *mən ʔayy žiha, kiif, šloon.* In what way is that better? *mən ʔayy žiha haada ʔaḥsan?*

that way - **1.** *heek.* I didn't mean it that way. *ʔana maa ɛaneeta heek.* **2.** *ɛala haṭ-ṭariiqa.* You won't get anywhere that way. *ɛala haṭ-ṭariiqa b-ḥayaatak maa btəṣal la-natiiže.*

this way or that way - **1.** *mən hoon ʔaw mn ᵊhniik.* You can go this way or that way. *fiik ᵊtruuḥ mən hoon ʔaw mn ᵊhniik.* **2.** *heek ʔaw heek.* You can do it this way or that way. *fiik taɛməla heek ʔaw heek.*

out of the way - *maḥduuf, mənɛəzel.* This place is somewhat out of the way. *hal-maḥall nooɛan maa maḥduuf.*

to get out of the way - **1.** *qaam (i qayamaan// nqaam) mn ᵊl-wəšš* (or *mn ᵊṭ-ṭariiq*). I finally got those boxes out of the way. *w-ʔaxiiran qəmt has-sanadiiq mn ᵊl-wəšš.* -- Thank heaven, we got that problem out of the way. *l-ḥamdəlla qəmna haš-šaġle mn ᵊṭ-ṭariiq.* **2.** *raaḥ (u ø) mn ᵊl-wəšš, raaḥ mn ᵊṭ-ṭariiq.* Get out of my way! *ruuḥ mən wəšši!*

under way - *žaari.* Negotiations are now under way. *l-ᵊmfaawaḍaat žaarye hallaq.*

to get under way - *bada (a ø) yəmši.* The project is slowly getting under way. *šwayye šwayye l-mašruuɛ ɛam yəbda yəmši.*

to give way - **1.** *nḥall.* The rope's giving way. *l-ḥabᵊl ɛam yənḥall.* **2.** *xafas (e/o xafᵊs).* I felt the board slowly giving way under me. *ḥasseet ᵊl-looḥ šwayye šwayye ɛam yəxfes mən-taḥti.*

to go out of one's way - **1.** *ṭaleɛ (a ø) ɛan ṭariiqo.* I'd appreciate a lift, but I don't want you to go out of your way. *bkuun mamnuunak ɛat-tawṣiile, laaken maa bəddi-yàak təṭlaɛ ɛan ṭariiqak.* **2.** *ġallab ḥaalo, ɛazzab ḥaalo.* I don't want you to go out of your way for my sake. *maa briidak ᵊtġalleb ḥaalak mənšaani.* **3.** *ɛəmel kəll žahdo.* We went out of our way to make him feel at home. *ɛməlna kəll žahᵊdna ḥatta nxallii yəšɛor kaʔənno b-beeto.*

to make one's way - **1.** *šaqq (ə ø) ṭariiqo, fataḥ (a ø) ṭariiqo.* You'll have to make your way through this crowd with your elbows. *laazem ᵊtšəqq ṭariiqak b-ᵊkwaaɛak b-haz-zaḥme.* **2.** *dabbar ḥaalo.* He'll make his way in life all right. *bidabber ḥaalo bᵊl-ḥayaat maa byənxaaf ɛaléе.*

to make way - *fataḥ (a fatᵊḥ) ṭariiq, šaqq (ə šaqq) ṭariiq.* Make way for the doctor. *ftaḥu ṭariiq ləl-ḥakiim.* -- Make way! *ftaḥu ṭariiq.*

we - *nəḥna.*

weak - **1.** *ḍɛiif* pl. *ḍɛaaf.* He's felt very weak since his illness. *šaaɛer ᵊb-ḥaalo ktiir ᵊḍɛiif mən waqᵊt maraḍo.* -- He could only speak in a weak voice. *maa qəder yəḥki ʔəlla b-ṣooṭ ᵊḍɛiif.* -- She has weak eyes. *baṣára ḍɛiif.* **2.** *ḍɛiif, waahi.* That was a rather weak argument. *hayye kaanet ḥəžže ḍɛiife šwayye.* **3.** *xafiif.* Would you like your tea weak or strong? *bətḥəbb ᵊš-šaay tabaɛak xafiif wəlla tqiil?* **4.** *naašef.* He received my proposal with a weak smile. *tqabbal ʔəqtiraaḥi b-ʔəbtisaame naašfe.*

**In a weak moment he accepted the job. *b-saaɛet ḍaɛᵊf qəbel ᵊš-šaġle.*

weakness - **1.** *ḍaɛᵊf.* Everybody can see the weakness of your argument. *kəll waaḥed fii yšuuf ḍaɛᵊf ḥəžžtak.* **2.** *nəqṭet˜* (pl. *nəqaṭ˜*) *ḍaɛᵊf.* He has many weaknesses. *fii ɛando ktiir nəqaṭ ḍaɛᵊf.* -- She has a weakness for candy. *ɛanda nəqṭet ḍaɛᵊf tižaah ᵊs-sakaaker.*

wealth - *sarwe, ġəna* (m.). I read a number of articles about the fabulous wealth of his family. *qareet ɛəddet maqaalaat ɛan ᵊs-sarwe l-haaʔile tabaɛ ɛeelto.* **2.** *baḥᵊr.* We have a wealth of information on that subject. *fii ɛanna baḥᵊr mn ᵊl-maɛluumaat ɛan hal-mawḍuuɛ.*

wealthy - *ġani** pl. *ʔaġniya* and *ġanaaya, zangiil* pl. *zanagiil.* He married a wealthy widow. *džawwaz ʔarmale ġaniyye.*

weapon - *slaaḥ* pl. *ʔasliḥa.* All weapons have to be turned over to the police. *kəll ᵊl-ʔasliḥa laazem tətsallam ləš-šərṭa.*

wear - *ḍayaan.* As for wear, you needn't have any worry. *mən žihet ᵊḍ-ḍayaan laa ykən-lak fəkre.*

**That car will take a lot of wear and tear. *has-sayyaara btəlqa daɛk ᵊktiir.*

**The cuffs are showing signs of wear. *l-qalbaat ᵊmbayyen ɛaleehon laḥa yənhəru.*

**There's still a lot of wear left in these shoes. *ləssa haṣ-ṣabbaaṭ byəlqa ktiir.*

men's wear - *malaabes rəžžaaliyye* (pl.). They carry only men's wear. *fii ɛandon bass malaabes rəžžaaliyye.*

to wear - **1.** *ləbes (e ləbᵊs//ltabas).* He never wears a hat. *maa byəlbes bərneeṭa ʔabadan.* -- What did she wear? *šuu kaanet laabse?* **2.** *ləqi (a ø).* This coat didn't wear well. *hal maanṭo maa ləqi mniiḥ.*

worn - *məhri*.* My coat is pretty worn. *kabbuudi məhri mniiḥ.* -- The rug doesn't look worn at all. *muu mbayyen ɛas-səžžaade ʔənno məhriyye ʔabadan.*

to wear down - **1.** *hara (i hari//nhara,* also *htara).* Walking on concrete will wear your heels down very rapidly. *l-maši ɛal-ʔarḍ ᵊl-baṭoon byəhrii-lek ᵊkɛaab kəndərtek b-sərɛa.* **2.** *ʔanhak.* We finally wore him down. *w-ʔaxiiran ʔanhaknáa.*

to wear off - *hamed (a hmuud), xəmed (a xmuud).* Wait till the excitement wears off. *stanna ḥatta yəhmad ᵊl-ḥamaas.*

to wear oneself out - *halak (e ø) ḥaalo.* Just don't wear yourself out! *laa təhlek ḥaalak yaa!*

to wear out - *hara (i hari//nhara,* also *htara).* These bad roads can wear out a tire in no time. *haṭ-ṭəroq ᵊl-ɛaaṭle btəhri l-kawašiik mətᵊl lamḥ ᵊl-baṣar.* -- He wears out his shoes very fast. *byəhri ṣababiiṭo b-sərɛa.*

worn-out - **1.** *mahruum.* He looks worn-out. *mbayyen ɛaléе mahruum.* **2.** *halkaan.* I'm all worn out from the trip. *ʔana halkaan tamaam mn ᵊs-safra.* **3.** *daayeb.* The gears are all worn-out. *l-ᵊmsan-nanaat kəllon daaybiin.* **4.** *məhri*.* Throw that worn-out cord away, it's dangerous. *kəbb haš-šriiṭ ᵊl-məhri, fii xaṭar.* **5.** *faareṭ.* The washing machine is so worn out that we have to get a new one. *l-ġassaale faarṭa la-daraže ʔənno laazəmna waaḥde ždiide.*

weary - *taɛbaan.* I feel very weary at times. *bḥəss ᵊb-ḥaali taɛbaan ᵊktiir mən waqt la-waqᵊt.*

weasel - *ʔəbᵊn˜ ɛərᵊs* pl. *banaat˜ ɛərᵊs.*

weather - *ṭaqᵊs, žaww.* How is the weather? *kiif ᵊṭ-ṭaqᵊṣ?*

**I'm a little under the weather today. *ʔana l-yoom muu ɛala baɛḍi.*

to weather - *tḥammal.* How did you weather the storm? *kiif ᵊtḥammalt ᵊl-ɛaaṣfe?*

to **weave** - *ḥayyak (ḥyaake).* The children wove this rug at school. *l-ᵊwlaad ḥayyaku has-səžžaade bᵊl-madrase.*

weaver - *ḥaayek* pl. *-iin, ḥayyaak* pl. *-iin.*

web - **1.** *šabake* pl. *-aat.* Have you seen that beautiful spider's web in the garden? *šəfᵊt haš-šabaket ᵊl-ɛankabuut ᵊl-ḥəlwe bᵊž-žneene?* **2.** *ʔaḥabiil* (pl.). It's all a web of lies. *kəlla ʔaḥabiil kəzᵊb.*

wedding - **1.** *ɛərᵊs* pl. *ɛraas.* I was at the wedding but not at the reception. *ḥḍərt ᵊl-ɛərs bass maa rəḥt ɛal-ʔəstəqbaal.* -- It was a quiet wedding. *kaan ɛərᵊs basiiṭ.* **2.** *ḥaflet˜* (pl. *-aat˜*) *ɛərᵊs.* We had a good time at the wedding. *nbaṣaṭna ktiir b-ḥaflet ᵊl-ɛərᵊs.*

wedding ring - *xaatem˜* (pl. *xawaatem˜*) *ᵊzwaaž.*

wedge - *ʔəsfiin* and *sfiin* pl. *ʔasafiin.*

Wednesday - *(yoom˜) ᵊl-ʔarᵊbɛa.*

weed - *ɛəšᵊb* pl. *ʔaɛšaab.* The whole garden is full of weeds. *ž-žneene kəlla malaane ʔaɛšaab.*

to weed - *ɛaššab.* I've got to weed the garden. *laazem ɛaššeb ᵊž-žneene.*

week - *žəmɛa* pl. *žəmaɛ, ʔəsbuuɛ* pl. *ʔasabiiɛ.* I'll be back in three weeks. *bəržaɛ baɛᵊd tlatt žəmaɛ.* -- We meet every week. *mnəžtəmeɛ kəll žəmɛa.* -- I go to Beirut twice a week. *bruuḥ la-beeruut marrteen bᵊž-žəmɛa.* -- He'll come a week from tomorrow. *byəži baɛd žəmɛa mən (taariix) bəkra.*

by the week - *bᵊž-žəmɛa, bᵊž-žəmɛiyye.* They pay their employees by the week. *byədfaɛu la-mwaẓ-ẓafiinon bᵊž-žəmɛa.*

weekend - *ɛəṭlet˜* (pl. *ɛəṭal˜*) *ʔaaxer˜ ᵊl-ʔəsbuuɛ.* We decided to spend the weekend at the lake. *qarrarna mmaḍḍi ɛəṭlet ʔaaxer ᵊl-ʔəsbuuɛ ɛand ᵊl-buḥayra.*

weekly - 1. *ʔəsbuuɛiyye* pl. *-aat.* He publishes a weekly. *byənšor ʔəsbuuɛiyye.* 2. *ʔəsbuuɛi*.* Is your weekly report ready? *taqriirak ᵊl-ʔəsbuuɛi ḥaaḍer šii?* 3. *ʔəsbuuɛiyyan.* This magazine appears weekly. *hal-mažalle btəṭlaɛ ʔəsbuuɛiyyan.*

to weep - *bəki (i bəke).* She wept bitter tears. *bəkyet mən ḥarqet qalba.*

weeping willow - *ṣafṣaafe* coll. *ṣafṣaaf* pl. *-aat.*

to weigh - 1. *zaan (i zeen//nzaan), wazan (-yuuzen wazᵊn//nwazan).* Please weigh this package for me. *baḷḷa zən-li hal-baakeet.* -- I weighed myself the other day at the doctor's. *wazant ḥaali hadaak ᵊl-yoom ɛand ᵊl-ḥakiim.* -- He always weighs his words carefully. *daayman biziin kalaamo mniiḥ.* 2. *wazan (-yuuzen wazᵊn).* This piece of meat weighs two kilos. *haš-šaqfet ᵊl-laḥme btuuzen kiiloyeen (or wazna kiiloyeen).*

**The responsibility weighs heavily on me. *l-masʔuuliyye taqlaane ɛaliyyi.*

weight - 1. pl. only *ʔawaaq.* The weights are under the scale. *l-ʔawaaq taḥt ᵊl-miizaan.* 2. *wazᵊn* pl. *ʔawzaan.* Did you put down the weight of the package? *qayyadᵊt wazn ᵊl-baakeet šii?* -- His opinion carries great weight. *raʔyo ʔəlo wazn ᵊkbiir.* 3. *ʔahammiyye.* Don't attach too much weight to what he says. *laa tɛalleq ʔahammiyye ktiir ɛala kalaamo.*

weights and measures - *mayaziin w-makayiil* (pl.).

weight lifting - *rafᵊɛ˜ ʔəsqaal, ḥamᵊl˜ ʔəsqaal.*

to lose weight - *nəḥef (a nəḥᵊf).* When I was sick I lost a lot of weight. *waqᵊt kənt ᵊḍɛiif ᵊnḥəft ᵊktiir.*

weighty - *xaṭiir.* I had weighty reasons for changing my mind. *kaan ɛandi ʔasbaab xaṭiira lamma ġayyarᵊt fəkri.*

weird - *məstahžan.* That's a weird story. *waḷḷa hayy qəṣṣa məstahžane.*

welcome - 1. *tarḥiib.* They gave us a warm welcome. *raḥḥabu fiina tarḥiib ḥaarr.* 2. *ʔahla w-sahla, ʔahlan wa-sahlan.* Welcome to Damascus! *ʔahla w-sahla ləš-šaam!* -- You're always welcome here. *ʔahla w-sahla fiik daayman.*

**Welcome home! *l-ḥamdəlla ɛas-salaame!*

**Thank you. - You're (quite) welcome. *šəkran.* - *ɛafwan* or *baṣiiṭa* or *laa šəkᵊr ɛala waažeb.*

**You're always welcome to use my car. *sayyaarti daayman taḥᵊt ʔamrak.*

**That is the most welcome news I've heard in months. *haada ʔasarr xabar sməɛto mən ʔəšhor.*

**His visit was a welcome interruption in our work. *zyaarto ʔažet ᵊb-waqta ka-ʔəstiraaḥa ʔəlna mn ᵊš-šəġᵊl.*

to welcome - 1. *raḥḥab b-, ʔahhal w-sahhal b-.* They welcomed us with open arms. *raḥḥabu fiina b-ḥafaawe* or *ʔahhalu w-sahhalu fiina ktiir.* 2. *raḥḥab b-.* He welcomed the opportunity to go abroad. *raḥḥab b-fərṣet safaro ləl-xaarež.*

to weld - *laḥam (e/o lḥaam//ltaḥam* and *nlaḥam).* Show him how to weld the two pipes together. *waržii kiif təlḥem ᵊl-buuriyeen sawa.*

welder - *laḥḥaam* pl. *-e.*

well - *biir* pl. *byaar(a).* They're digging a well back of the house. *ɛam yəḥᵊfru biir b-qafa l-beet.*

well - 1. *mniiḥ.* He knows Arabic well. *byaɛref ɛarabi mniiḥ.* -- He looks well preserved for his age. *huwwe ləssaato mḥaafeẓ ᵊmniiḥ bᵊn-nəsbe la-ɛəmro.* 2. *ṭayyeb.* Well, just as you say. *ṭayyeb, mətᵊl-ma bəddak.* -- Well, how are things? *ṭayyeb, kiif ᵊl-ʔaḥwaal?* 3. *xeer, ha!* Well, where did you come from?! *xeer, mneen ᵊʔžiit ʔənte?!*

**I'm not feeling well. *šaayef ḥaali muu ɛala baɛdi.*

**How well do you know him? *qaddeeš mada maɛrəftak fii?*

**There were well over a thousand people. *kaan fii ʔalf šaxᵊṣ w-quul ʔaktar.*

**Leave well enough alone. *maššii ḥaala, xalliiha mətᵊl-ma hiyye.*

**Well done, my friend! *braavo ɛaleek, yaa ʔaxi!*

as well as - 1. *w-kamaan.* He knows German as well as several other languages. *byaɛref ʔaḷmaani w-kamaan ɛəddet luġaat ġeera.* 2. *mətᵊl-ma.* He talks German as well as I do. *byəḥki ʔaḷmaani mətᵊl-ma bəḥki ʔana* or ***byəḥki ʔaḷmaani mətli.*

very well - 1. *ktiir ᵊmniiḥ.* He did it very well. *saawaaha ktiir ᵊmniiḥ.* -- The new business is doing very well. *š-šəġl ᵊž-ždiid maaši ktiir ᵊmniiḥ.* -- The patient is doing very well today. *l-mariiḍ ḥaalto ktiir ᵊmniiḥa l-yoom.* 2. *ṭayyeb.* Very well, you may go now. *ṭayyeb, fiik ᵊtruuḥ hallaq.* 3. *maa fii maaneɛ.* Please let me do it. - Very well. *bətražžaak xalliini ʔana saawiiha.* - *maa fii maaneɛ.*

**He couldn't very well refuse to come. *maa kaan ᵊb-ʔəmkaano yərfoḍ yəži.*

to get well - *ṭaab (i ø), tɛaafa, ṣaḥḥ (ə ø).* First I must get well again. *ʔawwal šii laazem ṭiib.* -- I hope you get well soon. *nšaaḷḷa tətɛaafa ɛan qariib* or ***mɛaafa nšaaḷḷa!*

well-behaved - *mrabba mniiḥ.* She's a well-behaved child. *hiyye ṭəfle mrabbaaye mniiḥ.*

well-being - *maṣlaḥa, manfaɛa, xeer.* I'm only concerned about your well-being. *ʔana kəll-ma hunaalek məhtamm ᵊb-maṣlaḥtak.*

well-done - *məstəwi mniiḥ.* The meat is well-done. *l-laḥᵊm məstəwi mniiḥ.*

well-known - *maɛruuf.* He's a well-known actor in the Middle East. *huwwe mmassel maɛruuf bᵊš-šarq ᵊl-ʔawṣaṭ.*

well-off: He is quite well-off. *ʔaḥwaalo mniiḥa.* -- He's well-off there. *maaši ḥaalo hniik.* -- He doesn't know when he's well-off. *qadd-ma kaan maaši ḥaalo ɛeeno maa btəšbaɛ.*

well-to-do - *fooq ᵊr-riiḥ.* His parents are well-to-do. *ʔahlo fooq ᵊr-riiḥ.*

**He comes from a well-to-do family. *huwwe mən ɛeele ʔaḷḷa mənɛem ɛaleeha.*

west - 1. *ġarᵊb.* The wind comes from the west. *l-hawa byəži mn ᵊl-ġarᵊb.* -- Their home faces west. *beeton ᵊmwaažeh ᵊl-ġarᵊb.* 2. *naaḥ˜ ᵊl-ġarᵊb, žihet˜ ᵊl-ġarᵊb.* The arrow points west. *s-sahᵊm biʔaššer naaḥ ᵊl-ġarᵊb.* -- They went west. *raaḥu žihet ᵊl-ġarᵊb.*

west of - *ġarb˜..., ġarbi˜...* Our house is west of the railroad tracks. *beetna ġarb ᵊs-səkke l-ḥadiidiyye.*

western - 1. *ġarbi*.* They live in the western part of the country. *saakniin bᵊl-qəsm ᵊl-ġarbi mən l-ᵊblaad.* -- The author is equally familiar with Eastern and Western civilization. *l-ᵊmʔallef ɛala ʔəṭṭilaaɛ mətsaawi ɛal-ḥaḍaara š-šarqiyye wᵊl-ġarbiyye.* 2. *ʔafranži*.* I've never seen him in western clothes. *b-ḥayaati maa šəfto laabes ʔawaaɛi ʔafranžiyye.* 3. *fəlᵊm˜* (pl. *ʔaflaam˜*) *kaawbooy.* Once in a while I enjoy going to a western. *ʔaḥyaanan bənbəṣeṭ b-ᵊmšaahadt fəlᵊm kaawbooy.*

wet - 1. *mabluul.* My socks are wet. *žraabaati mabluuliin.* 2. *məmṭer.* We had a wet summer. *ʔəžaana ṣeefiyye məmᵊṭra.* 3. *ṭari*.* Watch out, the paint is still wet. *ʔoɛa, ᵊd-dhaan ləssɛa ṭari* (or ***ləssɛa maa našef*).

to get wet - *nball, tbalbal, taštaš.* I got wet through and through. *nballeet ləl-ɛaḍᵊm.*

whale - *ḥuut(e)* pl. *ḥuwat* and *ḥwaat* and *ḥiitaan.*

wharf - *rṣiif˜* (pl. *ʔərᵊṣfet˜*) *marfaʔ.*

what - 1. *šuu.* What would you like for supper? *šuu žaaye ɛala baalak ɛal-ɛaša?* -- What's that to you? *šuu bihəmmak ʔənte?* or *šuu daxalak ʔənte?* -- What's the color of the gloves? *šuu loon l-ᵊkfuuf?* 2. *ʔeeš, šuu.* On what do you base your accusation? *ɛala ʔeeš ɛam təbni ʔəttihaamak?* -- With what do you open this box? *b-ʔeeš ᵊbtəftaḥ has-sanduuq?* 3. *šuu, ʔanu.* What things are missing? *šuu l-ʔašya l-mafquude?* or *ʔanu l-ʔašya l-mafquude?* -- Do you know what train we're supposed to take? *btaɛref ʔanu treen mafruuḍ fiina naaxod?* or *btaɛref šuu t-treen yalli mafruuḍ fiina naaxdo?* 4. *qaddeeš.* What time is it? *qaddeeš ᵊs-saaɛa?* 5. *yalli, halli.* That's just what I wanted to avoid. *haada tamaam yalli kənt raayed ʔətfaadda.* -- Thank you for these pretty gloves. They're just what I needed. *šəkran ɛal-ᵊkfuuf ᵊl-ḥəlwiin. haada yalli kaan laazəmni b-ɛeeno.* 6. *məlla.* What nonsense!

məlla ʔakᵊl hawa! -- What a lie! *məlla kəzbe!* -- What a man! *məlla rəžžaal!* 7. *qaddeeš, maa* + elative. What a big boy he is! *maašaalla, qaddeeš qəṭᵊƐto kbiire haṣ-ṣabi!* or *maašaalla maa ʔakbar(ha) qəṭƐet haṣ-ṣabi!* -- What a nice day we had yesterday! *qaddeeš nhaar ᵊmbaareh kaan həlu!* or *maa ʔahla nhaar ᵊmbaareh!* -- What beautiful flowers you have in your garden! *yaa Ɛeeni qaddeeš həlwiin haz-zhuur (halli) b-ᵊžneentak!* or *yaa Ɛeeni maa ʔahla haz-zhuur b-ᵊžneentak!* 8. *kəll šii fii...* The burglar took what money he could find. *l-haraami ʔaxad kəll šii fii maṣaari laqaaha.* -- I'll be glad to help out with what money I have with me. *b-kəll suruur məstaƐədd saaƐed b-kəll šii fii maṣaari maƐi.*

**I'll tell you what: you wait here and I'll go alone. *smaaƐ la-qəl-lak: ʔənte ntəẓer hoon w-ʔana bruuh la-haali.*

**I'll tell you what: you're plain lazy, that's all. *bəddak ᵊṣ-ṣaraaha? ʔənte kaslaan w-bass.*

**What with all I have to do, I can't be bothered with such silly things. *b-kəll halli b-raasi maa byəmkənni ʔəšġel haali b-heek tawaafeh.*

**I don't know what's what any more. *maa Ɛədt ʔaƐref kuuƐi mən buuƐi.*

what about - *šuu ṣaar b-*. What about me? *w-ʔana, šuu ṣaar fiyyi?* -- What about that job you applied for? *šuu ṣaar b-haš-šaġle halli qaddamt-əlla ṭalab?* -- What about your date? *šuu ṣaar ᵊb-mawᵊƐdak?*

what...for - 1. *leeš.* What did you do that for? *leeš ᵊƐməlt haš-šii?* 2. *la-ʔeeš, la-šuu.* What do you need this for? *la-ʔeeš bəddak haš-šii?*

what if - *šuu biṣiir ʔiza.* What if your friends don't get here at all? *šuu biṣiir ʔiza maa ʔəžu rəfaqaatak ʔabadan?*

what is more - 1. *fooq haad, fooq haš-šii, bᵊl-ʔiḍaafe la-haš-šii.* (And) what's more, he is very smart. *fooq haad huwwe ktiir zaki.* 2. *bᵊz-zaat.* I'm leaving, and what's more, today! *ʔana taarek, wᵊl-yoom bᵊz-zaat!*

what of it - *w-šuu ṣaar yaƐni?* He didn't get there in time, but what of it? *maa wəṣel la-hniik Ɛal-waqᵊt, w-šuu ṣaar yaƐni?*

and what not - *w-maa tayassar.* I've underwear and dresses and what not in that closet. *Ɛandi ʔawaaƐi w-ᵊrwaab w-maa tayassar ᵊb-hal-ᵊxzaane.*

so what - *w-šuu Ɛaléé?* All right, I haven't done it. So what? *ṭayyeb, maa saaweeta. w-šuu Ɛaléé?*

whatever - 1. *šuu-ma, mahma.* Whatever he does is all right with me. *šuu-ma byaƐmel* (or *mahma Ɛəmel*) *maa fii Ɛandi maaneƐ.* 2. *šuu-ma, ʔeeš-ma.* Do whatever you want. *Ɛmeel šuu-ma bəddak.* 3. *ʔabadan, mnoob.* I have no money whatever. *maa fii Ɛandi maṣaari ʔabadan.* 4. *kəll šii fii...* She's lost whatever respect she had for him. *ḍayyaƐet kəll šii fii ʔəhtiraam kaan Ɛanda ʔəlo.*

**Whatever made you do that? *šuu qaam Ɛaleek taƐmel haš-šii?*

whatever you say - 1. *qadd-ma btəʔmor.* How much do I owe you? - Whatever you say. *qaddeeš ṭələƐ-lak maƐi? - qadd-ma btəʔmor.* 2. *matᵊl-ma bəddak, matᵊl-ma bətriid.* Why don't we go to the beach? - Whatever you say, I don't care. *leeš maa mənruuh Ɛal-bahᵊr? - matᵊl-ma bəddak, maa btəfreq maƐi.*

whatsoever - *ʔayy ... ʔabadan, ʔayy ... mnoob.* She has no regard for others whatsoever. *maa Ɛanda ʔayy ʔəƐtibaar ləl-ġeer ʔabadan.*

wheat - *qamᵊh, hənṭa.*

wheel - 1. *duulaab* pl. *dawaliib, Ɛažale* pl. *-aat.* This wheel needs to be tightened. *had-duulaab laazmo šadd.* 2. *dərkəsyoon* pl. *-aat.* I'm dog-tired, I've been at the wheel for six hours. *ʔana halkaan mn ᵊt-taƐab, ṣar-li sətt saaƐaat wara d-dərkəsyoon.*

**We can take turns at the wheel if you want to. *fiina nətnaawab bᵊs-swaaqa ʔiza bəddak.*

**He's a big wheel in diplomatic circles. *ʔəlo wazno bᵊl-ʔawṣaaṭ ᵊd-dəblumaasiyye.*

to wheel - *daraž (o ø), karaž (o karᵊž).* Wheel the baby carriage into the garage. *droož Ɛarabiit ᵊl-walad ləl-garaaž.*

to wheel around - *daar (u ø) Ɛala kaƐbo.* He wheeled around suddenly and fired. *daar Ɛala kaƐbo fažʔatan w-qawwaṣ.*

when - 1. *ʔeemta.* When can I see you again? *ʔeemta bšuufak marra taanye?* 2. *lamma, waqᵊt-ma, waqᵊt, waqt-əlli.* When the work is done you can go. *lamma byəxloṣ ᵊš-šəġᵊl fiik ᵊtruuh.* -- When he calls up, tell him I'm not home. *waqᵊt bitalfen qəl-lo ʔana maa-li bᵊl-beet.* -- I wasn't home when he called. *maa kənt bᵊl-beet waqt-əlli talfan.*

**There are times when I enjoy being alone. *fii ʔiyyaam byəži Ɛala baali ʔəbqa la-haali.*

whenever - *ʔeemta-ma.* Come to see us whenever you have time. *taƐa zuurna ʔeemta-ma biṣiir Ɛandak waqᵊt.*

**Whenever did you find time to write? *kiif ṣaar Ɛandak waqᵊt təktob?*

where - 1. *ween, feen.* Where is the nearest hotel? *ween ʔaqrab ʔoteel?* -- Where are you? *weenak?* -- Where does the difference lie? *ween ᵊl-farᵊq?* -- Where shall I put those old newspapers? *ween hətt haž-žaraayed ᵊl-Ɛətaq?* 2. *la-ween, ween.* Where are you going? *(la-)ween raayeh?* -- Where is this letter going? *(la-)ween raayeh hal-maktuub?* 3. *mneen.* Where did you buy that hat? *mneen štareet hal-bərneeṭa?* -- Where did you catch that cold? *mneen ʔəžaak har-rašᵊh?* 4. *b-maṭrah-ma, b-mahall-ma.* We found him just where we expected him to be. *laqeenda b-maṭrah-ma kənna mətwaqqƐiin nlaaqii.* -- They will be sent where they are needed most. *laha yənbəƐtu b-mahall-ma fii ʔəlon haaže ʔaktar šii.*

**This is the house where I used to live. *haada l-beet yalli kənt saaken fii.*

where...from - *mneen.* Where is that smell coming from? *mneen žaaye har-riiha?* -- Where did you get that pen from? *mneen žəbt hal-qalam?*

**Where I come from it sometimes rains for weeks. *bᵊl-balad yalli Ɛəšᵊt fiiha ʔahyaanan ᵊl-maṭar btənzel la-məddet ʔasabiiƐ.*

wherever - *ween-ma, feen-ma, b-maṭrah-ma, b-mahall-ma.* Wherever you are, don't forget to write me. *ween-ma bətkuun laa tənsa maa təktəb-li.* -- Wherever you go in this part of the country you'll find good roads. *b-mahall-ma bətruuh ᵊb-hal-manṭiqa mən l-ᵊblaad bətlaaqi ṭoroq ᵊmniiha.*

whether - 1. *ʔiza kaan, ʔiza.* I'd like to know whether he's coming. *bhəbb ʔaƐref ʔiza (kaan) huwwe žaaye.* 2. *ʔiza, n-.* Whether you like it or not, I'll go ahead and do it. *ʔiza Ɛažabak walla laʔ* (or *n-Ɛažabak w-ᵊn-maa Ɛažabak*) *laha saawiiha.*

whey - *maṣᵊl.*

which - 1. *ʔanu* (m. f. and pl.), *ʔani* (f. only), *ʔanon* (pl. only). Which bag did you pick out? *ʔanu* (or *ʔani*) *šanta naqqeet?* -- Which instrument do you play best? *ʔanu ʔaale bədəqq Ɛaleeha ʔahsan šii?* -- Which are her children? *ʔanon ᵊwlaada?* -- Which is my pen? *ʔanu stilooyi?* -- Which one do you want? *ʔanu waahed bəddak?* 2. *yalli, halli.* Please return the book (which) you borrowed. *mən faḍlak ražžeƐ l-ᵊktaab yalli stƐərto.* -- The hat (which) I wanted is gone. *l-bərneeṭa halli kaan bəddi-ydaha raahet.*

**I picked a pencil which doesn't work. *naqqeet qalam maa byəktob.*

**It was an explosion (which) I'll never forget. *kaan ʔənfižaar ᵊb-hayaati maa bənsda.*

whichever - *ʔayy, ʔanu* (cf. **which** above). Take whichever seat you want. *xood ʔayy kərsi bəddak(-yda)* or ***xood ᵊl-kərsi yalli bəddak-yda.*

while - 1. *bərha, lahẓa.* You'll have to wait a while. *laazem təstanna šii bərha.* 2. *mədde, waqᵊt.* It took me a while to get used to it. *ləzəmni mədde hatta tƐawwadt Ɛaleeha.* -- For a while, I thought he was crazy. *haakmətni mədde hassabto mažnuun.* 3. *been-ma, ʔasnaaʔ-ma.* He called while we were out. *talfan been-ma kənna barra* (or ***talfan w-nəhna barra*). -- While you eat I'll take the children to school. *been-ma taakol baaxod ʔana l-ᵊwlaad Ɛal-madrase.* -- I want to arrive while it's still light. *bəddi ʔəṣal ʔasnaaʔ-ma tkuun ᵊd-dənye ləssaaha nhaar* (or ***bəddi ʔəṣal wᵊd-dənye ləssaaha nhaar*). 4. *been-ma, bayna-ma.* Some people live in luxury, while others starve. *fii naas Ɛaayšiin luuks been-ma l-ġeer žuuƐaaniin.*

once in a while - *mən waqt la-waqᵊt.* Once in a while I go to a movie. *mən waqt la-waqᵊt bruuh Ɛas-siinama.*

to be worth while - *haraz (e ø).* It isn't worth while. *maa btəhrez.*

to while away - *maḍḍa, ṣaraf (o ṣarᵊf), qatal (e/o qatᵊl).* I'm whiling away my time playing golf. *Ɛam maḍḍi waqti b-ləƐb ᵊl-goolf.*

whip - (with long lash) *qamše* pl. *-aat,* (usually of leather) *kərbaaž* pl. *karabiiž.* He snapped the whip. *ṭaqq ᵊl-qamše.*

to whip - 1. *ḍarab (o ḍarᵊb//nḍarab) bᵊl-kərbaaž (bᵊl-qamše).* He whipped the horse mercilessly.

ḍarab l-ᵊḥsaan bᵊl-qamše biduun raḥme. 2. *xafaq (o xafᵊq//nxafaq).* I'm whipping cream for the cake. *ɛam ʔaxfoq kreem lǝl-gaato.*

whipped cream - *kreem šaanṭii.*

whiskers - 1. *šawaareb* (pl.). A cat's whiskers are very sensitive. *šawaareb ᵊl-qaṭṭa ḥassaase ktiir.* 2. *daqᵊn* pl. *dquun(e).* Go shave off your whiskers. *ruuḥ qǝšš daqnak.*

whiskey - *wǝski.*

whisper - *hamᵊs, wašwaše.* His throat was so sore that he could only talk in a whisper. *ḥalqo kaan mǝltǝ́heb la-daraže ʔǝnno kaan kalaamo hamᵊs.*

to whisper - *wašwaš, hamas (o hamᵊs).* She whispered it in my ear. *wašwašǝt-li-yǝ́aha b-ʔǝdni.*

whistle - 1. *ṣǝffeera* pl. *-aat.* He signaled to us with his whistle. *ɛaṭaana ʔišaara b-ṣǝffeerto.* 2. *ṣafra* pl. *-aat.* The signal was one long and one short whistle. *l-ʔišaara kaanet ṣafra ṭawiile w-ṣafra qaṣiire.*

to whistle - 1. *ṣaffar.* Who's whistling? *miin ɛam yṣaffer?* 2. *ṣafar (o ṣfiir).* All night long, we heard the wind whistling in the trees. *ṭuul ᵊl-leele, smaɛna ṣfiir ᵊl-hawa been ᵊš-šažar.*

white - *ʔabyaḍ* f. *beeḍa* pl. *biiḍ.* She wore a white dress. *kaanet laabse roob ʔabyaḍ.*

white of eggs - *bayaaḍ˜ ᵊl-beeḍ.* I put in the whites of four eggs. *ḥaṭṭeet bayaaḍ ʔarbaɛ beeḍaat.*

whitewash - *ṭraaš, ṭarᵊš.* The whitewash is peeling off the walls. *ṭ-ṭraaš ɛam yǝqšor mǝn ɛal-ḥiiṭaan.*

to whitewash - *ṭaraš (o ṭarᵊš//nṭaraš).* How long will it take you to whitewash the garage? *qaddeeš byaaxdak la-ṭǝtroš ᵊl-garaaž?*

whitish - *ɛala ʔabyaḍ.* What's that whitish liquid there? *šuu has-saaʔel yalli ɛala ʔabyaḍ?*

Whitsuntide - *ɛiid˜ ᵊl-ɛanṣara.*

who - 1. *miin.* Who used this book last? *miin ʔaaxer waaḥed ᵊstaɛmal hal-ᵊktaab?* -- Whom do you want? *miin bǝddak?* 2. *miin, meen.* Who did you give it to? *la-miin ɛaṭeeta?* -- Who are you looking for? *ɛala miin ɛam ᵊddawwer?* 3. *yalli, halli.* Did you notice the man who just passed by? *laaḥaẓt ᵊz-zalame yalli hallaq maraq?* -- The friend to whom I gave it needed it badly. *ṣ-ṣadiiq yalli ɛaṭeeto-yǝ́aha kaan mǝḥtǝ́ž-la ktiir.* -- Where are the two with whom you went to school? *ween ᵊt-tneen halli rǝḥᵊt maɛon ɛal-madrase?*

**The other day I saw a man who looked very much like your brother. *hadaak ᵊl-yoom šǝfᵊt zalame byǝšbah ʔaxuuk ᵊktiir.*

**Here's a man on whom you can depend. *hayy rǝžžaal fiik tǝɛtǝ́med ɛalée.*

**I still don't know who's who around here. *lǝssaani maa baɛref ᵊl-waaḥed mn ᵊt-taani hoon.*

whoever - *miin-ma.* Whoever wants it may have it. *miin-ma bǝddo-yǝ́aha fii yaaxǝ́da.* -- Tell it to whoever you want. *quula la-miin-ma bǝddak.*

whole - 1. *kaamel.* I intend to stay a whole month. *naawi ʔǝbqa šahᵊr kaamel.* 2. *kǝll˜ ᵊl-, kǝll-* + pron. suff., *b-kaamel-* + pron. suff. I haven't been out of the house the whole week. *maa ṭlǝɛᵊt barraat ᵊl-beet kǝll ᵊž-žǝmɛa* (or *ž-žǝmɛa kǝlla* or *ž-žǝmɛa b-kaamǝ́la*). -- The whole village was flooded last winter. *kǝll ᵊḍ-ḍeeɛa ṭaafet ᵊš-šǝtwiyye l-maaḍye.* 3. *ṣḥiiḥ.* I can't swallow the pill whole. *maa bǝqder ʔǝblaɛ ᵊl-ḥabbe ṣḥiiḥa.*

**It's a whole lot cheaper than you'd think. *ʔarxaṣ b-ᵊktiir mǝmma bǝdǝnn.*

as a whole - *ka-kǝll.* You have to consider the theory as a whole. *laazem tǝɛtǝ́ber ᵊn-naẓariyye ka-kǝll.*

on the whole - *ɛal-ᵊɛmuum.* On the whole, I agree with you. *ɛal-ᵊɛmuum ʔana bwaafeq maɛak.*

wholesale - *bᵊž-žǝmle.* They sell only wholesale. *bibiiɛu bass bᵊž-žǝmle.*

wholesale price - *sǝɛr˜* (pl. *ʔasɛaar˜*) *ᵊž-žǝmle.* What's the wholesale price? *šuu sǝɛr ᵊž-žǝmle?*

wholesaler - *taažer˜* (pl. *tǝžžaar˜*) *žǝmle, taažer bᵊž-žǝmle.*

wholly - *ɛat-tamaam, kǝlliyyan.* This is not a wholly satisfactory solution, but it'll do. *hal-ḥall muu mǝrḍi ɛat-tamaam, laaken byǝmši ḥaalo.* -- The causes of lung cancer are not yet wholly understood. *ʔasbaab saraṭaan ᵊr-riʔa lǝssaata muu mafhuume ɛat-tamaam.*

whooping cough - *saɛle šahhaaqa.*

whore - *šarmuuṭa* pl. *šaramiiṭ, qaḥbe* pl. *-aat, šlǝkke* pl. *-aat, ɛaahra* pl. *-aat.*

whose - 1. *miin.* Whose watch is this? *saaɛet miin hayy?* 2. *la-miin, la-meen, tabaɛ˜ miin.* Whose is it? *la-miin hayy?* 3. *yalli, halli.* There's the lady whose bag you found yesterday. *hayy ᵊs-sǝtt yalli laqeet šantaayǝ́ta mbaareḥ.* -- Go to the people whose job it is to do it. *ruuḥ lǝl-ʔašxaaṣ halli šaġlǝ́ton ysaawuuha.*

**That reminds me of a man whose brother went with me to college. *haada bizakkǝrni b-rǝžžaal ʔaxúu raaḥ maɛi ɛaž-žaamɛa.*

why - *leeš.* Why is the train so crowded this morning? *leeš ᵊt-treen kǝll hal-qadd maɛžuuq ᵊl-yoom ᵊṣ-ṣǝbᵊḥ?* -- Why, what do you mean? *leeš, šuu bṭǝqṣod?*

**Have you eaten yet? - Why, yes! *ʔakalt šii? - ʔee naɛam!*

**Aren't you coming with us? - Why, yes! *maa-lak raayeḥ maɛna? - mbala!*

**Why, no. *laʔ ʔabadan.*

**Why, there you are! *hah, leekak!*

that's why - *mǝnšaan heek.* That's why I didn't call you. *mǝnšaan heek maa ttaṣalᵊt fiik.*

wick - *ftiile* pl. *-aat* and *fataayel.*

wide - 1. *waaseɛ.* Is the coat wide enough for you? *l-maanṭo waaseɛ ɛaleek ᵊkfaaye?* -- That discovery has opened up a wide field of research. *hal-ʔǝktišaaf fataḥ ḥaqᵊl waaseɛ lǝl-ʔabḥaas.* 2. *ɛariiḍ.* I like the wide streets in the city. *bḥǝbb ᵊš-šawaareɛ ᵊl-ɛariiḍa b-hal-balad.* 3. *kbiir.* We have a wide selection of shoes. *fii ɛanna taškiilet ṣababiiṭ ᵊkbiire.*

**The window is two feet wide. *š-šǝbbaak ɛarḍo qadameen.*

**Open the windows wide. *ftaaḥ ᵊš-šababiik ɛal-ʔaaxiir.*

**He left the door wide open. *tarak ᵊl-baab maftuuḥ ɛala mǝṣraaɛeeno.*

**You won't find one like him in the whole wide world. *law dǝrt ᵊd-dǝnye mǝn ʔawwǝ́la la-ʔaaxǝ́ra maa bǝtlaaqi waaḥed mǝtlo.*

wide-awake - 1. *fǝteḥ.* He's a wide-awake fellow. *huwwe waaḥed fǝteḥ.* 2. *waɛyaan ᵊmniiḥ, ṣaḥyaan ᵊmniiḥ.* At four in the morning I was already wide awake. *s-saaɛa ʔarbɛa ṣabaaḥan kǝnt waɛyaan ᵊmniiḥ.*

to look **wide-eyed** - *baḥlaq.* He looked at me wide-eyed. *baḥlaq fiyyi.*

to **widen** - 1. *wassaɛ, ɛarraḍ.* They're going to widen our street. *laḥa ywassɛu šaarǝɛna.* 2. *wassaɛ.* These arguments will only widen the gulf that already exists between them. *hal-ʔaxᵊd wᵊr-radd muu huwwe ʔǝlla la-tawsiiɛ huwwet ᵊl-xilaaf ᵊl-mawžuud beenaaton.*

widespread - 1. *šaayeɛ, mǝntǝ́šer.* How widespread is this view? *qaddeeš hal-fǝkra šaayɛa?* 2. *baaleġ, šaamel, ɛala niṭaaq waaseɛ.* The hail storm caused widespread damage. *zoobaɛt ᵊl-barad sabbabet xaṣaayer baalġa.*

widow - *ʔarmale* pl. *ʔaraamel.*

widower - *ʔarmal* pl. *ʔaraamel.*

widowhood - *tarammol.*

width - *ɛarḍ.* Measure the width and length of the room. *qiis ɛarḍ w-ṭuul ᵊl-ʔuuḍa.* -- The room is nine feet in width. *l-ʔuuḍa tǝsɛ ᵊqdaam ɛarḍ.* -- I need two widths of this material. *laazǝmni ɛarḍeen mǝn hal-ᵊqmaaš.*

wife - *zawže* pl. *-aat, mara* pl. *nǝswaan, madaam (madaam(e)t˜)* pl. *-aat.* She's the wife of a famous actor. *hiyye zawžet ᵊmmassel mašhuur.* -- Where is your wife? *ween madaamtak?*

wild - 1. *mǝtwaḥḥeš.* There are no wild animals in these woods. *maa fii ḥaywaanaat mǝtwaḥḥše b-hal-ġaabe.* 2. *ṭaayeš.* The children are too wild. *l-ᵊwlaad ṭaayšiin ᵊktiir.* 3. *muuḥeš.* It's wild country up there. *hal-ʔaraaḍi hniik muuḥše.* 4. *barri*.* Do you like wild strawberries? *bǝtḥǝbb l-ᵊfreez ᵊl-barri?* 5. *žnuuni*.* He's always full of wild plans. *daayman byǝṭlaɛ ᵊb-mašariiɛ ᵊžnuuniyye.*

**I'm not wild about it. *maa-li qaatel ḥaali ɛaleeha.*

**My boy is wild about ice cream. *ʔǝbni bižǝnn* (or *bimuut*) *ɛal-buuẓa.*

**The mob went wild. *r-ruɛaaɛ fǝltu.*

wilds - *barriyye.* They have a farm way out in the wilds. *ɛandon mazraɛa bɛiide bᵊl-barriyye.*

to run wild - 1. *twaḥḥaš.* The dog has run wild since his master died. *l-kalb ᵊtwaḥḥaš mǝn waqᵊt maat ṣaaḥbo.* 2. *fannak.* They just let the children run wild. *ɛam yfalltu l-ᵊwlaad yfannku.*

wildcat - *qaṭṭa* (pl. *qaṭaaṭ*) *barriyye.*

will - 1. *ʔiraade.* He has a strong will. *ɛando*

ʔiraade qawiyye. -- You came here of your own free will. *ʔžiit la-hoon ʔənte b-maṭlaq̄ ʔiraadtak.* -- Don't underestimate his will power. *laa təstahwen ᵊb-quwwet ʔiraadto.* **2.** *wṣiyye* pl. *waṣaaya.* He died without leaving a will. *maat biduun-ma yətrok ᵊwṣiyye.*

at will - *ɛala keef-* + pron. suff. They come and go at will. *biruuḥu w-ᵊbyəžu ɛala keefon* (or ***mətᵊl-ma bəddon).*

to will - *waṣṣa.* He willed all his property to the church. *waṣṣa kəll ʔamlaako ləl-ᵊkniise.*

I will, you will, etc. - no equivalent as auxiliary: I'll meet you at three o'clock. *bšuufak ᵊs-saaɛa tlaate.* -- They'll be surprised to see you here. *raḥa (or bəddon) yəstaġᵊrbu wužuudak hoon.* -- Will you please reserve a room for me? *btəḥžəz-li ʔuuḍa mən faḍlak?* -- He'll go for days without smoking. *fii yḍaayen ʔiyyaam bala tadxiin.* -- This theater will hold a thousand people. *hat-tyaatro byəsaɛ ʔalf šaxᵊṣ.* -- It won't work. *maa laḥa təštəġel.* -- Won't you come in for a minute? *tfət-lak šii daqiiqa?* -- I won't be a minute. *maa laḥa ġiib daqiiqa.* -- We would rather live in the city. *mənfaḍḍel ᵊnɛiiš bᵊl-madiine.* -- I thought that would happen. *ʔana ftakart ʔənno haš-šii bəddo yṣiir.* -- She wouldn't be comforted. *maa xallet ḥada ywaasiiha.* -- What would you like to drink? *šuu bətḥəbb təšrab?* -- I take it you won't be able to see him today. - Yes, I will. *šaayəf-lak maa laḥa təqder ᵊtšuufo l-yoom. - mbala, bəqder.*

willing - **1.** *məst(a)ɛədd.* I'm willing to try anything. *ʔana məstɛədd* (or ***ʔana ɛala ʔəstəɛdaad) žarreb ḥayyalla šii.* **2.** *hani** pl. *-iyyiin* and *hanaaya.* He's a willing worker. *huwwe šaġġiil hani.*

willow - *ṣafṣaafe* coll. *ṣafṣaaf* pl. *-aat.* There's a willow by the brook. *fii ṣafṣaafe ɛala kətf ᵊs-saaqye.*

willy-nilly: Willy-nilly I had to say yes. *n-ḥabbeet w-ᵊn-maa ḥabbeet nžabart quul ʔee.* -- She had to resign willy-nilly. *nžabret təstaɛfi n-ɛažžba walla laʔ.*

to **wilt** - *dəbel (a dabalaan).* The flowers will wilt very fast in this heat. *z-zhuur laḥa yədbalu b-sərɛa b-haš-šoob.*

to **win** - **1.** *rəbeḥ (a rəbᵊḥ), kəseb (a kasᵊb).* I'm going to win this game. *laḥa ʔərbaḥ hal-ləɛbe.* -- Last night I won almost 50 pounds at poker. *leelt ᵊmbaareḥ ksəbᵊt taqriiban xamsiin leera bᵊl-booker.* **2.** *faaz (u fooz), rəbeḥ, kəseb.* Which team do you think will win? *ʔanu fariiq btəɛtəqed bəddo yfuuz?* **3.** *faaz b-, rəbeḥ, kəseb.* He won the election. *faaz bᵊl-ʔəntixaabaat.* **4.** *rabbaḥ, kassab.* That must have won you his admiration. *haš-šii laazem ykuun rabbaḥak ʔəɛžaabo.*

to win back - *ražžaɛ.* I lost a hundred pounds, but I won it all back later in the evening. *xṣərt miit leera, laaken ražžaɛta kəlla baɛdeen bᵊl-leel.*

to win over to - *rəbeḥ (a ø) la-, kəseb (a ø) la-, žalab (e/o žalᵊb) la-.* I've won him over to our side. *rbəḥto la-ṭarafna.*

wind - *hawa* pl. *ʔəhᵊwye, riiḥ* (m. and f.) pl. *ryaaḥ.* There was a violent wind last night. *ṭəleɛ hawa qawi ᵊmbaareḥ bᵊl-leel.*

**There's something in the wind. *fii šii bᵊž-žaww.*

**I got wind of it yesterday. *driit fiiha mbaareḥ.*

**That took the wind out of his sails. *haš-šii naffas-lo manafiixo.*

to get winded - *nqaṭaɛ nafaso.* I get winded easily. *byənqəṭeɛ nafasi qawaam.*

to **wind** - **1.** *ɛarwaž, tɛarwaž.* The road winds through the mountains. *ṭ-ṭariiq biɛarwež bᵊž-žbaal.* **2.** *laff (ə laff//nlaff).* Wind it around my finger. *ləff-əlli-yḍaha ḥawaali ʔəṣbaɛti.* **3.** *rabaṭ (o rabᵊṭ//nrabaṭ).* I forgot to wind my watch. *nsiit ʔərboṭ saaɛti.*

to wind up - **1.** *laff (ə laff//nlaff).* Will you help me wind up this yarn? *bətsaaɛədni ləff hal-xeeṭ šii?* **2.** *xallaṣ, naha (i ø).* They gave him two weeks' time in which to wind up his affairs. *ɛaṭu maddet žəmᵊɛteen la-yxalleṣ ʔašġaalo.*

windmill - *ṭaaḥuun(et)˜ (pl. ṭawaḥiin˜) hawa.*

window - **1.** *šəbbaak* pl. *šababiik.* Please open the windows wide. *balla ftaaḥ ᵊš-šababiik ɛal-ʔaaxiir.* **2.** *giišẽe* (f.) pl. *giišeeyaat, šəbbaak* pl. *šababiik, ṭaaqa* pl. *-aat.* Inquire at Window Three. *stafhem mn ᵊl-giišẽe t-taalte.* **3.** *waažha* pl. *-aat, vətriin* pl. *-aat.* I saw a beautiful dress in the window. *šəfᵊt fəṣṭaan ḥəlu bᵊl-waažha.*

window frame - *bərwaaz˜ šəbbaak* pl. *barawiiz˜ šababiik.*

window shade - *bərdaaye (pl. baraadi) žarraar.*

window sill - *barṭoošet˜ šəbbaak* pl. *baraṭiiš˜ šababiik.*

windowpane - *looḥ˜ (pl. lwaaḥ˜) balloor.*

windpipe - *qaṣabe (pl. -aat) hawaaʔiyye.*

windshield - *balloor qəddaamaani.*

windshield wiper - *massaaḥet˜ (pl. -aat˜) balloor.*

windy - *məhwi.* That's a windy corner. *hal-qərne məhᵊwye.* -- Do you think it's too windy for tennis today? *btəɛtəqed ʔənno ṭ-ṭaqᵊṣ məhwi ktiir mənšaan ᵊt-tanəs ᵊl-yoom?*

wine - *nbiit, nbiid.* Do you prefer a dry wine? *bətfaḍḍel ᵊnbiit seek?*

wing - **1.** *ž(i)naaḥ* pl. *-aat* and *ʔažniḥa.* The pigeon broke its wing. *l-ḥammaame kasret žnaaḥa.* -- The office is in the left wing of the building. *l-maktab bᵊž-žnaaḥ ᵊš-šmaali tabaɛ ᵊl-binaaye.* -- The left wing of the party is growing steadily. *ž-žinaaḥ ᵊl-yasaari tabaɛ ᵊl-ḥəzᵊb ɛam yəqwa b-ʔəṭṭiraad.* -- She took him under her wing. *ḥaṭṭəto taḥt ᵊžnaaḥaata.* -- Some fifty cadets got their wings at the graduation ceremony. *ḥawaali xamsiin mən ṭəllaab ᵊl-kəlliyye ž-žawwiyye ḥəṣlu ɛala ʔažnəḥton b-ḥaflet ᵊt-taxarrož.* **2.** *kuuliis* pl. *kawaliis.* I watched the play from the wings. *tfarražᵊt ɛat-tamsiiliyye mən wara l-kawaliis.*

wink - *ġamze* pl. *-aat.* She gave me a knowing wink. *ġamzətni ġamzet waaḥde fahmaane.*

**I didn't sleep a wink. *maa ġamḍə̆t-li ɛeen.*

to wink (at) - *ġamaz (o ġamᵊz).* Did she wink at you? *ġamᵊztak šii?*

winner - *rabḥaan* pl. *-iin, raabeḥ* pl. *-iin, kasbaan* pl. *-iin, faaʔez* pl. *-iin.*

winter - **1.** *šəte.* It can be very cold here in winter. *ʔiyyaam byəḥkom bard ᵊktiir bᵊš-šəte hoon.* **2.** *šətwiyye* pl. *-aat.* They spend the summer in the mountains and the winter in Beirut. *biməḍḍu ṣ-ṣeefiyye bᵊž-žbaal wᵊš-šətwiyye b-beeruut.* **3.** *šətwi*.* I need a new winter coat. *laazəmni maanṭo šətwi ždiid.* -- I don't care very much for winter sports. *maa-li maraaq ᵊktiir bᵊr-riyaaḍa š-šətwiyye.*

winter resort - *mašta* pl. *mašaati.*

to **wipe** - **1.** *naššaf.* I'll wash the dishes if you wipe them. *ʔana bəžli ṣ-ṣḥuun ʔiza ʔənte bət-naššəfon.*

to wipe (off) - *masaḥ (a masᵊḥ//mmasaḥ).* First let me wipe off the dust. *ʔawwal šii xalliini ʔəmsaḥ ᵊl-ġabra.*

to wipe out - *masaḥ (a masᵊḥ//mmasaḥ), maḥa (i maḥi//mmaḥa).* The earthquake wiped out the whole town. *z-zalzale masḥet ᵊl-balad mən ʔasaasa.*

wire - **1.** *šriiṭ* pl. *šaraayeṭ.* The wire isn't strong enough. *š-šriiṭ muu qawi kfaaye.* **2.** *tallaġraaf* pl. *-aat, barq̄iyye* pl. *-aat.* Send him a wire. *bɛat-lo tallaġraaf.*

**Hold the wire, please! *xalliik ɛal-xaṭṭ mən faḍlak!*

**I had to pull a lot of wires to get it. *qəmt ᵊktiir mən raas haad w-ḥaṭṭeet ɛala raas haad la-ḥṣəlt ɛaleeha.*

by wire - *barq̄iyyan, tallaġraafiyyan.* I'll let you know by wire. *bxabbrak barq̄iyyan.*

barbed wire - *ʔaslaak šaaʔike* (pl.).

to wire - **1.** *baɛat (a ø) barq̄iyye, ʔabraq̄.* He wired me to meet him at the station. *baɛə̆t-li barq̄iyye* (or *ʔabrə̆q̄-li) laaqii bᵊl-ᵊmḥaṭṭa.* **2.** *madd (ə madd//mmaddet) ᵊl-kahraba b-.* It took three electricians a whole day to wire the house. *ʔaxdet tlətt kahrabžiyye yoom b-kaamlo la-ymaddu l-kahraba bᵊl-beet.* -- Who is doing the wiring in your house? *miin ɛam ymədd ᵊl-kahraba b-beet-kon?*

wisdom - *ḥəkme.*

wisdom tooth - *ḍərs˜ (pl. draas˜) ɛaqᵊl.*

wise - *ḥakiim* pl. *-iin* and *ḥəkamaaʔ.* You have made a very wise decision. *saaweet q̄araar ᵊktiir ḥakiim.* -- It was a wise man indeed who said... *kaan laa šakk ražol ḥakiim halli qaal...*

**Don't be such a wise guy! *haaže falsafe ktiir!*

to put one wise - *fattaḥ ᵊɛyuun˜ ḥada.* Don't you think we ought to put him wise? *maa btəɛtəqed ṣaar laazem nfattəḥ-lo ɛyuuno?*

wish - **1.** *rəġbe* pl. *-aat.* My wishes are easily satisfied. *rəġbaati taḥqiiqa saḥᵊl.* **2.** *tamanni* pl. *-yaat.* Best wishes for the New Year! *ʔaṭyab ᵊt-tamanniyaat bᵊl-ɛaam ᵊž-ždiid!* or ***kəll* *səne w-ʔənte saalem.*

to wish - *tmanna.* We wished him luck on his trip. *tmanneenda-lo safra saᶜiide.* -- I wish you many happy returns (of the day). *bətmannda-lak ʔiyyaam kəlla saᶜaade w-rafaahiyye.* -- I wouldn't wish it to happen to my worst enemy. *maa kənt bətmannaaha tṣiir la-ʔaladd ʔaᶜdaaʔi.* -- He wishes he were 20 years younger. *byətmanna law kaan ʔazġar ᶜəšriin səne.* -- What do you wish for most? *šuu btətmanna ʔaktar šii?*

**Did you wish that on me? *ʔənte ᶜallaqᵊtni hal-ᶜalqa?*

I wish - **1.** *ya-reet, ᶜala waah* (invar.). I wish I could stay longer. *ya-reet(ni) ʔəqder ʔəbqa ʔaktar mən heek.* -- I wish she were with us now. *ya-reet(a) kaanet maᶜna hallaq.* -- I wish you'd eat more, you're too thin. *ya-reet(ak) taakol ʔaktar mən heek, ʔənte naḥiif ᵊktiir.* **2.** *bəddi.* I wish you'd hurry up and finish your dinner! *bəddi-ydak təstaᶜžel w-ᵊtxalleṣ ᶜašaak!*

wit - *sərᶜet˜ badiiha.* What I like about him especially is his wit. *šuu byəᶜžəbni fii b-ṣuura xaaṣṣa huwwe sərᶜet badiihto.*

**He's no great wit. *huwwe muu ktiir ṭariif ᵊl-maᶜšar.*

**I'm at my wit's end. *nafdet kəll ḥiyali.*

wits - **1.** *ṣawaab.* She was out of her wits with fright. *ṭaar ṣawaaba mn ᵊl-xoof.* **2.** *ᶜaqᵊl.* You have to keep your wits about you. *laazem txalli ᶜaqlak ᵊb-raasak.*

witch - *saaḥra* pl. *-aat.* In former times they used to burn witches alive. *bᵊl-ᵊᶜṣuur ᵊl-maadye kaanu yəḥᵊrqu s-saaḥraat w-hənne ṭayybiin.*

**That old witch upstairs has caused me enough trouble. *hal-bənt ᵊl-ḥaraam fooq sabbabə́t-li wažaᶜ raas ᵊkfaaye.*

witchcraft - *səḥᵊr.*

with - **1.** *maᶜ.* I'll have lunch with him today. *bətġadda maᶜo l-yoom.* -- He took the book with him. *ʔaxad l-ᵊktaab maᶜo.* -- I don't have it with me. *maa maᶜi-ydaha.* -- Do you want something to drink with your meal? *bəddak təšrab maᶜ ʔaklak?* -- With all the work he's done he still isn't finished. *maᶜ kəll ᵊš-šəġᵊl yalli štaġal ləssa maa xalaṣ.* **2.** *b-.* I don't think you can open it with a screw driver. *maa bəᶜtəqed fiik təftaḥa b-ᵊmfakk.* -- What are you going to do with that old radio? *šuu laḥa taᶜmel b-har-raadyo l-ᶜatiiq?* -- What am I going to do with you? *šuu saawi fiik?* -- With pleasure. *b-kəll suruur* or *b-kəll mamnuuniyye.* -- The place was crawling with ants. *l-maḥall kaan ᶜam yəġli bᵊn-namᵊl.* **3.** *ᶜand.* He's staying with us. *naazel ᶜanna.* **4.** *mən.* She was green with envy. *wəšša kaan ʔaṣfar mən ḥasad.* **5.** *bᵊn-nəsbe la-.* With him it's all a matter of money. *bᵊn-nəsbe ʔəlo l-masʔale kəlla masʔalt maṣaari.* **6.** *ᶜala.* The responsibility rests with him. *l-masʔuuliyye waaqᶜa ᶜalée.*

to withdraw - **1.** *saḥab (a saḥᵊb//nsaḥab).* I withdraw the motion. *bəsḥab ᵊl-ʔəqtiraaḥ.* -- Only this morning I withdrew 200 pounds from my account. *ləssa l-yoom ᶜala bəkra saḥabᵊt miiteen leera mən ᵊḥsaabi.* -- All right, I withdraw what I said. *ṭayyeb, bəsḥab halli ḥakeeto.* **2.** *nsaḥab.* Let's withdraw to a quiet corner. *xalliina nənsə́ḥeb la-šii qərne haadye.* **3.** *nsaḥab, traažaᶜ.* The patrol withdrew under enemy fire. *d-dooriyye nsaḥbet taḥᵊt niiraan ᵊl-ᶜaduww.*

to wither - *dəbel (a dabalaan).* The leaves are withering on the branches. *l-ᵊwraaq ᶜam tədbal ᶜal-ᵊġṣaan.*

within - **1.** *ḍəmᵊn, b-.* I expect an answer within three days. *bənṭəẓer žawaab ḍəmᵊn tlətt iyyaam.* **2.** *ḍəmᵊn, daaxel, žuwwaat.* Speeding is forbidden within the city limits. *s-sərᶜa mamnuuᶜa ḍəmn ᵊḥduud ᵊl-balad.*

**The letters came within a few days of each other. *l-makatiib ʔəžet b-farᵊq kam yoom been ᵊl-waaḥed wᵊt-taani.*

**We live within easy walking distance of the theater. *saakniin laḥšet ḥažar ᶜan ᵊl-masraḥ.*

**Please stay within call. *mən faḍlak xalliik ᵊb-maḥall nəqder nnaadi-lak ʔeemta maa bəddna.*

without - **1.** *biduun, bala.* Can I get in without a ticket? *bəqder fuut biduun bileet?* -- He left without permission. *raaḥ biduun ʔəzᵊn.* **2.** *biduun-ma, bala-ma.* She left the room without saying a word. *tarket ᵊl-ʔuuḍa biduun-ma təḥki kəlme.*

**It goes without saying that you're invited. *maa bədda ḥaki ʔənte maᶜzuum.*

witness - *šaahed* pl. *šhuud.* Next witness, please. *š-šaahed ᵊt-taani mən faḍlak.*

**As God is my witness, I didn't do it. *ʔaḷḷa yəšhad ᶜaliyyi ʔana maa saaweeta.*

to witness - *šaahad, ᶜaayan.* A huge crowd witnessed the game. *fii žamᶜ ᵊkbiir šaahad l-ᵊmbaarda.* -- Did you witness the accident? *šaahadt ᵊl-ḥaades?*

witty - *ṭariif* pl. *-iin* and *ṭarafa.* He's very witty. *huwwe ktiir ṭariif.* -- That was a very witty remark. *kaanet ᵊmlaaḥaẓa ktiir ṭariife.*

wolf - **1.** *diib* pl. *dyaab.* He's a wolf in sheep's clothing. *huwwe diib b-ᵊlbaas xaaruuf.* **2.** *nəswanži* pl. *-iyye.* He has the reputation of being a wolf. *ṣiito nəswanži.*

woman - **1.** *mara (dual tənteen nəswaan)* pl. *nəswaan.* Is that woman reliable? *hal-mara fiik təᶜtə́med ᶜaleeha?* **2.** (chiefly Muslim women) *ḥarme* pl. *ḥariim, mara* pl. *nəswaan.* The women in this country are gradually discarding the veil. *l-ḥariim ᵊb-hal-ᵊblaad ᶜam yqiimu l-ᵊḥžaab šwayye šwayye.*

women's - *nəswaani*, nisaaʔi*, səttaati*.* Which floor are women's clothes on? *b-ʔanu ṭaabeq l-ʔawaaᶜi n-nəswaaniyye?*

old woman - *ᶜažuuz* pl. *ᶜažaayez.* He acts like an old woman. *byətṣarraf taṣarrof ᶜažaayez.*

womb - *raḥᵊm* pl. *ʔarḥaam.*

wonder - *məᶜžze* pl. *-aat, ᶜəžbe* and *ᶜažiibe* pl. *ᶜažaayeb.* That medicine works wonders. *had-dawa bisaawi məᶜᵊžzaat.* -- It's a wonder that you got here at all. *ᶜəžbe ʔənno ṣaar w-ᵊwṣəlt la-hoon.*

**No wonder it's cold. The window is open. *šloon maa bəddo ykuun bard wᵊš-šəbbaak maftuuḥ?*

**No wonder he flunked the exam; he didn't open a book. *šloon maa bəddo yəṣqoṭ bᵊl-faḥᵊṣ w-huwwe maa fataḥ ᵊktaab?*

to wonder - **1.** *staġrab, tᶜažžab.* I shouldn't wonder if it were true. *maa kənt bəstaġreb law kaanet ṣaḥiiḥa.* **2.** *tsaaʔal.* I often wonder whether it's worth while. *marraat ʔana bətsaaʔal ʔiza kaanet məḥᵊrze.* **3.** *fakkar, ftakar.* I was just wondering what you were doing when you called me up. *ʔana kənt ᶜam fakker yaa-tdra šuu ᶜam ᵊtsaawi waqt daqqeet-ə́lli talifoon.* -- What is it? - I was just wondering what you were doing. *šuu fii? - kənᵊt ᶜam ʔəftə́ker yaa-tdra šuu ᶜam taᶜmel.*

I wonder - *yaa-tdra, ʔabṣar.* I wonder what he'll do now. *yaa-tdra šuu raḥa ysaawi hallaq?* -- I wonder where he is. *yaa-tdra weeno?* -- I wonder if she has written him. *ʔabṣar (ʔiza) katbə́t-lo šii?* -- I wonder whether they're still here. *yaa-tdra ləssaahon hoon?*

wonderful - *təḥfe* (invar.). She's a wonderful girl. *hiyye bənᵊt təḥfe.* -- It's a wonderful opportunity for you. *hayy fərṣa təḥfe ʔəlak.*

wood - **1.** *xašab* pl. *ʔaxšaab.* What kind of wood is this? *šuu nooᶜ hal-xašab haada?* **2.** *ḥaṭab.* Go out and gather some wood. *ruuḥ ᵊžmaaᶜ-ᵊlna šwayyet ḥaṭab.*

woods - *ġaabe* pl. *-aat, ḥərᵊš* pl. *ʔaḥraaš.* Is there a path through the woods? *fii šii mamarr bᵊl-ġaabe?*

wood carver - *ḥaffaar˜* (pl. *-iin˜*) *xašab.*

wood carving - *ḥafr˜ xašab.*

piece of wood - *xašabe* pl. *-aat, šaqfet˜* (pl. *šəqaf˜*) *xašab(e),* (firewood) *ḥaṭabe* pl. *-aat, šaqfet˜* (pl. *šəqaf˜*) *ḥaṭab.*

**He isn't out of the woods yet. *ləssa maa xalaṣ mn ᵊl-mašaakel.*

wooden - *xašabi*, xašab* (invar.). The pan has a wooden handle. *l-maqlaaye ʔəla ʔiid xašabiyye* (or *ʔiid xašab*).

woodland - *ġaabaat* (pl.).

woodpecker - *naqqaar˜* (pl. *-iin˜*) *xašab.*

woodshed - *taxšiibe* pl. *-aat.*

woodworm - *suuse* coll. *suus* pl. *-aat.*

wool - *ṣuuf* pl. *ʔaṣwaaf.* The blanket is made of pure wool. *l-ᵊḥraam maᶜmuul mən ṣuuf ṣərᵊf.*

**You can't pull the wool over my eyes. *maa fiik təlᶜab ᶜaliyyi.*

woolen - *ṣuufi*, ṣuuf* (invar.). I bought a woolen sweater. *štareet kanze ṣuufiyye* (or *kanze ṣuuf* or ***kanzet ṣuuf*).

woolens - *ʔaṣwaaf* (pl.). Did you put moth balls in your woolens? *ḥaṭṭeeti naftaliin bᵊl-ʔaṣwaaf tabaᶜek?*

word - **1.** *kəlme* pl. *-aat.* We have to learn fifty new words for tomorrow. *laazem nəḥfaẓ xamsiin kəlme ždiide la-bəkra.* -- How do you spell that word?

kiif bəthažži hal-kəlme? -- In a word, no. *b-kəlme waaḥde, laʔ.* -- He gave his word that he would finish the job. *ɛaṭa kəlᵊmto ʔənno bixalleṣ ᵊš-šaġle.* -- I don't want to hear another word. *maa bəddi ʔəsmaɛ w-laa kəlme taanye.* -- May I have a word with you? *məmken ʔəḥki maɛak kəlme?* -- He doesn't let you get a word in edgewise. *maa bixallīi-lak mažaal təḥki kəlme.* -- You can't translate that sentence word for word. *maa btəqder ᵊttaržem haž-žəmle kəlme kəlme.* -- All right, repeat after me word by word. *ṭayyeb, ɛiid baɛdən mənni kəlme kəlme.* **2.** *kəlme, kalaam, qool.* He's a man of his word. *huwwe rəžžaal ɛand kəlᵊmto.* -- I said that without really meaning it, but he took me at my word. *qəlta ɛafwan, laaken qaam ʔaxadni ɛala kalaami.* -- You can take his word for it. *fiik təɛtəmed ɛala kalaamo.* -- He's a pious man in word and deed. *huwwe rəžžaal ṣaaleḥ bᵊl-qool w-bᵊl-fəɛᵊl.* **3.** *xabar.* They sent word they couldn't come. *baɛatu xabar ʔənno muu qadraaniin yəžu.* -- Have you had any word from your son lately? *ʔəžaak šii xabar mən ʔəbnak b-hal-ʔiyyaam?*

**See if you can put in a good word for me. *šuuf ʔiza fiik tətwaṣṣəṭ-li b-haš-šaġle.*

words - 1. *kalaam.* I'll never forget his words when he got the news. *b-ḥayaati maa bənsa kalaamo waqᵊt saməɛ ᵊl-xabar.* -- Mark my words! *ɛallem ɛala kalaami!* -- I don't mince my words. *ʔana maa bwaari b-kalaami.* -- If you make such bold predictions you may have to eat your words. *ʔiza btəṭlaɛ ᵊb-heek tanabbuʔaat ᵊkbiire məmken təlḥas kalaamak baɛdeen.* **2.** *kəlmaat* (pl.). I remember the tune, but I forget the words. *ɛam ʔədzakkar ᵊn-naġme, bass maa-li mədzakker kəlmaata.*

by word of mouth - *ɛan ṭariiq˜ ᵊl-ḥaki.* I only have these facts by word of mouth. *ḥəṣəlt ɛala hal-maɛluumaat ɛan ṭariiq ᵊl-ḥaki bass.*

in other words - *b-ɛibaara taanye, b-taɛbiir ʔaaxar, b-kəlme ʔəxra.* In other words, you don't like the idea. *b-ɛibaara taanye, maa-lak ḥaabeb ᵊl-fəkra.*

to word: How do you want to word the telegram? *kiif bəddak ɛibaaret* (or *ṣiiġet*) *ᵊt-tallaġraaf?* -- The ambassador delivered a strongly worded protest. *s-safiir qaddam ʔəḥtižaaž šadiid ᵊl-lahže.* -- The Foreign Ministry released a carefully worded statement. *wazaaret ᵊl-xaaržiyye ʔaṣdaret bayaan kəlmaato mnaqqaaye b-ᵊɛnaaye.*

work - 1. *šəġᵊl* pl. *ʔašġaal.* New public works are being planned. *fii ʔašġaal ɛaamme ždiide taḥt ᵊt-taṣmiim.* **2.** *šəġᵊl, ɛamal.* The work isn't interesting. *š-šəġᵊl maa bišawweq.* -- Do you like your work? *ḥaabeb šəġlak?* -- We have a lot of work these days. *fii ɛanna šəġl ᵊktiir hal-ʔiyyaam.* -- I'm up to my ears in work. *ġaaṭes bᵊš-šəġᵊl la-qaraqiiṭ ʔadaani.* **3.** *mʔallaf* pl. *-aat.* All of his works are very popular. *kəll ᵊmʔallafaato maḥbuube ktiir.* -- I haven't read his latest work yet. *ləssa maa qareet ʔaaxer ᵊmʔallaf ʔəlo.*

**It took a lot of work to convince him that we were right. *ḥtažna la-žahᵊd qawi ḥatta qanaɛnda ʔənno kənna ɛala ḥaqq.*

works - 1. *ʔawaayel* (pl.). My watch needs a new works. *saaɛti laazəma ʔawaayel ᵊždiide.* **2.** *maɛmal* pl. *maɛaamel.* There was an explosion at the gas works. *ṣaar fii ʔənfižaar ᵊb-maɛmal ᵊl-ġaaz.* **3.** *maṣlaḥa* pl. *maṣaaleḥ.* The water works were shut down. *maṣlaḥt ᵊl-miyaah ᵊtsakkaret.*

work of art - *ɛamal fanni* pl. *ʔaɛmaal fanniyye.* That's a work of art. *haada ɛamal fanni.*

out of work - *bala ɛamal, bala šəġᵊl, baṭṭaal, ɛaaṭel ɛan ᵊl-ɛamal.* He's been out of work since the factory closed. *ṣar-lo bala ɛamal mən waqᵊt sakkaret ᵊl-fabriika.*

to work - 1. *štaġal (šəġᵊl).* I work from eight to five. *bəštəġel mn ᵊt-tmaane ləl-xamse.* -- How long has he been working at his trade? *qaddeeš ṣar-lo byəštəġel b-ṣanᵊɛto?* -- The mechanic is just working on your car now. *l-miikaniiki ɛam yəštəġel hallaq ɛala sayyaartak.* -- The doctor worked over him for an hour. *l-ḥakiim štaġal ɛalée saaɛa.* -- We're working on him to give us the day off. *ɛam nəštəġel ɛalée yaɛṭiina hal-yoom fərṣa.* -- The elevator doesn't work. *l-ʔaṣanṣoor maa-lo ɛam yəštəġel.* **2.** *məši (i ø).* Come off it, that trick doesn't work with me. *ṭlaaɛ mənha, hal-ḥiile maa btəmši ɛaliyyi.* -- It doesn't always work. *maa btəmši ɛala ṭuul.* **3.** *šaġġal.* He works his employees very hard. *bišaġġel məstaxdamiino ktiir ᵊktiir.* -- Do you know how to work an adding machine? *btaɛref ᵊtšaġġel ʔaale ḥaasbe?*

**He has gradually worked himself up from office boy to vice president. *fataḥ ṭariiqo mən ʔaazen la-naaʔeb raʔiis b-kaddo w-ɛaraq ᵊžbiino.*

**I had to work my way through the crowd. *nžabarᵊt ʔəftaḥ ṭariiqi bᵊl-ɛažqa.*

**He worked his way through college. *štaġal w-ṣaraf ɛala ḥaalo bᵊž-žaamɛa.*

to work loose - *nḥall.* We almost had an accident when the steering wheel worked loose. *kaan laḥa yṣiir maɛna ʔaksiḍaan lamma d-dərkəsyoon nḥall.*

to work out - *ḥaḍḍar, rattab, waḍḍab.* We've been trying to work out a plan for such an emergency. *ṣar-ᵊlna məddе ɛam ᵊnžarreb ᵊnḥaḍḍer xəṭṭa la-ṭaareʔ mən han-nooɛ.*

**How do you think this idea would work out? *yaa-tára šuu byəṭlaɛ mən taṭbiiq hal-fəkra?*

**How did things work out? *kiif ᵊl-ʔawḍaaɛ məšyet?*

to set to work - 1. *baašar bᵊš-šəġᵊl.* He set to work immediately. *baašar bᵊš-šəġᵊl ḥaalan.* **2.** *šaġġal.* We'll set him to work as soon as he arrives. *mənšaġġlo mən waṣᵊlto.*

workday - *yoom˜* (pl. *ʔiyyaam˜*) *ɛamal, yoom˜ šəġᵊl.*

worker - 1. *šaġġiil* pl. *-e* and *-iin.* He's a good worker. *huwwe šaġġiil ᵊmniiḥ.* **2.** *šaġġiile* pl. *-aat.* She's a good worker. *hiyye šaġġiile mniiḥa.* **3.** *ɛaamel* pl. *ɛəmmaal.* The Steel Workers' Union has called for a strike. *naqaabet ɛəmmaal ᵊl-fuulaaz daɛet la-ʔəḍraab.*

working class - *ṭ-ṭabaqa l-ɛaamle, ṭab(a)qet˜ ᵊl-ɛəmmaal.*

working hours - *saaɛaat˜ ɛamal* (pl.), *saaɛaat˜ dawaam* (pl.). May I call you during working hours? *məmken talfən-lak ʔasna saaɛaat ᵊl-ɛamal?*

workman - *ɛaamel* pl. *ɛəmmaal, šaġġiil* pl. *-e.*

workshop - *warše* pl. *-aat* and *wəraš.*

world - 1. *ɛaalam, dənye* and *dənya.* He's traveled all over the world. *saafar ᵊb-kəll ʔanḥaaʔ ᵊl-ɛaalam.* -- The world has changed a lot these past 50 years. *l-ɛaalam ᵊtġayyar ᵊktiir b-hal-xamsiin səne l-ʔaxiire.* -- A child's world is very small. *dənya ṭ-ṭəfᵊl ṣġiire ktiir.* -- Even if he resigns, it still won't be the end of the world. *ḥatta w-ʔiza staɛfa, muu laḥa təxrab ᵊd-dənye.* **2.** *ɛaalam.* He's a famous name in the world of sports. *huwwe ɛalam mašhuur b-ɛaalam ᵊr-riyaaḍa.* -- She's known throughout the Arab world. *hiyye maɛruufe b-kəll ᵊl-ɛaalam ᵊl-ɛarabi.* -- The Free World has its share of economic problems too. *l-ɛaalam ᵊl-ḥərr ʔəlo ḥəṣṣto mn ᵊl-mašaakel ᵊl-ʔᵊqtiṣaadiyye kamaan.* **3.** *dənye.* It will do him a world of good to get away from home. *byəntəfeɛ qadd ᵊd-dənye ʔiza ġab-lo šwayye ɛan ᵊl-beet.* -- My father thinks the world of you. *ʔabi biqaddrak qadd ᵊd-dənye.* -- I wouldn't hurt him for the world. *maa bəʔzi w-law ɛaṭuuni maal ᵊd-dənye.* **4.** *ɛaalami*.* More and more people are dreaming of a world government. *ɛam yəzdaad ɛadad ᵊn-naas yalli ɛam yəḥlamu b-ᵊḥkuume ɛaalamiyye.* -- My father was wounded in World War II. *ʔabi nžaraḥ bᵊl-ḥarb ᵊl-ɛaalamiyye t-taanye.* **5.** *duwali*.* The World Bank is contributing 50 million dollars. *l-bank ᵊd-duwali ɛam ysaahem b-xamsiin malyoon dolaar.*

**Where in the world have you been? *mənšaan ʔaḷḷa, lək ween kənᵊt?*

worm - *duude* coll. *duud* pl. *-aat* and *diidaan.* Do you use worms for bait? *bəthəṭṭ duud mənšaan ᵊṭ-ṭəɛᵊm?*

worry - *hamm* pl. *hmuum, ġamm* pl. *ġmuum.* Her son gave her a great deal of worry. *ʔəbna sabbáb-la hamm ᵊktiir.*

to worry - 1. *qalaq (e qalaq).* His silence worries me. *skuuto byəqləqni.* **2.** *šaġal (e šaġalaan) baal˜...* The future doesn't worry him. *l-məstaqbal muu šaaġəl-lo baalo.* -- I won't let that worry me. *maa bxalli haš-šii yəšġəl-li baali.* -- Don't worry! *laa təšġel baalak!* -- You have nothing to worry about. *maa fii šii təšġel baalak ɛalée.* -- I really can't worry about that. *bᵊl-ḥaqiiqa maa fiini ʔəšġel baali b-haš-šii.*

worried - *mahmuum, mašġuul˜ ᵊl-baal.* Why are you so worried? *leeš hal-qadd mahmuum?* -- I'm worried because I haven't heard from him in a week. *ʔana mašġuul ᵊl-baal* (or *mašġuul baali*) *laʔənno maa ʔəžaani mənno xabar mən žəmɛa.*

**She looked at him with a worried expression on her face. *ṭṭallaɛet ɛalée w-wəšša kəllo ġamm w-hamm.*

worse - *ʔalɛan.* He's feeling worse this morning. *šaaɛer b-ḥaalo ʔalɛan ᵊl-yoom ɛala bəkra.* -- He's even worse off now. *w-ḥatta waḍɛo ʔalɛan hallaq.*
**It's snowing worse than ever. *naazel talᵊž ʔalɛan mən kəll marra.*
**He's none the worse for it. *maa ʔəžda mənha ʔayy ḍarar.*
from bad to worse - *mən sayyeʔ la-ʔaswaʔ, mən laɛne la-ʔalɛan.* His business is going from bad to worse. *tižaarto maašye mən sayyeʔ la-ʔaswaʔ.*
to get worse - *ltaɛan, ntaḥas.* Things are getting worse instead of better. *l-ʔawḍaaɛ ɛam təltáɛen ɛawaaḍ-ma ɛam təthassan.* -- Her condition is getting worse and worse. *ḥaaláta ɛam təntáḥes ʔaktar w-ʔaktar.*

worship - *ɛbaade.* We differ in our ways of worship. *mnəxtélef ᵊb-ṭəroq ᵊɛbaadətna.*
to worship - *ɛabad (o ɛbaade//nɛabad).* He worshipped her. *ɛabdáa.*

worst - *ʔaɛṭal, ʔanḥas, ʔalɛan, ʔaswaʔ.* But wait, I haven't told you the worst. *stanna šwayye, ləssa maa xabbartak ᵊl-ʔaɛṭal.* -- The worst is yet to come. *l-ʔanḥas žaaye ɛaṭ-ṭariiq ləssa.* -- We're over the worst of it. *žtəzna l-ʔalɛan* or *žtəzna ʔalɛan marḥale.* -- I got the worst piece. *ʔaxadᵊt ʔaɛṭal šaqfe.* -- It's the worst accident I can remember. *hayy ʔalɛan ʔaksiḍaan bədzakkára.* -- Of the three he's worst off. *mn ᵊt-tlaate waḍɛo ʔalɛan waaḥed.* -- Unemployment is worst in winter. *l-baṭaale ʔalɛan maa tkuun b-faṣl ᵊš-šəte.*
**He got the worst of the argument. *ṭaleɛ maġluub bᵊl-ᵊmžaadale.*
at (the) worst - *b-ʔaswaʔ˜ ᵊl-ḥaalaat, b-ʔalɛan˜ ᵊl-ḥaalaat, b-ʔanḥas˜ ᵊl-ḥaalaat.* At worst, the storm may last a week. *b-ʔaswaʔ ᵊl-ḥaalaat ᵊl-ɛaaṣfe bəddum žəmɛa.*
if worst comes to worst - *b-ʔaswaʔ˜ ᵊl-ḥaalaat, b-ʔalɛan˜ ᵊl-ḥaalaat, b-ʔanḥas˜ ᵊl-ḥaalaat.* If worst comes to worst, we can always sell our property. *b-ʔaswaʔ ᵊl-ḥaalaat fiina nbiiɛ məlᵊkna.*

worth - *qiime.* He didn't appreciate her true worth. *maa qaddar qiimáta ḥaqq qadra.*
**Did you get your money's worth out of that trip? *ḥarzet has-safra maṣruufak?*
**We certainly got our money's worth out of our car. *ʔakiid waḷḷa məṣriyyaatna maa raaḥet ḍyaaɛa b-has-sayyaara.*
**Give me fifty piasters' worth of peanuts. *ɛaṭiini b-xamsiin qərᵊš fəstoq ɛabiid.*
**I'll make it worth your while. *bxalliik təntáfeɛ mənha.*
to be worth - 1. *kaan (b)yəswa.* That horse is worth five hundred dollars. *hal-ᵊḥṣaan byəswa xamᵊs miit dolaar.* -- (I think) he's easily worth a million. *(bẓənn) byəswa malyoon ɛal-ʔaqall.* -- That house is worth every penny we put into it. *hal-beet byəswa kəll qərᵊš ḥaṭṭéenda fii.* 2. *ḥaraz (e ø).* It's worth the trouble. *btəḥrez (ᵊl-ġalabe).* -- It's worth (while) trying. *btəḥrez l-ᵊmḥaawale.* -- Was it worth your while? *yaa-tára ḥarzet šii bᵊn-nəsbe ʔəlak?* -- Is the book worth reading? *l-ᵊktaab byəḥrez yənqára* (or *btəḥrez ᵊqraayto)?* -- That mosque is really worth seeing. *haž-žaameɛ bᵊl-ḥaqiiqa byəḥrez yənšaaf* (or *btəḥrez šoofto).*

worthless - *bala qiime.* That bracelet is worthless, you might as well throw it away. *has-swaara bala qiime* (or ***maa-la qiime* or ***maa btəswa nḥaase),* *maa fii xṣaara tkəbba.* -- His advice proved completely worthless. *naṣiiḥto ṭaleɛet bala qiime bᵊl-marra.*

worthy - 1. *məḥrez.* This money is for a worthy cause. *hal-maṣaari la-ġaraḍ məḥrez.* 2. *žadiir.* She's certainly worthy of the honor. *mən kəll bədd hiyye žadiira bᵊš-šaraf.*

wound - *žərᵊḥ* pl. *žruuḥ(a).* It will be a couple of months before the wound in his leg is healed. *bədda l-masʔale šahreen ḥatta yəlʔem ᵊž-žərḥ ᵊb-saaqo.*
to wound - *žaraḥ (a žarᵊḥ//nžaraḥ).* Several men were wounded in the brawl. *fii ɛəddet ᵊržaal ᵊnžaraḥu bᵊl-ᵊxnaaqa.*

wrap - *laḥše* pl. *-aat.* Put on a wrap if you go outside. *ḥəṭṭi-lek laḥše ʔiza ṭaalɛa la-barra.*
to wrap (up) - *ṣarr (ə ṣarr//nṣarr), laff (ə laff//nlaff).* Shall I wrap it up for you? *ṣərr-əllak-yáaha?* -- Will you wrap this package as a gift, please? *baḷḷa ṣərr-ə́lli hal-baakeet ṣarret ᵊhdiyye.* -- The chocolate comes wrapped in waxpaper. *š-šakaleeṭa bətkuun maṣruura b-waraq ᵊmšammaɛ.*
**I have the scholarship just about wrapped up. *l-mənḥa taqriiban ṣaaret ᵊb-žeebti.*
wrapped up in - *makbuub ɛala.* He's all wrapped up in his work. *makbuub ɛal-ʔaaxiir ɛala ɛamalo.*

wrapping paper - *waraq˜ ṣarr, waraq˜ laff.*

wrath - *ġaḍab.*

wreath - *ʔəkliil* and *kliil* pl. *ʔakaliil.*

wreck - 1. *ḥiṭaam.* The ship's wreck is still visible under the water. *ləssa ḥiṭaam ᵊl-baaxra byənšaaf taḥt ᵊl-mayy.* 2. *ʔanqaaḍ* (pl.). The bodies are still buried in the wreck. *ž-žəsas ləssaaton taḥt ᵊl-ʔanqaaḍ.* 3. *ʔaksiḍaan* pl. *-aat.* Were any killed in the wreck? *ḥada qətel bᵊl-ʔaksiḍaan?*
**He's a complete wreck. *faareṭ ɛal-mazbuuṭ huwwe.*
to wreck - *xarrab//txarrab.* The car was completely wrecked. *s-sayyaara txarrabet ɛal-ʔaaxiir.* -- The explosion wrecked the whole plant. *l-ʔənfižaar xarrab ᵊl-fabriika kəlla.*

wrench - 1. (single or double-head) *məftaaḥ˜* (pl. *mafatiiḥ˜*) *šaqq.* 2. (Stillson) *məftaaḥ ʔəngliizi* pl. *mafatiiḥ ʔəngliiziyye.* 3. (monkey wrench) *bahbahaane* pl. *-aat.*

to **wrestle** - 1. *tṣaaraɛ.* I used to wrestle with my brother when we were boys. *kənt ᵊtṣaaraɛ ʔana w-ʔaxi lamma kənna wlaad.* 2. *ɛaarak.* I've been wrestling with this problem for hours. *ṣar-li ɛam ɛaarek (b-)hal-məšᵊkle saaɛaat.*

wrestler - *mṣaareɛ* pl. *-iin.*

wrestling - *mṣaaraɛa.* Don't miss the wrestling match tonight on television. *laa txalliiha tfuutak ᵊmbaaraat l-ᵊmṣaaraɛa bᵊt-televəzyoon l-leele.*

to **wring** - 1. *ɛaṣar (o/e ɛaṣᵊr//nɛaṣar).* Wring the towels well before you hang them on the line. *ɛṣoor ᵊl-bašakiir ᵊmniiḥ qabᵊl-ma tənšəron ɛal-ḥabᵊl.* 2. *farrak.* Just standing there and wringing your hands won't help a bit. *waqᵊftak hoon w-tafriikak ʔideek muu laha yfiid šii.*

wrinkle - *tažɛiide* pl. *-aat* and *tažaɛiid, žaɛde* pl. *-aat.* Her face is full of wrinkles. *wəšša malaan tažaɛiid.*
to wrinkle - 1. *qaṭṭab.* He wrinkled his forehead. *qaṭṭab ᵊžbiino.* 2. *žaɛlak//džaɛlak.* You'll wrinkle your suit if you don't hang it up properly. *bədžaɛlek badᵊltak ʔiza maa bətɛalláqa mazbuuṭ.* 3. *džaɛlak.* This silk wrinkles easily. *hal-ḥariir byədžaɛlak b-ᵊshuule.*

wrist - *rəsᵊġ* pl. *rsuuġa.* She broke her wrist. *kasret rəsġa.*
wrist watch - *saaɛet˜* (pl. *-aat˜*) *ʔiid.* My wrist watch is gone. *saaɛet ʔiidi xtafet.*

to **write** - 1. *katab (o ktaabe, ktiibe//nkatab).* Write your name on the first line. *ktoob ʔəsmak b-ʔawwal ṣaṭᵊr.* -- This pen writes well. *hal-qalam byəktob ɛaal.* 2. *kaatab, raasal.* He's been writing me for years. *ṣar-lo sniin ɛam ykaatəbni.*
to write down - *katab (o ktaabe, ktiibe//nkatab), qayyad//tqayyad.* Write down that telephone number before you forget it. *ktoob han-nəmret ᵊt-talifoon qabᵊl-ma tənsaaha.*
to write each other - *tkaatabu, traasalu.* We've been writing each other regularly for quite a while. *ṣar-ᵊlna mədde ɛam nətkaatab b-ʔəntiẓaam.*
to write off - *ḥazaf (e/o ḥazᵊf//nḥazaf), nasax (a nasᵊx//ntasax).* You'd better write that off as a bad debt. *ʔaḥsán-lak təḥzə́fa deen mayyet.*
to write out - *katab (o ktaabe, ktiibe//nkatab).* Please write out that check for me before I go. *baḷḷa ktəb-li haš-šakk qabᵊl-ma ruuḥ.*

writer - 1. *kaateb* pl. *kəttaab.* My son wants to become a writer. *ʔəbni bəddo yṣiir kaateb.* 2. *kaatbe* pl. *-aat.* My daughter is a writer. *bənti kaatbe.*

writing - 1. *xaṭṭ* pl. *xṭuuṭ, ktaabe, ktiibe.* I can't read his writing. *maa bəqder ʔəqra xaṭṭo.* 2. *ktaabe, ktiibe.* I don't get around to writing. *maa ɛam yṣiir maɛi waqᵊt ləl-ᵊktaabe.* -- The walls were covered with Arabic writing I couldn't read. *l-ḥiiṭaan kaanet malaane ktaabe ɛarabiyye maa ɛrəfᵊt ʔəqraaha.* -- I'm looking for some writing paper. *ɛam dawwer ɛala waraq ᵊktiibe.*
in writing - *xaṭṭan, kitaabatan, maktuub.* I'd like to have that in writing. *bəddi haš-šii xaṭṭan.*

wrong - 1. *xaṭaʔ.* He admitted that he was in the wrong. *ɛtaraf ʔənno kaan ɛala xaṭaʔ* (or ***...kaan məxṭe* or ***...kaan ᵊl-ḥaqq ɛalée).* 2. *ʔaza.* You'll regret the wrong you do to others. *btəndam ɛal-ʔaza halli bətsabbabo ləl-ġeer.* 3. *ġalaṭ* (invar.). I must have added the figures up wrong again. *laazem kuun žamaεt ᵊl-ʔarq̈aam ġalaṭ taani marra.* -- You're heading in the wrong direction. *ʔənte raayeḥ b-ʔəttižaah ġalaṭ.* -- You got me all wrong. *fhəmᵊtni ġalaṭ.* -- You did it wrong again. *saaweeta ġalaṭ taani marra.* -- I must have dialed the wrong number. *laazem kuun ḍarabᵊt nəmra ġalaṭ.* -- You gave me the wrong book. *εaṭeetni l-ᵊktaab ᵊl-ġalaṭ.* -- I entered by the wrong door. *fətt ᵊmn ᵊl-baab ᵊl-ġalaṭ.* -- He was driving on the wrong side of the street. *kaan εam ysuuq εala žihet ᵊš-šaareε ᵊl-ġalaṭ.*

**He got out on the wrong side of the bed. *tṣabbaḥ bᵊš-šeeṭaan.*

to be wrong - *ʔaxṭaʔ, ġəleṭ (a ġalaṭ).* I'm afraid you're wrong. *bẓənn-ə́llak ʔənte maxṭeʔ.* -- There she's wrong. *b-han-naaḥye hiyye ġalṭaane.* -- I'll admit that I was completely wrong about him. *bəεtə́ref ʔənni kənt ġalṭaan tamaam b-ḥaqqo.* -- I was wrong about the time of the ceremony. *kənᵊt ġalṭaan ᵊb-waqt ᵊl-ʔəḥtifaal.*

**Something is wrong with the telephone. *fii šii xarbaan bᵊt-talifoon.*

**Is anything wrong with you? *šə-bak, fii šii ḥaakmak ᵊl-yoom?*

**There's nothing wrong with that radio. *har-raadyo maa fii šii.*

**Do you think there's something wrong with that man? *btəεtə́qed fii šii muriib b-has-zalame?*

**You know what's wrong with this country? There isn't enough rain. *btaεref šuu εəllet˜ (or mṣiibet˜) hal-ᵊblaad? qəllet ᵊl-maṭar.*

to go wrong - **1.** *ʔəža bᵊl-εakᵊs.* Everything went wrong yesterday. *kəll šii mbaareḥ ʔəža bᵊl-εakᵊs.* **2.** *ntazaε, xəreb (a ø).* Something's gone wrong at the power plant. *fii šii ntazaε b-ᵊmḥaṭṭet tawliid ᵊl-kahraba.*

to wrong - *ẓalam (o ẓəlᵊm//nẓalam).* He felt wronged. *šaεar ᵊb-ḥaalo maẓluum (or nẓalam).* -- She thinks she's been wronged. *btəftə́ker ḥaala maẓluume.*

wrought iron - *ḥadiid ᵊmṭaaweε.*

wry - *maεuuž.* He has all kinds of wry notions in his head. *raaso malaan ʔafkaar maεuuže.*

**She made a wry face when I mentioned his name. *barmet buuza lamma zakarᵊt ʔəsmo.*

X

X-ray - **1.** *ʔašəεεet˜ rondžen* (pl.). Who discovered the X ray? *miin ᵊktašaf ʔašəεεet rondžen?* **2.** *ṣuuret˜* (pl. *ṣuwar˜*) *ʔašəεεa.* May I see the X ray? *məmken šuuf ṣuuret ᵊl-ʔašəεεa?*

X-ray treatment - *tadaawi bᵊl-ʔašəεεa.* X-ray treatments are quite expensive. *t-tadaawi bᵊl-ʔašəεεa˜ ġaali ktiir.*

to X-ray - *ṣawwar bᵊl-ʔašəεεa.* The dentist X-rayed my teeth. *ḥakiim ᵊs-snaan ṣawwar-li snaani bᵊl-ʔašəεεa.*

Y

yacht - *yaxt* pl. *yxuut(e).*

yard - *yard* pl. *-aat.* I'd like to have five yards of broadcloth. *bəddi xamᵊs yardaat žuux.*

yard - *saaḥa* pl. *-aat, fasḥa* pl. *-aat.* The house has a yard for the children to play in. *l-beet fii saaḥa mənšaan l-ᵊwlaad yəlεabu fiiha.*

freight yard - *mḥaṭṭet˜* (pl. *-aat˜*) *šaḥᵊn.* Where is the freight yard? *ween ᵊmḥaṭṭet ᵊš-šaḥᵊn?*

lumber yard - *məstawdaε˜* (pl. *-aat˜*) *xašab, dabbo˜* (pl. *dabboyaat˜*) *xašab.* You may be able to get that at the lumber yard. *bižuuz ᵊtlaaqi haš-šii b-məstawdaε ᵊl-xašab.*

yarn - **1.** *xiiṭaan* (pl.), *ġazᵊl.* I'll take six balls of that green yarn. *baaxod sətt kabakiib mən hal-xiiṭaan ᵊl-xəḍᵊr.* **2.** *xuraafe* pl. *-aat.* As children we liked the yarns he used to tell us. *waqᵊt kənna wlaad kənna nənbə́ṣeṭ bᵊl-xuraafaat yalli kaan yəḥkii-lna-ydaha.*

to **yawn** - *ttaawab (mtaawabe).*

year - *səne* pl. *sniin,* (with diminutive connotations) *sanawaat.* He's thirty years old. *εəmro tlaatiin səne.* -- What's a B.A.? It takes only a few years. But a doctorate - that takes years and years. *šuu l-bii ʔee yaεni? bədda bass sanawaat. bass ᵊd-doktoorda bədda sniin ṭawiile.* -- Do you know how to convert Christian into Muslim years? *btaεref ᵊtḥawwel ᵊs-səne l-miilaadiyye ləs-səne l-həžriyye?* -- Next year will be a leap year. *s-səne ž-žaaye bətkuun səne kabiise.* -- Muslims count by lunar years, not solar years. *l-məsᵊlmiin biʔarrxu bᵊs-səne l-q̈amariyye, muu bᵊs-səne š-šamsiyye.*

**He's well on in years. *huwwe mətqaddem bᵊl-εəmᵊr.*

year in, year out - *səne baεᵊd səne, səne wara səne.* Year in, year out, the same routine. *səne baεᵊd səne nafs ᵊr-ruutiin.*

all year round - *ṭuul ᵊs-səne.* They live in the city all year round. *byəsᵊknu bᵊl-balad ṭuul ᵊs-səne.*

for years - **1.** *mn ᵊsniin.* I haven't seen him for years. *maa šəfto mn ᵊsniin* or ****ṣar-li sniin maa šəfto.* **2.** *sniin w-ᵊsniin.* You can study that for years and never get anywhere. *fiik tədros haš-šii sniin w-ᵊsniin w-muu laḥa təṣal la-natiiže.* **3.** *b-ᵊsniin.* That bridge won't be finished for years. *haž-žəsᵊr maa byəxloṣ b-ᵊsniin.*

in years - **1.** *mn ᵊsniin.* I haven't seen him in years. *maa šəfto mn ᵊsniin* or ****ṣar-li sniin maa šəfto.* **2.** *la-sniin w-ᵊsniin.* They'll remember him in years to come. *biḍallu mədzakkriino la-sniin w-ᵊsniin.*

last year - *εaamnawwal, s-səne l-maaḍye.* I saw him in Cairo last year. *šəfto εaamnawwal bᵊl-q̈aahira.*

next year - *s-səne ž-žaaye.* I'll be abroad next year. *bkuun barraat l-ᵊblaad ᵊs-səne ž-žaaye.*

the year before last - *ʔawwal εaamnawwal.* The year before last I was in Switzerland. *ʔawwal εaamnawwal kənt b-ᵊswiisra.*

that year - *hadiik ᵊs-səne, sənta.* That year we had a bad drought. *hadiik ᵊs-səne ṣaar εanna maḥᵊl malεuun.*

this year - *has-səne, s-səne.* What are you going to do this year? *šuu raḥa taεmel has-səne?*

two years ago - *ʔawwal εaamnawwal.* Two years ago I made the Pilgrimage. *ḥažžeet ʔawwal εaamnawwal.*

yearly - **1.** *bᵊs-səne, sanawiyyan.* How much is it yearly? *qaddeeša bᵊs-səne?* **2.** *sanawi*.* My uncle pays us a yearly visit. *εammi byaεmə́l-lna zyaara sanawiyye* or ****εammi bizuurna bᵊs-səne marra.* -- His yearly income is no more than 6,000 pounds. *daxlo s-sanawi maa byədžaawaz sətt aalaaf leera.*

yeast - *xamiire* pl. *-aat* and *xamaayer.*

yell - *εyaaṭa* pl. *-aat, ṣarxa* pl. *-aat.* Did you hear that yell? *sməεt hal-ᵊεyaaṭa?*

to yell - *εayyaṭ, ṣarax (a ṣraax).* We heard someone yelling for help. *sməεna waaḥed εam yεayyeṭ lən-nažde.*

yellow - **1.** *ʔaṣfar* f. *ṣafra* pl. *ṣəfᵊr.* She's wearing a yellow dress. *laabse fəsṭaan ʔaṣfar.* -- Most of Asia is inhabited by the yellow race. *məεẓam səkkaan ʔaasya mn ᵊl-εərq̈ ᵊl-ʔaṣfar.* **2.** *ṣafaar.* Put in the yellows of three eggs. *ḥəṭṭi ṣafaar tlətt beeḍaat.* **3.** *žabaan* pl. *žəbana.* You're just yellow, that's why you don't want to do it. *ʔənte žabaan, mən heek maa-lak raayed taεmə́la.*

yellow fever - *ḥəmma ṣafraaʔ.*

yellowish - *εala ʔaṣfar, εala ṣafaar.* The towel has a yellowish color. *l-baškiir loono εala ʔaṣfar.*

Yemen - **1.** (country) *l-yaman.* **2.** (adj.) *yamani*.*

Yemeni - *yamani** pl. *-iyyiin* and *-iyye.*

yes - *ʔee, naεam.* She answered yes. *žaawabet ʔee.* -- Yes, I'll be glad to go. *naεam, bruuḥ ᵊb-kəll* *suruur.* -- She said yes to my question. *qaalə́t-li naƐam Ɛala su?aali.* -- Did you understand me? - Yes, madam! *fahmaan Ɛaliyyi? - naƐam yaa madaam!* (or *?ee naƐam!*) -- Did you understand me? - Yes, sir! *fahmaan Ɛaliyyi? - naƐam yaa siidi!* (or *?ee naƐam!*).

yesterday - *mbaareḥ, mbaarḥa.* I saw him only yesterday. *ləssa mbaareḥ šəfto.*

the day before yesterday - *?awwal əmbaareḥ, ?awwalt əmbaareḥ.* He left the day before yesterday. *saafar ?awwal əmbaareḥ.*

yet - **1.** *walla ləssa.* Did you see the new play yet? *šəft ət-tamsiiliyye ž-ždiide walla ləssa?* -- Have you selected anything yet? *naqqeet šii walla ləssa?* **2.** *ləssa, ləssa-* + pron. suff., *ləssaat-* + pron. suff. Haven't you read the book yet? *ləssa* (or *ləssaak* or *ləssaatak*) *maa qareet l-əktaab?* -- He hasn't come yet. *ləssa* (or *ləssda* or *ləssaato*) *maa ?əža.* -- I'll get him yet! *ləssa* (or *ləssaani* or *ləssaat(n)i*) *bəl əqṭo!* -- The day will yet come when I can give him a piece of my mind! *ləssa byəži l-yoom halli bwarži fii nžuum əd-dahər.* **3.** *bass, laaken.* He didn't want to go, yet he had to. *maa kaan ḥaabeb yruuḥ, bass ənžabar.* **4.** *maƐ zaalek, maƐ haada.* And yet you can't help liking him. *w-maƐ zaalek maa fiik ?əlla tḥəbbo.*

**I've yet to see it myself. *laazem šuufa b-zaati.*

as yet - *la-ḥadd hallaq.* As yet, we haven't had any news of her. *la-ḥadd hallaq maa ?əžaana mənha xabar.*

yield - *maḥṣuul* pl. *maḥaṣiil.* What is the yield per feddan here? *qaddeeš maḥṣuul əl-faddaan hoon?*

to yield - **1.** *darr (ə ø).* His business doesn't yield much profit. *tižaarto maa bəddərr ?arbaaḥ əktiir.* **2.** *ṭaalaƐ, Ɛaṭa (-yaƐṭi ø).* None of our experiments has yielded concrete results so far. *w-laa waaḥde mən tažaarəbna ṭaalaƐet ?ayy nataayež maḥsuuse la-hallaq.* **3.** *sallam.* I'll yield on this point. *bsallem b-han-nəqṭa.* -- I won't yield. *maa bsallem ?abadan.*

Y.M.C.A. - *žamƐiyyet~ əš-šəbbaan əl-masiiḥiyyiin.*

yoghurt - *laban.*

yoke - *niir* pl. *nyaar.*

yoke of oxen - *faddaan* pl. *fadadiin.*

yokel - *ḍiyaƐi** pl. *-iyye, žəl əf* (invar.), *žaaye* (pl. *žaayiin*) *mən wara l-baqar.* What's that yokel doing here? *šuu haḍ-ḍiyaƐi* (or *haž-žəl əf* or *haž-žaaye mən wara l-baqar*) *Ɛam yaƐmel hoon?*

yolk - *ṣafaar~ beeḍa* coll. *ṣafaar~ beeḍ* pl. *ṣafaar~ beeḍaat.* Stir in five yolks. *xfəqi ṣafaar xaməs beeḍaat.*

you - *?ənte* f. *?ənti* pl. *?əntu.*

young - *ẓġiir* pl. *ẓġaar.* He's still young. *ləssaato ẓġiir.* -- His mother is still young for her age. *?əmmo ləssaaha ẓġiire bən-nəsbe la-Ɛəmra.* -- He's too young for that job. *huwwe ẓġiir əktiir Ɛala haš-šaġle.* -- My sister is much younger than I. *?əxti ?aẓġar mənni b-əktiir.* -- He's the youngest of the children. *huwwe ?aẓġar waaḥed mən l-əwlaad.*

**The night is still young. *l-leel ləssda b-?awwalo.*

**I never worked very hard in my younger days. *b-ḥayaati maa taƐabət ḥaali ?iyyaam šbuubiiti.*

**Our cat had young ones two days ago. *qaṭṭətna žaabet əwlaad ?awwal əmbaareḥ.*

young girl, young lady - *šaabbe* pl. *-aat, ṣabiyye* pl. *ṣabaaya.* Do you know that young girl over there in the corner? *btaƐref haš-šaabbe hniik bəl-qərne?*

young man - *šabb* pl. *šabaab.* Who's that young man? *miin haš-šabb?*

young people - *šabaab w-ṣabaaya.* The young people had a lot of fun. *š-šabaab wəṣ-ṣabaaya nbaṣaṭu ktiir.* -- There were only young people there. *maa kaan fii ġeer šabaab w-ṣabaaya hniik.*

youngster - *ṣabi* pl. *ṣəbyaan,* (m. and f.) *walad* pl. *wlaad.*

your - **1.** *-ak (-k)* f. *-ek (-ki)* pl. *-kon.* Is this your seat, Miss? *haada maḥallek yaa ?aanise?* -- Wash your hands before dinner. *ġassel ?ideek qabl əl-Ɛaša.* **2.** *tabaƐak* f. *tabaƐek* pl. *tabaƐkon, šiitak* f. *šiitek* pl. *šiitkon.* I talked to your secretary. *ḥakeet maƐ əs-sək ərteera tabaƐak.* -- What did you do with your old radio? *šuu saaweet bər-raadyo tabaƐak əl-Ɛatiiq?*

yours - *tabaƐak* f. *tabaƐek* pl. *tabaƐkon, šiitak* f. *šiitek* pl. *šiitkon.* Whose seat is this? - Yours, of course. *la-miin hal-maḥall? - tabaƐak, maƐluum.* -- Is this doll yours? *hal-ləƐbe tabaƐek?*

**My bag is bigger than yours. *šantaayti ?akbar mən šantaaytak.*

**Is he a friend of yours? *huwwe waaḥed mən əṣḥaabak?*

**I've found my umbrella. Now where is yours? *laqeet šamsiiti. ween šamsiitak ?ənte?*

yourself - **1.** *la-ḥaalak* f. *la-ḥaalek* pl. *la-ḥaalkon, b-nafsak* f. *b-nafsek* pl. *b-nafskon, b-zaatak* f. *b-zaatek* pl. *b-zaatkon.* Why don't you do it yourself? *leeš maa btaƐməla la-ḥaalak?* -- You yourselves have to decide. *?əntu b-nafskon laazem ətqarrəru.* **2.** *ḥaalak (-ek, -kon), nafsak (-ek, -kon).* Did you hurt yourself? *?azeet ḥaalak šii?* -- You must learn to depend on yourself. *laazem tətƐallam tətƐəmed Ɛala nafsak.* -- You have only yourselves to blame. *maa-lkon ?əlla tluumu ḥaalkon.*

**Watch yourself when you cross the street. *?oƐa(k) w-?ənte Ɛam təqṭaƐ əš-šaareƐ* (f. *?oƐek w-?ənti Ɛam təqṭaƐi š-šaareƐ*).

**Help yourself. *tfaḍḍal* (f. *tfaḍḍali*).

by yourself - **1.** *la-ḥaalak (-ek, -kon), la-waḥdak (-ek, -kon).* Did you repair the engine all by yourself? *ṣallaḥt əl-motoor la-ḥaalak?* **2.** *la-ḥaalak (-ek, -kon), waḥdak (-ek, -kon).* You spent the whole Sunday by yourself? *maḍḍeet kəll əl-?aḥad la-ḥaalak?*

youth - **1.** *šbuubiyye, šabaab.* He had to work hard in his youth. *nžabar yətƐab əktiir b-əšbuubiito.* **2.** *šabaab* (pl.). What can you do? Youth is thoughtless. *šuu btaƐmel? š-šabaab ṭaayšiin.* -- Where is the International Youth Festival going to be held this year? *ween raḥa ykuun mahražaan əš-šabaab əl-Ɛaalami has-səne?*

Yugoslav - *yəġoslaavi** pl. *-iyyiin* and *-iyye.*

Yugoslavia - *yəġoslaavya.*

Yugoslavian - *yəġoslaavi**.

Y.W.C.A. - *žamƐiyyet~ əš-šaabbaat əl-masiiḥiyyaat.*

Z

zealot - *mətƐaṣṣeb* pl. *-iin.*

zebra - *ḥmaar waḥši* pl. *ḥamiir waḥšiyye, ḥmaar~ zarad.*

zenith - *samt~ ər-raas.*

zero - *ṣəfər* pl. *ṣfaar* and *ṣfuura.* Add another zero. *ziid ṣəfər taani.* -- It's five degrees below zero. *daražet əl-ḥaraara xamse taḥt əṣ-ṣəfər.*

zigzag - *mƐarwaž.* The destroyer changed to a zigzag course. *l-əmdammra ġayyaret w-mašyet b-?əttižaah əmƐarwaž.*

zinc - *zənk, tuutye.*

Zionism - *ṣ-ṣahyuuniyye.*

Zionist - *ṣahyuuni** pl. *-iyyiin* and *ṣahaayne.*

zipper - *saḥḥaab* pl. *-aat.*

zone - *manṭiqa* pl. *manaaṭeq.*

zoo - *žneenet~* (pl. *žanaayen~*) *ḥaywaan(aat), ḥadiiqet~* (pl. *ḥadaayeq~*) *ḥaywaan(aat).*

zoological - *zoolooži**.

zoologist - *zoolooži** pl. *-iyyiin.*

zoology - *zooloožya, Ɛəlm~ əl-ḥayawaan.*

zucchini - *kuusaaye* coll. *kuusa* pl. *kuusayaat.*

Zurich - *zuuriix.*

CPSIA information can be obtained at www.ICGtesting.com
Printed in the USA
BVOW05s2152211016

465731BV00005B/31/P

9 781589 011052